To Mike with best wishes

Forty Years of Stock Car Racing

Big Bucks and Boycotts

1965 - 1971

Third of a four volume series

By Greg Fielden

Also by Greg Fielden:

The Beginning, 1949-1958, Volume I
The Superspeedway Boom, 1959-1964, Volume II
and scheduled for release early 1990,
The Modern Era, 1972-1989, Volume IV

The Galfield Press

PO Box 3210, Pinehurst, NC 28374

About the Author . . .

Born in Charlotte, NC, the 36 year old author, Greg Fielden, is recognized as the premier historian of Winston Cup Grand National Stock Car Racing.

He has served as Historian and Statistician in the television booths of all major networks as well as the cable stations.

Fielden has written the four volume series, "**Forty Years of Stock Car Racing**" to provide racing fans with a chronicle of the history of the sport. This series has been acclaimed by Motorsports writers as a most important contribution to the literature of motorsports racing.

The series will be completed with the 500-plus page, "**The Modern Era, 1972-1989, Volume IV**", to be released in early 1990.

The author resides at 715 5th Avenue, S, Surfside Beach, SC 29575

"Forty Years of Stock Car Racing, Volume III, Big Bucks and Boycotts, 1965-1971

Copyright © 1989 by Gregory Lawrence Fielden

First Printing, June 1989

ISBN 0-9621580-3-8

Published by The Galfield Press

Manufactured in the United States of America

er Photo: The Winged cars of Chrysler Corporation,
at North Carolina Motor Speedway, Rockingham,
olina

Credits

The author wishes to extend a special thanks to P.J. Hollebrand and Fletcher Williams
for their invaluable assistance in compiling data for this publication

Elizabeth Baker
Fred Bince
Terry Brotherton
Allan E Brown
Ken Clapp
Richard Cole
Irma Combs
Phil Combs
Paul Dalton
Dorothy Davis
Larry Eanes
Chris Economaki
Ernie Elkins
Cynthia Fielden
Larry Fielden

Patricia Fielden
Tim and Frances Flock
Gene Granger
Sam Gulino
Jerry Haislip
Bill Hennecy
Bob Hoffman
Jim Hunter
Larry Jendras, Jr
Houston Lawing
Fran Lennert
Jon Lennert
Tony Martin
Jeanie and Morris Metcalfe
Graham Niven

Don O'Reilly
Howard O'Reilly
Doris Roberts
Hank Schoolfield
Mary Stacy
Mitzi Teague
Paul Vinson
Bob Weeks
Chip Williams

And my sincere appreciation
to NASCAR and its Photo
Department, particularly
Bob Costanzo and
T. Taylor Warren

And our appreciation to the Public Relations staffs
at all race tracks on the Winston Cup Circuit

Dedication

This series of books is dedicated to
those individuals who paid the ultimate price
in NASCAR Winston Cup Grand National Stock Car Racing,
the sport they loved

Larry Mann
Lou Figaro
Clint McHugh
Bobby Myers
Joe Weatherly
Jimmy Pardue
Buren Skeen
Billy Foster
Friday Hassler
Tiny Lund
Terry Schoonover

Frank Arford
John McVitty
Cotton Priddy
Gwyn Staley
Fireball Roberts
Billy Wade
Harold Kite
Talmadge Prince
Larry Smith
Ricky Knotts
Bruce Jacobi

Preface

In the mid to late 1969's and the early 1970's NASCAR Winston Cup Grand National racing was beset with turmoil. The four major groups involved in the sport (NASCAR, the drivers and owners, the sponsors and the fans) seemed not to be going in the same direction.

The most pressing problem was the fact that speed technology had surpassed safety technology. The automobile manufacturers had developed sophisticated speed machines which were not safe on existing tires and tracks.

The manufacturers had long been convinced that winning stock car races increased the sale of their vehicles. The saying was, "Win on Sunday. Sell on Monday." Winning stock car races was the premium priority at Ford and Chrysler.

In late 1964, NASCAR President Bill France issued a new set of rules for 1965. These new rules put a lid on the exotic machinery, particularly the engines which were designed and built for racing rather than street vehicles.

Chrysler balked at the new rules and announced they would boycott the 1965 season. This boycott took favorite drivers Richard Petty, David Pearson, Paul Goldsmith, Bobby Isaac and others off the NASCAR tracks. Attendance plummeted. The fans were not amused.

Chrysler came back in late 1965, but in 1966 Ford pulled its own boycott. Attendance remained down. This was the era of Big Bucks and Boycotts with both the bucks and the boycotts coming from factories.

These problems were largely settled by rules changes in which NASCAR was joined by other sanctioning bodies. Thus international rules for stock car racing were settled.

But the Big Bucks and Boycotts continued. In 1969 the drivers organized the Professional Drivers Association. This new organization boycotted the first Talladega 500 in 1969, claiming tires provided by Firestone and Goodyear were unsafe on the new track. The charge was true, but behind the boycott lay a long standing feeling that the drivers were not getting their share of the pot.

By 1970 the Independent (non-factory sponsored) drivers and owners were stretching their own muscles. This backbone of racing objected to "deal" money from promoters to "star" drivers. At one race in 1971, the independents pulled out after the green flag, leaving Richard Petty leading only four cars at the checkered.

The Big Bucks and Boycotts era was a much troubled period of time. Spectators were reluctant to spend their money not knowing who would be racing and how long they would race.

The real solution to the turmoil came in 1971. This was the entry of the R.J. Reynolds Tobacco company. Through its Winston brand of cigarettes, RJR became the sponsor of the total season with $100,000 up for grabs based on point standings. The competitors had never seen a six-figure sum dangling before them before the season started.

R. J. Reynolds joined NASCAR in a well-timed move. The manufacturers had gotten out of racing after the 1970 season, and the sport was in recession. Over the period of the next few years, the sport of stock car racing would scramble to its feet and begin to build the lofty status it enjoys today.

Table of Contents

The 1965 Season

Chrysler Cuts Out - -

Curtis Comes Home

Volume three of a four volume series . . Big Bucks and Boycotts   1965 - 1971

1965

The 1964 NASCAR Grand National season had produced electrifying high speeds, record attendance figures, the emergence of a popular champion and widespread media exposure.

But problems persisted. The element of danger cut deeply into the vein of the sport. Three leading drivers -- Joe Weatherly, Fireball Roberts and Jimmy Pardue had paid the ultimate price for the sport they loved.

Halfway through the 1964 season, outcries could be heard from drivers.

"It's reached the point at the superspeedways where it's a big relief when a race ends and you're okay, no matter where you finished," said Buck Baker. "It's become a pretty jumpy game."

Junior Johnson, regarded as the bravest of the brave, remarked, "We haven't learned enough to keep the cars handling safely at the speeds we now travel. And the

NASCAR President Bill France introduced 1965 rules which disallowed the Chrysler Hemi engine. "No manufacturer is favored; none penalized," he said

tire companies are having trouble developing compounds that will give adequate wear."

Fred Lorenzen, Ford's majestic prince, went one step further. "The speeds are just too fast," he said. "I'll never run another race unless they slow the speeds down."

By the summer of 1964, sanctioning NASCAR knew they had to address the issue. Executive manager Pat Purcell said, "I don't know what the answer will be. But in my opinion, we have simply got to find something to do."

For over two months, NASCAR President Bill France and his aides worked to find a solution which would keep drivers, owners and the factory sponsors happy -- and to cut speeds. On Monday, October 19, 1964, NASCAR announced a new set of rules for the 1965 season. New specifications, designed to slow the big Grand National cars and provide extra safety measures, took aim on the very expensive "limited production" engines.

The general rules for the 1965 NASCAR Grand National season:

1.**Engine:** Maximum size, 428 cubic inches of production design.

2.**Elimination of certain engines:** hemispherical combustion chamber and hi-rise cylinder heads, roller cams and roller tappets.

3.**Wheelbase:** 119 inches on superspeedways and 116 inches on short tracks and road courses.

4.**Carburetor:** one 4-barrel carburetor, 1 11/16 inch opening.

5.**Rubber lined gas tanks:** fuel cell, now under scrutiny by NASCAR, may be made mandatory if they pass the safety test.

The rules, effective January 1, 1965, excluded Chrysler's hemi-head and the Ford's hi-riser engines, and called for a longer wheelbase car on superspeedways.

Bill France said the rules were formulated ".... after a tremendous amount of research and consideration touching all phases of stock car racing. We believe that in finalizing these specifications for 1965, we have taken steps that will provide independents enough latitude so they can compete against the factory drivers.

"Those who prefer to use General Motors equipment will not be handicapped," France added.

Immediately, Ford Motor Co. approved the rule changes. "NASCAR is to be congratulated for its effort to speed progress in development of improved stock components," said Leo C. Beebe, Ford Division Special Vehicles Manager. "We believe the automobiles in stock car events should be as representative as possible of regular production models. By eliminating special high performance engines, NASCAR has provided manufacturers with greater opportunities to apply lessons learned on the tracks to improve passenger cars."

NASCAR's announcement, somewhat predictably, sent rumblings through the Chrysler front offices. "Racing has always prided itself of being progressive," said Bob Anderson of Chrysler. "Here we are backing up. Any engine takes a couple of years of experimentation to develop its full potential. I cannot speak for the corporation, but we will certainly go over the rules closely in Detroit. It could mean we won't be at Daytona."

The United States Auto Club, a rival of NASCAR in late model stock car racing, balked at Bill France's announcement. "We will operate under the same rules in 1965 as we did in 1964," said Henry Banks, USAC Competition Director. "It has always been our policy to give at least a one year notice and in many instances two years before making major changes in engine specifications. We feel that changing specifications without adequate notice works a hardship on our personnel and on the manufacturers."

Essentially, USAC said that the Plymouth and Dodge automobiles with the powerful hemi engines would be welcome on all tracks.

Under NASCAR rules, the Chrysler teams would have to run the Plymouth Fury and the Dodge Polara *without* the hemi engine on superspeedway tracks. "The Fury and Polara were designed as strictly luxury autos," said Ronney Householder, Director of Competition for Chrysler . "They're big with a lot of gadgets and fancy stuff. Weight distribution on these cars was meant for highway comfort, not racing. Aerodynamically, we would be dead. The new rules NASCAR announced has put us out of business down South."

Smokey Yunick, the maestro of the mechanical

world, analyzed the rules and offered his opinion. "The way I interpret it, the 1965 rules will not handicap the Ford as much as it will its competition," said Yunick, who did not field a car in 1964. "I don't look for the Fords to slow down much. The Chrysler people should be hurt, in the beginning at least. They have to go with a bigger car with less horsepower. Ford should have the upper hand. The new rules won't help the independents. The factory money is just too much."

Ten days later, on October 29, 1964, Householder issued a prepared statement:

Chrysler's Ronney Householder blasted new NASCAR rules

"The 1964 stock car season attracted the largest crowds and paid the biggest purses in history. The season has been a credit to all who participated. Plymouth and Dodge cars with the 426 c.i. hemi engines and their drivers, gave a good account of themselves in all sanctioned competitive events and contributed greatly to the season's success.

"The standard practice of all competitive sanctioning bodies is to make major rule changes after thorough discussion with owners, drivers, track owners and equipment manufacturers; and to provide a minimum of one full year's notice prior to adoption. The new NASCAR rules for the 1965 season as announced on October 19, 1964, do not permit an orderly development and testing program for replacement of equipment already programmed. The new rules interrupt the continuity of engineering cars for safety and performance and they are not consistent with racing's tradition of bringing the best and newest engineering equipment to the race track. We also believe the rules will work to the disadvantage of many car owners, some drivers, crews and track owners.

"The effect of the new NASCAR rules will be to arbitrarily eliminate from NASCAR competition the finest performance cars on the 1964 circuit, including the car of the Grand National champion. Under these new rules, the equipment running on NASCAR tracks in 1965 will be inferior to the best the automotive industry can produce for this purpose.

"Accordingly, unless NASCAR rules for 1965 are

modified or suspended for a minimum of 12 months to permit an orderly transition to new equipment, we have no alternative but to withdraw from NASCAR sanctioned events and concentrate our efforts in USAC, IMCA, NHRA, SCCA and other sanctioning bodies in 1965. In any case, the outstanding Dodge and Plymouth hemi-head cars will be racing wherever track owners want the public to see championship performances by stock car equipment."

Following Householder's statement and Chrysler's effective withdrawal, Bill France went on the offensive and explained the reasons for making abrupt changes in the rules. "We are at a crossroads," France said. "The hemi and hi-riser engines do not resemble the volume production engines one associates with 'stock'. Ford now has a single OverHead Cam engine they hoped to use as a racing engine. Chrysler is prepared to build 12 double OverHead Cam engines for racing purposes. We could not allow this to happen.

"We have been criticized for not announcing the rules one year in advance," he continued. "Try to find out from the auto makers a year in advance what they intend to build and you have an idea what we are up against.

"The 1965 NASCAR specifications were designed to provide fair competition among all 1965 American standard size production automobiles. If the Chrysler Corporation feels that its standard 426 c.i. wedge engines are not competitive with other comparable size cars of other American car makers, then I would be the last to criticize Chrysler on its withdrawl from NASCAR racing," continued France.

"NASCAR racing is first of all competitive. NASCAR's major aims through the years has been to match American automobiles of like performance capabilities in races of speed and endurance. The 1965 NASCAR specifications were drawn but for one purpose: to bring together cars with similar engine size, length, width and weight. No manufacturer is favored; none penalized," said France.

This statement seemed to be inviting Chrysler to boycott the 1965 season. However, the NASCAR President felt he had an ace up his sleeve. He was banking on General Motors coming back into the sport actively, and that would stave off any harm done by a Chrysler boycott.

"By the time the boys get around to you," France told a group of concerned promoters prior to a 150-miler at Augusta, GA on November 1, 1964, "everything will be worked out okay. I'm the one who is liable to take a beating at the Daytona 500 in February. Everything will be peachy-creamy." France left the meeting confident that General Motors would be back in force, which would smooth over any frayed edges the Chrysler boycott might create.

During November and December, the war of wills continued. Neither Chrysler nor Bill France wanted the boycott to continue; however neither party was willing to back down.

Rumors to the effect that General Motors would return to racing seemed unfounded. It was known that many in GM would have liked to go racing, but the "no racing" policy prevailed. And at that time, coming out of a brutal strike, the policy makers at GM were certainly concerned with more important business than stock car racing.

General Motors Vice President Lewis C. Goad made a public statement in December. "Racing may be dramatic and it may be exciting, but it does not add anything to the kind of proving ground testing that GM describes as all around the clock, all around the calendar, all around the country and all around the car," he said. "Racing tests the qualities of the car and driver, but it does not test the performance of passenger cars in normal use on streets and highways."

Chrysler said it would send factory backed drivers and teams to the USAC circuit. At the same time, Ford announced it would field industry supported cars in NASCAR races only. What that meant was that NASCAR would be all Ford, and USAC all Chrysler. With both sides apparently unwilling to compromise, the NASCAR drivers who had deals with Chrysler, began squirming. None of them really wanted to run USAC.

Cotton Owens: *"I have to go where I can make a living. That means I go where I get factory support."*

Richard Petty: *"I definitely won't switch to USAC. I couldn't make a living running stocks in that group because they don't run for enough money. Basically, it amounts to us going back to 1963, running against 1965 equipment."*

Ray Fox: *"I'm sitting tight and just trying to keep my people together. We keep hoping Bill will make some changes in his plans. One thing I know, I won't race at all -- not without backing."*

Buck Baker: *"I'm still going to race in NASCAR. I've been doing it for 18 years and I've never gone hungry. Racing is my business and I don't know anywhere I could race and make more money than I've made in NASCAR."*

Bud Moore: *"I have several irons in the fire, but none are getting hot."*

Bill France: *"People have always run Dodges and Plymouths in our races and they still will."*

But, by the time January rolled around, no one had backed down. The cold war was still going on and very little movement came from the General Motors camp.

Right after the new year, Billy Wade and Richard Petty were conducting tire tests at Daytona International Speedway for Goodyear. In spite of the prospect of some drivers being on the sidelines, many of them were going through routines and conducting business as usual -- in case a compromise would be reached.

Wade, 1963 Grand National Rookie of the Year and winner of four straight races in 1964, was on a 10 lap test session on January 5. As Wade's Bud Moore Mercury headed into the first turn, a tire blew out. Wade hit the concrete wall, nose-dived onto the apron, then slid back up the banking and struck the wall again. When attendants reached the 34 year-old Houston native, he was dead.

Less than three weeks later, Larry Thomas of Trinity, NC, a promising driver who had taken over the Burton-Robinson factory Plymouth when Jimmy Pardue was killed in tire tests in September of 1964, died in a highway accident. He was traveling along I-75 when his car struck the rear of another vehicle. Thomas' Plymouth jumped the guard rail and tumbled down an embankment. It was presumed that Thomas fell asleep at the wheel.The Burton-Robinson team folded its operation after losing two of their drivers in tragic accidents four months apart.

The Motor Trend 500 at Riverside was run on January 17 -- with no factory backed Plymouths or Dodges in the field. Ford products swept the first eight positions.

With Daytona's Speedweeks just over two weeks away, it was clear that Chrysler was prepared to sit out the entire year. France's hopes of a General Motors return were fleeing quickly. A GM representative squelched all existing rumors in late January: "The handwriting is on the wall," the high-ranking GM official stated. "The back door is not only not open, but it is being closely guarded. If there were any plans of racing through the back door, they have been changed. Anybody caught trying it would get their head chopped off."

France had one last gasp. He still thought General Motors cars could grace the NASCAR tracks in 1965, but he changed his angle. "I think our new rules will make it possible for dealer participation in racing," he said. "They can modify the GM cars and be very competitive. I don't anticipate any all-out factory support like Ford and Chrysler, but individuals can compete in their cars under the new rules."

Supporting France's statement was word that Buck Baker would drive Oldsmobiles on the Grand National circuit in 1965. "We will have up to four new Oldsmobiles, each with a 425 c.i. engine," said Baker. Sponsorship was coming from the Hoff Cadillac-Olds dealership in Norfolk, VA.

It was also reported that France had purchased a 1965 Plymouth Fury that had ended up in Baker's garage in Charlotte. And wealthy sportsman Sam Fletcher of Ft. Wayne, IN had entered a 1965 Plymouth Fury in the Daytona 500 with Johnny Allen listed as driver. Famed mechanic Red Vogt was tabbed as crew chief.

But the heavy hitters in Chrysler's camp were set to race elsewhere. Defending Grand National champ Richard Petty was going to do some drag racing in the South. "I'd be like a fish out of water anywhere other than the South," said Petty. "Neither Dad nor I like to travel. We'll be racing a Plymouth Barracuda on the quarter-mile."

Paul Goldsmith, David Pearson and Bobby Isaac would race on the USAC trail. Jim Paschal went back to chicken farming. LeeRoy Yarbrough and Earl Balmer went looking for rides anywhere.

When the Grand Nationals began checking into Daytona International Speedway for the Daytona 500, France saw the Fords were there en masse. But virtually everyone else was missing. "What this boils down to is that the Chrysler people are a bunch of lousy sports," France said angrily. "I think NASCAR should be complimented for setting up the rules and sticking by them."

In the rain-shortened Daytona 500, Ford Motor Co.

Richard Petty's Plymouth Barracuda which he drove in drag races in early 1965

vehicles took the first 13 spots. Baker's Oldsmobile had been demolished in a first lap crash in the 100-mile qualifying race. Johnny Allen drove his big Fury to a 23rd place finish -- having been lapped 19 times in the 114 laps he completed. The few independent Dodge and Plymouth cars and the General Motors vehicles were rendered non-competitive.

During Speedweeks, Bill France eased up slightly on his rules stance -- the first hint that he might back down. "If Chrysler makes a production line hemi engine that is optional equipment for Plymouth Furys and Dodges Polaras and makes it reasonably priced, then it will be approved for racing in NAS-CAR."

Promoters Bob Colvin and Clay Earles felt the pinch of the Chrysler boycott

Although France took one step back, Chrysler's Ronney Householder stood firm. "The hemi engine will not fit in a Fury or Polara," he insisted. "We designed the Belvederes and Coronets for the hemi engines in 1965. This was done long before the rules came out. It is physically impossible for us to install a hemi in those big cars. You can't just push a button on the assembly line and expect things to come out like they do in a pop-corn machine."

Attendance for the Daytona 500 was 58,682 -- down from 69,738 in 1964.

However, attendance was booming where Richard Petty showed up with his hopped-up Barracuda. On Sunday, February 28, 1965, Petty pulled his car into the Southeastern Dragway in Dallas, GA. A crowd of 10,000 was on hand, well beyond capacity. The largest throng before Petty had agreed to come was about 2,500.

Southeastern Dragway was a typical small operation. There were no bleachers or grandstands. The crowd lined up elbow-to-elbow on the edge of the strip. A dirt embankment and a wire fence was all that protected the spectators.

Petty lined his car up in the right lane for a duel with Arnie Beswick of Morrison, IL. When the green lights flashed, Beswick peeled out of the starting blocks. Petty's car stuttered with a transmission problem.

"The transmission was loaded up so bad it wouldn't go," Petty said later. "He had me beat. When I finally got it started, it took off in low gear."

Just as Petty slapped his car into second gear, a wheel leaned badly and the car veered toward the middle of the track. Petty fought the wheel and the car swerved back toward the crowd. The bright blue car slammed into the dirt embankment, went straight up in the air, jumped the wire fence where the crowd was standing and landed on its nose among the spectators.

Rescue workers rushed to the panic stricken area. They reached Petty, who was badly shaken. The first words from Petty were, "Never mind about me. Look after the people I've hit."

A wheel flew off Petty's car and struck eight year-old Wayne Dye of Austell, GA. The child was dead on arrival at Paulding Memorial Hospital in Dallas.

Seven other people were injured in the crash. Emory Allen, 24, of Blueridge, GA, was transported to University Hospital in Atlanta with critical head injuries.

Petty, who suffered from shock, later pieced the tragic events together. "I guess it was up to about 60 (mph) when I went from low gear to second. When you run in low (gear), there's not a lot of weight on the front wheels.

"When I changed gears, the wheels came down strong. I felt something give and I let off the gas, but I couldn't hold it."

*   *   *

In the early season Grand National events, spectators were merely trickling through the turnstiles. Attendance was off at virtually all the speedways. Nelson Weaver, President of Atlanta International Raceway, said his track planned to "remain neutral" in the disagreement between NASCAR and Chrysler, but issued an ultimatum as well. "We are in the final year of a five year contract with NASCAR," said Weaver. "We will not enter a new one until we have reached a decision about this matter. Our commitments are made through June 13 and we cannot change them. But our first responsibility is to our fans -- to give them the best racing that is possible. If our evaluation of the current situation indicates we might better serve our fans by making changes, then we shall give serious consideration to making these changes after June 13."

"Any announcement Mr. Weaver might have at this time is a little premature," replied France. "I still feel that the move I made was necessary to eliminate the high cost, low volume engine. I'm sure no other association could field as fine an array of cars as NASCAR. Chrysler could have a competitive car in our races, but they won't do it. They're trying to hurt us."

Whether or not the hurt was intended, nearly all the promoters felt the sting of half empty grandstands and uncontested Ford shows.

Bob Colvin, *Darlington Raceway: "We have to slow the cars down some. They are too fast for the drivers and too fast for the tracks. The method of slowing them down must come from NAS-CAR. But it would be my thinking that cutting displacement would be the best way."*

Carl Moore, *Vice President, Bristol International Speedway: "I've got to think that racing is suffering because of the Chrysler pull out. We've been selling out at our track in past years, but our advance sales are way down.*

France informed the restless promoters that relief would come by spring -- and that relief was spelled C-h-e-v-r-o-l-e-t. Big Bill had one last card to play.

News leaked out of Daytona Beach that respected car builder Ray Fox was going to put a pair of 1965 Chevrolets on the NASCAR Grand National circuit.

Reports said that Jim Rathmann, winner of the 1960 Indianapolis 500 and owner of a large Florida Chevrolet dealership, was the financial source for the project. Rathmann reportedly sent out 700 inquiries seeking other dealership support. Response was, however, weak.

Bristol Vice President Carl Moore said the Chrysler boycott was hurting advance ticket sales

"The factory isn't going to help us one bit," Fox confessed. "One dealer we wrote in North Carolina -- I believe it was in Charlotte -- wrote that he wasn't interested in racing. They are selling plenty of cars, so they apparently don't care for the publicity racing can provide.

"I don't know how many races we will be able to run, " Fox added. "I'll tell you one thing, we will run with anything on the track. We'll run the new 396 c.i. engine bored out to 427 c.i. And that engine will send Ford back to the drawing board. In order to run though, we may have to pass the hat through the stands."

Jim Rathmann ruffled some feathers in a prepared statement: "The only reason Fords are winning races is that they don't run fast enough to blow up. We wouldn't be getting in this business if we couldn't run faster than Fords."

The first Chevrolet was delivered to Fox on March 24. It was 11 days before the Atlanta 500 was scheduled. "I couldn't get it ready in time for Atlanta," said Fox. "The publicity people at Atlanta said I'd have it there, but I never said that. That was their way of just selling tickets."

Other news from Atlanta during the rain-out (it was eventually run on April 11) was that Buck Baker was ditching his Oldsmobile, another dealership backed entry. "We just can't do enough with this car," said the two-time Grand National champ. "I think I'll get a Chevy and let this buffalo roam on its own. It won't run worth a lick."

It wasn't until May 8 at Darlington that the new Chevrolets hit the track. There were two entered, but neither one was the Fox car. Baker had his new Chevy ready, and Jim Paschal, a defector from the Plymouth ranks, showed up in a Friedkin Enterprises Chevy wrenched by Bill Thomas.

In qualifying, the Chevys faded poorly. Paschal started 25th and Baker lined up 27th. Both were lapped twice in the first 37 laps, moments before a pit reporter for the Darlington Raceway radio network interviewed Bill France.

"I'm real pleased to see these Chevrolets doing so well," said France. "Buck Baker and Jim Paschal are doing a fine job out there."

Paschal was running in eighth place when a broken crankshaft put him out on lap 195. Baker finished 10th, 11 laps behind winner Junior Johnson.

Richard Petty had been a trackside spectator at Darlington. In a pre-race introduction, he received the biggest ovation from the crowd of 15,000 -- half what it was in 1964.

"Those stands are practically empty," said Richard. Lee Petty had an observation; "Racing is worse now than ever before," he said. "It's obvious that the attendance is hurting at all the major tracks this year because of the lack of competition."

One promoter who requested anonymity, said, "We might as well face it. This is going to be a bad year. We might as well write it off right now."

The Chevrolets did not offer Ford any competition in the Rebel 300. The last hope for France was that when the Ray Fox car arrived, it would crowd the Fords toward the front of the pack. However, funds were short. One source said, "What Rathmann got from the Chevy dealers wouldn't buy you lunch."

The Fox Chevy finally arrived trackside at Charlotte the week of the World 600. In fact, it was accompanied by three others -- the Paschal and Baker cars, plus another one slated to be driven by Sportsman driver Ned Setzer. LeeRoy Yarbrough was tabbed to drive the Fox car.

LeeRoy got in a couple of practice laps, but it failed to make it through inspection. NASCAR Chief Inspector Norris Friel determined that the Fox car did not pass the ground clearance rule of 6 1/2 inches. "It's been in the rules for years," said Friel. "Everybody else gets their cars up to where they are supposed to be. They all come down the pike and I treat them all the same. I don't give a damn what kind of car the man has."

Fox, angry at being turned away, argued, "If they wanted to go by the books so close, they would not allow a single one of those factory Fords to race."

After qualifying had closed, Richard Howard and A.C. Goines of Charlotte Motor Speedway met behind closed doors with Bill France. At that meeting, it was decided that Yarbrough would be allowed to start the race even though he had not made a qualification attempt. He started 44th in the World 600, ahead of three other drivers who had qualified but failed to earn a starting berth.

The other Chevrolets started 13th, 17th and 19th.

"I hope and pray the Chevys run well," said Ford driver Fred Lorenzen. "They mean so much to NASCAR racing right now."

The long awaited Ray Fox Chevrolet finally made its debut in the World 600

None of the Chevrolets led the World 600. Yarbrough made a crowd-pleasing charge from the rear of the field into the top 10, but engine problems kayoed him after 309 laps. Paschal and Baker also fell out with blown engines. Setzer finished sixth, 18 laps behind winner Lorenzen.

Bill France's last hope had fizzled. The Chevrolets, even with expert mechanic Ray Fox turning the wrenches, were not competitive. The Fords were sweeping the top spot in NASCAR and the Plymouths and Dodges reigned supreme in USAC. The Chevrolets were not competitive with either sanctioning body.

Les Richter, General Manager of Riverside International Raceway, had watched the proceedings with a close eye. In the late spring, he threw a gauntlet. "First, the auto moguls of Daytona Beach and Indianapolis should get together and cut out this bickering," said Richter. "The United States Auto Club has the Indy Car image and the Daytona Beach people are the championship form of stock car racing. There is friction between them. But if they bury the hatchet, they could have mutual benefits."

A few days after the World 600, Bill France met with USAC's Henry Banks in New York. There they resolved their long standing differences and adopted similar rules for their stock car racing divisions. The closer the specifications were in NASCAR and USAC, the less vulnerable they would be to the whims of the auto industry. The rule changes, announced on June 21 were:

1. A minimum weight limit of 9.36 pounds per cubic inch displacement for a car ready to run with a full load of fuel, oil and water (i.e.: a 427 c.i. car must weigh 3,996.7 pounds).
2. The hemi engine will be permitted on NASCAR tracks of over one mile in the Plymouth Fury, the Dodge 880 and Dodge Polara.
3. The hemi engine will be permitted in the Plymouth Belvedere and Dodge Coronet on all USAC tracks and on NASCAR tracks of one mile or less and road courses.

Favorable reaction was heard from the auto makers. Robert M. Rodger, Special Car Manager for Chrysler, said, "We regard the recent agreement by NASCAR and USAC as commendable and we congratulate them. However, no hemi powered '65 Fury or Polara has ever been built in production nor have such cars received design, tooling or testing programs to make them suitable for safe high speeds of NASCAR superspeedways. For these reasons, Chrysler Corporation does not plan to enter factory supported Furys or Polaras in these events."

Leo C. Beebe of Ford commented, "we have always encouraged NASCAR and USAC to provide similar specifications. We are encouraged."

The second half of the 1965 NASCAR Grand National season got underway at Daytona for the annual Firecracker 400. Although Chrysler's head men said it was "impossible" to fit a hemi engine in a Plymouth Fury, Buck Baker did it. He bolted a hemi engine in the Plymouth that Bill France had bought him back in the winter and put son Buddy in it. Young Baker did a masterful job -- finishing second to A.J. Foyt. None of the factory supported Chrysler cars entered the race.

It wasn't until July 25 at Bristol that the Chrysler factory cars were back in force. For the remainder of the year, they entered 18 short track races and won six of them; Petty won four times and Pearson twice.

While the NASCAR-USAC agreement was a step in the right direction, the superspeedway promoters still were mired in the dilemma of an all Ford show. They were faced with the perplexity that the race fans just might save their spending dollars and attend the short tracks. Bill France had changed the rules, but Chrysler wasn't biting on the big tracks.

On Saturday July 31, 1965, Bill France was in Atlanta to keep an eye on the USAC Indy Car proceedings at

Atlanta International Raceway. Nelson Weaver, President of the track, had said publicly that he might not sign with NASCAR in 1966. Weaver had booked an Indy Car event at his facility.

Interestingly, there were a number of other gentlemen in Atlanta. Bob Colvin of Darlington Raceway and A.C. Goines and Richard Howard of Charlotte Motor Speedway were also in town. So was Bill France, Jr. and Pat Purcell of NASCAR.

Something was cooking.

The six men met in downtown Atlanta. At the meeting, Colvin, Goines and Howard convinced Big Bill that only one measure could be taken this late in the year to salvage most of the ill feelings. The fans had been unhappy; so were the promoters and track officials. There was an immensely popular man who had been tucked safely away in suspension for four years -- Curtis Turner. And he just might be the savior of 1965.

The meeting was electric and tense. Turner was still a sore spot with Bill France. In 1961, Turner had led the Federation of Professional Athletes, an organization affiliated with the Teamsters Union. France emerged victorious in the dispute. Turner and Tim Flock lost all driving rights within the boundaries of the NASCAR sanction.

A couple hundred miles up the road, Concord Speedway was hosting a 100-mile stock car race sanctioned by Grand American Racing Association, a fledgling operation who had perhaps the biggest drawing card in the South -- Curtis Morton Turner.

Turner was in the infield of the half mile dirt track a few hours before race time -- relaxing in his air-conditioned, telephone-equipped Lincoln Continental. The phone rang and Colvin delivered the message that Turner had been hoping to hear for four years. Purcell spoke briefly with Turner, assuring him that he had been reinstated by NASCAR.

Curtis Turner was reinstated by Bill France in August 1965. "I feel like a man who just got out of jail," he said

Curtis Turner's comeback was complete after American 500 victory

Turner packed away his helmet and loaded up the Continental. "Let's get out of here," he said to his companions. "This is not a NASCAR track and from now on, I'm legal."

France issued an official statement from Atlanta. "We feel that Curtis Turner has paid the penalty for his activities by sitting out four years of NASCAR racing," said France. "We welcome him back."

"I feel like a man who just got out of jail," said Turner.

Turner felt Ford's welcome mat would be out for him. However, Ford said there would not be room for a one team expansion for the remainder of 1965. Talks with John Holman and Ford's John Cowley didn't generate a ride. "They think I'm too old," Turner said dejectedly. "They think I'm washed up."

With no Ford ride available, Turner went looking elsewhere. With the help of Joe Littlejohn, promoter at Piedmont Interstate Fairgrounds in Spartanburg, SC, Turner was seated in the Petty Engineering Plymouth for a 100-miler on August 14.

Turner was one of the quickest in pre-race practice sessions. The wall-to-wall crowd of 8,000 cheered their approval.

As qualifying got underway, Turner was one of the favorites for the pole. As he whipped off the fourth turn to take the green flag, the throng rose to their feet. Going into the first turn, the rear end broke loose on the Plymouth and smashed the wall - rear end first. He was out for the evening. It was a tremendous disappointment for the fans -- and Turner.

Turner's next effort was at Darlington, where he was slated to drive a Plymouth owned by Sam Fletcher. The car had run poorly twice at Daytona and had been parked ever since. Turner started eighth but couldn't keep up with the leading Fords. He retired on lap 51 with wheel bearing failure.

After Turner departed, he was greeted by Ford's Jacque Passino and John Cowley. There they informed Turner that a Wood Brothers Ford would be at his disposal for the remaining big races in 1965. Martinsville, North Wilkesboro, Charlotte and the inaugural event at Rockingham were on the schedule.

For two races, Turner drove a back-up Junior Johnson Ford. He qualified second at Hickory, but fell out after just 22 laps with overheating problems. He started fourth at Richmond, but once again overheating troubles put him out early.

Turner crashed with Bobby Isaac in the early going at Martinsville, then finished fifth at North Wilkesboro.

In the National 400 at Charlotte, Turner led for 13 laps and eventually finished third behind Fred Lorenzen and Dick Hutcherson. He had been engaged in a monumental struggle in the late stages. With just over a lap to go, Turner got caught in a squeeze with A.J. Foyt and spun out.

The unveiling of the North Carolina Motor Speedway at Rockingham had a full field of cars. The Chrysler factory cars were back in force, along with all the strong Ford teams. Turner started sixth on the grid and scrambled to victory. He led 239 of the 500 laps. The 41 year-old veteran passed upstart Cale Yarborough with 27 laps to go and picked up first place money of $13,090. "There's no question about it," said Cale, "he can still drive a race car. He proved that out there today."

NASCAR Grand National racing, which suffered dearly in 1965, ended the year on a high note.

Two other important developments came in 1965. Goodyear Tire & Rubber Co. came out with a new tire -- the Goodyear Lifesaver Inner Tire. "We want a tire for race cars that will insure the driver of some measure of control if he blows a tire," said Goodyear Racing Division Field Manager Chuck Blanchard. "This new tire is not the answer to a dream, but it does have many distinct advantages."

And that rubber lined fuel tank which NASCAR was studying closely, became mandatory within a year. The Firestone fuel cell was designed to cut down on fires in accidents where fuel tanks were split.

"I think you should always be interested in new things," said Harvey S. Firestone, company President. "For instance, we're always interested in the safety of our race drivers. We have set up a special research department now to develop an indestructible gas tank for race cars. There is no profit in this but we're sincerely interested in giving more protection to our good friends so we don't lose fellows like Fireball Roberts and Eddie Sachs."

During the 1965 season, Ford set a record which may never be approached. Cars with the Ford nameplate won 32 consecutive Grand National races from February 12 through July 25. For the year, they won 48 out of the 55 races.

Race No. 1

Gurney 3-For-3 in Motor Trend 500; 1 Spectator Killed

RIVERSIDE, CA (Jan. 17) -- Road racer Dan Gurney annexed his third straight Motor Trend 500 at Riverside International Raceway as the 1965 NASCAR season got underway without the top drivers employed by Chrysler Corporation.

Gurney wheeled his Wood Brothers Ford into the lead 55 laps from the finish and beat Junior Johnson to post his third Grand National career victory -- all coming on the 2.7-mile road course. Johnson finished 27 seconds behind Gurney and took the early lead in the 1965 point standings. Gurney entered the race on his international license and did not earn any NASCAR points.

Third place went to Marvin Panch with Darel Dieringer fourth. Gene Davis finished fifth..

Parnelli Jones, driving a Bill Stroppe Mercury, led the first 36 laps. Johnson led briefly before making a pit stop with Gurney inheriting the lead. The Costa Mesa, CA driver led all but 20 laps after taking the lead from Johnson.

"I never really strained the car," said the winner. "It ran beautifully all day and I was in good position, so I didn't have to stand on it at any time."

A.J. Foyt, driving a Holman-Moody Ford, was challenging Johnson for second place with 16 laps left. Foyt got his car off into the dirt in turn nine and flipped end over end. The Houston, TX USAC driver was transported to Riverside Community Hospital complaining of chest pains. He suffered a broken back and a fractured left heel. Doctors said he was in "fair" condition.

One spectator was killed in a freak accident. Dick Powell spun his Pontiac between turns one and two and slid to a safe halt on a dirt embankment. When Powell spun, spectators watching the race on a fork-lift, lurched to see the spin. The sudden shift in weight caused the fork-lift to roll down a hill. Ronald Pickle, 20, of San Diego, was killed and three other spectators injured when the fork-lift toppled over.

Ned Jarrett started third on the grid and ran with the leaders for nearly half the race. In the 94th lap, Jarrett's Ford burst into flames during a pit stop. Pit road occupants did some fast stepping as the rescue squad put out the fire. "Those people at Riverside did a tremendous job in putting out the fire," said Jarrett.

A crowd of 61,474 watched Gurney average 87.708 mph on the warm, sunny afternoon.

Grand National Race No. 1
185 Laps at Riverside Int'l Raceway
Riverside, CA
"Motor Trend 500"
500 Miles on 2.7-mile Paved Road Course
January 17, 1965

Fin	St	No.	Driver	Team / Car	Laps	Money	Status
1	11	121	Dan Gurney	Wood Bros '65 Ford	185	$13,625	Running
2	1	27	Junior Johnson	Johnson '65 Ford	185	7,310	Running
3	5	21	Marvin Panch	Wood Bros '65 Ford	184	4,075	Running
4	16	06	Darel Dieringer	'65 Ford	181	2,625	Running
5	15	5	Gene Davis	Bill Groves '64 Mercury	177	1850	Running
6	35	98	Eddie Gray	'64 Mercury	176	1,300	Running
7	8	45	Scotty Cain	'64 Mercury	172	1,175	Running
8	37	17	Sam Stanley	'64 Mercury	172	1,050	Running
9	18	88	Buck Baker	Baker '64 Dodge	171	1,025	Running
10	12	00	A J Foyt	Holman-Moody '65 Ford	169	1,035	Crash
11	17	12	Jerry Grant	'63 Ford	167	830	Running
12	22	4	Roy Tyner	'64 Chevrolet	164	650	Running
13	38	0	Nat Reeder	'64 Chevrolet	100	625	Fuel
14	23	6	Ed Brown	'64 Olds	151	605	Running
15	20	100	Dick Gulstrand	'63 Chevrolet	151	615	Running
16	36	711	Bob Conner	'63 Mercury	115	580	Clutch
17	28	71	Sam McQuagg	'63 Ford	97	575	Diff
18	6	9	Bill Amick	'64 Mercury	95	620	Engine
19	3	11	Ned Jarrett	Bondy Long '65 Ford	94	765	Fire
20	13	1	Skip Hudson	'64 Ford	90	635	Engine
21	33	43	Fritz Wilson	'64 Plymouth	84	550	Engine
22	21	60	Doug Cooper	Bob Cooper '64 Ford	80	540	Heating
23	14	76	Larry Frank	Frank '64 Ford	65	580	Running
24	4	28	Fred Lorenzen	Holman-Moody '65 Ford	55	625	Heating
25	25	58	Doug Moore	'64 Ford	51	525	Trans
26	30	84	Al Self	'64 Ford	49	500	Engine
27	9	611	Dick Brown	'65 Plymouth	47	525	Engine
28	10	33	Bob Bondurant	'64 Ford	47	520	Wheel Cy
29	41	2	Bobby Allison	Southern Racing '64 Ford	41	500	Heating
30	32	14	Joe Clark	'64 Mercury	41	500	Drive Sh
31	7	29	Dick Hutcherson	'65 Ford	40	525	Heating
32	2	15	Parnelli Jones	Bill Stroppe '64 Mercury	37	980	Valves
33	19	67	Jim Cook	'64 Mercury	36	550	Engine
34	39	19	Bob Thompson	'64 Mercury	26	500	Engine
35	40	18	Bill Boldt	'63 Mercury	19	500	Engine
36	31	20	Bill Meyer	'63 Ford	19	500	Engine
37	26	111	Johnny Steele	'63 Ford	16	500	Engine
38	34	10	Don Walker	'63 Ford	14	500	Trans
39	24	53	Bill Cantrell	'63 Chevrolet	2	500	Heating
40	42	38	Charles Powell	'62 Pontiac	1	500	Engine
41	29	48	Bruce Worrell	'63 Chevrolet	1	500	Trans
42	27	61	Dana Hall	'64 Pontiac	1	500	Trans

Time of Race: 5 hours, 41 minutes, 42 seconds
Average Speed: 87.708 mph
Pole Winner: Junior Johnson - 102.846
Fastest Qualifier: Dan Gurney - 103.500 mph
Lap Leaders: Parnelli Jones 1-36, Junior Johnson 37-38, Dan Gurney 39-81, Johnson 82-90, Gurney 91-116, A J Foyt 117-128, Gurney 129-185
Cautions: 2   Margin of Victory: 27 seconds   Attendance: 61,474

Race No. 2

Dieringer Nips Jarrett in Close Daytona Qualifier

DAYTONA BEACH, FL (Feb. 12) -- Darel Dieringer, wheeling a year-old Bud Moore Mercury, drove past Bobby Johns with six laps left and motored to victory in the opening 100-mile qualifying race at Daytona International Speedway. It was the third career win for the 38 year-old Indianapolis, IN veteran.

Ned Jarrett challenged Dieringer off the final corner, but ran out of room. He settled for second place, one car length behind. "I could have forced Darel down low on the last lap," said Jarrett. "But I don't race that way."

Third place went to Johns. Independent Larry Frank was fourth and H.B. Bailey pulled a surprise by taking fifth in a Pontiac. Fords took positions 2-4.

Only 12,000 fans were on hand. Many stayed away since the Chrysler products were not entered.

Ray Fox entered a big Dodge Polara with a hemi engine. Driver LeeRoy Yarbrough struggled to a 12th place finish.

The day before the Daytona 500, a loud popping noise could be heard when Fox cranked the engine. It did not make the green flag for the 500. Some people in the garage area said it was the work of a saboteur. Others said it was the work of someone within the Chrysler Corporation. Rumors were that Chrysler did not want the car to run in the 500.

Jarrett led the first 31 laps of the 40 lap sprint race. Johns took over on lap 32 and led until Dieringer found first place on lap 35.

Dieringer averaged 165.669 mph in a victory which was termed an "upset". Mercury Division of Ford Motor Co. had withdrawn factory support after the 1964 season.

The only Plymouth entered was a huge Fury, driven by Johnny Allen, owned by Sam Fletcher and set up by master mechanic Red Vogt. Allen only ran six laps before he pulled the car out of the race.

Grand National Race No. 2
40 Laps at Daytona Int'l Speedway
Daytona Beach, FL
100 Miles on 2.5-mile Paved Track
February 12, 1965

Fin	St	No.	Driver	Team / Car	Laps	Money	Status
1	1	16	Darel Dieringer	Bud Moore '64 Mercury	40	$1,100	Running
2	2	11	Ned Jarrett	Bondy Long '65 Ford	40	600	Running
3	3	7	Bobby Johns	Holman-Moody '65 Ford	40	400	Running
4	8	76	Larry Frank	Frank '64 Ford	39	300	Running
5	6	04	H B Bailey	Bailey '64 Pontiac	39	300	Running
6	15	82	Bunkie Blackburn	Casper Hensley '64 Pontiac	38	250	Running
7	9	12	Bobby Allison	Southern Racing '64 Ford	38	225	Running
8	7	60	Doug Cooper	Bob Cooper '64 Ford	37	200	Running
9	18	72	Jerry Grant	Friedkin Ent '63 Ford	37	150	Running
10	21	19	J T Putney	Herman Beam '65 Chevrolet	36	150	Running
11	11	44	Larry Hess	Hess '64 Ford	35	150	Running
12	17	3	LeeRoy Yarbrough	Ray Fox '64 Dodge	31	125	
13	19	55	Tiny Lund	Lyle Stelter '64 Ford	13	125	
14	4	29	Dick Hutcherson	Holman-Moody '65 Ford	12	100	
15	20	14	Johnny Allen	Sam Fletcher '65 Plymouth	6	100	
16	10	37	Bub Strickler	Strickler '64 Ford	5	100	
17	12	64	Elmo Langley	Langley '64 Ford	3	100	
18	14	81	Don Tilley	Joe Keistler '63 Dodge	2	100	
19	13	61	Berry Brooks	Bob Cooper '64 Pontiac	2	100	
20	5	49	G C Spencer	Spencer '64 Ford	1	100	
21	16	79	Joe Penland	Harold Rhodes '63 Chevrolet	1	100	

Time of Race: 36 minutes, 13 seconds
Average Speed: 165.669 mph
Pole Winner: Darel Dieringer - 171.151 mph
Lap Leaders: Ned Jarrett 1-31, Bobby Johns 32-34, Darel Dieringer 35-40
Cautions: None   Margin of Victory: 1 car length   Attendance: 12,000

Race No. 3

Johnson Edges Lorenzen; 13 Cars In First Lap Pile-Up

DAYTONA BEACH, FL (Feb. 12) -- Junior Johnson sped past Fred Lorenzen in the final lap and won the second 100-mile qualifier at Daytona International Speedway. It was a sweet victory for Johnson and crew chief Herb Nab. Johnson had hired Nab away from the Holman-Moody team over the winter.

Lorenzen came in second with Marvin Panch, Donald Tucker and Sam McQuagg filling out the top five.

The race was marred by a spectacular 13 car smash-up in the opening lap. Rookie Rod Eulenfeld lost control of his Ford in the

Darel Dieringer on quick pit stop in Daytona 100

fourth turn. His car dipped down onto the apron, then shot up into traffic. After being hit by several cars, Eulenfeld's car flipped and burst into flames. The Jacksonville, FL newcomer dashed to safety as cars were crashing around him.

Veteran Buck Baker suffered several broken ribs and a dislocated knee cap when his Oldsmobile was caught up in the melee. "I knew those guys had to be rookies because they panicked," huffed Baker from the Halifax Hospital. "They sat on the brakes and skidded all over the place. They froze. This is no place for a bunch of monkeys to be running 170 mph and freeze."

Rod Eulenfeld #71 took a wild ride in Daytona Qualifier

Many of the drivers in the wreck were freshman pilots looking to get in the Daytona 500 with the absence of the Chrysler teams.

The lead changed hands nine times among three drivers, with Lorenzen and Johnson pacing the field all the way except for two laps led by Earl Balmer. Balmer had been signed to replace the late Billy Wade, who was killed in a Bud Moore Mercury while testing tires on January 5.

Lorenzen thought he had won the race when he rode under the white flag to start the final lap. "When I passed Junior on the 39th lap and took the white flag," said Lorenzen, "I thought it was the checkered flag. It was a farce. I've got nobody to blame but myself."

Johnson averaged only 111.076 mph as 13 laps of yellow were used to clean up the first lap crash.

Race No. 4

Lorenzen Declared Victor In Damp Daytona 500

DAYTONA BEACH, FL (Feb. 14) -- Fred Lorenzen sloshed his way to victory in the seventh annual Daytona 500 at Daytona International Speedway. The race had been shortened to 332.5 miles due to a steady

Grand National Race No. 3
40 Laps at Daytona Int'l Speedway
Daytona Beach, FL
100 Miles on 2.5-mile Paved Track
February 12, 1965

Fin	St	No.	Driver	Team / Car	Laps	Money	Status
1	1	27	Junior Johnson	Johnson '65 Ford	40	$1,100	Running
2	2	28	Fred Lorenzen	Holman-Moody '65 Ford	40	600	Running
3	3	21	Marvin Panch	Wood Bros '65 Ford	40	400	Running
4	6	74	Donald Tucker	Don Snyder '63 Ford	38	300	Running
5	4	24	Sam McQuagg	Betty Lilly '65 Ford	38	300	Running
6	10	68	Bob Derrington	Derrington '64 Ford	37	250	Running
7	19	34	Wendell Scott	Scott '64 Ford	34	225	Running
8	7	15	Earl Balmer	Bud Moore '64 Mercury	27	200	
9	21	88	Neil Castles	Buck Baker '64 Dodge	27	150	
10	20	03	Reb Wickersham	Ray Underwood '64 Ford	15	150	
11	23	02	Roy Mayne	'65 Pontiac	14	150	
12	13	20	Jack Anderson	Ron Cory '64 Ford	13	125	
13	19	39	Robert Vaughn	Ronald Smith '63 Pontiac	4	125	
14	22	86	Buddy Baker	Buck Baker '65 Plymouth	2	100	
15	16	2	Jim Bray	Shorty Johns '65 Pontiac	2	100	
16	5	71	Rod Eulenfeld	Oscar Bowman '63 Ford	0	100	Crash
17	8	63	Bill DeCoster	Don House '63 Ford	0	100	Crash
18	9	59	Tom Pistone	Glen Sweet '64 Ford	0	100	Crash
19	11	42	Bill McMahan	Casper Hensley '63 Pontiac	0	100	Crash
20	12	35	Harold Painter	Lester Hunter '64 Dodge	0	100	Crash
21	14	10	Cale Yarborough	Gary Weaver '64 Ford	0	100	Crash
22	15	18	Ned Setzer	Toy Bolton '65 Chevrolet	0	100	Crash
23	17	31	Possum Jones	Sam Fogle '63 Ford	0	100	Crash
24	18	80	Earl Brooks	Allen McMillion '64 Pontiac	0	100	Crash
25	25	53	Pete Stewart	David Warren '63 Ford	0	100	Crash
26	26	87	Buck Baker	Baker '65 Olds	0	100	Crash
27	27	99	Herb Shannon	'64 Mercury	0	---	Crash
28	28	00	Jack Goodwin	'64 Mercury	0	---	Crash

Time of Race: 54 minutes, 1 second
Average Speed: 111.076 mph
Pole Winner: Fred Lorenzen - 170.551 mph
Lap Leaders: Junior Johnson 1-13, Fred Lorenzen 14-16, Johnson 17-21,
    Lorenzen 22. Johnson 23-24, Earl Balmer 25-26, Lorenzen 27-35, Johnson 36-38,
    Lorenzen 39, Johnson 40
Cautions: 1 for 13 laps   Margin of Victory: 1 car length   Attendance: 12,000

rainfall.

Lorenzen survived a brush with Marvin Panch with what turned out to be five laps to go and celebrated in victory lane nearly three hours later as nightfall shrouded the ceremonies. Darel Dieringer was credited with

Bobby Johns #7, Marvin Panch #21 and Bob Derrington #68 duel in Daytona 500

Grand National Race No. 4
200 Laps at Daytona Int'l Speedway
Daytona Beach, FL
"Daytona 500"
500 Miles on 2.5-mile Paved Track
February 14, 1965

Fin	St	No.	Driver	Team / Car	Laps	Money	Status
1	4	28	Fred Lorenzen	Holman-Moody '65 Ford	133	$27,100	Running
2	1	16	Darel Dieringer	Bud Moore '64 Mercury	132	12,900	Running
3	5	7	Bobby Johns	Holman-Moody '65 Ford	132	7,850	Running
4	16	15	Earl Balmer	Bud Moore '64 Mercury	132	4,350	Running
5	3	11	Ned Jarrett	Bondy Long '65 Ford	132	3,750	Running
6	6	21	Marvin Panch	Wood Bros '64 Ford	132	2,750	Running
7	26	29	Dick Hutcherson	Holman-Moody '65 Ford	130	2,175	Running
8	10	24	Sam McQuagg	Betty Lilly '65 Ford	130	1,900	Running
9	32	10	Cale Yarborough	Gary Weaver '64 Ford	128	1,500	Running
10	36	49	G C Spencer	Spencer '64 Ford	128	1,675	Running
11	13	12	Bobby Allison	Southern Racing '64 Ford	128	1,425	Running
12	9	04	H B Bailey	Bailey '64 Ford	126	1,425	Running
13	15	60	Doug Cooper	Bob Cooper '64 Ford	125	1,350	Running
14	19	19	J T Putney	Herman Beam '65 Chevrolet	125	1,225	Running
15	8	74	Donald Tucker	Don Snyder '63 Ford	124	1,275	Running
16	17	72	Jerry Grant	Friedkin Ent '63 Ford	123	1,170	Running
17	27	86	Neil Castles	Buck Baker '65 Plymouth	122	1,165	Running
18	12	68	Bob Derrington	Derrington '64 Ford	121	1,160	Running
19	21	44	Larry Hess	Hess '64 Ford	119	1,155	Running
20	14	34	Wendell Scott	Scott '64 Ford	118	1,150	Running
21	31	64	Elmo Langley	Langley '64 Ford	118	1,145	Running
22	33	81	Don Tilley	Joe Keistler '63 Dodge	117	1,140	Running
23	28	14	Johnny Allen	Sam Fletcher '65 Plymouth	114	1,135	Running
24	41	99	Herb Shannon	'64 Mercury	110	1,130	Engine
25	30	37	Bub Strickler	Strickler '64 Ford	73	1,225	Engine
26	20	03	Reb Wickersham	Ray Underwood '64 Ford	68	1,120	Running
27	11	82	Bunkie Blackburn	Casper Hensley '64 Pontiac	49	1,115	Crank Sh
28	2	27	Junior Johnson	Johnson '65 Ford	27	1,110	Crash
29	24	55	Tiny Lund	Lyle Stelter '64 Ford	12	1,105	Rock arm
30	22	02	Roy Mayne	'65 Pontiac	6	1,100	Distributor
31	23	20	Jack Anderson	Ron Cory '64 Ford	5	1,095	Trans
32	29	2	Jim Bray	Shorty Johns '64 Pontiac	4	1,090	Heating
33	43	35	Jeff Hawkins	Lester Hunter '64 Dodge	4	1,085	Handling
34	34	18	Ned Setzer	Toy Bolton '65 Chevrolet	3	1,080	Fuel Pmp
35	35	81	Berry Brooks	Bob Cooper '64 Pontiac	3	1,150	Oil Pres
36	42	26	Red Farmer	'64 Ford	3	1,070	Handling
37	37	53	Pete Stewart	David Warren '63 Ford	2	1,065	Handling
38	39	98	Jimmy Helms	'64 Ford	2	1,060	Clutch
39	40	08	Tom Pistone	'64 Ford	2	1,055	Clutch
40	18	88	Buddy Baker	Buck Baker '64 Dodge	2	1,050	Engine
41	7	76	Larry Frank	Frank '64 Ford	1	1,145	Oil Pres
42	38	79	Joe Penland	Harold Rhodes '63 Chevrolet	1	1,040	Piston
43	25	39	Robert Vaughn	Ronald Smith '63 Pontiac	1	1,035	Oil Pres

Time of Race: 2 hours, 22 minutes, 56 seconds
Average Speed: 141.539 mph
Pole Winner: Darel Dieringer - 171.151 mph
Lap Leaders: Junior Johnson 1-27, Marvin Panch 28-68, Fred Lorenzen 69-78,
    Panch 79-112, Bobby Johns 113, Panch 114-118, Lorenzen 119-133
Cautions: 3 for 43 laps (32 because of rain)   Margin of Victory: Under caution
Attendance: 58,682
* Race halted at 133 laps because of rain.

second place and Bobby Johns was third. Earl Balmer took fourth with Ned Jarrett fifth.

Panch, who spun out after tangling with Lorenzen, fell a lap off the pace and was paid sixth place money. "It was just one of those things that nobody could help," Panch said afterwards. "I thought I had enough room to pass but the hole closed up. I'm sure Freddy didn't chop me off intentionally."

Lorenzen, who led the last 15 laps, said, "I was running about six to eight feet off the rail. I didn't see

Marvin because our windshields were covered with rain. I didn't think he would try to pass me on the outside. He had plenty of room on the inside."

Junior Johnson appeared to be Lorenzen's toughest challenger. The Ronda, NC Ford driver charged into the lead at the drop of the green flag and had stretched his advantage when a tire blew on lap 27. The car shot up the banking and slugged the concrete wall. Debris was scattered over such a large area that it required 14 laps of yellow to clean up the track. Johnson was treated for a deep cut over his eye.

A heavy attrition rate depleted the field early. No less than 14 cars had retired in the first six laps of the race. Some observers felt there might not have been 10 cars left running if the race had gone the 500-mile distance.

Lorenzen averaged 141.539 mph for his 20th career Grand National victory.

Dieringer took a 764 point lead in the Grand National standings over Panch. Lorenzen moved up to third, 1,508 points out of first place.

Race No. 5
Jarrett Takes Spartanburg 100 By 22 Laps

SPARTANBURG, SC (Feb. 27) -- Ned Jarrett outlasted impressive newcomer Dick Hutcherson and ran away with the win in the 100-mile Grand National race

Grand National Race No. 5
200 Laps at Piedmont Interstate Fairgrounds
Spartanburg, SC
100 Miles on Half-mile Dirt Track
February 27, 1965

Fin	St	No.	Driver	Team / Car	Laps	Money	Status
1	5	11	Ned Jarrett	Bondy Long '65 Ford	200	$1,150	Running
2	4	49	G C Spencer	Spencer '64 Ford	178	700	Running
3	16	68	Bob Derrington	Derrington '64 Ford	177	450	Running
4	11	99	Gene Hobby	Hobby '64 Dodge	179	300	Running
5	1	29	Dick Hutcherson	Holman-Moody '64 Ford	160	275	Diff
6	7	18	Ned Setzer	Toy Bolton '65 Chevrolet	152	240	Sway bar
7	9	61	Doug Cooper	Bob Cooper '64 Ford	146	200	Running
8	8	34	Wendell Scott	Scott '64 Ford	144	175	Running
9	3	55	Tiny Lund	Lyle Stelter 64 Dodge	143	150	Running
10	6	45	Bud Moore	Louie Weathersby '65 Plym	104	140	Engine
11	2	26	Junior Johnson	Johnson '65 Ford	50	130	Heating
12	14	31	Darel Dieringer	Sam Fogle '65 Ford	43	120	Heating
13	10	10	Cale Yarborough	Gary Weaver '64 Pontiac	38	110	Diff
14	15	06	Danny Byrd	'63 Ford	35	100	H Gasket
15	12	81	Frank Weathers	Joe Keistler '65 Plymouth	4	100	Shocks
16	13	60	Berry Brooks	Bob Cooper '63 Dodge	2	100	Diff

Time of Race: 1 hour, 30 minutes, 26 seconds
Average Speed: 66.367 mph
Pole Winner: Dick Hutcherson - 70.644 mph
Lap Leaders: Junior Johnson 1-2, Dick Hutcherson 3-125, Ned Jarrett 126-150
    Hutcherson 151-160, Jarrett 161-200
Cautions: None   Margin of Victory: 22 laps   Attendance: 5,000

at the Piedmont Interstate Fairgrounds.

Jarrett crossed the finish line *22 laps* in front of runner-up G.C. Spencer. Third place Bob Derrington was 23 laps behind and rookie Gene Hobby 30 laps behind in fourth place. Fifth place went to Hutcherson, who was on the sidelines for the final 40 laps

Hutcherson of Keokuk, IA, put the Holman-Moody Ford on the pole. He swapped the lead four times with Jarrett and was holding down first place when the differential broke with 20 miles to go.

Only seven cars finished after 16 started the 200 lapper on the half-mile dirt track.

Junior Johnson started second and led the first two laps. But his Ford developed heating problems dropping him to 11th place at the finish.

Jarrett's whopping triumph came at an average speed of 66.367 mph before a crowd of 5,000.

Jarrett announced his intention to seek the Grand National title. "I've got three cars and I'm going to all the races," he said. "Some guys don't like the grind of running in all of them. A lot of the small tracks are just as challenging as the large ones. The little races keep you sharp for the big ones."

Race No. 6

Fire at Weaverville Fails To Stop Ned Jarrett

WEAVERVILLE, NC (Feb. 28) -- Spectators fought a raging fire as Ned Jarrett cruised to victory in the 100-mile Grand National race at Asheville-Weaverville Speedway. It was the second straight win for the 32 year-old Ford driver.

Dick Hutcherson came in second with Cale Yarborough third and G.C. Spencer fourth. Danny Byrd came from dead last in the 21 car field to nab fifth spot.

The race was slowed twice by caution flags. The first came out in the 103rd lap to allow fire fighters to battle a grass fire which had broken out along the backstretch. The green flag came back out when the fire was apparently contained.

The roaring race cars fanned the flames until they burned a strip 20 yards wide and 200 yards long down the backstretch and into the third turn. A number of the 6,500 spectators fought the blaze with shovels, blankets and seat cushions. The NASCAR fire fighters again went to the area and smothered the flames by the time the race ended.

Jarrett led all but one lap of the 200-lap contest, but was hard pressed by Hutcherson all the way.

Junior Johnson, starting fourth, chased his rivals for 176 laps. While running third the Johnson Ford gave up the ghost with a bad differential.

Rookie Berry Brooks smashed his Pontiac into the fourth turn wall after 124 laps. He was unhurt although his Pontiac was badly damaged.

Jarrett averaged 75.678 mph for his 39th career victory.

Grand National Race No. 6
200 Laps at Asheville-Weaverville Speedway
Weaverville, NC
100 Miles on Half-mile Paved Track
February 28, 1965

Fin	St	No.	Driver	Team / Car	Laps	Money	Status
1	1	11	Ned Jarrett	Bondy Long '65 Ford	200	$1,150	Running
2	3	29	Dick Hutcherson	Holman-Moody '65 Ford	200	700	Running
3	5	10	Cale Yarborough	Gary Weaver '64 Ford	197	450	Running
4	2	49	G C Spencer	Spencer '64 Ford	196	300	Running
5	21	08	Danny Byrd	'64 Ford	195	275	Running
6	7	19	J T Putney	Herman Beam '65 Chevrolet	189	240	Running
7	6	38	Neil Castles	Buck Baker '64 Dodge	186	200	Running
8	9	37	Bub Strickler	Strickler '64 Ford	185	175	Running
9	13	16	Ned Setzer	Toy Bolton '65 Chevrolet	180	150	Running
10	8	55	Tiny Lund	Lyle Stelter '64 Ford	180	140	Running
11	18	68	Bob Derrington	Derrington '64 Ford	177	130	Running
12	4	26	Junior Johnson	Johnson '65 Ford	176	120	Diff
13	14	99	Gene Hobby	Hobby '64 Dodge	173	110	Running
14	20	81	Frank Weathers	Joe Keistler '63 Dodge	171	100	Bell Hsng
15	16	61	Berry Brooks	Bob Cooper '64 Pontiac	124	100	Crash
16	12	31	Darel Dieringer	Sam Fogle '64 Ford	77	100	Fuel Pmp
17	19	34	Wendell Scott	Scott '63 Ford	63	100	Oil Pres
18	10	75	Gene Black	C L Crawford '64 Ford	50	100	Radiator
19	11	58	Doug Moore	Moore '64 Chevrolet	36	100	Diff
20	15	60	Doug Cooper	Bob Cooper '64 Ford	16	100	Engine
21	17	86	Buddy Baker	Buck Baker '65 Plymouth	9	100	Rear End

Time of Race: 1 hour, 19 minutes, 17 seconds
Average Speed: 75.678 mph
Pole Winner: Ned Jarrett - 84.230 mph
Lap Leaders: Ned Jarrett 1-104, Dick Hutcherson 105, Jarrett 106-200
Cautions: 2   Margin of Victory: Attendance: 6,500

Race No. 7

Johnson Ends 10 Year Jinx With Richmond 250 Win

RICHMOND, VA (March 7) -- Junior Johnson ended a personal jinx and grabbed first place in the Richmond 250 at the Atlantic Rural Fairgrounds. It was his first win at the half-mile dirt track, and the first race he has finished in the 1965 Grand National season.

Johnson, who has been competing at Richmond since 1955, scored an 18-second triumph over runner-up Buck Baker, who drove a wedge-powered Dodge.

J.T. Putney was six laps behind in third place. Curtis Crider was fourth and Bob Derrington fifth.

Dick Hutcherson, who won 60 races under the International Motor Contest Association (IMCA) as its champion in 1963 and 1964, had passed Johnson to take the lead in the 56th lap. He led for 18 laps and was running second when he crashed hard on lap 95. Hutcherson and Tiny Lund had gone into the first turn side-by-side. Hutcherson's Ford slipped into the loose dirt, tagged the wooden retaining wall and flipped over. No injuries were reported.

Twenty-two cars started the race and 10 were running at the finish. Elmo Langley, one of the 10 still chugging along when the checkered flag fell, was 104 laps behind Johnson and earned 13th place money.

Johnson averaged 61.416 mph before 12,000 spectators. It was his 39th career win, tying him with friendly rival Ned Jarrett.

Johnson admitted he didn't run flat out all the way. "Today, I decided to take it easier and see if I couldn't win a race on this track," said Johnson. "Here in past races, I've run hard and run myself out of car."

Grand National Race No. 7
250 Laps at Atlantic Rural Fairgrounds
Richmond, VA
"Richmond 250"
125 Miles on Half-mile Dirt Track
March 7, 1965

Fin	St	No.	Driver	Team / Car	Laps	Money	Status
1	1	26	Junior Johnson	Johnson '65 Ford	250	$2,200	Running
2	7	88	Buck Baker	Baker '64 Dodge	250	1,275	Running
3	19	19	J T Putney	Herman Beam '65 Chevrolet	242	900	Running
4	12	02	Curtis Crider	Crider '64 Mercury	238	600	Running
5	11	68	Bob Derrington	Derrington '63 Ford	237	450	Running
6	21	99	Gene Hobby	Hobby '64 Dodge	221	375	Running
7	2	31	Doug Cooper	Bob Cooper '63 Ford	217	300	Running
8	15	86	Neil Castles	Buck Baker '65 Plymouth	206	250	Oil Pres
9	8	72	Doug Yates	Yates '65 Plymouth	202	200	Spindle
10	4	49	G C Spencer	Spencer '64 Ford	191	200	Running
11	5	11	Ned Jarrett	Bondy Long '65 Ford	184	175	Diff
12	22	58	Doug Moore	Moore '64 Chevrolet	180	175	Running
13	13	64	Elmo Langley	Langley '64 Ford	146	175	Running
14	10	55	Tiny Lund	Lyle Stelter '64 Ford	135	150	Oil Pres
15	14	10	Cale Yarborough	Gary Weaver '64 Ford	124	150	Diff
16	3	29	Dick Hutcherson	Holman-Moody '65 Ford	95	125	Crash
17	16	37	Bub Strickler	Strickler '64 Ford	92	125	Crash
18	18	8	Larry Manning	Manning '63 Chevrolet	81	125	Diff
19	9	90	Sonny Hutchins	Junie Donlavey '64 Ford	65	125	Diff
20	6	34	Wendell Scott	Scott '63 Ford	47	125	Heating
21	20	61	Bob Cooper	Cooper '64 Pontiac	23	125	Fuel Tank
22	17	07	Danny Byrd	'64 Ford	1	125	Handling

Time of Race: 2 hours, 2 minutes, 7 seconds
Average Speed: 61.416 mph
Pole Winner: Junior Johnson - 67.847 mph
Lap Leaders: Junior Johnson 1-55, Dick Hutcherson 56-73, Doug Yates 74-86,
　　　Johnson 87-96, Ned Jarrett 97-140, Johnson 141-250
Cautions: 8 for 45 laps　　Margin of Victory: 18 seconds　　Attendance: 12,000

Grand National Race No. 8
167 Laps at Orange Speedway
Hillsboro, NC
150 Miles on .9-mile Dirt Track
March 14, 1965

Fin	St	No.	Driver	Team / Car	Laps	Money	Status
1	4	11	Ned Jarrett	Bondy Long '65 Ford	167	$1,400	Running
2	1	26	Junior Johnson	Johnson '65 Ford	166	1,000	Running
3	5	45	Bud Moore	Louie Weathersby '64 Plym	162	700	Running
4	11	64	Elmo Langley	Langley '64 Ford	161	575	Running
5	10	67	Buddy Arrington	Arrington '64 Dodge	160	425	Running
6	13	88	Buck Baker	Baker '64 Dodge	160	325	Running
7	8	27	Paul Lewis	Lewis '64 Ford	157	275	Running
8	12	31	Curtis Crider	Sam Fogle '63 Ford	157	225	Running
9	20	86	Neil Castles	Buck Baker '65 Plymouth	152	200	Running
10	9	19	J T Putney	Herman Beam '65 Chevrolet	149	175	Running
11	22	8	Larry Manning	Manning '63 Chevrolet	147	100	Running
12	2	29	Dick Hutcherson	Holman '65 Ford	144	100	Running
13	19	75	Gene Black	C L Crawford '64 Ford	141	100	Running
14	23	80	G T Nolan	Allen McMillion '63 Pontiac	139	100	Running
15	15	02	Darel Dieringer	Curtis Crider '63 Mercury	119	100	Heating
16	18	68	Bob Derrington	Derrington '64 Ford	58	100	Brakes
17	7	49	G C Spencer	Spencer '64 Ford	41	100	Diff
18	17	99	Gene Hobby	Hobby '64 Dodge	41	100	Crash
19	6	2	Fred Harb	Cliff Stewart '63 Pontiac	31	100	Engine
20	3	72	Doug Yates	Yates '65 Plymouth	23	100	Oil Pres
21	21	08	Cale Yarborough	'64 Ford	22	100	Engine
22	16	58	Doug Moore	Moore '64 Chevrolet	20	100	Diff
23	14	34	Wendell Scott	Scott '63 Ford	7	100	Heating

Time of Race: 1 hour, 39 minutes, 28 seconds
Average Speed: 90.663 mph
Pole Winner: Junior Johnson - 98.570 mph
Lap Leaders: Junior Johnson 1-137, Ned Jarrett 138-167
Cautions: 1 for 4 laps　　Margin of Victory: 1 lap plus　　Attendance: 7,500

Gene Hobby tumbles down the front stretch at Hillsboro

Race No. 8

Flat Tire Foils Johnson; Jarrett Pockets Hillsboro Win

HILLSBORO, NC (Mar. 14) -- Ned Jarrett breezed into the lead when a flat tire sent Junior Johnson to the pits and sped to victory in the 150-miler at Orange

Speedway. It was the 40th career victory for the Newton, NC Ford driver and vaulted him into second place in the NASCAR point standings.

Johnson wound up second, a lap off the pace. Bud Moore was five laps back in third spot. Elmo Langley was fourth and Buddy Arrington fifth.

Johnson put his yellow Ford on the pole and led the first 137 laps. The 33 year-old Ronda, NC star had lapped the field, but he lost two laps in the pits getting fresh rubber. Jarrett motored into the lead and led the final 30 laps. "There's no kidding myself," admitted Jarrett. "I couldn't have caught Junior. He was geared lower than I was and he could pull me bad off the corners. I hated to see him have trouble, but I was glad to get in first place."

Gene Hobby of Henderson, NC survived a frightful crack-up in the 44th lap. The rookie driver lost control of his Dodge and it struck the wooden retaining wall. The car got airborne and flipped five times down the front chute. Hobby was shaken but uninjured. "I guess I'm lucky," said Hobby. "That was a pretty bad spill, but at least I'm not hurt."

Dick Hutcherson ran wheel-to-wheel with Jarrett for second place most of the way. But brake failure sent Hutcherson to the pits for 30 laps and he wound up 12th in the final rundown.

A crowd of 7,500 watched as Jarrett averaged 90.663 mph on the .9-mile dirt oval.

Rookie Sam McQuagg leads pack of cars off fourth turn at Atlanta

Race No. 9

Panch-Foyt Team Snares Atlanta 500; Only 12 Finish

HAMPTON, GA (Apr. 11) -- Marvin Panch drove his Ford into a lap by himself, then let relief driver A.J.

Grand National Race No. 9
334 Laps at Atlanta Int'l Raceway
Hampton, GA
"Atlanta 500"
500 Miles on 1.5-mile Paved Track
April 11, 1965

Fin	St	No.	Driver	Team / Car	Laps	Money	Status
1	1	21	Marvin Panch*	Wood Bros '65 Ford	334	$18,420	Running
2	7	7	Bobby Johns	Holman-Moody '65 Ford	334	7,995	Running
3	4	11	Ned Jarrett	Bondy Long '65 Ford	330	4,700	Running
4	5	29	Dick Hutcherson	Holman-Moody '65 Ford	327	2,775	Running
5	22	88	Buddy Baker	Buck Baker '64 Dodge	325	1,850	Running
6	38	55	Tiny Lund	Lyle Stelter '64 Ford	322	1,250	Running
7	18	12	Bobby Allison	Southern Racing '64 Ford	321	1,200	Running
8	16	44	Larry Hess	Hess '64 Ford	310	1,050	Running
9	43	27	Paul Lewis	Lewis '64 Ford	310	950	Running
10	30	37	Bub Strickler	Strickler '64 Ford	309	850	Crash
11	27	17	Junior Spencer	Jerry Mullins '64 Ford	300	775	Running
12	11	49	G C Spencer	Spencer '64 Ford	299	700	Heating
13	24	77	Johnny Rutherford	'63 Ford	298	650	Engine
14	12	60	Doug Cooper	Bob Cooper '64 Ford	297	600	Running
15	28	68	Bob Derrington	Derrington '64 Ford	280	575	Running
16	17	28	Fred Lorenzen	Holman-Moody '65 Ford	250	800	Crash
17	10	24	Sam McQuagg	Betty Lilly '65 Ford	223	550	Heating
18	35	2	T C Hunt	Cliff Stewart '64 Pontiac	214	550	Engine
19	44	35	Cale Yarborough	Lester Hunter '63 Dodge	193	550	Crash
20	13	19	J T Putney	Herman Beam '65 Chevrolet	190	550	Crash
21	3	15	Earl Balmer	Bud Moore '64 Mercury	185	655	Engine
22	25	86	Neil Castles	Buck Baker '65 Plymouth	170	625	Oil Pres
23	37	56	Bill Morton	Curtis Larimer '64 Ford	142	550	Heating
24	8	76	Larry Frank	Frank '64 Ford	136	575	Engine
25	2	16	Darel Dieringer	Bud Moore '64 Mercury	132	850	Crash
26	40	52	E J Trivette	Jess Potter '63 Chevrolet	112	550	Engine
27	9	26	Junior Johnson	Johnson '65 Ford	110	575	Heating
28	23	87	Buck Baker	Baker '65 Olds	105	550	Diff
29	34	74	Donald Tucker	Don Snyder '63 Ford	98	550	Diff
30	6	41	A J Foyt	Wood Bros '65 Ford	91	575	Throttle
31	19	08	Danny Byrd	'64 Ford	63	575	Diff
32	14	04	H B Bailey	Bailey '64 Pontiac	48	550	Engine
33	29	9	Roy Tyner	Tyner '64 Chevrolet	47	550	Sway Bar
34	26	48	Jimmy Helms	'64 Ford	46	600	Oil Pres
35	39	34	Wendell Scott	Scott '64 Ford	29	550	Oil Pres
36	15	03	Reb Wickersham	Ray Underwood '64 Ford	26	500	H Gasket
37	20	59	Tom Pistone	Glen Sweet '64 Ford	24	525	Engine
38	21	67	Buddy Arrington	Arrington '64 Dodge	13	500	Clutch
39	36	18	Ned Setzer	Toy Bolton '65 Chevrolet	12	500	Sway Bar
40	32	39	Bob Vaughn	Ronald Smith '64 Pontiac	5	500	Oil Pres
41	41	96	Cotton Wallace	'63 Chevrolet	5	500	Tire Rub
42	31	10	Bernard Alvarez	Gary Weaver '64 Ford	2	500	Clutch
43	42	40	Bud Harless	Basil Whittaker '64 Pontiac	2	500	Handling
44	33	6	Jim Conway	'64 Ford	1	500	Clutch

Time of Race: 3 hours, 52 minutes, 17 seconds
Average Speed: 129.410 mph
Pole Winner: Marvin Panch - 145.581 mph
Lap Leaders: Darel Dieringer 1-40, Earl Balmer 41-46, Fred Lorenzen 47-70, Panch 71-103, Bobby Johns 104-107, Panch 108-177, Lorenzen 178-188, Panch 189-334
Cautions: 5 for 26 laps   Margin of Victory: 2 seconds   Attendance: 50,700
*Relieved by A J Foyt

Foyt usher the car into victory lane in the Atlanta 500 at Atlanta International Raceway. It was the 13th career win for Panch and the seventh time a relief driver had carried a car to victory lane in a NASCAR Grand National race.

Bobby Johns made up a lap late in the race and was 2.0-seconds behind the winning Wood Brothers Ford when the checkered flag fell. Ned Jarrett finished third and took the lead in the Grand National point standings. Dick Hutcherson was fourth and Buddy Baker fifth.

Foyt had started a second Wood Brothers Ford in the 500-miler, but left the race after 91 laps with a broken throttle linkage. Foyt took over Panch's car in the 212th lap and kept the car in front the rest of the way.

"I believe I could have finished the race, but my neck was hurting," said Panch. "I saw A.J. standing there all fresh and ready to go."

Panch had driven the red Ford into the lead on lap 189.

Darel Dieringer, who qualified second to Panch, led the first 40 laps. The Indianapolis veteran had fallen to sixth when he was tagged in the rear by Doug Cooper, sending his Mercury sliding out of control. Dieringer was forced to park the car and accept 25th place money. He completed 132 of the 334 laps on the 1.5-mile oval.

On a restart after a caution flag, Panch bumped into the lapped Chevrolet of J.T. Putney. Putney darted off the course on the backstretch and flipped three times. The car landed in a 14-foot deep ravine in the infield. Putney was not hurt.

Fred Lorenzen blew a tire and slammed nose-first into the concrete wall after 250 laps.

The caution was out five times for a total of 28 laps. Only 12 cars out of a starting field of 44 were still on the track when the race ended. Fourteen cars had departed before the 100-mile mark.

Veteran driver Buck Baker announced that he was going to ditch his cranky Oldsmobile in favor of a Chevy. "I told you guys last week this thing wouldn't run worth a lick," he told the news media. "It didn't run worth a lick. I'll be glad when I get that Chevy ready to go. And I'm going to get Buddy (Baker) a Chevy also. He showed me something out there today. Wouldn't you have liked to see him in a hemi-head engine in those last 100 miles. It would have been a race then."

Race No. 10

Dirt Track Demon Dick Hutcherson Dandy at Greenville

GREENVILLE, SC (Apr. 17) -- Dick Hutcherson held off a challenge from Ned Jarrett in a stretch duel and won the 100-mile Grand National event at Greenville-Pickens Speedway. It was the first NASCAR victory for the 33 year-old Keokuk, IA dirt track master.

Hutcherson took the lead in the 48th lap and led the rest of the way. Jarrett came in second, just one car length behind the winner. Buddy Baker took third place and Bud Moore, who won the pole in a lightly regarded Plymouth, was fourth. Fred Harb, who competed in only three races in 1964, continued his comeback bid by finishing fifth.

Hutcherson got the jump on Moore at the start and led the first 38 laps. Jeff Hawkins' Dodge stalled on the backstretch, bringing out the yellow. Hutcherson and Jarrett pitted, leaving Moore with the lead.

The Charleston, SC youngster held his Louie Weathersby Plymouth on the point for nine laps before Hutcherson grabbed the lead for good.

Hutcherson and Jarrett were poised to give the crowd a bumper-to-bumper sprint to the flag when the final restart came with 26 laps to go. Jarrett challenged at every turn, but was foiled by a late caution.

"I never drove harder to finish second in my life," declared runner-up Jarrett. "I thought I'd be able to take the lead from Dick again, but he really did a masterful job of driving."

Hutcherson, who won 29 IMCA races in 1964 -- all of them on dirt -- averaged 56.899 mph on the half-mile dirt track.

Grand National Race No. 10
200 Laps at Greenville-Pickens Speedway
Greenville, SC
100 Miles on Half-mile Dirt Track
April 17, 1965

Fin	St	No.	Driver	Team / Car	Laps	Money	Status
1	2	29	Dick Hutcherson	Holman-Moody '65 Ford	200	$1,000	Running
2	6	11	Ned Jarrett	Bondy Long '65 Ford	200	600	Running
3	12	86	Buddy Baker	Buck Baker '64 Dodge	197	400	Running
4	1	45	Bud Moore	Louie Weathersby '65 Plym	197	300	Running
5	11	2	Fred Harb	Cliff Stewart '64 Pontiac	193	275	Running
6	9	27	Paul Lewis	Lewis '64 Ford	192	240	Running
7	20	75	J T Putney	C L Crawford '64 Ford	188	200	Running
8	17	97	Henley Gray	Gene Cline '64 Ford	179	175	Running
9	18	20	Clyde Lynn	Lynn '64 Ford	175	150	Running
10	15	34	Wendell Scott	Scott '63 Ford	173	140	Running
11	24	80	G T Nolan	Allen McMillion '64 Pontiac	166	130	Running
12	10	60	Doug Cooper	Bob Cooper '64 Ford	157	120	Running
13	23	86	Neil Castles	Buck Baker '65 Plymouth	153	110	Dr Shaft
14	5	76	Larry Frank	Frank '64 Ford	83	100	Crash
15	19	68	Bob Derrington	Derrington '64 Ford	60	100	Tires
16	13	49	G C Spencer	Spencer '64 Ford	53	100	Diff
17	3	87	Buck Baker	Baker '65 Olds	49	100	R Housing
18	14	64	Elmo Langley	Langley '64 Ford	30	100	Diff
19	7	35	Jeff Hawkins	Lester Hunter '64 Dodge	29	100	Engine
20	21	52	E J Trivette	Jess Potter '63 Chevrolet	28	100	Engine
21	16	9	Roy Tyner	Tyner '63 Chevrolet	22	100	Axle
22	8	31	Cale Yarborough	Sam Fogle '64 Ford	16	100	Engine
23	4	55	Tiny Lund	Lyle Stelter '64 Ford	15	100	Engine
24	25	10	Bernard Alvarez	Gary Weaver '64 Ford	7	100	Handling
25	22	25	Jabe Thomas	Thomas '64 Ford	2	100	Shocks

Time of Race: 1 hour, 45 minutes, 27 seconds
Average Speed: 56.899 mph
Pole Winner: Bud Moore - 67.695 mph
Lap Leaders: Dick Hutcherson 1-38, Bud Moore 39-47, Hutcherson 48-200
Cautions: 3   Margin of Victory: 1 car length   Attendance:

Race No. 11

Johnson Pockets Wilkesboro Prize after Panch Crashes

N.WILKESBORO, NC (Apr. 18) -- Junior Johnson moved into the lead with 11 laps left and emerged victorious in the Gwyn Staley Memorial 400 at North Wilkesboro Speedway. It was the third win of the season for the 33 year-old chicken farmer from Ronda, NC.

Junior Johnson won at N. Wilkesboro. Here, he shakes hands with boxer Rocky Marciano

Bobby Johns wound up second, 7.0-seconds behind Johnson's Ford. Ned Jarrett finished third, Dick Hutcherson was fourth and Marvin Panch fifth.

Panch had taken the lead in the 370th lap when Johnson had to make an unscheduled pit stop to change a tire. Panch was comfortably ahead of Johnson when a tire popped on his Wood Brothers Ford and he smacked the wall.

Panch's 389 laps completed was good enough for fifth place.

"I ran over something on the track that caused the tire to blow," explained Panch. "However, Junior deserved to win the way he was running. He had the fastest car, and it's good he won before his homefolks."

Johnson led a total of 356 of the 400 laps on the .625-mile paved oval.

"I could never have caught Panch if he had not wrecked," said Johnson. "I hated to see Marvin wreck, but I'm real happy about winning here."

It was Johnson's first win at his hometown track since he won a 100-mile Grand National race on Oct. 19, 1958. Johnson also changed numbers for this event. His yellow Ford was adorned with the #26 instead of his customary #27. "I changed because I was getting tired of having bad luck with that #27," he said. "I was in #27 at Daytona and blew a tire and wrecked in the 27th lap. That was enough of that 27 stuff for me."

Johnson averaged 95.047 mph as three cautions for nine laps broke the action.

Grand National Race No. 11
400 Laps at N. Wilkesboro Speedway
North Wilkesboro, NC
"Gwyn Staley Memorial"
250 Miles on .625-mile Paved Track
April 18, 1965

Fin	St	No.	Driver	Team / Car	Laps	Money	Status
1	1	26	Junior Johnson	Johnson '65 Ford	400	$4,900	Running
2	6	7	Bobby Johns	Holman-Moody '65 Ford	400	2,125	Running
3	5	11	Ned Jarrett	Bondy Long '65 Ford	399	1,300	Running
4	4	29	Dick Hutcherson	Holman-Moody '65 Ford	393	850	Running
5	3	21	Marvin Panch	Wood Bros '65 Ford	389	675	Crash
6	19	15	Darel Dieringer	Bud Moore '64 Mercury	389	600	Running
7	2	28	Fred Lorenzen	Holman-Moody '65 Ford	388	550	Running
8	16	49	G C Spencer	Spencer '64 Ford	382	400	Running
9	25	10	Tiny Lund	Gary Weaver '64 Ford	381	350	Running
10	33	27	Paul Lewis	Lewis '64 Ford	377	300	Running
11	32	34	Wendell Scott	Scott '63 Ford	367	275	Running
12	9	17	Junior Spencer	Jerry Mullins '64 Ford	367	275	Running
13	27	37	Bub Strickler	Strickler '64 Ford	364	225	Running
14	13	52	E J Trivette	Jess Potter '63 Chevrolet	355	225	Running
15	34	25	Jabe Thomas	Thomas '64 Ford	347	200	Running
16	30	75	Gene Black	C L Crawford '64 Ford	339	175	Running
17	20	68	Bob Derrington	Derrington '63 Ford	339	175	Running
18	28	97	Henley Gray	Gene Cline '64 Ford	334	175	Running
19	8	60	Doug Cooper	Bob Cooper '64 Ford	248	200	Crash
20	24	88	Buddy Baker	Buck Baker '64 Dodge	248	150	Distributo
21	14	20	Clyde Lynn	Lynn '64 Ford	167	175	Trans
22	31	9	Roy Tyner	Tyner '64 Chevrolet	165	150	Trans
23	21	87	Buck Baker	Baker '65 Olds	131'	150	Crank Sh
24	11	53	J T Putney	David Warren '63 Ford	118	175	Diff
25	23	80	G T Nolan	Allen McMillion '64 Pontiac	105	150	Handling
26	17	81	Frank Weathers	Joe Keistler '63 Dodge	97	150	Oil Pres
27	15	31	Cale Yarborough	Sam Fogle '63 Ford	88	150	Oil Pres
28	12	56	Bill Morton	Curtis Larimer '63 Ford	72	175	Oil Pres
29	29	64	Elmo Langley	Langley '64 Ford	71	150	Engine
30	10	23	Buren Skeen	Reid Shaw '64 Ford	71	175	Heating
31	18	74	Donald Tucker	Don Snyder '64 Ford	54	150	Wheel
32	22	72	Doug Yates	Yates '65 Plymouth	46	150	Heating
33	7	67	Buddy Arrington	Arrington '64 Dodge	19	175	Engine
34	26	86	Neil Castles	Buck Baker '65 Plymouth	5	150	Trans

Time of Race: 2 hours, 37 minutes, 49 seconds
Average Speed: 95.047 mph
Pole Winner: Junior Johnson - 101.033 mph
Lap Leaders: Junior Johnson 1-164, Marvin Panch 165-168, Ned Jarrett 169-188, Johnson 189-369, Panch 370-389, Johnson 390-400
Cautions: 3 for 9 laps   Margin of Victory: 7 seconds   Attendance: 8,000

Race No. 12

'Martinsville Magic' Works For Lorenzen Again

MARTINSVILLE, VA (Apr. 25) -- Fred Lorenzen led the final 322 laps and won the Virginia 500 to notch his fourth straight victory at Martinsville Speedway. It was the second win of the season for the fair-haired Elmhurst, IL Ford driver.

Marvin Panch gave Lorenzen a strong chase near the

Grand National Race No. 12
500 Laps at Martinsville Speedway
Martinsville, VA
"Virginia 500"
250 Miles on Half-mile Paved Track
April 25, 1965

Fin	St	No.	Driver	Team / Car	Laps	Money	Status
1	2	28	Fred Lorenzen	Holman-Moody '65 Ford	500	$4,350	Running
2	3	21	Marvin Panch	Wood Bros '65 Ford	500	2,075	Running
3	5	29	Dick Hutcherson	Holman-Moody '65 Ford	494	1,250	Running
4	16	10	Tiny Lund	Gary Weaver '64 Ford	487	775	Running
5	12	67	Buddy Arrington	Arrington '64 Dodge	472	725	Running
6	13	64	Elmo Langley	Langley '64 Ford	471	625	Running
7	26	27	Paul Lewis	Lewis '64 Ford	469	575	Running
8	21	60	Doug Cooper	Bob Cooper '64 Ford	468	550	Engine
9	22	23	Buren Skeen	Reid Shaw '64 Ford	467	510	Running
10	6	11	Ned Jarrett	Bondy Long '65 Ford	458	475	Running
11	17	68	Bob Derrington	Derrington '63 Ford	450	450	Running
12	7	49	G C Spencer	Spencer '64 Ford	432	425	Crash
13	19	97	Henley Gray	Gene Cline '64 Ford	424	415	Running
14	18	20	Clyde Lynn	Lynn '64 Ford	419	405	Running
15	36	37	Darel Dieringer	Bub Strickler '64 Ford	404	370	Engine
16	14	34	Wendell Scott	Scott '63 Ford	392	385	Running
17	15	53	Curtis Crider	David Warren '64 Ford	390	375	Crank Sh
18	20	31	Cale Yarborough	Sam Fogle '64 Ford	384	440	Running
19	33	9	Roy Tyner	Tyner '63 Chevrolet	362	330	Trans
20	9	76	Larry Frank	Frank '64 Ford	344	345	Engine
21	24	74	Donald Tucker	Don Snyder '64 Ford	314	325	Running
22	1	26	Junior Johnson	Johnson '65 Ford	258	600	Crash
23	8	59	Tom Pistone	Glen Sweet '64 Ford	236	325	Engine
24	23	40	Bud Harless	Basil Whittaker '64 Pontiac	218	325	Wheel
25	10	90	Sonny Hutchins	Junie Donlavey '64 Ford	204	325	Radiator
26	4	7	Bobby Johns	Holman-Moody '65 Ford	176	325	Crash
27	31	99	Gene Hobby	Hobby '64 Dodge	93	275	Tires
28	25	87	Buck Baker	Baker '65 Olds	80	300	Engine
29	28	8	Larry Manning	Manning '63 Chevrolet	50	275	Crash
30	27	86	Neil Castles	Buck Baker '65 Plymouth	48	275	Brakes
31	11	17	Junior Spencer	Jerry Mullins '64 Ford	47	275	Brakes
32	35	80	G T Nolan	Allen McMillion '64 Pontiac	15	250	Brakes
33	29	56	Bill Morton	Curtis Larimer '64 Ford	7	250	Oil Pres
34	30	52	E J Trivette	Jess Potter '63 Chevrolet	6	250	Brakes
35	32	88	Buddy Baker	Buck Baker '64 Dodge	3	250	Trans
36	34	0	Terry Murchison	'64 Ford	2	250	Clutch

Time of Race: 3 hours, 44 minutes, 40 seconds
Average Speed: 66.765 mph
Pole Winner: Junior Johnson - 74.503 mph
Lap Leaders: Junior Johnson 1-60, Fred Lorenzen 61-73, Bobby Johns 74-88,
    Lorenzen 89-91, Johns 92, Johnson 93-178, Lorenzen 179-500
Cautions: 5 for 49 laps   Margin of Victory: 2 car lengths   Attendance: 10,000

Lorenzen gave credit to crew chief Jack Sullivan for coaching him during the 250-miler. "I was tempted to run with Junior early," said Lorenzen. "But Jack flashed me a sign that said 'think'. I settled down after that and waited for my chance."

Panch lost a lap in the pits midway through the race. His Wood Brothers team had attended a funeral for a family member and did not arrive at the track until the race was half over. "That lap I lost in the pits cost me the race," Panch lamented. "But I'm not knocking the crew. They worked hard and did a fine job."

Fred Lorenzen

Tom Pistone, who re-entered Grand National racing after a three year layoff, started eighth but was forced out of the race with a blown engine. "I'm just about out of money," said the Illinois Tiger. "That blown engine has all but washed me up."

Lorenzen averaged 66.765 mph for his 21st career NASCAR victory. A crowd of 10,000, about half what speedway management had been expecting, showed up for the race.

Race No. 13

Lund Outduels Jarrett In Rainy Columbia 100-Miler

COLUMBIA, SC (Apr. 28) -- Tiny Lund surged past Ned Jarrett in the 111th lap and was holding down first place when a thunder shower halted the 100-mile Grand National race at Columbia Speedway at 124 laps.

It was Lund's second career victory in big league NASCAR ranks and his first since the 1963 Daytona 500.

Jarrett was flagged in second place with Neil Castles third. Darel Dieringer came in fourth and Dick Hutcherson fifth.

Independents held the upper hand most of the way. Lund, wheeling a year-old Ford owned by Lyle Stelter, led on three occasions for 93 laps. Cale Yarborough qualified 10th in a Sam Fogle-owned Ford, but charged

end, but fell two car lengths short and settled for second place. Dick Hutcherson was third, Tiny Lund fourth and Buddy Arrington fifth.

Lorenzen paced himself in the early stages as Junior Johnson set the pace. Johnson led the first 61 laps but had to pit when a tire came apart after just 30 miles. He lost a lap and a half, but staged a blistering comeback. Thirty-two laps later -- on lap 93 --Johnson was back in front.

Johnson had pumped his lead up to 17 seconds by the 178th lap. As he was cruising along uncontested, the left front wheel collapsed and he went to the pits again. Returning to the track, Johnson started his no-tomorrow charge again and was in third place when another tire blew, sending his Ford into the wall.

Grand National Race No. 13
200 Laps at Columbia Speedway
Columbia, SC
"Columbia 200"
100 Miles on Half-mile Dirt Track
April 28, 1965

Fin	St	No.	Driver	Team / Car	Laps	Money	Status
1	4	55	Tiny Lund	Lyle Stelter '64 Ford	124	$1,000	Running
2	1	11	Ned Jarrett	Bondy Long '65 Ford	124	600	Running
3	18	86	Neil Castles	Buck Baker '65 Plymouth	122	400	Running
4	6	10	Darel Dieringer	Gary Weaver '65 Ford	121	300	Running
5	11	29	Dick Hutcherson	Holman-Moody '65 Ford	120	275	Running
6	12	9	Roy Tyner	Tyner '63 Chevrolet	118	240	Running
7	15	97	Henley Gray	Gene Cline '64 Ford	118	200	Running
8	13	68	Bob Derrington	Derrington '63 Ford	117	175	Running
9	9	34	Wendell Scott	Scott '63 Ford	114	150	Running
10	10	31	Cale Yarborough	Sam Fogle '64 Ford	113	140	Running
11	14	52	E J Trivette	Jess Potter '63 Chevrolet	110	130	Engine
12	7	79	Joe Penland	Harold Rhodes '63 Chevrolet	110	120	Crash
13	8	35	Jess Hawkins	Lester Hunter '64 Dodge	107	110	Running
14	5	88	Buddy Baker	Buck Baker '64 Dodge	102	100	Crash
15	16	75	J T Putney	C L Crawford '64 Ford	36	100	Wheel
16	17	53	David Warren	Warren '63 Ford	32	100	Brakes
17	2	49	G C Spencer	Spencer '64 Ford	32	100	Heating
18	3	45	Bud Moore	Louie Weathersby '65 Plym	5	100	Crash

Time of Race: 1 hour, 06 minutes, 55 seconds
Average Speed: 55.591 mph
Pole Winner: Ned Jarrett - 71.061 mph
Lap Leaders: Ned Jarrett 1-21, Tiny Lund 22-49, Cale Yarborough 50-52,
    Dick Hutcherson 53-54, Lund 55-105, Jarrett 106-110, Lund 111-124
Cautions: 6   Margin of Victory: 2 car lengths   Attendance: 7,300
* Race shortened to 124 laps because of rain

Grand National Race No. 14
500 Laps at Bristol Int'l Speedway
Bristol, TN
"Southeastern 500"
250 Miles on Half-mile Paved Track
May 2, 1965

Fin	St	No.	Driver	Team / Car	Laps	Money	Status
1	3	26	Junior Johnson*	Johnson '65 Ford	500	$4,550	Running
2	5	29	Dick Hutcherson	Holman-Moody '65 Ford	500	2,460	Running
3	7	11	Ned Jarrett	Bondy Long '65 Ford	500	1,730	Running
4	1	21	Marvin Panch	Wood Bros '65 Ford	487	1,375	Running
5	18	34	Wendell Scott	Scott '63 Ford	468	1,035	Running
6	10	17	Junior Spencer	Jerry Mulling '64 Ford	451	800	Crash
7	27	0	J T Putney	'65 Chevrolet	449	875	Running
8	11	25	Jabe Thomas	Thomas '64 Ford	444	650	Running
9	21	52	E J Trivette	Jess Potter '63 Chevrolet	442	550	Running
10	33	75	Gene Black	C L Crawford '64 Ford	436	500	Running
11	12	56	Darel Dieringer	Curtis Larimer '64 Ford	430	450	Running
12	29	53	Jimmy Helms	David Warren '63 Ford	428	425	Running
13	26	20	Clyde Lynn	Lynn '64 Ford	419	375	Running
14	19	68	Bob Derrington	Derrington '63 Ford	412	300	Running
15	23	58	Doug Moore	Moore '63 Chevrolet	377	260	Running
16	32	80	G T Nolan	Allen McMillion '64 Pontiac	363	260	Running
17	13	31	Cale Yarborough	Sam Fogle '63 Ford	359	320	Heating
18	30	86	Neil Castles	Buck Baker '65 Plymouth	323	260	Diff
19	28	99	Gene Hobby	Hobby '64 Dodge	295	260	Oil Leak
20	15	60	Doug Cooper	Bob Cooper '64 Ford	279	260	Engine
21	8	27	Paul Lewis	Lewis '64 Ford	185	260	Engine
22	9	49	C G Spencer	Spencer '64 Ford	164	260	Engine
23	6	59	Tom Pistone	Glen Sweet '64 Ford	160	260	Crash
24	4	7	Bobby Johns	Holman-Moody '65 Ford	123	285	Engine
25	16	40	Bud Harless	Basil Whittaker '64 Pontiac	87	275	Engine
26	22	97	Henley Gray	Gene Cline '64 Ford	51	275	Brakes
27	2	28	Fred Lorenzen	Holman-Moody '65 Ford	44	500	Crash
28	31	35	Jeff Hawkins	Lester Hunter '64 Dodge	43	250	Handling
29	24	38	Wayne Smith	Smith '65 Chevrolet	41	275	Bearing
30	17	64	Elmo Langley	Langley '64 Ford	31	275	H Gasket
31	25	74	Donald Tucker	Don Snyder '63 Ford	17	350	H Gasket
32	20	70	Joe Bill Adams	Adams '64 Ford	13	300	Clutch
33	14	88	Buddy Baker	Buck Baker '64 Dodge	8	290	Bearing

Time of Race: 3 hours, 20 minutes, 10 seconds
Average Speed: 74.937 mph
Pole Winner: Marvin Panch - 84.626 mph
Lap Leaders: Marvin Panch 1-9, Junior Johnson 10-140, Dick Hutcherson 141-142,
    Ned Jarrett 143-184, Johnson 185-231, Hutcherson 232-323, Jarrett 324-365,
    Hutcherson 366-438, Johnson 439-500
Cautions: 7 for 39 laps   Margin of Victory: 1 car length   Attendance: 18,500
*Relieved by Fred Lorenzen

Neil Castles came from 18th to finish third at Columbia

through the pack and led for three laps. Yarborough fell off the pace and wound up 10th, 11 laps behind.

G.C. Spencer qualified second, but was out of the race on lap 32 with overheating problems. Another independent, Bud Moore, started third and crashed in the fifth lap.

Six caution flags interrupted Lund's pace as he averaged 55.591 mph on the half-mile dirt track. A crowd of 7,300 showed up on the overcast evening.

Race No. 14

Johnson Makes up Deficit, Wins at Bristol -- Or Did He?

BRISTOL, TN (May 2) -- Junior Johnson emerged with the lead after a fender-framming episode with Dick Hutcherson 62 laps from the finish and was flagged the winner of the Southeastern 500 at Bristol

Fred Lorenzen and young fan Karen Carrier at Bristol

International Speedway. It was the fourth win of the season for the Ford driver.

Hutcherson wound up in second place, but the Keokuk, IA driver thought he had won. Ned Jarrett took third spot with Marvin Panch fourth and Wendell Scott fifth.

Johnson, who had lost a lap and a half when a tire blew after 265 laps, needed relief help from Fred Lorenzen for a 147 lap stretch. The two driver changes ate up extra pit time. The man from Ronda spent 117 laps making up the deficit before taking the lead for good.

Hutcherson claimed he won the race. "I may be a damn Yankee, but I'll always believe I won this race. No one will ever convince me I didn't," he growled. "I had a lap lead. When Lorenzen got out of the Johnson car and Junior climbed in, I took a two lap lead. At the finish, Johnson was just barely back in the lead lap."

Johnson, Hutcherson and Jarrett all finished nose-to-tail in an exciting finish that had the crowd of 18,500 on its feet. In a parting remark, Hutcherson said, "I think Robert E. Lee's grandson was scoring the race."

NASCAR Chief Scorer Joe Epton studied the score cards with Ralph Moody, co-owner of the Hutcherson Ford. Epton said Moody was satisfied with the official results.

Johnson won the race on tubeless tires, the first time that had ever been done in a NASCAR race. "We decided to take a chance on the tires," said Johnson. "You experiment a lot in racing. Sometimes you guess right and sometimes you guess wrong."

Jarrett upped his point lead to 748 points over Panch in the Grand National standings.

Johnson averaged 74.937 mph for his 41st career win.

Race No. 15

Protest Fails as Johnson's Rebel 300 Victory Upheld

DARLINGTON, SC (May 8) -- It took two days to become official, but Junior Johnson's Rebel 300 victory was upheld after NASCAR officials studied a protest by Bud Moore following the Darlington Raceway event. It was Johnson's fifth win of the season.

Darel Dieringer, driver of the Moore Mercury, wound up second, 3.0-seconds behind the winning Johnson Ford. Ned Jarrett came in third, Dick Hutcherson was fourth and Bobby Johns fifth.

Johnson clearly had the upper hand, leading for a total of 197 of the 219 laps on the 1.375-mile oval. But on Johnson's final pit stop, his car slid past his pit stall and the engine cut off. The pit crew, headed by Herb Nab, ran down and serviced the car. Then, they pushed the car until Johnson got started.

Under NASCAR rules, if a car goes past the assigned pit area, that car has to make another lap and stop in the proper space.

Dieringer held the lead until Johnson made the decisive pass with 12 laps remaining. Car owner Moore immediately filed a protest with NASCAR officials.

"If you go by the rule book," said Dieringer, "I won the race. It would be a tough break for Junior because he was outrunning me. But rules are rules."

NASCAR executives considered all angles and finally came up with a prepared statement two days later. *"Johnson did not violate the pit rule because the pit area below him was not being used,"* said the statement. *"The protest is hereby denied and Johnson is the winner of the race."*

Johnson lost the 1962 Southern 500 at this same facility when NASCAR discovered that Larry Frank had not been credited with a lap earlier in the race. "I don't see how they could have taken this win away from me," said Johnson. "I could have won the other race if I had known I needed to catch Frank.

Bub Strickler slides upside down in Rebel 300 as Jimmy Helms #53 passes

Grand National Race No. 15
219 Laps at Darlington Raceway
Darlington, SC
"Rebel 300"
300 Miles on 1.375-mile Paved Track
May 8, 1965

Fin	St	No.	Driver	Team / Car	Laps	Money	Status
1	3	26	Junior Johnson	Johnson '65 Ford	219	$10,490	Running
2	6	16	Darel Dieringer	Bud Moore '64 Mercury	219	6,155	Running
3	5	11	Ned Jarrett	Bondy Long '65 Ford	218	4,460	Running
4	4	29	Dick Hutcherson	Holman-Moody '65 Ford	217	2,925	Running
5	9	7	Bobby Johns	Holman-Moody '65 Ford	217	1,100	Running
6	14	88	Buddy Baker	Buck Baker '64 Dodge	215	1,500	Running
7	11	24	Sam McQuagg	Betty Lilly '65 Ford	213	1,250	Running
8	26	55	Tiny Lund	Lyle Stelter '64 Ford	213	1,000	Running
9	10	49	G C Spencer	Spencer '64 Ford	212	900	Running
10	27	87	Buck Baker	Baker '65 Chevrolet	208	800	Running
11	2	21	Marvin Panch	Wood Bros '65 Ford	201	770	Crash
12	20	52	E J Trivette	Jess Potter '63 Chevrolet	201	700	Running
13	16	86	Neil Castles	Buck Baker '65 Dodge	199	650	Running
14	30	35	Doug Cooper	Lester Hunter '64 Dodge	198	600	Running
15	18	34	Wendell Scott	Scott '63 Ford	198	550	Running
16	25	41	Jim Paschal	Toy Bolton '65 Chevrolet	190	500	Crank Sh
17	22	68	Bob Derrington	Derrington '63 Ford	180	450	Running
18	21	53	Jimmy Helms	David Warren '63 Ford	180	400	Running
19	19	44	Larry Hess	Hess '64 Ford	173	350	Running
20	15	37	Bub Strickler	Strickler '64 Ford	125	300	Crash
21	13	90	Sonny Hutchins	Junie Donlavey '64 Ford	106	350	Heating
22	28	14	Bunkie Blackburn	Sam Fletcher '65 Plymouth	102	300	Oil Leak
23	12	0	J T Putney	'65 Chevrolet	91	300	Engine
24	29	10	Cale Yarborough	Gary Weaver '64 Ford	82	300	Crash
25	1	28	Fred Lorenzen	Holman-Moody '65 Ford	56	415	Ignition
26	31	59	Tom Pistone	Glen Sweet '64 Ford	56	300	Steering
27	8	76	Larry Frank	Frank '64 Ford	40	340	Crash
28	23	9	Roy Tyner	Tyner '64 Chevrolet	30	300	Fuel Pump
29	17	17	Junior Spencer	Jerry Mullins '64 Ford	28	300	Crash
30	7	15	Earl Balmer	Bud Moore '64 Mercury	5	320	Crash
31	24	38	Wayne Smith	Smith '65 Chevrolet	3	300	Crash

Time of Race: 2 hours, 41 minutes, 32 seconds
Average Speed: 111.849 mph
Pole Winner: Fred Lorenzen - 138.133 mph
Lap Leaders: Fred Lorenzen 1, Junior Johnson 2-42, Marvin Panch 43,
  Cale Yarborough 44-46, Johnson 47-86, Dick Hutcherson 87, Johnson 88-136,
  Ned Jarrett 137-141, Darel Dieringer 142-147, Johnson 148-202, Dieringer 203-207,
  Johnson 208-219
Cautions: 6 for 50 laps   Margin of Victory: 3 seconds   Attendance: 15,000

Race No. 16

Jarrett Prevails in Tidewater 250

HAMPTON, VA (May 14) -- Ned Jarrett shook off a pesky Dick Hutcherson then sprinted to a one lap victory in the Tidewater 250 at Langley Field Speedway. It was the 41st career win for the current Grand National point leader.

Hutcherson fell off the pace in the late stages but still wound up second. Elmo Langley was third, Buddy Arrington fourth and Neil Castles fifth.

Hutcherson won the pole and led the first 101 laps. Jarrett was never more than a couple car lengths behind, and he finally made the pass on lap 102. Hutcherson made his only pit stop on lap 164 and fell a lap off the pace. Jarrett made a quick dash to the pits on lap 184 and got back out on the track just ahead of Hutcherson, who was still a lap down.

A trio of independents, G.C. Spencer, Doug Yates

Grand National Race No. 16
250 Laps at Langley Field Speedway
Hampton, VA
"Tidewater 250"
100 Miles on .4-mile Dirt Track
May 14, 1965

Fin	St	No.	Driver	Team / Car	Laps	Money	Status
1	2	11	Ned Jarrett	Bondy Long '65 Ford	250	$1,000	Running
2	1	29	Dick Hutcherson	Holman-Moody '65 Ford	249	600	Running
3	8	64	Elmo Langley	Langley '64 Ford	240	400	Running
4	9	6	Buddy Arrington	Arrington '64 Dodge	237	300	Running
5	10	86	Neil Castles	Buck Baker '65 Plymouth	233	275	Running
6	19	53	Jimmy Helms	David Warren '64 Ford	225	240	Running
7	11	34	Wendell Scott	Scott '63 Ford	223	200	Running
8	16	52	E J Trivette	Jess Potter '63 Chevrolet	218	175	Running
9	13	20	Clyde Lynn	Lynn '64 Ford	213	150	Running
10	21	8	Larry Manning	Manning '63 Chevrolet	212	140	Running
11	20	80	Worth McMillion	Allen McMillion '64 Pontiac	210	130	Running
12	12	68	Bob Derrington	Derrington '63 Ford	206	120	Running
13	14	97	Henley Gray	Gene Cline '64 Ford	180	110	A Frame
14	7	45	Bud Moore	Louie Weatherly '65 Plymouth	103	100	Engine
15	15	9	Roy Tyner	Tyner '64 Chevrolet	78	100	Engine
16	5	26	Junior Johnson	Johnson '65 Ford	67	100	Heating
17	18	99	Gene Hobby	Hobby '64 Dodge	29	100	Carbureto
18	17	67	Raymond Carter	Buddy Arrington '64 Dodge	13	100	Oil Pres
19	3	72	Doug Yates	Yates '64 Plymouth	0	100	Crash
20	6	55	Tiny Lund	Lyle Stelter '64 Ford	0	100	Crash
21	4	49	G C Spencer	Spencer '64 Ford	0	100	Crash

Time of Race: 1 hour, 43 minutes, 48 seconds
Average Speed: 57.815 mph
Pole Winner: Dick Hutcherson - 66.790 mph
Lap Leaders: Dick Hutcherson 1-101, Ned Jarrett 102-250
Cautions: 1 for 18 laps   Margin of Victory: 1 lap plus   Attendance:

Surely they won't take this one away."

Bub Strickler survived a wild upside-down ride through the first turn after his Ford climbed the wall. "I was riding along upside-down with glass, sparks of fire, hot oil and small bits of asphalt beating at my head," remarked Strickler. "But my helmet and face guard protected me. There's no telling what my face would look like if it had not been for my face shield."

Marvin Panch blew a tire and crashed late in the race. Earl Balmer went out after hitting the stalled Chevrolet of Wayne Smith early in the event.

Johnson averaged 111.849 for his 42nd career win.

and Tiny Lund all qualified in the top six. However, all three were eliminated in a first lap wreck.

Junior Johnson qualified fifth but parked his car after 67 laps with overheating problems.

Jarrett averaged 57.815 mph for his fourth win of the season.

Grand National Race No. 17
200 Laps at Bowman Gray Stadium
Winston-Salem, NC
50 Miles on Quarter-mile Paved Track
May 15, 1965

Fin	St	No.	Driver	Team / Car	Laps	Money	Status
1	1	26	Junior Johnson	Johnson '65 Ford	200	$850	Running
2	5	11	Ned Jarrett	Bondy Long '65 Ford	198	550	Running
3	2	29	Dick Hutcherson	Holman-Moody '65 Ford	196	430	Running
4	3	49	G C Spencer	Spencer '64 Ford	193	330	Running
5	4	23	Buren Skeen	Reid Shaw '64 Ford	193	285	Running
6	19	34	Wendell Scott	Scott '63 Ford	187	255	Running
7	7	64	Elmo Langley	Langley '64 Ford	186	220	Running
8	18	31	Cale Yarborough	Sam Fogle '63 Ford	185	165	Running
9	11	9	Roy Tyner	Tyner '64 Chevrolet	184	175	Running
10	9	20	Clyde Lynn	Lynn '64 Ford	180	140	Running
11	20	8	Larry Manning	Manning '63 Chevrolet	176	130	Running
12	14	52	E J Trivette	Jess Potter '63 Chevrolet	176	135	Running
13	15	97	Henley Gray	Gene Cline '64 Ford	173	125	Running
14	17	68	Bob Derrington	Derrington '63 Ford	173	100	Running
15	6	2	Fred Harb	Cliff Stewart '63 Pontiac	98	125	Handling
16	8	6	Buddy Arrington	Arrington '64 Dodge	60	100	Trans
17	13	53	Jimmy Helms	David Warren '63 Ford	55	100	Heating
18	10	86	Neil Castles	Buck Baker '65 Plymouth	39	115	Crash
19	12	70	Fred Goad	Joe Bill Adams '64 Ford	2	100	Brakes
20	16	67	Raymond Carter	Buddy Arrington '64 Dodge	1	100	Handling

Time of Race: 1 hour, 2 minutes, 37 seconds
Average Speed: 47.911 mph
Pole Winner: Junior Johnson - 49.261 mph
Lap Leaders: Junior Johnson 1-200
Cautions: None   Margin of Victory: 2 laps plus   Attendance: 8,500

Race No. 17

Johnson Romps at Bowman Gray; Mechanic Nab Fined

WINSTON-SALEM, NC (May 15) -- Junior Johnson led from start to finish and captured the 50-mile Grand National race at Bowman Gray Stadium for his sixth win of the year.

Following the race, NASCAR Inspector Dick Beaty wanted to inspect Johnson's winning Ford and he ordered crew chief Herb Nab to take it to the inspection station. Nab did as Beaty instructed, but moments later, the car was gone. Beaty said the car was removed without permission. Nab said a mechanic for the Johnson

team removed the car without his knowledge. Rumors had been circulating that 'bending the rules' had been escalating on NASCAR's premier stock car racing circuit.

Ned Jarrett finished second, two laps behind. He said he would not file a protest regarding the Johnson car, which was taken back to the team's trailer and removed from the speedway. "I don't want the race on a disqualification because the car was taken out," said Jarrett. "If it could have been inspected and it was illegal, then I'd want to be the winner."

Dick Hutcherson came in third, G.C. Spencer was fourth and Buren Skeen fifth.

A few days later, Nab was hit with a $100 fine by NASCAR for his actions.

Johnson averaged 47.911 mph in the caution-free 200 lapper.

Race No. 18

Spencer Fades; Johnson Nips Jarrett in Hickory 250

HICKORY, NC (May 16) -- Old crusty G.C. Spencer won the pole position and led in the early stages, but Junior Johnson came home the winner of the Hickory 250 at Hickory Speedway. It was the seventh win of the season for Johnson.

G. C. Spencer's rough luck continued at Hickory

Despite winning seven of his first 15 starts in the 1965 season, Johnson ranks only seventh in the standings, 6,208 points behind leader Ned Jarrett.

Jarrett was holding down a three second lead with two laps to go when a rear tire blew. Johnson eased into the lead as Jarrett finished on a rim throwing sparks. Third place went to Spencer, who led twice for 20 laps in the early going. Paul Lewis came in fourth and Buddy Baker fifth.

Baker had startled the veterans by charging his Oldsmobile into second place past the half-way point. Mechanical problems forced him into the pits for a lengthy stay and he wound up 10 laps behind.

"I couldn't have caught Ned at the end," admitted Johnson. "I was faster at the start but I wouldn't have won if he hadn't had trouble."

Spencer, 39, a veteran of 196 Grand National races, was bidding for his first big win. He was still in contention when a sputtering engine sent him to the pits for a three lap stay with just a handful of laps remaining.

Spencer is another driver affected by the Chrysler boycott, although he drives a Ford. "I was negotiating with Ford for a factory deal last winter," said Spencer. "The man in Detroit liked the idea. I though I had it sewed up. But the very next day, Chrysler pulled out and suddenly there was no deal. The Ford man said their present set-up of drivers would be sufficient for 1965."

Race No. 19

Balmer Charges Back from 4 Laps Down; Lorenzen Still Wins World 600

CHARLOTTE, NC (May 23) -- Fred Lorenzen staved off a furious rally by upstart driver Earl Balmer and won the World 600 at Charlotte Motor Speedway. It was Lorenzen's 10th superspeedway win and the third victory of the season.

Ned Jarrett #11, Paul Lewis #27, and Fred Lorenzen #28 race through fourth turn at Charlotte

Lorenzen scooted away from Balmer in the final showdown and won by 6.4-seconds. Dick Hutcherson came in third and took the lead in the Grand National point standings. Buddy Baker finished fourth and Pedro Rodriguez was fifth.

Balmer came into the pits in the 246th lap with a broken wheel. It took his Bud Moore team four laps to fix the problem. Balmer resumed the chase, but was hopelessly behind. Still, the Floyd Knobs, IN driver drove relentlessly, catching timely cautions and he sliced his deficit quickly.

Balmer moved into solid contention when the green flag flew after the final caution when Bob Derrington wrecked. Balmer nipped at Lorenzen's heels as the crowd of 50,000 stood in anticipation.

As Balmer made his move with seven laps to go, the lapped Ford of Donald Tucker blocked his path, sending the challenger up against the steel retaining barrier.

Grand National Race No. 18
250 Laps at Hickory Speedway
Hickory, NC
"Hickory 250"
100 Miles on .4-mile Dirt Track
May 16, 1965

Fin	St	No.	Driver	Team / Car	Laps	Money	Status
1	5	26	Junior Johnson	Johnson '65 Ford	250	$1,000	Running
2	3	11	Ned Jarrett	Bondy Long '65 Ford	250	600	Running
3	1	49	G C Spencer	Spencer '64 Ford	245	400	Running
4	6	27	Paul Lewis	Lewis '64 Ford	241	300	Running
5	7	87	Buddy Baker	Buck Baker '65 Olds	240	275	Running
6	11	86	Neil Castles	Buck Baker '65 Plymouth	238	240	Running
7	9	31	Cale Yarborough	Sam Fogle '63 Ford	235	200	Running
8	12	34	Wendell Scott	Scott '63 Ford	233	175	Running
9	23	70	Joe Bill Adams	Adams '64 Ford	231	150	Running
10	17	81	Frank Weathers	Joe Keistler '63 Dodge	229	140	Running
11	14	9	Roy Tyner	Tyner '64 Chevrolet	228	130	Running
12	19	8	Larry Manning	Manning '63 Chevrolet	228	120	Running
13	8	64	Elmo Langley	Langley '64 Ford	222	110	Crash
14	20	52	E J Trivette	Jess Potter '63 Chevrolet	209	100	Running
15	10	2	Fred Harb	Cliff Stewart '63 Pontiac	206	100	Axle
16	13	20	Clyde Lynn	Lynn '64 Ford	197	100	Running
17	21	97	Henley Gray	Gene Cline '64 Ford	155	100	Crash
18	2	29	Dick Hutcherson	Holman-Moody '65 Ford	136	100	Running
19	22	6	Buddy Arrington	Arrington '64 Dodge	82	100	Oil Pres
20	16	68	Bob Derrington	Derrington '63 Ford	62	100	Heating
21	4	45	Bud Moore	Louie Weathersby '65 Plym	47	100	Heating
22	18	53	Jimmy Helms	David Warren '63 Ford	37	100	H Gasket
23	24	99	Gene Hobby	Hobby '64 Dodge	21	100	Fuel Pres
24	15	67	Raymond Carter	Buddy Arrington '64 Dodge	15	100	Oil Pres

Time of Race: 1 hour, 23 minutes, 11 seconds
Average Speed: 72.130 mph
Pole Winner: G C Spencer - 76.312 mph
Lap Leaders: G C Spencer 1-16, Junior Johnson 17-24, Spencer 25-28,
   Ned Jarrett 29-174, Johnson 175-177, Jarrett 178-248, Johnson 249-250
Cautions: 2 for 9 laps   Margin of Victory: 1/4 lap   Attendance: 7,500

Grand National Race No. 19
400 Laps at Charlotte Motor Speedway
Charlotte, NC
"World 600"
600 Miles on 1.5-mile Paved Track
May 23, 1965

Fin	St	No.	Driver	Team / Car	Laps	Money	Status
1	1	28	Fred Lorenzen	Holman-Moody '65 Ford	400	$27,270	Running
2	6	15	Earl Balmer	Bud Moore '64 Mercury	400	10,900	Running
3	5	29	Dick Hutcherson	Holman-Moody '65 Ford	397	6,895	Running
4	14	88	Buddy Baker	Buck Baker '64 Dodge	392	4,250	Running
5	12	51	Pedro Rodriguez	Holman-Moody '65 Ford	391	3,425	Running
6	19	4	Ned Setzer	Toy Bolton '65 Chevrolet	382	2,525	Running
7	30	27	Paul Lewis	Lewis '64 Ford	380	2,250	Running
8	16	74	Donald Tucker	Don Snyder '63 Ford	352	1,750	Running
9	23	44	Larry Hess	Hess '64 Ford	348	1,500	Running
10	24	86	Neil Castles	Buck Baker '65 Plymouth	343	1,400	Running
11	29	37	Bub Strickler	Strickler '64 Ford	335	1,375	Crash
12	36	68	Bob Derrington	Derrington '63 Ford	331	1,350	Crash
13	38	53	Jimmy Helms	David Warren '63 Ford	321	1,300	Running
14	44	3	LeeRoy Yarbrough	Ray Fox '65 Chevrolet	309	1,250	Engine
15	41	66	Larry Manning	Manning '63 Chevrolet	308	1,225	Running
16	37	97	Henley Gray	Gene Cline '64 Ford	308	1,250	Running
17	32	52	E J Trivette	Jess Potter '63 Chevrolet	302	1,325	Running
18	2	16	Darel Dieringer	Bud Moore '64 Mercury	286	1,680	Engine
19	28	56	Bill Morton	Curtis Larimer '63 Ford	283	1,150	Engine
20	7	11	Ned Jarrett	Bondy Long '65 Ford	274	1,100	Engine
21	18	90	Sonny Hutchins	Junie Donlavey '64 Ford	244	1,125	Diff
22	4	7	Cale Yarborough	Banjo Matthews '65 Ford	232	1075	Crash
23	17	41	Jim Paschal	Toy Bolton '65 Chevrolet	211	1,125	Crash
24	9	26	Junior Johnson	Johnson '65 Ford	207	1,500	Engine
25	22	67	Buddy Arrington	Arrington '64 Dodge	187	1,000	Engine
26	43	70	Wendell Scott	Joe Bill Adams '64 Ford	179	950	Engine
27	27	63	Don Hume	Don House '63 Ford	146	950	Engine
28	33	19	J T Putney	Herman Beam '65 Chevrolet	142	1,000	Crash
29	11	49	G C Spencer	Spencer '64 Ford	121	925	Engine
30	10	76	Larry Frank	Frank '64 Ford	120	1,210	Ex Man
31	15	23	Buren Skeen	Reid Shaw '64 Ford	113	825	Crash
32	25	00	Tom Pistone	'64 Ford	94	900	Engine
33	3	21	Marvin Panch	Wood Bros '65 Ford	78	855	Crash
34	34	25	Jabe Thomas	Thomas '64 Ford	73	800	Crash
35	26	64	Elmo Langley	Langley '64 Ford	68	650	Clutch
36	39	62	Raymond Carter	Buddy Arrington '64 Dodge	58	600	Diff
37	21	49	Bunkie Blackburn	Sam Fletcher '65 Plymouth	53	625	Crank Sh
38	13	87	Buck Baker	Baker '65 Chevrolet	33	625	Engine
39	35	9	Roy Tyner	Tyner '64 Chevrolet	25	650	Tappett
40	31	13	Doug Cooper	Bob Cooper '65 Chevrolet	17	800	Drive Sh
41	8	3	Sam McQuagg	Betty Lilly '65 Ford	15	600	Crash
42	40	20	Clyde Lynn	Lynn '64 Ford	13	600	Crash
43	42	38	Wayne Smith	Smith '65 Chevrolet	9	600	Oil Pres
44	20	17	Junior Spencer	Jerry Mullins '64 Ford	9	625	Oil Leak

Time of Race: 4 hours, 55 minutes, 38 seconds
Average Speed: 121.722 mph
Pole Winner: Fred Lorenzen - 145.268 mph
Lap Leaders: Fred Lorenzen 1-16, Junior Johnson 17-24, Marvin Panch 25,
    Larry Frank 26-58, Lorenzen 59-81, Darel Dieringer 82-92, Lorenzen 93,
    Dieringer 94-105, Lorenzen 106, Dieringer 107-115, Lorenzen 116-127,
    Earl Balmer 128, Johnson 129-153, Lorenzen 154-182, Dieringer 183-192,
    Johnson 193-207, Balmer 208-210, Dieringer 211-212, Balmer 213-219,
    Dieringer 220-224, Lorenzen 225-272, Dieringer 273, Lorenzen 274-400.
Cautions: 11 for 80 laps   Margin of Victory: 6.4 seconds   Attendance: 50,000

Bub Strickler's Ford grinds to a halt on Charlotte's front chute

Lorenzen led for a total of 257 of the 400 laps. He and Darel Dieringer hooked up in a spine-tingling side-by-side duel which lasted nearly 10 laps. "I haven't dueled anybody like that since I ran with Richard Petty last year at Darlington," said Lorenzen.

Dieringer was knocked out of the race by a blown engine on lap 286.

Ray Fox entered a new 396 c.i. Chevrolet, but had problems getting the car past inspection. Charlotte Motor Speedway officials A.C.Goines and Richard Howard met with NASCAR President Bill France and convinced him that it was imperative that the Chevrolet compete in the 600.

LeeRoy Yarbrough, driver of the Fox car, started 44th and left the race on lap 309 with a blown engine.

Defending 600 champ Jim Paschal drove a Friedkin

Jabe Thomas' Ford leaps high in the air after running over loose wheel in World 600

Lorenzen broke away and cruised the final laps.

"The only time I was really scared was during the last few laps," confessed Lorenzen. "Here I was, out in front with victory just a few laps away. I started thinking and it scared me. I was afraid something would happen to my car -- like a tire blowing. There really wasn't any big reason to worry, and I shouldn't have been thinking anything like that."

Enterprises Chevy. He went 211 laps before blowing an engine.

Lorenzen averaged 121.722 mph as 80 laps were run under the yellow flag.

Ned Jarrett blew the engine in his Ford and lost the point lead to Hutcherson, who now leads by 608 points.

Race No. 20

Jarrett Wins Another Grand National Race by 22 Laps

SHELBY, NC (May 27) -- Ned Jarrett drove his Bondy Long Ford into the lead in the 176th lap and led the rest of the way to win the 100-miler at Cleveland County Fairgrounds. It was the fifth win of the season for the Newton, NC speedster.

Dick Hutcherson won the pole and led the first 175 laps. He was within 25 laps of winning his second race

of the season, but a broken axle sidelined his Holman-Moody Ford. Oddly, Hutcherson remained in second place for 22 laps as Jarrett motored on. All of the remaining cars were miles behind.

Bud Moore wound up in second place, 22 laps behind Jarrett. It was the second race of the year Jarrett had won by a 22-lap margin.

Hutcherson surprisingly took third place. He had already showered by the time the checkered flag fell. Doug Cooper came in fourth and Bob Derrington was fifth.

Twenty cars started the race and half of them were running at the finish. Dick Dixon was one driver still hanging in at the end although his Ford was 92 laps in arrears.

Jarrett averaged 63.909 mph for his 42nd career triumph.

Grand National Race No. 20
200 Laps at Cleveland County Fairgrounds
Shelby, NC
100 Miles on Half-mile Dirt Track
May 27, 1965

Fin	St	No.	Driver	Team / Car	Laps	Money	Status
1	3	11	Ned Jarrett	Bondy Long '65 Ford	200	$1,000	Running
2	8	45	Bud Moore	Louie Weathersby '65 Plym	178	600	Running
3	1	29	Dick Hutcherson	Holman-Moody '65 Ford	175	400	Axle
4	6	60	Doug Cooper	Bob Cooper '64 Ford	175	300	Running
5	12	68	Bob Derrington	Derrington '63 Ford	172	275	Running
6	16	86	Neil Castles	Buck Baker '65 Olds	172	240	Running
7	4	4	G C Spencer	Spencer '64 Ford	171	200	Diff
8	20	19	J T Putney	Herman Beam '65 Chevrolet	166	175	Running
9	10	52	E J Trivette	Jess Potter '63 Chevrolet	164	150	Running
10	13	97	Henley Gray	Gene Cline '64 Ford	159	140	Running
11	15	66	Larry Manning	Manning '63 Chevrolet	147	130	Running
12	5	27	Paul Lewis	Lewis '64 Ford	133	120	Heating
13	11	34	Wendell Scott	Scott '63 Ford	123	110	Heating
14	14	8	Dick Dixon	'63 Ford	108	100	Running
15	7	88	Buddy Baker	Buck Baker '64 Dodge	83	100	Axle
16	9	53	Jimmy Helms	David Warren '63 Ford	69	100	Trans
17	18	9	Roy Tyner	Tyner '63 Chevrolet	64	100	Engine
18	2	4	Ned Setzer	Toy Bolton '65 Chevrolet	63	100	Diff
19	17	87	Buck Baker	Baker '65 Chevrolet	41	100	Handling
20	19	78	Cale Yarborough	'63 Ford	12	100	Oil Pres

Time of Race: 1 hour, 33 minutes, 53 seconds
Average Speed: 63.909 mph
Pole Winner: Dick Hutcherson - 65.862 mph
Lap Leaders: Dick Hutcherson 1-175, Ned Jarrett 176-200
Cautions: Margin of Victory: 22 laps   Attendance:

Grand National Race No. 21
300 Laps at New Asheville Speedway
Asheville, NC
100 Miles on .333-mile Paved Track
May 29, 1965

Fin	St	No.	Driver	Team / Car	Laps	Money	Status
1	1	26	Junior Johnson	Johnson '65 Ford	300	$1,000	Running
2	2	11	Ned Jarrett	Bondy Long '65 Ford	296	600	Running
3	6	8	Dick Dixon	'63 Ford	284	400	Running
4	5	19	J T Putney	Herman Beam '65 Chevrolet	283	300	Running
5	8	39	Neil Castles	Buck Baker '65 Olds	278	275	Crash
6	16	9	Roy Tyner	Tyner '64 Chevrolet	276	246	Running
7	9	45	Bud Moore	Louie Weathersby '65 Plym	273	200	Running
8	10	75	Gene Black	C L Crawford '64 Ford	261	175	Running
9	11	52	E J Trivette	Jess Potter '63 Chevrolet	252	150	Running
10	15	97	Henley Gray	Gene Cline '64 Ford	249	140	Running
11	18	68	Bob Derrington	Derrington '63 Ford	246	130	Running
12	14	66	Larry Manning	Manning '63 Chevrolet	244	120	Wheel
13	13	53	Jimmy Helms	David Warren '63 Ford	233	110	Running
14	19	34	Wendell Scott	Scott '63 Ford	206	100	Running
15	17	00	Tom Pistone	'64 Ford	160	100	Trans
16	12	60	Doug Cooper	Bob Cooper '64 Ford	103	100	Crash
17	4	29	Dick Hutcherson	Holman-Moody '65 Ford	83	100	Diff
18	3	49	G C Spencer	Spencer '64 Ford	73	100	Engine
19	7	62	Buddy Arrington	Arrington '64 Dodge	52	100	Handling

Time of Race: 1 hour, 30 minutes 25 seconds
Average Speed: 66.293 mph
Pole Winner: Junior Johnson - 70.601 mph
Lap Leaders: Junior Johnson 1-300
Cautions: Margin of Victory: 2 laps-plus   Attendance:

Race No. 21

Johnson Outclasses Field In Asheville 100-Miler

ASHEVILLE, NC (May 29) -- Junior Johnson shoved his Ford into the lead at the drop of the green flag and was never headed as he won the 100-mile

Grand National race at the New Asheville Speedway. It was the eighth win of the year for Johnson.

The popular Wilkes County mountain man lapped the field by the 92nd lap and he was two laps up on runner-up Ned Jarrett when the checkered flag fell.

Dick Dixon, a newcomer from Connecticut, ran third in a two year old Ford. J.T. Putney came in fourth with Neil Castles fifth.

G.C. Spencer qualified a strong third, but left the race after 73 laps with a blown engine. Dick Hutcherson retired after 83 laps with differential problems. His point lead was cut to 336 over Jarrett.

Doug Cooper, who had painted his car green and placed the #13 on the doors for the World 600 only to experience an endless array of troubles, entered the car with a #60. The 1964 Rookie of the Year blew a tire and crashed after 104 laps. "Maybe the car didn't know that I took the #13 off the doors," muttered Cooper.

Johnson averaged 66.293 mph for his 45th career Grand National win.

Race No. 22

No Trouble For Jarrett In Harris 100

HARRIS, NC (May 30) -- Ned Jarrett took the lead from G.C. Spencer in the 24th lap and led the rest of the way to win the 100-miler at Harris Speedway. It was Jarrett's sixth win of the year.

Spencer, who started second and led the first 23 laps on the .3-mile paved oval, wound up second after running out of gas in the final two laps. He wound up four laps in arrears. Jarrett had lapped the field after 125 of the 334 laps and was never threatened after that.

Spencer and Dick Hutcherson engaged in a spirited duel for second place until Hutcherson dropped off the pace with mechanical woes. Dick Dixon finished third for the second race in a row. Hutcherson got fourth and J.T. Putney fifth.

Paul Lewis of Johnson City, TN earned the pole in his independent Ford. Lewis lasted only 16 laps before

Ned Jarrett

ignition problems put him out of the race.

Buddy Baker started third in his Dodge, but transmission problems ended his day after 60 laps.

Jarrett averaged 56.851 mph for his 43rd career win.

Grand National Race No. 22
334 Laps at Harris Speedway
Harris, NC
100 Miles on .3-Mile Paved Track
May 30, 1965

Fin	St	No.	Driver	Team / Car	Laps	Money	Status
1	5	11	Ned Jarrett	Bondy Long '65 Ford	334	$1,000	Running
2	2	49	G C Spencer	Spencer '64 Ford	330	600	Out Gas
3	17	8	Dick Dixon	'63 Ford	326	400	Running
4	4	29	Dick Hutcherson	Holman-Moody '65 Ford	325	300	Running
5	10	19	J T Putney	Herman Beam '65 Chevy	317	275	Running
6	14	60	Doug Cooper	Bob Cooper '64 Ford	315	240	Running
7	13	86	Neil Castles	Buck Baker '65 Plymouth	314	200	Running
8	20	9	Roy Tyner	Tyner '64 Chevrolet	300	175	Running
9	9	34	Wendell Scott	Scott '63 Ford	298	150	Running
10	12	97	Henley Gray	Gene Cline '64 Ford	295	140	Running
11	15	52	E J Trivette	Jess Potter '63 Chevrolet	293	130	Running
12	8	62	Buddy Arrington	Arrington '64 Dodge	289	120	Differen
13	16	75	Gene Black	C L Crawford '64 Ford	282	110	Running
14	11	53	Jimmy Helms	David Warren '63 Ford	260	100	Heating
15	18	66	Larry Manning	Manning '63 Chevrolet	90	100	Oil Pres
16	21	68	Bob Derrington	Derrington '63 Ford	63	100	Handling
17	3	88	Buddy Baker	Buck Baker '64 Dodge	60	100	Trans
18	7	45	Bud Moore	Louie Weathersby '65 Plym	22	100	Differen
19	1	27	Paul Lewis	Lewis '64 Ford	16	100	Ignition
20	22	00	Tom Pistone	'64 Ford	15	100	Engine
21	6	31	Cale Yarborough	Sam Fogle '63 Ford	10	100	Clutch
22	19	38	Wayne Smith	Smith '65 Chevrolet	7	100	Oil Pres

Time of Race: 1 hour, 45 minutes, 45 seconds
Average Speed: 56.851 mph
Pole Winner: Paul Lewis - 61.644 mph
Lap Leaders: G C Spencer 1-23, Ned Jarrett 24-334
Cautions: Margin of Victory: 4 laps plus   Attendance:

Race No. 23

Hutcherson Wins Nashville In Lone Factory Entry

NASHVILLE, TN (June 3) -- Dick Hutcherson of Keokuk, IA gunned his Ford into the lead at the outset and led all the way to win the 100-miler at the Nashville Fairgrounds Speedway. It was the second win of the season for the 33 year-old Ford driver.

Ned Jarrett's factory backed Bondy Long Ford was demolished in a highway accident en route to the track. The van which was towing the race car slid into a ditch during a violent thunderstorm between Harriman, TN and Crossville, TN. The van flipped on top of the racer, crushing it.

Jarrett was able to secure a Ford owned by Jabe

Grand National Race No. 23
200 Laps at Fairgrounds Speedway
Nashville, TN
100 Miles on Half-mile Paved Track
June 3, 1965

Fin	St	No.	Driver	Team / Car	Laps	Money	Status
1	2	29	Dick Hutcherson	Holman-Moody '65 Ford	200	$1,000	Running
2	4	25	Ned Jarrett	Jabe Thomas '64 Ford	199	600	Running
3	6	19	J T Putney	Herman Beach '65 Chevy	199	400	Running
4	5	34	Wendell Scott	Scott '63 Ford	196	300	Running
5	11	97	Henley Gray	Gene Cline '64 Ford	177	275	Running
6	9	60	Doug Cooper	Bob Cooper '64 Ford	176	240	Running
7	12	62	Raymond Carter	Buddy Arrington '64 Dodge	170	200	Running
8	3	49	G C Spencer	Spencer '64 Ford	128	275	No Tires
9	7	31	Cale Yarborough	Sam Fogle '63 Ford	78	150	D Shaft
10	13	17	Junior Spencer	Jerry Mullins '63 Ford	46	140	Clutch
11	10	68	Bob Derrington	Derrington '63 Ford	46	130	Clutch
12	1	00	Tom Pistone	'64 Ford	42	120	Engine
13	15	38	Wayne Smith	Smith '65 Chevrolet	12	110	Fender
14	14	89	Neil Castles	Buck Baker '65 Olds	5	100	Oil Pres
15	8	67	Buddy Arrington	Arrington '64 Dodge	1	100	Crash

Time of Race: 1 hour, 24 minutes 3 seconds
Average Speed: 71.386 mph
Pole Winner: Tom Pistone - 79.155 mph
Lap Leaders: Dick Hutcherson 1-200
Cautions: Margin of Victory: 1-lap plus   Attendance: 5,200

Ned Jarrett winging to victory at Birmingham

Thomas and finished second to Hutcherson, one lap off the pace. J.T. Putney came in third, Wendell Scott fourth and Henley Gray fifth.

Putney protested the finish, saying he had moved into second place when Jarrett slid high and grazed the wall with five laps to go. NASCAR officials said the caution flag came out for the Jarrett slide and that Putney had not made the pass until the yellow flag came out.

Putney had beaten Jarrett back to the caution flag, but there was no "racing back to the caution" rule in 1965.

Hutcherson averaged 71.386 mph as only seven cars finished out of a starting field of 15. A crowd of 5,200 was on hand to watch the first race ever staged at Nashville under the lights.

Race No. 24

Jarrett Captures Soggy Birmingham 100

BIRMINGHAM, AL (June 6) -- Ned Jarrett started from the pole and led all the way to win the rain-shortened 100-mile Grand National race at Birmingham International Raceway. The event was shortened to 108 laps (54 miles) by a rain storm described by local sports writer Clyde Bolton as a "junior typhoon".

Jarrett's Ford was 11 seconds in front of Dick Hutcherson when the squall hit. G.C. Spencer was flagged in third place. Tom Pistone came in fourth and Junior Spencer was fifth.

Rain had plagued the half mile paved track all day. Only a few cars qualified and Jarrett earned the pole with a speed of 71.575 mph. Hutcherson was forced to start 12th, having drawn that number out of a hat.

The first 33 laps were run under the caution flag.

Grand National Race No. 24
200 Laps at Birmingham Int'l Raceway
Birmingham, AL
"Birmingham 200"
100 Miles on Half-mile Paved Track
June 6, 1965

Fin	St	No.	Driver	Team / Car	Laps	Money	Status
1	1	11	Ned Jarrett	Bondy Long '65 Ford	108	$1,000	Running
2	12	29	Dick Hutcherson	Holman-Moody '65 Ford	108	600	Running
3	2	49	G C Spencer	Spencer '64 Ford	108	400	Running
4	16	00	Tom Pistone	'64 Ford	108	300	Running
5	4	17	Junior Spencer	Jerry Mullins '64 Ford	107	275	Running
6	9	31	Cale Yarborough	Sam Fogle '63 Ford	107	240	Running
7	5	09	Bobby Allison	'64 Ford	107	200	Running
8	8	67	Buddy Arrington	Arrington '64 Dodge	105	175	Running
9	6	62	Raymond Carter	Arrington '64 Dodge	104	150	Running
10	3	68	Bob Derrington	Derrington '63 Ford	102	140	Running
11	10	97	Henley Gray	Gene Cline '64 Ford	100	130	Running
12	11	60	Doug Cooper	Bob Cooper '64 Ford	98	120	Running
13	13	19	J T Putney	Herman Beam '64 Ford	88	110	Engine
14	15	34	Wendell Scott	Scott '63 Ford	75	100	Rear End
15	7	38	Wayne Smith	Smith '65 Chevrolet	49	100	Oil Leak
16	14	89	Neil Castles	Buck Baker '65 Olds	7	100	Rod

*Race Shortened to 108 laps due to rain

Time of Race: 57 minutes, 29 seconds
Average Speed: 56.364 mph
Pole Winner: Ned Jarrett - 71.575 mph
Lap Leaders: Ned Jarrett 1-108
Cautions: 1 for 33 laps   Margin of Victory: Red flag   Attendance:

When the green flag flew on lap 34, Jarrett stretched his advantage. Hutcherson sliced his way through the traffic and was running second by lap 65. Spencer started second and ran behind Jarrett until Hutcherson made the pass for runner-up honors.

On lap 108, Jarrett slowed suddenly as the rain hit the backstretch. He made it around to the front chute where the red flag was out. After an hour, officials declared it an official Grand National race.

Bobby Allison drove a Ford to a seventh place finish at his hometown track.

Race No. 25

Panch Outlasts Johnson For Dixie 400 Win

HAMPTON, GA (June 13) -- Marvin Panch, who admitted he thought about pulling out of the Dixie 400 "a half dozen times", came back and won his second straight race at the Atlanta International Raceway. It was Panch's 14th career win on the NASCAR Grand National tour.

Panch's Wood Brothers Ford was hampered by overheating problems but the Oakland, CA native was given a reprieve by eight caution flags which consumed 98 laps. "My car was running hot -- about 230 degrees -- but everytime it would reach the danger point, a caution would come out and the temperature would drop," said Panch. "With 60 miles to go, the Wood boys signaled me to turn it loose, so I did. We're lucky it made it to the finish."

Junior Johnson's Ford didn't quite make it to the end. After leading on seven occasions for 111 laps, Johnson's car blew an engine with just over three laps remaining. He was running second at the time, only a scant car length behind Panch.

Rookie Jesse Samples, 23 year-old youngster out of Atlanta, hit the oil deposited by Johnson's car and slid into the retaining wall. The car spun down and whacked the Pure Oil sign at the entrance to pit road. The car flipped over and straddled the pit wall. The Pure sign toppled and fire was spitting from the torn down electrical wires.

Samples was treated for cuts and bruises, but was otherwise uninjured.

Panch led Darel Dieringer across the finish line under caution. Third place went to Ned Jarrett while Johnson managed to come in fourth. Fifth place went to Buddy

Baker.

A crowd of 25,000 turned out in sunny weather to watch Chevrolet's big blast back into stock car racing. LeeRoy Yarbrough, manning the Ray Fox Chevy, started 12th but hustled up through the pack. The Jacksonville, FL driver swept past Dieringer in the 31st lap to take the lead. Yarbrough led for 36 laps before making a pit stop.

Grand National Race No. 25
267 Laps at Atlanta Int'l Raceway
Hampton, GA
"Dixie 400"
400 Miles on 1.5-mile Paved Track
June 13, 1965

Fin	St	No.	Driver	Team / Car	Laps	Money	Status
1	2	21	Marvin Panch	Wood Brothers '65 Ford	267	$12,300	Running
2	4	16	Darel Dieringer	Bud Moore '64 Mercury	267	6,770	Running
3	7	11	Ned Jarrett	Bondy Long '65 Ford	267	3,730	Running
4	8	26	Junior Johnson	Johnson '65 Ford	265	2,975	Engine
5	14	88	Buddy Baker	Buck Baker '64 Dodge	263	1,675	Running
6	13	49	G C Spencer	Spencer '64 Ford	261	1,225	Running
7	39	27	Paul Lewis	Lewis '64 Ford	260	1,100	Running
8	5	29	Dick Hutcherson	Holman-Moody '65 Ford	256	1,025	Running
9	29	34	Wendell Scott	Scott '63 Ford	254	925	Running
10	15	35	Buddy Arrington	Lester Hunter '64 Dodge	253	800	Running
11	40	67	Bill DeCosta	Arrington '64 Dodge	252	700	Running
12	27	03	Reb Wickersham	Ray Underwood '65 Ford	249	675	Engine
13	11	06	Cale Yarborough	Kenny Myler '64 Ford	249	655	Running
14	24	19	J T Putney	Herman Beam '65 Chevy	249	575	Running
15	30	60	Sam McQuagg	Bob Cooper '64 Ford	249	545	Running
16	28	46	Roy Mayne	Tom Hunter '65 Chevy	245	590	Running
17	26	68	Bob Derrington	Derrington '63 Ford	245	535	Running
18	17	44	Larry Hess	Hess '64 Ford	245	530	Running
19	22	52	E J Trivette	Jess Potter '63 Chevy	244	575	Running
20	35	62	Raymond Carter	Arrington '64 Dodge	243	520	Running
21	18	17	Jabe Thomas	Jerry Mullins '64 Ford	242	515	Running
22	41	25	Junior Spencer	Jabe Thomas '64 Ford	240	510	Running
23	1	28	Fred Lorenzen	Holman-Moody '65 Ford	214	855	Engine
24	36	75	Gene Black	C L Crawford '64 Ford	207	500	Running
25	33	96	Jesse Samples	'63 Chevrolet	198	495	Crash
26	10	7	Bobby Johns	Holman-Moody '65 Ford	190	590	Engine
27	6	76	Larry Frank	Frank '64 Ford	181	485	Crash
28	25	97	Henley Gray	Gene Cline '64 Ford	175	480	Differen
29	3	15	Earl Balmer	Bud Moore '64 Mercury	168	525	Crash
30	20	86	Neil Castles	Buck Baker '65 Plymouth	165	470	Engine
31	9	41	Jim Paschal	Friedkin Ent. '65 Chevy	140	465	S. Bar
32	38	87	Buck Baker	Baker '65 Chevrolet	127	460	Fuel pmp
33	16	74	Donald Tucker	Don Snyder '63 Ford	124	455	Gasket
34	12	3	LeeRoy Yarbrough	Ray Fox '65 Chevrolet	112	675	Engine
35	21	18	Stick Elliott	Toy Bolton '65 Chevrolet	112	520	Ball Jt.
36	23	56	Bill Morton	Curtis Larimer '64 Ford	97	465	Engine
37	37	9	Roy Tyner	Tyner '64 Chevrolet	79	435	Engine
38	42	09	Bobby Allison	'64 Ford	69	430	Engine
39	19	13	Doug Cooper	Bob Cooper '65 Chevrolet	31	425	Crash
40	31	00	Tom Pistone	'64 Ford	14	420	Engine
41	34	70	Fred Goad	Joe Bill Adams '64 Ford	7	415	Engine
42	32	38	Wayne Smith	Smith '65 Chevrolet	6	410	Clutch

Time of Race: 3 hours, 38 minutes, 13 seconds
Average Speed: 110.120 mph
Pole Winner: Fred Lorenzen - 143.407 mph
Lap Leaders: Marvin Panch 1-8, Junior Johnson 9-23, Bobby Johns 24, Darel Dieringer 25-30, LeeRoy Yarbrough 31-66, Johnson 67-73, Fred Lorenzen 74-99, Johnson 100-101, Johns 102-110, Johnson 111-122, Dieringer 123-167, Johnson 168-169, Johns 170, Johnson 171-198, Ned Jarrett 199-201, Johnson 202-246, Panch 247-267.
Cautions: 8 for 98 laps   Margin of Victory: Under caution   Attendance: 25,000

Yarbrough later fell out after 112 laps with a blown engine. Doug Cooper, in another '65 Chevy, crashed after 31 laps. He was driving a #13 and it was the second time in three races he had wrecked the car.

Fred Lorenzen won the pole but was never a factor. The engine in Lorenzen's Holman-Moody Ford blew after 214 laps, leaving him with a 23rd place finish.

Panch led only 29 laps -- the final 29. He averaged 110.120 mph.

Jarrett took a 202 point lead in the Grand National point standings. Former leader Dick Hutcherson struggled to finish eighth, losing 490 points to Jarrett.

Buddy Baker #88 finished 5th in Atlanta's Dixie 400 in '64 Dodge

Race No. 26

Hutch Handles Field at Greenville; Jarrett Hurt

GREENVILLE, SC (June 19) -- Dick Hutcherson took the lead when leader Bud Moore threw a wheel and coasted home first in the 100-mile Grand National race at Greenville-Pickens Speedway. Point leader Ned Jarrett was taken to the hospital with back and neck injuries after his car was crunched in the 67th lap.

Jarrett, who saw his point lead over Hutcherson sliced to just 10 points, had led the first 66 laps. On a restart following the day's first caution, Jarrett gunned his car -- but it suddenly lost power going into the first turn. The speeding pack plowed into his car countless times. Jarrett crawled out of the car and walked slowly to the pit area. A few minutes later, he collapsed. He was transported to Greenville General Hospital. Doctors said he suffered a severely bruised vertebra and a wrenched back.

"The caution came out on lap 60 and I went into the pits to get gas," said Jarrett, who spent four days in the hospital. "We later found out that water got in the fuel line, and it didn't get to the carburetor until the race restarted."

Moore took the lead when Jarrett was sidelined and padded his lead each turn of the half mile dirt track. With just 50 laps to go, the right front wheel came off his Louie Weathersby Plymouth and he was out of the race.

Hutcherson cruised into the lead and led the final 50

Grand National Race No. 26
200 Laps at Greenville-Pickens Speedway
Greenville, SC
100 Miles on Half-mile Dirt Track
June 19, 1965

Fin	St	No.	Driver	Team / Car	Laps	Money	Status
1	2	29	Dick Hutcherson	Holman-Moody '65 Ford	200	$1,000	Running
2	5	18	Stick Elliott	Toy Bolton '65 Chevrolet	197	600	Running
3	9	19	J T Putney	Herman Beam '65 Chevrolet	196	400	Running
4	15	9	Roy Tyner	Tyner '64 Chevrolet	190	300	Running
5	14	62	Buddy Arrington	Arrington '64 Dodge	188	275	Running
6	17	89	Neil Castles	Buck Baker '65 Olds	188	240	Running
7	11	34	Wendell Scott	Scott '64 Ford	180	200	Running
8	18	80	G T Nolan	Allen McMillion '64 Pontiac	169	175	Running
9	3	45	Bud Moore	Louie Weathersby '65 Plym	150	150	Spindle
10	19	68	Bob Derrington	Derrington '63 Ford	126	140	Running
11	4	31	Elmo Henderson	Sam Fogle '63 Ford	101	130	A Frame
12	8	38	Wayne Smith	Smith '65 Chevrolet	96	120	Fender
13	1	11	Ned Jarrett	Bondy Long '65 Ford	66	110	Crash
14	13	60	Doug Cooper	Bob Cooper '64 Ford	65	100	Crash
15	6	06	Cale Yarborough	Kenny Myler '64 Ford	62	100	Crash
16	20	35	Jeff Hawkins	Lester Hunter '64 Dodge	47	100	Heating
17	12	97	Henley Gray	Gene Cline '64 Ford	29	100	Differen
18	7	49	G C Spencer	Spencer '64 Ford	25	100	Differen
19	10	00	Tom Pistone	'64 Ford	14	100	Engine
20	16	52	E J Trivette	Jess Potter '63 Chevrolet	9	100	Brakes

Time of Race: 1 hour, 48 minutes, 33 seconds
Average Speed: 55.274 mph
Pole Winner: Ned Jarrett - 65.574 mph
Lap Leaders: Ned Jarrett 1-66, Bud Moore 67-150, Dick Hutcherson 151-200.
Cautions: 4   Margin of Victory: 3 laps-plus   Attendance:

laps, giving Ford its 24th straight Grand National win.

Stick Elliott finished second, three laps behind Hutcherson. J.T. Putney was third, Roy Tyner fourth and Buddy Arrington fifth.

Hutcherson averaged 55.274 mph for his third win of the year.

G.C. Spencer was fifth.

Spencer led the first three laps before Lund set sail. Hutcherson began closing the gap at the halfway point and made the final pass 81 laps from the finish.

Jarrett, who was released from the hospital the day before the race, drove while wearing a back brace. He suffered neck and back injuries in a pile-up at Greenville only five days earlier.

Buren Skeen, a Modified hot-shot out of Denton, NC, qualified seventh but crashed his Ford in the 133rd lap. He was not hurt.

Hutcherson averaged 59.701 mph for his second straight win.

Grand National Race No. 27
200 Laps at Rambi Raceway
Myrtle Beach, SC
100 Miles on Half-mile Dirt Track
June 24, 1965

Fin	St	No	Driver	Team / Car	Laps	Money	Status
1	1	29	Dick Hutcherson	Holman-Moody '65 Ford	200	$1,000	Running
2	22	11	Ned Jarrett	Bondy Long '65 Ford	200	600	Running
3	3	55	Tiny Lund	Lyle Stelter '64 Ford	195	400	Running
4	4	06	Cale Yarborough	Kenny Myler '64 Ford	193	300	Running
5	2	49	G C Spencer	Spencer '64 Ford	183	275	Ball Jt.
6	14	89	Neil Castles	Buck Baker '65 Olds	183	240	Running
7	13	68	Bob Derrington	Derrington '63 Ford	173	200	Running
8	12	52	E J Trivette	Jess Potter '63 Chevrolet	173	175	Running
9	20	53	Jimmy Helms	David Warren '63 Ford	166	150	Running
10	21	9	J T Putney	Roy Tyner '64 Chevrolet	161	140	Running
11	18	99	Gene Hobby	Hobby '64 Dodge	157	130	Differen
12	7	23	Buren Skeen	Reid Shaw '64 Ford	133	120	Crash
13	8	31	Doug Cooper	Sam Fogle '63 Ford	124	110	Wiring
14	11	97	Henley Gray	Gene Cline '64 Ford	95	100	Headers
15	9	64	Hop Holmes	'64 Ford	71	100	Engine
16	15	34	Wendell Scott	Scott '63 Ford	45	100	Engine
17	16	73	Arthur Page	'64 Ford	43	100	Heating
18	6	45	Bud Moore	Louie Weathersby '65 Plym	38	100	Steering
19	10	18	Stick Elliott	Toy Bolton '65 Chevrolet	15	100	Ball Jt.
20	5	00	Tom Pistone	'64 Ford	9	100	Heating
21	19	51	Jimmy Vaughn	'64 Dodge	8	100	Heating
22	17	88	Buddy Baker	Buck Baker '64 Dodge	4	100	Heating

Time of Race: 1 hour, 40 minutes, 30 seconds
Average Speed: 59.701 mph
Pole Winner: Dick Hutcherson - 66.421 mph
Lap Leaders: G C Spencer 1-3, Tiny Lund 4-119, Dick Hutcherson 120-200.
Cautions: Margin of Victory: Attendance:

Grand National Race No. 28
200 Laps at Valdosta 75 Speedway
Valdosta, GA
100 Miles on Half-mile Dirt Track
June 27, 1965

Fin	St	No.	Driver	Team / Car	Laps	Money	Status
1	5	06	Cale Yarborough	Kenny Myler '64 Ford	200	$1,000	Running
2	11	19	J T Putney	Herman Beam '64 Ford	197	600	Running
3	2	49	G C Spencer	Spencer '64 Ford	196	400	Engine
4	9	18	Stick Elliott	Toy Bolton '65 Chevrolet	196	300	Running
5	21	31	Harvey Jones	Sam Fogle '63 Ford	195	275	Running
6	14	52	E J Trivette	Jess Potter '63 Chevrolet	191	240	Running
7	15	9	Roy Tyner	Tyner '64 Ford	191	200	Running
8	13	89	Neil Castles	Buck Baker '65 Olds	189	175	Running
9	7	68	Bob Derrington	Derrington '63 Ford	184	150	Running
10	6	00	Tom Pistone	'64 Ford	175	140	Running
11	19	97	Henley Gray	Gene Cline '64 Ford	166	130	Running
12	1	29	Dick Hutcherson	Holman-Moody '65 Ford	161	120	Rear End
13	3	11	Ned Jarrett	Bondy Long '65 Ford	160	110	Running
14	16	99	Gene Hobby	Hobby '64 Dodge	133	100	Running
15	12	34	Wendell Scott	Scott '63 Ford	116	100	Differen
16	4	55	Tiny Lund	Lyle Stelter '64 Ford	85	100	Axle
17	8	88	Buddy Baker	Buck Baker '64 Dodge	15	100	Clutch
18	20	38	Wayne Smith	Smith '65 Chevrolet	12	100	Differen
19	18	87	Buck Baker	Baker '65 Chevrolet	3	100	Fuel Pmp
20	17	64	Elmer Gilliam	'64 Ford	1	100	Push Rod
21	10	53	Jimmy Helms	David Warren '63 Ford	1	100	Engine

Time of Race: 1 hour, 41 minutes, 56 seconds
Average Speed: 58.862 mph
Pole Winner: Dick Hutcherson - 64.54 mph
Lap Leaders: Dick Hutcherson 1-161, G C Spencer 162-182, Cale Yarborough 183-200.
Cautions: Margin of Victory: 3-laps plus   Attendance:

Race No. 27

Hutcherson Takes Point Lead With Myrtle Beach Win

MYRTLE BEACH, SC (June 24) -- Dick Hutcherson took the lead from Tiny Lund in the 120th lap and sped to victory in the 100-miler at Rambi Raceway. The Keokuk, IA driver took the Grand National point lead by a narrow six points over Ned Jarrett, who finished second after starting 22nd.

Third place went to Lund, who led for 116 laps in his Lyle Stelter Ford. Cale Yarborough finished fourth and

Race No. 28

Cale Yarborough Gets First GN Win in Valdosta 100

VALDOSTA, GA (June 27) -- Cale Yarborough, 24 year-old youngster out of Timmonsville, SC, inherited the lead with 18 laps to go and claimed his first Grand

National victory in the 100-miler at Valdosta 75 Speedway.

Yarborough, driving a Ford owned by Kenny Myler, started fifth and took a back seat to Dick Hutcherson and G.C. Spencer in the early going. Hutcherson, started on the pole but retired his Holman-Moody Ford behind pit wall after 161 laps with rear end trouble.

Cale Yarborough gets first Grand National victory

Spencer, driving his own year-old Ford, moved into the lead and appeared headed for his first Grand National win. However, a water hose broke, causing his car to overheat. Yarborough sailed into the lead and wound up three laps ahead of runner-up J.T. Putney. Spencer limped a few more circuits, finally departing with a blown engine. He still managed to get third place money based on the 196 laps he completed. Spencer was two laps ahead of Yarborough when the misfortune struck. "I don't reckon I'm ever going to win a Grand National race," said the dejected Spencer. "Something always happens to me."

Stick Elliott finished in fourth place and Harvey Jones fifth.

The race had been scheduled for the previous night, but rain stopped the action after 25 laps. Yarborough had been unable to get to the track, having been grounded by poor weather in a Charlotte airport. Sam McQuagg drove Yarborough's car when the race was originally started.

Curiously, race officials and sanctioning NASCAR decided to have a complete restart -- instead of picking up where they left off. Had officials picked up the race on lap 26 -- which is the customary procedure in rain interrupted events -- McQuagg would have gotten credit for the win since he started the car.

Yarborough averaged 58.862 mph. His first win came in his 78th Grand National start.

Race No. 29
Hemi Ban Lifted; Foyt Wins Firecracker 400 in Fleet Ford

DAYTONA BEACH, FL (July 4) -- A.J. Foyt's Ford, surviving a wreck-filled Firecracker 400, carried

Grand National Race No. 29
160 Laps at Daytona Int'l Speedway
Daytona Beach, FL
"Firecracker 400"
400 Miles on 2.5-mile Paved Track
July 4, 1965

Fin	St	No.	Driver	Team / Car	Laps	Money	Status
1	11	41	A J Foyt	Banjo Matthews '65 Ford	160	$8,500	Running
2	12	86	Buddy Baker	Buck Baker '65 Plymouth	160	5,400	Running
3	14	49	G C Spencer	Spencer '64 Ford	158	4,200	Running
4	28	19	J T Putney	Herman Beam '65 Chevrolet	153	2,525	Running
5	24	88	Neil Castles	Buck Baker '64 Dodge	152	1,725	Running
6	27	46	Roy Mayne	Tom Hunter '65 Chevrolet	152	1,525	Running
7	15	44	Larry Hess	Hess '64 Ford	151	1,300	Running
8	19	03	Reb Wickersham	Ray Underwood '65 Ford	151	1,200	Running
9	23	75	Gene Black	C L Crawford '64 Ford	149	1,175	Running
10	30	57	Lionel Johnson	Clay Esteridge '64 Ford	144	1,000	Running
11	38	55	Tiny Lund	Lyle Stelter '64 Ford	139	700	Running
12	1	21	Marvin Panch*	Wood Brothers '65 Ford	136	1,000	Heating
13	29	34	Wendell Scott	Scott '63 Ford	135	550	Running
14	32	53	Jimmy Helms	David Warren '63 Ford	131	530	Running
15	26	79	Frank Warren	Harold Rhodes '63 Ford	129	600	Out of gas
16	16	1	Paul Lewis	Lewis '64 Ford	125	520	Running
17	3	27	Cale Yarborough	Banjo Matthews '65 Ford	108	515	Engine
18	9	16	Darel Dieringer	Bud Moore '64 Mercury	108	510	Crash
19	6	29	Dick Hutcherson	Holman-Moody '65 Ford	108	505	Crash
20	5	11	Ned Jarrett	Bondy Long '65 Ford	108	500	Crash
21	22	64	Elmo Langley	Langley '64 Ford	99	495	Engine
22	18	17	Junior Spencer	Jerry Mullins '64 Ford	84	565	Axle
23	40	6	Bub Strickler	'64 Ford	84	485	Crash
24	10	14	Nelson Stacey	Sam Fletcher '65 Plymouth	83	480	Fuel pmp
25	21	09	Bobby Allison	'64 Ford	56	550	Heating
26	8	26	Junior Johnson	Johnson '65 Ford	51	470	Quit
27	35	25	Jabe Thomas	Thomas '64 Ford	51	465	Fuel pmp
28	2	15	Earl Balmer	Bud Moore '64 Ford	47	460	Engine
29	4	24	Sam McQuagg	Betty Lilly '65 Ford	34	455	Rock. Arm
30	33	52	E J Trivette	Jess Potter '63 Chevrolet	32	450	Engine
31	7	28	Fred Lorenzen	Holman-Moody '65 Ford	25	545	Engine
32	17	87	Buck Baker	Baker '65 Chevrolet	24	440	Push rod
33	13	33	Bunkie Blackburn	Ray Fox '65 Chevrolet	20	435	Clutch
34	37	3	LeeRoy Yarbrough	Ray Fox '65 Chevrolet	9	430	Clutch
35	39	68	Bob Derrington	Derrington '63 Ford	8	425	Oil leak
36	31	38	Wayne Smith	Smith '65 Chevrolet	5	420	Axle
37	36	02	Doug Cooper	Bob Cooper '65 Chevrolet	0	415	Oil Press
38	20	00	Tom Pistone	'64 Ford	0	410	Crash
39	25	97	Henley Gray	Gene Cline '64 Ford	0	405	Crash
40	34	89	Ken White	Buck Baker '65 Olds	0	400	Clutch

Time of race: 2 hours, 39 minutes, 57 seconds
Average Speed: 150.046 mph
Pole Winner: Marvin Panch - 171.510 mph
Lap Leaders: Earl Balmer 1-5, Marvin Panch 6, Fred Lorenzen 7, Cale Yarborough 8, Junior Johnson 9-10, Yarborough 11-14, A J Foyt 15-17, Johnson 18-22, Yarborough 23-39, Foyt 40-42, Yarborough 43-71, Darel Dieringer 72, Panch 73-81, Yarborough 82-93, Panch 94, Dieringer 95-99, Yarborough 100-108, Panch 109-136, Foyt 137-160.
Cautions: 3 for 20 laps   Margin of Victory: Attendance: 33,467
*Relieved by Fred Lorenzen

its driver to his second straight victory in the Independence day classic at Daytona International Speedway. It was the first win of the 1965 season for Foyt in any kind of automobile. He had spent 45 days recovering from injuries suffered in the season opening Riverside 500-miler in January.

A.J. took the lead for good in the 137th lap when leader Fred Lorenzen, driving in relief of Marvin Panch, blew a head gasket and overheated. Earlier, Cale Yarborough blew an engine, taking three contend-

A. J. Foyt talks with Glen Wood before the Firecracker 400

Race No. 30

Johnson Jumps Past Jarrett, Takes Manassas 400

MANASSAS, VA (July 8) -- Junior Johnson raced past Ned Jarrett in the fifth lap and led the rest of the way to win the 150-mile Grand National race at Old Dominion Speedway. It was the ninth win of the year for the 34 year-old Ronda, NC Ford driver.

Dick Hutcherson finished in second place in the 400 lapper on the .375-mile oval. Ned Jarrett came in third with Cale Yarborough fourth and Dick Dixon fifth.

Buddy Baker brought out the night's only caution period. In the 254th lap, Baker's Dodge blasted through the wooden guard rail and landed in the

ers on a wild slide in the first turn. Ned Jarrett, Dick Hutcherson and Darel Dieringer spun in the oil and all were knocked out of the race.

Foyt, manning the only factory Ford to finish -- seven had entered -- wound up almost a lap in front of Buddy Baker, who was driving a Plymouth equipped with a hemi engine. NASCAR announced that the ban on the hemi engine would be lifted as of the Firecracker 400. The factory Chrysler teams stayed on the sidelines, citing that the hemi is not suited for the heavy Fury. The smaller wheelbase Plymouth Belvedere is still ineligible on the superspeedways.

Third place went to G.C. Spencer with J.T. Putney finishing fourth and Neil Castles fifth.

A pair of Ray Fox Chevrolets were expected to challenge the Fords, but both were out of the race early. LeeRoy Yarbrough, Fox's principle driver, went out after nine laps with clutch trouble. Bunkie Blackburn suffered a similar fate after 20 laps.

Junior Johnson quit in disgust after a squabble with NASCAR officials on pit road. On lap 50, Johnson pitted under green. The bumper of his Herb Nab-prepared Ford was beyond his designated pit area. NASCAR officials ordered him to make another lap and complete his pit stop within the marked off area of his pit.

Johnson made another lap, but was pinched in by two cars which were not properly placed in their pit area. Johnson backed into Dick Hutcherson's car, which was being serviced behind him. The 220-pound Johnson dismounted in a huff and stomped off.

Johnson had made an improper pit stop at Darlington in May and survived a protest. Johnson had won that race but prevailed in a challenge by runner-up Darel Dieringer.

The lead changed hands 19 times among seven drivers. A crowd of 33,467 watched Foyt average 150.046 mph. Wrecks took out six cars.

Grand National Race No. 30
400 Laps at Old Dominion Speedway
Manassas, VA
150 Miles on .375-mile Paved Track
July 8, 1965

Fin	St	No.	Driver	Team / Car	Laps	Money	Status
1	2	26	Junior Johnson	Johnson '65 Ford	400	$1,100	Running
2	3	29	Dick Hutcherson	Holman-Moody '65 Ford	400	625	Running
3	1	11	Ned Jarrett	Bondy Long '65 Ford	398	450	Running
4	6	06	Cale Yarborough	Kenny Myler '64 Ford	393	350	Running
5	8	8	Dick Dixon	'63 Ford	388	325	Running
6	9	64	Elmo Langley	Langley '64 Ford	385	290	Running
7	7	49	G C Spencer	Spencer '64 Ford	383	250	Running
8	13	31	Bud Moore	Sam Fogle '63 Ford	376	225	Running
9	11	87	Buck Baker	Baker '65 Chevrolet	371	200	Running
10	10	20	Clyde Lynn	Lynn '64 Ford	369	190	Running
11	16	89	Neil Castles	Buck Baker '65 Olds	367	180	Running
12	4	90	Sonny Hutchins	Junie Donlavey '64 Ford	365	170	Flagged
13	24	57	Lionel Johnson	Clay Esteridge '64 Ford	360	160	Running
14	15	53	Jimmy Helms	David Warren '63 Ford	354	150	Running
15	14	68	Bob Derrington	Derrington '63 Ford	354	135	Running
16	22	80	Worth McMillion	Allen McMillion '64 Pontiac	345	125	Running
17	20	60	Bob Cooper	Cooper '64 Ford	284	115	Flagged
18	17	99	Gene Hobby	Hobby '64 Dodge	231	110	Crash
19	21	52	E J Trivette	Jess Potter '63 Chevrolet	215	100	Differen
20	19	38	Wayne Smith	Smith '65 Chevrolet	213	100	Running
21	18	34	Wendell Scott	Scott '63 Ford	206	100	Engine
22	5	88	Buddy Baker	Buck Baker '64 Dodge	150	100	Crash
23	23	97	Henley Gray	Gene Cline '64 Ford	139	---	Crash
24	12	37	Darel Dieringer	Bub Strickler '64 Ford	38	---	RR Hub

Time of Race: 2 hours, 12 minutes, 2 seconds
Average Speed: 68.165 mph
Pole Winner: Ned Jarrett - 73.569 mph
Lap Leaders: Ned Jarrett 1-4, Junior Johnson 5-400.
Cautions: 1 for 8 laps   Margin of Victory: Attendance: 2,600

adjacent wooded area. He was unhurt.

A slim crowd of 2,600 showed up for the Thursday evening program. The race had been rained out from the night before.

Gene Hobby, who survived a terrible tumble at Hillsboro, NC in March, wrecked his Dodge in the 239th lap.

Johnson averaged 68.165 mph for his 46th career Grand National win.

Grand National Race No. 31
200 Laps at Old Bridge Stadium
Old Bridge, NJ
"Old Bridge 200"
100 Miles on Half-mile Paved Track
July 9, 1965

Fin	St	No.	Driver	Team / Car	Laps	Money	Status
1	2	26	Junior Johnson	Johnson '65 Ford	200	$1,000	Running
2	3	29	Dick Hutcherson	Holman-Moody '65 Ford	199	600	Running
3	1	21	Marvin Panch	Wood Brothers '65 Ford	199	400	Running
4	5	16	Darel Dieringer	Bud Moore ' 64 Mercury	198	300	Running
5	4	11	Ned Jarrett	Bondy Long '65 Ford	198	275	Running
6	6	8	Dick Dixon	'64 Ford	197	240	Running
7	9	55	Tiny Lund	Lyle Stelter '64 Ford	196	200	Running
8	19	88	Buddy Baker	Buck Baker ' 64 Dodge	191	175	Running
9	10	60	Bob Cooper	Cooper '64 Ford	188	150	Running
10	11	20	Clyde Lynn	Lynn '64 Ford	187	140	Running
11	18	89	Neil Castles	Buck Baker '65 Olds	186	130	Running
12	17	3	Al White	'64 Ford	184	120	Running
13	16	80	Worth McMillion	Allen McMillion '64 Pontiac	174	110	Running
14	15	99	Gene Hobby	Hobby '64 Dodge	158	100	Running
15	13	52	E J Trivette	Jess Potter '63 Chevrolet	144	100	Trans
16	7	49	G C Spencer	Spencer '64 Ford	133	100	Wtr. pmp
17	8	64	Elmo Langley	Langley '64 Ford	91	100	Trans
18	12	39	Bob Vaughn	Ronald Smith '64 Pontiac	50	100	Engine
19	20	53	Jimmy Helms	David Warren '63 Ford	30	100	H Gasket
20	14	31	Cale Yarborough	Sam Fogle '63 Ford	18	100	Engine

Time of Race: 1 hour, 23 minutes, 14 seconds
Average Speed: 72.087 mph
Lap Leaders: Marvin Panch 1-7, Junior Johnson 8-36, G C Spencer 37-59, Panch 60-141, Johnson 142-200.
Pole Winner: Marvin Panch - 77.286 mph
Cautions: for 16 laps   Margin of Victory: Attendance:

Race No. 31

Johnson's 10th Comes At Old Bridge; Eyes Record

OLD BRIDGE, NJ (July 9) -- Junior Johnson passed Marvin Panch with 59 laps remaining and registered a one lap victory in the Old Bridge 200 at Old Bridge Speedway. Johnson's 10th win in 21 starts for the

Grand National Race No. 32
250 Laps at Islip Speedway
Islip, NY
50 Miles on .2-mile Paved Track
July 14, 1965

Fin	St	No.	Driver	Team / Car	Laps	Money	Status
1	1	21	Marvin Panch	Wood Brothers '65 Ford	250	$1,000	Running
2	4	29	Dick Hutcherson	Holman-Moody '65 Ford	249	600	Running
3	6	11	Ned Jarrett	Bondy Long '65 Ford	246	400	Running
4	7	06	Cale Yarborough	Kenny Myler '64 Ford	245	300	Running
5	8	8	Dick Dixon	'64 Ford	242	275	Running
6	2	55	Tiny Lund	Lyle Stelter '64 Ford	242	240	Running
7	14	34	Wendell Scott	Scott '63 Ford	235	200	Running
8	19	31	J T Putney	Sam Fogle '63 Ford	233	175	Running
9	17	89	Neil Castles	Buck Baker '65 Olds	233	150	Running
10	11	68	Bob Derrington	Derrington '63 Ford	225	140	Running
11	20	52	E J Trivette	Jess Potter '63 Chevrolet	224	130	Running
12	10	60	Bob Cooper	Cooper '64 Ford	202	210	Differen
13	3	49	G C Spencer	Spencer '64 Ford	115	110	Differen
14	5	26	Junior Johnson	Johnson '65 Ford	112	100	Crash
15	9	88	Buck Baker	Baker '64 Dodge	72	100	Trans
16	18	39	Bob Vaughn	Ronald Smith '64 Pontiac	49	100	Fuel pmp
17	15	64	Buddy Baker	Elmo Langley '64 Ford	48	100	Trans
18	13	00	Tom Pistone	'64 Ford	44	100	Heating
19	16	53	Jimmy Helms	David Warren '63 Ford	33	100	Brakes
20	22	3	Al White	'64 Ford	30	100	Clutch
21	12	20	Clyde Lynn	Lynn '64 Ford	27	100	Engine
22	21	99	Gene Hobby	Hobby '64 Dodge	9	100	Wheel

Time of Race: 1 hour, 8 minutes, 26 seconds
Average Speed: 43.838 mph
Pole Winner: Marvin Panch - 51.246 mph
Lap Leaders: Marvin Panch 1-250.
Cautions: Margin of Victory: 1-lap plus   Attendance:

1965 season has put him within striking distance of Tim Flock's all time NASCAR record of 18 Grand National victories in a single season.

"I hadn't really thought about the record," said Johnson. "It would be nice to beat it, but that's not our goal. We're just picking races and trying to win as many as we can."

Dick Hutcherson finished second and boosted his point lead to 108 points over Ned Jarrett, who finished fifth. Panch came in third with Darel Dieringer fourth.

Panch won the pole and led the first seven laps. Johnson led for 29 laps on the half-mile paved track before G. C. Spencer took over on lap 37. Spencer, the veteran out of Johnson City, TN who has been giving a good account of himself in tired, worn out equipment, led for 23 laps before Panch went back in front.

Panch dominated until lap 141 when Johnson made the final pass.

Spencer retired with water pump failure in the 133rd lap.

Johnson averaged 72.087 mph for his 47th career win, only seven shy of Lee Petty's career mark of 54 Grand National wins.

Race No. 32

Panch Takes Islip; Johnson Survives Fiery Wreck

ISLIP, NY (July 14) -- Marvin Panch breezed to an easy win at Islip Speedway when Junior Johnson was eliminated in a fiery wreck. It was Panch's third victory of the 1965 season.

Johnson had moved in to challenge Panch for first place in the 112th lap of the 250-lapper of the .2-mile paved oval. As Johnson tried to make a pass down the backstretch, the throttle hung open on his Ford and he plowed through the steel guard rail. His car bounced into a telephone pole and landed on its wheels in flame. Johnson scrambled out. He was treated for a knot on his elbow at a trackside first aid station.

Panch went unchallenged the rest of the way finishing a lap ahead of runner-up Dick Hutcherson. It was Hutcherson's third straight second place finish. Ned Jarrett was third, Cale Yarborough fourth and Dick Dixon fifth.

Wendell Scott had a rough afternoon, spinning out three times on the tight track. The Danville, VA Ford driver still managed to wind up seventh in the field of 22.

Panch averaged 43.838 mph for his 15th career Grand National win.

Race No. 33

Panch Perfect in Watkins Glen 151.8-Miler

WATKINS GLEN, NY (July 18) -- Marvin Panch pushed his Wood Brothers Ford around Junior Johnson's disabled Ford in the 14th lap and went unchallenged the rest of the way in the 151.8-mile Grand National race at Watkins Glen Raceway. It was the fourth victory of the season for the 39 year-old veteran.

Ned Jarrett, in second place, finished nearly a lap behind the fleet Panch. Buddy Baker, admittedly lacking in road racing artistry, ran well and took third spot. Cale Yarborough was fourth and Tiny Lund fifth.

Jarrett led the first lap, but Johnson took over the second time around on the 2.3-mile road course. Johnson was steadily pulling away when the engine blew in his butter-colored Ford on lap 13. Panch grabbed the lead at that point and was never pressured.

Grand National Race No.33
66 Laps at Watkins Glen Raceway
Watkins Glen, NY
151.8 Miles on 2.3-mile Paved Road Course
July 18, 1965

Fin	St	No.	Driver	Team / Car	Laps	Money	Status
1	3	21	Marvin Panch	Wood Brothers '65 Ford	66	$1,425	Running
2	2	11	Ned Jarrett	Bondy Long '65 Ford	66	650	Running
3	5	88	Buddy Baker	Buck Baker '64 Dodge	64	490	Running
4	8	06	Cale Yarborough	Kenny Myler '64 Ford	63	415	Running
5	10	55	Tiny Lund	Lyle Stelter '64 Ford	58	385	Running
6	17	46	Walt Hansgen	'64 Ford	58	355	Running
7	13	64	Elmo Langley	Langley '64 Ford	56	300	Running
8	19	3	Al White	'64 Ford	54	225	Running
9	4	89	Neil Castles	Buck Baker '65 Olds	54	240	Running
10	7	68	Bob Derrington	Derrington '63 Ford	54	235	Running
11	12	53	Jimmy Helms	David Warren '63 Ford	50	225	Oil Pres
12	1	29	Dick Hutcherson	Holman-Moody '65 Ford	42	220	Running
13	14	00	Tom Pistone	'64 Ford	34	205	Engine
14	9	34	Wendell Scott	Scott '63 Ford	27	150	Engine
15	6	26	Junior Johnson	Johnson '65 Ford	13	175	Engine
16	18	31	Bob Grossman	Sam Fogle '63 Ford	13	175	Differen
17	16	20	J T Putney	Clyde Lynn '64 Ford	7	175	Engine
18	15	99	Gene Hobby	Hobby '64 Dodge	1	175	Handling
19	11	52	E J Trivette	Jess Potter '63 Chevrolet	0	175	Crash

Time of Race: 1 hour, 32 minutes, 46 seconds
Average Speed: 98.182 mph
Pole Winner: No Time trials
Lap Leaders: Ned Jarrett 1, Junior Johnson 2-13, Marvin Panch 14-66.
Cautions: None   Margin of Victory: Attendance:

Doug Cooper of Gastonia, NC was injured when his Ford left the track and flipped six times in a practice session the day before the race. Cooper's Ford was demolished and the driver suffered a brain concussion, back and arm injuries. He was listed in 'fair' condition at Schuyler Memorial Hospital in Montour Falls, NY.

Panch averaged 98.182 mph for his second road racing victory. His last Grand National win on a road course came on November 11, 1956 at Lancaster, CA.

Race No. 34

Jarrett Wins Volunteer 500; Regains Point Lead

BRISTOL, TN (July 25) -- Ned Jarrett survived the rain and the wrecks to win the Volunteer 500 at Bristol International Speedway. It was the eighth win of the season for the 32 year-old Newton, NC Ford driver, putting him back on top of the Grand National point standings.

Grand National Race No. 34
500 Laps at Bristol Int'l Speedway
Bristol, TN
"Volunteer 500"
250 Miles on Half-mile Paved Track
July 25, 1965

Fin	St	No.	Driver	Team / Car	Laps	Money	Status
1	6	11	Ned Jarrett	Bondy Long '65 Ford	500	$4,315	Running
2	9	29	Dick Hutcherson	Holman-Moody '65 Ford	500	2,275	Running
3	8	24	Sam McQuagg	Betty Lilly '65 Ford	494	1,650	Running
4	15	41	Jim Paschal	Friedkin Ent. '65 Chevrolet	494	1,125	Running
5	16	87	Buck Baker	Baker '65 Chevrolet	484	1,025	Running
6	20	17	Junior Spencer	Jerry Mullins '64 Ford	483	800	Running
7	26	34	Wendell Scott	Scott '63 Ford	479	800	Running
8	28	74	Donald Tucker	Don Snyder '63 Ford	476	675	Running
9	32	68	Bob Derrington	Derrington '63 Ford	471	575	Running
10	14	19	J T Putney	Herman Beam '64 Ford	470	540	Running
11	31	75	Gene Black	C L Crawford '64 Ford	461	475	Running
12	24	67	Buddy Arrington	Arrington '64 Dodge	444	400	Running
13	36	80	Worth McMillion	Allen McMillion '64 Pontiac	429	350	Running
14	10	16	Darel Dieringer	Bud Moore '64 Mercury	400	535	Engine
15	21	03	Reb Wickersham	Ray Underwood '65 Ford	395	260	Engine
16	7	1	Paul Lewis	Lewis '64 Ford	346	260	Engine
17	2	43	Richard Petty	Petty Engineering '64 Plym	338	560	Differen
18	25	40	Bud Harless	Basil Whittaker '64 Pontiac	320	360	Engine
19	11	49	G C Spencer	Spencer '64 Ford	201	260	Gas tank
20	1	28	Fred Lorenzen	Holman-Moody '65 Ford	188	635	Handling
21	22	56	Neil Castles	Curtis Larimer '64 Ford	186	260	D. Shaft
22	4	27	Cale Yarborough	Banjo Matthews '65 Ford	183	285	Engine
23	3	26	Junior Johnson	Johnson '65 Ford	155	385	Crash
24	13	55	Tiny Lund	Lyle Stelter '64 Ford	153	320	Engine
25	23	18	Stick Elliott	Toy Bolton '65 Chevrolet	150	250	Engine
26	19	23	Buren Skeen	Reid Shaw '64 Ford	106	250	Engine
27	33	57	Lionel Johnson	Clay Esteridge '64 Ford	96	275	Differen
28	34	97	E J Trivette	Gene Cline '64 Ford	72	275	Crash
29	35	53	Jimmy Helms	David Warren '63 Ford	72	250	Crash
30	17	88	Buddy Baker	Buck Baker '64 Dodge	61	275	Wtr. Hose
31	27	25	Jabe Thomas	Thomas '64 Ford	43	285	Crash
32	18	09	Bobby Allison	'64 Ford	39	250	Heating
33	30	64	Elmo Langley	Langley '64 Ford	33	275	H. Gasket
34	29	62	Raymond Carter	Buddy Arrington '64 Dodge	32	275	Vibration
35	5	21	Marvin Panch	Wood Brothers '65 Ford	8	275	Crash
36	12	6	David Pearson	Cotton Owens '65 Dodge	8	250	Crash

Time of Race: 4 hours, 2 minutes, 37 seconds
Average Speed: 61.826 mph
Pole Winner: Fred Lorenzen - 84.348
Lap Leaders: Junior Johnson 1-81, Fred Lorenzen 82-83, Ned Jarrett 84-88,
    Darel Dieringer 89-133, Johnson 134-155, Dieringer 156-309, Jarrett 310-345,
    Dieringer 346-400, Jarrett 401-500.
Cautions: 8 for 167 laps.   Margin of Victory: 20 seconds   Attendance: 27,750

fifth place when the cars fused together, sending both hard into the third turn retaining barrier. Both drivers were shaken and bruised, but unhurt.

Pearson was walking back to the pits when he met Glen Wood, owner of the car Panch was driving. An argument occurred, spiced with plenty of arm-waving. As the argument grew more heated, Wood took a swing at Pearson. Pearson ducked and cocked his arm, but others intervened and led Pearson off in the other direction.

Richard Petty, who made his return at Bristol, signs autographs for fans

Richard Petty's Plymouth never led, but he offered stout challenges. At the 338 lap mark, Petty pulled his car into the pits with differential problems. A few laps earlier, he had been involved in a five car melee when Tiny Lund's blown engine sent a pack of cars spinning. J.T. Putney's Chevrolet delivered a solid shot into Petty's rear bumper.

Jarrett moved into a 28 point lead over Hutcherson in the race for the NASCAR title. Jarrett, winner of the championship in 1961, almost didn't make it to the end of the race. "I was sick to my stomach," Jarrett said afterwards. "The fumes got so bad in the car that it actually made me sick. I decided I'd just keep on going as long as I could. I said a little prayer with about 100 laps to go. This race seemed like forever."

With all the caution flags (8) and red flags (4), it took nearly six hours to complete the 500 laps.

Other drivers taken out by crashes were Junior Johnson, Jabe Thomas, E.J.Trivette and Jimmy Helms. Jarrett averaged 61.826 mph as Ford notched its 32nd consecutive Grand National triumph.

Crashes and periods of rain forced eight caution flags which consumed 167 laps of the 500 lap event. Jarrett took the lead for keeps on lap 401 when leader Darel Dieringer lost the engine in his Mercury.

Dick Hutcherson crowded Jarrett in the closing stages, finishing 20 seconds behind before 27,750 spectators. Sam McQuagg, rookie out of Columbus, GA, wound up third. Jim Paschal was fourth in his new Chevy and Buck Baker was fifth.

The 250-miler marked a return for Chrysler factory cars in NASCAR racing. David Pearson, driving Cotton Owens' Dodge, started 12th but whipped through the field early. He was challenging Marvin Panch for

Race No. 35

Petty Outlasts Johnson; Wins Nashville 400 by 6 Laps

NASHVILLE, TN (July 31) -- Richard Petty took the lead with 49 laps remaining when Junior Johnson lost an engine and won the Nashville 400 in a runaway. It was Petty's second start of the 1965 Grand National season and his 37th career victory.

A wall-to-wall crowd of 14,343

Richard won first '65 race at Nashville

turned out for the second Ford-Chrysler battle of the much troubled 1965 season. Johnson took command on lap 287 and led until his Ford erupted in a cloud of smoke on lap 351. Petty's blue Plymouth Belvedere equipped with a hemi engine, rolled into the lead and never looked back.

Ned Jarrett finished second and Buddy Arrington third. J.T. Putney and G.C. Spencer rounded out the top five.

Dick Hutcherson wound up 15th in the 24 car field, falling victim to engine problems after 158 laps. He fell 288 points behind Jarrett in the battle for the Grand National title.

The 28 year-old Petty averaged 72.383 mph as he ended Ford's 32 race win streak. "I'm worn out," said an exhausted Petty. "That's the first time I've run that long in a long time. I'm about give out."

Richard was so pooped that he didn't kiss Sally Harrison, Miss Nashville Speedway. "I wasn't able to," he said. "I figured if I couldn't do it right, I'd rather not do it at all."

In another development, NASCAR President Bill France reinstated Curtis Turner after a four year suspension. Turner had been involved in a 1961 effort to organize the drivers into a Teamsters affiliated union.

Grand National Race No. 35
400 Laps at Fairgrounds Speedway
Nashville, TN
"Nashville 400"
200 Miles on Half-mile Paved Track
July 31, 1965

Fin	St	No.	Driver	Team / Car	Laps	Money	Status
1	1	43	Richard Petty	Petty Engineering '65 Plym	400	$2,350	Running
2	3	11	Ned Jarrett	Bondy Long '65 Ford	394	1,100	Running
3	13	67	Buddy Arrington	Arrington '64 Dodge	382	750	Running
4	11	19	J T Putney	Herman Beam ' 65 Chevrolet	381	500	Running
5	4	49	G C Spencer	Spencer '64 Ford	374	475	Running
6	21	89	Neil Castles	Buck Baker '65 Olds	356	450	Running
7	14	68	Bob Derrington	Derrington '63 Ford	356	425	Running
8	2	26	Junior Johnson	Johnson '65 Ford	351	375	Engine
9	17	75	Gene Black	C L Crawford '64 Ford	333	325	Running
10	19	53	Jimmy Helms	David Warren '63 Ford	323	300	Flat tire
11	15	52	E J Trivette	Jess Potter '63 Chevrolet	301	270	Running
12	18	97	Henley Gray	Gene Cline '64 Ford	281	240	Running
13	10	34	Wendell Scott	Scott '63 Ford	272	220	Fan belt
14	6	1	Paul Lewis	Lewis '64 Ford	194	200	Engine
15	5	29	Dick Hutcherson	Holman-Moody '65 Ford	158	170	Engine
16	12	64	Elmo Langley	Langley '64 Ford	138	150	Engine
17	9	17	Junior Spencer	Jerry Mullins '64 Ford	91	130	Crash
18	16	38	Wayne Smith	Smith '65 Chevrolet	60	120	Fan belt
19	7	88	Buddy Baker	Buck Baker '64 Dodge	28	100	Differen
20	22	59	Tom Pistone	'64 Ford	28	100	Crash
21	20	9	Roy Tyner	Tyner '65 Chevrolet	23	100	Differen
22	8	87	Buck Baker	Baker '65 Chevrolet	20	100	Oil Pan
23	24	23	Boyd Adams	'63 Ford	15	100	Gas Tank
24	23	62	Raymond Carter	Buddy Arrington '64 Dodge	2	100	Ball Jt.

Time of Race: 2 hours, 45 minutes, 47 seconds
Average Speed: 72.383 mph
Pole Winner: Richard Petty - 82.117 mph
Lap Leaders: Richard Petty 1-286, Junior Johnson 287-351, Petty 352-400.
Cautions: 1 for 13 laps   Margin of Victory: 6-laps plus   Attendance: 14,343

Race No. 36

Pearson Falters; Jarrett Grabs Win at Shelby Fairgrounds

SHELBY, NC (Aug. 5) -- Ned Jarrett took the lead in the 127th lap when David Pearson made a long pit stop and outran the field by four laps to win the 100-miler at Cleveland County Fairgrounds. It was his ninth win of the year.

Pearson started on the pole and led the first 126 laps. The Spartanburg, SC Dodge driver made a routine pit stop, but his car stalled. By the time his Cotton Owens crew got him restarted, he was a lap and a half off the pace.

Pearson drove relentlessly and dramatically made up the deficit. He had moved to within 3.5-seconds of leader Jarrett when the left front wheel collapsed with 16 laps to go.

Jarrett breezed home four laps ahead of runner-up Richard Petty. Dick Hutcherson was third, 11 laps off the pace. Neil Castles was fourth in a Buck Baker Oldsmobile, a vehicle in which Baker termed a "buffalo" earlier in the year. Pearson's 184 laps completed was good enough for fifth place.

A crowd of 6,000 showed up, but only 14 cars were

on the starting grid. Jarrett averaged 64.748 mph as nine cars finished the 200 lapper on the half-mile dirt track.

Jarrett drove a brand new Ford -- only out of the shop three hours at race time.

Richard Petty won Western North Carolina 500 in an unpainted, unnumbered Plymouth

Grand National Race No. 36
200 Laps at Cleveland County Fairgrounds
Shelby, NC
100 Miles on Half-Mile Dirt Track
August 5, 1965

Fin	St	No.	Driver	Team / Car	Laps	Money	Status
1	3	11	Ned Jarrett	Bondy Long '65 Ford	200	$1,000	Running
2	4	43	Richard Petty	Petty Engineering '64 Plym	196	600	Running
3	2	29	Dick Hutcherson	Holman-Moody '65 Ford	189	400	Running
4	9	89	Neil Castles	Buck Baker '65 Olds	185	300	Running
5	1	6	David Pearson	Cotton Owens '65 Dodge	184	275	Ball Jt.
6	7	68	Bob Derrington	Derrington '63 Ford	180	240	Running
7	6	53	Jimmy Helms	David Warren '63 Ford	176	200	Running
8	10	20	Clyde Lynn	Lynn '64 Ford	170	175	Running
9	11	97	Henley Gray	Gene Cline '64 Ford	165	150	Running
10	13	75	G C Spencer	Spencer '64 Ford	162	140	Running
11	8	34	Wendell Scott	Scott '63 Ford	146	130	Axle
12	14	51	Jimmy Vaughn	'64 Dodge	50	120	Oil Pan
13	12	38	J T Putney	Wayne Smith '65 Chevrolet	15	110	Clutch
14	5	18	Stick Elliott	Toy Bolton '65 Chevrolet	14	100	Rear End

Time of Race: 1 hour, 32 minutes, 40 seconds
Average Speed: 64.748 mph
Pole Winner: David Pearson - 67.797 mph
Lap Leaders: David Pearson 1-126, Ned Jarrett 127-200.
Cautions: 2 for 5 laps   Margin of Victory: 4-laps plus   Attendance: 6,000

Race No. 37

Johnson Wrecks Again; Petty Picks Western N.C. Prize

WEAVERVILLE, NC (Aug. 8) -- Richard Petty led 305 of the final 306 laps and cruised to a two lap victory in the Western North Carolina 500 at Asheville-Weaverville Speedway. It was Petty's second win in four starts since returning to the NASCAR Grand National circuit.

Junior Johnson was leading once again when a tire blew, sending his Ford into the concrete retaining wall on lap 194. It was the fifth straight race Johnson has failed to finish -- and he crashed in three of them.

Ned Jarrett finished second, Dick Hutcherson third, Buddy Baker fourth, and Cale Yarborough fifth.

David Pearson's Dodge led twice for 89 laps, but he went out after 398 laps with a broken axle. "As soon as Pearson went out, I slowed up," said Petty. "I knew I

had a couple of laps on the others, so I backed off and paced myself the rest of the way."

Jarrett crept to a 350 point lead in the Grand National point standings.

Five cautions and a rain shower held Petty's average speed to 74.343 mph. It was his 38th career win on the stock car major league tour.

Grand National Race No. 37
500 Laps at Asheville-Weaverville Speedway
Weaverville, NC
"Western North Carolina 500"
250 Miles on Half-mile Paved Track
August 8, 1965

Fin	St	No.	Driver	Team / Car	Laps	Money	Status
1	1	43	Richard Petty	Petty Engineering '65 Plym	500	$3,200	Running
2	2	11	Ned Jarrett	Bondy Long '65 Ford	498	1,650	Running
3	5	29	Dick Hutcherson	Holman-Moody '65 Ford	495	1,200	Running
4	9	88	Buddy Baker	Buck Baker '64 Dodge	488	900	Running
5	13	06	Cale Yarborough	Kenny Myler '64 Ford	487	800	Running
6	8	87	Buck Baker	Baker '65 Chevrolet	485	700	Running
7	11	19	J T Putney	Herman Beam '65 Chevrolet	479	650	Running
8	14	34	Wendell Scott	Scott '63 Ford	469	600	Running
9	12	17	Junior Spencer	Jerry Mullins '64 Ford	443	500	Running
10	27	38	Wayne Smith	Smith '65 Chevrolet	442	400	Running
11	19	52	E J Trivette	Jess Potter '63 Chevrolet	441	380	Running
12	24	64	Elmo Langley	Langley '64 Ford	436	375	Engine
13	18	68	Bob Derrington	Derrington '63 Ford	430	325	Running
14	6	49	G C Spencer	Spencer '64 Ford	425	275	Engine
15	4	6	David Pearson	Cotton Owens '65 Dodge	398	250	Axle
16	15	20	Clyde Lynn	Lynn '64 Ford	374	250	Wtr Pump
17	7	1	Paul Lewis	Lewis '64 Ford	254	250	Engine
18	3	26	Junior Johnson	Johnson '65 Ford	193	250	Crash
19	10	10	LeeRoy Yarbrough	Gary Weaver '64 Ford	154	250	Differen
20	26	9	Darel Dieringer	Roy Tyner '65 Chevrolet	136	250	Oil Leak
21	23	67	Buddy Arrington	Arrington '64 Dodge	120	250	Lug bolts
22	21	97	Henley Gray	Gene Cline '64 Ford	95	250	Trans
23	22	53	Jimmy Helms	David Warren '63 Ford	78	250	Trans
24	17	89	Neil Castles	Buck Baker '65 Olds	10	250	Engine
25	25	0	Roy Tyner	Tyner '65 Chevrolet	7	250	Lug bolts
26	16	62	Darrell Bryant	Buddy Arrington '64 Dodge	1	100	D. Shaft
27	20	46	Roy Mayne	Tom Hunter '65 Chevrolet	1	100	Axle

Time of Race: 3 hours, 21 minutes, 46 seconds
Average Speed: 74.343 mph
Pole Winner: Richard Petty - 86.455 mph
Lap Leaders: Ned Jarrett 1-8, Junior Johnson 9-39, David Pearson 40-127, Richard Petty 128-167, Johnson 168-193, Petty 194-262, Pearson 263, Petty 264-500.
Cautions: 5 for ____ laps   Margin of Victory: 2-laps plus   Attendance: 7,500

Race No. 38

Hutcherson Hangs It Out In Rough Maryville 100

MARYVILLE, TN (Aug. 13) -- Dick Hutcherson survived a rollicking 100-miler over Smoky Mountain Raceway's choppy surface and grabbed his fifth win of the year. A one day postponement due to heavy rains left the half-mile dirt track rougher than a cob.

Hutcherson took the lead in the 170th lap when a broken ball joint forced leader David Pearson from the race. Hutcherson wound up four laps ahead of Buddy Baker to win the $1,000 top prize. "That's the roughest ride I've ever taken in a race car," declared Hutcherson. "I really earned my money tonight."

Third place went to Richard Petty, who was five laps behind. A broken shock absorber and a shattered windshield knocked Petty off the pace in the waning laps.

Jim Hunter of Knoxville, TN finished fourth in his first Grand National start. Fifth place went to Paul

Lewis, who blew an engine while running second with 14 laps to go.

Twenty-four cars started the race but only nine finished. All of the cars took a terrible beating in the 200 lapper. LeeRoy Yarbrough's Dodge broke an A-frame on the pot-holed track. Roy Tyner's Chevy broke a sway bar, Buck Baker took his Chevy to the pits with a broken control arm and Wendell Scott's Ford bounced over the holes so much that his radiator split.

Dick Hutcherson

Hutcherson averaged 65.455 mph and reduced Ned Jarrett's point lead to 270 points. Jarrett started on the pole but finished a distant sixth.

Grand National Race No. 38
200 Laps at Smoky Mountain Raceway
Maryville, TN
100-Miles on Half-mile Dirt Track
August 13, 1965

Fin	St	No.	Driver	Team / Car	Laps	Money	Status
1	3	29	Dick Hutcherson	Holman-Moody '65 Ford	200	$1,000	Running
2	11	88	Buddy Baker	Buck Baker '64 Dodge	196	600	Running
3	2	43	Richard Petty	Petty Engineering '64 Plym	195	400	Running
4	10	82	Jim Hunter	Casper Hensley '64 Pontiac	191	300	Running
5	5	1	Paul Lewis	Lewis '64 Ford	186	275	Engine
6	1	11	Ned Jarrett	Bondy Long '65 Ford	186	240	Running
7	18	68	Bob Derrington	Derrington '63 Ford	179	200	Running
8	8	19	J T Putney	Herman Beam '65 Chevrolet	177	175	Running
9	4	6	David Pearson	Cotton Owens '65 Dodge	169	150	Ball Jt.
10	16	20	Clyde Lynn	Lynn '64 Ford	168	140	Running
11	20	89	Neil Castles	Buck Baker '65 Olds	157	130	Running
12	12	64	Elmo Langley	Langley '64 Ford	143	120	Differen
13	15	34	Wendell Scott	Scott '63 Ford	122	110	Radiator
14	7	49	G C Spencer	Spencer '64 Ford	113	100	Steering
15	6	87	Buck Baker	Baker '65 Chevrolet	51	100	Con. Arm
16	24	53	Jimmy Helms	David Warren '63 Ford	45	100	H. Gasket
17	9	17	Junior Spencer	Jerry Mullins '64 Ford	40	100	Radiator
18	23	9	Roy Tyner	Tyner '65 Chevrolet	37	100	Sway bar
19	14	52	E J Trivette	Jess Potter '63 Chevrolet	30	100	Valve
20	17	0	William Gardner	Roy Tyner '65 Chevrolet	30	100	Battery
21	19	99	LeeRoy Yarbrough	Gene Hobby '64 Dodge	25	100	A frame
22	13	67	Pee Wee Ellwanger	Buddy Arrington '64 Dodge	20	100	Lug bolts
23	21	97	Henley Gray	Gene Cline '64 Ford	14	100	Differen
24	22	62	Buddy Arrington	Arrington '64 Dodge	1	100	Bell hsng.

Time of Race: 1 hour, 31 minutes, 40 seconds
Average Speed: 65.455 mph
Pole Winner: Ned Jarrett - 77.620 mph
Lap Leaders: Richard Petty 1- , David Pearson   -169, Dick Hutcherson 170-200.
Cautions: Margin of Victory: 4-laps plus   Attendance:

Race No. 39

Jarrett Wrecks Coming Out of Pits; Wins at Spartanburg

SPARTANBURG, SC (Aug. 14) -- Ned Jarrett unintentionally triggered a four car collision that put him on the path to victory in the 100-mile Grand National race at the Piedmont Interstate Fairgrounds. It was the 10th win of the year for the dark-haired Newton, NC Ford pilot.

Jarrett pitted in the 113th lap during a caution flag. His Bondy Long crew had trouble getting the car serviced and the green flag restart began before he got out of the pits. As the pack of cars received the green, Jarrett was racing down pit road just about a lap behind. NASCAR official Dick Wall motioned for Jarrett to move out of the pits onto the track. Jarrett's angle onto the track was directly in the path of the leaders -- and David Pearson, LeeRoy Yarbrough, G.C. Spencer and Clyde Lynn all crashed.

Another caution flag immediately came out and Jarrett made it back into the lead lap.

Dick Hutcherson led for seven circuits before Jarrett took the lead for good in lap 121. Cale Yarborough finished second with Elmo Langley third. Wendell Scott was fourth and Spencer recovered from the accident to wind up fifth.

Hutcherson was running second when his Ford over-

Grand National Race No. 39
200 Laps at Piedmont Interstate Fairgrounds
Spartanburg, SC
100 Miles on Half-mile Dirt Track
August 14, 1965

Fin	St	No.	Driver	Team / Car	Laps	Money	Status
1	5	11	Ned Jarrett	Bondy Long '65 Ford	200	$1,000	Running
2	6	06	Cale Yarborough	Kenny Myler '64 Ford	198	600	Running
3	19	64	Elmo Langley	Langley '64 Ford	191	400	Running
4	20	34	Wendell Scott	Scott '63 Ford	187	300	Running
5	4	49	G C Spencer	Spencer '64 Ford	185	275	Running
6	12	68	Bob Derrington	Derrington '64 Ford	182	240	Running
7	9	62	Buddy Arrington	Arrington '64 Dodge	163	200	Handling
8	13	38	Wayne Smith	Smith '65 Chevrolet	150	175	Running
9	1	29	Dick Hutcherson	Bondy Long '65 Ford	143	150	Heating
10	2	6	David Pearson	Cotton Owens '65 Dodge	113	140	Crash
11	23	55	Tiny Lund	Lyle Stelter '64 Ford	106	130	Engine
12	3	31	LeeRoy Yarbrough	Sam Fogle '63 Ford	100	120	Crash
13	21	20	Clyde Lynn	Lynn '64 Ford	96	110	Crash
14	7	18	Stick Elliott	Toy Bolton '65 Chevrolet	89	100	Tie rod
15	17	51	Jimmy Vaughn	'64 Dodge	62	100	Brakes
16	16	97	Henley Gray	Gene Cline '64 Ford	45	100	Fender
17	22	67	Pee Wee Ellwanger	Buddy Arrington '64 Dodge	42	100	Oil Line
18	15	53	Jimmy Helms	David Warren '63 Ford	36	100	Heating
19	11	46	Roy Mayne	Tom Hunter '65 Chevrolet	33	100	Heating
20	14	52	E J Trivette	Jess Potter '63 Ford	26	100	Manifold
21	8	17	Junior Spencer	Jerry Mullins '64 Ford	23	100	Heating
22	10	02	Darel Dieringer	Bob Cooper '65 Chevrolet	4	100	Oil Press
23	18	99	J T Putney	Gene Hobby '64 Dodge	1	100	Brakes

Time of Race: 1 hour, 45 minutes, 24 seconds
Average Speed: 56.926 mph
Pole Winner: Dick Hutcherson - 66.890 mph
Lap Leaders: David Pearson 1-113, Dick Hutcherson 114-120, Ned Jarrett 121-200.
Cautions: Margin of Victory: 2-laps plus   Attendance:

heated after 143 laps.

Jarrett averaged 56.926 mph and bumped his point lead to 398 over Hutcherson.

Curtis Turner made his first Grand National appearance. The Roanoke, VA veteran, snubbed by Ford, was assigned to drive the #43 Plymouth normally driven by Richard Petty. Turner backed the car into the wall on his first qualifying lap and did not start the race.

Race No. 40

Hutcherson Holds Off Pearson For Augusta 200 Win

AUGUSTA, GA (Aug. 15) -- Dick Hutcherson got the lead in the 42nd lap with the help of his speedy Holman-Moody pit crew and outran David Pearson and Ned Jarrett in a stirring duel at Augusta International Speedway.

The first of two caution flags came out in the 40th lap when Tiny Lund blew his engine. Hutcherson, running second, pitted along with all the lead cars. His pit crew, headed by Ralph Moody, was quickest and 'Hutch' returned to the track first.

The 32 year-old Keokuk, IA driver was able to hold his lead the rest of the way.

Pearson made a second pit stop during another yellow flag and made a run for Hutcherson in the final laps. His Dodge was just 2.75-seconds behind Hutcherson's Ford when the checkered flag fell on the 100-miler.

Jarrett was a close third. LeeRoy Yarbrough came in fourth and G.C. Spencer fifth.

Jarrett led the first 41 laps from the pole slot. It was strictly a three car race all the way. Richard Petty did not enter his Plymouth.

Hutcherson averaged 71.499 mph.

Grand National Race No. 40
200 Laps at Augusta Int'l Speedway
Augusta, GA
100-Miles on Half-mile Paved Track
August 15, 1965

Fin	St	No.	Driver	Team / Car	Laps	Money	Status
1	2	29	Dick Hutcherson	Holman-Moody '65 Ford	200	$1,000	Running
2	3	6	David Pearson	Cotton Owens '65 Dodge	200	600	Running
3	1	11	Ned Jarrett	Bondy Long '65 Ford	200	400	Running
4	12	10	LeeRoy Yarbrough	Gary Weaver '64 Ford	199	300	Running
5	21	49	G C Spencer	Spencer '64 Ford	196	375	Running
6	6	06	Cale Yarborough	Kenny Myler '64 Ford	194	240	Running
7	17	95	Buddy Baker	'64 Pontiac	192	200	Running
8	4	87	Buck Baker	Baker '65 Chevrolet	191	175	Running
9	16	34	Wendell Scott	Scott '63 Ford	191	150	Running
10	23	46	Roy Mayne	Tom Hunter '65 Chevrolet	190	140	Running
11	7	67	Buddy Arrington	Arrington '64 Dodge	185	130	Running
12	13	89	Neil Castles	Buck Baker '65 Olds	183	120	Running
13	22	64	Elmo Langley	Langley '64 Ford	176	110	Axle
14	19	62	Pee Wee Ellwanger	Buddy Arrington '64 Dodge	138	100	Engine
15	8	68	Bob Derrington	Derrington '63 Ford	127	100	Fuel pmp
16	9	97	Henley Gray	Gene Cline '64 Ford	89	100	Differen
17	20	17	Junior Spencer	Jerry Mullins '64 Ford	60	100	H Gasket
18	15	9	Roy Tyner	Tyner '65 Chevrolet	43	100	Heating
19	5	55	Tiny Lund	Lyle Stelter '64 Ford	41	100	Oil Line
20	10	52	E J Trivette	Jess Potter '63 Chevrolet	39	100	Fuel Pmp
21	11	0	William Gardner	Roy Tyner '65 Chevrolet	31	100	Differen
22	14	38	J T Putney	Wayne Smith '65 Chevrolet	17	100	Oil Leak
23	24	31	Darel Dieringer	Sam Fogle '63 Ford	9	100	Steering
24	18	53	Jimmy Helms	David Warren '63 Ford	1	100	D Shaft

Time of Race: 1 hour, 23 minutes, 55 seconds
Average Speed: 71.499 mph
Pole Winner: Ned Jarrett - 81.118 mph
Lap Leaders: Ned Jarrett 1-41, Dick Hutcherson 42-200.
Cautions: 2 for 12 laps.   Margin of Victory: 2.75-seconds   Attendance: 12,000

Race No. 41

Pearson Posts First '65 Win In Sandlapper 200

COLUMBIA, SC (Aug. 19) -- David Pearson seemingly came out of nowhere and won the Sandlapper

Curtis Turner made first comeback at Columbia but crashed in qualifying

200 at Columbia Speedway for his first win in over 11 months. It was also the first win for the Dodge nameplate since Pearson's car owner Cotton Owens won a race at Richmond on September 14, 1964.

Pearson took the lead in the 157th lap and held off Richard Petty by 10 car lengths to win the $1,000 top prize. Dick Hutcherson, who led for 94 laps, wound up third. Tiny Lund came in fourth and Cale Yarborough was fifth.

Point leader Ned Jarrett crashed in the final lap and wound up seventh. Hutcherson cut Jarrett's point lead to 334 points.

Pearson struggled to keep up for the first half of the race. During a pit stop, his Owens crew adjusted the chassis and he came on like a bolt of lightning. "I was falling back when the race first started," explained Pearson. "It was buzzing (spinning) off the corners. When we changed the wedge, I had the fastest car on the track."

J.T. Putney, Tom Pistone and Bob Derrington were eliminated in a three car tangle on the front chute in the second lap. No one was injured, but the cars were heavily damaged.

Pearson's 12th career win came at an average speed of 57.361 mph.

Race No. 42

Hutcherson's 'Easy Ride' Nets Moyock 300 Victory

MOYOCK, NC (Aug. 24) -- Dick Hutcherson drove his Ford past Richard Petty in the 32nd lap and led the rest of the way to win the Moyock 300 at Dog Track Speedway. It was the seventh win of the year for Hutcherson, and he pulled to within 286 points of

---

Grand National Race No. 41
200 Laps at Columbia Speedway
Columbia, SC
"Sandlapper 200"
100 miles on Half-mile Dirt Track
August 19, 1965

Fin	St	No.	Driver	Team / Car	Laps	Money	Status
1	6	6	David Pearson	Cotton Owens '65 Dodge	200	$1,000	Running
2	5	43	Richard Petty	Petty Engineering '65 Plym	200	800	Running
3	1	29	Dick Hutcherson	Holman-Moody '65 Ford	200	400	Running
4	4	55	Tiny Lund	Lyle Stelter '64 Ford	198	300	Running
5	10	06	Cale Yarborough	Kenny Myler '64 Ford	197	275	Running
6	11	10	LeeRoy Yarbrough	Gary Weaver '64 Ford	194	240	Running
7	3	11	Ned Jarrett	Bondy Long '65 Ford	191	200	Crash
8	18	34	Wendell Scott	Scott '63 Ford	190	175	Running
9	12	89	Neil Castles	Buck Baker '65 Olds	189	150	Running
10	23	87	Buck Baker	Baker '65 Chevrolet	188	140	Running
11	8	18	Stick Elliott	Toy Bolton '65 Chevrolet	188	130	Running
12	16	9	Darel Dieringer	Roy Tyner '65 Chevrolet	187	120	Running
13	17	31	Sam Smith	Sam Fogle '63 Ford	108	110	Crash
14	9	52	E J Trivette	Jess Potter '63 Chevrolet	71	100	Battery
15	22	88	Buddy Baker	Buck Baker '64 Dodge	56	100	Crash
16	13	97	Henley Gray	Gene Cline '64 Ford	32	100	Brakes
17	2	26	Junior Johnson	Johnson '65 Ford	26	100	Throttle
18	7	64	Bud Moore	Elmo Langley '64 Ford	23	100	Rear End
19	15	51	Jimmy Vaughn	'64 Dodge	15	100	Engine
20	14	53	Jimmy Helms	David Warren '63 Ford	14	100	Trans
21	21	38	J T Putney	Wayne Smith '65 Chevrolet	2	100	Crash
22	19	59	Tom Pistone	Glen Sweet '64 Ford	2	100	Crash
23	20	68	Bob Derrington	Derrington '63 Ford	2	---	Crash

Time of Race: 1 hour, 44 minutes, 36 seconds
Average Speed: 57.361 mph
Pole Winner: Dick Hutcherson - 71.343 mph
Lap Leaders: Junior Johnson 1-26, Dick Hutcherson 27-115, David Pearson 116-151, Hutcherson 152-156, Pearson 157-200.
Cautions: 4 for 38 laps   Margin of Victory: 10 car lengths   Attendance:

Grand National Race No. 42
300 Laps at Dog Track Speedway
Moyock, NC
"Moyock 300"
100 Miles on .333-mile Paved Track
August 24, 1965

Fin	St	No.	Driver	Team / Car	Laps	Money	Status
1	3	29	Dick Hutcherson	Holman-Moody '65 Ford	300	$1,000	Running
2	2	11	Ned Jarrett	Bondy Long '65 Ford	300	600	Running
3	1	43	Richard Petty	Petty Engineering '65 Plym	300	600	Running
4	4	55	Tiny Lund	Lyle Stelter '64 Ford	298	300	Running
5	7	90	Sonny Hutchins	Junie Donlavey '64 Ford	297	275	Running
6	5	88	Buddy Baker	Buck Baker '64 Dodge	292	240	Running
7	10	87	Buck Baker	Baker '65 Chevrolet	289	200	Running
8	6	8	Dick Dixon	'64 Ford	287	175	Running
9	16	64	Darel Dieringer	Elmo Langley '64 Ford	282	150	Running
10	12	89	Neil Castles	Buck Baker '65 Olds	274	140	Running
11	14	68	Bob Derrington	Derrington '63 Ford	263	130	Running
12	11	53	Jimmy Helms	David Warren '63 Ford	256	120	Running
13	15	80	Allen McMillion	McMillion '64 Pontiac	236	110	Running
14	17	34	Wendell Scott	Scott '63 Ford	168	100	Spindle
15	9	20	Clyde Lynn	Lynn '64 Ford	124	100	Handling
16	8	06	Cale Yarborough	Kenny Myler '64 Ford	90	100	Alternator
17	13	97	Henley Gray	Gene Cline '64 Ford	22	100	Steering
18	18	59	Tom Pistone	Glen Sweet '64 Ford	1	100	LF Hub

Time of Race: 1 hour, 35 minutes, 10 seconds
Average Speed: 63.047 mph
Pole Winner: Richard Petty - 68.493 mph
Lap Leaders: Richard Petty 1-31, Dick Hutcherson 32-300.
Cautions: Margin of Victory: Attendance: 5,400

standings leader Ned Jarrett.

Jarrett finished second and Petty third. Tiny Lund was fourth as fifth place went to Sonny Hutchins.

"My car was handling easy and I never had to floorboard it at all," said Hutcherson. "I just leaned back, took it easy and the car did the rest."

Petty won the pole and led the first 31 laps. He held second to Hutcherson until Jarrett passed him on lap 115. The top three cars ran in that order until the finish of the 300-lapper on the .333-mile paved track.

Eighteen cars started the race and 13 finished. Hutcherson averaged 63.047 mph before a crowd of 5,400.

Grand National Race No. 43
200 Laps at Baltimore-Washington Speedway
Beltsville, MD
100 Miles on Half-mile Paved Track
August 25, 1965

Fin	St	No.	Driver	Team / Car	Laps	Money	Status
1	1	11	Ned Jarrett	Bondy Long '65 Ford	200	$1,000	Running
2	2	55	Tiny Lund	Lyle Stelter '64 Ford	198	600	Running
3	19	37	Darel Dieringer	Bub Strickler '64 Ford	198	400	Running
4	3	8	Dick Dixon	'63 Ford	197	300	Running
5	7	34	Wendell Scott	Scott '63 Ford	191	275	Running
6	17	89	Neil Castles	Buck Baker '65 Olds	186	240	Running
7	11	84	Burt Robbins	Elmo Langley '64 Ford	186	200	Running
8	15	80	Worth McMillion	Allen McMillion '64 Pontiac	177	175	Running
9	13	20	Clyde Lynn	Lynn '64 Ford	166	150	Running
10	16	39	Bob Vaughn	Ronald Smith '64 Pontiac	60	140	Fender
11	5	06	Cale Yarborough	Kenny Myler '64 Ford	58	130	Heating
12	14	29	Dick Hutcherson	Holman-Moody '65 Ford	52	120	H Gasket
13	4	64	Elmo Langley	Langley '64 Ford	47	110	Differen
14	6	59	Tom Pistone	Glen Sweet '64 Ford	34	100	Vibration
15	8	53	Jimmy Helms	David Warren '63 Ford	32	100	Trans
16	12	97	Henley Gray	Gene Cline '64 Ford	27	100	Differen
17	9	57	Lionel Johnson	Clay Esteridge '64 Ford	26	100	Radiator
18	18	99	Buddy Baker	Gene Hobby '64 Dodge	16	100	Clutch
19	10	68	Bob Derrington	Derrington '63 Ford	14	100	Differen
--	--	43	Richard Petty	Petty Engineering '65 Plym	---	200	DNS

Time of Race: 1 hour, 20 minutes, 54 seconds
Average Speed: 74.165 mph
Pole Winner: Ned Jarrett - 79.260 mph
Lap Leaders: Ned Jarrett 1-200
Cautions: Margin of Victory: 2-laps plus   Attendance:

Race No. 43
Jarrett Leads All the Way at Baltimore-Washington Speedway

BELTSVILLE, MD (Aug 25) -- Ned Jarrett romped to his 11th win of the season by leading all the way in the 100-miler at the new Baltimore-Washington Speedway.

Dick Hutcherson, Jarrett's primary nemesis in the point race, fell out early and dropped 462 points behind in the standings.

Tiny Lund started second and ran in that position most of the evening. He finished second, just ahead of third place Darel Dieringer, who was driving a Ford entered by privateer Bub Strickler. Fourth at the stripe was Dick Dixon, who has registered seven top 10 finishes in eight starts since joining the Grand National ranks. Fifth place went to Wendell Scott.

Richard Petty blew the engine in his Plymouth in a practice session and did not start.

Hutcherson started back in 14th after a poor qualifying effort. He left the race in the 52nd lap with a blown head gasket.

Only nine cars finished and Jarrett averaged 74.165 mph for his 48th career Grand National victory.

Race No. 44
Johnson Ends Skid; Snares Myers Brothers Memorial

WINSTON-SALEM, NC (Aug. 28) -- Junior Johnson passed pole sitter Richard Petty in the second lap and streaked to a big win in the Myers Brothers Memorial event at Bowman Gray Stadium.

It was the 11th win of the year for the Ronda, NC chicken rancher but his first in his last nine starts on the Grand National tour.

Petty wound up second, four and a half laps behind the fleet Johnson Ford. Dick Hutcherson was third, Ned Jarrett fourth and Cale Yarborough fifth.

Johnson broke into a healthy advantage immediately after he passed Petty, and only a scrape with a spinning G.T. Nolan interrupted his effortless drive.

Johnson was unable to attend the victory lane ceremonies. Track Manager Alvin Hawkins said Johnson was near exhaustion afterwards and he took several minutes to get to his feet.

It was Johnson's 48th career win on the Grand National trail, locking him in a three-way tie for second on the all-time list. Lee Petty, who retired in 1964, leads with 54 victories. Johnson, Jarrett and the retired Herb Thomas all have 48 apiece.

Johnson averaged 46.632 mph for his third straight win on the flat quarter-mile oval.

Grand National Race No. 44
250 Laps at Bowman Gray Stadium
Winston-Salem, NC
"Myers Brothers Memorial"
62.5 Miles on Quarter-mile Paved Track
August 28, 1965

Fin	St	No.	Driver	Team / Car	Laps	Money	Status
1	2	26	Junior Johnson	Johnson '65 Ford	250	$1,000	Running
2	1	43	Richard Petty	Petty Engineering '65 Plym	246	800	Running
3	3	29	Dick Hutcherson	Holman-Moody '65 Ford	245	400	Running
4	6	11	Ned Jarrett	Bondy Long '65 Ford	243	300	Running
5	7	06	Cale Yarborough	Kenny Myler '64 Ford	240	275	Running
6	5	2	Fred Harb	Cliff Stewart '64 Pontiac	238	240	Running
7	8	23	Buren Skeen	Reid Shaw '64 Ford	234	200	Running
8	15	89	Neil Castles	Buck Baker '65 Olds	231	175	Running
9	10	20	Clyde Lynn	Lynn '64 Ford	230	150	Running
10	14	68	Bob Derrington	Derrington '63 Ford	225	140	Running
11	12	52	E J Trivette	Jess Potter '63 Ford	217	130	Running
12	11	84	Elmo Langley	Langley '64 Ford	136	120	Flat tire
13	13	38	Wayne Smith	Smith '65 Chevrolet	62	110	Heating
14	16	80	G T Nolan	Allen McMillion '64 Pontiac	59	100	Flat tire
15	17	99	Darrell Bryant	Gene Hobby '64 Dodge	44	100	Fuel pmp
16	9	34	Wendell Scott	Scott '63 Ford	34	100	Heating
17	4	59	Tom Pistone	Glen Sweet '64 Ford	4	100	Ignition
18	20	64	Buddy Baker	Elmo Langley '64 Ford	3	100	Handling
19	18	97	Henley Gray	Gene Cline '64 Ford	3	100	Handling
20	19	53	Jimmy Helms	David Warren '63 Ford	2	100	Brakes

Time of Race: 1 hour, 20 minutes, 25 seconds
Average Speed: 46.632 mph
Pole Winner: Richard Petty - 50.195 mph
Lap Leaders: Richard Petty 1, Junior Johnson 2-250.
Cautions: Margin of Victory: 4-laps plus   Attendance: 15,000

Race No. 45

Jarrett Wins Southern 500 by 14 Laps; Buren Skeen Dies

DARLINGTON, SC (Sept. 6) -- Ned Jarrett coaxed his overheating Ford to victory in the fabled Southern 500 at Darlington Raceway -- a wreck-filled event which mortally wounded Denton, NC rookie driver Buren Skeen.

Skeen, 28, died nine days after he suffered multiple internal injuries and a basal skull fracture in an early crash. Skeen's Ford went out of control in the second lap and was slammed broadside by Reb Wickersham's Ford. Skeen's bucket seat was knocked to the right side of the car. Rescue workers took nearly 20 minutes to get him out of the car. He never regained consciousness in his nine day fight for life. Wickersham was shaken badly and spent one night in the hospital for observation.

Jarrett took the lead in the 326th lap when a double-whammy sent leaders Fred Lorenzen and Darel

Grand National Race No. 45
364 Laps at Darlington Raceway
Darlington, SC
"Southern 500"
500 Miles on 1.375-mile Paved Track
September 6, 1965

Fin	St	No.	Driver	Team / Car	Laps	Money	Status
1	10	11	Ned Jarrett	Bondy Long '65 Ford	364	$21,060	Running
2	14	86	Buck Baker*	Baker '65 Plymouth	350	9,170	Running
3	5	16	Darel Dieringer	Bud Moore '64 Mercury	345	7,200	Differen
4	33	46	Roy Mayne	Tom Hunter '65 Chevrolet	345	3,225	Running
5	24	67	Buddy Arrington	Arrington '64 Dodge	344	2,400	Running
6	22	04	H B Bailey	Bailey '64 Pontiac	340	1,750	Running
7	31	18	Stick Elliott	Toy Bolton '65 Chevrolet	336	1,500	Running
8	41	79	Frank Warren	Harold Rhodes '63 Ford	334	1,250	Running
9	19	19	J T Putney	Herman Beam '65 Chevrolet	328	1,000	Running
10	44	57	Wendell Scott	Clay Esteridge '64 Ford	320	900	Running
11	2	28	Fred Lorenzen	Holman-Moody '65 Ford	319	1,550	Engine
12	37	53	Jimmy Helms	David Warren '63 Ford	316	800	Running
13	42	68	Bob Derrington	Derrington '63 Ford	311	775	Running
14	18	1	Paul Lewis	Lewis '64 Ford	308	750	Running
15	39	38	Wayne Smith	Smith '65 Chevrolet	304	725	Running
16	40	52	E J Trivette	Jess Potter '63 Chevrolet	302	700	Running
17	16	7	Bobby Johns	Shorty Johns '64 Pontiac	301	695	Differen
18	32	63	Don Hume	Hume '63 Ford	298	650	Running
19	6	29	Dick Hutcherson	Holman-Moody '65 Ford	293	625	Engine
20	20	49	G C Spencer	Spencer '64 Ford	293	620	Vapor lk.
21	35	44	Larry Hess	Hess '64 Ford	261	615	Clutch
22	7	41	Jim Paschal	Friedkin Ent. '65 Chevrolet	230	710	H Gasket
23	34	07	Bud Harless	Harless '64 Ford	222	605	Engine
24	38	75	Gene Black	C L Crawford '64 Ford	197	600	Oil Press
25	30	72	Neil Castles	Bill Champion '64 Ford	173	595	Crash
26	15	64	Elmo Langley	Langley '64 Ford	156	590	H Gasket
27	25	3	LeeRoy Yarbrough	Ray Fox '65 Chevrolet	134	635	Differen
28	17	87	Buddy Baker	Buck Baker '65 Chevrolet	123	580	Engine
29	11	24	Sam McQuagg	Betty Lilly '65 Ford	118	1,015	Crash
30	9	27	Cale Yarborough	Banjo Matthews '65 Ford	118	830	Crash
31	12	33	Bunkie Blackburn	Ray Fox '65 Chevrolet	109	695	Crash
32	4	15	Earl Balmer	Bud Moore '64 Mercury	94	580	Crash
33	29	62	Doug Cooper	Bob Cooper '65 Chevrolet	85	555	Differen
34	13	17	Junior Spencer	Jerry Mullins '64 Ford	79	620	Engine
35	8	14	Curtis Turner	Sam Fletcher '65 Plymouth	51	545	W Bearing
36	27	4	Bobby Wawak	'64 Mercury	46	560	Engine
37	3	21	Marvin Panch	Wood Brothers '65 Ford	42	605	Engine
38	43	97	Henley Gray	Gene Cline '64 Ford	29	530	Clutch
39	26	55	Tiny Lund	Lyle Stelter '64 Ford	25	555	A Frame
40	28	25	Bud Moore	Jabe Thomas '64 Ford	9	520	Oil Press
41	36	00	Burt Robbins	'64 Ford	3	515	Crash
42	21	23	Buren Skeen	Reid Shaw '64 Ford	2	510	Crash
43	23	03	Reb Wickersham	Ray Underwood '65 Ford	2	505	Crash
44	1	26	Junior Johnson	Johnson '65 Ford	1	750	Ignition

Time of Race: 4 hours, 19 minutes, 9 seconds
Average Speed: 115.878 mph
Pole Winner: Junior Johnson - 137.571 mph
Lap Leaders: Fred Lorenzen 1-32, Darel Dieringer 33-45, Earl Balmer 46,
    Bobby Johns 47-48, Jim Paschal 49-51, Cale Yarborough 52-53, Dieringer 54-86,
    Balmer 87, Sam McQuagg 88-118, Dieringer 119-121, Lorenzen 122,
    Paschal 123-128, Ned Jarrett 129-144, Lorenzen 145-147, Dieringer 148-166,
    Lorenzen 167, Dieringer 168-227, Lorenzen 228-232, Jarrett 233-239,
    Dieringer 240-287, Lorenzen 288-302, Dieringer 303-325, Jarrett 326-364.
Cautions: 7 for 44 laps   Margin of Victory: 14-laps plus   Attendance: 50,000
*Relieved by Buddy Baker

Dieringer to the pits with terminal problems. Lorenzen, driving a carefully programmed pace, still led for a total of 57 laps. He had moved to the front when Dieringer made his final pit stop on lap 287. When Lorenzen pitted on lap 302, Dieringer again picked up first place.

On lap 319 of the 364-lap event, Lorenzen pulled into

the pits with a blown engine; and at that precise moment smoke began pouring from the underside of Dieringer's Mercury. Dieringer limped a few more laps. Jarrett passed him for good with 39 laps left.

Jarrett's Bondy Long Ford finished 14 laps (19.25 miles) ahead of runner-up Buck Baker, who was in a hemi powered Plymouth Fury. Dieringer's 345 laps completed was good enough for third place money. Roy Mayne was 20 laps back in fourth, and fifth place went to Buddy Arrington, 24 laps behind.

Jarrett was driving the only factory backed machine to finish the race. "I was saying a prayer every lap for the last 20 laps," said Jarrett. "Don't underestimate the power of prayer. I had already conceded that I couldn't win unless something happened to Fred and Darel. I backed off to about 117 mph in the last 20 laps to let the car cool off. It ran at about 220 degrees. At one time I was afraid they might black flag me for going too slow."

Rescue workers attempt to remove Buren Skeen from his wrecked Ford after Southern 500 crash

Cale Yarborough's Ford becomes airborne after tangling with Sam McQuagg

Yarborough sails over the first turn wall at Darlington

Dick Hutcherson blew an engine on lap 293 and wound up 19th, falling 2,534 points behind Jarrett in the Grand National point standings.

Junior Johnson won the pole but went only one lap before ignition trouble sidelined his Ford. Curtis Turner made his return to Grand National racing in a Sam Fletcher owned Plymouth. He started eighth, but went out on lap 51 with a wheel bearing problem.

Cale Yarborough survived a spectacular flight over the guard rail in the 118th lap. As the Timmonsville,SC driver battled Sam McQuagg for the lead, the two cars side-swiped -- sending Yarborough's Ford high into the air. He completely cleared the guard rail, flipped a half-dozen times and came to rest against a light pole at the foot of the parking lot. McQuagg got pinched against the guard rail. Neither driver was hurt.

Before the race, pole sitter Johnson was fined when his Ford was found with an illegal locked rear end.

Jarrett averaged 115.878 mph.

Race No. 46

Petty Edges Pearson at Hickory; Turner Out Early

HICKORY, NC (Sept. 10) -- Richard Petty took the lead with 40 laps to go and held off David Pearson in a stretch run to win the Buddy Shuman Memorial at Hickory Speedway. It was the third win of the year for the Randleman, NC Plymouth driver.

Pearson finished second, 3.0 seconds behind Petty. Ned Jarrett was third and Junior Johnson fourth. Fifth place went to J.T. Putney.

Johnson was holding down first place in his Ford when a tire went flat, forcing him to the pits. He lost two laps and never made it up.

Curtis Turner qualified a Junior Johnson Ford in the second position -- next to Johnson -- but went only 35 laps before the car overheated. He was sacked with a 22nd place finish in the field of 26.

Dick Hutcherson led a single lap, but fell out with differential problems on lap 194 of the 250 lapper on the .4-mile dirt track. He fell to 2,826 points behind Jarrett and saw virtually any hope of winning the title vanish.

Local Sportsman driver Jack Ingram entered his first Grand National race and wound up last. The Asheville, NC driver pulled his Ford off the track early with handling problems.

Petty averaged 74.365 mph for his 39th career victory.

Grand National Race No. 46
250 Laps at Hickory Speedway
Hickory, NC
"Buddy Shuman Memorial"
100 Miles on .4-Mile Dirt Track
September 10, 1965

Fin	St	No.	Driver	Team / Car	Laps	Money	Status
1	5	43	Richard Petty	Petty Engineering '65 Plym	250	$1,200	Running
2	4	6	David Pearson	Cotton Owens '65 Dodge	250	600	Running
3	7	11	Ned Jarrett	Bondy Long '65 Ford	248	400	Running
4	1	26	Junior Johnson	Johnson '65 Ford	248	300	Running
5	8	19	J T Putney	Herman Beam '65 Chevrolet	246	275	Running
6	17	49	G C Spencer	Spencer '64 Ford	244	240	Running
7	6	1	Paul Lewis	Lewis '64 Ford	242	200	Running
8	13	02	Doug Cooper	Bob Cooper '65 Chevrolet	241	175	Running
9	24	55	Tiny Lund	Lyle Stelter '64 Ford	238	150	Running
10	10	9	Darel Dieringer	Roy Tyner '64 Chevrolet	235	140	Running
11	14	68	Bob Derrington	Derrington '63 Ford	232	130	Running
12	22	88	Buddy Baker	Buck Baker '64 Dodge	231	120	Running
13	20	38	Wayne Smith	Smith '65 Chevrolet	230	110	Running
14	25	89	Neil Castles	Buck Baker '65 Olds	230	100	Running
15	3	29	Dick Hutcherson	Holman-Moody '65 Ford	194	100	Differen
16	12	00	Elmo Langley	'64 Ford	67	100	Differen
17	16	53	Jimmy Helms	David Warren '63 Ford	56	100	Oil Press
18	23	75	Gene Black	C L Crawford '64 Ford	53	100	Oil Line
19	9	34	Wendell Scott	Scott '63 Ford	51	100	Engine
20	11	59	Tom Pistone	Glen Sweet '64 Ford	38	100	Oil Press
21	15	20	Clyde Lynn	Lynn '64 Ford	35	100	Crash
22	2	2	Curtis Turner	Junior Johnson '65 Ford	35	100	Heating
23	21	99	Joe Holder	Gene Hobby '64 Dodge	35	100	Trans
24	19	97	Henley Gray	Gene Cline '64 Ford	31	100	Crash
25	18	62	Buddy Arrington	Arrington '64 Dodge	16	100	Engine
26	26	64	Jack Ingram	Elmo Langley '64 Ford	4	100	Handling

Time of Race: 1 hour, 20 minutes, 41 seconds
Average Speed: 74.365 mph
Pole Winner: Junior Johnson - 74.766 mph
Lap Leaders: Junior Johnson 1-24, Dick Hutcherson 25, Johnson 26-161, David Pearson 162-169, Johnson 170-174, Pearson 175-187, Johnson 188-210, Richard Petty 211-250.
Cautions: None   Margin of Victory: 3 seconds   Attendance: 12,500.

Race No. 47
Hutcherson Beats Spencer by 8 Laps at New Oxford

NEW OXFORD, PA (Sept. 14) -- Dick Hutcherson outlasted Richard Petty and David Pearson to score a decisive victory in the Pennsylvania 200 Classic at Lincoln Speedway. It was the eighth win of the year for

Grand National Race No. 47
200 Laps at Lincoln Speedway
New Oxford, PA
"Pennsylvania 200 Classic"
100 Miles on Half-mile Dirt Track
September 14, 1965

Fin	St	No.	Driver	Team / Car	Laps	Money	Status
1	2	29	Dick Hutcherson	Holman-Moody '65 Ford	200	$1,000	Running
2	5	49	G C Spencer	Spencer '64 Ford	192	600	Running
3	3	6	David Pearson	Cotton Owens '65 Dodge	190	400	Engine
4	4	11	Ned Jarrett	Bondy Long '65 Ford	190	300	Running
5	12	86	Buddy Baker	Buck Baker '64 Dodge	189	275	Running
6	9	59	Tom Pistone	Glen Sweet '64 Ford	188	240	Running
7	7	06	Cale Yarborough	Kenny Myler '64 Ford	186	200	Running
8	28	62	Buddy Arrington	Arrington '64 Dodge	178	175	Running
9	27	46	Roy Mayne	Tom Hunter '65 Chevrolet	177	150	Running
10	19	89	Neil Castles	Buck Baker '65 Olds	175	140	Running
11	21	34	Wendell Scott	Scott '63 Ford	173	130	Running
12	26	52	E J Trivette	Jess Potter '63 Chevrolet	171	120	Running
13	18	97	Henley Gray	Gene Cline '64 Ford	169	110	Running
14	20	75	Gene Black	C L Crawford '64 Ford	157	100	Running
15	11	37	Darel Dieringer	Bub Strickler '64 Ford	136	100	Hub
16	8	00	Elmo Langley	'64 Ford	119	100	Wheel
17	16	20	Clyde Lynn	Lynn '64 Ford	107	100	Running
18	15	53	Jimmy Helms	David Warren '63 Ford	106	100	Brakes
19	1	43	Richard Petty	Petty Engineering '65 Plym	101	300	Suspen.
20	24	311	Al White	'64 Ford	80	100	Fender
21	6	87	Buck Baker	Baker '65 Chevrolet	76	100	Clutch
22	17	68	Bob Derrington	Derrington '63 Ford	75	100	Engine
23	13	31	LeeRoy Yarbrough	Sam Fogle '63 Ford	66	---	Brakes
24	22	55	Tiny Lund	Lyle Stelter '64 Ford	61	---	Hub
25	14	02	Dan Warwick	Bob Cooper '65 Chevrolet	51	---	Fender
26	10	18	Stick Elliott	Toy Bolton '65 Chevrolet	31	---	Heating
27	23	9	Roy Tyner	Tyner '65 Chevrolet	6	---	Suspen.
28	25	64	Bert Robbins	Elmo Langley '64 Ford	3	---	Clutch

Time of Race: 1 hour, 12 minutes, 38 seconds
Average Speed: 82.607 mph
Pole Winner: Richard Petty - 86.705 mph
Lap Leaders: Richard Petty 1-78, Dick Hutcherson 79-200.
Cautions: Margin of Victory: 8-laps plus   Attendance:

the rookie Grand National driver out of Keokuk, IA.

G.C. Spencer came in second, eight laps behind Hutcherson's Holman-Moody Ford. Pearson fell out with 10 laps remaining and still got third place money. Ned Jarrett came in fourth and Buddy Baker fifth.

Petty earned the pole for the 30th time in his career and led the opening 78 laps. Hutcherson, who started second, dogged Petty until he made the pass on lap 79. He led the rest of the way.

Petty departed on lap 101 when his Plymouth snapped an A-frame and broke some shock absorbers. Pearson was running second when his engine blew in the final laps.

Twenty-eight cars started the race and 14 finished. Only 22 starters got paid for their efforts. LeeRoy Yarbrough, Tiny Lund, Stick Elliott and Roy Tyner all failed to earn any prize money.

Hutcherson covered the 100 miles at an 82.607 mph clip.

Grand National Race No. 48
400 Laps at Old Dominion Speedway
Manassas, VA
150 Miles on .375-Mile Paved Track
September 17, 1965

Fin	St	No.	Driver	Team / Car	Laps	Money	Status
1	2	43	Richard Petty	Petty Engineering '65 Plym	400	$1,300	Running
2	1	11	Ned Jarrett	Bondy Long '65 Ford	399	625	Running
3	4	86	Buddy Baker	Buck Baker '64 Dodge	396	450	Running
4	6	55	Tiny Lund	Lyle Stelter '64 Ford	396	350	Running
5	9	59	Tom Pistone	Glen Sweet '64 Ford	393	325	Running
6	3	64	Elmo Langley	Langley '64 Ford	388	290	Running
7	18	02	Dan Warwick	Elmo Langley '64 Ford	381	250	Running
8	10	89	Neil Castles	Buck Baker '65 Olds	379	225	Running
9	13	37	Darel Dieringer	Bub Strickler '64 Ford	379	200	Running
10	12	46	Roy Mayne	Tom Hunter '65 Chevrolet	378	190	Running
11	14	57	Lionel Johnson	Clay Esteridge '64 Ford	375	180	Running
12	20	18	Stick Elliott	Toy Bolton '65 Chevrolet	375	170	Running
13	17	62	Buddy Arrington	Arrington '64 Dodge	372	160	Running
14	5	90	Sonny Hutchins	Junie Donlavey '64 Ford	371	150	Running
15	27	38	Wayne Smith	Smith '65 Chevrolet	367	135	Running
16	21	52	E J Trivette	Jess Potter '63 Chevrolet	357	125	Running
17	16	06	Cale Yarborough	Kenny Myler '64 Ford	356	115	Running
18	22	75	Gene Black	C L Crawford '64 Ford	349	110	Running
19	23	68	Bob Derrington	Derrington '63 Ford	343	100	Running
20	24	20	Clyde Lynn	Lynn '64 Ford	338	100	Running
21	29	53	Jimmy Helms	David Warren '63 Ford	336	100	Running
22	7	34	Wendell Scott	Scott '63 Ford	314	100	Running
23	8	49	G C Spencer	Spencer '64 Ford	297	---	Differen
24	25	97	Henley Gray	Gene Cline '64 Ford	145	---	Heating
25	15	31	LeeRoy Yarbrough	Sam Fogle '63 Ford	68	---	Trans
26	30	9	Roy Tyner	Tyner '65 Chevrolet	65	---	Differen
27	11	87	Buck Baker	Baker '65 Chevrolet	52	---	Clutch
28	28	80	Worth McMillion	Allen McMillion '64 Pontiac	51	---	Ignition
29	26	66	Red Foote	Larry Manning ' '64 Chevrolet	17	---	Heating
30	19	00	Bert Robbins	'64 Ford	11	---	A-frame

Time of Race: 2 hours, 12 minutes, 34 seconds.
Average Speed: 67.890 mph
Pole Winner: Ned Jarrett - 73.851 mph
Lap Leaders: Ned Jarrett 1- , Elmo Langley , -------- Richard Petty - 400.
Cautions:　　Margin of Victory: 1-lap plus　　Attendance:

Race No. 48

Petty Passes Langley; Wins 400 Lapper at Manassas

MANASSAS, VA (Sept. 17) -- Richard Petty scooted past Elmo Langley before the mid-point of the race and led the rest of the way to win the Grand National 150-miler at Old Dominion Speedway. It was the fourth win of the year for the defending NASCAR champion.

Ned Jarrett finished second a lap behind. Buddy Baker grabbed third place with Tiny Lund fourth and Tom Pistone fifth.

Jarrett led the early laps before Langley sped into the lead. The Landover, MD veteran ran surprisingly well until he faded to a sixth place finish.

G.C. Spencer, an independent driver operating on a limited budget, ran 297 laps before his Ford developed differential trouble. He finished 23rd, one spot behind the paying positions. "It hurts to pull the car all the way up here and run that many laps and not get paid anything," said Spencer.

Dick Hutcherson, his hopes for the championship all but gone, did not enter the race.

Petty averaged 67.890 mph for his 40th career win.

Grand National Race No. 49
300 Laps at Atlantic Rural Fairgrounds
Richmond, VA
"Capital City 300"
150 Miles on Half-mile Dirt Track
September 18, 1965

Fin	St	No.	Driver	Team / Car	Laps	Money	Status
1	2	6	David Pearson	Cotton Owens '65 Dodge	300	$2,300	Running
2	10	15	Darel Dieringer	Bud Moore '64 Mercury	299	1,525	Running
3	7	26	Junior Johnson	Johnson '65 Ford	298	1,200	Running
4	19	19	J T Putney	Herman Beam '65 Chevrolet	298	875	Running
5	26	89	Neil Castles	Buck Baker '65 Olds	278	710	Running
6	13	00	Bert Robbins	'64 Ford	276	525	Running
7	23	34	Wendell Scott	Scott '63 Ford	274	400	Running
8	31	52	E J Trivette	Jess Potter '63 Chevrolet	263	300	Running
9	36	57	Lionel Johnson	Clay Esteridge '64 Ford	252	250	Running
10	35	68	Bob Derrington	Derrington '63 Ford	250	250	Running
11	20	20	Clyde Lynn	Lynn '64 Ford	248	225	Running
12	14	64	Elmo Langley	Langley '64 Ford	246	225	Running
13	37	99	Gene Hobby	Hobby '64 Dodge	238	225	Running
14	33	97	Henley Gray	Gene Cline '64 Ford	237	225	Running
15	25	1	Paul Lewis	Lewis '64 Ford	221	200	Engine
16	6	86	Buddy Baker	Buck Baker '64 Dodge	220	200	Differen
17	22	53	Jimmy Helms	David Warren '63 Ford	219	200	Engine
18	21	02	Doug Cooper	Bob Cooper '65 Chevrolet	210	175	Sway bar
19	3	11	Ned Jarrett	Bondy Long '65 Ford	208	175	Engine
20	8	41	Jim Paschal	Friedkin Ent. '65 Chevrolet	193	175	Timing
21	12	46	Roy Mayne	Tom Hunter '65 Chevrolet	187	175	Differen
22	24	62	Buddy Arrington	Arrington '64 Dodge	179	150	Lug bolt
23	11	49	G C Spencer	Spencer '64 Ford	178	150	A-Frame
24	15	87	Buck Baker	Baker '65 Chevrolet	170	170	Oil leak
25	1	29	Dick Hutcherson	Holman-Moody '65 Ford	162	150	Crash
26	34	75	Gene Black	C L Crawford '64 Ford	154	150	Crash
27	28	66	Red Foote	Larry Manning '64 Chevrolet	149	150	Wheel
28	16	90	Sonny Hutchins	Junie Donlavey '64 Ford	139	150	Heating
29	27	18	Stick Elliott	Toy Bolton '65 Chevrolet	118	150	Radiator
30	30	9	Roy Tyner	Tyner '65 Chevrolet	107	150	D Shaft
31	32	80	Worth McMillion	Allen McMillion '64 Pontiac	103	150	Oil pan
32	29	38	Wayne Smith	Smith '65 Chevrolet	88	150	Heating
33	9	55	Tiny Lund	Lyle Stelter '64 Ford	85	150	Crash
34	18	43	LeeRoy Yarbrough	Petty Engineering '65 Plym	81	150	Crash
35	5	59	Tom Pistone	Glen Sweet '64 Ford	80	150	Crash
36	4	2	Curtis Turner	Junior Johnson '65 Ford	66	150	Heating
37	17	06	Cale Yarborough	Kenny Myler '64 Ford	28	150	Heating

Time of Race: 2 hours, 27 minutes, 35 seconds.
Average Speed: 60.983 mph
Pole Winner: Dick Hutcherson - 67.340 mph
Lap Leaders: Dick Hutcherson 1-2, David Pearson 3-82, Junior Johnson 83,
　　Ned Jarrett 84-99, Pearson 100-116, Hutcherson 117-161, Pearson 162-166,
　　Jarrett 167-208, Pearson 209, Dieringer 210-281, Pearson 282-300.
Cautions:　　Margin of Victory: 1-lap plus　　Attendance: 14,000

Race No. 49

More Sour Luck Foils Dieringer; Pearson Wins Richmond

RICHMOND, VA (Sept. 18) --Perennial 'bridesmaid' Darel Dieringer suffered another agonizing twist of fate when a blown tire knocked him from the lead with just 19 laps left, opening the door for David Pearson to win the Capital City 300 at Atlantic Rural Fairgrounds. It was the second win of the season for the Dodge driver.

Dieringer, who had led for 72 laps in his Bud Moore Mercury, got fresh rubber and managed to finish second, a lap behind. It was the fourth runner-up finish for the Indianapolis, IN driver in the 1965 season.

Third place went to Junior Johnson. J.T. Putney was fourth and Neil Castles fifth.

Johnson led only one lap in the race, but he offered a serious challenge in the late stages. The Ronda, NC Ford pilot ran circles around his rivals and made up a two lap deficit -- only to pit in the final laps with worn tires. He wound up third, two laps off the pace.

Dick Hutcherson, whose luck has eluded him in recent weeks, started on the pole and led twice for 47 laps. He was leading when he crashed with Gene Black in the 162nd lap. Title-bound Ned Jarrett started third but fell out with engine problems after 208 laps. His point lead grew to 3,194 points over Hutcherson with six races remaining.

Pearson's 13th career Grand National win came at an average speed of 60.983 mph before 14,000 spectators. The race had been postponed from Sept. 12 by rains.

LeeRoy Yarbrough drove Richard Petty's Plymouth, but was kayoed in a peculiar accident in the 80th lap. During a caution flag, Yarbrough slid into a utility pole in the infield. The radiator was smashed and Yarbrough walked back to the pits.

Race No. 50

Johnson Leads 481 Laps To Win Old Dominion 500

MARTINSVILLE, VA (Sept. 26) -- Junior Johnson bolted out of the starting blocks and took off from the field as he romped to victory in the Old Dominion 500 at Martinsville Speedway. It was victory number 12 of

				Grand National Race No. 50			
				500 Laps at Martinsville Speedway			
				Martinsville, VA			
				"Old Dominion 500"			
				250 Miles on Half-mile Paved Track			
				September 26, 1965			

Fin	St	No.	Driver	Team / Car	Laps	Money	Status
1	3	26	Junior Johnson	Johnson '65 Ford	500	$4,625	Running
2	1	43	Richard Petty	Petty Engineering '65 Plym	499	2,400	Running
3	4	6	David Pearson	Cotton Owens '65 Dodge	497	1,250	Running
4	10	11	Ned Jarrett	Bondy Long '65 Ford	495	775	Running
5	8	21	Marvin Panch	Wood Brothers '65 Ford	495	725	Running
6	7	29	Dick Hutcherson	Holman-Moody '65 Ford	495	675	Running
7	21	59	Tom Pistone	Glen Sweet '64 Ford	491	650	Running
8	13	10	Tiny Lund	Gary Weaver '64 Ford	485	525	Running
9	9	17	Junior Spencer	Jerry Mullins '64 Ford	483	500	Running
10	16	90	Sonny Hutchins	Junie Donlavey '64 Ford	480	475	Running
11	18	88	Buddy Baker	Buck Baker '64 Dodge	477	450	Running
12	17	67	Buddy Arrington	Arrington '64 Dodge	476	425	Running
13	25	89	Neil Castles	Buck Baker '65 Olds	470	415	Running
14	31	38	Wayne Smith	Smith '65 Chevrolet	458	380	Running
15	28	68	Bob Derrington	Derrington '63 Ford	457	370	Running
16	27	52	E J Trivette	Jess Potter '63 Chevrolet	449	385	Running
17	23	02	Doug Cooper	Bob Cooper '65 Chevrolet	437	385	Running
18	34	53	Jimmy Helms	David Warren '63 Ford	432	340	Running
19	33	75	Darel Dieringer	C L Crawford '64 Ford	420	330	Running
20	19	25	Jabe Thomas	Thomas '64 Ford	397	345	W. Bear.
21	5	28	Fred Lorenzen	Holman-Moody '65 Ford	365	350	Fuel pmp
22	24	56	Paul Lewis	Curtis Larimer '64 Ford	340	325	Oil line
23	36	32	O E Horn	'64 Ford	330	300	Brakes
24	12	27	Cale Yarborough	Banjo Matthews '65 Ford	214	325	Wheel
25	20	34	Wendell Scott	Scott '63 Ford	162	325	Engine
26	29	62	Pee Wee Ellwanger	Buddy Arrington '64 Dodge	145	275	Crash
27	26	9	Roy Tyner	Tyner ' 65 Chevrolet	141	300	Crash
28	15	19	J T Putney	Herman Beam '65 Chevrolet	138	300	Brakes
29	22	87	Buck Baker	Baker '65 Chevrolet	108	325	Brakes
30	30	97	Henley Gray	Gene Cline '64 Ford	80	275	Axle
31	6	47	Curtis Turner	Wood Brothers '65 Ford	45	275	Crash
32	2	35	Bobby Isaac	Nichels Eng '65 Dodge	45	350	Crash
33	37	18	Stick Elliott	Toy Bolton '65 Chevrolet	43	250	Valve
34	14	64	Elmo Langley	Langley '64 Ford	32	275	Crash
35	32	66	Red Foote	Larry Manning '64 Chevrolet	15	270	Trans
36	35	20	Clyde Lynn	Lynn '64 Ford	10	275	W Bear.
37	11	49	G C Spencer	Spencer '64 Ford	1	250	Crash

Time of Race: 3 hours, 43 minutes, 41 seconds
Average Speed: 67.056 mph
Pole Winner: Richard Petty - 74.503 mph
Lap Leaders: Junior Johnson 1-284, Richard Petty 285-292, Johnson 293-424, Petty 425-435, Johnson 436-500.
Cautions: 3 for 19 laps   Margin of Victory: 1 1/2 laps   Attendance: 20,000

the season for the Ronda, NC Ford star.

Johnson led virtually all the way. The only 19 laps which he didn't lead was when he brought his Holly Farms sponsored car into the pits for routine service.

Richard Petty, leader when Johnson pitted each time, wound up second a lap behind. David Pearson came in third with Ned Jarrett fourth and Marvin Panch fifth.

Johnson's crew chief Herb Nab was credited with the 'hot' set-up that gave Johnson an overwhelming advantage. Nab noticed the half mile paved track was exceptionally oily after a Modified-Sportsman race on Saturday. He made some radical chassis adjustments and switched to a soft tire compound -- and Johnson was

Field rounds turn in Martinsville's Old Dominion 500

Race No. 51

Johnson Outduels Lorenzen For Wilkes 400 Flag

N.WILKESBORO, NC (Oct. 3) -- Junior Johnson took the lead from Cale Yarborough in the 317th lap and led the rest of the way to win the Wilkes 400 at North Wilkesboro Speedway. The triumph was Johnson's 13th of the season and the 50th of his illustrious career.

Yarborough, driving Banjo Matthews' Ford, wound up second, two laps behind. Third place went to Ned

untouchable when the race started.

"I could've driven harder," drawled Johnson. "But I didn't have to."

Curtis Turner, who landed a Wood Brothers ride, tangled with Bobby Isaac in the early going. Isaac was making his first start of the year in a Nichels Engineering Dodge. Isaac was attempting to pass Turner but clipped Turner's rear quarter panel.

Turner dismounted and grabbed Isaac by the collar. "I want to know if you wrecked me on purpose," yelled Turner.

"No, I didn't wreck you on purpose," replied Isaac. "Why would I do that? I don't even know you."

Curtis Turner and Bobby Isaac walk back to pits after crash

Turner calmed down a little a few minutes later. "I guess he just came in too hard and lost it," said the Roanoke, VA lumberman. "It doesn't seem like he would have done anything like that on purpose when it was going to wreck him too."

Johnson's victory was his 49th, tying him for second on the all time list with Ned Jarrett. Retired Lee Petty is tops with 54 wins.

Johnson averaged 67.056 mph as only 19 laps were run under the caution flag.

Grand National Race No. 51
400 Laps at N. Wilkesboro Speedway
N. Wilkesboro, NC
"Wilkes 400"
250 Miles on .625-mile Paved Track
October 3, 1965

Fin	St	No.	Driver	Team / Car	Laps	Money	Status
1	5	26	Junior Johnson	Johnson '65 Ford	400	$4,475	Running
2	6	27	Cale Yarborough	Banjo Matthews '65 Ford	398	2,125	Running
3	7	11	Ned Jarrett	Bondy Long '65 Ford	398	1,275	Running
4	4	6	David Pearson	Cotton Owens '65 Dodge	397	825	Running
5	11	47	Curtis Turner	Wood Brothers '65 Ford	396	675	Running
6	8	21	Marvin Panch	Wood Brothers '65 Ford	396	525	Running
7	10	17	Junior Spencer	Jerry Mullins '64 Ford	394	475	Running
8	21	59	Tom Pistone	Glen Sweet '64 Ford	393	500	Running
9	12	49	G C Spencer	Spencer '64 Ford	392	400	Running
10	17	88	Buddy Baker	Buck Baker '64 Dodge	389	325	Running
11	19	19	J T Putney	Herman Beam '65 Chevrolet	387	300	Running
12	16	87	Buck Baker	Baker '65 Chevrolet	386	275	Running
13	22	34	Wendell Scott	Scott '63 Ford	375	300	Running
14	15	64	Elmo Langley	Langley '64 Ford	349	225	Running
15	24	02	Doug Cooper	Bob Cooper '65 Chevrolet	349	200	Running
16	23	46	Roy Mayne	Tom Hunter '65 Chevrolet	318	225	Engine
17	33	75	Gene Black	C L Crawford '64 Ford	311	175	Running
18	14	10	Darel Dieringer	Gary Weaver '64 Ford	308	200	Clutch
19	1	28	Fred Lorenzen	Holman-Moody '65 ford	219	550	Engine
20	29	52	E J Trivette	Jess Potter '63 Chevrolet	215	200	Differen
21	28	38	Wayne Smith	Smith '65 Chevrolet	211	175	Steering
22	18	56	Paul Lewis	Curtis Larimer '63 Ford	198	175	Engine
23	31	53	Jimmy Helms	David Warren '63 Ford	174	150	Vibration
24	26	25	Jabe Thomas	Thomas '64 Ford	154	175	Oil leak
25	20	7	Bobby Johns	Shorty Johns '64 Pontiac	119	175	Push rod
26	34	81	Frank Weathers	Joe Keistler '63 Dodge	119	150	Handling
27	25	89	Neil Castles	Buck Baker '65 Olds	98	175	Axle
28	13	06	Sam McQuagg	Kenny Myler '64 Ford	93	175	Gas tank
29	32	97	Henley Gray	Gene Cline '64 Ford	82	150	Crash
30	27	68	Bob Derrington	Derrington '63 Ford	82	175	A-frame
31	30	9	Roy Tyner	Tyner '65 Chevrolet	35	175	Engine
32	3	29	Dick Hutcherson	Holman-Moody '65 Ford	14	175	Crash
33	2	43	Richard Petty	Petty Engineering '65 Plym	14	450	Crash
34	9	35	Bobby Isaac	Nichels Eng. '65 Dodge	14	175	Crash
35	35	67	Buddy Arrington	Arrington '64 Dodge	13	150	Crash

Time of Race: 2 hours, 48 minutes, 55 seconds
Average Speed: 88.801 mph
Pole Winner: Fred Lorenzen - 101.580 mph
Lap Leaders: Fred Lorenzen 1-190, Junior Johnson 191-310, Cale Yarborough 311-316, Johnson 317-400.
Cautions: 5 for 36 laps   Margin of Victory: 2-plus laps   Attendance: 15,000

Jarrett, David Pearson was fourth and Curtis Turner fifth. It was the first race which Turner has finished since making his NASCAR comeback. "At least I finished one. Now I hope I can win one," said Turner.

Three top contenders were taken out in a 14th lap crash. Buddy Arrington's Dodge blew its engine, oiling the first turn. Dick Hutcherson, Bobby Isaac and Richard Petty were all eliminated in the wild scramble.

Fred Lorenzen, who hasn't won a Grand National race in five months, rebounded with a solid performance. He led the first 190 laps. "I got beat so bad at Martinsville that I was determined to get back in the right groove," said Lorenzen. "I hadn't been paying enough attention to my racing business. I told my crew that we were going to buckle down -- not be embarrassed any more."

Lorenzen was running in second place when the engine blew in his Ford. "Freddy and Cale were both outrunning me in the first half of the race," said Johnson. "We made adjustments though. We put more bite in the car and we could run with 'em. Racin' with Freddy was just like the old days."

The race ended under the caution flag when Doug Cooper's Chevrolet spun with two laps to go.

Johnson averaged 88.801 mph before a sell-out audience of 15,000.

Race No. 52

Lorenzen Prevails in Thrilling National 400; Kite Killed

CHARLOTTE, NC (Oct. 17) -- Fred Lorenzen outdueled a trio of rivals in a crowd-pleasing stretch run and won the spine-tingling National 400 at Charlotte Motor Speedway. Lorenzen emerged from a three-abreast battle for the lead to capture his 11th superspeedway race -- an event marred by the death of Har-

*Rock Harn #32, Sonny Hutchins #90 and Frank Warren #79
crash in National 400 at Charlotte*

Grand National Race No. 52
267 Laps at Charlotte Motor Speedway
Charlotte, NC
"National 400"
400 Miles on 1.5-mile Paved Track
October 17, 1965

Fin	St	No.	Driver	Team / Car	Laps	Money	Status
1	1	28	Fred Lorenzen	Holman-Moody '65 Ford	267	$9,920	Running
2	10	29	Dick Hutcherson	Holman-Moody '65 Ford	267	5,225	Running
3	6	47	Curtis Turner	Wood Brothers '65 Ford	267	3,340	Running
4	9	11	Ned Jarrett	Bondy Long '65 Ford	266	2,390	Running
5	17	3	LeeRoy Yarbrough	Ray Fox '65 Chevrolet	265	1,630	Running
6	8	41	A J Foyt	Banjo Matthews '65 Ford	265	1,930	Running
7	5	41	Earl Balmer	Bud Moore '64 Mercury	262	1,055	Wheel
8	20	04	H B Bailey	Bailey '64 Pontiac	257	975	Running
9	32	1	Paul Lewis	Lewis '64 Ford	256	900	Running
10	33	14	Iggy Katona	Sam Fletcher '65 Plymouth	251	850	Running
11	39	46	Roy Mayne	Tom Hunter '65 Chevrolet	251	800	Running
12	19	44	Larry Hess	Hess '64 Ford	248	800	Running
13	42	52	E J Trivette	Jess Potter '63 Chevrolet	248	750	Running
14	30	97	Henley Gray	Gene Cline '64 Ford	239	725	Running
15	28	84	Buddy Arrington	Elmo Langley '64 Ford	237	700	Running
16	43	75	Gene Black	C L Crawford '64 Ford	235	680	Running
17	29	38	Wayne Smith	Smith '65 Chevrolet	217	660	Crash
18	21	02	Doug Cooper	Bob Cooper '65 Chevrolet	215	865	Heating
19	44	57	Lionel Johnson	Clay Esteridge '64 Ford	210	620	Running
20	7	24	Sam McQuagg	Betty Lilly '65 Ford	209	625	Crash
21	3	16	Darel Dieringer	Bud Moore '64 Mercury	199	910	Wheel
22	12	49	G C Spencer	Spencer '64 Ford	188	570	Ball Jt.
23	13	86	Buddy Baker	Buck Baker '65 Plymouth	188	560	Running
24	41	63	Don Hume	Hume '63 Ford	183	550	Engine
25	40	88	Neil Castles	Buck Baker '64 Dodge	157	540	Wheel
26	18	87	Buck Baker	Baker '65 Chevrolet	123	555	A-Frame
27	15	64	Elmo Langley	Langley '64 Ford	114	520	Engine
28	26	18	Stick Elliott	Toy Bolton '65 Chevrolet	105	510	Shocks
29	14	17	Junior Spencer	Jerry Mullins '64 Ford	93	500	Crash
30	36	35	Jeff Hawkins	Lester Hunter '64 Dodge	92	515	Engine
31	34	34	Wendell Scott	Scot ' 63 Ford	89	505	D. Shaft
32	4	26	Junior Johnson	Johnson '65 Ford	63	500	Heating
33	31	4	Jim Paschal	Toy Bolton '65 Chevrolet	53	535	Oil Press
34	2	27	Cale Yarborough	Banjo Matthews '65 Ford	47	780	Engine
35	16	21	Marvin Panch	Wood Brothers '65 Ford	41	545	Rock. arm
36	11	J T Putney	Herman Beam '65 Chevrolet	16	440	Crash
37	37	7	Bobby Johns	Shorty Johns '64 Pontiac	16	460	Crash
38	38	10	Rene Charland	Gary Weaver '64 Ford	8	455	Oil Press
39	35	59	Tom Pistone	Glen Sweet '64 Ford	1	450	Handling
40	22	32	Rock Harn	'64 Ford	1	445	Crash
41	23	90	Sonny Hutchins	Junie Donlavey '64 Ford	1	440	Crash
42	24	01	Harold Kite	'65 Plymouth	1	410	Crash
43	25	79	Frank Warren	Harold Rhodes '63 Chevrolet	1	405	Crash
44	27	53	Jimmy Helms	David Warren '63 Ford	1	400	Crash

Time of Race: 3 hours, 21 minutes, 44 seconds
Average Speed: 119.117 mph
Pole Winner: Fred Lorenzen - 147.773 mph
Fastest Qualifier: Marvin Panch - 147.895 mph
Lap Leaders: Cale Yarborough 1-17, Darel Dieringer 18-29, Yarborough 30-39,
    A J Foyt 40-74, LeeRoy Yarbrough 75-80, Foyt 81-98, Fred Lorenzen 99,
    Curtis Turner 100-101, Dick Hutcherson 102, Earl Balmer 103-108, Turner 109-121,
    Dieringer 122-155, Ned Jarrett 156-163, Foyt 164-168, Dieringer 169, Foyt 170-172,
    Dieringer 173, Foyt 174-214, Turner 215-216, Lorenzen 217-224, Foyt 225-234,
    Lorenzen 235-241, Foyt 242, Lorenzen 243-247, Foyt 248, Lorenzen 249, Foyt 250-254,
    Lorenzen 255-267.
Cautions: 6 for 47 laps.   Margin of Victory: 3 car lengths   Attendance: 50,000

old Kite, who was making his first Grand National start in over nine years.

Kite was killed in the second lap when his out of control Plymouth was nailed by a speeding Jimmy Helms in the third turn. The 43 year-old East Point, GA driver, winner of the first February Speedweek Grand National race at Daytona in 1950, died almost instantly of massive internal injuries and a severed leg. Helms was treated for cuts and bruises and released from the track-side hospital.

The accident occurred as a pack of cars were dicing for position early in the race. Rock Harn, Sonny Hutchins and Frank Warren tangled and skidded into the retaining barrier. Kite slid sideways to miss the wreck and slid down off the banking. Helms, ducking below chaos in the upper groove, dived low and squarely struck Kite's drivers door.

Lorenzen, bidding to end a five month winless

Dick Hutcherson #29, Fred Lorenzen #28 and Curtis Turner #41 three-abreast in final laps at Charlotte

slump, and A.J.Foyt treated the crowd of 50,000 to a tremendous white-knuckle struggle for 44 laps. Dick Hutcherson, Lorenzen's teammate on the Holman-Moody team, and Curtis Turner were following in the leaders' shadow.

With six laps to go, Foyt made a stab at Lorenzen on the high side entering turn three. His Ford darted up high, wiggled a little and then caught the guard rail. Foyt rode the barrier for 100 yards before spinning out. Hutcherson squeaked by. Turner spun his car to avoid Foyt.

Lorenzen scooted out to a lead and beat Hutcherson by three car lengths. Ned Jarrett got fourth place and LeeRoy Yarbrough fifth. Foyt recovered and finished sixth.

Jarrett's fourth place finish enabled him to clinch the 1965 NASCAR Grand National championship.

Smokey Yunick entered a '65 Chevy with Bunkie Blackburn as driver. After an assortment of problems, the car was withdrawn.

Cale Yarborough led for 27 of the first 47 laps, but the Timmonsville, SC youngster was out of the race

early with engine problems.

Lorenzen averaged 119.117 mph as 47 laps were run under the caution flag.

Grand National Race No. 53
112 Laps at Orange Speedway
Hillsborough, NC
100 Miles on .9-mile Dirt Track
October 24, 1965

Fin	St	No	Driver	Team / Car	Laps	Money	Status
1	1	47	Dick Hutcherson	Holman-Moody '65 Ford	112	$1,000	Running
2	8	59	Tom Pistone	Glen Sweet '64 Ford	109	600	Running
3	4	43	Jim Paschal	Petty Engineering '64 Plym	109	400	Running
4	6	06	Cale Yarborough	Kenny Myler '64 Ford	106	300	Running
5	9	56	Paul Lewis	Lewis '64 Ford	105	275	Running
6	5	6	David Pearson	Cotton Owens ' 65 Dodge	102	240	Running
7	19	9	Darel Dieringer	Roy Tyner '65 Chevrolet	100	200	Running
8	11	68	Bob Derrington	Derrington '63 Ford	98	175	Running
9	20	80	Worth McMillion	Allen McMillion '64 Pontiac	97	150	Running
10	13	89	Neil Castles	Buck Baker '65 Olds	95	140	Running
11	7	88	Buddy Baker	Buck Baker '64 Dodge	93	130	Fan belt
12	16	20	Clyde Lynn	Lynn '64 Ford	90	120	Running
13	10	31	Ned Setzer	Sam Fogle '63 Ford	70	110	Running
14	17	34	Wendell Scott	Scott '63 Ford	63	100	Crash
15	2	26	Junior Johnson	Johnson '65 Ford	59	100	A-Frame
16	3	11	Ned Jarrett	Bondy Long '65 Ford	56	100	Engine
17	18	2	G C Spencer	Cliff Stewart '63 Pontiac	29	100	Engine
18	14	62	Buddy Arrington	Arrington '64 Dodge	26	100	A-Frame
19	15	38	Wayne Smith	Smith '65 Chevrolet	11	100	Clutch
20	12	97	Jimmy Helms	Gene Cline '64 Ford	1	100	Brakes

Time of Race: 1 hour, 9 minutes, 9 seconds
Average Speed: 87.462 mph
Pole Winner: Dick Hutcherson - 98.810 mph
Lap Leaders: David Pearson 1-24, Junior Johnson 25-59, Dick Hutcherson 60-112.
Cautions: 3 for 14 laps   Margin of Victory: 3-laps plus   Attendance: 4,500.

Race No. 53

Hutcherson First-to-Last-to-First at Hillsborough

HILLSBOROUGH, NC (Oct. 24) -- Determined Dick Hutcherson shook off an early setback and won going away in the 100-mile Grand National race at Orange Speedway. It was the ninth win of the year for the factory backed Ford rookie -- although he is ineligible for the rookie of the year award.

Pole sitter Hutcherson ran side-by-side with Junior Johnson for the first lap on the .9-mile dirt oval. Johnson's left front bumper sliced Hutcherson's right front tire and the Keokuk, IA driver had to make an unscheduled pit stop. He was a lap behind when he returned to the track.

At the finish, Hutcherson was three laps ahead of the field as independent Tom Pistone earned runner-up honors. Jim Paschal, in a Petty Engineering Plymouth, came in third. Cale Yarborough was fourth and Paul Lewis fifth.

David Pearson led the first 24 laps, driving under the Hutcherson-Johnson rubdown in the first lap. Johnson got his Ford sorted out and chased down Pearson, taking the lead on lap 25. Johnson was building his lead when the A-frame broke on lap 57, causing the car to sag with the left front wheel at a 45-degree angle.

Despite the fact that he was able to maintain his lead, NASCAR officials blackflagged Johnson after 59 laps. He was unable to make repairs and settled for a 15th place finish in the field of 20. Pearson fell off the pace with mechanical problems and wound up sixth, 10 laps behind.

The caution was out three times for 14 laps. Hutcherson averaged 87.462 mph for the 112-lap race. Only 4,500 spectators showed up at the historic facility.

Race No. 54

Comeback Complete; Turner Tames New Rockingham Track

ROCKINGHAM, NC (Oct. 31) --Curtis Turner, making his seventh start on the Grand National tour since his reinstatement, drove the Wood Brothers Ford to an 11-second victory in the inaugural American 500 at the new North Carolina Motor Speedway. It was the 17th career win for the 41 year-old Roanoke, VA veteran, but his first since March 8, 1959 when he won a 100-miler at Concord, NC

Cale Yarborough finished second, Marvin Panch was third and G.C. Spencer fourth as Ford swept the top four positions in the much ballyhooed return of Plymouth and Dodge factory cars on superspeedways. Jim Paschal with relief help from Richard Petty, wound up fifth after experiencing ignition problems.

Turner, who started fourth and led on eight occasions for a total of 239 laps, got around Yarborough with 27 laps remaining. After many of the contenders were taken out by an assortment of troubles, Turner and Cale were left in a lap by themselves.

Yarborough had to make a late pit stop, which allowed Turner to pick up first place. When he returned to the track he was 17 seconds behind. He cut the deficit to 11 seconds at the finish line.

Turner, who said he was "driving as hard as I could go", tagged the wall twice -- once in the final stretch run with Yarborough. "I was running hard through the

turns, drove into a little dust on the track and hit the wall," explained Turner. "But that didn't make any difference. The car was running beautifully all day."

Petty started on the pole, but crashed his Plymouth in a five car wreck on lap 59. David Pearson and Gene Black were also involved. On lap 126, Petty took the driving chores for Paschal, who had started ninth in another Petty Plymouth.

Grand National Race No. 54
500 Laps at North Carolina Motor Speedway
Rockingham, NC
"American 500"
500 Miles on 1-mile Paved Track
October 31, 1965

Fin	St	No.	Driver	Team / Car	Laps	Money	Status
1	4	41	Curtis Turner	Wood Brothers '65 Ford	500	$13,090	Running
2	7	27	Cale Yarborough	Banjo Matthews '65 Ford	500	6,450	Running
3	5	21	Marvin Panch	Wood Brothers '65 Ford	498	4,010	Running
4	17	49	G C Spencer	Spencer '64 Ford	490	2,450	Running
5	9	42	Jim Paschal*	Petty Engineering '65 Plym	486	2,000	Running
6	13	19	J T Putney	Herman Beam '65 Chevrolet	482	1,300	Running
7	8	29	Dick Hutcherson	Holman-Moody '65 Ford	475	1,150	Running
8	15	64	Elmo Langley	Langley '64 Ford	468	1,100	Running
9	25	87	Buck Baker	Baker '65 Chevrolet	468	1,150	Running
10	24	56	Paul Lewis	Curtis Larimer '64 Ford	459	1,000	Running
11	21	44	Larry Hess	Hess '64 Ford	457	845	Running
12	18	7	Bobby Johns	Shorty Johns '64 Pontiac	448	870	Running
13	41	83	Worth McMillion	Allen McMillion '65 Pontiac	439	810	Running
14	36	38	Wayne Smith	Smith '65 Chevrolet	434	805	Running
15	35	97	Jimmy Helms	Gene Cline '64 Ford	434	785	Running
16	12	11	Ned Jarrett	Bondy Long '65 Ford	425	720	W. bear.
17	38	68	Bob Derrington	Derrington '63 Ford	414	730	Running
18	19	25	Jabe Thomas	Thomas '64 Ford	408	715	Running
19	30	88	Neil Castles	Buck Baker '64 Dodge	408	675	Running
20	34	34	Wendell Scott	Scott '63 Ford	385	680	Running
21	10	35	Bobby Isaac	Nichels Eng. '65 Dodge	341	735	Engine
22	29	79	Frank Warren	Harold Rhodes '63 Chevrolet	305	625	Valve
23	11	24	Sam McQuagg	Betty Lilly '65 Ford	254	640	Engine
24	14	86	Buddy Baker	Buck Baker '65 Plym	253	605	Crash
25	3	6	David Pearson	Cotton Owens '65 Dodge	234	645	Engine
26	42	9	Roy Tyner	Tyner '65 Chevrolet	228	590	Gr. Seal
27	6	28	Fred Lorenzen	Holman-Moody '65 Ford	214	585	Engine
28	22	57	Lionel Johnson	Clay Esteridge '64 Ford	200	580	Clutch
29	16	17	Junior Spencer	Jerry Mullins '64 Ford	194	575	A-Frame
30	37	52	E J Trivette	Jess Potter '63 Ford	183	600	Fuel leak
31	27	46	Roy Mayne	Tom Hunter '65 Chevrolet	166	590	Axle
32	2	26	Junior Johnson	Johnson '65 Ford	154	1,100	Engine
33	20	18	Stick Elliott	Toy Bolton '65 Chevrolet	113	555	Oil press
34	26	59	Tom Pistone	Glen Sweet '64 Ford	90	600	Engine
35	32	02	Doug Cooper	Bob Cooper '65 Chevrolet	79	645	Engine
36	1	43	Richard Petty	Petty Engineering '65 Plym	58	1,240	Crash
37	40	89	Darrell Bryant	Buck Baker '65 Olds	57	555	No tires
38	28	75	Gene Black	C L Crawford '64 Ford	52	530	Crash
39	39	1	Rene Charland	'64 Ford	18	550	Oil Press
40	33	63	Don Hume	Hume '63 Ford	13	570	Brakes
41	43	67	Buddy Arrington	Arrington '64 Dodge	5	515	Oil leak
42	23	48	John Sears	L G DeWitt '64 Ford	1	510	Crash
43	31	10	Darel Dieringer	Gary Weaver '64 Ford	0	705	Crash

Time of Race: 4 hours, 54 minutes, 17 seconds
Average Speed: 101.942 mph
Pole Winner: Richard Petty - 116.260 mph
Lap Leaders: Junior Johnson 1-45, Curtis Turner 46, Marvin Panch 47-48, Johnson 49-81,
    Bobby Isaac 82, Johnson 83-89, Isaac 90-99, Turner 100-145, Panch 146-175,
    Turner 176-275, Jim Paschal 276-359, Turner 360-364, Johnson 365-378,
    Turner 379-438, Cale Yarborough 439-473, Turner 474-500.
Cautions: 8 for 55 laps   Margin of Victory: 11 seconds   Attendance: 35,000
*Relieved by Richard Petty

Junior Johnson #26, Richard Petty #43 and eventual winner Curtis Turner #41 battle early in inaugural American 500 at Rockingham

Petty was two laps down, but dashed around the one-mile oval with abandon. He grabbed first place in the 276th lap and proceeded to lap the field. Ignition problems spoiled a celebrated return for the Chrysler team.

Junior Johnson and Bobby Isaac ran hub-to-hub for first place for 50 laps. They traded the lead four times. Johnson eventually left after 54 laps with a blown engine; and Isaac popped his engine on lap 341.

After the race, Johnson hinted at retirement and said he would seriously consider putting Isaac in his car.

A crowd of 35,000 watched Turner average 101.942 mph. Ford Motor Co. had considered boycotting the race. They contended that their big Galaxies "can't run with those compact cars. There's no comparison."

Race No. 55

Jarrett Wins $1,111 For Taking Moyock 300

Bobby Isaac won pole in first start in the Junior Johnson Ford

MOYOCK, NC (Nov. 7) -- Ned Jarrett took the lead from Bobby Isaac in the 246th lap and led the rest of the way to win the 1965 season finale 100-mile Grand National race at Dog Track Speedway. It was Jarrett's 13th win of the season and his

Grand National Race No. 55
300 Laps at Dog Track Speedway
Moyock, NC
"Tidewater 300"
100 Miles on .333-mile Paved Track
November 7, 1965

Fin	St	No.	Driver	Team / Car	Laps	Money	Status
1	2	11	Ned Jarrett	Bondy Long '65 Ford	300	$1,111	Running
2	1	26	Bobby Isaac	Junior Johnson '65 Ford	299	600	Running
3	15	87	Buddy Baker	Buck Baker '65 Chevrolet	297	400	Running
4	4	42	Jim Paschal	Petty Engineering '65 Plym	297	300	Running
5	3	59	Tom Pistone	Glen Sweet '64 Ford	295	275	Running
6	14	02	Doug Cooper	Bob Cooper '65 Chevrolet	293	240	Running
7	5	19	J T Putney	Herman Beam '65 Chevrolet	291	200	Running
8	10	06	Sam McQuagg	Kenny Myler '64 Ford	291	175	Running
9	6	88	Neil Castles	Buck Baker '64 Dodge	289	150	Running
10	20	48	John Sears	L G DeWitt '64 Ford	280	140	Running
11	18	68	Bob Derrington	Derrington '63 Ford	268	130	Running
12	24	80	Worth McMillion	Allen McMillion '64 Pontiac	265	120	Running
13	19	38	Wayne Smith	Smith '65 Chevrolet	257	110	Running
14	21	89	Goldie Parsons	Buck Baker '65 Olds	242	100	Running
15	13	9	Roy Tyner	Tyner '65 Chevrolet	233	100	Differen
16	7	7	Bobby Johns	Shorty Johns '65 Pontiac	200	100	Running
17	11	1	Gil Hearne	'64 Ford	172	100	Brakes
18	17	00	Bill Champion	'64 Ford	109	100	Differen
19	23	44	Jim Tatum	Larry Hess '64 Ford	103	100	Differen
20	22	99	Joe Holder	Gene Hobby ' 64 Dodge	100	100	Steering
21	9	64	Elmo Langley	Langley '64 Ford	81	100	Steering
22	12	34	Wendell Scott	Scott '63 Ford	32	100	Radiator
23	8	18	Darel Dieringer	Toy Bolton '65 Chevrolet	24	---	Ignition
24	16	62	Buddy Arrington	Arrington '64 Dodge	15	---	Heating
25	25	83	G T Nolan	Allen McMillion '64 Pontiac	2	---	Ignition

Time of Race: 1 hour, 34 minutes, 5 seconds
Average Speed: 63.773 mph
Pole Winner: Bobby Isaac - 68.143 mph
Lap Leaders: Bobby Isaac 1-56, Ned Jarrett 57- , Isaac - , Jim Paschal - ,
   Jarrett - , Isaac -245, Jarrett 246-300.
Cautions: Margin of Victory: 1-lap plus   Attendance:

earnings of $1,111 left him one dollar ahead of Fred Lorenzen in the regular season winnings.

Jarrett sealed up his second NASCAR driving championship, finishing 3,034 points ahead of runner-up

Dick Hutcherson, who did not enter. Jarrett's winnings for the regular season plus post season awards, came to $93,624.40.

Jarrett and Isaac, the front row starters, battled close for almost the entire distance. Isaac, in his first assignment for the Junior Johnson Ford team, led the first 56 laps from the pole. Jarrett got by on lap 57 and the two drivers staged a door-to-door battle. Jarrett pulled away in the end and won by more than a lap.

Third place went to Buddy Baker, Jim Paschal was fourth and Tom Pistone fifth.

Driving as a teammate to Buddy Baker was Gloria "Goldie" Parsons, a 24 year-old blond out of Clemmons, NC. Parsons was driving an Oldsmobile from the Buck Baker stable and she spun out twice. Parsons wound up 14th in the field of 25 -- 58 laps behind the winner. "Buck told me to stay to the inside and keep out of trouble," said the perky Parsons. "That's what I tried to do."

Jarrett averaged 63.773 mph for the 300 lapper on the .333-mile paved track. It was his 50th career Grand National win, tying him for second place with Junior Johnson.

1965 NASCAR Season
Final Point Standings - Grand National Division

Rank	Driver	Points	Starts	Wins	Top 5	Top 10	Winnings
1	Ned Jarrett	38,824	54	13	42	45	$93,624.40
2	Dick Hutcherson	35,790	52	9	32	37	57,850.50
3	Darel Dieringer	24,696	35	1	10	15	52,213.63
4	G.C. Spencer	24,314	47	0	14	25	29,774.72
5	Marvin Panch	22,798	20	4	12	14	64,026.29
6	Bob Derrington	21,394	51	0	3	19	20,119.90
7	J.T. Putney	20,928	40	0	10	24	22,328.75
8	Neil Castles	20,848	51	0	6	28	22,328.75
9	Buddy Baker	20,672	42	0	12	17	26,836.21
10	Cale Yarborough	20,192	46	1	13	21	26,586.21
11	Wendell Scott	19,902	52	0	4	21	18,638.93
12	Junior Johnson	18,486	36	13	18	19	62,215.29
13	Fred Lorenzen	18,448	17	4	5	6	80,614,61
14	Paul Lewis	18,118	24	0	3	13	13,246.21
15	E.J. Trivette	13,450	39	0	0	7	13,247.95
16	Larry Hess	13,148	10	0	0	3	9,259.14
17	Buck Baker	13,136	31	0	3	12	21,579.14
18	Jimmy Helms	12,996	39	0	0	4	12,049.14
19	Doug Cooper	12,920	30	0	1	9	12,379.14
20	Bobby Johns	12,842	13	0	5	5	24,929.14
21	Tiny Lund	12,820	30	1	8	17	11,750
22	Buddy Arrington	11,744	31	0	6	9	11,600
23	Earl Balmer	11,636	9	0	2	4	19,045
24	Sam McQuagg	11,460	15	0	2	5	10,555
25	Elmo Langley	10,982	34	0	3	9	10,555
26	Henley Gray	9,552	38	0	1	7	8,320
27	Roy Mayne	8,838	15	0	1	5	9,060
28	Junior Spencer	8,436	21	0	2	7	9,345
29	H.B. Bailey	7,340	5	0	1	3	5,000
30	Wayne Smith	7,326	25	0	0	2	6,790
31	Donald Tucker	7,118	9	0	1	3	5,680
32	Tom Pistone	6,598	33	0	4	8	10,050
33	Bub Strickler	6,540	10	0	0	2	5,275
34	Bobby Allison	6,152	8	0	0	3	4,780
35	Jim Paschal	6,046	10	0	4	4	7,805
36	Roy Tyner	5,882	28	0	1	6	6,505
37	LeeRoy Yarbrough	5,852	14	0	2	3	5,905
38	Richard Petty	5,638	14	4	10	10	16,450
39	Curtis Turner	5,542	7	1	3	3	17,440
40	David Pearson	5,464	14	0	8	11	8,925
41	Clyde Lynn	5,414	24	0	0	9	4,545
42	Gene Black	4,970	18	0	0	4	6,080
43	Ned Setzer	4,828	8	0	0	3	4,805
44	Stick Elliott	4,332	14	0	2	3	4,985
45	Reb Wickersham	4,322	7	0	0	2	4,410
46	Frank Warren	3,814	4	0	0	1	2,880
47	Worth McMillion	3,794	10	0	0	2	2,590
48	Lionel Johnson	3,510	8	0	0	2	3,105
49	Paul "Bud" Moore	3,216	14	0	3	7	3,434
50	Sonny Hutchins	3,118	10	0	1	2	3,780

The 1966 Season

Balks, Boycotts --
and the Yellow Banana

Volume three of a four volume series . . Big Bucks and Boycotts   1965 - 1971

1966

As the 1965 Grand National season drew to a close, NASCAR was licking a few wounds. The Chrysler boycott had produced a box office disaster. Attendance figures at the major NASCAR tracks were a far cry from the record wrecking year of 1964.

On Monday, December 13, 1965, Bill France was at the Chrysler manufacturing plant to check on volume production. "I saw more hemi engines made today than Ferrari makes cars in a year," he remarked. Chrysler was back in the fold. NASCAR approved the powerful Chrysler hemi engine since it had become a production item.

Under the 1966 rules the 426 c.i. hemi would be allowed in intermediate and full size cars on short tracks and road courses. It would, however, be allowed on superspeedways only if they were bolted into a big Plymouth Fury or Dodge Polara. If the Chrysler teams wanted to run the smaller Belvedere, Coronet or Charger on the super tracks, they would have to use a 405 c.i hemi. These rules were actually the result of a recommendation by the Automobile Competition Committee of the United States (ACCUS), the American arm of the International Automobile Federation (FIA).

France felt these specifications, approved by both NASCAR and USAC, would be met with approval of both Chrysler and Ford -- and he kept hoping General Motors would slide back in.

But the problem was not solved. At the moment France stood at the Chrysler production line on December 13th, Ford Motor Co. made an announcement of its own. NASCAR Ford teams would utilize a new single OverHead Cam engine and would be out in force to defend their impressive laurels of 1965. All of France's efforts to achieve a balance between Ford and Chrysler as to the speed capabilities of each was crumbling.

The Ford announcement was made without previous notification to the sanctioning bodies. It was common practice for a manufacturer to obtain approval of new equipment before announcing intent to use it.

On Friday, December 17, 1965, NASCAR and USAC jointly said they would not permit the use of the OHC, citing lack of production. "I asked Ford officials if someone could order 50 OHC engines," said France. "The man told me they weren't available. If Ford is sincere about the OHC becoming a production engine, they will still make it available to the public without being able to use it in racing."

Henry Banks, Competition Director of USAC, said "Ford put the cart ahead of the horse. They should have gotten it approved before they announced they were going to use it."

Things got sticky just before the holidays. Ford's Leo C. Beebe said that they would not be able to field factory backed cars for Riverside or Daytona. Beebe added that Ford's plans had been based on the use of the OHC engine and since it was denied, "it will be impossible for us to prepare factory sponsored vehicles for the early stock car races at Riverside and Daytona."

Fearing another long term walkout, France discussed the situation with Ford officials. In a joint announcement on Christmas day, NASCAR and USAC said that Ford had agreed to continue its support of stock car racing without interruption. France said the OHC "will be looked upon as an experimental engine in 1966 and it will be reviewed for eligibility in 1967."

France left the door open for Ford if they mass produced the OHC.

Recently retired Junior Johnson, who had signed Bobby Isaac to drive his Ford in the 1966 Grand National season, said NASCAR was splitting hairs with regard to the rules. "There isn't anything production about a stock car," he growled. "A production car wouldn't last three laps at Daytona and there's never been a production engine raced in NASCAR with any success. Who does France think he's kidding?"

In late December, Ford took Fred Lorenzen to Daytona for a private testing session. The OHC engine was strapped into a big Ford Galaxie and Lorenzen turned some laps in the 178 mph range. "We had no problems," said Lorenzen. "It was really moving."

Ford's Dan Gurney racked up his fourth straight Motor Trend 500 victory at Riverside in January -- keeping Ford's unblemished record intact. But the factory Fords had difficulty keeping up with the heavy-hitting Chryslers on the big banks of Daytona. They were beaten badly in both 100-mile qualifiers and the Daytona 500. In 280 laps of racing at Daytona, Ford automobiles led only 67 laps. Ford Motor Co. executives were faced with the harsh reality that they would be in for a long year if their OHC was not approved.

The NASCAR President said "Ford is acting like children" when they pulled out of Grand National racing

Five days after Speedweeks ended, Ford said that a street version of its 427 c.i. OHC was now available as a production item. Donald N. Frey, Ford Division General Manager, said, "They (NASCAR) said they would reconsider the OverHead Cam when it went into production. In making the engine available to the public, we hope to qualify it for the stock car circuit."

Frey said the basic configuration of the OHC 'street' was the same as the racing version, except carburetion. Some other components had been altered "to provide smoother, safer operation on public roads," he added.

Rather then being dragged into another no-win situation, France said he would leave the final decision to ACCUS, the United States arm of the International Automobile Federation, the world governing body of auto racing.

On April 6, ACCUS announced approval of Ford's OHC engine -- with a handicap. In the past, NASCAR had handicapped certain engines -- but it had been governed by displacement. In 1966, it would be in weight as well as displacement.

The displacement in 1966 was 427 cubic inches. And there was a general 4,000 minimum weight limit on NASCAR Grand National cars. That computed to about 9.36 pounds per cubic inch.

If Ford wanted to use the OHC engine, the car would have to weigh 4,423.7 pounds or 10.36 pounds per c.i. The rule for the other engines with 427 cubic inch displacement would remain at 9.36 pounds per c.i. or a minimum weight of 3,996.72 pounds.

Problem solved? No. Ford officials contended the weight handicap was unfair -- and it would place undue loads on the tires. NASCAR's France said the new ruling would be subject to adjustments if tests showed it to be unfair, "but no adjustments will be made until it has been tested," said France.

The three main provisions of the new rules were:

1. *Ford's new OHC engine, previously not permitted, is allowed in competition with a weight handicap. The new engine is permitted in cars with 119 inch wheelbase (Galaxie).*
2. *Ford's Wedge engine is permitted with 2 four-barrel carburetors instead of 1 in all cars (116-119 inch wheelbase).*
3. *Chrysler's hemi remains with 1 four barrel carburetor, and is allowed in all cars (116" - 119") on all tracks.*

Ford immediately announced that it was pulling out of three short track races at Columbia, SC, Greenville, SC and Winston-Salem, NC. Their principle drivers Ned Jarrett, Bobby Isaac and Curtis Turner would be instructed not to compete in the three races held over a five day period.

"Ford hadn't planned on running the OHC in any of the three places," countered France. "The weight rule has absolutely nothing to do with these races. Ford is acting like children. I don't understand it."

On Friday April 15, as teams were checking into North Wilkesboro Speedway for the Gwyn Staley Memorial, Ford announced that it was beginning a boycott of NASCAR stock car racing. Attempts for an eleventh hour compromise by NASCAR fell through.

"We can't be competitive under these new rules," announced Ford President Henry Ford II. "We are giving away too much to the Chryslers. And besides that, the safety factor in this is quite important. We couldn't keep wheels on the car at this weight."

The next day, France met in Charlotte with 20 Grand National promoters. "The meeting was very cordial," said France. "Most of the time we discussed the 1967 rules, trying to set up regulations that would satisfy everyone including the independents. On the OHC, we have to make a test of it to see if our restrictions are correct. Until then, we can't do anything. We survived the 1957 AMA resolution and we can survive this."

Ford's announcement brought varied responses from the auto racing gallery.

Fred Lorenzen, Ford driver: *"Ford has backed me from the start. I can't and won't switch now."*

Cale Yarborough, Ford driver: *"Ford helped me when I needed them. I'm going to stick with them."*

Ned Jarrett, Ford driver and defending Grand National champion: *"We just can't keep treating the spectators the way we have the past couple of seasons."*

Bob Colvin, President of Darlington Raceway: *"Ford's squawking might just be laying the groundwork for an 'I told you so' attitude later in case the OHC doesn't work out. I don't think Ford can afford to pull out for good."*

Carl Moore, President Bristol International Speedway: *"Ford has spent millions in this 'Total Performance' ad campaign. I don't think they will allow that to go down the drain."*

Bobby Isaac, Ford driver: *"I'm just like a faucet. They turn me on, I go racing. They turn me off, I stop."*

Richard Petty, Plymouth driver: *"The car companies to me are like Russia, Red China and the United States sitting down at a big table and saying 'let's stop playing war'. An agreement is almost impossible."*

Thomas Binford, USAC President: *"The action by Ford certainly is not with the 'Total Performance' image they have advocated and advertised. The ACCUS members have tried to buy OHC engines to conduct a thorough and unbiased test with regard to the new regulations. But the search has proved futile. There seems to be no OHC engines available to purchase. Ford Motor Co. has presented no new evidence regarding the capabilities of the OHC, nor have they permitted access to the engine for testing. There is no justification for altering the rule. It will stand as announced. The decision to increase the weight to 1 pound per c.i. over the present 9.36 was not arrived at overnight. A good many formulas were discussed. It has always been our feeling that power-to-weight is an important factor of competition, and we arrived at our decision in an effort to keep the competition fair."*

Ford Motor Co. ordered all of its factory equipment be shipped to the Holman-Moody shops in Charlotte. Ford refused to allow their contracted teams to operate as independents.

Hank Schoolfield, editor and publisher of Southern MotoRacing, editorialized in his column: *"The sport has become large, but it is not grown up. It will not grow up, nor will it escape from such problems as the present one as long as it can be controlled by car makers. It will be controlled by car makers as long as its rules are such that winning can be accomplished only with special, high-performance equipment that is controlled by car makers.*

"Such control has been exercised for several years,

with the sport's welfare tottering on the ability of its organizers to tightrope along a very thin thread of appeasements and adjustments to keep the car makers happy.

"For the sport to regain control of itself, it must eliminate the car maker's control by making rules that will permit only the equipment that is equally available to all contestants."

As Ford began its self-imposed exile, they didn't draw much sympathy from the auto racing public. Tom Pistone, an independent out of Chicago who always seemed to be down to his last dollar, was giving the factory Chrysler drivers fits on the short track. Pistone, in a two year-old Ford, won the pole at Columbia and finished third. He finished second at Winston-Salem, and very nearly won the Virginia 500 at Martinsville.

Dick Hutcherson was caught in Ford boycott; yet won 3 races in abbreviated season

"Ford should feel ashamed if they can't build a car better than Tom Pistone," said Plymouth's Paul Goldsmith. "Tom had the fastest car at Martinsville."

While his Ford was competitive on the short tracks, Pistone felt he needed more horses to run up front on the superspeedways. "I wanted to run an OHC at Darlington in the Rebel 400," said Pistone. "Even with the extra weight, I wanted to give it a go. I tried to buy one from Holman-Moody, but they wouldn't sell me one. I'm not sure if they *wouldn't* or *couldn't* sell me one."

Tom Pistone's strong runs in self-owned Ford did not help Ford Motor Company's image in the eyes of the public

J. Elsie Webb, President of North Carolina Motor Speedway at Rockingham, announced on May 11 that the promoters were backing France in this latest dispute. "We have now left it up to Ford," said Webb. "We stand completely behind Mr. France. We want Mr. Ford to know the number of people he is hurting by his decision to stay out of racing. The little man, the average stockholder at each of the speedways, the Ford dealers, the racing fan and of course the sport itself."

Clay Earles, President of Martinsville Speedway, was ruffled by the prospect of another long term struggle, and a starting field devoid of the super stars. "We might as well plow up our race tracks and plant them with vegetable crops if we can't get some assurance that the top drivers will compete in Grand National events," he said. "No amount of promotion is going to help you if you haven't got the top men in the sport in your race."

On the other hand, Alvin Hawkins, promoter at Bowman Gray Stadium in Winston-Salem, said the level of competition is better on the short tracks when the factory teams are not present. "Personally," said Hawkins, "I don't care if they never get things settled. When their business is bad, our business is good."

Reporter Joe Whitlock observed: "There have been a few unpredictable moments, a few unsuccessful races, a handful of disappointing conferences and more than enough unanswered questions. The muddled situation created by Ford's April withdrawl could have produced chaos. But promoters went to work promoting, and the fans, once convinced Ford was the villain, responded."

It was only a matter of time before the Ford drivers began a mutiny. Curtis Turner was the first -- making an announcement that he would leave Ford and drive for Smokey Yunick in the Rebel 400. "I've only got a few years left to drive," said Turner. "Others may be able to sit around, but I've got to make the most of what time I have left. I need to be racin'."

Turner started eighth in the Yunick Chevrolet at Darlington, but went out with broken wheel bolts on lap 150.

Marvin Panch and Ned Jarrett followed shortly after Darlington. "Racing is my business," said Panch. "I am not under contract to Ford Motor Co. and I have a family to feed." Lee Petty, patriarch of Petty Enterprises, said a Plymouth would be readied for Panch to drive in the World 600 at Charlotte.

Ned Jarrett quit Ford also. "I will have to sever my relationship with Ford," said Jarrett. "I really hate to. But I just feel I should be out there running. I'm missing too much money by not racing. Besides, the fans

should not be deprived to seeing the defending Grand National champion another year."

Jarrett worked out a deal with Henley Gray to drive in the 600.

Panch won the World 600 in Cinderella fashion.

By the second week in July, Ford was still on the sidelines -- and Chrysler was doing most of the winning. There was word that Ford was contemplating making a return. Their boycott was not having the same effects on racing that Chrysler's withdrawl did a year earlier.

Ford and the tire companies went to Daytona to test the OHC and the rubber compounds. "What works on a Chrysler doesn't necessarily work on a Ford," said H.A. "Humpy" Wheeler, Southeastern Manager of Firestone's racing division. "The trees are shaking and there is a possibility Ford might be back before the year is out. We want to be prepared. We all have to get to work or we'll get behind the 8-ball. It's going to be a heck of a challenge to keep something on the car."

On July 13, Junior Johnson and Bobby Isaac both tested Johnson's Ford at Daytona. LeeRoy Yarbrough tested a Dodge Charger. On July 18, Dick Hutcherson tested the Holman-Moody Ford for Goodyear tires.

NASCAR arranged a private meeting with Ford officials. Fred Langley, General Manager of East Tennessee Motor Co in Knoxville, acted as mediator. "Ford's OHC engine should *never* have been approved for racing," said Langley, whose company had been involved in racing for several years. "Ford should have stayed in stock car racing this year with the Wedge engine. The company should have kept the OHC out until it was sold as a regular production line item and met NASCAR specifications. As soon as it was available to the public, then NASCAR could have no other action than approve it for use without the weight handicap."

Following Langley's surprising slap at the parent company, he made another announcement. "We at East Tennessee Motor Co. will sponsor Dick Hutcherson for the rest of 1966," added Langley. "I see no reason why Dick will not be competitive with any other car on the track."

Although Hutcherson's mount could not be readied by the August 7 Dixie 500, there was another

Junior Johnson brought his Ford to Atlanta in August. The car, which carried a variety of nicknames, created an uproar by passing NASCAR's technical inspection

Ford at Atlanta International Raceway.

It was Junior Johnson's 1966 Ford Galaxie. Fred Lorenzen was listed as driver, replacing Isaac. It was causing quite a stir. One wag quipped, "There's something over there in the garage area. I'm not sure what it is. It's some kind of yellow creation from the Wilkes County Chicken Coop."

The car was a yellow Ford entered by

Fred Lorenzen, driving Junior Johnson's "Yellow Banana", leads Darel Dieringer's Mercury down the front chute at Atlanta. Note the chopped roof of the Johnson Ford

Junior Johnson Racing. It was supposed to carry some resemblance bestowed by the original car maker -- Ford Motor Co. But somewhere along the line, it missed the boat.

Bob Hoffman, Editor of Southern MotorSports Journal, said, "The car's roof line had been lowered so much that (driver) Freddy Lorenzen was forced to lower his seat in order to see out the windshield."

Hank Schoolfield remarked, "It looked weird enough to be put together by a committee."

The Johnson Ford was a unique specimen of an "American family sedan". The roof had been chopped and lowered. The front windshield was sloped back. The front fenders hovered over the front tires. The rear deck lid rose up in the air, and the car looked like a four-wheel vacuum cleaner.

The car became known as the *"Yellow Banana"* . And it *passed* NASCAR inspection. So did Smokey Yunick's Chevrolet. Standing beside the black and gold Chevelle, it almost seemed that it was a miniature of sorts -- smaller than the production line model. A cluster of innovative technology was tucked neatly under the sheet metal. Wheels were off-centered and the roof line had been blessed with a handcrafted 'spoiler'.

While Johnson's Ford and Yunick's Chevrolet didn't run into any obstacles at the inspection station, three other cars did. A Ford owned by Bernard Alvarez and scheduled to be driven by Ned Jarrett, was turned away. There was not the time nor the manpower to correct every item needed to get clearance from Norris Friel, NASCAR's chief Technical Director.

LeeRoy Yarbrough and car owner Jon Thorne were sent packing when NASCAR found blocks of wood in the springs. The wood could fall out during the race, thus lowering the front of the car and creating an aerodynamic gem.

Cotton Owens, owner of the Dodge David Pearson

had put into the Grand National point lead, watched all of this curiously. He went back to his garage stall and began to do a little creating himself. He rigged a device where Pearson could pull a cable and lower the front of the car during the race.

Friel blew the whistle on Owens. He told the blond-thatched Owens to get it within the boundaries of the rule book or hit the highway.

Owens withdrew his car in protest and put the season championship in jeopardy. "It's a pretty bitter pill to swallow," said Owens. "The device lowered the car about a half-inch. This was the only way we could be competitive with these other two *funny* cars. You have to fight fire with fire. On top of it all, NASCAR lets those other two cars race.

"This may cause me and David to lose the championship," he added. "But somebody has got to stand up for what is right."

Pearson publicly backed Owens. "Instead of lowering the body like the others did," said Pearson, "we should have lowered the whole car. We were a quarter-inch too low. Big deal. If they're going to cheat, we can too. If they go legal, so will we. If that Ford is legal, then it looks like we'll have to fix our Dodge just like it."

Bobby Johns, who had been released from Holman-Moody's factory Ford team, had entered a family operated Chevrolet in the Dixie 500. He was holding court with a gang of newsmen. "If Freddy and that Ford win this race," said an angered Johns, "then it will be the biggest injustice in the history of NASCAR. It's the truth. Somebody should have said it before now. That Ford is strictly illegal and everybody knows it. I don't think the fans will appreciate that race car because it doesn't look like one.

"Everybody knows I have no love for Holman-Moody," Johns continued. "It's a fact that Lorenzen

Bobby Johns complained loudly about the "Yellow Banana"

was running a 27-gallon gas tank in the 1965 Daytona 500. I was legal on the same team. I should have won the race. I think we should all race on the same basis. If you're in a fight and your opponent has a glove filled with lead, who's going to win? It's very obvious to the eye what a laugh that car is."

Johnson and Lorenzen didn't acknowledge that anything was different with their car. "It's a Ford Galaxie," said Johnson. "All I can say is that Johns has an awfully big mouth."

Lorenzen, a one-time warrior with Johnson on the tracks, said, "This car looks the same as all of Junior's car have looked for the past five years. The car hasn't been around for awhile and everyone's forgotten what it looks like."

Turner won the pole in Yunick's Chevy at a record 148.331 mph; Lorenzen qualified third. In the race, they both fell out within nine laps of each other. Turner was victim to a faulty distributor on lap 130, and Lorenzen slugged the retaining wall on lap 139. Turner had led for 60 laps before his departure. Lorenzen had led for 24 laps.

The Atlanta fiasco caused concern among some other promoters. "If those cars don't look right when they come to Darlington for the Southern 500," said Raceway President Bob Colvin, "they're going back home. We won't even let 'em in the track to change the looks of it. It might help our race to let some of these guys in -- especially if it's a big name driver. But I'm looking at it from the view point of what's good for racing."

Bill France admitted the cars in question did not conform entirely to the rule book. However, he was not going to shut the door on some much-needed contestants due to what he called "gray areas".

"I admit the rules were bent at Atlanta," explained France. "After Fred Lorenzen drove Johnson's car in Atlanta, it sort of opened the door for any of the other Ford drivers to return to racing if they wanted to. The entire deal happened at the last minute and there was not time to prepare another body for the car. We are going to make every effort to stick to the rule book and everybody knows it. Junior knows it. He is rebuilding the Ford and putting a new body on it."

Ford came back in force a few days after the Dixie 500. Curtis Turner had been hired to drive the Junior Johnson Ford. Word came from sponsor Holly Farms that the swashbuckling Turner would have to exert a better image for the sponsor -- and that included wearing a driver's suit.

So, on August 18, 1966, Turner showed up at Columbia, SC to drive the Johnson Ford wearing a three-piece suit. Neatly dressed in pressed trousers, tie and sport jacket, Turner drove to a third place finish in the 100-miler on the half-mile dirt track. He led the first 134 laps, and the crowd of 8,954 cheered the ol' master. "Holly Farms told me that I was gonna have to wear a suit," said Turner. "They didn't specify what kind of suit, so I wore my best. You've gotta look good, you know."

Cotton Owens and David Pearson pulled out of Atlanta over rules hassle

Turner was later released from his assignment with Johnson when he got into a bumping match with Bobby Allison at Winston-Salem on August 27.

In 1965, Chrysler boycotted the NASCAR Grand National circuit -- and it produced a wide range of despair among the track owners, promoters and sanctioning NASCAR. In 1966, Ford tried the same tactic, but they were unable to secure the sympathies of the spectators. By late 1966, Ford and Chrysler were battling before large gatherings of racing fans.

Things were - generally - back to normal.

Race No. 1

Petty Wins Augusta; Isaac Does a Slow Burn

AUGUSTA, GA (Nov. 14, 1965) -- Richard Petty took the lead in the 263rd lap when Tiny Lund's Ford fell victim to mechanical problems and won the 1966 Grand National lid-lifter at Augusta Speedway.

Bobby Isaac, taking his second outing in Junior Johnson's Ford, finished second after making up three laps in the second half of the race. Ned Jarrett was a

Junior Johnson and Bobby Isaac formed Ford's newest team. Isaac finished second in '66 season opener at Augusta

close third, Jim Paschal finished fourth with Roy Mayne fifth.

Isaac had taken the lead in the opening lap. The Catawba, NC driver was widening his lead when he slid high in the first turn of the 11th lap. He bounced off the guard rail, bending a fender on his right front tire. Isaac pitted and lost three laps while crew chief Herb Nab wrestled with the bent metal. Isaac was running 30th when he got back in the race.

Petty led for a 94 lap stretch before Tiny Lund clawed his way to the front. Lund, behind the wheel of an independent Ford owned by Lyle Stelter, was late arriving at the track and posted no practice or qualifying time. He started dead last but came on like gangbusters. Lund was pulling away from Petty when the distributor failed on his car. Petty breezed into the lead for good.

"Tiny was going real good and he's a hard man to pass," said Petty. "I think I could have eventually gotten by him, but we'll never know for sure."

After Lund fell out, Isaac charged his way through the field three times and he was challenging Petty for the victory flag in the end. "I get the finest job in the world that a race driver could have," said Isaac. "I'm in a car that could run off and hide from everybody -- and I run into the wall."

Petty averaged 73.569 mph as 22 laps were run under the caution flag.

Grand National Race No. 1
300 Laps at Augusta Speedway
Augusta, GA
"Georgia Cracker 300"
150 Miles on Half-mile Paved Track
November 14, 1965

Fin	St	No.	Driver	Team / Car	Laps	Money	Status
1	1	42	Richard Petty	Petty Engineering '65 Plym	300	$1,700	Running
2	2	26	Bobby Isaac	Junior Johnson '65 Ford	300	850	Running
3	3	11	Ned Jarrett	Bondy Long '65 Ford	300	820	Running
4	6	10	Jim Paschal	Gary Weaver '64 Ford	297	515	Running
5	12	46	Roy Mayne	Tom Hunter '65 Chevrolet	296	490	Running
6	27	6	David Pearson	Cotton Owens '65 Dodge	295	465	Running
7	7	7	Bobby Johns	Shorty Johns '64 Pontiac	295	440	Running
8	26	18	Darel Dieringer	Toy Bolton '65 Chevrolet	293	425	Running
9	9	06	Cale Yarborough	Kenny Myler '64 Ford	291	390	Running
10	22	48	John Sears	L G DeWitt '64 Ford	286	380	Running
11	16	89	Neil Castles	Buck Baker '65 Olds	283	370	Running
12	18	79	Frank Warren	Harold Rhodes '63 Chevrolet	281	355	Running
13	17	38	Wayne Smith	Smith '65 Chevrolet	277	340	Running
14	28	34	Wendell Scott	Scott '63 Ford	276	320	Running
15	14	88	Buddy Baker	Buck Baker '64 Dodge	275	300	Running
16	10	02	Doug Cooper	Bob Cooper '65 Chevrolet	271	190	Running
17	19	83	Worth McMillion	Allen McMillion '64 Pontiac	269	150	Running
18	25	97	Henley Gray	Gene Cline '64 Ford	269	150	Running
19	4	59	Tom Pistone	Glen Sweet '64 Ford	265	150	Engine
20	30	55	Tiny Lund	Lyle Stelter '64 Ford	263	150	Distrib
21	21	80	Allen McMillion	McMillion '64 Pontiac	250	150	Running
22	24	68	Bob Derrington	Derrington '63 Ford	233	150	Running
23	8	25	Jabe Thomas	Thomas '64 Ford	232	---	Running
24	15	1	Gil Hearne	'64 Ford	229	---	Steering
25	20	9	Roy Tyner	Tyner '65 Chevrolet	169	---	Oil Pres
26	11	19	J T Putney	Herman Beam '65 Chevrolet	102	---	Engine
27	13	87	Buck Baker	Baker '65 Chevrolet	67	---	Engine
28	23	44	Larry Hess	Hess '64 Ford	40	---	Ball Jt.
29	29	56	Don Tilley	Curtis Larimer '64 Ford	15	---	Engine
30	5	64	Elmo Langley	Langley '64 Ford	14	---	Engine

Time of Race: 2 hours, 2 minutes, 2 seconds
Average Speed: 73.569 mph
Pole Winner: Richard Petty - 82.987 mph
Lap Leaders: Bobby Isaac 1-11, Richard Petty 12-105, Tiny Lund 106-200, Jim Paschal 201-216, Lund 217-262, Petty 263-300
Cautions: 3 for 22 laps   Margin of Victory: Attendance:

Race No. 2

Gurney Grabs 4th Straight Riverside 500-Miler

RIVERSIDE, CA (Jan. 23) -- Quick pit work by the Wood Brothers gave Dan Gurney an insurmountable lead and he breezed to victory in the fourth annual Motor Trend 500 at Riverside International Raceway. The 33 year-old Costa Mesa, CA international road racer took the lead for good in the 84th lap and wound up one minute and 10 seconds ahead of runner-up David Pearson.

Gurney made six pit stops in the five hour marathon. The Wood Brothers headed by Glen, Leonard, Delano and Ray Lee, serviced Gurney's Ford in two minutes flat. Pearson's Dodge made seven pit stops and his Cotton Owens team did the work in three minutes and 51 seconds. It was more than the difference in the outcome of the race.

Dan Gurney won 4th straight Riverside 500

"The Woods really make a science of the pit work," declared Gurney. "Sometimes I don't know how they do it, they're so smooth. I'd sure like to have these guys with me at Indianapolis."

Paul Goldsmith finished third, Curtis Turner was fourth and Dick Hutcherson fifth.

Turner provided many thrills for the 73,331 spectators who jammed the desert countryside. The 41 year-old Ford driver led on three occasions for 27 laps, but he was involved in several off-track skirmishes. While battling Pearson for second, the two cars got together and Turner sailed into a fence. He pitted, got the fender pried off the wheel and returned to the fray.

Several laps later, Turner spun backwards into the concrete wall. His car was leaking fuel and NASCAR officials gave him the black flag twice. Turner got back in the race again and was only two laps off the winner's pace when the checkered flag fell.

Gurney started second and led for 148 of the 185 laps on the 2.7-mile road course. The Motor Trend 500 marked the 10th Grand National start for Gurney -- four of which have ended in victory.

Junior Johnson entered two cars. Drivers Bobby Isaac and A.J. Foyt went out with mechanical problems seven laps apart. Richard Petty lasted 105 laps before the engine blew in his Plymouth; and Cale Yarborough went out with transmission failure after 103 laps.

Gurney averaged 97.952 mph -- a new 500-mile record on the huge road course.

Race No. 3

Goldsmith Grabs Glory From Petty in 100-mile Qualifier

DAYTONA BEACH, FL (Feb. 25) -- Paul Goldsmith of St. Claire Shores, MI whipped his Nichels Engineering Plymouth around Richard Petty in the last 100 yards and won the first 100-mile qualifying race at Daytona International Speedway by an eyelash. It was the first win in Grand National competition for the 38 year-old veteran since Feb. 23, 1958 when he won the final event on the old Beach and Road course at Daytona.

Petty, who led for 25 of the 40 laps, was second. Don White, one of Goldsmith's team mates, came in third with Marvin Panch fourth. Fifth place went to

Grand National Race No. 2
185 Laps at Riverside International Raceway
Riverside, CA
"Motor Trend 500"
500 Miles on 2.7-mile Paved Road Course
January 23, 1966

Fin	St	No.	Driver	Team / Car	Laps	Money	Status
1	2	121	Dan Gurney	Wood Brothers '66 Ford	185	$18,445	Running
2	1	6	David Pearson	Cotton Owens '65 Dodge	185	8,395	Running
3	6	99	Paul Goldsmith	Nichels Eng. '65 Plymouth	183	5,055	Running
4	3	41	Curtis Turner	Wood Brothers '66 Ford	183	3,445	Running
5	10	29	Dick Hutcherson	Holman-Moody '66 Ford	182	2,120	Running
6	9	56	Jim Hurtubise	Norm Nelson '65 Plymouth	182	1,335	Running
7	12	22	Billy Foster	'64 Dodge	181	1,275	Running
8	8	11	Ned Jarrett	Bondy Long '66 Ford	178	1.575	Running
9	14	1	Norm Nelson	Nelson '65 Plymouth	176	1,000	Running
10	19	18	Ron Hornaday	'64 Mercury	171	900	Running
11	16	4	Jerry Grant	Friedkin Ent. '65 Chevrolet	171	850	Running
12	34	24	Bobby Allison	Betty Lilly '65 Ford	169	650	Running
13	23	2	John Steele	Kyle Gibson '64 Mercury	164	625	Running
14	5	98	Don White	Nichels Eng. '65 Dodge	162	680	Running
15	27	10	Don Walker	'64 Ford	154	590	Ignition
16	25	71	Mario Andretti	Bondy Long '66 Ford	154	580	Crash
17	38	63	Walt Price	'65 Buick	154	575	Running
18	44	61	J T Putney	'65 Olds	150	570	Running
19	41	68	Bob Derrington	Derrington '63 Ford	146	565	Running
20	40	8	Jerry Oliver	'65 Chevrolet	144	560	Gear shift
21	17	48	James Hylton	Bud Hartje '65 Dodge	128	630	Crash
22	30	7	Jack McCoy	'64 Dodge	123	540	Crash
23	35	45	Carl Cardey	'64 Ford	119	530	Ball Jt.
24	18	33	Clem Proctor	'64 Ford	114	600	Engine
25	7	43	Richard Petty	Petty Engineering '65 Plym	105	550	Engine
26	11	27	Cale Yarborough	Banjo Matthews '66 Ford	103	650	Trans
27	29	89	Cliff Garner	'64 Mercury	98	500	Crash
28	31	00	Dick Gulstrand	'64 Chevrolet	65	500	Differen
29	15	26	Bobby Isaac	Junior Johnson '66 Ford	55	550	H Gasket
30	4	21	Marvin Panch	Wood Brothers '66 Ford	45	600	Trans
31	13	47	A J Foyt	Junior Johnson '66 Ford	45	575	Trans
32	21	198	Eddie Gray	'64 Mercury	43	500	Engine
33	24	126	Carl Joiner	'63 Chevrolet	41	500	Oil Leak
34	32	55	Tiny Lund	Lyle Stelter '65 Ford	34	500	Engine
35	22	9	Skip Hudson	'65 Chevrolet	30	500	Differen
36	20	145	Scotty Cain	'64 Mercury	20	525	Trans
37	36	3	Bruce Worrell	'63 Plymouth	15	500	Engine
38	42	16	Jim Cook	'64 Olds	14	500	Oil Press
39	33	34	Clyde Pickett	'64 Ford	11	500	Trans
40	26	74	Gene Black	'66 Ford	4	500	Engine
41	28	06	Dave James	'65 Plymouth	4	500	Engine
42	37	14	Joe Clark	'64 Mercury	4	500	Oil Press
43	39	111	Arley Scranton	'64 Mercury	3	500	Crash
44	43	38	Charles Powell	'64 Ford	1	500	Differen

Time of Race: 5 hours, 5 minutes, 58 seconds
Average Speed: 97.952 mph
Pole Winner: David Pearson - 106.078 mph
Lap Leaders: David Pearson 1-9, Dan Gurney 10-37, Curtis Turner 38-55, Gurney 56, Turner 57-58, Gurney 59-65, Turner 66-72, Gurney 73-82, Pearson 83, Gurney 84-185.
Cautions: 2 for ____ laps   Margin of Victory: 1 minute and 10 seconds
Attendance: 73,331

Grand National Race No. 3
40 Laps at Daytona Int'l Speedway
Daytona Beach, FL
100 Miles on 2.5-Mile Paved Track
February 25, 1966

Fin	St	No.	Driver	Team / Car	Laps	Money	Status
1	8	99	Paul Goldsmith	Nichels Eng. '65 Plymouth	40	$1,100	Running
2	1	43	Richard Petty	Petty Enterprises '66 Plym	40	600	Running
3	6	07	Don White	Nichels Eng. '65 Dodge	40	400	Running
4	5	21	Marvin Panch	Wood Brothers '66 Ford	40	300	Running
5	2	28	Fred Lorenzen	Holman-Moody '66 Ford	40	300	Running
6	12	98	Sam McQuagg	Nichels Eng. '66 Dodge	40	250	Running
7	10	71	Gordon Johncock	K&K Insurance '65 Dodge	40	225	Running
8	4	16	Darel Dieringer	Bud Moore '64 Mercury	40	200	Running
9	11	9	Larry Frank	Nichels Eng. '66 Plymouth	40	150	Running
10	9	27	Cale Yarborough	Banjo Matthews '66 Ford	40	150	Running
11	3	41	Curtis Turner	Wood Brothers '66 Ford	39	150	Running
12	7	48	James Hylton	Bud Hartje '65 Dodge	39	125	Running
13	14	46	Roy Mayne	Tom Hunter '66 Chevrolet	39	125	Running
14	20	23	Calvin Kelly	Hubert Howard '64 Ford	37	100	Running
15	28	61	Ned Setzer	Toy Bolton '66 Chevrolet	37	100	Running
16	24	97	Henley Gray	Gray '66 Ford	37	100	Running
17	25	38	Wayne Smith	Smith '66 Chevrolet	36	100	Running
18	33	08	Bob Derrington	Bub Strickler '64 Ford	36	100	Running
19	27	88	Buddy Baker	Buck Baker '65 Chevrolet	36	100	Running
20	18	44	Larry Hess	Hess '64 Ford	36	100	Running
21	16	0	Johnny Allen	Reid Shaw '64 Ford	35	100	Running
22	32	06	Gene Petro	Charles Johnson '64 Ford	35	100	Running
23	14	33	Johnny Rutherford	Curtis Satterfield '66 Chevy	35	100	Running
24	21	76	Ronnie Chumley	'64 Pontiac	34	100	Running
25	23	10	Tiny Lund	Gary Weaver '64 Ford	33	---	Running
26	19	93	Blackie Watt	Harry Neal '64 Ford	29	---	Engine
27	30	78	Nick Rampling	Ron Staughton '64 Chevrolet	27	---	Heating
28	31	75	Doug Cooper	'64 Ford	25	---	Ignition
29	22	32	Rock Harn	A T Mulherin '64 Ford	33	---	Engine
30	15	25	Jabe Thomas	Jeff Handy '64 Ford	21	---	Wheel
31	17	57	Lionel Johnson	Clay Esteridge '64 Ford	21	---	Heating
32	26	95	Gene Cline	Cline '64 Ford	6	---	Handling
33	29	85	Neil Castles	Buck Baker '65 Plymouth	5	---	Engine

Time of Race: 37 minutes, 24 seconds
Average Speed: 160.427 mph
Pole Winner: Richard Petty - 175.165 mph
Lap Leaders: Richard Petty 1-12, Darel Dieringer 13-15, Petty 16-17,
Paul Goldsmith 18-28, Petty 29-39, Goldsmith 40.
Cautions: 1 for 3 laps   Margin of Victory: 1 car length   Attendance: 22,000

Grand National Race No. 4
40 Laps at Daytona Int'l Speedway
Daytona Beach, FL
100 Miles on 2.5-Mile Paved Track
February 25, 1966

Fin	St	No.	Driver	Team / Car	Laps	Money	Status
1	6	3	Earl Balmer	Ray Fox '65 Dodge	40	$1,000	Running
2	4	56	Jim Hurtubise	Norm Nelson '65 Plymouth	40	600	Running
3	1	29	Dick Hutcherson	Holman-Moody '66 Ford	40	400	Running
4	2	12	LeeRoy Yarbrough	Jon Thorne '66 Dodge	40	300	Running
5	5	11	Ned Jarrett	Bondy Long '66 Ford	40	500	Running
6	10	6	David Pearson	Cotton Owens '66 Dodge	40	250	Running
7	8	26	Bobby Isaac	Junior Johnson '66 Ford	40	225	Running
8	11	14	Jim Paschal	Friedkin Ent. '66 Plymouth	40	200	Running
9	14	49	G C Spencer	Spencer '65 Plymouth	39	150	Running
10	15	79	Frank Warren	Harold Rhodes '64 Chevrolet	39	150	Running
11	9	47	A J Foyt	Junior Johnson '66 Ford	38	150	Running
12	16	36	H B Bailey	Bailey '66 Pontiac	38	125	Running
13	18	64	Elmo Langley	Langley-Woodfield '65 Chev	38	125	Running
14	23	34	Wendell Scott	Scott '64 Ford	38	100	Running
15	22	72	Bill Champion	Champion '64 Ford	38	100	Running
16	33	87	Neil Castles	Buck Baker '66 Olds	38	100	Running
17	27	55	Paul Connors	Lyle Stelter '64 Ford	38	100	Running
18	19	04	John Sears	L G DeWitt '64 Ford	37	100	Running
19	20	19	J T Putney	Putney '65 Chevrolet	37	100	Running
20	12	13	Mario Andretti	Smokey Yunick '66 Chevrolet	37	100	Running
21	30	67	Jim Malloy	'66 Ford	37	100	Running
22	21	90	Sonny Hutchins	Junie Donlavey '64 Ford	36	100	Running
23	25	74	Gene Black	Black '64 Ford	36	100	Running
24	31	00	Jack Goodwin	'66 Buick	35	100	Running
25	29	53	Jimmy Helms	David Warren '64 Ford	34	---	Running
26	17	18	Stick Elliott	Toy Bolton '66 Chevrolet	33	---	Running
27	26	45	Blaine Kaufman	Bill Seifert '64 Ford	33	---	Running
28	3	22	Bunkie Blackburn	Bob Rosenthal '65 Chevrolet	29	---	Heating
29	24	7	Bub Strickler	Shorty Johns '64 Pontiac	25	---	Distrib
30	28	09	Cy Fairchild	Larry DeBeau '64 Ford	18	---	Flagged
31	7	24	Bobby Allison	Betty Lilly '65 Ford	16	---	Engine
32	32	50	T L Blakely	Jim Bangsberry '66 Chevy	10	---	Vibration
33	13	03	Rene Charland	Ed Ackerman '64 Ford	3	---	Engine

Time of Race: 39 minutes, 1 second
Average Speed: 153.191 mph
Pole Winner: Dick Hutcherson - 174.317 mph
Lap Leaders: Dick Hutcherson 1-6, Mario Andretti 7, Bunkie Blackburn 8-11,
Jim Hurtubise 12-24, Hutcherson 25-39, Earl Balmer 40.
Cautions: 1 for 7 laps   Margin of Victory: 4 car lengths   Attendance: 22,000

Fred Lorenzen.

Chrysler Corp. cars led all but three laps; Darel Dieringer paced the action for three laps in his two year-old Mercury under yellow. Dieringer drifted back and finished eighth.

Johnny Rutherford, sensation of the 1963 Speedweek preliminary events, drove a Curtis Satterfield Chevrolet. But the Ft. Worth, TX driver had trouble getting up to speed and finished 23rd, five laps off the pace.

Goldsmith averaged 160.427 mph for his seventh career Grand National win.

Race No. 4
Earl Balmer Blasts Past Hutcherson For Last Lap Win

DAYTONA BEACH, FL (Feb. 25) --Earl Balmer of Floyd Knobs, IN bolted past Dick Hutcherson in the final lap and won the second 100-mile qualifying race at Daytona International Speedway. Balmer, driving the Ray Fox Dodge, led only the final lap to gain his first Grand National win.

Jim Hurtubise, famed USAC driver, was a close second in a Plymouth owned by Norm Nelson. Hutcherson, who led 21 laps, fell to third in the last lap shuffle. LeeRoy Yarbrough was fourth as Ned Jarrett came in fifth. NASCAR point leader David Pearson was sixth.

Hutcherson took the lead from Hurtubise in the 25th lap. He was still leading as the pack of cars rode under the white flag. Balmer made his move down the backstretch of lap 40. The slipstream helped Balmer race into the lead as Hutcherson's Ford bobbled momentarily. Hutch grazed the third turn wall, ricocheted off and sideswiped Hurtubise. Both drivers maintained control in a dazzling display of nerve and skill. Balmer outraced the duo to claim a four car-length win.

Mario Andretti drove a new Smokey Yunick Chevrolet and led briefly, but fell off the pace and wound up 20th, three laps down.

Paul Goldsmith and Earl Balmer share spotlight after winning Daytona Qualifiers

Neil Castles of Charlotte drove a Buck Baker Olds into 16th place. Oddly, he competed in the first qualifier as well, going out after five laps with engine failure. Castles became the first driver to compete and earn championship points in both Daytona qualifiers.

Balmer averaged 153.191 mph as seven laps were run under the caution flag.

Race No. 5

Petty Overcomes Troubles; Wins 2nd Daytona 500

DAYTONA BEACH, FL (Feb. 27) --Richard Petty overcame a series of tire problems, fought his way back into contention and became the first man to win the Daytona 500 twice. The 29 year-old Plymouth driver grabbed the lead in the 113th lap and was in front when a heavy thundershower ended the eighth annual

Richard Petty makes pit stop en route to Daytona 500 win

Grand National Race No. 5
200 Laps at Daytona Int'l Speedway
Daytona Beach, FL
"Daytona 500"
500 Miles on 2.5-Mile Paved Track
February 27, 1966

Fin	St	No.	Driver	Team / Car	Laps	Money	Status
1	1	43	Richard Petty	Petty Enterprises '66 Plym	198	$28,150	Running
2	19	27	Cale Yarborough	Banjo Matthews '66 Ford	197	12,800	Running
3	12	6	David Pearson	Cotton Owens '66 Dodge	196	7,950	Running
4	9	28	Fred Lorenzen	Holman-Moody '66 Ford	196	4,250	Running
5	11	98	Sam McQuagg	Nichels Eng. '66 Dodge	195	3,600	Running
6	6	56	Jim Hurtubise	Norm Nelson '66 Plymouth	195	2,700	Running
7	10	11	Ned Jarrett	Bondy Long '66 Ford	195	2,100	Running
8	8	12	LeeRoy Yarbrough	Jon Thorne '66 Dodge	193	1,750	Running
9	23	48	James Hylton	Bud Hartje '65 Dodge	193	1,500	Running
10	17	9	Larry Frank	Nichels Eng. '66 Plymouth	192	1,425	Running
11	16	14	Jim Paschal	Friedkin Ent. '66 Plymouth	192	1,350	Running
12	15	16	Darel Dieringer	Bud Moore '66 Mercury	192	1,275	Running
13	28	34	Wendell Scott	Scott '65 Ford	184	1,250	Running
14	37	19	J T Putney	Putney '65 Chevrolet	184	1,225	Running
15	43	25	Jabe Thomas	Jeff Handy '64 Ford	182	1,200	Running
16	20	79	Frank Warren	Harold Rhodes '64 Chevrolet	177	1,170	Running
17	31	97	Henley Gray	Gray '66 Ford	172	1,165	Running
18	3	99	Paul Goldsmith	Nichels Engineering '66 Plym	153	2,060	Running
19	33	38	Wayne Smith	Smith '66 Chevrolet	148	1,155	Fuel line
20	44	24	Bobby Allison	Betty Lilly '65 Ford	143	1,150	Engine
21	14	26	Bobby Isaac	Junior Johnson '66 Ford	141	1,145	Crash
22	32	87	Buck Baker	Baker '66 Olds	136	1,140	Ignition
23	45	0	Johnny Allen	Red Shaw '64 Ford	132	1,135	Heating
24	18	49	G C Spencer	Spencer '65 Plymouth	139	1,130	Engine
25	21	41	Curtis Turner	Wood Brothers '66 Ford	122	1,125	W'shield
26	7	21	Marvin Panch	Wood Brothers '66 Ford	119	1,820	W'shield
27	5	07	Don White	Nichels Eng. '65 Dodge	115	1,115	Ignition
28	42	33	Johnny Rutherford	Curtis Satterfield '66 Chevy	115	1,110	Crash
29	13	71	Gordon Johncock	K&K Insurance '65 Dodge	112	1,105	Engine
30	29	61	Ned Setzer	Toy Bolton '66 Chevrolet	110	1,100	Wheel
31	48	93	Blackie Watt	Harry Neal '64 Ford	107	1,095	Piston
32	36	88	Buddy Baker	Buck Baker "65 Chevrolet	69	1,090	Oil leak
33	22	47	A J Foyt	Junior Johnson '66 Ford	46	1,085	H Gasket
34	35	04	John Sears	L G DeWitt '64 Ford	40	1,080	H Gasket
35	2	29	Dick Hutcherson	Holman-Moody '66 Ford	38	1,075	W'shield
36	40	22	Bunkie Blackburn	Bob Rosenthal '65 Chevy	36	1,070	Engine
37	39	13	Mario Andretti	Smokey Yunick '66 Chevrolet	31	1,065	Crash
38	30	72	Bill Champion	Champion '64 Ford	29	1,060	H Gasket
39	46	57	Lionel Johnson	Clay Esteridge '64 Ford	28	1,055	Engine
40	47	18	Stick Elliott	Toy Bolton '66 Chevrolet	28	1,050	Trans
41	4	3	Earl Balmer	Ray Fox '65 Dodge	21	1,045	Engine
42	38	44	Larry Hess	Hess '64 Ford	19	1,040	Engine
43	25	46	Roy Mayne	Tom Hunter '66 Chevrolet	13	1,035	Trans
44	49	76	Ronnie Chumley	'64 Pontiac	8	1,030	Engine
45	26	64	Elmo Langley	Langley-Woodfield '65 Chevy	4	1,025	Oil Press
46	27	23	Calvin Kelly	Hubert Howard '64 Ford	4	1,020	Clutch
47	50	90	Sonny Hutchins	Junie Donlavey '64 Ford	3	1,015	Oil Press
48	34	08	Bub Strickler	Strickler '64 Ford	2	1,010	Clutch
49	24	36	H B Bailey	Bailey '66 Pontiac	1	1,005	Engine
50	41	03	Rene Charland	Ed Ackerman '64 Ford	1	1,000	Vibration

Time of Race: 3 hours 4 minutes, 54 seconds
Average Speed: 160.927 mph
Pole Winner: Richard Petty - 175.163 mph
Lap Leaders: Richard Petty 1-6, Paul Goldsmith 7-11, Petty 12-17, Goldsmith 18-33,
     Dick Hutcherson 34-35, Marvin Panch 36-40, Cale Yarborough 41-67,
     Goldsmith 68-78, Yarborough 79-81, Jim Hurtubise 82-85, Goldsmith 86-96,
     Petty 97-106, Panch 107-109, Yarborough 110-112, Petty 113-198.
Margin of Victory: 1-lap plus   Cautions: 4 for 22 laps   Attendance: 90,000.

running of the Daytona International Speedway event two laps shy of the scheduled distance.

Cale Yarborough's Ford took second place with David Pearson third in a Dodge. Fred Lorenzen crossed the line in fourth place and Sam McQuagg, newly appointed driver of the Nichels Engineering Dodge, finished fifth.

Tire problems took the spotlight in the $110,000 contest. Flying chunks of rubber from disintegrating tires smashed windshields of three contenders. Dick Hutcherson, Curtis Turner and Marvin Panch all had to withdraw from the race with broken windshields. Petty's tire problems began as early as the 18th lap. He pitted for fresh rubber and dropped a lap off the pace.

Petty spent the middle portions of the race battling back into contention. The Randleman, NC charger got up to first place three laps before the half-way point. Once he got the lead, he was untouchable, leading the final 86 laps.

"We changed compounds and it made me a little slower," said Petty, who was wheeling a 405 c.i. hemi powered Plymouth Belvedere. "But we had beautiful tire wear the rest of the way."

Jim Hurtubise had one of the fastest cars on the track, but he experienced numerous flat tires and finally finished sixth.

Turner, who was in contention when his misfortunes put him out after 122 laps, pointed his finger at Hurtubise for most of the flying rubber. "The left rear tire on one damn hemi Plymouth put three Fords out of the race," steamed Turner.

Yarborough led for 33 laps, but was no match for Petty in the stretch run. "I knew a win wasn't for me as long as Richard stayed in there the way he was running," confessed Cale.

A crowd of 90,000 watched Petty take his 42nd career win at an average speed of 160.627 mph.

Four caution flags broke the action as the lead changed hands 14 times among six drivers.

David Pearson #6 passes Larry Frank #9 in Daytona 500

Grand National Race No. 6
500 Laps at North Carolina Motor Speedway
Rockingham, NC
"Peach Blossom 500"
500 Miles on 1-Mile Paved Track
March 13, 1966

Fin	St	No.	Driver	Team / Car	Laps	Money	Status
1	1	99	Paul Goldsmith	Nichels Eng. '66 Plymouth	500	$14,340	Running
2	8	27	Cale Yarborough	Banjo Matthews '66 Ford	500	7,875	Running
3	19	24	Bobby Allison	Betty Lilly '65 Ford	488	4,250	Running
4	27	55	Harold Smith	Lyle Stelter '64 Ford	480	2,675	Running
5	24	04	John Sears	L G DeWitt '64 Ford	478	1,750	Running
6	26	46	Roy Mayne	Tom Hunter '66 Chevrolet	475	1,800	Running
7	14	64	Elmo Langley	Langley-Woodfield '64 Ford	472	1,150	Running
8	2	6	David Pearson	Cotton Owens '66 Dodge	470	1,340	Running
9	35	97	Henley Gray	Gray '66 Ford	465	1,095	Running
10	38	83	Worth McMillion	Allen McMillion '64 Pontiac	452	1,030	Running
11	13	19	J T Putney	Putney '66 Chevrolet	440	845	Lug Bolt
12	29	87	Neil Castles	Buck Baker '66 Olds	430	820	Running
13	15	88	Buddy Baker	Buck Baker '65 Chevrolet	424	795	Engine
14	16	20	Clyde Lynn	Lynn '64 Ford	424	770	Engine
15	32	02	Doug Cooper	Bob Cooper '65 Plymouth	423	945	Engine
16	44	70	J D McDuffie	McDuffie '64 Ford	420	725	Running
17	6	21	Marvin Panch	Wood Brothers '66 Ford	402	705	Crash
18	3	41	Curtis Turner	Wood Brothers '66 Ford	376	770	Crash
19	12	48	James Hylton	Bud Hartje '65 Dodge	302	675	Engine
20	17	14	Jim Paschal	Friedkin Ent. '66 Plymouth	276	910	Engine
21	25	1	Paul Lewis	Lewis '65 Plymouth	275	735	Engine
22	33	10	Tiny Lund	Larry DeBeau '64 Ford	267	725	Engine
23	42	74	Gene Black	Black '64 Ford	266	630	W bearing
24	39	38	Wayne Smith	Smith '66 Chevrolet	221	630	Engine
25	22	67	Buddy Arrington	Arrington '64 Dodge	196	595	Oil Press
26	10	28	Fred Lorenzen	Holman-Moody '66 Ford	193	760	Engine
27	28	33	Bub Strickler	Curtis Satterfield '65 Chevy	148	585	Crash
28	43	95	Gene Cline	Cline '64 Ford	147	590	Brakes
29	5	29	Dick Hutcherson	Holman-Moody '66 Ford	132	575	Crash
30	9	98	Sam McQuagg	Nichels Eng. '66 Dodge	131	790	Engine
31	37	9	Roy Tyner	Tyner '66 Chevrolet	101	600	Heating
32	18	12	LeeRoy Yarbrough	Jon Thorne '66 Dodge	89	700	Ignition
33	21	34	Wendell Scott	Scott '65 Ford	79	555	Engine
34	23	50	Bunkie Blackburn	Jim Bangsberry '66 Chevy	53	550	Handling
35	11	43	Darel Dieringer	Petty Enterprises '66 Plym	52	545	Crash
36	7	11	Ned Jarrett	Bondy Long '66 Ford	35	1,040	Engine
37	4	26	Bobby Isaac	Junior Johnson '66 Ford	34	585	Crash
38	30	61	Leroy Bolton	Toy Bolton '66 Chevrolet	27	530	Steering
39	41	77	Joel David	Harold Mays '65 Plymouth	17	545	Handling
40	36	85	Harold Dunnaway	'65 Plymouth	14	560	Ignition
41	20	59	Tom Pistone	Pistone '64 Ford	13	515	Trans
42	40	45	Tex McCullough	Bill Seifert '64 Ford	5	535	W bearing
43	34	7	Bobby Johns	Shorty Johns '66 Chevrolet	4	555	Clutch
44	31	49	G C Spencer	Spencer '65 Plymouth	1	900	H Gask

Time of Race: 4 hours, 59 minutes, 55 seconds
Average Speed: 100.027 mph
Pole Winner: Paul Goldsmith - 116.684 mph
Lap Leaders: Paul Goldsmith 1-24, Bobby Isaac 25-34, Goldsmith 35, Curtis Turner 36-40, LeeRoy Yarbrough 41-57, Jim Paschal 58-88, Sam McQuagg 89-114, David Pearson 115-127, Cale Yarborough 128, Paschal 129-130, Pearson 131-141, Fred Lorenzen 142-165, Turner 166, Goldsmith 167, Yarborough 168-236, Pearson 237 Yarborough 238-284, Turner 285-286, Yarborough 287, Goldsmith 288-308, Turner 309-312, Yarborough 313-366, Goldsmith 367-378 Marvin Panch 379-395, Goldsmith 396-446, Yarborough 447-451, Goldsmith 452-500.
Cautions: 10 for 70 Laps   Margin of Victory: 3.82 seconds   Attendance: 40,000

Race No. 6
Goldsmith Wins Peach Blossom 500 with 10 Stops

ROCKINGHAM, NC (Mar. 13) -- Paul Goldsmith slid under Cale Yarborough in the 452nd lap and led

Paul Goldsmith kept his Plymouth out front to win the Peach Blossom 500 at Rockingham

the rest of the way to win the inaugural Peach Blossom 500 at North Carolina Motor Speedway. It was Goldsmith's second win of the season, moving him into third place in the point standings.

Yarborough, whose Ford was crunched badly in an earlier wreck, wound up second, 3.82-seconds behind Goldsmith's Plymouth. Third place went to rookie Bobby Allison. Harold Smith came in fourth, 20 laps behind. Big John Sears nabbed fifth spot.

Goldsmith made 10 pit stops in the 500-miler on the one mile banked paved track. The St.Claire Shores, MI driver, who has taken up residence in Munster, IN, averaged 100.027 mph in the five hour event.

"I had to make an unscheduled pit stop at about the 80th lap," said the winner. "Some car had knocked my gas cap off. And my powerful hemi mill was pumping the gas out. After that, I ran as hard as I could. I was dirt-trackin' it in the corners, and that was causing more tire wear."

Yarborough led the most laps -- 177 -- but couldn't muster a challenge to Goldsmith in the final battle. "I couldn't keep up," said Cale. "I'm happy I was able to finish second. But it is still heartbreaking to get so close and miss the victory." It was the third straight runner-up finish Yarborough has posted on a superspeedway. He has yet to win a big one.

Bobby Isaac, driving Junior Johnson's Ford, passed Goldsmith in the 25th lap. He had quickly pulled away when Bub Strickler spun in front of him on lap 35. Isaac had nowhere to go except into Strickler. The two tangled with Isaac having the worst of it. He was out of the race while Strickler continued on only to spin out two more times.

Curtis Turner led for 12 laps, but was sidelined by a wreck in lap 376.

Only three of 13 factory backed machines finished. David Pearson was in the pits for 30 laps to replace a faulty distributor, but came back to finish eighth. The other factory backed cars finished 1-2.

Richard Petty did not race due to surgery on the fourth finger of his left hand. He was on the sidelines lending support to his replacement driver Darel Dieringer, who crashed after 52 laps.

Race No. 7

Hutch Hurries Past Pearson; Takes Southeastern 500

BRISTOL, TN (Mar. 20) -- Dick Hutcherson escaped a rash of wrecks and blown engines and coasted home first in the Southeastern 500 at Bristol International Speedway. It was the first win of the year for the 34 year-old Ford driver and the 10th of his career.

Independent Paul Lewis came in second, four laps behind. James Hylton finished third, Elmo Langley fourth and Sam McQuagg fifth.

Of the 10 factory backed cars that started the race, only two finished -- Hutcherson and McQuagg, who was slowed by a crash and was 11 laps behind.

Grand National Race No. 7
500 Laps at Bristol Int'l Speedway
Bristol, TN
"Southeastern 500"
250 Miles on Half-Mile Paved Track
March 20, 1966

Fin	St	No.	Driver	Team / Car	Laps	Money	Status
1	6	29	Dick Hutcherson	Holman-Moody '66 Ford	500	$4,150	Running
2	11	1	Paul Lewis	Lewis '65 Plymouth	496	1,825	Running
3	17	48	James Hylton	Bud Hartje '65 Dodge	494	1,550	Running
4	16	64	Elmo Langley	Langley-Woodfield '64 Ford	492	1,125	Running
5	7	98	Sam McQuagg	Nichels Eng. '66 Dodge	489	1,000	Running
6	19	74	Gene Black	Black '64 Ford	477	800	Running
7	27	45	Bill Seifert	Seifert '64 Ford	458	725	Running
8	30	34	Wendell Scott	Scott '65 Ford	455	675	Engine
9	24	97	Henley Gray	Gray '66 Ford	453	650	A Frame
10	9	49	G C Spencer	Spencer '65 Plymouth	452	500	Engine
11	26	20	Clyde Lynn	Lynn '64 Ford	446	485	A Frame
12	28	95	Gene Cline	Cline '64 Ford	446	425	A Frame
13	18	0	Johnny Allen	Reid Shaw '64 Ford	431	350	Engine
14	29	63	Larry Manning	Bob Adams '65 Plymouth	397	350	A Frame
15	1	6	David Pearson	Cotton Owens '66 Dodge	396	1,350	T Chain
16	22	73	Walter Wallace	Joan Petre '64 Ford	379	300	Differen
17	32	70	J D McDuffie	McDuffie '64 Ford	374	300	A Frame
18	5	21	Marvin Panch	Wood Brothers '66 Ford	328	425	Engine
19	14	11	Ned Jarrett	Bondy Long '66 Ford	320	590	Differen
20	4	43	Jim Paschal	Petty Enterprises '65 Plym	281	325	Oil Filter
21	3	9	Paul Goldsmith	Nichels Eng. '65 Plymouth	256	325	Alternator
22	2	28	Fred Lorenzen	Holman-Moody '66 Ford	250	350	Engine
23	13	26	Bobby Isaac	Junior Johnson '66 Ford	203	560	Crash
24	8	27	Cale Yarborough	Banjo Matthews '66 Ford	179	300	Engine
25	21	2	Johnny Steele	Kyle Gibson '64 Mercury	161	275	Engine
26	10	19	J T Putney	Putney '66 Chevrolet	65	275	Engine
27	12	67	Buddy Arrington	Arrington '64 Dodge	63	275	Lug Bolts
28	15	24	Bobby Allison	Betty Lilly '65 Ford	49	300	Engine
29	25	38	Wayne Smith	Smith '66 Chevrolet	10	325	Ignition
30	20	04	John Sears	L G DeWitt '64 Ford	9	275	Engine
31	23	96	Sonny Lamphear	Homer O'Dell '64 Ford	5	275	Oil Press
32	31	52	E J Trivette	Bill Church '66 Chevrolet	2	300	Trans

Time of Race: 3 hours, 34 minutes, 26 seconds
Average Speed: 69.952 mph
Pole Winner: David Pearson - 86.248 mph
Lap Leaders: David Pearson 1-142, Fred Lorenzen 143, Pearson 144-242,
    Marvin Panch 243-287, Pearson 288-331, Dick Hutcherson 332-337, Pearson 338-382,
    Hutcherson 383-500.
Cautions: 7 for 92 laps   Margin of Victory: 4 laps-plus   Attendance: 25,000

Sam McQuagg #98 spins in front of Paul Lewis #1. Both recovered in Bristol 500-lapper with Lewis finishing 2nd and McQuagg 5th

David Pearson started his Dodge on the pole and led 330 of the first 382 laps. He was seemingly on his way to victory when he slowed and pitted on lap 383. Hutcherson took the lead at that point and led the rest of the way.

Bobby Isaac crashed the Junior Johnson Ford

"When David went out, I knew all I had to do was finish the 500 laps to win it," said Hutcherson. "We had blown an engine on Thursday and another one of Friday. I backed off and just coasted home."

Hutcherson was seven laps in front when Pearson finally pulled behind pit wall with a broken timing chain.

Bobby Isaac was involved in his third straight wreck. He lost control of his Ford in the 203rd lap and knocked down part of the protective railing. He was not hurt in the mishap. Other top

Jim Paschal, subbing for Richard Petty, blows an engine at Bristol

contenders Jim Paschal, subbing for Richard Petty, Ned Jarrett, Marvin Panch and Cale Yarborough all went out with various problems.

Seven caution flags broke the action as 92 laps were run under the yellow flag. Only seven cars

Dick Hutcherson rides under checkered flag at Bristol

finished out of a starting field of 32.

The Wood Brothers brought a radical Ford for Curtis Turner to drive. It was called a "Fairlane" -- but it had a Galaxie front end. NASCAR officials turned thumbs down on the car at the inspection station.

Hutcherson averaged 69.952 mph before 25,000 spectators.

Race No. 8

Jim Hurtubise Laps Field to Win Atlanta 500

HAMPTON, GA (Mar. 27) -- Jim Hurtubise took the lead just past the halfway point when Richard Petty lost an engine and outran Fred Lorenzen to win the seventh annual Atlanta 500 at Atlanta International Raceway. It was the first NASCAR win for the 32 year-old N. Tonawanda, NY Plymouth driver. It came in his 11th start, dating back to 1957 when he first competed in a Grand National race.

Fred Lorenzen, who was battling Hurtubise for top honors, fell a lap off the pace with an ill-timed pit stop. He finished second. Third place went to Dick Hutcherson with Paul Goldsmith fourth and Jim Paschal fifth.

Petty won the pole and clearly had the upper hand for most of the way. He led 131 of the first 185 laps. Once he went out, Hurtubise and Lorenzen, with brief interludes from Curtis Turner, settled the race between themselves.

Bobby Isaac wheeled a motor scooter around before Atlanta 500.

Hurtubise and Lorenzen swapped first place five times in the last 100 miles. Lorenzen had made his final pit stop about 80 miles from the finish as Hurtubise stayed on the track. Hurtubise had lapped his rival, but was due for his final stop. The yellow flag came out on lap 295 for oil on the track from Ned Jarrett's blown engine. Hurtubise was able to make his final pit stop under yellow and kept his full lap advantage over Lorenzen.

"The car felt good," Hurtubise said of his Norm Nelson Plymouth. "It had developed a vibration about two-thirds of the way through the race. I slacked off for a while, but it vibrated at high and low speeds. So I decided to tromp on it and get the show over with."

Lorenzen tipped his hat to his former rival on the USAC circuit. "He deserved to win," said Lorenzen. "That guy was running the last five laps as hard as he ran the first five."

Car owner Nelson said Hurtubise "doesn't know what it is to slow up. Wide open is the only pace he knows."

The lead changed hands 23 times among nine drivers. Hurtubise averaged 131.247 mph before an audience announced at 71,000.

Hurtubise later admitted that his team had the Plymouth rigged with a device to lower the body during the event. "I carried a big monkey wrench with me," said 'Herk'. "On caution laps, I'd crank a bolt and lower the body so it would cut the air better. After the race was over, I drove real slow on the backstretch. I slung the wrench into the infield. I didn't want anybody to see that wrench in the car when I got to victory lane. They might have suspected something."

Race No. 9
Point Leader Pearson Hums at Hickory

HICKORY, NC (Apr. 3) -- David Pearson edged past Curtis Turner in the 199th lap and led the final 52 laps to win the Hickory 250 at Hickory Speedway. It was the first win of the season for Pearson, who has led the point race from the second event of the season.

Turner, driving a new intermediate Ford Fairlane -- NASCAR's first look at the smaller vehicle -- chased Pearson close for the final laps. He wound up 4.0-seconds behind Pearson's Dodge at the stripe. Third place went to Bobby Isaac with Ned Jarrett fourth and

Grand National Race No. 8
334 Laps at Atlanta Int'l Raceway
Hampton, GA
"Atlanta 500"
500 Miles on 1.5-mile Paved Track
March 27, 1966

Fin	St	No.	Driver	Team / Car	Laps	Money	Status
1	5	56	Jim Hurtubise	Norm Nelson '66 Plym	334	$17,920	Running
2	3	28	Fred Lorenzen	Holman-Moody '66 Ford	333	8,290	Running
3	2	29	Dick Hutcherson	Holman-Moody '66 Ford	333	4,825	Running
4	4	99	Paul Goldsmith	Nichels Eng '66 Plymouth	331	2,750	Running
5	17	14	Jim Paschal	Friedkin Ent '66 Plymouth	330	1,925	Running
6	14	27	Cale Yarborough	Banjo Matthews '66 Ford	329	1,250	Running
7	18	98	Sam McQuagg	Nichels Eng '66 Dodge	327	1,150	Running
8	11	07	Don White	Nichels Eng '65 Dodge	326	1,115	Running
9	28	55	Tiny Lund	Lyle Stelter '64 Ford	318	975	Running
10	19	24	Bobby Allison	Betty Lilly '66 Ford	315	875	Running
11	22	79	Frank Warren	Harold Rhodes '64 Chevrolet	313	750	Running
12	31	19	J T Putney	Putney '66 Chevrolet	309	850	Running
13	8	41	Curtis Turner	Wood Brothers '66 Ford	305	700	Engine
14	9	6	David Pearson	Cotton Owens '65 Dodge	304	715	Running
15	20	48	James Hylton	Bud Hartje '65 Ford	301	575	Engine
16	6	21	Marvin Panch	Wood Brothers '66 Ford	297	550	Engine
17	36	1	Paul Lewis	Lewis '65 Plymouth	296	600	Running
18	7	11	Ned Jarrett	Bondy Long '66 Ford	290	1,050	Engine
19	25	71	Gordon Johncock	K&K Insurance '65 Dodge	278	685	Engine
20	42	20	Clyde Lynn	Lynn '64 Ford	278	550	Running
21	4	12	LeeRoy Yarbrough	Jon Thorne '66 Dodge	273	555	Engine
22	38	53	Jimmy Helms	David Warren '64 Ford	268	600	Running
23	34	52	Wayne Woodward	Bill Church '65 Chevrolet	258	640	Running
24	15	59	Tom Pistone	Pistone '64 Ford	220	550	Engine
25	1	43	Richard Petty	Petty Ent '66 Plymouth	185	1,530	Engine
26	29	46	Roy Mayne	Tom Hunter '66 Chevrolet	162	550	Headers
27	37	38	Wayne Smith	Smith '66 Chevrolet	156	610	Oil cooler
28	40	73	Buddy Arrington	Joan Petre '64 Ford	88	580	Engine
29	10	26	Bobby Isaac	Junior Johnson '66 Ford	73	600	Crash
30	16	64	Elmo Langley	Langley-Woodfield '65 Ford	66	550	Ignition
31	23	44	Larry Hess	Hess '66 Ford	58	550	Engine
32	13	49	G C Spencer	Spencer '65 Plymouth	58	550	Handling
33	30	18	Stick Elliott	Toy Bolton '66 Chevrolet	48	550	Clutch
34	24	04	John Sears	L G DeWitt '64 Ford	39	550	Engine
35	21	7	Bobby Johns	Shorty Johns '66 Chevrolet	34	550	Oil Leak
36	32	57	Lionel Johnson	Clay Esteridge '64 Ford	28	625	Engine
37	33	9	Roy Tyner	Truett Rodgers '65 Chevrolet	20	600	Engine
38	39	25	Jabe Thomas	Jeff Handy '64 Ford	11	540	Steering
39	43	86	Neil Castles	Buck Baker '66 Chevrolet	6	500	Engine
40	41	97	Henley Gray	Gray '66 Ford	2	500	Engine
41	27	67	E J Trivette	Buddy Arrington '64 Dodge	2	525	Steering
42	44	95	Gene Cline	Cline '64 Ford	2	500	Engine
43	36	87	Buddy Baker	Buck Baker '66 Olds	1	570	Engine
44	35	74	Bunkie Blackburn	Gene Black '64 Ford	1	580	Engine

Time of Race: 3 hours, 49 minutes, 2 seconds
Average Speed: 131.247 mph
Pole Winner: Richard Petty - 147.742 mph
Lap Leaders: Richard Petty 1-31, Jim Hurtubise 32, Don White 33-40, Petty 41-43, David Pearson 44-46, Petty 47-77, Gordon Johncock 78-80, Hurtubise 81-85, LeeRoy Yarbrough 86, Curtis Turner 87, Hurtubise 88-89, Turner 90, Hurtubise 91-96, Turner 97-104, Johncock 105-113, Petty 114-153, Hurtubise 154-156, Ned Jarrett 157-158, Petty 159-184, Hurtubise 185-209, Fred Lorenzen 210-219, Hurtubise 220-258, Lorenzen 259-276, Hurtubise 277-334.
Cautions: 5 for 31 laps.   Margin of Victory: 1-lap plus   Attendance: 71,000

Paul Goldsmith fifth. Goldsmith was driving a Plymouth owned by privateer Bob Cooper.

Elmo Langley earned his first career pole position, led for a single lap, and finished sixth.

Jarrett led for 138 straight laps, but he fell off the pace in the closing stages. He was two laps behind.

Cale Yarborough drove a Bill Seifert-owned Ford, but retired with overheating problems after 121 laps.

Pearson averaged 68.428 mph for his 14th career victory.

Grand National Race No. 9
250 Laps at Hickory Speedway
Hickory, NC
"Hickory 250"
100 Miles on .4-mile Dirt Track
April 3, 1966

Fin	St	No.	Driver	Team / Car	Laps	Money	Status
1	4	6	David Pearson	Cotton Owens '64 Dodge	250	$1,000	Running
2	2	41	Curtis Turner	Wood Brothers '66 Ford	250	600	Running
3	5	26	Bobby Isaac	Junior Johnson '66 Ford	248	400	Running
4	3	11	Ned Jarrett	Bondy Long '66 Ford	248	500	Running
5	8	02	Paul Goldsmith	Bob Cooper '65 Plymouth	247	275	Running
6	1	64	Elmo Langley	Langley-Woodfield '64 Ford	246	240	Running
7	14	70	J D McDuffie	McDuffie '64 Ford	238	200	Running
8	10	61	Leroy Bolton	Toy Bolton '66 Chevrolet	237	175	Running
9	21	9	Roy Tyner	Truett Rodgers '65 Chevrolet	237	150	Running
10	16	43	Richard Petty	Petty Enterprises '65 Plym	236	140	Running
11	9	66	Wayne Woodward	Woodward '66 Chevrolet	235	130	Running
12	13	19	J T Putney	Putney '65 Chevrolet	234	120	Running
13	24	97	Henley Gray	Gray '66 Ford	228	110	Running
14	20	34	Wendell Scott	Scott '65 Ford	226	100	Running
15	19	20	Clyde Lynn	Lynn '64 Ford	224	100	Running
16	11	18	Stick Elliott	Toy Bolton '66 Chevrolet	212	100	Running
17	17	88	Buddy Baker	Buck Baker '65 Chevrolet	202	100	Running
18	12	55	Tiny Lund	Lyle Stelter '64 Ford	123	100	Engine
19	22	45	Cale Yarborough	Bill Seifert '64 Ford	121	100	Heating
20	23	53	Jimmy Helms	David Warren '64 Ford	96	100	Differen
21	25	95	Gene Cline	Cline '64 Ford	96	100	Flat tire
22	6	59	Tom Pistone	Pistone '64 Ford	89	100	Heating
23	18	74	Gene Black	Black '64 Ford	87	100	Heating
24	15	77	Joel Davis	Harold Mays '65 Plymouth	84	100	Heating
25	7	04	John Sears	L G DeWitt '64 Ford	65	100	Engine
26	26	87	Buck Baker	Baker '66 Olds	21	100	Heating

Time of Race: 1 hour, 27 minutes, 41 seconds
Average Speed: 68.428 mph
Pole Winner: Elmo Langley - 75.117 mph
Lap Leaders: Curtis Turner 1-3, Elmo Langley 4, Ned Jarrett 5-142, David Pearson 143-163, Richard Petty 164-170, Turner 171-198, Pearson 199-250.
Cautions: 6 for 29 laps   Margin of Victory: 4.0 seconds   Attendance: 14,000

Race No. 10
Ford Begins Boycott;
Pearson Best at Columbia

COLUMBIA, SC (Apr. 7) -- Ford Motor Co. pulled their factory backed drivers out of NASCAR Grand National racing, and Dodge's David Pearson led the final 99 laps to win the 100-miler at Columbia Speed-

Grand National Race No. 10
200 Laps at Columbia Speedway
Columbia, SC
100 Miles on Half-mile Dirt Track
April 7, 1966

Fin	St	No.	Driver	Team / Car	Laps	Money	Status
1	6	6	David Pearson	Cotton Owens '64 Dodge	200	$1,000	Running
2	9	02	Paul Goldsmith	Bob Cooper '65 Plymouth	200	600	Running
3	1	59	Tom Pistone	Pistone '64 Ford	198	400	Running
4	2	19	J T Putney	Putney '66 Chevrolet	198	300	Running
5	4	04	John Sears	L G DeWitt '64 Ford	195	275	Running
6	18	43	Richard Petty	Petty Enterprises '65 Plym	195	240	Running
7	20	9	Roy Tyner	Truett Rodgers '66 Chevrolet	193	200	Running
8	15	61	Leroy Bolton	Toy Bolton '66 Chevrolet	191	175	Running
9	16	34	Wendell Scott	Scott '65 Ford	187	150	Running
10	8	97	Henley Gray	Gray '65 Ford	183	140	Running
11	14	66	Wayne Woodward	Woodward '66 Chevrolet	182	130	Running
12	17	20	Clyde Lynn	Lynn '64 Ford	182	120	Running
13	21	95	Gene Cline	Cline '64 Ford	181	110	Running
14	11	70	J D McDuffie	McDuffie '64 Ford	181	100	Running
15	19	86	Neil Castles	Buck Baker '65 Plymouth	178	100	Running
16	12	77	Joel Davis	Harold Mays '65 Plymouth	170	100	Running
17	24	45	Jim Tatum	Bill Seifert '64 Ford	169	100	Running
18	5	18	Stick Elliott	Toy Bolton '66 Chevrolet	161	100	Engine
19	23	53	Jimmy Helms	David Warren '64 Ford	123	100	Heating
19	3	88	Buddy Baker	Buck Baker '66 Chevrolet	95	100	Crash
21	22	74	Bill Seifert	Gene Black '65 Ford	63	100	Brakes
22	13	64	Elmo Langley	Langley-Woodfield '64 Ford	63	100	Engine
23	7	87	Buck Baker	Baker '66 Olds	16	---	Wtr pump
24	10	55	Tiny Lund	Lyle Stelter '64 Ford	13	---	Heating

Time of Race: 1 hour, 31 minutes, 30 seconds
Average Speed: 65.574 mph
Pole Winner: Tom Pistone - 72.202 mph
Lap Leaders: Tom Pistone 1-53, David Pearson 54-84, J T Putney 85, Paul Goldsmith 86-101, Pearson 102-200.
Cautions: 8 for 19 laps   Margin of Victory: 1 car length   Attendance: 11,000

way. A crowd of 11,000 showed up -- the most ever according to promoter Buddy Gooden -- for the 200 lap battle on the half-mile dirt track.

Paul Goldsmith finished second, just one car length behind Pearson. Tom Pistone was third, J.T. Putney was fourth and John Sears fifth.

Pistone, driving a self-owned two year-old Ford, surprisingly won the pole position and led the first 53 laps. Pearson took the lead at that point and led most of the way. Goldsmith was in front for 16 laps and Putney led a single lap.

Factory backed Ford drivers Ned Jarrett, Curtis Turner, and Bobby Isaac along with car owner Ralph Moody, watched the race from the pit area.

Richard Petty had a rough night. He went over the turn and slid down a dirt embankment during qualifying, damaging his braking system. Petty started 18th in the field of 24 and finished sixth, five laps back.

The first five qualifiers were all independents. In a most unusual session of time trials, Pistone, Putney, Buddy Baker, Sears and Stick Elliott occupied the top five starting spots. Baker crashed in the 95th lap and Elliott's engine blew on lap 161.

Pearson averaged 65.574 mph for his second straight win.

Race No. 11

Pearson Gets 3rd in Row At Greenville-Pickens

GREENVILLE, SC (Apr. 9) -- David Pearson won his third straight Grand National race at Greenville-Pickens Speedway.

Pearson passed Tiny Lund in the 85th lap and led the rest of the way in the 100-miler on the half-mile dirt track. Richard Petty finished in second place and Lund was third despite falling out with two laps to go. Neil Castles grabbed fourth place and Jeff Hawkins was fifth.

Lund led the first 39 laps in his Ford. Pearson made the pass on lap 40 and led through the 81st lap when J.T. Putney spun to bring out the yellow. Surprisingly, Lund's Lyle Stelter pit crew got him out ahead of the factory crews. Lund led only three laps before Pearson sailed into the lead for good.

Paul Goldsmith chased Pearson and Lund in the early going, but fell out on lap 50 when his Bob Cooper Plymouth developed electrical problems.

Pearson's 17th career victory came at an average speed of 65.850 mph. The caution flag was out three times for a total of 11 laps.

Race No. 12

Pearson Bags 4th in Row at Winston-Salem

WINSTON-SALEM, NC (Apr 11) -- David Pearson passed Tom Pistone in the seventh lap and drove his Dodge to victory in the 50-mile event at Bowman Gray Stadium. It was the fourth win in a row for the Spartanburg, SC veteran -- tying him with the late Billy Wade for the most Grand National wins in a row.

Cotton Owens, Pearson's car owner, entered a two year old Dodge in the 200 lapper on the quarter mile track. The car had been previously used as a "show car". With Pearson leading the NASCAR point standings, Owens felt he needed another "race ready" car at his disposal.

Grand National Race No. 11
200 Laps at Greenville-Pickens Speedway
Greenville, SC
100 Miles on Half-mile Dirt Track
April 9, 1966

Fin	St	No.	Driver	Team / Car	Laps	Money	Status
1	2	6	David Pearson	Cotton Owens '64 Dodge	200	$1,000	Running
2	9	43	Richard Petty	Petty Enterprises '65 Plym	199	600	Running
3	1	55	Tiny Lund	Lyle Stelter '64 Ford	194	400	Differen
4	14	86	Neil Castles	Buck Baker '65 Plymouth	192	300	Running
5	8	23	Jess Hawkins	Hubert Howard '64 Ford	192	275	Running
6	16	97	Henley Gray	Gray '66 Ford	185	240	Running
7	4	19	J T Putney	Putney '66 Chevrolet	182	200	Running
8	15	20	Clyde Lynn	Lynn '64 Ford	180	175	Running
9	7	04	John Sears	L G DeWitt '64 Ford	180	150	Running
10	20	95	Gene Cline	Cline '64 Ford	175	140	Running
11	24	74	Gene Black	Black '65 Ford	169	130	Running
12	22	45	Jim Tatum	Bill Seifert '64 Ford	168	120	Running
13	21	89	Max Ledbetter	Buck Baker '65 Olds	140	110	Running
14	6	87	Buck Baker	Baker '66 Olds	134	100	Differen
15	19	53	Jimmy Helms	David Warren '64 Ford	123	100	Differen
16	18	9	Roy Tyner	Truett Rodgers '66 Chevrolet	118	100	Differen
17	23	66	Wayne Woodward	Woodward '66 Chevrolet	117	100	Heating
18	17	70	J D McDuffie	McDuffie '64 Ford	74	100	Brakes
19	11	59	Tom Pistone	Pistone '64 Ford	72	100	Brakes
20	10	34	Wendell Scott	Scott '65 Ford	58	100	Engine
21	25	77	Joel Davis	Harold Mays '64 Plymouth	57	100	Brakes
22	3	02	Paul Goldsmith	Bob Cooper '65 Plymouth	50	100	Wiring
23	12	73	Buddy Arrington	Joan Petre '64 Ford	40	100	H Gasket
24	5	88	Buddy Baker	Buck Baker '66 Chevrolet	28	100	H Gasket
25	13	64	Elmo Langley	Langley-Woodfield '64 Ford	17	100	Heating

Time of Race: 1 hour, 31 minutes, 7 seconds
Average Speed: 65.850 mph
Pole Winner: Tiny Lund - 68.208 mph
Lap Leaders: Tiny Lund 1-39, David Pearson 40-81, Lund 82-84, Pearson 85-200.
Cautions: 3 for 11 laps   Margin of Victory: 1-lap plus   Attendance:

Grand National Race No. 12
200 Laps at Bowman Gray Stadium
Winston-Salem, NC
50 Miles on Quarter-mile Paved Track
April, 11, 1966

Fin	St	No.	Driver	Team / Car	Laps	Money	Status
1	1	6	David Pearson	Cotton Owens '64 Dodge	200	$850	Running
2	2	59	Tom Pistone	Pistone '64 Ford	200	550	Running
3	5	43	Richard Petty	Petty Enterprises '65 Plym	198	425	Running
4	3	24	Bobby Allison	Betty Lilly '66 Ford	198	330	Running
5	4	64	Elmo Langley	Langley-Woodfield '64 Ford	197	305	Running
6	16	0	Cale Yarborough	Reid Shaw '64 Ford	195	265	Running
7	9	04	John Sears	L G DeWitt '64 Ford	190	220	Running
8	10	21	Hank Thomas	'64 Ford	188	165	Running
9	18	87	Buck Baker	Baker '66 Olds	187	150	Running
10	12	70	J D McDuffie	McDuffie '64 Ford	180	155	Running
11	20	20	Clyde Lynn	Lynn '64 Ford	177	130	Running
12	6	19	J T Putney	Putney '65 Chevrolet	174	140	Running
13	11	97	Henley Gray	Gray '66 Ford	168	110	Out Gas
14	13	95	Gene Cline	Cline '64 Ford	95	100	Flat tire
15	15	74	Gene Black	Black '64 Ford	50	100	Brakes
16	8	86	Neil Castles	Buck Baker '65 Plymouth	48	100	Differen
17	14	38	Wayne Smith	Smith '66 Chevrolet	33	115	Crash
18	17	34	Wendell Scott	Scott '65 Ford	32	115	Engine
19	7	9	Roy Tyner	Truett Rodgers '65 Chevrolet	10	115	Trans
20	21	45	Jim Tatum	Bill Seifert '64 Ford	8	100	Oil Press
21	22	53	Jimmy Helms	David Warren '64 Ford	5	100	D Shaft
22	19	73	Buddy Arrington	Joan Petre '64 Ford	1	100	Engine

Time of Race: 58 minutes, 20 seconds
Average Speed: 51.341 mph
Pole Winner: David Pearson - 54.479
Lap Leaders: Tom Pistone 1-6, David Pearson 7-200.
Cautions: 1 for 4 laps   Margin of Victory: Attendance: 4,200

David Pearson got 4th win in a row at Winston-Salem

Pistone was in the same lap with Pearson and finished second. Richard Petty scraped past Bobby Allison in the final five miles to take third. Allison was fourth and Elmo Langley was fifth.

Plymouth-driving Petty and independent Chevrolet driver J.T. Putney engaged in a fender framming episode much of the race. In the 64th lap, Petty and Putney came together in a battle for fourth, which Petty won only briefly. After making the pass, Petty had to pit for a fender rubbing a tire. He lost almost two laps in the pits.

Petty caught back up to Putney with 30 laps to go. Petty nudged Putney's bumper, sending him high in the third turn. Petty completed the pass to move into fourth.

Putney, of Arden, NC, went into the first turn full throttle, narrowly missing Petty's rear bumper. Rather than collecting Petty's bumper, Putney smashed into the wall. Oddly, the accident did not bring out the caution flag.

One caution for a two car spin didn't keep Pearson from setting a 50-mile Grand National record of 51.341 mph. A crowd of 4,200 was on hand.

Race No. 13

Paschal Leads Most of the Way; Romps at N.Wilkesboro

N.WILKESBORO, NC (Apr. 17) --Jim Paschal of High Point, NC pushed his Friedkin Enterprises Plymouth into the lead for good on lap 348 and went on to win the Gwyn Staley Memorial 400 at North Wilkesboro Speedway. It was Paschal's 20th career Grand National triumph, but his first since he won the 1964 World 600 at Charlotte.

Paschal started on the pole and led for 308 of the 400 laps on the .625-mile paved oval. G.C. Spencer finished second, six laps behind. David Pearson got credit for third place although the engine blew in his Dodge in the final laps. Wendell Scott came in fourth and Henley Gray was fifth.

A crowd of 6,000 -- less than half the normal atten-

Grand National Race No. 13
400 Laps at N. Wilkesboro Speedway
N. Wilkesboro, NC
"Gwyn Staley Memorial"
250 Miles on .625-mile Paved Track
April 17, 1966

Fin	St	No.	Driver	Team / Car	Laps	Money	Status
1	1	14	Jim Paschal	Friedkin Enterprises '66 Plym	400	$4,950	Running
2	7	49	G C Spencer	Spencer '65 Plymouth	394	2,225	Running
3	2	6	David Pearson	Cotton Owens '66 Dodge	382	1,350	Engine
4	26	34	Wendell Scott	Scott '65 Ford	378	825	Running
5	25	97	Henley Gray	Gray '66 Ford	375	625	Running
6	15	04	John Sears	L G DeWitt '64 Ford	371	525	Running
7	29	70	J D McDuffie	McDuffie '64 Ford	370	475	Running
8	35	86	Neil Castles	Buck Baker '65 Plymouth	362	400	Running
9	27	45	Bill Seifert	Seifert '64 Ford	357	375	Running
10	32	95	Gene Cline	Cline '64 Ford	350	300	Running
11	4	43	Richard Petty	Petty Enterprises '65 Plym	347	400	Running
12	36	92	Hank Thomas	W S Jenkins '64 Ford	345	250	Running
13	18	66	Wayne Woodward	Woodward '65 Chevrolet	331	250	Differen
14	9	74	Buddy Baker	Gene Black '64 Ford	317	225	Running
15	17	46	Roy Mayne	Tom Hunter '66 Chevrolet	287	200	Running
16	30	38	Wayne Smith	Smith '66 Chevrolet	267	200	Engine
17	6	98	Sam McQuagg	Nichels Eng '66 Dodge	266	200	Engine
18	20	25	Jabe Thomas	Jeff Handy '64 Ford	246	200	Differen
19	24	63	Larry Manning	Bob Adams '65 Plymouth	245	200	Running
20	28	20	Clyde Lynn	Lynn '64 Ford	239	200	Differen
21	14	64	Elmo Langley	Langley-Woodfield '64 Ford	228	175	Engine
22	19	73	Buddy Arrington	Joan Petre '64 Ford	210	175	Differen
23	37	9	Roy Tyner	Truett Rodgers '65 Chevrolet	198	150	Differen
24	11	99	Paul Goldsmith	Nichels Eng '65 Plymouth	193	250	Brakes
25	33	53	Jimmy Helms	David Warren '64 Ford	152	150	Flat tire
26	5	24	Bobby Allison	Betty Lilly '66 Ford	146	175	Engine
27	23	87	Buck Baker	Baker '66 Olds	143	200	Engine
28	22	7	Bobby Johns	Shorty Johns '66 Chevrolet	112	250	Heating
29	16	77	Joel Davis	Harold Mays '64 Plymouth	111	175	Differen
30	8	02	Doug Cooper	Bob Cooper '65 Plymouth	92	175	Differen
31	12	19	J T Putney	Putney '66 Chevrolet	89	50	Engine
32	10	40	Eddie Yarboro	'65 Dodge	77	25	Differen
33	13	1	Paul Lewis	Lewis '65 Plymouth	49	25	Engine
34	34	35	Max Ledbetter	'65 Olds	47	---	Oil Leak
35	21	48	James Hylton	Bud Hartje '65 Dodge	30	150	Engine
36	31	60	Ernest Eury	Joan Petre '64 Chevrolet	22	---	Steering
37	3	59	Tom Pistone	Pistone '64 Ford	5	25	Crash

Time of Race: 2 hours, 50 minutes, 22 seconds
Average Speed: 89.045 mph
Pole Winner: Jim Paschal - 102.693 mph
Lap Leaders: Jim Paschal 1-117, Richard Petty 118-123, Paschal 124-144, Petty 145-189, Paschal 190-306, Petty 307-347, Paschal 348-400.
Cautions: 8 for 48 laps   Margin of Victory: 6-laps plus   Attendance: 6,000

dance -- watched the event in the wake of the highly publicized Ford boycott.

Richard Petty started fourth on the grid and gave Paschal a run for his money. The Randleman, NC Plymouth ace led 92 laps and was leading in the 347th lap when the engine cut loose.

Only 14 cars in the field of 37 finished the 250-miler. Tom Pistone started third, but wrecked his

G.C. Spencer finished second at North Wilkesboro

Ford in the fifth lap. Paul Goldsmith ran in the top five most of the way before failing brakes sidelined his Plymouth.

Paschal's triumph was the first for the semi-factory backed Plymouth team owned by Tom Friedkin. "We've been figuring we were about due," said the 39 year-old Paschal. "Richard was running real well, too. I don't know what would have happened if his car had lasted. I had planned to make my move near the end, but I'm not sorry it didn't come to that."

Petty admitted it would have been a hard fought two-car showdown. "I doubt if either one of us could have passed the other without a little banging around," said Petty. "The pressure would have gotten tremendous at the finish."

Paschal averaged 89.045 mph in becoming the eighth different winner of the 1966 Grand National season.

Race No. 14

Upset-Minded Pistone Blows; Paschal Takes Virginia 500

MARTINSVILLE, VA (Apr. 24) -- Jim Paschal took the lead with less than 100 laps to go and won a disputed Virginia 500 at Martinsville Speedway. Paul Goldsmith had been flagged in first place, but after a scoring re-check, Paschal was officially given the nod.

Paschal's official margin of victory was 12 seconds over Goldsmith. Paschal's crew chief Bill Ellis had requested a recount of the scoring cards. Forty-five minutes later, Paschal was given the first place check of $4,550.

Richard Petty was five laps back in third, Elmo Langley was fourth and G.C. Spencer fifth.

Tiger Tom Pistone had the crowd of 10,500 on its feet as he charged from 20th starting position to fifth in the first 10 miles. With only one caution flag in the entire race, premium was placed

Tom Pistone #59 surprised everyone by taking the independent Ford to the point at Martinsville

on the pit crews. Pistone's throw-together pit crew consisting of two young sons and some volunteers from a tire company, lost time during green flag pit stops. But the little dynamo from Chicago never let up.

Pistone took the lead from David Pearson in the 232nd lap and led for 42 laps before making his second pit stop. He returned to the track running nearly a lap behind, but he charged his two year old Ford up into second when the engine came apart.

"When I get in a car that will go," said Pistone, "I can't help myself. I've just got to let it all hang out. My goal now is to finish a race.

"All the money in China couldn't buy the feeling I had when I was leading," he added. "It was simply

Grand National Race No. 14
500 Laps at Martinsville Speedway
Martinsville, VA
"Virginia 500"
250 Miles on Half-mile Paved Track
April 24, 1966

Fin	St	No.	Driver	Team / Car	Laps	Money	Status
1	1	14	Jim Paschal	Friedkin Ent '66 Plymouth	500	$4,550	Running
2	2	99	Paul Goldsmith	Nichels Eng '65 Plymouth	500	2,150	Running
3	4	43	Richard Petty	Petty Enterprises '66 Plym	495	1,250	Running
4	6	64	Elmo Langley	Langley-Woodfield '64 Ford	488	775	Running
5	21	49	G C Spencer	Spencer '65 Plymouth	486	725	Running
6	24	1	Paul Lewis	Lewis '65 Plymouth	485	675	Running
7	23	24	Bobby Allison	Betty Lilly '66 Ford	483	575	Running
8	22	48	James Hylton	Bud Hartje '65 Dodge	476	535	Running
9	5	6	David Pearson	Cotton Owens '66 Dodge	474	575	Running
10	28	88	Buddy Baker	Buck Baker '65 Chevrolet	469	450	Running
11	27	87	Buck Baker	Baker '66 Olds	467	425	Running
12	18	16	Johnny Wynn	'64 Mercury	464	425	Running
13	25	77	Joel Davis	Harold Mays '65 Plymouth	462	390	Running
14	34	9	Roy Tyner	Truett Rodgers '65 Chevrolet	453	380	Engine
15	17	97	Henley Gray	Gray '66 Ford	450	395	Running
16	3	98	Sam McQuagg	Nichels Eng '66 Dodge	449	435	Engine
17	37	83	Worth McMillion	Allen McMillion '65 Pontiac	444	350	Running
18	12	34	Wendell Scott	Scott '65 Ford	439	365	Running
19	7	7	Bobby Johns	Shorty Johns '66 Chevrolet	437	355	Differen
20	36	38	Wayne Smith	Smith '66 Chevrolet	429	320	Running
21	39	35	J T Putney	'65 Olds	419	300	Running
22	20	59	Tom Pistone	Pistone '64 Ford	357	450	Engine
23	10	72	Bill Champion	Champion '64 Ford	315	325	U Joint
24	19	02	Doug Cooper	Bob Cooper '65 Plymouth	290	350	Differen
25	14	70	J D McDuffie	McDuffie '64 Ford	251	325	Clutch
26	38	95	Gene Cline	Cline '64 Ford	242	275	Differen
27	16	53	Jimmy Helms	David Warren '64 Ford	170	300	Brakes
28	29	92	Hank Thomas	W S Jenkins '64 Ford	167	275	Wheel
29	15	25	Jabe Thomas	Jeff Handy '64 Ford	158	300	Differen
30	13	20	Clyde Lynn	Lynn '64 Ford	130	300	Differen
31	32	73	Pee Wee Ellwanger	Joan Petre '64 Ford	127	250	Differen
32	30	18	Stick Elliott	Toy Bolton '66 Chevrolet	124	250	Brakes
33	11	45	Bill Seifert	Seifert '64 Ford	69	275	Brakes
34	9	66	Wayne Woodward	Woodward '66 Chevrolet	68	275	Differen
35	33	86	Neil Castles	Buck Baker '65 Plymouth	43	250	Oil Leak
36	26	67	Buddy Arrington	Arrington '64 Dodge	36	275	Vibration
37	8	04	John Sears	L G DeWitt '64 Ford	18	275	Engine
38	35	5	Bob Derrington	'65 Plymouth	4	250	Vibration
39	40	96	Hugh Lamphear	Homer O'Dell '64 Ford	4	250	Clutch
40	31	50	Edward Jordan	'64 Ford	1	250	Handling

Time of Race: 3 hours, 36 minutes, 54 seconds
Average Speed: 69.156 mph
Pole Winner: Jim Paschal - 76.345 mph
Laps Leaders Jim Paschal 1-152, Paul Goldsmith 153-156, David Pearson 157-231, Tom Pistone 232-273, Paschal 274-391, Goldsmith 392-402, Paschal 403-500.
Cautions: 1 for 6 laps   Margin of Victory: 12 seconds   Attendance: 10,500

Jim Paschal won Virginia 500 after a scoring re-check

great. I just wish the car had lasted."

Paschal was adamant in victory lane. "I was confident I had won," he said. "It wouldn't have made any difference at the end if I knew I was in second. I was running as hard as I could. If they decide that I was second, I'm not going to raise any fuss about it. I just want them to check to be sure. I think they'll find a mistake, though."

Goldsmith said, "Whatever the officials decide will be right, I'm sure."

Point leader David Pearson finished ninth. He still held a 2,902 point lead over second ranking Goldsmith.

Pistone wound up 22nd, worth $450.

Paschal averaged 69.156 mph for his 21st career win.

Race No. 15

Slim Crowd Watches Petty Pancake Rebel 400 Field

DARLINGTON, SC (Apr. 30) -- Richard Petty started on the pole and ran away from the field to win the Rebel 400 at Darlington Raceway by three laps. It was Petty's third win of the year and the 43rd of his career.

Paul Goldsmith nosed past David Pearson in the late stages and finished second. Pearson got third despite a cracked wheel. Bunkie Blackburn was fourth and G.C. Spencer fifth.

The effects of the Ford boycott began to tell at the turnstiles. Only 12,000 showed up for the 400 miler, and 5,000 of those were Boy Scouts admitted free.

Petty was never seriously challenged as he led 271 of the 291 laps. Pearson was in front for 16 laps, Spencer led two laps under yellow, and Goldsmith and Darel Dieringer each led one lap.

Dieringer was driving a small Mercury Comet prepared by Bud Moore. The Indianapolis, IN driver started second and led for one lap during an exchange of pit stops. Engine failure put him out of action after 218 laps.

Grand National Race No.15
291 Laps at Darlington Raceway
Darlington, SC
"Rebel 400"
400 Miles on 1.375-mile Paved Track
April 30, 1966

Fin	St	No.	Driver	Team / Car	Laps	Money	Status
1	1	43	Richard Petty	Petty Enterprises '66 Plym	291	$12,115	Running
2	7	99	Paul Goldsmith	Nichels Eng '65 Plymouth	288	6,570	Running
3	11	6	David Pearson	Cotton Owens '65 Dodge	288	4,145	Running
4	9	3	Bunkie Blackburn	Ray Fox '65 Dodge	283	2,225	Running
5	10	49	G C Spencer	Spencer '65 Plymouth	283	1,670	Running
6	5	14	Jim Paschal	Friedkin Ent '66 Plymouth	278	1,250	Running
7	15	64	Elmo Langley	Langley-Woodfield '64 Ford	275	1,000	Running
8	26	87	Buck Baker	Baker '66 Olds	275	900	Running
9	17	48	James Hylton	Bud Hartje '65 Dodge	270	965	Running
10	12	1	Paul Lewis	Lewis '65 Plymouth	270	840	Running
11	23	4	John Sears	L G DeWitt '64 Ford	266	750	Running
12	14	19	J T Putney	Putney '66 Chevrolet	262	725	Running
13	28	97	Henley Gray	Gray '66 Ford	257	700	Running
14	36	86	Neil Castles	Buck Baker '65 Plymouth	253	675	Running
15	30	77	Joel Davis	Harold Mays '65 Plymouth	252	650	Running
16	19	24	Bobby Allison	Betty Lilly '66 Ford	246	645	W Bearing
17	13	7	Bobby Johns	Shorty Johns '66 Chevrolet	242	600	Engine
18	16	18	Stick Elliott	Toy Bolton '66 Chevrolet	239	575	Crank
19	25	46	Roy Mayne	Tom Hunter '66 Chevrolet	236	550	Running
20	29	30	Walter Ballard	Ballard '64 Ford	234	525	Running
21	24	88	Buddy Baker	Buck Baker '66 Chevrolet	220	500	Engine
22	2	16	Darel Dieringer	Bud Moore '66 Mercury	218	490	Engine
23	3	71	Earl Balmer	K&K Insurance '65 Dodge	186	520	Oil Pan
24	33	74	Gene Black	Black '64 Ford	184	470	Axle
25	8	22	Curtis Turner	Smokey Yunick '65 Chevrolet	150	460	Lug Bolts
26	34	25	Wendell Scott	Scott '65 Ford	144	450	Heating
27	22	67	Buddy Arrington	Arrington '64 Dodge	97	445	Engine
28	31	38	Wayne Smith	Smith '66 Chevrolet	75	440	Clutch
29	4	12	LeeRoy Yarbrough	Jon Thorne '66 Dodge	65	445	Engine
30	6	98	Sam McQuagg	Nichels Eng '66 Dodge	54	430	Heating
31	21	55	Tiny Lund	Lyle Stelter '64 Ford	54	425	Clutch
32	18	02	Doug Cooper	Bob Cooper '65 Plymouth	44	460	Engine
33	35	9	Roy Tyner	Truett Rodgers '66 Chevrolet	29	415	Trans
34	20	59	Tom Pistone	Pistone '64 Ford	4	410	Oil Press
35	27	66	Wayne Woodward	Woodward '66 Chevrolet	3	405	Engine
36	32	96	Sonny Lamphear	Homer O'Dell '64 Ford	0	400	Engine

Time of Race: 3 hours, 1 minute, 53 seconds
Average Speed: 131.993 mph
Pole Winner: Richard Petty - 140.815 mph
Lap Leaders: Richard Petty 1-36, Paul Goldsmith 37, G C Spencer 38-39, David Pearson 40-45, Petty 46-100, Dieringer 101, Petty 102-291.
Cautions: 1 for 5 laps   Margin of Victory: 3-plus laps
Attendance: 7,000 (plus 5,000 free Boy Scouts)

Curtis Turner resigned from the Ford camp and accepted an offer to drive Smokey Yunick's Chevrolet. "I've got only two or three years left," said Turner, "and I need to be racin'." Turner started eighth in the field of 36, but departed on lap 150 with broken lug bolts.

Earl Balmer qualified the K&K Insurance Dodge owned by Nord Krauskopf third fastest and ran with the leaders until a hole in his oil pan forced him behind pit wall at the 186 lap mark.

Petty said he charged nearly all the way. "I ran flat out until the last 30 laps," he remarked. "We practiced with our race set up and were really strong. I expected a little more competition from (Jim) Paschal and (Lee-Roy) Yarbrough. Apparently, they had their troubles."

Richard Petty won easily in Darlington's Rebel 400

Paschal faded to a sixth place finish and Yarbrough went out early with a blown engine.

Goldsmith saluted Petty. "He was the fastest and everything went right for him," said the former motorcycle champion. "When it's your day to win, there's nothing going to stop you -- and it was Richard Petty's day. I only wish we could have made things a little more interesting for him."

Petty averaged 131.993 mph in the briskly paced contest.

Grand National Race No. 16
250 Laps at Langley Field Speedway
Hampton, VA
"Tidewater 250"
100 Miles on .4-mile Dirt Track
May 7, 1966

Fin	St	No.	Driver	Team / Car	Laps	Money	Status
1	1	43	Richard Petty	Petty Enterprises '66 Plym	250	$1,000	Running
2	3	48	James Hylton	Bud Hartje '65 Dodge	250	600	Running
3	8	86	Neil Castles	Buck Baker '66 Plymouth	246	400	Running
4	4	64	Elmo Langley	Langley-Woodfield '64 Ford	244	300	Running
5	6	59	Tom Pistone	Pistone '64 Ford	244	275	Running
6	13	06	Johnny Wynn	John McCarthy '64 Mercury	243	240	Running
7	14	34	Wendell Scott	Scott '65 Ford	243	200	Running
8	18	9	Roy Tyner	Truett Rodgers '66 Chevrolet	233	175	D Shaft
9	7	19	J T Putney	Putney '66 Chevrolet	226	150	Running
10	10	2	Clyde Lynn	Lynn '64 Ford	222	140	Running
11	11	97	Henley Gray	Gray '66 Ford	203	130	Crash
12	12	45	Bill Seifert	Seifert '64 Ford	195	120	Crash
13	2	4	John Sears	L G DeWitt '64 Ford	194	110	Running
14	22	80	Worth McMillion	Allen McMillion '65 Pontiac	153	100	A Frame
15	19	53	Jimmy Helms	David Warren '64 Ford	69	100	Oil Press
16	17	87	Buck Baker	Baker '66 Olds	52	100	Brakes
17	9	96	Sonny Lamphear	Homer O'Dell '64 Ford	35	100	Throttle
18	15	25	Jabe Thomas	Jeff Handy '64 Ford	30	100	Trans
19	5	6	David Pearson	Cotton Owens '64 Dodge	26	100	Ignition
20	21	51	Bob Derrington	Derrington '65 Chevrolet	17	100	Handling
21	16	55	Tiny Lund	Lyle Stelter '64 Ford	13	100	T. Chain
22	20	30	Edward Jordan	'64 Ford	2	100	Ignition

Time of Race: 1 hour, 38 minutes, 49 seconds
Average Speed: 60.616 mph
Pole Winner: Richard Petty - 66.821 mph
Lap Leaders: John Sears 1-73, Richard Petty 74-250
Cautions: Margin of Victory: 16 seconds   Attendance: 5,000

Race No. 16

Sears Fastest in Tidewater 250 -- But Petty Wins

HAMPTON, VA (May 7) -- Richard Petty took the lead from an ailing John Sears in the 73rd lap and scored his second straight win in the Tidewater 250 at Langley Field Speedway. It was the fourth win of the year for the Randleman Rocket.

James Hylton wound up second, 16 seconds behind Petty. The Inman, SC rookie driver was in a Dodge owned by Bud Hartje. Neil Castles came in third with Elmo Langley fourth and Tom Pistone fifth.

Sears of Ellerbe, NC, started second and jumped Petty at the start. The 29 year-old Ford driver put his lightly regarded car up front for the first 73 laps. He was doing an excellent job of holding Petty off when mechanical problems sent him to the pits for a long stop. Sears got back in the race and wound up 13th, 56 laps behind.

Langley pressured Petty in the middle portions of the 100-miler, pulling along side the heavy favorite on several occasions. A blown tire knocked the Landover, MD Ford driver six laps off the pace near the end.

Bill Seifert was shaken up in a weird accident. Seifert's Ford popped a tire and struck the guard rail. Seifert's car was partially sticking through the rail. Henley Gray's Ford ran into the debris, blew a tire and hit Seifert's machine, pushing it down a steep embankment. The Skyland, NC driver spent one night in the hospital after x-rays proved negative.

Petty averaged 60.616 mph for his 44th career Grand National victory. A crowd of 5,000 was on hand.

Race No. 17

Petty Outruns Pistone for Speedy Morelock 200 Victory

MACON, GA (May 10) -- Richard Petty prevailed in a see-saw battle with Tom Pistone and won the Speedy Morelock 200 at Middle Georgia Raceway. It was the third straight win for Petty on NASCAR's major league stock car racing tour.

Pistone fell a lap off the pace when he made a lengthy pit stop, but charged around Petty late in the race. He wound up 19 seconds behind when the checkered flag fell. Bobby Allison came in third, James Hylton was fourth and Neil Castles fifth. Only 15 cars showed up for the 100-miler.

Darel Dieringer was entered in Bud Moore's Mercury Comet and he moved into the lead on lap six. He was running in third place when the engine blew on lap 135.

A crowd of 7,500 watched Petty average 82.023 mph.

Eleven cars of the 15 starters were running at the finish. Elmo Langley ran strong in the early going before a skipping engine set him back to eighth in the final rundown.

Grand National Race No. 17
200 Laps at Middle Georgia Raceway
Macon, GA
"Speedy Morelock 200"
100 Miles on Half-mile Paved Track
May 10, 1966

Fin	St	No.	Driver	Team / Car	Laps	Money	Status
1	1	43	Richard Petty	Petty Enterprises '66 Plym	200	$1,000	Running
2	2	59	Tom Pistone	Pistone '64 Ford	200	600	Running
3	4	24	Bobby Allison	Betty Lilly '66 Ford	197	400	Running
4	6	48	James Hylton	Bud Hartje '65 Dodge	193	300	Running
5	9	86	Neil Castles	Buck Baker '66 Plymouth	184	275	Running
6	11	06	Johnny Wynn	John McCarthy '64 Mercury	184	240	Running
7	15	97	Henley Gray	Gray '66 Ford	184	200	Running
8	5	64	Elmo Langley	Langley-Woodfield '64 Ford	184	175	Running
9	8	77	Joel Davis	Harold Mays '65 Plymouth	183	150	Running
10	7	87	Buck Baker	Baker '66 Olds	180	140	Running
11	13	51	Bob Derrington	Derrington '65 Chevrolet	175	130	Running
12	12	25	Buddy Baker	Jeff Handy '64 Ford	149	120	Engine
13	14	30	Edward Jordan	'64 Ford	144	110	Fender
14	3	16	Darel Dieringer	Bud Moore '66 Mercury	135	100	Engine
15	10	34	Wendell Scott	Scott '65 Ford	3	100	Engine

Time of Race: 1 hour, 13 minutes, 9 seconds
Average Speed: 82.023 mph
Pole Winner: Richard Petty - 85.026 mph
Lap Leaders: Richard Petty 1-5, Darel Dieringer 6-34, Petty 35- , Tom Pistone - , Petty -200.
Cautions: None   Margin of Victory: 19 seconds   Attendance: 7,500

Race No. 18

Factory Drivers Not Allowed; Dieringer Wins All-Independent Show at Monroe

MONROE, NC (May 13) -- Factory backed Chrysler drivers were told to stay at home and Darel Dieringer won an all-independent 125-mile Grand National race at Starlite Speedway. It was the third career win for the 39 year-old driver.

Grand National Race No. 18
250 Laps at Starlite Speedway
Monroe, NC
125 Miles on Half-mile Dirt Track
May 13, 1966

Fin	St	No.	Driver	Team / Car	Laps	Money	Status
1	20	0	Darel Dieringer	Reid Shaw "64 Ford	250	$1,000	Running
2	10	20	Clyde Lynn	Lynn '64 Ford	242	600	Running
3	14	34	Wendell Scott	Scott '65 Ford	238	400	Running
4	9	86	Neil Castles	Buck Baker '65 Plymouth	237	300	Running
5	13	97	Henley Gray	Gray '66 Ford	230	275	Running
6	15	60	Ernest Eury	Joan Petre '64 Chevrolet	223	240	Running
7	21	74	Gene Black	Black '64 Ford	213	200	Running
8	12	77	Joel Davis	Harold Mays '65 Plymouth	206	175	Differen
9	2	64	Elmo Langley	Langley-Woodfield '64 Ford	155	150	Differen
10	19	30	Bob Derrington	'64 Ford	136	140	Differen
11	6	70	J D McDuffie	McDuffie '64 Ford	132	130	Crash
12	22	96	Sonny Lamphear	Homer O'Dell '64 Ford	126	120	Heating
13	16	06	Johnny Wynn	John McCarthy '64 Mercury	102	110	Oil Press
14	18	51	Bunk Moore	Bob Derrington '65 Chevrolet	101	100	Heating
15	7	19	J T Putney	Putney '66 Chevrolet	99	100	Axle
16	17	87	Buck Baker	Baker '66 Olds	86	100	Differen
17	4	40	Charles Triplett	'65 Dodge	85	100	Differen
18	24	59	Tom Pistone	Pistone '64 Ford	84	100	Heating
19	5	4	John Sears	L G DeWitt '64 Ford	84	100	Differen
20	25	55	Tiny Lund	Lyle Stelter '64 Ford	79	100	Axle
21	23	95	Gene Cline	Cline '64 Ford	70	100	Axle
22	1	48	James Hylton	Bud Hartje '65 Dodge	50	100	Tie rod
23	11	02	Doug Cooper	Bob Cooper '65 Plymouth	32	---	Oil Line
24	3	73	Buddy Baker	Joan Petre '64 Ford	29	---	Heating
25	8	9	Roy Tyner	Truett Rodgers '66 Chevrolet	20	---	Trans

Time of Race: 1 hour, 39 minutes, 46 seconds
Average Speed: 60.140 mph
Pole Winner: James Hylton - 65.099 mph
Lap Leaders: Elmo Langley 1- , James Hylton - , John Sears -72, Darel Dieringer 73-250.
Cautions: 3 for ___ laps   Margin of Victory: 8-laps plus   Attendance: 2,500

Dieringer took the lead from John Sears in the 73rd lap and led the rest of the way on the choppy half-mile dirt track. At the finish, he was eight laps in front of runner-up Clyde Lynn. Third place went to Wendell Scott, Neil Castles was fourth and Henley Gray fifth.

Sears fell out in the 84th lap with differential trouble.

Rookie James Hylton earned his first pole position and led early in the race. However, a tie-rod broke on his Dodge and he was out by the 50th lap. Only seven cars finished the race. Rain had fallen during the event, but not hard enough to bring out the yellow flag.

Elmo Langley started second and led the early laps. Differential problems sent his Ford to the sidelines in the 155th lap and he got credit for ninth in the final rundown. Six cars were knocked out with differential failure.

Only 2,500 spectators showed up for the experimental event.

Dieringer was driving a Ford owned by Reid Shaw, who was entering only his fourth race since his former driver Buren Skeen was killed in the 1965 Southern

500 at Darlington. "It certainly feels good to win instead of running second," said Dieringer, the perennial bridesmaid of the '65 season. "I didn't even have this ride until last night. The boys worked real hard on race day to get it ready."

Dieringer averaged 60.140 mph for his first win in 15 months.

Race No. 19

Pistone's Flat Tires Pave Way For Pearson's Richmond Win

RICHMOND, VA (May 15) -- David Pearson took the lead in the 119th lap and sped to victory in the Richmond 250 at Atlantic Rural Fairgrounds. It was the fifth win of the year for the Spartanburg, SC Dodge driver and the 16th victory in 19 races for the powerful Chrysler Corp.

Richard Petty came in second, two laps behind. J.T. Putney was third with Darel Dieringer fourth and Paul Goldsmith fifth.

Excessive tire wear played havoc with the 30-car field. Tom Pistone, who won his third career pole in his independent Ford, led the first 22 laps before blowing a tire and hitting the wall. He lost two laps in the pits and was never able to make up the deficit. Pistone blew a second tire and fell hopelessly behind -- and finally went out with engine failure on lap 160.

"We knew the tires situation would be bad," said winner Pearson. "It was pretty much the way we expected. In fact, I slowed down there toward the end of the race to keep from having any more tire wear."

Quick pit work in the Cotton Owens-led pits was a major factor in Pearson's runaway victory. On two routine pit stops under the green flag, Owens was able to change two tires and add a full load of fuel in 21 and 22 seconds respectively. "There's no doubt this is the best pit bunch I've ever had," said the crusty Owens. "We've been together some time now and they seem to get better all the

David Pearson - Richmond winner

time."

Curtis Turner started 13th on the grid in Smokey Yunick's Chevelle -- a surprise entry. But engine failure after 27 laps put the black and gold car behind pit wall.

Pearson averaged 66.539 mph before a sparse turnout of 4,500.

Grand National Race No. 19
250 Laps at Atlantic Rural Fairgrounds
Richmond, VA
"Richmond 250"
125 Miles on Half-mile Dirt Track
May 15, 1966

Fin	St	No.	Driver	Team / Car	Laps	Money	Status
1	4	6	David Pearson	Cotton Owens '64 Dodge	250	$2,050	Running
2	10	43	Richard Petty	Petty Enterprises '66 Plym	248	1,250	Running
3	6	19	J T Putney	Putney '66 Chevrolet	244	950	Running
4	7	0	Darel Dieringer	Reid Shaw '64 Ford	242	700	Running
5	12	99	Paul Goldsmith	Nichels Eng '65 Plymouth	241	550	Running
6	9	4	John Sears	L G DeWitt '64 Ford	241	375	Running
7	20	86	Neil Castles	Buck Baker '65 Plymouth	231	300	Running
8	18	97	Henley Gray	Gray '66 Ford	219	250	Running
9	15	20	Clyde Lynn	Lynn '64 Ford	216	200	Running
10	23	80	Worth McMillion	Allen McMillion '64 Pontiac	216	200	Running
11	27	9	Roy Tyner	Truett Rodgers '66 Chevrolet	216	175	Running
12	24	83	G T Nolan	Allen McMillion '66 Pontiac	215	175	Running
13	19	70	J D McDuffie	McDuffie '64 Ford	207	175	Running
14	22	34	Wendell Scott	Scott '65 Ford	200	150	Running
15	16	65	Larry Manning	'65 Ford	175	150	Engine
16	1	59	Tom Pistone	Pistone '64 Ford	151	125	Engine
17	3	64	Elmo Langley	Langley-Woodfield '64 Ford	137	125	Differen
18	8	87	Buck Baker	Baker '66 Olds	125	125	Engine
19	25	30	Bob Derrington	'64 Ford	114	125	Engine
20	2	48	James Hylton	Bud Hartje '65 Dodge	101	125	Engine
21	26	60	Ernest Eury	Joan Petre '64 Chevrolet	93	125	A Frame
22	17	69	Mack Hanbury	'64 Ford	28	125	D Shaft
23	13	22	Curtis Turner	Smokey Yunick '65 Chevrolet	27	125	Engine
24	14	55	Tiny Lund	Lyle Stelter '64 Ford	27	125	Engine
25	29	95	Gene Cline	Cline '64 Ford	24	125	Differen
26	21	72	Bill Champion	Champion '64 Ford	19	125	Heating
27	5	02	Doug Cooper	Bob Cooper '65 Plymouth	14	125	Trans
28	11	06	Johnny Wynn	John McCarthy '64 Mercury	8	125	Oil Press
29	28	45	Jim Tatum	Bill Seifert '64 Ford	6	125	Heating
30	30	93	Bill Seifert	Harry Neal '64 Ford	1	125	Oil Press

Time of Race: 1 hour, 52 minutes, 43 seconds
Average Speed: 66.539 mph
Pole Winner: Tom Pistone - 70.978 mph
Lap Leaders: Tom Pistone 1-22, David Pearson 23-71, Elmo Langley 72-74, Pearson 75-109, Richard Petty 110-118, Pearson 119-250.
Cautions: 2 for 14 laps   Margin of Victory: 2-laps plus   Attendance: 4,500

Race No. 20

Panch Boycotts Boycott; Wins World 600 in Petty Plymouth

CHARLOTTE, NC (May 22) -- Marvin Panch boycotted the Ford boycott, joined forces with the Petty Enterprises team and outlasted a host of faster rivals to win the seventh annual World 600 at Charlotte Motor

Grand National Race No. 20
400 Laps at Charlotte Motor Speedway
Charlotte, NC
"World 600"
600 Miles on 1.5-mile Paved Track
May 22, 1966

Fin	St	No.	Driver	Team / Car	Laps	Money	Status
1	7	42	Marvin Panch *	Petty Enterprises '65 Plym	400	$26,060	Running
2	20	49	G C Spencer	Spencer '65 Plymouth	398	10,980	Running
3	19	31	Don White	Nichels Eng '66 Dodge	394	7,045	Running
4	18	48	James Hylton	Bud Hartje '65 Dodge	391	4,325	Running
5	37	87	Neil Castles	Buck Baker '66 Olds	371	3,440	Running
6	32	86	Paul Connors	Buck Baker '64 Dodge	370	2,600	Running
7	40	34	Wendell Scott	Scott '65 Ford	370	2,025	Running
8	22	11	Ned Jarrett	Henley Gray '66 Ford	362	2,375	Engine
9	29	93	Blackie Watt	Harry Neal '64 Ford	351	1,585	Running
10	13	88	Buck Baker	Baker '66 Chevrolet	348	1,450	Running
11	28	46	Roy Mayne	Tom Hunter '66 Chevrolet	333	1,400	Engine
12	34	68	Larry Manning	Bob Derrington '65 Plymouth	322	1,370	Engine
13	42	20	Clyde Lynn	Lynn '64 Ford	313	1,300	Engine
14	17	99	Paul Goldsmith	Nichels Eng '66 Plymouth	303	2,155	Engine
15	3	71	Earl Balmer	K&K Insurance '65 Dodge	301	1,400	Engine
16	44	53	Jimmy Helms	David Warren '64 Ford	297	1,225	Running
17	4	6	David Pearson	Cotton Owens '66 Dodge	295	2,250	Crash
18	39	95	Gene Cline	Cline '64 Ford	291	1,180	Running
19	15	67	Buddy Arrington	Arrington '64 Dodge	273	1,150	Engine
20	33	72	Bill Champion	Champion '64 Ford	256	1,180	Oil Leak
21	2	14	Jim Paschal	Friedkin Ent '66 Plymouth	240	1,300	Engine
22	1	43	Richard Petty	Petty Enterprises '66 Plym	236	1,320	Engine
23	26	18	Stick Elliott	Toy Bolton '66 Chevrolet	237	1,125	Engine
24	27	4	John Sears	L G DeWitt '64 Ford	157	1,075	Engine
25	12	64	Elmo Langley	Langley-Woodfield '64 Ford	144	1,050	Crash
26	11	55	Tiny Lund	Lyle Stelter '64 Ford	140	1,050	Engine
27	14	90	Sonny Hutchins	Junie Donlavey '64 Ford	129	975	Engine
28	38	38	Wayne Smith	Smith '66 Chevrolet	122	935	Axle
29	6	98	Sam McQuagg	Nichels Eng '66 Dodge	112	925	Engine
30	30	73	Earl Brooks	Joan Petre '64 Ford	92	875	Engine
31	21	79	Frank Warren	Harold Rhodes '64 Chevrolet	89	860	Engine
32	25	59	Tom Pistone	Pistone '64 Ford	84	935	Trans
33	31	5	Harold Smith	'64 Ford	76	925	Engine
34	23	36	H B Bailey	Bailey '66 Pontiac	70	775	Engine
35	36	06	Johnny Wynn	John McCarthy '64 Mercury	63	725	Engine
36	10	1	Paul Lewis	Lewis '65 Plymouth	54	820	Crash
37	5	3	Buddy Baker	Ray Fox '65 Dodge	51	1,000	Engine
38	43	96	Sonny Lamphear	Homer O'Dell '64 Ford	29	675	D Shaft
39	9	16	Darel Dieringer	Bud Moore '66 Mercury	21	790	Differen
40	35	19	J T Putney	Putney '66 Chevrolet	20	690	Engine
41	8	24	Curtis Turner	Betty Lilly '66 Ford	19	645	Engine
42	41	74	Gene Black	Black '64 Ford	6	635	Engine
43	16	22	Bobby Allison	Smokey Yunick '65 Chevrolet	3	630	Engine
44	24	33	Joel Davis	Curtis Satterfield '66 Chevy	1	625	Gas Tank

*Relieved by Richard Petty
Time of Race: 4 hours, 26 minutes, 35 seconds
Average Speed: 135.042 mph
Pole Winner: Richard Petty - 148.637 mph
Fastest Qualifier: Paul Goldsmith - 149.491 mph
Lap Leaders: Richard Petty 1-2, David Pearson 3-7, Petty 8, Buddy Baker 9-44,
  Paul Lewis 45-47, Pearson 48-90, Jim Paschal 91-97, Earl Balmer 98-100,
  Pearson 101-170, Paul Goldsmith 171-221, Petty 222-224, Goldsmith 225-279,
  Pearson 280-295, Goldsmith 296-301, Marvin Panch 302-400.
Cautions: 5 for 18 laps   Margin of Victory: 2-laps plus   Attendance: 45,000

attrition-filled contest. Don White was third, James Hylton fourth and Neil Castles fifth.

Only 11 cars in the field of 44 were running at the finish -- and Panch was the only one of the 11 who led in the 400 lapper. Richard Petty, who started on the pole and led only three laps, relieved Panch on lap 358 and ushered the car into victory lane. "My seat was rubbing right where I was burned in that wreck at Daytona a few years ago (1963)," said Panch. "I saw Richard standing by so I let him relieve me."

Petty, whose Plymouth had fallen out on lap 236 with engine problems, said, "Panch put the car in front and all I did was keep it there."

Panch started seventh and did not take the lead until the 302nd lap. He took first place when Paul Goldsmith pitted with a blown engine. He was never threatened after that.

Goldsmith led for 112 laps despite losing almost two laps on a 50-second pit stop. The St.Claire Shores, MI Plymouth driver charged through the pack and into the lead only to see his hopes dashed in a puff of smoke.

David Pearson led for 134 laps, but his Dodge was taken out in the 295th lap when a wheel broke, sending him into the wall. His wheel sailed over the guard rail, inflicting considerable damage to four vehicles sitting in the parking lot.

Pack of cars zoom through 4th turn at Charlotte

Other leaders ran into an assortment of problems. Buddy Baker, leading for the first time on a superspeedway, gunned his Ray Fox Dodge into the lead on lap nine and led until the first caution flag came out. Baker's car was out of the race seven laps later with a blown engine. Earl Balmer, wheeling the K&K Insurance Dodge, was in strong contention when his engine blew late in the going.

Ned Jarrett ended his association with Ford Motor Co. and entered an independent Ford owned by Henley Gray. The defending Grand National champ was in contention when the engine let go with just a few laps remaining.

Speedway. It was the 17th career victory for the 40 year-old veteran, but his first in almost a year.

Panch, member of the Ford factory team since 1962, explained why he discontinued his support of the Ford walkout in a rules hassle. "Lee Petty offered me a ride in his car, so I just had to take it," said Panch.

G.C. Spencer finished second, two laps behind in an

David Pearson's Dodge gets out of control after losing a wheel in World 600

A crowd of 45,000 watched the uneventful race, which was run at a record speed of 135.042 mph.

Pearson held a commanding lead in the Grand National point standings, 2,504 points over runner-up Goldsmith.

Grand National Race No. 21
300 Laps at Dog Track Speedway
Moyock, NC
100 Miles on .333-mile Paved Track
May 29, 1966

Fin	St	No.	Driver	Team / Car	Laps	Money	Status
1	2	6	David Pearson	Cotton Owens '64 Dodge	301	$1,000	Running
2	10	55	Tiny Lund	Lyle Stelter '64 Ford	300	600	Running
3	4	48	James Hylton	Bud Hartje '65 Dodge	298	400	Running
4	13	4	John Sears	L G DeWitt '64 Ford	294	300	Running
5	14	34	Wendell Scott	Scott '65 Ford	291	275	Running
6	15	92	Hank Thomas	W S Jenkins '64 Ford	288	240	Running
7	16	20	Clyde Lynn	Lynn '64 Ford	278	200	Running
8	17	70	J D McDuffie	McDuffie '64 Ford	278	175	Running
9	25	83	Worth McMillion	Allen McMillion '66 Pontiac	276	150	Running
10	18	87	Ray Hill	Buck Baker '66 Chevrolet	273	140	Running
11	24	80	G T Nolan	Allen McMillion '65 Pontiac	265	130	Running
12	11	88	Paul Connors	Buck Baker '66 Olds	260	120	Running
13	20	5	Larry Manning	'65 Plymouth	259	110	Running
14	7	69	Mack Hanbury	'64 Ford	192	100	Differen
15	12	86	Neil Castles	Buck Baker '65 Plymouth	179	100	Crash
16	5	64	Elmo Langley	Langley-Woodfield '64 Ford	171	100	Suspen
17	21	53	Jimmy Helms	David Warren '64 Ford	98	100	Ignition
18	1	43	Richard Petty	Petty Enterprises '65 Plym	84	100	Ignition
19	19	9	Roy Tyner	Truett Rodgers '66 Chevrolet	75	100	Trans
20	8	73	Buddy Baker	Joan Petre '64 Ford	75	100	Crash
21	9	0	Darel Dieringer	Reid Shaw '64 Ford	45	100	Heating
22	3	59	Tom Pistone	Pistone '64 Ford	43	100	Trans
23	22	58	Gene Hobby	Hobby '64 Dodge	27	---	Heating
24	6	19	J T Putney	Putney '66 Chevrolet	13	---	Engine
25	23	96	Bill Stiles	Homer O'Dell '64 Ford	4	---	Crash

Time of Race: 1 hour, 37 minutes, 14 seconds
Average Speed: 61.913 mph
Pole Winner: Richard Petty - 69.164 mph
Lap Leaders: Richard Petty 1-84, David Pearson 85-301
Cautions: Margin of Victory: 1-lap plus   Attendance:
*301 Laps were run due to scoring error

Race No. 21

Pearson Master in Moyock 300

MOYOCK, NC (May 29) -- David Pearson pushed his Dodge past Richard Petty in the 85th lap and sped to victory in the 100-mile Grand National event at Dog Track Speedway. The race, scheduled for 100-miles on the .333-mile paved oval, was actually a 301 lapper due to a scoring mix-up.

Pearson beat runner-up Tiny lund by a full lap for his sixth win of the season. All six of Pearson's triumphs have been in the two year-old Cotton Owens Dodge, which was once a show car. The outdated car has been beaten only once in 1966.

James Hylton came in third place with John Sears fourth and Wendell Scott fifth.

Petty started on the pole and jumped to an early lead. With Pearson in hot pursuit, the ignition failed in Petty's Plymouth on lap 84, knocking him from the race.

Crowd favorite Tom Pistone, who has given the Chrysler factory teams fits with his self-owned, unsponsored two year-old Ford on the short track, qualified third. However, the diminutive Chicago veteran once again ran into mechanical difficulties. He retired on lap 43 with transmission failure.

J.T. Putney started sixth in his Chevelle, but engine problems put him out after just 13 laps.

Pearson averaged 61.913 mph for his 19th career NASCAR victory.

Race No. 22

Pearson Uses Weatherly Trick To Win Asheville 300

ASHEVILLE, NC (June 2) -- David Pearson used an old trick mastered by the late Joe Weatherly, overcame tedious mechanical obstacles and won the Asheville 300 at the New Asheville Speedway.

Pearson took the lead in the 10th lap and led the rest of the way. But it was not as easy as it appears. The throttle hung open on lap 180 of the 300-lapper, nearly sending the Spartanburg, SC Dodge driver into the wall.

However, Pearson employed a tactic perfected by

Grand National Race No. 22
300 Laps at New Asheville Speedway
Asheville, NC
"Asheville 300"
100 Miles on .333-mile Paved Track
June 2, 1966

Fin	St	No.	Driver	Team / Car	Laps	Money	Status
1	2	6	David Pearson	Cotton Owens '64 Dodge	300	$1,000	Running
2	3	19	J T Putney	Putney '66 Chevrolet	299	600	Running
3	11	4	John Sears	L G DeWitt '64 Ford	286	400	Running
4	6	48	James Hylton	Bud Hartje '65 Dodge	285	300	Running
5	8	92	Hank Thomas	W S Jenkins '64 Ford	284	275	Running
6	14	34	Wendell Scott	Scott '65 Ford	282	240	Running
7	12	97	Henley Gray	Gray '66 Ford	281	200	Running
8	22	70	J D McDuffie	McDuffie '64 Ford	278	175	Running
9	9	87	Buck Baker	Baker '66 Olds	273	150	Running
10	19	20	Clyde Lynn	Lynn '64 Ford	262	140	Running
11	5	64	Elmo Langley	Langley-Woodfield '64 Ford	262	130	Running
12	16	93	Blackie Watt	Harry Neal '64 Ford	261	120	Running
13	18	35	Max Ledbetter	'65 Olds	234	110	Running
14	13	18	Stick Elliott	Toy Bolton '66 Chevrolet	169	100	Engine
15	21	45	Bill Tatum	Bill Seifert '64 Ford	153	100	Engine
16	20	9	Roy Tuner	Truett Rodgers '65 Chevrolet	103	100	Trans
17	1	43	Richard Petty	Petty Enterprises '65 Plym	89	100	Crash
18	10	02	Doug Cooper	Bob Cooper '65 Plymouth	51	100	Steering
19	4	00	Jack Ingram	'64 Dodge	14	100	Fuel line
20	7	73	Buddy Baker	Joan Petre '64 Ford	12	100	Differen
21	15	86	Neil Castles	Buck Baker '65 Plym	8	100	Engine
22	19	53	Jimmy Helms	David Warren '64 Ford	8	100	Engine

Time of Race: 1 hour, 32 minutes, 20 seconds
Average Speed: 64.917 mph
Pole Winner: Richard Petty - 72.964 mph
Lap Leaders: Richard Petty 1-9, David Pearson 10-300.
Cautions: Margin of Victory: 1-lap plus   Attendance: 7,000

Newcomer J.D. McDuffie started last in the 22 car field, but scooted up through the pack to finish eighth.

Pearson drove his Dodge to an average speed of 64.917 mph on the .333-mile paved oval.

Race No. 23
Lund's Failure Leaves Langley With First GN Win

Elmo Langley nabbed first GN victory at Spartanburg

SPARTANBURG, SC (June 4) -- Elmo Langley drove his low budget Ford into the lead with 40 laps to go and finished well ahead of the field to win the 100-mile Grand National event at the Piedmont Interstate Fairgrounds. It was the first big league win for the 36 year-old Landover, MD driver. The win came in

David Pearson's Dodge won at Asheville

Weatherly, who won a race at Concord, NC on May 6, 1962 by cutting the ignition switch entering each turn, then flipping it back on for the straightaways to gain speed. "I'm about wore out," said Pearson. "I had to do that twice a lap for 120 laps."

Pearson outran Chevrolet independent J.T. Putney by a full lap to register his seventh win of the season. John Sears came in third, James Hylton was fourth and Hank Thomas fifth.

Richard Petty won the pole for the 42nd time in his career and led the first 10 laps in his Plymouth. He was running second when a tire blew, sending him into the guard rail after 89 laps.

Grand National Race No. 23
200 Laps at Piedmont Interstate Fairgrounds
Spartanburg, SC
100 Miles on Half-mile Dirt Track
June 4, 1966

Fin	St	No.	Driver	Team / Car	Laps	Money	Status
1	6	64	Elmo Langley	Langley-Woodfield '64 Ford	200	$1,000	Running
2	11	86	Neil Castles	Buck Baker '65 Dodge	196	600	Running
3	5	02	Doug Cooper	Bob Cooper '65 Plymouth	195	400	Running
4	12	77	Joel Davis	Harold Mays '64 Plymouth	190	300	Running
5	14	70	J D McDuffie	McDuffie '64 Ford	189	275	Running
6	13	93	Blackie Watt	Harry Neal '64 Ford	188	240	Running
7	19	97	Henley Gray	Gray '66 Ford	182	200	Running
8	2	55	Tiny Lund	Lyle Stelter '64 Ford	170	175	Differen
9	7	96	Sonny Lamphear	Homer O'Dell '64 Ford	156	150	Differen
10	17	35	Max Ledbetter	'65 Olds	155	140	Running
11	16	60	Ernest Eury	Joan Petre '64 Chevrolet	143	130	Air Filter
12	3	59	Tom Pistone	Pistone '64 Ford	107	120	Heating
13	8	4	John Sears	L G DeWitt '64 Ford	90	110	Clutch
14	4	19	J T Putney	Putney '66 Chevrolet	89	100	Crash
15	22	61	Stick Elliott	Toy Bolton '66 Chevrolet	87	100	Shocks
16	1	6	David Pearson	Cotton Owens '64 Dodge	62	100	Engine
17	18	9	Roy Tyner	Truett Rodgers '65 Chevrolet	42	100	Trans
18	10	34	Wendell Scott	Scott '65 Ford	32	100	Crash
19	15	53	Jimmy Helms	David Warren '64 Ford	26	100	W bearing
20	9	73	Buddy Baker	Joan Petre '64 Ford	26	100	Heating
21	20	20	Clyde Lynn	Lynn '64 Ford	22	100	Axle
22	21	45	Bill Tatum	Bill Seifert '64 Ford	7	100	Engine

Time of Race: 1 hour, 39 minutes, 55 seconds
Average Speed: 60.050 mph
Pole Winner: David Pearson - 68.027 mph
Lap Leaders: Tiny Lund 1-160, Elmo Langley 161-200.
Cautions: Margin of Victory: 4-laps plus   Attendance:

his 141st start.

Langley started sixth and worked his way up to second behind Tiny Lund. Lund, who sped past pole sitter David Pearson in the first lap, was pulling away when the differential burned out on his Ford. Langley breezed into the lead and wound up four laps ahead of Neil Castles, who came in second. Doug Cooper was third, Joel Davis fourth and J.D. McDuffie fifth as independents stole the show.

Pearson was running second when his Dodge developed engine problems in the 62nd lap. Tom Pistone started third and ran with the leaders until his Ford overheated just past the half way point. J.T. Putney started a strong fourth, but wrecked his Chevrolet on lap 89.

Lund led the first 160 laps and struggled 10 more laps before he pulled his car behind the wall. He got credit for eighth in the final rundown..

Langley averaged 60.050 mph.

Race No. 24

Pearson Outduels Pistone; Wins East Tennessee 200

MARYVILLE, TN (June 9) -- David Pearson rolled around a smoking Tom Pistone in the 73rd lap and cruised to victory in the East Tennessee 200 at Smoky Mountain Raceway. It was the eighth win of the season for the point-leading Dodge driver.

Pistone won the pole in his battle-scarred Ford and led the first 72 laps. Steam began pouring from the car after 70 laps, and the Chicago veteran came down pit road on lap 72. He got back out on the track and went 24 more laps before calling it quits with overheating problems.

Pearson went unchallenged the rest of the way. "It was easy enough," said Pearson. "Tell you the truth, after Pistone went out, there wasn't much competition."

Buck Baker squeaked past Paul Lewis and won runner-up honors. Elmo Langley took fourth and Doug Cooper was fifth.

Richard Petty was not entered in the 100-miler. Darel Dieringer drove a Buck Baker Plymouth, but went out on lap 140 with a blown engine. Tiny Lund qualified a disappointing 17th and went out before the half way point with ignition troubles.

Pearson's 21st career win came at an average speed of 71.986 mph. Two cautions for seven laps broke the pace, and 4,500 spectators were on hand for the event.

Grand National Race No. 24
200 Laps at Smoky Mountain Raceway
Maryville, TN
"East Tennessee 200"
100 Miles on Half-mile Dirt Track
June 9, 1966

Fin	St	No.	Driver	Team / Car	Laps	Money	Status
1	4	6	David Pearson	Cotton Owens '64 Dodge	200	$1,000	Running
2	14	87	Buck Baker	Baker '66 Olds	198	600	Running
3	2	1	Paul Lewis	Lewis '65 Plymouth	198	400	Running
4	7	64	Elmo Langley	Langley-Woodfield '64 Ford	197	300	Running
5	9	02	Doug Cooper	Bob Cooper '65 Plymouth	196	275	Running
6	12	93	Blackie Watt	Harry Neal '64 Ford	194	240	Running
7	5	4	John Sears	L G DeWitt '64 Ford	193	200	Running
8	3	48	James Hylton	Bud Hartje '65 Dodge	191	175	Running
9	8	73	Buddy Baker	Joan Petre '64 Ford	191	150	Running
10	15	86	Neil Castles	Buck Baker '64 Dodge	185	140	Running
11	11	97	Henley Gray	Gray '66 Ford	182	130	Running
12	6	20	Clyde Lynn	Lynn '64 Ford	178	120	Running
13	24	53	Jimmy Helms	David Warren '64 Ford	178	110	Running
14	23	9	Roy Tyner	Truett Rodgers '66 Chevrolet	173	100	Running
15	20	06	Johnny Wynn	John McCarthy '64 Mercury	172	100	Running
16	21	74	Gene Black	Black '64 Ford	168	100	Running
17	18	34	Wendell Scott	Scott '65 Ford	158	100	Running
18	13	88	Darel Dieringer	Buck Baker '65 Plumouth	140	100	Engine
19	1	59	Tom Pistone	Pistone '64 Ford	96	100	Heating
20	17	55	Tiny Lund	Lyle Stelter '64 Ford	94	100	Ignition
21	19	70	J D McDuffie	McDuffie '64 Ford	66	100	Crash
22	25	96	Sonny Lamphear	Homer O'Dell '64 Ford	39	100	Oil Press
23	22	35	Max Ledbetter	'65 Olds	15	---	Differen
24	16	95	Jim Hunter	Gene Cline '64 Ford	8	---	Heating
25	26	45	J T Putney	Bill Seifert '64 Ford	6	---	Engine
26	10	61	Stick Elliott	Toy Bolton '66 Chevrolet	6	---	D Shaft

Time of Race: 1 hour, 23 minutes 21 seconds
Average Speed: 71.986 mph
Pole Winner: Tom Pistone - 78.947 mph
Lap Leaders: Tom Pistone 1-72, David Pearson 73-200.
Cautions: 2 for 7 laps   Margin of Victory: 2-laps plus   Attendance: 4,500

Race No. 25
Flat Tire Flattens Pearson; Petty Wins Fireball 300

Richard Petty won Fireball 300 at Weaverville

WEAVERVILLE, NC (June 12) -- Richard Petty roared around David Pearson's limping Dodge on the last turn of the last lap and won the Fireball 300 at Asheville-Weaverville Speedway. It was the sixth win of the season for Petty.

Pearson had passed Petty in the 183rd lap and built up a two lap lead when he dashed into the pits on lap 294 to get a few gulps of fuel. Pearson exited and still maintained his big lead, but he ran over a piece of debris and cut down the right rear tire. Pearson elected to stay on the track and try to beat Petty in a three-mile run. Petty closed the gap dramatically and finally caught Pearson in the last lap.

"I was lucky to win this one," admitted Petty. "I got way behind when I made an unscheduled pit stop (on lap 182), thinking I had a flat tire. The crew changed all the tires and nothing was wrong with any of them. I guess it was my own ignorance."

Pearson said he tried to beat Petty on the flat tire "because if I'd have pit, he would have passed me for sure. I almost made it."

Petty beat Pearson by 5.0-seconds. Third place went to Paul Lewis with Buck Baker fourth and John Sears fifth.

Ned Jarrett was running fifth in his Henley Gray Ford when brake failure put him out after 150 laps.

Petty averaged 81.423 mph before 6,200 spectators.

Race No. 26

Lund Edges Hylton in Photo Finish at Beltsville

BELTSVILLE, MD (June 15) -- Tiny Lund took the lead after two factory drivers went to the sidelines and held off rookie James Hylton by a whisker to win the Beltsville 200 at Beltsville Speedway. It was the third career win for the 36 year-old Harlan, IA Ford driver.

Lund, starting seventh in the field of 31, worked his way into contention as factory drivers Richard Petty and David Pearson shared the spotlight early. Pearson went out with rear end problems in the 33rd lap and Petty blew his engine after 71 laps. Lund, who owns a fish camp in Cross, SC, drove his car into the lead and was never headed.

Hylton, a rookie who moved into second place in the

Grand National Race No. 25
300 Laps at Asheville-Weaverville Speedway
Weaverville, NC
"Fireball 300"
150 Miles on Half-mile Paved Track
June 12, 1966

Fin	St	No.	Driver	Team / Car	Laps	Money	Status
1	1	43	Richard Petty	Petty Enterprises '66 Plym	300	$1,400	Running
2	2	6	David Pearson	Cotton Owens '66 Dodge	300	1,000	Running
3	4	1	Paul Lewis	Lewis '65 Plymouth	298	700	Running
4	16	87	Buck Baker	Baker '66 Olds	290	575	Running
5	12	4	John Sears	L G DeWitt '64 Ford	289	425	Running
6	5	48	James Hylton	Bud Hartje '65 Dodge	285	325	Running
7	8	19	J T Putney	Putney '66 Chevrolet	280	275	Running
8	28	18	Stick Elliott	Toy Bolton '66 Chevrolet	279	225	Running
9	20	92	Hank Thomas	W S Jenkins '64 Ford	277	300	Running
10	18	86	Neil Castles	Buck Baker '65 Dodge	273	175	Running
11	6	64	Elmo Langley	Langley-Woodfield '64 Ford	273	100	Running
12	21	34	Wendell Scott	Scott '65 Ford	270	100	Running
13	23	70	J D McDuffie	McDuffie '64 Ford	270	100	Running
14	27	9	Roy Tyner	Truett Rodgers '66 Chevrolet	266	100	Running
15	7	55	Tiny Lund	Lyle Stelter '55 Ford	264	100	Running
16	15	93	Blackie Watt	Harry Neal '64 Ford	262	100	Running
17	19	06	Johnny Wynn	John McCarthy '64 Mercury	261	100	Running
18	10	02	Doug Cooper	Bob Cooper '65 Plymouth	261	100	Running
19	17	20	Clyde Lynn	Lynn '64 Ford	260	100	Running
20	26	95	Henley Gray	Gene Cline '64 Ford	237	100	Running
21	22	53	Jimmy Helms	David Warren '64 Ford	224	100	Ignition
22	29	96	Sonny Lamphear	Homer O'Dell '64 Ford	213	100	Ignition
23	13	73	Buddy Baker	Joan Petre '64 Ford	210	100	Heating
24	3	16	Darel Dieringer	Bud Moore '66 Mercury	180	100	Oil Press
25	24	40	Eddie Yarboro	'65 Dodge	164	---	Differen
26	9	97	Ned Jarrett	Henley Gray '66 Ford	150	200	Brakes
27	14	77	Joel Davis	Harold Mays '64 Plymouth	18	---	Heating
28	14	46	Roy Mayne	Tom Hunter '66 Chevrolet	9	---	Crash
29	25	35	Max Ledbetter	'65 Olds	9	---	Engine

Time of Race: 1 hour, 50 minutes, 32 seconds
Average Speed: 81.423 mph
Pole Winner: Richard Petty - 86.455 mph
Lap Leaders: Richard Petty 1-134, David Pearson 135-141, Petty 142-182, Pearson 183-299, Petty 300
Cautions: None   Margin of Victory: 5.0 seconds   Attendance: 6,200

Grand National Race No. 26
200 Laps At Beltsville Speedway
Beltsville, MD
"Beltsville 200"
100 Miles on Half-mile Paved Track
June 15, 1966

Fin	St	No.	Driver	Team / Car	Laps	Money	Status
1	7	55	Tiny Lund	Lyle Stelter '64 Ford	200	$1,000	Running
2	6	48	James Hylton	Bud Hartje '65 Dodge	200	600	Running
3	16	92	Hank Thomas	W S Jenkins '64 Ford	195	400	Running
4	12	4	John Sears	L G DeWitt '64 Ford	195	300	Running
5	14	97	G C Spencer	Henley Gray '66 Ford	193	275	Running
6	20	93	Blackie Watt	Harry Neal '64 Ford	192	240	Running
7	11	06	Johnny Wynn	John McCarthy '64 Mercury	192	200	Running
8	22	86	Neil Castles	Buck Baker '65 Dodge	192	175	Running
9	18	74	Don Israel	Gene Black '64 Ford	188	150	Running
10	23	9	Roy Tyner	Truett Rodgers '66 Chevrolet	186	140	Running
11	31	83	Worth McMillion	Allen McMillion '65 Pontiac	185	130	Running
12	10	73	Buddy Baker	Joan Petre '64 Ford	184	120	Running
13	24		Edgar Wallen	'64 Chevrolet	179	110	Running
14	19	70	J D McDuffie	McDuffie '64 Ford	178	100	Running
15	4	2	Bobby Allison	J D Bracken '65 Chevrolet	174	100	Differen
16	5	64	Elmo Langley	Langley-Woodfield '64 Ford	173	100	Running
17	13	02	Doug Cooper	Bob Cooper '65 Plymouth	167	100	Differen
18	17	20	Clyde Lynn	Lynn '64 Ford	148	100	Differen
19	28	57	Lionel Johnson	Clay Esteridge '64 Ford	120	100	Ignition
20	15	03	Gil Hearne	Ed Ackerman '64 Ford	90	100	Vibration
21	1	43	Richard Petty	Petty Enterprises '66 Plym	71	100	Engine
22	8	90	Sonny Hutchins	Junie Donlavey '64 Ford	54	100	Differen
23	29	75	Gene Black	Black '64 Ford	53	---	Steering
24	25	53	Jimmy Helms	David Warren '64 Ford	49	---	Oil Press
25	26	95	Henley Gray	Gene Cline '64 Ford	42	---	Differen
26	9	87	Buck Baker	Baker '66 Olds	38	---	Differen
27	2	6	David Pearson	Cotton Owens '66 Dodge	33	---	Differen
28	21	72	Bill Champion	Champion '64 Ford	31	---	Oil Leak
29	3	59	Tom Pistone	Pistone '64 Ford	21	---	Clutch
30	30	58	Joe Holder	'64 Dodge	2	---	Oil Press
31	27	34	Wendell Scott	Scott '65 Ford	2	---	Engine

Time of Race: 1 hour, 21 minutes, 44 seconds
Average Speed: 73.409 mph
Pole Winner: Richard Petty - 80.250 mph
Lap Leaders: Richard Petty 1- , David Pearson -33, Petty 34-71, Tiny Lund 72-200.
Cautions: Margin of Victory: 2 feet   Attendance:

Rookie James Hylton finished a close 2nd at Beltsville

point standings, made a charge at Lund in the final lap. Hylton got his Dodge up beside in a sprint to the wire, but lost by about two feet.

Third place went to Hank Thomas. John Sears was fourth and G.C. Spencer fifth.

Bobby Allison had a lock on third place in his J.D. Bracken Chevrolet, but spun out when the rear end snapped with 22 laps to go. He got credit for 15th in the final order.

It was Allison's first start in a Chevrolet since leaving the Betty Lilly Ford team.

Point lead Pearson was one of nine drivers failing to earn a single dollar in prize money. General NASCAR guidelines require the first 22 finishers receive a slice of the payoff. Nine additional cars started the Beltsville race.

Lund averaged 73.409 mph in his Lyle Stelter-owned Ford.

Race No. 27

Pearson Wins Greenville 100 After Delayed Start

GREENVILLE, SC (June 25) -- Officials delayed the start so pole sitter David Pearson's team could make repairs, then he romped to victory in the 100-mile Grand National race at Greenville-Pickens Speedway. It was the ninth win of the year for the 31 year-old Dodge driver.

Pearson led all 200 trips around the half mile dirt track, but nearly didn't make the start of the race. On his second qualifying lap, the Cotton Owens Dodge which Pearson was driving broke an axle. Owens and his crew hustled to make repairs but they were not ready in time for the scheduled start. Speedway officials waited to start the race until Pearson was ready. The remainder of the field, consisting entirely of independents, howled in protest.

Tom Pistone finished second to Pearson, four laps behind. "I wonder if they would have held up the race if it were me trying to fix an axle," muttered Pistone. Third place went to Elmo Langley. Stick Elliott came across the line in fourth place and Henley Gray was fifth.

Tiny Lund and John Sears pressured Pearson early.

Grand National Race No. 27
200 Laps at Greenville-Pickens Speedway
Greenville, SC
100 Miles on Half-mile Dirt Track
June 25, 1966

Fin	St	No.	Driver	Team / Car	Laps	Money	Status
1	1	6	David Pearson	Cotton Owens '64 Dodge	200	$1,000	Running
2	6	59	Tom Pistone	Pistone '64 Ford	196	600	Running
3	7	74	Elmo Langley	Gene Black '64 Ford	192	400	Running
4	17	61	Stick Elliott	Toy Bolton '66 Chevrolet	189	300	Running
5	8	97	Henley Gray	Gray '66 Ford	188	275	Running
6	18	70	J D McDuffie	McDuffie '64 Ford	186	240	Running
7	13	06	Johnny Wynn	John McCarthy '64 Mercury	185	200	Running
8	2	4	John Sears	L G DeWitt '64 Ford	170	175	Running
9	9	95	Jeff Hawkins	Gene Cline '64 Ford	168	150	Differen
10	3	55	Tiny Lund	Lyle Stelter '64 Ford	147	140	Engine
11	10	86	Neil Castles	Buck Baker '65 Dodge	121	130	Running
12	14	9	Roy Tyner	Truett Rodgers '66 Chevrolet	115	120	Running
13	12	20	Clyde Lynn	Lynn '64 Ford	68	110	Differen
14	5	73	Buddy Baker	Joan Petre '64 Ford	47	100	Engine
15	4	0	Bryant Wallace	Reid Shaw '64 Ford	39	100	Heating
16	15	75	Bud Moore	Gene Black '64 Ford	35	100	Crash
17	11	53	Jimmy Helms	David Warren '64 Ford	9	100	Heating
18	16	96	Sonny Lamphear	Homer O'Dell '64 Ford	5	100	Heating

Time Of Race: 1 hour, 30 minutes, 31 seconds
Average Speed: 66.286 mph
Pole Winner: David Pearson - 69.3645 mph
Lap Leaders: David Pearson 1-200
Cautions: 1 for _____ laps   Margin of Victory: 4-plus laps   Attendance:

Lund fought overheating problems and had to slacken his pace. He eventually fell out after 147 laps with a blown engine. Sears dropped off the pace due to a long pit stop and finished eighth.

Buddy Baker drove a Ford owned by Joan Petre and challenged early. But the hefty Charlotte driver was out of action after 68 laps.

Bud Moore started back in 15th spot, but whipped his Ford up into fourth place when the steering froze, putting him into the wall on lap 35.

Pearson averaged 66.286 mph for his 22nd career victory.

Race No. 28

Sam McQuagg's Dodge "Spoils" Day for Firecracker 400 Rivals

DAYTONA BEACH, FL (July 4) -- Sam McQuagg drove his Nichels Engineering Dodge Charger -- equipped with a rear deck spoiler -- into the lead at the start and led virtually all the way to win the Firecracker 400 at Daytona International Speedway. It was the first

Sam McQuagg won Firecracker 400

to make sure I was not partying. Well, Smokey never called. I wasted a whole evening."

McQuagg started fourth on the grid, but had the lead by the backstretch of the first lap. For the entire 160-lap affair on the 2.5-mile tri-oval, McQuagg was hard to handle, leading all but 34 laps.

"This is the greatest thing that has ever happened to me," said the jubilant McQuagg. "I've dreamed about winning on a big track, but I never dreamed out loud about it. I never thought I'd be in victory lane this soon after going Grand National."

McQuagg's first start was two years ago in the 1964 Firecracker 400.

LeeRoy Yarbrough won the pole for only the second time in his career. The Jacksonville, FL Dodge driver was able to run with McQuagg in the early stages, but he was out of the race after 126 laps with sus-

Grand National victory for the 29 year-old Columbus, GA sophomore, and it came in his 31st NASCAR start.

McQuagg's Dodge -- and the new slope-backed Chargers in the hands of others -- were surprisingly stable on the speedy banks of Daytona. Throughout the early portion of the 1966 season, Dodge teams said the new aerodynamic

John Sears exits turn four at Daytona

pension troubles.

Richard Petty qualified second, but did not lead a lap. On lap 86, the engine in Petty's '64 Plymouth blew,

Mario Andretti in a Cotton Owens Dodge

Charger had a tendency to "lift" off the grounds at high speeds. The rear deck spoiler kept the cars on the ground this time.

Darel Dieringer came in second in his Bud Moore Mercury. The car ran out of gas in the final lap and coasted across the finish line 66 seconds behind the winner. Jim Paschal came in third, Curtis Turner was fourth and Jim Hurtubise fifth.

Smokey Yunick, owner of the Chevrolet Turner drove, gave his pilot an ultimatum before the race. "Smokey told me to be in bed by 10:00 pm the night before the race," said Turner. "Said he'd call just

Richard Petty is clobbered by Earl Balmer at Daytona

Grand National Race No. 28
160 Laps at Daytona Int'l Speedway
Daytona Beach, FL
"Firecracker 400"
400 Miles on 2.5-mile Paved Track
July 4, 1966

Fin	St	No.	Driver	Team / Car	Laps	Money	Status
1	4	98	Sam McQuagg	Nichels Eng '66 Dodge	160	$13,600	Running
2	12	16	Darel Dieringer	Bud Moore '66 Mercury	160	8,870	Running
3	13	14	Jim Paschal	Friedkin Ent '66 Plymouth	159	5,985	Running
4	3	13	Curtis Turner	Smokey Yunick '66 Chevrolet	159	3,100	Running
5	6	56	Jim Hurtubise	Norm Nelson '66 Plymouth	158	1,550	Running
6	7	31	Don White	Nichels Eng 66 Dodge	156	1,250	Running
7	19	04	Marvin Panch	Friedkin Ent '65 Plymouth	154	1,475	Running
8	20	24	Tiny Lund	Betty Lilly '66 Ford	153	1,375	Running
9	14	48	James Hylton	Bud Hartje '65 Dodge	153	1,300	Running
10	32	4	John Sears	L G DeWitt '64 Ford	152	1,200	Running
11	9	3	Buddy Baker	Ray Fox '65 Dodge	151	830	Engine
12	16	79	Frank Warren	Harold Rhodes '64 Chevrolet	150	740	Running
13	23	64	Elmo Langley	Langley-Woodfield '64 Ford	149	650	Running
14	27	2	Bobby Allison	J D Bracken '65 Chevrolet	149	655	Running
15	11	6	David Pearson	Cotton Owens '66 Dodge	148	475	Running
16	22	55	Harold Smith	Lyle Stelter '64 Ford	147	595	Running
17	34	44	Larry Hess	Hess '64 Ford	146	615	Running
18	36	89	Eddie MacDonald	'64 Chevrolet	144	585	Running
19	40	34	Wendell Scott	Scott '65 Ford	143	580	Running
20	25	93	Blackie Watt	Harry Neal '64 Ford	139	750	Running
21	37	70	J D McDuffie	McDuffie '64 Ford	133	570	Running
22	33	06	Johnny Wynn	John McCarthy '64 Mercury	132	590	Running
23	35	97	Henley Gray	Gray '66 Ford	126	585	Running
24	1	12	LeeRoy Yarbrough	Jon Thorne '66 Dodge	126	530	Suspen
25	26	00	Roy Mayne	'65 Dodge	112	525	Running
26	39	53	Jimmy Helms	David Warren '64 Ford	111	445	H Gasket
27	5	99	Paul Goldsmith	Nichels Eng '66 Plymouth	110	490	W'shield
28	28	02	Doug Cooper	Bob Cooper '65 Plymouth	96	460	Engine
29	2	43	Richard Petty	Petty Enterprises '64 Plym	86	530	Crash
30	10	71	Earl Balmer	K&K Insurance '65 Dodge	94	400	Crash
31	8	5	Mario Andretti	Cotton Owens '66 Dodge	78	395	Engine
32	30	8	Wayne Smith	Smith '66 Chevrolet	78	440	W'shield
33	21	86	Buck Baker	Baker '66 Chevrolet	54	410	Crash
34	24	39	Bunkie Blackburn	J H Crawford '66 Chevrolet	29	380	Oil Press
35	17	49	G C Spencer	Spencer '66 Plymouth	28	375	Suspen
36	29	67	Buddy Arrington	Arrington '64 Dodge	25	370	Oil Press
37	31	19	J T Putney	Putney '66 Chevrolet	20	365	Valve
38	15	7	Bobby Johns	Shorty Johns '66 Chevrolet	16	360	Crash
39	38	25	Jabe Thomas	Jeff Handy '64 Ford	13	355	Oil Press
40	18	33	Joel Davis	Curtis Satterfield '64 Chev	4	350	D Shaft

Time of Race: 2 hours, 36 minutes, 2 seconds
Average Speed: 153.813 mph
Pole Winner: Leeroy Yarbrough - 176.660 mph
Lap Leaders: Sam McQuagg 1-8, LeeRoy Yarbrough 9, McQuagg 10-18, Yarbrough 19-26, McQuagg 27-32, Jim Paschal 33-39, Yarbrough 40, McQuagg 41-59, Paschal 60-64, McQuagg 65-88, Jim Hurtubise 89, Buddy Baker 90-95, Curtis Turner 96-97, McQuagg 98-126, Baker 127-128, Hurtubise 129, McQuagg 130-160.
Cautions: 4 for 23 laps   Margin of Victory: 1 Minute, 6 seconds   Attendance: 46,200

sending him into a wild slide in turn one. Earl Balmer nailed Petty broadside. "My crankshaft broke and came out of the bottom end," explained Petty. "It locked the rear wheels and wedged into the steering so I couldn't steer. A rod went through the front tire, blowing it. Crankcase oil spilled out on the track and I spun into it. Then Earl Balmer hits me." Both drivers were shaken but uninjured.

Mario Andretti drove a Cotton Owens Dodge but went only 78 laps before his engine blew. Andretti's teammate David Pearson struggled to finish 15th.

McQuagg averaged 153.813 mph before 46,200 spectators.

Race No. 29

Langley Wins 2nd of Year Before Small Crowd of 1,459

MANASSAS, VA (July 7) -- Elmo Langley drove his Ford past Bobby Allison in the 176th lap and went on to post a seven lap victory in the 150-miler at Old Dominion Speedway. It was the second win of the year for the Landover, MD veteran.

No factory backed drivers were on hand. David Pearson and Richard Petty, principle Chrysler Corp. drivers, both refused to show up without "deal" money. Promoter Al Gore said he was not going to pay any drivers additional money.

The 400 lapper on the .375-mile paved oval attracted only 1,459 paying spectators. Although the attendance was slim, the action on the track was red hot.

Pole sitter Bobby Allison led twice for 39 laps, but transmission problems in his J.D.Bracken Chevelle balked late in the race. Prior to Allison's departure, Tiny Lund seemed headed for victory when the engine

Grand National Race No. 29
400 Laps at Old Dominion Speedway
Manassas, VA
150 Miles on .375-mile Paved Track
July 7, 1966

Fin	St	No.	Driver	Team / Car	Laps	Money	Status
1	2	64	Elmo Langley	Langley-Woodfield '64 Ford	400	$1,100	Running
2	5	4	John Sears	L G DeWitt '64 Ford	393	625	Running
3	6	48	James Hylton	Bud Hartje '65 Dodge	393	450	Running
4	11	63	Larry Manning	Bob Adams '65 Plymouth	393	350	Running
5	7	87	Buck Baker	Baker '66 Olds	392	325	Running
6	18	86	Neil Castles	Buck Baker '64 Dodge	381	290	Running
7	19	97	Henley Gray	Gray '66 Ford	380	250	Running
8	16	88	Ray Hill	Buck Baker '66 Chevrolet	370	225	Running
9	21	93	Blackie Watt	Harry Neal '64 Ford	358	200	Running
10	15	34	Wendell Scott	Scott '65 Ford	346	190	Running
11	22	83	Worth McMillion	Allen McMillion '66 Pontiac	304	180	Running
12	10	20	Clyde Lynn	Lynn '64 Ford	280	175	Heating
13	23	70	J D McDuffie	McDuffie '64 Ford	207	160	Brakes
14	13	5	Edgar Wallen	'64 Chevrolet	196	150	Engine
15	1	2	Bobby Allison	J D Bracken '65 Chevrolet	183	135	Trans
16	3	55	Tiny Lund	Lyle Stelter '64 Ford	166	125	Engine
17	9	57	Lionel Johnson	Clay Esteridge '64 Ford	131	115	Heating
18	24	00	Roy Mayne	'65 Dodge	129	110	Oil Leak
19	14	25	Jabe Thomas	Jeff Handy '64 Ford	115	100	Vibration
20	8	73	Buddy Baker	Joan Petre '64 Ford	112	100	Crash
21	17	53	Jimmy Helms	David Warren '64 Ford	109	100	Manifold
22	20	94	Don Biederman	Ron Stotten '64 Ford	86	100	Heating
23	12	06	Johnny Wynn	John McCarthy '64 Mercury	65	---	Brakes
24	4	67	Buddy Arrington	Arrington '64 Dodge	28	---	Axle

Time of Race: 2 hours, 12 minutes, 12 seconds
Average Speed: 68.079 mph
Pole Winner: Bobby Allison - 73.973 mph
Lap Leaders: Elmo Langley 1-6, Bobby Allison 7-39, Tiny Lund 40-159, Allison 160-175, Langley 176-400.
Cautions: 2 for _____ laps   Margin of Victory: 7-laps plus   Attendance: 1,459

blew in his Ford.

Langley started on the outside front row and led the first six laps. He fell behind the Allison-Lund struggle until he breezed into the lead before the halfway point.

John Sears finished second, seven laps behind the winner. Third place went to James Hylton, Larry Manning was fourth and Buck Baker fifth.

Buddy Arrington qualified an impressive fourth, but he was the first driver out of the race.

Two caution flags slowed Langley's average speed to 68.079 mph.

Grand National Race No. 30
52 Laps at Bridgehampton Raceway
Bridgehampton, NY
148.2-miles on 2.85-mile Paved Road Course
July 10, 1966

Fin	St	No.	Driver	Team / Car	Laps	Money	Status
1	1	6	David Pearson	Cotton Owens '65 Dodge	52	$1,375	Running
2	2	48	James Hylton	Bud Hartje '65 Dodge	52	775	Running
3	3	22	Marvin Panch	'64 Ford	51	570	Running
4	21	144	Roy Hallquist	'64 Ford	51	350	Running
5	4	64	Elmo Langley	Langley-Woodfield '64 Ford	51	350	Running
6	7	88	Buck Baker	Baker '66 Chevrolet	50	315	Running
7	28	55	Tiny Lund	Lyle Stelter '64 Ford	50	250	Running
8	6	4	John Sears	L G DeWitt '64 Ford	50	250	Running
9	19	00	Roy Mayne	'65 Dodge	49	200	Running
10	10	93	Blackie Watt	Harry Neal '64 Ford	48	195	Running
11	8	86	Ray Hill	Buck Baker '64 Dodge	48	205	Running
12	26	34	Wendell Scott	Scott '65 Ford	48	170	Running
13	11	87	Neil Castles	Buck Baker '64 Olds	47	165	Running
14	16	25	Jabe Thomas	Jeff Handy '64 Ford	47	160	Running
15	18	97	Henley Gray	Gray '66 Ford	45	155	Running
16	9	06	Johnny Wynn	John McCarthy '64 Mercury	45	175	Running
17	13	70	J D McDuffie	McDuffie '64 Ford	45	145	Running
18	17	20	Clyde Lynn	Lynn '64 Ford	44	135	Running
19	22	53	Jimmy Helms	David Warren '64 Ford	44	130	Running
20	5	19	J T Putney	Putney '66 Chevrolet	27	165	Bad gas
21	12	94	Don Biederman	Ron Stotten '64 Chevrolet	21	125	Running
22	23	73	Buddy Baker	Joan Petre '64 Ford	18	125	Oil Press
23	15	2	Bobby Allison	J D Bracken '65 Chevrolet	11	---	Oil Leak
24	25	9	Roy Tyner	Truett Rodgers '66 Chevrolet	11	---	Valve
25	14	15	Lyle Stelter	Stelter '64 Ford	7	---	Spun
26	27	44	Larry Hess	Hess '66 Rambler	5	---	Rock Arm
27	20	96	Sonny Lamphear	Homer O'Dell '64 Ford	2	---	Heating
28	24	11	Ned Jarrett	Larry Hess '64 Ford	1	200	Bearing

Time of Race: 1 hour, 42 minutes, 16 seconds
Average Speed: 86.949 mph
Pole Winner: David Pearson - won qualifying race
Lap Leaders: David Pearson 1-16, James Hylton 17-22, Pearson 23-52
Cautions: None   Margin of Victory: 1 minute, 40 seconds   Attendance: 9,000

Race No. 30

Pearson Outduels Hylton For Victory at Bridgehampton

BRIDGEHAMPTON, NY (July 10) -- David Pearson led all but six laps and shook a pesky James Hylton in the closing stages to win the 148.2-mile Grand National event at the Bridgehampton Raceway. It was the 10th win of the season for the title-bound Pearson.

Rookie Hylton led six laps in the early going, then faded near the end. He still wound up second, one minute and 40 seconds behind Pearson's Dodge. Third place went to Marvin Panch, who drove an independent Ford. Roy Hallquist was fourth and Elmo Langley fifth.

Richard Petty, who was slated to start second, blew the engine in his Plymouth at the finish of the qualifying race. He was unable to start the feature. That left Pearson as the only factory backed entrant, and he had little trouble disposing the field in the 52-lapper on the 2.85-mile road course.

Ned Jarrett started near the rear of the field and lasted only one lap before mechanical problems intervened. Tiny Lund started last in the 28 car field, but managed a seventh place finish.

Pearson averaged 86.949 mph for his first victory on a road course.

Race No. 31

Little Engine; Big Surprise -- Allison Wins Oxford in Chevy

OXFORD, ME (July 12) -- Bobby Allison, Hueytown, AL driver, led most of the way and finished a lap ahead of the field to win the 100-mile Grand National race at Oxford Plains Speedway. Manning a small Chevelle powered by a 327 c.i. engine, Allison started on the pole and led all the way except for a few laps when Tiny Lund was in front.

It was the first Grand National win for a Chevrolet since December 1, 1963 when Wendell Scott on at Jacksonville, FL.

"I think a new wrinkle has started," Allison said about his lightweight, small engine car. "We're pleased in two ways. It handled well right off the trailer. And secondly, it blew right by all the hot dogs."

Under NASCAR rules, each race car must weigh 9.36 pounds per cubic inch. Cars with the big bore 426 c.i. engines must weigh 3,997.36 pounds. Allison's little 327 only has to tip the scales at 3,060.72 pounds.

Allison wound up a lap ahead of runner-up Lund. Richard Petty finished third, Neil Castles was fourth and James Hylton fifth. Point leader David Pearson was seventh, five laps down.

Allison averaged 56.782 mph in winning his first Grand National event.

Grand National Race No. 31
300 Laps at Oxford Plains Speedway
Oxford, ME
100 Miles on .333-mile Paved Track
July 12, 1966

Fin	St	No.	Driver	Team / Car	Laps	Money	Status
1	1	2	Bobby Allison	J D Bracken '65 Chevrolet	300	$1,100	Running
2	7	55	Tiny Lund	Lyle Stelter '64 Ford	299	675	Running
3	2	43	Richard Petty	Petty Enterprises '66 Plym	299	450	Running
4	15	87	Neil Castles	Buck Baker '66 Olds	297	325	Running
5	5	48	James Hylton	Bud Hartje '65 Dodge	297	315	Running
6	4	19	J T Putney	Putney '66 Chevrolet	296	280	Running
7	3	6	David Person	Cotton Owens '65 Dodge	295	240	Running
8	8	4	John Sears	L G DeWitt '64 Ford	288	215	Running
9	21	93	Blackie Watt	Harry Neal '64 Ford	287	190	Running
9	19	20	Clyde Lynn	Lynn '64 Ford	284	180	Running
11	14	88	Buck Baker	Baker '66 Chevrolet	284	170	Running
12	17	34	Wendell Scott	Scott '65 Ford	281	160	Running
13	22	86	Ray Hill	Buck Baker '64 Dodge	273	155	Running
14	18	144	Roy Hallquist	'64 Ford	237	145	Running
15	10	03	Rene Charland	Ed Ackerman '64 Ford	192	140	Engine
16	11	15	Mario Caruso	Lyle Stelter '64 Ford	167	130	Differen
17	26	97	Henley Gray	Gray '66 Ford	135	125	Differen
18	20	70	J D McDuffie	McDuffie '64 Ford	116	120	Trans
19	27	73	Ernie Gahan	'64 Ford	114	115	Differen
20	24	53	Jimmy Helms	David Warren '64 Ford	97	115	Differen
21	16	22	Marvin Panch	'64 Ford	69	100	Trans
22	25	9	Roy Tyner	Truett Rodgers '66Chevrolet	60	115	Engine
23	9	00	Buddy Baker	'65 Dodge	49	---	Trans
24	6	64	Elmo Langley	Langley-Woodfield '64 Ford	39	---	Radiator
25	12	94	Don Biederman	Ron Stotten '64 Chevrolet	29	---	Heating
26	13	11	Ned Jarrett	Larry Hess '64 Ford	17	200	Engine
27	23	06	Johnny Wynn	John McCarthy '64 Mercury	3	---	Heating

Time of Race: 1 hour, 45 minutes, 40 seconds
Average Speed: 56.782 mph
Pole Winner: Bobby Allison - 65.681 mph
Lap Leaders: Bobby Allison 1- , Tiny Lund - , Allison -300.
Cautions: 4 for 25 laps   Margin of Victory: 1-lap plus   Attendance: 13,000

Race No. 32

Fists Fly at Fonda; Pearson Wins 11th of Year

FONDA, NY (July 14) -- David Pearson avoided a five car crash in the early laps and outdueled Richard Petty to win the 100-mile Grand National event at Fonda Speedway. It was the 11th win of the season for the Spartanburg, SC driver.

Pearson took the lead from Petty in the 163rd lap and led the rest of the way. Petty was mounting a serious challenge with four laps to go when he spun out. He recovered to finish second. Rene Charland was third, Roy Hallquist fourth and Buck Baker fifth.

J.T. Putney started on the outside front row and jumped into the lead at the start. Putney kept his Chevrolet in the lead until he swung wide off the second turn and went over the banking. The Arden, NC driver tried to keep control, maintaining speed along a service road

J.T. Putney led early, but was "knocked out" by Tiny Lund

running between the backstretch and the old section of the Erie Canal. When he pulled his car back onto the track surface, he was directly in the path of the on-rushing Tiny Lund. Lund hit Putney squarely in the door. Bobby Allison and Lyle Stelter were also collected in the mishap.

When Lund got back to the pit area, he approached Putney and landed a solid right hand on his jaw. Putney fell unconscious. He was taken to the hospital where he was revived and released.

NASCAR officials fined Lund $100. NASCAR Executive Manager Lin Kuchler said the punishment would have been more severe "if there had not been evidence of provocation. But it wasn't excusable for Lund to take a swing at him, even if he was provoked."

In warm-ups, Lund went into a turn too hard and went over the banking. "Next thing I knew," said Lund, "was that I was driving past gravestones in an old cemetery."

The lead changed hands eight times among four drivers. Tom Pistone had taken the lead from Pearson on lap 84 and was leading at the 114 lap mark when his engine overheated.

Tiny Lund drove through a graveyard, then slugged J.T. Putney

Pearson averaged 61.010 mph for his 24th career win.

Race No. 33

Hylton Runs Out of Gas; Allison Annexes Islip Event

ISLIP, NY (July 16) -- Bobby Allison sneaked his Chevrolet in through the back door and won the 60-mile Grand National race at Islip Speedway. It was the second win of the season for Allison and his small 327 c.i. engine.

James Hylton, who led from the 147th lap until seven

Grand National Race No. 32
200 Laps at Fonda Speedway
Fonda, NY
100 Miles on Half-mile Dirt Track
July 14, 1966

Fin	St	No.	Driver	Team / Car	Laps	Money	Status
1	12	6	David Pearson	Cotton Owens '65 Dodge	200	$1,100	Running
2	1	43	Richard Petty	Petty Enterprises '66 Plym	200	675	Running
3	26	03	Rene Charland	Ed Ackerman '64 Ford	199	450	Running
4	10	144	Roy Hallquist	'64 Ford	196	300	Running
5	9	87	Buck Baker	Baker '66 Olds	193	275	Running
6	16	48	James Hylton	Bud Hartje '65 Dodge	192	240	Running
7	15	70	J D McDuffie	McDuffie '64 Ford	191	200	Running
8	14	20	Clyde Lynn	Lynn '64 Ford	191	175	Running
9	23	34	Wendell Scott	Scott '65 Ford	181	150	Running
10	24	97	Henley Gray	Gray '66 ford	181	140	Running
11	27	93	Blackie Watt	Harry Neal '64 Ford	179	130	Running
12	19	88	Ray Hill	Buck Baker '65 Chevrolet	177	120	Running
13	20	78	Nick Rampling	'66 Plymouth	176	110	Running
14	21	31	Al White	'64 Mercury	175	100	Running
15	7	64	Elmo Langley	Langley-Woodfield '64 Ford	172	100	Running
16	13	4	John Sears	L G DeWitt '64 Ford	147	100	Axle
17	22	53	Jimmy Helms	David Warren '64 Ford	133	100	Heating
18	31	94	Don Biederman	Ron Stotten '64 Chevrolet	127	100	Crash
19	6	00	Buddy Baker	'65 Dodge	117	100	Axle
20	5	59	Tom Pistone	Pistone '64 Ford	114	100	Heating
21	25	9	Roy Tyner	Truett Rodgers '66 Chevrolet	92	100	Engine
22	18	86	Neil Castles	Buck Baker '64 Dodge	78	100	Axle
23	11	06	Johnny Wynn	John McCarthy '64 Mercury	68	---	H Gasket
24	28	73	Bub Strickler	Joan Petre '64 Ford	57	---	Heating
25	3	15	Tiny Lund	Lyle Stelter '64 Ford	33	---	Crash
26	2	19	J T Putney	Putney '66 Chevrolet	32	---	Crash
27	8	2	Bobby Allison	J D Bracken '65 Chevrolet	32	---	Crash
28	17	55	Lyle Stelter	Stelter '64 Ford	31	---	Crash
29	4	11	Ned Jarrett	Larry Hess '64 Ford	21	---	Crash
30	30	96	Sonny Lamphear	Homer O'Dell '64 Ford	4	---	Heating
31	29	44	Larry Hess	Hess '66 Rambler	1	---	Engine

Time of Race: 1 hour, 38 minutes, 21 seconds
Average Speed: 61.010 mph
Pole Winner: Richard Petty - 71.514 mph
Lap Leaders: J T Putney 1-31, Richard Petty 32-44, David Pearson 45-83,
   Tom Pistone 84-115, Petty 116-119, Pearson 120-156, Petty 157-162, Pearson 163-200
Cautions: Margin of Victory: Attendance:

Grand National Race No. 33
300 Laps at Islip Speedway
Islip, NY
60 Miles on .2-mile Paved Track
July 16, 1966

Fin	St	No.	Driver	Team / Car	Laps	Money	Status
1	7	2	Bobby Allison	J D Bracken '65 Chevrolet	300	$1,100	Running
2	3	48	James Hylton	Bud Hartje '65 Dodge	298	675	Running
3	11	11	Ned Jarrett	Larry Hess '64 Ford	297	650	Running
4	4	6	David Pearson	Cotton Owens '65 Dodge	295	300	Running
5	2	64	Elmo Langley	Langley-Woodfield '64 Ford	290	275	Running
6	14	86	Neil Castles	Buck Baker '64 Dodge	290	240	Running
7	21	87	Ray Hill	Buck Baker '66 Olds	289	200	Running
8	10	4	John Sears	L G DeWitt '64 Ford	287	175	Running
9	13	20	Clyde Lynn	Lynn '64 Ford	283	150	Running
10	25	97	Henley Gray	Gray '66 Ford	277	140	Running
11	19	31	Al White	'64 Mercury	274	130	Running
12	22	78	Nick Rampling	'66 Plymouth	269	120	Running
13	18	34	Wendell Scott	Scott '65 Ford	267	110	Running
14	16	94	Don Biederman	Ron Stotten '64 Chevrolet	239	100	Heating
15	8	43	Richard Petty	Petty Enterprises '66 Plym	202	100	W Bearing
16	20	93	Blackie Watt	Harry Neal '64 Ford	194	100	Flat tire
17	1	59	Tom Pistone	Pistone '64 Ford	184	100	W Bearing
18	6	22	Marvin Panch	'64 Ford	116	100	Trans
19	15	06	Johnny Wynn	John McCarthy '64 Mercury	104	100	Flat tire
20	28	9	Roy Tyner	Truett Rodgers '66 Chevrolet	77	100	Brakes
21	24	70	J D McDuffie	McDuffie '64 Ford	77	100	Trans
22	12	44	Roy Hallquist	'64 Ford	63	100	Trans
23	17	55	Tiny Lund	Lyle Stelter '64 Ford	57	---	Radiator
24	23	03	Rene Charland	Ed Ackerman '64 Ford	57	---	Differen
25	9	88	Buck Baker	Baker '66 Chevrolet	39	---	Oil Press
26	29	96	Jack Soper	Homer O'Dell '64 Ford	25	---	Heating
27	26	73	Al DeAngelo	Joan Petre '64 Ford	23	---	Engine
28	27	53	Jimmy Helms	David Warren '64 Ford	16	---	Oil Press
29	5	00	Buddy Baker	'65 Dodge	16	---	Trans

Time of Race: 1 hour, 16 minutes, 8 seconds
Average Speed: 47.285 mph
Pole Winner: Tom Pistone - 55.919 mph
Lap Leaders: Tom Pistone 1-146, James Hylton 147-292, Bobby Allison 293-300.
Margin of Victory: 2-laps plus   Cautions: Attendance: 10,000

laps remained in the 300 lapper, was holding a comfortable margin when he sputtered to the pits -- his fuel tank empty. Allison drove into the lead and was two laps ahead of Hylton when the checkered flag fell.

Ned Jarrett came in third, David Pearson was fourth and Elmo Langley fifth.

Allison was not expected to enter the race on the .2-mile paved oval. His car had been badly damaged in a race at Fonda, NY two days earlier. Allison's J.D. Bracken pit crew worked 18 hours rebuilding the car. Many other drivers chipped in -- and one who offered assistance was Hylton.

Tom Pistone, the snake-bitten Chicago driver, started on the pole and led the first 146 laps. He was forced to make a pit stop when his brakes overheated, setting fire to the car. He got back out on the track but ran only a few laps before retiring with wheel bearing failure.

Allison averaged 47.285 mph and moved into ninth place in the NASCAR point standings.

Pearson leads by a 3,312 point margin over second place Hylton.

Race No. 34

Late Race Surge by Goldsmith Nets Volunteer 500 Victory

BRISTOL, TN (July 24) -- Paul Goldsmith ran down Jim Paschal in the last five laps and stole the glory in the Volunteer 500 at Bristol International Speedway. It was the third win of the season for the 38 year-old Plymouth chauffeur.

Paschal was driving for Richard Petty, who called for relief on lap 376 due to neck cramps. Paschal was left with a three lap lead, two of which he lost in the pits during the driver change.

"I had been just riding it out," said Goldsmith. "Then when Petty's car got caught in the pits, I got interested in winning the race. I was running a pace near the end

Paul Goldsmith won Volunteer 500 in final laps

Grand National Race No. 34
500 Laps at Bristol Int'l Speedway
Bristol, TN
"Volunteer 500"
250-miles on Half-mile Paved Track
July 24, 1966

Fin	St	No.	Driver	Team / Car	Laps	Money	status
1	4	99	Paul Goldsmith	Nichels Eng '66 Plymouth	500	$5,400	Running
2	3	43	Richard Petty*	Petty Enterprises '66 Plym	500	2,950	Running
3	2	6	David Pearson	Cotton Owens '66 Dodge	496	2,150	Running
4	8	1	Paul Lewis	Lewis '65 Plymouth	492	1,200	Running
5	13	2	Bobby Allison	J D Bracken '65 Chevrolet	490	1,060	Running
6	14	64	Elmo Langley	Langley-Woodfield '64 Ford	481	940	Running
7	11	4	John Sears	L G DeWitt '64 Ford	469	800	Running
8	17	18	Stick Elliott	Toy Bolton '66 Chevrolet	465	775	Running
9	23	97	Henley Gray	Gray '66 Ford	464	725	Running
10	21	93	Blackie Watt	Harry Neal '64 Ford	461	650	Running
11	22	92	Hank Thomas	W S Jenkins '64 Ford	459	625	Running
12	26	88	Neil Castles	Buck Baker '66 Chevrolet	454	625	Running
13	29	74	Earl Brooks	Gene Black '64 Ford	454	585	Running
14	36	70	J D McDuffie	McDuffie '64 Ford	454	545	Running
15	27	19	J T Putney	Putney '66 Chevrolet	445	550	Oil Leak
16	34	20	Clyde Lynn	Lynn '64 Ford	440	515	Running
17	25	59	Tom Pistone	Pistone '64 Ford	439	545	Running
18	28	73	Buzz Gregory	Joan Petre '64 Ford	437	500	Running
19	20	06	Johnny Wynn	John McCarthy '64 Mercury	410	450	Running
20	35	95	Bill Seifert	Seifert '64 Ford	409	440	Running
21	15	11	Ned Jarrett	Bernard Alvarez '64 Ford	386	905	Differen
22	10	49	G C Spencer	Spencer '65 Plymouth	385	420	Engine
23	12	02	Doug Cooper	Bob Cooper '65 Plymouth	361	405	Engine
24	9	48	James Hylton	Bud Hartje '65 Dodge	341	400	Lug Bolts
25	30	63	Larry Manning	Bob Adams '65 Plymouth	296	420	Trans
26	5	14	Jim Paschal	Friedkin Ent '65 Plymouth	291	410	Engine
27	32	34	Wendell Scott	Scott '65 Ford	264	400	Engine
28	33	38	Wayne Smith	Smith '66 Chevrolet	258	390	Differen
29	18	46	Roy Mayne	Tom Hunter '66 Chevrolet	250	355	Differen
30	1	47	Curtis Turner	Toy Bolton '66 Chevrolet	209	445	Engine
31	24	00	Buddy Baker	'65 Dodge	181	225	U Joint
32	19	87	Buck Baker	Baker '66 Olds	151	125	Engine
33	16	72	Bill Champion	Champion '64 Ford	97	150	Differen
34	6	98	Sam McQuagg	Nichels Eng '66 Dodge	82	125	Brakes
35	7	16	Darel Dieringer	Bud Moore '66 Mercury	50	125	Oil Leak
36	31	79	Frank Warren	Harold Rhodes '64 Chevrolet	0	150	Distrib

Time of Race: 3 hours, 12 minutes, 24 seconds   *Relieved by Jim Paschal
Average Speed: 77.963 mph
Pole Winner: Curtis Turner - 84.309 mph
Lap Leaders: Turner 1-80, Goldsmith 81-159, Petty 160-495, Goldsmith 496-500.
Cautions: 2 for 24 laps   Margin of Victory: 3 car lengths   Attendance: 18,000

that I don't think could have been matched -- regardless of who was in that #43 car."

When the race was over, Paschal apologized to car owner Lee Petty for losing the race. "I'm sorry, Lee. I did the best I could."

"That's all anybody can ask for, Jim," replied Lee.

Another member of the Petty team clocked Paschal turning laps faster than Petty had earlier. But Goldsmith caught his second wind and won by a three car length margin.

David Pearson came in third, Paul Lewis was fourth and Bobby Allison fifth.

Curtis Turner started a Toy Bolton owned Chevrolet on the pole and led the first 80 laps. A loss of oil pressure sent Turner to the pits for a long stay. He was many laps behind when the car finally blew an engine well past the half way point.

A crowd of 18,000 watched Goldsmith average 77.963 mph for his ninth career Grand National win. The lead changed hands only three times in the 500 lapper on the half-mile paved oval.

Curtis Turner #47 won pole for Volunteer 500 in Toy Bolton Chevy. Richard Petty finished 2nd in his Plymouth

Race No. 35

Paul Lewis Comes from 27th To First in Smoky 200

MARYVILLE, TN (July 28) -- Paul Lewis of John-

Paul Lewis got first Grand National victory at Maryville

son City, TN authored a bold charge through the pack and notched his first Grand National victory in the Smoky 200 at Smoky Mountain Raceway. The 33 year-old Plymouth driver finished 2.0-seconds ahead of runner-up David Pearson.

Lewis, the sixth driver of the year to post his initial Grand National

triumph, started 27th in the field of 29 after missing the qualifying session. He took the lead from Pearson in the 137th lap and held off his favored rival to win the $1,000 top prize.

J.T. Putney wound up third after starting second. Doug Cooper was fourth and Bobby Allison fifth.

Buddy Baker started on the pole for the first time in his career. The 25 year-old Charlotte driver led the first 17 laps in his Dodge before giving way to Pearson for 98 laps. Baker trailed Pearson closely until he made a

Buddy Baker won first career pole but crashed in Smoky 200

crowd-pleasing pass on lap 116. The 6'5" second-generation driver was holding off Pearson when a tie-rod broke, sending his Dodge into the wall on lap 134.

Pearson took over and led until Lewis made the decisive pass on lap 137.

Lewis' victory enabled him to move into 27th place in

Grand National Race No. 35
200 Laps at Smoky Mountain Raceway
Maryville, TN
"Smoky 200"
100 miles on Half-mile Dirt Track
July 28, 1966

Fin	St	No.	Driver	team / Car	Laps	Money	Status
1	27	1	Paul Lewis	Lewis '65 Plymouth	200	$1,000	Running
2	3	6	David Pearson	Cotton Owens '65 Dodge	200	600	Running
3	2	19	J T Putney	Putney '66 Chevrolet	199	400	Running
4	11	02	Doug Cooper	Bob Cooper '65 Plymouth	195	300	Running
5	18	2	Bobby Allison	J D Bracken '65 Chevrolet	194	275	Running
6	4	48	James Hylton	Bud Hartje '65 Dodge	194	240	Running
7	8	4	John Sears	L G DeWitt '64 Ford	192	200	Running
8	10	93	Blackie Watt	Harry Neal '64 Ford	191	175	Running
9	13	97	Henley Gray	Gray '66 Ford	190	150	Running
10	16	06	Johnny Wynn	John McCarthy '64 Mercury	189	140	Running
11	14	87	Buck Baker	Baker '66 Olds	188	130	Running
12	28	34	Wendell Scott	Scott '65 Ford	188	120	Running
13	19	88	Neil Castles	Buck Baker '66 Chevrolet	188	110	Running
14	9	18	Stick Elliott	Toy Bolton '66 Chevrolet	183	100	Running
15	20	74	Earl Brooks	Gene Black '64 Ford	183	100	Running
16	26	53	Jimmy Helms	David Warren '64 Ford	175	100	Running
17	23	61	Joel Davis	Toy Bolton '66 Chevrolet	171	100	Running
18	6	20	Clyde Lynn	Lynn '64 Ford	171	100	Running
19	22	70	J D McDuffie	McDuffie '64 Ford	157	100	Running
20	29	94	Don Biederman	Ron Stotten '64 Chevrolet	155	100	Running
21	15	86	Darel Dieringer	Buck Baker '64 Dodge	137	100	Engine
22	1	00	Buddy Baker	'65 Dodge	134	100	Crash
23	17	73	Buzz Gregory	Joan Petre '64 Ford	126	---	Running
24	24	3	Buddy Arrington	'65 Dodge	87	---	Fuel pmp
25	12	11	Ned Jarrett	Larry Hess '64 Ford	78	200	Heating
26	5	64	Elmo Langley	Langley-Woodfield '64 Ford	46	---	Differen
27	25	25	Jabe Thomas	Jeff Handy '64 Ford	34	---	Engine
28	21	35	L D Ottinger	'65 Olds	32	---	Fender
29	7	43	Richard Petty	Petty Enterprises '66 Plym	17	---	Steering

Time of Race: 1 hour, 25 minutes, 56 seconds
Average Speed: 69.822 mph
Pole Winner: Buddy Baker - 77.821 mph
Lap Leaders: Buddy Baker 1-17, David Pearson 18-115, Baker 116-134, Pearson 135-136, Paul Lewis 137-200.
Cautions: Margin of Victory: 2 seconds   Attendance: 6,000

the point standings. Lewis, who began his big league career in 1960, got his first win in his 89th Grand National start. He averaged 69.822 mph.

Race No. 36

Petty Leads From Start to Finish at Nashville; Pearson Fails to Show

NASHVILLE, TN (July 30) -- Richard Petty zipped into the lead at the outset and led all the way to win the 200-mile Grand National race at Fairgrounds Speedway. It was the seventh win of the season for the 29 year-old Plymouth pilot.

A crowd of 15,161 fought boredom as Petty sprinted to a five lap victory. Veteran Buck Baker wound up second in his Oldsmobile and Bobby Allison was third. Allison had posed as Petty's most serious threat in the early going, but a leaking head gasket forced him to slack off. Fourth place went to Henley Gray and John Sears was fifth.

"I had to run pretty hard early in the race, but then Allison started smoking real badly and had to slow down," said Petty. "That took most of the pressure off."

After the race, more fans were milling around the Allison Chevelle than winner Petty. "It is gratifying to receive this much attention from the fans," remarked Allison.

Darel Dieringer sparked a four car wreck in the opening lap. Dieringer, driving the Betty Lilly Ford formerly driven by Allison, broke loose in the third turn. Johnny Wynn was also involved, knocking both out of the race.

Petty was the only factory supported driver to start the race. Jim Paschal was on hand, but engine failure put his Plymouth out after a practice session. David Pearson had a disagreement concerning "deal" money and did not show. Pearson's car owner Cotton Owens explained, "We're making all the races we can and not robbing anyone for deal money," he said. "But the scale of our operation makes it necessary for us to make sure we at least make expenses. Otherwise, we just have to miss some of the races."

Petty averaged 71.770 mph for his 47th career win.

Race No. 37

Petty Nips Baker at Atlanta; Rule Book Tossed Out

HAMPTON, GA (Aug 7) -- Richard Petty ignored a resounding controversy and nipped Buddy Baker in a stirring duel to win the Dixie 400 at Atlanta International Raceway. It was the fourth superspeedway win for the famed Plymouth driver.

Sam McQuagg finished third, James Hylton was fourth and Jerry Grant fifth. The 267-lap event on the 1.5-mile oval unquestionably took a back seat to the week long controversy sparked by the entry of two cars -- a Junior Johnson Ford with Fred Lorenzen making his active return, and a Chevelle built by Smokey Yunick manned by Curtis Turner.

Johnson's Ford, which had a variety of nicknames ranging from "Yellow Banana" and "Junior's Joke" to the "Magnifluxed Monster", was a unique specimen unlike any other Ford in the country. The front end sloped downward, the roofline was lowered, the windows were narrowed and the front windshield was placed in a very aerodynamic position. Additionally, the rear deck lifted up in the air considerably.

Yunick's car was similarly departed from the appearance bestowed by its original maker. The front of the body shell was neatly handcrafted. There was a raised lip at the rear of the roofline and the wheels were positioned off-center in the body cutaways.

Somehow, they made it through in-

Smokey Yunick had a unique Chevy at Atlanta

Grand National Race No. 36
400 Laps at Fairgrounds Speedway
Nashville, TN
200 Miles on Half-mile Paved Track
July 30, 1966

Fin	St	No.	Driver	Team / Car	Laps	Money	Status
1	1	43	Richard Petty	Petty Enterprises '66 Plym	400	$2,750	Running
2	13	87	Buck Baker	Baker '66 Olds	395	1,400	Running
3	2	2	Bobby Allison	J D Bracken '65 Chevrolet	394	850	Running
4	19	74	Henley Gray	Gene Black '66 Ford	383	500	Running
5	14	4	John Sears	L G DeWitt '64 Ford	383	475	Running
6	18	88	Neil Castles	Buck Baker '66 chevrolet	378	450	Running
7	20	20	Clyde Lynn	Lynn '64 Ford	378	425	Running
8	8	97	Coo Coo Marlin	Henley Gray '66 Ford	375	375	Running
9	16	34	Wendell Scott	Scott '65 Ford	375	325	Running
10	9	48	James Hylton	Bud Hartje '65 Ford	352	300	Throttle
11	26	44	Larry Hess	Hess '64 Ford	320	275	Running
12	15	18	Stick Elliott	Toy Bolton '66 Chevrolet	308	240	Engine
13	3	49	G C Spencer	Spencer '65 Plymouth	287	220	Differen
14	27	61	Joel Davis	Toy Bolton '66 Chevrolet	268	200	Oil Leak
15	21	3	Buddy Arrington	'64 Dodge	262	170	Differen
16	7	39	Friday Hassler	J H Crawford '66 Chevrolet	256	150	D Shaft
17	6	64	Elmo Langley	Langley-Woodfield '64 Ford	250	130	A Frame
18	23	38	Wayne Smith	Smith '66 Chevrolet	220	120	Engine
19	25	94	Don Biederman	Ron Stotten '64 Chevrolet	214	100	Oil Leak
20	11	19	J T Putney	Putney '66 Chevrolet	171	100	Engine
21	28	9	Roy Tyner	Truett Rodgers '66 Chevrolet	141	100	Oil Leak
22	4	1	Paul Lewis	Lewis '65 Plymouth	100	100	Engine
23	24	70	J D McDuffie	McDuffie '64 Ford	54	100	Heating
24	5	02	Doug Cooper	Bob Cooper '65 Plymouth	49	100	Engine
25	17	53	Marty Robbins	David Warren '64 Ford	48	100	Oil Leak
26	22	93	Blackie Watt	Harry Neal '64 Ford	21	100	Radiator
27	12	06	Johnny Wynn	John McCarthy '64 Mercury	2	100	Crash
28	10	24	Darel Dieringer	Betty Lilly '66 Ford	0	100	Crash

Time of Race: 2 hours, 47 minutes, 11 seconds
Average Speed: 71.770 mph
Pole Winner: Richard Petty - 82.493 mph
Lap Leaders: Richard Petty 1-400.

Cautions: 4 for 41 laps   Margin of Victory: 5-laps plus   Attendance: 15,161

Fred Lorenzen tags the wall at Atlanta

led for 24 laps early in the race. He crashed into the third turn wall on lap 139, putting him out of the race. When he wrecked, one member of the media quipped, "It's pretty hard to drive a banana at 145 mph."

Despite the return of Ford, Lorenzen and the Yunick car sitting on the pole, only 25,000 spectators showed up. Petty averaged a record 130.244 mph as 37 laps were run under the caution flag.

spection. On the other hand, David Pearson, LeeRoy Yarbrough and Ned Jarrett were sent packing when their cars failed to get the seal of approval from NASCAR Technical Director Norris Friel.

Jarrett and car owner Bernard Alvarez arrived trackside with a new Ford Fairlane. Friel handed them a long list of things that were declared unacceptable. Rather than attempting to fix every item, Jarrett and Alvarez went home.

Yarbrough's Jon Thorne-owned Dodge was ruled illegal when NASCAR inspectors discovered blocks of wood lodged in the front springs. The wood could fall out during the race, the inspectors reasoned, which would lower the body of the car. NASCAR ruled the purple Dodge out of the race and did not permit Thorne and Yarbrough to make corrections to the car.

Pearson's Cotton Owens Dodge was rigged with a device that would enable the driver to pull a cable and lower his car after the race had started. "I refused to change my car for reasons of principle," huffed Owens. "The principle involved was NASCAR allowing two cars to flaunt the rules while blowing the whistle on others. I realize that Lorenzen and Turner are valuable as drawing cards, but that didn't make what happened right."

Hylton picked up 2,200 points on Pearson in the battle for the 1966 NASCAR Grand National championship. Pearson's lead stood at 1,990 after 37 races.

Petty held off the upstart Baker in a thrilling duel. Baker, driving the Ray Fox Dodge, led for 62 laps and trailed Petty in close fashion for the final 46 laps. Third place McQuagg was seven laps behind at the finish.

Turner started on the pole and led the first 35 laps. The Roanoke, VA leadfoot was knocked out of the race with distributor problems. Lorenzen started third and

Grand National Race No. 37
267 Laps at Atlanta Int'l Raceway
Hampton, GA
"Dixie 400"
400 Miles on 1.5-mile Paved Track
August 7, 1966

Fin	St	No.	Driver	Team / Car	Laps	Money	Status
1	5	43	Richard Petty	Petty Enterprises '66 Plym	267	$13,525	Running
2	6	3	Buddy Baker	Ray Fox '66 Dodge	267	8,345	Running
3	9	98	Sam McQuagg	Nichels Eng '66 Dodge	260	3,505	Running
4	17	48	James Hylton	Bud Hartje '65 Dodge	259	3,000	Running
5	16	04	Jerry Grant	Friedkin Ent '65 Plymouth	255	1,925	Running
6	20	67	Buddy Arrington	Arrington '64 Dodge	254	1,425	Running
7	38	34	Wendell Scott	Scott '65 Ford	251	1,330	Running
8	13	89	Eddie MacDonald	Buck Baker '65 Chevrolet	251	1,075	Running
9	33	87	Buck Baker	Baker '66 Olds	249	980	Running
10	21	2	Bobby Allison	J D Bracken '65 Chevrolet	248	860	Running
11	14	51	Bob Derrington	Derrington '65 Chevrolet	242	790	Running
12	29	19	J T Putney	Putney '66 Chevrolet	241	745	Running
13	26	06	Johnny Wynn	John McCarthy '64 Mercury	233	630	Running
14	28	44	Larry Hess	Hess '64 Ford	226	600	Running
15	27	97	Henley Gray	Gray '66 Ford	216	595	Running
16	10	16	Darel Dieringer	Bud Moore '66 Mercury	211	740	Engine
17	39	73	Jimmy Helms	David Warren '64 Ford	209	655	Running
18	25	46	Roy Mayne	Tom Hunter '66 Chevrolet	207	580	Running
19	30	88	Neil Castles	Buck Baker '66 Chevrolet	183	625	Engine
20	41	95	E J Trivette	Gene Cline '64 Ford	183	620	Running
21	23	18	Stick Elliott	Toy Bolton '66 Chevrolet	149	565	Radiator
22	42	70	J D McDuffie	McDuffie '64 Ford	148	600	Trans
23	3	26	Fred Lorenzen	Junior Johnson '66 Ford	139	630	Crash
24	1	13	Curtis Turner	Smokey Yunick '66 Chevrolet	130	1,200	Distrib
25	11	7	Bobby Johns	Shorty Johns '66 Chevrolet	117	530	Engine
26	7	14	Jim Paschal	Friedkin Ent '66 Plymouth	108	565	Engine
27	34	49	G C Spencer	Spencer '65 Plymouth	106	635	Engine
28	8	42	Marvin Panch	Petty Enterprises '65 Plym	98	430	Clutch
29	19	33	Eldon Yarbrough	Curtis Satterfield '65 Chevy	74	500	Engine
30	18	64	Elmo Langley	Langley-Woodfield '64 Ford	67	495	Engine
31	22	79	Frank Warren	Harold Rhodes '64 Chevrolet	66	465	Engine
32	37	74	Earl Brooks	Gene Black '64 Ford	58	550	Oil Press
33	12	39	Bunkie Blackburn	J H Crawford '65 Chevrolet	52	480	Radiator
34	31	38	Wayne Smith	Smith '66 Chevrolet	44	475	Engine
35	2	71	Earl Balmer	K&K Insurance '65 Dodge	41	470	Crash
36	35	24	Tiny Lund	Betty Lilly '66 Ford	41	515	Engine
37	40	65	Darrell Bryant	Buddy Arrington '64 Dodge	17	445	Oil Press
38	24	4	John Sears	L G DeWitt '64 Ford	15	380	Engine
39	4	99	Paul Goldsmith	Nichels Eng '66 Plymouth	14	400	Distrib
40	32	09	Friday Hassler	'66 Chevrolet	13	395	H Gasket
41	36	20	Clyde Lynn	Lynn '64 Ford	12	465	Engine
42	15	63	Larry Manning	Bob Adams '65 Plymouth	11	460	Engine

Time of Race: 3 hours, 4 minutes, 30 seconds
Average Speed: 130.244 mph
Pole Winner: Curtis Turner - 148.331 mph
Lap Leaders: Curtis Turner 1-35, Darel Dieringer 36-46, Fred Lorenzen 47-48, Jerry Grant 49, Dieringer 50-53, Jim Paschal 54-68, Turner 69-90, Richard Petty 91, Turner 92, Petty 93-101, Turner 102-103, Petty 104, Lorenzen 105, Petty 106-118, Lorenzen 119-139, Buddy Baker 140-200, Petty 201-230, Baker 231, Petty 232-267.
Cautions: 6 for 37 laps   Margin of Victory: 2.0 seconds   Attendance: 25,000

Race No. 38

Pearson Holds Off Petty and Turner in Columbia Thriller

COLUMBIA, SC (Aug. 18) -- David Pearson took the lead from Bobby Allison in the 168th lap and sped to victory in the 100-mile Grand National race at Columbia Speedway. It was the 12th win of the season for the curly-headed Spartanburg Dodge driver.

Richard Petty finished second on Pearson's bumper as the race ended under the caution flag for J.D. McDuffie's wreck. Curtis Turner was third, James Hylton came in fourth and Dick Hutcherson was fifth.

Turner drove in the 200-lapper on the half-mile dirt track wearing a three-piece business suit. "Holly Farms (sponsor for the Junior Johnson-owned Ford) told me that I was gonna drive for them and I would have to wear a suit," said the 42 year-old as he loosened his tie after the race. "They wanted me to be a gentleman driver and I figure this is the first step. You've gotta look good, you know."

Turner started second and led the first 134 laps. A long pit stop pushed him back in the field, but he hustled his way back up into contention until McDuffie's spin.

Petty led for two laps before Allison grabbed command. Allison was holding off his rivals until his engine went sour in the final 33 laps. He wound up 11th, 10 laps behind.

Tom Pistone survived a solo wreck in the 17th lap. Pistone's Ford whacked the guard rail and sailed completely over the retaining barrier. He landed unhurt in a patch of trees.

Pearson averaged 66.128 mph as a crowd of 8,954 were on hand.

Grand National Race No. 38
200 Laps at Columbia Speedway
Columbia, SC
100 Miles on Half-mile Dirt Track
August 18, 1966

Fin	St	No.	Driver	Team / Car	Laps	Money	Status
1	4	6	David Pearson	Cotton Owens '65 Dodge	200	$1,000	Running
2	3	42	Richard Petty	Petty Enterprises '66 Plym	200	600	Running
3	2	26	Curtis Turner	Junior Johnson '66 Ford	200	400	Running
4	6	48	James Hylton	Bud Hartje '65 Dodge	198	300	Running
5	7	29	Dick Hutcherson	Holman-Moody '66 Ford	198	275	Running
6	5	64	Elmo Langley	Langley-Woodfield '64 Ford	195	340	Running
7	16	09	Friday Hassler	'66 Chevrolet	195	200	Running
8	9	73	Buddy Baker	Joan Petre '64 Ford	195	175	Running
9	10	4	John Sears	L G DeWitt '64 Ford	193	150	Running
10	11	60	Doug Cooper	Bob Cooper '65 Plymouth	191	140	Running
11	1	2	Bobby Allison	J D Bracken '65 Chevrolet	190	130	Running
12	14	70	J D McDuffie	McDuffie '64 Ford	184	120	Crash
13	13	34	Wendell Scott	Scott '65 Ford	183	110	Running
14	12	74	Buster Sexton	Gene Black '64 Ford	183	100	Running
15	21	97	Henley Gray	Gray '66 Ford	173	100	Running
16	24	9	Roy Tyner	Truett Rodgers '66 Chevrolet	173	100	Running
17	20	44	Larry Hess	Hess '66 Rambler	170	100	Running
18	19	55	Tiny Lund	Lyle Stelter '64 Ford	169	100	Running
19	15	94	Don Biederman	Ron Stotten '64 Chevrolet	167	100	Running
20	22	95	Bill Seifert	Seifert '64 Ford	166	100	Running
21	23	61	Joel Davis	Toy Bolton '66 Chevrolet	157	100	Running
22	18	20	Clyde Lynn	Lynn '64 Ford	147	100	Engine
23	8	06	Johnny Wynn	John McCarthy '64 Mercury	120	---	Engine
24	25	65	Buddy Arrington	Arrington '65 Dodge	65	---	Ignition
25	17	02	Doug Cooper	Bob Cooper '65 Plymouth	41	---	Engine
26	26	59	Tom Pistone	Pistone '64 Ford	17	---	Crash

Time of Race: 1 hour, 30 minutes, 44 seconds
Average Speed: 66.128 mph
Pole Winner: Bobby Allison - 73.469 mph
Lap Leaders: Curtis Turner 1-134, Richard Petty 135-136, Bobby Allison 137-167, David Pearson 168-200.
Cautions: 2 for ___ laps   Margin of Victory: 1 car length   Attendance: 8,954

Race No. 39

Junior Ends Retirement; Darel Takes Western NC 500

WEAVERVILLE, NC (Aug. 21) -- Darel Dieringer took advantage of misfortunes that struck down two race leaders and won the Western North Carolina 500 at Asheville-Weaverville Speedway. It was Dieringer's second win of the season.

Dieringer took the lead when overheating problems sent leader Richard Petty to the pits in the 342nd lap. The Indianapolis, IN Mercury driver outran G.C. Spencer by eight laps to tack down the $3,150 prize. Petty struggled 17 more laps before calling it quits. Third place went to James Hylton, John Sears was fourth and Friday Hassler fifth.

Junior Johnson ended his retirement which lasted almost a year, and won the pole in his rebuilt Ford Fairlane. Johnson led the first 118 laps as no one in the 30 car field could keep close to him. During an exchange of pit stops, Johnson fell to fourth behind Dieringer, Petty and Dick Hutcherson. However, by lap 143, he was back in the lead.

Johnson made an unscheduled trip to the pits on lap 219 and turned the race over to Petty and Dieringer. Johnson let Curtis Turner in his car after the distributor was replaced, but he pulled out on lap 321 with engine failure.

Turner had started third in a Toy Bolton Chevrolet, but spun when the engine blew in the eighth lap.

"I guess you might say I outlasted 'em today," said a tired but happy Dieringer in victory lane. "I slowed up in the end. It just wears you out to slow up so much. Don't let anybody tell you that stroking is easy. To me, it's the hardest way to win a race."

Johnson vowed that he was retiring for good this time. "That's all, I'm going back into retirement," said the 35 year-old Ronda, NC charger. "Curtis will be driving the car from now on."

Dieringer averaged 76.700 mph for his fifth career Grand National victory.

of the year.

Petty started second and jumped into an early lead. He was leading Allison by a few car lengths when the engine in his Plymouth exploded as he motored down the backstretch. Petty left valve springs and rods scattered on the backstretch on the half mile paved track when his engine blew. "I haven't had one come apart like that in a long time," said Petty.

Allison cruised into first place and was leading Elmo Langley by a narrow margin when Langley retreated to the pits on lap 163. Allison was left in a lap by himself.

Langley earned second place money. James Hylton was third, Buck Baker fourth and Tiny Lund fifth.

Point leader David Pearson did not show since his Cotton Owens team did not get any deal money. As a result, only 3,000 spectators watched Allison average 68.899 mph.

Grand National Race No. 39
500 Laps at Asheville-Weaverville Speedway
Weaverville, NC
"Western North Carolina 500"
250 Miles on Half-mile Paved Track
August 21, 1966

Fin	St	No.	Driver	Team / Car	Laps	Money	Status
1	2	16	Darel Dieringer	Bud Moore '66 Mercury	500	$3,150	Running
2	6	49	G C Spencer	Spencer '65 Plymouth	492	1,750	Running
3	13	48	James Hylton	Bud Hartje '65 Dodge	486	1,250	Running
4	16	4	John Sears	L G DeWitt '64 Ford	478	900	Running
5	15	09	Friday Hassler	'66 Chevrolet	470	800	Running
6	22	34	Wendell Scott	Scott '65 Ford	468	700	Running
7	12	1	Paul Lewis	Lewis '65 Plymouth	460	650	Engine
8	9	2	Bobby Allison	J D Bracken '65 Chevrolet	457	600	Running
9	26	38	Wayne Smith	Smith '66 Chevrolet	450	500	Running
10	27	95	Clyde Lynn	Gene Cline '64 Ford	440	400	Running
11	18	65	Buddy Arrington	Arrington '65 Dodge	432	380	Running
12	24	93	Blackie Watt	Harry Neal '64 Ford	431	375	Running
13	5	6	David Pearson	Cotton Owens '66 Dodge	426	325	Engine
14	23	88	Neil Castles	Buck Baker '66 Chevrolet	424	275	Running
15	8	11	Ned Jarrett	Bondy Long '66 Ford	420	450	Engine
16	29	35	Max Ledbetter	'65 Olds	415	200	Running
17	14	02	Bob Cooper	Cooper '65 Plymouth	375	200	Engine
18	4	42	Richard Petty	Petty Enterprises '66 Plym	369	200	Heating
19	1	26	Junior Johnson*	Johnson '66 Ford	321	700	Engine
20	25	10	Paul Burnhaver	Gary Weaver '64 Ford	291	200	Trans
21	10	19	J T Putney	Putney '66 Chevrolet	254	200	Brakes
22	11	64	Elmo Langley	Langley-Woodfield '64 Ford	204	200	Running
23	19	97	Henley Gray	Gray '66 Ford	195	200	Crash
24	30	70	J D McDuffie	McDuffie '64 Ford	194	200	Crash
25	7	29	Dick Hutcherson	Holman-Moody '66 Ford	168	200	Engine
26	20	87	Doug Cooper	Buck Baker '66 Olds	167	150	Axle
27	21	75	Earl Brooks	Gene Black '64 Ford	153	150	Differen
28	17	73	Buddy Baker	Joan Petre '64 Ford	140	150	Clutch
29	28	61	Joel Davis	Toy Bolton '66 Chevrolet	53	150	Engine
30	3	47	Curtis Turner	Toy Bolton '66 Chevrolet	3	150	Engine

Time of Race: 3 hours, 15 minutes, 34 seconds
Average Speed: 76.700 mph
Pole Winner: Junior Johnson - 86.831 mph
Lap Leaders: Junior Johnson 1-118, Darel Dieringer 119-136, Richard Petty 137-141,
    Dick Hutcherson 142, Johnson 143-219, Petty 220-334, Dieringer 335-336,
    Petty 337-341, Dieringer 342-500.
Cautions: 3 for 23 laps.   Margin of Victory: 8-laps plus   Attendance: 14,300
*Relieved by Curtis Turner

Grand National Race No. 40
200 Laps at Beltsville Speedway
Beltsville, MD
"Maryland 200"
100 Miles on Half-mile Paved Track
August 24, 1966

Fin	St	No.	Driver	Team / Car	Laps	Money	Status
1	1	2	Bobby Allison	J D Bracken '65 Chevrolet	200	$1,000	Running
2	3	64	Elmo Langley	Langley-Woodfield '64 Ford	199	600	Running
3	4	48	James Hylton	Bud Hartje '65 Dodge	196	400	Running
4	10	87	Buck Baker	Baker '66 Olds	195	300	Running
5	5	55	Tiny Lund	Lyle Stelter '64 Ford	194	275	Running
6	8	73	Buddy Baker	Joan Petre '64 Ford	193	240	Running
7	9	75	Earl Brooks	Gene Black '64 Ford	192	200	Running
8	16	65	Buddy Arrington	Arrington '65 Dodge	189	175	Running
9	13	20	Clyde Lynn	Lynn '64 Ford	187	150	Running
10	6	4	John Sears	L G DeWitt '64 Ford	185	140	Engine
11	20	70	J D McDuffie	McDuffie '64 Ford	183	130	Running
12	15	95	Bill Seifert	Seifert '64 Ford	176	120	Running
13	18	00	Jimmy Helms	'64 Ford	173	110	Running
14	12	34	Wendell Scott	Scott '65 Ford	170	100	Running
15	22	50	Edgar Wallen	'64 Chevrolet	149	100	Running
16	11	61	Joel Davis	Toy Bolton '66 Chevrolet	145	100	Vibration
17	14	97	Henley Gray	Gray '66 Ford	126	100	Differen
18	17	94	Don Biederman	Ron Stotten '64 Chevrolet	122	100	Oil Press
19	7	92	Hank Thomas	W S Jenkins '64 Ford	86	100	Heating
20	2	42	Richard Petty	Petty Enterprises '66 Plym	30	100	Engine
21	21	63	Larry Manning	Bob Adams '65 Plymouth	17	100	Vibration
22	19	93	Blackie Watt	Harry Neal '64 Ford	2	100	Oil Press

Time of Race: 1 hour, 26 minutes, 5 seconds
Average Speed: 68.899 mph
Pole Winner: Bobby Allison - 79.330 mph
Lap Leaders: Richard Petty 1-30, Bobby Allison 31-200.
Cautions: Margin of Victory: 1-lap plus   Attendance: 3,000

Race No. 40
Allison Chevelle Tops in Maryland 200

BELTSVILLE, MD (Aug. 24) -- Bobby Allison took the lead when engine failure put Richard Petty out of the hunt and drove to a one lap victory in the Maryland 200 at Beltsville Speedway. It was Allison's third win

Race No. 41
Hair-raising Allison-Turner Feud Spices Myers Memorial

WINSTON-SALEM, NC (Aug. 27) -- Flamboyant Bobby Allison and crusty veteran Curtis Turner engaged in a frightful, crowd-stirring, car-smashing contest as David Pearson drove to victory in the Myers Brothers Memorial event at Bowman Gray Stadium.

Pearson took the lead in the 219th lap and beat Richard Petty by 10 seconds to post his 13th win of the season.

While there was a degree of action in the battle for the lead, all eyes of the overflow crowd of 15,000 were on Allison and Turner, who rammed their machines into each other with relentless abandon.

Curtis Turner and Bobby Allison got in a war
at Winston-Salem

The seed was planted early when Turner hooked Allison's rear bumper, spinning him out on lap eight of the 250-lapper on the quarter-mile oval. Allison lost a lap in the process, but rejoined the fray running with the leaders.

Pearson had led the first 97 laps. Turner, driving Junior Johnson's Ford, passed Pearson on lap 98. At that point, Allison was trying to pass Turner to get back in the lead lap. Tom Pistone stuck his nose into the action, battling Turner for the lead. Petty and Pearson followed in hot pursuit.

Turner was doing a masterful job of blocking his rivals on the tight track. Pistone made a stab at the lead, but Turner blocked his outside pass. Allison dived under Turner as the cars went three abreast into the third turn.

Pistone banged into the retaining wall as Turner and Allison came together. Turner's car spun as Petty took the lead.

Turner returned to the track and was moving slowly, waiting on Allison's Chevrolet. Allison sensed the ambush and didn't fall into it. Allison cut back and hit Turner's Ford in the rear. After that, it was men versus machines continuously for about 10 laps.

Much of the banging occurred under the yellow flag. Curiously, NASCAR officials did not warn either driver. Turner spun Allison, and Allison came back and spun Turner. Turner waited on Allison once again for another shot at his adversary. Allison aimed his limping automobile at Turner and buried the front of his car into Turner's car. At that point, NASCAR officials ejected

both from the race -- an academic decision since both cars were wrecked beyond running order.

The battered cars came to a halt on the front chute -- and many of the fans jumped over the fence and rushed onto the track. Police officers quickly restored order and kept Allison and Turner at a distance.

Each driver was fined $100 for "rough driving". Johnson, owner of Turner's car, was irritated after the fracas. "If that happens again," Johnson told Turner, "I'll pay the $100 fine and let you pay for fixing the race car."

Allison played the event down. "It was necessary to warn and fine us," he said later. "We know better than anyone the consequences of rough driving at high speeds. The thing between Turner and myself began and ended at Bowman Gray Stadium."

James Hylton finished third, five laps behind the leaders. Fourth place went to John Sears and Pistone survived his encounter with the guard rail to finish fifth.

Pearson averaged 45.928 mph.

Grand National Race No. 41
250 Laps at Bowman Gray Stadium
Winston-Salem, NC
"Myers Brothers Memorial"
62.5 Miles on Quarter-mile Paved Track
August 27, 1966

Fin	St	No.	Driver	Team / Car	Laps	Money	Status
1	2	6	David Pearson	Cotton Owens '65 Dodge	250	$1,000	Running
2	1	42	Richard Petty	Petty Enterprises '66 Plym	250	600	Running
3	8	48	James Hylton	Bud Hartje '65 Dodge	245	400	Running
4	7	4	John Sears	L G DeWitt '64 Ford	245	300	Running
5	5	59	Tom Pistone	Pistone '64 Ford	240	275	Running
6	14	34	Wendell Scott	Scott '65 Ford	240	240	Running
7	17	20	Clyde Lynn	Lynn '64 Ford	235	200	Running
8	15	70	J D McDuffie	McDuffie '64 Ford	233	175	Running
9	20	97	Henley Gray	Gray '66 Ford	223	150	Running
10	12	40	Eddie Yarboro	'65 Dodge	215	140	Running
11	11	94	Don Biederman	Ron Stotten '64 Chevrolet	209	130	Heating
12	18	60	Ernest Eury	'64 Chevrolet	207	120	Running
13	24	50	Larry Manning	'64 Chevrolet	203	110	Running
14	13	61	Joel Davis	Toy Bolton '66 Chevrolet	194	100	Running
15	6	64	Elmo Langley	Langley-Woodfield '64 Ford	169	100	Axle
16	21	00	Buddy Baker	'64 Ford	153	100	Oil Press
17	4	26	Curtis Turner	Junior Johnson '66 Ford	114	100	Crash
18	3	2	Bobby Allison	J D Bracken '65 Chevrolet	111	100	Crash
19	22	95	Bill Seifert	Seifert '64 Ford	96	100	Brakes
20	19	15	Paul Dean Holt	Lyle Stelter '64 Ford	50	100	Ball Jt.
21	9	92	Hank Thomas	W S Jenkins '64 Ford	32	100	Axle
22	10	65	Buddy Arrington	Arrington '65 Dodge	25	100	Gas tank
23	16	38	Wayne Smith	Smith '66 Chevrolet	12	100	Engine
24	23	73	Jimmy Helms	Joan Petre '64 Ford	6	100	Fuel pmp

Time of Race: 1 hour, 21 minutes, 39 seconds
Average Speed: 45.928 mph
Pole Winner: Richard Petty - 54.348 mph
Lap Leaders: David Pearson 1-97, Curtis Turner 98-105, Richard Petty 106-218, Pearson 219-250.

Cautions: 3 for 16 laps   Margin of Victory: 10 seconds   Attendance: 15,000

Race No. 42

Dieringer Dances to Victory in Darlington Southern 500

DARLINGTON, SC (Sept. 5) -- Daring Darel Dieringer rode a wave of fortune by taking the lead seven laps from the finish to win the 17th annual Southern 500 at Darlington Raceway.

Dieringer, driving Bud Moore's compact Mercury Comet, roared into the lead when a flat tire deflated Richard Petty's hopes. It was the first superspeedway win of Dieringer's career.

Petty finished second, nearly a lap behind as he struggled the final 10 laps with a leaking tire. David Pearson took third spot, Marvin Panch was fourth and Fred Lorenzen fifth.

The lead changed hands 28 times with Petty and Dieringer leading most of the way. Petty put his Plymouth into the lead for 137 laps of the 334 laps. He had taken the lead from Dieringer on lap 293 and was pulling away when his misfortune struck. Dieringer, who led for 105 laps, had started third and was never out of the hunt.

The 40 year-old Dieringer won $20,900, including $1,500 for being the highest finishing independent. The Darlington Raceway had posted bonus money for the non factory-backed teams.

"I would have been happy with second this year," said Dieringer. "Petty's bad luck let me sneak in here. It was a sure bet I couldn't have caught him."

Petty survived a brush with Earl Balmer in the 189th lap. Balmer, running seventh four laps down, was leading the onrushing Petty into the first turn. Petty tapped the rear of Balmer's Dodge and sent him into the wall. The errant car climbed the guard rail, teetered on the sliver of steel and spewed debris and gasoline into the open scaffold press box. The 100-125 press members were sitting just 15 feet from the track surface.

Bobby Allison #2, Darel Dieringer #16 and Paul Lewis #1 race through 1st turn at Darlington

"We were diving for cover like soldiers seeking the sanctuary of a fox hole," said reporter Tom Higgins of the *Charlotte Observer*.

The inside of Balmer's left front wheel caught the tip of the guard rail, tossing the car back onto the track. He ripped 100 feet of steel guard rail onto the track and splintered eight fence posts.

"I don't know what happened," said a shaken Balmer afterwards. "My car hadn't handled well for several laps. I didn't see Petty at all. I thought sure as hell I was going into that press box. All I could

Earl Balmer splinters guard rail at Darlington after nearly going into press box

Grand National Race No. 42
364 Laps at Darlington Raceway
Darlington, SC
"Southern 500"
500 Miles on 1.375-mile Paved Track
September 5, 1966

Fin	St	No.	Driver	Team / Car	Laps	Money	Status
1	3	16	Darel Dieringer	Bud Moore '66 Mercury	364	$20,900	Running
2	2	43	Richard Petty	Petty Enterprises '66 Plym	364	8,975	Running
3	13	6	David Pearson	Cotton Owens '66 Dodge	361	4,700	Running
4	14	42	Marvin Panch	Petty Enterprises '66 Plym	360	2,725	Running
5	9	28	Fred Lorenzen	Holman-Moody '66 Ford	360	2,300	Running
6	11	14	Jim Paschal	Friedkin Ent '66 Plymouth	360	2,595	Running
7	10	29	Dick Hutcherson	Holman-Moody '65 Ford	358	1,280	Running
8	1	12	LeeRoy Yarbrough	Jon Thorne '66 Dodge	358	1,650	Running
9	5	98	Sam McQuagg	Nichels Eng '66 Dodge	358	900	Running
10	18	49	G C Spencer	Spencer '66 Plymouth	358	1,180	Running
11	7	21	Cale Yarborough	Wood Brothers '66 Ford	356	700	Running
12	21	1	Paul Lewis	Lewis '65 Plymouth	353	925	Running
13	20	11	Ned Jarrett	Bondy Long '66 Ford	350	1,375	Running
14	12	26	Curtis Turner	Junior Johnson '66 Ford	348	600	Crash
15	16	48	James Hylton	Bud Hartje '65 Dodge	348	800	Running
16	4	99	Paul Goldsmith	Nichels Eng '66 Plymouth	345	605	Engine
17	19	36	H B Bailey	Bailey '66 Pontiac	341	840	Running
18	23	64	Elmo Langley	Langley-Woodfield '64 Ford	336	710	Running
19	25	19	J T Putney	Putney '66 Chevrolet	333	725	Running
20	40	4	John Sears	L G DeWitt '64 Ford	327	695	Running
21	44	44	Larry Hess	Hess '64 Ford	326	665	Running
22	38	97	Henley Gray	Gray '66 Ford	323	660	Running
23	36	88	Neil Castles	Buck Baker '66 Chevrolet	321	655	Running
24	43	34	Wendell Scott	Scott '65 Ford	317	650	Running
25	37	72	Bill Champion	Champion '64 Ford	308	645	Running
26	30	79	Frank Warren	Harold Rhodes '64 Chevrolet	305	590	Engine
27	26	20	Bunkie Blackburn	'64 Mercury	287	615	Running
28	24	24	Tiny Lund	Betty Lilly '66 Ford	248	580	Engine
29	28	09	Friday Hassler	'66 Chevrolet	196	575	W Bearing
30	6	71	Earl Balmer	K&K Insurance '65 Dodge	185	470	Crash
31	31	93	Blackie Watt	Harry Neal '64 Ford	172	465	Engine
32	42	75	Earl Brooks	Gene Black '66 Ford	120	510	Engine
33	8	3	Buddy Baker	Ray Fox '65 Dodge	97	455	Throttle
34	32	89	Eddie MacDonald	Buck Baker '65 Chevrolet	97	450	Engine
35	22	47	Stick Elliott	Toy Bolton '66 Chevrolet	78	445	Valve
36	33	2	Bobby Allison	J D Bracken '65 Chevrolet	71	640	Engine
37	17	7	Bobby Johns	Shorty Johns '66 Chevrolet	56	535	Engine
38	39	51	Bob Derrington	Derrington '65 Chevrolet	51	480	Cam
39	29	67	Buddy Arrington	Arrington '65 Dodge	50	425	Engine
40	34	38	Wayne Smith	Smith '66 Chevrolet	26	520	Engine
41	27	87	Buck Baker	Baker '66 Olds	22	435	Engine
42	35	25	Doug Cooper	Jeff Handy '64 Ford	16	460	Engine
43	15	04	Jerry Grant	Friedkin Ent '65 Plymouth	7	405	Trans
44	41	73	Jimmy Helms	Joan Petre '64 Ford	1	450	D Shaft

Time of Race: 4 hours, 21 minutes, 31 seconds
Average Speed: 114.830 mph
Pole Winner: LeeRoy Yarbrough - 140.058 mph
Lap Leaders: Paul Goldsmith 1-5, Richard Petty 6, LeeRoy Yarbrough 7-41,
   Curtis Turner 42-53, Sam McQuagg 54-76, Darel Dieringer 77-87,
   Dick Hutcherson 88, Petty 89-96, Cale Yarborough 97-105, Dieringer 106-109,
   Yarborough 110-126, David Pearson 127, Goldsmith 128, Dieringer 129-163,
   Goldsmith 164-166, Petty 167-180, Yarborough 181-187, Marvin Panch 188-193,
   Dieringer 194, Panch 195-202, Petty 203-215, Dieringer 216-245, Petty 246-249,
   Dieringer 250-261, Petty 262-287, Dieringer 288-292, Petty 293-357, Dieringer 358-364
Cautions: 8 for 80 laps   Margin of Victory: Attendance: 65,000

time the press members abandoned the facility. In unison, they issued a written ultimatum and delivered it to Raceway President Bob Colvin.

"We the undersigned do hereby notify Darlington Raceway that we will not endanger our lives in the future by covering Darlington events from the existing press location. We hereby request that the location of the press box be moved to a site affording better safety facilities and a better view of the race track. We are of the opinion that the present press box at the track is without equal in racing from a standpoint of peril to human life. And we refuse to assume the responsibility for this condition in order to serve the Raceway," read the petition.

Curtis Turner and Bobby Allison, principles in the fender-smashing episode at Winston-Salem the week before, failed to finish. Turner, wheeling Junior Johnson's Ford, led for 11 laps in the early stages before wrecking on lap 348. Allison started far back in 33rd and was never a factor. He withdrew after 71 laps with a blown engine.

A crowd of 65,000 watched Dieringer average 114.830 mph.

James Hylton #48, Earl Brooks #75 and Paul Goldsmith #99 duel at Darlington

Race No. 43

Water Truck Foils Johnson; Pearson Wins at Hickory

HICKORY, NC (Sept. 9) -- David Pearson took the lead in the 71st lap, broke out of a two car battle when a utility truck blocked Junior Johnson, and won the Buddy Shuman Memorial at Hickory Speedway. It was the 14th win of the season for Pearson.

Johnson announced that he was coming out of retire-

think of was 'Oh, those poor people up there'."

Petty went on his way with a crunched front bumper. "I caused all that confusion," remarked the big-hearted Petty. "I was trying to pass him going into the number one turn. I don't think he saw me and he tried to move up in the groove. That's when I hit him. It was only a tap, but it was enough."

The caution flag was out for 28 laps, and in the mean-

Grand National Race No. 43
250 Laps at Hickory Speedway
Hickory, NC
"Buddy Shuman Memorial"
100 Miles on .4-mile Dirt Track
September 9, 1966

Fin	St	No.	Driver	Team / Car	Laps	Money	Status
1	2	6	David Pearson	Cotton Owens '65 Dodge	250	$1,000	Running
2	1	42	Richard Petty	Petty Enterprises '66 Plym	249	600	Running
3	3	1	Paul Lewis	Lewis '65 Plymouth	248	400	Running
4	9	48	James Hylton	Bud Hartje '65 Dodge	242	300	Running
5	7	92	Hank Thomas	W S Jenkins '64 Ford	240	275	Running
6	11	34	Wendell Scott	Scott '65 Ford	236	240	Running
7	5	2	Bobby Allison	J D Bracken '65 Chevrolet	235	200	Running
8	17	20	Clyde Lynn	Lynn '64 Ford	219	175	Running
9	6	4	John Sears	L G DeWitt '64 Ford	219	150	Running
10	16	95	Bill Seifert	Gene Cline '64 Ford	217	140	Running
11	8	26	Junior Johnson*	Johnson '66 Ford	212	130	Crash
12	4	64	Elmo Langley	Langley-Woodfield '64 Ford	212	120	Running
13	19	97	Henley Gray	Gray '66 Ford	211	110	Running
14	14	19	J T Putney	Putney '66 Chevrolet	203	100	Running
15	15	70	J D McDuffie	McDuffie '64 Ford	183	100	Running
16	18	15	Paul Dean Holt	Lyle Stelter '64 Ford	74	100	Axle
17	13	73	Buddy Baker	Joan Petre '64 Ford	67	100	Fire
18	10	87	Buck Baker	Baker '66 Olds	56	100	Ignition
19	20	96	Neil Castles	Homer O'Dell '64 Ford	20	100	Engine
20	21	59	Tom Pistone	Pistone '64 Ford	14	100	Heating
21	12	0	Darel Dieringer	Reid Shaw '64 Ford	3	100	Heating

Time of Race: 1 hour, 25 minutes, 4 seconds
Average Speed: 70.533 mph
Pole Winner: Richard Petty - 76.923 mph
Lap Leaders: David Person 1-15, Junior Johnson 16-70, Pearson 71-250.
Cautions: 5 for 14 laps   Margin of Victory: 1-lap plus   Attendance: 10,000
*Relieved by Dick Hutcherson

ment once again to replace Curtis Turner in his own Ford for the 250-lapper on the .4-mile dirt track. Johnson started eighth, but it took him only 16 laps to take the lead. The crowd of 10,000 cheered approvingly as Johnson built up a healthy lead by lap 70.

At that point, Johnson bent the fender on a tire during some close quarter racing. He rolled down pit road with a flat tire, but a freakish occurrence kept him from getting into his pit stall.

Buddy Baker's Ford had caught on fire, burning the grassy pit area. A water truck had positioned itself to fight the blaze, blocking Johnson's path to his pit. By the time he got the tire changed, he was two laps behind.

Johnson climbed out in disgust and turned the driving chores over to Dick Hutcherson, who was just spectating before his impromptu assignment. Hutcherson was running fourth when he lost control in the fourth turn and slammed into the guard rail. The car flipped high in the air and came down on its roof.

It was the sixth race for the Johnson car since he broke out of a boycott by Ford -- and the fourth time it has been wrecked. Hutcherson was the fourth driver to take control of the car. Bobby Isaac, who started the year in the Johnson Ford but was fired, said, "They'll

be at least 10 drivers in and out of that car. I was just the first. There will be a whole parade of drivers for that car."

Richard Petty settled for second place in the 100-miler, a lap behind Pearson. Paul Lewis came in third, James Hylton was fourth and Hank Thomas fifth.

Pearson averaged 70.533 mph in his Cotton Owens Dodge.

Race No. 44

Johnson, Petty Falter; Pearson Wins Again At Richmond

RICHMOND, VA (Sept. 11) -- David Pearson drove his Dodge into the lead when mechanical failure dropped Richard Petty from the lead and went on to post his 15th win of the season in the Capital City 300

Grand National Race No. 44
300 Laps at Atlantic Rural Fairgrounds
Richmond, Va
"Capital City 300"
150 Miles on Half-mile Dirt Track
September 11, 1966

Fin	St	No.	Driver	Team / Car	Laps	Money	Status
1	1	6	David Pearson	Cotton Owens '66 Dodge	300	$2,350	Running
2	10	87	Buck Baker	Baker '66 Olds	295	1,600	Running
3	5	1	Paul Lewis	Lewis '65 Plymouth	295	1,250	Running
4	8	47	Curtis Turner	Toy Bolton '66 Chevrolet	292	875	Running
5	11	64	Elmo Langley	Langley-Woodfield '64 Ford	286	710	Running
6	25	95	Bill Seifert	Seifert '64 Ford	264	525	Running
7	14	34	Wendell Scott	Scott '65 Ford	264	400	Running
8	20	17	Bob Cooper	'66 Chevrolet	259	300	Running
9	16	92	Hank Thomas	W S Jenkins '64 Ford	242	250	Engine
10	4	48	James Hylton	Bud Hartje '65 Dodge	237	250	Running
11	22	50	Darrell Bryant	'64 Chevrolet	226	225	Spindle
12	3	42	Richard Petty	Petty Enterprises '66 Plym	220	225	Differen
13	19	20	Clyde Lynn	Lynn '64 Ford	188	225	Running
14	27	96	Jimmy Helms	Homer O'Dell '64 Ford	183	225	Engine
15	2	26	Junior Johnson	Johnson '66 Ford	176	200	Engine
16	6	19	J T Putney	Putney '66 Chevrolet	171	200	A Frame
17	24	97	Henley Gray	Gray '66 Ford	164	200	Crash
18	21	88	Neil Castles	Buck Baker '66 Chevrolet	134	175	Oil Pan
19	7	4	John Sears	L G DeWitt '64 Ford	127	175	Rear End
20	13	2	Bobby Allison	J D Bracken '65 Chevrolet	114	175	D Shaft
21	23	15	Paul Dean Holt	Lyle Stelter '64 Ford	87	175	Sway bar
22	9	16	Darel Dieringer	Bud Moore '64 Mercury	80	150	Crash
23	17	67	Buddy Arrington	Arrington '65 Dodge	67	150	Radiator
24	15	70	J D McDuffie	McDuffie '64 Ford	40	150	Engine
25	12	72	Bill Champion	Champion '64 Ford	27	150	Battery
26	18	63	Larry Manning	Bob Adams '65 Plymouth	19	150	Oil Press
27	26	83	Worth McMillion	Allen McMillion '65 Pontiac	12	150	Engine
28	28	58	Gene Hobby	Hobby '64 Dodge	7	---	Flagged
29	29	80	G T Nolan	Allen McMillion '64 Pontiac	6	---	Flagged

Time of Race: 2 hours, 23 minutes, 7 seconds
Average Speed: 62.886 mph
Pole Winner: David Pearson - 70.644 mph
Lap Leaders: David Pearson 1-87, Junior Johnson 88-118, Pearson 119-193, Richard Petty 194-220, Pearson 221-300.
Cautions: 5 for 29 laps.   Margin of Victory: 5-laps plus   Attendance: 10,000

at the Atlantic Rural Fairgrounds.

Pearson outdistanced runner-up Buck Baker by five laps to win $2,350. Paul Lewis was third, Curtis Turner came in fourth and Elmo Langley fifth.

Petty had taken the lead in the 194th lap and was holding a narrow advantage over Pearson when the differential failed in his Plymouth. Pearson took the lead for the final time on lap 221 and led the rest of the way.

Junior Johnson started second and led for 31 laps in the 150-miler. A blown engine sent Johnson to the showers on lap 176. It was the sixth time in seven outings since August that the Johnson Ford has failed to finish.

Turner, recently fired from the Johnson ride, went back to the lightly regarded Toy Bolton Chevrolet and ran a strong fourth.

Darel Dieringer was unhurt in a spectacular crash. His Mercury darted out of control in the 81st lap, clobbered the wooden board fence and flipped. The car, with its right front wheel torn off, landed upside down on the track surface.

Pearson averaged 62.886 mph for his fourth win in his last seven starts.

Race No. 45

Hutcherson Recovers From Johnson Jostle; Wins Joe Weatherly Memorial 150

HILLSBOROUGH, NC (Sept. 18) -- Dick Hutcherson survived a brush with Junior Johnson and roared to victory in the Joe Weatherly Memorial 150 at Orange Speedway. It was the second win of the season for the

Wendell Scott #34 kicks up dust at Hillsboro

Grand National Race No. 45
167 Laps at Orange Speedway
Hillsborough, NC
"Joe Weatherly Memorial 150"
150 Miles on .9-mile Dirt track
September 18, 1966

Fin	St	No.	Driver	Team / Car	Laps	Money	Status
1	1	29	Dick Hutcherson	Holman-Moody '66 Ford	167	$1,400	Running
2	5	6	David Pearson	Cotton Owens '65 Dodge	167	1,000	Running
3	4	1	Paul Lewis	Lewis '65 Plymouth	165	700	Running
4	3	48	James Hylton	Bud Hartje '65 Dodge	163	575	Running
5	6	4	John Sears	L G DeWitt '64 Ford	163	425	Running
6	7	64	Elmo Langley	Langley-Woodfield '64 Ford	154	325	Running
7	11	88	Neil Castles	Buck Baker '66 Olds	151	275	Running
8	8	34	Wendell Scott	Scott '65 Ford	146	225	Running
9	9	67	Buddy Arrington	Arrington '65 Dodge	144	200	Running
10	10	20	Clyde Lynn	Lynn '64 Ford	141	175	Running
11	14	97	Henley Gray	Gray '66 Ford	141	100	Running
12	23	92	Hank Thomas	W S Jenkins '64 Ford	141	100	Running
13	21	94	Don Biederman	Ron Stotten '64 Chevrolet	136	100	Running
14	12	60	Ernest Eury	'64 Chevrolet	135	100	Running
15	13	50	Mike Page	'64 Chevrolet	132	100	Running
16	17	63	Larry Manning	Bob Adams '65 Plymouth	109	100	Running
17	18	73	Buddy Baker	Joan Petre '64 Ford	57	100	Brakes
18	16	59	Tom Pistone	Pistone '64 Ford	52	100	Heating
19	15	95	Bill Seifert	Seifert '64 Ford	51	100	Differen
20	2	26	Junior Johnson	Johnson '66 Ford	28	100	A Frame
21	22	38	Wayne Smith	Smith '66 Chevrolet	16	100	Fuel line
22	19	15	Paul Dean Holt	Lyle Stelter '64 Ford	2	100	H Gasket
23	20	70	J D McDuffie	McDuffie '64 Ford	1	100	Oil Press

Time of Race: 1 hour, 39 minutes, 32 seconds
Average Speed 90.603 mph
Pole Winner" Dick Hutcherson - 95.716 mph
Lap Leaders: Dick Hutcherson 1-10, Junior Johnson 11-20, Hutcherson 21-167.
Cautions: None   Margin of Victory: 6 seconds   Attendance: 6,500

Keokuk, IA Ford driver.

David Pearson took second place, 6.0-seconds behind the winner. Paul Lewis came in third, James Hylton was fourth and John Sears fifth.

Johnson started second and took the lead in the 11th lap after a brush with leader Hutcherson. Johnson, who recently ended a retirement to drive his own car in light of "stupid driver mistakes" on the part of his other drivers, led through lap 20. Johnson limped to the pits

Ned Jarrett #11 and Dick Hutcherson in close battle at Hillsboro

with a sagging right front wheel.

Eight laps later, Johnson was out of the race with suspension problems. Curtis Turner, one of the drivers who had been fired by Johnson in 1966, was in the pit area watching the race. He told a bystander, "Go tell Junior he's fired. He put a dent in the door."

Hutcherson survived a scare in the late stages. He made a routine pit stop for fuel and his pit crew left the gas cap off. He was forced to make an additional stop to have another one secured in place. He got out just in front of Pearson and outran him the rest of the way.

"It's good to see Ford win again (it was Ford's first win in 16 races) and it's even better because I was driving it," beamed Hutch from victory lane. "I could increase my margin over David any time I needed to."

Hutcherson's 11th career win came at an average speed of 90.603 mph.

Race No. 46

Lorenzen Disqualified, Then Ruled Winner at Martinsville

MARTINSVILLE, VA (Sept. 25) -- Fred Lorenzen drove his Holman-Moody Ford to a five lap victory in the Old Dominion 500 at Martinsville Speedway, then watched as NASCAR officials disqualified his car for having an enlarged fuel tank. Three days later, NASCAR reversed their decision and Lorenzen pocketed the $4,350 first place check.

Fred Lorenzen takes checkered flag at Martinsville

It was simply another peculiar series of events in the controversial 1966 Grand National season.

Lorenzen outlasted Bobby Allison's speedy Chevrolet and crossed the finish line five laps ahead of Darel

Grand National Race No. 46
500 laps at Martinsville Speedway
Martinsville, VA
"Old Dominion 500"
250 Miles on Half-mile Paved Track
September 25, 1966

Fin	St	No.	Driver	Team / Car	Laps	Money	Status
1	2	28	Fred Lorenzen	Holman-Moody '66 Ford	500	$4,350	Running
2	21	16	Darel Dieringer	Bud Moore '66 Mercury	495	2,100	Running
3	17	2	Bobby Allison	J D Bracken '65 Chevrolet	494	1,425	Engine
4	10	29	Dick Hutcherson	Holman-Moody '66 Ford	492	775	Running
5	14	48	James Hylton	Bud Hartje '65 Dodge	490	725	Running
6	20	1	Paul Lewis	Lewis '65 Plymouth	490	700	Running
7	16	4	John Sears	L G DeWitt '64 Ford	482	575	Running
8	25	19	J T Putney	Putney '66 Chevrolet	479	525	Running
9	22	46	Roy Mayne	Tom Hunter '66 Chevrolet	475	500	Running
10	37	88	Neil Castles	Buck Baker '66 Chevrolet	471	450	Running
11	32	86	Buck Baker	Baker '64 Dodge	467	425	Running
12	7	21	Cale Yarborough	Wood Brothers '66 Ford	464	425	Differen
13	31	38	Wayne Smith	Smith '66 Chevrolet	458	390	Running
14	1	26	Junior Johnson	Johnson '66 Ford	453	580	Differen
15	24	97	Henley Gray	Gray '66 Ford	453	395	Running
16	39	95	Bill Seifert	Seifert '64 Ford	439	360	Running
17	38	35	Max Ledbetter	'65 Olds	425	350	Running
18	11	98	Sam McQuagg	Nichels Eng '66 Dodge	347	365	Steering
19	12	09	Friday Hassler	'65 Chevrolet	346	355	Axle
20	27	73	Buddy Baker	Joan Petre '64 Ford	330	345	Clutch
21	4	11	Ned Jarrett	Bondy Long '66 Ford	327	650	Clutch
22	33	70	J D McDuffie	McDuffie '64 Ford	296	300	Oil Press
23	3	43	Richard Petty	Petty Enterprises '66 Plym	263	375	Ignition
24	19	25	Jabe Thomas	Jeff Handy '64 Ford	260	325	Brakes
25	36	10	Paul Burnhaver	'64 Dodge	257	300	Ignition
26	28	17	Jimmy Trull	'66 Chevrolet	247	247	Differen
27	5	99	Paul Goldsmith	Nichels Eng '66 Plymouth	229	325	Brakes
28	34	20	Clyde Lynn	Lynn '64 Ford	204	275	Engine
29	35	61	Joel Davis	Toy Bolton '66 Chevrolet	179	275	Differen
30	30	92	Hank Thomas	W S Jenkins '64 Ford	170	275	Differen
31	15	47	Curtis Turner	Toy Bolton '66 Chevrolet	161	275	Oil Press
32	23	67	Buddy Arrington	Arrington '64 Dodge	134	285	Differen
33	13	64	Elmo Langley	Langley-Woodfield '64 Ford	128	275	Oil Pump
34	6	14	Jim Paschal	Friedkin Ent '66 Plymouth	112	275	D Shaft
35	9	6	David Pearson	Cotton Owens '66 Dodge	92	275	Oil Press
36	26	94	Don Biederman	Ron Stotten '64 Chevrolet	90	250	Engine
37	18	75	Earl Brooks	Gene Black '65 Ford	50	275	Crash
38	29	34	Wendell Scott	Scott '65 Ford	37	250	Oil Press
39	40	60	Ernest Eury	'64 Chevrolet	44	250	Ignition
40	8	49	G C Spencer	Spencer '65 Plymouth	8	275	Radiator

Time of Race: 3 hours, 36 minutes, 50 seconds
Average Speed: 69.177 mph
Pole Winner: Junior Johnson - 75.598 mph
Lap Leaders: Junior Johnson 1-50, Fred Lorenzen 51-109, Bobby Allison 110-182, Ned Jarrett 183-209, Allison 210-354, Johnson 355-387, Lorenzen 388-500.
Cautions: 4 for 26 laps   Margin of Victory: 5-laps plus   Attendance: 15,000

Dieringer's ailing Mercury. Allison, whose engine blew with six laps remaining, got credit for third place. Dick Hutcherson was fourth and James Hylton fifth.

As Lorenzen was going through the ceremonial interview in the press box following the 250-miler, a statement was delivered upstairs. Penciled on a piece of paper was the message: *"Statement from Norris Friel: We checked and found an illegal tank. We had a request to check the tank. Statement from Johnny Bruner: The car automatically disqualified itself according to the rules. Darel Dieringer is the winner. Lorenzen finished 40th."*

Lorenzen howled in protest, "It isn't fair that they disqualify me," he said. "I drove hard out there today. The tank was sealed in the car at Darlington by NASCAR officials and if my tank holds too much, the other cars do too.

"It's that new type of gas tank we had to start using at Darlington," Lorenzen said of the new Firestone Fuel Cell. "It has a rubber bladder, and maybe it's possible it stretched a little. They'd better check the first five cars. Their's might have stretched, too."

Co-owner Ralph Moody requested that NASCAR inspect the fuel cells of the first five finishers. "I wanted NASCAR to check the first five cars, but they told me they didn't have enough gas to do so," said Moody. "Where are the top NASCAR officials anyway? I guess they've gone home. This will turn out to be another typical NASCAR operation. I'm getting fed up with it all."

Lorenzen's fuel cell was measured at 23.1 gallons, 1.1 gallons more than rules permit. Despite Bruner's statement that Dieringer was the winner due to Lorenzen's disqualification, official word didn't come until three days later.

Lin Kuchler, Executive Manager of NASCAR, released a statement on September 28th, 72 hours after the race had ended. *"After a complete and thorough examination of all the evidence, the National Stock Car Racing Commission has reached the following conclusions: The fuel cell in Fred Lorenzen's car in the Martinsville race was a cell made by Firestone Tire and Rubber Co. according to the specifications outlined in the NASCAR rules governing fuel cells. The original dimensions set forth in the rules were maintained. There is no indication that the fuel cell had been tampered with in any manner. There was every indication Holman-Moody abided by the rules. Therefore, it is the decision of the National Stock Car Racing Commission to overrule the disqualification of Fred Lorenzen and declare him the winner."*

Lorenzen led twice for 172 laps and took the lead for the final time on lap 358. Allison's lightweight Chevrolet picked off the giants one-by-one and led for 218 laps. But his three pit stops averaged 55.6-seconds apiece and he lost a total of six laps. Allison made up four of them when his rivals pitted, and made up two more on the track. He was gaining on Lorenzen when the engine blew in the final laps of the race.

"He had a bomb out there," Lorenzen confessed. "If he hadn't had any trouble, he would have won the race."

Junior Johnson led twice for 83 laps, but his Ford was the victim of differential failure after 453 laps. Point leader David Pearson fell out early and wound up 35th. He still held a 2,580 point lead over rookie Hylton.

Lorenzen averaged 69.177 mph for his 24th career Grand National victory.

Race No. 47

Hutcherson's Patience Nets Wilkes 400 Victory

N.WILKESBORO, NC (Oct. 2) -- Dick Hutcherson, biding his time as two early leaders ran themselves into mechanical problems, motored to victory in the Wilkes 400 at North Wilkesboro Speedway. It was the third win of the year for Hutcherson and the Holman-Moody Ford team.

The 34 year-old Keokuk, IA dirt track master took the lead for the first time in the 307th lap when Fred Lorenzen blew the engine in his Ford. Hutcherson finished

Grand National Race No. 47
400 Laps at N.Wilkesboro Speedway
N.Wilkesboro, NC
"Wilkes 400"
250 Miles on .675-mile Paved Track
October 2, 1966

Fin	St	No.	Driver	Team / Car	Laps	Money	Status
1	4	29	Dick Hutcherson	Holman-Moody '66 Ford	400	$4,325	Running
2	11	6	David Pearson	Cotton Owens '66 Dodge	400	2,225	Running
3	7	1	Paul Lewis	Lewis '65 Plymouth	400	1,325	Running
4	35	14	Jim Paschal	Friedkin Ent '66 Plymouth	397	800	Running
5	15	48	James Hylton	Bud Hartje '65 Dodge	395	625	Running
6	17	47	Curtis Turner	Toy Bolton '66 Chevrolet	391	525	Running
7	25	46	Roy Mayne	Tom Hunter '66 Chevrolet	389	475	Running
8	14	4	John Sears	L G DeWitt '64 Ford	389	425	Running
9	13	09	Friday Hassler	'66 Chevrolet	387	375	Running
10	16	73	Buddy Baker	Joan Petre '64 Ford	385	325	Running
11	19	34	Wendell Scott	Scott '65 Ford	382	300	Running
12	21	59	Tom Pistone	Pistone '64 Ford	381	350	Engine
13	31	97	Henley Gray	Gray '66 Ford	375	275	Running
14	26	86	Neil Castles	Buck Baker '64 Dodge	375	250	Running
15	22	67	Buddy Arrington	Arrington '64 Dodge	371	275	Running
16	27	20	Clyde Lynn	Lynn '64 Ford	368	225	Running
17	24	75	Earl Brooks	Gene Black '65 Ford	467	225	Running
18	33	95	Bill Seifert	Gene Cline '64 Ford	361	225	Running
19	6	21	Cale Yarborough	Wood Brothers '66 Ford	355	225	Engine
20	34	60	Ernest Eury	'64 Chevrolet	354	225	Running
21	30	63	Larry Manning	Bob Adams '65 Plymouth	323	200	Running
22	32	35	Max Ledbetter	'65 Olds	312	200	Lug Bolts
23	3	28	Fred Lorenzen	Holman-Moody '66 Ford	307	725	Engine
24	5	16	Darel Dieringer	Bud Moore '66 Mercury	212	200	Crash
25	29	25	Jabe Thomas	Jeff Handy '64 Ford	210	200	Differen
26	2	43	Richard Petty	Petty Enterprises '66 Plym	186	275	Ignition
27	20	94	Don Biederman	Ron Stotten '64 Chevrolet	134	200	Differen
28	1	26	Junior Johnson	Johnson '66 Ford	129	425	Engine
29	8	64	Elmo Langley	Langley-Woodfield '64 Ford	111	200	H Gasket
30	10	2	Bobby Allison	J D Bracken '65 Chevrolet	92	200	Engine
31	18	87	Buck Baker	Baker '66 Olds	83	175	Clutch
32	12	19	J T Putney	Putney '66 Chevrolet	60	175	Differen
33	23	61	Joel Davis	Toy Bolton '66 Chevrolet	55	200	Trans
34	9	49	G C Spencer	Spencer '65 Plymouth	38	175	Engine
35	28	38	Wayne Smith	Smith '66 Chevrolet	29	175	D Shaft

Time of Race: 2 hours, 48 minutes, 31 seconds
Average Speed: 89.012 mph
Pole Winner: Junior Johnson - 103.069 mph
Lap Leaders: Junior Johnson 1-76, Fred Lorenzen 77-111, Johnson 112-128,
    Lorenzen 129-306, Dick Hutcherson 307-400.
Cautions: 5 for 52 laps   Margin of Victory: 12 seconds   Attendance: 15,000

12 seconds in front of runner-up David Pearson despite slacking off dramatically in the final 12 laps with overheating troubles. "I knew at one time I had a couple of laps on David and the rest of the guys," explained Hutcherson, "so I decided to slow down and try to finish."

Dick Hutcherson's Ford en route to Wilkes 400 triumph

Paul Lewis was sniffing Pearson's tailpipes and came across the finish line third. Jim Paschal came from 35th starting position to nail down fourth spot and James Hylton was fifth.

Junior Johnson started on the pole for the 37th time on a short track -- a NASCAR record. The Ronda, NC Ford driver led the first 76 laps before Lorenzen took the lead. Johnson went into the lead again on lap 112 and was leading in the 128th lap when his engine blew. It was the ninth time in the last 10 starts that the Johnson car had failed to finish.

Lorenzen led for 178 laps until he pitted with a blown engine. Hutcherson, who started fourth, breezed into the lead and held it to the finish.

Richard Petty started next to Johnson in the front row, but lasted only 186 laps before ignition failure put his Plymouth out of action.

Hutcherson's 12th career win came at an average speed of 89.012 mph.

Race No. 48

Yarbrough Stomps Big Field To Win National 500

CHARLOTTE, NC (Oct. 16) -- LeeRoy Yarbrough of Jacksonville, FL led 301 laps and easily disposed of the National 500 field, notching his first superspeedway victory at Charlotte Motor Speedway. The 28 year-old Dodge driver finished 18 seconds in front of Darel Dieringer to pocket the $17,455 first prize.

Yarbrough started 17th on the grid, but zipped into

seventh by the second lap. It was clearly evident that Yarbrough's purple Jon Thorne Dodge Charger was the class of the field. He took the lead for the first time on lap 19 and led the rest of the way with the exception of routine pit stops.

"I've always known a race car could perform this way, and that it would be possible to have the fastest car in the field and nothing go wrong," said Yarbrough. "But I've never experienced it. I've had the

Grand National Race No. 48
334 Laps at Charlotte Motor Speedway
Charlotte, NC
"National 500"
500 Miles on 1.5-mile Paved Track
October 16, 1966

Fin	St	No.	Driver	Team / Car	Laps	Money	Status
1	17	12	LeeRoy Yarbrough	Jon Thorne '66 Dodge	334	$17,455	Running
2	18	15	Darel Dieringer	Junior Johnson '66 Ford	334	7,670	Running
3	7	99	Paul Goldsmith	Nichels Eng '66 Plymouth	334	4,205	Running
4	2	26	Gordon Johncock	Junior Johnson '66 Ford	334	2,865	Running
5	8	71	Earl Balmer	K&K Insurance '66 Dodge	332	1,975	Running
6	11	42	Marvin Panch	Petty Enterprises '66 Plym	329	1,550	Running
7	19	1	Paul Lewis	Lewis '65 Plymouth	328	1,250	Running
8	20	48	James Hylton	Bud Hartje '65 Dodge	320	1,150	Crash
9	29	4	John Sears	L G DeWitt '64 Ford	319	1,075	Running
10	14	6	David Pearson	Cotton Owens '66 Dodge	314	1,025	Running
11	25	33	Jack Bowsher	Bowsher '66 Ford	313	1,025	Engine
12	34	19	J T Putney	Putney '66 Chevrolet	313	935	Running
13	35	86	Neil Castles	Buck Baker '64 Dodge	313	905	Running
14	22	5	Butch Hartman	Hartman '65 Dodge	307	875	Running
15	9	56	Jim Hurtubise	Norm Nelson '66 Plym	306	905	Crash
16	40	38	Wayne Smith	Smith '66 Chevrolet	305	825	Running
17	42	34	Wendell Scott	Scott '65 Ford	302	790	Running
18	43	75	Henley Gray	Gene Black '65 Ford	296	765	Running
19	41	51	George England	Tinker Faulkner '65 Chevy	293	745	Running
20	28	47	Stick Elliott	Toy Bolton '66 Chevrolet	290	735	Engine
21	37	30	Iggy Katona	'65 Dodge	286	715	Running
22	13	31	Don White	Nichels Eng '66 Dodge	272	715	Engine
23	44	20	Clyde Lynn	Lynn '64 Ford	265	685	Running
24	12	14	Jim Paschal	Friedkin Ent '66 Plymouth	262	710	Engine
25	1	28	Fred Lorenzen	Holman-Moody '66 ford	248	800	Engine
26	6	21	Cale Yarborough	Wood Brothers '66 Ford	207	750	W bearing
27	39	05	Donnie Allison	Robert Harper '65 Chevrolet	186	655	Engine
28	31	55	Tiny Lund	Lyle Stelter '64 Ford	161	720	Engine
29	32	46	Roy Mayne	Tom Hunter '66 Chevrolet	144	685	Steering
30	21	64	Elmo Langley	Langley-Woodfield '64 Ford	141	635	Engine
31	30	09	Friday Hassler	'66 Chevrolet	130	615	Engine
32	33	87	Buck Baker	Baker '66 Olds	124	630	Engine
33	24	79	Frank Warren	Harold Rhodes '64 Chevrolet	114	585	Engine
34	27	49	G C Spencer	Spencer '65 Plymouth	98	600	Radiator
35	5	3	Buddy Baker	Ray Fox '65 Dodge	97	600	Engine
36	3	13	Curtis Turner	Smokey Yunick '66 Chevrolet	93	635	Engine
37	26	11	Ned Jarrett	Bondy Long '66 Ford	73	1.095	Valve
38	4	43	Richard Petty	Petty Enterprises '66 Plym	48	580	Suspen
39	38	44	Larry Hess	Hess '64 Ford	41	550	Crash
40	16	98	Sam McQuagg	Nichels Eng '66 Dodge	35	620	Engine
41	36	7	Bobby Johns	Shorty Johns '66 Chevrolet	28	545	Oil leak
42	15	29	Dick Hutcherson	Holman-Moody '66 Ford	17	535	Crash
43	10	27	A J Foyt	Banjo Matthews '66 Ford	12	580	Engine
44	23	67	Buddy Arrington	Arrington '64 Dodge	7	525	Engine

Time of Race: 3 hours, 49 minutes, 55 seconds
Average Speed: 130.576 mph
Pole Winner: Fred Lorenzen - 150.533 mph
Fastest Qualifier: LeeRoy Yarbrough - 151.101 mph
Lap Leaders: Curtis Turner 1-9, Cale Yarborough 10-18, LeeRoy Yarbrough 19-48, Paul Goldsmith 49, Yarbrough 50-105, Gordon Johncock 106-111, Darel Dieringer 112-115, Yarbrough 116-160, Johncock 161-162, Yarbrough 163-201, Johncock 202, Yarbrough 203-302, Dieringer 303, Yarbrough 304-334.
Cautions: 6 for 46 Laps   Margin of Victory: 18 seconds   Attendance: 55,000

LeeRoy Yarbrough #12 ducks inside Fred Lorenzen in National 500. Yarbrough won his first superspeedway race

fastest car before, but always had trouble."

Dieringer, driving a Junior Johnson Ford, finished second after leading for five laps. Paul Goldsmith came in third and Gordon Johncock was fourth in another Johnson Ford. Fifth place went to Earl Balmer.

Johncock posed as a threat, leading for nine laps and always being in the shadow of the lead. The USAC

Trophy looks good on LeeRoy who won impressively

Indy Car driver lost valuable time on a pit stop. The motor died and it took five minutes before the Johnson crew could get the car rolling again. Although two laps down, Johncock charged like a mad man -- making up lost distance. His hard charging led one veteran pit road rail bird to comment, "Johncock is the squirreliest driver I've seen in a long time. But you've got to say one thing -- he runs the hell out of a race car."

Fred Lorenzen started on the pole, but never led. The Elmhurst, IL Ford pilot departed after the engine failed on lap 248. Curtis Turner, driving Smokey Yunick's

Chevrolet, led the first nine laps before yielding to Cale Yarborough. Turner lasted only 93 laps before he went behind pit wall with a blown engine.

Yarborough led for nine laps, but he was out after 207 laps with a bad wheel bearing. Richard Petty, who has been silent since his Dixie 400 victory at Atlanta in August, went only 48 laps when he pulled out of the race with suspension failure.

Donnie Allison, younger brother of Bobby Allison, drove in his first Grand National race and wound up 27th in a Ford.

Yarbrough's third career Grand National triumph came at an average speed of 130.576 mph. It was the first career win for car owner Jon Thorne of Valdosta, GA.

Race No. 49

Lorenzen Survives Protest; Wins American 500

ROCKINGHAM, NC (Oct. 30) -- The 1966 NAS-CAR Grand National season ended with a flurry of protests as Fred Lorenzen finished first in the American 500 at North Carolina Motor Speedway. It was the 12th career superspeedway win for the blond bachelor out of Elmhurst, IL, putting him one behind the late Fireball Roberts, who won 13 superspeedway events.

Lorenzen took the lead in the 201st lap and led the final 300 laps in the 500-miler on the one-mile paved oval. Don White, driving a Ray Nichels Dodge, came in second, four laps behind. Car owner Nichels protested the Lorenzen car. He handed $100 to NAS-CAR's Johnny Bruner. "Lorenzen got over 100 miles on a tank of gas," said Nichels. "We get around 80. Naturally, we're curious."

Nichels not only protested the gas tank, but the engine and weight of the car as well.

John Holman, Lorenzen car owner, jumped into the fracas, "If they're going to have an inspection," he growled, "then let's get five cars and do it the way it should be done." Holman forked over $400 to protest the next four cars. Oddly, three of them were factory backed Fords. "Here's another $100. Let's go get the #43 car (driven by Richard Petty). If some people are going to be ornery, then let's get everyone in the act."

Bruner turned down Holman's $100 for the Petty car. "Petty fell out of the race and he had already left the grounds," said Bruner. "If he had protested earlier, we'd have held Petty up."

Each of the first five cars were carefully examined and all declared 'legal'.

Ned Jarrett came in third, Cale Yarborough was fourth and Junior Johnson fifth.

Jarrett announced his retirement before the race and was honored in a pre-race ceremony. "When I quit, I'll still be champion," he said. "Sure, the 1966 winner will be determined in the final race, but I'm champion through that race and that's the way I want to go out."

Jarrett had one alarming occurrence in the race. While trying to unfasten his shoulder harness to lean out the window and wipe dirt off his windshield, he triggered the fire extinguisher in the cockpit of his car. Carbon monoxide filled the car and Jarrett had to make an unscheduled pit stop. "That stuff about gagged me," he said later. "It also embarrassed me."

Ned Jarrett, driving in his final race, triggered the fire extinguisher during American 500 at Rockingham

For White, a USAC driver with close ties to Nichels Engineering, it was only his 13th NASCAR start, and his third runner-up finish. He finished second in two straight races at Savannah, GA and Columbia, SC in 1955.

Petty and Lorenzen were the only leaders in the 500-mile marathon. Petty poked the nose of his Plymouth into the lead for 180 laps, but he departed after 320 laps with a blown engine.

"I don't know who would have won if Petty had lasted," admitted Lorenzen. "He could pull me coming off the turns, but I believe I was going a little further in the turns than he was. So I guess we were pretty equal."

Bobby Isaac made his return in a Cotton Owens Dodge, but retired after 293 laps with a vibration. David Pearson, principle driver on the Owens Dodge team, finished seventh and locked up the driving championship. Pearson finished 1,950 points in front of 1966 Rookie of the Year James Hylton

LeeRoy Yarbrough and Dick Hutcherson were

Grand National Race No. 49
500 Laps at North Carolina Motor Speedway
Rockingham, NC
"American 500"
500 Miles on 1-Mile Paved Track
October 30, 1966

Fin	St	No.	Driver	Team / Car	Laps	Money	Status
1	1	28	Fred Lorenzen	Holman-Moody '66 Ford	500	$14,550	Running
2	8	31	Don White	Nichels Eng '66 Dodge	496	7,350	Running
3	18	11	Ned Jarrett	Bondy Long '66 Ford	496	4,700	Running
4	12	21	Cale Yarborough	Wood Brothers '66 Ford	494	2,250	Running
5	25	47	Junior Johnson	Johnson '66 Ford	494	1,475	Running
6	7	3	Buddy Baker	Ray Fox '65 Dodge	492	2,700	Running
7	13	6	David Person	Cotton Owens '66 Dodge	488	1,100	Running
8	5	14	Jim Paschal	Friedkin Ent '66 Plymouth	485	2,050	Running
9	27	05	Donnie Allison	Robert Harper '65 Chevrolet	478	1,525	Running
10	20	48	James Hylton	Bud Hartje '65 Dodge	475	1,150	Running
11	31	19	J T Putney	Putney '66 Chevrolet	471	1,125	Running
12	16	49	G C Spencer	Spencer '65 Plymouth	468	940	Running
13	14	15	Darel Dieringer	Junior Johnson '66 Ford	464	905	Alternat
14	29	1	Buddy Arrington	Paul Lewis '65 Plymouth	463	805	Running
15	19	33	Jack Bowsher	Bowsher '66 Ford	462	685	Engine
16	33	79	Frank Warren	Harold Rhodes '64 Chevrolet	455	925	Running
17	37	87	Buck Baker	Baker '66 Olds	452	850	Running
18	38	97	Henley Gray	Gray '66 Ford	450	805	Running
19	22	64	Elmo Langley	Langley-Woodfield '64 Ford	449	725	Engine
20	34	46	Roy Mayne	Tom Hunter '66 Chevrolet	447	810	Running
21	35	44	Larry Hess	Hess '64 Ford	442	795	Engine
22	43	94	Don Biederman	Ron Stotten '64 Chevrolet	440	710	Running
23	32	09	Friday Hassler	'66 Chevrolet	438	825	Engine
24	30	38	Wayne Smith	Smith '66 Chevrolet	438	725	Running
25	42	45	Clyde Lynn	Bill Seifert '64 Ford	417	690	Running
26	36	70	J D McDuffie	McDuffie '64 Ford	402	755	Running
27	3	26	Gordon Johncock	Junior Johnson '66 Ford	375	605	Engine
28	2	43	Richard Petty	Petty Enterprises '66 Plym	320	650	Engine
29	15	42	Paul Lewis	Petty Enterprises '66 Plym	308	670	Engine
30	26	5	Bobby Isaac	Cotton Owens '65 Dodge	293	615	Vibration
31	11	98	Sam McQuagg	Nichels Eng '66 Dodge	270	585	Engine
32	9	71	Earl Balmer	K&K Insurance '65 Dodge	188	655	Oil Press
33	4	29	Dick Hutcherson	Holman-Moody '66 Ford	127	550	Crash
34	10	13	Curtis Turner	Smokey Yunick '66 Chevrolet	126	595	Engine
35	40	59	Wendell Scott	Tom Pistone '64 Ford	119	540	Engine
36	21	4	John Sears	L G DeWitt '64 Ford	110	535	Engine
37	6	99	Paul Goldsmith	Nichels Eng '66 Plymouth	80	530	Cont. arm
38	24	7	Bobby Johns	Shorty Johns '66 Chevrolet	78	525	Carb
39	17	12	LeeRoy Yarbrough	Jon Thorne '66 Dodge	67	595	Crash
40	39	86	Neil Castles	Buck Baker '64 Dodge	58	555	Distrib
41	28	2	Bobby Allison	J D Bracken '65 Chevrolet	57	510	Engine
42	44	53	Don Tilley	George Elliott '64 Ford	48	505	Steering
43	41	22	Tommy Bostick	'65 Chevrolet	42	500	Engine
44	23	55	Tiny Lund	Lyle Stelter '64 Ford	2	500	Clutch

Time of Race: 4 hours, 47 minutes, 30 seconds,
Average Speed: 104.348 mph
Pole Winner: Fred Lorenzen - 115.988 mph
Fastest Qualifier: LeeRoy Yarbrough - 116.054 mph
Lap Leaders: Fred Lorenzen 1, Richard Petty 2-6, Lorenzen 7-8, Petty 9-13, Lorenzen 14-25, Petty 26-70, Lorenzen 71-91, Petty 92-131, Lorenzen 132, Petty 133, Lorenzen 134-141, Petty 142-147, Lorenzen 148-151, Petty 152-164, Lorenzen 165-176, Petty 177-184, Lorenzen 185-196, Petty 197-205, Lorenzen 206-232, Petty 233-280, Lorenzen 281-500.
Cautions: 4 for 35 laps   Margin of Victory: 4-laps plus   Attendance: 35,000

eliminated by wrecks. Curtis Turner and Gordon Johncock were taken out by engine problems.

Junior Johnson competed in his final race. Following the event, he hung up his helmet for good.

Lorenzen averaged 104.348 mph for his 25th career win.

1966 NASCAR Season
Final Point Standings - Grand National Division

Rank	Driver	Points	Starts	Wins	Top 5	Top 10	Winnings
1	David Pearson	35,638	42	15	26	33	$78,193.60
2	James Hylton	33,688	41	0	20	32	38,722.10
3	Richard Petty	22,952	39	8	20	22	85,465.11
4	Henley Gray	22,468	46	0	4	18	21,900.96
5	Paul Goldsmith	22,078	21	3	11	11	54,608.53
6	Wendell Scott	21,702	45	0	3	17	23,051.62
7	John Sears	21,432	46	0	11	30	25,191.35
8	J.T. Putney	21,208	39	0	4	9	18,652.72
9	Neil Castles	20,446	41	0	7	17	19,034.09
10	Bobby Allison	19,910	34	3	10	15	23,419.09
11	Elmo Langley	19,116	47	2	12	20	22,454.69
12	Darel Dieringer	18,214	25	3	7	9	52,529.09
13	Ned Jarrett	17,616	21	0	5	8	23,254.09
14	Jim Paschal	16,404	18	2	6	10	30,984.09
15	Sam McQuagg	16,068	16	1	4	7	29,529.09
16	Paul Lewis	15,352	21	1	9	14	17,826.06
17	Marvin Panch	15,308	14	1	4	6	38,431.06
18	Cale Yarborough	15,188	14	0	3	3	24,076.06
19	G.C. Spencer	15,028	20	0	6	9	26,721.06
20	Clyde Lynn	14,856	41	0	10	15	13,221.06
21	Buck Baker	14,504	34	0	7	13	13,860
22	Buddy Baker	14,302	41	0	1	7	21,325
23	Fred Lorenzen	12,454	11	2	6	6	36,310
24	Curtis Turner	12,266	21	0	5	6	16,890
25	Roy Mayne	11,074	18	0	1	5	9,940
26	LeeRoy Yarbrough	10,528	9	1	2	4	23,925
27	J.D. McDuffie	9,572	36	0	1	9	8,545
28	Dick Hutcherson	9,392	14	3	8	9	22,985
29	Tiny Lund	9,332	31	1	5	10	11,880
30	Blackie Watt	8,518	20	0	0	9	7,000
31	Frank Warren	8,334	11	0	0	1	6,740
32	Buddy Arrington	7,636	20	0	0	3	8,510
33	Wayne Smith	7,442	23	0	0	1	9,835
34	Jimmy Helms	6,530	29	0	0	0	5,815
35	Stick Elliott	6,358	19	0	1	3	7,335
36	Earl Balmer	5,794	9	1	2	2	7,935
37	Tom Pistone	5,788	28	0	6	6	7,765
38	Johnny Jack Wynn	5,644	22	0	0	5	4,650
39	Larry Manning	4,964	12	0	1	1	3,920
40	Larry Hess	4,928	13	0	0	0	5,290
41	Roy Tyner	4,248	26	0	0	4	4,435
42	Hank Thomas	4,180	14	0	3	7	3,530
43	Bill Seifert	4,128	15	0	0	4	3,830
44	Bob Derrington	4,122	9	0	0	1	2,730
45	Joel Davis	4,066	20	0	1	3	4,685
46	Paul Connors	3,986	3	0	0	1	2,820
47	Jabe Thomas	3,820	13	0	0	0	3,580
48	Doug Cooper	3,808	20	0	3	4	5,185
49	Junior Johnson	3,750	7	0	1	1	3,610
50	Larry Frank	3,738	2	0	0	2	1,575

The 1967 Season

A Squabble, The Streak
And Richard Becomes The 'King'

Volume three of a four volume series . . Big Bucks and Boycotts   1965 - 1971

1967

The 1965 and 1966 NASCAR Grand National seasons were marred by manufacturers boycotts -- costly walkouts involving some of the sport's biggest names. The Chrysler boycott in 1965, which pulled Richard Petty, David Pearson, Bobby Isaac, Paul Goldsmith and others off the tour, was particularly damaging for NASCAR and the sport of stock car racing. The Ford withdrawl in 1966, taking Fred Lorenzen, Dick Hutcherson, Marvin Panch and Ned Jarrett out of action, had equally wasteful results.

The 1967 season got underway without the specter of another boycott. The Ford and Chrysler camp came to Daytona for Speedweeks with their guns fully loaded -- although Chrysler had said earlier that the parent company was going to cut back its aid to the NAS-CAR teams. With all the top guns on hand, the Daytona 500 drew 94,250 paying spectators -- an all-time record. Maybe the 1967 season would go on without a hitch.

Mario Andretti scored an upset triumph in the 500. Driving a Holman-Moody Ford, the USAC Indy Car star outdistanced Lorenzen to bag the $48,900 first prize. Andretti's feat gave Ford two 500-mile victories within a month. Parnelli Jones had won the Motor Trend 500 at Riverside in a Bill Stroppe Ford combed by the Wood Brothers.

Through the first nine races of the 1967 season, Plymouth and Dodge cars won six of them. Ford had won

only three events, but all of them were highly publicized affairs -- the Riverside race, the Daytona 500 and a Daytona qualifier. Chrysler, supposedly heavy favorites at Daytona, had dominated the Big D since 1964. But this time they were being left in the wake of the speedier and healthier Fords. Some of the Chrysler executives subscribed to the old adage that *"if we ain't winnin', then they must be cheatin'."* Things took an all too familiar twist just before the April 2nd Atlanta 500.

Two headline makers in 1967 - Fred Lorenzen and Richard Petty

From its offices in Detroit, Chrysler sent word that the company was disturbed with the pre-race inspection procedure by sanctioning NAS-CAR. They felt a number of components used by the Ford teams had not met the minimum production standards, and that the new 'templates' which measured the contour of the automobiles were not being strictly enforced.

"We will withdraw from the Atlanta 500 if NASCAR does not uphold its rules regarding engine eligibility, minimum production standards and cylinder heads," said Bob Rodger, Special Vehicles Manager of Chrysler six days before the Atlanta 500.

The controversy stemmed from Ford's use of a new intake manifold and cylinder head system. Rodger contended the new Ford parts were illegal because they did not meet the minimum production requirements -- that is 500 units manufactured and available through dealers and parts outlets.

Lin Kuchler, Executive Director of NASCAR, said the new Ford manifold and exhaust systems were simply an improvement over those formerly used, and they were generally available as required by the rules.

"Since the 427 c.i. engine has been standard Ford racing equipment for almost two years," Kuchler stated, "there is no question that the basic engine meets our rules. And since the new parts now are standard equipment to go with the already approved engine, there is no controversy as far as we're concerned."

Chrysler factory teams Ray Nichels, Cotton Owens and Nord Krauskopf filed entries for the Atlanta 500 on a contingency basis: They would not compete unless NASCAR ruled the Ford parts illegal.

Kuchler wired the three and said NASCAR did not accept conditional entries. "I told them they could show up ready to race, and we'd enforce the rules. And I also told them we consider that the new Ford parts meet our rules. If they don't intend to race, they should stay home."

Chrysler did not receive support from most of the teams they had contracted for 1967. "I have been told that it will be appreciated if we consider not running Atlanta," said Bill Ellis, car builder and crew chief for the Friedkin Enterprises Plymouth team. "But we can't take appreciation to the bank. We'll race at Atlanta."

Richard Petty, who sat out virtually all of the 1965 season, had no intention of being handcuffed to the sidelines again. "We race for a living," said Petty. "They are having a race in Atlanta. We'll be there. In fact, we'll take two cars. If we get a notion, we'll take three cars."

When the race teams were scheduled to arrive at Atlanta International Raceway, Chrysler's Rodger issued another statement, "Drivers of Dodge and Plymouth cars have decided to compete at Atlanta without protest," he said. "The decision was made when NASCAR officials agreed they will reconsider their position on earlier protests concerning NASCAR rules infractions and interpretations." No mention was made of the unwillingness of most Chrysler teams to join the parent company.

NASCAR President Bill France didn't entirely agree with the contents of Rodger's statement. "We agreed to discuss the rules," said France, "but not to reconsider our decision on the Ford engines. It is as legal as the Chrysler engine. We have our own interpretation and Chrysler has its interpretation."

Ford won another biggie in the Atlanta 500. Ford cars led for 317 of the 334 laps and Cale Yarborough beat Dick Hutcherson by over a lap.

Ford was cleaning up on the superspeedways, but they were nowhere to be found for the bulk of the Grand National schedule -- the short track 100 and 150-milers.

Richard Petty's Plymouth won 27 races in 1967

In the 17 Grand National events between the Atlanta 500 and Daytona's July 4 Firecracker 400, Richard Petty won 10 times. Plymouth cars won 14 of the 17 events -- and during that span, 12 of the contests ranged from 100 to 150 miles.

Junior Johnson, whose Ford won the 250-miler at North Wilkesboro with Darel Dieringer aboard, pleaded with Ford Motor Co. to give him and other teams the go ahead to race in the 100-milers. "You learn something new in racing every time you race," said Johnson. "Whether you're racing 500 miles on a superspeedway or two laps on a dirt track, you pick up little things. I know all the arguments against running all the races, but I don't agree with them. Every time we go up against Petty in a major race, we're up against the education he has gotten in several smaller races that we didn't attend. If we get permission from Ford to go racing against Petty in all the races, we'll stop his streak."

When the teams arrived trackside at Daytona for Firecracker 400 preparations, NASCAR greeted the competitors with a rigid inspection. Of the 50 cars which entered the race, only one passed inspection the first time -- the Bud Moore Mercury driven by LeeRoy Yarbrough. Most of the cars which failed inspection did not fit the templates. "We've got to get back to *stock* in stock car racing," said Bill France. "We warned the teams we were going to crack down for the Firecracker. Apparently, nobody believed us."

Petty was one who had to make more than one trip to the inspection area. The templates left far too many gaps when measuring the lines of the blue Plymouth. "Finally," said Petty, "I just gave the fender a good kick and it fell into place so it would fit the template."

Mario Rossi, mechanic for Jon Thorne's semi-independent team, thought NASCAR was walking along a pretty thin line. "We were about an eighth of an inch off and we had to go take a hammer and beat out a $20,000 race car," said Rossi.

Darel Dieringer said NASCAR's action was not a surprise. "There were some things going on," said Dieringer. "Everybody knew it and it was getting out of hand. Nobody is opposed to strict enforcement of the rules. As long as NASCAR keeps it up, everybody will be happy. When somebody sneaks away with something, it's going to start all over again."

Richard Petty confers with his crew chief and brother, Maurice

All of the top teams eventually made it through inspection at Daytona. Cale Yarborough racked up another big track victory, leading a 1-2-3-4 sweep for Fords.

After the Firecracker, however, the 1967 season belonged to Richard Petty.

The 30 year-old Petty had already won 11 races by the mid-point of the '67 campaign. Two of the triumphs were on superspeedways -- the Rebel 400 at Darlington and the Carolina 500 at Rockingham. Nine of the victories were on short tracks, including Martinsville, Weaverville and Richmond where he had ample competition.

Immediately after the Firecracker, Rapid Richard went on a rampage. He won a 300-miler on Trenton's 1.5-mile paved track. He finished second to Bobby Allison at Oxford, ME. Then he reeled off three wins in a row at Fonda, NY, Islip, NY and Bristol. Petty lost to Hutcherson in a close event at Maryville, TN, then won Nashville. A blown engine while leading put him out of the Dixie 500 at Atlanta; Hutcherson won again.

Then the lights went out for everyone but the Level Cross, NC gang. On August 12, 1967 at Bowman Gray Stadium in Winston-Salem, NC, Petty began a winning streak which borders on the unbelievable. For two months, Petty was unbeatable. Undefeated. Won 10 races in a row. A King of stock car racing was rising to the top.

And as his star beamed brighter, so did that of NASCAR Grand National stock car racing. "I know of no other driver in NASCAR history who has brought more recognition to the sport," said Bill France. "In bringing the spotlight into focus on the Petty team, he is also bringing added recognition to NASCAR. They have worked many years to achieve success. I'm proud

he is setting his records as a member of NASCAR."

"We're not doing anything different from what we did last year," Petty said modestly. "We've just been running good and getting a lot of breaks. It's essential to winning, no matter what kind of competition you're against. We've been prepared to win like we are this year ever since I can remember. But we could never get the breaks. This year we are.

"Most of the credit for our success should go to Maurice (his brother), Dale Inman, Smoky McCloud, Tom Cox and Alex Yoder," continued Petty. "Oh yes, don't forget about the Old Man (Lee Petty). He still has a lot to do with this operation."

Petty said his success was the product of good, solid teamwork. "We've got a durn good mechanical crew," said Petty. "We nearly always go into a race with the fastest car, or one that is competitive. If the car holds up, then I haven't done my job properly if I don't win. When the equipment is equal to the competition and it lasts, you can count on winning or coming close. Either that or the driver is not doing his job."

As the Petty victories were mounting up, the Ford camp became restless. Car owner Banjo Matthews was assigned to find a 'diamond in the rough' -- a hungry and aggressive youngster. "My objective is to find a young fellow who has ability, personality, good habits; a person who will be a credit to racing with whom I can work," said Matthews. "We need someone who has a desire to get into Grand National racing, but has never had the opportunity."

Bosco Lowe was picked to drive Banjo Matthews Ford in a few short track races

Ford, the acknowledged leader in uncovering raw, natural talent, needed to find another Fred Lorenzen. On April 24, 1967, Lorenzen announced his retirement from stock car racing. Holman-Moody had withdrawn Lorenzen's entry at North Wilkesboro and Martinsville in the spring when he was unable to compete due to stomach ulcers. "I want to go out while I'm on top," Lorenzen said in his farewell speech. "I've won everything that you can win and there's no way to go but down."

Jacques H. Passino, Special Vehicles Manager for

Ford, praised Lorenzen: "No man since Barney Old-field has contributed more to the performance image of Ford products than Fred Lorenzen. Over the years, Freddy has shown himself to be a serious dedicated professional who chooses his races carefully, leaves nothing to chance and gives an all-out effort each time."

Ford had called Lorenzen back in the winter of 1960 when he was down to his last penny. They offered him a seat in the primary Holman-Moody car -- and the rest became history. He became an instant success.

Now, Ford was looking for another 'diamond in the rough'. Bosco Lowe and Swede Savage were saddled in factory backed Fords at Hickory on September 8.

Lowe, 24-year old Sportsman driver, started 10th in the Matthews Ford and finished seventh --17 laps behind winner Petty. Savage, 21, who had been toying with motorcycles in California, drove a Holman-Moody Ford. He started eighth, but blew his engine on lap 226. The Ford effort had come up short as the Petty beat went on.

Later that month, the Ford big-wheels gathered in Dearborn. Topic of discussion was how to stop Petty's winning streak. From the stormy meeting came word that Darel Dieringer had been fired from the Junior Johnson Ford. The reason: "He's not pushing the button."

Dieringer had driven Johnson's Ford in 16 Grand National events. He won once, finished second three times and third three times. Six times he was taken out with engine failure, including the last three he drove. "If I'm not pushing the button," said Dieringer, "what does that say about their engines that have been blowing up?"

LeeRoy Yarbrough was hired to replace Dieringer at the Wilkes 400 at North Wilkesboro Speedway on October 1.

Jacques Passino and nine other top Ford executives were on hand at North Wilkesboro to keep an eye on the Ford effort -- and the fleet Petty. Reporter Bob Moore of *the Charlotte Observer* wrote, "Ten closely-knit gentlemen have thrown the second largest automobile company into a state of confusion. The company has pushed the button, lettered P-A-N-I-C."

Early in the race, David Pearson, Lorenzen's replacement in the primary Holman-Moody car, lost an engine on lap 17. Lorenzen climbed down from Johnson's rig and spoke privately with Pearson, who was then led down to the Johnson pits. Lorenzen felt that Johnson should wave Yarbrough in the pits and replace him with Pearson. After a brief conference, Pearson headed back to the Holman-Moody pits. And Yarbrough stayed in the Johnson car. He brought it home third, behind Petty and Dick Hutcherson.

"I saw Ford's big boss standing on top of Junior Johnson's truck," said Petty. "I knew those Ford drivers were going to be showing what they could do. I

laid back in the early going. It was awfully hectic up there in the lead pack. When it opened up, I went."

Petty led for 256 of the 400 laps and won going away. It was Petty's 10th straight win and his 27th of the year.

The National 500 at Charlotte Motor Speedway was the next event on the 1967 slate. Ford wasn't giving up -- and there were only three races left in the year. A total of nine factory backed Fords came to Charlotte in an effort to stop the Petty Plymouth. On Thursday, the Johnson Ford with LeeRoy Yarbrough at the wheel, took itself out of the 500. During a shake-down session, the fire extinguisher went off in the car. Blinded by the carbon monoxide, Yarbrough crashed heavily. "The thing exploded," said LeeRoy. "I couldn't see a thing. The windows became fogged and I rolled one down hoping I could see something. But with my safety belt on, I couldn't get my head out the window and I didn't have any idea where I was. I tried to steer it to the outside wall to get an idea where I was."

Yarbrough's heavy lick left the engine, radiator the frame and other parts scattered all over the banking. Yarbrough was a spectator for the race. NASCAR rules did not allow a back-up car to be brought to the track.

The week had gotten off to a shaky start. And for Ford, it went downhill from there.

Whitey Gerkin, one of the outsiders Ford had brought to Charlotte, crashed his car in the second lap. Gordon Johncock, driving Bud Moore's Mercury, wrecked in the 28th lap.

Mario Andretti, Jack Bowsher and David Pearson were wiped out in a big collision on lap 192. A.J. Foyt, who replaced Bosco Lowe in Banjo Matthews' car, lost his engine on lap 212. Donnie Allison blew his engine on lap 284, and Cale Yarborough cooked his engine with 33 laps to go. Dick Hutcherson was the only industry-supported Ford driver to survive the race -- and he finished third.

Ford failed once again to ring the victory bell. Petty didn't win either, dropping several laps off the pace because of an early wreck. He parked the car later with a blown engine.

Buddy Baker won the race in a Dodge. It was his first Grand National victory.

The third annual American 500 was scheduled October 29 at Rockingham. Ford brought in Jimmy Clark, the Formula 1 maestro from Scotland, and 10 other factory drivers.

Latest addition to the Ford camp was a unit headed by retired Fred Lorenzen. During all the in-house bickering at Ford's headquarters, Lorenzen had gotten into the act. He had certain ideas, and he aired them freely. Ford didn't bite. They felt his obstinate ideas were insufficient to produce favorable results.

Lorenzen persistently nagged Ford enough so that a one line conversation went something like this: "If you think you can do better, take a car to Rockingham and do it."

Ten days before the American 500, Lorenzen went to work -- rounding up a car, crew and driver. He borrowed a Ford from Holman-Moody -- a car that Mario Andretti had used as a back-up. He got a 396 cubic inch engine from the Charlotte-based shops, obtained the services of J.C. "Jake" Elder, and then telephoned Bobby Allison. "I've had my eye on Bobby for some time," said Lorenzen. "He runs so smooth and he has experience. I wanted him because I thought he could get the job done. I knew he would be my choice for driver -- if I could get him."

Allison had been struggling for most of 1967. He won three races in a lightly regarded Chevrolet in 1966, which earned him a ride in Bud Moore's Mercury at the start of the 1967 season. Moore and Allison enjoyed only mediocre success. When David Pearson left Cotton Owens' Dodge team to fill the vacancy on the Holman-Moody team when Lorenzen retired, Allison hooked up with Owens. It wasn't long before he won a 100-miler at Birmingham, AL. It would be Owens' last win of the year.

During the Firecracker 400 at Daytona, in which Allison finished seventh, he was criticized for what some observers felt was a conservative driving style. "I have always raced as hard as my equipment would permit," countered Allison. "I was insulted when some people hinted that I wasn't driving all out in the Firecracker 400. I've always raced to win and I always will as long as I stay in this business."

The annual Northern tour followed Daytona. Owens had no intentions of dragging his car up the east coast when he wasn't involved in the point battle. Allison wanted to race, so he asked permission from Owens to take his J.D. Bracken-owned Chevelle up north. Owens said it was all right with him.

Allison peeled off a victory at Oxford,

Richard Petty became "The King" in 1967

ME on July 11. When Allison returned to Hueytown, he had a message waiting on his desk. Owens had phoned that Chrysler executives had spoken with him

and were upset at Allison winning a race in a Chevrolet. Allison was fired for driving in -- and winning -- a Grand National race in which his Dodge wasn't entered.

Bobby Allison became an instant hero late in the 1967 season

When Lorenzen called, Allison was itching to get back into another front line car. He had some personal scores to settle. More importantly, he just wanted to race.

Fords qualified 1-2-3-4 for the American 500. Pearson was on the pole and Bowsher was second. Allison put the #11 Lorenzen car into third place and Cale Yarborough was fourth.

After Allison turned in the quick qualifying time, Lorenzen told members of the media, "You can color this car gone."

Allison felt the car was capable of winning right off the trailer. From the first practice lap in the car," said Allison, "I felt this was a car I could win with. I had confidence in the car and complete confidence in Lorenzen's ability to run the crew. He knows what he's doing. Those victories he took as a driver prove that beyond doubt."

Allison led the American 500 on six occasions for a total of 164 laps. He finished a lap ahead of runner-up Pearson. Petty was taken out in a pit road accident with Pearson before the half-way point.

Lorenzen had called the shots -- all of them -- from the pits. "He directed Allison on the track much like a TV director handles the start of his show," said Chris Economaki. "He wrote a long list of orders for Allison to follow, which he did."

Lorenzen told Allison to *"Slow Down"* late in the race. Allison slackened his pace from 112 mph to 108. *"Slow Down Some More"* read the next pit board from Lorenzen. Allison slowed down to 104 mph and crossed under the checkered flag with both hands clasped above his head -- off of the steering wheel.

Joining the internationally acclaimed Jimmy Clark was Jochen Rindt, who was listed as Clark's designated relief driver. Clark's engine blew on lap 149 -- he was five laps behind at the time -- and Rindt never got a chance to get behind the wheel.

Italian Grand Prix driver Ludovico Scarfiotti had been assigned to drive a back-up Friedkin Enterprises Plymouth in the American 500. But the experienced road racer was having difficulty with the big stock cars on the high banks of North Carolina Motor Speedway.

Scarfiotti complained to NASCAR President Bill France about the car. France had a hand in the negotiations to get Scarfiotti to Rockingham. He had expected a competitive car for his debut in NASCAR Grand National racing. He was able to get the car up to only about 110 mph. France donned a helmet and climbed in the car. Within a few laps, France was turning laps in the upper 109 mph bracket. His impromptu performance ended Scarfiotti's complaints.

Scarfiotti never drove in the race. Crew chief Bill Ellis was visibly upset about having to make four trips to the inspection area before the car was finally approved. He said after all the added work he did to the car, it wouldn't be a safe race car. Ellis withdrew the car.

Ford had finally broken its drought. Lorenzen and Allison got the green light to race in the final event of the 1967 season.

The Western North Carolina 500 at Asheville-Weaverville Speedway was the scene of perhaps the most exciting race of the year. Allison's Ford and Petty's Plymouth, near equal in speed, fought each over the half-mile battleground. On lap 479 of the 500-lapper, Petty dove under Allison in the first turn. The King emerged with the lead as Allison wrestled for control. Allison caught back up on lap 494 and put a 'slide job' on Petty as he took the lead for good.

"Those 500 laps took five years off my life," said a quivering Lorenzen afterwards. "But as far as I'm concerned, Bobby Allison has a life time job."

The 1967 season was uninterrupted by another boycott -- although it was a real possibility in the spring. As the season progressed, Richard Petty became a King. And by the end of the year, Bobby Allison had arrived on the NASCAR front. The seeds for one of the most thrilling long-term rivalries had been planted.

Race No. 1
Petty Passes Hutcherson; Pockets Prize in Augusta 300

AUGUSTA, GA (Nov. 13, 1966) -- Richard Petty got around Dick Hutcherson in the 78th lap and hustled to victory in the Augusta 300 at Augusta Raceway. It was the first event of the 1967 NASCAR Grand National season.

Paul Lewis, privateer who has been crowding the factory backed drivers for several months, finished second, three laps behind. David Pearson came in third, James Hylton was fourth and Tiny Lund came in fifth.

"That's as good a way to start the season as I know," said the 29 year-old Petty.

Elmo Langley finished eighth after a scare in practice. Langley sped into the third turn in a shake-down session, slipped out of the groove and banged into the guard rail. Langley's Ford clipped a telephone pole, rode the top of the rail and somehow came back down onto the speedway surface. While he was grinding the undercarriage on the guard rail, the frightened driver got a look at the 100-foot drop outside the third turn. "I wasn't sure which way I was going," said the Landover, MD Ford driver. "I've never seen anything that looked so far down."

Rising star Friday Hassler qualified 4th at Augusta but blew engine early

Friday Hassler qualified his Chevrolet in fourth spot. The Chattanooga, TN driver went out in spectacular fashion when his engine blew, setting the rear portion of the car on fire. Hassler jumped out and ran to safety.

LeeRoy Yarbrough crashed his Chevrolet in the 185th lap without injury.

Petty's 49th career win came at an average speed of 71.809 mph

Race No. 2
Parnelli Wins at Riverside; Billy Foster Killed

RIVERSIDE, CA (Jan 29) -- Parnelli Jones won the rain-delayed Motor Trend 500 at Riverside International Raceway, ending Dan Gurney's four race win streak. It

Grand National Race No. 1
300 Laps at Augusta Raceway
Augusta, GA
"Augusta 300"
150 Miles on Half-mile Paved Track
November 13, 1966

Fin	St	No.	Driver	Team / Car	Laps	Money	Status
1	3	43	Richard Petty	Petty Enterprises '66 Plym	300	$1,735	Running
2	6	1	Paul Lewis	Lewis '65 Plymouth	297	1,170	Running
3	2	6	David Pearson	Cotton Owens '66 Dodge	297	1,050	Running
4	10	48	James Hylton	Bud Hartje '65 Dodge	296	645	Running
5	11	55	Tiny Lund	Lyle Stelter '64 Ford	289	605	Running
6	7	59	Tom Pistone	Pistone '64 Ford	278	345	Running
7	22	75	Earl Brooks	Gene Black '66 Ford	276	275	Running
8	13	64	Elmo Langley	Langley-Woodfield '64 Ford	276	375	Running
9	18	73	Curly Mills	Joan Petre '64 Ford	274	230	Running
10	19	25	Jabe Thomas	Jeff Handy '64 Ford	269	200	Running
11	20	34	Wendell Scott	Scott '65 Ford	269	125	Running
12	21	94	Don Biederman	Ron Stotten '64 Chevrolet	266	100	Running
13	17	97	Henley Gray	Gray '66 Ford	246	140	Engine
14	8	2	Bobby Allison	J D Bracken '65 Chevrolet	241	120	Running
15	5	14	Jim Paschal	Friedkin Ent '66 Plymouth	151	125	Oil Pan
16	9	4	John Sears	L G DeWitt '64 Ford	146	120	Engine
17	1	29	Dick Hutcherson	Holman-Moody '66 Ford	142	175	Engine
18	16	70	J D McDuffie	McDuffie '64 Ford	137	150	Engine
19	23	61	Joel Davis	Toy Bolton '66 Chevrolet	129	100	Differen
20	14	33	LeeRoy Yarbrough	'66 Chevrolet	59	185	Crash
21	12	19	J T Putney	Putney '66 Chevrolet	55	220	Distrib
22	15	87	Neil Castles	Buck Baker '66 Olds	47	165	Engine
23	25	9	Roy Tyner	Truett Rodgers '66 Chevrolet	19	100	Engine
24	24	45	Buster Sexton	Bill Seifert '64 Ford	15	100	Ball Jt.
25	4	39	Friday Hassler	Red Sharp '66 Chevrolet	7	25	Engine

Time of Race: 2 hours, 5 minutes, 20 seconds
Average Speed: 71.809 mph
Pole Winner: Dick Hutcherson - 84.112 mph
Lap Leaders: Dick Hutcherson 1-77, Richard Petty 78-300.
Cautions: 2 for ___ laps   Margin of Victory: 3-laps plus   Attendance: 2,000

was the first Grand National win for the 33 year-old Torrence, CA driver since May 30, 1959 when he won on a dirt track event in Los Angeles.

Jones passed Gurney in the 86th lap and led the last 100 laps on the 2.7-mile road course. Gurney was in hot pursuit of leader Jones when he was penalized one lap for passing the pace car during a caution flag. The Costa Mesa driver fell out on lap 143 with a blown engine.

Jones, wheeling the Bill Stroppe Mercury serviced by the Wood Brothers, finished two laps and 25 seconds in front of runner-up Paul Goldsmith's Plymouth. Norm Nelson was third, Don White fourth and James Hylton fifth.

Billy Foster, USAC driver out of Victoria, B.C., Canada, was killed instantly in a practice session on Friday, January 20. His Rudy Hoerr-owned Dodge smashed hard into the turn nine wall after brake failure. Dr. Irving Omphroy, Raceway physician, said the 1965 USAC Rookie of the Year "died upon impact with the wall. As far as I can tell, he died instantly." Foster became the 15th man to die in a NASCAR Grand National car.

Jones averaged 91.080 mph in the five and a half

hour endurance contest. "This race was the hardest on equipment of any I've driven," said Jones. Only 12 cars finished the race.

Pole winner Dick Hutcherson crashed his Bondy Long Ford into a spinning Frank Burnett in the 14th lap Hutcherson was sidelined by the crash; Burnett continued only to fall out later with a blown engine.

Fred Lorenzen was leading the race on January 22 when rain began falling in the California desert. The red flag came out and Lorenzen's left front tire went flat. When the race was resumed seven days later, Lo-

renzen got the tire changed under caution and got back into the race. He put his Ford solidly into contention but went out on lap 141 with engine failure.

LeeRoy Yarbrough flipped his Jon Thorne Dodge several times in the 38th lap. He was not hurt.

Race No. 3

LeeRoy Staves Off A.J. In 100-Mile Thriller

DAYTONA BEACH, FL (Feb. 24) -- LeeRoy Yarbrough drove his Jon Thorne Dodge around A.J. Foyt with five laps to go and held on for a one car length victory in the first 100-mile Grand National qualifier at Daytona International Speedway. It was the fourth career win for Yarbrough and the second for 21 year-old car owner Thorne.

Grand National Race No. 2
185 Laps at Riverside Int'l Raceway
Riverside, CA
"Motor Trend 500"
500 Miles on 2.7-mile Road Course
January 22 & 29, 1967

Fin	St	No.	Driver	Team / Car	Laps	Money	Status
1	6	115	Parnelli Jones	Bill Stroppe '67 Ford	185	$18,720	Running
2	11	99	Paul Goldsmith	Nichels Eng '66 Plymouth	183	8,600	Running
3	15	11	Norm Nelson	Nelson '67 Plymouth	183	5,250	Running
4	12	31	Don White	Nichels Eng '66 Dodge	183	3,325	Running
5	17	48	James Hylton	Bud Hartje '65 Dodge	178	2,175	Running
6	29	18	Bruce Worrell	Bob Bristol '64 Mercury	174	1,650	Running
7	21	451	Scotty Cain	Bill Clinton '66 Ford	171	1,400	Running
8	2	6	David Pearson	Cotton Owens '67 Dodge	170	1,950	Running
9	16	114	Mario Andretti	Holman-Moody '67 Ford	164	1,000	Engine
10	41	78	Charles Prickett	Don Dostinich '66 Chevrolet	162	1,000	Running
11	32	8	Jerry Oliver	'65 Chevrolet	160	800	Running
12	39	80	Bo Reeder	'64 Ford	159	700	Running
13	27	24	Jack Harden	Betty Lilly '66 Ford	157	675	Running
14	3	16	Dan Gurney	Bill Stroppe '67 Mercury	143	990	Engine
15	5	28	Fred Lorenzen	Holman-Moody '67 Ford	141	735	Engine
16	36	94	Don Biederman	Ron Stotten '64 Chevrolet	133	630	Wheel
17	44	55	Don Noel	Noel '67 Ford	131	625	Spun
18	22	145	John Martin	'65 Plymouth	110	620	Engine
19	13	14	Jim Paschal	Friedkin Ent '67 Plymouth	106	625	Clutch
20	31	88	Clyde Prickett	Dan Dostinich '66 Chevrolet	104	610	Distrib
21	4	43	Richard Petty	Petty Enterprises '66 Plym	103	680	Radiator
22	8	26	Lloyd Ruby	Junior Johnson '67 Ford	96	565	Engine
23	38	61	Jim Cook	Cos Cancilla '65 Olds	92	530	Engine
24	20	2	Bobby Allison	J D Bracken '66 Chevrolet	92	500	Trans
25	23	7	Jack McCoy	Charles Bell '66 Dodge	88	575	Differen
26	7	27	A J Foyt	Banjo Matthews '67 Ford	87	555	Engine
27	19	97	Henley Gray	Gray '66 Ford	87	580	Engine
28	9	04	Jerry Grant	Friedkin Ent '67 Plymouth	74	520	Radiator
29	24	19	J T Putney	Putney '66 Chevrolet	70	525	Crash
30	42	143	Frank Burnett	Burnett '65 Plymouth	60	500	Engine
31	34	3	Joe Clark	'65 Plymouth	52	500	Engine
32	35	63	Walt Price	'65 Buick	51	500	Engine
33	43	79	Randy Dodd	'65 Chevrolet	47	500	Differen
34	10	12	LeeRoy Yarbrough	Jon Thorne '66 Dodge	38	650	Crash
35	33	4	Cliff Garner	J R VanCurren '64 Mercury	25	500	Engine
36	30	96	Ray Elder	Elder '65 Dodge	23	500	D Shaft
37	14	15	Curtis Turner	Bill Stroppe '67 Mercury	15	550	Crash
38	25	1	Marvin Porter	Carl Dane '67 Ford	15	500	Sway bar
39	1	29	Dick Hutcherson	Bondy Long '67 Ford	14	1,000	Crash
40	28	23	Johnny Steele	'64 Mercury	13	500	Engine
41	38	9	Roy Tyner	Truett Rodgers '66 Chevrolet	9	500	Clutch
42	40	03	Tom Roa	'65 Pontiac	9	500	Clutch
43	18	85	Gordon Johncock	R L Diestler '67 Plymouth	1	600	Trans
44	26	45	Carl Cardey	'65 Ford	0	500	Engine

Time of Race: 5 hours, 29 minutes, 3 seconds
Average Speed: 91.080 mph
Pole Winner: Dick Hutcherson - 106.951 mph
Lap Leaders: David Pearson 1-3, Parnelli Jones 4-18, Dan Gurney 19-24, Jones 25-35, A J Foyt 36-40, Paul Goldsmith 41-46, Fred Lorenzen 47-50, Richard Petty 51-55, Gurney 56-85, Jones 86-185.
Cautions: Margin of Victory: 2 laps and 25 seconds.   Attendance:

Grand National Race No. 3
40 Laps at Daytona Int'l Speedway
Daytona Beach, FL
100 Miles on 2.5-mile Paved Track
February 24, 1967

Fin	St	No	Driver	Team / Car	Laps	Money	Status
1	3	12	LeeRoy Yarbrough	Jon Thorne '67 Dodge	40	$1,350	Running
2	4	27	A J Foyt	Banko Matthews '67 Ford	40	650	Running
3	7	99	Paul Goldsmith	Nichels Eng '67 Plymouth	40	400	Running
4	6	3	Buddy Baker	Ray Fox '67 Dodge	40	400	Running
5	11	42	Tiny Lund	Petty Enterprises '66 Plym	39	300	Running
6	16	14	Jim Paschal	Friedkin Ent '67 Plymouth	39	250	Running
7	2	6	David Pearson	Cotton Owens '67 Dodge	39	425	Running
8	10	37	Charlie Glotzbach	K&K Insurance '65 Dodge	39	200	Running
9	9	48	James Hylton	Bud Hartje '65 Dodge	39	150	Running
10	18	68	Gary Bettenhausen	Harry Ranier '66 Ford	38	150	Running
11	5	71	Bobby Isaac	K&K Insurance '67 Dodge	38	150	Running
12	15	0	Ramo Stott	Stott '66 Plymouth	37	125	Running
13	19	04	Coo Coo Marlin	Charlie Hughes '65 Chevy	37	125	Running
14	20	41	Dorus Wisecraver	Ted Sidwell '66 Ford	36	100	Running
15	13	16	Bobby Allison	Bud Moore '67 Mercury	35	100	Running
16	27	64	Elmo Langley	Langley-Woodfield '66 Ford	35	100	Running
17	26	79	Frank Warren	Harold Rhodes '66 Chevrolet	35	100	Running
18	8	7	Bobby Johns	Shorty Johns '66 Chevrolet	35	100	Running
19	24	62	Ken Spikes	Harold Collins '67 Pontiac	35	100	Running
20	12	05	Donnie Allison	Robert Harper '66 Chevrolet	29	100	Crash
21	17	49	G C Spencer	Spencer '67 Plymouth	28	100	Crash
22	25	38	Wayne Smith	Smith '66 Chevrolet	24	100	Rock arm
23	21	09	Don Biederman	'66 Chevrolet	19	100	Flagged
24	28	80	Bob Pickell	Cozze Brothers '66 Chev	13	100	Rock arm
25	23	75	Earl Brooks	Gene Black '66 Ford	12	100	Engine
26	22	24	Jack Harden	Betty Lilly '66 Ford	6	100	Engine
27	14	10	Jim Hurtubise	Norm Nelson '67 Plymouth	4	100	W'shield
28	1	13	Curtis Turner	Yunick-Rich '66 Chevrolet	1	100	Quit

Time of Race: 36 minutes, 36 seconds
Average Speed: 163.934 mph
Pole Winner: Curtis Turner - 180.831 mph
Lap Leaders: A J Foyt 1, David Pearson 2-4, Foyt 5-6, Pearson 7-11, LeeRoy Yarbrough 12-14, Pearson 15, Foyt 16-21, Paul Goldsmith 22, Foyt 23-24, Goldsmith 25, Foyt 26-31, Yarbrough 32-33, Foyt 34-35, Yarbrough 36-40.
Cautions: 1   Margin of Victory: 1 car length   Attendance: 20,000

Grand National Race No. 4
40 Laps at Daytona Int'l Speedway
Daytona Beach, FL
100-Miles on 2.5 mile Paved Track
February 24, 1967

Fin	St	No.	Driver	Team / Car	Laps	Money	Status
1	6	28	Fred Lorenzen	Holman-Moody '67 Ford	40	$1,350	Running
2	3	26	Darel Dieringer	Junior Johnson '67 Ford	40	650	Running
3	2	21	Cale Yarborough	Wood Brothers '67 Ford	40	400	Running
4	7	29	Dick Hutcherson	Bondy Long '67 Ford	40	300	Running
5	1	43	Richard Petty	Petty Enterprises '67 Plym	40	300	Running
6	4	11	Mario Andretti	Holman-Moody '67 Ford	40	250	Running
7	5	2	Don White	Nichels Eng '67 Dodge	40	225	Running
8	16	1	Paul Lewis	A J King '67 Dodge	39	200	Running
9	15	90	Sonny Hutchins	Junie Donlavey '67 Ford	39	150	Running
10	11	31	Innes Ireland	Ray Fox '66 Dodge	39	150	Running
11	13	85	Gordon Johncock	R L Diestler '67 Plymouth	38	150	Running
12	17	4	John Sears	L G DeWitt '66 Ford	37	125	Running
13	23	00	Neil Castles	Emory Gilliam '65 Plymouth	37	125	Running
14	27	76	Red Farmer	Ben Arnold '66 Ford	37	100	Running
15	8	36	H B Bailey	Bailey '66 Pontiac	36	100	Running
16	22	78	Joel Davis	Earl Ivey '66 Chevrolet	35	100	Running
17	9	39	Friday Hassler	Red Sharp '66 Chevrolet	35	100	Running
18	97	97	Henley Gray	Gray '67 Ford	34	100	Running
19	24	34	Wendell Scott	Scott '65 Ford	34	100	Running
20	26	20	Clyde Lynn	Lynn '66 Ford	33	100	Running
21	21	54	Tom Raley	John Miller '65 Ford	30	100	Running
22	20	45	Blackie Watt	'66 Chevrolet	30	100	Running
23	12	51	George England	Tom Hixon '65 Chevrolet	25	100	Flagged
24	10	15	Sam McQuagg	Bud Moore '67 Mercury	20	100	Suspen
25	18	19	J T Putney	Putney '66 Chevrolet	21	100	Engine
26	14	40	Jerry Grant	Friedkin Ent '67 Plymouth	5	100	Engine
27	19	46	Roy Mayne	Tom Hunter '65 Chevrolet	3	100	Engine
28	25	89	Don Stives	Ron Smith '65 Dodge	1	100	Handling

Time of Race: 34 minutes, 22 seconds
Average Speed: 174.587 mph
Pole Winner: Richard Petty - 179.068 mph
Lap Leaders: Cale Yarborough 1-3, Mario Andretti 4, Yarborough 5-6, Richard Petty 7-8, Yarborough 9, Andretti 10-23, Yarborough 24, Andretti 25, Yarborough 26-29, Andretti 30, Yarborough 31, Andretti 32-33, Darel Dieringer 34-35, Dick Hutcherson 36-37, Fred Lorenzen 38-40.
Cautions: none   Margin of Victory: Attendance: 20,000

Foyt finished second and complained that Tiny Lund had blocked him in the final lap. Paul Goldsmith was third, Buddy Baker fourth and Lund a lap down in fifth.

Foyt had attempted a slingshot around Yarbrough as the pack entered the third turn of the final lap. Lund's presence in the lower groove thwarted Foyt's plan. Foyt also accused Yarbrough of passing him during a brief caution flag. He threatened to withdraw from the Daytona 500.

Foyt cornered a NASCAR official and told him of his intention to pull out of the 500. "What are you going to do?" he asked. "Well," the official drawled, "I guess we'll just move everybody up one notch in the

LeeRoy Yarbrough

starting field." After cooling off, Foyt decided to stay and compete in the Daytona 500.

Curtis Turner started on the pole and pulled his Chevrolet off the track after one lap. "This Chevy is ready for the 500," Turner said. "No use in running today."

Bobby Isaac made his debut with the K&K Insurance team headed by Harry Hyde and wound up 11th after starting fifth.

Yarbrough averaged 163.934 mph and won $1,350.

Race No. 4

Lorenzen Goes Non-Stop To Win Second Daytona 100

DAYTONA BEACH, FL (Feb. 24) Fred Lorenzen rode most of the way in the slipstream of the leaders, then forged to the front with three laps remaining and won the second 100-mile qualifying race at Daytona International Speedway at 174.587 mph.

Lorenzen's Holman-Moody Ford ran out of gas in the second turn of the final lap and coasted across the finish line comfortably ahead of runner-up Darel Dieringer. Cale Yarborough came in third, Dick Hutcherson was fourth and Richard Petty fifth.

The lead changed hands 15 times among six drivers in the torrid struggle. Lorenzen took a back seat to the early race between Yarborough, Petty and Mario Andretti. When his rivals had to pit for a few splashes of fuel, Lorenzen drove into

Fred Lorenzen won Daytona 100. It was his final Grand National victory

the lead and made the full 100-miles without a pit stop. "It ran dry on the last lap," said Lorenzen. "I was doing all the drafting I could, but I still wasn't sure I'd make it all the way."

Andretti finished sixth in another Holman-Moody Ford.

Other USAC entries included Gordon Johncock, who finished 11th; and Don White, who ran seventh in a Nichels Engineering Dodge.

International road racer Innes Ireland drove a back-up Ray Fox Dodge and finished a credible 10th.

Race No. 5

Mario Andretti Runs Away and Wins Daytona 500

DAYTONA BEACH, FL (Feb. 26) -- Mario Andretti of Nazareth, PA led the USAC brigade and scored an upset victory in the ninth annual Daytona 500 in a Holman-Moody Ford. It was the first NASCAR win for the 26 year-old open wheel veteran.

Mario Andretti pulls Holman-Moody Ford into victory lane

Andretti started in 12th spot in the 50 car field and didn't take the lead for the first time until the 23rd lap. Andretti kept his blue Ford among the leaders for the entire distance and led more laps than any other driver.

Andretti took the lead for keeps on lap 168 and built his advantage to 22 seconds over running mate Fred Lorenzen when the ninth and final caution came out with two laps to go. Richard Petty, running in seventh place, blew his engine -- spraying the surface with oil.

Lorenzen took second place and James Hylton was third. Tiny Lund was fourth despite sitting in the pits the final lap with an empty fuel tank. Jerry Grant took fifth place.

Andretti and Lorenzen were the only drivers in the lead lap when the green flag came out following a caution on lap 168. Lund lined up third, a lap down.

"I think Freddy and Tiny were messing around with each other and I slipped away," said Andretti, a two-time USAC champion. "I was just about out of gas. That last caution flag helped out. I pedaled around in fourth gear those last two laps.

Curtis Turner, who won the pole, led twice for six laps. The Roanoke, VA leadfoot went out on lap 144 with a blown engine. He was one lap behind at the time.

Don White, wheeling a Ray Nichels Dodge, spun wildly in the 46th lap, triggering a first turn pile-up involving H.B.Bailey, Ramo Stott and John Sears. Three laps later, Dick Hutcherson nosed into the retaining

Grand National Race No. 5
200 Laps at Daytona Int'l Speedway
Daytona Beach, FL
"Daytona 500"
500 Miles on 2.5-mile Paved Track
February 26, 1967

Fin	St	No.	Driver	Team / Car	Laps	Money	Status
1	12	11	Mario Andretti	Holman-Moody '67 Ford	200	$48,900	Running
2	4	28	Fred Lorenzen	Holman-Moody '67 Ford	200	15,950	Running
3	19	48	James Hylton	Bud Hartje '65 Dodge	199	10,925	Running
4	11	42	Tiny Lund	Petty Enterprises '66 Plym	198	6,675	Out gas
5	43	40	Jerry Grant	Friedkin Ent '67 Plymouth	197	4,725	Running
6	6	26	Darel Dieringer	Junior Johnson '67 Ford	196	3,900	Running
7	18	90	Sonny Hutchins	Junie Donlavey '67 Ford	195	3,100	Running
8	2	43	Richard Petty	Petty Enterprises '67 Plym	193	3,750	Engine
9	42	10	Jim Hurtubise	Norm Nelson '67 Plymouth	192	2,500	Running
10	26	00	Neil Castles	Emory Gilliam '65 Plymouth	191	2,425	Running
11	44	05	Donnie Allison	Robert Harper '66 Chevrolet	188	3,350	Running
12	24	4	John Sears	L G DeWitt '66 Ford	188	2,275	Running
13	47	46	Roy Mayne	Tom Hunter '66 Chevrolet	185	2,250	Differen
14	29	41	Dorus Wisecraver	Ted Sidwell '66 Ford	183	2,225	Running
15	38	34	Wendell Scott	Scott '65 Ford	176	2,200	Running
16	7	99	Paul Goldsmith	Nichels Eng '67 Plymouth	175	2,170	Engine
17	36	97	Henley Gray	Gray '67 Ford	173	2,165	Running
18	30	36	H B Bailey	Bailey '66 Pontiac	171	3,160	Running
19	23	71	Bobby Isaac	K&K Insurance '67 Dodge	166	2,155	Oil Leak
20	33	64	Elmo Langley	Langley-Woodfield '66 Ford	165	2,150	Running
21	40	20	Clyde Lynn	Lynn '66 Ford	165	2,145	Running
22	41	15	Sam McQuagg	Bud Moore '67 Mercury	163	2,140	Engine
23	25	0	Ramo Stott	Stott '66 Plymouth	163	1,135	Running
24	15	6	David Pearson	Cotton Owens '67 Dodge	159	4,730	Engine
25	1	13	Curtis Turner	Yunick-Rich '67 Chevrolet	143	6,425	Engine
26	32	78	Joel Davis	Earl Ivey '66 Chevrolet	141	1,120	Hub
27	20	31	Innes Ireland	Ray Fox '66 Dodge	126	1,115	Engine
28	9	3	Buddy Baker	Ray Fox '67 Dodge	120	1,400	Engine
29	46	19	J T Putney	Putney '66 Chevrolet	119	1,105	Running
30	22	85	Gordon Johncock	R L Diestler '67 Plymouth	112	1,100	Engine
31	21	68	Gary Bettenhausen	Harry Ranier '66 Ford	82	1,095	Heating
32	13	14	Jim Paschal	Friedkin Ent '67 Plymouth	77	1,090	Engine
33	17	37	Charlie Glotzbach	K&K Insurance '65 Dodge	74	1,085	Fuel pmp
34	3	12	LeeRoy Yarbrough	Jon Thorne '67 Dodge	71	1,480	Engine
35	39	62	Ken Spikes	Harold Collins '67 Pontiac	65	1,075	Engine
36	10	29	Dick Hutcherson	Bondy Long '67 Ford	46	1,070	Crash
37	5	27	A J Foyt	Banjo Matthews '67 Ford	44	1,765	Clutch
38	14	2	Don White	Nichels Eng '67 Dodge	43	1,060	Crash
39	8	21	Cale Yarborough	Wood Brothers '67 Ford	42	1,055	Suspen
40	31	16	Bobby Allison	Bud Moore '67 Mercury	34	1,000	Oil Leak
41	49	80	Bob Pickell	Cozze Brothers '66 Chevy	22	950	Axle
42	28	76	Red Farmer	Ben Arnold '66 Ford	21	900	Engine
43	37	7	Bobby Johns	Shorty Johns '66 Chevrolet	18	850	Distrib
44	45	49	G C Spencer	Spencer '67 Plymouth	15	800	Engine
45	50	45	Blackie Watt	'66 Chevrolet	15	750	Heating
46	16	1	Paul Lewis	A J King '67 Dodge	5	700	Hub
47	35	79	Frank Warren	Harold Rhodes '66 Chevrolet	5	650	Oil Leak
48	34	39	Friday Hassler	Red Sharp '66 Chevrolet	4	600	Crash
49	48	51	George England	Tom Hixon '65 Chevrolet	2	550	Engine
50	27	04	Coo Coo Marlin	Charlie Hughes '65 Chevrolet	1	500	Trans

Time of Race: 3 hours, 24 minutes, 11 seconds.
Average Speed: 146.926 mph
Pole Winner: Curtis Turner - 180.831 mph
Lap Leaders: Curtis Turner 1, LeeRoy Yarbrough 2-3, A J Foyt 4-10, Yarbrough 11-13, Buddy Baker 14-16, Yarbrough 17-19, Baker 20, Yarbrough 21-22, Mario Andretti 23-39, Baker 40-41, Darel Dieringer 42-43, Baker 44-48, Dieringer 49, David Pearson 50-53, Tiny Lund 54, Andretti 55-76, Pearson 77-81, Turner 82-86, Pearson 87-91, Dieringer 92, Pearson 93-94, Dieringer 95, Pearson 96, Andretti 97, Dieringer 98, Andretti 99-114, Fred Lorenzen 115-123, Dieringer 124-126, Andretti 127-135, Pearson 136-142, Andretti 143, Pearson 144, Andretti 145-152, Pearson 153-158, Andretti 159-163, Lorenzen 164-167, Andretti 168-200.
Cautions: 6 for 54 Laps   Margin of Victory: Under caution   Attendance: 94,250

wall in the same spot. "I've never hit anything harder in my life," said a shaken Hutcherson.

David Pearson had passed Andretti in the 153rd lap and put a little daylight between his Dodge and Andret-

Petty Enterprises crew services King Richard in Daytona 500

ti's Ford. However, the engine let go in Pearson's car on lap 159, putting him out of the race.

LeeRoy Yarbrough had the hot set-up early in the race, putting his Jon Thorne Dodge into the lead on four occasions before falling victim to a blown engine on lap 71.

Hylton's consistency has put him into a 916 point lead over Lorenzen in the Grand National point standings.

A crowd of 94,250 watched Andretti average 146.926 mph.

Race No. 6

Petty Outduels Dieringer; Nabs 50th GN Win

WEAVERVILLE, NC (Mar. 5) -- Richard Petty pushed his Plymouth past Darel Dieringer in the 234th

Curtis Turner's engine blows in Daytona 500

Grand National Race No. 6
300 Laps at Asheville-Weaverville Speedway
Weaverville, NC
"Fireball 300"
150 Miles on Half-mile Paved Track
March 5, 1967

Fin	St	No.	Driver	Team / Car	Laps	Money	Status
1	2	43	Richard Petty	Petty Enterprises '67 Plym	300	$1,800	Running
2	1	26	Darel Dieringer	Junior Johnson '67 Ford	298	1,050	Running
3	4	2	Bobby Allison	J D Bracken '66 Chevrolet	297	700	Running
4	6	6	David Pearson	Cotton Owens '66 Dodge	295	775	Running
5	5	4	John Sears	L G DeWitt '66 Ford	289	425	Running
6	9	19	J T Putney	Putney '66 Chevrolet	287	325	Running
7	16	00	Paul Lewis	Emory Gilliam '65 Dodge	286	275	Running
8	8	64	Elmo Langley	Langley-Woodfield '66 Ford	279	225	Running
9	17	20	Clyde Lynn	Lynn '66 Ford	275	200	Running
10	11	34	Wendell Scott	Scott '65 Ford	274	175	Running
11	20	45	Bill Seifert	Seifert '65 Ford	273	100	Running
12	18	97	Henley Gray	Gray '66 Ford	262	100	Running
13	13	31	Paul Dean Holt	Ralph Murphy '66 Ford	244	100	Running
14	14	91	Jim Conway	Neil Castles '65 Plymouth	215	100	Trans
15	21	38	Wayne Smith	Smith '66 Chevrolet	157	100	Differen
16	22	9	Roy Tyner	Truett Rodgers '66 Chevrolet	128	100	Differen
17	19	46	Roy Mayne	Tom Hunter '66 Chevrolet	109	100	Differen
18	12	09	Neil Castles	'66 Chevrolet	100	100	Clutch
19	10	75	Earl Brooks	Gene Black '66 Ford	93	100	Lug Bolt
20	15	48	James Hylton	Bud Hartje '65 Dodge	88	100	Engine
21	7	88	Buck Baker	Baker '66 Olds	51	100	Engine
22	3	14	Jim Paschal	Friedkin Ent '65 Plymouth	41	100	Wiring

Time of Race: 1 hour, 47 minutes, 58 seconds
Average Speed: 83.360 mph
Lap Leaders: Darel Dieringer 1-103, Richard Petty 104-115, Dieringer 116-118,
Bobby Allison 119-143, Petty 144-214, Dieringer 215-233, Petty 234-300.
Cautions: 1 for 5 laps   Margin of Victory: 2-laps plus   Attendance: 9,500

lap and steadily pulled away to win the Fireball 300 at Asheville-Weaverville Speedway. It was Petty's second win of the season and the 50th of his career.

Dieringer, driving the Junior Johnson Ford, started on the pole and led the first 103 laps. Petty engaged in a lead swapping duel with the Indianapolis veteran, and had upped his margin to two laps when the checkered flag fell.

Bobby Allison was third in a Chevrolet. David Pearson came in fourth and John Sears was fifth.

A crowd of 9,500 watched the 29 year-old Petty average 83.360 mph -- a 150 mile record on a half mile track. "I've had cars run better up here," said Petty, "but never one that handled better. Darel pulled even with me on the straights, but I could leave him in the turns."

Third fastest qualifier Jim Paschal wound up last after he experienced electrical problems after just 41 laps. Point leader James Hylton was credited with 20th after his Dodge developed engine trouble on lap 88. Despite his misfortune, the 31 year-old sophomore padded his lead in the standings to 1,036 points over the idle Fred Lorenzen.

Petty stood third in the point race, 894 behind Lorenzen.

Race No. 7

Pearson Prevails in Bristol Cliff-Hanger

BRISTOL, TN (Mar. 19) -- David Pearson, behind by two laps with nine miles remaining, inherited the lead after two front runners encountered late race misfortunes, and won the Southeastern 500 at Bristol International Speedway. It was the first win of the year for the 32 year-old defending Grand National champion.

Grand National Race No. 7
500 Laps at Bristol Int'l Speedway
Bristol, TN
"Southeastern 500"
250 Miles on half-mile Paved Track
March 19, 1967

Fin	St	No.	Driver	Team / Car	Laps	Money	Status
1	14	6	David Pearson	Cotton Owens '67 Dodge	500	$5,290	Running
2	7	21	Cale Yarborough	Wood Brothers '67 Ford	500	3,050	Running
3	1	26	Darel Dieringer	Junior Johnson '67 Ford	497	2,700	Running
4	25	00	Neil Castles	Emory Gilliam '65 Plymouth	485	1,400	Running
5	4	29	Dick Hutcherson	Bondy Long '67 Ford	482	1,125	Engine
6	18	64	Elmo Langley	Langley-Woodfield '66 Ford	476	800	Running
7	16	05	Donnie Allison	Robert Harper '67 Chevrolet	472	725	Running
8	30	45	Bill Seifert	Seifert '65 Ford	462	675	Running
9	24	34	Wendell Scott	Scott '65 Ford	455	625	Running
10	32	09	Max Ledbetter	'66 Chevrolet	441	575	Running
11	31	80	Bob Pickell	Cozze Brothers '66 Chevrolet	432	550	Running
12	35	58	Jimmy Helms	'65 Plymouth	430	490	Running
13	17	39	Friday Hassler	Red Sharp '66 Chevrolet	393	485	Trans
14	12	48	James Hylton	Bud Hartje '65 Dodge	390	445	Battery
15	2	28	Fred Lorenzen	Holman-Moody '67 Ford	341	475	Engine
16	11	1	Paul Lewis	A J King '67 Dodge	307	415	Engine
17	6	14	Jim Paschal	Friedkin Ent '67 Plymouth	289	395	Engine
18	26	97	Henley Gray	Gray '66 Ford	255	425	Engine
19	9	2	Bobby Allison	J D Bracken '66 Chevrolet	242	350	Engine
20	23	20	Clyde Lynn	Lynn '66 Ford	229	340	Engine
21	19	88	Buck Baker	Baker '67 Olds	199	330	Engine
22	8	99	Paul Goldsmith	Nichels Eng '67 Plymouth	165	320	Ignition
23	27	75	Earl Brooks	Gene Black '66 Ford	159	340	Oil Leak
24	13	12	LeeRoy Yarbrough	Jon Thorne '67 Dodge	146	360	Ignition
25	5	49	G C Spencer	Spencer '66 Plymouth	136	320	Heating
26	21	24	Jack Harden	Betty Lilly '66 Ford	106	285	Engine
27	15	19	J T Putney	Putney '66 Chevrolet	89	300	Engine
28	29	38	Wayne Smith	Smith '66 Chevrolet	75	290	Engine
29	10	4	John Sears	L G DeWitt '66 Ford	61	255	Engine
30	20	81	Jack Ingram	Tom Ingram '65 Chevrolet	49	245	Engine
31	34	9	Roy Tyner	Truett Rodgers '66 Chevrolet	36	245	Differen
32	22	46	Roy Mayne	Tom Hunter '66 Chevrolet	16	200	Engine
33	36	85	Jim Hunter	'65 Chevrolet	7	200	Engine
34	3	43	Richard Petty	Petty Enterprises '67 Plym	6	225	Crash
35	28	63	Larry Manning	Bob Adams '66 Ford	4	225	Engine
36	33	86	Joe Ed Neubert	'65 Chevrolet	4	225	Engine

Time of Race: 3 hours, 17 minutes, 32 seconds
Average Speed: 75.937 mph
Pole Winner: Darel Dieringer - 87.124 mph
Lap Leaders: Darel Dieringer 1-2, Richard Petty 3-6, Dick Hutcherson 7-54,
Jim Paschal 55-113, Hutcherson 114-124, David Pearson 125-188, Dieringer 189-207,
Hutcherson 208-211, Dieringer 212-292, Hutcherson 293-381, Cale Yarborough 382-425
Hutcherson 426-482, Yarborough 483-494, Pearson 495-500.
Cautions: 6 for 59 laps   Margin of Victory: 7 seconds   Attendance: 23,000

Cale Yarborough crossed the finish line 7.0-seconds behind Pearson's Dodge. He had lost the lead when a tire was cut with six laps remaining. Third place went to Darel Dieringer, Neil Castles was fourth and Dick Hutcherson fifth.

Hutcherson had led for 67 laps and was nursing a lap lead on Yarborough and two on Pearson. As he was cruising to victory, his engine blew on lap 482, sending him into the guard rail. As the yellow came out, Pearson was able to make up a lap on Yarborough, who took the lead with 18 laps to go.

Yarborough ran over some debris that

Joe Ed Neubert #86 spins as Richard Petty narrowly misses

popped a right front tire on his Wood Brothers Ford. He elected to try to finish the race running on the innerliner. Yarborough led through the 494th lap when Pearson made the decisive pass.

"I thought I was running second behind Hutcherson," remarked Pearson. "My crew had me second and Cale third. I went after him just in case. When I passed him so easy, I knew he had some kind of trouble."

Yarborough, who has only one Grand National victory to his credit, sat on a stack of tires afterwards. "There wouldn't have been any question about it if my right front tire hadn't gone flat," he moaned. "David could never have passed me."

Point leader James Hylton experienced problems for the second race in a row. A dead battery felled his Dodge after 390 laps. He finished 14th.

Pearson averaged 75.937 mph before 23,000 spectators.

Race No. 8

Pearson Wins Greenville; Paschal Runs Out of Gas

GREENVILLE, SC (Mar. 25) -- David Pearson led all but two laps but didn't seal the victory until the final mile and a half in the 100-mile Grand National event at Greenville-Pickens Speedway. It was the 30th career win for the Spartanburg, SC Dodge driver.

Jim Paschal had put his Plymouth within shouting distance of Pearson in the final stretch battle, but ran out of gas with three laps to go. Paschal limped to a halt in the third turn and watched as Pearson took the victory flag uncontested.

Paschal received second place money based on the 197 laps he completed on the half-mile dirt track. John Sears finished third, Buddy Baker was fourth and James Hylton fifth.

Richard Petty started sixth and led two laps. He was involved in a pit road collision with Dick Hutcherson, and later spun out and withdrew from the race.

Hutcherson won the pole for the 16th time in his career and was running second when the right front wheel folded on lap 186. He was paid for seventh place.

Pearson averaged 61.824 mph before 8,300 spectators.

David Pearson won at Greenville, then split with car owner Cotton Owens

Grand National Race No. 8
200 Laps at Greenville-Pickens Speedway
Greenville, SC
100 Miles on Half-mile Dirt Track
March 25, 1967

Fin	St	No.	Driver	team / Car	Laps	Money	Status
1	2	6	David Pearson	Cotton Owens '66 Dodge	200	$1,200	Running
2	5	14	Jim Paschal	Friedkin Ent '65 Plymouth	197	600	Out / gas
3	4	4	John Sears	L G DeWitt '66 Ford	197	400	Running
4	7	47	Buddy Baker	Toy Bolton '66 Chevrolet	191	300	Running
5	9	48	James Hylton	Bud Hartje '65 Dodge	190	275	Running
6	3	64	Elmo Langley	Langley-Woodfield '66 ford	189	240	Running
7	1	29	Dick Hutcherson	Bondy Long '67 Ford	186	200	Wheel
8	12	09	Neil Castles	'66 Chevrolet	184	175	Running
9	13	76	Curly Mills	Don Culpepper '66 Ford	183	150	Running
10	15	34	Wendell Scott	Scott '65 Ford	182	140	Running
11	14	20	Clyde Lynn	Lynn '66 Ford	182	130	Running
12	10	10	Dick Johnson	Bill Champion '66 Ford	178	120	Running
13	11	97	Henley Gray	Gray '66 Ford	177	110	Running
14	20	45	Bill Seifert	Seifert '66 Ford	172	100	Running
15	17	75	Earl Brooks	Gene Black '66 Ford	165	100	Running
16	23	32	Larry Miller	Miller '65 Dodge	151	100	Running
17	21	58	George Poulos	'65 Plymouth	147	100	Running
18	19	00	Bill Vanderhoff	Emory Gilliam '65 Plymouth	114	100	Out / gas
19	6	43	Richard Petty	Petty Enterprises '67 Plym	95	100	Crash
20	16	31	Bill Ervin	Ralph Murphy '66 Ford	65	100	Crash
21	8	2	Bobby Allison	J D Bracken '65 Chevrolet	59	100	Rear End
22	18	35	Harold Stockton	'65 Olds	23	100	Clutch
23	22	44	Larry Hess	Hess '66 Rambler	5	100	Engine

Time of Race: 1 hour, 37 minutes, 3 seconds
Average Speed: 61.824 mph
Pole Winner: Dick Hutcherson - 70.313 mph
Lap Leaders: David Pearson 1-74, Richard Petty 75-76, Pearson 77-200.
Cautions: Margin of Victory: 3-laps plus   Attendance: 8,300

Race No. 9

Flat Flattens Petty; Allison Wins at Winston-Salem

WINSTON-SALEM, NC (Mar. 27) -- Bobby Allison took the lead in the 128th lap when a flat tire sent Richard Petty to the pits and won the 50-mile Easter Monday Grand National race at Bowman Gray Stadium. It was the first win of the season for the Hueytown, AL Chevrolet driver.

Petty pitted to get fresh rubber, but fell three laps behind. He wound up second, two laps off the pace. Third place went to John Sears with Clyde Lynn fourth and James Hylton fifth.

David Pearson showed muscle early by passing Allison for the lead in the eighth lap. His white Dodge led until the 36th lap when it slowed on the backstretch. Petty took the lead and fended off his rivals until his tire troubles.

Pearson limped to the 48th lap when he pulled out

with a broken axle. He got credit for 15th place in the field of 19.

Rookie George Poulos tangled with Allison during the early stages. But Allison held his car firm and continued on his way. Poulos was trying to pull off the track when his Plymouth dropped oil pressure. The pit area at Bowman Gray is outside the retaining walls.

Allison won the 50-miler at an average speed of 49.248 mph on the flat quarter-mile oval. A crowd of 9,000 was on hand.

Grand National Race No. 9
200 Laps at Bowman Gray Stadium
Winston-Salem, NC
50 Miles on Quarter-mile Paved Track
March 27, 1967

Fin	St	No.	Driver	Team / Car	Laps	Money	Status
1	1	2	Bobby Allison	J D Bracken '65 Chevrolet	200	$820	Running
2	2	43	Richard Petty	Petty Enterprises '67 Plym	198	550	Running
3	17	4	John Sears	L G DeWitt '66 Ford	196	430	Running
4	5	20	Clyde Lynn	Lynn '66 Ford	195	320	Running
5	6	48	James Hylton	Bud Hartje '65 Dodge	192	300	Running
6	11	45	Bill Seifert	Seifert '65 Ford	189	255	Running
7	12	97	Henley Gray	Gray '66 Ford	187	215	Running
8	10	89	Don Stives	Ron Smith '66 Chevrolet	187	185	Running
9	8	34	Wendell Scott	Scott '65 Ford	180	165	Running
10	13	40	Eddie Yarboro	'65 Dodge	124	140	Clutch
11	19	32	Larry Miller	Miller '65 Dodge	92	130	Clutch
12	9	75	Earl Brooks	Gene Black '65 Ford	89	135	Engine
13	3	14	Jim Paschal	Friedkin Ent '65 Plymouth	74	160	Clutch
14	7	88	Buck Baker	Baker '66 Olds	52	125	Engine
15	4	6	David Pearson	Cotton Owens '65 Dodge	48	300	Axle
16	16	35	Harold Stockton	'65 Olds	46	100	Brakes
17	18	76	Curly Mills	Don Culpepper '66 Ford	15	100	Wtr Pmp
18	15	00	Neil Castles	Emory Gilliam '65 Plymouth	14	100	Oil Press
19	14	57	George Poulos	'65 Plymouth	5	100	Oil Press

Time of Race: 1 hour, 55 seconds
Average Speed: 49.248 mph
Pole Winner: Bobby Allison - 53.476 mph
Lap Leaders: Bobby Allison 1-7, David Pearson 8-36, Richard Petty 37-127, Allison 128-200.
Cautions: 1 for 8 laps   Margin of Victory: 2-laps plus   Attendance: 9,000

Race No. 10

Petty, Andretti Fade; Cale Collects Atlanta 500 Prize

HAMPTON, GA (Apr.2) -- Cale Yarborough led for 301 of the 334 laps and cruised to an easy win in the Atlanta 500 at Atlanta International Raceway. It was the second career win for the Timmonsville, SC Ford driver but his first on a superspeedway.

Yarborough, 28, started on the pole and thoroughly dominated the $76,315 event. The only drivers capable of keeping Yarborough in sight were Mario Andretti and Richard Petty. Petty led for a 17 lap segment after

Mario Andretti leads tight pack through turn at Atlanta

Grand National Race No. 10
334 Laps at Atlanta Int'l Raceway
Hampton, GA
"Atlanta 500"
500 Miles on 1.5-mile Paved Track
April 2, 1967

Fin	St	No.	Driver	Team / Car	Laps	Money	Status
1	1	21	Cale Yarborough	Wood Brothers '67 Ford	334	$21,035	Running
2	9	29	Dick Hutcherson	Bondy Long '67 Ford	333	8,600	Running
3	10	3	Buddy Baker	Ray Fox '67 Dodge	332	4,900	Running
4	13	37	Charlie Glotzbach	K&K Insurance '65 Dodge	327	2,750	Running
5	11	71	Bobby Isaac	K&K Insurance '67 Dodge	326	1,875	Running
6	25	48	James Hylton	Bud Hartje '65 Dodge	326	1,325	Running
7	26	39	Friday Hassler	Red Sharp '66 Chevrolet	325	1,200	Running
8	32	4	John Sears	L G DeWitt '66 Ford	324	1,175	Engine
9	14	16	Bobby Allison	Bud Moore '67 Mercury	324	950	Running
10	17	49	G C Spencer	Spencer '67 Plymouth	324	925	Running
11	29	19	J T Putney	Putney '66 Chevrolet	323	750	Running
12	20	05	Donnie Allison	Robert Harper '66 Chevrolet	322	725	Running
13	23	90	Sonny Hutchins	Junie Donlavey '67 Ford	318	550	Running
14	36	67	Buddy Arrington	Arrington '65 Dodge	313	670	Running
15	8	14	Jim Paschal	Friedkin Ent '67 Plymouth	307	550	Running
16	30	10	Bill Champion	Champion '66 Ford	307	550	Running
17	16	1	Paul Lewis	A J King '67 Dodge	284	550	Running
18	12	15	Sam McQuagg	Bud Moore '67 Mercury	277	575	Suspen
19	22	11	Mario Andretti	Holman-Moody '67 ford	261	550	Crash
20	6	42	Tiny Lund	Petty Enterprises '67 Plym	246	550	Running
21	4	6	David Pearson	Cotton Owens '67 Dodge	224	1,075	Ignition
22	2	43	Richard Petty	Petty Enterprises '67 Plym	215	710	Engine
23	7	26	Darel Dieringer	Junior Johnson '67 Ford	195	580	Engine
24	18	2	Don White	Nichels Eng '67 Ford	193	600	W'shield
25	40	38	Wayne Smith	Smith '66 Chevrolet	184	580	Engine
26	28	64	Elmo Langley	Langley-Woodfield '66 Ford	175	575	Engine
27	5	27	A J Foyt	Banjo Matthews '67 Ford	174	575	Engine
28	3	28	Fred Lorenzen	Holman-Moody '67 Plym	173	615	Crash
29	33	46	Roy Mayne	Tom Hunter '66 Chevrolet	171	650	Differen
30	31	12	LeeRoy Yarbrough	Jon Thorne '66 Dodge	162	700	Engine
31	19	99	Paul Goldsmith	Nichels Eng '67 Plymouth	153	575	Heating
32	38	66	Bay Darnell	'65 Plymouth	123	600	Differen
33	34	24	Jack Harden	Betty Lilly '66 Ford	120	640	Crash
34	37	00	Neil Castles	Emory Gilliam '65 Plymouth	114	610	Suspen
35	15	7	Bobby Johns	Shorty Johns '66 Chevrolet	80	550	Engine
36	27	79	Frank Warren	Harold Rhodes '67 Chevrolet	54	525	Trans
37	35	03	Eldon Yarbrough	Harold Mays '65 Chevrolet	46	580	Heating
38	24	5	John Martin	R L Diestler '67 Plymouth	44	500	Oil Leak
39	42	20	Clyde Lynn	Lynn '66 Ford	13	500	Engine
40	41	34	Wendell Scott	Scott '65 Ford	10	500	Engine
41	21	85	Gordon Johncock	R L Diestler '67 Ford	9	500	Crash
42	43	0	Dick Johnson	'66 Ford	5	500	Engine
43	44	45	Bill Seifert	Seifert '65 Ford	4	500	Engine
44	39	33	Blackie Watt	'65 Chevrolet	2	540	Engine

Time of Race: 3 hours, 49 minutes, 3 seconds
Average Speed: 131.238 mph
Pole Winner: Cale Yarborough - 148.996 mph
Lap Leaders: Cale Yarborough 1-60, Darel Dieringer 61-67, Fred Lorenzen 68-69,
    Yarborough 70-99, Lorenzen 100, Yarborough 101-151, Mario Andretti 152-157,
    Yarborough 158-179, Richard Petty 180-196, Yarborough 197-334.
Cautions: 6 for 39 laps   Margin of Victory: 1-lap plus   Attendance: 70,000

Cale made a pit stop, but was felled by a blown engine.

Andretti thrilled the audience of 70,000 with his rim-riding style, picking a groove mere inches from the outside guard rail. The USAC speed merchant passed Yarborough for the lead in a daring maneuver on lap 152. Six laps later, Andretti blew a tire and slid into the wall. Andretti went back into the race after a long pit stop, but fell victim to another wall banger on lap 265.

Dick Hutcherson drove a steady race and finished second. Buddy Baker continued to turn heads with a sparkling third place effort. Charlie Glotzbach and Bobby Isaac took fourth and fifth in team K&K Insurance Dodges.

Curtis Turner's Chevy lies crumpled after practice spill at Atlanta

Fred Lorenzen and A. J. Foyt left the race in a spectacular incident on lap 174. Foyt's Ford uncorked an engine and Lorenzen went into a long slide after hitting the oil slick. Foyt came to rest against the guard rail and Lorenzen piled into the inside steel rail. Neither driver was hurt.

Yarborough, who averaged 131.238 mph, won by nearly three miles, but he said he "won by about three inches on Wednesday."

Curtis Turner was shaking down his Smokey Yunick

Paul Lewis rounds turn in Atlanta 500

Chevrolet when he lost control just after passing Yarborough. The car darted out of control, struck the outside retaining barrier and became airborne.

Yarborough whipped off the fourth turn and watched Turner's car sail over his roof. Turner flipped end-over-end three times, the barrel-rolled another six times. Turner was taken to a hospital, examined and released. "I have so many bruises that I can't find a place to lay on to sleep at night," he remarked a day later.

"I saw Turner's car flipping in front of me and suddenly it was gone," said Cale. "I knew it was in the air right above my head. It hit the pavement right behind me. He couldn't have missed me by more than three inches."

A week after the race, Yunick announced that he and Turner were parting ways. "We've been friends too long," said the famed mechanic. "I don't want to build the car that kills Curtis Turner. I want him to retire so we can still be friends."

Point leader James Hylton finished sixth and sprang to a 4,098 point lead in the Grand National point standings. Petty moved into second, dropping Lorenzen to third.

Race No. 11
Petty Laps Field in Sandlapper 200

COLUMBIA, SC (Apr. 6) -- Richard Petty outran Jim Paschal in a race long duel and took top honors in the Sandlapper 200 at Columbia Speedway. It was Petty's third win of the season and put him within three victories of his father, Lee, NASCAR's all-time race winner.

Petty led on four occasions for a total of 131 laps and beat runner-up Paschal by better than a lap. Dick Hutcherson survived a brush with rookie Larry Miller in the final laps and grabbed third place. James Hylton came in fourth and Neil Castles was fifth.

Petty and Paschal, both driving Plymouths, were the

Grand National Race No. 11
200 Laps at Columbia Speedway
Columbia, SC
"Sandlapper 200"
100 Miles on Half-mile Dirt Track
April 6, 1967

Fin	St	No.	Driver	Team / Car	Laps	Money	Status
1	2	43	Richard Petty	Petty Enterprises '67 Plym	200	$1,000	Running
2	3	14	Jim Paschal	Friedkin Ent '67 Plymouth	199	600	Running
3	1	29	Dick Hutcherson	Bondy Long '67 Ford	198	400	Running
4	6	48	James Hylton	Bud Hartje '65 Dodge	197	300	Running
5	13	88	Neil Castles	Buck Baker '66 Olds	193	275	Running
6	9	34	Wendell Scott	Scott '65 Ford	188	240	Running
7	12	78	Joel Davis	Earl Ivey '66 Chevrolet	187	200	Running
8	5	64	Elmo Langley	Langley-Woodfield '66 Ford	187	175	Running
9	15	45	Bill Seifert	Seifert '66 Ford	186	150	Running
10	16	97	Henley Gray	Gray '66 Ford	183	140	Running
11	14	32	Larry Miller	Miller '65 Plymouth	178	130	Running
12	7	76	Tiny Lund	Don Culpepper '66 Ford	177	120	Running
13	8	10	Dick Johnson	Bill Champion '66 Ford	166	110	Flagged
14	17	35	Harold Stockton	'66 Olds	156	100	Running
15	19	58	George Poulos	'65 Plymouth	128	100	Running
16	4	4	John Sears	L G DeWitt '66 Ford	100	100	Heating
17	11	20	Clyde Lynn	Lynn '66 Ford	53	100	Differen
18	18	9	Roy Tyner	Truett Rodgers '66 Chevrolet	50	100	Differen
19	10	2	Bobby Allison	J D Bracken '65 Chevrolet	11	100	Engine

Time of Race: 1 hour, 31 minutes, 40 seconds
Average Speed: 65.455 mph
Pole Winner: Dick Hutcherson - 74.166 mph
Lap Leaders: Richard Petty 1-5, Jim Paschal 6-11, Petty 12-42, Paschal 43-60, Petty 61-72, Paschal 73-79, Petty 80-200.
Cautions: Margin of Victory: 1-lap plus   Attendance: 6,000

only drivers to lead the 200 lapper on the half-mile dirt track. Hutcherson won the pole and was always in contention, but never led.

Bobby Allison started in the middle of the pack and went out early when his Chevrolet ran into mechanical problems. He finished last in the 19 car field. John Sears qualified a strong fourth in his L. G. DeWitt Ford, but overheating difficulties ended his bid for his first Grand National win.

Petty averaged 65.455 mph before 6,000 spectators.

David Pearson was on hand for the 100-miler, but did not have a car to drive. Car owner Cotton Owens had entered a Dodge, but withdrew at the last moment. Pearson received no word about the withdrawl, and was reportedly miffed with the situation.

Race No. 12
Petty Survives Tire-Killing Hickory 250

HICKORY, NC (Apr.9) -- Richard Petty made six pit stops in a 100-mile Grand National event yet still emerged victorious in the tire-popping contest at Hickory Speedway. It was the fourth win of the season for the Randleman, NC Plymouth pilot.

Dick Hutcherson came in second, James Hylton was third, Jim Paschal fourth and Bobby Allison fifth.

A hard, abrasive dirt track and fast speeds overtaxed the available tires, and winner Petty used 16 tires in winning the 100-miler -- in all probability a record. "I don't think I've ever had to use that many tires in a 100-mile race," commented Petty afterwards.

With the leaders experiencing tire problems, six different drivers led the Hickory 250 on the .4-mile oval. Allison was in front the longest -- 105 laps before he fell off the pace with a sputtering engine in the late stages. The Hueytown, AL Chevrolet chauffeur took the lead for the first time on lap 73 -- after he charged from a two lap deficit. Allison had blown a tire and slapped the retaining wall, putting him well behind the leaders.

Petty led for a total of 83 laps, point leader Hylton led 48 laps and Hutcherson was in front for 41 laps. Roy Mayne and John Sears led briefly during caution periods.

The caution was out five times for 22 laps, lowering Petty's winning speed of 69.699 mph

Grand National Race No. 12
250 Laps at Hickory Speedway
Hickory, NC
"Hickory 250"
100 Miles on .4-mile Dirt Track
April 9, 1967

Fin	St	No.	Driver	Team / Car	Laps	Money	Status
1	1	43	Richard Petty	Petty Enterprises '67 Plym	250	$1,000	Running
2	2	29	Dick Hutcherson	Bondy Long '67 Ford	248	600	Running
3	9	48	James Hylton	Bud Hartje '65 Dodge	247	400	Running
4	7	14	Jim Paschal	Friedkin Ent '65 Plymouth	246	300	Running
5	4	2	Bobby Allison	J D Bracken '65 Chevrolet	245	275	Running
6	14	45	Bill Seifert	Seifert '65 Ford	235	240	Running
7	3	4	John Sears	L G DeWitt '66 Ford	234	200	Engine
8	21	78	Joel Davis	Earl Ivey '66 Chevrolet	226	175	Running
9	16	67	Buddy Arrington	Arrington '65 Dodge	223	150	Out / gas
10	5	18	J T Putney	Putney '66 Chevrolet	221	140	Running
11	13	34	Wendell Scott	Scott '65 Ford	217	130	Running
12	11	09	Roy Mayne	'66 Chevrolet	217	120	Running
13	8	64	Elmo Langley	Langley-Woodfield '66 Ford	215	110	Running
14	17	35	Harold Stockton	'65 Olds	202	100	Running
15	20	57	George Poulos	'65 Plymouth	196	100	Running
16	19	32	Larry Miller	Miller '65 Dodge	191	100	Running
17	15	88	Neil Castles	Buck Baker '66 olds	177	100	Engine
18	12	75	Earl Brooks	Gene Black '66 Ford	104	100	Crash
19	6	10	Dick Johnson	Bill Champion '66 Ford	84	100	Crash
20	10	20	Clyde Lynn	Lynn '66 Ford	50	100	Differen
21	18	76	Curly Mills	Don Culpepper '66 Ford	28	100	Crash
22	23	38	Wayne Smith	Smith '66 Chevrolet	25	100	Engine
23	22	9	Roy Tyner	Truett Rodgers '66 Chevrolet	20	100	Trans

Time of Race: 1 hour, 26 minutes, 5 seconds
Average Speed: 69.699 mph
Pole Winner: Richard Petty - 79.120 mph
Lap Leaders: Dick Hutcherson 1-32, Richard Petty 33-50, Hutcherson 51,
John Sears 52, Roy Mayne 53-55, James Hylton 56-72, Bobby Allison 73-177,
Petty 178-206, Hutcherson 207-214, Petty 215-250.
Cautions: 5 for 22 laps   Margin of Victory: 2-laps plus   Attendance: 4,000

Race No. 13

Dieringer All the Way in Gwyn Staley 400; Pearson Quits Owens

N.WILKESBORO, NC (Apr. 16) -- Darel Dieringer drove his Junior Johnson Ford into the lead in the first lap and led all the way to win the Gwyn Staley Memorial 400 at North Wilkesboro Speedway. The overwhelming triumph was the seventh career win for the 40 year-old Indianapolis veteran driver.

Cale Yarborough was a lap back in second place in the uneventful contest. Dick Hutcherson came in third, Jim Paschal was fourth and Paul Lewis fifth.

David Pearson pulled his Cotton Owens Dodge behind the wall with overheating problems on lap 134. The following day, the defending Grand National champion announced he was leaving the Owens team. "We've had a lot of tough luck so far this year," said Owens. "I think it's best we go our separate ways."

Darel Dieringer led all the way

Despite six caution flags which bunched the field, Dieringer effortlessly pulled away from the field on every restart. "I'm glad we were able to win so impressively in Johnson's home country," said Dieringer. "We all wanted to win this one real bad. I'm proud I could do my share as the driver."

Johnson's Ford weighed in at 3,500 pounds -- the absolute minimum allowed under NASCAR power-to-weight rules. Johnson unveiled a small 374 cubic inch engine. "We are reaching speeds where the 427 is at a disadvantage in fuel consumption and tire wear," said Johnson. "In a long distance race, where you have to make several pit stops for fuel and tires, the lighter car is better."

Glen Wood, owner of Yarborough's runner-up Ford, said he knew he didn't have a chance the day before the race. "We were racing for second place," said the mild-mannered former driver. "We knew we couldn't beat him unless he had trouble. He didn't have trouble, so we finished where we figured we would."

Dieringer averaged 93.594 mph before 9,400 spectators.

Grand National Race No. 13
400 Laps at N.Wilkesboro Speedway
N.Wilkesboro, NC
"Gwyn Staley Memorial 400"
250 Miles on .675-mile Paved Track
April 16, 1967

Fin	St	No.	Driver	Team / Car	Laps	Money	Status
1	1	26	Darel Dieringer	Junior Johnson '67 Ford	400	$5,150	Running
2	4	21	Cale Yarborough	Wood Brothers '67 Ford	399	2,275	Running
3	8	29	Dick Hutcherson	Bondy Long '67 Ford	396	1,325	Running
4	14	14	Jim Paschal	Friedkin Ent '67 Plymouth	396	825	Running
5	6	1	Paul Lewis	A J King '67 Dodge	392	625	Running
6	10	2	Bobby Allison	J D Bracken '65 Chevrolet	391	525	Running
7	2	43	Richard Petty	Petty Enterprises '67 Plym	389	500	Running
8	9	4	John Sears	L G DeWitt '66 Ford	387	425	Running
9	12	48	James Hylton	Bud Hartje '65 Dodge	386	400	Running
10	16	11	J T Putney	Putney '66 Chevrolet	378	325	Running
11	21	20	Clyde Lynn	Lynn '66 Ford	376	425	Running
12	15	87	Buck Baker	Baker '66 Ford	369	275	Suspen
13	23	34	Wendell Scott	Scott '65 Ford	368	300	Running
14	24	45	Bill Seifert	Seifert '65 Ford	368	250	Running
15	34	76	Tiny Lund	Don Culpepper '66 Ford	364	200	Running
16	22	63	Larry Manning	Manning '66 Ford	362	300	Running
17	28	38	Wayne Smith	Smith '66 Chevrolet	357	225	Running
18	13	64	Elmo Langley	Langley-Woodfield '66 Ford	325	225	Clutch
19	25	09	Max Ledbetter	'66 Chevrolet	319	225	Running
20	19	46	Roy Mayne	Tom Hunter '66 Chevrolet	291	225	Differen
21	31	57	George Poulos	'65 Plymouth	271	175	Differren
22	27	97	Henley Gray	Gray '66 Ford	270	200	Throttle
23	30	01	Paul Dean Holt	Dennis Holt '66 Ford	210	200	Differen
24	32	75	Earl Brooks	Gene Black ' 66 Ford	203	175	Engine
25	20	18	Dick Johnson	Johnson '66 Ford	178	200	Engine
26	5	6	David Pearson	Cotton Owens '67 Dodge	134	200	Heating
27	18	67	Buddy Arrington	Arrington '65 Dodge	126	200	Heating
28	7	99	Paul Goldsmith	Nichels Eng '67 Plymouth	95	200	Ignition
29	26	40	Eddie Yarboro	'65 Dodge	85	200	D Shaft
30	17	25	Sam McQuagg	Don Robertson '67 Ford	50	175	Heating
31	29	35	Harold Stockton	'65 Olds	49	175	Engine
32	14	39	Friday Hassler	Red Sharp '66 Chevrolet	31	175	Clutch
33	11	49	G C Spencer	Spencer '66 Plymouth	4	250	Engine
34	33	32	Larry Miller	Miller '65 Dodge	1	150	Brakes

Time of Race: 2 hours, 40 minutes, 16 seconds
Average Speed: 93.594 mph
Pole Winner: Darel Dieringer - 104.603 mph
Lap Leaders: Darel Dieringer 1-400.
Cautions: 6 for 33 laps   Margin of Victory: 1-lap plus   Attendance: 9,400

Race No. 14
Late Race Kick Lifts Petty Over Cale at Martinsville

MARTINSVILLE, VA (Apr. 23) -- Richard Petty passed Cale Yarborough with 20 laps to go and sprinted to a close victory in the Virginia 500 at Martinsville Speedway. It was the fifth win of the season for Petty.

Yarborough held command most of the way, leading for 259 of the 500 laps on the half-mile paved track. He was holding a 4.5-second cushion over Petty when John Sears blew his engine on lap 473. Yarborough, running close behind Sears, slipped in the oil and slapped the concrete wall.

The caution came out but neither Petty nor

Yarborough pitted -- each placing track position as the main priority. When the green came out, Petty passed Yarborough easily and got to the finish line first by 9.0-seconds.

Third place went to independent J.T. Putney. Dick Hutcherson led 122 laps and finished fourth after rear end problems knocked him off the pace in the late stages. Paul Goldsmith came in fifth.

"Those last 20 laps was the only time I had an advantage all day," remarked Petty. "It looked to me like the fender was on his tire. I knew I could get him in the last laps because I could smell the rubber burning."

Point leader James Hylton lost 220 points to Petty in the battle for the championship, but still held a lead of

Grand National Race No. 14
500 Laps at Martinsville Speedway
Martinsville, VA
"Virginia 500"
250 Miles on Half-mile Paved Track
April 23, 1967

Fin	St	No.	Driver	Team / Car	Laps	Money	Status
1	2	43	Richard Petty	Petty Enterprises '67 Plym	500	$4,450	Running
2	4	21	Cale Yarborough	Wood Brothers '67 Ford	500	2,300	Running
3	21	11	J T Putney	Putney '66 Chevrolet	491	1,300	Running
4	3	99	Dick Hutcherson	Bondy Long '67 Ford	488	925	Running
5	6	99	Paul Goldsmith	Nichels Eng '67 Plymouth	488	725	Running
6	13	48	James Hylton	Bud Hartje '65 Dodge	436	675	Running
7	19	64	Elmo Langley	Langley-Woodfield '66 Ford	483	575	Running
8	26	87	Buck Baker	Baker '66 Ford	483	525	Running
9	17	67	Buddy Arrington	Arrington '65 Dodge	480	500	Running
10	16	20	Clyde Lynn	Lynn '66 Ford	470	475	Running
11	27	45	Bill Seifert	Seifert '65 Ford	468	450	Running
12	11	4	John Sears	L G DeWitt '66 Ford	461	425	Engine
13	31	97	Henley Gray	Gray '66 Ford	460	390	Running
14	28	38	Wayne Smith	Smith '66 Chevrolet	454	380	Running
15	37	76	Tiny Lund	Don Culpepper '66 Ford	440	370	Running
16	36	57	George Poulos	'65 Plymouth	400	360	Running
17	25	18	Dick Johnson	Johnson '66 Ford	365	375	Engine
18	15	7	Bobby Johns	Shorty Johns '66 Chevrolet	279	365	Radiator
19	10	05	Donnie Allison	Robert Harper '66 Chevrolet	271	355	Engine
20	5	16	Bobby Allison	Bud Moore '67 Mercury	264	370	Crash
21	24	34	Wendell Scott	Scott '65 Ford	259	325	Crash
22	20	54	Tom Raley	Raley '65 Ford	188	325	H Gasket
23	30	46	Roy Mayne	Tom Hunter '66 Chevrolet	170	300	Crash
24	8	49	G C Spencer	Spencer '66 Plymouth	169	325	Oil Leak
25	32	62	Ken Spikes	Harold Collins '67 Pontiac	141	300	Tie rod
26	12	39	Friday Hassler	Red Sharp '66 Chevrolet	123	300	Trans
27	18	63	Larry Manning	Bob Adams '66 Ford	106	300	D Shaft
28	29	80	Ray Hill	Cozze Brothers '66 Chevrolet	91	275	Differen
29	7	15	Sam McQuagg	Bud Moore '67 Mercury	71	300	Oil Pan
30	22	25	Jabe Thomas	Don Robertson '67 Ford	64	325	Brakes
31	33	75	Earl Brooks	Gene Black '66 Ford	63	250	Engine
32	14	10	Bill Champion	Champion '67 Ford	48	275	Brakes
33	23	90	Sonny Hutchins	Junie Donlavey '67 Ford	15	285	Engine
34	9	14	Jim Paschal	Friedkin Ent. 67 Plymouth	15	275	Crash
35	34	81	Tom Ingram	Ingram '66 Chevrolet	14	250	Vibration
36	1	26	Darel Dieringer	Junior Johnson '67 Ford	4	400	Crash
37	35	32	Larry Miller	Miller '65 Dodge	3	250	Flagged

Time of Race: 3 hours, 42 minutes, 24 seconds
Average Speed: 67.446 mph
Pole Winner: Darel Dieringer - 77.319 mph
Lap Leaders: Darel Dieringer 1, Cale Yarborough 2-141, Dick Hutcherson 142-237, Richard Petty 238-268, Hutcherson 269-287, Petty 288-343, Hutcherson 344, Petty 345-354, Yarborough 355-386, Hutcherson 387-392, Yarborough 393-479, Petty 480-500.
Cautions: 8 for 57 laps   Margin of Victory: 9 seconds   Attendance: 12,500

3,810 points.

Darel Dieringer started on the pole in Junior Johnson's potent Ford. He led the first lap then bounced off the guard rail into the path of Jim Paschal. Yarborough took the lead and proceeded to lead through lap 141.

Ralph Moody withdrew his Ford while driver Fred Lorenzen was still nursing a stomach ulcer.

Bobby Allison, driving Bud Moore's Mercury,

Richard Petty takes to the high groove around Virginia 500 rivals

crashed in the 266th lap. Sam McQuagg, in another Moore Mercury, went out on lap 171 with a hole in his oil pan.

A crowd of 12,500 watched Petty win at an average speed of 67.446 mph.

Grand National Race No. 15
200 Laps at Savannah Speedway
Savannah, GA
100 Miles on Half-mile Paved Track
April 28, 1967

Fin	St	No.	Driver	Team / Car	Laps	Money	Status
1	5	2	Bobby Allison	J D Bracken '65 Chevrolet	200	$1,000	Running
2	2	43	Richard Petty	Petty Enterprises '67 Plym	200	600	Running
3	4	14	Jim Paschal	Friedkin Ent '67 Plymouth	198	400	Running
4	6	64	Elmo Langley	Langley-Woodfield '66 Ford	194	300	Out / gas
5	8	20	Clyde Lynn	Lynn '66 Ford	194	275	Running
6	10	34	Wendell Scott	Scott '65 Ford	193	240	Running
7	7	75	Earl Brooks	Gene Black '66 Ford	189	200	Running
8	3	48	James Hylton	Bud Hartje '65 Dodge	187	175	Running
9	13	45	Bill Seifert	Seifert '65 Ford	184	150	Running
10	9	97	Henley Gray	Gray '66 Ford	177	140	Running
11	16	78	Joel Davis	Earl Ivey '66 Chevrolet	170	130	Running
12	15	01	Paul Dean Holt	Dennis Holt '67 Ford	159	120	Running
13	11	88	Buck Baker	Baker '66 Olds	156	110	Crash
14	12	57	George Poulos	'65 Plymouth	156	100	Running
15	1	4	John Sears	L G DeWitt '66 Ford	107	100	Differen
16	14	18	Dick Johnson	Johnson '66 Ford	82	100	Clutch

Time of Race: 1 hour, 29 minutes, 49 seconds
Average Speed: 66.802 mph
Pole Winner: John Sears - 72.173 mph
Lap Leaders: John Sears 1-3, Richard Petty 4-69, James Hylton 70-85, Bobby Allison 86-200.
Cautions: Margin of Victory: 16 seconds   Attendance: 3,700

Race No. 15
Allison's Chevy First at Savannah; Named to Drive Owens Dodge

SAVANNAH, GA (Apr. 28) -- Bobby Allison took the lead from James Hylton in the 86th lap and led the rest of the way to win the 100-miler at Savannah Speedway. It was Allison's fifth career Grand National win, but his first on a dirt track. "Did you know that this is the first race, including heats, that I have ever won on dirt?" asked Allison as he was swarmed by fans and a handful of media representatives.

Allison finished 16 seconds ahead of Richard Petty. Jim Paschal was third, Elmo Langley fourth despite running out of gas, and Clyde Lynn was fifth.

Hylton started third and showed some early muscle as he passed Petty for the lead on lap 70. He led for 16 laps before losing the lead to Allison's Chevrolet. Hylton was still in contention when he spun his Dodge on lap 183 and was hit by Buck Baker. Petty had to swerve off the track to avoid a collision and lost much ground to Allison.

The Hylton-Baker mishap did not bring out the caution flag. "Buck was purely a victim," said Hylton. "I got up in the loose stuff and spun it around."

Only hours before he won the race, Allison was tabbed as new driver for the Cotton Owens Dodge team, replacing the departed David Pearson.

John Sears won pole at Savannah, but fell out early

A slim crowd of 3,700 watched Allison take the Savannah prize at a 66.802 mph clip.

John Sears won his first career pole and led the first three laps. The 6'2", 270-pound Ellerbe, NC resident went out on lap 107 with rear end problems.

Grand National Race No. 16
250 Laps at Virginia State Fairgrounds
Richmond, VA
"Richmond 250"
125-miles on Half-mile Dirt Track
April 30, 1967

Fin	St	No.	Driver	Team / Car	Laps	Money	Status
1	1	43	Richard Petty	Petty Enterprises '67 Plym	250	$2,150	Running
2	4	6	Bobby Allison	Cotton Owens '67 Dodge	250	1,300	Running
3	2	29	Dick Hutcherson	Bondy Long '67 Ford	247	950	Running
4	7	48	James Hylton	Bud Hartje '65 Dodge	241	700	Running
5	15	20	Clyde Lynn	Lynn '66 Ford	231	550	Running
6	24	83	Worth McMillion	Allen McMillion '66 Pontiac	229	375	Running
7	18	45	Bill Seifert	Seifert '66 Ford	227	300	Running
8	17	75	Earl Brooks	Gene Black '66 Ford	223	250	Running
9	3	14	Jim Paschal	Friedkin Ent '67 Plymouth	218	200	Engine
10	22	9	Roy Tyner	Truett Rodgers '66 Chevrolet	211	200	Running
11	5	4	John Sears	L G DeWitt '66 Ford	194	175	Differen
12	20	01	Paul Dean Holt	Dennis Holt '67 Ford	194	175	Running
13	13	99	Paul Goldsmith	Nichels Eng '67 Plymouth	121	175	Brakes
14	12	64	Elmo Langley	Langley-Woodfield '66 Ford	105	150	Crash
15	19	54	Tom Raley	Raley '66 Ford	104	150	Engine
16	16	67	Buddy Arrington	Arrington '65 Dodge	93	125	D Shaft
17	14	18	Dick Johnson	Johnson '66 ford	87	125	Engine
18	11	11	J T Putney	Putney ' 66 Chevrolet	81	125	Suspen
19	6	2	Sam McQuagg	J D Bracken '65 Chevrolet	63	125	Sway bar
20	8	34	Wendell Scott	Scott '65 Ford	46	125	Engine
21	21	57	George Poulos	'65 Plymouth	16	125	Flagged
22	23	38	Wayne Smith	Smith '66 Chevrolet	9	125	Rear End
23	10	5	Jim Wright	'66 Dodge	9	125	Crash
24	9	87	Buck Baker	Baker '66 Ford	8	125	Fuel line

Time of Race: 1 hour, 53 minutes, 40 seconds
Average Speed: 65.982 mph
Pole Winner: Richard Petty - 70.038 mph
Lap Leaders: Dick Hutcherson 1-12, Richard Petty 13-76, Hutcherson 77-110,
    Petty 111-136, Bobby Allison 137-149, Petty 150-250.
Cautions: 6 for 32 laps   Margin of Victory: 20 seconds   Attendance: 6,000

Race No. 16

Petty Outraces Allison; Wins 54th at Richmond

RICHMOND, VA (Apr. 30) -- Richard Petty passed a spinning Bobby Allison in the 150th lap and galloped to victory in the Richmond 250 for his record-tying 54th career Grand National victory. Richard's father Lee, holder of the all-time win record, greeted his son in victory lane. "I've enjoyed having that record," said Lee. "I'm just glad that it's staying in the family."

Allison wound up second in his Cotton Owens Dodge, 20 seconds behind the winner. The Hueytown, AL driver, taking his maiden voyage in the highly regarded mount, spun out twice and failed in his quest to give car owner Owens his sixth straight win at the half-mile dirt track..

Allison was leading at the time of his second spin. He scooped up second running Dick Hutcherson in the process as Petty sped into the lead. Hutcherson got stuck in a ditch and lost three laps. Allison continued, but didn't have enough speed to catch Petty.

Hutcherson finished in third place. James Hylton was fourth and Clyde Lynn fifth.

Sam McQuagg, former running-mate with Allison on the Bud Moore team, was assigned to drive the J.D. Bracken Chevrolet which Allison has campaigned the last two years. The Columbus, GA driver went 63 laps before a sway bar broke on the car, putting him out of action.

Petty averaged 65.982 mph for his sixth win of the year. He still trailed winless Hylton in the NASCAR standings by 3,654 points.

Ford racing great Fred Lorenzen announced his retirement from NASCAR, citing stomach ulcers. "I haven't been feeling well lately, and it takes a lot out of you," said an emotional Lorenzen. "I guess every athlete wants to quit when he is on top. I know I'm slowing down and have been a little more cautious in the last year and a half. I added all these things up and decided that now is the time to quit." said the 32 year-old driver.

Race No. 17

Petty's Hemi Hums at Darlington; Records Record 55th

DARLINGTON, SC (May 13) -- Richard Petty ran into the wall on lap 89, but it didn't prevent him from setting an all-time victory record in Darlington Raceway's Rebel 400. Petty led 266 of the 291 laps and finished more than a lap in front of David Pearson, who was making his first start in the Holman-Moody Ford.

Petty's triumph was the 55th of his career -- pushing him one past retired Lee Petty in the all-time victory column. "There have been a lot of fuss lately over me tying or breaking Daddy's record of 54 victories," said Richard. "We've never even thought of it that way. As far as we're concerned, the Petty family has 109 wins."

Pearson was foiled when he was gobbled up in a three car wreck on lap 31. After leading the first 12 laps, Pearson settled back into third place. On lap 31, Buddy Baker, running second, tapped the rear of

Wendell Scott's Ford, sending him out of control. Scott's car slid up the banking and was hit by Pearson. Pearson pitted and his Holman-Moody pit crew tore

David Pearson and Richard Petty wheel to wheel at Darlington

off the left front quarter panel, and the Spartanburg driver was back on his way.

Petty banged into the guard rail on lap 89 while holding a good lead, He made a pit stop and returned to the track running fourth. In a short span of seven laps, Petty was back in the lead.

Dick Hutcherson finished third, Bobby Allison was fourth and Sam McQuagg fifth.

Six cars were eliminated in a wild crash as the rebel flag (Darlington begins its races with the rebel flag, rather than the customary green flag) was waved. Friday Hassler's Chevrolet nearly climbed into the grandstand when it was rear ended by Buck Baker. Jabe Thomas, Roy Mayne, Frank Warren and J.T. Putney,

Friday Hassler's Chevy climbs the wall at the start of Rebel 400 at Darlington

Grand National Race No. 17
291 Laps at Darlington Raceway
Darlington, SC
"Rebel 400"
400 Miles on 1.375-mile Paved Track
May 13, 1967

Fin	St	No	Driver	Team / Car	Laps	Money	status
1	2	43	Richard Petty	Petty Enterprises '67 Plym	291	$14,090	Running
2	1	17	David Pearson	Holman-Moody '67 Ford	290	8,285	Running
3	9	29	Dick Hutcherson	Bondy Long '67 Ford	285	5,005	Running
4	11	6	Bobby Allison	Cotton Owens '67 Dodge	285	2,775	Running
5	8	16	Sam McQuagg	Bud Moore '67 Mercury	283	2,175	Running
6	13	1	Paul Lewis	A J King '67 Dodge	280	1,650	Running
7	6	99	Paul Goldsmith	Nichels Eng '67 Plymouth	280	1,350	Running
8	10	37	Bobby Isaac	K&K Insurance '65 Dodge	277	1,240	Running
9	23	64	Elmo Langley	Langley-Woodfield '66 Ford	269	1,125	Running
10	29	38	Wayne Smith	Smith '66 Chevrolet	259	1,050	Running
11	25	10	Bill Champion	Champion '66 Ford	257	975	Running
12	31	34	Wendell Scott	Scott '65 Ford	250	925	Running
13	28	45	Don Biederman	Bill Seifert '65 Ford	247	900	Running
14	7	14	Jim Paschal	Friedkin Ent '67 Plymouth	246	875	Engine
15	19	05	Armond Holley	Robert Harper '66 Chevrolet	237	850	Engine
16	35	20	Clyde Lynn	Lynn '66 Ford	236	800	Running
17	36	09	Neil Castles	'66 Chevrolet	234	775	Running
18	21	4	John Sears	L G DeWitt '66 Ford	233	750	Running
19	12	48	James Hylton	Bud Hartje '66 Dodge	219	720	Running
20	30	18	Dick Johnson	Johnson '67 Ford	158	675	Crash
21	33	97	Henley Gray	Gray '66 Ford	154	650	Engine
22	3	21	Earl Balmer	Wood Brothers '67 Ford	102	625	Crash
23	32	63	Larry Manning	Bob Adams '66 Ford	52	600	Crash
24	4	3	Buddy Baker	Ray Fox '67 Dodge	45	610	Oil Press
25	27	80	Gary Sain	Cozze Brothers '66 Chevrolet	40	575	Push rod
26	34	62	Ken Spikes	Harold Collins '67 Pontiac	36	560	Heating
27	15	2	Donnie Allison	J D Bracken '66 Chevrolet	22	550	Engine
28	26	67	Buddy Arrington	Arrington '65 Dodge	20	540	Clutch
29	17	49	G C Spencer	Spencer '67 Plymouth	18	650	Oil Press
30	5	26	Darel Dieringer	Junior Johnson '67 Ford	15	530	Engine
31	16	87	Buck Baker	Baker '66 Ford	1	525	Crash
32	14	39	Friday Hassler	Red Sharp '66 Chevrolet	0	525	Crash
33	18	11	J T Putney	Putney '66 Chevrolet	0	555	Crash
34	20	79	Frank Warren	Harold Rhodes '66 Chevrolet	0	510	Crash
35	22	46	Roy Mayne	Tom Hunter '66 Chevrolet	0	525	Crash
36	24	25	Jabe Thomas	Don Robertson '67 Ford	0	500	Crash

Time of Race: 3 hours, 10 minutes, 56 seconds
Average Speed: 125.738 mph
Pole Winner: David Pearson - 144.536 mph
Lap Leaders: David Pearson 1-12, Buddy Baker 13-15, Richard Petty 16-31,
   Bobby Allison 32-33, Petty 34-36, Jim Paschal 37, Petty 38-89, Allison 90-91,
   Sam McQuagg 92-93, Pearson 94-95, Petty 96-99, Pearson 100, Petty 101-291.
Cautions: 5 for 31 laps   Margin of Victory: 1-lap plus   Attendance: 23,000

along with Hassler and Baker, were out of the race.

Veteran Baker was miffed moments after the crash. "That #39 car (driven by Hassler) stopped in front of me," said an irritated Baker. "I could do nothing but run all over him. I don't understand the folks that run racing. It seems they go out and get some of these drivers out of the cotton fields."

Hassler had his own version, "When we got up to about 100 mph, everybody in front of me started stopping. I slowed down, but apparently the guy behind me didn't do a very good job of stopping."

Earl Balmer drove the Wood Brothers Ford in place of Cale Yarborough, who was practicing for the Indianapolis 500. Balmer started third, but crashed on lap 102.

Petty averaged 125.738 mph before 23,000 fans.

Race No. 18

Paschal Ends 13-Month Slump With Beltsville 200 Victory

BELTSVILLE, MD (May 19) -- Jim Paschal took the lead from Richard Petty in the 171st lap and scored a 5.0-second victory in the Beltsville 200 at Beltsville Speedway. It was the first win for the 40 year-old High Point, NC veteran since April 24, 1966 when he won at Martinsville.

Petty, who passed Paschal once on the track, had a flat tire and made one extra pit stop. Three caution flags kept the field bunched, but Petty was unable to handle

Friedkin Enterprises pit crew services Jim Paschal

Paschal in the final stretch run.

Bobby Allison finished third -- on the bumper of Petty. Donnie Allison wound up fourth and Paul Lewis was fifth.

Petty won the pole for the 52nd time in his career and led the first 97 laps. Oil on the track from Earl Brooks' blown engine brought out the yellow flag. The leaders went to the pits for tires and fuel. Paschal's pit crew, headed by Bill Ellis, was the quickest. Paschal returned to the track with the lead.

Petty got around Paschal on lap 117 and led until the flat tire sent him to the pits again.

Paschal's 22nd career win came at an average speed of 71.036 mph. A crowd of 8,245 filled the wooden bleachers at the half-mile paved track.

Race No. 19

Petty Prevails Over Allison In Tidewater 250

HAMPTON, VA (May 20) -- Richard Petty posted his eighth win of the season in the Tidewater 250 at Langley Field Speedway. The Plymouth driver, who has won six of his last nine starts on the Grand National tour, moved to within 1,814 points of point leader James Hylton, who is still looking for his first career victory.

Bobby Allison finished second in the Cotton Owens Dodge, 6.0-seconds behind Petty. Hylton was four laps back in third place. Elmo Langley took fourth

Grand National Race No. 18
200 Laps at Beltsville Speedway
Beltsville, MD
"Beltsville 200"
100 Miles on Half-mile Paved Track
May 19, 1967

Fin	St	No.	Driver	Team / Car	Laps	Money	Status
1	3	14	Jim Paschal	Friedkin Ent '67 Plymouth	200	$1,000	Running
2	1	43	Richard Petty	Petty Enterprises '67 Plym	200	600	Running
3	2	6	Bobby Allison	Cotton Owens '67 Dodge	200	400	Running
4	4	2	Donnie Allison	J D Bracken '65 Chevrolet	198	300	Running
5	5	00	Paul Lewis	Emory Gilliam '65 Dodge	195	275	Running
6	10	4	John Sears	L G DeWitt '66 Ford	194	240	Running
7	7	48	James Hylton	Bud Hartje '65 Dodge	194	200	Running
8	12	20	Clyde Lynn	Lynn '66 Ford	182	175	Running
9	13	67	Buddy Arrington	Arrington '65 Dodge	173	150	Engine
10	14	07	George Davis	Davis '67 Chevrolet	152	140	Running
11	8	34	Wendell Scott	Scott '65 Ford	145	130	Engine
12	11	75	Earl Brooks	Gene Black '65 Ford	77	120	Engine
13	6	64	Elmo Langley	Langley-Woodfield '66 Ford	57	110	Differen
14	9	45	Bill Seifert	Seifert '65 Ford	37	100	Trans
15	16	01	Paul Dean Holt	Dennis Holt '67 Ford	16	100	Differen
16	15	97	Henley Gray	Gray '66 Ford	2	100	Oil Press

Time of Race: 1 hour, 23 minutes, 26 seconds
Average Speed: 71.036 mph
Pole Winner: Richard Petty - 80.286 mph
Lap Leaders: Richard Petty 1-97, Jim Paschal 98-116, Petty 117-170, Paschal 171-200.
Cautions: 3 for ___ laps   Margin of Victory: 5 seconds   Attendance: 8,245

Grand National Race No. 19
250 Laps at Langley Field Speedway
Hampton, VA
"Tidewater 250"
100 Miles on .4-mile Dirt Track
May 20, 1967

Fin	St	No.	Driver	Team / Car	Laps	Money	Status
1	1	43	Richard Petty	Petty Enterprises '67 Plym	250	$1,000	Running
2	5	6	Bobby Allison	Cotton Owens '67 Dodge	250	600	Running
3	8	48	James Hylton	Bud Hartje '65 Dodge	246	400	Running
4	6	64	Elmo Langley	Langley-Woodfield '66 Ford	233	300	Running
5	3	2	Donnie Allison	J D Bracken '65 Chevrolet	230	275	Running
6	9	34	Wendell Scott	Scott '65 Ford	228	240	Running
7	11	20	Clyde Lynn	Lynn '66 Ford	227	200	Running
8	12	45	Bill Seifert	Seifert '65 Ford	222	175	Running
9	2	4	John Sears	L G DeWitt '66 Ford	185	150	Ball Jt
10	7	00	Paul Lewis	Emory Gilliam '65 Dodge	146	140	Fan belt
11	4	14	Jim Paschal	Friedkin Ent '67 Plymouth	141	130	Wiring
12	10	67	Buddy Arrington	Arrington '65 Dodge	106	120	Lug bolts
13	13	01	Paul Dean Holt	Dennis Holt '67 Ford	14	110	Oil Press
14	16	97	Henley Gray	Gray '66 Ford	12	100	Oil Press
15	15	75	Earl Brooks	Gene Black '65 Ford	2	100	Oil Press
16	14	18	Dick Johnson	Johnson '66 Ford	1	100	Time gear

Time of Race: 1 hour, 29 minutes, 57 seconds
Average Speed: 66.704 mph
Pole Winner: Richard Petty - 68.214 mph
Lap Leaders: John Sears 1-18, Richard Petty 19-152, Bobby Allison 153-161, Petty 162-250.
Cautions: Margin of Victory: 6 seconds   Attendance: 6,800

place money and Donnie Allison was fifth.

Petty started on the pole, but took an immediate back seat to independent John Sears. The huge Ellerbe, NC Ford driver paced the action for the first 18 laps, drawing cheers from the crowd of 6,800 as he kept Petty, Allison and Jim Paschal at bay.

Petty finally got by on lap 19 and held the lead through the 152nd lap when he pitted. Allison took the lead for nine laps then made his pit stop. That gave Petty the lead again and he was never headed.

Sears fell out in the final laps with a broken ball joint and wound up ninth in the field of 16. Paschal fell out on lap 141 with electrical problems.

Petty averaged 66.704 mph for his 56th career win.

Race No. 20

Paschal Plows Into Fence -- Wins World 600

CHARLOTTE, NC (May 28) -- Jim Paschal threw away a three lap lead late in the race, but held his ill-handling Plymouth ahead of a pair of hungry challengers to win the eighth annual World 600 at Charlotte Motor Speedway.

Paschal started 10th and had moved into the lead as early as the 37th lap. Most of his rivals had a newly designed Firestone tire on their car -- a soft compound tire which ran quick but chunked rubber. As Paschal lumbered around on his Goodyears, he built up a three lap lead with 150 miles to go. It was a cakewalk.

Jim Paschal led 335 of 400 laps to win World 600

But as he motored through the fourth turn on lap 339, Paschal lost control of his Friedkin Enterprises Plymouth and rode the wall for 300 feet. "I got up in the marbles and had nowhere to go," explained Paschal. "It was all my fault."

The caution came out and Paschal went to the pits on

Grand National Race No. 20
400 Laps at Charlotte Motor Speedway
Charlotte, NC
"World 600"
600 Miles on 1.5-mile Paved Track
May 28, 1967

Fin	St	No.	Driver	Team / Car	Laps	Money	Status
1	10	14	Jim Paschal	Friedkin Ent '67 Plymouth	400	$28,450	Running
2	3	17	David Pearson	Holman-Moody '67 Ford	400	12,530	Running
3	4	6	Bobby Allison	Cotton Owens '67 Dodge	400	7,670	Running
4	5	43	Richard Petty	Petty Enterprises '67 Plym	397	4,875	Running
5	9	42	Tiny Lund	Petty Enterprises '67 Plym	396	4,000	Running
6	14	29	Dick Hutcherson	Bondy Long '67 Ford	395	3,125	Running
7	6	3	Buddy Baker	Ray Fox '67 Dodge	394	2,620	Running
8	17	01	Ramo Stott	Stott '67 Plymouth	388	2,075	Running
9	16	48	James Hylton	Bud Hartje '65 Dodge	385	1,950	Running
10	29	11	J T Putney	Putney '67 Chevrolet	383	1,825	Running
11	12	71	Bobby Isaac**	K&K Insurance '67 Dodge	377	1,880	Running
12	18	79	Frank Warren	Harold Rhodes '66 Chevrolet	375	1,725	Running
13	44	92	Bobby Wawak	Wawak '66 Plymouth	372	1,700	Running
14	24	47	Stick Elliott	Toy Bolton '66 Chevrolet	370	1,650	Running
15	19	64	Elmo Langley	Langley-Woodfield '66 Ford	365	1,570	Running
16	20	87	Buck Baker	Baker '66 Ford	364	1,525	Running
17	23	67	Buddy Arrington	Arrington '65 Dodge	360	1,525	Running
18	34	34	Wendell Scott	Scott '65 Ford	351	1,470	Engine
19	43	20	Clyde Lynn	Lynn '66 Ford	347	1,450	Running
20	38	24	Jack Harden	Betty Lilly '66 Ford	344	1,375	Running
21	42	38	Wayne Smith	Smith '66 Chevrolet	340	1,405	Running
22	2	26	Darel Dieringer	Junior Johnson '67 Ford	322	1,505	Engine
23	22	39	Friday Hassler	Red Sharp '66 Chevrolet	322	1,375	Oil leak
24	39	51	George England	Tom Hixon '66 Chevrolet	321	1,400	Running
25	28	25	Jabe Thomas	Don Robertson '67 Ford	308	1,250	Engine
26	13	12	Donnie Allison	Jon Thorne '67 Dodge	305	1,300	Engine
27	11	99	Paul Goldsmith*	Nichels Eng '67 Plymouth	266	1,425	Engine
28	27	4	Henley Gray	L G DeWitt '66 Ford	266	1,175	Oil Press
29	35	10	Bill Champion	Champion '66 Ford	262	1,160	Engine
30	40	76	Roy Tyner	Don Culpepper '66 Ford	260	1,200	Engine
31	32	1	Paul Lewis	A J King '67 Dodge	218	1,195	Oil Leak
32	8	16	Sam McQuagg	Bud Moore '67 Mercury	207	1,075	Engine
33	21	90	Sonny Hutchins	Junie Donlavey '67 Ford	179	1,150	Trans
34	37	46	Roy Mayne	Tom Hunter '66 Chevrolet	170	1,025	Engine
35	15	49	G C Spencer	Spencer '67 Plymouth	165	1,025	Lug bolts
36	36	06	Neil Castles	Castles '65 Dodge	163	975	Heating
37	26	0	E J Trivette	A C Rakestraw '67 Dodge	129	550	Engine
38	41	80	Gary Sain	Cozze Brothers '66 Chevy	79	990	Heating
39	31	7	Bobby Johns	Shorty Johns '66 Chevrolet	68	1,000	Oil Leak
40	33	02	Johnny Allen	Harold Mays '66 Chevrolet	66	925	Engine
41	1	21	Cale Yarborough	Wood Brothers '67 Ford	58	2,450	Steering
42	7	37	Charlie Glotzbach	K&K Insurance '65 Dodge	49	825	Brakes
43	25	81	Tom Ingram	Ingram '66 Chevrolet	44	810	Fuel pmp
44	30	00	Armond Holley	Emory Gilliam '65 Dodge	31	775	Engine

Time of Race: 4 hours, 25 minutes, 2 seconds
Average Speed: 135.832 mph
Pole Winner: Cale Yarborough - 154.385 mph
Lap Leaders: Cale Yarborough 1-24, Darel Dieringer 25-36, Jim Paschal 37-44, Paul Goldsmith 45-53, Bobby Isaac 54, Paul Lewis 55-58, Buddy Baker 59-62, Paschal 63-97, Goldsmith 98-105, Paschal 106-157, Goldsmith 158-159, Paschal 161-400.
Caution Flags: 5 for 32 laps   Margin of Victory: 5 seconds   Attendance: 70,000
*Relieved by Charlie Glotzbach   **Relieved by Sam McQuagg

lap 340. He lost his entire three lap advantage while crew chief Bill Ellis repaired the car. "We couldn't see Jim hit the wall," said Ellis. "But when he came down the straightaway I saw smoke coming off his wheels and I knew he had hit something."

Miraculously, Paschal kept his ill-handling vehicle ahead of Bobby Allison and David Pearson over the last 57 lap stretch of green flag racing. "He had been running a steady 150 mph before the wreck," said El-

Buck Baker #87 bucks traffic in third turn at Charlotte

out on lap 58 with steering problems related to the bout with the retaining barrier. Darel Dieringer started second and led for 12 laps but spun out near the midway point. He finally called it quits with a blown engine on lap 322.

Paul Goldsmith blew his engine on lap 266, and Sam McQuagg fell victim to a similar fate on lap 207.

Paschal, who led for a total of 335 of the 400 laps, averaged 135.832 mph.

Recently retired Fred Lorenzen was on hand filing reports for the *Charlotte News* . "I thought all reporters had it pretty easy," said Lorenzen. "But this stuff is real work. I had to take out about every other line I wrote to keep from stepping on someone's toes and making them mad at me. I don't know how you keep from doing that."

lis. "After that, he slipped to 141 and I could tell he had his hands full. He pumped it back up to 148 in the last 10 laps. I'll never understand how he held that car on the track."

Pearson finished second, 5.0-seconds behind Paschal. Allison was a close third. Richard Petty used 12 tires in the first 40 laps and slackened his pace to finish fourth. Fifth place went to Tiny Lund, driving another Petty Plymouth. The two Petty cars used 73 tires in the 600-miler. Point leader James Hylton wound up ninth and held an 814 point lead over Petty in the Grand National standings.

Cale Yarborough led for 24 laps from the pole, but he clobbered the third turn wall after a tire let go. He was

Race No. 21

Paschal Wrecks Again -- and Wins Again at Asheville

ASHEVILLE, NC (June 2) -- Old pro Jim Paschal, coming off a World 600 victory when he hit the wall shortly before the finish, pulled the trick again to win the Asheville 300 at Asheville Speedway.

Paschal was holding down a solid lead when his Plymouth slipped into the steel railing on lap 180. The misfortune sent him to the pits for a lengthy stay. He emerged from the pits running fifth.

By the 258th lap, the 40 year-old veteran had slashed his way through the pack and took the lead for good.

"I don't know what to say about all of this," smiled Paschal. "I'm not running into these walls on purpose. I'd like to win one without running into anything."

Donnie Allison, driving the J.D. Bracken Chevrolet, finished a strong second. He trailed Paschal by 8.0-seconds when the checkered flag fell. Third place went to Richard Petty, James Hylton was fourth and Buddy Arrington fifth.

Jack Ingram, rising Sportsman star out of Asheville, started second and ran with the leaders early. A blown tire sent his Chevrolet into the fence on lap 122, knocking him out of the race.

Neil Castles carried a movie camera on the trunk of his Dodge, filming racing scenes for the Hollywood production "Speedway" starring Elvis Presley. Castles had to make many pit stops to get aditional film

Paschal's 24th career win came at an average speed of 63.080 mph. A crowd of 7,240 watched the Friday night show.

out."

The caution flag was out only once for Buddy Arrington's opening lap wreck. After that, Petty led for 242 of the 500 laps on the half mile paved oval.

Petty averaged 80.321 mph for his 57th career Grand National win.

Grand National Race No. 21
300 Laps at Asheville Speedway
Asheville, NC
"Asheville 300"
100 Miles on .333-mile Paved Track
June 2, 1967

Fin	St	No.	Driver	team / Car	Laps	Money	Status
1	5	14	Jim Paschal	Friedkin Ent '67 Plymouth	300	$1,000	Running
2	3	2	Donnie Allison	J D Bracken '66 Chevrolet	300	600	Running
3	1	43	Richard Petty	Petty Enterprises '67 Plym	298	400	Running
4	4	48	James Hylton	Bud Hartje '65 Dodge	297	300	Running
5	7	67	Buddy Arrington	Arrington '65 Dodge	281	275	Running
6	10	80	Gary Sain	Cozze Brothers '66 Chevy	273	240	Running
7	9	97	Henley Gray	Gray '66 Ford	272	200	Running
8	14	35	Max Ledbetter	'65 Olds	266	175	Running
9	12	40	Eddie Yarboro	'65 Dodge	264	150	Running
10	11	01	Paul Dean Holt	Dennis Holt '67 Ford	241	140	Running
11	13	32	Larry Miller	Miller '65 Dodge	143	130	Crash
12	2	81	Jack Ingram	Tom Ingram '66 Chevrolet	122	120	Crash
13	15	57	George Poulos	'65 Plymouth	92	110	Flagged
14	6	4	Elmo Langley	Langley-Woodfield '66 Ford	79	100	Engine
15	8	07	George Davis	Davis '66 Chevrolet	36	100	D Shaft
16	18	8	Ed Negre	Negre '67 Ford	19	100	Differen
17	16	45	Bill Seifert	Seifert '65 Ford	10	100	H Gasket
18	17	25	Jabe Thomas	Don Robertson '67 Ford	5	100	Ignition

Time of Race: 1 hour, 35 minutes, 7 seconds
Average Speed: 63.080 mph
Pole Winner: Richard Petty - 73.710 mph
Lap Leaders: Richard Petty 1-21, James Hylton 22-32, Donnie Allison 33-112, Jim Paschal 113-180, D.Allison 181-257, Paschal 258-300.
Cautions: Margin of Victory: 8 seconds   Attendance: 7,240

Race No. 22

Long Pit Stop Costs Paschal; Petty Wins Macon 300

MACON, GA (June 6) -- Richard Petty took the lead from Jim Paschal just past the halfway point and won the Macon 300 at Middle Georgia Raceway. The five lap victory was the ninth of the season for the 29 year-old Plymouth driver.

Paschal, who led for 58 laps, lost his lead when he pitted for gas and tires on lap 151. His Bill Ellis pit crew took 27 seconds to change two tires and add two cans of fuel. He got back on the track a lap behind and blew his engine 25 laps later.

James Hylton finished in second place and Elmo Langley was third. Bobby Allison drove George Davis' Chevrolet to fourth place. Doug Cooper finished fifth.

"It was a pretty easy win," said Petty. "But things would have been more interesting if Jim hadn't fallen

Grand National Race No. 22
300 Laps at Middle Georgia Raceway
Macon, GA
"Macon 300"
150 Miles on Half-mile Paved Track
June 6, 1967

Fin	St	No.	Driver	Team / Car	Laps	Money	Status
1	1	43	Richard Petty	Petty Enterprises '67 Plym	300	$1,400	Running
2	11	48	James Hylton	Bud Hartje '65 Dodge	295	1,000	Running
3	9	4	Elmo Langley	L G DeWitt '66 Ford	292	700	Running
4	10	07	Bobby Allison	George Davis '67 Chevrolet	290	575	Running
5	5	02	Doug Cooper	Bob Cooper '66 Chevrolet	286	425	Running
6	12	97	Henley Gray	Gray '66 Ford	278	325	Running
7	15	45	Bill Seifert	Seifert '65 Ford	275	275	Running
8	13	25	Jabe Thomas	Don Robertson '67 Ford	274	225	Running
9	24	34	Wendell Scott	Scott '65 Ford	263	200	Running
10	3	39	Friday Hassler	Red Sharp '66 Chevrolet	258	175	Differen
11	18	01	Paul Dean Holt	Dennis Holt '67 Ford	257	100	Running
12	4	49	G C Spencer	Spencer '67 Chevrolet	236	100	Engine
13	2	14	Jim Paschal	Friedkin Ent '67 Plymouth	176	100	Engine
14	19	40	Eddie Yarboro	'65 Dodge	176	100	Clutch
15	6	05	Armond Holley	Robert Harper '66 Chevrolet	96	100	Trans
16	17	52	Jack Etheridge	Etheridge '65 Ford	54	100	Heating
17	21	31	Bill Ervin	Ralph Murphy '66 Ford	53	100	Brakes
18	7	87	Buddy Baker	Buck Baker '66 Ford	27	100	Differen
19	8	11	J T Putney	Putney '66 Chevrolet	25	100	Radiator
20	22	57	George Poulos	'65 Plymouth	25	100	Engine
21	16	62	Ken Spikes	Harold Collins '67 Pontiac	24	100	Radiator
22	20	35	Max Ledbetter	'66 Olds	2	100	Axle
23	23	32	Larry Miller	Miller '65 Dodge	0	100	Hub
24	14	67	Buddy Arrington	Arrington '65 Dodge	0	100	Crash

Time of Race: 1 hour, 32 minutes, 3 seconds
Average Speed: 80.321 mph
Pole Winner: Richard Petty - 86.538 mph
Lap Leaders: Richard Petty 1-93, Jim Paschal 94-151, Petty 152-300.
Cautions: 1 for 3 laps   Margin of Victory: 5-laps plus   Attendance: 7,330

Race No. 23

East Tennessee 200 Falls To Rapid Richard

MARYVILLE, TN (June 8) -- Richard Petty took a back seat in qualifying, but came on strong in the race and won the East Tennessee 200 at Smoky Mountain Raceway for his 10th win of the year. The latest victory for the 6'2", 195-pounder gave him a solid shot at beating Tim Flock's all-time season win total of 18 set in 1955.

"I ain't thinkin' about the record," said Petty. "All

I'm thinking about now is winning my next race."

Petty took the lead from Dick Hutcherson in the 128th lap and led the rest of the way. Jim Paschal finished in second place, a half lap behind the winner. Hutcherson got third place, Friday Hassler was fourth and Elmo Langley fifth.

Petty started sixth on the grid, but had the lead by the 46th lap. Hutcherson led on two occasions for 83 laps, but was no match for the Hemi-powered Plymouth at the end of the 200 lapper.

Jim Hunter, a local Sportsman racer, led the qualifying trials in a major upset. He put his Chevrolet through the timing lights at 79.051 mph -- a record for the half mile dirt track. Another rookie, Joe Ed Neubert, qualified third.

Hunter, competing in only his fourth Grand National race, wound up 12th after leading the race with mechanical problems on lap 184. Neubert finished sixth in his Chevrolet, three laps off the pace.

A crowd of 8,550 watched Petty win with a speed of 72.919 mph.

Race No. 24

Paschal Flagged Winner; Allison Gets Money in Birmingham 100

BIRMINGHAM, AL (June 10) -- Bobby Allison was declared the winner of the 100-mile Grand National race at Birmingham International Speedway a half hour after the checkered flag fell. Allison crossed the finish line just in front of Jim Paschal, who was flagged the winner of the 160-lapper. Trackside scorers said Allison was barely in the lead lap, finishing third.

Cotton Owens, owner of the Allison Dodge, protested. NASCAR officials studied the score cards and said Allison's scorer had missed him on one lap. It was the sixth time Allison had driven the Owens Dodge -- and the first time he has reached victory circle.

Paschal got credit for second place, one car length back. Richard Petty came in third, James Hylton was fourth and Friday Hassler fifth.

A partisan crowd of 8,230 cheered Allison's sixth career Grand National triumph.

Paschal started on the pole for the 12th time in his career and led the first 140 laps on the newly paved .625-mile oval. Allison, who started fourth, led only the final 20 laps.

Allison averaged 88.999 mph in the event, which lasted just over an hour.

Grand National Race No. 23
200 Laps at Smoky Mountain Raceway
Maryville, TN
"East Tennessee 200"
100 Miles on Half-mile Dirt Track
June 8, 1967

Fin	St	No.	Driver	Team / Car	Laps	Money	Status
1	6	43	Richard Petty	Petty Enterprises '67 Plym	200	$1,000	Running
2	8	14	Jim Paschal	Friedkin Ent '67 Plymouth	200	600	Running
3	2	29	Dick Hutcherson	Bondy Long '67 Ford	200	400	Running
4	5	39	Friday Hassler	Red Sharp '66 Chevrolet	199	300	Running
5	7	4	Elmo Langley	L G DeWitt '66 Ford	199	275	Running
6	3	86	Joe Ed Neubert	'65 Chevrolet	197	240	Running
7	10	48	James Hylton	Bud Hartje '65 Dodge	196	200	Running
8	13	20	Clyde Lynn	Lynn '66 Ford	191	175	Running
9	9	49	G C Spencer	Spencer '66 Plymouth	189	150	Running
10	11	97	Henley Gray	Gray '66 Ford	187	140	Running
11	14	07	George Davis	Davis '66 Chevrolet	186	130	Running
12	1	85	Jim Hunter	'65 Chevrolet	176	120	Seal
13	19	32	Larry Miller	Miller '65 Dodge	169	110	Running
14	17	35	Max Ledbetter	'66 Olds	166	100	Running
15	4	2	Donnie Allison	J D Bracken '65 Chevrolet	133	100	Fuel pmp
16	16	45	Bill Seifert	Seifert '65 Ford	130	100	Battery
17	18	31	Bill Ervin	Ralph Murphy '66 Ford	114	100	Heating
18	12	01	Paul Dean Holt	Dennis Holt '67 Ford	99	100	Oil Press
19	20	57	George Poulos	'65 Plymouth	56	100	Steering
20	15	34	Wendell Scott	Scott '65 Ford	51	100	Spindle

Time of Race: 1 hour, 22 minutes, 17 seconds
Average Speed: 72.919 mph
Pole Winner: Jim Hunter - 79.051 mph
Lap Leaders: Dick Hutcherson 1-45, Richard Petty 46-89, Hutcherson 90-123, Petty 124-200.
Cautions: Margin of Victory: Half-lap   Attendance: 8,550

Grand National Race No. 24
160 Laps at Birmingham
International Speedway
Birmingham, AL
100 Miles on .625-mile Paved Track
June 10, 1967

Fin	St	No.	Driver	Team / Car	Laps	Money	Status
1	4	6	Bobby Allison	Cotton Owens '67 Dodge	160	$1,000	Running
2	1	14	Jim Paschal	Friedkin Ent '67 Plymouth	160	600	Running
3	2	43	Richard Petty	Petty Enterprises '67 Plym	160	400	Running
4	5	48	James Hylton	Bud Hartje '65 Dodge	158	300	Running
5	3	39	Friday Hassler	Red Sharp '66 Chevrolet	157	275	Running
6	7	4	John Sears	L G DeWitt '66 Ford	156	240	Running
7	9	04	George Davis	Davis '66 Chevrolet	153	200	Running
8	8	20	Clyde Lynn	Lynn '66 Ford	150	175	Running
9	11	76	Earl Brooks	Gene Black '66 Ford	149	150	Running
10	10	97	Henley Gray	Gray '66 Ford	149	140	Running
11	14	34	Wendell Scott	Scott '65 Ford	147	130	Running
12	13	18	Dick Johnson	Johnson '67 Ford	146	120	Running
13	12	45	Bill Seifert	Seifert '65 Ford	145	110	Running'
14	15	01	Paul Dean Holt	Dennis Holt '67 Ford	141	100	Running
15	6	2	Donnie Allison	J D Bracken '65 Chevrolet	130	100	Sway bar
16	18	57	George Poulos	'65 Plymouth	126	100	Running
17	17	31	Bill Ervin	Ralph Murphy '66 Ford	122	100	Heating
18	16	32	Larry Miller	Miller '65 Dodge	122	100	Running

Time of Race: 1 hour 7 minutes, 25 seconds
Average Speed: 88.999 mph
Pole Winner: Jim Paschal - 94.142 mph
Lap Leaders: Jim Paschal 1-140, Bobby Allison 141-160.
Cautions: Margin of Victory: 1 car length   Attendance: 8,230.

Race No. 25

After 24 Starts and 11 Wins, Petty Takes Point Lead

ROCKINGHAM, NC (June 18) -- Richard Petty out-ran Buddy Baker and won the second annual Carolina 500 at North Carolina Motor Speedway for his 11th win of the year. The victory and the 2,700 points that went with winning moved Petty into the point lead for the first time this year.

Baker, giving the Ray Fox Dodge a strong run, wound up second, a lap off the pace. Dick Hutcherson finished third, Cale Yarborough was fourth and Darel Dieringer fifth.

Bobby Allison leads Richard Petty in Carolina 500

It was strictly a two car show with Petty and Baker battling in the spotlight. Petty led nine times for 249 laps and Baker paced the field five times for 214 laps. "I was worried about Baker," Petty confessed. "He was the only one who could run with me. He was actually faster than I was on the straightaways."

Petty's Plymouth and Baker's Dodge winged away from the factory Fords in the 500-lapper on the one-mile banked oval. Ford Motor Co. representatives suggested the use of a set of gears that would restrict high rpm's in hopes they would finish the grueling affair. "We've been scattering engines all over the speedways in the big races," said Junior Johnson, owner of Die-ringer's Fairlane. "They (Ford officials) figured we've been turning them too much. So we use a higher gear for less rpm's, and the cars won't run."

Only 14 cars finished out of the 44 that took the green flag. LeeRoy Yarbrough, who quit the Jon Thorne Dodge team to take the wheel of Bud Moore's Mercury, led for 11 laps but fell out with a blown head gasket on lap 353.

Bobby Isaac retired with rear end problems; David Pearson left with engine troubles, and Bobby Allison

blew an engine as many of the hot dogs succumbed to the punishment in the four hour, 46 minute marathon.

Petty averaged 104.682 mph as he took a 90-point lead over James Hylton, who finished eighth. A crowd of 22,000 turned out in sunny, warm weather.

Grand National Race No. 25
500 Laps at North Carolina Motor Speedway
Rockingham, NC
"Carolina 500"
500 Miles on 1-mile Paved Track
June 18, 1967

Fin	St	No.	Driver	Team / Car	Laps	Money	Status
1	2	43	Richard Petty	Petty Enterprises '67 Plym	500	$16,175	Running
2	3	3	Buddy Baker	Ray Fox '67 Dodge	499	9,700	Running
3	1	29	Dick Hutcherson	Bondy Long '67 Ford	498	5,200	Running
4	4	21	Cale Yarborough	Wood Brothers '67 Ford	496	2,650	Running
5	10	26	Darel Dieringer	Junior Johnson '67 Ford	494	1,875	Running
6	17	1	Paul Lewis	A J King '67 Dodge	488	1,375	Running
7	11	37	Charlie Glotzbach	K&K Insurance '65 Dodge	485	1,225	Running
8	15	48	James Hylton	Bud Hartje '65 Dodge	482	1,150	Running
9	14	4	John Sears	L G DeWitt '66 Ford	477	1,100	Engine
10	5	14	Jim Paschal	Friedkin Ent '67 Plymouth	473	1,050	Running
11	42	63	Bill Dennis	Bob Adams '66 Ford	456	1,025	Running
12	8	99	Paul Goldsmith	Nichels Eng '67 Plymouth	453	1,000	Differen
13	24	20	Clyde Lynn	Lynn '66 Ford	449	785	Running
14	32	76	Earl Brooks	Don Culpepper '66 Ford	437	720	Running
15	38	01	Paul Dean Holt	Dennis Holt '67 Ford	401	710	Running
16	7	71	Bobby Isaac	K&K Insurance '67 Dodge	382	700	Differen
17	21	87	Buck Baker	Baker '66 Ford	351	690	Engine
18	6	16	LeeRoy Yarbrough	Bud Moore '67 Mercury	349	680	H Gasket
19	44	91	Neil Castles	Castles '66 Plymouth	325	675	Axle
20	36	8	Ed Negre	Negre '67 Ford	322	670	Running
21	12	17	David Pearson	Holman-Moody '67 Ford	307	1,165	Engine
22	31	9	Roy Tyner	Truett Rodgers '66 Chevrolet	283	660	Clutch
23	41	02	Doug Cooper	Bob Cooper '66 Chevrolet	276	650	Carb
24	18	64	Elmo Langley	Langley-Woodfield '66 Ford	235	695	Engine
25	16	92	Bobby Wawak	Wawak '65 Plymouth	222	640	A Frame
26	27	46	Roy Mayne	Tom Hunter '66 Chevrolet	220	680	Engine
27	29	97	Henley Gray	Gray '66 Ford	211	605	Engine
28	43	25	Jabe Thomas	Don Robertson '67 Ford	194	600	Engine
29	30	45	Bill Seifert	Seifert '65 Ford	171	595	Differen
30	34	34	Wendell Scott	Scott '65 Ford	159	590	Engine
31	13	49	G C Spencer	Spencer '67 Plymouth	148	585	Ignition
32	40	74	Tiny Lund	Turkey Minton '67 Chevrolet	139	580	Trans
33	23	18	Dick Johnson	Johnson '67 Ford	136	575	Brakes
34	28	38	Wayne Smith	Smith '66 Chevrolet	75	595	Trans
35	26	03	Johnny Allen	Harold Mays '66 Chevrolet	71	640	Differen
36	9	6	Bobby Allison	Cotton Owens '67 Dodge	70	660	Engine
37	37	07	George Davis	Davis '66 Chevrolet	34	555	Engine
38	22	79	Frank Warren	Harold Rhodes '66 Chevrolet	31	550	Engine
39	33	67	Buddy Arrington	Arrington '65 Dodge	23	545	Engine
40	20	7	Bobby Johns	Shorty Johns '66 Chevrolet	11	540	Heating
41	39	62	Ken Spikes	Harold Collins '67 Pontiac	9	535	Crash
42	35	9	Gary Sain	Cozze Brothers '66 Chevrolet	7	530	Crash
43	19	05	Armond Holley	Robert Harper '66 Chevrolet	3	550	Crash
44	25	11	J T Putney	Putney '66 Chevrolet	2	500	Crash

Time of Race: 4 hours, 46 minutes, 35 seconds
Average Speed: 104.682 mph
Pole Winner: Dick Hutcherson - 116.486 mph
Lap Leaders: Richard Petty 1-15, LeeRoy Yarbrough 16-25, Petty 26-36, Yarbrough 37, Buddy Baker 38-87, Petty 88-115, Dick Hutcherson 116-135, Petty 136-159, Paul Goldsmith 160, Petty 161, Baker 162-188, Petty 189-230, Baker 231-358, Petty 359, Baker 360-366, Petty 367, Baker 368-369, Petty 370-399, Hutcherson 400-404, Petty 405-500.

| Cautions: 9 for 45 laps | Margin of Victory: 1-lap plus | Attendance: 22,000 |

Race No. 26

Petty Grabs Gold at Greenville; 3 Flip in First Lap

GREENVILLE, SC (June 24) -- Richard Petty steered clear of a triple-flip in the opening lap, then staved off Dick Hutcherson to win the 100-mile Grand National race at Greenville-Pickens Speedway. It was Petty's 25th start and his 12th win of the year in what has all indications of a record-wrecking year.

Dick Hutcherson wound up second. Elmo Langley was third five laps back. Clyde Lynn was fourth and Doug Cooper fifth.

Top threats Jim Paschal, John Sears and Cooper were all victims of a first lap fiasco. The three drivers, starting on the outside of the first three rows, charged into the first turn. Before the race, the area had been saturated by a water truck, which had lost power and leaked several gallons of water. All three cars shot straight over the banking and flipped outside the track. Miraculously, only Paschal and late arriving Wendell Scott were sidelined.

A crowd of 6,300 watched Petty lead all 200 laps and average 61.781 mph for his 60th career victory.

James Hylton, second in the point standings, did not start the race and fell 490 points behind Petty in the Grand National standings.

Race No. 27

Paschal Tops Petty in GN Return to Montgomery

MONTGOMERY, AL (June 27) -- The NASCAR Grand National Circuit returned to the Montgomery Speedway for the first time in 11 years, and a crowd of 5,210 turned out to cheer Jim Paschal's fourth win of the year. It also marked the 11th win for the Plymouth nameplate in the last 12 races.

Paschal pushed his Friedkin Enterprises entry around Petty in the 61st lap and led the rest of the way. He padded his advantage to a half-lap when the checkered flag fell. Petty wound up second and Bobby Allison was third. James Hylton finished fourth and Elmo Langley picked up fifth place money

It was the first NASCAR Grand National event

Grand National Race No. 26
200 Laps at Greenville-Pickens Speedway
Greenville, SC
100 Miles on Half-mile Dirt Track
June 24, 1967

Fin	St	No.	Driver	Team / Car	Laps	Money	Status
1	1	43	Richard Petty	Petty Enterprises '67 Plym	200	$1,000	Running
2	3	29	Dick Hutcherson	Bondy Long '67 Ford	200	600	Running
3	7	64	Elmo Langley	Langley-Woodfield '64 Ford	195	400	Running
4	11	20	Clyde Lynn	Lynn 66 Ford	192	300	Running
5	6	02	Doug Cooper	Bob Cooper '67 Chevrolet	191	275	Running
6	8	91	Neil Castles	Castles '66 Plymouth	186	240	Running
7	18	32	Larry Miller	Miller '65 Plymouth	179	200	Running
8	4	4	John Sears	L G DeWitt '66 Ford	178	175	Running
9	12	75	Jimmy Helms	Gene Black '66 Ford	177	150	Running
10	5	49	G C Spencer	Spencer '66 Plymouth	165	140	Engine
11	15	31	Bill Ervin	Ralph Murphy '65 Ford	158	130	Oil Press
12	20	57	George Poulos	'65 Plymouth	152	120	Running
13	13	8	Ed Negre	Negre '67 Ford	139	110	Engine
14	17	35	Max Ledbetter	'65 Olds	123	100	Engine
15	9	97	Henley Gray	Gray '66 Ford	108	100	No tires
16	10	45	Bill Seifert	Seifert '65 Ford	62	100	Heating
17	19	94	Don Biederman	Ron Stotten '67 Chevrolet	28	100	Oil Press
18	16	01	Paul Dean Holt	Dennis Holt '67 Ford	26	100	Engine
19	21	88	Ken Rice	Buck Baker '66 Olds	2	100	Engine
20	2	14	Jim Paschal	Friedkin Ent '67 Plymouth	1	100	Crash
21	14	34	Wendell Scott	Scott '65 Ford	1	100	Crash

Time of Race: 1 hour, 37 minutes, 7 seconds
Average Speed: 61.781 mph
Pole Winner: Richard Petty - 69.498 mph
Lap Leaders: Richard Petty 1- , Dick Hutcherson - , Petty -200.
Cautions: 2 for ___ laps   Margin of Victory: Attendance: 6,300

Grand National Race No. 27
200 Laps at Montgomery Speedway
Montgomery, AL
100 Miles on Half-mile Paved Track
June 27, 1967

Fin	St	No.	Driver	Team / Car	Laps	Money	Status
1	3	14	Jim Paschal	Friedkin Ent '67 Plymouth	200	$1,000	Running
2	1	43	Richard Petty	Petty Enterprises '67 Plym	200	600	Running
3	2	6	Bobby Allison	Cotton Owens '67 Dodge	198	400	Running
4	6	48	James Hylton	Bud Hartje '65 Dodge	196	300	Running
5	5	64	Elmo Langley	Langley-Woodfield '66 Ford	193	275	Running
6	8	39	Friday Hassler	Red Sharp '66 Chevrolet	189	240	Running
7	14	97	Henley Gray	Gray '66 Ford	186	200	Running
8	16	91	Neil Castles	Castles '65 Plymouth	184	175	Running
9	9	20	Clyde Lynn	Lynn '66 Ford	182	150	Engine
10	20	45	Bill Seifert	Seifert '65 Ford	180	140	Running
11	21	88	Buck Baker	Baker '67 Olds	166	130	Running
12	17	01	Paul Dean Holt	Dennis Holt '67 Ford	120	120	Differen
13	12	07	George Davis	Davis '66 Chevrolet	118	110	Axle
14	10	18	Dick Johnson	Johnson '66 Ford	80	100	Differen
15	11	25	Jabe Thomas	Don Robertson '67 Ford	46	100	Engine
16	7	74	Tiny Lund	Turkey Minton '67 Chevrolet	24	100	Oil Leak
17	15	94	Don Biederman	Ron Stotten '66 Chevrolet	21	100	Crash
18	13	34	Wendell Scott	Scott '65 Ford	17	100	Engine
19	4	2	Donnie Allison	J D Bracken '65 Chevrolet	14	100	Engine
20	19	31	Bill Ervin	Ralph Murphy '66 Ford	4	100	W bearing
21	18	57	George Poulos	'65 Plymouth	0	100	Differen

Time of Race: 1 hour, 22 minutes, 50 seconds
Average Speed: 72.435 mph
Pole Winner: Richard Petty - 77.088 mph
Lap Leaders: Richard Petty 1-60, Jim Paschal 61-200.
Cautions: Margin of Victory: Half-lap   Attendance: 5,210

staged at the half-mile oval since September 9, 1956 when Buck Baker won in a Chrysler. Baker finished 11th this outing in an Oldsmobile.

Paschal's 25th career victory came at an average speed of 72.435 mph as another two-car battle left all other competitors far behind. The 40 year-old Paschal has been racing for half his life, but says he has not entertained the idea

Jim Paschal

of quitting. "I'll continue racing if I can keep learning about it," he said. "I'm serious about that. I've learned more racing in the last three years than I did in all of the 17 years before that. And to keep up with the advances, I'll have to learn more in the next three years than I have in the last 20."

Race No. 28

Cale Leads Ford Sweep in Frantic Firecracker 400

DAYTONA BEACH, FL (July 4) -- Cale Yarborough won a dizzying, high speed dash to the finish line in the Firecracker 400 to post his second superspeedway win of the year. The 400-mile event at Daytona International Speedway ended in a 180 mph climax that took over eight and a half hours to complete.

Heavy rain storms interrupted the race twice -- one delay was for four and a half hours. Most of the

Buddy Baker led Firecracker 400 early but departed with suspension trouble

Grand National Race No. 28
160 Laps at Daytona Int'l Speedway
Daytona Beach, FL
"Firecracker 400"
400 Miles on 2.5-mile Paved Track
July 4, 1967

Fin	St	No.	Driver	Team / Car	Laps	Money	Status
1	2	21	Cale Yarborough	Wood Brothers '67 Ford	160	$15,725	Running
2	8	29	Dick Hutcherson	Bondy Long '67 Ford	160	8,395	Running
3	1	26	Darel Dieringer	Junior Johnson '67 Ford	160	5,905	Running
4	7	17	David Pearson	Holman-Moody '67 Ford	160	3,525	Running
5	4	71	Bobby Isaac	K&K Insurance '67 Dodge	159	1,950	Running
6	10	16	LeeRoy Yarbrough	Bud Moore '67 Mercury	158	1,525	Running
7	11	6	Bobby Allison	Cotton Owens '67 Dodge	158	1,325	Running
8	12	48	James Hylton	Bud Hartje '65 Dodge	157	1,225	Running
9	15	14	Jim Paschal	Friedkin Ent '67 Plymouth	156	1,125	Running
10	16	12	Donnie Allison	Jon Thorne '67 Ford	155	1,025	Running
11	3	43	Richard Petty	Petty Enterprises '67 Plym	153	750	Running
12	21	79	Frank Warren	Harold Rhodes '66 Chevrolet	152	800	Running
13	20	24	Jack Harden	Betty Lilly '67 Ford	149	575	Running
14	14	99	Paul Goldsmith	Nichels Eng '67 Plymouth	144	580	Engine
15	24	38	Wayne Smith	Smith '66 Chevrolet	92	575	Engine
16	28	01	Paul Dean Holt	Dennis Holt '67 Ford	82	570	Engine
17	26	76	Earl Brooks	Don Culpepper '66 Ford	76	565	Engine
18	6	37	Sam McQuagg	K&K Insurance '65 Dodge	57	535	W bearing
19	17	87	Buck Baker	Baker '66 Ford	57	530	Engine
20	34	34	Wendell Scott	Scott '65 Ford	41	525	Heating
21	19	25	Jabe Thomas	Don Robertson '67 Ford	38	520	Differen
22	18	64	Elmo Langley	Langley-Woodfield '66 Ford	37	515	Engine
23	31	4	John Sears	L G DeWitt '66 Ford	34	530	Engine
24	22	92	Bobby Wawak	Wawak '65 Plymouth	29	580	Suspen
25	27	18	Dick Johnson	Johnson '67 Ford	23	525	Carb
26	38	7	Bobby Johns	Shorty Johns '66 Chevrolet	22	495	Heating
27	9	11	Mario Andretti	Holman-Moody '67 Ford	20	490	Crash
28	5	3	Buddy Baker	Ray Fox '67 Dodge	17	1,485	Suspen
29	23	46	Roy Mayne	Tom Hunter '66 Chevrolet	13	505	Engine
30	25	05	Armond Holley	Robert Harper '66 Chevrolet	11	500	Trans
31	35	45	Bill Seifert	Seifert '65 Ford	6	470	Engine
32	13	27	A J Foyt	Banjo Matthews '67 Ford	5	515	W bearing
33	39	68	Gary Bettenhausen	Harry Ranier '66 Ford	4	435	Crash
34	33	94	Don Biederman	Ron Stotten '66 Chevrolet	4	455	Vibration
35	30	20	Clyde Lynn	Lynn '66 Ford	3	475	Engine
36	29	16	Neil Castles	Castles '65 Dodge	3	470	Engine
37	36	97	Henley Gray	Gray '66 Ford	3	440	Engine
38	37	52	Jack Etheridge	Etheridge '65 Ford	2	435	Ignition
39	32	10	Bill Champion	Champion '66 Ford	0	455	Engine

Time of Race: 2 hours, 47 minutes, 9 seconds
Average Speed: 143.583 mph
Pole Winner: Darel Dieringer - 179.802 mph
Lap Leaders: Buddy Baker 1-5, Bobby Isaac 6, Baker 7-9, David Pearson 10,
  Baker 11-16, Pearson 17-22, Bobby Allison 23-27, Pearson 28,
  Cale Yarborough 29, Pearson 30-39, Yarborough 40, Pearson 41-46, Yarborough 47-48,
  Sam McQuagg 49, Isaac 50-59, Yarborough 60, Darel Dieringer 61-63, Pearson 64-69,
  Isaac 67-71, Pearson 72-73, Isaac 74-86, Yarborough 87, Isaac 88-92, Yarborough 93-94,
  Pearson 95-98, Yarborough 99-103, Dieringer 104, Pearson 105-123, Dieringer 124-130,
  Yarborough 131-135, Pearson 136-139, Dieringer 140-141, Yarborough 142,
  Dieringer 143-144, Yarborough 145-147, Dieringer 148, Yarborough 149-151,
  Dieringer 152, Yarborough 153-156, Dick Hutcherson 157-159, Yarborough 160.
Cautions: 4 for 43 laps   Margin of Victory: 100 yards   Attendance: 46,000

46,000 spectators had been long gone.

Yarborough, driving the Wood Brothers Ford, made a nerve-stabbing pass of Dick Hutcherson in the final lap and beat two challengers by an eyelash. Hutcherson wound up second. Darel Dieringer crossed the line in third place. David Pearson fell out of the lead pack nine laps from the finish and came home fourth. Fifth place went to Bobby Isaac.

Yarborough was leading with four laps to go when

A.J. Foyt drove the Banjo Matthews Ford at Daytona but went only 5 laps

pass, and he just turned into me."

Goldsmith was philosophical: "A winning driver is working his car to the hilt and is always bordering on a spin-out. But that's the way it is at Daytona."

NASCAR officials cracked down on the inspection procedure three days before the race. Of the 50 entries, 49 had to have additional body work done. "This happens at every track," said mechanic Mario Rossi of the Jon Thorne team. "We were an eighth of an inch off and we have to get a hammer and beat on a $20,000 race car."

LeeRoy Yarbrough's Bud Moore Mercury was the only car in the field which did not flunk the initial inspection.

he slowed and allowed Hutcherson to take the lead. "I'd have stopped on the backstretch if necessary to keep from being the leader on the last lap," said Cale.

Hutcherson led the charge under the white flag, but he too, lifted his right foot on the back straight. "It seemed like I nearly stopped trying to make a couple of those other guys pass," said Hutch. "I slowed so much that they had to hit me in the fanny."

Hutcherson was a sitting duck on the last lap. Yarborough, with Dieringer in tow, swept past in the third turn. Yarborough blocked Dieringer's bid off the fourth

Richard Petty in the pits during Firecracker 400

turn. Hutcherson nabbed second place by inches.

Mario Andretti and Paul Goldsmith brushed each other in the 20th lap, sending the USAC star into a long slide. Andretti thumped the wall and came to a halt in the grassy area between the track and pit road.

"Goldsmith squeezed me out," Andretti said. "There wasn't anything I could do. I was up by his door to

Race No. 29

Trenton's Northern 300 Won by Richard Petty

TRENTON, NJ (July 9) -- Richard Petty prevailed in a race long struggle with Darel Dieringer and grabbed his 13th win of the season in the Northern 300 at Trenton Speedway.

Petty's electric blue Plymouth led for 244 of the 300 laps, but he was hard pressed by Dieringer, who was at the keyboard of Junior Johnson's Ford. The lead changed hands eight times among Petty, Dieringer and Jim Paschal, who led for a single lap.

Dieringer finished second, 28 seconds behind. Paschal wound up third, three laps behind. Paul Goldsmith finished fourth and Elmo Langley was fifth.

Bobby Allison put his J.D. Bracken

Richard Petty's 13th win of the year came at Trenton, NJ

Chevrolet into contention until a blown tire sent him to the pits. The Hueytown, AL driver eventually wound up ninth, 25 laps off the pace due to overheating problems in the late stages.

One caution flag for three laps held Petty's winning speed to 95.322 mph. The 30 year-old Randleman Rocket took the lead for the final time in the 254th lap and led the rest of the way.

For most of the race, Petty and Dieringer had the crowd of 19,500 on its feet. They diced for the lead in reckless abandon in heavy traffic. "It was a case where we both wanted to lead at the time," said Petty. "Neither one of us wanted to back off and we were having a good race."

Thirty-six cars started the race and 16 finished. The victory was Petty's 61st of his career.

Grand National Race No. 29
300 Laps at Trenton Speedway
Trenton, NJ
"Northern 300"
300 Miles on 1-mile Paved Track
July 9, 1967

Fin	St	No.	Driver	Team / Car	Laps	Money	Status
1	1	43	Richard Petty	Petty Enterprises '67 Plym	300	$4,350	Running
2	3	26	Darel Dieringer	Junior Johnson '67 Ford	300	1,965	Running
3	2	14	Jim Paschal	Friedkin Ent '67 Plymouth	297	1,310	Running
4	4	99	Paul Goldsmith	Nichels Eng '67 Plymouth	293	700	Running
5	9	64	Elmo Langley	Langley-Woodfield '66 Ford	288	625	Running
6	7	4	John Sears	L G DeWitt '66 Ford	286	600	Running
7	19	87	Buck Baker	Baker '66 Ford	280	550	Running
8	18	06	Neil Castles	Castles '65 Dodge	279	510	Running
9	16	2	Bobby Allison	J D Bracken '65 Chevrolet	276	550	Running
10	6	48	James Hylton	Bud Hartje '65 Dodge	275	450	Running
11	35	24	Jack Harden	Betty Lilly '66 Ford	275	400	Running
12	10	20	Clyde Lynn	Lynn '66 Ford	272	400	Running
13	11	34	Wendell Scott	Scott '65 Ford	270	390	Running
14	31	07	George Davis	Davis '67 Chevrolet	265	350	Running
15	22	45	Bill Seifert	Seifert '65 Ford	264	370	Running
16	30	63	Bill Dennis	Bob Adams '66 Ford	260	335	Running
17	17	92	Bobby Wawak	Wawak '65 Dodge	216	375	Clutch
18	8	79	Frank Warren	Harold Rhodes '66 Chevrolet	200	340	Engine
19	13	18	Dick Johnson	Johnson '67 Ford	170	330	Engine
20	33	11	J T Putney	Putney '66 Chevrolet	166	295	Heating
21	28	31	Bill Ervin	Ralph Murphy '66 Ford	108	275	Brakes
22	21	97	Henley Gray	Gray '66 Ford	96	300	Suspen
23	5	49	G C Spencer	Spencer '67 Plymouth	92	325	Engine
24	34	88	Al Tasnady	Buck Baker '67 Olds	89	275	Oil Leak
25	23	94	Don Biederman	Ron Stotten '66 Chevrolet	86	300	Engine
26	14	38	Wayne Smith	Smith '66 Chevrolet	77	275	Engine
27	15	57	George Poulos	'65 Plymouth	68	275	Suspen
28	24	01	Paul Dean Hoit	Dennis Holt '67 Ford	55	275	Heating
29	25	12	Larry Miller	Miller '65 Dodge	42	275	Differen
30	26	55	Tiny lund	Lyle Stelter '66 Ford	39	250	Heating
31	27	76	Earl Brooks	Don Culpepper '66 Ford	24	225	Engine
32	12	8	Ed Negre	Negre '67 Ford	16	250	Engine
33	20	1	Jabe Thomas	Don Robertson '67 Ford	8	250	Engine
34	32	9	Roy Tyner	Truett Rodgers '66 Chevrolet	4	225	Engine
35	29	91	Elmer Gilliam	Neil Castles '65 Plymouth	4	225	Differen
36	36	89	Don Stiles	Ron Smith '66 Ford	0	225	D Shaft

Time of Race: 3 hours, 8 minutes, 50 seconds
Average Speed: 95.322 mph
Pole Winner: Richard Petty - 101.208 mph
Lap Leaders: Richard Petty 1-11, Darel Dieringer 12-38, Petty 39-79, Jim Paschal 80, Petty 81-154, Dieringer 155-163, Petty 164-234, Dieringer 235-253, Petty 254-300.
Cautions: 4 for ___ laps   Margin of Victory: 28 seconds   Attendance: 19,500

Race No. 30

Allison Wins Maine 100; Loses Owens Dodge Ride

OXFORD, ME (July 11) -- Bobby Allison hauled the J.D. Bracken Chevrolet to the Oxford Plains Speedway and won the 100-miler, but the victory was costly as he was squeezed out of the factory backed Dodge owned by Cotton Owens.

Allison's fourth win of the season netted him $1,150, but it could cost him thousands. "I wanted to run these Northern races," said Allison. "But Cotton told me he wasn't going to bring his Dodge. I asked him if it was alright if I ran the races in the Chevy. He said 'sure'. But when the news hit that I had won in a Chevrolet, the powers to be at Chrysler must have told Cotton to let me go. I'm very upset about it."

Grand National Race No. 30
300 Laps at Oxford Plains Speedway
Oxford, ME
"Maine 300"
100 Miles on .333-mile Paved Track
July 11, 1967

Fin	St	No.	Driver	Team / Car	Laps	Money	status
1	2	2	Bobby Allison	J D Bracken '65 Chevrolet	300	$1,150	Running
2	4	43	Richard Petty	Petty Enterprises '67 Plym	299	700	Running
3	3	14	Jim Paschal	Friedkin Ent '67 Plymouth	297	450	Running
4	1	48	James Hylton	Bud Hartje '65 Dodge	297	325	Running
5	10	06	Neil Castles	Castles '65 Dodge	294	315	Running
6	9	11	J T Putney	Putney '66 Chevrolet	292	280	Running
7	12	20	Clyde Lynn	Lynn '66 Ford	291	240	Running
8	13	88	Buck Baker	Baker '67 Olds	289	215	Running
9	11	64	Elmo Langley	Langley-Woodfield '66 Ford	288	190	Running
10	14	92	Bobby Wawak	Wawak '66 Ford	282	180	A Frame
11	16	07	George Davis	Davis '66 Chevrolet	279	170	Running
12	15	8	Ed Negre	Negre '67 Ford	277	160	Running
13	19	34	Wendell Scott	Scott '65 Ford	271	155	Heating
14	6	87	Buck Baker	Baker '66 Ford	241	145	Engine
15	7	4	John Sears	L G DeWitt '66 Ford	235	140	Engine
16	24	01	Paul Dean Holt	Dennis Holt '67 Ford	200	130	Wheel
17	8	55	Tiny Lund	Lyle Stelter '66 Ford	173	125	Differen
18	28	9	Roy Tyner	Truett Rodgers '66 Chevrolet	164	120	Engine
19	23	38	Wayne Smith	Smith '66 Chevrolet	146	115	Running
20	17	18	Dick Johnson	Johnson '66 Ford	138	115	Differen
21	18	02	Doug Cooper	Bob Cooper '67 Chevrolet	106	115	Oil Line
22	21	45	Bill Seifert	Seifert '66 Ford	99	115	Heating
23	20	91	Fats Caruso	Neil Castles '65 Plymouth	96	100	Wheel
24	29	94	Don Biederman	Ron Stotten '67 Chevrolet	90	100	Heating
25	27	32	Larry Miller	Miller '65 Dodge	54	100	Fuel line
26	26	57	George Poulos	'65 Plymouth	20	100	Crash
27	22	97	Henley Gray	Gray '66 Ford	44	100	Crash
28	5	49	G C Spencer	Spencer '66 Plymouth	12	100	Axle
29	25	31	Bill Ervin	Ralph Murphy '66 Ford	6	100	U Joint
30	30	76	Earl Brooks	Don Culpepper '66 Ford	1	100	Oil Line

Time of Race: 1 hour, 37 minutes, 15 seconds
Average Speed: 61.697 mph
Pole Winner: James Hylton - 66.043 mph
Lap Leaders: 8 lead changes among Bobby Allison, James Hylton, Richard Petty and Jim Paschal.
Cautions: 2 for 4 laps   Margin of Victory: 1-lap plus   Attendance: 10,000

Allison beat Richard Petty by over a lap. Third place went to Jim Paschal, James Hylton was fourth and Neil Castles fifth.

Sophomore Hylton won the pole in record time and led in the early stages, but he was three laps off the pace at the end of the 300 lapper.

A crowd of 10,000 braved threatening skies to watch Allison average a record 61.697 mph.

Two brief cautions for a total of four laps broke the action. Two spin-outs by George Davis brought out the yellow flag, although a pair of separate wrecks by George Poulos and Henley Gray did not warrant a caution flag.

Race No. 31
Petty Avoids Mishaps; Wins Fonda Hundred

FONDA, NY (July 13) -- Richard Petty took the lead in the 117th lap and sprinted to a one lap victory in the 100-mile Grand National race at Fonda Speedway. It was the 14th win of the 1967 NASCAR season for Petty, making his a virtual cinch to top Tim Flock's all-time mark of 18 wins in a single season.

Bobby Allison led for 58 laps and wound up second. He survived a tangle with J.T. Putney which knocked him out of the lead lap. G.C. Spencer came in third, John Sears was fourth and James Hylton fifth.

Tiny Lund started second and led the first 24 laps in his independent Ford. After losing first place to Petty in the 25th lap, Lund spun out. He was running in the top five when he left the race with a broken axle on lap 144.

Allison led up to the 116th lap when he pitted his Chevrolet. He returned to the track and was running second when he hit a spinning Putney on lap 135. Both continued with Putney finishing sixth.

A total of 20 laps were run under the yellow flag. Bobby Wawak and George Davis were eliminated in single car crashes.

A crowd of 7,200 watched Petty win at a speed of 65.826 mph.

Grand National Race No. 31
200 Laps at Fonda Speedway
Fonda, NY
100 Miles on Half-mile Dirt Track
July 13, 1967

Fin	St	No.	Driver	Team / Car	Laps	Money	Status
1	1	43	Richard Petty	Petty Enterprises '67 Plym	200	$1,150	Running
2	4	2	Bobby Allison	J D Bracken '65 Chevrolet	199	700	Running
3	6	49	G C Spencer	Spencer '66 Plymouth	197	450	Running
4	9	4	John Sears	L G DeWitt '66 Ford	196	300	Running
5	8	48	James Hylton	Bud Hartje '65 Dodge	196	275	Running
6	5	11	J T Putney	Putney '66 Chevrolet	195	240	Running
7	15	91	Neil Castles	Castles '65 Plymouth	193	200	Running
8	10	88	Buck Baker	Baker '67 Olds	189	175	Running
9	21	20	Clyde Lynn	Lynn '66 Ford	189	150	Running
10	16	45	Bill Seifert	Seifert '66 Ford	187	140	Running
11	26	97	Henley Gray	Gray '66 Ford	187	130	Running
12	18	31	Bill Ervin	Ralph Murphy '66 Ford	171	120	Running
13	12	34	Wendell Scott	Scott '65 Ford	168	110	Running
14	20	01	Paul Dean Holt	Dennis Holt '67 Ford	155	100	Running
15	19	57	George Poulos	'65 Plymouth	151	100	Running
16	2	55	Tiny Lund	Lyle Stelter '66 Ford	140	100	Axle
17	3	14	Jim Paschal	Friedkin Ent '67 Plymouth	143	100	Differen
18	27	94	Don Biederman	Ron Stotten '67 Chevrolet	125	100	Cont arm
19	30	32	Larry Miller	Miller '65 Dodge	112	100	Radiator
20	28	38	Wayne Smith	Smith '66 Chevrolet	96	100	Engine
21	24	07	George Davis	Davis '66 Chevrolet	94	100	Crash
22	17	76	Earl Brooks	Don Culpepper '66 Ford	91	100	Heating
23	7	64	Elmo Langley	Langley-Woodfield '66 Ford	68	100	Engine
24	11	02	Doug Cooper	Bob Cooper '67 Chevrolet	65	100	Oil Line
25	25	9	Roy Tyner	Truett Rodgers '66 Chevrolet	60	100	Clutch
26	13	8	Ed Negre	Negre '67 Ford	49	100	Ball Jt.
27	14	92	Bobby Wawak	Wawak '66 Plymouth	29	100	Crash
28	29	87	Ken Rice	Buck Baker '66 Ford	10	100	Engine
29	23	06	Elmer Gilliam	Neil Castles '65 Dodge	3	100	Oil Leak
30	22	18	Dick Johnson	Johnson '66 Ford	2	100	A Frame

Time of Race: 1 hour, 31 minutes, 9 seconds
Average Speed: 65.826 mph
Pole Winner: Richard Petty - 72.173 mph
Lap Leaders: Tiny Lund 1-24, Richard Petty 25-58, Bobby Allison 59-116, Petty 117-200.
Cautions: 5 for 20 laps   Margin of Victory: 1-lap plus   Attendance: 7,200

Race No. 32
Petty Concludes Northern Swing With Islip Victory

ISLIP, NY (July 15) -- Mid-race leaders Bobby Allison and James Hylton faltered in the late stages and Richard Petty cruised home first by three laps in the Islip 300 at Islip Speedway. It was the 15th win in 30 starts for the 30 year-old Plymouth pilot.

Petty led the final 20 laps despite a faulty transmission. "I had nothing but high gear for the second half of the race," said Petty. "I wouldn't have won unless Allison had trouble."

Allison had taken the lead from John Sears in the 221st lap and was headed for his fifth win of the year. But he was involved in a collision with Wendell Scott with 20 laps to go, which sent him to the pits for seven laps.

Petty drove into the lead and wound up three laps ahead of Hylton. G.C. Spencer was third with Sears fourth. Jim Paschal came in fifth. Allison fell to sixth.

Hylton had taken the lead on lap 120 of the 300 lapper and was leading on lap 183 when his Dodge spun out. The Inman, SC driver recovered but was never in contention after that.

Despite Petty's dominance of the 1967 Grand National season, he held only a 784 point lead over winless Hylton in the NASCAR standings.

Grand National Race No. 32
300 Laps at Islip Speedway
Islip, NY
"Islip 300"
60 Miles on .2-mile Paved Track
July 15, 1967

Fin	St	No.	Driver	Team / Car	Laps	Money	Status
1	1	43	Richard Petty	Petty Enterprises '67 Plym	300	$1,150	Running
2	2	48	James Hylton	Bud Hartje '65 Dodge	297	800	Running
3	5	49	G C Spencer	Spencer '66 Plymouth	297	500	Running
4	4	4	John Sears	L G DeWitt '66 Ford	295	300	Running
5	10	14	Jim Paschal	Friedkin Ent '67 Plymouth	294	275	Running
6	3	2	Bobby Allison	J D Bracken '65 Chevrolet	293	240	Running
7	8	11	J T Putney	Putney '66 Chevrolet	292	200	Running
8	9	64	Elmo Langley	Langley-Woodfield '66 Ford	290	175	Running
9	6	20	Clyde Lynn	Lynn '66 Ford	287	150	Running
10	12	07	George Davis	Davis '66 Chevrolet	284	100	Running
11	11	88	Buck Baker	Baker '67 Olds	274	130	Oil Press
12	16	34	Wendell Scott	Scott '65 Ford	271	120	Ball Jt.
13	14	55	Tiny Lund	Lyle Stelter '66 Ford	187	110	Ball Jt.
14	19	91	Neil Castles	Castles '65 Plymouth	162	100	W bearing
15	20	31	Bill Ervin	Ralph Murphy '66 Ford	143	100	Fender
16	23	94	Don Biederman	Ron Stotten '67 Chevrolet	137	100	Brakes
17	17	97	Henley Gray	Gray '66 Ford	124	100	Heating
18	25	32	Larry Miller	Miller '65 Dodge	121	100	Engine
19	24	57	George Poulos	'65 Plymouth	118	100	Crash
20	18	45	Bill Seifert	Seifert '66 Ford	117	100	Crash
21	21	38	Wayne Smith	Smith '66 Chevrolet	112	100	Trans
22	7	92	Bobby Wawak	Wawak '66 Plymouth	111	100	Crash
23	15	76	Earl Brooks	Don Culpepper '66 Ford	50	---	Radiator
24	29	18	Dick Johnson	Johnson '66 Ford	49	---	Crash
25	13	9	Roy Tyner	Truett Rodgers '66 Chevrolet	42	---	Trans
26	22	02	Doug Cooper	Bob Cooper '67 Chevrolet	24	---	Oil Leak
27	26	8	Ed Negre	Negre '67 Ford	15	---	Radiator
28	28	87	Ken Rice	Buck Baker '66 Ford	10	---	Handling
29	27	06	Elmer Gilliam	Neil Castles '65 Dodge	2	---	Steering

Time of Race: 1 hour, 24 minutes, 51 seconds
Average Speed: 42.428 mph
Pole Winner: Richard Petty - 51.136 mph
Lap Leaders: Richard Petty 1-46, Bobby Allison 47-119, James Hylton 120-183,
   John Sears 181-220, Allison 221-280, Petty 281-300.
Cautions: 5 for 29 laps   Margin of Victory: 3-laps plus   Attendance: 4,100

Race No. 33

Petty Loses 3 Laps; Stages Comeback to Win at Bristol

BRISTOL, TN (July 23) -- Richard Petty overcame a series of misfortunes, but staged a miraculous comeback and won the Volunteer 500 at Bristol International Speedway. It was the 16th victory of the season for the Petty Enterprises team.

Dick Hutcherson's Ford finished in second place, three-quarters of a lap back. Darel Dieringer came in third, Jim Paschal was fourth and James Hylton fifth.

Petty started on the pole for the 13th time of the season and jumped out to an early lead. On lap 56, Petty's Plymouth came down pit road with a cut tire. The Petty crew changed all four tires and sent their driver back on the track -- two laps behind.

David Pearson picked up the lead and held first place in the Holman-Moody Ford until lap 114 when he slowed abruptly with engine problems. Hutcherson took the lead when Pearson fell off the pace and led until lap 181 when Petty, lapping the half-mile paved track at an alarming rate, forged back into the lead.

Petty led for just two laps when he came into the pits for routine service. During the pit stop, his crew left the gas cap dangling by the chain. Petty was held at the end of pit road. By the time Petty's crew had trotted down pit road to secure the cap, he had lost another lap.

It was just another minor hinderance to Petty -- who had scampered back into the lead lap by the 256th circuit. By that time, only Hutcherson was left in the lead lap and Petty had little trouble disposing his Ford rival.

"I think we've got an edge on some of the other

Grand National Race No. 33
500 Laps at Bristol Int'l Speedway
Bristol, TN
"Volunteer 500"
250 Miles on Half-mile Paved Track
July 23, 1967

Fin	St	No.	Driver	Team / Car	Laps	Money	Status
1	1	43	Richard Petty	Petty Enterprises '67 Plym	500	$6,050	Running
2	6	29	Dick Hutcherson	Bondy Long '67 Ford	500	3,250	Running
3	2	26	Darel Dieringer	Junior Johnson '67 Ford	498	2,300	Running
4	4	14	Jim Paschal	Friedkin Ent '67 Plymouth	492	1,325	Running
5	13	48	James Hylton	Bud Hartje '65 Dodge	486	1,100	Running
6	25	06	Neil Castles	Castles '65 Dodge	480	950	Running
7	18	64	Elmo Langley	Langley-Woodfield '66 Ford	477	700	Running
8	14	39	Friday Hassler	Red Sharp '66 Chevrolet	476	725	Running
9	21	4	John Sears	L G DeWitt '66 Ford	470	625	Running
10	19	87	Buck Baker	Baker '66 Ford	469	550	Running
11	20	68	Buddy Baker	Harry Ranier '66 Ford	465	525	Engine
12	24	20	Clyde Lynn	Lynn '66 Ford	454	490	Running
13	32	97	Henley Gray	Gray '66 Ford	450	485	Running
14	27	76	Earl Brooks	Don Culpepper '66 Ford	449	495	Running
15	26	11	J T Putney	Putney '66 Chevrolet	445	500	Running
16	7	16	LeeRoy Yarbrough	Bud Moore '67 Mercury	407	415	Engine
17	22	10	Bill Champion	Champion '66 Ford	394	395	H Gasket
18	28	18	Dick Johnson	Johnson '66 Ford	344	400	Steering
19	16	49	G C Spencer	Spencer '67 Plymouth	311	375	Differen
20	15	81	Bobby Johns	Shorty Johns '66 Chevrolet	304	365	Engine
21	35	94	Wendell Scott	Ron Stotten '66 Chevrolet	298	330	Ball Jt.
22	30	67	Buddy Arrington	Arrington '65 Dodge	234	345	Engine
23	33	40	Eddie Yarboro	'65 Dodge	214	330	Battery
24	23	24	Jack Harden	Betty Lilly '67 Ford	191	300	Differen
25	9	12	Donnie Allison	J D Bracken '66 Chevrolet	158	295	H Gasket
26	10	99	Paul Goldsmith	Nichels Eng '67 Plymouth	151	485	Valve
27	8	6	Sam McQuagg	Cotton Owens '67 Dodge	150	275	Vibration
28	5	17	David Pearson	Holman-Moody '67 Ford	116	540	Valve
29	31	38	Wayne Smith	Smith '66 Chevrolet	106	280	Heating
30	17	2	Bobby Allison	J D Bracken '65 Chevrolet	83	275	Trans
31	34	02	Doug Cooper	Bob Cooper '67 Chevrolet	80	275	D Shaft
32	11	53	Bobby Isaac	Activated Angels '67 Dodge	76	250	Clutch
33	3	21	Cale Yarborough	Wood Brothers '67 Ford	59	275	Engine
34	36	25	Jabe Thomas	Don Robertson '67 Ford	30	250	Engine
35	29	9	Roy Tyner	Truett Rodgers '66 Chevrolet	15	275	Oil Press
36	12	74	Tom Pistone	Turkey Minton '67 Chevrolet	14	250	Engine

Time of Race: 3 hours, 10 minutes, 35 second
Average Speed: 78.705 mph
Pole Winner: Richard Petty - 86.621 mph
Lap Leaders: Richard Petty 1-56, David Pearson 57-114, Dick Hutcherson 115-181,
   Petty 182-183, Hutcherson 184-255, Petty 256-258, Hutcherson 259-310, Petty 311-312,
   Hutcherson 313-318, Petty 319-418, Hutcherson 419-438, Petty 439-500.
Cautions: 6 for 42 laps   Margin of Victory: 3/4 lap   Attendance: 20,400

Wendell Scott listens to Volunteer 500 on a radio after being sidelined by a bad ball joint

teams," said Maurice Petty, crew chief for his older brother. "But we haven't got any real secret. The difference is between the seat and the steering wheel. We have the best driver."

Sam McQuagg, who was driving the Cotton Owens Dodge, started eighth and went out on lap 151 with a vibration. Bobby Allison, driving a Chevrolet since his dismissal from the Owens team, left early with transmission problems.

Petty averaged 78.705 mph as six caution flags consumed 42 laps.

Race No. 34

Allison Fails 3 Laps Short; Hutcherson Wins at Maryville

MARYVILLE, TN (July 27) -- Dick Hutcherson took the lead three laps from the finish and grabbed his first win of the year in the Smoky Mountain 200 at Smoky Mountain Raceway. It was the first Grand National victory for the Keokuk, IA veteran since October 2, 1965 when he won at North Wilkesboro.

Richard Petty wound up in second place with Jim Hunter, surprising rookie out of Knoxville, coming home third. James Hylton got fourth place money and Bobby Allison was fifth.

Allison suffered a heartbreaker. After starting 10th in his J.D. Bracken Chevrolet, the Alabama star whipped his car into a patented broadside on the half-mile dirt track and was challenging Hutcherson for the lead before the half way point. Allison had gone into the lead on lap 186 when Hutcherson spun out. Allison was headed for victory when his car died on the backstretch with three laps to go. Ignition failure was the culprit.

"I never gave up," said Hutcherson. "I knew all along I had the fastest car, but after I spun, I had to wait for something to happen to Bobby."

Jim Paschal and Bobby

Dick Hutcherson

Grand National Race No. 34
200 Laps at Smoky Mountain Raceway
Maryville, TN
"Smoky Mountain 200"
100 Miles on Half-mile Dirt Track
July 27, 1967

Fin	St	No.	Driver	Team / Car	Laps	Money	Status
1	1	29	Dick Hutcherson	Bondy Long '67 Ford	200	$1,050	Running
2	7	43	Richard Petty	Petty Enterprises '67 Plym	200	600	Running
3	9	85	Jim Hunter	'65 Chevrolet	199	400	Running
4	13	48	James Hylton	Bud Hartje '65 Dodge	199	300	Running
5	10	2	Bobby Allison	J D Bracken '65 Chevrolet	197	275	Ignition
6	11	4	John Sears	L G DeWitt '66 Ford	197	240	Running
7	8	39	Friday Hassler	Red Sharp '66 Chevrolet	197	200	Running
8	6	64	Elmo Langley	Langley-Woodfield '66 Ford	196	175	Running
9	18	20	Clyde Lynn	Lynn '66 Ford	190	150	Running
10	22	91	Neil Castles	Castles '65 Plymouth	190	140	Running
11	27	45	Bill Seifert	Seifert '66 Ford	187	130	Running
12	17	51	George Hixon	Tom Hixon '66 Chevrolet	187	120	Running
13	25	97	Henley Gray	Gray '66 Ford	185	110	Running
14	24	34	Wendell Scott	Scott '65 Ford	184	100	Running
15	21	94	Don Biederman	Ron Stotten '66 Chevrolet	183	100	Running
16	20	76	Earl Brooks	Don Culpepper '66 Ford	182	100	Running
17	26	9	Roy Tyner	Truett Rodgers '66 Chevrolet	182	100	Running
18	33	88	Buck Baker	Baker '67 Olds	179	100	Running
19	23	07	George Davis	Davis '66 Chevrolet	170	100	Running
20	19	18	Dick Johnson	Johnson '66 Ford	164	100	Running
21	31	31	Bill Ervin	Ralph Murphy '66 Ford	163	100	Running
22	5	14	Jim Paschal	Friedkin Ent '67 Plymouth	157	100	Crash
23	16	92	Bobby Wawak	Wawak '65 Dodge	152	---	Crash
24	32	35	Max Ledbetter	'66 Olds	144	---	Running
25	4	49	G C Spencer	Spencer '67 Plym	68	---	Suspen
26	29	54	Tom Raley	Raley '66 Ford	57	---	Gas tank
27	15	02	Doug Cooper	Bob Cooper '66 Chevrolet	53	---	Crash
28	2	86	Joe Ed Neubert	'65 Chevrolet	53	---	Crash
29	12	74	Tom Pistone	Turkey Minton '66 Chevrolet	50	--	Crash
30	3	6	Sam McQuagg	Cotton Owens '67 Dodge	46	---	Brakes
31	30	01	Paul Dean Holt	Dennis Holt '67 Ford	44	---	Heating
32	14	00	Paul Lewis	Emory Gilliam '65 Dodge	17	---	Crash
33	28	8	Ed Negre	Negre '67 Ford	13	---	Distrib

Time of Race: 1 hour, 31 minutes, 14 seconds
Average Speed: 65.765 mph
Pole Winner: Dick Hutcherson - 79.540 mph
Lap Leaders: Dick Hutcherson 1- 186, Bobby Allison 187-197, Hutcherson 198-200.
Cautions: Margin of Victory: Attendance: 5,400

Wawak were taken out by a crash in the 158th lap.

Biggest surprise in qualifying was Joe Ed Neubert, who ran second quickest in his Chevrolet. Neubert, of Knoxville, was eliminated in a 54th lap crash with Tom Pistone and Doug Cooper.

Hutcherson averaged 65.765 mph for his 13th caree Grand National victory.

Race No. 35
Petty Survival of the Fittest At Nashville

NASHVILLE, TN (July 29) -- Richard Petty took the lead from Friday Hassler with just over 100 laps to go and sped to victory in the Nashville 400 at Fairgrounds Speedway. It was the 17th win of the season and the ninth in the last 14 Grand National races for the toothy Petty.

Petty breezed to a five lap victory after four top contenders ran aground with a multitude of problems. "I was doing plenty wrong," said Petty. "But they done wronger."

James Hylton got credit for finishing second with John Sears third, Sam McQuagg fourth and Clyde Lynn fifth.

Dick Hutcherson won the pole and led on two occasions before being foiled by engine problems. Jim Paschal led in the early going for 16 laps but he slid into the wall when G.C. Spencer blew his engine.

Bobby Allison and Hassler, both in Chevrolets, put themselves in contention by planning only one pit stop in the 400 lapper on the half mile paved oval. In contrast, Petty made seven pit stop en route to the victory.

Allison was leading on lap 260 when he blew his engine. Hassler led for a short time before falling to Petty's brute speed. The Chattanooga, TN driver was running second to Petty when his engine let go in the final 35 laps.

Petty survived a 360 degree spin in the 234th lap. He also changed 12 tires on his way to the $2,050 triumph. A crowd of 13,751 watched the curly-haired Petty win his 65th career race at a speed of 70.866 mph.

Race No. 36
Hutcherson Outlasts Petty; Gets First Big Track Win

HAMPTON, GA (Aug. 6) -- Dick Hutcherson outlasted Top Gun Richard Petty and won the Dixie 500 at

Grand National Race No. 35
400 Laps at Fairgrounds Speedway
Nashville, TN
"Nashville 400"
200 Miles on Half-mile Paved Track
July 29, 1967

Fin	St	No.	Driver	Team / Car	Laps	Money	Status
1	2	43	Richard Petty	Petty Enterprises '67 Plym	400	$2,050	Running
2	8	48	James Hylton	Bud Hartje '65 Dodge	395	1,500	Running
3	11	4	John Sears	L G DeWitt '66 Ford	390	900	Running
4	6	6	Sam McQuagg	Cotton Owens '67 Dodge	390	500	Running
5	14	20	Clyde Lynn	Lynn '66 Ford	375	475	Running
6	24	51	George England	Tom Hixon '66 Chevrolet	369	450	Running
7	20	94	Don Biederman	Ron Stotten '66 Chevrolet	364	425	Running
8	9	39	Friday Hassler	Red Sharp '66 Chevrolet	363	375	Engine
9	26	45	Bill Seifert	Seifert '66 Ford	345	325	Running
10	21	35	Max Ledbetter	'66 Olds	322	300	Running
11	1	29	Dick Hutcherson	Bondy Long '67 Ford	305	270	Engine
12	29	34	Wendell Scott	Scott '65 Ford	300	240	Engine
13	15	97	Henley Gray	Gray '66 Ford	269	220	Running
14	5	2	Bobby Allison	J D Bracken '65 Chevrolet	260	200	Engine
15	19	38	Wayne Smith	Smith '66 Chevrolet	235	170	Clutch
16	22	88	Buck Baker	Baker '67 Olds	139	150	Engine
17	13	04	Coo Coo Marlin	Cunningham '66 Chevrolet	120	130	Heating
18	18	07	George Davis	Davis '66 Chevrolet	118	120	Crash
19	23	9	Roy Tyner	Truett Rodgers '66 Chevrolet	104	100	W bearing
20	27	31	Bill Ervin	Ralph Murphy '65 Ford	69	100	Heating
21	31	92	Bobby Wawak	Wawak '65 Dodge	58	100	Ignition
22	17	76	Earl Brooks	Don Culpepper '66 Ford	52	100	Crash
23	28	8	Ed Negre	Negre '67 Ford	46	100	Oil Leak
24	12	06	Neil Castles	Castles '66 Dodge	45	100	Steering
25	3	14	Jim Paschal	Friedkin Ent '67 Plymouth	44	100	Steering
26	4	49	G C Spencer	Spencer '67 Plymouth	36	100	Engine
27	25	18	Dick Johnson	Johnson '66 Ford	36	100	Crash
28	32	24	Jack Harden	Betty Lilly '67 Ford	34	100	Crash
29	30	01	Paul Dean Holt	Dennis Holt '67 Ford	24	100	D Shaft
30	7	74	Tom Pistone	Turkey Minton '67 Chevrolet	21	100	Engine
31	10	64	Elmo Langley	Langley-Woodfield '66 Ford	21	100	Crash
32	16	91	Walter Wallace	Neil Castles '65 Plymouth	11	100	Vibration

Time of Race: 2 hours, 49 minutes, 20 seconds
Average Speed: 70.866 mph
Pole Winner: Dick Hutcherson - 84.260 mph
Lap Leaders: Dick Hutcherson 1-21, Jim Paschal 22-36, Hutcherson 37- , Bobby Allison - , Richard Petty - , Allison -260, Friday Hassler 261- , Petty -400.
Cautions: 8 for 50 laps   Margin of Victory: 5-laps plus   Attendance: 13,751

Atlanta International Raceway for his first superspeedway victory.

Paul Goldsmith, who was three laps down with 70 laps to go, wound up second in the same lap with the winner. Third place went to LeeRoy Yarbrough with Donnie Allison fourth and Bud Moore fifth.

Petty, who has thoroughly dominated the 1967 season, was poised to hang another jewel on his chain of success. The Randleman, NC veteran led on three occasions for 127 laps. He had just passed Hutcherson for the lead on 261 when his engine blew. It was the first time in 26 events that Petty has failed to finish.

Hutcherson led the final 73 laps. "I was starting to wonder if I was ever going to win a big one," said a happy Hutcherson. "We've been so close so many times. It would have been a heck of a race if Richard's car had held up. I was ready to race him and my car was just as fast as his."

Grand National Race No. 36
334 Laps At Atlanta Int'l Raceway
Hampton, GA
"Dixie 500"
500 Miles on 1.5-mile Paved Track
August 6, 1967

Fin	St	No.	Driver	Team / Car	Laps	Money	Status
1	8	29	Dick Hutcherson	Bondy Long '67 Ford	334	$16,500	Running
2	12	99	Paul Goldsmith	Nichels Eng '67 Plymouth	334	7,900	Running
3	6	16	LeeRoy Yarbrough	Bud Moore '67 Mercury	331	4,725	Running
4	13	12	Donnie Allison	Jon Thorne '67 Ford	323	2,550	Running
5	15	53	Bud Moore	Activated Angels '67 Dodge	323	1,925	Running
6	21	4	John Sears	L G DeWitt '66 Ford	318	1,535	Running
7	26	06	Neil Castles	Castles '67 Dodge	312	1,250	Running
8	20	0	G C Spencer	A C Rakestraw '65 Dodge	311	1,125	Running
9	27	46	Roy Mayne	Tom Hunter '66 Chevrolet	310	1,075	Running
10	29	92	Bobby Wawak	Wawak '65 Plymouth	309	1,020	Running
11	18	37	Bobby Allison	K&K Insurance '67 Dodge	303	1,025	Engine
12	17	63	Bill Dennis	Bob Adams '66 Ford	296	975	Running
13	35	45	Bill Seifert	Seifert '66 Ford	289	890	Running
14	34	34	Wendell Scott	Scott '66 Ford	288	865	Running
15	31	33	Blackie Watt	Harold Mays '66 Chevrolet	283	845	Running
16	38	97	Henley Gray	Gray '66 Ford	266	800	Running
17	2	43	Richard Petty	Petty Enterprises '67 Plym	262	1,485	Engine
18	1	26	Darel Dieringer	Junior Johnson '67 Ford	256	900	Engine
19	7	17	David Pearson	Holman-Moody '67 Ford	238	1,225	Steering
20	23	87	Buck Baker	Baker '66 Ford	227	725	Engine
21	33	20	Clyde Lynn	Lynn '66 Ford	206	705	Rear End
22	16	79	Frank Warren	Harold Rhodes '66 Ford	176	680	Engine
23	3	3	Buddy Baker	Ray Fox '67 Dodge	175	1,110	Crash
24	42	64	Elmo Langley	Langley-Woodfield '66 Ford	167	660	Engine
25	14	48	James Hylton	Bud Hartje '65 Dodge	165	650	Suspen
26	37	62	Roy Tyner	Harold Collins '67 Pontiac	143	655	Engine
27	36	76	Earl Brooks	Don Culpepper '66 Ford	134	645	Engine
28	4	14	Jim Paschal	Friedkin Ent '67 Plymouth	133	745	Crash
29	9	21	Cale Yarborough	Wood Brothers '67 Ford	132	1,150	Crash
30	41	94	Don Biederman	Ron Stotten '66 Chevrolet	102	600	Crash
31	5	6	Sam McQuagg	Cotton Owens '67 Dodge	99	615	Ignition
32	32	25	Jabe Thomas	Don Robertson '67 Ford	90	600	Manifold
33	11	71	Bobby Isaac	K&K Insurance '65 Dodge	84	595	Engine
34	28	10	Bill Champion	Champion '66 Ford	56	580	Engine
35	22	02	Doug Cooper	Bob Cooper '66 Chevrolet	54	580	Trans
36	44	54	Dr. Don Tarr	Tom Raley '65 Ford	47	540	H Gasket
37	10	72	Charlie Glotzbach	K&K Insurance '65 Dodge	44	605	W bearing
38	30	51	George England	Tom Hixon '66 Chevrolet	31	550	Clutch
39	39	9	Ken Spikes	Truett Rodgers '66 Chevrolet	28	525	Engine
40	43	01	Paul Dean Holt	Dennis Holt '67 Ford	23	530	Engine
41	24	11	J T Putney	Putney '66 Chevrolet	19	540	Engine
42	40	8	Ed Negre	Negre '67 Ford	17	510	Engine
43	19	7	Bobby Johns	Shorty Johns '66 Chevrolet	10	555	Rear End
44	25	39	Friday Hassler	Red Sharp '66 Chevrolet	5	525	Rear End

Time of Race: 3 hours, 47 minutes, 14 seconds
Average Speed: 132.286 mph
Pole Winner: Cale Yarborough - 150.669 mph
Lap Leaders: Buddy Baker 1-33,
  Charlie Glotzbach 34-37,
  Richard Petty 38-89,
  Jim Paschal 90-104, Yarborough 105-130,
  Baker 131-133, Dick Hutcherson 134-141,
  Baker 142-173, Hutcherson 174-178,
  Petty 179-252, Hutcherson 253-260,
  Petty 261, Hutcherson 262-334.
Cautions: 6 for 38 laps
 Margin of Victory:
Attendance: 36,000

Tires were a major factor in the 500 miler. The tire companies were caught short of a workable compound -- and race teams were furnished only one set of tires. After that, crews had to scrounge around for tires to finish the event. "I didn't know what to expect from the tires," said Hutcherson. "We cut a tire door in the floorboard so I could see how critical wear was."

NASCAR President Bill France issued a statement after the race. "Sometimes it takes an emergency to make us aware of the valuable assets we normally take for granted," he said. "There was a shortage of tires at Atlanta. Because of a long labor strike at Firestone and a short but damaging strike at Goodyear, the supply was very low. Goodyear gathered up tires from points throughout the United States and chartered 15 flights to Atlanta. We all owe Goodyear a debt of gratitude for the extreme efforts they made to assure a safe race."

Bobby Allison hitched a ride with Nord Krauskopf's K&K Insurance Dodge team and finished 11th after blowing an engine late. Teammate Bobby Isaac suffered a similar fate on lap 84.

Hutcherson, who started eighth, averaged 132.286 mph before a crowd of 36,000.

Petty's point lead grew to 1,874 points over James Hylton, who fell out on lap 165 with suspension failure.

Race No. 37
Petty Ties Flock's Record in Myers Brothers Memorial

WINSTON-SALEM, NC (Aug. 12) -- Richard Petty started on the pole and led all 250 laps to gain his 18th win of the 1967 NASCAR season at Bowman Gray Stadium. The victory tied Tim Flock's 1955 record for

Announcer Bob Montgomery interviews Dixie 500 winner Dick Hutcherson

the most Grand National triumphs in a single season. Petty's 18th victory came in his 36th 1967 start.

Petty went the entire 250 laps without a pit stop and wound up three laps ahead of Jim Paschal, who made one pit stop. Bobby Allison, who was beset with a flat tire and a spin, finished third just behind Paschal. John Sears came in fourth and James Hylton was fifth.

A crowd of 8,500 watched Petty make history. Reporter Jesse Outlar wrote that Petty's accomplishment "is remarkable from any angle. It would be like the Falcons winning the NFL championship; Hank Aaron batting .600; or a Novi winning the Indianapolis 500. Race drivers simply are not suppose to win half the races."

Despite all the hoopla surrounding Petty from the start of the year, his point lead is uncomfortable at best. His lead stands at 1,938 points -- a small margin considering up to 4,000 points are awarded to the winner of a superspeedway race. Hylton ranks second, using consistency to place high in the standings.

Petty averaged 50.893 mph in the caution free event.

Race No. 38
Petty Wedges Past Allison; Cops 19th at Columbia

COLUMBIA, SC (Aug. 17) -- Richard Petty took the lead with 12 laps remaining and won the 100-mile

Grand National event at Columbia Speedway. It was his 19th win of the season.

Petty and Allison swapped the lead four times during the 200 lapper on the half mile dirt track. Allison had pushed his Chevrolet around Petty in the 53rd lap and led his Plymouth rival most of the way. In the late stages, Petty hugged Alli-

Petty's record-breaking 19th win of the year came at Columbia

son's rear bumper and made the decisive pass on lap 189. Two laps after losing the lead, Allison thumped

Grand National Race No. 37
250 Laps at Bowman Gray Stadium
Winston-Salem, NC
"Myers Brothers Memorial"
62.5 Miles on Quarter-mile Paved Track
August 12, 1967

Fin	St	No.	Driver	Team / Car	Laps	Money	Status
1	1	43	Richard Petty	Petty Enterprises '67 Plym	250	$1,00	Running
2	3	14	Jim Paschal	Friedkin Ent '67 Plymouth	247	600	Running
3	2	2	Bobby Allison	J D Bracken '65 Chevrolet	247	400	Running
4	4	4	John Sears	L G DeWitt '66 Ford	245	300	Running
5	5	48	James Hylton	Bud Hartje '65 Dodge	243	275	Running
6	6	20	Clyde Lynn	Lynn '66 Ford	239	239	Running
7	10	64	Elmo Langley	Langley-Woodfield '66 Ford	236	200	Running
8	13	34	Wendell Scott	Scott '65 Ford	231	175	Running
9	7	11	J T Putney	Putney '66 Chevrolet	229	150	Running
10	12	02	Doug Cooper	Bob Cooper '66 Chevrolet	222	140	Running
11	9	88	Buddy Baker	Buck Baker '66 Chevrolet	183	130	Oil Leak
12	8	38	Wayne Smith	Smith '66 Chevrolet	153	120	Rear End
13	14	91	Neil Castles	Castles '65 Plymouth	142	110	Rear End
14	11	07	George Davis	Davis '66 Chevrolet	114	100	Crash
15	15	45	Bill Seifert	Seifert '65 Ford	86	100	Trans
16	18	9	Roy Tyner	Truett Rodgers '66 Chevrolet	53	100	Rear End
17	16	18	Dick Johnson	Johnson '67 Ford	32	100	Trans
18	17	40	Eddie Yarboro	'65 Dodge	2	100	Handling

Time of Race: 1 hour, 13 minutes, 41 seconds
Average Speed: 50.893 mph
Pole Winner: Richard Petty - 53.160 mph
Lap Leaders: Richard Petty 1-250.
Cautions: None   Margin of Victory: 3-laps plus   Attendance: 8,500.

Grand National Race No. 38
200 Laps at Columbia Speedway
Columbia, SC
100 Miles on Half-mile Dirt Track
August 17, 1967

Fin	St	No.	Driver	Team / Car	Laps	Money	Status
1	1	43	Richard Petty	Petty Enterprises '67 Plym	200	$1,000	Running
2	3	4	John Sears	L G DeWitt '66 Ford	199	600	Running
3	9	64	Elmo Langley	Langley-Woodfield '66 Ford	197	400	Running
4	5	2	Bobby Allison	J D Bracken '66 Chevrolet	197	300	Running
5	8	48	James Hylton	Bud Hartje '65 Dodge	196	275	Running
6	15	20	Clyde Lynn	Lynn '66 Ford	191	240	Running
7	19	02	Doug Cooper	Bob Cooper '66 Chevrolet	184	200	Running
8	20	76	Earl Brooks	Don Culpepper '66 Ford	182	175	Running
9	14	97	Henley Gray	Gray '66 Ford	181	150	Running
10	13	34	Wendell Scott	Scott '66 Ford	178	140	Running
11	21	35	Harold Stockton	'65 Olds	150	130	Running
12	17	9	Roy Tyner	Truett Rodgers '66 Chevrolet	143	120	Running
13	23	31	Bill Ervin	Ralph Murphy '66 Ford	109	110	Engine
14	18	91	Neil Castles	Castles '65 Plymouth	101	100	Lug bolt
15	4	55	Tiny Lund	Lyle Stelter '66 Ford	96	100	Engine
16	16	07	George Davis	Davis '67 Chevrolet	73	100	Suspen
17	2	6	Buddy Baker	Cotton Owens '67 Dodge	69	100	Axle
18	22	57	George Poulos	'65 Plymouth	67	100	Crash
19	12	54	Tom Raley	Raley '66 Ford	65	100	Trans
20	6	14	Jim Paschal	Friedkin Ent '67 Plymouth	55	100	Crash
21	10	45	Bill Seifert	Seifert '66 Ford	52	100	Heating
22	7	18	Dick Johnson	Johnson '67 Ford	12	100	Crash
23	24	75	Jackie Fox	Gene Black '66 Ford	6	---	Wtr hose
24	11	29	Dick Hutcherson	Bondy Long '67 Ford	3	---	Engine

Time of Race: 1 hour, 33 minutes, 21 seconds
Average Speed: 64.274 mph
Pole Winner: Richard Petty - 74.968 mph
Lap Leaders: Richard Petty 1-2, Bobby Allison 3-37, Petty 38-52, Allison 53-188, Petty 189-200.
Cautions: 5 for ___ laps   Margin of Victory: 1-lap plus   Attendance: 6,800

the wall and limped home fourth, three laps behind.

John Sears finished second, a lap off the pace. Elmo Langley came in third. James Hylton was fifth, a lap behind Allison.

Buddy Baker qualified second in the Cotton Owens Dodge and ran well in the early going. His day came to an end in the 69th lap when an axle broke. Jim Paschal crashed in the 55th lap and Tiny Lund went out on lap 96 with a blown engine.

Petty's 67th career Grand National win came at an average speed of 64.274 mph. A crowd of 6,800 watched the event.

Race No. 39

Petty's 20th Comes in Savannah Cakewalk

SAVANNAH, GA (Aug. 25) -- Richard Petty continued his amazing record-wrecking spree by winning the 100-mile Grand National race at Savannah Speedway. It was Petty's third straight and his 20th victory of the season.

Petty staved off an early challenge from Dick

Hutcherson and wound up five laps in front of Elmo Langley. Tom Pistone was third, Neil Castles was fourth and George Davis fifth.

James Hylton, second in the point standings, finished seventh in a determined display -- driving the final 40 laps with a broken axle.

Hutcherson fell off the pace following a five lap pit stop to repair a crumpled fender. Pistone, driving a Turkey Minton Chevrolet, picked up second place but

Grand National Race No. 39
200 laps at Savannah Speedway
Savannah, GA
100 Miles on Half-mile Paved Track
August 25, 1967

Fin	St	No.	Driver	Team / Car	Laps	Money	Status
1	1	43	Richard Petty	Petty Enterprises '67 Plym	200	$1,000	Running
2	6	64	Elmo Langley	Langley-Woodfield '66 Ford	195	600	Running
3	5	74	Tom Pistone	Turkey Minton '67 Chevrolet	194	400	Running
4	18	91	Neil Castles	Castles '65 Plymouth	190	300	Running
5	14	07	George Davis	Davis 66 Chevrolet	186	275	Running
6	20	76	Earl Brooks	Don Culpepper '66 Ford	174	240	Running
7	2	48	James Hylton	Bud Hartje '65 Dodge	173	200	Running
8	12	20	Clyde Lynn	Lynn '66 Ford	162	175	Running
9	17	57	George Poulos	'65 Plymouth	159	150	Running
10	4	29	Dick Hutcherson	Bondy Long '67 Ford	150	140	Spindle
11	7	02	Doug Cooper	Bob Cooper '66 Chevrolet	147	130	Running
12	16	01	Bill Ervin	Dennis Holt '67 Ford	135	120	Running
13	13	52	Jack Etheridge	Etheridge '65 Ford	104	110	A Frame
14	3	2	Bobby Allison	J D Bracken '65 Chevrolet	72	100	Sway bar
15	10	9	Roy Tyner	Truett Rodgers '66 Chevrolet	66	100	Differen
16	15	45	Bill Seifert	Seifert '66 Ford	52	100	Ignition
17	8	88	Buddy Baker	Buck Baker '67 Olds	47	100	Radiator
18	9	00	Bud Moore	Emory Gilliam '65 Dodge	33	100	Ball Jt.
19	11	97	Henley Gray	Gray '66 Ford	19	100	Heating
20	19	94	Don Biederman	Ron Stotten '66 Chevrolet	17	100	Oil Pres

Time of Race: 1 hour, 32 minutes, 15 seconds
Average Speed: 65.041 mph
Pole Winner: Richard Petty - 71.942 mph
Lap Leaders: Richard Petty 1-200.
Cautions: Margin of Victory: 5-laps plus   Attendance: 5,000

Grand National Race No. 40
364 Laps at Darlington Raceway
Darlington, SC
"Southern 500"
500 Miles on 1.375-mile Paved Track
September 4, 1967

Fin	St	No.	Driver	Team / Car	Laps	Money	Status
1	1	43	Richard Petty	Petty Enterprises '67 Plym	364	$26,900	Running
2	11	17	David Pearson*	Holman-Moody '67 Ford	359	10,825	Running
3	4	42	G C Spencer	Petty Enterprises '67 Plym	359	6,175	Running
4	10	72	Charlie Glotzbach	K&K Insurance '67 Dodge	356	3,325	Running
5	12	53	Bud Moore	Activated Angels '67 Dodge	355	2,725	Running
6	14	71	Bobby Isaac	K&K Insurance '67 Dodge	351	1,800	Running
7	6	12	Donnie Allison	Jon Thorne '67 Ford	350	1,650	Running
8	15	48	James Hylton	Bud Hartje '65 Dodge	348	1,500	Running
9	13	14	Jim Paschal	Friedkin Ent '67 Plymouth	347	1,400	Engine
10	28	79	Frank Warren	Harold Rhodes '66 Chevrolet	338	1,300	Running
11	18	4	John Sears	L G DeWitt '66 Ford	335	1,250	Running
12	33	06	Neil Castles	Castles '65 Dodge	334	1,350	Running
13	25	59	Roy Mayne	'66 Chevrolet	334	1,175	Running
14	27	76	Earl Brooks	Don Culpepper '66 Ford	330	1,075	Running
15	30	67	Buddy Arrington	Arrington '65 Dodge	229	1,000	Running
16	16	7	Bobby Johns	Shorty Johns '66 Chevrolet	326	950	Running
17	38	19	E J Trivette	Roy Dutton '66 Ford	320	950	Running
18	39	45	Bill Seifert	Seifert '65 Ford	314	900	Running
19	36	97	Henley Gray	Gray '66 Ford	312	850	Running
20	42	94	Don Biederman	Ron Stotten '66 Chevrolet	297	825	Running
21	44	9	Ken Spikes	Truett Rodgers '66 Chevrolet	277	800	Running
22	29	34	Wendell Scott	Scott '66 Ford	266	725	Engine
23	34	11	J T Putney	Putney '66 Chevrolet	259	700	Engine
24	17	26	Darel Dieringer	Junior Johnson '67 Ford	254	750	Engine
25	22	87	Doug Cooper	Buck Baker '66 Ford	231	650	Engine
26	5	99	Paul Goldsmith	Nichels Eng '67 Plymouth	192	640	Crash
27	43	01	Dr. Don Tarr	Dennis Holt '67 Ford	170	680	Oil Line
28	24	10	Bill Champion	Champion '66 Ford	131	720	Running
29	32	24	Bobby Mausgrover	Betty Lilly '67 Ford	125	610	Oil Pan
30	2	3	Buddy Baker	Ray Fox '67 Dodge	123	675	Crash
31	21	36	H B Bailey	Bailey '66 Pontiac	115	590	Crash
32	19	2	Bobby Allison	J D Bracken '65 Chevrolet	111	605	Engine
33	26	38	Wayne Smith	Smith '66 Chevrolet	108	620	Water pm
34	23	64	Elmo Langley	Langley-Woodfield '66 Ford	107	560	Crash
35	3	6	Sam McQuagg	Cotton Owens '67 Dodge	79	580	Crash
36	7	29	Dick Hutcherson	Bondy Long '67 Ford	78	550	Crash
37	37	20	Clyde Lynn	Lynn '66 Ford	61	590	Crash
38	35	62	Roy Tyner	Harold Collins '67 Pontiac	42	580	Engine
39	8	16	LeeRoy Yarbrough	Bud Moore '67 Mercury	33	525	Engine
40	20	55	Tiny Lund	Lyle Stelter '66 Ford	26	520	Engine
41	41	75	Bob Cooper	Gene Black '66 Ford	24	565	Oil Leak
42	31	25	Jabe Thomas	Don Robertson '67 Ford	17	510	Engine
43	40	31	Ed Negre	Ralph Murphy '66 Ford	8	555	Engine
44	9	21	Cale Yarborough	Wood Brothers '67 Ford	3	620	Engine

Time of Race: 3 hours, 50 minutes, 15 seconds
Average Speed: 130.423 mph
Pole Winner: Richard Petty - 143.436 mph
Lap Leaders: Buddy Baker 1-6, Richard Petty 7-54, David Pearson 55-66, Petty 67-127, Donnie Allison 128, Petty 129-364.
Cautions: 3 for 25 laps   Margin of Victory: 5-laps plus   Attendance: 57,000
*Relieved by Cale Yarborough

ran out of gas with five laps to go.

Bobby Allison started third and ran with the leaders until a sway bar broke on his Chevrolet, putting him out after 72 laps.

A crowd of 5,000 watched Petty win at an average speed of 65.041 mph.

Race No. 40

Petty Leads All But 19 Laps In Southern 500 Victory

DARLINGTON, SC (Sept. 4) -- Richard Petty continued his winning ways by dominating the Southern 500 at Darlington Raceway, leading for 345 of the 364 laps. It was Petty's 21st win of the season and the 69th of his career.

Petty started on the pole and led virtually all the way after Buddy Baker had led the opening six laps. It was clearly evident to the 57,000 spectators that unless mechanical problems intervened, the race was in Petty's control.

Finishing second, five laps behind, was David Pearson's Ford with relief driver Cale Yarborough at the keyboard. G.C.Spencer, driving a Petty Enterprises Plymouth, wound up third, losing second place to Yarborough two laps from the finish. Charlie Glotzbach came in fourth and Bud Moore was fifth.

"This has to be the climax of the season," said Petty.

"Even if we win the rest of the races, this is the biggest thrill. We've been trying to win this race for 18 years. Daddy was never able to win the Southern 500. I could name nearly a dozen Southern 500s Daddy or I should have won."

Sam McQuagg survived a frightening tumble in the 81st lap. The Columbus, GA Dodge driver clipped

McQuagg's badly mangled Dodge sits in the Darlington garage

fenders with Dick Hutcherson, sending McQuagg into the concrete pit wall. The car flipped end-over-end and then side-over-side about eight times. McQuagg groggily climbed out of the car, walked away, then collapsed. He was treated and released from a local hospital.

Chuck Looney and Mike Bailey, members of Bobby Allison's pit crew, were slightly injured by flying chunks of concrete.

Baker was eliminated in a grinding three car crash in the 125th lap. H.B. Bailey spun in the first turn and was hit by Elmo Langley and Baker. All three were out of the race.

Rookie Donnie Allison finished sixth in the Jon Thorne Ford and won the Fireball Roberts Rookie of the Race award.

Petty averaged a record 130.423 mph, topping Roberts' 1963 time of 129.784 mph.

One Ford driver, who requested anonymity, said, "Nobody can touch Petty. Everybody used to say that Fred Lorenzen was the luckiest guy in the world. Baloney. Richard could ride around with one hand tied behind his back and still win. Nobody is that good. Nobody."

Sam McQuagg flipped the Cotton Owens Dodge at Darlington after tangling with Dick Hutcherson

Race No. 41

Allison Blows; Petty Takes 5th Straight at Hickory

HICKORY, NC (Sept. 8) -- Richard Petty zoomed into the lead when engine failure sent Bobby Allison to the showers and won the Buddy Shuman Memorial at Hickory Speedway. It was the 22nd victory of the season for the 30 year-old "king" of stock car racing.

Rookie Jack Ingram, a Sportsman driver out of Asheville, finished second in a Chevrolet. Jim Paschal came in third, James Hylton was fourth and Elmo Langley fifth. Petty drove the final two laps on a flat tire.

Petty took back seat most of the way, but outlasted his speedier rivals on the .4-mile paved oval. Dick Hutcherson won the pole and led three times for 17 laps, but was taken out when he rear-ended Jim

Jack Ingram finished second to Petty at Hickory

Paschal's Plymouth on lap 141. Paschal was in strong contention until a sputtering engine dropped him two laps off the pace.

Allison thrilled the crowd of 11,000 by blasting around Petty in the 217th lap of the 250-lapper. He was inching away from the heavy favorite when smoke belched from his J.D. Bracken Chevrolet.

Ford Motor Co. had two surprise entries in an attempt to quench the Petty domination. Swede Savage was assigned to man a Holman-Moody Ford and started eighth. Engine failure put him out after 226 laps.

Sportsman driver Bosco Lowe got a ride in Banjo Matthews' Ford, and he managed to finish 10th, 17 laps behind.

Petty's 70th career victory came at an average speed of 71.414 mph.

Race No. 42

Rapid Richard's Rampage Continues at Richmond

RICHMOND, VA (Sept. 10) -- Richard Petty took the lead in the 138th lap and led the rest of the way to

Grand National Race No. 41
250 Laps at Hickory Speedway
Hickory, NC
"Buddy Shuman Memorial"
100 Miles on .4-mile Paved Track
September 8, 1967

Fin	St	No.	Driver	Team / Car	Laps	Money	Status
1	2	43	Richard Petty	Petty Enterprises '67 Plym	250	$1,500	Running
2	6	81	Jack Ingram	Tom Ingram '66 Chevrolet	249	600	Running
3	3	14	Jim Paschal	Friedkin Ent '67 Plym	248	400	Running
4	4	48	James Hylton	Bud Hartje '65 Dodge	245	300	Running
5	9	64	Elmo Langley	Langley-Woodfield '66 Ford	244	275	Running
6	13	25	Jabe Thomas	Don Robertson '67 Ford	237	240	Running
7	33	74	Tom Pistone	Turkey Minton '67 Chevrolet	234	200	Running
8	23	76	Earl Brooks	Don Culpepper '66 Ford	234	175	Running
9	16	38	Wayne Smith	Smith '66 Chevrolet	234	150	Running
10	7	27	Bosco Lowe	Banjo Matthews '66 Ford	233	140	Running
11	12	06	Neil Castles	Castles '65 Dodge	231	130	Running
12	22	02	Bob Cooper	Cooper '67 Chevrolet	229	120	Running
13	20	19	E J Trivette	Roy Dutton '66 Ford	229	110	Running
14	10	20	Clyde Lynn	Lynn '66 Ford	228	100	Running
15	27	97	Henley Gray	Gray '66 Ford	228	100	Running
16	8	111	Swede Savage	Holman-Moody '67 Ford	226	100	Engine
17	18	45	Bill Seifert	Seifert '65 Ford	226	100	Running
18	5	2	Bobby Allison	J D Bracken '65 Chevrolet	223	100	Engine
19	26	35	Max Ledbetter	'65 Olds	215	100	Running
20	31	94	Don Biederman	Ron Stotten '66 Chevrolet	206	100	Running
21	29	57	George Poulos	'65 Plymouth	194	100	Running
22	30	01	Paul Dean Holt	Dennis Holt '67 Ford	175	100	Crash
23	28	31	Bill Ervin	Ralph Murphy '66 Ford	143	100	Shocks
24	1	29	Dick Hutcherson	Bondy Long '67 Ford	141	100	Crash
25	32	49	G C Spencer	Spencer '67 Plymouth	135	---	Oil Press
26	15	54	Tom Raley	Raley '65 Ford	130	---	Engine
27	11	88	Doug Cooper	Buck Baker '66 Olds	87	---	Trans
28	21	34	Wendell Scott	Scott '66 Ford	51	---	Engine
29	24	75	Jackie Fox	Gene Black '66 Ford	51	---	Steering
30	19	07	George Davis	Davis '66 Chevrolet	50	---	Crash
31	25	12	Johnny Steele	'67 Ford	39	---	Engine
32	17	40	Eddie Yarboro	'65 Dodge	4	---	Crash
33	14	4	John Sears	L G DeWitt '66 Ford	2	---	Engine

Time of Race: 1 hour, 24 minutes, 1 seconds
Average Speed: 71.414 mph
Pole Winner: Dick Hutcherson - 86.538 mph
Lap Leaders: Dick Hutcherson 1-14, Jim Paschal 15-52, Hutcherson 53-54, Paschal 55-105, Richard Petty 106-116, Hutcherson 117, Bobby Allison 118-186, Petty 187-217, Allison 218-222, Petty 223-250.
Cautions: 6 for 44 laps   Margin of Victory: 1-lap plus   Attendance: 11,000

win the Capital City 300 at the muddy Virginia State Fairgrounds. It was the sixth win in a row for the record-setting Plymouth driver.

Dick Hutcherson came from 19th starting slot to finish second and Paul Goldsmith was third. Sam McQuagg came in fourth and James Hylton was fifth.

Rains on Saturday and Sunday morning forced officials to determine the starting positions via a draw. It was a stroke of fortune for Petty, who had crashed his car in a practice session. Petty drew the number two position, beside Earl Brooks, who drew the pole.

The lead changed hands nine times among six drivers. Petty was in front for a total of 182 of the 300 laps. The caution was out 10 times for a total of 71 laps.

Most serious accident of the day involved Bobby Allison, whose Chevrolet tore out a section of fence and flipped down the front chute. The badly broken car came to rest at the base of the scoring stand. Closest to the remains of the car was Judy Allison, wife of the driver. Allison was stunned but otherwise okay.

"I don't know what I'm going to do now," said Allison. "I've had so much crummy luck this season that I've lost a lot of my spirit."

Brooks, of Lynchburg, VA, led the first 24 laps -- all but two were run under caution. The Ford driver eventually wound up 16th, 127 laps behind Petty.

Local Modified and Sportsman star Ray Hendrick got a ride in a Cotton Owens Dodge, but a blown engine put him out after 107 laps.

Petty averaged 57.631 mph before a crowd of 11,000.

Grand National Race No. 42
300 Laps at Virginia State Fairgrounds
Richmond, VA
"Capital City 300"
150 Miles on Half-mile Dirt Track
September 10, 1967

Fin	St	No.	Driver	Team / Car	Laps	Money	Status
1	2	43	Richard Petty	Petty Enterprises '67 Plym	300	$2,450	Running
2	19	29	Dick Hutcherson	Bondy Long '67 Ford	300	1,540	Running
3	12	99	Paul Goldsmith	Nichels Eng '67 Plym	299	1,210	Running
4	10	6	Sam McQuagg	Cotton Owens '67 Dodge	289	875	Rear End
5	20	48	James Hylton	Bud Hartje '65 Dodge	285	710	Running
6	18	34	Wendell Scott	Scott '66 Ford	274	525	Running
7	29	83	Worth McMillion	Allen McMillion '66 Pontiac	268	400	Running
8	25	19	E J Trivette	Roy Dutton '66 Chevrolet	264	300	Running
9	24	97	Henley Gray	Gray '66 Ford	260	250	Running
10	17	07	George Davis	Davis '66 Chevrolet	247	250	Running
11	21	57	George Poulos	'65 Plymouth	246	225	Running
12	5	64	Elmo Langley	Langley-Woodfield '66 Ford	203	225	Axle
13	9	45	Bill Seifert	Seifert '66 Ford	202	225	A Frame
14	26	38	Wayne Smith	Smith '66 Chevrolet	202	225	Trans
15	30	12	Johnny Steele	'67 Ford	197	200	Engine
16	1	76	Earl Brooks	Don Culpepper '66 Ford	173	200	Running
17	14	63	Melvin Bradley	Bob Adams '66 Ford	169	200	Frame
18	13	11	J T Putney	Putney '66 Ford	165	175	Trans
19	6	2	Bobby Allison	J D Bracken '65 Chevrolet	128	175	Crash
20	8	4	John Sears	L G DeWitt '66 Ford	125	175	Engine
21	15	5	Ray Hendrick	Cotton Owens '66 Dodge	107	175	Engine
22	23	31	Bill Ervin	Ralph Murphy '66 Ford	102	150	Tie Rod
23	4	25	Jabe Thomas	Don Robertson '67 Ford	102	150	A Frame
24	22	01	Paul Dean Holt	Dennis Holt '67 Ford	100	150	Trans
25	16	02	Doug Cooper	Bob Cooper '66 Chevrolet	94	150	Differen
26	25	75	Harold Fagan	Bob Gilreath '66 Ford	91	150	Oil Press
27	28	94	Don Biederman	Ron Stotten '66 Chevrolet	79	150	Sway bar
28	3	91	Neil Castles	Castles '65 Plymouth	30	---	Crash
29	7	54	Tom Raley	Raley '66 Ford	10	---	Crash
30	11	20	Clyde Lynn	Lynn '66 Ford	10	---	Crash

Time of Race: 2 hours, 36 minutes, 10 seconds
Average Speed: 57.631 mph
Pole Winner: No Time Trials (drew for position)
Lap Leaders: Earl Brooks 1-24, Richard Petty 25, Paul Goldsmith 26-89, Dick Hutcherson 90, Bobby Allison 91-96, Petty 97-101, Sam McQuagg 110-123, Hutcherson 124-137, Petty 138-300.
Cautions: 10 for 71 laps   Margin of Victory: Attendance: 11,000

Grand National Race No. 43
300 Laps at Beltsville Speedway
Beltsville, MD
"Maryland 300"
150 Miles on Half-mile Paved Track
September 15, 1967

Fin	St	No.	Driver	Team / Car	Laps	Money	Status
1	1	43	Richard Petty	Petty Enterprises '67 Plym	300	$1,400	Running
2	3	2	Bobby Allison	J D Bracken '65 Chevrolet	298	1,000	Running
3	2	14	Jim Paschal	Friedkin Ent '67 Plymouth	298	700	Running
4	6	48	James Hylton	Bud Hartje '65 Dodge	292	575	Running
5	4	4	John Sears	L G DeWitt '66 Ford	286	425	Running
6	15	06	Neil Castles	Castles '65 Dodge	284	325	Running
7	11	02	Bob Cooper	Cooper '66 Chevrolet	284	275	Running
8	18	07	George Davis	Davis '66 Chevrolet	283	225	Running
9	20	30	Bobby Mausgrover	'66 Ford	273	200	Running
10	13	76	Earl Brooks	Don Culpepper '66 Ford	271	175	Running
11	16	88	Doug Cooper	Buck Baker '67 Olds	270	100	Running
12	14	20	Clyde Lynn	Lynn '66 Ford	268	100	Running
13	24	25	Jabe Thomas	Don Robertson '67 Ford	265	100	Running
14	28	19	E J Trivette	Roy Dutten '66 Ford	264	100	Running
15	10	64	Elmo Langley	Langley-Woodfield '66 Ford	236	100	H Gasket
16	19	45	Bill Seifert	Seifert '66 Ford	225	100	Clutch
17	8	34	Wendell Scott	Scott '66 Ford	211	100	Oil Press
18	12	10	Bill Champion	Champion '66 Ford	177	100	Ball Jnt
19	23	01	Paul Dean Holt	Dennis Holt '67 Ford	152	100	Crash
20	7	49	G C Spencer	Spencer '67 Plymouth	124	100	Ignition
21	30	31	Bill Ervin	Ralph Murphy '66 Ford	107	100	Oil Press
22	25	9	Roy Tyner	Truett Rodgers '66 Chevrolet	96	100	Rear End
23	29	12	Johnny Steele	'67 Ford	83	100	Oil Press
24	9	55	Tiny Lund	Lyle Stelter '66 Ford	59	100	Rear End
25	22	54	Tom Raley	Raley '66 Ford	44	---	Engine
26	26	75	Harold Fagan	Bob Gilreath '66 Ford	14	---	Oil Leak
27	17	63	Melvin Bradley	Bob Adams '66 Ford	10	---	Oil Leak
28	21	94	Don Biederman	Ron Stotten '66 Chevrolet	7	---	Oil Leak
29	5	90	Sonny Hutchins	Junie Donlavey '67 Ford	5	---	Engine
30	27	97	Henley Gray	Gray '66 Ford	1	---	Housing

Time of Race: 1 hour, 57 minutes, 33 seconds
Average Speed: 76.563 mph
Pole Winner: Richard Petty - 81.044 mph
Lap Leaders: Richard Petty 1-28, Bobby Allison 29-42, Petty 43-45, Allison 46-112, Petty 113-117, Allison 118-165, Petty 166-300.
Cautions: Margin of Victory: 2-laps plus   Attendance: 6,000

Race No. 43

More Bad Luck For Bobby; Another Win For Richard

BELTSVILLE, MD (Sept. 15) -- Foul luck reared its ugly head once again at Bobby Allison, and Richard Petty continued his mesmerizing streak in the Maryland 300 at Beltsville Speedway. It was the seventh win in a row for Petty -- and the 24th of the 1967 season.

Allison wound up second despite long pit stops, a blackflag for a loose gas cap and a blown tire. He was two laps behind in his patched-up Chevrolet, which was badly damaged five days earlier in a wreck at Richmond.

Third place went to Jim Paschal, James Hylton was fourth and John Sears fifth.

The race was strictly a Petty-Allison show. Allison passed Petty for the first time in the 29th lap. The two drivers traded the lead five more times before Petty gained the upper hand for good on lap 166.

Allison had built up a lap lead on Petty when he made his first pit stop on lap 160. He returned to the track still in first place, but NASCAR officials noticed his gas cap was not secured. They gave him the blackflag on lap 165. Allison pitted and lost the lead.

The Hueytown, AL driver had worked his way back into contention, but a blown tire ended his hopes on lap 191. From then on, Petty cruised to the finish with a two lap lead.

Petty averaged 76.563 mph for his 72nd career Grand National victory. A crowd of 6,000 was on hand at the half mile paved track.

Race No. 44

Petty Slips By Wild Wrecks; Wins Hillsborough 150

HILLSBOROUGH, NC (Sept. 17) -- Richard Petty dodged two early wrecks and slipped past Tiny Lund to win the Hillsborough 150 at Orange Speedway. It was the eighth win in a row for the Randleman Rocket.

Dick Hutcherson, who led the first 68 laps, wound up in second place. Buddy Baker finished third, James Hylton was fourth and G.C. Spencer fifth

Lund passed Hutcherson in the 69th lap and led for 11 laps when he pitted with transmission problems. Petty motored into the lead, never to be headed.

Jack Harden, an engineer with the space agency in Huntsville, AL, survived a terrible tumble into the woods on lap 12. His new Ford went over the bank and landed deep in the wooden area surrounding the track. He was placed on a stretcher and taken to the hospital with back injuries.

On lap 34, Paul Dean Holt flipped end-over-end on the front chute after tangling with Earl Brooks and Bill Ervin. Holt was removed to the hospital with neck injuries.

Petty made an unscheduled pit stop early and fell almost a lap behind. Baker had skidded high and tossed mud onto Petty's front windshield. "I couldn't see a thing," said Petty. "I figured it would be best to pit and get that mud off so I could see."

Petty averaged 81.574 mph before a slim turnout of 5,600.

Grand National Race No. 44
167 Laps at Orange Speedway
Hillsborough, NC
"Hillsborough 150"
150 Miles on .9-mile Dirt Track
September 17, 1967

Fin	St	No.	Driver	Team / Car	Laps	Money	Status
1	1	43	Richard Petty	Petty Enterprises '67 Plym	167	$1,500	Running
2	2	29	Dick Hutcherson	Bondy Long '67 Ford	167	1,050	Running
3	3	6	Buddy Baker	Cotton Owens '67 Dodge	165	700	Running
4	5	48	James Hylton	Bud Hartje '65 Dodge	164	575	Running
5	6	49	G C Spencer	Spencer '67 Plymouth	164	425	Running
6	7	64	Elmo Langley	Langley-Woodfield '66 Ford	161	325	Running
7	4	2	Bobby Allison	J D Bracken '65 Chevrolet	160	275	Running
8	12	02	Bob Cooper	Cooper '66 Chevrolet	153	225	Running
9	8	4	John Sears	L G DeWitt '66 Ford	153	200	Running
10	13	20	Clyde Lynn	Lynn '66 Ford	152	175	Running
11	17	19	E J Trivette	Roy Dutton '66 Ford	149	100	Running
12	28	83	G T Nolan	Allen McMillion '66 Pontiac	144	100	Running
13	15	25	Jabe Thomas	Don Robertson '67 Ford	143	100	Running
14	23	75	Harold Fagan	Bob Gilreath '66 Ford	133	100	Running
15	14	88	Doug Cooper	Buck Baker '67 Olds	100	100	Trans
16	9	55	Tiny Lund	Lyle Stelter '66 Ford	83	100	Trans
17	19	57	George Poulos	'65 Plymouth	79	100	Clutch
18	20	12	Johnny Steele	'67 Ford	70	100	Oil Press
19	18	38	Wayne Smith	Smith '66 Chevrolet	68	100	Engine
20	24	9	Roy Tyner	Truett Rodgers '66 Chevrolet	64	100	Rear End
21	26	45	Bill Seifert	Seifert '66 Ford	60	100	Oil Press
22	22	97	Henley Gray	Gray '66 Ford	52	100	Trans
23	25	8	Ed Negre	Negre '67 Ford	36	100	Battery
24	16	01	Paul Dean Holt	Dennis Holt '67 Ford	33	100	Crash
25	11	76	Earl Brooks	Don Culpepper '66 Ford	33	---	Crash
26	21	31	Bill Ervin	Ralph Murphy '66 Ford	32	---	Crash
27	27	34	Wendell Scott	Scott '66 Ford	28	---	Engine
28	10	30	Jack Harden	'66 Ford	11	---	Crash

Time of Race: 1 hour, 50 minutes, 33 seconds
Average Speed: 81.574 mph
Pole Winner: Richard Petty - 94.159 mph
Lap Leaders: Dick Hutcherson 1-68, Tiny Lund 69-79, Richard Petty 80-167.
Cautions: 3 for 33 laps   Margin of Victory: Attendance: 5,600

Race No. 45

Petty Wins Old Dominion 500 By 4 Laps

MARTINSVILLE, VA (Sept. 24) -- Richard Petty guided his electric blue Plymouth around a smoking Paul Goldsmith in the 306th lap and sped to victory in the Old Dominion 500 at Martinsville Speedway. It was the 26th win of the season for Petty and his ninth Grand National triumph in a row.

Dick Hutcherson finished a distant second, four laps behind the unbeatable Petty. David Pearson came in third, James Hylton was fourth and Jim Paschal fifth.

Paul Goldsmith started third and stormed into the lead in the 20th lap. The 39 year-old Plymouth driver stretched his lead by a wide margin -- putting two laps on Petty at one point. But his Nichels Engineering mount popped its engine on lap 305. Petty was left in a

Cale Yarborough #21 and Jim Paschal #14 up front for the start of the Old Dominion 500

Grand National Race No. 45
500 Laps at Martinsville Speedway
Martinsville, VA
"Old Dominion 500"
250 Miles on Half-mile Paved Track
September 24, 1967

Fin	St	No.	Driver	Team / Car	Laps	Money	Status
1	5	43	Richard Petty	Petty Enterprises '67 Plym	500	$4,400	Running
2	6	29	Dick Hutcherson	Bondy Long '67 Ford	496	2,075	Running
3	9	17	David Pearson	Holman-Moody '67 Ford	495	1,475	Running
4	12	48	James Hylton	Bud Hartje '65 Ford	493	775	Running
5	2	14	Jim Paschal	Friedkin Ent '67 Plymouth	493	800	Running
6	21	1	Swede Savage	Holman-Moody '66 Ford	479	750	Running
7	14	49	G C Spencer	Spencer '67 Plymouth	478	575	Running
8	18	20	Clyde Lynn	Lynn '66 Ford	467	525	Running
9	34	11	J T Putney	Putney '66 Chevrolet	406	475	Running
10	27	40	Eddie Yarboro	'65 Dodge	449	475	Running
11	25	39	Friday Hassler	Red Sharp '66 Chevrolet	447	450	Running
12	29	76	Earl Brooks	Don Culpepper '66 Ford	446	400	Running
13	23	34	Wendell Scott	Scott '66 Ford	444	425	Running
14	38	97	Henley Gray	Gray '66 Ford	442	380	Running
15	36	45	Bill Seifert	Seifert '65 Ford	434	370	Running
16	32	63	Dr. Don Tarr	Bob Adams '66 Ford	404	360	Battery
17	16	4	John Sears	L G DeWitt '66 Ford	377	375	Engine
18	20	9	Roy Tyner	Truett Rodgers '66 Chevrolet	310	365	Differen
19	3	99	Paul Goldsmith	Nichels Eng '67 Plymouth	306	705	Differen
20	17	64	Elmo Langley	Langley-Woodfield '66 Ford	249	345	Engine
21	11	6	Buddy Baker	Cotton Owens '67 Dodge	241	325	Trans
22	7	2	Bobby Allison	J D Bracken '65 Chevrolet	222	325	Engine
23	30	25	Jabe Thomas	Don Robertson '67 Ford	214	300	Trans
24	10	12	Donnie Allison	Jon Thorne '67 Ford	207	325	Engine
25	40	24	Bobby Mausgrover	Betty Lilly '67 Ford	178	300	Brakes
26	22	06	Neil Castles	Castles '65 Dodge	149	325	Oil Press
27	28	88	Doug Cooper	Buck Baker '67 Olds	144	275	Clutch
28	1	21	Cale Yarborough	Wood Brothers '67 Ford	120	425	Engine
29	31	38	Wayne Smith	Smith '66 Chevrolet	94	275	Crash
30	33	94	Don Biederman	Ron Stotten '66 Chevrolet	82	275	Trans
31	26	92	Bobby Wawak	Wawak '65 Plymouth	75	275	Engine
32	39	19	E J Trivette	Roy Dutton '66 Ford	63	250	Oil Leak
33	24	07	George Davis	Davis '66 Chevrolet	61	275	Brakes
34	8	74	Tom Pistone	Turkey Minton '66 Chevrolet	49	275	Heating
35	13	16	LeeRoy Yarbrough	Bud Moore '67 Mercury	28	275	Trans
36	4	26	Darel Dieringer	Junior Johnson '67 Ford	23	300	Engine
37	15	10	Bill Champion	Champion '67 Ford	21	275	Oil Press
38	37	62	Ken Spikes	Harold Collins '67 Pontiac	6	250	W bearing
39	35	54	Tom Raley	Raley '65 Ford	4	250	Engine
40	19	67	Larry Manning	Buddy Arrington '65 Dodge	4	275	Oil Leak

Time of Race: 3 hours, 35 minutes, 30 seconds
Average Speed: 69.605 mph
Pole Winner: Cale Yarborough - 77.386 mph
Lap Leaders: Jim Paschal 1-19, Paul Goldsmith 20-305, Richard Petty 306-500.
Cautions: 7 for 43 laps   Margin of Victory: 4-laps plus   Attendance: 13,600

lap by himself and he cruised to an easy victory.

"Goldy was really running," said Petty. "I don't know if I could have caught him or not. He was just flat outrunning me."

Hutcherson had to settle for runner-up honors for the eighth time this year. "Doesn't anything ever go wrong with him?" asked Hutch."This is the sixth time I've finished second to Petty. I guess you might say I'm best of the rest."

Tom Pistone made a crowd-pleasing charge into third place in the early going, but left the race after 49 laps with overheating problems. Pistone was one of three drivers to use a soft tire compound -- the others were Paschal, who led the first 19 laps and Goldsmith, who led for 286 straight laps. "I've been running some Sportsman races about three times a week and I know what's going good on the short tracks," said Pistone. "I knew those tires would work best here. Goldsmith noticed how well I was doing on them and he went all the way back to Indiana to get some for his car."

Swede Savage drove a Holman-Moody Ford into sixth place in his second Grand National start.

Petty averaged 69.605 mph as the caution flew seven times for 43 laps.

Race No. 46
Petty Wins 10th Straight Before Ford Racing Brass

N.WILKESBORO, NC (Oct. 1) -- With several of the top racing officials from Ford Motor Co. looking on, Richard Petty continued his phenomenal winning streak by taking the Wilkes 400 at North Wilkesboro Speedway. It was the 10th win in a row for Petty and his 27th of the season.

Petty took the lead in the 181st lap and scampered uncontested to the first place prize of $4,725. Dick Hutcherson finished second for the ninth time this year and LeeRoy Yarbrough was third in the Junior Johnson Ford. Bobby Allison survived overheating problems to

10 in a row for Richard

finish fourth and Jim Paschal was fifth.

Jacques Passino, Ford's Director of racing, joined John Holman and Ralph Moody in the pit area -- to get a first hand look at the incredible Petty success story. "I saw Ford's big boss standing on top of Junior Johnson's truck," said Petty. "I knew those Ford drivers were going to be showing what they could do. I don't mind racing like that."

Passino's appearance was the outgrowth of some closed door meetings in Detroit. Out of that meeting came word that Darel Dieringer had been fired from the Johnson Ford and Yarbrough was hired to replace him.

The lead changed hands six times among five drivers. Petty didn't lead until the 107th lap. He took the lead from Bobby Allison and led all but 38 of the last 294 laps.

Petty's point lead grew to 3,918 points over second place James Hylton. Petty's seasonal earnings rose to $126,150, a new NASCAR record. Fred Lorenzen pocketed $122,587.28 in prize and point money in 1963.

Petty's 75th career triumph came at an average speed of 94.837 mph. A crowd of 9,800 was on hand in sunny autumn weather.

Race No. 47

Buddy Baker Whips Star-Studded Field and Petty to Win National 500

CHARLOTTE, NC (Oct. 15) -- Buddy Baker outran and outclassed an all-star cast to win the National 500 at Charlotte Motor Speedway. Baker's victory, his first in 215 Grand National starts, ended Richard Petty's winning streak at 10.

Baker pushed his Ray Fox Dodge around Cale Yarborough in the 257th lap and led the rest of the way.

Buddy Baker drafts Richard Petty at Charlotte. Baker went on to win his first race, snapping Petty's 10 race win streak

---

Grand National Race No. 46
400 Laps at N.Wilkesboro Speedway
N.Wilkesboro, NC
"Wilkes 400"
250 Miles on .625-mile Paved Track
October 1, 1967

Fin	St	No.	Driver	Team / Car	Laps	Money	Status
1	5	43	Richard Petty	Petty Enterprises '67 Plym	400	$4,725	Running
2	1	29	Dick Hutcherson	Bondy Long '67 Ford	398	2,400	Running
3	2	26	LeeRoy Yarbrough	Junior Johnson '67 Ford	398	1,300	Running
4	7	2	Bobby Allison	J D Bracken '65 Chevrolet	398	1,125	Running
5	3	14	Jim Paschal	Friedkin Ent '67 Plymouth	398	650	Running
6	12	74	Tom Pistone	Turkey Minton '67 Chevrolet	389	525	Running
7	21	06	Cale Yarborough	Castles '65 Dodge	386	600	Running
8	15	1	Swede Savage	Holman-Moody '67 Ford	386	425	Running
9	16	4	John Sears	L G DeWitt '66 Ford	372	375	Running
10	28	63	Melvin Bradley	Bob Adams '66 Ford	370	325	Running
11	29	34	Wendell Scott	Scott '66 Ford	369	300	Running
12	24	02	Bob Cooper	Cooper '66 Chevrolet	369	275	Running
13	27	45	Bill Seifert	Seifert '66 Ford	368	275	Running
14	30	0	Eddie Yarboro	'65 Dodge	362	250	Running
15	33	38	Wayne Smith	Smith '66 Chevrolet	356	200	Running
16	23	88	Doug Cooper	Buck Baker '67 Olds	328	250	Engine
17	22	11	J T Putney	Putney '66 Chevrolet	300	300	Engine
18	9	48	James Hylton	Bud Hartje '65 Ford	236	300	Engine
19	13	49	G C Spencer	Spencer '67 Plymouth	235	225	Engine
20	19	9	Earl Brooks	Truett Rodgers '66 Chevrolet	215	225	Rear End
21	6	99	Paul Goldsmith	Nichels Eng '67 Plymouth	173	200	Engine
22	25	20	Clyde Lynn	Lynn '66 Ford	144	200	Rear End
23	17	64	Elmo Langley	Langley-Woodfield '66 Ford	120	200	Oil Press
24	10	6	Buddy Baker	Cotton Owens '67 Dodge	114	225	Engine
25	31	97	Henley Gray	Gray '66 Ford	107	175	Steering
26	14	81	Jack Ingram	Tom ingram '66 Chevrolet	86	200	Rear End
27	26	25	Jabe Thomas	Don Robertson '67 Ford	83	200	Trans
28	34	94	Don Biederman	Ron Stotten '66 Chevrolet	71	175	Rear End
29	20	07	George Davis	Davis '66 Chevrolet	57	200	Clutch
30	18	92	Bobby Wawak	Wawak '65 Plymouth	37	200	Rear End
31	8	40	Jerry Grant	Friedkin Ent '67 Plymouth	36	175	Engine
32	32	8	Ed Negre	Negre '67 Ford	36	150	Throttle
33	11	53	Bud Moore	Activated Angels '67 Dodge	28	175	Handling
34	4	17	David Pearson	Holman-Moody '67 Ford	17	425	Engine
35	35	75	Harold Fagan	Bob Gilreath '66 Ford	16	150	Engine

Time of Race: 2 hours, 38 minutes, 10 seconds
Average Speed: 94.837 mph
Pole Winner: Dick Hutcherson - 104.312 mph
Lap Leaders: Dick Hutcherson 1-20, Jim Paschal 21-29, Paul Goldsmith 30-48,
    Bobby Allison 49-106, Richard Petty 107-142, Allison 143-180, Petty 181-400.
Cautions: 3 for 20 laps   Margin of Victory: 2-laps plus   Attendance: 9,800

Bobby Isaac finished second with Dick Hutcherson, Charlie Glotzbach and G.C. Spencer rounding out the top five.

Petty's bid ended in the 41st lap when Paul Goldsmith blew an engine and lurched sideways in the second turn. Petty, running close behind, hit Goldsmith -- ripping the passenger door off his car. "It wouldn't run after that," said Petty. "It felt like there was a parachute hangin' off my car." Petty eventually fell out with a blown engine on lap 268.

`   The 44 car field was spiced with several USAC drivers. Ford had imported five internationally known drivers in an effort to end the Petty-Plymouth reign. None of the additional entries finished the race.

Baker led for 160 laps and was thrilled over his first win in nine years on the stock car racing major league circuit. "When I went under that checkered flag," remarked Baker, "I let out a yell you could have heard in Concord. This is the greatest day of my life. Maybe it will give me a mental boost. Now I know how to win."

Baker started fourth on the grid and was able to miss several crashes. "I was behind a few of the wrecks, but I had time to slow down," he said.

Whitey Gerkin's Ford crashed early at Charlotte

Among those kayoed by wrecks included Whitey Gerkin, Gordon Johncock, Paul Goldsmith, and a four car tangle which put out Mario Andretti, Jack Bowsher, Jim Paschal and David Pearson.

LeeRoy Yarbrough wrecked Junior Johnson's Ford in a practice session when the fire extinguisher went off, blinding the Jacksonville, FL driver. NASCAR rules said that a back-up car would not be permitted to start the race, so Yarbrough spectated.

Curtis Turner made his return to racing, wheeling the Turkey Minton Chevrolet. Clutch failure knocked him out on lap 82.

The lead changed hands 22 times among seven drivers and only 14 cars finished. Runner-up Isaac, on the come-back trail after losing factory rides with both Ford and Chrysler, was pleased with his team's performance. "For strictly an independent team, I don't think it would have been possible to do any better," said the Catawba, NC driver.

Baker averaged 130.317 mph before 60,000 spectators.

Grand National Race No. 47
334 Laps at Charlotte Motor Speedway
Charlotte, NC
"National 500"
500 Miles on 1.5-mile Paved Track
October 15, 1967

Fin	St	No.	Driver	Team / Car	Laps	Money	Status
1	4	3	Buddy Baker	Ray Fox '67 Dodge	334	$18,950	Running
2	15	71	Bobby Isaac	K&K Insurance '67 Dodge	333	9,480	Running
3	8	29	Dick Hutcherson	Bondy Long '67 Ford	332	5,860	Running
4	9	72	Charlie Glotzbach	K&K Insurance '65 Dodge	329	4,250	Running
5	21	42	G C Spencer	Petty Enterprises '67 Plym	328	3,375	Running
6	22	2	Don White	Nichels Eng '67 Dodge	324	2,595	Running
7	30	92	Bobby Wawak	Wawak '65 Plymouth	317	2,125	Running
8	27	06	Neil Castles	Castles '65 Dodge	315	1,775	Running
9	32	69	Buddy Arrington	Arrington '65 Dodge	311	1,575	Running
10	1	21	Cale Yarborough	Wood Brothers '67 Ford	301	2,100	Engine
11	38	22	J T Putney	Putney '66 Chevrolet	300	1,500	Running
12	41	19	Henley Gray	Roy Dutton '66 Ford	297	1,395	Running
13	14	37	Bobby Allison	K&K Insurance '67 Dodge	294	1,350	Engine
14	24	79	Frank Warren	Harold Rhodes '66 Chevrolet	292	1,310	Running
15	13	12	Donnie Allison	Jon Thorne '67 Ford	284	1,325	Engine
16	25	4	John Sears	L G DeWitt '66 Ford	278	1,250	Engine
17	37	38	Wayne Smith	Smith '66 Chevrolet	274	1,225	Running
18	5	43	Richard Petty	Petty Enterprises '67 Plym	268	1,225	Engine
19	6	6	Darel Dieringer	Cotton Owens '67 Dodge	257	1,350	Trans
20	26	90	Sonny Hutchins	Junie Donlavey '67 Ford	247	1,150	Engine
21	36	9	Roy Tyner	Truett Rodgers '66 Chevrolet	227	1,125	Running
22	2	27	A J Foyt	Banjo Matthews '67 Ford	212	1,175	Engine
23	44	20	Clyde Lynn	Lynn '66 Ford	208	1,100	Differen
24	7	17	David Pearson	Holman-Moody '67 Ford	191	1,680	Crash
25	11	14	Jim Paschal	Friedkin Ent '67 Plymouth	190	1,125	Crash
26	20	1	Jack Bowsher	Bowsher '67 Ford	190	1,100	Crash
27	17	11	Mario Andretti	Holman-Moody '67 Ford	182	975	Crash
28	35	49	Wendell Scott	G C Spencer '67 Plymouth	182	950	Clutch
29	19	53	Bud Moore	Activated Angels '67 Dodge	124	925	Throttle
30	28	64	Elmo Langley	Langley-Woodfield '66 Ford	109	900	Engine
31	23	97	Red Farmer	Henley Gray '67 Ford	104	900	Engine
32	33	46	Larry Manning	Tom Hunter '66 Chevrolet	102	875	Crash
33	42	84	Dub Simpson	'66 Ford	89	865	Radiator
34	18	74	Curtis Turner	Turkey Minton '67 Chevrolet	82	800	Clutch
35	40	45	Bill Seifert	Seifert '66 Ford	78	825	Engine
36	29	39	Friday Hassler	Red Sharp '66 Chevrolet	58	750	Engine
37	39	67	Larry Hess	Buddy Arrington '65 Dodge	53	800	Engine
38	3	99	Paul Goldsmith	Nichels Eng '67 Plymouth	41	750	Crash
39	34	02	Bob Cooper	Cooper '66 Chevrolet	40	685	Trans
40	31	0	Don Schisler	'67 Dodge	36	740	Engine
41	43	24	Bobby Mausgrover	Betty Lilly '67 Ford	34	690	Oil Leak
42	12	16	Gordon Johncock	Bud Moore '67 Mercury	28	720	Crash
43	10	48	James Hylton	Bud Hartje '65 Dodge	19	760	Oil Press
44	16	54	Whitey Gerkin	'67 Ford	2	625	Crash

Time of Race: 3 hours, 50 minutes, 4 seconds
Average Speed: 130.317 mph
Pole Winner: Cale Yarborough - 154.872 mph
Lap Leaders: Cale Yarborough 1-31, Darel Dieringer 32-43, Bobby Isaac 44, Dieringer 45-56, Yarborough 57-68, Dieringer 69-79, David Pearson 80-85, Yarborough 86-112, A J Foyt 113, Buddy Baker 114-135, Yarborough 136, Baker 137-149, Yarborough 150-153, Pearson 154-157, Isaac 158-173, Dick Hutcherson 174-175, Yarborough 176-181, Hutcherson 182-186, Yarborough 187-193, Isaac 194-206, Baker 207-253, Yarborough 254-256, Baker 257-334.
Cautions: 9 for 64 laps   Margin of Victory: 1-lap plus   Attendance: 60,000

Race No. 48

Lorenzen Picks Allison; New Team Wins American 500

ROCKINGHAM, NC (Oct. 29) --Ford Motor Co, in an all-out effort to end the Richard Petty-Chrysler domination of the 1967 NASCAR season, assigned Fred Lorenzen to head a new team out of the Holman-Moody shops. Lorenzen, who retired from active competition in April, spoke about his new assignment: "I got a call and was informed I could have any car and driver I wanted for the American 500. I lined up the equipment I wanted and I knew Bobby Allison would be my choice for driver -- if I could get him."

Allison, the 29 year-old hot shot out of Hueytown, AL, was available and he masterfully guided the Lorenzen car into victory lane in his first start at North Carolina Motor Speedway.

Bobby Allison celebrates in victory lane at Rockingham

Allison took the lead in the 389th lap when leader Cale Yarborough blew an engine, and finished a lap ahead of Holman-Moody running mate David Pearson. "From the first practice lap in the car," said Allison, "I knew I had a car I could win with. I had confidence in the car and complete confidence in Lorenzen's ability to run the crew."

Pearson wound up a lap and 10 seconds behind. Paul Goldsmith finished third, A.J. Foyt was fourth and Gordon Johncock fifth.

Richard Petty was taken out by a pit road mishap on lap 191. Petty and Pearson locked bumpers during a log-jam on pit road -- and Petty's Plymouth spun into the wall. Several crewmen servicing Donnie Allison's Ford suffered abrasions.

Allison was in the hunt for the $16,300 first prize all afternoon. He led on six occasions for a total of 164 laps and dodged a number of on track skirmishes. Second fastest qualifier Jack Bowsher plowed into the spinning cars of Bobby Wawak and Earl Brooks on lap 17. All three were eliminated.

A timing chain broke on Bobby Isaac's Dodge as he exited the second turn on lap 56. He abruptly lost power, triggering a massive pile-up involving James

Grand National Race No. 48
500 Laps at North Carolina Motor Speedway
Rockingham, NC
"American 500"
500 Miles on 1-mile Paved Track
October 29, 1967

Fin	St	No.	Driver	Team / Car	Laps	Money	Status
1	3	11	Bobby Allison	Holman-Moody '67 Ford	500	$16,300	Running
2	1	17	David Pearson	Holman-Moody '67 Ford	499	10,150	Running
3	9	99	Paul Goldsmith	Nichels Eng '67 Plymouth	499	5,250	Running
4	10	27	A J Foyt	Banjo Matthews '67 Ford	498	2,800	Running
5	7	16	Gordon Johncock	Bud Moore '67 Mercury	497	1,875	Running
6	18	53	Bud Moore	Activated Angels '67 Dodge	488	1,350	Running
7	21	4	John Sears	L G DeWitt '66 Ford	481	1,200	Running
8	37	55	Tiny Lund	Lyle Stelter '66 Ford	472	1,200	Running
9	28	64	Elmo Langley	Langley-Woodfield '66 Ford	462	1,100	Running
10	36	45	Bill Seifert	Seifert '65 Ford	457	1,110	Running
11	22	97	Red Farmer	Henley Gray '66 Ford	448	1,025	Running
12	27	49	Ed Negre	G C Spencer '67 Plymouth	446	1,000	Running
13	6	29	Dick Hutcherson	Bondy Long '67 Ford	441	885	Engine
14	8	26	LeeRoy Yarbrough	Junior Johnson '67 Ford	405	755	Spring
15	17	54	Whitey Gerkin	'67 Ford	405	785	Crash
16	4	21	Cale Yarborough	Wood Brothers '67 Ford	388	700	Crash
17	35	07	George Davis	Davis '67 Chevrolet	382	760	Running
18	39	34	Wendell Scott	Scott '66 Ford	377	710	Engine
19	11	3	Buddy Baker	Ray Fox '67 Dodge	324	700	Engine
20	38	87	J T Putney	Buck Baker '66 Ford	307	710	Engine
21	31	06	Neil Castles	Castles '65 Dodge	286	790	Spun
22	14	6	Darel Dieringer	Cotton Owens '67 Dodge	267	760	Engine
23	42	20	Clyde Lynn	Lynn '66 Ford	252	650	Engine
24	26	39	Friday Hassler	Red Sharp '66 Chevrolet	249	670	Engine
25	13	12	Donnie Allison	Jon Thorne '67 Ford	245	640	Engine
26	33	10	Bill Champion	Champion '66 Ford	236	720	Engine
27	23	2	Don White	Nichels Eng '67 Dodge	214	605	Engine
28	5	43	Richard Petty	Petty Enterprises '67 Plym	191	600	Crash
29	32	79	Frank Warren	Harold Rhodes '66 Chevrolet	147	695	Engine
30	34	66	Jimmy Clark	Holman-Moody '67 Ford	144	665	Engine
31	25	7	Bobby Johns	Shorty Johns '66 Chevrolet	126	635	Clutch
32	19	72	Charlie Glotzbach	K&K Insurance '65 Dodge	80	605	T Chain
33	29	44	James Sears	L G DeWitt '66 Ford	72	505	Ball Jt
34	34	88	Doug Cooper	Buck Baker '67 Olds	59	650	Engine
35	12	14	Jim Paschal	Friedkin Ent '67 Plymouth	56	535	Crash
36	16	71	Bobby Isaac	K&K Insurance '67 Dodge	56	560	T Chain
37	17	42	G C Spencer	Petty Enterprises '67 Plym	56	555	Crash
38	20	48	James Hylton	Bud Hartje '65 Dodge	55	550	Crash
39	43	38	Wayne Smith	Smith '66 Chevrolet	52	545	Crash
40	40	9	Roy Tyner	Truett Rodgers '66 Chevrolet	33	540	Oil Press
41	44	32	Jabe Thomas	Don Robertson '67 Ford	21	535	Steering
42	2	1	Jack Bowsher	Bowsher '67 Ford	17	605	Crash
43	30	92	Bobby Wawak	Wawak '65 Plymouth	16	675	Crash
44	41	76	Earl Brooks	Don Culpepper '66 Ford	15	500	Crash

Time of Race: 5 hours, 4 minutes, 49 seconds
Average Speed: 98.420 mph
Pole Winner: David Pearson - 117.120 mph
Lap Leaders: David Pearson 1, Jack Bowsher 2-12, Bobby Allison 13-17, Dick Hutcherson 18-31, Allison 32-33, A J Foyt 34-58, Gordon Johncock 59, Whitey Gerkin 60-61, Red Farmer 62-68, Richard Petty 69-83, Cale Yarborough 84-85, Petty 86-143, Yarborough 144-149, Allison 150-151, Hutcherson 152-154, Yarborough 155-195, Lee-Roy Yarbrough 196-198, Yarborough 199-201, Pearson 202-236, Hutcherson 237-287, Allison 288-323, Yarborough 324-331, Allison 332-338, Yarborough 339-340, Hutcherson 341, Yarborough 342-388, Allison 389-500.
Cautions: 9 for 81 laps   Margin of Victory: 1-lap plus   Attendance: 53,378.

Hylton, Wayne Smith and G.C. Spencer. Hylton was removed from his car and sent to Richmond Memorial Hospital with a concussion and head injuries. Smith was taken to the hospital with neck injuries. Spencer and Isaac were not hurt.

Jimmy Clark, the Formula I champ out of Scotland, was seated in a Holman-Moody Ford with Jochen

Rindt listed a relief driver. Clark started 24th and worked his way up to 12th before the engine let go. The only problem Clark seemed to encounter was "I couldn't find the bloody brake pedal when I went into the turns."

Only 13 of the 44 cars that started the race finished. The caution was out nine times for a total of 81 laps. A crowd of 53,378 watched Allison average 98.420 mph. It was his fifth win of the year.

Grand Prix driver Jimmy Clark #66 competed in American 500

Race No. 49

Allison Beats Petty in Car Bumping Western NC 500

WEAVERVILLE, NC (Nov. 5) -- Bobby Allison prevailed in a fender-bending Western North Carolina 500 at Asheville-Weaverville Speedway, putting an exciting climax on the 1967 NASCAR Grand National season. It was the second win in a row for Allison and crew chief Fred Lorenzen.

Allison took the lead with seven laps to go with a car-jarring pass -- and he outran Richard Petty by a car length to the checkered flag. David Pearson was third, Dick Hutcherson fourth and Friday Hassler fifth.

Only six cars finished the 250-miler, witnessed by 3,500 spectators who braved a chilly afternoon in the Carolina mountains. Eighth place finisher Doug Cooper was 150 laps behind the winner, but still running at the end.

Allison, who won the pole, and Petty locked horns on several occasions during the 500 lapper. The lead changed hands 22 times among four drivers, with Allison and Petty sharing the spotlight. Petty made a pass on Allison with 22 laps to go that sent Allison's gold Ford skidding up toward the wall. When Allison caught Petty in the final laps, he pushed Petty up in the marbles and made the decisive pass.

Respective pit crews nearly came to blows in the pit area. "I guess when you've won as much as I have, everyone takes pot shots at you," said Petty.

"We were racing for the win," countered Allison. "He put me out of the groove more than once, and I did the same thing to him. Things like that happen on short tracks when you have two cars that are equal and two

Grand National Race No. 49
500 Laps at Asheville-Weaverville Speedway
Weaverville, NC
"Western North Carolina 500"
250 Miles on Half-mile Paved Track
November 5, 1967

Fin	St	No.	Driver	Team / Car	Laps	Money	Status
1	1	11	Bobby Allison	Holman-Moody '67 Ford	500	$3,250	Running
2	6	43	Richard Petty	Petty Enterprises '67 Plym	500	2,300	Running
3	3	17	David Pearson	Holman-Moody '67 Ford	500	1,500	Running
4	4	66	Dick Hutcherson	Holman-Moody '67 Ford	490	900	Running
5	11	39	Friday Hassler	Red Sharp '66 Chevrolet	471	800	Engine
6	26	4	John Sears	L G DeWitt '66 Ford	413	700	Engine
7	29	35	Max Ledbetter	'65 Olds	396	650	Running
8	22	88	Doug Cooper	Buck Baker '66 Olds	350	600	Engine
9	23	20	Clyde Lynn	Lynn '66 Ford	285	500	Engine
10	9	74	Tom Pistone	Turkey Minton '67 Chevrolet	226	400	Crash
11	15	9	Roy Tyner	Truett Rodgers '66 Chevrolet	202	380	Crash
12	5	16	Cale Yarborough	Bud Moore '67 Mercury	196	375	Trans
13	12	49	G C Spencer	Spencer '67 Plymouth	147	325	Engine
14	17	67	Don Schisler	Buddy Arrington '65 Dodge	140	275	Crash
15	21	22	J T Putney	Putney '66 Chevrolet	130	200	Crash
16	20	45	Bill Seifert	Seifert '66 Ford	123	200	Engine
17	28	94	Don Biederman	Ron Stotten '66 Chevrolet	115	200	Oil Press
18	14	06	Neil Castles	Castles '65 Dodge	100	200	Radiator
19	7	27	Bosco Lowe	Banjo Matthews '67 Ford	100	200	W bearing
21	16	02	Bob Cooper	Cooper '66 Chevrolet	96	200	Engine
22	13	64	Elmo Langley	Langley-Woodfield '66 Ford	80	200	Engine
23	30	6	Darel Dieringer	Cotton Owens '67 Dodge	61	200	Oil Press
24	27	75	Harold Fagan	Bob Gilreath '66 Ford	55	200	Engine
25	18	34	Wendell Scott	Scott '66 Ford	52	200	Crash
26	25	93	Walson Gardner	Gardner '67 Ford	47	150	Crash
27	2	26	LeeRoy Yarbrough	Junior Johnson '67 Ford	22	650	Brakes
28	8	40	Jim Paschal	Friedkin Ent '67 Plymouth	7	150	Engine
29	10	2	Paul Lewis	J D Bracken '65 Chevrolet	5	150	Crash
30	19	19	Henley Gray	Roy Dutton '66 Ford	5	150	Crash

Time of Race: 3 hours, 16 minutes, 37 seconds
Average Speed: 76.291 mph
Pole Winner: Bobby Allison - 90.407 mph
Lap Leaders: Bobby Allison 1-121, Dick Hutcherson 122-124, David Pearson 125-214, Richard Petty 215-231, Allison 232-234, Pearson 235-255, Petty 256, Pearson 257, Petty 258-269, Pearson 270-271, Petty 272-314, Allison 315-316, Petty 317, Pearson 318-328, Petty 329=333, Allison 334-416, Pearson 417-430, Petty 431, Pearson 432, Allison 433-478, Petty 479-493, Allison 494-500.
Cautions: 10 for 73 laps   Margin of Victory: 1 car length   Attendance: 3,500

drivers who want to win badly."

Lorenzen was overjoyed at becoming 2-for-2 as a crew chief. "As far as I'm concerned," he spouted, "Allison has a life-time job."

Allison averaged only 76.291 mph as 73 laps were run under the caution flag. Bosco Lowe, teaming up with Banjo Matthews, spun early and eventually fell out with a burned wheel bearing. LeeRoy Yarbrough pulled Junior Johnson's Ford out in the 22nd lap with no brakes. Cale Yarborough, driving Bud Moore's Mercury, departed with transmission failure.

Hutcherson was driving a Holman-Moody Ford in what was his final race as a driver. He and team owner Bondy Long had a falling out after the American 500. Hutch accepted an offer to head up David Pearson's Ford team for the 1968 season.

Petty won his second NASCAR Grand National championship by 6,028 points over James Hylton.

1967 NASCAR Season
Final Point Standings - Grand National Division

Rank	Driver	Points	Starts	Wins	Top 5	Top 10	Winnings
1	Richard Petty	42,472	48	27	38	40	$150,196.10
2	James Hylton	36,444	46	0	26	39	49,731.50
3	Dick Hutcherson	33,658	33	2	22	25	85,159.28
4	Bobby Allison	30,812	45	6	21	27	58,249.64
5	John Sears	29,078	41	0	9	25	28,936.74
6	Jim Paschal	27,624	45	4	20	25	60,122.28
7	David Pearson	26,302	22	2	11	13	72,650.40
8	Neil Castles	23,218	36	0	4	16	20,682.32
9	Elmo Langley	22,286	45	0	10	24	23,897.52
10	Wendell Scott	20,700	45	0	0	11	19,509.76
11	Paul Goldsmith	20,402	21	0	7	8	38,731.14
12	Darel Dieringer	20,194	18	1	8	9	34,709.24
13	Clyde Lynn	20,016	44	0	5	22	19,519.24
14	Bobby Isaac	19,698	12	0	3	5	24,474.24
15	Buddy Baker	18,600	21	1	7	8	46,949.24
16	Donnie Allison	18,298	20	0	4	7	17,613.15
17	Henley Gray	17,502	43	0	0	12	15,986.16
18	J.T. Putney	16,752	29	0	1	10	15,686.16
19	Tiny Lund	16,292	19	0	4	5	17,331.16
20	Cale Yarborough	16,228	16	2	7	8	57,911.16
21	G.C. Spencer	15,240	29	0	5	10	20,225.
22	Bill Seifert	14,676	41	0	0	12	11,905.
23	Charlie Glotzbach	11,444	9	0	3	5	14,790.
24	Frank Warren	9,992	12	0	0	1	9,185.
25	Earl Brooks	9,952	34	0	0	8	8,610.
26	Buddy Arrington	9,768	15	0	1	5	7,720.
27	Buck Baker	9,450	20	0	0	5	7,560.
28	Wayne Smith	9,372	28	0	0	2	10,225.
29	Fred Lorenzen	9,268	5	1	2	2	17,875.
30	Roy Mayne	9,262	14	0	0	1	8,830.
31	Bobby Wawak	9,078	14	0	1	3	8,070.
32	Friday Hassler	8,820	21	0	3	9	10,265.
33	Paul Lewis	8,492	14	0	3	8	8,620.
34	Sonny Hutchins	8,448	7	0	0	2	6,385.
35	Paul "Bud" Moore	7,812	6	0	2	3	7,200.
36	Sam McQuagg	7,400	14	0	3	3	9,845.
37	LeeRoy Yarbrough	7,012	15	1	3	4	15,325.
38	Don Biederman	5,850	22	0	0	1	5,935.
39	Ramo Stott	5,676	3	0	0	1	3,335.
40	George Davis	5,434	21	0	1	6	4,400.
41	Jack Harden	5,254	10	0	0	0	4,450.
42	Paul Dean Holt	5,006	23	0	0	1	4,220.
43	Roy Tyner	4,936	27	0	0	1	8,170.
44	Bill Champion	4,040	11	0	0	0	6,205.
45	Dick Johnson	3,954	23	0	0	0	5,070.
46	George Poulos	3,780	23	0	0	1	3,040.
47	Bill Dennis	3,730	3	0	0	0	2,335.
48	Doug Cooper	3,666	21	0	2	4	5,665.
49	Ed Negre	3,578	14	0	0	0	3,805.

The 1968 Season

Ford Motor Co. Flexes Muscles -- NASCAR, MIS Ink Multi Year Pact

Volume three of a four volume series . . Big Bucks and Boycotts   1965 - 1971

1968

Ford Motor Company took it on the chin during the 1967 NASCAR Grand National season. Although their talented teams and drivers had won half of the ten oval track super-speedway events, it was Richard Petty and Plymouth who grabbed virtually all the headlines. An imposing 10 race victory string, 27 wins for the year and his second championship in three full seasons had made Petty the darling of the stock car racing world. The Ford squad was able to handle most of the other factory backed Chrysler teams, but they had run into a roadblock

Ford's John Holman built an empire. Ford had a banner year in 1968

when it came to the Level Cross gang. "The Pettys are two years ahead of all the other Chrysler teams," reflected Dodge driver Buddy Baker. "And they are one year ahead of the Fords."

Ford entered the 1968 season determined to regain their position as top dog on NASCAR's racing circuit by sending at least one, and perhaps two teams after the championship. Ford had not previously sent their factory-backed teams into the small track events, thinking that races of 250 miles or more were the ones that got the most publicity and would therefore return them greater exposure for their money.

Then, the rampaging Petty began winning super-speedway races as well as 250-milers on short tracks. His smashing 27 victories put Ford in a bad light. And Ford's top brass didn't want a repeat of that situation.

Dick Hutcherson, one of Ford's top drivers from 1965-1967, was ushered into retirement at the close of the '67 campaign. His new assignment was to head David Pearson's Holman-Moody effort to crowd Petty's quest for a third title. The immediately successful Fred Lorenzen-Bobby Allison combo shifted over to Bondy Long's outfit in Camden, SC. Their deal was to run all the races through the March 31st Atlanta 500 (the first seven races). At that time Ford would evaluate their position in the point standings. If Allison was ranking high, there would be a good chance he would get the green light to run all the races -- something Allison had always wanted to do.

Bobby Allison started the year in a Bondy Long Ford, but quit midway through the year

"I just hope to be able to run all the races," said Allison. "I want to go after the Grand National championship. Maybe we can do well enough so that Ford sends us to every race. I don't want to run just some of the races."

Cale Yarborough, LeeRoy Yarbrough, Donnie Allison and a host of USACers in selected major events would make up the rest of the big-moneyed Ford team.

Chrysler, too, was busy preparing for 1968 season. Joining Petty in all the events would be the K&K Insurance Dodge team owned by Nord Krauskopf, directed by Harry Hyde and driven by Bobby Isaac. "We've been a shoestring independent for two years now," said Hyde. "Now we're going to have some factory help and we'll have a chance to get our operation in high gear. Nord told me when we started (in 1966) that this was a three year project. The first year would be filled with mistakes. The second year we would devote our effort to making corrections. And the third year we would be set up for winning.

"Bobby is a better driver than we've had the car prepared for," added Hyde. "He can drive a lot harder when we make it feel right for him. We'll be able to do that this year."

Isaac would make a run for the title for the first time in his career. "I think we've got a good chance to win some races," he said. "Don't count us out of the championship, either."

Perennial independent contender James Hylton would be getting small packages from Dodge. "We like the way James operates," said Ronney Householder, head of Chrysler's racing effort.

"No more stroking for me," said a happy Hylton. "Now I can really race."

Plymouth driver Jim Paschal got the ax from Chrysler, who wanted young, aggressive drivers who were willing to push the button and run up front. Paschal had just come off one of his most productive seasons -- winning four Grand National events including the World 600 at Charlotte. Bill Ellis, crew chief for the Friedkin Enterprises team which the 41 year-old High Point, NC veteran had driven for, thought Chrysler's move was surprising. "I thought we did extremely well last year for what was basically an independent team," said Ellis. "Paschal is one of the most consistent race drivers I've ever seen. And he was great to work with. I guess factory officials wanted to go with younger drivers. They want young bucks who are eager to run up front. That wasn't Jim's style. He could run with anybody when it was necessary, but he didn't punish the equipment."

Although Charlie Glotzbach was supposed to be

headed to the Friedkin Enterprises team, Jerry Grant, a USAC driver out of California, filled Paschal's seat. Glotzbach shifted over to the Cotton Owens Dodge

Paul Goldsmith landed the Valleydale sponsorship which enabled him to race in 1968

when Chrysler was unsuccessful in luring Donnie Allison off the Ford team. Darel Dieringer, 41, joined the Mario Rossi Plymouth team and planned to compete in major events.

Although Chrysler spoke in terms of hiring young drivers, Dieringer and Grant were both over 40. Isaac was 35.

Ray Nichels Engineering, principle distributor of Chrysler racing parts, had announced that he may not field a car on the NASCAR trail in 1968. That might have left veteran Paul Goldsmith off the tour. However, just before the 1968 Grand National season started, Nichels and Goldsmith announced the acquisition of a pair of sponsors -- Frosty Morn Meats and Valleydale Packers. The sponsorship enabled the venerable team to remain intact.

Junior Johnson, one of Ford's leading team owners, had only won one Grand National race in 1966 and 1967. LeeRoy Yarbrough was lined up to drive his car, and Johnson was happy about that. "LeeRoy is a charger," said Johnson, "and I like that. These drivers who lay back and save their equipment while waiting for the front runners to make mistakes or go out with mechanical trouble aren't my idea of real race drivers. The only way to race is get out front and stay there. There's a lot of pressure on the guy running in the lead, and a lot of guys can't take the pressure."

Across the FoMoCo hall, Lorenzen -- always noted as being a thinker who enjoyed tremendous success as a driver -- stood up and offered another view point. "It is the smart driver who wins races," insisted Lorenzen. "Look at Bobby Allison. He's a fine driver and he's smart. He'll be a winner."

While Ford and Chrysler were stepping up their involvement in racing, General Motors still showed no movement joining in the fun. Edward M. Cole, President of General Motors, admitted he was a reluctant

The "Y" Boys, Cale Yarborough #21 and LeeRoy Yarbrough #26, dominated the big tracks in 1968

party to the corporation's anti-racing policies. Cole indicated that General Motors would stay out of racing because it feared provoking federal safety standards. "It is a very difficult position, the interest the government has in safety," he said. "I don't know whether you can equate safety and racing together in the same project."

As the Ford teams began to shake down their new products at Daytona in February, speeds were spiraling upwards at an alarming rate. The new fastback Ford Torinos and Mercury Montegos were slicing through the wind -- and producing speeds near 190 mph. "I blinked a bit and almost lost it," said Cale Yarborough, who was seated in the Wood Brothers Mercury. "Now I get all my blinking done on the straightaways so I can keep my eyes wide open through the turns."

Mario Andretti's Ford cut loose in a long slide in one of the opening days of practice. His Holman-Moody Ford slid up the banking and struck the retaining wall. For the Nazareth, PA star, it was the latest in a series of mishaps in NASCAR events. "I don't think I like this so much anymore," muttered Andretti. "It's not fun."

Yarborough won the pole for the Daytona 500 with a speed of 189.222 mph, leading a virtual sweep for the fast Fords. Only Petty's Plymouth blocked a top seven sweep for the Ford products. Yarborough's electrifying time shattered the old record of 180.813 set by Curtis Turner in 1967 in a Smokey Yunick Chevrolet.

Yunick was back at Daytona in 1968 with Gordon Johncock listed as driver of a black and gold Chevelle. But the car was late in arriving and never made it through inspection.

Acting Technical Director Bill Gazaway gave Yunick a list of nine items that needed surgical work. They were:

1. *The frames did not conform to the general appearance of frames on other Chevelles.*
2. *Rocker panels cut away to make room for exhaust pipe clearance. Not allowed.*
3. *Floor area not in standard position. Floor being elevated made room for a higher driveshaft tunnel.*
4. *A-frames not properly located.*
5. *Fuel cell vent line not properly located.*
6. *Door handles not standard. Roll bar installation interferes with inner handles and non-standard handles do not protrude from car, thus offering less drag.*
7. *Screw jack covers are behind rear window allowing weight adjustments to be made during pit stops without opening trunk.*
8. *Front tread width does not conform to rules.*
9. *Doors not removable. Must be able to be removed by inspectors.*

During the lengthy tear-down, Gazaway's inspectors had disassembled much of Yunick's car. Among other things, the fuel tank had been drained and removed from the car in order to measure its contents.

Yunick studied the hand-written 9-item list without emotion. After a few moments, he turned and said, "Better make that 10!"

At which point the master mechanic climbed into his car and -- without a fuel tank -- drove off.

*   *   *

Yarborough went on to lead the Fords to an impressive triumph in the Daytona 500. Only one Chrysler product finished in the top five.

Cale nosed out LeeRoy Yarbrough in the exciting finish -- after LeeRoy had mistakenly made a pit stop late in the race. He had misread a message from Junior Johnson's pit board.

The 'Yarbs' had another private battle in the Atlanta 500. LeeRoy had made a late race pass on a restart, but he was immediately blackflagged by NASCAR for jumping the gun. Cale won again -- and LeeRoy suffered another slow burn.

Yarbrough's ill-luck continued at North Wilkesboro. While holding a commanding lead with five miles remaining, his engine blew.

Within weeks, Johnson changed his number from 26 to 98. Three years earlier, Johnson had traded 27 for 26 due to bad luck he experienced in his driving days.

"If you add 13 and 13," Johnson reasoned, "it makes 26. And we've been having double tough luck this season. When you aren't winning you have to make changes. Since everybody is doing a good job, it wouldn't make sense to fire anybody. So we changed the number."

Yarbrough's luck took a turn for the better. He won the Northern 300 at Trenton, NJ, and he won the Dixie 500 at Atlanta International Raceway.

When Cale and LeeRoy weren't pocketing the big dollars on the superspeedways, David Pearson was racking up on the short tracks. During a 13 race span in the early spring, Pearson's Holman-Moody Ford had won seven of them.

Ford had won 12 of the first 17 Grand National races in 1968, including all on the superspeedways and road courses.

Ford's power play had produced immediate results. The Chrysler teams found themselves lagging behind.

"Chrysler people have got to stop singing songs (in reference to musical commercials) and start designing some parts that will get the job done," said Paul Goldsmith.

"You can't go racing when you're only half ready," said Plymouth team manager and crew chief Bill Ellis. "I can't get parts from Chrysler on time. Some owners can get parts when they need them; others can't."

Even Lee Petty had something to say. "Ford is spending 10 times as much money as we (Chrysler) are, and

Cale and LeeRoy were the top two Ford performers in 1968

they are winning races."

Another Chrysler team owner remarked, "Ford is improving engines and building new ones and better ones all the time. We're still working with the same stuff we had in 1964. When you talk with somebody at Chrysler about this situation, there seems to be an attitude of 'we don't need you; you need us'. It looks like a lean year for the Chrysler products."

Ford Motor Co. had done extensive engine research the past several months. One of the major changes in Ford's procedure was to create an engine department for each and every factory backed team. That had been different in 1967. Junior Johnson said Ford "blew 27 races last year."

The engines would arrive at the track, Johnson pointed out, "and we would pick out the ones we wanted," Johnson said. "The engines were all built at Holman-Moody, supposedly with engineers overseeing the operation. Our engines were as fast as Chryslers, but they didn't last.

"Ford was concerned about it too," Johnson continued. "Ford is strong on performance and if something is wrong they want to know about it and correct it. That is why they spend money on competitive performance tests."

Bobby Allison led the point standings after the Daytona 500. In the following event, the Southeastern 500 at Bristol, he blew an engine early and wound up last. He fell 23 points behind Richard Petty in the point standings. Ford had told Long to keep his car at home the following week. Allison was not going to be able to go for the point championship. "They pulled me out before we got to Atlanta," said Allison. "We were told that if we were doing good in the points as of Atlanta, we'd probably get to run them all. It didn't work out that way."

Allison still stood fifth in the point standings after the Atlanta 500 -- even though he had been forced to miss two races. Shortly after that, Lorenzen stopped showing up at the races. The crew chief had been on a leave of absence.

In July, Lorenzen left the Long team. "Freddy's health has gone from bad to worse," said car owner Long in a prepared statement. "He just can't take it any longer."

Inside reports indicated that Ford released Lorenzen. And Lorenzen didn't admit to having any more problems with his ulcers. "My health is good," he said. "No more stomach problems. I'm not associated with Ford any more. I'm lonely. I don't know what to do with my time. I'd like to race again."

Before Lorenzen's departure, Allison had quit the operation. "I accepted this ride all along with the understanding that I would run all the races," said Allison. "Then I hear it's down to 22 races. Now it's down to 15. I want to race more than 15 times a year."

Allison dusted off his J.D. Bracken-owned Chevrolet and went racing. He finished second in the Carolina 500 at Rockingham, and won a 300-lapper on the Islip, NY small oval.

When he first brought the Chevy to the tracks, Allison mentioned a "silent sponsor", but he did not elaborate.

The rumor mill said that a St.Louis Chevrolet dealership was going to pay the bills -- and then be reimbursed entirely by General Motors. Smokey Yunick admitted that behind the scenes pressures were placed on him to put one of his engines in the Allison car. Yunick said one of the GM executives had said, "It would be appreciated if you can break an engine loose for Bobby."

The Allison team never got one of Smokey's beefed up motors. By autumn, he had given up on the Chevrolet. "It has become impossible to field a competitive car with the Chevrolet," said Allison. "We've reached the point where we can't hope for better than fourth or fifth, and that is relying on others to fall out. That's not my kind of racing."

With that statement, Allison accepted an offer to finish out the season in Friedkin Enterprises Plymouths. Jerry Grant had been long gone. Modified and Sportsman hero Ray Hendrick drove the car in a four events; and ol' pro Curtis Turner drove the car in six races.

Chrysler cars won only three of 10 superspeedway events in 1968. Cale Yarborough won four in his Mercury. LeeRoy Yarbrough, Donnie Allison and David Pearson won one each.

Pearson and Petty each won 16 Grand National events in the 49-race season. Isaac won three times, all on short tracks.

But the point battle was among the closest ever. Pearson and Isaac battled nip and tuck for the championship, which Pearson wound up winning by 126 points.

While the action was hot and heavy on the track, some interesting things were going on elsewhere. On May 23, 1968, ground breaking ceremonies for an elaborate speedway were taking place in Talladega, AL. Dr. James L. Hardwick, Mayor of Talladega, turned the first spade of dirt for the construction of the new Alabama International Motor Speedway. Bill France was going to build a track -- a little bit bigger and a little bit faster than his Daytona International Speedway. Scheduled opening of the $5 million project was September of 1969.

There was a facility in Michigan which had already been built. Lawrence LoPatin (pronounced *Lo-Pay-tin*, rhymes with *go scatin'*) formed a corporation, sold $3-million worth of public stock and got the Michigan International Speedway off and running.

Larry LoPatin, President of American Raceways, Inc. and Michigan International Speedway

LoPatin, whose self-description was "I'm a fat slob who knows how to put pieces together", was not an auto racing enthusiast. A Detroit industrialist, LoPatin saw a chance to make millions in the auto racing business. "I'm profit-oriented," he once said. "Not just dealing in fun and games."

Within a few months, he was "up to my eyeballs" in the sport, and admitted that he had grown to like auto racing. After forming American Raceways, Inc., it was his plan to build and operate more than a dozen major racing facilities all across the nation.

"Prior to my total involvement to automobile racing, my impressions of the sport were that it was highly fragmented in terms of facility ownership, extremely complex in terms of the racing establishment, and sadly lacking in approach from the fans point of view -- with the exception of Daytona International Speedway." said LoPatin. "My first prophesy regarding the super tracks, therefore, is that they will be designed, developed and constructed with the idea of accommodating, attracting and servicing the fans."

Within a year he owned 47 percent of Riverside International Raceway. He then merged Riverside with Atlanta International Raceway in which he obtained 19 percent of the stock with an option to buy an additional 52 percent. He had begun construction on Texas Inter-

Michigan International Speedway under construction. Shortly after completion, the 2-mile track joined NASCAR as part of a 10-year contract

national Speedway in College Station, TX and had plans to build a giant complex in New Jersey.

LoPatin's Michigan track opened on October 13, 1968. The first race was a 250-mile USAC Indy Car race. A crowd of 55,000 turned out for the show and he turned a profit of $94,523 in his first outing. USAC Competition Director Henry Banks was angered when he found out that the race took in $500,000 in receipts, yet LoPatin only paid a purse of $75,000.

LoPatin had been seeking a long-term contract with USAC and Banks -- a multi year deal which was unheard of in auto racing. The 42 year-old LoPatin planned to develop what he called 'franchise racing'. "Our organization will have 20-25 major races by 1971," he promised. "There are just so many Sundays in a year, so securing dates is most important. Long range contracts with sanctioning bodies will enable us to operate a more stable program.

"Dates are a very precious commodity in the racing industry," added LoPatin. "I want all the dates I can get."

USAC's Banks was reluctant to jump into a long term contract with someone he didn't fully understand.

Bill France just happened to be at Michigan International Speedway on October 13 during the inaugural event. France wanted to check this LoPatin guy out for himself.

Within 48 hours, the two made a joint announcement: Michigan International Speedway and NASCAR had signed a *10 year contract*.

"We waited for months for USAC to move on dates," declared LoPatin. "Then Bill France comes to our opening race on Oct. 13. He said he wanted to see me about some things. The first thing Monday morning he was on my doorstep. When he left Tuesday afternoon, we had fashioned one of the longest deals in racing history -- two major NASCAR late model stock car races a year for 10 years."

The contract also stated that LoPatin's Texas track would be the guaranteed site for the 1969 Grand National finale.

LoPatin had gotten just what he wanted -- a long term deal with a major sanctioning body.

The France-LoPatin pact was a bombshell -- but not as earth shattering as the one which came out of Randleman, NC on Monday, November 25, 1968. Upon completion of the 1968 NASCAR season, Petty said he was switching to Ford after 10 years with Plymouth. "Ford has a vast storehouse of knowledge," said Petty. "Much more than Chrysler has. "The name of the game is money. If I could get a better deal, I'd take it. Even if it was working in a super market."

Ronney Householder, Director of Chrysler's racing efforts, said, "His leaving creates a big hole in our operation. The offer from Ford had to have been fantastic. I really didn't think Ford could afford Petty."

The 31 year-old Petty said his contract with Ford was not the deciding factor. "My relationship with Ford is on a year-to-year basis," he said. "I won't be getting much more money from Ford than I was getting with Chrysler, but I honestly feel like the potential for winning more money is much, much greater with Ford.

"I want to run just as many races as I possibly can," added Petty. "But more importantly, I want to win as many races as I can. I feel like running a Ford will give me that opportunity."

Race No. 1

Sheriff Busts Up Moonshine Still; '68 Opener Goes on Schedule

MACON, GA (Nov. 12, 1967) -- Bobby Allison held off a late surge by Richard Petty and won the Middle Georgia 500 at Middle Georgia Raceway to take an early lead in the point standings. The 1968 NASCAR Grand National season opener was unaffected by the discovery of an elaborate moonshine operation, which was hidden beneath the Raceway.

Allison posted his third straight win for the Holman-Moody Ford team with retired Fred Lorenzen serving as crew chief. The 29 year-old Hueytown, AL speedster took the lead in the 452nd lap and led the rest of the way. Petty finished second, a lap behind. Tiny Lund came in third, Red Farmer was fourth and Dub Simpson fifth.

David Pearson had taken the lead from Allison in the 374th lap and built up a sizable lead when his Holman-Moody Ford popped an engine with 27 miles remaining. Petty made a charge at Allison after spending five laps in the pits with mechanical problems early on.

"I doubt I would have been able to catch Pearson if he had finished," admitted Allison.

The 267-mile event went on as scheduled even though Federal and State officers located a huge moonshine still neatly tucked under the .534-mile facility. Peach County Sheriff Reggie Mullis called it "one of the most well-built stills ever operated."

The officer said the still was located under the Middle Georgia Raceway with the only entrance through a ticket booth at the north end of the track. Mullis said agents climbed down a 35 foot ladder leading from the trap door. There they found a 125 foot tunnel where the still was located.

"This is one of the most cleverly run moonshine operations I have ever seen," said one Federal agent. Following an investigation, it was discovered that the still was capable of producing 200 gallons of actual whiskey every five days.

At the end of the tunnel, there was a 2,000 gallon cooker, a 1,200 gallon box fermenter and a 750 gallon gas fuel tank for cooking. The operators had installed yellow lights to keep bugs out of the mash.

Authorities put the still out of operation a couple of weeks before the race. Most of the 6,800 spectators who attended the race were unaware the still was ever located at their hometown track.

Track President H. Lamar Brown, Jr. was charged with possession of apparatus for the distillery of illegal liquor.

The case came to trial on December 12, 1968, with Brown being found not guilty after a two hour deliberation by the jury.

			Grand National Race No. 1			
			500 Laps at Middle Georgia Raceway			
			Macon, GA			
			"Middle Georgia 500"			
			267 Miles on .534-mile Paved Track			
			November 12, 1967			

Fin	St	No.	Driver	Team / Car	Laps	Money	Status
1	2	11	Bobby Allison	Holman-Moody '67 Ford	500	$3,300	Running
2	6	43	Richard Petty	Petty Enterprises '67 Plym	499	2,040	Running
3	12	55	Tiny Lund	Lyle Stelter '66 Ford	491	1,275	Running
4	19	97	Red Farmer	Farmer '67 Ford	476	900	Running
5	27	88	Dub Simpson	Buck Baker '67 Olds	470	800	Running
6	17	64	Elmo Langley	Langley-Woodfield '66 Ford	468	725	Running
7	11	39	Friday Hassler	Red Sharp '66 Chevrolet	462	675	Running
8	22	20	Clyde Lynn	Lynn '66 Ford	459	600	Running
9	21	02	Bob Cooper	Cooper '66 Chevrolet	457	500	Running
10	28	21	Bill Seifert	'66 Ford	456	400	Running
11	3	17	David Pearson	Holman-Moody '67 Ford	451	500	Engine
12	30	95	E J Trivette	'66 Ford	447	375	Running
13	16	4	John Sears	L G DeWitt '66 Ford	436	350	Running
14	20	25	Jabe Thomas	Don Robertson '67 Ford	374	275	Running
15	29	93	Wilson Gardner	Gardner '67 Ford	362	200	Differen
16	8	37	Bobby Isaac	K&K Insurance '67 Dodge	320	230	Engine
17	1	26	LeeRoy Yarbrough	Junior Johnson '67 Ford	252	400	Engine
18	14	06	Neil Castles	Castles '65 Dodge	250	225	Engine
19	9	27	Bosco Lowe	Banjo Matthews '67 Ford	220	225	Differen
20	4	14	Jim Paschal	Friedkin Ent '67 Plymouth	171	275	Engine
21	5	16	Cale Yarborough	Bud Moore '67 Mercury	164	250	H Gasket
22	10	74	Tom Pistone	Turkey Minton '67 Chevrolet	154	225	Oil Pan
23	7	40	Charlie Glotzbach	Friedkin Ent '67 Plymouth	151	235	Differen
24	15	49	G C Spencer	Spencer '67 Plymouth	143	225	Differen
25	13	2	Paul Lewis	J D Bracken '65 Chevrolet	128	225	Valve
26	25	19	Henley Gray	Gray '66 Ford	102	150	Heating
27	26	34	Wendell Scott	Scott '66 Ford	73	150	Oil Press
28	18	87	Buck Baker	Baker '66 Ford	60	150	Oil Press
29	24	07	George Davis	Davis '66 Chevrolet	56	150	T Chain
30	23	73	Rod Eulenfeld	'66 Chevrolet	55	150	Engine

Time of Race: 3 hours, 17 minutes, 40 seconds
Average Speed: 81.001 mph
Pole Winner: LeeRoy Yarbrough - 94.323 mph
Lap Leaders: LeeRoy Yarbrough 1-62, Tom Pistone 63-97, Yarbrough 98-121,
    Bobby Allison 122-196, David Pearson 197-226, Allison 227-373, Pearson 374-451,
    Allison 452-500.
Cautions: 6 for ___ laps   Margin of Victory: 1-lap plus   Attendance: 6,800

Race No. 2

Allison Pays Petty; Petty Beats Allison at Montgomery

MONTGOMERY, AL (Nov. 26, 1967) -- Late entrant Richard Petty drove his Plymouth around a sputtering Bobby Allison in the 143rd lap and won the 100-mile Grand National event at Montgomery Speedway. Petty showed up only after he received a sizable amount of "show money" from the promoters. Allison is one of the promoters at the half-mile paved track.

Allison finished second, the first time in four races he has failed to put the Holman-Moody Ford into victory lane. Bobby Isaac came in third, Tom Pistone was fourth and Paul Lewis fifth.

Petty and Allison, who have been involved in a few fender benders in recent weeks, met in victory circle. "Let's say we get along fine on the track," said Petty. "I'm not so sure about off the track, but it's a thing of the past."

Petty led the first 96 laps from the pole, but fell a lap behind after making a green flag pit stop. Allison led from lap 97 through the 142nd lap, but lost a cylinder late in the race. Petty had little trouble overcoming the deficit and won by almost a lap.

LeeRoy Yarbrough chased Petty and Allison early, but brake failure put his Junior Johnson Ford out on lap 123. David Pearson left the race after 102 laps with suspension problems.

A crowd of 6,000 watched Petty win his 76th career race at an average speed of 70.644 mph.

Grand National Race No. 2
200 Laps at Montgomery Speedway
Montgomery, AL
100 Miles on Half-mile Paved Track
November 26, 1967

Fin	St	No.	Driver	Team / Car	Laps	Money	Status
1	1	43	Richard Petty	Petty Enterprises '67 Plym	200	$1,200	Running
2	2	11	Bobby Allison	Holman-Moody '67 Ford	200	600	Running
3	7	37	Bobby Isaac	K&K Insurance '67 Dodge	196	400	Running
4	8	74	Tom Pistone	Turkey Minton '67 Chevrolet	196	300	Running
5	5	2	Paul Lewis	J D Bracken '65 Chevrolet	195	275	Running
6	17	06	Neil Castles	Castles '65 Dodge	193	240	Running
7	6	39	Friday Hassler	Red Sharp '66 Chevrolet	191	200	Running
8	12	87	Buck Baker	Baker '66 Ford	190	175	Running
9	14	20	Clyde Lynn	Lynn '66 Ford	188	150	Running
10	18	25	Jabe Thomas	Don Robertson '67 Ford	188	140	Running
11	25	34	Wendell Scott	Scott '6 Ford	185	130	Running
12	15	64	Elmo Langley	Langley-Woodfield '66 Ford	185	120	Running
13	21	19	Henley Gray	Gray '66 Ford	182	110	Running
14	26	95	E J Trivette	'66 Ford	166	100	Flat tire
15	30	58	Phil Wendt	'66 Chevrolet	182	100	Engine
16	27	9	Bill Vanderhoof	Truett Rodgers '66 Chevrolet	151	100	Running
17	28	31	Bill Ervin	Ralph Murphy '66 Ford	149	100	Running
18	11	09	Roy Tyner	'66 Pontiac	134	100	Differen
19	24	94	Don Beiderman	Ron Stotten '66 Chevrolet	129	100	Heating
20	3	26	LeeRoy Yarbrough	Junior Johnson '67 Ford	123	100	Brakes
21	20	45	Bill Seifert	Seifert '66 Ford	118	100	Valve
22	4	17	David Pearson	Holman-Moody '67 Ford	102	100	Frame
23	9	21	John Sears	L G DeWitt '66 Ford	39	---	Differen
24	23	76	Ben Arnold	Don Culpepper '66 Ford	39	---	Engine
25	13	21	Bosco Lowe	'67 Ford	38	---	Engine
26	22	88	Dub Simpson	Buck Baker '67 Olds	38	---	Brakes
27	19	02	Bob Cooper	Cooper '66 Chevrolet	35	---	Sway bar
28	29	01	Paul Dean Holt	Dennis Holt '67 Ford	30	---	Heating
29	10	97	Red Farmer	Farmer '67 Ford	28	---	Spring
30	16	93	Walson Gardner	Gardner '67 Ford	26	---	Engine

Time of Race: 1 hour, 24 minutes, 56 seconds
Average Speed: 70.644 mph
Pole Winner: Richard Petty - 79.964 mph
Lap Leaders: Richard Petty 1-96, Bobby Allison 97-142, Petty 143-200.
Cautions: 4 for 20 laps   Margin of Victory: Attendance: 6,000

Race No. 3
Dan By The Riverside;
Gurney Wins Again

RIVERSIDE, CA (Jan. 21) -- Dan Gurney shook off the effects of a blown tire and a long pit stop and roared to his fifth Motor Trend 500 victory at Riverside International Raceway. It was the 12th NASCAR Grand

Grand National Race No. 3
186 Laps at Riverside Int'l Raceway
Riverside, CA
"Motor Trend 500"
500 Miles on 2.7-mile Paved Road Course
January 21, 1968

Fin	St	No.	Driver	Team / Car	Laps	Money	Status
1	1	121	Dan Gurney	Wood Brothers '68 Ford	186	$21,250	Running
2	2	17	David Pearson	Holman-Moody '68 Ford	186	9,600	Running
3	3	115	Parnelli Jones	Bill Stroppe '68 Ford	186	5,600	Running
4	12	29	Bobby Allison	Bondy Long '68 Ford	185	3,250	Running
5	7	21	Cale Yarborough	Wood Brothers '68 Ford	184	2,225	Running
6	14	3	Al Unser	Rudy Ho'err '67 Dodge	182	1,550	Running
7	10	37	Bobby Isaac	K&K Insurance '67 Dodge	182	1,370	Running
8	16	06	Dave James	'67 Plymouth	171	1.250	Running
9	17	45	Scotty Cain	Bill Clinton '66 Ford	167	1,150	Running
10	4	43	Richard Petty	Petty Enterprises '67 Plym	163	1,650	Engine
11	20	61	Jim Cook	Cos Cancilla '67 Olds	162	1,000	Running
12	35	19	Henley Gray	Gray '66 Ford	150	900	Running
13	30	20	Clyde Lynn	Lynn '66 Ford	148	800	Running
14	31	88	Clyde Pickett	Dan Dostinich '67 Chevrolet	140	700	Running
15	24	7	Jack McCoy	Charles Bell '67 Dodge	118	725	Engine
16	36	92	Guy Jones	'66 Ford	109	650	Engine
17	37	143	Frank Burnett	'65 Plymouth	92	640	Gas Tank
18	40	08	Sam Rose	Rose '67 Mercury	92	630	Lug bolt
19	22	1	Don White	Nichels Eng '68 Dodge	90	705	Brakes
20	21	41	Norm Nelson*	Friedkin Ent '68 Plymouth	87	720	Engine
21	38	111	Ed Brown	'67 Ford	73	615	Fuel pmp
22	11	44	Jerry Grant	Friedkin Ent '67 Plymouth	71	760	Crash
23	9	22	Darel Dieringer	Mario Rossi '68 Plymouth	69	625	Engine
24	25	18	Harold Hardesty	Bob Bristol '66 Ford	67	575	Crash
25	15	6	Buddy Baker	Cotton Owens '67 Dodge	59	575	Clutch
26	27	00	Frank Jones	'65 Chevrolet	55	520	Differen
27	8	11	Mario Andretti	Holman-Moody '68 Ford	41	540	Engine
28	39	8	Jerry Oliver	'66 Chevrolet	39	510	Differen
29	29	25	Vallie Engelauf	'66 Chevrolet	38	505	Trans
30	19	96	Ray Elder	Fred Elder '65 Dodge	37	500	Fuel pmp
31	42	2	Johnny Steele	Kyle Gibson '67 Ford	33	500	Crash
32	32	38	Don Noel	'67 Ford	31	575	Engine
33	33	15	Paul Dorrity	Glen Dorrity '67 Chevrolet	28	500	Differen
34	13	48	James Hylton	Hylton Eng '67 Dodge	21	575	Engine
35	34	9	Roy Tyner	Tyner '66 Ford	19	500	Clutch
36	26	5	Bill Small	'65 Chevrolet	16	500	Trans
37	5	26	LeeRoy Yarbrough	Junior Johnson '68 Ford	14	575	Oil Pan
38	28	98	Bob Link	Link '67 Ford	14	500	Sway bar
39	23	99	Jerry Titus	'66 Ford	5	500	H Gasket
40	44	80	Bo Reeder	'67 Ford	4	500	Differen
41	41	09	Carl Joiner	'67 Pontiac	3	500	Heating
42	18	4	John Sears	L G DeWitt '66 Ford	2	500	Engine
43	6	27	A J Foyt	Banjo Matthews '68 Ford	0	550	Engine
44	43	46	Joe Clark	'65 Plymouth	0	500	H Gasket

Time of Race: 4 hours, 57 minutes, 55 seconds
Average Speed: 100.598 mph
Pole Winner: Dan Gurney - 110.971 mph
Lap Leaders: Parnelli Jones 1-24, Dan Gurney 25-26, Mario Andretti 27-29,
    David Pearson 30-32, Jones 33-44, Pearson 45, Gurney 46-47, Jones 48,
    Gurney 49-79, Pearson 80-85, Jones 86-88, Gurney 89-145, Jones 146-153,
    Gurney 154-158, Jones 159, Gurney 160-186.
Cautions: Margin of Victory: 36 seconds   Attendance: 73,000

National start for the 37 year-old Costa Mesa, CA driver and the fifth time he has earned a trip to victory lane.

Gurney took the lead for keeps in the 160th lap and wound up 36 seconds in front of runner-up David Pearson. Third place went to Parnelli Jones, Bobby Allison was fourth and Cale Yarborough fifth. Fords swept the first five positions.

Gurney, driving the Wood Brothers Ford, started on the pole and led for 124 of the 186 laps on the 2.7- mile road course. While holding a 52 second lead over Jones, Gurney blew a rear tire on lap 145 and dashed to the pits. Glen Wood noticed that fragments of rubber were wrapped around the rear axle and it took one minute and 25 seconds to complete the stop. Gurney returned to the track in third place, but it took only 15 laps for him to work his way back into the lead.

A.J. Foyt's Riverside jinx continued as his Banjo Matthews Ford suffered a blown engine before he completed a lap. Mario Andretti, Norm Nelson, Don White and three other top ranked USAC drivers ran into mechanical problems and failed to finish.

Richard Petty was running sixth with 15 laps to go when the engine blew in his Plymouth, sending him into the turn six wall. He got credit for 10th place based on the 163 laps he completed.

Jerry Grant spun his Plymouth off the course in the 72nd lap. It appeared to be a solo mishap and the hefty Californian started to climb out of his car. A moment later, he was hit hard by Vallie Engelauf. Grant complained of back injuries, and was treated at a local hospital.

Gurney completed the 500 miles in just under five hours and averaged 100.598 mph.

Allison held the point lead by a slim 16 points over Petty in the NASCAR driver standings.

For the first time in a NASCAR Grand National race, a number of cars were equipped with a safety screen over the driver's window opening. The factory Fords all had a wire mesh screen to protect the driver. The idea came from Charlie Gray of Ford's Special Vehicles Department.

Race No. 4

Yarborough Nips Yarbrough In Close Daytona 500 Finish

DAYTONA BEACH, FL (Feb. 25) -- Cale Yarborough squeezed past LeeRoy Yarbrough with four laps to go and held on to win the 10th annual Daytona 500 by one second. Yarborough's triumph, his third on a superspeedway, gave Ford Motor Co. a sweep of the first three spots in the classic at Daytona International Speedway.

Yarborough was running second behind Yarbrough after the 11th caution flag. When the green flag came out on lap 179, Cale was trapped in traffic and LeeRoy scooted to a healthy lead. With 10 laps to go, Cale was 3.2-seconds behind. Within five laps, he was on LeeRoy's tailpipes and he made the all-important pass on lap 197. "I knew I could take him if the yellow didn't come out," said the 28 year-old Yarborough. "Our Mercury ran like a gem. Once I got by him, I knew he couldn't do any better than second place."

LeeRoy led six times for 62 laps, but had to settle for runner-up honors. Bobby Allison finished third with Al Unser fourth and David Pearson fifth.

Cale Yarborough won Daytona 500 in Wood Brothers Mercury

The caution flag was waved a record 11 times for no less than 150 miles. The frequency of the caution flag caused two pace cars -- both Chevrolet Camaros -- to overheat. A third pace car had to be brought in to lead the single file formation.

Cale had to overcome a number of problems en route to the $47,250 victory. As early as the 14th lap, the Timmonsville, SC driver was in the pits with a skipping motor. Two laps later, he was back in the pits with ignition problems. Mechanic Leonard Wood corrected the problems, but not before Cale had lost a lap. Due to the many cautions, he was able to get back into the lead lap before the half way point.

Mario Andretti, defending champion, led for 17 laps

Richard Petty drove a black-topped Plymouth at Daytona

but was knocked out in a wild crash with John Sears and Buddy Baker on lap 105. No injuries were reported. Since winning the Daytona 500 in 1967, Andretti has been involved in three straight crashes. Baker, upset at being taken out of the race, remarked in disgust, "That guy takes out one or two contenders every time he races down here. He just lost it. He had a chance to let up and correct it, but he kept standing on it. When he swung around directly in front of me, there was nothing I could do," said Baker.

A crowd of 94,800 watched Yarborough average 143.251 mph.

Veteran car builder Smokey Yunick entered a Chevrolet with Gordon Johncock listed as driver. However, the car ran into a roadblock at the inspection station. NASCAR officials combed the car exceptionally close and declared the car had to undergo extensive surgical work in order to obtain eligibility for the race.

Inspectors took the fuel tank from the car, drained it and measured its contents closely. Officials indicated the car's body had not fit the templates and that a peculiar joint was located in the front suspension. NASCAR gave Yunick a list of nine items to change on the car.

When handed the list, Yunick muttered, "Better make that 10". He hopped in the car -- without a gas tank -- and drove off.

The 125-mile qualifying races were rained out on Friday. The day dawned dark, gray and wet. The weather broke for about 40 minutes, and Bill France wanted the drivers to buckle up and prepare to start racing. Most of

Grand National Race No. 4
200 Laps at Daytona Int'l Speedway
Daytona Beach, FL
"Daytona 500"
500 Miles on 2.5-mile Paved Track
February 25, 1968

Fin	St	No.	Driver	Team / Car	Laps	Money	Status
1	1	21	Cale Yarborough	Wood Brothers '68 Mercury	200	$47,250	Running
2	3	26	LeeRoy Yarbrough	Junior Johnson '68 Mercury	200	17,525	Running
3	6	29	Bobby Allison	Bondy Long '68 Ford	200	10,150	Running
4	8	6	Al Unser	Cotton Owens '68 Dodge	200	6,250	Running
5	4	17	David Pearson	Holman-Moody '68 Ford	199	4,750	Running
6	9	99	Paul Goldsmith	Nichels Eng '68 Plymouth	199	4,500	Running
7	23	22	Darel Dieringer	Mario Rossi '68 Dodge	199	4,100	Running
8	2	43	Richard Petty	Petty Enterprises '68 Plym	198	4,350	Running
9	5	16	Tiny Lund	Bud Moore '68 Mercury	197	2,500	Running
10	27	32	Andy Hampton	Harry Ranier '67 Dodge	193	2,525	Running
11	67	67	Buddy Arrington	Arrington '67 Dodge	186	2,350	Running
12	19	27	A J Foyt	Banjo Matthews '68 Ford	183	2,350	Trans
13	34	84	Bob Senneker	'66 Chevrolet	182	3,200	Running
14	25	20	Clyde Lynn	Lynn '67 Mercury	182	2,200	Running
15	40	45	Bill Seifert	Seifert '67 Ford	181	2,100	Running
16	15	5	Butch Hartman	Hartman '68 Dodge	180	2,275	Running
17	42	34	Wendell Scott	Scott '66 Ford	179	2,045	Running
18	24	46	Larry Manning	Tom Hunter '66 Chevrolet	179	2,110	Running
19	49	19	Henley Gray	Gray '66 Ford	175	2,025	Running
20	35	30	Dave Marcis	Larry Wehrs '66 Chevrolet	175	2,015	Running
21	38	73	Rod Eulenfeld	Julian Kline '66 Chevrolet	174	2,000	Running
22	10	37	Sam McQuagg	K&K Insurance '67 Dodge	171	1,140	Engine
23	44	96	Charles Burnett	Ray Buckner '66 Ford	146	1,135	Flagged
24	31	79	Frank Warren	Harold Rhodes '66 Chevrolet	143	1,130	Heating
25	17	64	Elmo Langley	Langley-Woodfield '66 Ford	141	1,125	Heating
26	37	25	Jabe Thomas	Don Robertson '67 Ford	126	1,120	Heating
27	29	56	Jim Hurtubise	Lyle Stelter '66 Mercury	123	1,125	Crash
28	50	11	Don Biederman	James Brown '66 Ford	123	1,110	Engine
29	20	11	Mario Andretti	Holman-Moody '68 Mercury	105	1,580	Crash
30	13	3	Buddy Baker	Ray Fox '68 Dodge	103	1,700	Crash
31	28	4	John Sears	L G DeWitt '67 Ford	101	1,145	Crash
32	21	15	Charlie Glotzbach	Friedkin Ent '68 Plymouth	91	1,140	Engine
33	41	75	Earl Brooks	Gene Black '66 Ford	89	1,085	Crash
34	33	10	Bill Champion	Champion '66 Ford	79	1,080	Heating
35	39	18	Dick Johnson	Bob Casperson '67 Ford	63	1,075	Engine
36	11	71	Bobby Isaac	K&K Insurance '68 Dodge	56	1,070	Engine
37	16	7	Bobby Johns	Shorty Johns '66 Chevrolet	55	1,065	Ignition
38	47	90	Sonny Hutchins	Junie Donlavey '67 Ford	53	1,060	Engine
39	32	02	Bob Cooper	Cooper '67 Chevrolet	52	1,055	Engine
40	7	66	Donnie Allison	Holman-Moody '68 Ford	48	1,000	Crash
41	43	51	Stan Meserve	Margo Hamm '67 Dodge	34	950	Brakes
42	26	14	Jerry Grant	Friedkin Ent '68 Plymouth	32	1,000	Crash
43	30	97	Red Farmer	Farmer '67 Ford	24	850	Engine
44	14	48	James Hylton	Hylton Eng '67 Dodge	24	800	Crash
45	45	0	Dr. Don Tarr	Tarr '67 Chevrolet	23	750	H Gasket
46	46	2	Paul Lewis	Bracken & Bracken '67 Dodge	14	700	Engine
47	48	9	Roy Tyner	Tyner '67 Pontiac	8	1,650	Engine
48	12	1	Bud Moore	Activated Angels '68 Dodge	7	600	Crash
49	18	36	H B Bailey	Bailey '66 Pontiac	6	550	Engine
50	36	06	Dub Simpson	Neil Castles '67 Dodge	0	500	Oil Press

Time of Race: 3 hours, 23 minutes, 44 seconds
Average Speed: 143.251 mph
Pole Winner: Cale Yarborough - 189.222 mph
Lap Leaders: Cale Yarborough 1-12, David Pearson 13-22, Richard Petty 23-26,
　Al Unser 27, LeeRoy Yarbrough 28-34, Buddy Baker 35-36, Yarbrough 37-40, Baker 41
　Yarbrough 42-46, Mario Andretti 47-48, Butch Hartman 49-51, Baker 52-68,
　Yarbrough 69-71, Andretti 72-76, Bobby Allison 77-78, Andretti 79-88,
　Yarbrough 89-143, Yarbrough 144-166, Allison 167-171, Yarbrough 172-176,
　Yarbrough 177-196, Yarbrough 197-200.
Cautions: 11 for 60 laps　　Margin of Victory: 1 second　　Attendance: 94,800.

the drivers refused to get in their cars. They said the track was still wet and in no condition to race on.

France drove his personal car into the garage area and immediately a crowd surrounded him. "Are there any

David Pearson and LeeRoy Yarbrough lead pack of Fords out of turn 2 at Daytona

per and it proved to be the quickest way around the half-mile paved track. "I tried passing Richard low on the first lap and it worked," said Pearson. "After that, I pretty well knew I could pass anybody like that if I had to."

Petty, who led for a total of 108 laps, said he gave out toward the end of the race. "The car had

of you guys who want to race?" France asked loudly. The only driver to raise his hand was rookie Dave Marcis. "Line up your cars and we'll get started. We'll pay the full purse and if the hot-shots don't want to run, they can go back to the garage area."

Some drivers walked toward their cars; others stood firm. The confrontation never came as a heavy rain hit the track again within a half hour.

Race No. 5

Pearson Wins Southeastern 500; His First in a Ford

BRISTOL, TN (Mar. 17) -- David Pearson took the lead with 31 laps to go and won the Southeastern 500 at Bristol International Speedway. It was the first victory for the 33 year-old Spartanburg, SC driver since he joined Holman-Moody 10 months ago.

Richard Petty wound up second, 3.0-seconds behind. LeeRoy Yarbrough finished third, Darel Dieringer was fourth and Bobby Isaac came in fifth.

Pearson took the low groove throughout the 500 lap-

3-abreast in Southeastern 500 -- Dave Marcis #30, Richard Petty #43 and Buddy Baker #3

what it took to win, but the driver didn't," he conceded. "I gave out. I was so tired I wasn't driving as sharp as you need to here. I kept getting into the turns too hard and got into trouble."

Petty scraped the retaining wall on a number of occasions, which allowed Pearson to take a free ride home.

The caution flag was out 11 times for a total of 81 laps. Jerry Grant, who replaced Jim Paschal in the Friedkin Enterprises Plymouth, crashed early in the race for the third straight race.

The lead changed hands 21 times among four drivers. Cale Yarborough led for 48 laps but departed on lap 237 with rear gearing failure.

Point leader Bobby Allison finished last in the 36 car field, falling victim to a blown engine after just 41 laps. Richard Petty took a 13 point lead over Pearson in the Grand National point standings as Allison dropped to third.

Race No. 6

Pearson Beats Glotzbach In Richmond 250

RICHMOND, VA (Mar. 24) -- David Pearson won his fifth race in the last six tries at the Virginia State

Richard Petty finished 2nd at Bristol

Grand National Race No. 5
500 Laps at Bristol Int'l Speedway
Bristol, TN
"Southeastern 500"
250 Miles on Half-mile Paved Track
March 17, 1968

Fin	St	No.	Driver	Team / Car	Laps	Money	Status
1	2	17	David Pearson	Holman-Moody '68 Ford	500	$5,725	Running
2	1	43	Richard Petty	Petty Enterprises '68 Plym	500	4,125	Running
3	4	26	LeeRoy Yarbrough	Junior Johnson '68 Ford	499	2,100	Running
4	5	22	Darel Dieringer	Mario Rossi '68 Plymouth	492	1,325	Running
5	11	71	Bobby Isaac	K&K Insurance '67 Dodge	491	900	Running
6	29	1	Bud Moore	A J King '68 Dodge	491	800	Running
7	15	09	Jack Ingram	Roy Tyner '66 Chevrolet	481	700	Running
8	16	10	Bill Champion	Champion '66 Ford	469	650	Running
9	17	64	Elmo Langley	Langley-Woodfield '66 Ford	468	625	Running
10	32	2	Earl Brooks	'66 Ford	467	550	Running
11	36	06	Neil Castles	Castles '67 Plymouth	467	525	Running
12	19	45	Bill Seifert	Seifert '66 Ford	454	490	Running
13	20	30	Dave Marcis	Larry Wehrs '66 Chevrolet	449	460	Running
14	23	20	Clyde Lynn	Lynn '67 Mercury	445	445	Rear End
15	22	50	Wendell Scott	G C Spencer '66 Plymouth	436	425	Running
16	27	02	Bob Cooper	Cooper '66 Chevrolet	430	415	Running
17	21	25	Jabe Thomas	Don Robertson '67 Ford	427	395	Running
18	34	01	Paul Dean Holt	Dennis Holt '67 Ford	412	375	Running
19	26	31	Bill Ervin	Newman Long '66 Ford	396	350	Running
20	24	19	Henley Gray	Gray '66 Ford	392	340	Running
21	33	18	Dick Johnson	Bob Casperson '67 Ford	338	330	Ball Jt.
22	35	93	Walson Gardner	Gardner '67 Ford	295	320	Engine
23	10	3	Buddy Baker	Ray Fox '67 Dodge	245	305	Heating
24	3	21	Cale Yarborough	Wood Brothers '68 Ford	237	325	Rear End
25	28	48	James Hylton	Hylton Eng '67 Dodge	227	295	Driver ill
26	18	39	Friday Hassler	Red Sharp '66 Chevrolet	206	285	Sway bar
27	31	95	Doug Cooper	Henley Gray '66 Ford	206	275	Ball jt.
28	9	16	Tiny Lund	Bud Moore '68 Mercury	199	265	Engine
29	12	4	John Sears	L G DeWitt '67 Ford	191	255	Rear End
30	6	27	Donnie Allison	Banjo Matthews '68 Ford	114	245	Rear End
31	25	76	Roy Tyner	Don Culpepper '66 Ford	104	200	Oil Leak
32	14	49	G C Spencer	Spencer '67 Plymouth	91	200	Crash
33	7	14	Jerry Grant	Friedkin Ent '68 Plymouth	72	200	Crash
34	13	99	Paul Goldsmith	Nichels Eng '68 Plymouth	60	200	D Shaft
35	30	51	Stan Meserve	Margo Hamm '67 Dodge	54	200	Engine
36	8	29	Bobby Allison	Bondy Long '68 Ford	41	200	Engine

Time of Race: 3 hours, 14 minutes, 11 seconds
Average Speed: 77.247 mph
Pole Winner: Richard Petty - 88.582 mph
Lap Leaders: David Pearson 1-34, Richard Petty 35-45, Pearson 46-95, Petty 96,
    LeeRoy Yarbrough 97-123, Cale Yarborough 124-167, Petty 168,
    Yarborough 169-172, Petty 173-209, Pearson 210, Petty 211-213, Yarborough 214-284,
    Pearson 285-311, Yarbrough 312-315, Pearson 316-348, Petty 349-403,
    Yarbrough 404-469, Pearson 470-500.
Cautions: 11 for 81 laps
Margin of Victory: 3 seconds
Attendance: 19,800.

"I didn't use but half the horsepower I had," said Pearson. "If you try to goose it all the way around, you burn up your tires in 20 laps."

Owens said his new driver "is the best one I've had since Pearson. He drove a beautiful race". Bobby Allison, Darel Dieringer and Sam McQuagg had driven for Owens since Pearson quit a year ago.

Bobby Isaac started on the pole for the second time in his career and led the first nine laps. He was involved in a spin with Wayne Smith and lost 40 laps in the pits getting repairs. He returned and finished 13th in the field of 20.

Pearson averaged 65.217 mph before 11,200 spectators.

Grand National Race No. 6
250 Laps at Virginia State Fairgrounds
Richmond, VA
"Richmond 250"
125 Miles on Half-mile Dirt Track
March 24, 1968

Fin	St	No.	Driver	Team / Car	Laps	Money	Status
1	16	17	David Pearson	Holman-Moody '68 Ford	250	2,300	Running
2	2	6	Charlie Glotzbach	Cotton Owens '67 Dodge	249	1,275	Running
3	4	64	Elmo Langley	Langley-Woodfield '66 Ford	237	950	Running
4	8	88	Neil Castles	Castles '67 Olds	237	700	Running
5	11	20	Clyde Lynn	Lynn '66 Ford	232	550	Running
6	12	25	Jabe Thomas	Don Robertson '67 Ford	229	375	Running
7	20	9	Roy Tyner	Tyner '67 Pontiac	227	300	Running
8	9	45	Bill Seifert	Seifert '66 Ford	224	250	Running
9	10	34	Wendell Scott	Scott '66 Ford	223	200	Running
10	13	19	Henley Gray	Gray '66 Ford	220	200	Running
11	18	95	Harold Fagan	Henley Gray '66 Ford	215	175	Running
12	19	09	Bill Vanderhoff	Roy Tyner '66 Chevrolet	214	175	Running
13	1	37	Bobby Isaac	K&K Insurance '67 Dodge	201	175	Running
14	14	01	Paul Dean Holt	Dennis Holt '67 Ford	196	150	Flat tire
15	15	31	Bill Ervin	Newman Long '66 Ford	180	150	Brakes
16	6	4	John Sears	L G DeWitt '66 Ford	150	125	Sway bar
17	3	43	Richard Petty	Petty Enterprises '68 Plym	137	325	Engine
18	17	38	Wayne Smith	Smith '66 Chevrolet	60	125	Crash
19	7	10	Bill Champion	Champion '66 Ford	59	125	Suspen
20	5	06	Buck Baker	Neil Castles '67 Plymouth	30	125	Oil Press

Time of Race: 1 hour, 55 minutes, 55 seconds
Average Speed: 65.217 mph
Pole Winner: Bobby Isaac - 67.822 mph
Lap Leaders: Bobby Isaac 1-9, Charlie Glotzbach 10-41, David Pearson 42-44,
    Glotzbach 45-73, Pearson 74-89, Richard Petty 90-137, Glotzbach 138-155,
    Pearson 156-250.
Cautions: Margin of Victory: 1-lap plus   Attendance: 11,200

Fairgrounds and took the lead in the NASCAR point standings. It was the 32nd career triumph for the Spartanburg, SC Ford driver.

Charlie Glotzbach, taking his first ride in the Cotton Owens Dodge, wound up in second place. Elmo Langley finished third, Neil Castles was fourth and Clyde Lynn fifth.

Pearson gunned his way past Glotzbach in the 156th lap and led the rest of the way. Richard Petty had taken the lead from Pearson in the 90th lap and was pulling away when his Plymouth blew an engine on lap 137. Glotzbach took over at that point but was able to hold Pearson off for only 18 laps.

Race No. 7

Protests Fly; Cale Takes Controversial Atlanta 500

HAMPTON, GA (Mar. 31) -- Cale Yarborough drove the Wood Brothers Mercury to a controversial victory in the Atlanta 500 at Atlanta International

Grand National Race No. 7
334 Laps at Atlanta Int'l Raceway
Hampton, GA
"Atlanta 500"
500 Miles on 1.5-mile Paved Track
March 31, 1968

Fin	St	No.	Driver	Team / Car	Laps	Money	Status
1	4	21	Cale Yarborough	Wood Brothers '68 Mercury	334	$20,680	Running
2	1	26	LeeRoy Yarbrough	Junior Johnson '68 Mercury	334	9,360	Running
3	7	27	Donnie Allison	Banjo Matthews '68 Ford	333	5,415	Running
4	3	6	Charlie Glotzbach	Cotton Owens '68 Dodge	332	3,225	Running
5	14	2	Darel Dieringer	Mario Rossi '68 Plymouth	332	2,300	Running
6	12	43	Richard Petty	Petty Enterprises '68 Plym	331	1,775	Running
7	10	3	Buddy Baker	Ray Fox '68 Dodge	331	1,200	Running
8	5	71	Bobby Isaac	K&K Insurance '68 Dodge	330	1,075	Running
9	19	37	Sam McQuagg	K&K Insurance '68 Dodge	329	1,000	Running
10	15	5	Butch Hartman	Hartman '68 Dodge	327	850	Running
11	13	56	Jim Hurtubise	Lyle Stelter '68 Mercury	322	750	Running
12	6	16	Tiny Lund	Bud Moore '68 Mercury	322	700	Running
13	26	39	Friday Hassler	Red Sharp '67 Chevrolet	319	700	Running
14	22	79	Frank Warren	Harold Rhodes '66 Chevrolet	318	600	Running
15	18	48	James Hylton	Hylton Eng '67 Dodge	313	625	Running
16	28	30	Dave Marcis	Larry Wehrs '66 Chevrolet	304	575	Running
17	24	64	Elmo Langley	Langley-Woodfield '66 Ford	299	550	Running
18	38	20	Clyde Lynn	Lynn '67 Mercury	294	600	Running
19	9	29	Bobby Allison	Bondy Long '68 Ford	291	1,165	Crash
20	34	0	Dr Don Tarr	Tarr '66 Chevrolet	284	640	Running
21	25	50	Serge Adam	'66 Ford	235	625	Clutch
22	41	88	Dub Simpson	Buck Baker '67 Olds	213	550	Engine
23	43	25	Jabe Thomas	Don Robertson '67 Ford	174	550	Engine
24	17	4	John Sears	L G DeWitt '67 Ford	167	625	Crash
25	36	34	Wendell Scott	Scott '66 Ford	129	620	Oil Press
26	31	06	Neil Castles	Castles '67 Plymouth	110	700	A Frame
27	16	1	Bud Moore	A J King '68 Dodge	91	550	Engine
28	20	2	G C Spencer	'67 Dodge	86	575	Engine
29	33	52	Tony Tantarelli	'67 Ford	74	650	A Frame
30	35	96	Charles Burnett	James Brown '66 Ford	69	630	Clutch
31	2	17	David Pearson	Holman-Moody '68 Ford	54	625	Crash
32	11	99	Paul Goldsmith	Nichels Eng '68 Plym	48	675	Handling
33	23	02	Bob Cooper	Cooper '66 Chevrolet	29	550	Engine
34	30	38	Wayne Smith	Smith '67 Chevrolet	22	550	D Shaft
35	32	76	Roy Tyner	Don Culpepper '66 Ford	20	550	Engine
36	44	23	Earl Brooks	Don Robertson '66 Ford	18	500	Heating
37	39	80	E J Trivette	E C Reid '66 Chevrolet	17	540	Rear End
38	42	8	Ed Negre	Negre '67 Ford	11	500	Engine
39	27	7	Bobby Johns	Shorty Johns '67 Chevrolet	11	525	Heating
40	21	97	Red Farmer	Farmer '67 Ford	7	500	Quit
41	8	14	Jerry Grant	Friedkin Ent '68 Plymouth	6	500	Engine
42	40	58	Phil Wendt	'66 Chevrolet	6	530	Engine
43	29	45	Bill Seifert	Seifert '66 Ford	5	500	Quit
44	37	19	Henley Gray	Gray '66 Ford	4	500	Quit

Time of Race: 3 hours, 59 minutes, 24 seconds
Average Speed: 125.564 mph
Pole Winner: LeeRoy Yarbrough - 155.646 mph
Fastest Qualifier: Bobby Allison - 155.806 mph
Lap Leaders: LeeRoy Yarbrough 1-22, Cale Yarborough 23-24, James Hylton 25-29, Yarbrough 30-55, Sam McQuagg 56-60, Donnie Allison 61-62, Yarbrough 63-94, D.Allison 95-115, Yarbrough 116-155, Yarbrough 156-157, Bobby Allison 158-177, Yarbrough 178-237, B.Allison 238-259, Yarbrough 260-300, Yarbrough 301-305, Yarbrough 306-334.
Cautions: 11 for 73 laps   Margin of Victory: 9 seconds   Attendance: 73,000

Bobby and Donnie Allison with Miss Atlanta International Raceway, Kay Wilson

for a stop-and-go penalty. Cale scooted to a big advantage and crossed the finish line 9.0-seconds ahead for his second win of the year.

Behind Yarbrough was Donnie Allison in third. Charlie Glotzbach was fourth and Darel Dieringer took fifth.

The scenario went like this. Starting single-file on all restarts (there was no double-file restarts in 1968), the lapped car of Frank Warren headed the field. Cale and LeeRoy were next in line. Warren gunned his Chevrolet off the fourth turn, but he said "my car bogged down and they came around me like bandits -- Cale on the outside and LeeRoy on the inside. The green was not out, but I had started. The way I see it, that means the race had restarted," said Warren.

Johnson, who spent several minutes in an arm-flaring episode on pit road with NASCAR's Johnny Bruner, angrily said, "If LeeRoy passed Cale illegally, then Cale passed Warren illegally. I can't outrun Chrysler, Ford and NASCAR too. They (NASCAR) are a bunch of crooks. We protested, but it's not worth a dime."

Johnson filed a formal protest, but sanctioning NASCAR disallowed it two days later. Cale's $20,680 victory was upheld.

Jim Foster, assistant to NASCAR President Bill France, explained the ruling, "Due to the fact that LeeRoy had jumped the gun on two previous restarts in the race, NASCAR warned his crew that if he did it again, he would be black-flagged," said Foster.

Cale supported NASCAR's ruling. "LeeRoy definitely passed me while the caution was still out," he said. "I think the decision was made right."

Raceway.

Runner-up LeeRoy Yarbrough was black-flagged from the lead just 33 laps from the finish for allegedly jumping the green flag following the day's 11th and final caution flag. Yarbrough, driving Junior Johnson's Mercury, failed to obey the consultation flag for five laps. Finally, after NASCAR officials convinced Johnson to flag his driver in the pits, LeeRoy whipped in

Yarborough led most of the way, pushing his maroon and white Mercury in front five times for 172 laps.

Bobby Allison, driving Bondy Long's Ford, led for 42 laps but crashed into the homestretch wall on lap 291. He was running in third place at the time.

Track officials said 73,000 spectators showed up to watch Cale average 125.564 mph.

Race No. 8

Pearson, Isaac, Ingram Fade; Petty Wins at Hickory

HICKORY, NC (Apr. 7) -- Richard Petty came on strong in the late stages and won the 100-mile Grand National event at Hickory Speedway. It was the second win of the season for the defending NASCAR champion.

David Pearson led for 59 laps, but fought handling problems when his tires heated up. He settled for second place. Bobby Isaac led for 116 laps, but faded to third. Friday Hassler finished fourth and James Hylton was fifth despite blowing his engine in the final lap.

Jack Ingram, highly touted Sportsman racer out of Asheville, qualified a lightly regarded two year-old Chevrolet in the second spot. He held third place in the early going, keeping ahead of Petty in a stirring duel. Ingram fell eight laps off the pace and wound up seventh.

"You've got to handle to win on any short track," said Petty. "And we were sure handling today. The real key was that my car would stick when I went low in the turns. I was able to pass Pearson and Isaac without much trouble."

Petty was driving a Plymouth with a 404 c.i. engine, and under NASCAR rules, was permitted to shave 200 pounds off his car. "A lighter car gets through the turns quicker," noted Petty. "It was a pretty easy win."

Petty's 77th career Grand National win came at an average speed of 79.435 mph. A crowd of 10,000 was on hand.

Petty increased his point lead to 85 points over independent Clyde Lynn.

Grand National Race No. 8
250 Laps at Hickory Speedway
Hickory, NC
100 Miles on .4-mile Paved Track
April 7, 1968

Fin	St	No.	Driver	Team / CAr	Laps	Money	Status
1	4	43	Richard Petty	Petty Enterprises '67 Plym	250	$1,200	Running
2	1	17	David Pearson	Holman-Moody '68 Ford	250	600	Running
3	3	71	Bobby Isaac	K&K Insurance '67 Dodge	250	400	Running
4	6	39	Friday Hassler	Red Sharp '66 Chevrolet	246	300	Running
5	7	48	James Hylton	Hylton Eng '67 Dodge	244	275	Engine
6	10	4	John Sears	L G DeWitt '66 Ford	243	240	Running
7	2	0	Jack Ingram	'66 Chevrolet	242	200	Running
8	22	76	Roy Tyner	Don Culpepper '66 Ford	239	175	Running
9	14	45	Bill Seifert	Seifert '66 Ford	237	150	Running
10	8	64	Elmo Langley	Langley-Woodfield '66 Ford	235	140	Running
11	13	20	Clyde Lynn	Lynn '66 Ford	232	130	Running
12	15	19	Henley Gray	Gray '66 Ford	229	120	Running
13	5	49	G C Spencer	Spencer '67 Plymouth	222	110	Differen
14	17	25	Jabe Thomas	Don Robertson '67 Ford	222	100	Running
15	9	06	Neil Castles	Castles '67 Plymouth	122	100	Engine
16	12	88	Buck Baker	Baker '67 Olds	115	100	Engine
17	16	03	Wayne Smith	James Cook '66 Chevrolet	106	100	Differen
18	21	09	Bob Cooper	Cooper '66 Chevrolet	99	100	Heating
19	11	34	Wendell Scott	Scott '66 Ford	72	100	Oil Press
20	18	01	Paul Dean Holt	Dennis Holt '67 Ford	38	100	Oil Press
21	20	9	Bill Vanderhoff	Roy Tyner '67 Pontiac	31	100	Coil
22	19	1	Jim Vandiver	'66 Chevrolet	5	100	D SHaft

Time of Race: 1 hour, 15 minutes, 32 seconds
Average Speed: 79.435 mph
Pole Winner: David Pearson - 86.975 mph
Lap Leaders: David Pearson 1-8, Bobby Isaac 9-124, Richard Petty 125-135,
  Pearson 136-186, Petty 187-250.
Cautions: 2 for 19 laps   Margin of Victory 1/2 lap   Attendance: 10,000.

Race No. 9

Post Entry Petty Wins Greenville; Loses Half of Point Lead

GREENVILLE, SC (Apr. 13) -- Richard Petty took the lead from Bobby Isaac in the 161st lap and went on to win the 100-miler at Greenville-Pickens Speedway. But the defending Grand National champ stood still in the point race.

Petty had failed to submit a written entry for the race and did not get the 50 points for winning the race. His point lead was cut from 85 to 42 points over second place Clyde Lynn.

Isaac finished second in the 100-miler and held onto third place in the point standings, one point behind Lynn. Charlie Glotzbach took third place with Roy Tyner fourth and Tiny Lund fifth.

NASCAR has decided to enforce an old rule requiring drivers to file written entries to both the race promoter and the sanctioning body.

David Pearson won the pole and led for 76 of the first 79 laps. After dropping to second place, a tire blew on Pearson's Holman-Moody Ford, sending him into the wall. He wound up 14th in the final order, completing 144 laps.

Six caution flags held Petty's winning speed to 63.347 mph. He finished three laps ahead of Isaac, who lost his brakes before the half-way point.

Grand National Race No. 9
200 Laps at Greenville-Pickens Speedway
Greenville, SC
100 Miles on Half-mile Dirt Track
April 13, 1968

Fin	St	No.	Driver	Team / Car	Laps	Money	Status
1	3	43	Richard Petty	Petty Enterprises '68 Plym	200	$1,200	Running
2	2	37	Bobby Isaac	K&K Insurance '67 Dodge	197	600	Running
3	6	6	Charlie Glotzbach	Cotton Owens '67 Dodge	197	400	Running
4	10	9	Roy Tyner	Tyner '67 Pontiac	195	300	Running
5	4	56	Tiny Lund	Lyle Stelter '66 Ford	195	275	Running
6	23	45	Bill Seifert	Seifert '66 Ford	191	240	Running
7	9	88	Buck Baker	Baker '67 Olds	188	200	Running
8	12	34	Wendell Scott	Scott '66 Ford	188	175	Running
9	15	20	Clyde Lynn	Lynn '66 Ford	187	150	Running
10	7	64	Elmo Langley	Langley-Woodfield '66 Ford	171	140	Throttle
11	18	01	Paul Dean Holt	Dennis Holt '67 Ford	163	130	Running
12	13	02	Bob Cooper	Cooper '66 Chevrolet	157	120	Rear End
13	11	25	Jabe Thomas	Don Robertson '67 Ford	152	110	Running
14	1	17	David Pearson	Holman-Moody '68 Ford	144	100	Crash
15	16	95	Jeff Hawkins	Henley Gray '66 Ford	107	100	Ignition
16	5	4	John Sears	L G DeWitt '66 Ford	91	100	Sway bar
17	8	3	Buddy Baker	Ray Fox '67 Dodge	77	100	Distrib
18	21	19	Henley Gray	Gray '66 Ford	72	100	Axle
19	19	31	Bill Ervin	Newman Long '66 Ford	56	100	Ignition
20	14	06	Neil Castles	Castles '67 Plymouth	42	100	D Shaft
21	17	8	Ed Negre	Negre '67 Ford	33	100	Oil Press
22	22	76	Ben Arnold	Don Culpepper '66 Ford	31	100	Oil Press
23	20	09	Bill Vanderhoff	Roy Tyner '66 Chevrolet	27	---	Heating

Time of Race: 1 hour, 34 minutes, 43 seconds
Average Speed: 63.347 mph
Pole Winner: David Pearson - 67.848 mph
Lap Leaders: David Pearson 1-71, Richard Petty 72-74, Pearson 75-79, Petty 80-89, Bobby Isaac 90-160, Petty 161-200.
Cautions: 6 for ___ laps   Margin of Victory: 3-laps plus   Attendance: 6,800

Bobby Isaac won at Columbia

Race No. 10
Isaac Ends Four Year Famine; Takes Point Lead with Win At Columbia

COLUMBIA, SC (Apr. 18) -- Bobby Isaac of Catawba, NC ended a 50 month winless skid and took the Grand National point lead with a 100-mile victory at Columbia Speedway. The 35 year-old driver pushed his K&K Insurance Dodge around Richard Petty in the 15th lap and led the rest of the way.

Charlie Glotzbach finished second in the Cotton Owens Dodge and James Hylton was third. Buddy Baker finished fourth and Richard Petty came in fifth.

For the second straight race, Petty did not earn any points since he failed to turn in an entry blank. He lost his point lead to Isaac, who moved seven points ahead. Clyde Lynn, an independent out of Christiansburg, VA, ranked a close third, one point behind Petty. David Pearson, who struggled to finish seventh, held fourth spot, just 40 points out of first place. Isaac's Dodge, set

Grand National Race No. 10
200 Laps at Columbia Speedway
Columbia, SC
100 Miles on Half-mile Dirt Track
April 18, 1968

Fin	St	No.	Driver	Team / Car	Laps	Money	Status
1	6	37	Bobby Isaac	K&K Insurance '67 Dodge	200	$1,000	Running
2	10	6	Charlie Glotzbach	Cotton Owens '67 Dodge	200	600	Running
3	3	48	James Hylton	Hylton Eng '67 Dodge	200	400	Running
4	7	3	Buddy Baker	Ray Fox '67 Dodge	199	300	Running
5	1	43	Richard Petty	Petty Enterprises '68 Plym	198	475	Running
6	2	4	John Sears	L G DeWitt '66 Ford	197	240	Running
7	4	17	David Pearson	Holman-Moody '68 Ford	197	200	Running
8	13	64	Elmo Langley	Langley-Woodfield '66 Ford	196	175	Running
9	5	56	LeeRoy Yarbrough	Lyle Stelter '66 Ford	195	150	Running
10	9	06	Neil Castles	Castles '67 Plymouth	191	140	Running
11	15	20	Clyde Lynn	Lynn '66 Ford	191	130	Running
12	11	88	Buck Baker	Baker '67 Olds	188	120	Running
13	16	34	Wendell Scott	Scott '66 Ford	183	110	Running
14	18	9	Roy Tyner	Tyner '67 Pontiac	180	100	Running
15	14	25	Jabe Thomas	Don Robertson '67 Ford	176	100	Running
16	17	19	Henley Gray	Gray '66 Ford	173	100	Running
17	23	09	Bill Vanderhoff	Roy Tyner '66 Chevrolet	78	100	Rear End
18	12	45	Bill Seifert	Seifert '66 Ford	63	100	Engine
19	21	95	Harold Fagan	Henley Gray '66 Ford	62	100	Engine
20	22	76	Ben Arnold	Don Culpepper '66 Ford	56	100	Vibration
21	20	31	Paul Dean Holt	Newman Long '66 Ford	52	100	Vibration
22	19	8	Ed Negre	Negre '67 Ford	51	100	Rear End
23	8	02	Bob Cooper	Cooper '66 Chevrolet	42	---	Alternator

Time of Race: 1 hour 24 minutes, 5 seconds
Average Speed: 71.358 mph
Pole Winner: Richard Petty - 75.282 mph
Lap Leaders: Richard Petty 1-14, Bobby Isaac 15-200.
Cautions: 4 for ___ laps   Margin of Victory: Attendance: 6,500

up by Harry Hyde, was clearly the fastest car on the track. On lap 138, he ran out of gas and coasted to the pits, but his lead was big enough that he didn't lose first place.

Glotzbach got by Hylton for second in a late race pass.

Isaac's first Grand National victory since Feb. 21, 1964, came at an average speed of 71.358 mph.

Race No. 11

Pearson Wins Gwyn Staley Memorial; 17 Engines Blow

N.WILKESBORO, NC (Apr. 21) -- David Pearson slipped into the lead 10 laps from the finish when Lee-Roy Yarbrough blew an engine, and won the Gwyn

Paul Goldsmith pits at North Wilkesboro

Staley Memorial 400 at North Wilkesboro Speedway. It was the third victory of the year for the 33 year-old Ford driver.

Yarbrough was well on his way to victory. The Jacksonville, FL Ford pilot had led for 129 laps and was holding a 10 second lead when the engine blew to pieces. His car skidded into the retaining wall, taking Bobby Isaac's Dodge with him. Pearson ducked under the incident and cruised to an easy win.

Pearson finished a lap ahead of runner-up Buddy Baker. Isaac recovered from his brush with the steel rail and came in third. Darel Dieringer, with relief help from Richard Petty, was fourth and Yarbrough got credit for fifth.

"We knew we weren't going to outrun the contenders," said Pearson, whose Holman-Moody Ford ran on

only seven cylinders for a good portion of the race. "We just rode it out. My pit crew won this race. They got me on the track first after every pit stop."

Yarbrough and car owner Junior Johnson were disconsolate after another heart-breaking loss. "It beats anything I've ever seen," said Johnson. "We keep going to the well, but we keep coming away thirsty. It's plumb unreal."

Fifteen cars in the starting field finished the race. A total of 17 cars were knocked out of the event by engine failures -- an unusually high number.

Pearson averaged 90.425 mph before a crowd of 13,500.

Grand National Race No. 11
400 Laps at N.Wilkesboro Speedway
N.Wilkesboro, NC
"Gwyn Staley Memorial"
250 Miles on .625-mile Paved Track
April 21, 1968

Fin	St	No.	Driver	Team / Car	Laps	Money	Status
1	1	17	David Pearson	Holman-Moody '68 Ford	400	$5,100	Running
2	12	3	Buddy Baker	Ray Fox '68 Dodge	399	2,275	Running
3	3	71	Bobby Isaac	K&K Insurance '67 Dodge	399	1,325	Running
4	4	22	Darel Dieringer*	Mario Rossi '68 Plymouth	396	825	Running
5	2	98	LeeRoy Yarbrough	Junior Johnson '68 Ford	391	750	Engine
6	14	4	John Sears	L G DeWitt '67 Ford	390	525	Running
7	8	14	Jerry Grant	Friedkin Ent '68 Plymouth	390	475	Running
8	22	76	Roy Tyner	Don Culpepper '66 Ford	386	500	Running
9	21	06	Neil Castles	Castles '67 Plymouth	381	500	Running
10	19	20	Clyde Lynn	Lynn '67 Mercury	377	325	Running
11	24	28	Earl Brooks	Clyde Lynn '66 Ford	362	300	Running
12	29	19	Henley Gray	Gray '66 Ford	362	275	Running
13	15	02	Bob Cooper	Cooper '66 Chevrolet	361	275	Engine
14	26	34	Wendell Scott	Scott '66 Ford	359	250	Running
15	17	25	Jabe Thomas	Don Robertson '67 Ford	342	225	Running
16	18	50	Eddie Yarboro	'66 Plymouth	338	225	Engine
17	33	95	Harold Fagan	Henley Gray '66 Ford	338	200	Running
18	30	51	Stan Meserve	Margo Hamm '67 Dodge	333	225	Running
19	20	88	Buck Baker	Baker '67 Olds	326	225	Engine
20	23	45	Bill Seifert	Seifert '66 Ford	308	250	Engine
21	32	01	Paul Dean Holt	Dennis Holt '67 Ford	265	175	Engine
22	9	49	G C Spencer	Spencer '67 Plymouth	257	200	Engine
23	10	48	James Hylton	Hylton Eng '67 Dodge	248	200	Engine
24	13	12	Jim Hurtubise	Tom Pistone '68 Mercury	243	200	Crash
25	27	38	Wayne Smith	Smith '66 Chevrolet	215	200	Rear End
26	6	43	Richard Petty	Petty Enterprises '68 Plym	210	500	Engine
27	7	99	Paul Goldsmith	Nichels Eng '68 Plymouth	144	250	Engine
28	28	46	Larry Manning	Tom Hunter '66 Chevrolet	117	200	Rear End
29	5	29	Bobby Allison	Bondy Long '68 Ford	97	200	Engine
30	31	09	Bill Vanderhoff	Roy Tyner '67 Pontiac	97	175	Engine
31	25	64	Elmo Langley	Langley-Woodfield '66 Ford	71	175	Engine
32	35	0	Dr Don Tarr	Tarr '66 Chevrolet	62	150	Engine
33	11	08	Jack Ingram	Giachetti Bros '66 Chevrolet	57	250	Engine
34	16	39	Friday Hassler	Red Sharp '66 Chevrolet	30	175	Engine
35	34	31	Leonard Brock	Newman Long '66 Ford	1	175	Engine

Time of Race: 2 hours, 45 minutes, 33 seconds
Average Speed: 90.425 mph
Pole Winner: David Pearson - 104.993 mph
Lap Leaders: David Pearson 1-32, Bobby Isaac 33, Richard Petty 34-59,
    Paul Goldsmith 60-76, Bobby Allison 77-96, Goldsmith 97-106, Petty 107-118,
    Pearson 119-208, Petty 209, Pearson 210-257, LeeRoy Yarbrough 258-260.
    Pearson 261, Yarbrough 262-390, Pearson 391-400.
Cautions: 10 for 67 laps   Margin of Victory: 1-lap plus   Attendance: 13,500
*Relieved by Richard Petty

Race No. 12

Cale's Mercury Masters Martinsville Field

MARTINSVILLE, VA (Apr. 28) -- Cale Yarborough drove his Mercury into the lead 51 laps from the finish and won the Virginia 500 at Martinsville Speedway. It was the third win of the season for the stubby 29 year-old Timmonsville, SC leadfoot.

Yarborough held off David Pearson in a stretch duel

Grand National Race No. 12
500 Laps at Martinsville Speedway
Martinsville, VA
"Virginia 500"
250 Miles on Half-mile Paved Track
April 28, 1968

Fin	St	No.	Driver	Team / Car	Laps	Money	Status
1	3	21	Cale Yarborough	Wood Brothers '68 Mercury	500	$5,476	Running
2	1	17	David Pearson	Holman-Moody '68 Ford	500	2,797	Running
3	5	27	Donnie Allison	Banjo Matthews '68 Ford	498	1,245	Running
4	8	26	LeeRoy Yarbrough	Junior Johnson '68 Ford	498	800	Running
5	7	12	Tom Pistone	Pistone '68 Ford	497	725	Running
6	12	1	Bud Moore	A J King '68 Dodge	494	675	Running
7	9	16	Tiny Lund	Bud moore '68 Mercury	494	575	Running
8	11	4	John Sears	L G DeWitt '67 Ford	489	525	Running
9	10	48	James Hylton	Hylton Eng '67 Dodge	489	500	Running
10	14	64	Elmo Langley	Langley-Woodfield '66 Ford	485	475	Running
11	23	06	Neil Castles	Castles '67 Plymouth	479	460	Running
12	30	44	Blaine Kauffman	'67 Chevrolet	461	400	Running
13	34	80	E J Trivette	E C Reid '66 Chevrolet	459	390	Running
14	39	19	Henley Gray	Gray '66 Ford	459	380	Running
15	2	43	Richard Petty	Petty Enterprises '68 Plym	449	1,004	Rear End
16	15	71	Bobby Isaac	K&K Insurance '67 Dodge	432	385	Running
17	37	01	Paul Dean Holt	Dennis Holt '67 Ford	388	380	Running
18	24	39	Friday Hassler	Red Sharp '66 Chevrolet	381	365	Engine
19	18	34	Wendell Scott	Scott '66 Ford	370	355	Oil Press
20	20	25	Jabe Thomas	Don Robertson '67 Ford	349	345	A Frame
21	16	49	G C Spencer	Spencer '67 Plymouth	335	325	Ignition
22	17	20	Clyde Lynn	Lynn '66 Ford	328	325	Oil Line
23	28	76	Roy Tyner	Don Culpepper '66 Ford	309	300	Engine
24	29	46	Larry Manning	Tom Hunter '66 Chevrolet	268	300	Rear End
25	19	70	J D McDuffie	McDuffie '67 Buick	237	325	Heating
26	4	29	Bobby Allison	Bondy Long '68 Ford	235	375	Engine
27	26	02	Bob Cooper	Cooper '66 Chevrolet	217	300	Oil Press
28	22	10	Bill Champion	Champion '66 Ford	148	325	Crash
29	21	90	Sonny Hutchins	Junie Donlavey '67 Ford	133	375	Rear End
30	32	51	Stan Meserve	Margo Hamm '67 Dodge	126	275	Steering
31	13	3	Buddy Baker	Ray Fox '67 Dodge	109	275	Trans
32	25	28	Earl Brooks	Clyde Lynn '66 Ford	103	275	Brakes
33	27	45	Bill Seifert	Seifert '66 Ford	94	275	Engine
34	36	09	Bill Vanderhoff	Roy Tyner '66 Chevrolet	72	250	Oil Leak
35	6	14	Paul Goldsmith	Friedkin Ent '68 Plymouth	63	275	Crash
36	35	95	Harold Fagan	Henley Gray '66 Ford	62	250	Brakes
37	38	8	Ed Negre	Negre '67 Ford	47	250	Wheel
38	33	38	Wayne Smith	Smith '67 Chevrolet	18	250	Engine
39	40	88	Buck Baker	Baker '67 Olds	15	250	Oil Leak
40	31	0	Dr Don Tarr	Tarr '66 Chevrolet	14	250	Clutch

Time of Race: 3 hours, 44 minutes, 56 seconds
Average Speed: 66.686 mph
Pole Winner: David Pearson - 78.230 mph
Lap Leaders: David Pearson 1-66, LeeRoy Yarbrough 67-86, Richard Petty 87-101,
  Pearson 102-131, Petty 132-160, Bobby Allison 161-208, Petty 209-244,
  Pearson 245,Petty 246-449, Cale Yarborough 450-500.
Cautions: 10 for 72 laps   Margin of Victory: 50 yards   Attendance: 19,000

and reached the checkered flag 50 yards in front. Donnie Allison finished third, LeeRoy Yarbrough was fourth and Tom Pistone fifth.

Richard Petty had built up a sizable lead when his Plymouth succumbed to rear gearing failure with 51 laps left. Yarborough took the lead at that point and kept his Wood Brothers mount in first place the rest of the way.

Petty's 449 laps was good enough for 15th place. Despite finishing far down in the order, John Holman filed a protest against the blue Plymouth. He posted $100 tear-down fee and watched as NASCAR inspectors combed the engine. "He was beating us pretty bad to-day," explained the famed racing entrepreneur. "So we will look just to keep every-body on their toes."

When in-formed that Holman had

Clyde Lynn rounds turn in Virginia 500

protested his car, Petty responded, "Go tell that fat rascal that we'll tear it down if he'll stand there and watch."

Holman accepted Petty's ultimatum and watched as the two hour inspection took place. NASCAR inspectors found nothing wrong with the car and pronounced it 'legal'.

Point leader Bobby Isaac finished sixth, 68 laps down. He was involved in a spin and spent several laps in the pits. He still held an eight point lead over Pearson in the Grand National standings. Clyde Lynn ranked third, 34 points behind Isaac.

A crowd of 19,000 watched Yarborough take his sixth career Grand National victory at an average speed of 66.686 mph.

Race No. 13

Isaac Outduels Pistone; Pads Point Lead With Augusta Win

AUGUSTA, GA (May 3) -- Bobby Isaac passed Tom Pistone in the 139th lap and led the rest of the way to win the Dixie 250 at Augusta Speedway. It was the second win of the season for the Catawba, NC Dodge driver.

Buddy Baker wound up in second place, a lap behind. Pistone was third, falling a lap off the pace when he spun out with 40 laps to go. James Hylton got fourth and Buck Baker was fifth.

Bobby Isaac

A crowd of 4,500 watched Isaac and Richard Petty battle bumper-to-bumper for the first 86 laps. Petty was running a close second when the axle broke in his Plymouth.

Pistone, who started third in his Mercury, picked up the challenge. He engaged in a tight duel with Baker, which allowed Isaac to sprint to a big lead.

Pistone led for eight laps when Isaac was in the pits.

David Pearson was not entered and fell to third place in the point standings. Isaac moved to a 39 point lead over Clyde Lynn, who came from 20th spot to finish sixth.

LeeRoy Yarbrough was a late entrant. He qualified a Lyle Stelter Ford second in the grid, but left after 158 laps with rear gearing failure. He got credit for 15th in the field of 23.

Isaac's Dodge won the 125 miler at a 73.099 mph clip.

Race No. 14

Pearson Leads All But One Lap in Fireball 300 Victory

WEAVERVILLE, NC (May 5) -- David Pearson started on the pole and romped to a two lap victory in the Fireball 300 at Asheville-Weaverville Speedway. It was the fourth win of the year for the 5'11" Spartanburg Ford driver.

Pearson finished two laps in front of runner-up Bobby Isaac, who survived a brush with Buddy Baker

Grand National Race No. 13
250 Laps at Augusta Speedway
Augusta, GA
"Dixie 250"
125 Miles on Half-mile Paved Track
May 3, 1968

Fin	St	No.	Driver	Team / Car	Laps	Money	Status
1	1	71	Bobby Isaac	K&K Insurance '67 Dodge	250	$1,100	Running
2	7	3	Buddy Baker	Ray Fox '67 Dodge	249	700	Running
3	3	12	Tom Pistone	Pistone '68 Mercury	249	600	Running
4	5	48	James Hylton	Hylton Eng '67 Dodge	244	500	Running
5	17	87	Buck Baker	Baker '67 Olds	239	425	Running
6	20	20	Clyde Lynn	Lynn '67 Mercury	238	350	Running
7	8	79	Frank Warren	Harold Rhodes '67 Chevrolet	233	325	Crash
8	11	34	Wendell Scott	Scott '66 Ford	229	275	Running
9	14	25	Jabe Thomas	Don Robertson '67 Ford	228	225	Running
10	21	96	Bob Moore	James Brown '66 Ford	227	200	Running
11	23	01	Paul Dean Holt	Dennis Holt '67 Ford	200	130	Running
12	9	64	Elmo Langley	Langley-Woodfield '66 Ford	188	120	Engine
13	10	06	Neil Castles	Castles '67 Plymouth	175	110	Engine
14	6	4	John Sears	L G DeWitt '67 Ford	170	100	Rear End
15	2	55	LeeRoy Yarbrough	Lyle Stelter '67 Ford	158	100	Rear End
16	19	70	J D McDuffie	McDuffie '67 Buick	125	100	Rear End
17	13	09	Roy Tyner	Tyner '67 Pontiac	87	100	Rear End
18	4	43	Richard Petty	Petty Enterprises '68 Plym	86	300	Axle
19	16	19	Henley Gray	Gray '66 Ford	54	100	Heating
20	22	95	Harold Fagan	Henley Gray '66 Ford	54	100	Suspen
21	18	45	Bill Seifert	Seifert '66 Ford	30	100	Crash
22	12	02	Bob Cooper	Cooper '66 Chevrolet	20	100	Engine
23	15	51	Stan Meserve	Margo Hamm '67 Dodge	17	100	Ignition

Time of Race: 1 hour, 42 m minutes, 36 seconds
Average Speed: 73.099 mph
Pole Winner: Bobby Isaac - 83.877 mph
Lap Leaders: Bobby Isaac 1-130, Tom Pistone 131-138, Isaac 139-250.
Cautions: Margin of Victory: 1-lap plus   Attendance: 4,500

Grand National Race No. 14
300 Laps at Asheville-Weaverville
Speedway
Weaverville, NC
"Fireball 300"
150 Miles on Half-mile Paved Track
May 5, 1968

Fin	St	No.	Driver	Team / Car	Laps	Money	Status
1	1	17	David Pearson	Holman-Moody '68 Ford	300	$1,400	Running
2	4	71	Bobby Isaac	K&K Insurance '67 Dodge	298	1,000	Running
3	2	43	Richard Petty	Petty Enterprises '68 Plym	297	900	Running
4	7	48	James Hylton	Hylton Eng '67 Dodge	295	575	Running
5	26	64	Elmo Langley	Langley-Woodfield '66 Ford	291	425	Running
6	14	20	Clyde Lynn	Lynn '68 Ford	291	325	Running
7	16	25	Jabe Thomas	Don Robertson '67 Ford	278	275	Running
8	17	95	Harold Fagan	Henley Gray '66 Ford	259	225	Running
9	13	19	Henley Gray	Gray '66 Ford	257	200	Running
10	15	51	Stan Meserve	Margo Hamm '67 Dodge	243	175	Running
11	10	76	Roy Tyner	Don Culpepper '66 Ford	225	100	Engine
12	11	5	Pete Hamilton	Rocky Hinton '68 Ford	215	100	Wheel
13	5	4	John Sears	L G DeWitt '67 Ford	207	100	Push rod
14	21	06	Neil Castles	Castles '67 Plymouth	197	100	Crash
15	12	45	Bill Seifert	Seifert '66 Ford	119	100	Crash
16	28	28	Earl Brooks	Clyde Lynn '67 Mercury	148	100	Valve
17	18	46	Max Ledbetter	Tom Hunter '66 Chevrolet	134	100	Rear End
18	9	3	Buddy Baker	Ray Fox '67 Dodge	106	100	Crash
19	27	70	J D McDuffie	McDuffie '67 Ford	98	100	Oil Press
20	3	12	Tom Pistone	Pistone '68 Mercury	81	100	Engine
21	19	93	Walson Gardner	Gardner '67 Ford	74	100	Engine
22	23	0	Dr Don Tarr	Tarr '66 Chevrolet	63	100	Oil Press
23	24	34	Wendell Scott	Scott '66 Ford	61	100	Engine
24	25	88	Buck Baker	Baker '67 Olds	51	100	Rear End
25	22	08	Jack Ingram	Giachetti Bros '66 Chevrolet	25	---	Engine
26	20	01	Paul Dean Holt	Dennis Holt '67 Ford	15	---	Engine
27	6	49	G C Spencer	Spencer '67 Plymouth	13	---	Suspen
28	8	75	Gene Black	Black '66 Ford	4	---	Engine

Time of Race: 1 hour, 59 minutes, 44 seconds
Average Speed: 75.167 mph
Pole Winner: David Pearson - 89.708 mph
Lap Leaders: David Person 1-86, Buddy Baker 87, Pearson 88-300.
Cautions: 6 for 45 laps   Margin of Victory: 2-laps plus   Attendance: 7,800

Buddy Baker looks at his wrecked Dodge at Weaverville

early in the race. Richard Petty lost three laps in the pits during a four tire change, and wound up third. James Hylton came in fourth and Elmo Langley was fifth.

Baker, behind the wheel of the Ray Fox Dodge, led lap 87 as Pearson pitted under the yellow flag. Baker had passed Isaac on the restart to gain second place and hooked up in a heated duel. Isaac tucked the nose of his car under Baker in the second turn and slapped sheet metal with the big Charlotte driver. The cars separated, but Baker plowed into the wall in the fourth turn on lap 106. He was out of the race.

Bill Seifert banged into the wall and was hit broadside by Neil Castles with just less than 100 laps to go. Both cars were badly damaged.

Pearson averaged 75.167 mph for his 34th career win. The 300 lapper on the half-mile paved track was postponed two months due to snow back in March.

Race No. 15

Lightweight Ford Nets Rebel 400 Victory for Pearson

DARLINGTON, SC (May 11) -- David Pearson, driving a Ford powered by a small 396 c.i. engine, won the Rebel 400 at Darlington Raceway for his first superspeedway victory in almost seven years. "I had almost forgotten what it feels like to win a big track race," confessed Pearson.

Pearson finished 18 seconds in front of runner-up Darel Dieringer, who was driving Mario Rossi's Plymouth. Richard Petty came in third, Buddy Baker was fourth and LeeRoy Yarbrough fifth.

According to NASCAR's power-to-weight ratio, Pearson's car was allowed to weigh 293 pounds less than cars with larger engines. "Raw power is not the key to winning at this track," said Holman-Moody crew chief Dick Hutcherson.. "We figured we could

Grand National Race No. 15
291 Laps at Darlington Raceway
Darlington, SC
"Rebel 400"
400 Miles on 1.375-mile Paved Track
May 11, 1968

Fin	St	No.	Driver	Team / Car	Laps	Money	Status
1	2	17	David Pearson	Holman-Moody '68 Ford	291	$13,700	Running
2	3	22	Darel Dieringer	Mario Rossi '68 Plymouth	291	7,620	Running
3	11	43	Richard Petty	Petty Enterprises '68 Plym	291	5,330	Running
4	6	3	Buddy Baker	Ray Fox '67 Dodge	290	2,675	Running
5	1	26	LeeRoy Yarbrough	Junior Johnson '68 Ford	287	2,225	Running
6	13	48	James Hylton	Hylton Eng '67 Dodge	285	1,600	Running
7	12	71	Bobby Isaac	K&K Insurance '67 Dodge	284	1,300	Running
8	14	4	John Sears	L G DeWitt '67 Ford	278	1,200	Running
9	17	1	Bud Moore	A J King '68 Dodge	277	1,100	Running
10	15	64	Elmo Langley	Langley-Woodfield '66 Ford	263	1,000	Running
11	18	10	Bill Champion	Champion '66 Ford	260	950	Running
12	20	80	E J Trivette	E C Reid '66 Chevrolet	256	900	Running
13	34	09	Wendell Scott	Roy Tyner '66 Chevrolet	252	850	Running
14	24	0	Dr Don Tarr	Tarr '66 Chevrolet	242	825	Crash
15	8	14	Curtis Turner	Friedkin Ent '68 Plymouth	241	800	Engine
16	27	28	Earl Brooks	Clyde Lynn '66 Ford	241	875	Running
17	26	19	Henley Gray	Gray '66 Ford	240	875	Running
18	22	52	Lennie Waldo	Elmer Buxton '67 Ford	239	700	Running
19	29	30	Clyde Lynn	Lynn '67 Mercury	236	755	Running
20	9	21	Cale Yarborough	Wood Brothers '68 Mercury	222	725	Engine
21	28	01	Paul Dean Holt	Dennis Holt '67 Ford	207	715	Running
22	30	95	Harold Fagan	Henley Gray '66 Ford	207	670	Running
23	4	29	Bobby Allison	Bondy Long '68 Ford	201	575	Clutch
24	16	99	Paul Goldsmith	Nichels Eng '68 Dodge	182	600	Engine
25	32	51	Stan Meserve	Margo Hamm '67 Dodge	171	560	Trans
26	19	25	Jabe Thomas	Don Robertson '67 Ford	166	500	Engine
27	23	38	Wayne Smith	Smith '66 Chevrolet	163	490	Rear End
28	10	6	Charlie Glotzbach	Cotton Owens '68 Dodge	148	480	Oil Press
29	5	27	Donnie Allison	Banjo Matthews '68 Ford	90	470	Crash
30	25	76	Roy Tyner	Don Culpepper '66 Ford	68	610	Oil Leak
31	21	8	Ed Negre	Negre '67 Ford	57	450	Trans
32	7	16	Tiny Lund	Bud Moore '68 Mercury	44	440	Lug bolt
33	33	88	Neil Castles	Buck Baker '67 Olds	4	430	Engine
34	31	44	Larry Hess	Hess '67 Rambler	0	460	Engine

Time of Race: 3 hours, 54 seconds
Average Speed: 132.699 mph
Pole Winner: LeeRoy Yarbrough - 148.850 mph
Lap Leaders: David Pearson 1-18, LeeRoy Yarbrough 19-27, Buddy Baker 28-58,
    Cale Yarborough 59-62, Paul Goldsmith 63-64, Baker 65-107,
    Charlie Glotzbach 108-115, Baker 116-157, Pearson 158-204, Richard Petty 205-218,
    Pearson 219-232, Petty 233-239, Pearson 240-291.
Cautions: 4 for 23 laps   Margin of Victory: 18 seconds   Attendance: 22,500.

sacrifice a little speed on the straightaway in order to get lighter for handling in the turns. Some of those cars with the 427 c.i. engines were melting tires right and left."

Pearson was out front four times for 131 laps and had better than a lap on the field when he slacked off in the final laps.

Baker survived a number of skirmishes en route to fourth place. Bobby Allison spun around after being tapped by Baker. Charlie Glotzbach clobbered the wall after another bump from the Charlotte driver.

"I was terrible," said Baker. "My dad (Buck Baker) won three times here, and I've wanted to win a race here for as long as I can remember. I guess I just tried too hard."

Allison later fell out with clutch failure, and

Curtis Turner pits the Friedkin Enterprises Plymouth in Rebel 400

Glotzbach dropped out with no oil pressure. Baker had led 116 laps after starting sixth.

Curtis Turner made his return to Grand National racing in the Friedkin Enterprises Plymouth. The 44 year-old Roanoke, VA driver had replaced Jerry Grant in the Bill Ellis-engineered car and ran in the top 10 all day. A blown engine put him out late in the event.

Bobby Isaac finished seventh and still held the point lead by 39 points over Pearson. Petty ranked a close third, 14 points behind Pearson.

Pearson averaged 132.699 mph before a relatively small trackside audience of 22,500.

Grand National Race No. 16
300 Laps at Beltsville Speedway
Beltsville, MD
"Beltsville 300"
150 Miles on Half-mile Paved Track
May 17, 1968

Fin	St	No.	Driver	Team / Car	Laps	Money	Status
1	2	17	David Pearson	Holman-Moody '68 Ford	300	$1,400	Running
2	7	71	Bobby Isaac	K&K Insurance '67 Dodge	299	1,000	Running
3	8	3	Buddy Baker	Ray Fox '67 Dodge	297	700	Running
4	5	48	James Hylton	Hylton Eng '67 Dodge	297	575	Running
5	6	4	John Sears	L G DeWitt '67 Ford	285	425	Running
6	10	25	Jabe Thomas	Don Robertson '67 Ford	282	325	Engine
7	23	06	Neil Castles	Castles '67 Plymouth	282	275	Running
8	19	09	Roy Tyner	Tyner '66 Chevrolet	273	225	Running
9	4	10	Bill Champion	Champion '66 Ford	269	200	Running
10	21	19	Henley Gray	Gray '66 Ford	267	175	Running
11	15	28	Earl Brooks	Brooks '66 Ford	262	100	Running
12	17	01	Paul Dean Holt	Dennis Holt '67 Ford	246	100	Running
13	13	64	Elmo Langley	Langley-Woodfield '66 Ford	171	100	Engine
14	1	43	Richard Petty	Petty Enterprises '68 Plym	158	300	Engine
15	14	70	J D McDuffie	McDuffie '67 Buick	122	100	Oil Leak
16	9	55	Tom Pistone	Lyle Stelter '66 Ford	115	100	Quit
17	11	07	George Davis	Davis '67 Chevrolet	112	100	Rear End
18	16	8	Ed Negre	Negre '67 Ford	101	100	Clutch
19	3	5	Pete Hamilton	Rocky Hinton '68 Ford	85	100	Crash
20	22	88	Buck Baker	Baker '67 Olds	82	100	Steering
21	12	20	Clyde Lynn	Lynn '67 Mercury	14	100	Crash
22	20	95	Harold Fagan	Henley Gray '66 Ford	10	100	H Gasket
23	18	34	Wendell Scott	Scott '66 Ford	3	100	Oil Press

Time of Race: 2 hours, 15 seconds
Average Speed: 74.844 mph
Pole Winner: Richard Petty - 83.604 mph
Lap Leaders: Richard Petty 1-158, David Pearson 159-230, Bobby Isaac 231-242, Pearson 243-300.
Cautions: Margin of Victory: 1 lap & 5 seconds   Attendance: 8,700

Race No. 16

Pearson's Ford Best in Beltsville 300

BELTSVILLE, MD (May 17) -- David Pearson passed Bobby Isaac with 58 laps to go and sprinted to an easy victory in the Beltsville 300 at Beltsville Speedway. It was the sixth win of the season for the Ford driver.

Isaac's Dodge finished second, a lap and five seconds behind. Buddy Baker came in third, James Hylton was fourth and John Sears fifth.

Richard Petty won the pole and took off like a bolt of lightning -- leading the first 158 laps. Petty was leaving his rivals rapidly when the engine came unglued, leaving Pearson and Isaac to settle the outcome.

Pete Hamilton, driving the Rocky Hinton Ford, qualified a strong third and was in contention for the first few laps. However, the Dedham, MA rookie slapped the wall on lap 86, putting him out of the race.

Pearson pulled to within 36 points of point leader Isaac with his 74.844 mph triumph.

Race No. 17

Pearson Hustles to Fourth in Row at Langley Field

HAMPTON, VA (May 18) -- David Pearson outran Richard Petty and pocketed his fourth straight Grand National win in the Tidewater 250 at Langley Field Speedway. The victory pulled Pearson to within 35 points of standings leader Bobby Isaac, who finished second.

Buddy Baker wound up a lap behind in third. James Hylton was fourth and Pete Hamilton fifth.

The lead changed hands seven times in the 250-lapper on the .4-mile paved track, with Pearson leading three times for 125 laps. He took the lead for the final time in the 188th lap.

Petty brushed the wall shortly after Pearson made the pass and lost two laps in the pits. He came back strong and was making up lost ground when a puff of smoke appeared from under the blue Plymouth on lap 226. He struggled to continue, falling well off the pace. Petty pulled his car into the pits four laps from the finish and had to settle for sixth place.

John Sears qualified in sixth spot but crashed his Ford when the engine let go on lap 113.

Pearson's 37th career victory came at an average speed of 71.457 mph.

Grand National Race No. 17
250 Laps at Langley Field Speedway
Hampton, VA
"Tidewater 250"
100 Miles on .4-mile Paved Track
May 18, 1968

Fin	St	No.	Driver	Team / Car	Laps	Money	Status
1	2	17	David Pearson	Holman-Moody '68 Ford	250	$1,000	Running
2	3	71	Bobby Isaac	K&K Insurance '67 Dodge	250	600	Running
3	4	3	Buddy Baker	Ray Fox '67 Dodge	249	400	Running
4	8	48	James Hylton	Hylton Eng '67 Dodge	246	300	Running
5	7	5	Pete Hamilton	Rocky Hinton '68 Ford	243	275	Running
6	1	43	Richard Petty	Petty Enterprises '68 Plym	242	440	Engine
7	5	55	Tom Pistone	Lyle Stelter '66 Ford	239	200	Running
8	10	10	Elmo Langley	Bill Champion '66 Ford	239	175	Running
9	9	20	Clyde Lynn	Lynn '67 Mercury	238	150	Running
10	15	06	Neil Castles	Castles '67 Plymouth	238	140	Running
11	17	88	Bobby Mausgrover	Buck Baker '67 Olds	230	130	Running
12	18	34	Wendell Scott	Scot '67 Ford	229	120	Flat tire
13	14	95	Harold Fagan	Henley Gray '66 Ford	212	110	Running
14	20	25	Jabe Thomas	Don Robertson '67 Ford	175	100	Running
15	19	09	Roy Tyner	Tyner '66 Chevrolet	128	100	Fuel line
16	6	4	John Sears	L G DeWitt '67 Ford	112	100	Engine
17	11	8	Ed Negre	Negre '67 Ford	76	100	Quit
18	12	01	Paul Dean Holt	Dennis Holt '67 Ford	73	100	Quit
19	16	28	Earl Brooks	Brooks '66 Ford	4	100	Steering
20	13	19	Henley Gray	Gray '66 Ford	1	100	Engine

Time of Race: 1 hour, 23 minutes, 58 seconds
Average Speed: 71.457 mph
Pole Winner: Richard Petty - 80.801 mph
Lap Leaders: David Pearson 1-55, Richard Petty 56-60, Pearson 61-67, Petty 68-137, Buddy Baker 138-156, Petty 157-187, Pearson 188-250.
Cautions: ___ for 25 laps   Margin of Victory: Attendance: 10,000

Race No. 18

Baker Sloshes Way to Rain-Shortened World 600 Victory

Grand National Race No. 18
400 Laps at Charlotte Motor Speedway
Charlotte, NC
"World 600"
600 Miles on 1.5-mile Paved Track
May 26, 1968

Fin	St	No.	Driver	Team / Car	Laps	Money	Status
1	12	3	Buddy Baker	Ray Fox '68 Dodge	255	$27,780	Running
2	1	27	Donnie Allison	Banjo Matthews '68 Ford	255	12,975	Running
3	2	98	LeeRoy Yarbrough	Junior Johnson '68 Mercury	254	9,290	Running
4	4	17	David Pearson	Holman-Moody '68 Ford	254	6,300	Running
5	14	71	Bobby Isaac	K&K Insurance '68 Dodge	253	5,475	Running
6	10	6	Charlie Glotzbach	Cotton Owens '68 Dodge	252	4,025	Running
7	7	16	Tiny Lund	Bud Moore '68 Mercury	252	3,525	Running
8	21	48	James Hylton	Hylton Eng '67 Dodge	251	3,125	Running
9	8	14	Curtis Turner	Friedkin Ent '68 Plymouth	251	2,525	Running
10	17	37	Sam McQuagg	K&K Insurance '67 Dodge	250	2,025	Running
11	16	4	John Sears	L G DeWitt '67 Ford	250	1,950	Running
12	13	15	Jerry Grant	Friedkin Ent '68 Plymouth	248	1,955	Running
13	22	2	Paul Lewis	'67 Dodge	247	1,900	Running
14	24	39	Friday Hassler	Red Sharp '66 Chevrolet	245	1,800	Running
15	39	55	Harold Smith	Lyle Stelter '66 Ford	244	1,850	Running
16	25	08	Dr Don Tarr	E C Reid '66 Chevrolet	242	1,685	Running
17	37	80	E J Trivette	E C Reid '66 Chevrolet	241	1,625	Running
18	20	64	Elmo Langley	Langley-Woodfield '66 Ford	240	1,525	Running
19	36	52	Lenie Waldo	Elmer Buxton '67 Ford	239	1,550	Running
20	40	25	Jabe Thomas	Don Robertson '67 Ford	239	1,600	Running
21	23	79	Frank Warren	Harold Rhodes '66 Chevrolet	238	1,550	Running
22	33	06	Neil Castles	Castles '67 Plymouth	235	1,525	Running
23	43	34	Wendell Scott	Scott '67 Ford	235	1,500	Running
24	30	28	Clyde Lynn	Earl Brooks '66 Ford	235	1,425	Running
25	29	95	Harold Fagan	Henley Gray '66 Ford	235	1,400	Running
26	44	96	Bob Moore	Roy Buckner '66 Ford	234	1,420	Running
27	26	58	Phil Wendt	'66 Chevrolet	230	1,350	Running
28	5	29	Bobby Allison	Bondy Long '68 Ford	229	1,520	Engine
29	35	10	Bill Champion	Champion '66 Ford	229	1,310	Running
30	42	19	Henley Gray	Gray '66 Ford	227	1,330	Running
31	32	45	Bill Seifert	Seifert '68 Ford	213	1,325	Running
32	9	22	Darel Dieringer	Mario Rossi '68 Plymouth	212	1,225	Crash
33	34	76	Roy Tyner	Don Culpepper '66 Ford	212	1,225	Running
34	41	38	Wayne Smith	Smith '68 Chevrolet	205	1,240	Running
35	27	30	Dave Marcis	Larry Wehrs '66 Chevrolet	202	1,150	Running
36	28	46	Larry Manning	Tom Hunter '66 Chevrolet	199	1,125	Running
37	19	90	Sonny Hutchins	Junie Donlavey '67 Ford	190	1,100	Trans
38	6	43	Richard Petty	Petty Enterprises '68 Plym	186	1,705	Ignition
39	15	1	Bud Moore	A J King '68 Dodge	182	1,205	Trans
40	38	02	Bob Cooper	Cooper '66 Chevrolet	153	1,025	Oil Leak
41	11	99	Paul Goldsmith	Nichels Eng '68 Dodge	91	1,125	Engine
42	31	12	Earl Balmer	Tom Pistone '68 Mercury	59	1,075	Handling
43	18	49	G C Spencer	Spencer '67 Plymouth	56	950	Valve
44	3	21	Cale Yarborough	Wood Brothers '68 Mercury	45	1,220	Crash

Time of Race: 3 hours, 4 minutes, 14 seconds
Average Speed: 104.207 mph
Pole Winner: Donnie Allison - 159.223 mph
Lap Leaders: Cale Yarborough 1-44, Donnie Allison 45-47, Jerry Grant 48, D.Allison 49-69, LeeRoy Yarbrough 70-100, Buddy Baker 101-142, Yarbrough 143-152, D.Allison 153, Richard Petty 154, Bud Moore 155-160, Baker 161-162, Moore 163-180, Baker 181-204, Bobby Allison 205-217, Yarbrough 218-225, Baker 226-255.
Cautions: 6 for 110 laps   Margin of Victory: Under caution   Attendance: 60,000
**Race shortened to 255 laps due to rain.

CHARLOTTE, NC (May 26) -- Buddy Baker followed the pace car the final 36 laps and was declared the winner of the rain-shortened World 600 at Charlotte Motor Speedway. Efforts to beat the elements were finally halted at 7:00 pm with 382.5 of the scheduled 600 miles completed.

The event was red-flagged twice by heavy rain storms, and 110 laps were run under the caution flag. Rain started falling on lap 98 of the scheduled 400 lapper, and although there was no chance to get all 600 miles in the books, NASCAR officials elected to run as much under caution to reach the half-way point.

Baker drove a heads-up race, leading for 92 laps. He was in position to win the race when the contest was red-flagged six and a half hours after it began. "Someone, I believe it was Marvin Panch, told me a long time ago that the head on a guy's shoulders was put there for a purpose," said Baker. "After the last two races here at Charlotte, I'm beginning to see what he means. I have run easy in only two races since I've been running for Ray Fox, and I've won them both. That must mean something."

Baker wound up just ahead of Donnie Allison's Ban-

Buddy Baker #3 battles with Bobby Allison and Bud Moore in World 600

jo Matthews Ford. LeeRoy Yarbrough was third, David Pearson came in fourth and Bobby Isaac was fifth.

Cale Yarborough poked the Wood Brothers Mercury into the lead at the outset and threatened to lap the field before the first pit stop. He had stretched his advantage to over a half lap when a tire blew, sending his car into the wall hard off turn two. Yarborough was out of the race and had to accept last place money.

Little Bud Moore of Charleston, SC provided a surprise in the middle stages, putting his A.J. King Dodge up front after slashing way through the field. Moore spun out once and eventually left with transmission failure after 182 laps.

Curtis Turner drove a steady race and wound up ninth in his Plymouth.

Baker averaged a record low 104.207 mph as 84 laps were run single file while rain was falling. NASCAR Executive Vice-President Lin Kuchler defended the decision to try to get the race in despite the weather. "Once the race starts,"said Kuchler, "we make every effort to get it in. The reason we do this is because in addition to the spectators, many of the competitors prefer to struggle it out. There is a tremendous cost involved to postpone a race."

Race No. 19

Petty All the Way at Asheville; Pit Crews Fight After Race

ASHEVILLE, NC (May 31) -- Richard Petty led all

300 laps and took first place in the Asheville 300 at Asheville Speedway. It was his fourth win of the year.

Petty fended off David Pearson in the early going then scampered to a one lap win over Buddy Baker. Third place went to Bobby Isaac with James Hylton fourth and Elmo Langley fifth.

Petty won the pole at record speed and held his Plymouth in front of Pearson's Ford through the first 39 laps. As Pearson was lapping Stan Meserve for the third time, the two cars tangled, sending Pearson into the wall. Meserve spun into the infield.

Angry words were exchanged between Pearson and Meserve. The "jaw" session seemed to die down when apparently a member of Meserve's pit crew ran onto the track and hit Pearson from behind. The pits emptied and several fist-swinging incidents broke out. "I turned around and saw everybody swinging," said NASCAR Field Manager Johnny Bruner.

Petty had boosted his margin to three laps when a right front tire blew with seven laps left. He pitted for fresh rubber and still had a lap on runner-up Baker.

A crowd of 3,500 watched Petty's 79th career race at an average speed of 65.741 mph.

Grand National Race No. 19
300 Laps at Asheville Speedway
Asheville, NC
"Asheville 300"
100 Miles on .333-mile Paved Track
May 31, 1968

Fin	St	No.	Driver	Team / Car	Laps	Money	Status
1	1	43	Richard Petty	Petty Enterprises '68 Plym	300	$1,200	Running
2	4	3	Buddy Baker	Ray Fox '67 Dodge	299	600	Running
3	3	71	Bobby Isaac	K&K Insurance '67 Dodge	296	400	Running
4	5	48	James Hylton	Hylton Eng '67 Dodge	292	300	Running
5	8	64	Elmo Langley	Langley-Woodfield '66 Ford	288	275	Running
6	12	28	Earl Brooks	Brooks '66 Ford	286	240	Running
7	6	4	John Sears	L G DeWitt '67 Ford	284	200	Running
8	7	70	J D McDuffie	McDuffie '67 Buick	281	175	Running
9	9	25	Jabe Thomas	Don Robertson '67 Ford	267	160	Running
10	21	19	Henley Gray	Gray '67 Ford	261	145	Running
11	15	8	Ed Negre	Negre '67 Ford	259	130	Running
12	11	09	Roy Tyner	Tyner '66 Chevrolet	256	120	Running
13	18	75	Gene Black	Black '67 Ford	248	110	Running
14	20	01	Paul Dean Holt	Dennis Holt '67 Ford	234	100	Running
15	13	45	Bill Seifert	Seifert '67 Ford	139	100	Steering
16	14	20	Clyde Lynn	Lynn '66 Ford	111	100	Differen
17	17	34	Wendell Scott	Scott '67 Ford	105	100	Rear End
18	19	69	Dave Mote	'66 Chevrolet	81	100	Oil Press
19	23	06	Neil Castles	Castles '67 Plymouth	74	100	Heating
20	16	02	Bob Cooper	Cooper '66 Chevrolet	39	100	Oil Pres
21	2	17	David Pearson	Holman-Moody '68 Ford	38	100	Crash
22	10	51	Stan Meserve	Margo Hamm '67 Dodge	35	100	Crash
23	22	31	Lee Brock	Newman Long '66 Ford	1	---	Crash

Time of Race: 1 hour, 31 minutes, 16 seconds
Average Speed: 65.741 mph
Pole Winner: Richard Petty - 74.349 mph
Lap Leaders: Richard Petty 1-300,
Cautions: Margin of Victory: 1-lap plus   Attendance: 3,500.

Race No. 20

Pearson Manhandles Macon Field; Wins 8th of Year

MACON, GA (June 2) -- David Pearson led 235 laps en route to victory in the Macon 300 Grand National race at Middle Georgia Raceway. It was the eighth time the Spartanburg Ford driver has earned the trip to victory lane in the 1968 season.

Bobby Isaac finished second and held a 49 point lead in the Grand National standings. Third place went to Richard Petty with James Hylton fourth and Tiny Lund fifth.

Curtis Turner finished sixth in another strong perfor-mance in the Friedkin Enterprises Plymouth.

Isaac led the first 11 laps before Pearson took over. Toward the middle portions of the event, Petty led for a stretch of 54 laps. Pearson got around his Plymouth rival and won by more than a half lap.

Buddy Baker started seventh, but withdrew his Ray Fox Dodge on lap 79. The team did not earn any prize money for the 26th position they were credited with.

One caution for 10 laps held Pearson's speed down to 79.342 mph on the half mile paved track. The track, which had been measured at .563-mile, had been re-measured at a half mile for this event.

The fresh pavement tore up badly in the latter portions of the race. Track owner and promoter Lamar Brown, Jr. said the the track would require a $30,000 repair job. He accepted the misfortune philosophically: "We might as well finish tearing it up good," he said. "We will have a big demolition derby on July 19. That ought to do it."

Grand National Race No. 20
300 Laps at Middle Georgia Raceway
Macon, GA
"Macon 300"
150 Miles on Half-mile Paved Track
June 2, 1968

Fin	St	No.	Driver	Team / Car	Laps	Money	Status
1	1	17	David Pearson	Holman-Moody '68 Ford	300	$1,400	Running
2	2	71	Bobby Isaac	K&K Insurance '67 Dodge	300	1,000	Running
3	4	43	Richard Petty	Petty Enterprises '68 Plym	300	900	Running
4	10	48	James Hylton	Hylton Eng '67 Dodge	297	575	Running
5	3	16	Tiny Lund	Bud Moore '68 Mercury	292	425	Running
6	6	14	Curtis Turner	Friedkin Ent '68 Plymouth	291	325	Running
7	16	28	Earl Brooks	Brooks '66 Ford	282	275	Running
8	19	20	Clyde Lynn	Lynn '66 Ford	280	225	Running
9	20	70	J D McDuffie	McDuffie '67 Buick	276	200	Running
10	9	06	Neil Castles	Castles '67 Plymouth	275	160	Running
11	13	34	Wendell Scot	Scott '67 Ford	269	100	Running
12	21	96	Bob Moore	Roy Buckner '66 Ford	266	100	Running
13	26	01	Paul Dean Holt	Dennis Holt '67 Ford	256	100	Running
14	14	25	Jabe Thomas	Don Robertson '67 Ford	243	100	Running
15	18	51	Stan Meserve	Margo Hamm '67 Dodge	237	100	Bearing
16	17	09	Roy Tyner	Tyner '66 Chevrolet	176	100	Bearing
17	30	19	Henley Gray	Gray '66 Ford	155	100	Quit
18	28	95	Harold Fagan	Henley Gray '66 Ford	151	100	Oil Press
19	24	75	Gene Black	Black '66 Ford	143	100	Tie rod
20	15	45	Bill Seifert	Seifert '68 Ford	137	100	Heating
21	5	4	John Sears	L G DeWitt '67 Ford	135	100	Engine
22	11	64	Elmo Langley	Langley-Woodfield '66 Ford	133	100	Engine
23	9	39	Friday Hassler	Red Sharp '66 Chevrolet	132	100	Rear End
24	17	88	Serge Adam	Buck Baker '67 Olds	109	100	Oil Press
25	12	02	Bob Cooper	Cooper '66 Chevrolet	79	---	Heating
26	7	3	Buddy Baker	Ray Fox '67 Dodge	79	---	Quit
27	27	31	Leonard Brock	Newman Long '66 Ford	15	---	A Frame
28	22	8	Ed Negre	Negre '67 Ford	14	---	Disq
29	25	87	Bobby Mausgrover	Buck Baker '66 Chevrolet	13	---	Oil Press
30	23	69	David Mote	'66 Chevrolet	8	---	Fuel pmp

Time of Race: 1 hour, 53 minutes, 26 seconds
Average Speed: 79.342 mph
Pole Winner: David Pearson - 86.873 mph
Lap Leaders: David Pearson led 235 laps; Richard Petty led 54 laps; Bobby Isaac led 11 laps.
Cautions: 1 for 10 laps   Margin of Victory: Attendance: 3,500

Race No. 21

Pearson, Isaac Falter; Petty Wins at Maryville

MARYVILLE, TN (June 6) -- Richard Petty outlasted David Pearson and Bobby Isaac and won the 100-miler at the newly renovated Smoky Mountain Raceway. It was the fifth win of the season for the curly-haired Plymouth driver.

Rookie Pete Hamilton pulled the biggest surprise by taking second in a Rocky Hinton Ford wrenched by Turkey Minton. James Hylton came in third, ol' pro Curtis Turner was fourth and John Sears was fifth.

Pearson led the first 59 laps from the pole. Isaac made a pass for the lead on lap 60 and held it until Petty

Pete Hamilton with crew chief Turkey Minton. The new team finished 2nd at Maryville

took first place on lap 100. Pearson went behind the wall with engine problems on lap 119 and Isaac left on lap 134 with a busted oil pan.

Buddy Baker, another contender, blew a tire and hit the retaining wall hard. He was taken to Blount Memorial Hospital for observation. Bud Moore was running in fourth place with 14 laps to go when his Dodge popped a tire and wrecked. He got credit for eighth in the final order.

Petty struggled in the first half of the race, then his crew made chassis changes on a pit stop. "When I finally got to running good, I looked around and nobody was left to race with," said Petty.

Petty's 80th career victory came at an average speed of 76.743 mph.

Grand National Race No. 21
200 Laps at Smoky Mountain Raceway
Maryville, TN
100 Miles on Half-mile Paved Track
June 6, 1968

Fin	St	No.	Driver	Team / Car	Laps	Money	Status
1	4	43	Richard Petty	Petty Enterprises '68 Plym	200	$1,200	Running
2	6	5	Pete Hamilton	Rocky Hinton '68 Ford	199	600	Running
3	7	48	James Hylton	Hylton eng '67 Dodge	199	400	Running
4	5	14	Curtis Turner	Friedkin Ent '68 Plymouth	195	300	Running
5	10	4	John Sears	L G DeWitt '66 Ford	192	275	Running
6	20	64	Elmo Langley	Langley-Woodfield '66 Ford	191	240	Running
7	18	20	Clyde Lynn	Lynn '66 Ford	189	200	Running
8	3	1	Bud Moore	A J King '68 Dodge	183	175	Crash
9	12	25	Jabe Thomas	Don Robertson '67 Ford	183	155	Running
10	16	19	Henley Gray	Gray '66 Ford	183	145	Running
11	14	34	Wendell Scott	Scott '67 Ford	178	135	Running
12	13	51	Stan Meserve	Margo Hamm '67 Dodge	175	120	Running
13	17	75	Gene Black	Black '66 Ford	169	110	Running
14	2	71	Bobby Isaac	K&K Insurance '67 Dodge	134	100	Oil Pan
15	1	17	David Pearson	Holman-Moody '68 Ford	119	100	Valve
16	11	28	Earl Brooks	Brooks '66 Ford	114	100	Oil Press
17	15	01	Paul Dean Holt	Dennis Holt '67 Ford	108	100	Rear End
18	21	06	Neil Castles	Castles '67 Plymouth	90	100	Heating
19	8	3	Buddy Baker	Ray Fox '67 Dodge	75	100	Crash
20	19	09	Roy Tyner	Tyner '66 Chevrolet	31	100	Ignition
21	9	39	Friday Hassler	Red Sharp '66 Chevrolet	1	100	Axle

Time of Race: 1 hour, 18 minutes, 11 seconds
Average Speed: 76.743 mph
Pole Winner: David Pearson - 88.583 mph
Lap Leaders: David Pearson 1-59, Bobby Isaac 60-99, Richard Petty 100-200.
Cautions: Margin of Victory: 1-lap plus   Attendance: 9,800

Race No. 22

Petty Perfect at Birmingham; Pearson Disqualified

BIRMINGHAM, AL (June 8) -- Richard Petty led all but one lap and won the 100-mile Grand National event at Birmingham Speedway.

Grand National Race No. 22
160 Laps at Birmingham Speedway
Birmingham, AL
100 Miles on .625-mile Paved Track
June 8, 1968

Fin	St	No.	Driver	Team / Car	Laps	Money	Status
1	2	43	Richard Petty	Petty Enterprises '68 Plym	160	$1,200	Running
2	3	71	Bobby Isaac	K&K Insurance '67 Dodge	160	600	Running
3	6	48	James Hylton	Hylton Eng '67 Dodge	158	400	Running
4	5	39	Friday Hassler	Red Sharp '66 Chevrolet	157	300	Running
5	4	2	Bobby Allison	J D Bracken '66 Chevrolet	157	275	Running
6	9	64	Elmo Langley	Langley-Woodfield '66 Ford	155	240	Running
7	7	4	John Sears	L G DeWitt '67 Ford	153	200	Running
8	10	25	Jabe Thomas	Don Robertson '67 Ford	153	175	Running
9	12	76	Roy Tyner	Don Culpepper '66 Ford	152	155	Running
10	14	06	Neil Castles	Castles '67 Plymouth	152	145	Running
11	17	20	Clyde Lynn	Lynn '66 Ford	149	135	Running
12	11	34	Wendell Scott	Scott '67 Ford	148	120	Running
13	13	28	Earl Brooks	Brooks '66 Ford	146	110	Running
14	16	15	Bill Seifert	Seifert '68 Ford	145	100	Running
15	15	19	Henley Gray	Gray '66 Ford	141	100	Running
16	8	51	Stan Meserve	Margo Hamm '67 Dodge	70	100	Heating
17	18	01	Paul Dean Holt	Dennis Holt '67 Ford	41	100	Trans
18	1	17	David Pearson	Holman-Moody '68 Ford	159	100	Disqual

Time of Race: 1 hour, 7 minutes, 18 seconds
Average Speed: 89.153 mph
Pole Winner: David Pearson - 97.784 mph
Lap Leaders: Richard Petty 1-86, Bobby Allison 87, Petty 88-160.
Cautions: 2 for ___ laps   Margin of Victory: Attendance: 5,245.

Bobby Isaac finished in second place with James Hylton third. Friday Hassler and Bobby Allison rounded out the top five.

David Pearson had crossed the finish line in third place, but he was disqualified because his Holman-Moody Ford was shod with tires of a different tread design than which it started the race. NASCAR rules say the tires and the tread design must match on all four wheels.

Allison, who was back in his trusty J.D. Bracken Chevrolet after quitting the factory backed Ford of Bondy Long, led for a single lap and thrilled the audience of 5,245. The Hueytown, AL driver had a lock on second place when he ran over a piece of metal, cutting both right side tires with 18 laps to go. He fell to fifth in the final rundown.

Allison quit the Long team when he was told the Birmingham race would not be on the team's schedule. "When I took this ride, I had a deal for 32 races," said Allison. "Then it went down to 22. Next thing I knew it was reduced to 15 races. I want to race. Just sitting around has driven me nuts. I want to drive in front of my hometown fans, so I quit the Ford and brought the Chevy out of the closet."

Petty's average speed of 89.153 mph was slowed by two brief caution flags.

Race No. 23

Allison Wonderland in Rockingham's Carolina 500

ROCKINGHAM, NC (June 16) -- Donnie Allison of Hueytown, AL scored his first Grand National victory and saved the day for Ford in a 1-2 brother finish in the Carolina 500 at North Carolina Motor Speedway. The 28 year-old sophomore driver, wheeling the Banjo Matthews Ford, beat older brother Bobby by two laps in a heat-searing 500-miler on the 1-mile paved track.

A third Allison, Eddie, served as crew chief for the second place Chevrolet and the third place Dodge driven by James Hylton. Fourth place went to Richard Brickhouse, who was competing in his first Grand National event and his first on a paved track. Roy Tyner finished fifth.

Donnie Allison

Donnie took the lead from Richard Petty, who was driving in relief of Darel Dieringer, in the 372nd lap. Attrition took out most of the contenders, and at one time Allison held a four lap lead on the field.

Bobby, back in the saddle of the J.D. Bracken Chevrolet, had quit the factory Ford team of Bondy Long in a dispute over the frequency the car would be raced for the remainder of the 1968 season.

Swede Savage, 21 year-old newcomer out of San Bernadino, CA, took Allison's place in the Fred Lorenzen engineered car and worked his way up to second place before clutch failure ended his hopes. Savage had been penalized twice for passing on the yellow flag. At one point, Lorenzen flashed a pit board message to Savage which read: *"Don't Not Pass"*.

Point leader Bobby Isaac was eliminated in a wreck in the 295th lap, but he was able to extend his point lead to 83 points over David Pearson, who departed 150 laps earlier with a blown engine. Only 14 cars finished the race.

Grand National Race No. 23
500 Laps at North Carolina Motor Speedway
Rockingham, NC
"Carolina 500"
500 Miles on 1-mile Paved Track
June 16, 1968

Fin	St	No.	Driver	Team / Car	Laps	Money	Status
1	7	27	Donnie Allison	Banjo Matthews '68 Ford	500	$16,675	Running
2	13	2	Bobby Allison	J D Bracken '66 Chevrolet	498	9,650	Running
3	17	48	James Hylton	Hylton Eng '67 Dodge	494	5,150	Running
4	16	03	Richard Brickhouse	Dub Clewis '67 Plymouth	470	2,650	Running
5	23	76	Roy Tyner	Don Culpepper '66 Ford	469	1,850	Running
6	21	25	Jabe Thomas	Don Robertson '67 Ford	464	1,300	Running
7	30	70	J D McDuffie	McDuffie '67 Buick	463	1,200	Running
8	25	4	John Sears	L G DeWitt '67 Ford	457	1,225	Running
9	33	20	Clyde Lynn	Lynn '66 Ford	457	1,200	Running
10	28	30	Dave Marcis	Larry Wehrs '66 Chevrolet	456	1,050	Running
11	32	06	Neil Castles	Castles '67 Plymouth	448	1,150	Running
12	37	19	Henley Gray	Gray '66 Ford	445	1,060	Running
13	10	29	Swede Savage	Bondy Long '68 Ford	343	935	Clutch
14	38	50	Eddie Yarboro	Yarboro '66 Plymouth	418	805	Oil Press
15	36	93	Walson Gardner	Gardner '67 Ford	406	780	Crash
16	24	51	Stan Meserve	Margo Hamm '67 Dodge	406	700	D Shaft
17	44	87	Buck Baker	Baker '68 Chevrolet	395	890	Running
18	39	34	Wendell Scott	Scott '67 Ford	380	720	Running
19	12	22	Darel Dieringer*	Mario Rossi '68 Plymouth	379	675	Engine
20	6	6	Charlie Glotzbach**	Cotton Owens '68 Dodge	372	670	Ignition
21	29	10	Bill Champion	Champion '66 Ford	368	665	Heating
22	15	79	Frank Warren	Harold Rhodes '66 Chevrolet	324	660	Crash
23	20	64	Elmo Langley	Langley-Woodfield '66 Ford	316	650	Crash
24	8	71	Bobby Isaac	K&K Insurance '67 dodge	295	645	Crash
24	31	5	Pete Hamilton	Rocky Hinton '68 Ford	260	790	Crash
26	3	43	Richard Petty	Petty Enterprises '68 Plym	236	1,115	Oil Press
27	11	16	Tiny Lund	Bud Moore '68 Mercury	234	630	Crash
28	1	98	LeeRoy Yarbrough	Junior Johnson '68 Ford	217	750	Clutch
29	4	99	Paul Goldsmith	Nichels Eng '68 Dodge	201	595	Idler arm
30	2	17	David Pearson	Holman-Moody '68 Ford	142	665	Engine
31	22	80	E J Trivette	E C Reid '66 Chevrolet	139	585	Oil Press
32	5	21	Cale Yarborough	Wood Brothers '68 Mercury	129	580	Engine
33	18	49	G C Spencer	Spencer '67 Plymouth	120	625	Engine
34	42	46	Larry Manning	Tom Hunter '66 Chevrolet	114	570	Heating
35	35	07	George Davis	Davis '66 Chevrolet	96	645	Crash
36	26	38	Wayne Smith	Smith '68 Chevrolet	88	610	Clutch
37	40	8	Ed Negre	Negre '67 Ford	87	585	Heating
38	9	3	Buddy Baker	Ray Fox '68 Dodge	78	650	Lug Bolts
39	34	45	Bill Seifert	Seifert '68 Ford	66	635	Engine
40	43	75	Paul Dean Holt	Dennis Holt '67 Ford	56	540	Oil Line
41	14	1	Bud Moore	A J King '68 Dodge	27	535	Engine
42	27	11	Earl Brooks	'66 Ford	23	555	Oil Pan
43	19	39	Friday Hassler	Red Sharp '66 Chevrolet	16	550	Sway bar
44	41	88	Bobby Mausgrover	Buck Baker '67 Olds	4	500	Rear End

Time of Race: 5 hours, 2 minutes, 0 seconds
Average Speed: 99.338 mph
Pole Winner: LeeRoy Yarbrough - 118.644 mph
Lap Leaders: LeeRoy Yarbrough 1-86, Paul Goldsmith 87-101, Yarbrough 102-109, Goldsmith 110-130, Yarbrough 131, Goldsmith 132-147, Yarbrough 148-172, Darel Dieringer 173, Bobby Isaac 174, Dieringer 175-185, Isaac 186-201, Dieringer 202-307, Donnie Allison 308-324, Dieringer 325-336, D.Allison 337-338, Dieringer 339-340, D.Allison 341, Dieringer 342-350, D.Allison 351-355, Dieringer 356-371, D.Allison 372-500.
Cautions: 8 for 74 laps   Margin of Victory: 2-laps plus   Attendance: 40,000
*Relieved by Richard Petty   **Relieved by Paul Goldsmith

Swede Savage took the wheel of the Bondy Long-Fred Lorenzen Ford at Rockingham

Richard Brickhouse finished 4th in Carolina 500. It was his first Grand National start and his first race on a paved track

"I was in a position that all race drivers dream about," said Donnie. "Leading the race by a couple of laps in a car that was the class of the field. It's a beautiful feeling."

Car owner Matthews said the victory secured his position with Ford Motor Co. "If I had failed to win one this year," said the former driver, "I would have probably gotten the ax. I didn't expect to get another chance this year, but Ford has showed a lot of faith in me."

Allison averaged 99.338 mph in the five hour marathon. A crowd of 40,000 braved 95 degree heat.

Race No. 24

Petty Beats Pearson On Greenville Dirt Track

GREENVILLE, SC (June 22) -- Richard Petty scooted past David Pearson with 30 laps remaining and won a close 100-mile Grand National race at Greenville-Pickens Speedway. It was the seventh win of the season for the Randleman, NC Plymouth driver.

Pearson's Ford wound up second, 4.0-seconds behind the winner. John Sears came in third with Clyde Lynn fourth and Jabe Thomas fifth.

Petty started second in the 22 car field, but never led until the final 15 miles. Pearson led the first 52 laps before making a pit stop during a caution flag. Buddy Baker moved to the front for five laps before Pearson assumed command again.

Pearson kept his Holman-Moody Ford in the lead until Petty ran him down in the late stages. "I had new tires on and I think David had only new tires on the outside," explained Petty. "I couldn't see his tires, but I could see him sliding. I ran into him two or three times,

but each time I backed off so he could get straightened out."

Petty made the last pass when Pearson slid high in the first turn. "I just couldn't hold it down," he said. "Petty was holding it down better than I was in the turns."

Point leader Bobby Isaac blew an engine on lap 14 and wound up last. Pearson closed to within 69 points in the chase for the Grand National title.

Rookie Stan Meserve, racing for the first time on a dirt track, flipped his Dodge three times in the 105th lap. He was shaken but unhurt.

Baker pulled his Ray Fox Dodge out of the race with brake failure on lap 60.

A crowd of 7,200 watched Petty take his 82nd career win at an average speed of 64.609 mph.

Grand National Race No. 24
200 Laps at Greenville-Pickens Speedway
Greenville, SC
100 Miles on Half-mile Dirt Track
June 22, 1968

Fin	St	No.	Driver	Team / Car	Laps	Money	Status
1	2	43	Richard Petty	Petty Enterprises '68 Plym	200	$1,200	Running
2	1	17	David Pearson	Holman-Moody '68 Ford	200	600	Running
3	5	4	John Sears	L G DeWitt '66 Ford	195	400	Running
4	11	20	Clyde Lynn	Lynn '66 Ford	194	300	Running
5	6	25	Jabe Thomas	Don Robertson '67 Ford	193	275	Running
6	10	70	J D McDuffie	McDuffie '67 Buick	191	240	Running
7	17	93	Elmo Langley	Langley-Woodfield '66 Ford	187	200	Running
8	12	34	Wendell Scott	Scott '67 Ford	183	175	Running
9	14	19	Henley Gray	Gray '66 Ford	175	150	Running
10	22	9	Roy Tyner	Tyner '66 Chevrolet	175	140	Running
11	8	87	Sam Waldrop	Buck Baker '68 Chevrolet	171	130	Running
12	20	01	Paul Dean Holt	Dennis Holt '67 Ford	164	120	Running
13	21	8	Ed Negre	Negre '67 Ford	157	110	Flat tire
14	9	75	Bryant Wallace	Gene Black '66 Ford	118	100	Lug bolts
15	7	88	Buck Baker	Baker '67 Olds	117	100	Rear End
16	18	51	Stan Meserve	Margo Hamm '67 Dodge	98	100	Crash
17	13	28	Earl Brooks	Brooks '66 Ford	95	100	Crash
18	16	45	Bill Seifert	Seifert '68 Ford	87	100	Valve
19	15	95	Cecil Gordon	Henley Gray '66 Ford	85	100	Brakes
20	3	3	Buddy Baker	Ray Fox '68 Dodge	60	100	Brakes
21	19	06	Neil Castles	Castles '67 Plymouth	40	100	Gas Line
22	4	71	Bobby Isaac	K&K Insurance '67 Dodge	14	100	Engine

Time of Race: 1 hour, 32 minutes, 52 seconds
Average Speed: 64.609 mph
Pole Winner: David Pearson - 68.834 mph
Lap Leaders: David Pearson 1-52, Buddy Baker 53-57, Pearson 58-169, Richard Petty 170-200.
Cautions: 6 for 18 laps   Margin of Victory: 4 seconds   Attendance: 7,200

Race No. 25
Cale Routs Rivals in Firecracker 400 Runaway

DAYTONA BEACH, FL (July 4) -- Cale Yarborough led all but 18 laps and blew away the competition in the 10th annual Firecracker 400 at Daytona International

Cale and Betty Jo Yarborough celebrate Firecracker 400 victory

Speedway. It was the seventh career win for the 29 year-old Mercury driver, and his third straight at the 2.5-mile Big D.

LeeRoy Yarbrough finished second, two full laps behind. David Pearson came in third, Darel Dieringer was fourth and Tiny Lund fifth as Ford Motor Co. products took four of the top five spots.

"This is the easiest race I've ever won, and also the cleanest," said Cale. "I'd like to compliment the drivers in slower cars for the great job they did of staying out of the way of the faster cars."

The 160-lapper was accident free and only two cautions broke the action -- both as the result of blown engines.

Wood Brothers service Cale Yarborough in Firecracker 400. Cale won the race, his 3rd straight at Daytona

"Three of my four pit stops were under the green flag," said Yarborough. "I found out later that the Wood boys put me back on the track in about 20 seconds. Most of the other crews were taking 22-26

seconds. At 185 mph, you can cover a lot of ground in four seconds."

Charlie Glotzbach won the pole and was holding down third place with three laps to go when a tire exploded on his Dodge. Glotzbach limped to the pits, but crew chief Cotton Owens couldn't get the car back on the track. The mishap dropped Glotzbach from third to ninth.

Point leader Bobby Isaac lost two positions when he was penalized a lap for passing the pace car. He wound up eighth and watched as Pearson closed to within 54 points in the Grand National standings.

Richard Petty qualified second and led for five laps in the early going. However, his Plymouth was knocked out when the engine blew on lap 132.

Grand National Race No. 25
160 Laps at Daytona Int'l Speedway
Daytona Beach, FL
"Firecracker 400"
400 Miles on 2.5-mile Paved Track
July 4, 1968

Fin	St	No.	Driver	Team / Car	Laps	Money	Status
1	4	21	Cale Yarborough	Wood Brothers '68 Mercury	160	$15,400	Running
2	3	98	LeeRoy Yarbrough	Junior Johnson '68 Mercury	158	8,545	Running
3	5	17	David Pearson	Holman-Moody '68 Ford	157	5,730	Running
4	9	22	Darel Dieringer	Mario Rossi '68 Plymouth	157	2,975	Running
5	10	16	Tiny Lund	Bud Moore '68 Mercury	157	1,875	Running
6	16	99	Paul Goldsmith	Nichels Eng '68 Dodge	156	1,525	Running
7	12	1	Bud Moore	A J King '68 Dodge	155	1,325	Running
8	11	71	Bobby Isaac	K&K Insurance '68 Dodge	155	1,225	Running
9	1	6	Charlie Glotzbach	Cotton Owens '68 Dodge	154	2,100	Blew tire
10	15	56	Jim Hurtubise	Lyle Stelter '68 Mercury	152	1,050	Crank
11	13	14	Jerry Grant	Friedkin Ent '68 Plymouth	152	775	Running
12	14	11	Mario Andretti	Holman-Moody '68 Ford	151	725	Running
13	19	48	James Hylton	Hylton Eng '67 Dodge	151	575	Running
14	21	4	John Sears	L G DeWitt '66 Ford	151	630	Running
15	8	7	Bobby Johns	Shorty Johns '66 Chevrolet	151	550	Running
16	18	75	Butch Hartman	Hartman '68 Dodge	150	545	Running
17	22	03	Richard Brickhouse	Dub Clewis '67 Plymouth	145	565	Running
18	24	64	Elmo Langley	Langley-Woodfield '68 Ford	140	560	Running
19	32	46	Larry Manning	Tom Hunter '68 Chevrolet	139	530	Running
20	27	76	Roy Tyner	Don Culpepper '66 Ford	135	550	Running
21	2	43	Richard Petty	Petty Enterprises '68 Plym	132	1,395	Engine
22	30	20	Clyde Lynn	Lynn '66 Ford	130	540	Running
23	35	25	Jabe Thomas	Don Robertson '67 Ford	127	510	Running
24	31	34	Wendell Scott	Scott '67 Ford	126	530	Running
25	25	80	E J Trivette	E C Reid '66 Chevrolet	126	525	Running
26	23	52	Lennie Waldo	Elmer Buxton '67 Ford	114	520	Running
27	29	69	David Mote	'66 Chevrolet	100	525	Running
28	33	10	Bill Champion	Champion '66 Ford	80	485	Engine
29	28	01	Paul Dean Holt	Dennis Holt '67 Ford	65	505	Heating
30	6	29	A J Foyt	Bondy Long '68 Ford	64	475	Steering
31	20	2	Bobby Allison	J D Bracken '66 Chevrolet	49	645	Axle
32	7	3	Buddy Baker	Ray Fox '68 Dodge	23	465	Rear End
33	37	45	Bill Seifert	Seifert '68 Ford	23	460	Trans
34	19	18	Dick Johnson	Johnson '67 Ford	22	455	Manifold
35	34	28	Earl Brooks	Brooks '66 Ford	15	450	Engine
36	26	38	Wayne Smith	Smith '68 Chevrolet	14	470	Rear End
37	36	70	J D McDuffie	McDuffie '67 Buick	1	440	Engine

Time of Race: 2 hours, 23 minutes, 30 seconds
Average Speed: 167.247 mph
Pole Winner: Charlie Glotzbach - 185.156 mph
Fastest Qualifier: LeeRoy Yarbrough 187.049 mph
Lap Leaders: LeeRoy Yarbrough 1-2, Cale Yarborough 3-5, Yarborough 6, Richard Petty 7-11, Yarborough 12, Yarborough 13-33, Yarborough 34-36, David Pearson 37-42, Yarborough 43-160.
Cautions: 2 for 14 laps   Margin of Victory: 2-laps plus   Attendance: 44,600

LeeRoy Yarbrough #98, Mario Andretti #11 and Bobby Isaac #71 find themselves in crowded pit road predicament at Daytona

A.J. Foyt drove the Bondy Long Ford but was never a factor. The famed USAC pilot parked the car with steering problems after 64 laps.

Donnie Allison crashed his Banjo Matthews Ford in a practice session the day before the race. It appeared repairs could be made, but Matthews noticed the frame had been bent. He withdrew from the event.

A crowd of 44,600 watched Yarborough set an event record of 167.247 mph.

The day after the race, Jim Hurtubise drove a front-engine Indy Car around the Daytona track at a record 191.938 mph. It was the first time the 190 mph barrier had been cracked.

Race No. 26

Allison Beats Factory Cars With Independent Chevy

ISLIP, NY (July 7) -- Bobby Allison of Hueytown, AL passed David Pearson with 28 laps to go and scored a popular upset win in the Islip 300 at Islip Speedway. The 30 year-old driver, who recently quit the factory Ford team, whipped three industry-supported cars in the 60-mile race on the .2-mile flat oval.

Pearson finished a close second in the Holman-Moody Ford. Buddy Baker was third in the Ray Fox Dodge and Richard Petty came in fourth. Fifth place went to James Hylton.

Bobby Isaac wound up sixth and clung to a 49 point lead over Pearson in the Grand National point standings.

Buddy Baker started on the pole for the first time in two years, and led the first 95 laps. Petty took charge on lap 96 and led through the 192nd lap when he had to make an unscheduled pit stop. Petty was trying to put a lap on Allison when the two cars tangled. A fender was bent in on Petty's right front tire and the long pit stop removed him from contention.

After the race, Maurice Petty and Dale Inman, crew members for Petty, attacked Allison. Petty was fined $250 and Inman was fined $100 for fighting by sanctioning NASCAR.

"I guess it was a blowoff of one of those things that builds up over a period of time," said Maurice. "It started last year at Asheville-Weaverville when Bobby roughed up Richard real bad and got away with it. You might say we settled an old score."

"I don't hold grudges," said Allison. "I think Maurice was led into the deal by Inman, who is a great crewman

Grand National Race No. 26
300 Laps at Islip Speedway
Islip, NY
"Islip 300"
60 Miles on .2-mile Paved Track
July 7, 1968

Fin	St	No.	Driver	Team / Car	Laps	Money	Status
1	5	2	Bobby Allison	J D Bracken '66 Chevrolet	300	$1,000	Running
2	2	17	David Pearson	Holman-Moody '68 Ford	300	600	Running
3	1	3	Buddy Baker	Ray Fox '68 Dodge	299	400	Running
4	3	43	Richard Petty	Petty Enterprises '68 Plym	298	500	Running
5	4	48	James Hylton	Hylton Eng '67 Dodge	294	275	Running
6	11	71	Bobby Isaac	K&K Insurance '67 Dodge	293	240	Running
7	8	64	Elmo Langley	Langley-Woodfield '67 Ford	291	200	Running
8	12	20	Clyde Lynn	Lynn '66 Ford	287	175	Running
9	10	4	John Sears	L G DeWitt '66 Ford	287	155	Running
10	13	06	Neil Castles	Castles '67 Plymouth	283	145	Running
11	17	34	Wendell Scott	Scott '66 Ford	277	135	Running
12	6	44	John Wingier	'67 Ford	275	120	Running
13	9	25	Jabe Thomas	Don Robertson '67 Ford	271	110	Running
14	21	87	Buck Baker	Baker '68 Chevrolet	258	100	Running
15	15	8	Ed Negre	Negre '67 Ford	231	100	Rear End
16	22	09	Bill Vanderhoff	Roy Tyner '66 Chevrolet	230	100	Brakes
17	14	28	Earl Brooks	Brooks '66 Ford	191	100	Quit
18	16	0	Frank Warren	Dr Don Tarr '66 Chevrolet	160	100	Fuel pmp
19	18	70	J D McDuffie	McDuffie '67 Buick	127	100	Brakes
20	7	49	G C Spencer	Spencer '67 Plymouth	110	100	Rear End
21	20	45	Bill Seifert	Seifert '68 Ford	109	100	Quit
22	19	76	Roy Tyner	Don Culpepper '66 Ford	74	100	Oil Press
23	23	01	Paul Dean Holt	Dennis Holt '67 Ford	62	100	Quit
24	25	69	David Mote	'66 Chevrolet	29	100	Shocks
25	24	75	Gene Black	Black '66 Ford	17	100	Trans

Time of Race: 1 hour, 14 minutes, 8 seconds
Average Speed: 48.561 mph
Pole Winner: Buddy Baker - 51.873 mph
Lap Leaders: Buddy Baker 1-95, Richard Petty 96-192, David Pearson 193-272, Bobby Allison 273-300.
Cautions: 1 for 3 laps   Margin of Victory: 6 car lengths   Attendance: 4,600

Maurice Petty was fined $250 for attacking Bobby Allison after Islip event

and loyal to the Pettys, but he is an agitator. They both got me. When I was down on the ground, someone kicked me in the back. Somebody told me it was Dale."

Allison said he had thought about taking some kind of action. "I was going to call the police and have Maurice and Dale arrested," said Allison. "Lin Kuchler was there and he talked me out of it."

It was Allison's 11th career victory, but his first since November 12, 1967 when he won at Macon, GA in a Holman-Moody Ford. He averaged 48.561 mph before 4,600 spectators.

Race No. 27

Allison Fantastic at Oxford, But Petty Wins Maine 300

Oxford, ME (July 9) -- Richard Petty took the lead with 38 laps to go and won the Maine 300 at Oxford Plains Speedway, but two time winner Bobby Allison stole the show in his independent Chevrolet.

Petty outran runner-up David Pearson by 12 seconds

to pocket the $1,350 first prize. Third place went to Buddy Baker with Allison fourth and Bobby Isaac fifth.

Allison started fourth and ran with the leaders for the first half of the race. A fuel filler tube was jarred from his car and he had to pit for quick repairs. His pit crew, headed by brother Eddie Allison, completed the work but he lost five laps. From that point on Allison drove like a wild man. He made up two laps on all of his factory backed rivals and wound up three laps off the pace.

The race was run caution free, and Petty averaged a record 63.717 mph. Neil Castles spun wildly through the first turn, narrowly missing several cars. His Plymouth came to a halt out of harm's way and no yellow was waved. Castles continued and was later eliminated with rear gearing failure.

A wall-to-wall crowd of 11,426 watched the 300 laper on the .333-mile paved oval.

Grand National Race No. 27
300 Laps at Oxford Plains Speedway
Oxford, ME
"Maine 300"
100 Miles on .333-mile Paved Track
July 9, 1968

Fin	St	No.	Driver	Team / Car	Laps	Money	Status
1	2	43	Richard Petty	Petty Enterprises '68 Plym	300	$1,350	Running
2	3	17	David Pearson	Holman-Moody '68 Ford	300	700	Running
3	1	3	Buddy Baker	Ray Fox '67 Dodge	297	450	Running
4	4	2	Bobby Allison	J D Bracken '66 Chevrolet	297	325	Running
5	5	71	Bobby Isaac	K&K Insurance '67 Dodge	292	315	Running
6	10	48	James Hylton	Hylton Eng '67 Dodge	291	280	Running
7	9	5	Pete Hamilton	Rocky Hinton '68 Ford	289	240	Running
8	6	4	John Sears	L G DeWitt '66 Ford	288	215	Running
9	17	70	J D McDuffie	McDuffie '67 Buick	284	190	Running
10	18	34	Wendell Scott	Scott '66 Ford	281	180	Running
11	23	28	Earl Brooks	Brooks '66 Ford	277	170	Running
12	16	8	Ed Negre	Negre '67 Ford	275	160	Running
13	22	45	Niles Gage	Bill Seifert '68 Ford	274	155	Running
14	15	06	Neil Castles	Castles '67 Plymouth	272	145	Rear End
15	24	01	Paul Dean Holt	Dennis Holt '67 Ford	255	140	Running
16	12	25	Jabe Thomas	Don Robertson '67 Ford	243	130	Running
17	19	09	Glen Luce	Roy Tyner '66 Chevrolet	223	125	Ignition
18	8	49	G C Spencer	Spencer '67 Plymouth	221	125	Heating
19	13	51	Stan Meserve	Margo Hamm '67 Dodge	169	120	Rear End
20	21	76	Roy Tyner	Don Culpepper '66 Ford	87	120	Carb
21	14	44	Don Wingier	'67 Chevrolet	82	100	Valve
22	26	87	Buck Baker	Baker '68 Chevrolet	79	100	Steering
23	25	75	Bill Seifert	Gene Black '66 Ford	53	100	Rear End
24	7	64	Elmo Langley	Langley-Woodfield '66 Ford	51	100	Rear End
25	20	0	Frank Warren	Dr Don Tarr '66 Chevrolet	18	100	Brakes
26	11	20	Clyde Lynn	Lynn '66 Ford	9	10	Rear End
27	27	69	David Mote	'66 Chevrolet	3	100	Ignition

Time of Race: 1 hour, 34 minutes, 10 seconds
Average Speed: 63.717 mph
Pole Winner: Buddy Baker - 67.835 mph
Lap Leaders: Buddy Baker 1-110, Richard Petty 111-259, David Pearson 260-262, Petty 263-300.
Cautions: None   Margin of Victory: 12 seconds   Attendance: 11,426

Race No. 28

Petty Dominates Fonda 200 For 9th Win of Year

FONDA, NY (July 11) -- Richard Petty pushed his Plymouth around rival David Pearson in the 21st lap and led the rest of the way to win the Fonda 200 at Fonda Speedway. It was the ninth win of the year for the 31 year-old Petty.

Buddy Baker finished in second place with Bobby Allison third. Bobby Isaac came in fourth and Pearson was fifth.

Isaac gained a single point on Pearson in the Grand National standings and now leads by 47 points.

Three caution flags for 19 laps held Petty's winning speed to 64.935 mph. Frank Warren started the fireworks when he spun in the third turn in the 44th lap. Buck Baker, Roy Tyner and John Sears were swept into the melee. Tyner and Warren were sidelined, but Baker and Sears got back into the race.

Sears was later kayoed in a crash with J.D. McDuffie. They got tangled up trying to avoid a spinning Isaac.

Grand National Race No. 28
200 Laps at Fonda Speedway
Fonda, NY
"Fonda 200"
100 Miles on Half-mile Paved Track
July 11, 1968

Fin	St	No.	Driver	Team / Car	Laps	Money	Status
1	2	43	Richard Petty	Petty Enterprises '68 Plym	200	$1,200	Running
2	4	3	Buddy Baker	Ray Fox '68 Dodge	200	600	Running
3	6	2	Bobby Allison	J D Bracken '66 Chevrolet	200	400	Running
4	3	71	Bobby Isaac	K&K Insurance '67 Dodge	197	300	Running
5	1	17	David Pearson	Holman-Moody '68 Ford	196	275	Running
6	8	48	James Hylton	Hylton Eng '67 Dodge	195	240	Running
7	10	64	Elmo Langley	Langley-Woodfield '66 Ford	192	200	Running
8	17	34	Wendell Scott	Scott '66 Ford	192	175	Running
9	14	20	Clyde Lynn	Lynn '66 Ford	191	155	Running
10	16	8	Ed Negre	Negre '67 Ford	188	145	Running
11	24	75	Gene Black	Black '66 Ford	178	135	Running
12	19	25	Jabe Thomas	Don Robertson '67 Ford	175	120	Running
13	12	87	Buck Baker	Baker '68 Chevrolet	174	110	Running
14	25	69	David Mote	'66 Chevrolet	173	100	Running
15	9	70	J D McDuffie	McDuffie '67 Buick	123	100	Crash
16	11	4	John Sears	L G DeWitt '66 Ford	123	100	Crash
17	21	28	Earl Brooks	Brooks '66 Ford	81	100	Oil Press
18	23	45	Bill Seifert	Seifert '68 Ford	74	100	Clutch
19	22	01	Paul Dean Holt	Dennis Holt '67 Ford	49	100	Hub
20	5	51	Stan Meserve	Margo Hamm '67 Dodge	46	100	Engine
21	20	0	Frank Warren	Dr Don Tarr '66 Chevrolet	43	100	Crash
22	7	49	G C Spencer	Spencer '67 Plymouth	41	100	Oil Press
23	15	76	Roy Tyner	Don Culpepper '66 Ford	41	100	Crash
24	18	44	Don Wingier	'67 Chevrolet	24	100	Trans
25	13	06	Neil Castles	Castles '67 Plymouth	17	100	Trans

Time of Race: 1 hour, 32 minutes, 24 seconds
Average Speed: 64.935 mph
Pole Winner: David Pearson - 73.800 mph
Lap Leaders: David Pearson 1-20, Richard Petty 21-200.
Cautions: 3 for 19 laps   Margin of Victory: Attendance: 8,000

Pearson was running second when he ran out of gas with 10 laps to go. The extra pit stop dropped him four laps off the pace.

A crowd of 8,000 was on hand to watch the third event of the annual NASCAR Northern tour.

Race No. 29

LeeRoy Breaks Jinx; Wins Northern 300 at Trenton

TRENTON, NJ (July 14) -- LeeRoy Yarbrough of Jacksonville, FL led all but 15 laps and won the Northern 300 at the Trenton Speedway. After finishing second in three superspeedway events in the 1968

Grand National Race No. 29
300 Laps at Trenton Speedway
Trenton, NJ
"Northern 300"
300 Miles on 1-Mile Paved Track
July 14, 1968

Fin	St	No.	Driver	Team / Car	Laps	Money	Status
1	1	98	LeeRoy Yarbrough	Junior Johnson '68 Ford	300	$2,900	Running
2	3	17	David Pearson	Holman-Moody '68 Ford	299	1,475	Running
3	8	2	Bobby Allison	J D Bracken '66 Chevrolet	299	1,025	Running
4	9	6	Charlie Glotzbach	Cotton Owens '68 Dodge	297	675	Running
5	7	5	Pete Hamilton	Rocky Hinton '68 Ford	294	625	Running
6	11	48	James Hylton	Hylton Eng '67 Dodge	289	600	Running
7	22	4	John Sears	L G DeWitt '67 Ford	287	575	Running
8	12	49	G C Spencer	Spencer '67 Plymouth	287	500	Running
9	13	64	Elmo Langley	Langley-Woodfield '66 Ford	281	475	Running
10	19	20	Clyde Lynn	Lynn '66 Ford	278	450	Running
11	17	25	Jabe Thomas	Don Robertson '67 Ford	278	425	Running
12	30	34	Wendell Scott	Scott '67 Ford	274	400	Running
13	16	18	Dick Johnson	Johnson '67 Ford	272	390	Running
14	18	45	Bill Seifert	Seifert '68 Ford	261	380	Running
15	15	10	Bill Champion	Champion '66 Ford	254	370	Engine
16	4	71	Bobby Isaac	K&K Insurance '67 Dodge	250	385	Engine
17	14	44	Blaine Kauffman	'67 Chevrolet	249	350	Oil Leak
18	2	22	Darel Dieringer	Mario Rossi '68 Dodge	231	415	Engine
19	28	70	J D McDuffie	McDuffie '67 Buick	195	330	Axle
20	6	3	Buddy Baker	Ray Fox '68 Dodge	191	320	Engine
21	23	87	Buck Baker	Baker '68 Chevrolet	168	310	Engine
22	5	43	Richard Petty	Petty Enterprises '68 Plym	162	625	Engine
23	20	28	Earl Brooks	Brooks '66 Ford	119	300	Crash
24	29	01	Paul Dean Holt	Dennis Holt '67 Ford	119	300	Clutch
25	34	51	Stan Meserve	Margo Hamm '67 Dodge	111	275	Rear End
26	21	06	Neil Castles	Castles '67 Plymouth	87	375	Ignition
27	24	0	Dr Don Tarr	Tarr '66 Chevrolet	74	275	Crash
28	36	11	Roy Hallquist	'67 Chevrolet	51	250	Vibration
29	10	90	Sonny Hutchins	Junie Donlavey '67 Ford	44	275	Axle
30	35	76	Roy Tyner	Don Culpepper '66 Ford	18	250	Engine
31	26	75	Gene Black	Black '66 Ford	3	250	Crash
32	25	8	Ed Negre	Negre '67 Ford	3	250	Crash
33	27	23	Harold Fagan	Don Robertson '66 Ford	3	250	Crash
34	32	69	David Mote	'66 Chevrolet	2	225	Sway bar
35	31	09	Bill Vanderhoff	Roy Tyner '66 Chevrolet	0	225	Rear End
36	33	07	George Davis	Davis '66 Chevrolet	0	225	Trans

Time of Race: 3 hours, 22 minutes, 4 seconds
Average Speed: 89.079 mph
Pole Winner: LeeRoy Yarbrough - 103.717 mph
Lap Leaders: LeeRoy Yarbrough 1, David Pearson 2, Yarbrough 3-38, Bobby Isaac 39, Richard Petty 40, Yarbrough 41-95, Petty 96, Yarbrough 97-133, Petty 134, Isaac 135, Petty 136-144, Yarbrough 145-300.
Cautions: 5 for 28 laps   Margin of Victory: 1-lap plus   Attendance: 16,800

Grand National season, Yarbrough's Junior Johnson Ford finally broke a winless spell that had lasted over a year.

Yarbrough won for the first time since February 24, 1967 when he won a 100-mile qualifying race at Daytona. The victory was Johnson's first as a car owner since April 16, 1967 when Darel Dieringer won at North Wilkesboro.

Yarbrough took the lead for good on lap 145 and stretched his advantage to over a lap. David Pearson finished second and Bobby Allison was third. Charlie Glotzbach came in fourth and Pete Hamilton was fifth.

Point leader Bobby Isaac was running second when the engine blew in his Dodge with 50 laps to go. The Catawba, NC veteran had his point lead sliced to just 20 points over Pearson.

A crowd of 16,800 watched Yarbrough's fifth career win come at an average speed of 89.079 mph.

Five caution flags for a total of 28 laps interrupted the action. The most serious incident occurred in the third lap when Gene Black spun and was hit broadside by Ed Negre. Harold "Frog" Fagan was also involved.

Black was taken to the hospital and later released.

Darel Dieringer, who qualified second, fell out on lap 231 when his engine blew. Richard Petty suffered a similar fate on lap 162.

Race No. 30

Calm Pearson Prevails in Steamy Volunteer 500

BRISTOL, TN (July 21) -- David Pearson played it cool in 95 degree heat and let a quartet of early challen-

Jabe Thomas crashes at Bristol

Grand National Race No. 30
500 Laps at Bristol Int'l Speedway
Bristol, TN
"Volunteer 500"
250 Miles on Half-mile Paved Track
July 21, 1968

Fin	St	No.	Driver	Team / Car	Laps	Money	Status
1	6	17	David Pearson	Holman-Moody '68 Ford	500	$5,175	Running
2	4	21	Cale Yarborough	Wood Brothers '68 Mercury	499	2,650	Running
3	3	29	Swede Savage	Bondy Long '68 Ford	498	1,700	Running
4	9	71	Bobby Isaac	K&K Insurance '67 Dodge	497	900	Running
5	18	39	Friday Hassler	Red Sharp '66 Chevrolet	488	800	Running
6	10	3	Buddy Baker	Ray Fox '68 Dodge	481	700	Engine
7	24	06	Neil Castles	Castles '67 Plymouth	467	650	Running
8	12	16	Tiny Lund	Bud Moore '68 Mercury	465	625	Engine
9	32	45	Bill Seifert	Seifert '68 Ford	464	600	Running
10	29	70	J D McDuffie	McDuffie '67 Buick	463	525	Running
11	20	64	Elmo Langley	Langley-Woodfield '66 Ford	460	540	Running
12	21	20	Clyde Lynn	Lynn '66 Ford	455	515	Running
13	33	46	Larry Manning	Tom Hunter '66 Chevrolet	437	460	Running
14	27	9	Roy Tyner	Tyner '67 Pontiac	421	445	Running
15	15	4	John Sears	L G DeWitt '67 Ford	407	425	Rear End
16	34	57	Ervin Pruitt	Pruitt '67 Dodge	403	415	Running
17	23	25	Jabe Thomas	Don Robertson '67 Ford	387	420	Crash
18	2	6	Charlie Glotzbach	Cotton Owens '68 Dodge	385	425	Engine
19	31	34	Wendell Scott	Scott '66 Ford	367	340	Wheel
20	28	93	Walson Gardner	Gardner '67 Ford	362	340	Engine
21	13	5	Pete Hamilton	Rocky Hinton '68 Ford	329	330	Engine
22	26	99	Eddie Yarboro	'66 Plymouth	298	320	Fan belt
23	7	99	Paul Goldsmith	Nichels Eng '68 Dodge	290	305	Rear End
24	8	43	Richard Petty	Petty Enterprises '68 Plym	236	800	Fan belt
25	16	2	Bobby Allison	J D Bracken '66 Chevrolet	212	295	Battery
26	11	22	Darel Dieringer	Mario Rossi '68 Plymouth	206	285	Lug bolt
27	22	28	Earl Brooks	Brooks '66 Ford	194	300	Oil pan
28	30	18	Dick Johnson	Johnson '67 Ford	187	265	Quit
29	19	08	Bob Burcham	E C Reid '66 Chevrolet	176	315	Engine
30	35	01	Paul Dean Holt	Dennis Holt '67 Ford	143	250	Oil Leak
31	17	49	G C Spencer	Spencer '67 Plymouth	135	250	Engine
32	1	98	LeeRoy Yarbrough	Junior Johnson '68 Ford	120	750	Engine
33	25	51	Stan Meserve	Margo Hamm '67 Dodge	81	250	Rear End
34	5	27	Donnie Allison	Banjo Matthews '68 Ford	63	275	Rear End
35	14	48	James Hylton	Hylton Eng '67 Dodge	35	250	Engine
36	36	03	Richard Brickhouse	Dub Clewis '67 Plymouth	8	250	Engine

Time of Race: 3 hours, 16 minutes, 34 seconds
Average Speed: 76.310 mph
Pole Winner: LeeRoy Yarbrough - 87.421 mph
Lap Leaders: Charlie Glotzbach 1-74, Pete Hamilton 75-85, David Pearson 86-113, Hamilton 114-116, Paul Goldsmith 117-182, Cale Yarborough 183, Goldsmith 184-271, Pearson 272-500.
Cautions: 13 for 92 laps   Margin of Victory 1 1/2 laps   Attendance: 20,000

gers burn themselves out in the Volunteer 500 at Bristol International Speedway.

Pearson started sixth in the 36 car field and rode patiently as LeeRoy Yarbrough, Charlie Glotzbach, Cale Yarborough and Paul Goldsmith set the early pace. As track temperatures soared to 140 degrees, most of the cars experienced trouble getting through the turns.

Pearson took the lead from Goldsmith in the 272nd lap and led the rest of the way. Yarborough finished second, a lap and a half back. Rookie Swede Savage was third, Bobby Isaac fourth and Friday Hassler fifth.

Glotzbach, in the Cotton Owens Dodge, and Yarbrough's Junior Johnson Ford broke away from the

David Pearson in Volunteer 500 victory lane

Race No. 31

Petty Holds Off 'Little Bud' In Maryville Thriller

MARYVILLE, TN (July 25) -- Richard Petty avoided an early pile-up and held off a late surge by Bud Moore to win the Smoky 200 at Smoky Mountain Raceway. It was the 10th win of the season for the lanky Petty.

Petty sneaked through a 39th lap crash triggered when Friday Hassler blew an engine. Leader Bobby Isaac slipped in the oil and slugged the retaining wall. Pete Hamilton crashed in the same incident. David Pearson and Moore spun around, but got back into the race.

Moore, taking his first ride since joining the Bondy Long team, dropped two laps off the pace, but came charging back. At the end of the 200 lapper, Moore's gold and white Ford was perched on Petty's rear bumper which had the crowd of 6,000 on its collective feet.

Pearson finished third and took a two-point lead over Isaac in the Grand National point standings. Buddy Baker finished fourth and James Hylton was fifth.

Sam McQuagg, who took over the A.J. King Dodge

pack early in a stirring two car duel. Yarbrough departed on lap 120 with engine failure, and Glotzbach pulled behind the wall with the same problem on lap 385. Goldsmith led twice for 154 laps but withdrew his Dodge on lap 290 with rear gearing failure.

Yarborough chased the leaders in the early stages and led for a single lap, but he had handling problems in the final 200 laps and could not challenge Pearson.

"After the track got hot and slick," said Pearson, "I could handle better than the others. You don't win races like this by trying to get away from the field in the first 100 laps."

Savage, driving the Bondy Long Ford, spun out once and did considerable "dirt tracking" en route to third place. Within a week, crew chief Fred Lorenzen resigned from the Long operation. Official reason from Ford was that Lorenzen was suffering from "nervous tension".

The caution flag was out a total of 13 times for 92 laps. Pearson averaged 76.310 mph before 20,000 spectators.

Pearson was able to inch within 16 points of standings leader Bobby Isaac.

Linda Vaughn and Bud Moore talk before a race. Moore finsihed a close 2nd to Richard Petty at Maryville

ride when Moore switched teams, wound up 11th after crashing in the final laps.

Bobby Allison started his Chevrolet ninth, but was never a factor. He pulled out of the race near the half-way point with no oil pressure.

The caution flag was out for a total of 39 laps, reducing Petty's winning speed to 71.513 mph.

Grand National Race No. 31
200 Laps at Smoky Mountain Raceway
Maryville, TN
"Smoky 200"
100 Miles on Half-mile Paved Track
July 25, 1968

Fin	St	No.	Driver	Team / Car	Laps	Money	Status
1	2	43	Richard Petty	Petty Enterprises '68 Plym	200	$1,200	Running
2	4	29	Bud Moore	Bondy Long '68 Ford	200	600	Running
3	3	17	David Pearson	Holman-Moody '68 Ford	199	400	Running
4	6	3	Buddy Baker	Ray Fox '68 Dodge	199	300	Running
5	8	48	James Hylton	Hylton Eng '67 Dodge	197	275	Running
6	10	64	Elmo Langley	Langley-Woodfield'66 Ford	192	240	Running
7	12	49	G C Spencer	Spencer '66 Plymouth	188	200	Running
8	13	28	Earl Brooks	Brooks '66 Ford	186	175	Running
9	23	20	Clyde Lynn	Lynn '66 Ford	184	155	Running
10	16	70	J D McDuffie	McDuffie '67 Buick	184	145	Running
11	11	1	Sam McQuagg	A J King '68 Dodge	173	135	Crash
12	19	01	Paul Dean Holt	Dennis Holt '67 Ford	160	120	Running
13	21	4	John Sears	L G DeWitt '67 Ford	158	110	Running
14	14	06	Neil Castles	Castles '67 Plymouth	134	100	A Frame
15	25	76	Ben Arnold	Don Culpepper '66 Ford	129	100	Oil Press
16	20	45	Bill Seifert	Seifert '68 Ford	112	100	Quit
17	9	2	Bobby Allison	J D Bracken '66 Chevrolet	102	100	Oil Press
18	24	9	Roy Tyner	Tyner '67 Pontiac	70	100	Brakes
19	18	19	Henley Gray	Gray '67 Ford	55	100	Quit
20	22	25	Jabe Thomas	Don Robertson '67 Ford	50	100	Oil Leak
21	15	51	Stan Meserve	Margo Hamm '67 Dodge	47	100	Rear End
22	1	71	Bobby Isaac	K&K Insurance '67 Dodge	42	100	Crash
23	7	5	Pete Hamilton	Rocky Hinton '68 Ford	40	100	Crash
24	5	39	Friday Hassler	Red Sharp '66 Chevrolet	38	100	Engine
25	17	18	Dick Johnson	Johnson '67 Ford	37	100	Exhaust
26	26	34	Wendell Scott	Scott '66 Ford	7	100	Engine

Time of Race: 1 hour, 23 minutes, 54 seconds
Average Speed: 71.513 mph
Pole Winner: Bobby Isaac - 86.538 mph
Lap Leaders: Bobby Isaac 1-39, Richard Petty 40-200.
Cautions: ___ for 39 laps   Margin of Victory: 1 car length   Attendance: 6,000

Race No. 32

Pearson Wins Rain-Shortened Nashville 400

NASHVILLE, TN (July 27) -- David Pearson took the lead with 68 laps to go and was three laps in front of the field when a heavy downpour ended the Nash-

ville 400 after 301 laps. It was the 10th win of the season for the Spartanburg Ford driver.

Petty started on the pole and led the first 131 laps. He made his first pit stop during a caution flag, leaving Person with the lead for two laps. Pearson pitted and lost a lap while crew chief Dick Hutcherson adjusted the wedge in the car.

Petty led for 100 laps as Pearson worked his way back into the lead lap. At the wheel of a better handling car, Pearson zoomed into first place on lap 234 and was never headed.

Petty was foiled by carburetor troubles and fell three laps off the pace. He still managed to finish second. Third place went to Bobby Allison. Bobby Isaac was fourth and Charlie Glotzbach finished fifth in an independent Dodge owned by Ervin Pruitt.

Once the rain hit, officials had no choice but to call the race off.

Pearson gained three points over Isaac in the point race, upping his lead to five points.

The victory was Pearson's 40th of his career. He averaged 72.980 mph before a crowd of 15,221.

Grand National Race No. 32
400 Laps at Fairgrounds Speedway
Nashville, TN
"Nashville 400"
200 Miles on Half-mile Paved Track
July 27, 1968

Fin	St	No.	Driver	Team / Car	Laps	Money	Status
1	3	17	David Pearson	Holman-Moody '68 Ford	301	$2,950	Running
2	1	43	Richard Petty	Petty Enterprises '68 Plym	298	1,700	Running
3	2	2	Bobby Allison	J D Bracken '66 Chevrolet	295	900	Running
4	4	71	Bobby Isaac	K&K Insurance '67 Dodge	294	500	Running
5	21	57	Charlie Glotzbach	Ervin Pruitt '67 Dodge	293	475	Running
6	5	64	Elmo Langley	Langley-Woodfield '66 Ford	285	450	Running
7	15	20	Clyde Lynn	Lynn '66 Ford	276	425	Running
8	16	76	Roy Tyner	Don Culpepper '66 Ford	266	375	Running
9	12	45	Bill Seifert	Seifert '68 Ford	247	325	Running
10	14	04	Jack Marlin	'66 Chevrolet	237	300	Running
11	10	70	J D McDuffie	McDuffie '67 Buick	226	270	Engine
12	6	48	James Hylton	Hylton Eng '67 Dodge	124	240	Crash
13	8	06	Neil Castles	Castles '67 Plymouth	123	220	Engine
14	20	51	Stan Meserve	Margo Hamm '67 Dodge	113	200	Engine
15	22	01	Paul Dean Holt	Dennis Holt '67 Ford	89	170	Rear End
16	9	4	John Sears	L G DeWitt '67 Ford	37	150	Ball Jt
17	7	49	G C Spencer	Spencer '67 Plymouth	27	130	Engine
18	17	25	Jabe Thomas	Don Robertson '67 Ford	23	120	Steering
19	13	28	Earl Brooks	Brooks '66 Ford	19	100	Quit
20	18	38	Wayne Smith	Smith '68 Chevrolet	12	100	Crash
21	19	9	Bill Vanderhoff	Roy Tyner '67 Pontiac	9	100	Rear End
22	11	34	Wendell Scott	Scott '66 Ford	9	100	Engine

Time of Race: 2 hours, 3 minutes, 44 seconds
Average Speed: 72.980 mph
Pole Winner: 85.066 mph
Lap Leaders: Richard Petty 1-131, David Pearson 132-133, Petty 134-233, Pearson 234-301.
Cautions: 6 for 42 laps   Margin of Victory: 3-laps plus   Attendance: 15,221
*Race shortened to 301 laps due to rain

Race No. 33

Luck Changes; LeeRoy Wins Atlanta's Dixie 500

HAMPTON, GA (Aug. 4) -- LeeRoy Yarbrough lost the Daytona 500 and the Atlanta 500 by little quirks of fate that can be traced to "bad luck". The Jacksonville, FL veteran's luck took a turn for the better as he drove Junior Johnson's Mercury to victory in the Dixie 500 at Atlanta International Raceway.

The 29 year-old Yarbrough took the lead from David Pearson with 40 laps to go and beat runner-up Bobby Isaac by 10 seconds to post his second career superspeedway triumph. "This race ran exactly as we planned," said the winner. "We figured last Wednesday that we could feel out the competition in the early stages and cool it until it came time to run for the checkered flag."

Car owner Johnson, whose legend grew as a driver who would 'charge' from flag to flag, told members of the media that he decided to change his strategy. "If you always go for broke," drawled Johnson, "sure enough, you go broke."

Third place went to Donnie Allison. Pearson finished fourth and Richard Petty was fifth.

Isaac took the point lead by a single point over Pearson in what has become the tightest battle for the Grand National championship in the history of NASCAR.

The lead changed hands 29 times among nine drivers. Charlie Glotzbach took the Cotton Owens Dodge to the front for 38 laps and was holding a 9-second lead when a tire blew on his car. The flapping rubber damaged the suspension components and the Georgetown, IN driver was out of the race by lap 155.

Cale Yarborough led on three occasions for 66 laps, but his Wood Brothers Mercury slammed into the wall on lap 265 after a tire let go. Pole winner Buddy Baker went out on lap 25 when the lug bolts stripped on his Ray Fox Dodge.

Yarbrough's sixth career win came at an average speed of 127.068 mph.

Several independent drivers were upset at Raceway management when they received only $50 in "deal

money", half what they normally get. Privateer Roy Tyner, who turns all of his appearance money over to the Holy Angels Nursery in Belmont, NC, sent a written message to the Nursery along with his $50. "Pray for the Atlanta International Raceway. They need it," said the note.

Grand National Race No. 33
334 Laps at Atlanta Int'l Raceway
Hampton, GA
"Dixie 500"
500 Miles on 1.5-mile Paved Track
August 4, 1968

Fin	St	No.	Driver	Team / Car	Laps	Money	Status
1	5	98	LeeRoy Yarbrough	Junior Johnson ;68 Ford	334	$17,260	Running
2	13	71	Bobby Isaac	K&K Insurance '68 Dodge	334	8,440	Running
3	9	27	Donnie Allison	Banjo Matthews '68 Ford	334	5,925	Running
4	4	17	David Pearson	Holman-Moody '68 Ford	334	3,005	Running
5	10	43	Richard Petty	Petty Enterprises '68 Plym	333	2,535	Running
6	17	48	James Hylton	Hylton Eng '68 Dodge	328	1,625	Running
7	11	29	Bud Moore	Bondy Long '68 Ford	328	1,350	Running
8	18	4	John Sears	L G DeWitt '67 Ford	327	1,275	Running
9	21	39	Friday Hassler	Red Sharp '66 Chevrolet	318	1,175	Running
10	33	49	G C Spencer	Spencer '67 Plymouth	316	1,125	Running
11	27	45	Bill Seifert	Seifert '68 Ford	310	1,125	Running
12	23	96	Bob Moore	Roy Buckner '66 Ford	306	1,025	Running
13	35	57	Roy Tyner	Ervin Pruitt '67 Dodge	303	950	Running
14	39	0	Dr Don Tarr	Tarr '66 Chevrolet	301	950	Running
15	34	32	Willie Crane	'68 Ford	300	875	Running
16	25	20	Clyde Lynn	Lynn '66 Ford	297	850	Running
17	6	16	Tiny Lund	Bud Moore '68 Mercury	295	825	Engine
18	2	21	Cale Yarborough	Wood Brothers '68 Mercury	265	1,230	Crash
19	22	10	Bill Champion	Champion '66 Ford	251	775	D Shaft
20	30	38	Wayne Smith	Smith '68 Chevrolet	217	750	Oil Line
21	12	99	Paul Goldsmith	Nichels Eng '68 Dodge	200	735	Engine
22	14	22	Darel Dieringer	Mario Rossi '68 Dodge	189	700	Engine
23	28	18	Earl Brooks	Dick Johnson '67 Ford	189	715	Engine
24	26	2	Bobby Allison	J D Bracken '66 Chevrolet	167	755	Rear End
25	3	6	Charlie Glotzbach	Cotton Owens '68 Dodge	152	660	Engine
26	7	1	Sam McQuagg	A J King '68 Dodge	122	660	Engine
27	32	19	Wendell Scott	Henley Gray '66 Ford	115	650	Heating
28	20	5	Pete Hamilton	Rocky Hinton '68 Ford	110	640	Rear End
29	38	51	Stan Meserve	Margo Hamm '67 Dodge	103	655	Ignition
30	19	64	Elmo Langley	Langley-Woodfield '66 Ford	90	645	Engine
31	24	61	Hoss Ellington	Ellington '67 Mercury	80	610	Suspen
32	37	03	Richard Brickhouse	Dub Clewis '67 Plymouth	77	650	Engine
33	15	80	E J Trivette	E C Reid '66 Chevrolet	66	590	Trans
34	16	97	Red Farmer	Farmer '67 Ford	56	690	Heating
35	31	52	Jabe Thomas	Elmer Buxton '67 Ford	53	580	Engine
36	1	3	Buddy Baker	Ray Fox '68 Dodge	25	725	Lug bolt
37	36	7	Bobby Johns	Shorty Johns '66 Chevrolet	23	645	Engine
38	8	56	Jim Hurtubise	Lyle Stelter '68 Mercury	21	565	Mtr mount
39	29	06	Neil Castles	Castles '67 Plymouth	5	585	Engine
40	40	70	J D McDuffie	McDuffie '67 Buick	4	550	Vibration

Time of Race: 3 hours, 56 minutes, 34 seconds
Average Speed: 127.068 mph
Pole Winner: Buddy Baker - 153.361 mph
Lap Leaders: Cale Yarborough 1-25, Paul Goldsmith 26, James Hylton 27-31, LeeRoy Yarbrough 32-51, Red Farmer 52, Richard Petty 53-56, Yarbrough 57-59, David Pearson 60, Yarbrough 61-70, Charlie Glotzbach 71-91, Yarborough 92-112, Pearson 113-131, Glotzbach 132-141, Pearson 142-144, Glotzbach 145-151, Pearson 152-159, Yarbrough 160-192, Bobby Isaac 193, Petty 194, Isaac 195, Pearson 196-217, Yarbrough 218-272, Petty 273, Pearson 274-276, Yarbrough 277-283, Isaac 284, Petty 285, Pearson 286-294, Yarbrough 295-334.
Cautions: 11 for 67 laps   Margin of Victory: 10 seconds   Attendance: 51,300

LeeRoy Yarbrough #98 broke his big track jinx with Dixie 500 victory

Race No. 34

Pearson Regains Point Lead With Close Columbia Win

COLUMBIA, SC (Aug. 8) -- David Pearson passed Bobby Isaac in the 126th lap and held off a late bid by Charlie Glotzbach to win the Sandlapper 200 at Columbia Speedway. It was the 11th win of the season for Pearson, and he moved back into the lead in the race for the Grand National championship.

Glotzbach emerged as a solid contender in the late stages and pulled along side of Pearson in the final lap. His bid fell short by a half-car length. Third place went to LeeRoy Yarbrough. Elmo Langley was fourth and Neil Castles fifth.

Bobby Isaac led for 53 laps and was holding down third place when his Dodge blew a tire on lap 184, sending him into the wall. He was credited with 11th place in the field of 24.

Buddy Baker started on the pole and led the first two laps. Little Bud Moore of Charleston, SC passed Baker in the third lap and led through lap 29. Baker got the lead back and led until the 73rd lap when Isaac grabbed the lead.

The spirited runs by Baker and Moore were interrupted by tire failures, which sent both cars into the wall. Moore's Bondy Long Ford crashed in the 61st lap, and Baker wrecked on lap 138.

John Sears survived a frightening crash in the 178th lap. The big Ellerbe, NC driver broke loose in the third turn, cleared the guard rail and tumbled end-over-end. Sears was shaken but unhurt.

Other contenders Richard Petty (hole in oil pan) and Bobby Allison (distributor) failed to go the distance on the half-mile dirt track.

Pearson's 41st career win came at an average speed of 67.039 mph.

Grand National Race No. 34
200 Laps at Columbia Speedway
Columbia, SC
"Sandlapper 200"
100 Miles on Half-mile Dirt Track
August 8, 1968

Fin	St	No.	Driver	Team / Car	Laps	Money	Status
1	10	17	David Pearson	Holman-Moody '68 Ford	200	$1,000	Running
2	7	6	Charlie Glotzbach	Cotton Owens '68 Dodge	200	600	Running
3	6	56	LeeRoy Yarbrough	Lyle Stelter '67 Ford	199	400	Running
4	14	64	Elmo Langley	Langley-Woodfield '66 Ford	198	300	Running
5	5	06	Neil Castles	Castles '67 Plymouth	197	275	Running
6	16	76	Tiny Lund	Don Culpepper '66 Ford	194	240	Running
7	20	20	Clyde Lynn	Lynn '66 Ford	192	200	Running
8	21	34	Wendell Scott	Scott '66 Ford	188	175	Running
9	13	25	Jabe Thomas	Don Robertson '67 Ford	187	150	Running
10	18	93	Walson Gardner	Gardner '67 Ford	187	140	Running
11	4	71	Bobby Isaac	K&K Insurance '67 Dodge	186	130	Engine
12	15	01	Paul Dean Holt	Dennis Holt '67 Ford	184	120	Running
13	9	4	John Sears	L G DeWitt '67 Ford	171	110	Crash
14	22	95	Henley Gray	Gray '66 Ford	165	100	Running
15	11	70	J D McDuffie	McDuffie '67 Buick	159	100	H Gasket
16	1	3	Buddy Baker	Ray Fox '68 Dodge	138	100	Crash
17	8	2	Bobby Allison	J D Bracken '66 Chevrolet	125	100	Distrib
18	19	45	Bill Seifert	Seifert '68 Ford	99	100	Vibration
19	17	8	Ed Negre	Negre '67 Ford	83	100	Rock shaf
20	23	28	Earl Brooks	Brooks '66 Ford	76	100	Heating
21	2	43	Richard Petty	Petty Enterprises '68 Plym	72	300	Oil Pan
22	12	9	Roy Tyner	Tyner '67 Pontiac	70	100	Heating
23	24	51	Stan Meserve	Margo Hamm '67 Dodge	68	---	Heating
24	3	29	Bud Moore	Bondy Long '68 Ford	61	---	Crash

Time of Race: 1 hour, 29 minutes, 30 seconds
Average Speed: 67.039 mph
Pole Winner: Buddy Baker - 74.196 mph
Lap Leaders: Buddy Baker 1-2, Bud Moore 3-29, Baker 30-72, Bobby Isaac 73-125, David Pearson 126-200.
Cautions: Margin of Victory: Half car length   Attendance: 7,000

Race No. 35

Pearson Beats Petty in Myers Brothers Memorial

WINSTON-SALEM, NC (Aug. 10) -- David Pearson took the lead from Richard Petty in the 140th lap and led the rest of the way to win the Myers Brothers Memorial event at Bowman Gray Stadium.

Grand National Race No. 35
250 Laps at Bowman Gray Stadium
Winston-Salem, NC
"Myers Brothers Memorial"
62.5 Miles on Quarter-mile Paved Track
August 10, 1968

Fin	St	No.	Driver	Team / Car	Laps	Money	Status
1	2	17	David Pearson	Holman-Moody '68 Ford	250	$1,000	Running
2	1	43	Richard Petty	Petty Enterprises '68 Plym	250	850	Running
3	3	71	Bobby Isaac	K&K Insurance '67 Dodge	246	400	Running
4	4	48	James Hylton	Hylton Eng '68 Dodge	244	300	Running
5	7	64	Elmo Langley	Langley-Woodfield '66 Ford	244	275	Running
6	9	20	Clyde Lynn	Lynn '66 Ford	240	240	Running
7	6	4	John Sears	L G DeWitt '66 Ford	239	200	Running
8	11	34	Wendell Scott	Scott '66 Ford	232	175	Running
9	16	25	Jabe Thomas	Don Robertson '67 Ford	230	150	Running
10	10	45	Bill Seifert	Seifert '68 Ford	229	140	Running
11	14	9	Roy Tyner	Tyner '67 Pontiac	209	130	Running
12	17	8	Ed Negre	Negre '67 Ford	206	120	Running
13	20	38	Wayne Smith	Smith '68 Chevrolet	159	110	Rear End
14	5	2	Bobby Allison	J D Bracken '66 Chevrolet	131	100	Engine
15	18	06	Neil Castles	Castles '67 Plymouth	113	100	Trans
16	8	70	J D McDuffie	McDuffie '67 Buick	62	100	Engine
17	12	01	Paul Dean Holt	Dennis Holt '67 Ford	37	100	Quit
18	19	76	Ben Arnold	Don Culpepper '66 Ford	17	100	Trans
19	15	28	Earl Brooks	Brooks '66 Ford	13	100	Heating
20	13	95	Henley Gray	Gray '66 Ford	12	100	Engine

Time of Race: 1 hour, 23 minutes, 27 seconds
Average Speed: 42.940 mph
Pole Winner: Richard Petty - 53.828 mph
Lap Leaders: Richard Petty 1-139, David Pearson 140-250.
Cautions: 5 for 34 laps   Margin of Victory: 3 seconds   Attendance: 12,000

Petty had started on the pole for the 75th time in his career and led the first 139 laps. He was holding a five car length led over Pearson when Bobby Allison, running directly in front of Petty's Plymouth, blew an engine. Allison hit the wall and Petty grazed the wall, opening the door for Pearson.

Pearson edged Petty by 3.0-seconds at the finish of the 250 lapper on the quarter-mile oval. Bobby Isaac finished third and fell nine points behind Pearson in the NASCAR point standings. James Hylton came in fourth and Elmo Langley was fifth.

The caution was out five times for a total of 34 laps, and Pearson averaged a non-record 42.940 mph. It was the 12th win of the season for the Ford driver.

Race No. 36

11 Races, 11 Faces -- Pearson Wins Western NC 500

WEAVERVILLE, NC (Aug.18) -- David Pearson enjoyed a Sunday drive and easily captured the 11th annual Western North Carolina 500 at Asheville-Weaverville Speedway for his 13th win of the year. Pearson became the 11th different winner in the 11 runnings of this late summer classic at the famous half-mile paved oval.

Bobby Isaac finished second and fell 11 points behind Pearson in the Grand National point standings. Neil Castles came from 20th starting spot to finish third and Roy Tyner was fourth. Fifth place went to Bill Seifert.

Isaac was fined by NASCAR officials for swerving toward pit steward Dick Wall. The incident occurred in the 39th lap when Pearson and Isaac pitted under caution. After getting fresh rubber, Pearson and Isaac pulled out of their respective pit areas together and were running nose-to-tail down pit lane. The pace car was approaching on the homestretch and Wall decided Pearson could beat the pace car out to remain on the lead lap. Wall waved Pearson on. But he flagged Isaac down, holding him up a lap.

Isaac pitted a second time during the caution flag and swerved his Dodge at Wall when exiting pit road. NASCAR Vice President Jim Foster said Isaac's actions "definitely were deliberate".

Isaac was still steaming after the race. "I wasn't trying to run him over," said Isaac. "I was just trying to wake him up. I had that pace car beat (several non-partisan observers agreed), but I get penalized a lap. It's a pretty fine line when a man figures down to inches in a 250 mile race."

NASCAR ranking officials Bill Gazaway and Lin Kuchler survived a close call when Earl Brooks' Ford blew a tire and tore down part of the pit wall on lap 145. Gazaway was struck by flying chunks of concrete, but was not seriously injured. Kuchler scrambled to safety.

Pearson led all but 44 of the 500 laps and won at an average speed of 73.686 mph.

Grand National Race No. 36
500 Laps at Asheville-Weaverville Speedway
Weaverville, NC
"Western North Carolina 500"
250 Miles on Half-mile Paved Track
August 18, 1968

Fin	St	No.	Driver	Team / Car	Laps	Money	Status
1	2	17	David Pearson	Holman-Moody '68 Ford	500	$2,150	Running
2	5	71	Bobby Isaac	K&K Insurance '67 Dodge	497	1,270	Running
3	20	06	Neil Castles	Castles '67 Plymouth	472	1,050	Running
4	18	9	Roy Tyner	Tyner '67 Pontiac	467	850	Running
5	22	45	Bill Seifert	Seifert '68 Ford	457	750	Running
6	26	25	Jabe Thomas	Don Robertson '67 Ford	446	650	Running
7	15	57	Ervin Pruitt	Pruitt '67 Dodge	446	600	Running
8	24	93	Walson Gardner	Gardner '67 Ford	438	550	Running
9	23	34	Wendell Scott	Scott '66 Ford	436	500	Running
10	6	1	Pete Hamilton	A J King '68 Dodge	418	420	Oil Pan
11	28	01	Paul Dean Holt	Dennis Holt '67 Ford	343	380	Heating
12	11	2	Bobby Allison	J D Bracken '66 Chevrolet	275	375	Trans
13	25	50	Eddie Yarboro	'66 Plymouth	271	325	Lug bolt
14	29	88	George England	Buck Baker '67 Olds	235	275	Rear End
15	21	8	Ed Negre	Negre '67 Ford	205	200	Crash
16	12	64	Elmo Langley	Langley-Woodfield '66 Ford	204	200	Engine
17	4	99	Paul Goldsmith	Nichels Eng '68 Dodge	198	225	Throttle
18	7	48	James Hylton	Hylton Eng '68 Dodge	198	200	Crash
19	10	08	Bob Burcham	E C Reid '66 Chevrolet	190	200	Engine
20	14	64	Earl Brooks	Brooks '66 Ford	136	200	Crash
21	16	20	Clyde Lynn	Lynn '66 Ford	132	200	Engine
22	1	22	Darel Dieringer	Mario Rossi '68 Plymouth	119	800	Engine
23	13	76	Tiny Lund	Don Culpepper '66 Ford	93	200	Vibration
24	17	51	Stan Meserve	Margo Hamm '67 Dodge	91	200	Heating
25	19	70	J D McDuffie	McDuffie '67 Buick	56	200	Engine
26	3	43	Richard Petty	Petty Enterprises '68 Plym	52	425	A Frame
27	27	38	Wayne Smith	Smith '68 Chevrolet	35	150	D Shaft
28	8	4	John Sears	L G DeWitt '67 Ford	33	150	Engine
29	9	49	G C Spencer	Spencer '67 Plymouth	14	150	Engine

Time of Race: 3 hours, 23 minutes, 34 seconds
Average Speed: 73.686 mph
Pole Winner: Darel Dieringer - 88.409 mph
Lap Leaders: Darel Dieringer 1-2, David Pearson 3-39, Paul Goldsmith 40-63, Pearson 64-128, Goldsmith 129-145, Pearson 146-147, Bobby Isaac 148, Pearson 149-500.
Cautions: 7 for 90 laps   Margin of Victory: 3-laps plus   Attendance: 10,500

Race No. 37

Petty's Plymouth Powerful at South Boston

S.BOSTON. VA (Aug 23) -- Richard Petty started on the pole and led all but two laps in winning the

100-mile Grand National event at South Boston Speedway. It was the 11th win of the season for Petty, but none have come on superspeedways.

Richard Petty won at South Boston, VA

Petty was never seriously challenged during the 267-lap contest on the .375-mile paved track. He made one pit stop, giving the lead briefly to Bobby Isaac.

David Pearson finished second to Petty. He was just 5.0-seconds behind at the finish, but never mustered a threat to take the lead. Isaac was third with Charlie Glotzbach and Buddy Baker filling the top five.

Local Modified star Ray Hendrick finished sixth in the Friedkin Enterprises Plymouth, a ride shared earlier in the year by Curtis Turner and Jerry Grant.

Bobby Allison qualified fifth in his J.D. Bracken

Grand National Race No. 37
267 Laps at South Boston Speedway
South Boston, VA
100 Miles on .375-Mile Paved Track
August 23, 1968

Fin	St	No.	Driver	Team / Car	Lap	Money	Status
1	1	43	Richard Petty	Petty Enterprises '68 Plym	267	$1,200	Running
2	3	17	David Pearson	Holman-Moody '68 Ford	267	600	Running
3	4	71	Bobby Isaac	K&K Insurance '67 Dodge	267	400	Running
4	6	6	Charlie Glotzbach	Cotton Owens '68 Dodge	265	300	Running
5	2	3	Buddy Baker	Ray Fox '68 Dodge	264	255	Running
6	8	15	Ray Hendrick	Friedkin Ent '68 Plymouth	263	240	Running
7	9	64	Elmo Langley	Langley-Woodfield '66 Ford	263	200	Running
8	7	4	John Sears	L G DeWitt '67 Ford	259	175	Running
9	11	20	Clyde Lynn	Lynn '66 Ford	253	150	Running
10	12	25	Jabe Thomas	Don Robertson '67 Ford	248	140	Running
11	16	51	Stan Meserve	Margo Hamm '67 Dodge	240	130	Running
12	10	70	J D McDuffie	McDuffie '67 Buick	219	120	Running
13	19	9	Roy Tyner	Tyner '67 Pontiac	132	110	Wtr Hose
14	15	34	Wendell Scott	Scott '66 Ford	113	100	Engine
15	18	06	Neil Castles	Castles '67 Plymouth	82	100	Axle
16	5	2	Bobby Allison	J D Bracken '66 Chevrolet	67	100	Rear End
17	13	45	Bill Seifert	Seifert '68 Ford	46	100	Engine
18	21	66	Larry Manning	'66 Chevrolet	36	100	Heating
19	17	01	Paul Dean Holt	Dennis holt '67 Ford	31	100	Trans
20	20	56	LeeRoy Yarbrough	Lyle Stelter '67 Mercury	22	100	Rear End
21	14	78	Earl Brooks	Brooks '67 Ford	17	100	Heating

Time of Race: 1 hour, 19 minutes, 8 seconds
Average Speed: 75.916 mph
Pole Winner: Richard Petty - 84.428 mph
Lap Leaders: Richard Petty 1-120, Bobby Isaac 121-122, Petty 123-267.
Cautions: Margin of Victory: 5 car lengths   Attendance: 7,000

Chevrolet. He ran in the top five until rear gearing problems put him out after 67 laps.

Pearson increased his narrow point lead to 12 points over Isaac.

Petty averaged a record 75.916 mph for his 86th career triumph.

Race No. 38

Pearson's 14th of Season Comes at Langley Field

HAMPTON, VA (Aug. 24) -- David Pearson led from start to finish and won the Crabber 250 at Langley Field Speedway. It was the 14th win of the season for the dark-haired Ford pilot.

Richard Petty finished a half lap behind in second place in the uneventful 100-miler. Bobby Isaac came in third, Bobby Allison was fourth and Ray Hendrick fifth.

Pearson gained two points on Isaac in the Grand National standings, increasing his lead to 14 points in the tight race for the championship.

Grand National Race No. 38
250 Laps at Langley Field Speedway
Hampton, VA
"Crabber 250"
100 Miles on .4-mile Paved Track
August 24, 1968

Fin	St	No.	Driver	Team / Car	Laps	Money	Status
1	1	17	David Pearson	Holman-Moody '68 Ford	250	$1,000	Running
2	3	43	Richard Petty	Petty Enterprises '68 Plym	250	800	Running
3	2	71	Bobby Isaac	K&K Insurance '67 Dodge	249	400	Running
4	9	2	Bobby Allison	J D Bracken '66 Chevrolet	247	300	Running
5	6	15	Ray Hendrick	Friedkin Ent '68 Plymouth	245	255	Running
6	5	4	John Sears	L G DeWitt '67 Ford	244	240	Running
7	8	64	Elmo Langley	Langley-Woodfield '66 Ford	244	200	Running
8	21	06	Neil Castles	Castles '67 Plymouth	241	175	Running
9	9	9	Roy Tyner	Tyner '67 Pontiac	240	150	Running
10	10	20	Clyde Lynn	Lynn '66 Ford	239	140	Running
11	11	70	J D McDuffie	McDuffie '67 Buick	239	130	Running
12	18	45	Bill Seifert	Seifert '67 Ford	232	120	Running
13	14	8	Ed Negre	Negre '67 Ford	231	110	Running
14	12	25	Jabe Thomas	Don Robertson '67 Ford	227	100	Running
15	24	34	Wendell Scott	Scott '67 Ford	224	100	Running
16	19	93	Walson Gardner	Gardner '67 Ford	214	100	Running
17	7	3	Buddy Baker	Ray Fox '68 Dodge	166	100	Quit
18	4	6	Charlie Glotzbach	Cotton Owens '68 Dodge	135	100	Heating
19	16	76	Earl Brooks	Don Culpepper '67 Ford	124	100	Quit
20	23	01	Paul Dean Holt	Dennis holt '67 Ford	119	100	Quit
21	22	51	Stan Meserve	Margo Hamm '67 Dodge	102	100	Engine
22	15	66	Larry Manning	'66 Chevrolet	101	100	Heating
23	20	56	LeeRoy Yarbrough	Lyle Stelter '67 Mercury	98	100	Clutch
24	13	10	Bill Champion	Champion '67 Ford	62	100	Clutch

Time of Race: 1 hour, 19 minutes, 23 seconds
Average Speed: 75.582 mph
Pole Winner: David Pearson 78.007 mph
Lap Leaders: David Pearson 1-250.
Cautions: None   Margin of Victory: Half-lap   Attendance: 7,600

A crowd of 7,600 watched the caution-free event. Only eight cars in the starting field of 24 fell out of the race, and three of those quit. Buddy Baker, driving the factory backed Ray Fox Dodge, went 166 laps before pulling out for no reason. Earl Brooks and Paul Dean Holt, a pair of independents, also quit. A minimum purse of $100 was paid to those drivers who finished 14th-24th.

Clyde Lynn announced he was quitting Grand National racing after the 1968 season

Clyde Lynn, third ranking driver in the point standings, announced that he would retire at the end of the season. Lynn said he was "tired of racing. I can't get any factory help and I haven't got a chance to win otherwise."

Pearson's 44th career win came at an average speed of 75.582 mph.

Race No. 39

Yarborough Nips Pearson in Close Southern 500 Finish

DARLINGTON, SC (Sept. 2) -- Cale Yarborough held a speedier David Pearson at bay on the tight and narrow Darlington Raceway and posted his first "home track" victory in the 19th Southern 500.

The $25,415 triumph was Yarborough's fourth superspeedway win of the season.

Passing was virtually impossible on the 1.375-mile ancient oval. Pearson followed Yarborough for several laps before making a stab at the lead on lap 320. Going into the one groove first turn, Pearson ducked under Yarborough's Mercury -- and the two cars fused

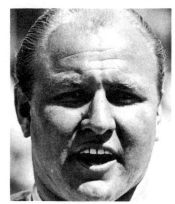

Cale Yarborough

together. Yarborough bounced off the steel guard rail and hit Pearson's Ford. Pearson looped his car onto the apron as the green flag racing conditions remained in effect.

Pearson lost a half lap, but resumed the chase.

Pearson was able to close the gap and was perched on Yarborough's bumper with six laps left. But Yarborough didn't leave any openings for his rival and crossed the finish line four car lengths ahead.

Grand National Race No. 39
364 Laps at Darlington Raceway
Darlington, SC
"Southern 500"
500 Miles on 1.375-mile Paved Track
September 2, 1968

Fin	St	No.	Driver	Team / Car	Laps	Money	Status
1	2	21	Cale Yarborough	Wood Brothers '68 Mercury	364	$25,415	Running
2	16	17	David Pearson	Holman-Moody '68 Ford	364	10,850	Running
3	7	3	Buddy Baker	Ray Fox '68 Dodge	362	6,200	Running
4	1	6	Charlie Glotzbach	Cotton Owens '68 Dodge	360	3,800	Running
5	8	99	Paul Goldsmith	Nichels Eng '68 Dodge	357	3,075	Running
6	13	14	Curtis Turner	Friedkin Ent '68 Plymouth	354	1,800	Running
7	18	2	Bobby Allison	J D Bracken '66 Chevrolet	352	2,200	Running
8	11	29	Bud Moore	Bondy Long '68 Ford	350	1,500	Running
9	23	39	Friday Hassler	Red Sharp '66 Chevrolet	343	1,400	Running
10	5	27	Donnie Allison	Banjo Matthews '68 Ford	342	2,350	Running
11	40	03	Richard Brickhouse	Dub Clewis '67 Plymouth	335	1,250	Running
12	15	64	Elmo Langley	Langley-Woodfield '66 Ford	334	1,150	Running
13	26	46	Larry Manning	Tom Hunter '66 Chevrolet	331	1,100	Running
14	36	19	Bill Seifert	Seifert '66 Ford	320	1,100	Running
15	37	34	Wendell Scott	Scott '67 Ford	316	1,050	Running
16	27	0	Dr Don Tarr	Tarr '66 Chevrolet	308	950	Running
17	25	61	Hoss Ellington	Ellington '67 Mercury	304	900	Running
18	28	18	Dick Johnson	Johnson '67 Ford	287	850	Running
19	43	9	Ben Arnold	Roy Tyner '67 Pontiac	284	825	Running
20	6	43	Richard Petty	Petty Enterprises '68 Plym	273	1,450	Engine
21	39	93	Paul Dean Holt	Dennis Holt '67 Ford	263	800	Running
22	24	80	E J Trivette	E C Reid '66 Chevrolet	205	725	Engine
23	14	36	H B Bailey	Bailey '67 Pontiac	181	700	Crash
24	34	20	Clyde Lynn	Lynn '68 Ford	156	725	Engine
25	35	57	Frank Warren	Ervin Pruitt '67 Dodge	144	700	Oil Press
26	12	15	James Hylton	Friedkin Ent '68 Plymouth	134	640	Heating
27	4	98	LeeRoy Yarbrough	Junior Johnson '68 Ford	127	3,305	Engine
28	3	22	Darel Dieringer	Mario Rossi '68 Plymouth	127	695	Crash
29	9	16	Tiny Lund	Bud Moore '68 Mercury	126	610	Crash
30	31	59	Jim Hurtubise	Tom Pistone '68 Mercury	121	800	Crash
31	41	5	Earl Brooks	'67 Ford	86	640	Trans
32	17	1	Pete Hamilton	A J King '68 Dodge	56	655	Crash
33	10	71	Bobby Isaac	K&K Insurance '68 Dodge	55	570	Crash
34	19	84	Roy Trantham	Trantham '68 Ford	55	560	Crash
35	42	52	Bobby Mausgrover	Elmer Buxton '67 Ford	51	605	Crash
36	32	25	Jabe Thomas	Don Robertson '67 Ford	51	650	Crash
37	20	4	John Sears	L G DeWitt '67 Ford	48	540	Crash
38	21	49	G C Spencer	Spencer '67 Plymouth	33	520	Oil Press
39	33	76	Roy Tuner	Don Culpepper '66 Ford	30	575	Engine
40	29	07	George Davis	Davis '67 Chevrolet	27	520	Battery
41	38	56	Serge Adam	Lyle Stelter '66 Ford	24	535	Sway bar
42	44	70	J D McDuffie	McDuffie '67 Buick	22	535	Oil Press
43	30	10	Bill Champion	Champion '67 Ford	17	505	Engine
44	22	7	Bobby Johns	Shorty Johns '67 Chevrolet	1	500	Clutch

Time of Race: 3 hours, 58 minutes, 5 seonds
Average Speed: 126.132 mph
Pole Winner: Charlie Glotzbach - 144.830 mph
Lap Leaders: Cale Yarborough 1-16, Richard Petty 17-18, Yarborough 19-22, Petty 23-27, LeeRoy Yarborough 28-126, Donnie Allison 127-130, Paul Goldsmith 131-151, D.Allison 152-174, Yarborough 175-177, David Pearson 178-203, Yarborough 204-259 D.Allison 260-274, Yarborough 275-364.
Cautions: 7 for 65 laps.   Margin of Victory: 4 car lengths   Attendance: 70,000

Buddy Baker finished third in the Ray Fox Dodge. The 27 year-old Charlotte veteran drove the final 400 miles with no brakes. Charlie Glotzbach wound up fourth, Paul Goldsmith was fifth and Curtis Turner sixth.

Cale Yarborough and Richard Petty lead pack of cars down front chute at Darlington

Yarborough led 20 of the first 22 laps, but made an unscheduled pit stop to change all four tires. His speedy Goodyear tires wore out early and he made the switch to Firestones. When he returned to the track, the Timmonsville, SC driver was two full laps behind.

"Even though we fell a couple of laps behind," said Cale, "the tire change was the key to our victory."

Pearson apologized to crew chief Dick Hutcherson for coming up second best in the prestigious affair. "I could run him down, but passing him was another matter," he said.

Pearson jumped out to a big lead in the Grand National point standings. Bobby Isaac was wiped out in a 55th lap crash. Rookie Bobby Mausgrover spun onto the apron in the first turn, then slid up into traffic. Isaac's Dodge crashed into Mausgrover's Ford,

Bobby Mausgrover #52 spins in front of Bobby Isaac #71 and Pete Hamilton #1 in Southern 500

inflicting heavy damage to both automobiles. Pete Hamilton, Roy Trantham, Jabe Thomas, H.B. Bailey and John Sears were also involved.

Isaac was credited with a 33rd place finish and fell 104 points behind Pearson.

Yarborough averaged 126.132 mph before 70,000 spectators.

Race No. 40

Pearson Edges Isaac in Buddy Shuman Memorial

HICKORY, NC (Sept. 6) -- David Pearson drove his Holman-Moody Ford around Bobby Isaac's Dodge in the 173rd lap and led the rest of the way to win the Buddy Shuman Memorial at Hickory Speedway. It was

Grand National Race No. 40
250 Laps at Hickory Speedway
Hickory, NC
"Buddy Shuman Memorial"
100 Miles on .4-mile Paved Track
September 6, 1968

Fin	St	No.	Driver	Team / Car	Laps	Money	Status
1	2	17	David Pearson	Holman-Moody '68 Ford	250	$1,000	Running
2	3	71	Bobby Isaac	K&K Insurance '67 Dodge	250	600	Running
3	5	3	Buddy Baker	Ray Fox '68 Dodge	249	400	Running
4	1	43	Richard Petty	Petty Enterprises '68 Plym	244	500	Running
5	8	64	Elmo Langley	Langley-Woodfield '66 Ford	244	275	Running
6	7	4	John Sears	L G DeWitt '66 Ford	243	240	Running
7	23	38	Wayne Smith	Smith '68 Chevrolet	239	200	Running
8	16	48	James Hylton	Hylton Eng '68 Dodge	238	175	Running
9	13	20	Clyde Lynn	Lynn '66 Ford	235	150	Running
10	12	9	Roy Tyner	Tyner '67 Pontiac	234	140	Running
11	19	06	Neil Castles	Castles '67 Plymouth	236	130	Running
12	22	25	Jabe Thomas	Don Robertson '67 Ford	220	120	Running
13	17	76	Ben Arnold	Don Culpepper '66 Ford	219	110	Running
14	21	5	Earl Brooks	'67 Ford	216	100	Running
15	14	34	Wendell Scott	Scott '66 Ford	203	100	Running
16	4	21	Cale Yarborough	Wood Brothers '68 Ford	168	600	Crash
17	6	2	Bobby Allison	J D Bracken '66 Chevrolet	130	100	Sway bar
18	10	70	J D McDuffie	McDuffie '67 Buick	121	100	Rear End
19	20	19	Cecil Gordon	Henley Gray '66 Ford	113	100	Battery
20	11	8	Ed Negre	Negre '67 Ford	99	100	Oil Leak
21	9	84	Roy Trantham	Trantham '68 Ford	70	100	Engine
22	15	95	Paul Dean Holt	Henley Gray '66 Ford	47	100	Flagged
23	18	45	Bill Seifert	Seifert '68 Ford	20	100	Oil Line

Time of Race: 1 hour, 14 minutes, 40 seconds
Average Speed: 80.357 mph
Pole Winner: Richard Petty - 85.868 mph
Lap Leaders: Richard Petty 1-13, Bobby Isaac 14-172, David Pearson 173-250.
Cautions: Margin of Victory: Attendance: 6,500

the 15th victory of the season for Pearson.

Isaac finished second after leading 159 of the 250 laps on the .4-mile paved track. Buddy Baker finished third and Richard Petty recovered from a bout with the retaining wall to finish fourth. Fifth place went to Elmo Langley.

Cale Yarborough started fourth and ran with the leaders in the early going. He was eliminated from the race when a tire blew, forcing his Wood Brothers Mercury into the wall. Cale wound up 16th in the field of 23, but he was listed as earning $600. He received $100 for 16th place and $500 appearance money. It was the first time the official money winnings included appearance money.

Pearson's 45th victory came at an average speed of 80.357 mph. A crowd of 6,500 showed up for the memorial event honoring NASCAR pioneer Buddy Shuman, who lost his life in a Hickory hotel fire in 1955.

Grand National Race No. 41
300 Laps at Virginia State Fairgrounds
Richmond, VA
"Capital City 300"
187.5-miles on .625-mile Paved Track
September 8, 1968

Fin	St	No.	Driver	Team / Car	Laps	Money	Running
1	1	43	Richard Petty	Petty Enterprises '68 Plym	300	$2,400	Running
2	2	17	David Pearson	Holman-Moody '68 Ford	300	1,490	Running
3	4	21	Cale Yarborough	Wood Brothers '68 Mercury	299	1,210	Running
4	6	2	Bobby Allison	J D Bracken '66 Chevrolet	299	875	Running
5	3	3	Buddy Baker	Ray Fox '68 Dodge	298	710	Running
6	5	71	Bobby Isaac	K&K Insurance '68 Dodge	297	525	Running
7	8	15	Ray Hendrick	Friedkin Ent 68 Plymouth	295	400	Running
8	7	48	James Hylton	Hylton Eng '68 Dodge	293	300	Running
9	9	64	Elmo LAngley	Langley-Woodfield '66 Ford	293	250	Running
10	10	20	Clyde Lynn	Lynn '66 Ford	284	250	Running
11	12	4	John Sears	L G DeWitt '67 Ford	279	225	Running
12	18	38	Wayne Smith	Smith '68 Chevrolet	273	225	Running
13	20	34	Wendell Scott	Scott '67 Ford	271	225	Running
14	16	57	Ervin Pruitt	Pruitt '67 Dodge	265	225	Running
15	24	76	Ben Arnold	Don Culpepper '67 Ford	262	200	Running
16	28	25	Jabe Thomas	Don Robertson '67 Ford	260	200	Running
17	21	19	Cecil Gordon	Henley Gray '67 Ford	257	200	Running
18	23	83	Worth McMillion	Allen McMillion '67 Pontiac	236	175	Running
19	23	93	Walson Gardner	Gardner '67 Ford	232	175	Running
20	22	95	Paul Dean Holt	Henley Gray '66 Ford	195	175	Quit
21	14	8	Ed Negre	Negre '67 Ford	157	175	Engine
22	11	10	Bill Champion	Champion '67 Ford	129	150	Crash
23	26	9	Roy Tyner	Tyner '67 Pontiac	128	150	Crash
24	24	66	Larry Manning	'67 Chevrolet	100	150	Crash
25	15	5	Earl Brooks	'67 Ford	86	150	Heating
26	25	06	Neil Castles	Castles '67 Plymouth	61	150	Wtr pmp
27	17	45	Bill Seifert	Seifert '68 Ford	53	150	Crash
28	13	70	J D McDuffie	McDuffie '67 Buick	12	---	Oil Press

Time of Race: 2 hours, 11 minutes, 20 seconds
Average Speed: 85.659 mph
Pole Winner: Richard Petty - 103.178 mph
Lap Leaders: Richard Petty 1-58, David Pearson 59-80, Petty 81-105, Pearson 106-116, Petty 117-140, Ray Hendrick 141-147, Pearson 148-154, Petty 155-178, Pearson 179-189, Buddy Baker 190-196, Pearson 197-205, Cale Yarborough 206-212, Pearson 213-216, Petty 217-300.
Cautions: 10 for 52 laps   Margin of Victory: Attendance: 13,000

Race No. 41

Petty Roars Back to Win Capital City 300 at Richmond

RICHMOND, VA (Sept. 8) -- Richard Petty overcame an unscheduled pit stop that dropped him a lap and a half off the pace, and roared back to win the Capital City 300 at the Virginia State Fairgrounds. It was the 12th win of the season for the Plymouth driver.

David Pearson finished in second place with Cale Yarborough third. Bobby Allison came in fourth, Buddy Baker was fifth and Bobby Isaac sixth.

Petty led for 215 of the 300 laps on the newly re-measured .625-mile oval. He started on the pole with a record 103.178 mph lap and led most of the early going. Petty was leading when he blew a tire on lap 179, forcing him to the pits.

Effective use of caution flags enabled Petty to climb back into contention. Once he got back in the lead lap, he ran down his opponents and won going away.

Local short track star Ray Hendrick led seven laps in the Friedkin Enterprises Plymouth before fading to seventh in the final rundown.

Baker and Isaac were involved in a mid-race collision. Isaac had to swerve his Dodge to miss an erratic backmarker. His car bounced off the wall into the path of Baker. The two cars hit hard, and it was miraculous that they both continued and finished well.

Petty averaged 85.659 mph for his 87th career victory. A turnaway crowd of 13,000 watched the 187.5-mile event.

Race No. 42

Isaac Wins Maryland 300; Pearson Disqualified

BELTSVILLE, MD (Sept. 13) -- Bobby Isaac passed David Pearson on lap 241 and went on to score a narrow victory in the Maryland 300 at Beltsville 300. It was the third win of the season for the 36 year-old Catawba, NC Dodge driver.

Pearson, who had blown the engine in his Holman-Moody Ford in a practice session, wound up second in a Ford owned by Roy Trantham and tuned by Turkey Minton. However, Pearson's second place effort was nullified following a post-race weigh-in. NASCAR

Grand National Race No. 42
300 Laps at Beltsville Speedway
Beltsville, MD
"Maryland 300"
150 Miles on Half-mile Paved Track
September 13, 1968

Fin	St	No.	Driver	Team / Car	Laps	Money	Status
1	3	71	Bobby Isaac	K&K Insurance '67 Dodge	300	$1,400	Running
2	4	2	Bobby Allison	J D Bracken '66 Chevrolet	298	1,000	Running
3	2	43	Richard Petty	Petty Enterprises '68 Plym	294	700	Running
4	6	49	G C Spencer	Spencer '67 Plymouth	294	750	Running
5	21	9	Roy Tyner	Tyner '67 Pontiac	285	425	Running
6	13	20	Clyde Lynn	Lynn '66 Ford	285	325	Running
7	10	07	George Davis	Davis '67 Chevrolet	285	275	Running
8	14	70	J D McDuffie	McDuffie '67 Buick	283	250	Running
9	12	25	Jabe Thomas	Don Robertson '67 Ford	280	225	Running
10	16	34	Wendell Scott	Scott '66 Ford	274	200	Running
11	17	5	Earl Brooks	'67 Ford	270	190	Running
12	5	48	James Hylton	Hylton Eng '67 Dodge	268	180	Running
13	19	19	Cecil Gordon	Henley Gray '66 Ford	250	170	Running
14	18	95	Paul Dean Holt	Henley Gray '66 Ford	222	160	Oil Press
15	8	06	Neil Castles	Castles '67 Plymouth	170	150	Oil Press
16	9	10	Bill Champion	Champion '67 Ford	166	140	Engine
17	11	45	Elmo Langley	Bill Seifert '68 Ford	149	130	Clutch
18	1	21	Cale Yarborough	Wood Brothers '68 Mercury	142	120	Crash
19	22	83	G T Nolan	Allen McMillion '67 Pontiac	123	110	Oil Press
20	7	4	John Sears	L G DeWitt '67 Ford	81	100	Engine
21	15	51	Stan Meserve	Margo Hamm '67 Dodge	38	100	Axle
22	23	64	Bill Seifert	Langley-Woodfield '66 Ford	8	100	Oil Leak
23	20	84	David Pearson	Roy Trantham '68 Ford	300	---	Disqual

Time of Race: 2 hours, 6 minutes, 42 seconds
Average Speed: 71.033 mph
Pole Winner: Cale Yarborough - 81.311 mph
Lap Leaders: Cale Yarborough 1-142, Bobby Isaac 143-300.
Margin of Victory: 2-laps plus   Cautions: Attendance: 7,300

followed by Richard Petty, G.C. Spencer and Roy Tyner.

Prior to the start of the race, the Trantham Ford was found to weigh 35 pounds under the 4,000-pound minimum. Dick Hutcherson inserted 35 pounds of weight and Pearson lined up 20th on the starting grid.

Cale Yarborough led the first 142 laps before he crashed into the wall. Isaac took the lead as Pearson worked his way up to second.

Harry Hyde, crew chief on the K&K Insurance Dodge, filed a protest against the Trantham-Pearson car. He said he noticed members of the Holman-Moody crew removing weight from the car after they had added the 35 pounds to be eligible to start.

NASCAR Vice-President Lin Kuchler commented on the ruling: "It is regrettable that occasionally any sporting association must take rigid disciplinary action. However, this is the only way NASCAR can hold the respect of the spectators, press and contestants."

Isaac's fourth career Grand National win came at a speed of 71.033 mph.

Bobby Isaac and Harry Hyde look over 426 c.i Dodge hemi engine

officials found that the Ford that Pearson drove was nearly 200 pounds below the minimum weight allowed. Pearson was stripped of the $1,000 second place pay-off, but more importantly, the 49 points which went with it. Isaac was able to cut his deficit to 55 points in the race for the 1968 NASCAR Grand National driving title.

Bobby Allison was credited with second place,

Grand National Race No. 43
167 Laps at Orange Speedway
Hillsborough, NC
"Hillsborough 150"
150 Miles on .9-mile Dirt Track
September 15, 1968

Fin	St	No.	Driver	Team / Car	Laps	Money	Status
1	1	43	Richard Petty	Petty Enterprises '68 Plym	167	$1,600	Running
2	12	48	James Hylton	Hylton Eng '67 Dodge	160	1,000	Running
3	11	57	Neil Castles	Ervin Pruitt '67 Dodge	152	700	Running
4	7	4	John Sears	L G DeWitt '66 Ford	150	575	Running
5	23	83	Worth McMillion	Allen McMillion '67 Pontiac	145	425	Running
6	10	2	Bobby Allison	J D Bracken '66 Chevrolet	145	325	Running
7	20	9	Roy Tyner	Tyner '67 Pontiac	140	275	Engine
8	15	5	Earl Brooks	'67 Ford	138	225	Running
9	8	45	Elmo Langley	Bill Seifert '68 Ford	137	200	Running
10	3	49	G C Spencer	Spencer '67 Plymouth	133	175	Battery
11	4	71	Bobby Isaac	K&K Insurance '67 Dodge	131	100	Running
12	2	17	David Pearson	Holman-Moody '68 Ford	120	100	Engine
13	6	15	Curtis Turner	Friedkin Ent '68 Plymouth	116	100	Engine
14	24	88	Ken Meisenhelder	Buck Baker '67 Olds	103	100	Flagged
15	13	70	J D McDuffie	McDuffie '67 Buick	85	100	Rear End
16	9	20	Clyde Lynn	Lynn '66 Ford	84	100	Spindle
17	14	25	Jabe Thomas	Don Robertson '67 Ford	64	100	Engine
18	21	95	Paul Dean Holt	Henley Gray '66 Ford	40	100	Brakes
19	17	34	Wendell Scott	Scott '66 Ford	35	100	Heating
20	16	19	Cecil Gordon	Henley Gray '66 Ford	12	100	Trans
21	5	3	Buddy Baker	Ray Fox '68 Dodge	5	100	D Shaft
22	22	64	Bill Seifert	Langley-Woodfield '66 Ford	4	100	Oil Leak
23	18	51	Stan Meserve	Margo Hamm '67 Dodge	2	100	Axle
24	19	06	Ray Hill	Neil Castles '67 Plymouth	1	100	Oil Press

Time of Race: 1 hour, 42 minutes, 51 seconds
Average Speed: 87.681 mph
Pole Winner: Richard Petty - 93.245 mph
Lap Leaders: Richard Petty 1-74, David Pearson 75-85, Petty 86, Pearson 87, Petty 88-167.
Cautions: 1 for 4 laps   Margin of Victory: 7-laps plus   Attendance: 6,700

Race No. 43

Richard Runs Rivals Ragged In Rough Hillsborough Event

Richard Petty and David Pearson in close quarters at Hillsborough's big dirt track

HILLSBOROUGH, NC (Sept. 15) -- Richard Petty scored his 13th win of the season in an awesome display of speed and durability in the Hillsborough 150 at Orange Speedway. Petty's electric blue Plymouth outlasted David Pearson and finished seven laps ahead of the field in what may be the final event at this historic .9-mile dirt oval.

James Hylton finished second and Neil Castles was third. Fourth place went to John Sears with Worth McMillion fifth.

Petty led for 155 of the 167 laps and lost the lead twice to Pearson. The two veteran campaigners thrilled the crowd of 6,700 to a fender slapping duel before Pearson's Ford blew its engine.

Pearson wound up 12th in the field of 24, but lost only one point to Bobby Isaac in the point race. Isaac lost over 30 laps on a lengthy pit stop to repair mechanical problems. The Catawba, NC Dodge driver got back on the track and finished 11th.

Curtis Turner started sixth in his Plymouth, but succumbed to engine problems after 116 laps. It would be the final Grand National appearance for the legendary Roanoke, VA driver, often regarded as the "Babe Ruth of Stock Car Racing".

Word leaked out that this historic dirt track, scene of some of the wildest events in NASCAR's history, might soon be a thing of the past. In recent years, the Orange Speedway has been given only one Grand National date. For the 1969 season, the new Alabama International Motor Speedway was said to have the inside line on the second weekend in September.

Race No. 44

Petty Steers Clear of Trouble; Wins Old Dominion 500

MARTINSVILLE, VA (Sept. 22) -- Richard Petty kept his Plymouth on the point for 324 of the 500 laps and walked away with a three laps victory in the Old Dominion 500 at Martinsville Speedway. It was Petty's 14th win of the year, but his first in a "major" event of 250 miles or more.

Grand National Race No. 44
500 Laps at Martinsville Speedway
Martinsville, VA
"Old Dominion 500"
250 Miles on Half-mile Paved Track
September 22, 1968

Fin	St	No.	Driver	Team / Car	Laps	Money	Status
1	6	43	Richard Petty	Petty Enterprises '68 Plym	500	$5,999	Running
2	1	21	Cale Yarborough	Wood Brothers '68 Mercury	497	2,700	Running
3	9	98	LeeRoy Yarbrough	Junior Johnson '68 Ford	497	1,244	Running
4	39	29	Bud Moore	Bondy Long '68 Ford	494	775	Running
5	8	71	Bobby Isaac	K&K Insurance '67 Dodge	494	725	Running
6	3	17	David Pearson	Holman-Moody '68 Ford	492	850	Running
7	7	14	Ray Hendrick	Friedkin Ent '68 Plymouth	492	575	Running
8	5	27	Donnie Allison	Banjo Matthews '68 Ford	491	550	Running
9	17	4	John Sears	L G DeWitt '66 Ford	488	500	Running
10	14	84	Roy Trantham	Trantham '68 Ford	485	475	Running
11	15	39	Friday Hassler	Red Sharp '66 Chevrolet	475	450	Running
12	24	9	Roy Tyner	Tyner '67 Pontiac	474	425	Running
13	26	38	Wayne Smith	Smith '68 Chevrolet	470	415	Running
14	13	2	Bobby Allison	J D Bracken '68 Chevrolet	468	415	Engine
15	28	34	Wendell Scott	Scott '66 Ford	465	370	Running
16	23	70	J D McDuffie	McDuffie '67 Buick	465	385	Running
17	21	30	Dave Marcis	Larry Wehrs '66 Chevrolet	462	499	Flat tire
18	33	51	Stan Meserve	Margo Hamm '67 Dodge	457	340	Running
19	27	50	Eddie Yarboro	West End Motors '66 Plym	455	330	Running
20	22	20	Clyde Lynn	Lynn '66 Ford	451	335	Running
21	12	48	James Hylton	Hylton Eng '67 Dodge	439	325	Running
22	2	3	Buddy Baker	Ray Fox '68 Dodge	436	400	Engine
23	31	25	Jabe Thomas	Don Robertson '67 Ford	417	300	Running
24	37	93	Walson Gardner	Gardner '67 Ford	408	300	Running
25	34	76	Earl Brooks	Don Culpepper '66 Ford	405	300	Rear End
26	35	83	Worth McMillion	Allen McMillion '67 Pontiac	391	275	Radiator
27	20	06	Neil Castles	Castles '67 Plymouth	374	375	Engine
28	29	18	Dick Johnson	Johnson '67 Ford	366	275	Oil Press
29	38	19	Henley Gray	Gray '66 Ford	325	275	Running
30	16	49	G C Spencer	Spencer '67 Plymouth	249	300	Ignition
31	30	0	Dr Don Tarr	Tarr '66 Chevrolet	237	250	Crash
32	19	64	Elmo Langley	Langley-Woodfield '66 Ford	235	275	Clutch
33	32	45	Bill Seifert	Seifert '68 Ford	192	250	Heating
34	4	1	Pete Hamilton	A J King '68 Dodge	154	319	Crash
35	10	22	Darel Dieringer	Mario Rossi '68 Plymouth	143	275	Clutch
36	40	66	Larry Manning	'66 Chevrolet	130	250	Heating
37	18	10	Bill Champion	Champion '67 Ford	96	275	Crash
38	36	47	Cecil Gordon	Bill Seifert '68 Ford	65	250	Oil Pan
39	11	6	Charlie Glotzbach	Cotton Owens '68 Dodge	21	275	Crash
40	25	57	Paul Dean Holt	Ervin Pruitt '67 Dodge	1	275	Oil Press

Time of Race: 3 hours, 47 minutes, 56 seconds
Average Speed: 65.808 mph
Pole Winner: Cale Yarborough - 77.279 mph
Lap Leaders: Cale Yarborough 1-19, Pete Hamilton 20-37, David Pearson 38-103, Hamilton 104, Bobby Allison 105, Pearson 106-138, Richard Petty 139-157, B.Allison 158-169, Pearson 170-193, Petty 194-259, Pearson 260-261, Petty 262-500.
Cautions: 7 for 60 laps   Margin of Victory: 3-laps plus   Attendance: 21,000

Dr. Don Tarr backs into pit wall in Old Dominion 500

Race No. 45

Petty "On the Stick", Wins Again at N. Wilkesboro

N.WILKESBORO, NC (Sept. 29) -- Richard Petty led virtually all the way and won the Wilkes 400 at North Wilkesboro Speedway. It was the 15th win of the season for the Plymouth driver, who won 27 races in 1967.

"This is beginning to feel like last year," grinned Petty in victory lane. "It's kind of late in the year. I've got to get on the stick."

Petty finished a lap ahead of David Pearson to pocket the $5,975 first place check. Third place went to

Cale Yarborough survived three crashes and finished second, pushing his seasonal money winnings to $130,706. LeeRoy Yarbrough came in third, Bud Moore was fourth and Bobby Isaac fifth. Point leader David Pearson came home sixth.

Pole winner Yarborough and second fastest qualifier Buddy Baker collided in the first turn of the first lap, sending the 40 car field scrambling for an opening. Baker was later involved in a crash with Moore, and his car caught fire in the pit area. Baker finally called it quits on lap 436 with a blown engine.

Charlie Glotzbach spun and hit the wall in the 21st lap. Upon impact with the concrete wall, Glotzbach's Dodge burst into flames. The Georgetown, IN driver quickly dismounted and ran to safety.

Pete Hamilton, 1967 National Sportsman champion, led twice for 19 laps in another fine run for the Dedham, MA rookie. He was kayoed on lap 154 when he crashed with Yarborough.

David Pearson leads Richard Petty at Martinsville

Petty and Pearson were the fastest drivers on the half mile paved oval, but Pearson was sacked with a long pit stop. "I wasn't worried about anybody but David," said Petty. "After he pitted for a long time, I just wanted to stay out of trouble. And there was plenty of that out there today."

The caution flag was out seven times for 60 laps -- all of them for wrecks and spin-outs. Petty averaged 65.808 mph for his 89th career Grand National win.

Grand National Race No. 45
400 Laps at N.Wilkesboro Speedway
N.Wilkesboro, NC
"Wilkes 400"
250 Miles on .625-mile Paved Track
September 29, 1968

Fin	St	No.	Driver	Team / Car	Laps	Money	Status
1	3	43	Richard Petty	Petty Enterprises '68 Plym	400	$5,975	Running
2	2	17	David Pearson	Holman-Moody '68 Ford	399	2,500	Running
3	6	98	LeeRoy Yarbrough	Junior Johnson '68 Mercury	399	1,450	Running
4	1	14	Bobby Allison	Friedkin Ent '68 Plymouth	397	1,150	Running
5	4	21	Cale Yarborough	Wood Brothers '68 Mercury	395	625	Running
6	9	22	Darel Dieringer	Mario Rossi '68 Plymouth	392	600	Running
7	5	71	Bobby Isaac	K&K Insurance '67 Dodge	391	475	Running
8	12	48	James Hylton	Hylton Eng '67 Dodge	390	425	Running
9	14	4	John Sears	L G DeWitt '66 Ford	389	375	Running
10	15	64	Elmo Langley	Langley-Woodfield '66 Ford	388	375	Running
11	13	49	G C Spencer	Spencer '67 Plymouth	388	350	Running
12	8	1	Pete Hamilton	A J King '68 Dodge	388	325	Running
13	16	30	Dave Marcis	Larry Wehrs '66 Chevrolet	377	300	Running
14	23	20	Clyde Lynn	Lynn '66 Ford	373	325	Rear End
15	20	25	Jabe Thomas	Don Robertson '67 Ford	367	275	Running
16	29	34	Wendell Scott	Scott '66 Ford	366	250	Running
17	7	3	Buddy Baker	Ray Fox '68 Dodge	354	275	Ignition
18	17	45	Bill Seifert	Seifert '68 Ford	352	275	Running
19	19	5	Earl Brooks	'66 Ford	350	275	Running
20	24	76	Stan Meserve	Don Culpepper '66 Ford	346	275	Running
21	28	50	Eddie Yarboro	West End Motors '66 Plym	329	250	Running
22	21	06	Neil Castles	Castles '67 Plymouth	265	325	Engine
23	11	84	Roy Trantham	Trantham '68 Ford	243	250	Vibration
24	10	6	Charlie Glotzbach	Cotton Owens '68 Dodge	224	275	Engine
25	22	57	Roy Tyner	Ervin Pruitt '67 Dodge	80	325	Heating
26	27	18	Dick Johnson	Johnson '67 Ford	25	250	Engine
27	30	47	Cecil Gordon	Bill Seifert '68 Ford	23	250	Oil Leak
28	18	38	Wayne Smith	Smith '68 Chevrolet	16	250	Engine
29	25	02	Walson Gardner	Bob Cooper '66 Chevrolet	2	250	Crash
30	26	70	J D McDuffie	McDuffie '67 Buick	1	250	Engine

Time of Race: 2 hours, 39 minutes, 24 seconds
Average Speed: 94.103 mph
Pole Winner: Bobby Allison - 104.525 mph
Lap Leaders: Bobby Allison 1-69, Richard Petty 70-122, David Pearson 123-127,
   LeeRoy Yarbrough 128-132, Richard Petty 133-229, Yarbrough 230, Petty 231-352,
   Yarbrough 353-354, Petty 355-400.
Cautions: 3 for 25 laps   Margin of Victory: 1-lap plus   Attendance: 16,000

LeeRoy Yarbrough with Bobby Allison fourth and Cale Yarborough fifth.

Allison, recently assigned to drive the Friedkin Enterprises Plymouth engineered by Bill Ellis, won the pole and led the first 69 laps. He was leading with Petty in hot pursuit when he overran the lapped car of Wendell Scott. The collision crunched the fender on the left front tire and the Hueytown, AL driver had to take an extended stay on pit road. He was never in contention after that.

Pearson and Yarbrough held the lead for brief stints when Petty made routine pit stops. No one ever passed Petty on the track during the 400-lapper.

Charlie Glotzbach was taken out in a spectacular crash on lap 229. The engine in his Cotton Owens Dodge blew and he slid backwards into the retaining fence. The orange Dodge was heavily damaged, but Glotzbach was unhurt.

Pearson extended his lead to 64 points in the Grand National standings over Bobby Isaac, who finished seventh.

Petty's 90th career win came at an average speed of 94.103 mph.

Race No. 46

Allison Loses in Pits; Pearson Wins Augusta 200

AUGUSTA, GA (Oct. 5) -- David Pearson took the lead in the 109th lap during a caution flag and held off Bobby Allison to win the Augusta 200 at Augusta Speedway. It was the 16th win of the season for the title-bound Spartanburg, SC Ford driver.

Allison started on the pole and led the first 108 laps. He lost first place when his Bill Ellis crew had difficulty changing two tires. He resumed the chase in third place and wound up second, 3.0-seconds behind the winner.

Third place went to Richard Petty, who had the fastest car on the track but couldn't make up lost time. Petty pitted for fresh rubber early -- on lap 22, and lost a lap. In the final analysis, he was in the lead lap running down both Pearson and Allison.

Bobby Isaac finished fourth and John Sears was fifth.

Independent Elmo Langley provided an early surprise. The Landover, MD Ford driver qualified fifth and was running fourth when his engine blew on lap 33.

A crowd of 4,300 watched Pearson claim his 46th career win at a 75.821 mph clip.

Grand National Race No. 46
200 Laps at Augusta Speedway
Augusta, GA
"Augusta 200"
100 Miles on Half-mile Paved Track
October 5, 1968

Fin	St	No.	Driver	Team / Car	Laps	Money	Status
1	3	17	David Pearson	Holman-Moody '68 Ford	200	$1,000	Running
2	1	14	Bobby Allison	Friedkin Ent '68 Plymouth	200	600	Running
3	2	43	Richard Petty	Petty Enterprises '68 Plym	200	600	Running
4	4	71	Bobby Isaac	K&K Insurance '68 Dodge	199	300	Running
5	7	4	John Sears	L G DeWitt '67 Ford	194	275	Running
6	8	57	James Hylton	Ervin Pruitt '67 Dodge	193	240	Running
7	6	30	Dave Marcis	Larry Wehrs '66 Chevrolet	189	200	Running
8	15	20	Clyde Lynn	Lynn '66 Ford	185	175	Running
9	12	70	J D McDuffie	McDuffie '67 Buick	184	150	Running
10	16	45	Bill Seifert	Seifert '68 Ford	181	140	Running
11	20	25	Jabe Thomas	Don Robertson '67 Ford	181	130	Running
12	17	09	Roy Tyner	Tyner '66 Chevrolet	177	120	Running
13	19	01	Paul Dean Holt	Dennis Holt '67 Ford	153	110	Running
14	21	02	Walson Gardner	Bob Cooper '66 Chevrolet	126	100	Ignition
15	10	76	Ben Arnold	Don Culpepper '66 Ford	102	100	Engine
16	11	51	Stan Meserve	Margo Hamm '67 Dodge	84	100	Rear End
17	18	8	Ed Negre	Negre '67 Ford	35	100	Heating
18	5	64	Elmo Langley	Langley-Woodfield '66 Ford	33	100	Engine
19	9	0	Frank Warren	Dr Don Tarr '66 Chevrolet	22	100	Heating
20	14	5	Earl Brooks	'67 Ford	3	100	Engine
21	13	34	Wendell Scott	Scott '67 Ford	1	100	Engine

Time of Race: 1 hour, 19 minutes, 8 seconds
Average Speed: 75.821 mph
Pole Winner: Bobby Allison - 84.822 mph
Lap Leaders: Bobby Allison 1-108, David Pearson 109-200.
Cautions: 1 for ___ laps   Margin of Victory: 3 seconds   Attendance: 4,300

Race No. 47

Chargin' Charlie Gets First Victory in National 500

CHARLOTTE, NC (Oct. 20) -- Flashy Charlie Glotzbach, often spectacular but previously unsuccessful, won the National 500 at Charlotte Motor Speedway for his first Grand National victory. It also ended an eight year famine for car owner Cotton Owens on superspeedways. Owens' only other big track triumph was in the 1960 Atlanta 500 with Bobby Johns at the helm of his Pontiac.

Glotzbach took the lead for keeps 33 laps from the finish and beat Paul Goldsmith by 7.0-seconds. The Georgetown, IN driver averaged a record 135.324 mph in the Owens Dodge, which had won the pole 11 days earlier. The race was rain-delayed and was finally staged in the shadow of Hurricane Gladys.

The cupboard was getting bare before Charlie Glotzbach won National 500

David Pearson finished third and pulled out to an 81 point lead over Bobby Isaac in the standings. Bobby Allison was fourth and Cale Yarborough fifth. Isaac finished ninth.

Goldsmith, bidding to end a two year losing streak, was in first place with 35 laps to go. He made his final pit stop, but swerved his car to miss a crewman working on another car. His Ray Nichels Dodge slid into a quagmirish infield and it took him several seconds to get out of the mud.

The Speedway had been the target of four days of heavy rains as the hurricane swept up the East coast.

Buddy Baker started third, but was out early when his Dodge crashed in the 18th lap. Rookie Hoss Ellington and part-time Grand National contestant Red Farmer also wrecked after tire failures.

"Our first win couldn't have come at a better time," said a happy Glotzbach. "The cupboard was getting pretty bare, after all the weird things that have happened to us. I had begun to think that bad luck was going to badger us from now on. But this wipes out all the bad breaks -- by a longshot."

Glotzbach, who first appeared on the NASCAR scene in 1960, got his first win in only his 36th start. The 1968 season was his first full year.

USAC stock car king Butch Hartman entered a Dodge and surprised some of the Southern stalwarts. He charged from 15th to take the lead in the 22nd lap. However, Hartman fell to an 11th place finish, 11 laps behind Glotzbach.

Donnie Allison #27 and Paul Goldsmith pair up on Charlotte's high banks

Grand National Race No. 47
334 Laps at Charlotte Motor Speedway
Charlotte, NC
"National 500"
500 Miles on 1.5-mile Paved Track
October 20, 1968

Fin	St	No.	Driver	Team / Car	Laps	Money	Status
1	1	6	Charlie Glotzbach	Cotton Owens '68 Dodge	334	$19,280	Running
2	7	99	Paul Goldsmith	Nichels Eng '68 Dodge	334	9,505	Running
3	2	17	David Pearson	Holman-Moody '68 Ford	334	6,800	Running
4	4	14	Bobby Allison	Friedkin Ent '68 Plymouth	332	4,195	Running
5	5	21	Cale Yarborough	Wood Brothers '68 Mercury	332	3,335	Running
6	14	27	Donnie Allison*	Banjo Matthews '68 Ford	331	2,770	Running
7	9	1	Pete Hamilton	A J King '68 Dodge	330	2,070	Running
8	11	22	Darel Dieringer	Mario Rossi '68 Plymouth	327	1,775	Running
9	8	71	Bobby Isaac	K&K Insurance '68 Dodge	326	1,700	Running
10	25	11	A J Foyt	Holman-Moody '68 Ford	325	1,600	Running
11	15	75	Butch Hartman	Hartman '68 Dodge	323	1,685	Running
12	32	32	Marty Robbins	'67 Dodge	312	1,525	Running
13	18	47	Elmo Langley	Bill Seifert '68 Ford	309	1,500	Running
14	24	4	John Sears	L G DeWitt '67 Ford	307	1,425	Running
15	35	06	Neil Castles	Castles '67 Plymouth	303	1,500	Running
16	22	39	Friday Hassler	Red Sharp '66 Chevrolet	301	1,325	Running
17	28	64	Bill Seifert	Langley-Woodfield '66 Ford	298	1,325	Running
18	27	10	Bill Champion	Champion '67 Ford	298	1,325	Running
19	37	34	Wendell Scott	Scott '67 Ford	298	1,215	Running
20	30	80	E J Trivette	E C Reid '66 Chevrolet	296	1,235	Running
21	38	20	Clyde Lynn	Lynn '66 Ford	283	1,275	Running
22	41	76	Ben Arnold	Don Culpepper '66 Ford	274	1,150	Running
23	21	30	Dave Marcis	Larry Wehrs '66 Chevrolet	230	1,150	Engine
24	44	25	Jabe Thomas	Don Robertson '67 Ford	193	1,175	Engine
25	20	18	Dick Johnson	Johnson '67 Ford	183	1,100	Shackle
26	17	97	Red Farmer	Farmer '67 Ford	178	1,100	Crash
27	42	5	Earl Brooks	'67 Ford	175	1,100	Engine
28	33	45	Cecil Gordon	Bill Seifert '68 Ford	161	1,025	Crank
29	36	8	Ed Negre	Negre '67 Ford	147	1,000	Flagged
30	43	9	Roy Tyner	Tyner '67 Pontiac	144	1,025	Trans
31	40	38	Wayne Smith	Smith '68 Chevrolet	144	1,000	Engine
32	6	43	Richard Petty	Petty Enterprises '68 Plym	135	1,450	Engine
33	12	84	Roy Trantham	Trantham '68 Ford	115	900	Brakes
34	29	61	Hoss Ellington	Ellington '67 Mercury	110	885	Crash
35	26	49	G C Spencer	Spencer '67 Plymouth	105	925	Engine
36	16	48	James Hylton	Hylton Eng '67 Dodge	83	875	Ignition
37	39	42	Lennie Waldo	'66 Ford	79	850	Engine
38	34	46	Roy Mayne	Tom Hunter '66 Chevrolet	77	775	H Gasket
39	19	7	Bobby Johns	Shorty Johns '66 Chevrolet	63	750	Engine
40	23	03	Richard Brickhouse	Dub Clewis '67 Plymouth	56	725	Fan pulley
41	13	98	LeeRoy Yarbrough	Junior Johnson '68 Ford	52	825	Quit
42	45	09	Bill Vanderhoff	Roy Tyner '66 Chevrolet	30	725	Oil Press
43	3	3	Buddy Baker	Ray Fox '68 Dodge	18	780	Crash
44	31	51	Stan Meserve	Margo Hamm '67 Dodge	18	625	Rear End
45	10	29	Bud Moore	Bondy Long '68 Ford	6	600	Quit

Time of Race: 3 hours, 42 minutes, 8 seconds
Average Speed: 135.234 mph
Pole Winner: Charlie Glotzbach - 156.060 mph
Fastest Qualifier: LeeRoy Yarbrough - 156.372 mph
Lap Leaders: Charlie Glotzbach 1-2, David Pearson 3-5, Glotzbach 6, Buddy Baker 7-16, Glotzbach 17-21, Butch Hartman 22-28, Pearson 29-45, Donnie Allison 46, Bobby Allison 47-70, D.Allison 71-75, Pearson 76-102, D.Allison 103-125, Pearson 126-135, Paul Goldsmith 136-138, Pete Hamilton 139-146, Pearson 147-189, Hamilton 190, Pearson 191-234, Cale Yarborough 235, Pearson 236-244, Glotzbach 245-256, Pearson 257, Glotzbach 258-296, Pearson 297, Goldsmith 298-300, Pearson 301, Glotzbach 302-334.
Cautions: 6 for 49 laps   Margin of Victory: 7 seconds   Attendance: 38,300
*Relieved by A J Foyt

A disappointing crowd of 38,300 watched nine drivers swap the lead 26 times. The caution was out six times for a total of 49 laps.

Earl Balmer attempted a comeback. The Floyd Knobs, IN veteran hooked up with Bud Moore, but he crashed the Mercury in practice.

Country singer Marty Robbins, pictured here with Glen Wood, finished 12th in National 500

Race No. 48

Pearson Clinches Title; Petty Wins American 500

ROCKINGHAM, NC (Oct. 27) -- Richard Petty ended a 13 month slump on superspeedways by taking first place in the American 500 at North Carolina Motor

Richard Petty and Winky Louise in Rockingham victory lane. It was Petty's only superspeedway win of the year

Speedway. The toothy 31 year-old Plymouth driver finished 16 seconds ahead of runner-up David Pearson, who clinched his second straight Grand National championship.

Petty passed Pearson in the 443rd lap and was never headed. LeeRoy Yarbrough finished in third place, Tiny Lund was fourth and Bobby Allison fifth.

Petty started fourth but dropped to ninth in the early laps. "Everybody was banging on each other," said Petty. "So I dropped back a little. The only guy I was worried about was Cale (Yarborough). But he wasn't around at the finish. It really doesn't matter now."

Yarborough was going for his fifth superspeedway win of the year. The Timmonsville, SC Mercury driver led on four occasions for 92 laps when his engine blew

Charlie Glotzbach #6 and Bud Moore #29 tangle on pit road at Rockingham

on lap 325. He was leading at the time he went out.

Bobby Isaac started third and delivered one of his strongest big track performances. A long pit stop to correct mechanical ills cost him all hopes of capturing his first championship. Eventually, the engine in his K&K Insurance Dodge let go in the final laps.

Top contenders Charlie Glotzbach and Bud Moore were taken out by a pit road crash on lap 53. A stray tire had rolled away from the Petty pits and Glotzbach swerved to miss it. By doing so, he pinched Moore into the steel pit wall, knocking Moore out of the race. NASCAR officials blackflagged Glotzbach, but car owner Cotton Owens ordered his driver to park the car rather than accept a penalty. "What happened couldn't be helped," huffed Owens. "We shouldn't be penalized for something which wasn't Charlie's fault. We quit!"

Petty had the race sewed up when he lapped Pearson with 42 laps to go. Prior to that, crew chief Maurice Petty gave his driver the 'E-Z' message on the pit board. "We couldn't get Richard to slow down," said

Grand National Race No. 48
500 Laps at North Carolina Motor Speedway
Rockingham, NC
"American 500"
500 Miles on 1-mile Paved Track
October 27, 1968

Fin	St	No.	Driver	Team / Car	Laps	Money	Status
1	4	43	Richard Petty	Petty Enterprises '68 Plym	500	$17,075	Running
2	2	17	David Pearson	Holman-Moody '68 Ford	500	9,775	Running
3	6	98	LeeRoy Yarbrough	Junior Johnson '68 Ford	498	5,225	Running
4	9	16	Tiny Lund	Bud Moore '68 Mercury	497	2,800	Running
5	8	14	Bobby Allison	Friedkin Ent '68 Plymouth	496	1,850	Running
6	14	91	Don White	Nichels Eng '68 Dodge	495	1,400	Running
7	17	48	James Hylton	Hylton Eng '68 Dodge	491	1,375	Running
8	16	84	G C Spencer	Roy Trantham '68 Ford	488	1,200	Running
9	20	03	Richard Brickhouse	Dub Clewis '67 Plymouth	480	1,100	Running
10	18	75	Butch Hartman	Hartman '68 Dodge	478	1,100	Running
11	19	4	John Sears	L G DeWitt '67 Ford	476	1,050	Running
12	28	39	Friday Hassler	Red Sharp '66 Chevrolet	466	1,000	Running
13	27	7	Bobby Johns	Shorty Johns '66 Chevrolet	446	975	Running
14	39	47	Bill Seifert	Seifert '68 Ford	444	950	Engine
15	41	20	Clyde Lynn	Lynn '66 Ford	433	935	Running
16	13	27	Donnie Allison	Banjo Matthews '68 Ford	430	920	Crash
17	3	71	Bobby Isaac	K&K Insurance '68 Dodge	427	930	Engine
18	44	45	Earl Brooks	Bill Seifert '68 Ford	427	890	Running
19	36	9	Roy Tyner	Tyner '67 Pontiac	420	945	Engine
20	35	93	Walson Gardner	Gardner '67 Ford	414	920	Flagged
21	38	19	Henley Gray	Gray '68 Ford	408	895	Running
22	42	18	Dick Johnson	Johnson '67 Ford	407	830	Running
23	43	25	Jabe Thomas	Don Robertson '67 Ford	400	815	Running
24	24	30	Dave Marcis	Larry Wehrs '66 Chevrolet	396	800	Engine
25	10	3	Buddy Baker	Ray Fox '68 Dodge	385	835	Engine
26	1	21	Cale Yarborough	Wood Brothers '68 Mercury	325	1,120	Engine
27	37	34	Wendell Scott	Scott '67 Ford	309	795	Running
28	22	10	Bill Champion	Champion '67 Ford	271	740	Engine
29	5	99	Paul Goldsmith	Nichels Eng '68 Dodge	270	725	Ignition
30	26	56	Tommy Gale	Lyle Stelter '67 Mercury	172	760	Crash
31	25	97	Red Farmer	Farmer '67 Ford	159	770	Rear End
32	29	06	Neil Castles	Castles '67 Plymouth	156	830	Engine
33	11	22	Darel Dieringer	Mario Rossi '68 Plymouth	148	690	Engine
34	12	1	Pete Hamilton	A J King '68 Dodge	145	650	Engine
35	31	70	J D McDuffie	McDuffie '67 Buick	95	735	Engine
36	34	76	James Sears	Don Culpepper '66 Ford	92	710	Crash
37	33	0	Dr Don Tarr	Tarr '66 Chevrolet	91	685	Crash
38	23	57	Ervin Pruitt	Pruitt '67 Dodge	90	590	Crash
39	40	80	E J Trivette	E C Reid '66 Chevrolet	87	605	Brakes
40	30	64	Elmo Langley	Langley-Woodfield '66 Ford	82	560	Engine
41	7	6	Charlie Glotzbach	Cotton Owens '68 Dodge	59	545	Quit
42	15	29	Bud Moore	Bondy Long '68 Ford	53	535	Crash
43	32	52	Dexter Gainey	Elmer Buxton '67 Ford	41	650	Flagged
44	21	11	Frank Gardner	Holman-Moody '68 Ford	1	515	Flagged

Time of Race: 4 hours, 45 minutes, 33 seconds
Average Speed: 105.060 mph
Pole Winner: Cale Yarborough - 118.717 mph
Lap Leaders: Cale Yarborough 1-13, Bobby Isaac 14-47, Yarborough 48-54, Isaac 55-86, Donnie Allison 87-97, Richard Petty 98-117, Isaac 118-169, Buddy Baker 170-175, Tiny Lund 176, Petty 177-209, Baker 210-241, Yarborough 242-252, Petty 253-264, Yarborough 265-325, Petty 326-359, David Pearson 360-378, Petty 379-437, Pearson 438-442, Petty 443-500.
Cautions: 6 for 46 laps   Margin of Victory: 16 seconds   Attendance: 32,000

Race No. 49
Cale Outlasts Isaac, Wins '68 Finale at Jefferson

JEFFERSON, GA (Nov. 3) -- Cale Yarborough shoved his Mercury past Bobby Isaac in the 150th lap and hustled to his sixth win of the year in the Peach State 200 at Jeffco Speedway.

Glen Wood and Cale Yarborough. Yarborough won the 1968 season finale at Jefferson, GA

Richard Petty trailed Yarborough by a half lap at the checkered flag. David Pearson finished third and was officially crowned 1968 NASCAR Grand National champion. James Hylton came in fourth and LeeRoy Yarborough was fifth.

Isaac led most of the way and was holding down second place when a tire blew, sending his Dodge into the wall. The accident occurred with nine laps remaining. Isaac got credit for ninth place in the final order. He finished 126 points behind Pearson in the final point tally.

Counting the post season awards for winning the championship, Pearson's total in-take was $133,064.75. Yarborough was the leading money winner with $138,051.30. Pearson won the championship, but Isaac's K&K Insurance team received first place point money of $12,653 because he started two more races than Pearson during the 1968 campaign. NASCAR pays the point money based on points and multiples. The points are multiplied by the starts, and the multiple factor is the basis for the point pay-off. It is the first time in NASCAR history that its champion did not collect first place money.

Yarborough won the pole at a record 90.694 mph, which established Jeffco Speedway as the fastest

Maurice. "I gave him the 'E-Z' sign, and what does he do? He stomps on the gas and laps Pearson."

Pearson managed to get back in the lead lap when Petty finally broke the throttle in the final laps.

Petty won the five hour race at an average speed of 105.060 mph. Attendance was tabbed at 32,000.

Grand National Race No. 49
200 Laps at Jeffco Speedway
Jefferson, GA
"Peach State 200"
100 Miles on Half-mile Paved Track
November 3, 1968

Fin	St	No.	Driver	Team / Car	Laps	Money	Status
1	3	21	Cale Yarborough	Wood Brothers '68 Mercury	200	$1,000	Running
2	7	43	Richard Petty	Petty Enterprises '68 Plym	200	800	Running
3	1	17	David Pearson	Holman-Moody '68 Ford	199	400	Running
4	6	48	James Hylton	Hylton Eng '68 Dodge	199	300	Running
5	10	56	LeeRoy Yarbrough	Lyle Stelter '67 Mercury	197	275	Running
6	8	4	John Sears	L G DeWitt '66 Ford	197	240	Running
7	9	39	Friday Hassler	Red Sharp '66 Chevrolet	197	200	Running
8	11	64	Elmo Langley	Langley-Woodfield '66 Ford	192	175	Running
9	2	71	Bobby Isaac	K&K Insurance '68 Dodge	191	150	Crash
10	12	06	Neil Castles	Castles '67 Plymouth	190	140	Running
11	19	20	Clyde Lynn	Lynn '66 Ford	186	130	Running
12	13	25	Jabe Thomas	Don Robertson '67 Ford	186	120	Running
13	22	70	J D McDuffie	McDuffie '67 Buick	184	110	Running
14	15	34	Wendell Scott	Scott '66 Ford	183	100	Running
15	14	96	Don Tomberlin	Roy Buckner '66 Ford	181	100	Running
16	23	19	Henley Gray	Gray '68 Ford	181	100	Running
17	21	80	E J Trivette	E C Reid '66 Chevrolet	179	100	Running
18	24	47	Bill Seifert	Seifert '68 Ford	178	100	Running
19	20	45	Cecil Gordon	Bill Seifert '68 Ford	178	100	Running
20	17	8	Ed Negre	Negre '67 Ford	177	100	Running
21	27	57	Ervin Pruitt	Pruitt '67 Dodge	172	100	Running
22	26	09	Stan Meserve	Roy Tyner '66 Chevrolet	168	100	Running
23	25	01	Paul Dean Holt	Dennis Holt '67 Ford	142	---	Ignition
24	18	52	Dexter Gainey	Elmer Buxton '66 Ford	101	---	Crash
25	16	5	Earl Brooks	'67 Ford	74	---	Crash
26	29	9	Roy Tyner	Tyner '67 Pontiac	71	---	Engine
27	5	14	Bobby Allison	Friedkin Ent '68 Plymouth	64	---	Engine
28	4	84	G C Spencer	Roy Trantham '68 Ford	28	---	Oil Press
29	28	31	Bill Ervin	Newman Long '66 Ford	4	---	Flagged

Time of Race: 1 hour, 17 minutes, 11 seconds
Average Speed: 77.737 mph
Pole Winner: David Pearson - 90.694 mph
Lap Leaders: Bobby Isaac 1- , James Hylton - , Isaac -149,
     Cale Yarborough 150-200.
Cautions: Margin of Victory: Half-lap   Attendance: 5,200.

half-mile track in the country. Asheville-Weaverville Speedway had held the honor based on Bobby Allison's pole time of 90.407 mph set last year.

Veteran G.C. Spencer qualified fourth, but left the race early with engine problems. Allison suffered engine failure in his Plymouth and went out on lap 64.

Yarborough's ninth career win came at an average speed of 77.737 mph. A crowd of 5,200 was on hand in chilly weather.

1968 NASCAR Season
Final Point Standings - Grand National Division

Rank	Driver	Points	Starts	Wins	Top 5	Top 10	Winnings
1	David Pearson	3,499	47	16	36	38	$133,064.75
2	Bobby Isaac	3,373	49	3	27	35	60,341.50
3	Richard Petty	3,123	49	16	32	35	99,534.60
4	Clyde Lynn	3,041	49	0	2	25	29,225.55
5	John Sears	3,017	49	0	5	24	29,178.75
6	Elmo Langley	2,823	48	0	6	28	25,831.85
7	James Hylton	2,719	41	0	16	27	32,607.50
8	Jabe Thomas	2,687	48	0	1	15	21,165.70
9	Wendell Scott	2,685	48	0	0	10	20,497.20
10	Roy Tyner	2,504	48	0	4	14	20,246.95
11	Bobby Allison	2,454	37	2	16	20	52,287.95
12	Neil Castles	2,330	44	0	4	15	19,506.35
13	Buddy Baker	2,310	38	1	16	18	56,022.95
14	Bill Seifert	2,175	44	0	1	9	18,402.95
15	Earl Brooks	1,957	40	0	0	5	14,232.95
16	LeeRoy Yarbrough	1,894	26	2	15	16	87,919.30
17	Cale Yarborough	1,804	21	6	12	12	138,051.30
18	Paul Dean Holt	1,723	39	0	0	0	8,985.30
19	Charlie Glotzbach	1,693	22	1	10	12	43,100.30
20	Henley Gray	1,559	30	0	0	6	12,565.30
21	Darel Dieringer	1,525	19	0	5	8	28,215
22	Tiny Lund	1,443	17	0	5	10	17,775
23	G.C. Spencer	1,401	26	0	1	6	10,120
24	J.D. McDuffie	1,370	32	0	0	9	8,335
25	Donnie Allison	1,307	13	1	5	8	50,815
26	Stan Meserve	1,274	31	0	0	1	7,475
27	Friday Hassler	1,224	20	0	3	8	12,000
28	Bill Champion	1,155	18	0	0	2	10,170
29	Paul "Bud" Moore	1,086	16	0	2	9	12,325
30	Paul Goldsmith	1,020	15	0	2	4	24,365
31	Ed Negre	928	23	0	0	1	4,985
32	Pete Hamilton	919	15	0	3	6	7,920
33	Wayne Smith	901	18	0	0	1	7,235
34	Dave Marcis	851	8	0	0	2	7,099
35	Dr. Don Tarr	827	12	0	0	0	7,510
36	E. J. Trivette	821	13	0	0	0	8,295
37	Dick Johnson	735	11	0	0	0	5,920
38	Bob Cooper	668	14	0	0	1	4,485
39	Buck Baker	650	17	0	1	3	3,580
40	Walson Gardner	640	14	0	0	2	4,275
41	Larry Manning	640	12	0	0	0	6,995
42	Frank Warren	611	10	0	0	1	5,365
43	Jerry Grant	559	7	0	0	1	5,665
44	Harold Fagan	531	12	0	0	1	3,680
45	Richard Brickhouse	514	7	0	1	2	7,190
46	Jim Hurtubise	504	6	0	0	1	4,490
47	Curtis Turner	456	6	0	1	4	5,850
48	Bobby Johns	453	7	0	0	0	5,010
49	Eddie Yarboro	447	6	0	0	0	2,255
50	Red Farmer	407	7	0	1	1	4,810

The 1969 Season

The Professional Drivers Association; and the Infamous Talladega Boycott

Volume three of a four volume series .. Big Bucks and Boycotts 1965 - 1971

1969

In 1961, NASCAR driver Curtis Turner met with some Teamster Union leaders in Chicago and quickly laid the groundwork to organize the race drivers into the Federation of Professional Athletes - a proposed affiliation with the Brotherhood of Teamsters. Within a week, Turner made an official announcement regarding a driver's union. Targeted benefits for members were better purses, more adequate insurance coverage, pension plans, a scholarship for children of deceased members and upgraded racing facilities. Turner's ideas were readily accepted among the NASCAR drivers, but he made a number of mistakes.

As part of the bargain, Turner was supposed to campaign for parimutuel betting on the races. There were a number of hardcore traditionalists who were dead set against opening the door to organized gambling.

Turner also made his announcement in haste, saying that a majority of drivers had signed up when in fact they had not. By allowing the entire auto racing industry in on his "secret", he found himself a lonesome target to NASCAR President Bill France's attack. When Turner needed the drivers to back him as a unit, he had only Tim Flock still standing beside him. Turner and Flock were suspended "for life", and the FPA fizzled out.

In August of 1969, there was another attempt to organize a drivers' association. Led by superstar Richard Petty, who surrounded himself with the biggest drawing cards in stock car racing, the drivers kept the lid on their private discussions.

On Thursday evening, August 14, three days before the inaugural Yankee 600 at Michigan International Speedway, eleven drivers met in Ann Arbor, MI. "Eleven of us -- all drivers -- formed it to begin with," said Petty. "It was an idea many people had been working with for a long time. We got together one night up in Michigan and agreed."

Before the meeting broke up, the Professional Drivers Association had been formed.

The main goals of the PDA were very similar to Curtis Turner's original guidelines of the FPA. "Our main goals are a retirement plan and insurance plan for drivers, the formation of a uniform pension plan, and driver and crew convenience at the tracks," said Petty. "If we can clean up the sport from the inside out, it will draw more people to the tracks. The promoters will make more money and can undertake the costs necessary to maintain a pension plan."

News didn't leak out right away. Nobody knew about the meeting or the nature of the discussions. "Before we transact any business," Petty said, "we want to recruit as many members as we possibly can so we can speak for everyone. We want to sign up all Grand National and Grand Touring (NASCAR's compact sedan circuit) drivers first. The Sportsman and Modified drivers will be invited to join if they want to. Then eventually, we'll open it up to everyone who wants to join."

Petty was elected President of the Professional Drivers Association with Cale Yarborough and Elmo Langley becoming Vice Presidents. On the board of directors were Bobby Allison, Buddy Baker, LeeRoy Yarbrough, David Pearson, Pete Hamilton, Charlie Glotzbach, Donnie Allison and James Hylton.

The group consisted of all the front line drivers except Bobby Isaac. He was not informed of the meeting. Some of the other charter members said Isaac, a loner, couldn't be trusted. In the feeling out process, Isaac had not showed any interest in a driver's organization.

Petty said the PDA had retained Lawrence Fleisher, a New York attorney, as its general counsel. Fleisher, a vigorous campaigner in organizing athletes in other professional sports, was also executive Vice President of Restaurants Associates in New York.

Petty, Yarborough and Langley issued a press release a few days before the race teams checked into

Darlington Raceway for the Southern 500.

Bill France expressed surprise at the news. "NASCAR has been pretty great to this bunch of people," stressed France. "Some of these fellows have gotten to be big heroes and they have apparently forgotten how they got there. I can't see why LeeRoy Yarbrough, for instance, would want such a group. He's won $150,000 this year alone. That's not too bad.

"We're not planning to change NASCAR," France continued. "We'll post our prize money and they're welcome to run if they want to. If not, that's their business. There are no contracts with NASCAR. But these fellows had better realize that they can't go very far without factory cars. And I'm sure the factories would put someone in their cars if they should think about a strike or something."

A strike?

"We have made absolutely no demands at all," said Petty. "There have been no strike threats made. The PDA will devote its efforts to the betterment of the sport by seeking to work in harmony with NASCAR, the promoters and others involved in auto racing. However, I want to make it clear that we have elected officers and an executive committee who, with counsel from our attorney, will determine future policies of our association."

Nevertheless, France felt something was up. Just around the corner was the grand opening of the Alabama International Motor Speedway in Talladega, AL, an 1,800 acre site that France had carefully groomed into what he hoped would be "the finest facility in the nation." The inaugural Talladega 500 was scheduled for September 14, 1969.

Construction on the Alabama International Motor Speedway got underway on May 23, 1968. On May 12, 1969, France invited newsmen to tour the yet unpaved 2.66-mile track in a tour bus. "Progress on the Speedway has been dramatic," beamed France. "Moss-

Thornton Construction, general contractors on the project, have stayed ahead of schedule since ground breaking a year ago."

Bobby Allison checked out the facility on several occasions. In early July, he issued some concern for the tires. "This can be a 200 mph track if the tire companies can make a tire that can stand it," said the Hueytown, AL driver. "One of the big limitations at Daytona is that once you get up to about 190 mph, a tire distorts so badly that it's crazy looking. I've been up beside other drivers at Daytona and their tires look strange at 190 mph."

Later that month, France said the track was 92 percent complete and testing could get underway in early August.

Bobby Allison was the first driver to get a first hand look at the new track. On July 24, he drove around the enormous oval in a passenger car. At the time, he said the track was "extremely rough". It was the first negative comment heard about Bill France's new baby.

The leading Ford and Mercury teams began rolling into Talladega the week of August 4. The Chrysler teams had elected to stay away from Talladega during initial testing of their new high-winged, snub-nosed Charger Daytona. Charlie Glotzbach, who had walked away from Cotton Owens' factory Dodge team in March over a disagreement with NASCAR, was itching to get back into the saddle. The Georgetown, IN veteran circled the 4.7-mile Chrysler testing grounds in Chelsea, MI at 193 mph. Additional sessions were aborted when the engine blew in his car.

Further tests for the Dodge Daytona were conducted at Daytona International Speedway. Glotzbach and Buddy Baker each turned laps at 192.6 in a brief session.

Over at France's new track, LeeRoy Yarbrough and Donnie Allison were shaking down their cars for Ford.

Bill France could not understand why LeeRoy Yarbrough joined the Professional Drivers Association

By early summer, the New Alabama International Motor Speedway was beginning to take shape

On Thursday, August 7, Yarbrough drove his Junior Johnson Ford around Talladega at 195.468 mph -- an unofficial world record on a closed course. Allison whipped Banjo Matthews' Ford around the high-banked oval at just a shade over 193 mph.

"This place is rough as a cob," Allison said after climbing out of his car. "It would be a beautiful speedway if it was smooth. The roughness bounces a car around so much that it feels like it's tearing the wheels off in the corners. Going into both corners and where the gate is on the backstretch is where it's so rough. And the only way they're going to fix it is to repave it."

After his record setting lap, Yarbrough said, "It's plenty fast. It ought to make International Speedway Corporation's stock go up."

Bill France donned a helmet and practiced at Talladega for the inaugural event

Yarbrough came back a week later and engaged in extensive tests on August 14 and 15. "We ran a heck of a test and the tires took a beating," said the Jacksonville, FL star. "They've got some improvements to make, but I guess any new speedway has. They've got some rough bumps."

Bobby Isaac and Glotzbach brought their Daytonas to Talladega the following week. Glotzbach spoke to track officials about the rough spots and was told they would be taken care of. Isaac said "it has a few really rough spots." Glotzbach and Isaac got their cars up in the 191-193 mph range.

Baker took the Cotton Owens Dodge to 195.250 on August 21. Bobby Allison, wheeling Mario Rossi's winged Dodge, eclipsed Yarbrough's mark with an electrifying 197.5 mph lap on August 25.

Biggest surprise of the testing sessions in late August was a red and black #53 Ford Talladega. The car had been prepared by Holman-Moody and driven earlier in the year by Bobby Unser and Mario Andretti in USAC stock car events. There was a new driver for the Talladega run. His name happened to be *Bill France.*

France was able to get the car up to about 175 mph. "It's a world record for a 59 year-old man," France said proudly.

When the drivers arrived at Darlington, the PDA members began signing up the remainder of the Grand National drivers. Isaac, who was shunned in the original meetings, was recruited, but he turned the PDA down. "If I wasn't good enough for them two weeks

ago," reasoned Isaac, "then I'm not good enough for them now."

Bobby Allison was cornered by several members of the media. "We formed an organization because we felt we were foolish in not forming one," he told them. "Every other major sport has its players organization. There are definitely things that we have grievances about. I don't feel the purses match the gate receipts on any of the big tracks and some little ones. And we have no pension plan. Insurance is inadequate. A guy devotes his life to racing, and he gets only $7,500 if he gets an arm torn off. If he gets killed, his wife gets $15,000. We've never had a voice in planning or scheduling. They might have a 500-mile race and two days later, a 100-miler a thousand miles away."

There was renewed speculation that the PDA was planning a boycott at some track in the near future. France expressed concerns about "New York interests".

The PDA wasn't issuing any statements publicly. During the pre-race proceedings at Darlington, several small groups of drivers were seen in private conferences. When they were confronted by a media representative, they clammed up.

Buddy Baker issued one public statement. "I think a lot of people, including the press, have the wrong conception of our association," he said. "We aren't going to start a bonfire like a lot of people think. We're not going to start a battle with NASCAR or boycott anything."

PDA President Petty made a similar statement. "We have no plans to boycott or strike any race track. Anything you've heard is strictly hearsay. We haven't talked about this whatsoever. We would like for you to keep in mind that anything that hurts racing, hurts us."

Larry LoPatin, President of American Raceways which operated four tracks hosting Grand National events, offered his opinion. "I think the sport has a long way to go before pressure groups start making demands from it. A driver's organization may be fine, but Bill France and Bill France, Jr. are no patsies. I believe their interests in the drivers is sincere," said LoPatin.

Petty wouldn't say exactly how many members the PDA had signed up, but it was most of the Grand National regulars and many of the Grand Touring competitors. Each member had paid the $200 initiation fee.

Eight days before the running of the first Talladega 500, Bill France filed an entry for the big race. He had

Richard Petty and Bill France "hashed it out" in open garage area before Talladega 500

his primary entry -- the #99 purple car. The quickest lap in the #88 was a staggering 199.987 mph, an unofficial world record. It made him an early favorite for the pole and a good bet to hit the 200 mph barrier.

In late Tuesday practice sessions, a few of the faster cars experienced tire problems. But it was not unlike similar first day shake-down sessions at other new tracks.

On Wednesday, September 10, teams got down to the fine tuning in the run for the pole. As practice continued, speeds began to creep up toward the magical 200 mph barrier. And some of the teams were alarmed at the number of tires that were coming apart.

Several of the teams left their cars in the garage during the first day qualifying. Only nine cars made the run against the clock. Glotzbach turned a lap of 199.466 mph to win the pole. The other qualifiers in order were: LeeRoy Yarbrough (199.350), Cale Yarborough (198.651), Buddy Baker (197.814), Richard Petty (196.964), Bobby Isaac (196.386), David Pearson (196.060), Bobby Johns (188.961) and James Hylton (187.401). Fifteen spots had been open.

Many of the tires had blistered and cracked in the two lap run against the clock. France quickly stepped in and waived the tire rule, which stated that a driver must start the race on the same set of tires he qualified.

Goodyear and Firestone representatives said they would bring in new tires on Thursday.

Twenty-one spots were open on the second day of time trials, but only four cars made runs through the

spoken with Bobby Allison at Richmond. "He asked me if he drove in the race," said Allison, "could he join the PDA. I think he's serious about it. He told me he had a car and he had filed an entry.

"My reaction to that?" Allison responded to questioning. "I'd say that he would be a foolish old man. He wants to get in the PDA any way he can."

If France became an active driver, it would open a legal avenue for him to join the Professional Drivers Association. Then he could elbow his way in on some of the meetings and find out what really was going on.

On Tuesday, September 9, teams began checking into Alabama International Motor Speedway. All of the Ford teams were there in force -- and there were seven winged Dodge Daytonas on hand. Two were entered by Nichels Engineering; driver Charlie Glotzbach would get his choice of the faster of the two.

Glotzbach shook down both Nichels Engineering Daytonas and found the royal blue #88 faster than

Richard Petty's Ford loaded on the trailer 24 hours before the start of the Talladega 500. Petty led the Professional Drivers Association boycott of the inaugural event at Alabama International Motor Speedway

timing lights. Bill Seifert (174.426), J.C. Spradley (164.307), Cecil Gordon (161.459) and Frank Warren (159.387) earned positions 10-13. The Allison brothers had not attempted a qualification. Neither had Dave Marcis; or John Sears; or Richard Brickhouse; or Bill France. Most of the teams had discovered the new tires shipped in overnight were not any better than the ones on Wednesday.

By Thursday night, tire company reps were in a frenzy. Phone calls were placed to the headquarters -- and both Goodyear and Firestone promised another compound would arrive via chartered plane on Friday.

Throughout the morning practice session, teams tried all available tire compounds. Although there was no marked improvement, 14 cars did take time trials. They ranged from Donnie Allison's 197.847 mph to Henley Gray's 145.067.

Many trackside conferences took place on Friday. As the sun was beginning to slide down the blue Alabama sky, an impromptu test session was arranged. Charlie Glotzbach's Dodge would mount all available Goodyear tires; and Donnie Allison's Ford would carry all the Firestones in controlled tests. Every four laps, the two daring drivers would come in the pits and change. "My heart was in my mouth the whole time," said Allison. "That was the most scared I've ever been in all my life."

Glotzbach was seated in his car, which broke an A-Frame during the test. "They ought to call this race," he said. "Nobody has any tires good for more than 15 laps."

Firestone officials studied the tires and made their decision. They would not mount a single tire on any car in the Talladega 500. They packed up their gear and headed out.

Goodyear was about to make the same decision. But Bill France convinced Goodyear's Public Relations Manager Dick Ralstin to hang around a little longer. After a private conference with France, Ralstin said Goodyear would bring in another tire by race time Sunday.

The Firestone pull-out and the uncertainty of Goodyear really settled the issue. Most of the drivers went to bed Friday night knowing they would not race in the Talladega 500.

Petty talked with several of the PDA members that night and virtually all of them were in favor of not racing on Sunday.

At 10:30 am Saturday, Petty and France met face-to-face in the garage area. Petty informed France of the PDA's decision not to compete. An argument followed -- a heated one at that. "There will be a race tomorrow," France yelled to Petty. "If you don't want to be in it, pack up and leave."

Petty loaded his Ford onto the trailer. Several other teams followed suit. By late morning, there were 12-14 cars loaded.

Shortly after lunch, Petty and France met again in the garage area. This time, Petty was joined by an array of fellow drivers. Petty tried to convince France that there was no alternative other than to postpone the race.

"What you hot-dogs do is your business," barked France. "But quit threatening the boys who want to race. If you want to go home, then go!"

"Wait a minute," Petty shot back. "That threatening goes both ways. Don't threaten us."

Donnie Allison stepped in and said to France, "Bill, look at the right front tire on Dave Marcis' car. It's shredded all to pieces and he was only running 185."

"If the tires shred at 190, " countered France, "then run 175 or 180. It's like flying. If you run into bad weather, you slow down."

LeeRoy Yarbrough stepped up and spoke in a hushed tone. "Bill, how would you like to attend a couple of funerals next week?"

"I'll take my chances on that," came his reply. "There will be a race tomorrow and we will pay the posted purse. If you aren't going to race, then leave."

On Saturday afternoon, the Grand Touring cars engaged in a 400-mile battle. Ken Rush of High Point, NC drove a Camaro to victory. There were no spin outs or crashes in the 400 miler. Nor were there any tire problems.

After the GT race, another dozen or so Grand National drivers had loaded their cars. But no one pulled out of the garage area. NASCAR officials had gone through the GT garage, telling the drivers to stick around. They may be needed on Sunday if worse came to worse.

As darkness spread over the sprawling facility Saturday afternoon, a booming voice was heard over the public address system. There was no mistaking this voice. It belonged to Bill France.

"All those who are not going to race, leave the garage area so those who are going to race can work on their cars."

It was now or never. This was the moment of truth.

Within a few moments, a truck motor cranked up. It was the Petty Enterprises truck. The headlights came on and the famous #43 was pulled from the garage area.

Others followed. A total of 32 cars were hauled out of the pit and garage area late Saturday afternoon. As the Grand Nationals were being towed out, the Grand Touring cars were being pulled into the primary garage. It was a hectic hour.

"Most of us felt the Talladega track is too rough and the tires we have are not safe to race at speeds around 200 mph," explained PDA President Petty. "It was just that simple. We stick our necks out every time we race. We aren't foolish enough to play Russian roulette. The track is rough and dangerous. We will not race on the track as it is now."

James Hylton was another who left the track. "If they

don't do something about this track, somebody's going to get killed. There's no tire that will stand up to speeds over 190 mph. I put three hard laps on mine and they came apart."

Richard Brickhouse, who had joined the PDA at Darlington, said as a member he wasn't given any choice. "We were told we couldn't race," said the sophomore driver. "The way they voted was by raising their hands. The majority raised their hands, so we were told the PDA was not going to race."

GT driver Buck Baker, who shunned the Chrysler and Ford boycotts in 1965 and 1966, offered his opinion, "Things must have gotten a little plush for a lot of these guys," said the crusty Baker. "They must want things a little better than they are. When I sign an entry blank, I'll race. I remember driving around holes in the track big enough to bury a man."

Bill France said all along there would be a Talladega 500 on September 14, 1969

The Talladega 500 went on as scheduled. A crowd of 62,000 showed up -- many of them drawn by curiosity. Each spectator was handed a written statement from Bill France. It read: *"I am very much surprised that some of our drivers and car owners would wait until the last day prior to a major race and withdraw their automobiles from a race. Track officials and NASCAR officials worked until the last moment to get the drivers to fulfill their obligations to the fans who traveled from some distance to see the event. Everyone expected they would race.*

"It would be unfair to the spectators who traveled to Talladega to see a race to postpone it. It would also be unfair to the drivers and car owners who wish to compete.

"Therefore, we will start the first annual Talladega 500 at 1:00 pm Sunday, as scheduled, lining up the Grand National cars in the order they qualified. We will allow the Grand Touring cars to start in the back of this field in order that they finished the 'Bama 400. We will pay the purse of $120,000 as advertised.

"Persons who attend the race, and those holding reserved seat tickets who do not attend, will be allowed to exchange them for tickets for a future race at Daytona Speedway or for a future race at Alabama International Motor Speedway.

"They can see two races for the price of one.

"This does not apply to press tickets, complimentary tickets or credentials.

Sincerely, Bill France.

Shortly before the race got underway, the PA announcer said, "Folks, this one is on the house."

The starting field for the Talladega 500 consisted of 13 Grand National cars. The remainder of the 36 car field was filled with Grand Touring automobiles.

Bobby Isaac sat on the pole in his K&K Insurance Dodge Daytona. Jim Vandiver, last minute replacement for Bobby Johns in the Ray Fox Dodge Charger, was on the outside rail position. Jim Hurtubise, started third in the L.G. DeWitt Ford. DeWitt, Vice-President of North Carolina Motor Speedway in Rockingham, had been encouraged by France to keep his car in the field. Regular driver John Sears, a PDA member, joined the walk-out.

Other Grand National drivers not honoring the boycott were Dr. Don Tarr, rookie Dick Brooks, Ramo Stott, Coo Coo Marlin, Roy Tyner, Homer Newland (an ARCA driver), Richard Brickhouse (who was seated in the Nichels Engineering Dodge Daytona), Les Snow (ARCA driver who hopped aboard Neil Castles' Dodge), privateer Earl Brooks, and Tiny Lund (last minute substitute for Bill France himself).

A promising driver, Brickhouse had been told that the #99 Dodge Daytona would be available for him to drive if he wanted it.

The 29 year-old Rocky Point, NC sophomore pilot stayed up nearly all night Saturday trying to make a decision whether to race or not. "If I had known or suspected a boycott," he said, "I never would have joined the PDA."

Brickhouse tried to get in touch with PDA President Petty Sunday morning. He was unable to contact him. So he had his resignation from the PDA announced over the Public Address.

"When I entered Grand National racing, my only objective was to make something good out of it," he said. "I wanted to get to the top if I was capable -- to make racing my profession. I have spent a great deal of money and a lot of time to do it. I have sacrificed.

"I can't afford to be a playboy. I can't afford to gamble. I came to Talladega to race. I have no intentions of jeopardizing my life or that of others. I will run a comfortable speed until it comes time to win the race."

Brickhouse won the first Talladega 500 finishing 7.0-seconds ahead of runner-up Vandiver. "I think anybody in my position would have done the same thing. All my life I've dreamed about driving a factory backed car. I couldn't pass up this opportunity," said Brickhouse.

Both Ford and Chrysler factory representatives left it up to each team owner whether to race or not. All team owners pulled their cars out with the factory backed drivers -- with the exception of Nord Krauskopf, whose driver Bobby Isaac said all along he wanted to race; and Ray Nichels, who provided his back-up car to Brickhouse.

Isaac led the first competitive lap at Talladega, but his Dodge experienced tire problems even at conservative speeds. He wound up fourth. Third place went to Stott, who was a last minute replacement for Brickhouse in the Ellis car.

France greeted Brickhouse in victory lane and congratulated him for winning his first Grand National event. Later, France issued a statement to the press: "This race reminded me of what the great Cannonball Baker (NASCAR's first National Commissioner) used to say, 'Quitters never win and winners never quit'. The guys who raced today were the real winners."

Wendell Scott had intentions of competing in the race, but his two year-old Ford was sabotaged before the race -- to the extent that he was unable to drive it.

Monday, September 15, Petty received countless telephone calls from other drivers and members of the media. He explained the action that the PDA took.

"We first discovered we were going to have trouble with tires on Wednesday," he said. "NASCAR right away lifted the tire rule. Rubber company officials started promising us a different tire. They brought in a bunch late Thursday and a couple of the boys took them out to test them. They didn't blister as bad, but they were filled with cracks after three or four laps. Three different tires were tried and each time, they proved unsatisfactory.

"Finally, the tire people told us they could have 170 of a new compound ready by race time on Sunday. This meant no scuffing in and no practice laps. In addition, they said they wouldn't mount any tires on any car that ran over 190 mph.

"We tried to talk to Bill France into postponing the race two or three weeks until the tire companies had a chance to come up with a tire that would work.

"We did things wrong at Talladega," admitted Petty. "But so did they (NASCAR). It was about 50-50, maybe 60-40 in our favor. We should have found a quiet place to talk instead of hashing it out in the garage area."

France said he thought about postponing the race. "I could have put it off until, say, November," he said. "But how do I know that they wouldn't have done the same thing again?"

At 4:30 pm, Thursday September 18, 1969, the PDA issued an official statement. The contents of the written draft, in its entirety:

"The Professional Drivers Association, whose members withdrew last Saturday (Sept. 13) from the "Talladega 500" restated the reasons why the drivers felt it was absolutely necessary to take this step.

"Drivers who drove and tested this new 2.66-mile racing surface had informed the president of NASCAR as early as July 24th, that the layout of the track was extremely rough. Since it was felt that the track could not be resurfaced in time for the race scheduled for Sept. 14, the drivers were led to believe that this dan-

gerous condition could be overcome with proper tires. The tire companies were aware of the problems after testing, and they promised to undertake all possible action to solve them.

"During the five days of practice and qualifications for the "Talladega 500", additional promises to correct the grave safety problems of the track were made to the drivers. In fact, six different types of tires were utilized during the preliminary runs without success. None was able to withstand speeds of 190 mph or over for more than eight laps. Moreover, tire failures were not restricted to any particular make of car. After a final special testing period Friday evening, one of the two tire companies withdrew its products completely from the race. The other tire company promised to solve the problem on Saturday with a new tire that would arrive Saturday afternoon.

"On Saturday, a spokesman for the remaining tire company was quoted as saying: "We will not guarantee that any tire we have available for the race will not come apart at full racing speeds."

"A meeting of the PDA was then held in order to bring the tire problem to the attention of its members who were planning to drive in the race. At that meeting it was clear that the only tires available for the race would be untested and without proper break-in.

"The result of the meeting was that all of the members present determined that they could not compete because, as Richard Petty, the elected President of the PDA stated: "This track is not ready to race on." Since full racing speeds could not be attained on the available tires, Petty stated: "There isn't a PDA member alive who will deliberately run behind another driver when his car can run faster. Every serious race driver wants to win, right from the start. If full racing speeds could not be risked, the race could not be run in a proper way."

"The meeting recommended to NASCAR that the race be postponed for several weeks so the roughness of the track could be repaired and proper tires supplied.

"Bill France, the track president, and also the president of NASCAR steadfastly refused to postpone the race, insisting that it go on under the conditions that existed, and with the available tires.

"In the face of this indifference to the safety of the drivers, the drivers asked: "How can Mr. France, president of NASCAR look out for the welfare of NASCAR drivers, when he owns the track?"

"The drivers pointed out that they gave up $100,000 in prize money in missing the race in order to establish the right of drivers to be protected from unsafe track conditions.

"The PDA regrets that many of the fans were inconvenienced and disappointed by the lack of its participants. However, the members felt that in view of the hazards involved it would be unfair to the drivers and their families to compete. The tire companies them-

selves admitted they had no tires that would withstand the punishment of this extremely rough racing surface for an undetermined number of laps at full speed. It was also the feeling of the members that a race of less the maximum capability of the race cars, as was ultimately staged, would be unfair to the fans and contribute to the deterioration of the sport.

"The membership of the PDA is open to all active race drivers who are interested in improving the sport and the quality of the drivers. Its purpose is the safety and general welfare of its members, as well as the entire racing fraternity.

"Our members are race drivers first and accept the risks involved, but when these life and death risks become both unreasonable and unnecessary then corrective action is essential.

"Despite this, Mr. France has been unwilling, since the race, to discuss the problems with the drivers and with their lawyer."

Bill France had a statement of his own, which was published in the NASCAR Newsletter:

"I would like to take this opportunity to explain to you some of the reasons the decision was made to run the Talladega 500 stock car race on September 14 on schedule, despite a boycott by a majority of the drivers who had entered and qualified their cars.

"NASCAR has two major responsibilities to consider: (1) NASCAR must see that the fans purchasing tickets see what was advertised and publicized if humanly possible. It is the responsibility of the sanctioning body, the track operators and the drivers to do everything humanly possible to see that a race is run as scheduled. (2) NASCAR must protect the drivers who wish to compete from being deprived of fair competition while guaranteeing that they will receive the posted awards that have been advertised and publicized.

"In refusing to postpone or cancel the race NASCAR and the speedway fulfilled obligations to the ticket purchasers and to the drivers.

"I have received numerous letters since the race. The ticket buyers, and a vast majority of our NASCAR members are in support of the action taken.

"I want to personally thank the NASCAR crew of officials, many who had to work all night Saturday to get a new field of cars ready, for their dedication to NASCAR and to the sport. I also want to thank the tire manufacturers and the other accessory companies for their efforts in servicing the cars.

"I feel the right decisions were made for the public. They went to Talladega to see a race and they saw one. In addition they will be allowed to exchange their rain checks for a future race at Talladega or Daytona.

"Sincerely, Bill France.

Before the ink was dry on each prepared statement, NASCAR had announced that the Wilkes 400 at North Wilkesboro Speedway had been postponed from September 21 to October 5. Track president Enoch Staley requested the change "to protect the public and speedway from anything like what happened last weekend at Talladega."

France's first step was to insert a clause that said the race cars, once entered in a NASCAR Grand National event, would have to race. If the original driver was not able to compete for any unforeseen reason, the car owner would agree to name a substitute driver. France flew to Detroit to discuss the proposal with the automotive factories. He was turned down by both Ford and Chrysler. "That was ridiculous," said a Chrysler spokesman. "Our cars would become property of the race track until the race was completed."

Within a few days, France and NASCAR announced that all entry blanks for future Grand National events would contain a "Good Faith to the Public" pledge.

On each entry blank the following was written:

"In signing this blank, both driver or drivers and car owner recognize their obligation to the public and race promoters or speedway corporation posting the prize money and conducting the event. Therefore, we agree to compete in the event if humanly possible unless the

Behind the 13 Grand National cars, 23 Grand Touring automobiles comprised the Talladega 500 field

event is postponed, cancelled or if the car fails to qualify for the starting field."

NASCAR's Vice-President Lin Kuchler made the official statement from Daytona Beach. "As the sanctioning organization," said Kuchler, "NASCAR has two major responsibilities. One is to see that the fans who purchase tickets see what was advertised and publicized. Second, there is the responsibility to the driver to see that the race is run on schedule under the rules and that the prize money is paid as advertised.

"In order to protect the public and the track operator from a situation such as the late-hour driver boycott at Talladega, the Good Faith to the Public pledge will be in all future entry blanks.

"If a driver does not want to sign the pledge and if there is any doubt in his mind about his willingness to compete, he should not enter the event," said Kuchler.

On September 24, 1969, the PDA had announced that members were having a meeting in Charlotte. All track promoters and Bill France were welcomed to attend.

The day before, September 23, France met with track promoters in Greensboro. At the meeting, the NASCAR president discussed the new entry blanks, but more importantly, he told them not to attend the PDA meeting in Charlotte.

Most promoters stayed away, but Richard Howard of Charlotte Motor Speedway, J. Elsie Webb of North Carolina Motor Speedway and Clay Earles of Martinsville Speedway went to the PDA meeting anyway. All three of them had races coming up in the immediate future and they felt it was in their best interests to be present.

"The Talladega incident is behind us all," declared Petty. "All PDA members plan to race in all the remaining events on the 1969 schedule. This meeting is called to clear the air about certain things."

Fifty-eight people attended the PDA meeting. Drivers and track promoters were welcome; the press was not. The 36 drivers present signed the new entry blanks for the upcoming races at Charlotte, Rockingham and Martinsville.

PDA Vice-President Elmo Langley was disappointed Bill France was not in attendance. "We were hoping he would care enough to attend the meeting," said Langley. Attorney Larry Fleisher said, "I don't know why Bill France is trying to avoid meeting with us."

"I had more important things to do," was France's reply.

*   *   *

There had been rumors that the drivers were planning a strike or boycott at Talladega -- to hurt France. But preconceived reasons -- if there were any -- were forgotten when the tire problems and track conditions gave the drivers a ready-made opportunity to balk. France then acted in the only way he felt he could. He adjusted in the face of controversy to give the public a race and a free ticket to a later show.

Chrysler's Bob Rodger designed the new Dodge Daytona

Race No. 1

Flu-Ridden Petty Wins Georgia 500 at Macon

MACON, GA (Nov. 17, 1968) -- Richard Petty, bed-ridden with the flu, decided to race at the last minute and won the Georgia 500 at Middle Georgia Raceway. The 250-miler on the half mile paved track put Petty on top of the early 1969 Grand National point standings.

Petty drove his Plymouth around David Pearson with 21 laps to go and beat his Ford rival to the finish line by 5.0-seconds. James Hylton came in third, Elmo Langley was fourth and John Sears fifth.

The event was a highly competitive affair as the lead changed hands 12 times among four drivers. Bobby Isaac started second and led for 61 laps before his

Dodge was sidelined by engine trouble after 315 laps. Bobby Allison led on three occasions for 61 laps, but his Plymouth went out on lap 252 with rear gearing failure. Darel Dieringer's Plymouth developed drive shaft problems and went out at the 119 lap mark.

Two caution flags for 16 laps slowed Petty's winning speed to 85.121 mph. Earl Brooks broke a wheel and plowed into the guard rail on lap 217. LeeRoy Yarbrough wrecked the Lyle Stelter Mercury on lap 322.

A crowd of 6,000 watched half of the starting field complete the distance.

Grand National Race No. 1
500 Laps at Middle Georgia Raceway
Macon, GA
250 Miles on Half-mile Paved Track
November 17, 1968

Fin	St	No.	Driver	Team / Car	Laps	Money	Status
1	5	43	Richard Petty	Petty Enterprises '68 Plym	500	$3,500	Running
2	1	17	David Pearson	Holman-Moody '68 Ford	500	2,345	Running
3	6	48	James Hylton	Hylton Eng '68 Dodge	490	1,375	Running
4	8	64	Elmo Langley	Langley-Woodfield '66 Ford	476	925	Running
5	12	4	John Sears	L G DeWitt '66 Ford	466	825	Running
6	7	39	Friday Hassler	Red Sharp '66 Chevrolet	462	725	Engine
7	21	06	Neil Castles	Castles '67 Plymouth	459	750	Running
8	17	47	Bill Seifert	Seifert '68 Ford	454	625	Running
9	25	19	Henley Gray	Gray '68 Ford	447	525	Running
10	20	76	Ben Arnold	Red Culpepper '66 Ford	442	425	Running
11	29	45	Cecil Gordon	Bill Seifert '68 Ford	439	380	Running
12	19	46	Roy Mayne	Tom Hunter '66 Chevrolet	423	400	Running
13	15	34	Wendell Scott	Scott '66 Ford	416	350	Running
14	27	93	Walson Gardner	Gardner '67 Ford	408	300	Running
15	30	9	Roy Tyner	Tyner '67 Pontiac	392	200	Running
16	10	56	LeeRoy Yarbrough	Lyle Stelter '67 Mercury	316	225	Crash
17	2	71	Bobby Isaac	K&K Insurance '68 Dodge	315	300	Engine
18	13	8	Ed Negre	Negre '67 Ford	294	225	Running
19	3	14	Bobby Allison	Friedkin Ent '68 Plymouth	252	275	Rear End
20	26	38	Wayne Smith	Smith '68 Chevrolet	222	225	Engine
21	9	49	G C Spencer	Spencer '67 Plymouth	210	225	Rear End
22	22	5	Earl Brooks	'67 Ford	189	250	Crash
23	23	57	Ervin Pruitt	Pruitt '67 Dodge	162	235	Rear End
24	18	80	E J Trivette	E C Reid '66 Chevrolet	140	225	Heating
25	4	22	Darel Dieringer	Mario Rossi '68 Plymouth	119	250	D Shaft
26	24	0	Dr Don Tarr	Tarr '66 Chevrolet	94	175	Rear End
27	14	96	Don Tomberlin	Roy Buckner '66 Ford	90	175	Engine
28	11	10	Bill Champion	Champion '66 Ford	81	175	Oil Leak
29	16	25	Jabe Thomas	Don Robertson '67 Ford	26	175	Engine
30	28	70	J D McDuffie	McDuffie '67 Buick	20	150	Engine

Time of Race: 3 hours, 8 minutes, 6 seconds
Average Speed: 85.121 mph
Pole Winner: David Pearson - 95.472 mph
Lap Leaders: David Pearson 1-2, Bobby Isaac 3-28, Pearson 29-31, Bobby Allison 32-57, Isaac 58-92, Allison 93-132, Richard Petty 133-219, Allison 220-222, Petty 223-360, Pearson 361, Petty 362-477, Pearson 478-479, Petty 480-500.
Cautions: 2 for 16 laps   Margin of Victory: 5 seconds   Attendance: 6,000

Race No. 2

Allison Nabs Petty With Last Lap Pass at Montgomery

MONTGOMERY, AL (Dec. 8, 1968) -- Bobby Allison, hopelessly out of the running with just nine laps to go, took advantage of a timely caution and nabbed Richard Petty at the finish line for victory in the Alabama 200.

The slim crowd of 2,800, braving a bitter, icy wind, watched stock car racing history as both Allison and Petty were taking their last tides in Plymouths. Petty had shocked the racing world by announcing he was switching to Ford, and Allison was expected to shift over to the Mario Rossi Dodge team for the 1969 season.

James Hylton finished in third place, Bobby Isaac was fourth and Neil Castles fifth.

Petty had taken first place from Allison in the 168th lap and was pulling away. On lap 191 of the 200 lapper, Roy Tyner blew the engine in his Pontiac, bringing out the second caution flag. Allison ducked in the pits and got two new tires on his car. Petty opted to take track position and keep the lead.

When the green flag came out with two laps to go, Allison rapidly made up the deficit and was sitting on Petty's rear bumper within a lap. Coming off the final turn, Allison dived inside of Petty and won by four feet.

"I ain't believin' this," said Allison, shaking his head. "We were out of it with 10 laps to go, and here I am in victory lane."

Petty was disappointed in failing to win his final start in a Plymouth. "I didn't figure he could catch up in one or two laps," he muttered, "but he did."

Allison averaged 73.200 mph for his 12th career Grand National win.

Grand National Race No. 2
200 Laps at Montgomery Speedway
Montgomery, AL
"Alabama 200"
100 Miles on Half-mile Paved Track
December 8, 1968

Fin	St	No.	Driver	Team / Car	Laps	Money	Status
1	3	14	Bobby Allison	Friedkin Ent '68 Plymouth	200	$1,000	Running
2	1	43	Richard Petty	Petty Enterprises '68 Plym	200	600	Running
3	4	48	James Hylton	Hylton Eng '68 Dodge	195	400	Running
4	2	71	Bobby Isaac	K&K Insurance '68 Dodge	193	300	Running
5	7	06	Neil Castles	Castles '67 Plymouth	188	275	Running
6	6	4	John Sears	L G DeWitt '67 Ford	187	240	Running
7	9	76	Ben Arnold	Red Culpepper '66 Ford	185	200	Running
8	16	19	Henley Gray	Gray '68 Ford	184	175	Running
9	13	47	Cecil Gordon	Bill Seifert '68 Ford	181	150	Running
10	17	30	Dave Marcis	Larry Wehrs '6 Chevrolet	180	140	Running
11	21	57	Ervin Pruitt	Pruitt '67 Dodge	178	130	Running
12	14	5	Earl Brooks	'67 Ford	174	120	Running
13	10	70	J D McDuffie	McDuffie '67 Buick	170	110	Running
14	18	25	Jabe Thomas	Don Robertson '67 Ford	170	100	Running
15	20	31	Bill Ervin	Newman Long '66 Ford	161	100	Running
16	19	45	Lee Gordon	Bill Seifert '68 Ford	160	100	Running
17	11	8	Ed Negre	Negre '67 Ford	155	100	Running
18	12	9	Roy Tyner	Tyner '67 Pontiac	143	100	Engine
19	15	34	Wendell Scott	Scott '66 Ford	110	100	Manifold
20	5	2	Red Farmer	J D Bracken '66 Chevrolet	101	100	Oil Pres
21	8	64	Elmo Langley	Langley-Woodfield '66 Ford	81	100	Clutch
22	22	09	Sherril Pruitt	Roy Tyner '66 Chevrolet	10	100	Heating

Time of Race: 1 hour, 21 minutes, 58 seconds
Average Speed: 73.200 mph
Pole Winner: Richard Petty - 80.899 mph
Lap Leaders: Richard Petty 1-9, Bobby Isaac 10-45, Petty 46-53, Isaac 54-67, Petty 68-143, Bobby Allison 144-167, Petty 168-199, Allison 200.
Cautions: 2 for 11 laps   Margin of Victory: 4 feet   Attendance: 2,800

Richard Petty and crew go over new #43 Ford.
Petty won his first outing at Riverside

Race No. 3

Petty's First Ford Ride Nets Riverside 500 Victory

RIVERSIDE, CA (Feb. 1) -- Richard Petty, admittedly a weakling on a road course, stayed on the Riverside International Raceway well enough to scramble to victory in the twice-delayed Motor Trend 500. It was the first time the 32 year-old Petty had driven a Ford on the NASCAR Grand National tour.

Petty, an acknowledged master of the oval tracks, once said he "couldn't get much experience on a road course because I can't stay on one long enough."

Petty encountered two close calls en route to his 93rd career win. He spun off the course twice, but held the lead for 103 of the 186 laps that made up the 500 miler.

A.J. Foyt, who won the pole and led the first 27 laps, finished second, 25 seconds behind Petty's electric blue Ford. David Pearson, with relief assistance from Parnelli Jones, was third. USAC's Al Unser was fourth and James Hylton fifth.

"The difference today was that I finished," said Petty, who scored his first road course win since he won at Bridgehampton, NY on July 21, 1963. "In other races, I've spent too much time off the track trying to get things fixed."

The race, twice rained out on Sundays by flood-brewing storms, was run on a Saturday afternoon before a crowd of 46,300.

Perennial favorite Dan Gurney, winner of this classic five times, never got untracked. The Costa Mesa, CA road racing specialist started third, but never led. He spun off the course once when he lost his brakes, and backed into a pile of hay bales in the ninth turn. He eventually went out on lap 66 with engine failure.

Cale Yarborough went out with mechanical problems on lap 81, and LeeRoy Yarbrough blew his engine with five laps to go. He still wound up sixth.

The event was run without a full course caution and Petty averaged a record 105.498 mph. Forty-four cars started the race and only 14 finished.

Race No. 4

Pearson From 15th to 1st in Opening 125-Mile Qualifier

DAYTONA BEACH, FL (Feb. 20) -- David Pearson, the first man to officially top the 190 mph barrier in a stock car at Daytona, started deep in the field but easily captured the first 125-mile qualifying race at Daytona International Speedway.

Pearson started his Holman-Moody Ford 15th on the grid with a time of 190.029 mph. It took the

Grand National Race No. 3
186 Laps at Riverside Int'l Raceway
Riverside, CA
"Motor Trend 500"
500 Miles on 2.7-mile Paved Road Course
February 1, 1969

Fin	St	No.	Driver	Team / Car	Laps	Money	status
1	4	43	Richard Petty	Petty Enterprises '69 Ford	186	$19,650	Running
2	1	1	A J Foyt	Jack Bowsher '69 Ford	186	10,200	Running
3	5	17	David Pearson*	Holman-Moody '69 Ford	184	6,775	Running
4	6	41	Al Unser	Robbins Electric '69 Dodge	183	3,825	Running
5	14	48	James Hylton	Hylton Eng '67 Dodge	177	2,450	Running
6	2	98	LeeRoy Yarbrough	Junior Johnson '69 Ford	177	2,050	Engine
7	16	96	Ray Elder	Fred Elder '67 Dodge	172	1,400	Running
8	15	45	Scotty Cain	Bill Clinton '69 Ford	170	1,450	Running
9	21	4	John Sears	L G DeWitt '67 Ford	169	1,350	Running
10	29	18	Harold Hardesty	Bob Bristol '66 Ford	163	1,250	Running
11	28	6	Ray Johnstone	Cos Cancilla '67 Olds	163	1,225	Running
12	23	61	Dick Bown	Mike Ober '69 Chevrolet	160	1,230	Running
13	19	06	Neil Castles	Castles '67 Plymouth	157	1,125	Running
14	33	19	Henley Gray	Harry Melton '68 Ford	152	1,000	Running
15	12	22	Bobby Allison	Mario Rossi '69 Dodge	151	1,100	Rear End
16	34	79	Randy Dodd	'67 Chevrolet	143	950	Rear End
17	42	9	Marvin Sjolin	'67 Mercury	132	925	Running
18	7	97	Mario Andretti	Holman-Moody '69 Ford	132	925	Engine
19	24	64	Elmo Langley	Langley '66 Ford	131	875	Engine
20	20	15	Paul Dorrity	Glen Dorrity '67 Chevrolet	129	850	Engine
21	30	0	Dr Don Tarr	Tarr '67 Chevrolet	110	825	Trans
22	9	12	Roger McCluskey	'69 Plymouth	100	825	Heating
23	32	25	Wendell Parnell	Michael's '66 Chevrolet	87	795	Engine
24	11	21	Cale Yarborough	Wood Brothers '69 Mercury	81	940	Engine
25	31	143	Frank Burnett	'67 Plymouth	80	785	Trans
26	3	121	Dan Gurney	Wood Brothers '69 Mercury	66	980	Engine
27	43	09	Sam Rose, Jr.	Sam Rose '67 Ford	65	775	Rear End
28	37	198	Robert Link	Link '67 Ford	62	775	Engine
29	35	70	J D McDuffie	McDuffie '67 Buick	50	775	Engine
30	17	04	Cliff Garner	'67 Plymouth	48	775	Engine
31	26	16	Jerry Oliver	'67 Oldsmobile	48	770	Trans
32	40	29	Ralph Arnold	'66 Ford	43	765	Engine
33	13	31	Don White	Nichels Eng '68 Dodge	41	835	Engine
34	18	90	Mary Kinert	Frank Townsend '67 Chevy	40	755	Trans
35	44	7	Jack McCoy	Ernie Conn '69 Dodge	27	750	Trans
36	38	74	Robert Hale	'66 Pontiac	24	750	Engine
37	10	11	Paunelli Jones	Holman-Moody '69 Ford	22	770	Engine
38	8	71	Bobby Isaac	K&K Insurance '69 Dodge	22	775	Trans
39	27	92	Guy Jones	'66 Ford	8	800	Engine
40	22	106	David James	'67 Plymouth	5	850	Rear End
41	25	32	Joe Frasson	Gary Sigman '69 Plymouth	3	825	Ignition
42	39	88	Jim Cook	Dan Dostinich '67 Chevrolet	3	750	Ignition
43	41	2	Johnny Steele	Steele '69 Ford	3	750	Oil Leak
44	36	8	Bob England	England '69 Chevrolet	1	750	Engine

Time of Race: 4 hours, 45 minutes, 37 seconds
Average Speed: 105.498 mph
Pole Winner: A J Foyt - 110.323 mph
Lap Leaders: A J Foyt 1-27, LeeRoy Yarbrough 28, Mario Andretti 29-31, Foyt 32-50, Yarbrough 51-57, Andretti 58-61, Foyt 62-77, Richard Petty 78-82, Yarbrough 83-88, Petty 89-186.
Cautions: None   Margin of Victory: 25 seconds   Attendance: 46,300.
* Relieved by Parnelli Jones

five positions in the 50 lap sprint race.

Buddy Baker, who won the pole for this preliminary event along with the Daytona 500 with a clocking of 188.901 mph, went only two laps before he pulled in the pits and quit. "I want to save my car for the 500," said Baker. "There was nothing to gain by running this race."

Of the 27 cars that started the race, 22 were running at the finish. Only three however, were on the lead lap. H.B. Ranier, whose background is in coal mining, entered two Dodges in the race. Andy Hampton crashed his car in the sixth lap, and Vic Elford wound up 11th.

LeeRoy Yarbrough, who lost his primary Junior Johnson Ford in a practice crash, drove a back-up Ford, but struggled to finish ninth. He was lapped twice.

Pearson averaged 152.181 mph for his 47th career Grand National victory.

Grand National Race No. 4
50 Laps at Daytona Int'l Speedway
Daytona Beach, FL
125 Miles on 2.5-mile Paved Track
February 20, 1969

Fin	St	No.	Driver	Team / Car	Laps	Money	Status
1	15	17	David Pearson	Holman-Moody '69 Ford	50	$1,200	Running
2	9	21	Cale Yarborough	Wood Brothers '69 Mercury	50	800	Running
3	6	27	Donnie Allison	Banjo Matthews '69 Ford	50	550	Running
4	16	11	A J Foyt	Jack Bowsher '69 Ford	49	500	Running
5	11	88	Benny Parsons	Russ Dawson '69 Ford	49	450	Running
6	5	67	Buddy Arrington	Arrington '69 Dodge	49	400	Running
7	3	48	James Hylton	Hylton Eng '69 Dodge	48	345	Running
8	2	1	Pete Hamilton	A J King '69 Dodge	48	325	Running
9	10	98	LeeRoy Yarbrough	Junior Johnson '69 Ford	48	325	Running
10	17	03	Richard Brickhouse	Dub Clewis '67 Plymouth	48	310	Running
11	26	8	Vic Elford	H B Ranier '69 Dodge	48	300	Running
12	8	36	H B Bailey	Bailey '69 Pontiac	48	290	Running
13	18	18	Dick Johnson	Johnson '68 Ford	47	280	Running
14	13	64	Elmo Langley	Langley '68 Ford	47	270	Running
15	7	39	Friday Hassler	Hassler '67 Chevrolet	46	260	Running
16	12	32	Dick Brooks	Brooks '69 Plymouth	46	255	Running
17	19	23	Don Biederman	Dennis Holt '67 Ford	45	245	Running
18	25	19	Henley Gray	Harry Melton '68 Ford	44	235	Running
19	23	57	Ervin Pruitt	Pruitt '67 Dodge	44	225	Running
20	22	0	Dr Don Tarr	Tarr '67 Chevrolet	44	220	Running
21	14	30	Dave Marcis	Milt Lunda '67 Chevrolet	43	215	Engine
22	21	82	Dick Poling	'67 Chevrolet	42	210	Running
23	4	7	Bobby Johns	Shorty Johns '67 Chevrolet	32	205	Running
24	20	69	Bill Kimmel	'69 Chevrolet	9	200	Axle
25	27	58	Andy Hampton	H B Ranier '69 Dodge	6	---	Crash
26	24	34	Wendell Scott	Scott '68 Ford	4	---	Engine
27	1	3	Buddy Baker	Ray Fox '69 Dodge	2	--	Quit

Time of Race: 49 minutes, 16 seconds
Average Speed: 152.181 mph
Pole Winner: Buddy Baker - 188.901 mph
Fastest Qualifier: David Pearson - 190.029 mph
Lap Leaders: Buddy Baker 1, Pete Hamilton 2-15, James Hylton 16-17, David Pearson 18-23, Cale Yarborough 24-42, Pearson 43-50.
Cautions: 2 for 15 laps   Margin of Victory: 12 car lengths   Attendance: 25,000

Spartanburg, SC speedster only 18 laps to get to the front. After making a couple of pit stops under the caution flag, Pearson ran down Cale Yarborough in a stretch run and won by 12 car lengths.

Yarborough finished in second place and Donnie Allison was third. A.J. Foyt was fourth and Benny Parsons, an ARCA champion making his first Grand National start, was fifth. Ford automobiles swept the first

Race No. 5

'Racer' Isaac Prevails in Second 125-Miler

DAYTONA BEACH, FL (Feb. 20) -- Bobby Isaac drove his K&K Insurance Dodge past Charlie Glotzbach in the 43rd lap and went on to win the second 125-mile qualifying race at Daytona International Speedway.

Glotzbach finished second, three car lengths behind Isaac. Paul Goldsmith was third, giving the Dodge teams a 1-2-3 finish. Bobby Unser was fourth in Smokey Yunick's Ford. Swede Savage was fifth in the Wood Brothers Mercury.

Bobby Allison led much of the early going in his Mario Rossi Dodge, but he retired on lap 31 with engine problems. He wound up 22nd in the field of 24, putting him near the rear of the field for the Daytona 500.

Although the 125-milers caused much apprehension before the start of the race, there were no accidents. "Some of the other guys don't like these qualifying races," said Isaac. "But I like them. You can practice for two weeks down here but you really don't know what the racing conditions will be until you go racing. I think the qualifying races are to our advantage. Besides, we came down here to race."

The caution flag was out twice for 16 laps, reducing Isaac's winning speed to 151.668 mph. It was the fifth career Grand National win for the Catawba, NC veteran.

Bobby Isaac wheels down pit road after winning 125-miler at Daytona

Fin	St	No.	Driver	Team / Car	Laps	Money	Status
1	1	71	Bobby Isaac	K&K Insurance '69 Dodge	50	$1,200	Running
2	2	6	Charlie Glotzbach	Cotton Owens '69 Dodge	50	800	Running
3	5	99	Paul Goldsmith	Nichels Eng '69 Dodge	50	550	Running
4	14	13	Bobby Unser	Smokey Yunick '69 Ford	50	500	Running
5	11	41	Swede Savage	Wood Brothers '68 Mercury	50	450	Running
6	10	43	Richard Petty	Petty Enterprises '69 Ford	49	400	Running
7	3	25	Jabe Thomas	Don Robertson '68 Plymouth	49	345	Running
8	4	96	Ray Elder	Fred Elder '69 Dodge	48	335	Running
9	15	29	Ramo Stott	'67 Plymouth	48	325	Running
10	16	06	Neil Castles	Castles '69 Plymouth	47	310	Running
11	20	45	Cecil Gordon	Bill Seifert '68 Ford	47	300	Running
12	13	76	Tommy Gale	Red Culpepper '68 Ford	46	290	Running
13	19	44	Dub Simpson	Giachetti Bros '67 Chevrolet	46	280	Running
14	22	53	Billy Taylor	Carl Miller '67 Plymouth	45	270	Running
15	7	10	Bill Champion	Champion '68 Ford	44	260	Running
16	21	33	Wayne Smith	Smith '69 Chevrolet	43	255	Running
17	12	47	Bill Seifert	Seifert '68 Ford	43	245	Running
18	23	70	J D McDuffie	McDuffie '67 Buick	43	235	Running
19	18	08	E J Trivette	E C Reid '69 Chevrolet	42	225	Running
20	8	80	Frank Warren	E C Reid '67 Chevrolet	41	220	W Bearing
21	6	4	John Sears	L G DeWitt '67 Ford	32	215	Engine
22	9	22	Bobby Allison	Mario Rossi '69 Dodge	31	210	Engine
23	17	75	George Bauer	'67 Dodge	27	205	Engine
24	24	26	Earl Brooks	Brooks '67 Ford	3	200	Engine

Grand National Race No. 5
50 Laps at Daytona Int'l Speedway
Daytona Beach, FL
125 Miles on 2.5-mile Paved Track
February 20, 1969

Time of Race: 49 minutes, 27 seconds
Average Speed: 151.668 mph
Pole Winner: Bobby Isaac - 188.726 mph
Fastest Qualifier: Paul Goldsmith 189.897 mph
Lap Leaders: - - - - - - - - - - - - - - - - - , Bobby Allison   -31, Charlie Glotzbach 32-42,
Bobby Isaac 43-50.
Cautions: 2 for 16 laps   Margin of Victory: 3 car lengths   Attendance: 25,000

Race No. 6

Tire Gamble Works; LeeRoy Whips Charlie in Daytona 500

DAYTONA BEACH, FL (Feb. 23) -- With the advantage of a soft compound tire he got on the final pit stop, LeeRoy Yarbrough ran down Charlie Glotzbach in the final lap and won the Daytona 500 at Daytona International Speedway.

Yarbrough, driving the Junior Johnson Ford, pitted for new tires on lap 181 of the 200 lap contest, and returned to the track 11 seconds behind the Glotzbach Dodge. Crew chief Herb Nab decided to place a soft compound tire on the left rear wheel -- affording better traction and more speed, but less durability. Glotzbach

LeeRoy Yarbrough #98 leads Swede Savage #41 and Richard Petty #43 in Daytona 500

made his final pit stop on lap 186 and took two regular compound tires.

"The tires made the difference," said a jubilant Yarbrough. "It was the pit crew's decision and they deserve credit for this victory. I was thinking I might run second again (he wound up a close second in 1968), but I saw I was gaining on him. I knew the car had the power when I needed it."

Glotzbach finished a car length behind in second place. "He just beat me," said the Georgetown, IN driver. "There's no defense that I know of against the

Charlie Glotzbach tried to slingshot LeeRoy Yarbrough off the final turn, but had to settle for 2nd in Daytona 500

slingshot. I wasn't going to run him off in the grass or put him in the wall. I finished second. I could've finished last."

Donnie Allison came in third. A.J. Foyt was fourth and pole sitter Buddy Baker was fifth.

Accidents took out a number of contestants, including defending champion Cale Yarborough, who clobbered the fourth turn wall on lap 103 after a tire failure.

Yarborough was badly shaken up but suffered nothing worse than a broken nose.

Bobby Unser parked the Smokey Yunick Ford against the wall after a blown tire. Paul Goldsmith, Swede Savage and Bobby Isaac also wrecked their factory cars.

Isaac trapped in behind a pack of slow cars, was hit by Richard Petty's Ford. "I just ran up on them," admitted Petty, who experienced handling problems and a batch of blistered tires in his first big track start in a Ford. "I guess I could have prevented it, but I didn't. It was a stupid mistake."

Isaac did not point the finger at Petty. "It wasn't his fault," said Isaac. "What the problem was those slower cars. That 8 car (Vic Elford) and the 03 car (Richard Brickhouse) were all over the track. Some people aren't watching their mirrors."

Yarbrough won $38,950 for taking his third superspeedway win. Things looked bleak four days earlier when the engine blew in a practice run, sending his car out of control and into the wall. He was forced to go to a back-up Junior Johnson Ford. "They are all about the same. Any one of his cars can win any race," said Yarbrough.

Yarbrough enjoyed a spectacular weekend, having won the Permatex 300 for Sportsman cars the day before. It was a tragic affair as aspiring youngster Don MacTavish was killed in a gruesome eighth lap wreck. Yarbrough won the 300 in a Bondy Long Ford, who has pulled out of Grand National racing due to tax reasons.

Grand National Race No. 6
200 Laps at Daytona Int'l Speedway
Daytona Beach, FL
"Daytona 500"
500 Miles on 2.5-mile Paved Track
February 23, 1969

Fin	St	No.	Driver	Team / Car	Laps	Money	Status
1	19	98	LeeRoy Yarbrough	Junior Johnson '69 Ford	200	$38,950	Running
2	4	6	Charlie Glotzbach	Cotton Owens '69 Dodge	200	18,425	Running
3	7	27	Donnie Allison	Banjo Matthews '69 Ford	199	13,275	Running
4	9	11	A J Foyt	Jack Bowsher '69 Ford	199	5,800	Running
5	1	3	Buddy Baker	Ray Fox '69 Dodge	198	10,050	Running
6	3	17	David Pearson	Holman-Moody '69 Ford	198	5,600	Running
7	11	88	Benny Parsons	Russ Dawson '69 Ford	197	2,450	Running
8	12	43	Richard Petty	Petty Enterprises '69 Ford	196	3,150	Running
9	50	58	Andy Hampton	H B Ranier '69 Dodge	191	2,500	Running
10	16	96	Ray Elder	Fred Elder '69 Dodge	190	2,935	Running
11	23	8	Vic Elford	H B Ranier '69 Dodge	188	2,650	Running
12	21	03	Richard Brickhouse	Dub Clewis '67 Plymouth	188	3,560	Running
13	31	39	Friday Hassler	Hassler '67 Chevrolet	187	3,460	Running
14	14	25	Jabe Thomas	Jabe Thomas '68 Plymouth	187	2,495	Running
15	15	48	James Hylton	Hylton '68 Dodge	185	2,445	Running
16	20	06	Neil Castles	Castles '69 Plymouth	185	2,385	Running
17	44	30	Dave Marcis	Milt Lunda '67 Chevrolet	181	2,260	Running
18	22	45	Bill Seifert	Seifert '68 Ford	179	2,335	Running
19	49	80	Frank Warren	E C Reid '67 Chevrolet	178	2,245	Running
20	29	64	Elmo Langley*	Langley '68 Ford	178	2,285	Running
21	43	75	George Bauer	'67 Dodge	176	2,205	Running
22	26	44	Dub Simpson	Giachetti Bros '67 Chevrolet	176	1,420	Running
23	30	10	Bill Champion	Champion '68 Ford	176	1,395	Running
24	38	19	Henley Gray	Marry Melton '68 Ford	173	1,355	Running
25	47	0	Dr Don Tarr	Tarr '67 Chevrolet	172	1,345	Running
26	37	08	E J Trivette	E C Reid '69 Chevrolet	171	1,345	Running
27	34	47	Cecil Gordon	Bill Seifert '68 Ford	171	1,360	Running
28	13	67	Buddy Arrington	Arrington '69 Dodge	170	1,610	Engine
29	48	34	Wendell Scott	Scott '68 Ford	168	1,105	Running
30	2	71	Bobby Isaac	K&K Insurance '69 Dodge	150	3,400	Crash
31	32	33	Wayne Smith	Smith '69 Chevrolet	148	1,350	Running
32	33	32	Dick Brooks	Brooks '69 Plymouth	140	1,345	Engine
33	18	29	Ramo Stott	'67 Plymouth	139	1,410	Engine
34	24	76	Ben Arnold**	Red Culpepper '68 Ford	133	1,370	Engine
35	39	26	Earl Brooks	Brooks '67 Ford	130	1,275	Heating
36	10	41	Swede Savage	Wood Brothers '68 Mercury	123	2,520	Crash
37	27	18	Dick Johnson	Johnson '68 Ford	104	1,345	Oil Leak
38	5	21	Cale Yarborough	Wood Brothers '69 Mercury	103	2,560	Crash
39	35	70	J D McDuffie	McDuffie '67 Buick	87	2,290	Crash
40	42	7	Bobby Johns	Shorty Johns '67 Chevrolet	67	1,205	Heating
41	6	99	Paul Goldsmith	Nichels Eng '69 Dodge	62	1,600	Crash
42	8	13	Bobby Unser	Smokey Yunick '69 Ford	56	1,400	Crash
43	40	22	Bobby Allison	Mario Rossi '69 Dodge	45	1,160	Engine
44	17	1	Pete Hamilton	A J King '69 Dodge	44	1,885	Crash
45	41	4	John Sears	L G DeWitt '67 Ford	41	965	Heating
46	45	69	Bill Kimmel	'69 Chevrolet	30	900	Engine
47	25	36	H B Bailey	Bailey '69 Pontiac	24	1,940	Engine
48	28	53	Billy Taylor	Carl Miller '67 Plymouth	20	870	Engine
49	46	82	Dick Poling	'67 Chevrolet	19	760	Engine
50	36	57	Roy Mayne	Ervin Pruitt '67 Dodge	9	725	Engine

Time of Race: 3 hours, 9 minutes, 56 seconds
Average Speed: 157.950 mph
Pole Winner: Buddy Baker - 188.901 mph
Fastest Qualifier: David Pearson - 190.029 mph
Lap Leaders: Buddy Baker 1-3, Cale Yarborough 4-20, Baker 21-25, James Hylton 26-27,
Baker 28-33, Donnie Allison 34-45, Baker 46, Bobby Unser 47, Baker 48-55,
A J Foyt 56, D.Allison 57-118, Charlie Glotzbach 119-138, D.Allison 139-145,
Glotzbach 146-154, D.Allison 155-160, LeeRoy Yarbrough 161-177,
Glotzbach 178-199, Yarbrough 200.
Cautions: 5 for 38 laps   Margin of Victory: 1 car length   Attendance: 101,800
*Relieved by John Sears   **Relieved by Tommy Gale

Petty struggled to finish eighth in his Ford, but he opened up a 39 point lead in the Grand National point standings over independent James Hylton, who finished 15th in a Dodge.

Richard Petty leads field through turn at Daytona

Race No. 7

Pearson Wins Rainy, Disputed Carolina 500

ROCKINGHAM, NC (Mar. 9) -- David Pearson led the final 130 laps and won the disputed Carolina 500 at North Carolina Motor Speedway. It was the second win of the season for Pearson and it moved him into second place in the point standings.

Pearson finished almost a lap in front of Bobby Allison, whose Mario Rossi team requested a scoring re-check. Third place went to Cale Yarborough, Paul Goldsmith was fourth and point leader Richard Petty fifth.

Pearson overcame a penalty and two scrapes with the guard rail to post his fifth career superspeedway triumph. Car owner Rossi wasn't so sure. "I honestly feel like we (Allison) won the race," he said. "When Pearson hit the wall Bobby passed him. About four laps later, the caution flag came out and Bobby made up a lap. When Bobby passed David at the end of the race, I believe it was for the lead."

NASCAR's Joe Epton studied the score cards and upheld Pearson's 48th career Grand National win.

During a caution flag early in the race, which lasted 22 laps, NASCAR officials tried to sort things out and figure out who was leading the race. The crew chiefs of virtually all of the contenders were yelling at chief steward Johnny Bruner; and the sanctioning body opted to keep the yellow flag out until proper running order could be determined.

Finally, the pace car picked up Yarborough, a decision that brought outrage among all pit road occupants and a few members of the media. Veteran scribe Benny Phillips wrote in his piece, "Even a computer couldn't have proven Cale was in the lead."

The remainder of the race was run in the specter of protest, but Pearson was clearly the class of the field.

He led on six occasions for 311 laps. "Actually, this was the easiest superspeedway race I have ever won. The car worked beautifully," said the winner.

Pearson was docked a lap in the early stages when he drove past the 'stop' sign at the end of pit road. "As far as having that lap taken," said Pearson, "it made me mad at first. But in the final outcome, things turned out the same. I don't know if I was guilty or not, but it doesn't make any difference now."

Petty spun out twice and was eight laps off the pace. "Well, look at it this way," said the good-natured Petty. "We've got the car handling great on the straightaways. Now all we have to do is get it to handle through the corners. At least we're half way there."

Pearson averaged 102.569 mph before 31,500 fans.

Race No. 8

Pit Miscue Halts Isaac; Pearson Beats One-Eyed Petty

AUGUSTA, GA (Mar. 16) -- David Pearson scampered into the lead on lap 120 when a series of pit miscues sidetracked Bobby Isaac, and won the Cracker 200 at Augusta Speedway. It was the third win of the year for the Holman-Moody Ford driver.

Pearson led the final 81 laps and beat one-eyed Richard Petty to the checkered flag. Petty was driving with a patch over his eye as the result of an accident at the

---

Grand National Race No. 7
500 Laps at North Carolina Motor Speedway
Rockingham, NC
"Carolina 500"
500 Miles on 1-mile Paved Track
March 9, 1969

Fin	St	No.	Driver	Team / Car	Laps	Money	Status
1	1	17	David Pearson	Holman-Moody '69 Ford	500	$16,150	Running
2	10	22	Bobby Allison	Mario Rossi '69 Dodge	500	9,500	Running
3	11	21	Cale Yarborough	Wood Brothers '69 Mercury	498	4,975	Running
4	12	99	Paul Goldsmith	Nichels Eng '69 Dodge	497	2,700	Running
5	5	43	Richard Petty	Petty Enterprises '69 Ford	492	1,850	Running
6	3	27	Donnie Allison	Banjo Matthews '69 Ford	491	1,425	Running
7	2	71	Bobby Isaac	K&K Insurance '69 Dodge	490	1,375	Running
8	14	4	John Sears	L G DeWitt '67 Ford	489	1,200	Running
9	13	48	James Hylton	Hylton Eng '67 Dodge	483	1,125	Running
10	22	61	Hoss Ellington	Ellington '67 Mercury	469	1,250	Running
11	28	39	Friday Hassler	Hassler '69 Chevrolet	462	1,025	Running
12	17	32	Dick Brooks	Brooks '69 Plymouth	451	1,200	Running
13	18	10	Bill Champion	Champion '68 Ford	448	975	Running
14	16	25	Jabe Thomas	Don Robertson '69 Plymouth	444	950	Running
15	31	82	Dick Poling	'67 Chevrolet	437	935	Running
16	42	8	Ed Negre	Negre '67 Ford	437	920	Running
17	24	76	Ben Arnold	Red Culpepper '68 Ford	429	905	Running
18	21	08	E J Trivette	E C Reid '69 Chevrolet	425	890	Running
19	19	67	Buddy Arrington	Arrington '69 Dodge	424	875	Running
20	23	34	Wendell Scott	Scott '68 Ford	423	860	Running
21	36	26	Earl Brooks	Brooks '67 Ford	415	915	Running
22	7	64	Elmo Langley	Langley '68 Ford	394	830	Running
23	6	98	LeeRoy Yarbrough	Junior Johnson '69 Ford	387	815	Rear End
24	35	9	Roy Tyner	Tyner '69 Pontiac	383	895	Engine
25	8	03	Richard Brickhouse	Dub Clewis '67 Plymouth	380	800	Engine
26	4	6	Charlie Glotzbach	Cotton Owens '69 Dodge	373	785	Heating
27	29	18	Dick Johnson	Johnson '68 Ford	371	770	Engine
28	25	49	G C Spencer	Spencer '67 Plymouth	307	830	Rear End
29	40	70	J D McDuffie	McDuffie '67 Buick	284	770	Engine
30	39	19	Henley Gray	Harry Melton '68 Ford	281	765	Engine
31	30	06	Neil Castles	Castles '68 Plymouth	266	860	Rear End
32	38	47	Cecil Gordon	Bill Seifert '68 Ford	266	745	Engine
33	20	80	Frank Warren	E C Reid '67 Chevrolet	265	680	Engine
34	37	23	James Sears	Paul Dean Holt '67 Ford	247	725	Engine
35	32	86	Dub Simpson	Neil Castles '67 Plymouth	243	775	Engine
36	33	45	Bill Seifert	Seifert '68 Ford	241	735	Engine
37	27	30	Dave Marcis	Milt Lunda '69 Dodge	202	645	Flagged
38	9	3	Buddy Baker	Ray Fox '689 Dodge	183	705	Engine
39	34	33	Wayne Smith	Smith '69 Chevrolet	126	680	Rear End
40	15	7	Bobby Johns	Shorty Johns '67 Chevrolet	59	600	D Shaft
41	26	90	Sonny Hutchins	Junie Donlavey '67 Ford	54	610	Vibration
42	41	0	Dr Don Tarr	Tarr '67 Chevrolet	48	545	Clutch
43	43	29	John Kennedy	'67 Dodge	28	525	Engine

Time of Race: 4 hours, 52 minutes, 22 seconds
Average Speed: 102.569 mph
Pole Winner: David Pearson - 119.619 mph
Lap Leaders: David Pearson 1-3, Donnie Allison 4-5, Pearson 6-20, Buddy Baker 21-46, LeeRoy Yarbrough 47, Buddy Baker 48-64, D.Allison 65-76, Charlie Glotzbach 77, D.Allison 78-88, Glotzbach 89-90, Baker 91-105, Cale Yarborough 106-161, Baker 162-175, Yarborough 176-182, Bobby Allison 183-185, Glotzbach 186, B.Allison 187-196, Pearson 197-207, Glotzbach 208-214, Pearson 215-289, Yarbrough 290-291, Pearson 292-368, Yarborough 369-370, Pearson 371-500.
Cautions: 10 for 82 laps   Margin of Victory: Attendance: 31,500.

Grand National Race No. 8
200 Laps at Augusta Speedway
Augusta, GA
"Cracker 200"
100 Miles on Half-mile Paved Track
March 16, 1969

Fin	St	No.	Driver	Team / Car	Laps	Money	Status
1	3	17	David Pearson	Holman-Moody '69 Ford	200	$1,200	Running
2	2	43	Richard Petty	Petty Enterprises '69 Ford	200	600	Running
3	1	71	Bobby Isaac	K&K Insurance '69 Dodge	200	400	Running
4	5	48	James Hylton	Hylton Eng '67 Dodge	196	350	Running
5	7	4	John Sears	L G DeWitt '67 Ford	195	325	Running
6	8	06	Neil Castles	Castles '69 Plymouth	191	300	Running
7	9	18	Dick Johnson	Johnson '68 Ford	186	275	Running
8	13	00	Don Biederman	'67 Chevrolet	183	270	Running
9	16	8	Ed Negre	Negre '67 Ford	182	265	Running
10	17	45	Bill Seifert	Seifert '68 Ford	181	260	Running
11	15	08	E J Trivette	E C Reid '69 Chevrolet	179	255	Running
12	20	19	Henley Gray	Harry Melton '68 Ford	178	250	Running
13	11	76	Ben Arnold	Red Culpepper '68 Ford	174	245	Running
14	14	34	Wendell Scott	Scott '67 Ford	172	240	Running
15	24	1	Pete Hazelwood	'68 Ford	167	235	Running
16	18	82	Dick Poling	'67 Chevrolet	165	230	Running
17	21	26	Earl Brooks	Brooks '67 Ford	163	225	Running
18	22	47	Cecil Gordon	Bill Seifert '68 Ford	158	220	Running
19	12	25	Jabe Thomas	Don Robertson '68 Plymouth	148	215	Running
20	19	93	Walson Gardner	Gardner '67 Ford	146	210	Running
21	10	10	Bill Champion	Champion '68 Ford	53	205	Oil Leak
22	23	70	J D McDuffie	N V Keith '67 Buick	51	200	Oil Press
23	4	30	Dave Marcis	Milt Lunda '69 Dodge	27	---	Engine
24	25	9	Roy Tyner	Tyner '69 Pontiac	17	---	Vibration
25	6	64	Elmo Langley	Langley '68 Ford	10	---	Engine

Time of Race: 1 hour, 17 minutes, 20 seconds
Average Speed: 77.586 mph
Pole Winner: Bobby Isaac - 86.901 mph
Lap Leaders: Bobby Isaac 1-119, David Pearson 120-200.
Cautions: 1 for 10 laps   Margin of Victory: Attendance: 5,100

Petty Enterprises shops in Level Cross, NC two days earlier. Isaac wound up third, James Hylton was fourth and John Sears was fifth.

Isaac won the pole and scooted away from the pack in the first half of the race. When he made his only scheduled pit stop on lap 120, the K&K Insurance Dodge crew headed by Harry Hyde had difficulty changing two tires. It took 28 seconds to replace the outside tires and Isaac got back on the track in third place. To add to the misfortune, NASCAR officials blackflagged Isaac to the pits once again to have his gas cap securely placed. He dropped almost two laps behind and was hopelessly out of contention.

Isaac made up over a lap on the field and finished third, in the same lap with the winner.

"I was just hoping to keep him in sight," said Pearson. "But he was gone. We won this race in the pits."

Dave Marcis, promising sophomore driver out of Wausau, WI, qualified fourth in his Dodge. But he left the race after 27 laps with a blown engine.

Pearson averaged 77.586 mph before a crowd of 5,100.

Race No. 9

Isaac, Pearson Fail; Allison Captures Southeastern 500

BRISTOL, TN (Mar. 23) -- Heart-breaking mechanical failures sent Bobby Isaac and David Pearson to the sidelines in the final 26 miles, opening the door for Bobby Allison to win the Southeastern 500 at Bristol International Speedway. It was the second win for Allison in the 1969 season, and it gave car owner Mario Rossi his first Grand National victory.

A standing room only crowd of 28,000 watched Allison's Dodge cross the finish line four laps in front of runner-up LeeRoy Yarbrough's Ford. Suspense and drama were packed into the final stages of the 250-miler. Isaac had won the pole and led for 299 laps. He was seemingly headed to victory when the radiator hose came off his Dodge on lap 448, causing the engine to blow.

Isaac was so disconsolate that he ran across the track, hopped over the guard rail and disappeared into the parking lot.

Pearson picked up the lead with Allison trailing by two laps. But a tell-tale stream of smoke became visible from under Pearson's Ford with 15 laps to go. Pearson made a pit stop and crew chief Dick Hutcherson lifted the hood. He quickly put it back in place and sent Pearson on his way. Pearson's car was able to hold first place until the 493rd lap, when Allison sped into the

Grand National Race No. 9
500 Laps at Bristol Int'l Speedway
Bristol, TN
"Southeastern 500"
250 Miles on Half-mile Paved Track
March 23, 1969

Fin	St	No.	Driver	Team / Car	Laps	Money	Status
1	4	22	Bobby Allison	Mario Rossi '69 Dodge	500	$5,025	Running
2	8	98	LeeRoy Yarbrough	Junior Johnson '69 Ford	496	3,000	Running
3	2	17	David Pearson	Holman-Moody '69 Ford	495	2,400	Engine
4	3	21	Cale Yarborough	Wood Brothers '69 Mercury	494	1,275	Running
5	10	27	Donnie Allison	Banjo Matthews '69 Ford	491	800	Running
6	6	30	Dave Marcis	Milt Lunda '69 Dodge	489	600	Running
7	9	43	Richard Petty	Petty Enterprises '69 Ford	484	575	Running
8	15	64	Elmo Langley	Langley '68 Ford	476	575	Running
9	17	39	Friday Hassler	Hassler '67 Chevrolet	468	530	Running
10	21	06	Neil Castles	Castles '68 Plymouth	465	620	Running
11	14	7	Bobby Johns	Shorty Johns '67 Chevrolet	459	535	Running
12	16	25	Jabe Thomas	Don Robertson '68 Plymouth	457	500	Running
13	12	48	James Hylton	Hylton Eng '67 Dodge	454	530	Running
14	1	71	Bobby Isaac	K&K Insurance '69 Dodge	448	1,180	Radiator
15	22	08	E J Trivette	E C Reid '69 Chevrolet	445	520	Running
16	24	19	Henley Gray	Harry Melton '68 Ford	439	485	Running
17	29	34	Wendell Scott	Scott '67 Ford	436	475	Running
18	20	18	Dick Johnson	Johnson '68 Ford	433	440	Running
19	7	6	Charlie Glotzbach	Cotton Owens '69 Dodge	429	430	Engine
20	18	10	Bill Champion	Champion '68 Ford	428	420	Running
21	30	26	Earl Brooks	Brooks '67 Ford	419	435	Running
22	26	45	Bill Seifert	Seifert '68 Ford	330	425	Engine
23	11	4	John Sears	L G DeWitt '67 Ford	279	450	Engine
24	25	80	Frank Warren	E C Reid '67 Chevrolet	256	405	Heating
25	28	00	Cecil Gordon	'67 Chevrolet	237	395	Tors'n ba
26	19	67	Buddy Arrington	Arrington '68 Dodge	125	365	Rear End
27	27	33	Wayne Smith	Smith '68 Chevrolet	65	380	Heating
28	13	49	G C Spencer	Spencer '67 Plymouth	63	370	Steering
29	5	3	Buddy Baker	Ray Fox '69 Dodge	28	360	Engine
30	23	70	J D McDuffie	McDuffie '67 Buick	27	360	Engine

Time of Race: 3 hours, 4 minutes, 9 seconds
Average Speed: 81.455 mph
Pole Winner: Bobby Isaac - 88.669 mph
Lap Leaders: Bobby Isaac 1-142, Bobby Allison 143-148, David Pearson 149-173, Isaac 174-273, Pearson 274, Isaac 275, Pearson 276-421, Isaac 422-447, Pearson 448-492, B.Allison 493-500.
Cautions: 4 for 32 laps   Margin of Victory: 4-laps plus   Attendance: 28,000

Bobby Allison #22 passes Cale Yarborough at Bristol

lead. Pearson's car finally coasted to a halt on lap 495.

Pearson got credit for third place. Cale Yarborough finished fourth and Donnie Allison was fifth. Pearson was able to close to within 25 points of leader Richard

Petty, who finished seventh.

"It happens all the time," said winner Allison in reference to the troubles that beset his two speedier rivals. "I figure I've lost more than I've won this way."

Allison averaged 81.455 mph for his 13th career victory.

Race No. 10

Controversy Flares; Cale Wins Atlanta 500

HAMPTON, GA (Mar. 30) -- Cale Yarborough withstood a late rally from David Pearson and won the controversial Atlanta 500 at Atlanta International Raceway. It was the first win of the season for the 30 year-old Timmonsville, SC Mercury driver.

Pearson finished 3.0-seconds behind Yarborough and gained runner-up honors. Paul Goldsmith came in third, Bobby Allison was fourth and Pete Hamilton fifth. Hamilton was subbing for Donnie Allison, who was felled by hepatitus a few days before the race.

Controversy flared at epic proportions during the entire week. Pole winner Pearson, Bobby Isaac and fastest qualifier Buddy Baker were all sent to the rear for the start when they changed tire brands. Swede Savage was also put at the back after making an 11th hour tire change.

Charlie Glotzbach ran over a jack during a pit stop and was penalized a lap. After falling out of the race on lap 142 with ignition problems, Glotzbach let go a verbal blast at the sanctioning body, vowing to quit NASCAR forever. "NASCAR is run like a communist organization," he growled. "It rules everything and the drivers have nothing to say about anything. I don't like the way NASCAR is operated and not many of the other drivers do either. They're afraid to say anything about it. I don't like it, and I'm getting out."

Runner-up Pearson complained that debris was laying on the backstretch "for 50 or 60 laps". He said he cut a

Grand National Race No. 10
334 Laps at Atlanta Int'l Raceway
Hampton, Ga
"Atlanta 500"
500 Miles on 1.5-mile Paved Track
March 30, 1969

Fin	St	No.	Driver	Team / Car	Laps	Money	Status
1	5	21	Cale Yarborough	Wood Brothers '69 Mercury	334	$21,590	Running
2	40	17	David Pearson	Holman-Moody '69 Ford	334	10,630	Running
3	6	99	Paul Goldsmith	Nichels Eng '69 Dodge	332	6,225	Running
4	2	22	Bobby Allison	Mario Rossi '69 Dodge	331	4,100	Running
5	21	27	Pete Hamilton	Banjo Matthews '69 Ford	329	3,225	Running
6	14	30	Dave Marcis	Milt Lunda '69 Dodge	320	2,550	Running
7	27	06	Neil Castles	Castles '69 Plymouth	314	2,150	Running
8	17	03	Richard Brickhouse	Dub Clewis '67 Plymouth	313	1,775	Running
9	7	43	Richard Petty	Petty Enterprises '69 Ford	312	1,700	Engine
10	10	67	Buddy Arrington	Arrington '69 Dodge	312	1,625	Running
11	8	98	LeeRoy Yarbrough	Junior Johnson '69 Mercury	303	1,575	Trans
12	32	46	Roy Mayne	Tom Hunter '67 Chevrolet	296	1,575	Running
13	31	76	Ben Arnold	Red Culpepper '68 Ford	292	1,525	Running
14	23	25	Jabe Thomas	Don Robertson '68 Plymouth	289	1,425	Running
15	33	00	Henley Gray	'67 Chevrolet	288	1,425	Running
16	25	70	J D McDuffie	McDuffie '67 Buick	284	1,300	Crash
17	26	10	Bill Champion	Champion '67 Ford	277	1,275	Running
18	12	47	Cecil Gordon	Bill Seifert '68 Ford	275	1,250	Crash
19	39	13	Swede Savage	Smokey Yunick '69 Ford	266	1,275	Engine
20	19	08	E J Trivette	E C Reid '69 Chevrolet	258	1,200	Running
21	3	64	Elmo Langley	Langley '68 Ford	233	1,200	Engine
22	4	80	Frank Warren	E C Reid '67 Chevrolet	221	1,175	Engine
23	38	71	Bobby Isaac	K&K Insurance '69 Dodge	202	1,165	Engine
24	29	45	Bill Seifert	Seifert '68 Ford	202	1,190	Oil LEak
25	16	7	Bobby Johns	Shorty Johns '67 Chevrolet	193	1,100	W Bearing
26	24	8	Ed Negre	Negre '67 Ford	190	1,125	Engine
27	36	23	Wendell Scott	Dennis Holt '67 Ford	187	1,100	Clutch
28	9	48	James Hylton	Hylton Eng '69 Dodge	181	1,225	Engine
29	18	39	Friday Hassler	Hassler '67 Chevrolet	181	1,000	Oil Leak
30	20	61	Hoss Ellington	Ellington '67 Mercury	174	950	Steering
31	15	4	John Sears	L G DeWitt '67 Ford	157	950	Engine
32	35	82	Dick Poling	'67 Chevrolet	154	975	D Shaft
33	1	6	Charlie Glotzbach	Cotton Owens '69 Dodge	142	960	Ignition
34	13	96	Don Tomberlin	Roy Buckner '68 Ford	125	850	Spun
35	22	49	G C Spencer	Spencer '68 Plymouth	105	875	Engine
36	37	3	Buddy Baker	Ray Fox '69 Dodge	100	1,175	Clutch
37	28	18	Dick Johnson	Johnson '68 Ford	89	775	Engine
38	34	2	John Kennedy	'67 Dodge	60	750	Oil Leak
39	30	44	Dub Simpson	Giachetti Bros '67 Chevrolet	55	725	Ignition
40	11	32	Dick Brooks	Brooks '69 Plymouth	38	700	Engine

Time of Race: 3 hours, 46 minutes, 10 seconds
Average Speed: 132.191 mph
Pole Winner: David Pearson - 156.794 mph
Fastest Qualifier: Buddy Baker - 158.730 mph
Lap Leaders: Charlie Glotzbach 1-2, Cale Yarborough 3-51, Bobby Isaac 52-54, David Pearson 55-60, Yarborough 61-107, Pearson 108-116, Yarborough 117-275, Pearson 276-277, Yarborough 278-315, Pearson 316-319, Yarborough 320-334.
Cautions: 5 for 53 laps   Margin of Victory: 3 seconds   Attendance: 85,000

Pete Hamilton spins through 4th turn at Atlanta

tire and spun because of the debris. Third place Goldsmith complained to officials that Pearson had passed the pace car illegally.

Aside from the controversy, Yarborough led 308 of the 334 laps, putting a record audience of 85,000 to sleep much of the way. It was a smashing success for the new Ford Boss 429 c.i. engine, which had been disallowed at Daytona and Rockingham until it had been delivered in sufficient quantities to dealerships across America. "We were three days behind when we came here," said Cale. "But we caught up today. This new Mercury and this new

Atlanta President, T. Jack Black and winner Cale Yarborough

Boss 429 engine worked like clock-work."

The record crowd came in great anticipation, but watched a rout instead. The early portions were frantic, with many of the front runners working their way from the back of the pack. Baker charged from 37th to ninth by the 10th lap; Isaac had come from 38th to second by lap 40. But neither Dodge driver was around at the finish.

Pearson started 40th, but had the lead by the 55th lap. Cale averaged 132.191 mph for his 10th career win.

Race No. 11

Isaac Makes Up Lap; Wins Columbia 200

COLUMBIA, SC (Apr. 3) -- Bobby Isaac overcame a lap deficit and roared to victory in the Columbia 200 NASCAR Grand National race at Columbia Speedway. It was the second victory of the season for the Catawba, NC Dodge pilot.

David Pearson finished second, 12 seconds behind Isaac. Richard Petty came in third, James Hylton was fourth and John Sears fifth.

The 100-miler on the half-mile dirt track was a hard fought battle as the lead changed hands seven times. Each of the top five finishers led at one stage or another. Isaac started on the pole and led the first 48 laps. During a pit stops, his car lost power and by the time crew chief Harry Hyde got it running, Isaac had fallen a lap behind.

Sears surprised the 8,200 spectators by leading for 14 straight laps.

Isaac, pitching his red Dodge into a picture perfect four wheel drift, made up his lap by the 89th circuit. He had moved back into the lead by lap 151.

Petty enjoyed one of his strongest runs of the 1969

Grand National Race No. 11
200 Laps at Columbia Speedway
Columbia, SC
"Columbia 200"
100 Miles on Half-mile Dirt Track
April 3, 1969

Fin	St	No.	Driver	Team / Car	Laps	Money	Status
1	1	71	Bobby Isaac	K&K Insurance '69 Dodge	200	$1,000	Running
2	2	17	David Pearson	Holman-Moody '69 Ford	200	800	Running
3	4	43	Richard Petty	Petty Enterprises '69 Ford	199	400	Running
4	6	48	James Hylton	Hylton Eng '67 Dodge	197	350	Running
5	5	4	John Sears	L G DeWitt '67 Ford	197	325	Running
6	7	64	Elmo Langley	Langley '68 Ford	194	300	Running
7	13	06	Neil Castles	Castles '69 Plymouth	194	275	Running
8	8	26	Earl Brooks	Brooks '67 Ford	193	270	Running
9	11	18	Dick Johnson	Johnson '68 Ford	189	265	Running
10	3	25	Jabe Thomas	Don Robertson '68 Plymouth	188	260	Running
11	15	19	Henley Gray	Harry Melton '68 Ford	184	255	Running
12	10	34	Wendell Scott	Scott '67 Ford	180	250	Running
13	16	76	Ben Arnold	Red Culpepper '68 Ford	174	245	Running
14	18	23	Paul Dean Holt	Dennis Holt '67 Ford	104	240	Engine
15	19	12	Pete Hazelwood	'67 Chevrolet	96	235	Engine
16	17	70	J D McDuffie	McDuffie '67 Buick	94	230	Engine
17	9	10	Bill Champion	Champion '68 Ford	87	225	Engine
18	12	80	E J Trivette	E C Reid '69 Chevrolet	55	220	W Bearing
19	21	51	Dub Simpson	'67 Plymouth	50	215	Heating
20	22	45	Bill Seifert	Seifert '68 Ford	49	210	Engine
21	14	30	Dave Marcis	Milt Lunda '69 Dodge	42	205	Heating
22	23	47	Cecil Gordon	Bill Seifert '68 Ford	27	200	Steering
23	20	9	Roy Tyner	Tyner '69 Pontiac	7	100	Crash
24	24	2	Jack Etheridge	'67 Mercury	7	100	Crash
25	25	82	Dick Poling	'67 Chevrolet	1	100	Rear End

Time of Race: 1 hour, 27 minutes, 31 seconds
Average Speed: 68.558 mph
Pole Winner: Bobby Isaac - 73.806 mph
Lap Leaders: Bobby Isaac 1-48, David Pearson 49, John Sears 50-63, James Hylton 64-68, Richard Petty 69-150, Isaac 151-165, Petty 166-167, Isaac 168-200.
Cautions: 4 for 21 laps   Margin of Victory: 12 seconds   Attendance: 8,200

season by leading twice for 84 laps. He lost the lead to Isaac on lap 168 and fell to third place.

Isaac averaged 68.558 mph for his sixth career Grand National triumph. The 100-miler was the first dirt track event staged during the 1969 championship season.

Race No. 12

Isaac Leads All the Way In Hickory 250

HICKORY, NC (Apr. 6) -- Bobby Isaac, rapidly becoming NASCAR's short track rabbit, started on the pole and led the entire distance to win the Hickory 250 at Hickory Speedway. It was the second straight Grand National win for the 36 year-old Dodge driver.

Richard Petty finished second, two laps behind the fleet K&K Insurance Dodge. Third place went to David Pearson. Dave Marcis notched his first top five finish

Grand National Race No. 12
250 Laps at Hickory Speedway
Hickory, NC
"Hickory 250"
100 Miles on .4-mile Paved Track
April 6, 1969

Fin	St	No.	Driver	Team / Car	Laps	Money	Status
1	1	71	Bobby Isaac	K&K Insurance '69 Dodge	250	$1,700	Running
2	5	43	Richard Petty	Petty Enterprises '69 Ford	248	1,300	Running
3	4	17	David Pearson	Holman-Moody '69 Ford	245	1,100	Engine
4	3	30	Dave Marcis	Milt Lunda '69 Dodge	244	700	Running
5	6	49	G C Spencer	Spencer '67 Plymouth	243	600	Running
6	8	06	Neil Castles	Castles '68 Plymouth	243	500	Running
7	9	25	Jabe Thomas	Don Robertson '68 Plymouth	237	400	Running
8	17	51	Ben Arnold	'67 Plymouth	236	350	Running
9	11	08	E J Trivette	E C Reid '69 Chevrolet	235	300	Running
10	14	70	J D McDuffie	N V Keith '67 Buick	232	280	Running
11	15	64	Elmo Langley	Langley '68 Ford	231	275	Running
12	10	18	Dick Johnson	Johnson '68 Ford	230	270	Running
13	18	34	Wendell Scott	Scott '67 Ford	228	265	Running
14	7	4	John Sears	L G DeWitt '67 Ford	225	260	Running
15	20	47	Cecil Gordon	Bill Seifert '68 Ford	224	255	Running
16	16	26	Earl Brooks	Brooks '67 Ford	214	250	Running
17	12	19	Henley Gray	Harry melton '68 Ford	138	245	Ball Jt
18	19	45	Bill Seifert	Seifert '68 Ford	126	240	Heating
19	2	48	James Hylton	Hylton Eng '69 Dodge	88	235	Ignition
20	13	10	Bill Champion	Champion '68 Ford	17	230	Engine

Time of Race: 1 hour, 15 minutes, 52 seconds
Average Speed: 79.086 mph
Pole Winner: Bobby Isaac - 85.612 mph
Lap Leaders: Bobby Isaac 1-250.
Cautions: 4 for 19 laps   Margin of Victory: 2-laps plus   Attendance: 8,200

Race No. 13

Isaac Spins, Then Wins Greenville 200 for 3rd Straight

GREENVILLE, SC (Apr. 8) -- Bobby Isaac spun from the lead in the second lap, then came back to score an overwhelming victory in the Greenville 200 at Greenville-Pickens Speedway. The triumph was Isaac's third straight on the Grand National tour.

Isaac had taken the lead at the start, but spun out in the fourth turn of the second lap. He went to the rear of the 24 car field, but worked his way up to the lead by the 40th lap.

After Isaac made a pit stop, independent Ford driver Elmo Langley showed his rear bumper to the field for 29 laps. Isaac wrestled the lead from Langley in the 102nd lap and led the rest of the way.

Grand National Race No. 13
200 Laps at Greenville-Pickens Speedway
Greenville, SC
"Greenville 200"
100 Miles on Half-mile Dirt Track
April 8, 1969

Fin	St	No.	Driver	Team / Car	Laps	Money	Status
1	2	71	Bobby Isaac	K&K Insurance '69 Dodge	200	$1,000	Running
2	3	48	James Hylton	Hylton Eng '69 Dodge	199	600	Running
3	1	17	David Pearson	Holman-Moody '69 Ford	198	600	Running
4	10	64	Elmo Langley	Langley '68 Ford	197	350	Running
5	4	43	Richard Petty	Petty Enterprises '69 Ford	197	325	Running
6	6	4	John Sears	L G DeWitt '67 Ford	197	300	Running
7	12	26	Earl Brooks	Brooks '67 Ford	191	275	Running
8	8	10	Bill Champion	Champion '68 Ford	191	270	Running
9	11	06	Neil Castles	Castles '68 Plymouth	191	265	Running
10	18	80	E J Trivette	E C Reid '67 Chevrolet	180	260	Running
11	16	34	Wendell Scott	Scott '67 Ford	180	255	Running
12	15	19	Henley Gray	Harry Melton '68 Ford	176	250	Running
13	17	25	Jabe Thomas	Don Robertson '68 Plymouth	172	245	Running
14	23	47	Cecil Gordon	Bill Seifert '68 Ford	170	240	Running
15	19	12	Pete Hazelwood	'68 Ford	161	235	Running
16	9	70	J D McDuffie	McDuffie '67 Buick	158	230	Rear End
17	22	45	Bill Seifert	Seifert '68 Ford	124	225	Crash
18	13	8	Ed Negre	Negre '67 Ford	118	220	Engine
19	5	18	Dick Johnson	Johnson '68 Ford	95	215	Crash
20	7	51	Dub Simpson	'67 Ford	85	210	Crash
21	20	08	Danny Turner	E C Reid '67 Chevrolet	84	205	Ignition
22	14	76	Ben Arnold	Red Culpepper '68 Ford	83	200	Heating
23	24	82	Dick Poling	'67 Chevrolet	64	---	Flagged
24	21	93	Walson Gardner	Gardner '67 Dodge	40	---	Engine

Time of Race: 1 hour, 33 minutes, 11 seconds
Average Speed: 64.389 mph
Pole Winner: Bobby Isaac - 70.359 mph
Lap Leaders: Bobby Isaac 1, David Pearson 2-4, James Hylton 5-17, Pearson 18-22,
    Richard Petty 23-39, Isaac 40-58, Elmo Langley 59-87, Isaac 88-90, Langley 91-101,
    Isaac 102-200.
Cautions: 5 for 27 laps   Margin of Victory: 1-lap plus   Attendance: 8,000

with a strong fourth place effort, and G.C. Spencer was fifth.

Pearson's narrow Grand National point lead was cut to four points over second place Petty. Isaac ranks seventh, 266 points behind Pearson.

James Hylton unveiled a new Dodge and qualified second. The Inman, SC top ranking independent ran at Isaac's tailpipes in the early laps, but went out on lap 88 with ignition failure. He got credit for 19th in the 20 car field when the final results were issued by sanctioning NASCAR.

The crowd of 8,200 watched the uneventful race, which Isaac won at an average speed of 79.086 mph.

David Pearson clobbered the wall at Hickory

James Hylton finished in second place after leading for 13 laps. David Pearson came in third with Langley fourth and Richard Petty fifth.

Pearson pulled to within two points of Petty in the NASCAR standings.

Dick Johnson, little known driver out of Sacramento, CA, qualified a strong fifth, but his Ford was taken out on lap 97 in a bout with the retaining wall. Dub Simpson, seventh fastest qualifier, slugged the wall in the 88th lap. Neither driver was injured.

A crowd of 8,000 watched Isaac garner his eighth career win at an average speed of 64.389 mph.

Grand National Race No. 14
500 Laps at Richmond Fairgrounds Raceway
Richmond, VA
"Richmond 500"
250 Miles on Half-mile Paved Track
April 13, 1969

Fin	St	No.	Driver	Team / Car	Laps	Money	Status
1	1	17	David Pearson	Holman-Moody '69 Ford	500	$3,650	Running
2	3	43	Richard Petty	Petty Enterprises '69 Ford	499	1,800	Running
3	12	64	Elmo Langley	Langley '68 Ford	483	1,075	Running
4	14	06	Neil Castles	Castles '69 Plymouth	475	775	Running
5	13	45	Bill Seifert	Seifert '68 Ford	465	675	Running
6	19	70	J D McDuffie	McDuffie '67 Buick	464	625	Running
7	7	10	Bill Champion	Champion '68 Ford	450	600	Clutch
8	17	80	E J Trivette	E C Reid '67 Chevrolet	438	575	Running
9	23	19	Henley Gray	Harry Melton '68 Ford	436	530	Running
10	25	12	Pete Hazelwood	'68 Ford	365	520	Engine
11	9	18	Dick Johnson	Johnson '68 Ford	362	535	Engine
12	6	25	Jabe Thomas	Don Robertson '68 Plymouth	361	525	Running
13	26	20	Ray Hendrick	'67 Chevrolet	351	490	Engine
14	27	9	Worth McMillion	Roy Tyner '69 Pontiac	328	480	Rear End
15	5	48	James Hylton	Hylton Eng '69 Dodge	281	495	Engine
16	24	23	Paul Dean Holt	Dennis Holt '67 Ford	235	460	Oil Leak
17	18	26	Earl Brooks	Brooks '67 Ford	212	475	Axle
18	8	4	John Sears	L G DeWitt '67 Ford	177	465	Engine
19	21	8	Ed Negre	Negre '67 Ford	167	430	Heating
20	4	90	Sonny Hutchins	Junie Donlavey '67 Ford	55	470	Rear End
21	15	47	Cecil Gordon	Bill Seifert '68 Ford	45	435	Crash
22	20	56	Dr Ed Hessert	Lyle Stelter '69 Mercury	40	425	Crash
23	10	67	Buddy Arrington	Arrington '69 Dodge	35	415	Engine
24	16	34	Wendell Scott	Scott '67 Ford	21	405	Engine
25	11	76	Ben Arnold	Red Culpepper '68 Ford	13	405	Engine
26	22	82	Dick Poling	'67 Chevrolet	13	365	Trans
27	2	71	Bobby Isaac	K&K Insurance '69 Dodge	7	455	Engine
28	28	1	John Kennedy	Bill Champion '67 Ford	1	345	Flagged

Time of Race: 3 hours, 23 minutes, 23 seconds
Average Speed: 73.752 mph
Pole Winner: David Pearson - 82.538 mph
Lap Leaders: David Pearson 1-55, John Sears 56-58, Pearson 59-73,
   James Hylton 74-133, Pearson 134-187, Richard Petty 188-208, Pearson 209-500.
Cautions: 6 for 40 laps   Margin of Victory: 1-lap plus   Attendance: 14,600

Race No. 14

Pearson Ties Petty for Point Lead with Richmond 500 Win

RICHMOND, VA (APR. 13) -- David Pearson, leading 415 of the 500 laps, dominated the Richmond 500

and moved into a tie for first place in the Grand National Point Standings.

Pearson pushed his Holman-Moody Ford around Richard Petty in the 209th lap and led the rest of the way at Richmond Fairgrounds Raceway.

Petty finished second, a lap off the pace. Elmo Langley was third, 17 laps behind as attrition depleted the 28 car field. Neil Castles came in fourth and Bill Seifert was fifth. Only nine cars finished the 250-miler.

Bobby Isaac, bidding for his fourth straight win, fell out after just seven laps with a blown engine.

"I was sorry to see Bobby fall out so early," said the 34 year-old Pearson. "He's been putting it to me the last three races and I felt I could blow him off today."

Pearson's sixth victory in his last eight starts at the half-mile oval came at an average speed of 73.752 mph.

James Hylton, popular privateer out of Inman, SC, provided Pearson with a stout challenge as he led for 60 straight laps. The engine in Hylton's yellow Dodge blew on lap 282, and he was out of the race.

Petty experienced more handling problems throughout the event. The electric blue Ford was pushing badly in the turns, and on one occasion he swung wide and hit the front stretch wall. "We'll get this thing turned around one of these days." said Petty.

Race No. 15

Snappy Pit Service Nets Allison Win at N.Wilkesboro

N.WILKESBORO, NC (Apr. 20) -- Quick pit work and a shot-in-the-dark chassis set up enabled Bobby Allison to post his second win of the season in the Gwyn Staley Memorial at North Wilkesboro Speedway.

After logging a mediocre qualifying time (11th fastest), Allison and his Mario Rossi Dodge team decided to try a new chassis set up. "We tried several set ups," said Allison. "Toward the end of the last day of practice, we went to one we had discussed but never tried. We didn't have time to try it out. It was strictly a shot-in-the-dark."

Allison motored around Buddy Baker in the 299th lap and led the rest of the way. He finished 8.0-seconds in front of runner-up LeeRoy Yarbrough's Mercury. David Pearson came in third and Baker was fourth. Each of the top four drivers completed all 400 laps around the .625-mile oval.

Fifth place went to James Hylton, who was in the Cotton Owens Dodge vacated by Charlie Glotzbach.

Allison ran with the lead pack the entire afternoon,

but said his pit crew made the difference. "They put me in front twice," remarked the Hueytown, AL veteran. "It was a close race all the way and the pit stops made the difference. We had a long day of pit stop practice last week and it really paid off."

Bobby Isaac started on the pole for the sixth time this year and led the first 89 laps. After losing the lead on pit stops, Isaac roared back and led for a 34 lap stretch just before the half way point. He was running second when ignition troubles sidelined his Dodge.

David Pearson "dirt tracks" his way through North Wilkesboro turn

Pearson took the lead in the Grand National point standings by an eight point margin over Richard Petty, who finished seventh. The Randleman, NC Ford driver was penalized for passing the pace car and eventually fell 12 laps off the pace.

Independent John Sears of Ellerbe, NC, who has been knocking on the door, was disgusted after his Ford went out with engine failure on lap 202. "To hell with driving a race car for a living," he fumed. "I think I'll see if I can get a job with the Salvation Army."

Allison took his 14th career win at an average speed of 95.268 mph. A crowd of 13,000 filled the front and backstretch grandstands.

Race No. 16

Petty, With Help from Hylton, Grabs Virginia 500 Flag

MARTINSVILLE, VA (Apr. 27) -- Richard Petty and James Hylton teamed to win the Virginia 500 at Martinsville Speedway, giving Petty his first official win in nearly three months. "Now I know how it feels to win again," declared Petty.

Grand National Race No. 15
400 Laps at N.Wilkesboro Speedway
N.Wilkesboro, NC
"Gwyn Staley Memorial 400"
250 Miles on .625-mile Paved Track
April 20, 1969

Fin	St	No.	Driver	Team / Car	Laps	Money	Status
1	11	22	Bobby Allison	Mario Rossi '69 Dodge	400	$5,125	Running
2	9	98	LeeRoy Yarbrough	Junior Johnson '69 Mercury	400	3,750	Running
3	10	17	David Pearson	Holman-Moody '69 Ford	400	2,100	Running
4	2	3	Buddy Baker	Ray Fox '69 Dodge	400	1,150	Running
5	3	6	James Hylton	Cotton Owens '69 Dodge	398	775	Running
6	12	14	Sam McQuagg	Bill Ellis '69 Plymouth	395	625	Running
7	4	43	Richard Petty	Petty Enterprises '69 Ford	388	600	Engine
8	14	67	Buddy Arrington	Arrington '69 Dodge	385	575	Running
9	13	64	Elmo Langley	Langley '68 Ford	384	555	Running
10	22	08	E J Trivette	E C Reid '69 Chevrolet	379	620	Running
11	21	51	Dub Simpson	'69 Chevrolet	375	660	Running
12	26	46	Roy Mayne	Tom Hunter '69 Chevrolet	373	525	Running
13	8	70	J D McDuffie	McDuffie '67 Buick	366	515	Running
14	15	18	Dick Johnson	Johnson '68 Ford	362	505	Running
15	30	34	Wendell Scott	Scott '67 Ford	361	495	Running
16	7	25	Jabe Thomas	Don Robertson '68 Plymouth	361	485	Running
17	24	33	Cecil Gordon	'68 Chevrolet	349	475	Running
18	19	32	Dick Brooks	Brooks '69 Plymouth	335	440	Engine
19	27	76	Ben Arnold	Red Culpepper '68 Ford	332	455	Ignition
20	6	4	Johns Sears	L G DeWitt '67 Ford	302	445	Engine
21	16	06	Neil Castles	Castles '68 Plymouth	283	435	Wtr pmp
22	20	10	Bill Champion	Champion '68 Ford	21	400	Oil Leak
23	1	71	Bobby Isaac	K&K Insurance '69 Dodge	219	640	Ignition
24	5	30	Dave Marcis	Milt Lunda '69 Dodge	153	405	Rear End
25	29	19	Henley Gray	Harry Melton '68 Ford	138	395	Quit
26	17	03	Richard Brickhouse	Dub Clewis '67 Plymouth	120	390	Rear End
27	28	80	Danny Turner	E C Reid '67 Chevrolet	62	380	Oil Leak
28	18	49	G C Spencer	Spencer '68 Plymouth	24	370	Axle
29	23	8	Ed Negre	Negre '67 Ford	14	385	Engine
30	25	45	Bill Seifert	Seifert '68 Ford	2	350	Quit

Time of Race: 2 hours, 37 minutes, 27 seconds
Average Speed: 95.268 mph
Pole Winner: Bobby Isaac - 106.731 mph
Lap Leaders: Bobby Isaac 1-89, David Pearson 90-91, Bobby Allison 92-129, Isaac 130-163, Allison 164-173, Buddy Baker 174-239, Allison 240-246, Pearson 247-265, Baker 266-267, Allison 268-271, Baker 272-298, Allison 299-400.
Cautions: 4 for 30 laps   Margin of Victory: 8 seconds   Attendance: 13,000

Petty led on four occasions for a total of 65 laps, including the final 39. But he almost didn't make it. "I had all but passed out there once," said NASCAR's winningest driver. "I needed some help. I was sure glad a guy as capable as Hylton was standing by."

Hylton drove the Petty Ford from lap 399 until lap 447. Petty took over and outran David Pearson in a stretch duel. Pearson's Ford, driven in relief by Cale Yarborough, wound up 3.0-seconds behind Petty. Bobby Allison came in third, LeeRoy Yarbrough was fourth and Buddy Arrington fifth.

Allison, in Mario Rossi's Dodge, started on the pole and seemed likely to notch his third straight 250-mile win. However, he lost three laps in the pits; two on long stops and one to replace a tire during an unscheduled visit to the pits. The former NASCAR Modified champ passed the leaders three times and was closing in on Petty and Yarborough when the checkered flag fell.

Richard Petty pits at Martinsville. The Randleman, NC driver won the Virginia 500

A rash of penalties were handed out by sanctioning NASCAR during the race -- in the wake of the Charlie Glotzbach outcry. Swede Savage, driving in place of Donnie Allison, was penalized for running over an air hose. Yarborough's Wood Brothers Mercury was held a lap for making an improper pit stop. Neil Castles was penalized a lap for passing the pace car.

To top it off, Dick Brooks was disqualified from the race after his 428th lap for running in the wrong direction on the track. The Porterville, CA rookie had spun out in the first turn. He drove his Plymouth back to the pits opposite traffic. NASCAR officials told him to park the car for the rest of the day.

Buddy Young of Fairfax, VA competed in his first Grand National race and finished ninth in a fine effort. Young began racing in 1967 in the Hobby division, then moved up to the Sportsman class in 1968. Fellow driver Sonny Hutchins asked Young, "What are you going to have next year, an Indy Car?"

Petty averaged 64.405 mph before a sell out crowd of 23,000. The caution flag was out eight times for 61 laps.

Race No. 17

Petty Hurt as Isaac Easily Wins Fireball 300

WEAVERVILLE, NC (May 4) -- Bobby Isaac led all but 17 laps and won the Fireball 300 at Asheville-Weaverville Speedway going away. Richard Petty was injured when his Ford popped a tire and smashed nearly head-on into the concrete retaining wall.

Isaac took the lead from David Pearson in the 67th lap

Grand National Race No. 16
500 Laps at Martinsville Speedway
Martinsville, VA
"Virginia 500"
250 Miles on Half-mile Paved Track
April 27, 1969

Fin	St	No.	Driver	Team / Car	Laps	Money	Status
1	6	43	Richard Petty*	Petty Ent '69 Ford	500	$10,275	Running
2	21	17	David Pearson**	Holman-Moody '69 Ford	500	5,050	Running
3	1	22	Bobby Allison	Mario Rossi '69 Dodge	500	2,840	Running
4	5	98	LeeRoy Yarbrough	Junior Johnson '69 Mercury	496	1,550	Running
5	10	67	Buddy Arrington	Arrington '69 Dodge	496	1,075	Running
6	18	06	Neil Castles	Castles '67 Plymouth	489	975	Running
7	11	27	Swede Savage	Banjo Matthews '69 Ford	485	875	Running
8	9	64	Elmo Langley	Langley '68 Ford	476	775	Running
9	26	38	Buddy Young	Fred Bear '67 Chevrolet	474	725	Running
10	29	08	E J Trivette	E C Reid '69 Chevrolet	474	675	Running
11	14	25	Jabe Thomas***	Don Robertson '69 Plymouth	468	665	Running
12	28	34	Wendell Scott	Scott '67 Ford	458	655	Running
13	27	76	Ben Arnold	Red Culpepper '68 Ford	456	645	Running
14	19	70	J D McDuffie	McDuffie '67 Buick	453	635	Running
15	40	19	Henley Gray	Harry Melton '68 Ford	449	625	Running
16	17	32	Dick Brooks	Brooks '69 Plymouth	428	615	Disqual
17	32	26	Earl Brooks	Brooks '67 Ford	423	605	Running
18	25	10	Bill Champion	Champion '68 Ford	422	595	Running
19	34	33	Wayne Smith	Smith '69 Chevrolet	420	585	Crash
20	12	4	John Sears	L G DeWitt '67 Ford	393	575	Oil Leak
21	35	8	Ed Negre	Negre '67 Ford	382	565	Heating
22	13	39	Friday Hassler	Hassler '67 Chevrolet	364	555	Ignition
23	2	71	Bobby Isaac	K&K Insurance '69 Dodge	281	630	Axle
24	16	18	Dick Johnson	Johnson '68 Ford	259	535	Crash
25	3	21	Cale Yarborough	Wood Brothers '69 Mercury	245	575	Crash
26	38	0	Frank Warren	Dr Don Tarr '67 Chevrolet	245	515	Trans
27	31	46	Roy Mayne	Tom Hunter '67 Chevrolet	238	505	Heating
29	23	90	Sonny Hutchins	Junie Donlavey '67 Ford	232	505	H Gasket
29	8	30	Dave Marcis	Milt Lunda '69 Dodge	221	485	Ignition
30	7	6	James Hylton	Cotton Owens '69 Dodge	213	475	Engine
31	39	93	Walson Gardner	Gardner '67 Ford	196	470	Steering
32	20	45	Bill Seifert	Seifert '69 Ford	169	465	Trans
33	22	03	Richard Brickhouse	Dub Clewis '67 Plymouth	142	485	Ignition
34	30	80	Danny Turner	E C Reid '67 Chevrolet	139	455	Trans
35	37	47	Cecil Gordon	Bill Seifert '67 Ford	123	450	Engine
36	33	56	Dr Ed Hessert	Lyle Stelter '67 Mercury	60	445	Brakes
37	4	3	Paul Goldsmith	Ray Fox '69 Dodge	40	465	Ignition
38	24	51	Dub Simpson	Bill Strong '69 Chevrolet	24	435	Oil Leak
39	36	23	Paul Dean Holt	Dennis Holt '67 Ford	11	430	Flagged
40	15	49	G C Spencer	Spencer '67 Plymouth	1	425	Engine

Time of Race: 3 hours, 52 minutes, 54 seconds
Average Speed: 64.405 mph
Pole Winner: Bobby Allison - 78.260 mph
Lap Leaders: Bobby Allison 1-142, LeeRoy Yarbrough 143-144, Allison 145-240, Richard Petty 241-247, Bobby Isaac 248-258, Allison 259-399, David Pearson 400-411, Petty 412-428, Pearson 429-449, Petty 450-451, Pearson 452-461, Petty 462-500.
Cautions: 8 for 61 laps   Margin of Victory 3 seconds   Attendance: 23,000
*Relieved by James Hylton **Relieved by Cale Yarborough ***Relieved by G C Spencer

and led the rest of the way. Pearson blew a tire on lap 114 and hit the wall, joining Petty on the sidelines.

With his two most powerful rivals out of the way, Isaac coasted to a one lap win over runner-up James Hylton. John Sears came in third, Neil Castles was fourth and Earl Brooks fifth. Buddy Young, making only his second big league start, wound up sixth.

The right front tire of Petty's Ford exploded and jerked the car into the wall. Reporter Bob Terrell said, "A harder lick has never been delivered to the concrete around Asheville-Weaverville."

The right front wheel was shoved back into the driver's compartment. Crew chief Maurice Petty and the entire pit crew, fearing Richard was injured, dashed across the track to aid their driver -- scurrying between race cars which were still streaking by.

Petty was helped from the car and complained of pains in his rib area.

Pearson had just gotten a pit board message which read, "Tires Good" from crew chief Dick Hutcherson. A lap later, the right front tire blew, sending his Ford into the wall. He was not hurt..

The victory was Isaac's fifth of the year. "I have fallen out of every race since I last won at Greenville," said Isaac, who cut his teeth on this half-mile track nearly 10 years ago. "Not only am I glad to win, heck, I'm just glad to finish."

Runner-up Hylton started last in the 25 car field because he was unable to make a qualification attempt.

Isaac averaged 72.581 mph before a crowd of 5,500.

Richard Petty creamed the wall in Fireball 300

Grand National Race No. 17
300 Laps at Asheville-Weaverville Speedway
Weaverville, NC
"Fireball 300"
150 Miles on Half-mile Paved Track
May 4, 1969

Fin	St	No.	Driver	Team / Car	Laps	Money	Status
1	1	71	Bobby Isaac	K&K Insurance '68 Dodge	300	$2,050	Running
2	25	48	James Hylton	Hylton Eng '68 Dodge	299	1,275	Running
3	4	4	John Sears	L G DeWitt '67 Ford	298	1,000	Running
4	5	06	Neil Castles	Castles '67 Plymouth	297	625	Running
5	19	26	Earl Brooks	Brooks '67 Ford	284	475	Running
6	9	38	Buddy Young	Fred Bear '67 Chevrolet	284	430	Running
7	12	32	Dick Brooks	Brooks '69 Plymouth	283	400	Running
8	8	10	Bill Champion	Champion '68 Ford	280	380	Running
9	13	70	J D McDuffie	McDuffie '67 Buick	277	360	Running
10	16	34	Wendell Scott	Scott '67 Ford	273	350	Running
11	14	45	Bill Seifert	Seifert '68 Ford	269	340	Running
12	23	47	Cecil Gordon	Bill Seifert '68 Ford	267	330	Running
13	20	19	Henley Gray	Harry Melton '67 Ford	263	320	Running
14	24	23	Paul Dean Holt	Dennis Holt '67 Ford	243	310	Oil Leak
15	17	80	E J Trivette	E C Reid '67 Chevrolet	238	300	Clutch
16	21	93	Walson Gardner	Gardner '67 Ford	234	290	Crash
17	10	25	Jabe Thomas	Don Robertson '68 Plymouth	219	285	Axle
18	11	76	Ben Arnold	Red Culpepper '68 Ford	213	280	Running
19	7	64	Elmo Langley	Langley '68 Ford	144	275	Flagged
20	15	82	Roy Mayne	'67 Chevrolet	137	270	D Shaft
21	2	17	David Pearson	Holman-Moody '69 Ford	114	615	Crash
22	22	46	Max Ledbetter	Tom Hunter '69 Chevrolet	91	260	Heating
23	3	43	Richard Petty	Petty Ent '69 Ford	52	330	Crash
24	18	8	Ed Negre	Negre '67 Ford	42	250	Heating
25	6	18	Dick Johnson	Johnson '68 Ford	15	250	Clutch

Time of Race: 2 hours, 4 minutes,
Average Speed: 72.581 mph
Pole Winner: Bobby Isaac - 90.361 mph
Lap Leaders: Bobby Isaac 1-49, David Pearson 50-66, Isaac 67-300.
Cautions: 3 for 34 laps   Margin of Victory: 1-lap plus   Attendance: 5,500

Race No. 18

Allison Crashes Out; LeeRoy Limps Home First in 'Rebel'

DARLINGTON, SC (May 10) -- LeeRoy Yarbrough emerged victorious in a wild finish in the Rebel 400 after leader Bobby Allison wiped out his Dodge against a tunnel abutment.

Yarbrough, who was a lap down with 30 laps to go, got the lead with four laps left as the result of a three car scramble that sent Allison into the wall. Allison bounced off the wall and collided with Yarbrough's Mercury. Both cars went spinning off the track. Allison wound up against a concrete structure, and Yarbrough looped his car without hitting anything.

Yarbrough limped to the pits where the Junior Johnson crew made quick repairs in order to get him back on the track. The race ended under the yellow flag with Cale Yarborough second and Paul Goldsmith third. Allison got fourth place and David Pearson came in fifth.

"I saw Bobby up against the rail and he was coming down," said Yarbrough. "I tried to get by him, but he hung me in the door. Then we both spun off.

"I was lucky, real lucky to continue on. Bobby wasn't that lucky," added Yarbrough.

Allison pointed his finger at Cale for causing the wreck. "It wasn't LeeRoy's fault. He had nothing to do with it. It was Cale's fault. He put me in the wall," said Allison.

LeeRoy Yarbrough crosses under the checkered flag at Darlington

Grand National Race No. 18
291 Laps at Darlington Raceway
Darlington, SC
"Rebel 400"
400 Miles on 1.375-mile Paved Track
May 10, 1969

Fin	St	No.	Driver	Team / Car	Laps	Money	Status
1	4	98	LeeRoy Yarbrough	Junior Johnson '69 Mercury	291	$14,700	Running
2	1	21	Cale Yarborough	Wood Brothers '69 Mercury	290	8,020	Running
3	3	99	Paul Goldsmith	Nichels Eng '69 Dodge	288	5,005	Running
4	8	22	Bobby Allison	Mario Rossi '69 Dodge	287	2,650	Crash
5	5	17	David Person	Holman-Moody '69 Ford	285	2,550	Running
6	20	18	Dick Johnson	Johnson '68 Ford	270	1,650	Running
7	17	49	G C Spencer	Spencer '69 Plymouth	270	1,400	Running
8	24	61	Hoss Ellington	Ellington '67 Mercury	268	1,200	Running
9	13	30	Dave Marcis	Milt Lunda '69 Dodge	268	1,125	Running
10	22	56	Gerald Chamberlain	Lyle Stelter '67 Mercury	267	1,050	Running
11	2	43	Richard Petty*	Petty Ent '69 Ford	263	1,050	D Shaft
12	15	25	Jabe Thomas	Don Robertson '68 Plymouth	258	925	Running
13	25	08	E J Trivette	E C Reid '69 Chevrolet	258	1,050	Running
14	29	8	Ed Negre	Negre '67 Ford	258	955	Running
15	31	34	Wendell Scott	Scott '67 Ford	253	910	Running
16	16	64	Elmo Langley	Langley '68 Ford	248	800	Running
17	33	45	Bill Seifert	Seifert '68 Ford	244	815	Running
18	35	47	Cecil Gordon	Bill Seifert '68 Ford	237	750	Running
19	30	0	Earl Brooks	Dr Don Tarr '67 Chevrolet	233	770	Running
20	18	39	Friday Hassler	Hassler '67 Chevrolet	225	700	Rear End
21	23	76	Ben Arnold	Red Culpepper '68 Ford	219	650	Crash
22	27	82	Roy Mayne	'67 Chevrolet	217	725	Running
23	14	03	Richard Brickhouse	Dub Clewis '67 Plymouth	151	600	Wtr pump
24	21	10	Bill Champion	Champion '64 Ford	147	590	Oil Leak
25	32	70	J D McDuffie	McDuffie '67 Buick	147	625	Clutch
26	9	71	Bobby Isaac	K&K Insurance '69 Dodge	138	635	Steering
27	26	38	Buddy Young	Fred Bear '67 Chevrolet	123	675	Clutch
28	12	4	John Sears	L G DeWitt '67 Ford	108	540	Trans
29	11	3	Neil Castles	Ray Fox '69 Dodge	102	560	Engine
30	19	32	Dick Brooks	Brooks '69 Plymouth	99	555	Engine
31	6	6	Buddy Baker	Cotton Owens '69 Dodge	63	525	Engine
32	10	48	James Hylton	Hylton Eng '69 Dodge	52	570	Crash
33	28	51	Dub Simpson	Bill Strong '69 Chevrolet	52	605	W Bearing
34	7	27	Donnie Allison	Banjo Matthews '69 Ford	19	510	Engine
35	36	9	Roy Tyner	Tyner '69 Pontiac	5	505	Engine
36	34	44	Bob Ashbrook	Giachetti Bros '67 Chevrolet	2	535	Engine

Time of Race: 3 hours, 2 minutes, 28 seconds
Average Speed: 131.572 mph
Pole Winner: Cale Yarborough - 152.293 mph
Lap Leaders: Richard Petty 1-2, Cale Yarborough 3-13, Donnie Allison 14-18, Yarbrough 19-30, Buddy Baker 31-48, Bobby Allison 49-57, Petty 58-103, B.Allison 104-279, LeeRoy Yarbrough 280-283, B.Allison 284-287, Yarbrough 288-291.
Cautions: 4 for 24 laps   Margin of Victory: 1-lap plus Under Caution   Attendance: 34,700
*Relieved by Donnie Allison

Yarborough claimed he never touched Allison in the incident. "Bobby just lost it, that's all," retorted Cale. "I thought we were friends. I don't like to be blamed for something I didn't do."

Allison virtually had the race sewed up, having led from lap 104 through lap 279. He was holding a lap lead on the field when he made his final pit stop under green. Just as he pulled down pit road, Donnie Allison, driving in relief of Richard Petty, blew his engine. The caution came out and Yarbrough made up his lap.

Allison led the restart on lap 286; Yarbrough lagging two car lengths behind, trapped in traffic. As the pack of cars sped into the first turn, Allison darted into the wall. Cale scooted under, but LeeRoy got tangled up with the leader.

A couple of days later, Allison viewed film of the incident and came to the conclusion that Cale did not hit him. "I owe Cale an apology," said Allison. "At the

Bobby Allison's Dodge was wiped out in late race crash at Darlington

time it appeared that he had hit me, but after looking at the film, I was wrong."

Buddy Baker left the Ray Fox Dodge team to take the seat of the Cotton Owens Dodge. Baker went out on lap 63 with a blown engine. Chrysler officials hired Neil Castles to drive the Fox car. Castles left the race after 102 laps with a blown engine.

Fox was disturbed at the turn of events. "Maybe I shouldn't even be here," he grumbled. "But if I was bigger, I'd challenge Baker to a fist fight."

Yarbrough averaged 131.572 mph before a Saturday crowd of 34,700.

Race No. 19

Isaac All the Way In Beltsville 300

BELTSVILLE, MD (May 16) -- Bobby Isaac of Catawba, NC started on the pole and led all the way to win the Beltsville 300 at Beltsville Speedway. It was the sixth win of the year for the leadfoot Dodge driver.

Neil Castles came from 22nd starting spot to finish second, two laps behind. John Sears came in third, Elmo Langley was fourth and James Hylton fifth.

David Pearson hounded Isaac the entire distance. But the defending Grand National champion blew his engine on lap 246, leaving Isaac riding freely the final 54 laps.

Isaac was quick to give his pit crew credit for the victory. "I made two pits stops under the yellow flag," said Isaac. "Harry (Hyde) and the boys got me out ahead of Pearson each time."

The K&K Insurance Dodge crew has often encountered lengthy pit stops in crucial situations. "Tonight they were the best," said Isaac.

Richard Petty did not enter the race due to rib injuries

he suffered at Weaverville two weeks earlier. He fell 64 points behind Pearson in the Grand National standings.

Isaac averaged 73.059 mph for his 10th career victory.

Race No. 20

Pearson Wins at Hampton as Isaac Runs Out of Gas

HAMPTON, VA (May 17) -- David Pearson took the lead with 15 laps to go when leader Bobby Isaac ran out of gas, and cruised to a big win in the Tidewater 375 at Langley Field Speedway.

Isaac tried to run the 375-lapper on the .4-mile track with only one pit stop. Crew chief Harry Hyde told Isaac to stay on the track during the only caution flag and he later ran out of gas in the shadow of the checkered flag.

"I knew Isaac had to pit again," said Pearson. "There wasn't any way he could have made it. I don't know why he didn't pit under caution. I couldn't believe it."

Grand National Race No. 19
300 Laps at Beltsville Speedway
Beltsville, MD
"Beltsville 300"
150 Miles on Half-mile Paved Track
May 16, 1969

Fin	St	No.	Driver	Team / Car	Laps	Money	Status
1	1	71	Bobby Isaac	K&K Insurance '69 Dodge	300	$2,500	Running
2	22	06	Neil Castles	Castles '67 Plymouth	298	1,500	Running
3	4	4	John Sears	L G DeWitt '67 Ford	295	1,000	Running
4	3	64	Elmo Langley	Langley '68 Ford	295	750	Running
5	5	48	James Hylton	Hylton Eng '69 Dodge	292	600	Running
6	9	49	G C Spencer	Spencer '68 Plymouth	292	500	Running
7	10	25	Jabe Thomas	Don Robertson '68 Plymouth	287	450	Running
8	12	80	E J Trivette	E C Reid '67 Chevrolet	280	425	Running
9	11	34	Wendell Scott	Scott '67 Ford	279	400	Running
10	20	18	Dick Johnson	Johnson '68 Ford	277	390	Running
11	13	10	Bill Champion	Champion '68 Ford	277	380	Running
12	16	26	Earl Brooks	Brooks '67 Ford	271	370	Running
13	2	17	David Pearson	Holman-Moody '69 Ford	246	560	Engine
14	6	30	Dave Marcis	Marcis '69 Dodge	184	350	Rear End
15	8	67	Buddy Arrington	Arrington '69 Dodge	169	340	Rear End
16	7	38	Buddy Young	Fred Bear '67 Chevrolet	85	330	Engine
17	18	47	Cecil Gordon	Bill Seifert '68 Ford	65	320	Vibration
18	19	19	Henley Gray	Harry Melton '68 Ford	37	310	Engine
19	17	70	J D McDuffie	McDuffie '67 Buick	27	300	Engine
20	15	45	Bill Seifert	Seifert '69 Ford	24	290	Quit
21	14	8	Ed Negre	Negre '67 Ford	24	280	Trans
22	21	15	Dr Ed Hessert	Hessert '68 Plymouth	14	270	Quit

Time of Race: 2 hours, 3 minutes, 12 seconds
Average Speed: 73.059 mph
Pole Winner: Bobby Isaac - 83.329 mph
Lap Leaders: Bobby Isaac 1-300.
Cautions: 3 for 29 laps   Margin of Victory: 2-laps plus   Attendance: 8,500

Grand National Race No. 20
375 Laps at Langley Field Speedway
Hampton, VA
"Tidewater 375"
150 Miles on .4-mile Paved Track
May 17, 1969

Fin	St	No.	Driver	Team / Car	Laps	Money	Status
1	1	17	David Pearson	Holman-Moody '69 Ford	375	$2,700	Running
2	4	48	James Hylton	Hylton Eng '69 Dodge	370	1,500	Running
3	3	30	Dave Marcis	Milt Lunda '69 Dodge	369	1,000	Running
4	2	71	Bobby Isaac	K&K Insurance '69 Dodge	368	750	Running
5	9	06	Neil Castles	Castles '67 Plymouth	366	600	Running
6	6	4	John Sears	L G DeWitt '67 Ford	365	500	Running
7	11	64	Elmo Langley	Langley '68 Ford	361	450	Running
8	8	14	Sam McQuagg	Bill Ellis '69 Plymouth	358	425	Running
9	5	67	Buddy Arrington	Arrington '69 Dodge	354	400	Running
10	17	34	Wendell Scott	Scott '67 Ford	339	390	Running
11	16	70	J D McDuffie	McDuffie '67 Buick	316	380	Running
12	12	25	Jabe Thomas	Don Robertson '68 Plymouth	315	370	Running
13	10	03	Richard Brickhouse	Dub Clewis '67 Plymouth	299	360	Running
14	7	49	G C Spencer	Spencer '68 Plymouth	200	350	Engine
15	20	45	Bill Seifert	Seifert '69 Ford	196	340	Quit
16	21	19	Henley Gray	Harry Melton '68 Ford	175	330	Trans
17	14	18	Dick Johnson	Johnson '68 Ford	160	320	Clutch
18	19	80	E J Trivette	E C Reid '67 Chevrolet	91	310	Engine
19	15	10	Bill Champion	Champion '68 Ford	62	300	Clutch
20	22	26	Earl Brooks	Brooks '67 Ford	58	290	Steering
21	13	8	Ed Negre	Negre '67 Ford	47	280	Engine
22	23	15	Dr Ed Hessert	Hessert '68 Plymouth	44	270	Engine
23	24	12	Pete Hazelwood	'68 Ford	21	260	Flagged
24	18	47	Cecil Gordon	Bill Seifert '68 Ford	16	250	Rear End

Time of Race: 1 hour, 58 minutes, 45 seconds
Average Speed: 75.789 mph
Pole Winner: David Pearson - 80.236 mph
Lap Leaders: David Pearson 1-40, Bobby Isaac 41-166, Pearson 167-226, Isaac 227-360, Pearson 361-375.
Cautions: 1 for 5 laps   Margin of Victory: 5-laps plus   Attendance: 7,500

Isaac lost seven laps in the pits while his crew tried to restart the car. He fell to fourth place in the final order. James Hylton came in second, five laps behind Pearson. Dave Marcis finished third. Neil Castles rounded out the top five.

Richard Petty sat out his second straight race and dropped to 104 points behind Pearson in the battle for the Grand National title.

Isaac was exhausted after the race. "I was so tired at the end I wasn't very upset about running out of gas," he said. "In a way, I was glad it was over."

Pearson averaged 75.789 mph and won $2,700.

Race No. 21

Yarbrough Ropes 600 Field; Gets 3rd Superspeedway Win

CHARLOTTE, NC (May 25) -- LeeRoy Yarbrough was in command most of the way and breezed to a two lap victory in the World 600 at Charlotte Motor Speedway. The $29,325 triumph was the third superspeedway win for the 30 year-old Jacksonville, FL Mercury driver.

Yarbrough took the lead for the final time in the 162nd lap and was never challenged the rest of the way. He wound up two laps in front of runner-up Donnie Allison, who was at the helm of the Banjo Matthews Ford. Donnie received relief help from borther Bobby for the final 100 miles. James Hylton powered his independent Dodge into third place and G.C. Spencer was fourth. Bobby Isaac fell out after 374 laps, but still was credited with a fifth place finish.

Yarbrough led for a total of 274 of the 400 laps as most of the factory backed entries fell by the wayside. Of the 10 factory backed cars in the race, only two finished.

David Pearson almost leaves the ballpark in World 600

Grand National Race No. 21
400 Laps at Charlotte Motor Speedway
Charlotte, NC
"World 600"
600 Miles on 1.5-mile Paved Track
May 25, 1969

Fin	St	No.	Driver	Team / Car	Laps	Money	Status
1	2	98	LeeRoy yarbrough	Junior Johnson '69 Mercury	400	$29,325	Running
2	1	27	Donnie Allison*	Banjo Matthews '69 Ford	398	14,755	Running
3	11	48	James Hylton	Hylton Eng '69 Dodge	382	9,670	Running
4	31	49	G C Spencer	Spencer '67 Plymouth	381	6,300	Running
5	10	71	Bobby Isaac	K&K Insurance '69 Dodge	374	5,375	Engine
6	22	37	Dr Don Tarr	Ray Fox '67 Dodge	373	4,100	Running
7	20	61	Hoss Ellington	Ellington '67 Mercury	368	3,525	Running
8	32	25	Jabe Thomas	Don Robertson '68 Plymouth	368	3,100	Running
9	14	39	Friday Hassler	Hassler '67 Chevrolet	367	2,575	Engine
10	16	64	Elmo Langley	Langley '68 Ford	367	2,150	Running
11	23	90	Sonny Hutchins	Junie Donlavey '67 Ford	361	2,075	Running
12	30	38	Buddy Young	Fred Bear '67 Chevrolet	359	1,975	Running
13	19	08	E J Trivette	E C Reid '69 Chevrolet	351	1,925	Running
14	44	9	Roy Tyner	Tyner '69 Pontiac	351	1,920	Running
15	43	70	J D McDuffie	McDuffie '67 Buick	348	1,875	Running
16	7	6	Buddy Baker	Cotton Owens '69 Dodge	347	1,775	Engine
17	33	15	Dr Ed Hessert	Hessert '68 Plymouth	341	1,775	Running
18	25	45	Bill Seifert	Seifert '69 Ford	338	1,685	Running
19	5	43	Richard Petty	Petty Ent '69 Ford	336	1,675	Engine
20	28	76	Ben Arnold	Red Culpepper '68 Ford	326	1,625	Running
21	34	47	Cecil Gordon	Bill Seifert '68 Ford	315	1,625	Running
22	15	67	Buddy Arrington	Arrington '69 Dodge	308	1,600	Engine
23	4	21	Cale Yarborough	Wood Brothers '69 Mercury	307	1,600	Hub
24	40	6	Earl Brooks	Brooks '67 Ford	305	1,600	Running
25	13	14	Sam McQuagg**	Bill Ellis '69 Plymouth	303	1,575	Engine
26	8	30	Dave Marcis	Milt Lunda '69 Dodge	272	1,475	Engine
27	9	99	Paul Goldsmith	Nichels Eng '69 Dodge	245	1,450	Steering
28	12	3	Neil Castles	Ray Fox '69 Dodge	153	1,525	Crash
29	21	4	John Sears***	L G DeWitt '69 Ford	150	1,500	Crash
30	39	96	Frank Warren	Warren '68 Ford	139	1,500	Heating
31	18	10	Bill Champion	Champion '68 Ford	135	1,350	Engine
32	38	84	Larry Hess	Elmo Langley '68 Ford	122	1,325	Engine
33	17	32	Dick Brooks	Brooks '69 Plymouth	112	1,300	Oil Pan
34	29	82	Roy Mayne	'69 Chevrolet	110	1,275	Engine
35	41	34	Wendell Scott	Scott '67 Ford	108	1,315	Engine
36	37	51	Dub Simpson	Bill Strong '69 Chevrolet	81	1,225	Rear End
37	26	18	Dick Johnson	Johnson '68 Ford	69	1,200	W Bearing
38	36	56	Gerald Chamberlain	Lyle Stelter '67 Mercury	57	1,175	Wiring
39	24	03	Richard Brickhouse	Dub Clewis '67 Plymouth	48	1,175	Carb fire
40	35	80	Henley Gray	E C Reid '67 Chevrolet	34	1,135	Sway Bar
41	6	22	Bobby Allison	Mario Rossi '69 Dodge	15	1,125	Radiator
42	3	17	David Pearson	Holman-Moody '69 Ford	13	1,750	Crash
43	27	40	John Kenney	Bill Champion '68 Ford	4	1,050	Crash
44	42	0	Ed Negre	Dr Don Tarr '67 Chevrolet	2	1,080	Trans

Time of Race: 4 hours, 27 minutes, 56 seconds
Average Speed: 134.361 mph
Pole Winner: Donnie Allison - 159.296 mph
Lap Leaders: Cale Yarborough 1-3, LeeRoy Yarbrough 4-29, Paul Goldsmith 30-37, James Hylton 38-39, Goldsmith 40-41, Bobby Isaac 42-47, Dave Marcis 48-53, Richard Petty 54-103, Yarbrough 104-105, Petty 106-150, Yarbrough 151-157, Isaac 158-161, Yarbrough 162-400.
Cautions: 5 for 45 laps   Margin of Victory: 2-laps plus   Attendance: 75,000
*Relieved by Bobby Allison   **Relieved by Richard Brickhouse
***Relieved by David Pearson

The last challenger to Yarbrough was Richard Petty, who had run second most of the event. But the engine blew in his Ford on lap 337, putting him behind the wall.

David Pearson was the first big name driver to go out of the race. On lap 13, Pearson's Ford darted up toward the wall and struck the rail with a glancing blow. His car lifted high in the air and teetered on top of the guard rail. Finally, the car came down into the track and spun to the infield. "I don't know what happened," said Pearson. "The first thing I knew I was on top of the guard rail -- looking down at the parking lot. I think I was all the way out and came back. I sure had a lot of help from the Man above."

J. C. Yarborough broke his leg in World 600 qualifying crash

Pearson later relieved John Sears and crashed when the engine blew. "I'm headed home now," remarked Pearson. "I'm going to get someone else to fly the plane. I'm afraid to fly it. I'm snakebit today."

The lead changed hands only 13 times before an audience of 75,000. Yarbrough was always near the front and said it "was the easiest race I've ever won. After Richard went out, Herb

Two 'Docs' - Don Tarr and Ed Hessert, spin in World 600

(Nab, crew chief) told me to slow down. I cut it to about 6,800 rpms. It was almost a perfect day," said Yarbrough.

Neil Castles drove the Ray Fox Dodge and was running ninth when he got tangled with Pearson on lap 155. After the race, Fox announced that he was quitting racing, turning in his factory deal with Dodge. The veteran car builder had become disenchanted when Buddy Baker left to join Cotton Owens.

Only 18 cars in the starting field of 44 were running at the finish. Yarbrough averaged 134.361 mph for his ninth career victory.

Despite his 19th place finish, Petty cut Pearson's point lead to 45 points after 21 races.

Race No. 22
Isaac Masters Macon for 7th Win of Season

MACON, GA (June 1) -- Bobby Isaac drove his Dodge around David Pearson in the 229th lap and hustled to victory in the Macon 300 at Middle Georgia Raceway. The 150-mile win was Isaac's seventh of the 1969 Grand National season.

Pearson chased Isaac most of the way and led for 19 laps. He was 4.0-seconds behind Isaac when the checkered flag fell. Richard Petty finished a distant third, John Sears was fourth and Neil Castles fifth.

Bobby Allison was back in action in his trusty Chevrolet, finishing sixth. Allison has always expressed interest in running all the races.

Pearson was able to tack on a single point to his standings lead. He now leads Petty by 46 points. Isaac ranks sixth, 366 points behind leader Pearson.

James Hylton qualified a strong fourth, but departed after 89 laps with rear gearing problems. Dave Marcis started fifth, but was beset by a lengthy pit stop and wound up 13th in the field of 24.

Isaac averaged 73.717 mph before a crowd of 6,500.

Grand National Race No. 22
300 Laps at Middle Georgia Raceway
Macon, GA
"Macon 300"
150 Miles on Half-mile Paved Track
June 1, 1969

Fin	St	No.	Driver	Team / Car	Laps	Money	Status
1	2	71	Bobby Isaac	K&K Insurance '69 Dodge	300	$2,500	Running
2	1	17	David Pearson	Holman-Moody '69 Ford	300	1,700	Running
3	3	43	Richard Petty	Petty Ent '69 Ford	299	1,000	Running
4	7	4	John Sears	L G DeWitt '67 Ford	295	750	Running
5	9	06	Neil Castles	Castles '67 Plymouth	295	600	Running
6	6	2	Bobby Allison	Allison '67 Chevrolet	294	500	Running
7	10	39	Friday Hassler	Hassler '67 Chevrolet	291	450	Running
8	11	64	Elmo Langley	Langley '68 Ford	291	425	Running
9	8	32	Dick Brooks	Brooks '69 Plymouth	283	400	Running
10	21	70	J D McDuffie	McDuffie '67 Buick	276	390	Running
11	16	34	Wendell Scott	Scott '67 Ford	275	380	Running
12	20	76	Ben Arnold	Red Culpepper '68 Ford	262	370	Running
13	5	30	Dave Marcis	Milt Lunda '69 Dodge	247	360	Running
14	22	0	Earl Brooks	Dr Don Tarr '67 Chevrolet	245	350	Running
15	23	96	Frank Warren	Warren '68 Ford	242	340	Running
16	15	10	Bill Champion	Champion '68 Ford	229	330	Hub
17	14	25	Jabe Thomas	Don Robertson '68 Plymouth	144	320	Axle
18	13	03	Richard Brickhouse	Dub Clewis '67 Plymouth	107	310	Rear End
19	18	45	Bill Seifert	Seifert '69 Ford	101	300	Heating
20	4	48	James Hylton	Hylton Eng '68 Dodge	89	290	Rear End
21	17	47	Cecil Gordon	Bill Seifert '68 Ford	35	280	Heating
22	19	08	E J Trivette	E C Reid '69 Chevrolet	26	270	Heating
23	12	18	Dick Johnson	Johnson '68 Ford	17	260	Engine
24	24	23	Paul Dean Holt	Dennis Holt '67 Ford	12	250	Flagged

Time of Race: 2 hours, 2 minutes, 5 seconds
Average Speed: 73.717 mph
Pole Winner: David Pearson - 87.946 mph
Lap Leaders: David Pearson 1-9, Bobby Isaac 10-116, Pearson 117-228, Isaac 229-300.
Cautions: 2 for 28 laps   Margin of Victory: 4 seconds   Attendance: 6,500

Race No. 23

Isaac Leads All but 4 Laps In Maryville 300 Victory

MARYVILLE, TN (June 5) -- Bobby Isaac, master of short track racing, gained his eighth victory of the season by romping to a six-lap win in the Maryville 300 at Smoky Mountain Raceway. Isaac has led 2,158 laps in the 1969 season, mostly on short tracks.

David Pearson started on the pole for the 46th time in his career, and led the first three laps. Isaac bolted past on lap four, leading all but one lap from that point on.

Pearson finished second with James Hylton third. Neil Castles was fourth and Elmo Langley took fifth.

Richard Petty started second and was holding down third place when a right front tire blew on his Ford, sending him into the wall on lap 60. Petty climbed from the wreckage slowly. He was not hurt.

Dave Marcis started fourth and was running fifth

David Pearson and Richard Petty on front row for Maryville 300

when the ignition failed in his Dodge. He got credit for 19th in the field of 23.

A jam-packed crowd of 9,200 watched Isaac take his 12th career win at an average speed of 81.706 mph.

Grand National Race No. 23
300 Laps at Smoky Mountain Raceway
Maryville, TN
"Maryville 300"
150 Miles on Half-mile Paved Track
June 5, 1969

Fin	St	No.	Driver	Team / Car	Laps	Money	Status
1	3	71	Bobby Isaac	K&K Insurance '69 Dodge	300	$1,400	Running
2	1	17	David Pearson	Holman-Moody '69 Ford	294	1,250	Running
3	9	48	James Hylton	Hylton Eng '69 Dodge	293	825	Running
4	11	06	Neil Castles	Castles '67 Plymouth	292	650	Running
5	7	64	Elmo Langley	Langley '68 Ford	287	500	Running
6	5	39	Friday Hassler	Hassler '67 Chevrolet	279	450	Running
7	8	25	Jabe Thomas	Don Robertson '68 Plymouth	275	425	Running
8	19	70	J D McDuffie	McDuffie '67 Buick	271	400	Running
9	18	08	E J Trivette	E C Reid '69 Chevrolet	270	370	Running
10	15	45	Bill Seifert	Seifert '69 Ford	267	350	Running
11	13	76	Ben Arnold	Red Culpepper '68 Ford	265	340	Running
12	22	26	Earl Brooks	Brooks '67 Ford	241	330	Spring
13	12	49	G C Spencer	Spencer '67 Plymouth	218	320	Lug Bolt
14	20	19	Henley Gray	Harry Melton '68 Ford	184	310	Quit
15	14	51	Dub Simpson	Bill Strong '69 Chevrolet	149	300	Engine
16	6	2	Bobby Allison	Allison '68 Chevrolet	129	290	Rear End
17	16	23	Paul Dean Holt	Dennis Holt '67 Ford	108	285	Engine
18	17	47	Cecil Gordon	Bill Seifert '68 Ford	75	280	Engine
19	4	30	Dave Marcis	Milt Lunda '69 Dodge	72	275	Ignition
20	2	43	Richard Petty	Petty Ent '69 Ford	60	270	Crash
21	10	18	Dick Johnson	Johnson '68 Ford	57	265	Fire
22	21	34	Wendell Scott	Scot '67 Ford	32	260	Engine
23	23	4	John Sears	L G DeWitt '67 Ford	0	255	Engine

Time of Race: 1 hour, 50 m minutes, 9 seconds
Average Speed: 81.706 mph
Pole Winner: David Pearson - 87.976 mph
Lap Leaders: David Pearson 1-3, Bobby Isaac 4-61, Pearson 62, Isaac 63-300.
Cautions: 1 for 8 laps   Margin of Victory: 6-laps plus   Attendance: 9,200

Race No. 24

Cale Nails LeeRoy in Final Lap Shoot-out at Michigan

BROOKLYN, MI (June 15) -- Cale Yarborough recovered from a last lap tangle with LeeRoy Yarbrough and went on to win the inaugural Motor State 500 at Michigan International Speedway.

A crowd of 46,238 were on their collective feet as the two 'Yarbs' roared into the final lap side-by-side. LeeRoy's Mercury slipped sideways after brushing Cale's car, and slammed into the wall. Yarborough wiggled through the turn, got straightened out and reached the finish line 5.0-seconds in front of David Pearson. Richard Petty scampered into third place. Yarbrough continued around the track, grinding his car against the wall. He came up a few hundred feet short of the finish line. He still got credit for fourth place. Charlie Glotzbach, making his return to racing, wound up fifth. Glotzbach was back behind the wheel of the Cotton Owens Dodge. Regular driver Buddy Baker had suffered a shoulder injury in a tire test at Daytona a few

Grand National Race No. 24
250 Laps at Michigan Int'l Speedway
Brooklyn, MI
"Motor State 500"
500 Miles on 2-mile Paved Track
June 15, 1969

Fin	St	No.	Driver	Team / Car	Laps	Money	Status
1	4	21	Cale Yarborough	Wood Brothers '69 Mercury	250	$17,625	Running
2	7	17	David Pearson	Holman-Moody '69 Ford	250	10,100	Running
3	5	43	Richard Petty	Petty Ent '69 Ford	250	5,875	Running
4	2	98	LeeRoy Yarbrough	Junior Johnson '69 Mercury	249	4,100	Crash
5	6	6	Charlie Glotzbach	Cotton Owens '69 Dodge	249	3,150	Running
6	8	99	Paul Goldsmith	Nichels Eng' 69 Dodge	248	2,500	Running
7	25	48	James Hylton	Hylton Eng '69 Dodge	244	2,102	Running
8	30	06	Neil Castles	Castles '69 Dodge	242	1,572	Running
9	11	4	John Sears	L G Dewitt '69 Ford	240	1,422	Running
10	31	25	Jabe Thomas	Don Robertson '68 Plymouth	227	1,452	Running
11	15	15	Dr Ed Hessert	Hessert '68 Plymouth	224	1,352	Running
12	26	34	Wendell Scott	Scott '67 Ford	216	1,302	Running
13	20	70	J D McDuffie	McDuffie '67 Buick	211	1,227	Running
14	13	61	Hoss Ellington	Ellington '67 Mercury	210	1,277	Steering
15	29	08	E J Trivette	E C Reid '69 Chevrolet	210	1,127	Running
16	23	47	Cecil Gordon	Bill Seifert '68 Ford	206	1,077	Running
17	32	44	Bob Ashbrook	Giachetti Bros '67 Ford	198	1,052	Running
18	34	19	Henley Gray	Harry Melton '68 Ford	193	977	Engine
19	38	30	Dave Marcis	Milt Lunda '69 Dodge	191	927	Engine
20	22	23	Paul Dean Holt	Dennis Holt '67 Ford	187	877	Engine
21	24	45	Bill Seifert	Seifert '68 Ford	183	877	Engine
22	27	26	Earl Brooks	Brooks '67 Ford	165	802	Running
23	16	76	Ben Arnold	Red Culpepper '68 Ford	155	727	Lug Bolts
24	10	32	Dick Brooks	Brooks '69 Plymouth	150	702	Engine
25	21	0	Dick Poling	Dr Don Tarr '67 Chevrolet	143	682	Engine
26	37	29	John Kennedy	Kennedy '678 Chevrolet	143	677	Engine
27	1	27	Donnie Allison	Banjo Matthews '69 Ford	115	775	Engine
28	3	71	Bobby Isaac	K&K Insurance '69 Dodge	94	695	Engine
29	33	18	Dick Johnson	Johnson '68 Ford	80	692	Clutch
30	9	22	Bobby Allison	Mario Rossi '69 Dodge	78	635	Engine
31	36	73	Bobby Wawak	'69 Dodge	74	657	Engine
32	35	38	Buddy Young	Fred Bear '67 Ford	62	652	Oil Line
33	28	2	Roy Tyner	Tyner '69 Pontiac	62	647	W Bearing
34	19	96	Frank Warren	Warren '68 Ford	55	642	H Gasket
35	17	10	Bill Champion	Champion '68 Ford	637	50	Engine
36	14	64	Elmo Langley	Langley '68 Ford	15	657	Engine
37	12	03	Richard Brickhouse	Dub Clewis '67 Plymouth	11	677	Crash
38	18	80	Wayne Gillette	E C Reid '67 Chevrolet	1	622	Rear End

Time of Race: 3 hours, 35 minutes, 26 seconds
Average Speed: 139.254 mph
Pole Winner: Donnie Allison - 160.135 mph
Lap Leaders: LeeRoy Yarbrough 1-13, John Sears 14, James Hylton 15-16,
    Donnie Allison 17-18, Bobby Allison 19, D.Allison 20-22, Yarbrough 23-55,
    David Pearson 56, Yarbrough 57-84, Yarbrough 85, Charlie Glotzbach 86-87,
    Yarbrough 88-96, Paul Goldsmith 97-100, D.Allison 101-104, Yarbrough 105-107,
    Yarbrough 108, Yarbrough 109-114, Yarbrough 115-119, Yarbrough 120,
    Yarbrough 121-122, Yarbrough 123, Pearson 124-171, Yarbrough 172-173,
    Yarbrough 174-180, Yarbrough 181-186, Yarbrough 187-203, Yarbrough 204,
    Pearson 205, Yarbrough 206-213, Pearson 214-220, Yarbrough 221-231,
    Yarbrough 232-243, Yarbrough 244-246, Yarbrough 247, Yarbrough 248-250.
Cautions: 7 for 35 laps   Margin of Victory: 5 car lengths   Attendance: 46,238

in the first NASCAR race at the two-mile oval operated by Larry LoPatin's American Raceways. "If they gave an Oscar for stock car racing's most thrilling event," wrote Benny Phillips, "then the Motor State 500 would take the lead by leaps and bounds."

Petty enjoyed his best finish on a superspeedway for the 1969 season. He was close behind the Cale-LeeRoy duel and said he expected a bump and grind finish. "I figured they'd wreck before they did," said Petty. "They were really racing and something like that was bound to happen."

Pole sitter Donnie Allison led on three occasions for nine laps, but his Banjo Matthews Ford fell victim to a blown engine after 115 laps. Bobby Isaac went out just before the half-way point with engine trouble, a fate that would strike Bobby Allison on lap 78.

Yarborough averaged 139.254 mph as seven cautions flags interrupted the brisk battle for 35 laps.

Race No. 25

Petty Wins at Kingsport As Isaac Blows Engine

KINGSPORT, TN (June 19) -- Richard Petty took the lead 41 laps from the finish and won the Kingsport 250 at Kingsport Speedway. It was the fourth win of the season for Petty, and the third time he has visited victory lane since he switched to Ford.

Bobby Isaac started on the pole and led for 187 of the first 210 laps. He was holding down a comfortable lead when the engine in his Dodge blew. Petty drove into the lead and was never headed.

John Sears came from 11th starting spot to gain runner-up honors. David Pearson came in third, Neil Castles was fourth and G.C. Spencer fifth.

Dave Marcis startled the veterans by qualifying second in his Milt Lunda Dodge. The 28 year-old Wausau, WI native mixed it up with the factory drivers until mechanical problems forced him to the sidelines after 158 laps.

By posting his 95th career Grand National victory, Petty inched to within 65 points of standings leader Pearson.

Castles, who briefly drove the Ray Fox factory Dodge a month ago, made a crowd-pleasing charge from 23rd to fourth at the finish. It was the second time this year that the 35 year-old Charlotte driver had started at the rear of the pack and notched a top four finish.

Petty, who led only the final 41 laps, averaged 73.619 mph before a crowd of 8,500.

days earlier.

"I think LeeRoy just went into the turn too hard and lost it," said Cale. "I don't fault him at all. He was trying his darnedest to win the race, just like I was."

After Yarbrough had walked back to the pit area, Ford's Ralph Moody approached him and told him to be careful what he said. "I guess we just bumped," LeeRoy explained. "I thought I had figured out a way to win the race, but it didn't happen that way."

The lead changed hands 35 times among nine drivers

Grand National Race No. 25
250 Laps at Kingsport Speedway
Kingsport, TN
"Kingsport 250"
100 Miles on .4-mile Paved Track
June 19, 1969

Fin	St	No.	Driver	Team / Car	Laps	Money	Status
1	3	43	Richard Petty	Petty Ent '69 Ford	250	$1,000	Running
2	11	4	John Sears	L G DeWitt '68 Ford	249	600	Running
3	4	17	David Pearson	Holman-Moody '69 Ford	248	600	Running
4	23	06	Neil Castles	Castles '67 Plymouth	247	350	Running
5	6	49	G C Spencer	Spencer '67 Plymouth	246	325	Running
6	10	64	Elmo Langley	Langley '68 Ford	241	300	Running
7	5	48	James Hylton	Hylton Eng '69 Dodge	239	275	Running
8	7	25	Jabe Thomas	Don Robertson '68 Plymouth	231	270	Running
9	8	76	Ben Arnold	Red Culpepper '68 Ford	228	265	Running
10	16	34	Wendell Scott	Scott '67 Ford	227	260	Running
11	1	71	Bobby Isaac	K&K Insurance '69 Dodge	212	255	Engine
12	12	26	Earl Brooks	Brooks '67 Ford	200	250	Running
13	22	04	Ken Meisenhelder	Meisenhelder '67 Olds	179	245	Running
14	2	30	Dave Marcis	Milt Lunda '69 Dodge	158	240	Fly wheel
15	20	70	J D McDuffie	McDuffie '67 Buick	155	235	Running
16	17	23	Paul Dean Holt	Dennis Holt '67 Ford	137	230	Ignition
17	19	47	Cecil Gordon	Bill Seifert '68 Ford	87	225	Clutch
18	9	08	E J Trivette	E C Reid '69 Chevrolet	65	220	Brakes
19	15	10	Bill Champion	Champion '68 Ford	65	215	Brakes
20	14	45	Bill Seifert	Seifert '69 Ford	39	210	Throttle
21	21	80	Wayne Gillette	E C Reid '67 Chevrolet	32	205	Engine
22	18	07	Coo Coo Marlin	Cunningham-Kelley '69 Chev	9	200	Rear End
23	13	38	Buddy Young	Fred Bear '67 Chevrolet	6	200	Oil Leak

Time of Race: 1 hour, 21 minutes, 30 seconds
Average Speed: 73.619 mph
Pole Winner: Bobby Isaac - 90.112 mph
Lap Leaders: Bobby Isaac 1-73, David Pearson 74-95, Isaac 96-209,
   Richard Petty 210-250.
Cautions: 5 for 35 laps   Margin of Victory: 1-lap plus   Attendance: 8,500

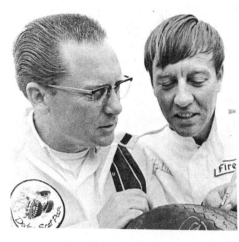

Harry Hyde and Bobby Isaac

Pearson was ordered to start at the rear of the field when he missed qualifying. The half-mile dirt track had been hit by a mid-afternoon rain storm, leaving it in less than desirable condition. Pearson and Hylton were two of the drivers who opted to wait until near the end of time trials to make their run against the clock.

Before they had a chance to make their runs, qualifying time had run out. Pearson started 20th in the field of 25 and charged through the pack. He was running sixth by the eighth lap, and led on two brief occasions

Race No. 26

Isaac's Dodge Survives Protest to Win at Greenville

GREENVILLE, SC (June 21) -- Bobby Isaac led all but three laps and won the Greenville 200 at Greenville-Pickens Speedway. The ninth victory of the season for the Catawba, NC Dodge driver was protested by Ralph Moody and Dick Hutcherson before the start of the race.

Johnny Bruner, Jr. confirmed the protest had been filed in writing before the race began. He supervised the engine teardown and declared the Harry Hyde built machine to be in perfect compliance with the NASCAR rules.

Isaac passed Pearson in the 109th lap and led the rest of the way. Pearson, in the Holman-Moody Ford, finished 9.0-seconds behind in second place. Richard Petty came in third, James Hylton was fourth and Neil Castles was fifth.

Grand National Race No. 26
200 Laps at Greenville-Pickens Speedway.
Greenville, SC
"Greenville 200"
100 Miles on Half-mile Dirt Track
June 21, 1969

Fin	St	No.	Driver	Team / Car	Laps	Money	Status
1	1	71	Bobby Isaac	K&K Insurance '69 Dodge	200	$1,000	Running
2	20	17	David Pearson	Holman-Moody '69 Ford	200	800	Running
3	2	43	Richard Petty	Petty Ent '69 Ford	200	400	Running
4	21	48	James Hylton	Hylton Eng '68 Dodge	196	350	Running
5	5	06	Neil Castles	Castles '67 Plymouth	195	325	Running
6	7	70	J D McDuffie	McDuffie '67 Buick	191	300	Running
7	10	26	Earl Brooks	Brooks '67 Ford	186	275	Running
8	11	08	E J Trivette	E C Reid '69 Chevrolet	183	270	Running
9	6	64	Elmo Langley	Langley '68 Ford	183	265	Running
10	25	57	Ervin Pruitt	Pruitt '67 Dodge	181	260	Running
11	17	19	Henley Gray	Harry Melton '68 Ford	180	255	Running
12	14	34	Wendell Scott	Scott '68 Ford	178	250	Running
13	13	04	Ken Meisenhelder	Meisenhelder '67 Olds	174	245	Running
14	15	76	Ben Arnold	Red Culpepper '68 Ford	167	240	Running
15	12	25	Jabe Thomas	Don Robertson '68 Plymouth	150	235	Rear End
16	9	10	Bill Champion	Champion '68 Ford	145	230	Axle
17	19	12	Pete Hazelwood	'67 Ford	133	225	Trans
18	16	47	Cecil Gordon	Bill Seifert '68 Ford	123	220	Quit
19	3	4	John Sears	L G DeWitt '68 Ford	62	215	Crash
20	23	45	Bill Seifert	Seifert '69 Ford	49	210	Steering
21	18	80	Wayne Gillette	E C Reid '67 Chevrolet	46	205	Oil Line
22	8	0	Dick Poling	Dr Don Tarr '67 Chevrolet	45	200	Axle
23	4	18	Dick Johnson	Johnson '68 Ford	42	---	Heating
24	22	82	Buster Sexton	'67 Chevrolet	9	---	Flagged
25	24	23	Paul Dean Holt	Dennis Holt '67 Ford	1	---	Engine

Time of Race: 1 hour, 37 minutes, 4 seconds
Average Speed: 61.813 mph
Pole Winner: Bobby Isaac - 66.030 mph
Lap Leaders: Bobby Isaac 1-66, David Pearson 67, Isaac 68-106, Pearson 107-108,
   Isaac 109-200.
Cautions: 5 for 29 laps   Margin of Victory: 9 seconds   Attendance: 9,300

for three laps.

Isaac was in control of the 100-miler from start to finish. He lost the lead only during yellow flag pit stops.

John Sears qualified third and ran second most of the early going. The independent Ford driver's day came to an end against the guard rail in the 62nd lap. Dick Johnson started fourth, but went out with overheating problems on lap 42.

Isaac's 13th career win came at an average speed of 61.813 mph.

Race No. 27

Pearson Nurses Overheating Ford to Victory at Raleigh

RALEIGH, NC (June 26) -- David Pearson nursed his ailing Holman-Moody Ford across the finish line three laps ahead of the field and won the North State 200 at State Fairgrounds Speedway. It was the sixth win of the season for the veteran Ford driver.

Pearson had taken the lead on lap 84 and built up a half lap advantage over the field late in the race. With 11 laps to go, Pearson's car suddenly slowed -- the victim of overheating problems. Second place Richard Petty, sensing he could catch the crippled Pearson, gunned his car but sailed over the first turn banking with eight laps to go. It took wreckers three laps to retrieve him from a ditch.

"My car got hot at the end," said the winner. "I guess I must have busted a water hose. But after I saw Richard go over the bank, I wasn't worried."

Petty got back in the race to finish second. James Hylton was third, 11 laps back. John Sears came in fourth with Elmo Langley fifth. Wendell Scott, popular independent out of Danville, VA, finished sixth.

Pearson got the jump on pole-sitter Bobby Isaac and led all but 18 laps. Petty led during an exchange of pit stops. Isaac was holding down third place when his Dodge suffered suspension failure on the rough dirt track. He got 10th in the final rundown.

Third-fastest qualifier Neil Castles broke an axle on the rutted surface after 40 laps. Only nine cars finished the race out of the 24 starters.

Pearson averaged 65.418 mph before a crowd of 7,100.

Grand National Race No. 27
200 Laps at State Fairgrounds Speedway
Raleigh, NC
"North State 200"
100 Miles on Half-mile Paved Track
June 26, 1969

Fin	St	No.	Driver	Team / Car	Laps	Money	Status
1	2	17	David Pearson	Holman-Moody '69 Ford	200	$1,200	Running
2	4	43	Richard Petty	Petty Ent '69 Ford	197	600	Running
3	5	48	James Hylton	Hylton Eng '67 Dodge	189	400	Running
4	8	4	John Sears	L G DeWitt '67 Ford	184	350	Running
5	7	64	Elmo Langley	Langley '68 Ford	183	325	Running
6	12	34	Wendell Scott	Scott '67 Ford	181	300	Running
7	10	26	Earl Brooks	Brooks '67 Ford	180	275	Running
8	13	08	E J Trivette	E C Reid '69 Chevrolet	167	270	Running
9	11	10	Bill Champion	Champion '68 Ford	163	265	Running
10	1	71	Bobby Isaac	K&K Insurance '69 Dodge	129	260	Spring
11	21	70	J D McDuffie	McDuffie '67 Buick	124	255	Engine
12	19	76	Ben Arnold	Red Culpepper '68 Ford	109	250	Heating
13	15	04	Ken Meisenhelder	Meisenhelder '67 Olds	108	245	Running
14	6	18	Dick Johnson	Johnson '68 Ford	89	240	A Frame
15	9	0	Dick Poling	Dr Don Tarr '67 Chevrolet	88	235	Heating
16	23	12	Pete Hazelwood	'67 Ford	61	230	Steering
17	22	19	Henley Gray	Harry Melton '68 Ford	55	225	A Frame
18	3	06	Neil Castles	Castles '69 Dodge	40	220	Axle
19	16	93	Walson Gardner	Gardner '67 Ford	20	215	Battery
20	17	21	Paul Dean Holt	'68 Ford	16	210	Engine
21	14	47	Cecil Gordon	Bill Seifert '68 Ford	14	205	Quit
22	20	45	Bill Seifert	Seifert '69 Ford	9	200	Quit
23	24	25	Jabe Thomas	Don Robertson '68 Plymouth	6	200	Engine
24	18	80	Wayne Gilette	E C Reid '67 Chevrolet	2	200	Quit

Time of Race: 1 hour, 31 minutes, 43 seconds
Average Speed: 65.418 mph
Pole Winner: Bobby Isaac - 72.942 mph
Lap Leaders: David Pearson 1-65, Richard Petty 66-83, Pearson 84-200.
Cautions: 4 for 12 laps   Margin of Victory: 3-laps plus   Attendance: 7,100

Race No. 28

'Secret Weapon' Helps LeeRoy to 'Firecracker' Win

DAYTONA BEACH, FL (July 4) -- A "secret weapon" employed by crew chief Herb Nab enabled LeeRoy Yarbrough to scamper to victory in the Medal of Honor Firecracker 400 at Daytona International Speedway.

Yarbrough drove his Junior Johnson Ford around Buddy Baker's Dodge with 17 laps remaining and posted an 0.9-second triumph in the Independence day classic. Baker had to settle for second after falling out of Yarbrough's draft in the final laps. Third place went to Donnie Allison with David Pearson fourth and Richard Petty fifth.

Yarbrough was in command most of the way, leading six times for 96 laps. While running in the lead, Yarbrough was able to shake any rival who attempted to ride along in the slingshot.

There was a subtle change in the script of Yarbrough's back-to-back wins at the Big D. Crew chief Nab moved the exhaust pipes the evening before the race. Instead of having the twin 3 1/2-inch pipes protruding from the side of the car, Nab positioned them to expel the hot fumes from under the rear bumper. "We didn't say anything about it," said Nab. "I just made the change for reasons I'd prefer not to explain."

LeeRoy Yarbrough celebrates Firecracker 400 victory with wife, Gloria and Union 76 Racestopper, Cheryl Johnson

Grand National Race No. 28
160 Laps at Daytona Int'l Speedway
Daytona Beach, FL
"Firecracker 400"
400 Miles on 2.5-mile Paved Track
July 4, 1969

Fin	St	No.	Driver	Team / Car	Laps	Money	Status
1	9	98	LeeRoy Yarbrough	Junior Johnson '69 Ford	160	$22,175	Running
2	11	6	Buddy Baker	Cotton Owens '69 Dodge	160	11,195	Running
3	2	27	Donnie Allison	Banjo Matthews '69 Ford	159	6,905	Running
4	3	17	David Pearson	Holman-Moody '69 Ford	156	4,050	Running
5	4	43	Richard Petty	Petty Ent '69 Ford	156	1,950	Running
6	10	30	Dave Marcis	Milt Lunda '69 Dodge	153	1,500	Running
7	23	03	Richard Brickhouse	Dub Clewis '67 Plymouth	151	1,325	Running
8	13	37	Dr Don Tarr	Ray Fox '67 Dodge	150	1,250	Running
9	14	48	James Hylton	Hylton Eng '69 Dodge	146	1,125	Running
10	29	36	H B Bailey	Bailey '69 Pontiac	144	1,000	Rear End
11	33	33	Wayne Smith	Smith '68 Chevrolet	143	975	Running
12	32	08	E J Trivette	E C Reid '69 Chevrolet	142	950	Running
13	27	96	Frank Warren	Warren '68 Ford	141	905	Running
14	20	64	Elmo Langley	Langley '68 Ford	141	900	Running
15	38	46	Roy Mayne	Tom Hunter '69 Chevrolet	141	875	Running
16	19	25	Jabe Thomas	Don Robertson '68 Plymouth	139	850	Heating
17	15	4	John Sears*	L G DeWitt '69 Ford	139	850	Running
18	37	9	Roy Tyner	Tyner '69 Pontiac	137	800	Running
19	36	0	Dick Poling	Dr Don Tarr '67 Chevrolet	134	775	Running
20	28	10	Bill Champion	Champion '68 Ford	134	750	Running
21	26	76	Ben Arnold	Red Culpepper '68 Ford	130	765	Running
22	8	22	Bobby Allison	Mario Rossi '69 Dodge	127	730	Crash
23	18	67	Buddy Arrington	Arrington '69 Dodge	118	720	Crash
24	21	61	Hoss Ellington	Ellington '67 Mercury	118	810	Crash
25	22	06	Neil Castles	Castles '69 Dodge	114	750	Engine
26	24	15	Dr Ed Hessert	Hessert '69 Plymouth	111	715	Crash
27	35	19	Henley Gray**	Harry Melton '68 Ford	105	680	Crash
28	16	32	Dick Brooks	Brooks '69 Plymouth	100	695	Running
29	6	71	Bobby Isaac	K&K Insurance '69 Dodge	63	685	Engine
30	25	7	Bobby Johns	Shorty Johns '67 Chevrolet	54	675	Engine
31	12	13	Joe Leonard	Smokey Yunick '69 Ford	47	720	Crash
32	5	3	Charlie Glotzbach	Ray Fox '69 Dodge	46	740	Engine
33	39	53	Paul Conners	'67 Dodge	31	635	Engine
34	7	99	Paul Goldsmith	Nichels Eng '69 Dodge	30	630	Crash
35	40	26	Earl Brooks	Brooks 67 Ford	30	625	Engine
36	17	45	Bill Seifert	Seifert '69 Ford	24	620	Quit
37	1	21	Cale Yarborough	Wood Brothers '69 Mercury	22	1,265	Engine
38	31	47	Cecil Gordon	Bill Seifert '68 Ford	21	610	Quit
39	30	23	Wendell Scott	Don Robertson '67 Ford	10	605	Rear End
40	34	09	J D McDuffie	E C Reid '69 Chevrolet	6	600	Oil Leak

Time of Race: 2 hours, 29 minutes, 11 seconds
Average Speed: 160.875 mph
Pole Winner: Cale Yarborough - 190.706 mph
Lap Leaders: David Pearson 1, Cale Yarborough 2-21, LeeRoy Yarbrough 22-31,
    Charlie Glotzbach 32, Yarborough 33-40, Buddy Baker 41-42, Glotzbach 43-45,
    Pearson 46-48, Yarbrough 49-76, Richard Petty 77-80, Yarbrough 81-112,
    Donnie Allison 113-116, Baker 117-130, Yarbrough 131, Baker 132-143,
    Yarbrough 144-160.

Cautions: 2 for 27 laps	Margin of Victory: 0.9 seconds	Attendance: 53,800

*Relieved by Neil Castles   **Relieved by Cecil Gordon

Although Nab didn't elaborate, it was obvious that the new positioning seriously affected any attempts to draft Yarbrough. "I tried drafting him for a few laps," said runner-up Baker. "But my car started overheating because of those hot fumes blowing in my radiator. And, I got a little groggy breathing those fumes. I had to back off in order to get my senses back."

Buddy Arrington was hospitalized after a spectacular crash on lap 127. Cecil Gordon, driving in relief of Henley Gray, spun his Ford on the backstretch. Arrington looped his Dodge and was hit by Hoss Ellington, ripping up both cars. Bobby Allison caught Ellington on the rebound.

Arrington suffered a ruptured spleen and several

Bobby Allison's Dodge and Hoss Ellington's Mercury lie battered on Daytona's backstretch

cracked ribs. Ellington cut his forehead, and Allison suffered a bruised knee.

Paul Goldsmith blew a tire and crashed in the 30th lap. Joe Leonard, driving Smokey Yunick's Ford, wrecked on lap 47.

Cale Yarborough set an all-time NASCAR qualifying record of 190.706 mph. He led for 20 laps in the early stages before popping his engine on lap 22.

After the race, sanctioning NASCAR slipped a new rule into the books, disallowing any exhaust pipes to be positioned at the rear of the car.

Race No. 29

Petty Wins Dover Inaugural; Pearson, Yarbrough Crash Out

DOVER, DE (July 6) -- Richard Petty took the led in the 222nd lap and breezed to a six lap victory in the Mason-Dixon 300 at the new Dover Downs International Speedway. It was the fifth win of the season for the 32 year-old Randleman, NC Ford driver.

Sonny Hutchins wound up second in the Junie

James Hylton finished 3rd in Mason-Dixon 300

Donlavey Ford. James Hylton came in third, John Sears was fourth and Elmo Langley fifth.

Only three factory backed cars entered the 300-miler. Pole sitter David Pearson led twice for 21 laps, but saw his hopes dashed when a tire separated, sending his Ford into the wall. He was not hurt in the 65th lap mishap, but his Holman-Moody Ford was a wipe out.

LeeRoy Yarbrough took the lead when Pearson went out. He led for 104 consecutive laps. After making a pit stop, he moved back into first place, but a tire failure put his Ford into the wall on lap 221.

LeeRoy Yarbrough blew tire and hit wall in Mason-Dixon 300

"It was strictly a three car race," said winner Petty. "After LeeRoy went out, I coasted the rest of the way." Petty said his biggest worry was the tire wear. "I blistered the right front tire three times," he noted.

Third place Hylton requested a recount of the score cards, claiming he finished second. Official ruling by NASCAR came two days later, and Sonny Hutchins' second-place finish was upheld.

The lead changed hands seven times among three drivers. Petty averaged 115.772 mph before 22,000 spectators.

Grand National Race No. 29
300 Laps at Dover Downs Int'l Speedway
Dover, DE
"Mason-Dixon 300"
300 Miles on 1-mile Paved Track
July 6, 1969

Fin	St	No.	Driver	Team / Car	Laps	Money	Status
1	3	43	Richard Petty	Petty Ent '69 Ford	300	$4,725	Running
2	4	90	Sonny Hutchins	Junie Donlavey '67 Ford	294	2,050	Running
3	9	48	James Hylton	Hylton Eng '69 Dodge	294	1,275	Running
4	8	4	John Sears	L G DeWitt '69 Ford	293	825	Running
5	25	84	Elmo Langley	Langley '68 Ford	287	725	Running
6	7	15	Dr Ed Hessert	Hessert '69 Plymouth	281	675	Running
7	17	34	Wendell Scott	Scott '67 Ford	277	650	Running
8	10	25	Bill Champion	Champion '68 Ford	275	600	Running
9	28	45	Bill Seifert	Seifert '68 Ford	273	585	Running
10	13	47	Cecil Gordon	Bill Seifert '68 Ford	273	595	Running
11	27	19	Henley Gray	Harry Melton '68 Ford	267	560	Running
12	16	70	J D McDuffie	McDuffie '67 Buick	265	575	Running
13	29	44	George Ashbrook	Giachetti Bros '67 Chevrolet	262	540	Running
14	32	06	Neil Castles	Castles '69 Dodge	261	530	Running
15	2	98	LeeRoy Yarbrough	Junior Johnson '69 Ford	223	620	Crash
16	5	49	G C Spencer	Spencer '68 Plymouth	210	560	Engine
17	23	04	Ken Meisenhelder	Meisenhelder '67 Olds	183	500	Rear End
18	12	76	Ben Arnold	Red Culpepper '68 Ford	155	515	Engine
19	18	0	Frank Warren	Dr Don Tarr '67 Chevrolet	128	505	Engine
20	20	11	Roy Hallquist	'68 Chevrolet	93	495	Oil Leak
21	30	57	Bobby Mausgrover	Ervin Pruitt '67 Dodge	82	460	D Shaft
22	19	26	Earl Brooks	Brooks '67 Ford	71	475	Engine
23	1	17	David Pearson	Holman-Moody '69 Ford	65	890	Crash
24	6	31	Buddy Young	Fred Bear '67 Chevrolet	65	455	Engine
25	31	9	Roy Tyner	Tyner '69 Pontiac	65	420	Rear End
26	14	64	Dub Simpson	Elmo Langley '68 Ford	62	440	Heating
27	22	40	Jabe Thomas	Bill Champion '67 Ford	56	410	Crash
28	24	82	George Davis	'67 Chevrolet	24	400	Quit
29	11	03	Richard Brickhouse	Dub Clewis '67 Plymouth	19	415	Engine
30	21	23	Paul Dean Holt	Don Robertson '67 Ford	7	380	Engine
31	26	86	Ed Negre	Neil Castles '67 Plymouth	2	370	Ignition
32	15	25	James Cox	Don Robertson '67 Plymouth	1	385	Engine

Time of Race: 2 hours, 35 minutes, 28 seconds
Average Speed: 115.772 mph
Pole Winner: David Pearson - 130.430 mph
Lap Leaders: David Pearson 1-5, LeeRoy Yarbrough 6-15, Richard Petty 16-42, Pearson 43-63, Yarbrough 64-167, Petty 168-211, Yarbrough 212-221, Petty 222-300.
Cautions: 4 for 27 laps   Margin of Victory: 6-laps plus   Attendance: 22,000

Race No. 30

Pearson Laps Field In Thompson 200

THOMPSON, CT (July 10) -- David Pearson took the lead when mechanical problems forced Richard Petty to the sidelines and won the Thompson 200 at the New Thompson Speedway. It was the seventh win of the season for the defending Grand National champion.

James Hylton finished second, a lap behind. John Sears came in third, followed by G.C. Spencer and Richard Brickhouse.

Pearson and Petty earned the front row starting spots. Pearson led the first lap by a fender, then Petty shoved his blue Ford into the lead. The Randleman, NC veteran led through the 96th lap when he made what appeared to be a routine pit stop.

However, the Petty Enterprises crew noticed fluid leaking from the rear end from a broken seal. Petty was out and Pearson trotted uncontested the rest of the way.

Wendell Scott was eliminated in a pit road crash with Dave Marcis. Marcis continued and finished 19th in the field of 31.

Rookie Buddy Young lost control of his Chevrolet and slammed into a dirt retaining bank. The Fairfax, VA driver got back in the race after a three lap visit to the pits. He finished seventh.

Pearson averaged 89.498 mph on the .625-mile-oval. A standing room only crowd of 12,000 was on hand.

Grand National Race No. 30
200 Laps at New Thompson Speedway
Thompson, CT
"Thompson 200"
125 Miles on .625-mile Paved Track
July 10, 1969

Fin	St	No.	Driver	Team / Car	Laps	Money	Status
1	1	17	David Pearson	Holman-Moody '69 Ford	200	$2,200	Running
2	3	48	James Hylton	Hylton Eng '69 Dodge	199	1,500	Running
3	4	4	John Sears	L G DeWitt '68 Ford	199	1,000	Running
4	7	49	G C Spencer	Spencer '68 Plymouth	197	900	Running
5	5	03	Richard Brickhouse	Dub Clewis'67 Plymouth	193	800	Running
6	9	06	Neil Castles	Castles '67 Plymouth	193	700	Running
7	8	31	Buddy Young	Fred Bear '67 Chevrolet	191	650	Running
8	12	15	Dr Ed Hessert	Hessert '68 Plymouth	189	600	Running
9	16	08	E J Trivette	E C Reid '69 Chevrolet	189	550	Running
10	14	45	Bill Seifert	Seifert '68 Ford	189	500	Running
11	19	70	J D McDuffie	McDuffie '67 Buick	187	475	Running
12	13	33	Wayne Smith	Smith '69 Chevrolet	179	450	Running
13	21	19	Henley Gray	Harry Melton '68 Ford	178	425	Running
14	17	10	Bill Champion	Champion '68 Ford	177	400	Running
15	26	47	Cecil Gordon	Bill Seifert '68 Ford	176	390	Running
16	20	76	Ben Arnold	Red Culpepper '68 Ford	173	380	Running
17	23	09	Dick Watson	E C Reid '67 Chevrolet	171	370	Brakes
18	24	26	Earl Brooks	Brooks '67 Ford	144	360	Running
19	6	30	Dave Marcis	Milt Lunda '69 Dodge	139	350	Running
20	11	84	Elmo Langley	Langley '68 Ford	139	340	Engine
21	31	34	Wendell Scott	Scott '67 Ford	128	330	Crash
22	10	25	Jabe Thomas	Don Robertson '68 Plymouth	118	320	Ignition
23	27	23	Paul Dean Holt	Don Robertson '67 Ford	310	98	Engine
24	18	11	Roy Hallquist	'68 Chevrolet	97	300	Engine
25	2	43	Richard Petty	Petty Ent '69 Ford	96	250	Rear End
26	15	0	Frank Warren	Dr Don Tarr '67 Chevrolet	67	250	Oil Line
27	25	04	Ken Meisenhelder	Meisenhelder '67 Olds	46	250	Oil Leak
28	28	57	Bobby Mausgrover	Ervin Pruitt '67 Dodge	45	250	Quit
29	22	64	Dub Simpson	Elmo Langley '68 Ford	17	250	Heating
30	30	86	Ed Negre	Neil Castles '69 Dodge	15	250	Ignition
31	29	82	Mark Sellers	'67 Chevrolet	1	250	Engine

Time of Race: 1 hour, 23 minutes, 8 seconds
Average Speed: 89.498 mph
Pole Winner: David Pearson - 99.800 mph
Lap Leaders: David Pearson 1, Richard Petty 2-96, Pearson 97-124, James Hylton 125-131, Pearson 132-200.
Cautions: 2 for 13 laps   Margin of Victory: 1-lap plus   Attendance: 12,000

Grand National Race No. 31
200 Laps at Trenton Speedway
Trenton, NJ
"Northern 300"
300 Miles on 1.5-mile Paved Track
July 13, 1969

Fin	St	No.	Driver	Team / Car	Laps	Money	Status
1	2	17	David Pearson	Holman-Moody '69 Ford	200	$5,300	Running
2	4	22	Bobby Allison	Mario Rossi '69 Dodge	199	2,050	Running
3	1	71	Bobby Isaac	K&K Insurance '69 Dodge	199	1,350	Running
4	6	48	James Hylton	Hylton Eng '69 Dodge	198	725	Running
5	5	14	LeeRoy Yarbrough	L G DeWitt '69 Ford	196	675	Running
6	8	30	Dave Marcis	Milt Lunda '69 Dodge	193	600	Running
7	13	03	Richard Brickhouse	Dub Clewis '67 Plymouth	189	550	Running
8	7	32	Dick Brooks	Brooks '69 Dodge	187	500	Running
9	28	84	Elmo Langley	Langley '68 Ford	187	475	Running
10	15	15	Dr Ed Hessert	Hessert '69 Plymouth	186	450	Running
11	31	06	Neil Castles	Castles '69 Dodge	186	425	Running
12	16	08	E J Trivette	E C Reid '69 Chevrolet	182	400	Running
13	27	34	Wendell Scott	Scott '67 Ford	178	390	Running
14	23	9	Roy Tyner	Tyner '69 Pontiac	176	380	Running
15	34	57	Bobby Mausgrover	Ervin Pruitt '67 Dodge	175	370	Running
16	24	26	Earl Brooks	Brooks '67 Ford	175	360	Running
17	20	47	Cecil Gordon	Bill Seifert '68 Ford	170	350	Running
18	12	25	Jabe Thomas	Don Robertson '68 Plymouth	169	340	Running
19	18	10	Bill Champion	Champion '68 Ford	154	330	Clutch
20	11	4	John Sears	L G DeWitt '67 Ford	148	320	Engine
21	21	0	Frank Warren	Dr Don Tarr '67 Chevrolet	140	300	Rear End
22	36	11	Roy Hallquist	'68 Chevrolet	70	275	Rear End
23	22	19	Henley Gray	Harry Melton '69 Ford	65	300	Sway Bar
24	10	90	Sonny Hutchins	Junie Donlavey '67 Ford	64	300	Engine
25	14	31	Buddy Young	Fred Bear '67 Chevrolet	56	300	Ignition
26	17	70	J D McDuffie	McDuffie '67 Buick	46	300	Engine
27	35	04	Ken Meisenhelder	Meisenhelder '67 Olds	41	250	Flagged
28	25	76	Ben Arnold	Red Culpepper '68 Ford	37	275	Heating
29	3	43	Richard Petty	Petty Ent '69 Ford	36	325	Engine
30	33	33	Wayne Smith	Smith '68 Chevrolet	21	275	Rear End
31	37	40	Phil Montague	Bill Champion '67 Ford	8	230	Flagged
32	32	86	Ed Negre	Neil Castles '67 Plymouth	7	255	Engine
33	9	49	G C Spencer	Spencer '68 Plymouth	5	255	Engine
34	19	45	Bill Seifert	Seifert '68 Ford	5	255	Engine
35	29	23	Paul Dean Holt	Don Robertson '67 Ford	3	255	Oil Leak
36	26	64	Dub Simpson	Elmo Langley '68 Ford	2	250	Quit
37	30	09	Wayne Gillette	E C Reid '67 Chevrolet	1	250	Engine

Time of Race: 2 hours, 28 minutes, 45 seconds
Average Speed: 121.008 mph
Pole Winner: Bobby Isaac - 132.668 mph
Lap Leaders: Bobby Isaac 1-38, James Hylton 39, LeeRoy Yarbrough 40-41, Isaac 42-101, David Pearson 102-104, Isaac 105-130, Pearson 131-155, Isaac 156-167, Pearson 168-200.
Cautions: 2 for 10 laps   Margin of Victory: 1-lap plus   Attendance: 12,000

Race No. 31

Isaac Fastest at Trenton, But Pearson Wins Northern 300

TRENTON, NJ (July 13) -- David Pearson outlasted the competition and came home first in the Northern 300 at Trenton Speedway. It was the eighth win of the year for the Spartanburg, SC Ford driver, and it boosted his point lead to 106 points over Richard Petty.

Pearson put his blue and gold Ford into the lead for keeps on lap 168 when Bobby Isaac had to make a pit stop for blistered tires. Isaac, who had suffered tire problems all day long, falling a lap behind at one point, came back strong. But ignition troubles forced him to the pits for two laps and he was never again in contention.

Bobby Allison wound up second with Isaac third, both a lap down. Fourth place went to James Hylton and fifth to LeeRoy Yarbrough. Yarbrough was driving a Ford owned by L.G. DeWitt. Junior Johnson had declined to enter the 300-miler on the kidney shaped track.

Richard Petty started third, but blew his engine on lap 38. Petty had already fallen two laps off the pace with recurring tire problems. He finished 29th in the field of 37.

A disappointing crowd of 12,000 watched the first race at the redesigned 1.5-mile track. Pearson averaged 121.008 mph for his 54th career Grand National triumph.

Grand National Race No. 32
300 Laps at Beltsville Speedway
Beltsville, MD
"Maryland 300"
150 Miles on Half-mile Paved Track
July 15, 1969

Fin	St	No.	Driver	Team / Car	Laps	Money	Status
1	1	43	Richard Petty	Petty Ent '69 Ford	300	$2,500	Running
2	4	17	David Pearson	Holman-Moody '69 Ford	300	1,700	Running
3	2	48	James Hylton	Hylton Eng '69 Dodge	299	1,000	Running
4	9	06	Neil Castles	Castles '67 Plymouth	296	750	Running
5	10	4	John Sears	L G DeWitt '68 Ford	294	600	Running
6	8	49	G C Spencer	Spencer '67 Plymouth	294	500	Running
7	6	31	Buddy Young	Fred Bear '67 Chevrolet	290	450	Running
8	11	45	Bill Seifert	Seifert '68 Ford	284	425	Running
9	18	70	J D McDuffie	McDuffie '67 Buick	281	400	Running
10	12	08	E J Trivette	E C Reid '69 Chevrolet	279	390	Running
11	15	47	Cecil Gordon	Bill Seifert '68 Ford	277	380	Running
12	22	26	Earl Brooks	Brooks '67 Ford	277	370	Running
13	14	19	Henley Gray	Harry Melton '68 Ford	260	360	Running
14	17	25	Jabe Thomas	Don Robertson '68 Plymouth	208	350	Oil Leak
15	24	57	Bobby Mausgrover	Ervin Pruitt '67 Dodge	89	240	Heating
16	21	15	Dr Ed Hessert	Hessert '68 Plymouth	73	330	Engine
17	3	71	Bobby Isaac	K&K Insurance '69 Dodge	60	320	Crash
18	23	0	Frank Warren	Dr Don Tarr '67 Chevrolet	43	310	Trans
19	16	76	Ben Arnold	Red Culpepper '67 Ford	38	300	Engine
20	7	03	Richard Brickhouse	Dub Clewis '67 Plymouth	29	290	Engine
21	19	34	Wendell Scott	Scott '67 Ford	18	280	Engine
22	20	09	Wayne Gillette	E C Reid '67 Chevrolet	5	270	Brakes
23	5	64	Elmo Langley	Langley '68 Ford	4	260	Engine
24	13	86	Bill Champion	Neil Castles '69 Dodge	3	250	Ignition

Time of Race: 1 hour, 56 minutes, 30 seconds
Average Speed: 77.253 mph
Pole Winner: Richard Petty - 82.094 mph
Lap Leaders: Richard Petty 1-3, James Hylton 4-13, Bobby Isaac 14-60, Petty 61-110, David Pearson 111-116, Hylton 117-123, Petty 124-159, Pearson 160-298, Petty 299-300.
Cautions: 2 for 9 laps   Margin of Victory: 15 seconds   Attendance: 4,800

Race No. 32

Petty Wins Disputed Maryland 300 at Beltsville

BELTSVILLE, MD (July 15) -- David Pearson was flagged the winner of the Maryland 300 at Beltsville Speedway, but it was Richard Petty who pocketed the $2,500 first place check.

Pearson had taken the lead in the 160th lap and appeared on his way to an easy win. He pulled into the pits for fuel on lap 298, allowing Petty to get back into the lead lap. When Pearson was delayed getting out of the pits, Petty motored into first place two laps from the finish.

Pearson got back out on the track and was three-quarters of a lap behind. However, he received the checkered flag from Johnny Bruner, Jr. Petty immediately protested and requested a check of the score cards.

Within an hour, the mistake was found and Petty was elevated to first place. "One of my scorers had missed a lap," he said. "Actually, I led from the 160th lap through the finish."

Pearson walked over to Petty and congratulated his Ford rival. "I didn't think I had won. I was trying to make it to the finish, but I ran out of gas. I had to pit."

Pearson had led laps 160-298, but he wound up 15 seconds behind Petty at the stripe.

James Hylton, who led for 17 laps, finished third. Neil Castles was fourth and John Sears fifth.

Bobby Isaac started third and passed Hylton for the lead in the 14th lap. The Catawba, NC Dodge driver stretched his advantage to almost a half lap when a tire blew. Isaac hit the wall and was out of the race.

Petty averaged 77.253 mph for his 97th career Grand National win.

Race No. 33

Pearson Misses Wrecks, Hits Victory Lane at Bristol

BRISTOL, TN (July 20) -- David Pearson tactfully missed a bundle of wrecks and won the Volunteer 500 at Bristol International Speedway by three laps. It was the ninth win of the season for the 34 year-old Ford driver.

With Richard Petty providing a crucial assist on the 104-degree afternoon, Pearson's Ford finished well ahead of runner-up Bobby Isaac. Third place went to Donnie Allison with Cale Yarborough in relief. James Hylton took fourth place and Cecil Gordon fifth.

Yarborough had won the pole and led the first 31 laps. On lap 32, Cale hooked the rear bumper of Jabe Thomas' Plymouth, setting off an eight car wreck. "I hit him, but I didn't mean to," Cale confessed. "I was trying to get by but there wasn't enough room."

Eliminated in the crash were Thomas, and Bobby Allison. Petty and Dick Brooks had their machines crippled.

Pearson, suffering from the flu, had led from laps 183-344 when he pitted and turned the wheel over to Petty. The tag team led the final 142 laps. Petty had blown an engine after 60 laps.

Only 10 cars finished the race, and 10th place Roy Tyner was 97 laps behind. Speedway management unveiled a new track with steeply banked turns. The pole speed increased about 15 mph over the top time in the spring.

Multi-car wreck on Bristol's new high-banked track

"If you ask me," said Petty, "they ruined a good race track. There's not enough room for the speeds we're running."

Rookie Dick Brooks said, "Looks like they tried to make a superspeedway out of a half mile track. I think they missed. This is a dangerous place and it's going to be rough on equipment. I think they were lucky to finish 10 cars."

Pearson averaged 79.737 mph and moved out to a 149 point lead in the Grand National standings. A crowd of 32,000 watched the race.

Grand National Race No. 33
500 Laps at Bristol Int'l Speedway
Bristol, TN
"Volunteer 500"
250 Miles on Half-mile Paved Track
July 20, 1969

Fin	St	No.	Driver	Team / Car	Laps	Money	Status
1	3	17	David Pearson*	Holman-Moody '69 Ford	500	$5,525	Running
2	7	71	Bobby Isaac	K&K Insurance '69 Dodge	497	3,150	Running
3	32	27	Donnie Allison**	Banjo Matthews '69 Ford	487	2,300	Running
4	9	48	James Hylton	Hylton Eng '69 Dodge	477	1,500	Running
5	24	47	Cecil Gordon	Bill Seifert '68 Ford	431	1,000	Running
6	14	76	Ben Arnold	Red Culpepper '68 Ford	430	925	Running
7	25	45	Bill Seifert	Seifert '69 Ford	429	800	Running
8	19	10	Bill Champion	Champion '68 Ford	429	750	Running
9	31	70	J D McDuffie	McDuffie '67 Buick	418	700	Running
10	30	9	Roy Tyner	Tyner '69 Pontiac	403	650	Running
11	6	98	LeeRoy Yarbrough	Junior Johnson '69 Ford	358	640	Engine
12	28	93	Walson Gardner	Gardner '67 Ford	255	630	Flagged
13	18	15	Dr Ed Hessert	Hessert '69 Plymouth	253	575	Engine
14	17	64	Elmo Langley	Langley '68 Ford	224	550	Engine
15	26	19	Henley Gray	Harry Melton '69 Ford	206	500	Quit
16	10	4	John Sears	L G DeWitt '67 Ford	194	535	Engine
17	15	06	Neil Castles	Castles '69 Dodge	147	450	Engine
18	12	49	G C Spencer	Spencer '67 Plymouth	136	465	Engine
19	21	34	Wendell Scott	Scott '67 Ford	121	430	Crash
20	8	30	Dave Marcis	Milt Lunda '69 Dodge	112	420	Heating
21	22	08	E J Trivette	E C Reid '69 Chevrolet	106	410	Crash
22	11	31	Buddy Young	Fred Bear '67 Chevrolet	86	440	Engine
23	2	43	Richard Petty	Petty Ent '69 Ford	60	440	Engine
24	1	21	Cale Yarborough	Wood Brothers '69 Mercury	57	1,080	Engine
25	13	32	Dick Brooks	Brooks '69 Plymouth	51	395	Crash
26	4	22	Bobby Allison	Mario Rossi '69 Dodge	32	390	Crash
27	5	6	Buddy Baker	Cotton Owens '69 Dodge	30	380	Crash
28	23	25	Jabe Thomas	Don Robertson '68 Plymouth	28	345	Crash
29	16	09	Wayne Gillette	E C Reid '67 Chevrolet	18	335	Heating
30	20	07	Coo Coo Marlin	Cunningham-Kelley '69 Chev	2	325	Engine
31	27	26	Earl Brooks	Brooks '67 Ford	2	325	Crash
32	29	57	Bobby Mausgrover	Ervin Pruitt '67 Dodge	2	325	Crash

Time of Race: 3 hours, 8 minutes, 7 seconds
Average Speed: 79.737 mph
Pole Winner: Cale Yarborough - 103.432 mph
Lap Leaders: Cale Yarborough 1-31, Bobby Allison 32, James Hylton 33-81, David Pearson 82-93, Bobby Isaac 94-96, Donnie Allison 97-182, Pearson 183-344, Isaac 345-357, LeeRoy Yarbrough 358, Pearson 359-500.
Cautions: 8 for 58 laps   Margin of Victory: 3-laps plus   Attendance: 32,000
*Relieved by Richard Petty   **Relieved by Cale Yarborough

Race No. 34

Petty Nips Isaac at Wire In Nashville 400

NASHVILLE, TN (July 26) -- Richard Petty held off Bobby Isaac in a stirring duel and won the Nashville 400 at Fairgrounds Speedway.

Isaac made up almost two laps in the last half of the

race and wound up second, a half car length behind Petty's Ford. James Hylton was third, John Sears fourth and Neil Castles fifth.

The lead changed hands only twice in the 400 lapper, and Petty was out front for all but two laps. On lap 130, Isaac pitted under the yellow flag and collapsed behind the wheel. Crew chief Harry Hyde dragged Isaac out of the car and flagged down Dave Marcis. By the time Marcis had hooked up the safety gear, he had lost a lap.

Within 70 laps, Isaac was back behind the wheel. "Never since I've been racing has the heat gotten to me like that," he said later.

Isaac rapidly made up lost ground and got back in the lead lap when he tapped Petty into a spin on lap 334. The final 10 laps had the crowd of 15,846 on its feet.

"I think I could have beaten Petty if I had been able to stay in the car," Isaac said.

Point leader David Pearson finished sixth, 24 laps back. His Ford lost a cylinder in the second half of the race.

Petty's 98th career Grand National triumph came at an average speed of 78.740 mph.

Race No. 35

Petty Smokes Field In Smoky 200

MARYVILLE, TN (July 27) -- Richard Petty, hitting stride in the summer months, drove his Ford to a narrow victory over David Pearson in the Smoky 200 at Smoky Mountain Raceway. It was the third win for Petty in the last four Grand National events, and it put him one win away from the magic 100-victory plateau.

Pearson started on the pole for the 49th time in his career and led for 28 laps. He made a run at Petty in the final laps but had to settle for second place. Neil Castles came in third with Elmo Langley fourth and James Hylton fifth.

Bobby Isaac, seeking to end a winless July, passed Pearson on lap 28 and built up a half lap lead. A blown tire sent Isaac's Dodge into the second turn wall on lap 72. He was out of the race.

Petty took the lead at that point and led all but one of

Grand National Race No. 34
400 Laps at Fairgrounds Speedway
Nashville, TN
"Nashville 400"
200 Miles on Half-mile Paved Track
July 26, 1969

Fin	St	No.	Driver	Team / Car	Laps	Money	Status
1	1	43	Richard Petty	Petty Ent '69 Ford	400	$3,000	Running
2	2	71	Bobby Isaac*	K&K Insurance '69 Dodge	400	1,700	Running
3	4	48	James Hylton	Hylton Eng '68 Dodge	387	950	Running
4	8	4	John Sears	L G DeWitt '68 Ford	384	550	Running
5	9	06	Neil Castles	Castles '67 Plymouth	379	500	Running
6	3	17	David Pearson	Holman-Moody '69 Ford	376	690	Running
7	7	07	Coo Coo Marlin	Cunningham-Kelley '69 Chev	357	480	Running
8	10	33	Wayne Smith	Smith '68 Chevrolet	351	470	Running
9	18	70	J D McDuffie	McDuffie '67 Buick	348	460	Running
10	6	64	Elmo Langley	Langley '68 Ford	265	450	Suspen
11	12	34	Wendell Scott	Scott '67 Ford	237	440	Crash
12	22	12	Pete Hazelwood	'68 Ford	228	430	Engine
13	11	10	Bill Champion	Champion '68 Ford	200	420	Crash
14	19	19	Henley Gray	Harry Melton '68 Ford	115	410	Quit
15	14	08	E J Trivette	E C Reid '69 Chevrolet	97	400	Suspen
16	20	47	Cecil Gordon	Bill Seifert '68 Ford	89	390	Fan Belt
17	23	25	Jabe Thomas	Don Robertson '68 Plymouth	66	380	Rear End
18	17	45	Bill Seifert	Seifert '69 Ford	66	370	Quit
19	5	30	Dave Marcis	Milt Lunda '69 Dodge	40	360	Ignition
20	21	04	Ken Meisenhelder	Meisenhelder '67 Olds	33	350	Ignition
21	15	76	Ben Arnold	Red Culpepper '68 Ford	14	340	Oil Leak
22	16	26	Earl Brooks	Brooks '67 Ford	13	330	Vibration
23	24	57	Bobby Mausgrover	Ervin Pruitt '67 Dodge	10	320	Suspen
24	13	09	Wayne Gillette	E C Reid '67 Chevrolet	5	310	Quit

Time of Race: 2 hours, 32 minutes, 24 seconds
Average Speed: 78.740 mph
Pole Winner: Richard Petty - 84.918 mph
Lap Leaders: Richard Petty 1-128, David Pearson 129-130, Petty 131-400.
Cautions: 5 for 18 laps   Margin of Victory: 1/2 car length   Attendance: 15,846
*Relieved by Dave Marcis

Grand National Race No. 35
200 Laps at Smoky Mountain Raceway
Maryville, TN
"Smoky 200"
100 Miles on Half-mile Paved Track
July 27, 1969

Fin	St	No.	Driver	Team / Car	Laps	Money	Status
1	3	43	Richard Petty	Petty Ent '69 Ford	200	$1,000	Running
2	1	17	David Pearson	Holman-Moody '69 Ford	200	800	Running
3	8	06	Neil Castles	Castles '67 Plymouth	195	400	Running
4	6	64	Elmo Langley	Langley '68 Ford	189	350	Running
5	4	48	James Hylton	Hylton Eng '68 Dodge	189	325	Running
6	13	47	Cecil Gordon	Bill Seifert '68 Ford	181	300	Running
7	21	33	Wayne Smith	Smith '68 Chevrolet	179	275	Running
8	7	4	John Sears	L G DeWitt '68 Ford	178	270	Running
9	18	45	Bill Seifert	Seifert '69 Ford	177	265	Running
10	10	76	Ben Arnold	Red Culpepper '68 Ford	177	260	Running
11	9	08	E J Trivette	E C Reid '69 Chevrolet	176	255	Running
12	16	19	Henley Gray	Harry Melton '68 Ford	175	250	Running
13	15	70	J D McDuffie	McDuffie '67 Buick	172	245	Running
14	12	34	Wendell Scott	Scott '67 Ford	170	240	Running
15	19	12	Pete Hazelwood	'68 Ford	164	235	Running
16	17	25	Jabe Thomas	Don Robertson '68 Plymouth	149	230	Running
17	5	30	Dave Marcis	Milt Lunda '69 Dodge	123	225	Engine
18	23	04	Ken Meisenhelder	Meisenhelder '67 Olds	97	220	Heating
19	2	71	Bobby Isaac	K&K Insurance '69 Dodge	72	215	Crash
20	14	09	Wayne Gillette	E C Reid '67 Chevrolet	61	210	Quit
21	22	57	Bobby Mausgrover	Ervin Pruitt '67 Dodge	35	205	Radiator
22	11	10	Bill Champion	Champion '68 Ford	30	200	Heating
23	20	26	Earl Brooks	Brooks '67 Ford	22	200	Heating

Time of Race: 1 hour, 12 minutes, 48 seconds
Average Speed: 82.417 mph
Pole Winner: David Pearson - 87.434 mph
Lap Leaders: David Pearson 1-27, Bobby Isaac 28-72, Richard Petty 73-129,
   Pearson 130, Petty 131-200.
Cautions: 1 for 7 laps   Margin of Victory: 1 car length   Attendance: 7,800

the remaining 128 laps.

A crowd of 7,800 watched Petty win at an average speed of 82.417 mph. Pearson maintained his comfortable point lead in the driver standings with a 143 point bulge over Petty.

Race No. 36

LeeRoy Leads Ford 1-2-3-4-5 Sweep in Atlanta's Dixie 500

HAMPTON, GA (Aug. 10) -- LeeRoy Yarbrough fought off a virus and drove his Ford to victory in the Dixie 500 at Atlanta International Raceway. It was the fifth superspeedway triumph of the season for the 30 year-old Jacksonville, FL veteran.

Yarbrough, who led 144 of the 334 laps, paced a 1-2-3-4-5 sweep for Ford automobiles. David Pearson finished 5.5 seconds behind Yarbrough. Richard Petty was third, Charlie Glotzbach fourth and Donnie Allison fifth. Glotzbach took a ride in Smokey Yunick's Ford.

Hoss Ellington spins in Dixie 500

Only two factory drivers failed to finish. Hard-luck Bobby Isaac blew the engine in his Dodge after 93 laps. Paul Goldsmith left the race after 147 laps when his fuel filler cap was jarred loose as he bumped Pearson on pit road.

The 10th chapter of this event was witnessed by only 14,300 spectators. The 500-miler had been rained out on August 3, and the following week heavily overcast skies greeted the sparse crowd.

Pearson's runner-up effort enabled him to boost his point lead to 146 over Petty.

Yarbrough's 11th career win came at an average speed of 133.001 mph. Car owner Junior Johnson said his team's success can be traced to two factors. "We've got a little better car than we had last year," he said, "and LeeRoy is a little better driver than he was last year."

LeeRoy Yarbrough and crew chief Herb Nab

Yarbrough took the lead from Petty with 32 laps remaining and was never headed. Although he was unchallenged in the final laps, Yarbrough said it was one of his most difficult drives. "I have been sick with the flu for about 10 days," he said. "I took a shot this morning and I feel a little better. But there were six guys out there today who were really determined to win. I can say this is as tough a race as I've run this year."

Pearson passed Petty for the runner-up slot with three laps left.

Race No. 37

Pearson Paddles to Victory In Soggy Yankee 600

BROOKLYN, MI (Aug. 17) -- After 78 laps of pacing and 87 laps of racing, David Pearson was declared the winner of the inaugural Yankee 600 at Michigan International Speedway. It was the 10th win of the season for the title-bound Pearson.

The scheduled 300-lap event on the two-mile oval was flagged to a halt after 165 laps had been completed. Two rain-enforced delays totaled about four hours. Nearly half of the laps were run under the caution flag,

Grand National Race No. 36
334 Laps at Atlanta Int'l Raceway
Hampton, GA
"Dixie 500"
500 Miles on 1.5-mile Paved Track
August 10, 1969

Fin	St	No.	Driver	Team / Car	Laps	Money	Status
1	2	98	LeeRoy Yarbrough	Junior Johnson '69 Ford	334	$18,620	Running
2	7	17	David Pearson	Holman-Moody '69 Ford	334	9,750	Running
3	3	43	Richard Petty	Petty Ent '69 Ford	334	6,100	Running
4	6	13	Charlie Glotzbach	Smokey Yunick '69 Ford	333	3,585	Running
5	5	27	Donnie Allison	Banjo Matthews '69 Ford	333	2,775	Running
6	9	22	Bobby Allison	Mario Rossi '69 Dodge	332	2,200	Running
7	1	21	Cale Yarborough	Wood Brothers '69 Mercury	331	2,560	Running
8	4	6	Buddy Baker	Cotton Owens '69 Dodge	331	1,555	Running
9	17	48	James Hylton	Hylton Eng '69 Dodge	327	1,550	Running
10	15	32	Dick Brooks	Brooks '69 Plymouth	313	1,475	Running
11	14	15	Dr Ed Hessert	Hessert '69 Plymouth	311	1,450	Running
12	23	06	Neil Castles	Castles '69 Dodge	310	1,475	Running
13	20	07	Coo Coo Marlin	Cunningham-Kelley '69 Chev	307	1,400	Running
14	38	29	John Kennedy	Kennedy '67 Chevrolet	302	1,425	Running
15	26	25	Jabe Thomas	Don Robertson '68 Plymouth	301	1,375	Running
16	22	47	Cecil Gordon	Bill Seifert '68 Ford	300	1,325	Running
17	36	33	Wayne Smith	Smith '68 Chevrolet	298	1,350	Running
18	39	08	E J Trivette	E C Reid '69 Chevrolet	297	1,250	Running
19	35	34	Wendell Scott	Scott '67 Ford	296	1,300	Running
20	27	10	Bill Champion	Champion '68 Ford	295	1,200	Running
21	40	04	Ken Meisenhelder	Meisenhelder '67 Olds	288	1,250	Running
22	34	57	Bobby Mausgrover	Ervin Pruitt '67 Dodge	279	1,225	Running
23	31	70	J D McDuffie	McDuffie '67 Buick	264	1,240	Engine
24	28	31	Buddy Young	Fred Bear '67 Chevrolet	264	1,025	Wtr pump
25	30	76	Ben Arnold	Red Culpepper '68 Ford	247	1,075	Engine
26	37	19	Henley Gray	Harry Melton '68 Ford	244	1,125	D Shaft
27	29	96	Frank Warren	Warren '68 Ford	207	1,175	Engine
28	12	64	Elmo Langley	Langley '68 Ford	192	1,050	Heating
29	24	09	Wayne Gillette	E C Reid '67 Chevrolet	187	975	Sway Bar
30	10	99	Paul Goldsmith	Nichels Eng '69 Dodge	147	1,000	Filler cap
31	11	30	Dave Marcis	Milt Lunda '69 Dodge	133	950	Engine
32	25	61	Hoss Ellington	Ellington '69 Ford	107	925	Crash
33	8	71	Bobby Isaac	K&K Insurance '69 Dodge	93	900	Engine
34	18	49	G C Spencer	Spencer '67 Plymouth	83	900	Engine
35	32	0	Earl Brooks	Dr Don Tarr '67 Chevrolet	82	925	Engine
36	33	51	Dub Simpson	Bill Strong '69 Chevrolet	78	875	Engine
37	21	8	Ed Negre	G C Spencer '67 Plymouth	62	800	Engine
38	13	45	Bill Seifert	Seifert '69 Ford	46	775	Engine
39	19	37	Dr Don Tarr	Ray Fox '67 Dodge	28	750	Clutch
40	16	39	John Sears	Friday Hassler '67 Chevrolet	3	725	Engine

Time of Race: 3 hours, 45 minutes, 35 seconds
Average Speed: 133.001 mph
Pole Winner: Cale Yarborough - 155.413
Lap Leaders: Cale Yarborough 1-49, Buddy Baker 50-52, Richard Petty 53-55,
    Paul Goldsmith 56, Yarborough 57-69, Charlie Glotzbach 70-72, Yarborough 73-93,
    Baker 94-96, Yarborough 97-110, David Pearson 111-122, Glotzbach 123-124,
    Pearson 125-165, LeeRoy Yarbrough 166-170, Petty 171-181, Yarborough 182-239,
    Petty 240-241, Yarborough 242-290, Pearson 291-292, Petty 293-302,
    Yarbrough 303-334.
Cautions: 3 for 31 laps   Margin of Victory: 5.5 seconds   Attendance: 14,300

Grand National Race No. 37
300 Laps at Michigan Int'l Speedway
Brooklyn, MI
"Yankee 600"
600 Miles on 2-mile Paved Track
August 17, 1969

Fin	St	No.	Driver	Team / Car	Laps	Money	Status
1	1	17	David Pearson	Holman-Moody '69 Ford	165	$21,950	Running
2	12	6	Buddy Baker	Cotton Owens '69 Dodge	165	10,880	Running
3	5	43	Richard Petty	Petty Ent '69 Ford	165	7,020	Running
4	2	21	Cale Yarborough	Wood Brothers '69 Mercury	165	3,675	Running
5	6	22	Bobby Allison	Mario Rossi '69 Dodge	165	2,775	Running
6	4	71	Bobby Isaac	K&K Insurance '69 Dodge	165	2,050	Running
7	14	14	Richard Brickhouse	Bill Ellis '69 Plymouth	165	1,750	Running
8	3	98	LeeRoy Yarbrough	Junior Johnson '69 Ford	165	1,575	Running
9	9	48	James Hylton	Hylton Eng '69 Dodge	165	1,475	Running
10	22	15	Dr Ed Hessert	Hessert '69 Plymouth	164	1,525	Running
11	24	39	Friday Hassler	Hassler '67 Chevrolet	164	1,450	Running
12	13	4	John Sears	L G DeWitt '69 Ford	163	1,400	Running
13	17	64	Elmo Langley	Langley '68 Ford	163	1,375	Running
14	10	88	Charlie Glotzbach	Nichels Eng '69 Dodge	162	1,350	Running
15	20	61	Hoss Ellington	Ellington '69 Ford	162	1,325	Running
16	26	31	Buddy Young	Fred Bear '67 Chevrolet	162	1,325	Running
17	19	5	Ron Grana	C J Grana '69 Ford	162	1,275	Running
18	16	37	Dr Don Tarr	Ray Fox '67 Dodge	162	1,250	Running
19	23	06	Neil Castles	Castles '69 Dodge	161	1,275	Running
20	8	30	Dave Marcis	Milt Lunda '69 Dodge	161	1,225	Running
21	44	25	Jabe Thomas	Don Robertson '68 Plymouth	161	1,175	Running
22	18	45	Bill Seifert	Seifert '68 Ford	160	1,150	Running
23	31	33	Wayne Smith	Smith '68 Chevrolet	158	1,125	Running
24	28	08	E J Trivette	E C Reid '69 Chevrolet	157	1,125	Running
25	38	01	Bill Massuch	Otis Patton '68 Ford	157	1,075	Running
26	32	47	Cecil Gordon	Bill Seifert '68 Ford	157	1,050	Running
27	39	34	Wendell Scott	Scott '67 Ford	156	1,025	Running
28	40	70	J D McDuffie	McDuffie '67 Buick	155	1,000	Running
29	29	29	John Kennedy	Kennedy '67 Chevrolet	155	1,000	Running
30	36	76	Ben Arnold	Red Culpepper '68 Ford	152	950	Running
31	15	32	Dick Brooks	Brooks '69 Plymouth	137	925	Running
32	27	8	Ed Negre	G C Spencer '67 Plymouth	136	925	Engine
33	21	27	Donnie Allison	Banjo Matthews '69 Ford	133	1,000	Engine
34	34	96	Frank Warren	Warren '68 Ford	128	850	Engine
35	25	10	Bill Champion	Champion '68 Ford	128	850	Engine
36	42	62	Homer Newland	Kaye Eng '69 Dodge	126	800	Running
37	30	36	H B Bailey	Bailey '69 Pontiac	97	775	Oil Leak
38	7	18	Benny Parsons	Russ Dawson '69 Ford	75	750	Engine
39	11	99	Paul Goldsmith	Nichels Eng '69 Dodge	60	725	Engine
40	41	87	Mel Gillette	'69 Olds	50	720	Engine
41	35	09	Wayne Gillette	E C Reid '67 Chevrolet	48	715	Clutch
42	37	19	Henley Gray	Harry Melton '68 Ford	41	710	Engine
43	43	26	Earl Brooks	Brooks '67 Ford	35	705	Crash
44	33	9	Roy Tyner	Tyner '69 Pontiac	5	700	Engine

Time of Race: 2 hours, 51 minutes, 25 seconds
Average Speed: 115.508 mph
Pole Winner: David Pearson - 161.714 mph
Lap Leaders: David Pearson 1-7, Bobby Isaac 8-17, Pearson 18-36,
    Richard Brickhouse 37, Cale Yarborough 38-46, Pearson 47, Buddy Baker 48-49,
    Paul Goldsmith 50-51, Baker 52, Goldsmith 53-55, Baker 56, Bobby Isaac 57-61,
    Bobby Allison 62-63, Dr Ed Hessert 64, Yarborough 65-68, Donnie Allison 69,
    Yarborough 70-75, D.Allison 76, Yarborough 77-87, D.Allison 88-90, Pearson 91-109,
    Richard Petty 110-121, B.Allison 122-126, Friday Hassler 127-129, LeeRoy
    Yarbrough 130-131, Yarborough 132, Pearson 133-165.
Cautions: 7 for 78 laps   Margin of Victory: 3 seconds   Attendance: 52,237
* Race shortened to 165 laps due to rain

disappointing a rain-soaked audience of 52,237.

Buddy Baker was flagged in second place with Richard Petty third. Cale Yarborough finished fourth and Bobby Allison rounded out the top five. The first nine cars were in the lead lap.

"I believe my car could have gone 600 miles and I'd be in the same place I'm sitting right now," Pearson said during the victory interview. "My car ran perfectly. Any time I wanted to move out, I had plenty to take me away from the others."

The final 20 laps were run under green, despite wet track conditions. "It was pretty wet in a few spots on the back chute," said the winner. "We should have run five or 10 more laps under caution before we restarted, but I think they were anxious to get those laps on the board."

The lead changed hands 26 times among a dozen drivers. Pearson led the final 33 laps and beat Baker by

3.0 seconds.

Paul Goldsmith competed in his final Grand National race. The 41 year-old veteran led twice for five laps, but fell out on lap 60 with a blown engine. "I plan on cutting back my racing activities," said Goldsmith.

Paul Goldsmith drove in his final Grand National race in Yankee 600

Charlie Glotzbach was hired to drive a Nichels Engineering Dodge as a running-mate to Goldsmith, and he finished 14th, three laps back. "I'll probably go with Paul and Ray from now on," said Glotzbach. "But I want to hear what Ford offers first. I'm looking to get back in NASCAR racing."

Benny Parsons, hot-shot from the ARCA ranks, competed in his third Grand National race. He started seventh but went out on lap 75 with engine trouble.

Pearson averaged only 115.508 mph for his sixth career superspeedway victory.

Race No. 38

Isaac Wins South Boston 100 For 10th of Year

S.BOSTON, VA (Aug. 21) -- Bobby Isaac led all but four laps and won the South Boston 100 at South Boston Speedway. It was the 10th win of the season for the 37 year-old Catawba, NC veteran.

David Pearson finished in second place with Richard Petty third. James Hylton survived a bumping match with Neil Castles to finish fourth. Elmo Langley came in fifth.

The 267-lapper on the .375-mile oval was the first short track race since the Professional Drivers Association formed a union a week earlier in Michigan. Three drivers -- Hoss Ellington, Ed Negre and Pete Hazelwood -- withdrew from the race, presumably in a form of protest over prize distribution. Independent drivers have long complained of weak prize money for position 6-10. A 10th place finish was worth only $60 more than last place. "There's only three drivers who make any money," reflected independent Castles. "The guy

who wins, the guy who finishes second -- and the man who runs dead last. The last place finisher never uses up any tires. Everybody else loses money."

Castles fell out on lap 187 due to ignition failure. In the middle stages, he and Hylton engaged in a spirited bumping duel.

Isaac averaged 76.906 mph before a crowd of 8,000.

Race No. 39

Petty Grabs 100th Career Win At Winston-Salem

WINSTON-SALEM, NC (Aug. 22) -- Richard Petty recovered from a first lap spin-out, then came on strong and won the Myers Brothers Stock Car Racing Spectacle at Bowman Gray stadium. The triumph was Petty's 100th in Grand National competition.

Bobby Isaac, who led all but nine laps, wound up second after he ran out of gas while holding a two lap

---

Grand National Race No. 38
267 Laps at South Boston Speedway
South Boston, VA
"South Boston 100"
100 Miles on .375-mile Paved Track
August 21, 1969

Fin	St	No.	Driver	Team / Car	Laps	Money	Status
1	1	71	Bobby Isaac	K&K Insurance '68 Dodge	267	$1,000	Running
2	3	17	David Pearson	Holman-Moody '69 Ford	267	800	Running
3	2	43	Richard Petty	Petty Ent '69 Ford	266	400	Running
4	6	48	James Hylton	Hylton Eng '68 Dodge	261	350	Running
5	5	64	Elmo Langley	Langley '68 Ford	259	325	Running
6	11	45	Bill Seifert	Seifert '68 Ford	252	300	Running
7	7	25	Jabe Thomas	Don Robertson '68 Plymouth	251	275	Running
8	14	08	E J Trivette	E C Reid '69 Chevrolet	250	270	Running
9	12	34	Wendell Scott	Scott '67 Ford	250	265	Running
10	9	10	Bill Champion	Champion '68 Ford	248	260	Running
11	13	47	Cecil Gordon	Bill Seifert '68 Ford	243	255	Running
12	19	70	J D McDuffie	McDuffie '67 Buick	242	250	Running
13	17	19	Henley Gray	Harry Melton '68 Ford	239	245	Running
14	21	26	Earl Brooks	Brooks '67 Ford	234	240	Running
15	24	06	Neil Castles	Castles '67 Plymouth	187	235	Ignition
16	22	12	Pete Hazelwood	'68 Ford	103	230	Quit
17	10	8	Ed Negre	G C Spencer '67 Plymouth	57	225	Quit
18	23	23	James Cox	Don Robertson '67 Ford	38	220	Brakes
19	20	57	Bobby Mausgrover	Ervin Pruitt '67 Dodge	35	215	Rear End
20	18	04	Ken Meisenhelder	Meisenhelder '67 Olds	27	210	Flat tire
21	16	76	Ben Arnold	Red Culpepper '68 Ford	26	205	Oil Leak
22	15	09	Wayne Gillette	E C Reid '67 Chevrolet	5	200	Clutch
23	8	61	Hoss Ellington	Ellington '69 Ford	4	200	Quit
24	4	4	John Sears	L G DeWitt '68 Ford	1	200	Oil Leak

Time of Race: 1 hour, 18 minutes, 1 second
Average Speed: 76.906 mph
Pole Winner: Bobby Isaac - 84.959 mph
Lap Leaders: Bobby Isaac 1-182, David Pearson 183, Richard Petty 184-186, Isaac 187-267.
Cautions: 2 for 13 laps   Margin of Victory: Attendance: 8,000

lead. David Pearson finished third with Elmo Langley fourth and James Hylton fifth.

Petty started on the pole, but spun after he hit Isaac's left rear bumper in the first lap. Petty spun around as the caution came out. He quickly righted his path without losing a lap.

Isaac pulled away from his factory backed rivals with ease and built up a two lap lead. Pearson and Petty each had made pit stops when their fuel supply ran low. Isaac tried to take his Dodge all the way without a pit stop, but he ran nine laps short. His pit stop took 10 seconds longer than Pearson and Petty, and he had to settle for second place.

"There has been so much publicity about me going for win number 100," said Petty. "But I wish it had come in a big race. This win ain't no bigger or smaller than any other I've won. They all count -- one at a time. The only thing I'm thinking of now is getting started on my second hundred."

Petty averaged 47.458 mph on the quarter-mile paved oval.

Race No. 40

Isaac, 5 Laps Down, Wins Western N.C. 500 by 4 Laps

WEAVERVILLE, NC (Aug. 24) -- Bobby Isaac rallied from five laps down and won the 12th annual Western North Carolina 500 at Asheville-Weaverville Speedway. The four lap victory was Isaac's 11th of the season.

Bobby Isaac

Isaac took the lead for good in the 386th lap when leader David Pearson made two unscheduled pit stops. He kept alive an event tradition by becoming the 12th different winner in the 12 runnings of this 250-miler.

Pearson finished second and rookie Dick Brooks was third, 13 laps back. Fourth place went to Elmo Langley and fifth to James Hylton although he was 33 laps behind.

Isaac won the pole and led on four occasions for 373 laps. Richard Petty's Ford moved to the front for a 43 lap stretch following a hot battle with his factory comrades. Isaac passed Petty in turn one on lap 120. Petty crashed into the wall while attempting to regain the lead from Isaac in the third turn. He was out for the day, but uninjured.

Isaac led all but three circuits from lap 121-324, but he lost his sizable advantage when he ran out of gas with 176 laps remaining. He coasted his Dodge into the pits, but the K&K Insurance crew headed by Harry Hyde had trouble getting the car restarted. The crew pushed Isaac's car out of the pits, but it stalled in the first turn. The caution flag came out.

Isaac lost five laps altogether.

After the race, the Holman-Moody team protested Isaac's victory -- claiming his crew had pushed the car down pit road farther than rules allow. Sanctioning NASCAR upheld Isaac's victory a day later.

Isaac averaged 80.450 mph as a crowd of 11,000 watched in sunny weather.

Grand National Race No. 39
250 Laps at Bowman Gray Stadium
Winston-Salem, NC
"Myers Brothers Stock Car Spectacle"
62.5 Miles on Quarter-mile Paved Track
August 22, 1969

Fin	St	No.	Driver	Team / Car	Laps	Money	Status
1	1	43	Richard Petty	Petty Ent '69 Ford	250	$1,000	Running
2	2	71	Bobby Isaac	K&K Insurance '69 Dodge	250	600	Running
3	3	17	David Pearson	Holman-Moody '69 Ford	250	600	Running
4	6	64	Elmo Langley	Langley '68 Ford	248	350	Running
5	4	48	James Hylton	Hylton Eng '68 Dodge	246	325	Running
6	5	4	John Sears	L G DeWitt '67 Ford	245	300	Running
7	7	06	Neil Castles	Castles '69 Dodge	244	275	Running
8	19	70	J D McDuffie	McDuffie '67 Buick	237	270	Running
9	11	34	Wendell Scott	Scott '67 Ford	236	265	Running
10	10	08	E J Trivette	E C Reid '69 Chevrolet	231	260	Running
11	21	25	Jabe Thomas	Don Robertson '68 Plymouth	227	255	Running
12	20	04	Ken Meisenhelder	Meisenhelder '67 Olds	221	250	Running
13	17	76	Ben Arnold	Red Culpepper '68 Ford	217	245	Running
14	9	10	Bill Champion	Champion '68 Ford	153	240	Brakes
15	22	19	Henley Gray	Harry Melton '68 Ford	93	235	Brakes
16	18	12	Pete Hazelwood	'68 Ford	91	230	Quit
17	14	8	Ed Negre	G C Spencer '67 Plymouth	82	225	Trans
18	13	45	Bill Seifert	Seifert '69 Ford	29	220	Quit
19	23	23	James Cox	Don Robertson '67 Ford	26	215	Oil Leak
20	24	33	Wayne Smith	Smith '68 Chevrolet	25	210	Engine
21	12	47	Cecil Gordon	Bill Seifert '68 Ford	24	205	Quit
22	16	26	Earl Brooks	Brooks '67 Ford	16	200	Quit
23	15	09	Wayne Gillette	E C Reid '67 Chevrolet	4	---	Quit
24	8	61	Hoss Ellington	Ellington '69 Ford	2	---	Quit

Time of Race: 1 hour, 19 minutes, 1 second
Average Speed: 47.458 mph
Pole Winner: Richard Petty - 54.253 mph
Lap Leaders: Bobby Isaac 1-241, Richard Petty 242-250.
Cautions: 3 for 17 laps   Margin of Victory: 4 seconds   Attendance: 10,500

Grand National Race No. 40
500 Laps at Asheville-Weaverville Speedway
Weaverville, NC
"Western North Carolina 500"
250 Miles on Half-mile Paved Track
August 24, 1969

Fin	St	No.	Driver	Team / Car	Laps	Money	Status
1	1	71	Bobby Isaac	K&K Insurance '69 Dodge	500	$2,800	Running
2	3	17	David Pearson	Holman-Moody '69 Ford	496	1,725	Running
3	7	32	Dick Brooks	Brooks '69 Plymouth	487	1,050	Running
4	10	64	Elmo Langley	Langley '68 Ford	481	850	Running
5	9	48	James Hylton	Hylton Eng '68 Dodge	467	750	Running
6	11	8	Ed Negre	G C Spencer '67 Plymouth	461	650	Running
7	19	25	Jabe Thomas	Don Robertson '68 Plymouth	454	600	Running
8	22	45	Bill Seifert	Seifert '69 Ford	451	550	Running
9	23	47	Cecil Gordon	Bill Seifert '68 Ford	450	530	Running
10	17	08	E J Trivette	E C Reid '69 Chevrolet	447	520	Running
11	18	76	Ben Arnold	Red Culpepper '68 Ford	420	510	Running
12	15	34	Wendell Scott	Scott '67 Ford	417	500	Running
13	14	70	J D McDuffie	McDuffie '67 Buick	407	490	Trans
14	6	06	Neil Castles	Castles '69 Dodge	398	500	Crash
15	4	30	Dave Marcis	Milt Lunda '69 Dodge	366	495	Rear End
16	8	4	John Sears	L G DeWitt '67 Ford	318	460	Rear End
17	27	23	James Cox	Don Robertson '68 Plymouth	315	450	Crash
18	21	19	Henley Gray	Harry Melton '68 Ford	256	440	Quit
19	20	09	Wayne Gillette	E C Reid '67 Chevrolet	188	430	Quit
20	12	49	G C Spencer	Spencer '67 Plymouth	158	420	Engine
21	13	10	Bill Champion	Champion '68 Ford	143	410	Clutch
22	5	98	LeeRoy Yarbrough	Junior Johnson '69 Ford	133	420	Engine
23	2	43	Richard Petty	Petty Ent '69 Ford	120	440	Crash
24	24	57	Bobby Mausgrover	Ervin Pruitt '67 Dodge	103	380	Oil Leak
25	25	12	Pete Hazelwood	'68 Ford	93	370	Oil Leak
26	26	26	Earl Brooks	Brooks '67 Ford	47	365	Ignition
27	16	61	Hoss Ellington	Ellington '69 Ford	8	355	Quit

Time of Race: 3 hours, 6 minutes, 27 seconds
Average Speed: 80.450 mph
Pole Winner: Bobby Isaac - 89.000 mph
Lap Leaders: Bobby Isaac 1-57, David Pearson 58-77, Richard Petty 78-120, Isaac 121-181, Pearson 182-184, Isaac 185-324, Pearson 325-385, Isaac 386-500.
Cautions: 4 for 17 laps   Margin of Victory: 4-laps plus   Attendance: 11,000

Grand National Race No. 41
367 Laps at Darlington Raceway
Darlington, SC
"Southern 500"
500 Miles on 1.375-mile Paved Track
September 1, 1969

Fin	St	No.	Driver	Team / Car	Laps	Money	Status
1	4	98	LeeRoy Yarbrough	Junior Johnson '69 Ford	230	$21,800	Running
2	5	17	David Pearson	Holman-Moody '69 Ford	230	12,250	Running
3	2	6	Buddy Baker	Cotton Owens '69 Dodge	230	6,700	Running
4	3	27	Donnie Allison	Banjo Matthews '69 Ford	227	3,325	Running
5	9	22	Bobby Allison	Mario Rossi '69 Dodge	225	2,750	Running
6	7	88	Charlie Glotzbach	Nichels Eng '69 Dodge	224	2,000	Running
7	11	32	Dick Brooks	Brooks '69 Plymouth	223	1,825	Running
8	14	31	Buddy Young	Fred Bear '67 Chevrolet	222	1,800	Running
9	6	43	Richard Petty	Petty Ent '69 Ford	220	1,600	Running
10	8	14	Richard Brickhouse	Bill Ellis '69 Dodge	220	2,000	Running
11	18	49	G C Spencer	Spencer '68 Plymouth	219	1,450	Running
12	15	61	Hoss Ellington	Ellington '69 Ford	218	1,350	Running
13	32	06	Neil Castles	Castles '69 Dodge	215	1,450	Running
14	35	46	Roy Mayne	Tom Hunter '69 Chevrolet	211	1,250	Running
15	22	96	Frank Warren	Warren '69 Ford	210	1,250	Running
16	31	25	Jabe Thomas	Don Robertson '68 Plymouth	209	1,475	Running
17	30	34	Wendell Scott	Scott '67 Ford	209	1,150	Running
18	24	47	Cecil Gordon	Bill Seifert '68 Ford	208	1,125	Running
19	25	15	Dr Ed Hessert	Hessert '69 Plymouth	208	1,175	Running
20	23	76	Ben Arnold	Red Culpepper '68 Ford	207	1,075	Running
21	10	4	John Sears	L G DeWitt '69 Ford	204	1,100	Engine
22	38	0	J C Spradley	'67 Chevrolet	203	1,075	Running
23	33	51	Dub Simpson	Bill Strong '69 Chevrolet	202	1,050	Running
24	28	10	Bill Champion	Champion '68 Ford	194	975	Running
25	34	70	J D McDuffie	McDuffie '67 Buick	193	1,000	Running
26	16	64	Elmo Langley	Langley '68 Ford	190	925	Crash
27	40	83	Earl Brooks	Wayne Smith '69 Chevrolet	183	900	Crash
28	12	48	James Hylton	Hylton Eng '69 Dodge	165	975	Engine
29	1	21	Cale Yarborough	Wood Brothers '69 Mercury	143	2,475	Crash
30	29	36	H B Bailey	Bailey '69 Pontiac	130	825	Engine
31	27	07	Coo Coo Marlin	Cunningham-Kelley -69 Chev	78	825	Engine
32	39	04	Ken Meisenhelder	Meisenhelder '67 Olds	47	825	Flagged
33	17	30	Dave Marcis	Milt Lunda '69 Dodge	43	975	Steering
34	13	7	Bobby Johns	Shorty Johns '67 Chevrolet	28	725	Crash
35	26	8	Ed Negre	G C Spencer '67 Plymouth	26	750	Crash
36	21	08	E J Trivette	E C Reid '69 Chevrolet	26	675	Crash
37	20	9	Roy Tyner	Tyner '69 Pontiac	26	650	Wtr Pump
38	19	45	Bill Seifert	Seifert '68 Ford	8	650	Engine
39	36	19	Henley Gray	Harry Melton '68 Ford	1	665	Engine
40	37	57	Bobby Mausgrover	Ervin Pruitt '67 Dodge	1	650	Engine

Time of Race: 2 hours, 59 minutes, 40 secons
Average Speed: 105.612 mph
Pole Winner: Cale Yarborough - 151.985 mph
Lap Leaders: Cale Yarborough 1-29, James Hylton 30-31, Dave Marcis 32-41, Yarborough 42-67, LeeRoy Yarbrough 68-93, Bobby Allison 94-97, Yarborough 98-119, Buddy Baker 120, Yarborough 121-138, Yarborough 139-142, Donnie Allison 143, Yarborough 144-159, David Pearson 160, Yarbrough 161-168, Pearson 169-194, Yarbrough 195-201, Pearson 202, Baker 203-213, Yarbrough 214-219, Pearson 220-229, Yarbrough 230.
Cautions: 7 for 85 laps   Margin of Victory: 1 car length   Attendance: 68,000
*Race shortened to 230 laps due to rain and darkness

Race No. 41

Yarbrough Wins Southern 500 With Last Lap Pass

DARLINGTON, SC (Sept. 1) -- LeeRoy Yarbrough muscled his way past David Pearson in the final lap and won the rain-abbreviated Southern 500 at Darlington Raceway. It was Yarbrough's sixth superspeedway win of the season and it pushed his season's earnings to $164,955.

The 20th running of the South's oldest big track event was shortened to 316 miles due to rain delays and impending darkness.

The final showdown was set up by pit stops in the 200th lap -- with what turned out to be 30 laps to go. Pearson's Holman-Moody crew put on a soft compound tire -- which gave him great speed for a short time, but weakening durability in a lengthy green flag run. Yarbrough pitted and had a harder tire put on his Ford.

Pearson raced past Yarbrough on lap 220 and stretched his advantage to about eight car lengths. But as the laps were winding down, Pearson started gliding in the turns; Yarbrough was closing the gap.

"We knew it was going to be a sprint race after it quit raining," said LeeRoy. "I had my work cut out. I was hoping to force David into making a little mistake. He went high in the third turn of the last lap and I took what he gave me. When I got in the lead, I shut the door on him. I'm as tickled about winning this race as anything I've done in my life."

Pearson accepted the runner-up finish, but couldn't conceal his disappointment. "The longer I ran on those soft tires the looser I got in the turns," said Pearson. "I was pushing it so hard that I finally hit the fence in the third turn. That's when he passed me."

Buddy Baker finished third and Donnie Allison was fourth despite being involved in three wrecks. Bobby Allison came in fifth.

Sophomore driver Richard Brickhouse lost eight laps in the pits with carburetor problems, but he roared back to finish 10th. Car owner Bill Ellis praised his new driver. "He'll mash the gas, no doubt about that," said Ellis. "Once we get a car to hold up under him, he's going to be tough."

Bobby and Donnie Allison crash in Southern 500

Donnie Allison was involved in a six car scramble in the 143rd lap. Also involved were Bobby Allison, Baker, Cale Yarborough and Charlie Glotzbach. "You know what a rain-shortened race is good for?" asked Donnie. "A bunch of banged up race cars. I've never seen anything like it. The wreck was unfortunate, but we were just racing."

Yarbrough averaged 105.612 mph for his 12th career Grand National win. Pearson upped his point lead to 214 points over Richard Petty, who finished ninth.

Race No. 42

Isaac Hot at Hickory; Holds Off Castles for 100-mile Win

HICKORY, NC (Sept. 5) -- Bobby Isaac got around Neil Castles in the 190th lap and led the rest of the way to win the Buddy Shuman Memorial at Hickory

Grand National Race No. 42
250 Laps at Hickory Speedway
Hickory, NC
"Buddy Shuman Memorial"
100 Miles on .4-mile Paved Track
September 5, 1969

Fin	St	No.	Driver	Team / Car	Laps	Money	Status
1	1	71	Bobby Isaac	K&K Insurance '69 Dodge	250	$1,700	Running
2	9	06	Neil Castles	Castles '69 Dodge	249	1,200	Running
3	2	43	Richard Petty	Petty Ent '69 Ford	247	900	Running
4	6	4	John Sears	L G DeWitt '69 Ford	246	700	Running
5	7	31	Buddy Young	Fred Bear '67 Chevrolet	245	600	Running
6	21	32	Dick Brooks	Brooks '69 Plymouth	244	500	Running
7	8	64	Elmo Langley	Langley '68 Ford	241	400	Running
8	16	8	E J Trivette	G C Spencer '67 Plymouth	237	350	Running
9	3	48	James Hylton	Hylton Eng '69 Dodge	236	300	Ignition
10	15	45	Bill Seifert	Seifert '69 Ford	236	280	Running
11	12	25	Jabe Thomas	Don Robertson '68 Plymouth	235	275	Running
12	10	70	J D McDuffie	McDuffie '67 Buick	234	270	Running
13	19	10	Bill Champion	Champion '68 Ford	230	265	Running
14	17	47	Cecil Gordon	Bill Seifert '68 Ford	229	260	Running
15	11	76	Ben Arnold	Red Culpepper '68 Ford	224	255	Running
16	13	34	Wendell Scott	Scott '67 Ford	204	250	Engine
17	18	57	Bobby Mausgrover	Ervin Pruitt '67 Dodge	177	245	Quit
18	5	49	G C Spencer	Spencer '67 Plymouth	122	240	Rear End
19	20	26	Earl Brooks	Brooks '67 Ford	41	235	Suspen
20	22	04	Ken Meisenhelder	Meisenhelder '67 Olds	18	230	Engine
21	4	17	David Pearson	Holman-Moody '69 Ford	1	425	Engine
22	14	19	Henley Gray	Harry Melton '68 Ford	1	220	Engine

Time of Race: 1 hour, 14 minutes, 31 seconds
Average Speed: 80.519 mph
Pole Winner: Bobby Isaac - 86.212 mph
Lap Leaders: Richard Petty 1-66, Bobby Isaac 67-160, Neil Castles 161-189, Isaac 190-250.
Cautions: 3 for 11 laps   Margin of Victory: 1-lap plus   Attendance: 6,000

Speedway. It was the 12th win of the year for Isaac, who began his racing career at this .4-mile oval 13 years earlier.

Castles, of Charlotte, started ninth but ran with the leaders all night. The 35 year-old Dodge driver led for 29 laps before being passed by Isaac.

"I would have loved to win this race named in honor of Buddy Shuman, who was like my foster father," said Castles. "But Isaac was just too strong."

Castles finished second, a lap off the pace. Richard Petty, who led the first 66 laps, wound up third. John Sears came in fourth and Buddy Young was fifth.

David Pearson started fourth but blew the engine in his Ford after just one lap. He finished 21st in the field of 22 and lost 18 points to Petty in the battle for the Grand National championship.

Isaac led for 155 of the 250 laps, but took a back seat in the early stages. "After the first few laps, Petty looked and sounded like he was pulling a lower gear," said Isaac. "I knew as long as the track was dry, he could handle me. But when the track got slick, he was spinning off the corners. Castles was faster than Petty at the end of the race."

Isaac averaged 80.519 mph as a crowd of 6,000 braved threatening weather.

Race No. 43

Allison Last To First At Richmond

RICHMOND, VA (Sept. 7) -- Eleventh-hour entrant Bobby Allison came from the rear of the field and posted a three lap victory in the Capital City 250 at Richmond Fairgrounds Raceway. It was the fourth win of the season for the Hueytown, AL Dodge driver.

Allison had blown an engine in a late practice session on Saturday. Car owner and crew chief Mario Rossi ordered a new engine from his Spartanburg, SC garage, but it didn't arrive until 10:00 am Sunday morning.

Allison's red and gold Dodge was rolled into the 25th starting spot moments before the pace lap began.

"If hard work has anything to do with it," said Rossi, "then we deserved this one. Some of the crew and myself haven't had three hours sleep in the last three days."

Bobby Allison and Mario Rossi came from last-to-first in Capital City 250

Allison took the lead from Richard Petty in the 171st lap and led the rest of the way in the 462-lap event on the .542-mile oval. Sonny Hutchins gained his second runner-up finish of the season. Bobby Isaac finished third, David Pearson fourth and John Sears fifth.

Mechanical problems foiled Pearson and Isaac, and rear end failure put Petty out. Allison breezed to a four lap lead at the mid-way point, but had to run like gangbusters to hold off a late gallop by LeeRoy Yarbrough.

Yarbrough, whose car was driven by Elmo Langley for about 100 laps, made up four laps on Allison only to lose the engine in his Ford 44 laps from the finish.

Allison and Yarbrough tangled twice on pit road, but no serious damage was inflicted to either car. Herb Nab, crew chief for Yarbrough, threatened to file a protest against Allison. After Yarbrough fell out, Nab reconsidered and did not file a protest.

Allison averaged 76.388 mph as the lead changed hands only three times. A crowd of 12,000 watched the race.

Grand National Race No. 43
462 Laps at Richmond Fairgrounds Raceway
Richmond, VA
"Capital City 250"
250 Miles on .542-mile Paved Track
September 7, 1969

Fin	St	No.	Driver	Team / Car	Laps	Money	Status
1	25	22	Bobby Allison	Mario Rossi '69 Dodge	462	$5,000	Running
2	8	90	Sonny Hutchins	Junie Donlavey '67 Ford	459	2,575	Running
3	3	71	Bobby Isaac	K&K Insurance '69 Dodge	456	1,775	Running
4	2	17	David Pearson	Holman-Moody '69 Ford	455	1,250	Running
5	6	4	John Sears	L G DeWitt '69 Ford	454	925	Running
6	5	48	James Hylton	Hylton Eng '69 Dodge	448	650	Running
7	13	47	Cecil Gordon	Bill Seifert '68 Ford	431	600	Running
8	15	34	Wendell Scott	Scott '67 Ford	430	575	Running
9	11	8	Ed Negre	G C Spencer '67 Plymouth	428	560	Running
10	4	98	LeeRoy Yarbrough*	Junior Johnson '69 Ford	419	570	Engine
11	14	76	Ben Arnold	Red Culpepper '68 Ford	418	535	Running
12	12	31	Buddy Young	Fred Bear '67 Chevrolet	418	525	Running
13	23	9	Roy Tyner	Tyner '69 Pontiac	411	490	Running
14	21	25	Jabe Thomas	Don Robertson '68 Plymouth	409	480	Running
15	17	08	E J Trivette	E C Reid '69 Chevrolet	397	495	Running
16	7	06	Neil Castles	Castles '69 Dodge	326	485	Lug Bolt
17	19	26	Earl Brooks	Brooks '67 Ford	322	475	Crash
18	18	10	Bill Champion	Champion '68 Ford	283	465	Crash
19	1	43	Richard Petty	Petty Ent '69 Ford	171	580	Rear End
20	22	57	Bobby Mausgrover	Ervin Pruitt '67 Dodge	159	420	Trans
21	9	64	Elmo Langley	Langley '68 Ford	90	435	Brakes
22	16	45	Bill Seifert	Seifert '69 Ford	58	425	Engine
23	10	54	Bill Dennis	Dennis '69 Chevrolet	54	415	Trans
24	20	32	Dick Brooks	Brooks '69 Plymouth	44	405	Axle
25	24	70	J D McDuffie	McDuffie '67 Buick	22	370	Engine

Time of Race: 3 hours, 16 minutes, 32 seconds
Average Speed: 76.388 mph
Pole Winner: Richard Petty - 91.257 mph
Lap Leaders: Richard Petty 1-137, Bobby Allison 138-144, Petty 145-171, Allison 172-462.
Cautions: 6 for 39 laps   Margin of Victory: 3-laps plus   Attendance: 12,000
*Relieved by Elmo Langley

Race No. 44

Brickhouse Boycotts Boycott; Wins Talladega 500 in Winged Dodge Daytona

TALLADEGA, AL (Sept. 14) -- Richard Brickhouse of Rocky Point, NC withdrew from the Professional Drivers Association, signed up with Ray Nichels and drove a new Dodge Daytona to an electrifying triumph in the inaugural Talladega 500 at the Alabama

International Motor Speedway. It was the first Grand National win for the 29 year-old Brickhouse.

Brickhouse was one of only eight pre-registered Grand National drivers to enter the race. The newly formed PDA, headed by Richard Petty, walked out of the new facility late Saturday due to what they said were unsafe track conditions. "This track is simply not ready to run on," declared PDA President Petty. "Most

Bobby Isaac leads the field down for the start of the first Talladega 500

of us felt the tires we have are not safe to race on at speeds of around 200 mph. It was just that simple."

Brickhouse, a sophomore driver who signed up with the PDA two weeks earlier, notified Petty and the rest of the PDA of his resignation via Public Address at the speedway. "I joined the PDA at Darlington," said Brickhouse, "but I didn't expect anything like this. I want to race, but also I don't want to make anybody mad. It was a mighty hard decision to make."

Brickhouse was told that the #99 Dodge Daytona was available if he wanted it. Regular driver Charlie Glotzbach had joined the boycott. "I felt a driver in my position, with the chance to drive a factory car, needed to race," confessed Brickhouse. "I think anybody in my

Grand National Race No. 44
188 Laps at Alabama Int'l Motor Speedway
Talladega, AL
"Talladega 500"
500 Miles on 2.66-mile Paved Track
September 14, 1969

Fin	St	No.	Driver	Team / Car	Laps	Money	Status
1	9	99	Richard Brickhouse	Nichels Eng '69 Dodge Day	188	$24,550	Running
2	2	3	Jim Vandiver	Ray Fox '69 Dodge	188	12,400	Running
3	12	14	Ramo Stott	Bill Ellis '69 Dodge	188	7,050	Running
4	1	71	Bobby Isaac	K&K Ins '69 Dodge Daytona	187	4,725	Running
5	5	32	Dick Brooks	Brooks '69 Plymouth	180	3,300	Running
6	11	26	Earl Brooks	Brooks '67 Ford	164	2,500	Running
7	23	7	Jimmy Vaughn	Vaughn '68 Camaro	159	2,000	Running
8	29	52	Billy Hagan	Hagan '68 Cougar	155	1,750	Running
9	13	53	Tiny Lund	Bill France '69 Ford	152	1,675	Clutch
10	6	07	Coo Coo Marlin	Cunningham-Kelley '69 Chev	150	1,600	Engine
11	18	81	Bill Ward	'68 Camaro	149	1,550	Running
12	24	17	Ernie Shaw	Shaw '68 Mustang	149	1,500	Running
13	35	1	Amos Johnson	'68 Camaro	147	1,450	Running
14	20	54	Bobby Fleming	Tommy Fleming '68 Camaro	146	1,400	Running
15	22	56	Ben Arnold	Jack Mercer '68 Camaro	135	1,375	Running
16	4	37	Dr Don Tarr	Ray Fox '67 Dodge	129	1,375	Engine
17	16	21	Frank Sessoms	Sessoms '68 Camaro	128	1,325	Running
18	28	87	Buck Baker	Baker '69 Firebird	108	1,300	Engine
19	21	90	Dick LAwrence	'68 Camaro	108	1,275	Running
20	14	0	Dr Wilbur Pickett	Flo Starr '68 Camaro	92	1,250	Engine
21	31	98	Larry Bock	'69 Dart	85	1,225	Engine
22	17	19	Stan Starr, Jr.	Starr & Son '68 Camaro	82	1,200	Steering
23	26	13	Richard Childress	Childress '68 Camaro	80	1,175	Axle
24	15	04	C B Gwyn	Gwyn '68 Cougar	73	1,150	Engine
25	3	4	Jim Hurtubise	L G DeWitt '69 Ford	63	1,125	Engine
26	32	31	Earle Canavan	Canavan '69 AMC Javelin	62	1,100	Engine
27	8	62	Homer Newland	Kaye Eng '69 Dodge	53	1,075	Engine
28	27	88	T C Hunt	Hunt '68 Camaro	53	1,050	Rear End
29	7	9	Roy Tyner	Tyner '69 Pontiac	33	1,025	Engine
30	34	46	J W King	'69 Mustang	26	1,000	Trans
31	19	41	Bobby Brewer	'68 Camaro	9	975	Engine
32	25	72	Al Straub	Straub '69 Mustang	9	950	Frame
33	10	06	Les Snow	Neil Castles '69 Dodge	2	925	Frame
34	36	47	Bob Burcham	'68 Camaro	2	900	Engine
35	33	74	Doug Easton	Al Straub '68 Mustang	0	875	D Shaft
36	30	16	Don Schisler	Bud Moore '69 Cougar	0	850	Engine

Time of Race: 3 hours, 15 minutes, 7 seconds
Average Speed: 153.778 mph
Pole Winner: Bobby Isaac - 196.386 mph
Fastest Qualifier: Charlie Glotzbach 199.466 mph
Lap Leaders: Bobby Isaac 1, Dr Don Tarr 2-3,
    Jim Vandiver 4, Tarr 5, Isaac 6-8, Tiny Lund 9-10,
    Richard Brickhouse 11-12, Isaac 13, Vandiver 14-17,
    Isaac 18-19, Ramo Stott 20, Dick Brooks 21-22,
    Vandiver 23-27, Lund 28-48, Brickhouse 49-50,
    Vandiver 51-52, Brickhouse 53-55, Vandiver 56-68,
    Brickhouse 59, Vandiver 60-61, Tarr 62-64,
    Vandiver 65-70, Isaac 71-75, Vandiver 76-80,
    Brickhouse 81-84, Vandiver 85-87, Brickhouse 88-97,
    Lund 98-101, Vandiver 102-118, Lund 119,
    Vandiver 120-129, Isaac 130, Vandiver 131-157,
    Stott 158-160, Vandiver 161-177,
    Brickhouse 178-188.
Cautions: 7 for 38 laps
Margin of Victory: 7 seconds
Attendance: 62,000

Richard Brickhouse #99 gets the checkered flag one lap and 3 car lengths ahead of Bobby Isaac

position would have done the same thing."

Brickhouse started ninth in the field of 36, which was filled by 23 Grand Touring cars which had competed in a 400-miler the day before. NASCAR and track President Bill France had said all along, "We will have a 500-mile race and we will pay the posted prize money."

Richard Brickhouse

With some 37 drivers walking out, France decided to give the ticket holders a free race. "The ticket stubs for this Talladega 500 can be turned in for any future race at Daytona or Talladega," said France.

A crowd of 62,000 watched the 500-miler. Primary conteners were Bobby Isaac, the only 'name' driver who was shunned by the PDA, Tiny Lund, driving a Bill France owned Ford, Jim Vandiver, a GT driver who accepted the driving seat in the Ray Fox Dodge, and Brickhouse were the primary contenders.

Brickhouse motored past Vandiver with 11 laps remaining and padded his advantage to 7.0-seconds when the checkered flag fell on racing history. Vandiver gained runner-up honors in only his second Grand National start. Ramo Stott, who was summoned to fill the vacancy in the Bill Ellis Dodge when Brickhouse shifted to the Nichels Engineering Dodge, finished third. Isaac, who started on the pole with a lap of 196.386 mph, finished fourth after suffering tire problems. Rookie Dick Brooks was fifth.

The caution flag came out every 25 laps so crews could change tires. In the five days of practice leading up to the event, tires had blistered and chunked as early

Bill France greets Talladega 500 winner Richard Brickhouse

as four laps. "I kept a lid on my speed most of the race," said Brickhouse. "But when I was behind in the late going, I pumped my speed up to about 198 mph to catch Vandiver. My pit crew was really worried about tires. Mack Howard (crew chief) came all the way out on the grass to tell me to slow down. I ran hard enough to win, then I backed off."

Vandiver responded brilliantly to his new assignment. The Charlotte driver led 13 times for 102 laps, but lost in the shuffle in the end. "That new Daytona is worth 5 mph, but I didn't have one," said Vandiver. "I had planned on running harder at the end, but I couldn't run that fast."

Isaac had two unscheduled pit stops that knocked him a lap off the pace. "I was just coolin' it," said Isaac. "But I still had the tires blister. I knew I could win the race, but when I fell a lap behind ..."

Dr. Don Tarr, driving a two-year old Ray Fox Dodge, surprised all the railbirds by charging to the front for six laps. The Miami physician turned in some lap speeds of about 195 mph, which startled the crusty Fox. "He's driving that car 20 mph faster than it will go," said Fox.

Tiny Lund, driving a car NASCAR President France bought to do some testing, led for 28 laps before clutch failure knocked him out after 152 laps. The engine in France's car was set back six inches -- but there was no rule book for this particular event.

Brickhouse averaged 153.778 mph for his first win, which came in his 26th big league start.

Race No. 45

Fans Cheer Isaac Victory at Columbia

COLUMBIA, SC (Sept. 18) -- A crowd of 6,500 cheered Bobby Isaac's victory in the Sandlapper 200 at Columbia Speedway. It was the 13th win of the season

David Pearson went through the fence at Columbia

for the veteran Dodge pilot -- and his popularity was apparent in the pre-race introduction.

The 37 year-old Isaac, the only 'name' driver to compete in the Talladega 500 four days earlier, took the lead in the 135th lap and led the rest of the way. He finished a half lap in front of runner-up Richard Petty. Third place went to James Hylton with John Sears fourth and Eldon Yarbrough fifth.

Isaac led the first three laps on the half-mile dirt track. Petty bolted past and led for 131 laps. Isaac wrestled the lead from Petty with 66 laps left and was never headed.

David Pearson blew a tire on lap 82 and sailed over the banking. His Ford crashed through a board fence surrounding the speedway property. "I knew my tire was going bald," said Pearson. "I was hoping for a caution so I could get it changed under yellow. I didn't figure I'd be the one to bring out the caution flag."

There were rumors of threats to drivers who did not honor the Talladega boycott, but the race was staged without any incidents. During the pre-race introductions, Isaac -- who did not participate in the boycott -- got the biggest ovation of the night.

Grand National Race No. 45
200 Laps at Columbia Speedway
Columbia, SC
"Sandlapper 200"
100 Miles on Half-mile Dirt Track
September 18, 1969

Fin	St	No.	Driver	Team / Car	Laps	Money	Status
1	2	71	Bobby Isaac	K&K Insurance '69 Dodge	200	$1,000	Running
2	1	43	Richard Petty	Petty Ent '69 Ford	200	600	Running
3	9	48	James Hylton	Hylton Eng '69 Dodge	196	400	Running
4	3	4	John Sears	L G DeWitt '69 Ford	195	350	Running
5	23	56	Eldon Yarbrough	Lyle Stelter '67 Ford	194	325	Running
6	13	64	Elmo Langley	Langley '68 Ford	190	300	Running
7	11	71	J D McDuffie	McDuffie '67 Buick	189	275	Running
8	17	34	Wendell Scott	Scott '67 Ford	187	270	Running
9	4	47	Cecil Gordon	Bill Seifert '68 Ford	187	265	Running
10	7	45	Bill Seifert	Seifert '68 Ford	186	260	Running
11	10	10	Bill Champion	Champion '68 Ford	181	255	Running
12	16	76	Ben Arnold	Red Culpepper '68 Ford	178	250	Running
13	12	25	Jabe Thomas	Don Robertson '67 Plymouth	176	245	Running
14	15	04	Ken Meisenhelder	Meisenhelder '67 Olds	175	240	Running
15	14	09	E J Trivette	E C Reid '67 Chevrolet	169	235	Running
16	18	19	Henley Gray	Harry Melton '68 Ford	169	230	Running
17	21	57	Johnny Halford	Ervin Pruitt '67 Dodge	166	225	Running
18	5	0	Frank Warren	Dr Don Tarr '67 Chevrolet	108	220	Suspen
19	6	17	David Pearson	Holman-Moody '69 Ford	82	415	Crash
20	20	06	Neil Castles	Castles '67 Plymouth	45	210	Axle
21	22	16	Paul Dean Holt	Dennis Holt '68 Mercury	34	205	Engine
22	8	8	Ed Negre	G C Spencer '67 Plymouth	13	200	Trans
23	19	08	Wayne Gillette	E C Reid '69 Chevrolet	3	---	Quit

Time of Race: 1 hour, 25 minutes, 26 seconds
Average Speed: 70.230 mph
Pole Winner: Richard Petty - 73.108 mph
Lap Leaders: Bobby Isaac 1-3, Richard Petty 4-134, Isaac 135-200.
Cautions: 2 for 15 laps   Margin of Victory: 1/2 lap   Attendance : 6,500

Grand National Race No. 46
500 Laps at Martinsville Speedway
Martinsville, VA
"Old Dominion 500"
250 Miles on Half-mile Paved Track
September 28, 1969

Fin	St	No.	Driver	Team / Car	Laps	Money	Status
1	6	43	Richard Petty	Petty Ent '69 Ford	500	$10,085	Running
2	1	17	David Pearson	Holman-Moody '69 Ford	500	5,190	Running
3	7	6	Buddy Baker	Cotton Owens '69 Dodge	496	2,675	Running
4	11	48	James Hylton	Hylton Eng '69 Dodge	496	2,525	Running
5	18	67	Buddy Arrington	Arrington '69 Dodge	489	1,075	Running
6	4	71	Bobby Isaac	K&K Insurance '69 Dodge	486	1,040	Running
7	38	20	Clyde Lynn	Lynn '67 Ford	478	875	Running
8	14	25	Jabe Thomas	Don Robertson '68 Plymouth	477	775	Running
9	13	64	Elmo Langley	Langley '68 Ford	476	725	Running
10	22	13	Jim Vandiver	'67 Chevrolet	474	700	Running
11	35	10	Bill Champion	Champion '68 Ford	466	665	Running
12	27	45	Bill Seifert	Seifert '69 Ford	459	655	Running
13	29	47	Cecil Gordon	Bill Seifert '68 Ford	450	645	Running
14	40	57	Johnny Halford	Ervin Pruitt '67 Dodge	449	635	Running
15	12	31	Buddy Young	Fred Bear '67 Chevrolet	446	625	Running
16	24	4	John Sears	L G DeWitt '69 Ford	444	615	Running
17	2	21	Cale Yarborough	Wood Brothers '69 Mercury	400	800	Engine
18	31	51	Dub Simpson	Bill Strong '69 Chevrolet	392	595	Running
19	36	34	Wendell Scott	Scott '67 Ford	387	585	Engine
20	5	98	LeeRoy Yarbrough	Junior Johnson '69 Ford	348	620	Engine
21	33	08	E J Trivette	E C Reid '69 Chevrolet	320	565	Axle
22	26	81	Dave Alonzo	'67 Ford	312	555	Engine
23	20	06	Neil Castles	Castles '69 Dodge	240	545	Engine
24	28	76	Ben Arnold	Red Culpepper '68 Ford	222	535	Brakes
25	3	22	Bobby Allison	Mario Rossi '69 Dodge	173	575	Wheel
26	17	54	Bill Dennis	Dennis '69 Chevrolet	153	515	Engine
27	32	15	Dr Ed Hessert	Hessert '69 Plymouth	136	505	Crash
28	23	61	Hoss Ellington	Ellington '69 Ford	120	505	Crash
29	19	39	Friday Hassler	Hassler '67 Chevrolet	115	485	Engine
30	39	19	Henley Gray	Harry Melton '68 Ford	112	475	Oil Press
31	8	27	Donnie Allison	Banjo Matthews '69 Ford	66	470	Engine
32	37	26	Earl Brooks	Brooks '67 Ford	59	465	Brakes
33	30	46	Roy Mayne	Tom Hunter '69 Chevrolet	49	460	Oil Leak
34	10	30	Dave Marcis	Milt Lunda '69 Dodge	34	435	Spring
35	21	32	Dick Brooks	Brooks '69 Plymouth	31	425	Hub
36	25	0	J D McDuffie	Dr Don Tarr '67 Chevrolet	25	445	Engine
37	16	49	G C Spencer	Spencer '67 Plymouth	16	440	Crash
38	34	9	Roy Tyner	Tyner '69 Pontiac	11	435	Engine
39	15	8	Ed Negre	G C Spencer '67 Plymouth	4	430	Oil Press
40	9	14	Richard Brickhouse	Bill Ellis '69 Dodge	2	425	Crash

Time of Race: 3 hours, 57 minutes, 37 seconds
Average Speed: 63.127 mph
Pole Winner: David Pearson - 83.197 mph
Lap Leaders: Cale Yarborough 1-125, David Pearson 126-129, LeeRoy Yarbrough 130,
    Pearson 131-151, Buddy Baker 152-250, Yarbrough 251-266, Bobby Isaac 267-304,
    Yarbrough 305-309, Baker 310-453, Pearson 454-464, Richard Petty 465-500.
Cautions: 11 for 61 laps   Margin of Victory: 6 seconds   Attendance: 20,000

Race No. 46

Petty Catches Beer Can and Top Prize at Martinsville

MARTINSVILLE, VA (Sept. 28) -- Richard Petty caught a beer can in the windshield and $10,085 in prize money by winning the Old Dominion 500 at Martinsville Speedway. It was the 10th win of the year for Petty.

Petty was trailing David Pearson late in the running. As he came off the fourth turn on lap 464, a fan tossed a beer can which hit Petty's Ford directly in the front windshield. The caution flag came out for debris on the track, allowing Petty to make up almost a lap deficit.

As Pearson pitted, Petty stayed on the track. He led the final 46 laps as Pearson was caught in traffic. Pearson wound up second, Buddy Baker was third and James Hylton fourth. Fifth place went to Buddy Arrington.

"Today was the worst I've ever seen for beer cans on the track," said Petty, who led the Talladega boycott. "I don't know if the Talladega deal had anything to do with that or not."

Pearson was helpless in traffic during the final run. "I could have run Richard down if I had had some brakes," he said.

Baker led twice for a total of 253 laps, but fell a lap off the pace when he lost a cylinder. "My car sure got to smoking there at the end," said Baker, not noted for his short track savvy. "There wasn't anybody who could handle me when I was running strong."

Bobby Isaac led for 38 laps. But he fell 18 laps off the pace when he had to pit for a brake repair. He still wound up sixth in the final order.

Isaac and Richard Brickhouse tangled fenders in the first lap and both spun. Brickhouse was out a lap later, but Isaac continued. "Something locked up in the rear end," said Brickhouse. "I didn't have any control over the car."

Petty's 101st career victory came at an average speed of 63.127 mph. The caution flag was out 11 times for 61 laps.

Race No. 47

Bottle Bottles Up Petty, Pearson Wins Wilkes 400

N.WILKESBORO, NC (Oct. 5) -- David Pearson took advantage of a fan's vandalism, reversed the script on Richard Petty and roared through a four lap traffic jam to win the Wilkes 400. The 250-mile event at North Wilkesboro Speedway was Pearson's 11th win of the year.

Pearson took the lead four laps from the finish after a caution flag was displayed when a spectator threw a brown beer bottle onto the track. The incident erased Petty's commanding lead.

Petty had led for 270 of the 400 laps, but watched as the caution wiped out his insurmountable lead.

Pearson knifed his way through the lapped cars of Dave Marcis and Buddy Baker, and passed leader Petty

to win the $5,750 first prize. On the restart with five laps to go, Marcis and Baker were running side-by-side. "I got in behind Baker," said Petty, "and David took what was left. I made the wrong choice because Marcis passed Baker -- and Pearson passed me."

Pearson, who never led until the final few laps, said, "I saw Marcis on the inside so I followed him. The inside is the quickest way around and Marcis had been getting off the turns quicker than Baker."

Pearson edged Petty by a single car length. Petty settled for second as Bobby Isaac came in third. LeeRoy Yarbrough finished fourth with Baker fifth. Marcis took sixth.

Richard Brickhouse and James Hylton got into a furious bumping match early in the race. Bill Ellis, who owns Brickhouse's Dodge, claimed Hylton's act was premeditated. "He's been looking for a factory ride for four years," said Ellis. "He came here with an old beat up car with one thing in mind -- to wreck or spin Richard out. He is mad that Richard is in line to get a factory ride since he won at Talladega."

Grand National Race No. 47
400 Laps at N.Wilkesboro Speedway
N.Wilkesboro, NC
"Wilkes 400"
250 Miles on .625-mile Paved Track
October 5, 1969

Fin	St	No.	Driver	Team / Car	Laps	Money	Status
1	2	17	David Pearson	Holman-Moody '69 Ford	400	$5,750	Running
2	3	43	Richard Petty	Petty Ent '69 Ford	400	3,000	Running
3	1	71	Bobby Isaac	K&K Insurance '69 Dodge	399	2,075	Running
4	6	98	LeeRoy Yarbrough	Junior Johnson '69 Ford	397	1,125	Running
5	4	6	Buddy Baker	Cotton Owens '69 Dodge	396	875	Running
6	7	30	Dave Marcis	Milt Lunda '69 Dodge	394	625	Running
7	5	14	Richard Brickhouse	Bill Ellis '69 Dodge	394	600	Running
8	8	32	Dick Brooks	Brooks '69 Plymouth	393	575	Running
9	10	49	G C Spencer	Spencer '67 Plymouth	392	580	Running
10	11	48	James Hylton	Hylton Eng '68 Dodge	391	545	Running
11	21	06	Neil Castles	Castles '69 Dodge	390	660	Running
12	17	8	J D McDuffie	G C Spencer '67 Plymouth	380	525	Running
13	14	31	Buddy Young	Fred Bear '67 Chevrolet	377	515	Running
14	23	9	Roy Tyner	Tyner '69 Pontiac	375	530	Running
15	26	47	Cecil Gordon	Bill Seifert '68 Ford	375	495	Running
16	12	64	Elmo Langley	Langley '68 Ford	372	485	Running
17	20	76	Ben Arnold	Red Culpepper '68 Ford	365	475	Running
18	24	45	Bill Seifert	Seifert '69 Ford	365	465	Running
19	28	34	Wendell Scott	Scott '67 Ford	355	455	Running
20	25	51	Dub Simpson	Bill Strong '69 Chevrolet	304	445	Engine
21	13	25	Jabe Thomas	Don Robertson '68 Plymouth	298	435	Running
22	29	81	E J Trivette	G C Spencer '67 Plymouth	224	425	Engine
23	18	10	Bill Champion	Champion '68 Ford	221	415	Clutch
24	19	57	Johnny Halford	Ervin Pruitt '69 Dodge	190	405	Axle
25	15	20	Clyde Lynn	Lynn '67 Ford	170	395	Oil Leak
26	30	26	Earl Brooks	Brooks '67 Ford	161	390	No Tires
27	16	67	Buddy Arrington	Arrington '69 Dodge	149	380	Throttle
28	27	19	Henley Gray	Harry Melton '68 Ford	71	370	Quit
29	9	4	John Sears	L G DeWitt '69 Ford	24	435	Brakes
30	22	33	Wayne Smith	Smith '68 Chevrolet	2	425	Engine

Time of Race: 2 hours, 40 minutes, 32 seconds
Average Speed: 93.429 mph
Pole Winner: Bobby Isaac - 106.032 mph
Lap Leaders: Bobby Isaac 1-121, Richard Petty 122-125, Buddy Baker 126-129, Petty 130-389, David Pearson 390, Petty 391-396, Pearson 397-400.
Cautions: 3 for 23 laps   Margin of Victory: 1 car length   Attendance: 11,000

Hylton said he was not trying to put Brickhouse out of the race. "If I was trying to wreck him," replied Hylton, "then I would *wreck* him. We both ran up on a slower car and we hit, that's all."

Brickhouse finished seventh; Hylton 10th.

Pearson averaged 93.429 mph before a crowd of 11,000. Track promoter Enoch Staley said the spectator who threw the bottle was arrested. He would be charged with "public drunkeness and other charges," Staley said.

Race No. 48

Donnie Allison Ends Famine; Wins Charlotte National 500

CHARLOTTE, NC (Oct. 12) -- Donnie Allison drove his Banjo Matthews Ford around Buddy Baker with five laps to go and sprinted to victory in the National 500 at Charlotte Motor Speedway. The Hueytown, AL

Eventual winner Donnie Allison leads Buddy Baker at Charlotte

driver ended a 16 month famine with his $20,280 win.

"Before this race, I was the only factory backed Ford driver without a big win," said Allison, who last won at Rockingham on June 16, 1968. "Ford Motor Co. never put an ounce of pressure on me. But I took a lot of ribbing because I hadn't won. I'm just glad to get one under the belt this year."

Bobby Allison finished in second place, making it the second time he has finished second to his brother in a Grand National race. Third place went to Baker, who had to pit for tires and fuel with five laps left. Charlie Glotzbach was fourth and David Pearson fifth.

Donnie beat Bobby by 16 seconds after Bobby had to make a late pit stop to replace a blistered front tire.

Grand National Race No. 48
334 Laps at Charlotte Motor Speedway
Charlotte, NC
"National 500"
500 Miles on 1.5-mile Paved Track
October 12, 1969

Fin	St	No.	Driver	Team / Car	Laps	Money	Status
1	3	27	Donnie Allison	Banjo Matthews '69 Ford	334	$20,280	Running
2	6	22	Bobby Allison	Mario Rossi '69 Dodge Day	334	10,465	Running
3	5	6	Buddy Baker	Cotton Owens '69 Dodge Day	334	6,550	Running
4	7	99	Charlie Glotzbach*	Nichels Eng '69 Dodge Day	334	4,025	Running
5	8	17	David Pearson	Holman-Moody '69 Ford	332	3,800	Running
6	13	32	Dick Brooks	Brooks '69 Plymouth	321	2,650	Running
7	21	06	Neil Castles	Castles '69 Dodge	320	2,125	Running
8	29	39	Friday Hassler	Hassler '69 Chevrolet	318	1,900	Running
9	22	37	Dr Don Tarr	Ray Fox '67 Dodge	318	1,760	Running
10	15	4	John Sears	L G DeWitt '69 Ford	315	1,685	Engine
11	44	48	James Hylton	Hylton Eng '69 Dodge Daytona	314	1,675	Running
12	28	33	Wayne Smith	Smith '69 Chevrolet	312	1,580	Running
13	17	64	Elmo Langley	Langley '68 Ford	307	1,535	Running
14	23	61	Hoss Ellington	Ellington '69 Ford	306	1,480	Running
15	34	29	John Kennedy	Kennedy '67 Chevrolet	301	1,425	Running
16	24	45	Bill Seifert	Seifert '69 Ford	298	1,380	Running
17	27	8	Wendell Scott	G C Spencer '67 Plymouth	297	1,355	Running
18	36	76	Ben Arnold	Red Culpepper '68 Ford	292	1,325	Running
19	38	47	Cecil Gordon	Bill Seifert '58 Ford	291	1,300	Running
20	35	51	Dub Simpson	Bill Strong '69 Chevrolet	291	1,275	Running
21	39	19	Henley Gray	Harry Melton '68 Ford	290	1,250	Running
22	16	10	Bill Champion	Champion '68 Ford	288	1,235	Running
23	42	09	Wayne Gillette	E C Reid '69 Chevrolet	281	1,200	Running
24	32	84	J D McDuffie	Elmo Langley '68 Ford	277	1,175	Clutch
25	1	21	Cale Yarborough	Wood Brothers '69 Mercury	260	1,510	Engine
26	31	25	Jabe Thomas	Don Robertson '68 Plymouth	240	1,150	Running
27	2	43	Richard Petty	Petty ent '69 Ford	239	1,260	Engine
28	10	30	Dave Marcis	Milt Lunda '69 Dodge Daytona	217	1,130	Engine
29	43	26	Earl Brooks	Brooks '67 Ford	201	1,025	Engine
30	20	49	G C Spencer	Spencer '67 Plymouth	191	1,100	Engine
31	19	9	Roy Tyner	Tyner '69 Pontiac	184	1,010	Engine
32	25	90	Sonny Hutchins	Junie Donlavey '67 Ford	175	980	Engine
33	33	08	E J Trivette	E C Reid '67 Chevrolet	170	950	Engine
34	37	13	Jimmy Lineberger	'67 Chevrolet	131	925	Crash
35	26	31	Buddy Young	Fred Bear '67 Chevrolet	109	905	Rear End
36	14	67	Buddy Arrington	Arrington '69 Dodge	103	885	Engine
37	45	88	Richard Brickhouse	Bill Ellis '69 Dodge Daytona	95	900	Engine
38	4	98	LeeRoy Yarbrough	Junior Johnson '69 Ford	94	875	Engine
39	30	07	Coo Coo Marlin	Cunningham-Kelley '69 Chev	90	850	Engine
40	12	1	A J Foyt	Jack Bowsher '69 Ford	88	875	W Bearing
41	9	71	Bobby Isaac	K&K Ins '69 Dodge Daytona	81	775	Engine
42	41	54	Bill Dennis	Dennis '69 Chevrolet	69	725	Engine
43	11	3	Jim Vandiver	Ray Fox '69 Dodge	64	825	Steering
44	40	82	Bob Cooper	'68 Chevrolet	55	675	Rear End
45	18	96	Frank Warren	Warren '68 Ford	21	660	Engine

Time of Race: 3 hours, 48 minutes, 32 seconds
Average Speed: 131.271 mph
Pole Winner: Cale Yarborough - 162.162 mph
Lap Leaders: Donnie Allison 1-25, Dave Marcis 26-31, Buddy Baker 32-97, Bobby Allison 98-114, D.Allison 115, B.Allison 116-117, Richard Petty 118-123, D.Allison 124-148, B.Allison 149-159, D.Allison 160-195, Petty 196, D.Allison 197-206, B.Allison 207-225, D.Allison 226-240, Baker 241, Cale Yarborogh 242-245, D.Allison 246, Yarborough 247-259, D.Allison 260, Baker 261-263, B.Allison 264-268, Baker 269-271, B.Allison 272-279, D.Allison 280-283, B.Allison 284, D.Allison 285-322, Baker 323-329, D.Allison 330-334.
Cautions: 9 for 50 laps   Margin of Victory: 16 seconds   Attendance: 50,000
*Relieved by Richard Brickhouse

Donnie started third, but grabbed the lead in the first lap. "When I went to the front early, I knew I could handle just about anyone if nothing happened," said Allison.

Cale Yarborough started on the pole with a record 162.162 mph lap, but didn't lead until the 242nd lap.

James Hylton #48 and G.C. Spencer #49 side-by-side in National 500

Cale's day came to an end on lap 260 when the engine blew in his Wood Brothers Mercury. Other top drivers who failed to go the distance were Richard Brickhouse, Bobby Isaac, A.J. Foyt, LeeRoy Yarbrough and Richard Petty.

The 500-miler was the first full-fledged battle between the Dodge Daytonas and the Ford Talladegas. Seven winged Dodges entered the race.

Allison averaged 131.271 mph before 50,000 spectators.

Race No. 49

Speedy Isaac Salvages Savannah Victory

SAVANNAH, GA (Oct. 17) -- Bobby Isaac took the lead in the fourth lap and led the rest of the way to win the 100-miler at Savannah Speedway. It was the 14th win of the year for the Dodge veteran.

Richard Petty finished in second place with David Pearson third. LeeRoy Yarbrough came in fourth and Elmo Langley fifth.

Isaac started on the pole, but lost the lead to Pearson at the start. Pearson led only the first three laps before Isaac assumed command.

Pearson's third place finish enabled him to hold a commanding 272 point lead over Petty in the Grand National point battle. Isaac ranks sixth, 899 points behind.

Twenty-three of the 29 cars that started the race were running at the finish. Two of the retirees withdrew

from the race.

J.C. Yarborough, Cale's little brother, started 16th and finished 21st. J.C. had broken his leg in a qualifying race for the World 600 in May. The 100-miler on the half-mile paved track was Yarborough's first start since his mishap.

Isaac averaged 78.482 mph for his 18th career Grand National win.

Grand National Race No. 49
200 Laps at Savannah Speedway
Savannah, GA
100 Miles on Half-mile Paved Track
October 17, 1969

Fin	St	No.	Driver	Team / Car	Laps	Money	Status
1	1	71	Bobby Isaac	K&K Insurance '69 Dodge	200	$1,000	Running
2	3	43	Richard Petty	Petty Ent '69 Ford	200	600	Running
3	2	17	David Pearson	Holman-Moody '69 Ford	200	600	Running
4	4	98	LeeRoy Yarbrough	Junior Johnson '69 Ford	198	350	Running
5	9	64	Elmo Langley	Langley '68 Ford	194	325	Running
6	7	48	James Hylton	Hylton Eng '69 Dodge	193	300	Running
7	6	06	Neil Castles	Castles '69 Dodge	192	275	Running
8	20	45	Bill Seifert	Seifert '69 Ford	190	270	Running
9	10	10	Bill Champion	Champion '68 Ford	189	265	Running
10	17	70	J D McDuffie	McDuffie '67 Buick	184	260	Running
11	22	25	Jabe Thomas	Don Robertson '68 Plymouth	183	255	Running
12	18	8	Ed Negre	G C Spencer '67 Plymouth	183	250	Running
13	13	76	Ben Arnold	Red Culpepper '68 Ford	181	245	Running
14	25	34	Wendell Scott	Scott '67 Ford	181	240	Running
15	23	26	Earl Brooks	Brooks '67 Ford	177	235	Running
16	19	19	Henley Gray	Harry Melton '68 Ford	175	230	Running
17	24	08	E J Trivette	E C Reid '69 Chevrolet	172	225	Running
18	21	04	Ken Meisenhelder	Meisenhelder '67 Olds	165	220	Running
19	15	47	Cecil Gordon	Bill Seifert '68 Ford	158	215	Running
20	27	03	Bill Shirey	Dub Clewis '67 Plymouth	157	210	Running
21	16	16	J C Yarborough	Dennis Holt '68 Mercury	157	205	Running
22	26	69	Larry Baumel	Auto Lad '69 Ford	148	200	Running
23	14	0	Frank Warren	Dr Don Tarr '67 Chevrolet	121	100	Running
24	5	30	Dave Marcis	Milt Lunda '69 Dodge	93	100	Rear End
25	11	32	Dick Brooks	Brooks '69 Plymouth	61	100	Oil Leak
26	8	4	John Sears	L G DeWitt '68 Ford	56	100	Rear End
27	12	57	Johnny Halford	Ervin Pruitt '67 Dodge	56	100	Brakes
28	28	12	Pete Hazelwood	'68 Ford	29	100	Quit
29	29	23	James Cox	Don Robertson '67 Ford	1	100	Quit

Time of Race: 1 hour, 16 minutes, 27 seconds
Average Speed: 78.482 mph
Pole Winner: Bobby Isaac - 86.095 mph
Lap Leaders: David Pearson 1-3, Bobby Isaac 4-200.
Cautions: 2 for 11 laps   Margin of Victory: Attendance: 5,700

Race No. 50

Caution-Free Augusta Event to Bobby Isaac

AUGUSTA, GA (Oct. 19) -- Bobby Isaac led all but two laps and won the 100-miler at Augusta Speedway with ease. It was the 15th win of the year for the quiet Dodge driver.

Isaac started on the pole and was in front all the way

except for two laps when he made a routine pit stop.

Isaac finished nearly a lap in front of Richard Petty's Ford. David Pearson came in third, LeeRoy Yarbrough was fourth and Elmo Langley fifth.

Richard Brickhouse spins into the wall at Rockingham

The 200 lapper was run without a caution flag, and Isaac was seldom challenged.

Yarbrough, going for the money winnings title, entered a rare 100-mile. But he was lapped twice.

A slim crowd of 4,500 watched Isaac average 78.740 mph. "I've won several races on the short tracks this year," said Isaac. "I just wish I could win a superspeedway race. Lord knows I've run well enough to win one. The breaks have never come my way. We'll win a big race one of these days."

Race No. 51

Yarbrough Takes 7th Super-speedway Win at Rockingham

ROCKINGHAM, NC (Oct. 26) -- LeeRoy Yarbrough continued his superspeedway assault by taking first place in the American 500.

Yarbrough shoved his Ford around David Pearson with 57 laps remaining and pulled away for an easy win. Pearson wound up second after dropping a lap off the pace. Buddy Baker was third, Dave Marcis fourth and John Sears fifth.

LeeRoy Yarbrough grabbed his 7th superspeedway win of the year in the American 500

The newly designed North Carolina Motor Speedway took its toll on drivers and cars. Only 17 of the 40 cars finished the race.

Charlie Glotzbach led the first 39 laps from the pole. The Georgetown, IN driver was taken out in a spectacular flaming slide when his engine blew after 281 laps.

Cale Yarborough smashed his Mercury into the wall on lap 168. Donnie Allison blasted the homestretch

Grand National Race No. 50
200 Laps at Augusta Speedway
Augusta, GA
100 Miles on Half-mile Paved Track
October 19, 1969

Fin	St	No.	Driver	Team / Car	Laps	Money	Status
1	1	71	Bobby Isaac	K&K Insurance '69 Dodge	200	$1,000	Running
2	3	43	Richard Petty	Petty Ent '69 Ford	200	600	Running
3	2	17	David Pearson	Holman-Moody '69 Ford	199	600	Running
4	4	98	LeeRoy Yarbrough	Junior Johnson '69 Ford	198	350	Running
5	8	64	Elmo Langley	Langley '68 Ford	195	325	Running
6	7	4	John Sears	L G DeWitt '68 Ford	194	300	Running
7	9	06	Neil Castles	Castles '69 Dodge	194	275	Running
8	15	0	Frank Warren	Dr Don Tarr '67 Chevrolet	188	270	Running
9	17	45	Bill Seifert	Seifert '69 Ford	188	265	Running
10	13	76	Ben Arnold	Red Culpepper '68 Ford	188	260	Running
11	19	47	Cecil Gordon	Bill Seifert '68 Ford	186	255	Running
12	22	10	Bill Champion	Champion '68 Ford	182	250	Running
13	21	08	E J Trivette	E C Reid '69 Chevrolet	179	245	Running
14	20	03	Bill Shirey	Dub Clewis '67 Plymouth	179	240	Running
15	5	30	Dave Marcis	Milt Lunda '69 Dodge	178	235	Engine
16	14	68	Larry Baumel	Auto Lad '69 Ford	176	230	Running
17	26	34	Wendell Scott	Scott '67 Ford	175	225	Running
18	25	19	Henley Gray	Harry Melton '68 Ford	175	220	Running
19	12	25	Jabe Thomas	Don Robertson '68 Plymouth	167	215	Running
20	18	16	J C Yarborough	Dennis Holt '68 Mercury	161	210	Running
21	24	26	Earl Brooks	Brooks '67 Ford	125	205	Engine
22	28	12	Pete Hazelwood	'68 Ford	125	200	Rear End
23	27	82	Mack Sellers	'67 Chevrolet	85	100	Running
24	11	29	John Kennedy	Kennedy '67 Chevrolet	78	100	Clutch
25	29	23	James Cox	Don Robertson '67 Ford	51	100	Steering
26	6	48	James Hylton	Hylton Eng '69 Dodge	45	100	Rear End
27	23	04	Ken Meisenhelder	Meisenhelder '67 Olds	30	100	Engine
28	10	8	Ed Negre	G C Spencer '67 Plymouth	10	100	Rear End
29	16	70	J D McDuffie	McDuffie '67 Buick	8	100	Engine

Time of Race: 1 hour, 16 minutes, 12 seconds
Average Speed: 78.740 mph
Pole Winner: Bobby Isaac - 85.689 mph
Lap Leaders: Bobby Isaac 1-139, Richard Petty 140-141, Isaac 142-200.
Cautions: None   Margin of Victory: Attendance: 4,500

wall head-on after hooking fenders with Glotzbach on lap 143. No drivers were injured.

Bobby Allison, driving one of only four winged Dodge Daytonas in the race, was running second in the early stages when he hit a spinning John Kennedy. The accident occurred in the 20th lap -- and Kennedy was already three laps off the pace.

Runner-up Pearson clinched the Grand National championship. His closest adversary Richard Petty, blew a tire and crashed in the 113th lap. Pearson padded his lead to 363 points with just three races left on the 1969 slate.

Yarbrough wiped out his primary car in a practice crash. Junior Johnson brought in a back-up, which Yarbrough promptly set a new track record of 137.732 mph in qualifying.

He started ninth and led seven times for 213 laps. "You needed a suit of armor out there today," commented Yarbrough. "There were wrecks and stuff flying all over the place."

It was the second time in the 1969 Grand National season that Yarbrough had driven a back-up car to

Charlie Glotzbach put his winged Dodge on the pole

Grand National Race No. 51
492 Laps at North Carolina Motor Speedway
Rockingham, NC
"American 500"
500 Miles on 1.017-mile Paved Track
October 26, 1969

Fin	St	No.	Driver	Team / Car	Laps	Money	Status
1	9	98	LeeRoy Yarbrough	Junior Johnson '69 Ford	492	$17,600	Running
2	4	17	David Pearson	Holman-Moody '69 Ford	491	10,725	Running
3	6	6	Buddy Baker	Cotton Owens '69 Dodge	485	5,350	Running
4	10	30	Dave Marcis	Milt Lunda '69 Dodge Daytona	472	2,850	Running
5	14	4	John Sears	L G DeWitt '69 Ford	465	2,070	Running
6	13	32	Dick Brooks	Brooks '69 Plymouth	157	1,700	Running
7	23	61	Hoss Ellington	Ellington '69 Ford	454	1,400	Running
8	24	8	Ed Negre	G C Spencer '67 Plymouth	445	1,300	Running
9	33	34	Wendell Scott	Scott '67 Ford	433	1,200	Running
10	31	06	Neil Castles	Castles '69 Dodge	431	1,200	Running
11	28	46	Roy Mayne	Tom Hunter '69 Chevrolet	430	1,125	Running
12	30	45	Bill Seifert	Seifert '69 Ford	429	1,100	Running
13	37	25	Jabe Thomas	Don Robertson '68 Plymouth	425	1,075	Running
14	35	47	Cecil Gordon	Bill Seifert '68 Ford	419	1,050	Running
15	21	10	Bill Champion	Champion '68 Ford	416	1,035	Running
16	8	71	Bobby Isaac	K&K Insurance '69 Dodge	391	1,020	T Chain
17	25	08	E J Trivette	E C Reid '69 Chevrolet	388	1,005	Suspen
18	32	57	Johnny Halford	Ervin Pruitt '67 Dodge	369	1,015	Running
19	39	69	Larry Baumel	Auto Lad '69 Ford	366	975	Engine
20	27	0	J D McDuffie	Dr Don Tarr '67 Chevrolet	329	960	Running
21	36	9	Earl Brooks	Roy Tyner '69 Pontiac	313	945	Wtr pump
22	22	41	Elmo Langley	Bill Champion '67 Ford	304	930	Brakes
23	1	99	Charlie Glotzbach	Nichels Eng '69 Dodge Day	281	1,265	Engine
24	17	49	G C Spencer	Spencer '67 Plymouth	240	975	Engine
25	40	51	Dub Simpson	Bill Strong '69 Chevrolet	239	885	W Bearing
26	18	31	Buddy Young	Fred Bear '67 Chevrolet	186	820	Crash
27	29	7	Bobby Johns	Shorty Johns '67 Chevrolet	183	830	Engine
28	15	48	James Hylton	Hylton '69 Dodge	174	740	Engine
29	3	21	Cale Yarborough	Wood Brothers '69 Mercury	168	750	Crash
30	5	27	Donnie Allison	Banjo Matthews '69 Ford	143	710	Crash
31	11	88	Richard Brickhouse	Bill Ellis '69 Dodge Daytona	124	720	Suspen
32	7	43	Richard Petty	Petty Ent '69 Ford	113	680	Crash
33	26	54	Ben Arnold	Bill Dennis '69 Chevrolet	105	665	Engine
34	38	44	Lennie Pond	Giachetti Bros '67 Chevrolet	73	650	Engine
35	12	67	Buddy Arrington	Arrington '69 Dodge	72	635	Rear End
36	19	64	Clyde Lynn	Elmo Langley '68 Ford	40	645	Heating
37	16	39	Friday Hassler	Hassler '67 Chevrolet	37	605	Engine
38	34	19	Henley Gray	Harry Melton '68 Ford	29	590	D Shaft
39	2	22	Bobby Allison	Mario Rossi '69 Dodge Day	20	650	Crash
40	20	29	John Kennedy	Kennedy '67 Chevrolet	17	560	Crash

Time of Race: 4 hours, 28 minutes, 12 seconds
Average Speed: 111.938 mph
Pole Winner: Charlie Glotzbach - 136.972 mph
Fastest Qualifier: LeeRoy Yarbrough 137.732 mph
Lap Leaders: Charlie Glotzbach 1-39, Cale Yarborough 40-52, LeeRoy Yarbrough 53-61, Yarbrough 62-65, Bobby Isaac 66-104, Richard Petty 105-110, Yarborough 111-130, David PEarson 131-137, Buddy Baker 138-144, Yarbrough 145-148, Isaac 149, Yarborough 150-167, Isaac 168-170, Glotzbach 171-181, Baker 182-187, Glotzbach 188-211, Baker 212-222, Yarbrough 223-264, Baker 265-274, Glotzbach 275-280, Pearson 281-326, Yarbrough 327-354, Pearson 355-356, Yarbrough 357-426, Pearson 427-435, Yarbrough 436-492.
Cautions: 7 for 66 laps   Margin of Victory: 1 1/2 lap   Attendance: 33,800

victory. He had manned a substitute car in the Daytona 500. "I felt pretty bad and felt our chances were slim when I crashed on Wednesday," said the 31 year-old Yarbrough. "But the new car felt pretty good. I felt if I could keep my nose clean during all those wrecks, we had a good shot to win."

Yarbrough averaged 111.938 mph for his 13th career win. A crowd of 33,800 watched the 500-miler.

Race No. 52

Isaac Outruns Pearson For Jeffco Victory

JEFFERSON, GA (Nov. 2) -- Bobby Isaac roared to his 16th win of the season by taking the 100-miler at Jeffco Speedway.

Isaac, 37, passed David Pearson in the 63rd lap and was never headed. Pearson came in second with Richard Petty, LeeRoy Yarbrough and Neil Castles rounding out the top five.

Pearson started on the pole and led the first 62 laps with Isaac in hot pursuit. Isaac made the decisive pass on lap 63.

"Our Dodge has been running real good on the short tracks," said Isaac. "If we stay out of trouble and steer away from mistakes, we usually win."

Pearson, who has already wrapped up the 1969 Grand National championship, said, "It's quite a relief to win the championship a third time. It is demanding and nerve wrecking. I don't intend on going through this again."

Of the 27 cars that started the race, 21 finished.

Isaac averaged 85.106 mph before 7,000 spectators.

Grand National Race No. 52
200 Laps at Jeffco Speedway
Jefferson, GA
"Jeffco 200"
100 Miles on Half-mile Paved Track
November 2, 1969

Fin	St	No.	Driver	Team / Car	Laps	Money	Status
1	2	71	Bobby Isaac	K&K Insurance '69 Dodge	200	$1,350	Running
2	1	17	David Pearson	Holman-Moody '69 Ford	200	950	Running
3	3	43	Richard Petty	Petty Ent '69 Ford	198	500	Running
4	4	98	LeeRoy Yarbrough	Junior Johnson '69 Ford	196	350	Running
5	5	06	Neil Castles	Castles '69 Dodge	191	325	Running
6	8	64	Elmo Langley	Langley '68 Ford	189	300	Running
7	7	39	Friday Hassler	Hassler '67 Chevrolet	188	275	Running
8	9	10	Bill Champion	Champion '68 Ford	188	270	Running
9	17	19	Henley Gray	Harry Melton '68 Ford	181	265	Running
10	12	25	Jabe Thomas	Don Robertson '68 Plymouth	180	260	Running
11	19	08	E J Trivette	E C Reid '69 Chevrolet	180	255	Running
12	20	47	Cecil Gordon	Bill Seifert '68 Ford	178	250	Running
13	18	70	J D McDuffie	McDuffie '67 Buick	178	245	Running
14	21	34	Wendell Scott	Scott '67 Ford	177	240	Out of gas
15	13	57	Johnny Halford	Ervin Pruitt '67 Dodge	177	235	Running
16	22	26	Earl Brooks	Brooks '67 Ford	176	230	Running
17	14	45	Bill Seifert	Seifert '69 Ford	173	225	Running
18	16	76	Ben Arnold	Red Culpepper '68 Ford	171	220	Running
19	10	69	Larry Baumel	Auto Lad '69 Ford	171	215	Running
20	11	4	John Sears	L G DeWitt '69 Ford	170	210	Running
21	26	12	Pete Hazelwood	'68 Ford	164	205	Running
22	6	30	Dave Marcis	Marcis '69 Dodge	160	200	Oil Leak
23	15	0	Frank Warren	Dr Don Tarr '67 Chevrolet	126	100	Trans
24	25	48	James Hylton	Hylton '69 Dodge	98	100	Crash
25	24	9	Roy Tyner	Tyner '69 Pontiac	97	100	Running
26	23	82	Mack Sellers	'67 Chevrolet	78	100	Quit
27	27	23	James Cox	Don Robertson '67 Ford	42	100	Quit

Time of Race: 1 hour, 10 minutes, 30 seconds
Average Speed: 85.106 mph
Pole Winner: David Pearson 89.565 mph
Lap Leaders: David Pearson 1-62, Bobby Isaac 63-200.
Cautions: 1 for 4 laps   Margin of Victory: Attendance: 7,000

Grand National Race No. 53
500 Laps at Middle Georgia Raceway
Macon, GA
"Georgia 500"
274 Miles on .548-mile Paved Track
November 9, 1969

Fin	St	No.	Driver	Team / Car	Laps	Money	Status
1	5	22	Bobby Allison	Mario Rossi '69 Dodge	500	$3,050	Running
2	3	17	David Pearson	Holman-Moody '69 Ford	500	2,025	Running
3	1	71	Bobby Isaac	K&K Insurance '69 Dodge	500	1,300	Running
4	10	4	John Sears	L G DeWitt '67 Ford	482	775	Running
5	14	10	Bill Champion	Champion '68 Ford	471	675	Running
6	4	43	Richard Petty	Petty Ent '69 Ford	469	650	Engine
7	16	47	Cecil Gordon	Bill Seifert '68 Ford	467	600	Running
8	15	76	Ben Arnold	Red Culpepper '68 Ford	464	575	Running
9	23	19	Henley Gray	Harry Melton '69 Ford	463	530	Running
10	6	48	James Hylton	Hylton Eng '69 Dodge	460	545	Running
11	17	45	Bill Seifert	Seifert '69 Ford	455	535	Running
12	26	89	Don Patton	'67 Chevrolet	441	500	Running
13	12	25	Jabe Thomas	Don Robertson '68 Plymouth	440	515	Running
14	19	34	Wendell Scott	Scott '67 Ford	410	505	Running
15	22	26	Earl Brooks	Brooks '67 Ford	409	470	Running
16	9	06	Neil Castles	Castles '67 Plymouth	381	485	Engine
17	29	12	Pete Hazelwood	'68 Ford	366	450	Flagged
18	21	08	E J Trivette	E C Reid '69 Chevrolet	314	440	Rear End
19	20	8	Ed Negre	G C Spencer '67 Plymouth	291	455	Engine
20	11	64	Elmo Langley	Langley '68 Ford	288	445	Clutch
21	18	57	Johnny Halford	Ervin Pruitt '67 Dodge	256	435	Engine
22	7	39	Friday Hassler	Hassler '67 Chevrolet	236	425	Engine
23	25	82	Roy Mayne	'67 Chevrolet	221	390	Axle
24	8	32	Dick Brooks	Brooks '69 Plymouth	210	405	Rear End
25	28	70	Don Biederman	'68 Ford	133	370	Clutch
26	27	23	James Cox	Don Robertson '67 Ford	132	365	Quit
27	24	0	Don Tarr	Tarr '67 Chevrolet	126	355	Wtr Pump
28	13	68	Larry Baumel	Auto Lad '69 Ford	99	370	Oil Leak
29	2	98	LeeRoy Yarbrough	Junior Johnson '69 Ford	64	435	Quit

Time of Race: 3 hours, 37 minutes, 8 seconds
Average Speed: 81.079 mph
Pole Winner: Bobby Isaac - 98.148 mph
Lap Leaders: David Pearson 1-83, Bobby Isaac 84-146, Pearson 147,
    Richard Petty 148-157, Bobby Allison 158, Isaac 159, Petty 160, Isaac 161-199,
    Petty 200-345, Isaac 346-349, Pearson 350-472, Allison 473-477, Pearson 478-488,
    Allison 489-500.
Cautions: 10 for 58 laps   Margin of Victory: 5 car lengths   Attendance: 10,000

Race No. 53

Yarbrough and Nab Square Off; Allison Wins at Macon

MACON, GA (Nov. 9) -- Bobby Allison took the lead from David Pearson with 12 laps to go and won the Georgia 500 at Middle Georgia Raceway for his fifth win of the year.

Allison had run among the leaders in the early going,

Bobby Allison #22 scoots into first place as Richard Petty and David Pearson tangle at Macon

Brooks fifth.

Buddy Baker, bidding for his third Grand National win, led on 13 occasions for 150 laps. He was holding down first place under caution when he flicked the "V" sign to his Cotton Owens pit crew on lap 228. While his concentration lapsed, Baker smacked the rear of Hylton's car, caving in the front of his own Dodge. The radiator was ruptured and Baker was out of the race a lap later.

Isaac took the lead for four laps, but lost first place to Allison on lap 234. Allison pitted for a flat tire two laps later, and Isaac motored on to victory.

Dodge officials were visibly upset when Baker crashed out under the yellow flag. The only race Dodge had won on the big tracks was a tainted 500-miler at Talladega. Crew chief and car owner Owens slung the pit board like a frisbee as he watched Baker take himself out of the race. "I was looking back at the pit crew," said Baker. "I made a mistake. I feel bad about it."

but fell a lap off the pace with 100 laps left. Pearson and Richard Petty, who were in a lap by themselves, hooked fenders on lap 420. Both cars spun around, allowing Allison to scoot back into the lead lap.

Pearson got his Ford restarted and assumed the lead. On the final restart, Allison heeled Pearson for several laps before making the pass on lap 489.

Pearson finished second, five car lengths behind the winner. Isaac finished third, John Sears was fourth and Bill Champion fifth. Petty wound up sixth after blowing his engine with 31 laps left.

LeeRoy Yarbrough qualified second and followed Pearson for the first 64 laps. During a caution flag, Yarbrough pitted and requested a tire change. Yarbrough waved off a suggested change of tire treads by crew chief Herb Nab.

Nab then refused to change the tires at all. When Yarbrough didn't get any new tires, he parked the car.

Allison averaged 81.079 mph for his 16th career Grand National win.

Race No. 54

Isaac Gets 1st Superspeedway Win in Season Finale at Texas

COLLEGE STATION, TX (Dec. 7) -- Bobby Isaac ended a six year famine on the superspeedways by taking his first big track win in the inaugural Texas 500 at Texas International Speedway. It was the 17th win of the season for the Dodge driver.

Isaac took the lead with 15 laps remaining and won by two laps over Donnie Allison's Ford. Benny Parsons came in third, James Hylton was fourth and Dick

Bobby Isaac won his first superspeedway race at Texas

Grand National Race No. 54
250 Laps at Texas Int'l Speedway
College Station, TX
"Texas 500"
500 Miles on 2-mile Paved Track
December 7, 1969

Fin	St	No.	Driver	Team / Car	Laps	Money	Status
1	7	71	Bobby Isaac	K&K Ins '69 Dodge Daytona	250	$15,640	Running
2	6	27	Donnie Allison	Banjo Matthews '69 Ford	248	8,200	Running
3	21	18	Benny Parsons	Russ Dawson '69 Ford	247	4,000	Running
4	11	48	James Hylton	Hylton Eng '69 Dodge Daytona	239	3,700	Running
5	12	32	Dick Brooks	Brooks '69 Plymouth	237	3,350	Running
6	9	96	Ray Elder	Fred Elder '69 Dodge Daytona	232	2,530	Running
7	25	7	Jack McCoy	Ernie Conn '69 Dodge Daytona	230	2,000	Running
8	1	6	Buddy Baker	Cotton Owens '69 Dodge Day	229	1,625	Crash
9	10	30	Dave Marcis	Milt Lunda '69 Dodge Daytona	225	1,375	Running
10	3	98	LeeRoy Yarbrough	Junior Johnson '69 Ford	222	1,375	Engine
11	23	47	Cecil Gordon	Bill Seifert '68 Ford	222	1,250	Running
12	30	25	Jabe Thomas	Don Robertson '68 Plymouth	222	1,200	Running
13	26	08	E J Trivette	E C Reid '69 Chevrolet	221	1,175	Running
14	35	57	Johnny Halford	Ervin Pruitt '67 Dodge	218	1,150	Running
15	17	39	Friday Hassler	Hassler '69 Chevrolet	217	1,130	Engine
16	18	06	Neil Castles	Castles '69 Dodge	217	1,120	Running
17	29	19	Henley Gray	Harry Melton '68 Ford	215	1,110	Running
18	34	34	Wendell Scott	Scott '67 Ford	212	1,100	Running
19	27	70	Don Biederman	'68 Ford	205	1,075	Running
20	31	36	H B Bailey	Bailey '69 Pontiac	195	1,050	Engine
21	24	43	Richard Petty	Petty Ent '69 Ford	192	1,025	Clutch
22	38	81	Dave Alonzo	'67 Plymouth	174	1,000	Running
23	8	22	Bobby Allison	Mario Rossi '69 Dodge Day	163	1,010	Engine
24	32	26	Earl Brooks	Brooks '67 Ford	146	950	Oil Leak
25	4	21	Cale Yarborough	Wood Brothers '69 Mercury	143	990	Crash
26	2	17	David Pearson	Holman-Moody '69 Ford	142	1,500	Clutch
27	28	64	Elmo Langley	Langley '68 Ford	110	880	Engine
28	19	74	Bill Shirey	Shirey '69 Plymouth	82	865	Engine
29	15	76	Ben Arnold	Red Culpepper '68 Ford	75	850	Clutch
30	14	8	Frank Warren	G C Spencer '67 Plymouth	73	840	Engine
31	13	10	Bill Champion	Champion '68 Ford	69	830	Engine
32	16	4	John Sears	L G DeWitt '69 Ford	60	820	Heating
33	5	99	Richard Brickhouse	Nichels Eng '69 Dodge Day	53	870	Engine
34	33	03	Joe Hines	Dub Clewis '67 Plymouth	38	800	Sway Bar
35	37	0	Ed Negre	Dr Don Tarr '67 Chevrolet	22	790	Steering
36	20	45	Bill Seifert	Seifert '69 Ford	14	780	Engine
37	22	69	Larry Baumel	Auto Lad '69 Ford	4	770	Engine
38	36	9	Roy Tyner	Tyner '69 Pontiac	2	760	Engine

Time of Race: 3 hours, 27 minutes, 56 seconds
Average Speed: 144.277 mph
Pole Winner: Buddy Baker - 176.284 mph
Lap Leaders: Buddy Baker 1-7, David Pearson 8-9, Baker 10-11, LeeRoy Yarbrough 12-13
   Baker 14-18, Donnie Allison 19, Baker 20-39, Pearson 40-41, Cale Yarbrough 42-47,
   Baker 48-58, Pearson 59-66, Baker 67-98, Pearson 99-103, D.Allison 104,
   Yarborough 105-114, Baker 115-137, Pearson 138-141, Baker 142-146,
   Pearson 147-156, Yarbrough 157-158, D.Allison 159-162, Baker 163-168,
   Yarbrough 169, Baker 170-173, Yarbrough 174-175, D.Allison 176-178, Baker 179,
   D.Allison 180-184, Yarbrough 185-189, Baker 190-193, Yarbrough 194-198,
   D.Allison 199, Baker 200-229, Bobby Isaac 230-233, D.Allison 234-235, Isaac 236-250.
Cautions: 3 for 29 laps   Margin of Victory: 2-laps plus   Attendance: 23,508

For Isaac, the victory ended a career void on the superspeedways. "I've been trying since 1963 to win a big race," said Isaac. "I've been close many times. This is the greatest day of my life."

David Pearson capped off his third title year by winning the Grand National championship by 357 points over Richard Petty. Pearson started second and led in the early stages. He departed on lap 142 with clutch trouble.

Petty started in 24th spot, but lost his clutch on lap 192. It would be the final appearance for Petty in a Ford. He announced that he would return to Plymouth in 1970. "We didn't win any superspeedway races this year," said Petty. "That's the name of the game. Plymouth is coming out with a SuperBird, and maybe we can cash in on some of the big track money. This has been a frustrating year."

Cale Yarborough was seriously injured when his Mercury blew a tire and slammed the concrete wall on lap 143. The Timmonsville, SC driver suffered a shattered shoulder blade, an injury doctors said would keep him out of action for nine months. "When this bone is broken this badly," said one doctor, "usually the patient is dead. It's a miracle he survived such a hard crash."

Isaac averaged 144.277 before a crowd of 23,508. Three days of rain forced track officials to close the infield. All fans in attendance had to occupy the grandstand seats.

1969 NASCAR Season
Final Point Standings - Grand National Division

Rank	Driver	Points	Starts	Wins	Top 5	Top 10	Winnings
1	David Pearson	4,170	51	11	42	44	$229,760
2	Richard Petty	3,813	50	10	31	38	129,906
3	James Hylton	3,750	52	0	27	39	114,416
4	Neil Castles	3,530	52	0	14	30	54,367
5	Elmo Langley	3,383	53	0	13	28	73,092
6	Bobby Isaac	3,301	50	17	29	33	92,074
7	John Sears	3,166	52	0	17	27	52,281
8	Jabe Thomas	3,103	51	0	0	12	44,989
9	Wendell Scott	3,015	51	0	0	11	47,451
10	Cecil Gordon	3,002	51	0	1	8	39,679
11	E.J. Trivette	2,988	49	0	0	15	35,896
12	Bill Champion	2,813	48	0	1	10	33,656
13	Bill Seifert	2,765	50	0	0	15	44,361
14	J.D. McDuffie	2,741	50	0	0	12	30,861
15	Ben Arnold	2,736	48	0	0	8	33,256
16	LeeRoy Yarbrough	2,712	30	7	16	21	193,211
17	Henley Gray	2,517	48	0	0	5	29,335
18	Earl Brooks	2,454	49	0	1	6	34,793
19	Dave Marcis	2,348	36	0	3	11	32,383
20	Bobby Allison	2,055	27	5	13	15	69,483
21	Dick Brooks	1,780	28	0	3	12	28,187
22	Buddy Baker	1,769	18	0	9	11	62,928
23	Cale Yarborough	1,715	19	2	7	8	74,240
24	Donnie Allison	1,662	16	1	10	11	78,055
25	Richard Brickhouse	1,660	24	1	2	9	45,637
26	G.C. Spencer	1,562	26	0	4	8	21,660
27	Ed Negre	1,465	30	0	0	4	15,160
28	Friday Hassler	1,421	18	0	0	7	17,690
29	Frank Warren	1,299	24	0	0	0	15,677
30	Hoss Ellington	1,210	15	0	0	4	16,552
31	Roy Tyner	1,191	21	0	0	1	12,302
32	Dr. Ed Hessert	1,113	18	0	0	7	17,690
33	Buddy Arrington	1,099	16	0	2	6	12,975
34	Dick Johnson	1,055	22	0	0	4	11,182
35	Buddy Young	981	21	0	1	5	15,542
36	Dub Simpson	959	20	0	0	0	12,915
37	Charlie Glotzbach	944	12	0	5	6	36,090
38	Roy Mayne	924	13	0	0	0	9,875
39	Wayne Smith	922	16	0	0	2	10,340
40	Paul Goldsmith	892	11	0	4	5	22,305
41	Dr. Don Tarr	855	12	0	0	3	13,720
42	Ken Meisenhelder	627	16	0	0	0	5,630
43	Pete Hazelwood	598	15	0	0	1	4,160
44	Sonny Hutchins	535	8	0	2	2	9,552
45	Wayne Gillette	509	15	0	0	0	5,827
46	Paul Dean Holt	485	14	0	0	0	4,442
47	Johnny Halford	465	8	0	0	0	4,200
48	Ray Elder	433	4	0	0	4	7,200
49	John Kennedy	417	8	0	0	0	6,462
50	Dick Poling	408	12	0	0	0	5,467

The   1970   Season

American   Raceways   Empire   Crumbles;
And   the   New   Carburetor   Plate

Volume three of a four volume series .. Big Bucks and Boycotts   1965 - 1971

1970

Shortly after the infamous boycott of the inaugural Talladega 500 by the Professional Drivers Association, Larry LoPatin publicly criticized NASCAR President Bill France. "This may be the end of an era," barked LoPatin, a Detroit financier who was elbowing his way into prominence as head of the multi speedway franchise American Raceways, Inc. "You can't run an organization without order. The Ford Tiny Lund drove at Talladega was illegal. The GT (Grand Touring) cars aren't eligible in Grand National racing. Would the same decision have been made if the NASCAR President was not the president of the track?"

LoPatin's American Raceways operated four tracks -- Michigan International Speedway, Atlanta International Raceway, Riverside International Raceway and Texas International Speedway. Work was underway on a fifth plant in New Jersey.

Within six weeks after the Talladega boycott, LoPatin removed Les Richter from his Executive Vice President position at ARI. Richter, a former All-Pro linebacker for the Los Angeles Rams, had openly sided with France and the drivers in separate areas during the dispute at Talladega. His services at ARI were terminated on October 29, 1969. "As a promoter," said LoPatin, "I felt he was off base in both areas. He involved himself in areas that were not his responsibility."

Richter's resignation, under pressure, was a signal that the long-predicted confrontation between stock car racing's established impresario France and the Johnny-come-lately LoPatin, was about to surface.

"It is unfortunate that my association with American Raceways has not been a happy one," remarked Richter. "But there was simply a conflict of objectives over the future of auto racing in the country and ARI's involvement in it."

In no time, France removed the December 7, 1969 season-ending Texas 500 from the Grand National schedule. NASCAR felt the $75,000 total purse posted by American Raceways, Inc. was far too low for a 500-miler on a two-mile superspeedway. Although no general rules regulated purses on big tracks, France said LoPatin would have to put up $100,000 in order to secure the event. "The Texas 500 is temporarily off the Grand National schedule until this difference is resolved," read NASCAR's official statement.

LoPatin reluctantly agreed to post awards of $93,150 for the event. With the contingency awards from accessory firms, the total purse was $100,000.

Three days of torrential rains just before the Texas 500 caused a major headache for track officials. The infield was virtually under water, and it had to be closed to the public. No vehicles other than emergency trucks were allowed in.

A slim crowd of 23,500, all of them sitting in the main grandstand, turned out for the inaugural event.

It was the fourth time in 1969 that a race staged by American Raceways, Inc. had been hit hard by foul weather. The Motor Trend 500 at Riverside had been rained out twice and finally staged before 46,300 spectators. It was a far cry from the 73,000 who attended the event in 1968.

The Dixie 500 at Atlanta was delayed a week by rain and finally presented under a dark, gray sky. Only 27,300 showed up. The Yankee 600 at Michigan was called off after 330 miles. Despite the poor weather, the attendance figure released by the Speedway was 52,237.

LoPatin was being gripped by severe money problems. "We cannot stand another year like we experienced in 1969," admitted LoPatin.

The first face-to-face meeting between LoPatin and France following the Talladega boycott was at the annual Ford Motorsports Banquet at Dearborn in late November. France and LoPatin were seen in a verbal, finger-pointing episode during a break in the ceremonies. France stormed out of the gala affair as dinner was being served. He was not present for the awards presentation which followed.

On December 17, 1969, NASCAR signed a pact with

ABC-Sports. The contract called for the American Broadcasting Co. to televise nine races in 1970 -- five of them live -- with options for 26 more in 1971 and 1972.

Stipulations of the $1,365,000 contract were that payments totaling $275,000 would be divided between the tracks hosting the televised event, the drivers, and a special fund to some of the tracks holding "major" events which were not televised. A notable exception were all of the events operated by American Raceways. No races were slated to be televised at any ARI facility -- and more importantly, they would not share in the money set aside to the other tracks.

Richard Howard, Chairman of the NASCAR Television Committee and ABC-Sports President Roone Arledge made the joint announcement. "This is certainly a major breakthrough for stock car racing," said Howard. "The popularity of the sport has risen tremendously in the last few years and now people all over the country will be able to enjoy NASCAR racing. This is a very substantial agreement. It will benefit the sport in many ways."

Arledge said that ABC-Sports was willing to gamble on stock car racing. "Auto racing has been one of the mainstays of ABC's *Wide World of Sports* since the program debuted nine years ago," said Arledge. "It has continued to be one of the best rated shows. Viewer interests in the sport confirm our belief that the time is ripe for automobile racing's expansion on television. We are confident of the success of our new package."

Bill France said there could be drawbacks to NASCAR on the network airwaves. "The problem for us is to condense a four hour event into a one and one-half hour program," said France. "The first portion of a race will be taped and a half hour or so of the highlights will be shown. Then it will cut to live coverage."

None of the races would be shown flag-to-flag, ABC said.

The same day the TV pact was signed, Richard Petty returned to Chrysler after a one year stint with Ford. "Guess you can say that we're headed back home," drawled Petty. "It'll be like rejoining family. The big reason is the new SuperBird (a virtual copy of the shark-nosed, high-winged Dodge Daytona, which debuted in late 1969). We feel Plymouth now has a car that will get the job done on the big tracks. Before, we felt like we were at a big disadvantage on the superspeedways.

"We had a one year contract with Ford which was renewable," continued Petty. "We chose not to renew it. The deal we have with Chrysler calls for us to run two

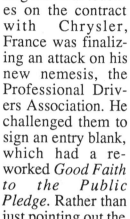

cars on the superspeedways and one car on all the smaller tracks. I will run the car on the short tracks and go for the point title."

Glenn E. White, general manager of the Chrysler-Plymouth Division, said his company was delighted to have Petty back in the fold. "Flags at over 3,400 dealer showrooms have been flying at half-staff since Petty left us a year ago," said White. "Now they are at full staff".

As Petty was putting the final touches on the contract with Chrysler, France was finalizing an attack on his new nemesis, the Professional Drivers Association. He challenged them to sign an entry blank, which had a reworked *Good Faith to the Public Pledge*. Rather than just pointing out the unwritten obligations the drivers had to the public, France spiced up the entry blanks with an ultimatum. And the first entry blank that went in the mail was for the Motor Trend 500 at Riverside, a la American Raceways.

The entry blank read: *"In consideration of the approval and acceptance by NASCAR and Riverside International Raceway of this entry and entry fee for the 1970 Motor Trend 500, and in consideration of the promises made by Riverside International Raceway with respect to, among other things, awards and promotions, the undersigned car owner of the described car further agrees with NASCAR and Riverside International Raceway: (1)-to start the described car in the 1970 Motor Trend 500 and qualifying events provided the described car qualifies or the appropriate NASCAR officials assign it a starting position, and (2)-to utilize, if necessary, a substitute driver for the described car if the driver executing the entry blank is for any reason unable or unwilling to drive this car in the 1970 Motor Trend 500 and qualifying events without the consent of the NASCAR Competition Director."*

That meant that once the entry blank was signed, NASCAR had complete control of the race car until the event was over. If there was another boycott, NASCAR could appoint a person of its choice to drive the car in the race.

Richard Petty, President of the PDA, Elmo Langley, Vice-President of the association, James Hylton and E.J. Trivette mailed in the entry blanks with the *Good Faith to the Public Pledge* scratched out.

"France wants to keep control of 110 percent of

Huge cranes sprouted up from the Talladega turns so ABC Sports could televise Alabama 500

racing," declared Petty, "and it can't be done. The sport has outgrown a one man operation."

"We disagree with the pledge," said Langley. "If this is binding, then NAS-CAR could put anyone in the car -- even an unqualified driver. I'm not going to let anybody else drive my car if I can't."

France stated the purpose behind the pledge. "NASCAR guarantees the money and the race," he said. "We have to guarantee the driver something. They should have to guarantee us something. We owe that much to the race promoter and to the fans who may purchase tickets months in advance. Somebody has to protect the public. Without the public, we have no sport."

The altered entry forms were not accepted. They were sent back to the four drivers.

Petty and Chrysler conferred about the situation. "Chrysler's advice was to go ahead and sign the blank since no one had any sort of intention of not racing," said Petty. "So, that's what we did."

It was a strategic victory for France. The unyielding position of France had been that he would not recognize or negotiate with the PDA. His contention was that the drivers are not employees of NASCAR and that there were no grounds for NASCAR to negotiate with a driver's union.

France still held the PDA's motives in high suspicion -- and he felt another boycott was entirely possible, particularly at his new Alabama International Motor Speedway in Talladega.

A series of tire tests were scheduled at Talladega throughout the winter months. In January, several of the tests were frozen out; temperatures were in the single digits.

LeeRoy Yarbrough was able to turn a lap of 199.916 mph during a three day test in late February.

On March 24, 1970, Buddy Baker went to Talladega to test Goodyear tires. He was driving a Chrysler-owned Dodge Daytona. On his 30th lap, Baker was clocked at 200.096 mph. After a 40 minute break, the Charlotte driver went back out and turned in a 200.336 mph lap. The very next time around, the electric timer caught him at 200.447 mph.

It was widely acclaimed as the first time a car had been driven past the 200 mph barrier on a closed

The Professional Drivers Association members backed down from a squabble over entry blanks and competed in the Motor Trend 500 at Riverside

course.

"It's hard to explain exactly what your train of thought does in a situation like this," said Baker. "You have to completely divorce yourself of any other thoughts -- you become part of the race car. It surprised me that a car running that fast could be as stable as ours was. I was in the bottom lane all the way around.

"I have the satisfaction of knowing I'm the first to crack 200," he added. "Nobody can take that away from me."

There was no mention -- from Baker or anybody else for that matter -- of a testing session which took place six and a half years earlier on October 9, 1963 at Goodyear's test track in San Angelo, TX. A.J. Foyt took his Sheraton-Thompson Indy Car to the giant five-mile facility and was timed at 200.4 mph by an electric eye timing devise. It broke the existing record of 186.329 mph held by Jim McElreath.

Foyt and chief mechanic George Bignotti snipped off part of the plexiglas windshield in order to reduce wind drag. "That made a difference," said Foyt. "In earlier runs that morning, we were running only 191-192 mph. We cut the windshield down and hit 200."

All of the Goodyear tests at Talladega in the early winter of 1970 seemed to indicate the tire problems had been licked. The turns had been repaved and every driver who tested had kind remarks about the new track. "I'm actually looking forward to running here in April," said Yarbrough.

The inaugural Alabama 500 was scheduled for Talladega on April 12. It also happened to be the first of the live presentations by ABC-Sports.

Written at the bottom of the NASCAR-ABC pact was a guard against another boycott. It said that if fewer than 10 of the preceding year's top 20 NASCAR drivers failed to compete, ABC's payment would be substantially reduced.

Although the Professional Drivers Association had assured everyone there would be no boycott of this event, France wasn't taking any chances. On Saturday, April 11, 1970, France booked a 50-lap, 133-mile "qualifying" race for ARCA cars. The event would determine starting positions for a 500-mile ARCA event slated for the 2.66-mile oval on June 14. Just in case the PDA had anything up their sleeve, France wanted some additional cars on site which he could substitute at the last moment if he had to.

A relatively small audience of 36,000 dotted the massive grandstands for the first Alabama 500. It was unclear how many of those exchanged the Talladega 500 ticket stubs from the year before and were admitted free. It was also unclear how much effect the live television coverage had on the trackside attendance.

ABC plugged into New York when the race was already half over. The highly competitive first half of the race was not aired. Few highlights were shown.

Goodyear introduced a new treadless tire, and there was a great deal of uncertainty and anxiety under the Goodyear tent. The lead changed hands five times in the first 10 laps. Buddy Baker averaged 195.030 mph through the opening 10 laps -- an all-time record.

Cale Yarborough, who started back in 21st after his Wood Brothers team lost three engines during qualifying, roared through the pack. He took the lead on lap

16. While leading, Cale was clocked at 199.060 mph in the 22nd lap. Before he had completed another lap, the right rear tire peeled off a strip of rubber down the middle of the tire. He pitted and got fresh rubber. Instructions from the Wood Brothers were to "slow down".

Charlie Glotzbach blew a tire -- but he said it was caused by running over a can thrown onto the track by a spectator. Bobby Allison said his front windshield had been broken by a foreign object that came from the grandstand. Yarborough nearly "had my head taken off" when a beer bottle exploded against his front windshield as he motored down the backstretch. "They ought to arrest that guy and give him a jail sentence to quit trying to kill people," Cale said angrily. "I'll tell you one thing, it wasn't a kid who did something like that. They've got more sense. It was some drunk."

In the late stages, Pete Hamilton, who was assigned to drive the back-up Petty Enterprises Plymouth Super-Bird, picked up the lead when Baker pitted. Baker got back onto the track and was closing in on Hamilton when his left front tire ripped apart with 13 laps left. Large chunks of rubber severed the oil cooler, spraying hot oil onto the engine. The car became engulfed in flames.

Baker spun the car in front of the main grandstand. The flames blew out during the long slide.

All of this was happening when ABC was in a commercial. A number of replays were shown when the network returned to the air.

Hamilton went on to win the Alabama 500 at an average speed of 152.321 mph. He had made 14 pit stops and used 28 tires.

A week later, the Gwyn Staley Memorial was televised live from North Wilkesboro Speedway. There was only one lead change during the entire 400 lapper, and it occurred long before the ABC cameras picked up the action. Richard Petty led every lap shown on TV, and most of the time, he was better than a lap up on the field.

The other three live televised races were the Rebel 400 at Darlington, Charlotte's World 600 and the Nashville 420. Richard Petty survived a nasty tumble at Darlington moments after ABC began it's live coverage. David Pearson went onto win by three laps.

Donnie Allison won the World 600 by two laps; and Bobby Isaac was two laps up on the field in the Nashville 420. All of the televised races events were runaways.

Meanwhile, attendance figures at the American Raceways tracks were reaching new lows. The Atlanta 500, rained out once again, drew only 22,000 on Easter Sunday. The two races at Riverside had drawn 43,200 and 18,500 respectively. The turnout for the June 14 event at Riverside was the most embarrassing figure in the track's history.

The Motor State 400 at Michigan attracted 47,600 -- a respectable figure. LoPatin had said earlier that the

Michigan event was a "make or break" race for his company.

On June 21, 1970, the Lone Star 400 scheduled for Texas International Speedway was cancelled. It was publicly announced that the reason it was taken off the schedule was because of the Goodyear tire strike. Goodyear had not had time to conduct tests.

The next American Raceways, Inc. event was August 2 at Atlanta. But there were rumblings going on at ARI, and there was no money. The board of directors at Atlanta and Riverside had been trying to get LoPatin removed.

The political maneuvers in the organization came to a head with the failure of American Raceways, Inc. to post the prize money for the August 2 Dixie 500, which ARI operated under a management contract that was tied to a loan agreement.

ARI had been unable to pay Investors Diversified Services a quarterly note of $100,000. LoPatin had wired Bill France with the message, "I might not be running things come Sunday (Aug. 2)." LoPatin had not posted ARI's $89,600 portion of the $103,000 purse. Four days before the Dixie 500 was scheduled to run, France removed it from the slate.

NASCAR guaranteed that a purse would be paid in full. If for any reason the track operators failed to post the prize money, NASCAR would then have to pay it.

Richard Howard, General Manager of Charlotte Motor Speedway, stepped in and posted the purse. "It would have been a black eye on the sport of NASCAR stock car racing to have this major event cancelled," said Howard. "It was in the best interests of the sport to have the money posted. So I did it."

The Dixie 500 went on schedule.

On Friday, July 31, Larry LoPatin resigned as President of American Raceways, Inc. Leslie Share, Executive Vice-President, LoPatin's closest aide, and Leo Margolian, Operating Manager, resigned under pressure.

"Michigan had been our money maker," said LoPatin. "Unfortunately, the weather has contributed to our losing money at other tracks. I feel that we built speedways which were real competition tracks and not just high speed ovals. I feel our pluses in auto racing were far over our negatives. I know my concept was right. The question is was my personality right for it."

Texas Real Estate developer Ben Parks was elected board chairman, and Les Richter president and chief operating manager.

As LoPatin fell from grace, Bernard Kahn, Sports Editor of the Daytona Beach News-Journal, offered another epitaph on LoPatin's tombstone: "His fall was long overdue. The Detroit promoter came in racing as a fast mouth looking for a fast buck."

During the summer months additional Goodyear tire tests were conducted at Alabama International Motor Speedway. The weather conditions at Talladega had been ideal in April during the Alabama 500. Yet there had been a few blow outs and several blistered tires during the race.

The second annual Talladega 500 was scheduled for August 23 -- in the height of the sweltering Alabama summer.

Ramo Stott won Talladega ARCA qualifying race before empty grandstands

Less than a month before the race, David Pearson and Charlie Glotzbach had tested Goodyear tires at Talladega. During one of the opening segments, Glotzbach's Dodge had worn out two right side tires in just nine laps. Pearson had even greater problems.

After just two and a half laps, both right side tires blew simultaneously as he sped into the third turn. The Ford lifted on two wheels and slid backwards into the wall. Miraculously, the car stayed upright and Pearson was not hurt. He was only going 192 mph at the time of the wreck. Speeds would be much greater in the qualifications and the race.

NASCAR issued a statement immediately after the tire test results. "Goodyear was using an experimental tire," they said. "Proven products aren't tested."

Bill France didn't believe there would be a problem. "If Goodyear has the same tires they had when Buddy Baker ran 200 mph, then there won't be any problems," said Big Bill.

Car owners Junior Johnson and Banjo Matthews said they were not going to enter the Talladega 500. "I have three cars in my shop," said Johnson. "If I went to Talladega, I'd probably need all three."

Neither Johnson nor Matthews entered their Fords. They had not entered the April 16 Alabama 500 either. Two of the most respected car builders had never run a lap in competition at Talladega.

Goodyear's Dick Ralstin acknowledged that there were problems. "The extra 10 mph (above speeds at Daytona) is the only factor we never have had before," he said. "It is critical. We are in a new era -- and it is experimental. This time we've got the heat to deal with."

After his wreck, Pearson delivered an outcry. "Something's got to be done before we race down there again," said the three-time Grand National champion. "The tire people have done a lot for racing and in time,

I'm sure they'll whip this problem, too. But until they do, something's got to be done.

"If there's not a suitable tire or something isn't done to cut the speeds, I'm going to ask John Holman (co-owner of his car) to withdraw our entry."

Goodyear came back for more tests a few weeks later. "There is a problem," admitted Ralstin. "If there wasn't, we wouldn't be going back to conduct further tests."

Glotzbach whipped his Dodge Daytona around the track at a speed of 198 mph on a relatively cool August afternoon. No problems were reported. The tests were jointly conducted by Goodyear and Dow Chemical Co. . Dow, Glotzbach's sponsor, was testing engine coolants and anti-freeze.

Bobby Isaac and Bobby Allison had also conducted tire tests. The two veteran drivers along with Pearson suggested some sort of carburetor restrictor plate. Mario Rossi, Allison's car owner, agreed. "Horsepower is directly associated with the size of the carburetor," said Rossi. We can figure out almost to the mile per hour how fast we'll run if they would make us use a smaller carburetor."

On Saturday August 8, NASCAR announced that beginning with the Yankee 400 at Michigan International Speedway (August 16), all Grand National cars would be required to use a plate between the carburetor and intake manifold with a maximum 1 1/4-inch venturi opening.

Prior to these changes, the venturi opening on the single four barrel carburetor allowed a maximum 1 11/16-inches.

NASCAR's Lin Kuchler and Bill Gazaway conferred with drivers, mechanics and manufacturer representatives for two weeks before announcing the changes.

"Drivers and car owners have told us that they have been on the ragged edge at most of the races this year and have had trouble keeping their equipment together," said Kuchler. "These changes should provide closer competition."

Cotton Owens, owner of the Dodge driven by Buddy Baker, spoke favorably about the new rules. "The change is the best thing that has happened to racing in a long time. Those guys have been over the ragged edge. This new ruling will give them a margin of safety."

Top speeds at Michigan during the Yankee 400 were in the 157 mph range -- a drop of over 5 mph from the highest speeds recorded in the Motor State 400 two months earlier. Only five cars suffered engine failure -- one-third the number in the June race.

Speeds dropped even more at Talladega. Bobby Isaac had established the all-time NASCAR qualifying record of 199.658 mph for the April 12 Alabama 500. Isaac was again on the pole for the Talladega 500, but his speed was 186.834 mph -- a drop of 13 mph. There were two fewer engine failures in the August event.

The Professional Drivers Association released a written statement that it supported NASCAR's latest rules. Back in May, the PDA hired L&M Enterprises -- a corporation formed by Carolina sports writer Leonard Laye and pro basketball star Larry Miller -- to handle the managerial duties. "We don't have the time and facilities needed," said Petty. "We are at an important stage in the progress of the PDA. We haven't had regular meetings and haven't kept things up."

Laye remarked, "The first thing we want is recognition. The first objective is to get through to Bill France -- but it's a long range objective."

It was in 1970 that the Automobile Research Corp. first came on the scene. Newspaper publisher Hank Schoolfield said, "It has a lot to do with racing and not so much to do with research."

By any name, the company was NASCAR President France's answer to the political threat of another driver boycott -- an arrangement to chop off some of the potential boycotting powers.

The Automobile Research Corp. set up a plan to pay each of the "top Grand National drivers", numbering from 20-25, $500 each to drive in selected superspeedway events. The contract stipulated that the cars must compete in at least half of each race unless a *serious* mechanical problem takes them out. The five tracks covered under the contract were Darlington, Talladega, Charlotte, Rockingham and Daytona. Twenty-two drivers signed up and guaranteed their participation in each of those 10 superspeedway events.

"I don't think this is intended to help the PDA," said Petty.

There was not much noise heard from the PDA the rest of the year.

On December 28, 1970, L. Mendel Rivers, NASCAR's National Commissioner, passed away in Birmingham, AL. He was 65.

Rivers, a veteran United States Congressman, was chairman of the House Committee on Armed Services. Rivers accepted the post as NASCAR Commissioner on July 15, 1969, and was the third man to serve in that capacity. He followed Harley Earl, a retired General Motors vice president, and Cannonball Baker, a legendary racing figure.

Near the end of the year, Chrysler announced that it was cutting back its racing effort. For 1971, they would only sponsor Petty Enterprises. Richard Petty would race a factory Plymouth and Buddy Baker would move from Cotton Owens' outfit to a Petty Dodge.

Left out of the picture was the K&K Insurance team and driver Bobby Isaac, who won the 1970 Grand National championship. Also cut off was Bobby Allison, who finished second in the point race.

Pete Hamilton, who won three superspeedway races for Petty Enterprises in 1970, got the ax. "We would like to keep Pete," said Petty. "But the word came from Chrysler.

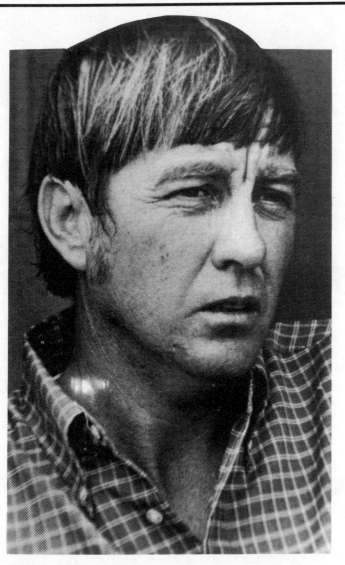

Bobby Isaac won the Grand National Championship, set a world closed course record of 201.104 mph, then lost his factory sponsorship

"Part of the bargain was that all of Chrysler's racing equipment would be moved from Nichels Engineering in Highland, IN to the Petty establishment in Level Cross, NC.

The announcement by Chrysler didn't set too well with Nord Krauskopf, owner of the K&K Insurance Co.

He sent his team, headed by Harry Hyde and Isaac, to Talladega on November 24. Order of the day was to top the all-time closed course record of 200.447 mph which Baker set in March.

Temperatures were in the 'teens the night before. Winds were howling up to 18 mph, and the mercury never got above 36 degrees. Nevertheless, Isaac took his Dodge Daytona onto the high banks, chasing after the elusive world record.

Isaac wheeled his high-winged Dodge Daytona 24 times around the Alabama International Speedway. In the 22nd lap, he clocked in at 201.104 mph. Four of his laps were faster than Baker's former record.

"Under the existing weather conditions," said Isaac, "I think it was about as fast as any human could drive a machine. Setting this record is the pinnacle of my career."

Hyde, who said team owner Krauskopf wanted the record because Chrysler had selected Baker to drive the only factory backed Dodge in 1971, "and he wanted to let someone know who the best Dodge team was this year. You've got to give credit to Isaac," added Hyde. "That little guy braved it pretty good out there today."

Race No. 1

A.J. Ends Skid; Wins Motor Trend 500 at Riverside

RIVERSIDE, CA (Jan. 18) -- A.J. Foyt ended a seven year famine on the twisting Riverside International Raceway by winning the Motor Trend 500. The 35 year-old veteran out of Houston, TX drove his Ford around Parnelli Jones 25 laps from the finish and won by 3.5-seconds. Roger McCluskey, driving a new Plymouth SuperBird, came in second. Third place went to LeeRoy Yarbrough with Donnie Allison fourth and Richard Petty fifth.

Dan Gurney, five-time winner of this annual event, started on the pole in the second Petty Enterprises entry. The popular Costa Mesa, CA driver never led, but managed to finish sixth.

Two spectacular accidents injured two drivers, both of them seriously. Buddy Young of Fairfax, VA, making his first start for the L.G. DeWitt team, tumbled

Buddy Young's Ford lies in a smoking heap after severe Riverside crash

end-over-end just past the start-finish line. Dick Brooks had blown an engine, laying a thick coat of oil on the track which Young couldn't avoid. The 27 year-old sophomore driver suffered a concussion and internal injuries in the mishap.

Jim Cook, 48 year-old driver out of Norwalk, CA, was critically injured when his Ford hit a concrete wall head on after he tried to avoid a pile-up. Cook's Ford was bent double and the transmission was thrown out. He was airlifted to Riverside Community Hospital with multiple head injuries and fractures of both arms and legs.

Parnelli Jones had earned the pole with a 113.310 mph qualifying lap, but was forced to start at the rear over a tire squabble. Jones, a Firestone dealer, had made his record run on limited edition tires, which

Grand National Race No. 1
193 Laps at Riverside Int'l Raceway
Riverside, CA
"Motor Trend 500"
500 Miles on 2.62-mile Paved Road Course
January 18, 1970

Fin	St	No.	Driver	Team / Car	Laps	Money	Status
1	3	11	A J Foyt	Jack Bowsher '70 Ford	193	$19,700	Running
2	13	1	Roger McCluskey	Norm Nelson '70 Plym S'Bird	193	9,000	Running
3	5	98	LeeRoy Yarbrough	Junior Johnson '70 Ford	193	6,275	Running
4	8	27	Donnie Allison	Banjo Matthews '70 Ford	190	4,475	Running
5	6	43	Richard Petty	Petty Ent '70 Plym SuperBird	186	3,000	Engine
6	1	42	Dan Gurney	Petty Ent '70 Plym SuperBird	180	2,400	Running
7	18	06	Neil Castles	Castles '69 Dodge Daytona	178	1,750	Running
8	17	39	Friday Hassler	James Hanley '69 Chevrolet	176	1,550	Running
9	22	116	Jerry Oliver	Cos Cancilla '70 Olds	176	1,400	Running
10	25	83	Dick Gulstrand	James Good '69 Chevrolet	170	1,350	Running
11	35	21	Parnelli Jones	Wood Brothers '70 Mercury	168	1,275	Clutch
12	34	321	Kevin Terris	Terris '69 Plymouth	165	1,250	Running
13	4	22	Bobby Allison	Mario Rossi '69 Dodge Daytona	164	1,225	Bell hous
14	20	30	Dave Marcis	Marcis '69 Dodge Daytona	163	1,200	Crash
15	43	09	Sam Rose	Rose '68 Ford	157	1,175	Running
16	21	81	Dave Alonzo	'68 Plymouth	150	1,150	Running
17	2	17	David Pearson	Holman-Moody '70 Ford	148	1,925	Trans
18	28	4	Dick Kranzler	Kranzler '68 Chevrolet	148	1,100	Running
19	42	15	Paul Dorrity	'68 Chevrolet	143	1,075	Engine
20	11	132	Joe Frasson	Mario Frasson '70 Dodge	142	1,050	Running
21	40	00	Frank James	Jim Calder '69 Chevrolet	137	1,025	Rear End
22	39	61	Dick Bown	Mike Ober '69 Chevrolet	135	1,025	Running
23	29	179	Randy Dodd	'69 Chevrolet	111	1,000	Clutch
24	36	96	Ray Elder	Fred Elder '69 Dodge Daytona	106	975	Engine
25	19	38	Jimmy Insolo	Marvin Rowley '68 Chevrolet	98	950	Engine
26	32	18	Jim Cook	'68 Ford	94	925	Crash
27	41	16	Steve Froines	'68 Olds	83	900	Crash
28	9	6	Sam Posey	Cotton Owens '69 Dodge	82	900	Engine
29	7	71	Bobby Isaac	K&K Ins '69 Dodge Daytona	77	885	Engine
30	37	7	Jack McCoy	Ernie Conn '69 Dodge	69	850	Oil Leak
31	33	23	G T Tallas	Tallas '69 Ford	49	840	Engine
32	44	40	Les Loeser	Loeser '68 Ford	38	830	Clutch
33	15	32	Dick Brooks	Brooks '69 Plymouth	37	895	Engine
34	12	31	Buddy Young	L G DeWitt '69 Ford	37	810	Crash
35	10	48	James Hylton	Hylton Eng '69 Dodge Daytona	34	820	Engine
36	24	64	Elmo Langley	Langley '68 Ford	29	800	Engine
37	26	126	Carl Joiner	Dean Thorne '69 Ford	23	800	Rear End
38	16	88	Don Noel	Noel-Lewis'68 Ford	18	800	Engine
39	14	93	Don White	Nichels Eng '69 Dodge Day	16	880	Brakes
40	31	144	Lothar Motschenbacher	'68 Chevrolet	7	800	Clutch
41	23	05	Frank Dieny	'68 Chevrolet	4	800	W bearing
42	38	45	Scotty Cain	Bill Clinton '69 Ford	3	800	Trans
43	27	80	Bob England	England '69 Chevrolet	3	800	Trans
44	30	79	Frank Warren	Warren '69 Plymouth	1	800	Engine

Time of Race: 5 hours, 11 minutes, 19 seconds
Average Speed: 97.450 mph
Pole Winner: Dan Gurney - 112.060 mph
Fastest Qualifier: Parnelli Jones - 113.310 mph
Lap Leaders: David Pearson 1-25, A J Foyt 26, Richard Petty 27-28, Pearson 29-34, LeeRoy Yarbrough 35, Foyt 36-42, Parnelli Jones 44, Donnie Allison 45-64, Foyt 65-66, Jones 67-84, D Allison 85-86, Pearson 87-94, Yarbrough 95, Roger McCluskey 96-97, Yarbrough 98, Jones 99-109, Yarbrough 110, Jones 111-168, Foyt 169-193.
Cautions: 6 for 31 laps   Margin of Victory: 3.5 seconds   Attendance: 43,200

NASCAR said were ineligible for competition. They were not available in sufficient quantity to meet NASCAR rules, the sanctioning body said.

Jones, behind the wheel of the Wood Brothers Mercury, came from 35th starting spot to lead by the 43rd lap. He had grabbed the upper hand and was pulling away when clutch failure put him out on lap 168. Foyt took the lead at that point and led the rest of the way.

A crowd of 43,200 watched Foyt win his third career

Richard Petty gets service in MotorTrend 500

Grand National race -- and his first since 1965 -- at an average speed of 97.450 mph.

Race No. 2

Cale Sets World Record of 183.295 mph in Daytona 125

DAYTONA BEACH, FL (Feb. 19) -- Cale Yarborough, who was expected to be on the sidelines for six to ninth months after a bad crack-up at Texas in December, roared back into action with a stunning victory in the 125-mile qualifying race at Daytona International Speedway.

The 30 year-old Timmonsville, SC veteran pushed his Wood Brothers Mercury past Pete Hamilton in the

Cale Yarborough leads Bobby Isaac in 125 mile qualifier

Grand National Race No. 2
50 Laps at Daytona Int'l Speedway
Daytona Beach, FL
125 Miles on 2.5-mile Paved Track
February 19, 1970

Fin	St	No.	Driver	Team / Car	Laps	Money	Status
1	1	21	Cale Yarborough	Wood Brothers '69 Mercury	50	$1,300	Running
2	5	71	Bobby Isaac	K&K Ins '69 Dodge Daytona	50	800	Running
3	4	98	LeeRoy Yarbrough	Junior Johnson '69 Ford	50	550	Running
4	3	27	Donnie Allison	Banjo Matthews '69 Ford	50	500	Running
5	6	40	Pete Hamilton	Petty Ent '70 Plym SuperBird	50	450	Running
6	7	43	Richard Petty	Petty Ent '70 Plym SuperBird	50	400	Running
7	18	32	Dick Brooks	Brooks '70 Plym SuperBird	48	345	Running
8	20	7	Ramo Stott	Stott '70 Plym SuperBird	48	335	Running
9	8	3	Jim Vandiver	Ray Fox '69 Dodge	48	325	Running
10	10	25	Jabe Thomas	Don Robertson '69 Plymouth	46	310	Running
11	22	23	James Hylton	Don Robertson '69 Plymouth	46	300	Running
12	27	37	Dr Don Tarr	Tarr '69 Dodge Daytona	46	290	Running
13	9	64	Elmo Langley	Langley '69 Mercury	45	280	Running
14	14	86	John Sears	Dennis Gallion '69 Dodge	44	270	Running
15	11	03	Tommy Gale	Walt Valerie '69 Ford	43	260	Running
16	12	10	Bill Champion	Champion '68 Ford	43	255	Running
17	19	20	Joe Hines, Jr	Hines '69 Dodge	43	245	Running
18	21	06	Neil Castles	Castles '69 Dodge Daytona	43	235	Running
19	28	33	Wayne Smith	Smith '69 Chevrolet	41	225	Running
20	25	69	Bill Kimmel	Kimmel '69 Chevrolet	41	220	Running
21	13	47	Raymond Williams	Bill Seifert '68 Ford	41	215	Running
22	29	51	Dub Simpson	Bill Strong '69 Chevrolet	39	210	Running
23	2	17	David Pearson	Holman-Moody '69 Ford	38	405	Steering
24	24	07	Coo Coo Marlin	Cunningham-Kelley '69 Chev	38	200	Running
25	16	62	Ron Keselowski	Kaye Eng '69 Dodge	35	---	Axle
26	23	95	Leonard Blanchard	'70 Ford	35	---	Running
27	17	76	Ben Arnold	Arnold '69 Ford	23	---	Engine
28	30	9	Roy Tyner	Tyner '69 Pontiac	18	---	Engine
29	15	74	Bill Shirey	Shirey '69 Plymouth	14	---	Engine
30	26	01	Arnold Bennett	Tire City '68 Ford	1	---	D Shaft

Time of Race: 40 minutes, 48 seconds
Average Speed: 183.295 mph
Pole Winner: Cale Yarborough - 194.015 mph
Lap Leaders: Cale Yarborough 1-10, Bobby Isaac 11-31, David Pearson 32-34, Pete Hamilton 35-36, Yarborough 37-50.
Cautions: None   Margin of Victory: 5.5 seconds   Attendance: 18,700.

37th lap and led the rest of the way.

Yarborough completed the 125 miles in just over 40 minutes and established an all-time race record of 183.295 mph. He had won the pole with another record performance -- 194.015 mph.

Bobby Isaac finished in second place. He made one pit stop -- a 20.4 second stay while his K&K Insurance team changed right side tires. Yarborough had pitted with Isaac, but took only 15 seconds. When the two leaders returned to the track, the separation was about five seconds. Isaac was unable to close on Yarborough and wound up 5.5 seconds behind at the checkered flag.

Third place went to LeeRoy Yarbrough with Donnie Allison fourth and Hamilton fifth.

"I think my car and Bobby's were about equal," said Yarborough. "The difference was the pit stop. We didn't change any tires and got out quicker. We had checked tire wear and knew we could run 50 laps on one set. In fact, I still have rubber left on my tires right now."

David Pearson, who started second, ran with the leaders and led for three laps. Four laps after making his only pit stop, he pulled behind the wall with steering problems.

The 125-miler was run without a caution flag. A crowd of 18,700 was on hand.

Grand National Race No. 3
50 Laps at Daytona Int'l Speedway
Daytona Beach, FL
125 Miles on 2.5-mile Paved Track
February 19, 1970

Fin	St	No.	Driver	Team / Car	Laps	Money	Status
1	2	99	Charlie Glotzbach	N'chls-G'smith '69 Dodge Day	50	$1,300	Running
2	1	6	Buddy Baker	Cotton Owens '69 Dodge Day	50	800	Running
3	4	22	Bobby Allison	Mario Rossi '69 Dodge Day	50	550	Running
4	5	55	Tiny Lund	John McConnell '69 Dodge Day	49	500	Running
5	15	14	Richard Brickhouse	Bill Ellis '70 Plym SuperBird	49	450	Running
6	6	96	Ray Elder	Fred Elder '69 Dodge Daytona	49	400	Running
7	20	88	Benny Parsons	Parsons '69 Ford	48	345	Running
8	18	39	Friday Hassler	James Hanley '69 Chevrolet	47	335	Running
9	21	05	Ron Grana	C J Grana '69 Ford	47	325	Running
10	23	93	Paul Feldner	'69 Dodge	47	310	Running
11	24	46	Roy Mayne	Tom Hunter '69 Chevrolet	47	300	Running
12	10	79	Frank Warren	Warren '69 Plymouth	47	290	Running
13	14	82	Joe Frasson	Mario Frasson '70 Dodge	47	280	Running
14	3	11	A J Foyt	Jack Bowsher '69 Ford	47	270	Running
15	13	24	Cecil Gordon	Gordon '68 Ford	46	260	Running
16	28	15	Dr Ed Hessert	Hessert '69 Dodge	45	255	Running
17	22	09	Dick Trickle	Fran Kelly '69 Ford	45	245	Running
18	19	08	E J Trivette	E C Reid '69 Chevrolet	45	235	Running
19	27	67	Dick May	Joyce Ronacher '69 Ford	45	225	Running
20	29	44	Bob Ashbrook	Giachetti Bros '70 Chevrolet	44	220	Running
21	16	89	Butch Hirst	Morris Davis '69 Ford	43	215	Running
22	26	63	Jimmy Crawford	Crawford Ent '70 Chevrolet	41	210	Running
23	7	30	Dave Marcis	Marcis '69 Dodge Daytona	22	205	Wtr pump
24	31	00	Harry Shipe	Joe Savoca 69 Ford	21	200	Clutch
25	12	5	Buddy Arrington	Arrington '69 Dodge Daytona	20	---	Heating
26	30	57	Johnny Halford	Ervin Pruitt '69 Dodge	20	---	Crash
27	9	45	Bill Seifert	Seifert '69 Ford	19	---	Crash
28	11	78	Talmadge Prince	Hodges-Prince '69 Dodge Day	18	---	Crash
29	8	59	Jim Hurtubise	Tom Pistone '70 Ford	14	---	Rear End
30	25	26	Earl Brooks	Brooks '69 Ford	11	---	Engine
31	17	70	J D McDuffie	McDuffie '69 Buick	4	---	Steering

Time of Race: 50 minutes, 46 seconds.
Average Speed: 147.734 mph
Pole Winner: Buddy Baker - 192.624 mph
Lap Leaders: Buddy Baker 1, Charlie Glotzbach 2-23, Bobby Allison 24, Baker 25-36, Glotzbach 37-50.
Cautions: 1 for 13 laps   Margin of Victory: 4.7 seconds   Attendance: 18,700

Race No. 3

Glotzbach Wins Qualifier; Talmadge Prince Killed

DAYTONA BEACH, FL (Feb. 19) -- Charlie Glotzbach made a triumphant return to racing and won the death-marred second 125-mile qualifying race at Daytona International Speedway.

It was the first start for the 31 year-old Georgetown, IN Dodge driver since being shot Nov. 30 by a disgruntled employee at his place of business.

Rookie Talmadge Prince of Dublin, GA, driving in his first Grand National race, was killed instantly in the 19th lap. Prince, who purchased James Hylton's Dodge Daytona a few weeks before Speedweeks, blew the engine in the first turn. The car slid sideways into the high speed groove where it was hit broadside by Bill Seifert. Johnny Halford grazed Prince's car, but he was unhurt.

Talmadge Prince #78 is passed by Charlie Glotzbach in Daytona 125. Glotzbach won the run, Prince was killed

Track physician A.A. Monaco said Prince died of a broken neck. He was dead when removed from the car. Seifert suffered cardiac contusions and a concussion.

Glotzbach swept past Buddy Baker with 14 laps to go and sprinted to a 4.7-second victory. "I just followed Buddy for awhile," said Glotzbach, who won for just the second time on the Grand National tour. "I noticed he was holding me up, so I went on by him."

Bobby Allison finished in third place and Tiny Lund was fourth. Fifth place went to Richard Brickhouse. West coaster Ray Elder was sixth, giving the winged Chrysler products a 1-2-3-4-5-6 sweep.

Glotzbach averaged 147.734 mph as 13 laps were run under the caution for the Prince incident.

Race No. 4

Hamilton Outruns Ol' Pro Pearson in Daytona 500

DAYTONA BEACH, FL (Feb.22) -- Newcomer Pete Hamilton of Dedham, MA outran veteran David Pearson in the final laps and won the Daytona 500, producing the biggest surprise in the 12 year history of this event.

Hamilton, recently assigned to drive a Petty Enterprises Plymouth SuperBird in major races on the 1970 Grand National schedule, sneaked past his favored rival with nine laps to go and beat Pearson by three car lengths to cash in on the $44,850 prize. Bobby Allison came in third with Charlie Glotzbach fourth and Bobby Isaac fifth.

The decisive strategy came on lap 187 after Dick Brooks blew an engine,

David Pearson #17 loses traction in 4th turn. The slip allowed Pete Hamilton #40 to win the Daytona 500

bringing out the yellow flag. Hamilton, who had led four laps earlier but had never showed an abundance of muscle, pitted and got four fresh tires from his Maurice Petty-led crew. Pearson, who had led all but one of the previous 44 laps, came in the pits and got two right side tires.

When the green flag came out, Hamilton motored into the lead with Pearson in hot pursuit. Pearson mounted

a final stab at Hamilton with two laps to go. Pearson's Ford wobbled in the fourth turn as Hamilton scampered to daylight.

"I was aware of the slingshot here," said Hamilton. "But I felt I could stay in front of David if I could get ahead of him. I thought my car was stronger than his after I took on fresh tires. We both got crossed up when he tried to slingshot me. Both of our cars were

Pete Hamilton drove the Petty Enterprises Plymouth SuperBird to an upset victory in Daytona 500

Grand National Race No. 4
200 Laps at Daytona Int'l Speedway
Daytona Beach, FL
"Daytona 500"
500 Miles on 2.5-mile Paved Track
February 22, 1970

Fin	St	No.	Driver	Team / Car	Laps	Money	Status
1	9	40	Pete Hamilton	Petty Ent '70 Plym SuperBird	200	$44,850	Running
2	31	17	David Pearson	Holman-Moody '69 Ford	200	17,650	Running
3	6	22	Bobby Allison	Mario Rossi '69 Dodge Day	199	9,950	Running
4	4	99	Charlie Glotzbach	Nchls-G'smith '69 Dodge Day	199	5,850	Running
5	3	71	Bobby Isaac	K&K Ins '69 Dodge Daytona	198	4,450	Running
6	10	14	Richard Brickhouse	Bill Ellis '70 Plym SuperBird	198	3,175	Running
7	34	59	Jim Hurtubise	Tom Pistone '70 Ford	197	2,575	Running
8	15	7	Ramo Stott	Stott '70 Plym SuperBird	194	2,525	Running
9	5	98	LeeRoy Yarbrough	Junior Johnson '69 Ford	193	2,175	Running
10	33	30	Dave Marcis	Marcis '69 Dodge Daytona	193	2,025	Running
11	12	96	Ray Elder	Fred Elder '69 Dodge Daytona	189	1,925	Running
12	35	06	Neil Castles	Castles '69 Dodge Daytona	188	1,825	Running
13	8	55	Tiny Lund	John McConnell '69 Dodge Day	187	1,860	Engine
14	14	88	Benny Parsons	Parsons '69 Ford	187	1,725	Running
15	16	39	Friday Hassler	James Hanley '69 Chevrolet	187	1,675	Running
16	22	46	Roy Mayne	Tom Hunter '69 Chevrolet	184	1,650	Running
17	27	86	John Sears	Dennis Gallion '69 Dodge	184	1,620	Running
18	40	07	Coo Coo Marlin	Cunningham-Kelley '69 Chev	182	1,610	Running
19	13	32	Dick Brooks	Brooks '70 Plym SuperBird	181	1,700	Engine
20	24	79	Frank Warren	Warren '69 Plymouth	181	1,590	Running
21	26	82	Joe Frasson	Mario Frasson '70 Dodge	175	1,675	Running
22	21	23	James Hylton	Don Robertson '69 Plymouth	174	1,190	Running
23	39	89	Butch Hirst	Morris Davis '69 Ford	172	1,185	Running
24	20	93	Paul Feldner	'69 Dodge	167	1,180	Running
25	19	25	Jabe Thomas	Don Robertson '69 Plymouth	140	1,175	Running
26	36	09	Dick Trickle	Fran Kelly '69 Ford	131	1,170	H Gasket
27	2	6	Buddy Baker	Cotton Owens '69 Dodge Day	122	2,265	Ignition
28	25	64	Elmo Langley	Langley '69 Mercury	109	1,160	Ignition
29	32	5	Buddy Arrington	Arrington '69 Dodge Daytona	77	1,255	Crash
30	18	05	Ron Grana	C J Grana '69 Ford	72	1,150	Engine
31	29	03	Tommy Gale	Walt Valerio '69 Mercury	70	1,115	Engine
32	28	11	A J Foyt	Jack Bowsher '69 Ford	58	1,240	Engine
33	37	95	Leonard Blanchard	'70 Ford	57	1,135	Heating
34	38	62	Ron Keselowski	Kaye Eng '69 Dodge	46	1,230	Valve
35	7	27	Donnie Allison	Banjo Matthews '69 Ford	41	1,225	Engine
36	23	37	Dr Don Tarr	Tarr '69 Dodge Daytona	41	1,120	Steering
37	1	21	Cale Yarborough	Wood Brothers '69 Mercury	31	7,465	Engine
38	17	3	Jim Vandiver	Ray Fox '69 Dodge	15	1,110	Clutch
39	11	43	Richard Petty	Petty Ent '70 Plym SuperBird	7	1,105	Engine
40	30	24	Cecil Gordon	Gordon '68 Ford	7	1,100	A Frame

Time of Race: 3 hours, 20 minutes, 32 seconds
Average Speed: 149.601 mph
Pole Winner: Cale Yarborough - 194.015 mph
Lap Leaders: Cale Yarborough 1-11, Charlie Glotzbach 12, Bobby Allison 13,
    Tiny Lund 14-16, Yarborough 17-31, LeeRoy Yarbrough 32, Buddy Baker 33,
    Ramo Stott 34-35, Bobby Isaac 36-38, Glotzbach 39-44, Isaac 45-60, Glotzbach 61-62,
    Pete Hamilton 63-65, Isaac 66-67, David Pearson 68-69, Isaac 70-78, Pearson 79-90,
    Glotzbach 91-117, Pearson 118-138, Hamilton 139, B.Allison 140-143,
    Pearson 144-174, B.Allison 175, Pearson 176-191, Hamilton 192-200.
Cautions: 6 for 45 laps   Margin of Victory: 3 car lengths   Attendance: 103,800

*Dick Brooks blew his engine late in the Daytona 500,
setting up Hamilton-Pearson duel*

Cut tires and unscheduled pit stops took Glotzbach, Isaac, Bobby Allison and LeeRoy Yarbrough out of the lead lap.

"I'm a young driver with a lot to learn," confessed Hamilton. "Winning one race doesn't prove you know it all."

Buddy Arrington suffered rib injuries when his Dodge Daytona slapped the backstretch wall on lap 89.

Buddy Baker's Dodge was equipped with a two-way radio hook-up with car owner Cotton Owens. Ignition failure knocked the Charlotte driver out after 122 laps.

Hamilton averaged 149.601 mph -- the exact speed that Marvin Panch won the 1961 Daytona 500. A record crowd of 103,800 watched Hamilton win his first Grand National race in his 20th start. He had been 1968 Rookie of the Year, but fell off the tour in 1969 when his car owner A.J.King got out of racing.

Race No. 5

Hylton Captures Richmond 500 in First Start For Ford

RICHMOND, VA (Mar.1) -- Perennial runner-up James Hylton overcame a six lap deficit and won the Richmond 500 at Richmond Fairgrounds Raceway. It was the first career win for the 34 year-old Inman, SC driver. He was making his first start in a Ford since switching from Dodge.

Richard Petty, who won the pole and led the first 303 laps, wound up second after losing nine laps to Hylton while his pit crew struggled with battery and distributor

out of shape."

Pearson swallowed a bitter pill with second place. "I just went sideways and couldn't get it back," he said of the challenge two laps from the end. "Those tires were hot and slick. We probably should have changed all four tires on that last stop."

Wrecks and mechanical failures eliminated most of the favorites. Richard Petty left the race early when his engine blew. Pole sitter Cale Yarborough popped his engine on the front chute on lap 31. Donnie Allison and A.J. Foyt fell by the wayside with engine problems.

James Hylton works on his Ford before Richmond 500

problems. Petty's Plymouth was easily the class of the field and made up three laps on Hylton. The final margin of victory was 15.1 seconds

Elmo Langley finished third, nine laps back. Bobby Isaac lost 16 laps in the pits and came home fourth. Fifth place went to Neil Castles.

Petty had lapped second place Isaac on lap 113. He was three laps up on Hylton and the rest of the independents. Eight laps before the half-way point, Petty was two laps ahead of Isaac and six laps up on everyone else.

Petty pitted on lap 303 and lost nine laps on two pit stops. Isaac took first place until his 16 second pit stop on lap 340. Hylton grabbed the lead when Isaac pitted and held off Petty's late charge. Petty got back in the lead lap with 13 laps to go.

"I've waited a long time for this," said the 1966 Rookie of the Year. "When I got into the Grand Nationals, I gave myself five years to win a race. This is my fifth year and it was worth the wait. It feels great to know you can win one."

Hylton's first big NASCAR win came in his 187th start. He had finished second 12 times before he cracked victory circle.

There were no factory backed Fords in the field. Ford Motor Co. had announced that after Daytona, factory teams would feel the pinch of a shift in policy in Dearborn.

Hylton averaged 82.044 mph as only one caution for seven laps slowed the action.

Race No. 6

Richard Spins, Wins and Grins at Rockingham

ROCKINGHAM, NC (Mar. 8) -- Richard Petty survived nine spin-outs and wrecks -- including two of his own -- and won the Carolina 500 at North Carolina Motor Speedway. It was the first win of the season for the 32 year-old driver, who returned to Plymouth after a one year stint with Ford.

Grand National Race No. 5
500 Laps at Richmond Fairgrounds Raceway
Richmond, VA
"Richmond 500"
271 Miles on .542-mile Paved Track
March 1, 1970

Fin	St	No.	Driver	Team / Car	Laps	Money	Status
1	3	48	James Hylton	Hylton Eng '69 Ford	500	$5,195	Running
2	1	43	Richard Petty	Petty Ent '70 Plymouth	500	2,970	Running
3	8	64	Elmo Langley	Langley '69 Ford	491	1,845	Running
4	2	71	Bobby Isaac	K&K Insurance '69 Dodge	485	1,220	Running
5	5	06	Neil Castles	Castles '69 Dodge	482	945	Running
6	15	51	Dub Simpson	Bill Strong '69 Chevrolet	470	670	Running
7	7	25	Jabe Thomas	Don Robertson '69 Plymouth	465	620	Running
8	10	9	Roy Tyner	Tyner '70 Pontiac	449	595	Running
9	19	74	Bill Shirey	Shirey '69 Plymouth	442	575	Running
10	12	34	Wendell Scott	Scott '69 Ford	438	565	Running
11	25	70	J D McDuffie	McDuffie '69 Buick	434	530	Running
12	9	76	Ben Arnold	Arnold '69 Ford	407	545	Running
13	4	30	Dave Marcis	Marcis '69 Dodge	299	560	Engine
14	6	54	Bill Dennis	Dennis '69 Chevrolet	263	525	Engine
15	26	72	Benny Parsons	L G DeWitt '69 Ford	260	490	D Shaft
16	20	77	John Kenney	Bob Freeman '68 Ford	232	505	Brakes
17	13	84	John Sears	Elmo Langley '68 Ford	228	495	Engine
18	17	10	Bill Champion	Champion '69 Ford	187	485	Heating
19	11	24	Cecil Gordon	Gordon '68 Ford	153	475	Trans
20	21	19	Henley Gray	Gray '69 Ford	115	440	Brakes
21	18	79	Frank Warren	Warren '69 Plymouth	100	455	Axle
22	16	33	Wayne Smith	Smith '69 Chevrolet	69	445	Engine
23	23	47	Bill Seifert	Seifert '69 Ford	50	410	Clutch
24	22	04	Ken Meisenhelder	Meisenhelder '69 Chevrolet	11	400	Suspen
25	24	67	Dick May	Joyce Ronacher '69 Ford	9	390	Oil Leak
26	14	57	Johnny Halford	Ervin Pruitt '69 Dodge	8	410	Oil Leak

Time of Race: 3 hours, 18 minutes, 11 seconds
Average Speed: 82.044 mph
Pole Winner: Richard Petty - 89.137 mph
Lap Leaders: Richard Petty 1-303, Bobby Isaac 304-340, James Hylton 341-500.
Cautions: 1 for 7 laps   Margin of Victory: 15.1 seconds   Attendance: 13,850

Petty put his wing-tailed SuperBird into the lead on lap 356 and led the rest of the way. Cale Yarborough wound up second in the Wood Brothers Mercury, three laps behind. Dick Brooks came in third with relief help from Neil Castles. Fourth place went to Bobby Allison with Pete Hamilton fifth.

The critical event of the day came on lap 409 of the

Richard Petty spun but won the Carolina 500

Richard Petty spins down pit road at Rockingham after clipping Cale Yarborough

Grand National Race No. 6
492 Laps at North Carolina Motor Speedway
Rockingham, NC
"Carolina 500"
500 Miles on 1.017-mile Paved Track
March 8, 1970

Fin	St	No.	Driver	Team / Car	Laps	Money	Status
1	8	43	Richard Petty	Petty Ent '70 Plym S'Bird	492	$16,715	Running
2	6	21	Cale Yarborough	Wood Brothers '70 Mercury	489	9,890	Running
3	5	32	Dick Brooks*	Brooks '70 Plym SuperBird	484	5,265	Running
4	1	22	Bobby Allison	Mario Rossi '69 Dodge Day	483	3,315	Running
5	7	40	Pete Hamilton	Petty Ent '70 Plym S'Bird	475	2,090	Running
6	12	30	Dave Marcis	Marcis '69 Dodge Daytona	470	1,565	Running
7	32	46	Roy Mayne	Tom Hunter '69 Chevrolet	460	1,465	Running
8	14	34	Wendell Scott	Scott '69 Ford	456	1,315	Running
9	15	64	Elmo Langley	Langley '69 Ford	454	1,215	Running
10	23	4	James Sears	L G DeWitt '69 Ford	448	1,390	Running
11	25	25	Jabe Thomas	Don Robertson '69 Plymouth	447	1,140	Running
12	18	24	Cecil Gordon	Gordon '68 Ford	438	1,115	Running
13	19	70	J D McDuffie	McDuffie '69 Buick	427	1,090	Running
14	3	71	Bobby Isaac	K&K Ins '69 Dodge Daytona	423	1,090	Running
15	35	76	Ben Arnold	Arnold '69 Ford	421	1,050	Running
16	34	65	Joe Phipps	Phipps '69 Chevrolet	401	1,035	Running
17	2	99	Charlie Glotzbach	Nchls-G'smith '69 Dodge Day	366	1,095	Ignition
18	24	48	James Hylton	Hylton Eng '69 Ford	345	1,005	Clutch
19	40	26	Earl Brooks	Brooks '69 Ford	345	990	Running
20	17	47	Raymond Williams	Bill Seifert '68 Ford	343	975	Running
21	9	72	Benny Parsons	L G DeWitt '69 Ford	330	960	Lug Bolt
22	22	37	Dr Don Tarr	Tarr '69 Dodge Daytona	298	995	Oil Leak
23	29	19	Henley Gray	Gray '69 Ford	257	930	Engine
24	28	57	Johnny Halford	Ervin Pruitt '69 Dodge	244	915	Engine
25	20	74	Bill Shirey	Shirey '69 Plymouth	242	900	Engine
26	33	68	Larry Baumel	Auto Lad '69 Mercury	211	810	Flagged
27	21	49	G C Spencer	Spencer '69 Plymouth	203	845	Oil Press
28	38	9	Roy Tyner	Tyner '70 Pontiac	181	755	Engine
29	11	98	LeeRoy Yarbrough	Junior Johnson '69 Ford	160	840	Crash
30	16	79	Frank Warren	Warren '69 Plymouth	119	725	Engine
31	13	39	Friday Hassler	James Hanley '69 Chevrolet	108	735	Crash
32	31	06	Neil Castles	Castles '69 Dodge Daytona	105	770	Crash
33	4	6	Buddy Baker	Cotton Owens '69 Dodge Day	95	680	Lug Bolts
34	39	23	James Cox	Don Robertson '69 Plymouth	85	665	Clutch
35	30	8	Ed Negre	Negre '69 Ford	85	650	Crash
36	36	51	Dub Simpson	Bill Strong '69 Chevrolet	73	635	Engine
37	10	59	Bunkie Blackburn	Tom Pistone '70 Ford	35	620	Crash
38	37	33	Wayne Smith	Smith '69 Chevrolet	29	605	Steering
39	27	84	John Sears	Elmo Langley '69 Ford	14	590	Rear End
40	26	10	Bill Champion	Champion '68 Ford	3	575	Crash

Time of Race: 4 hours, 18 minutes, 32 seconds
Average Speed: 116.117 mph
Pole Winner: Bobby Allison - 139.048 mph
Lap Leaders: Bobby Allison 1,Bobby Isaac 2-32, Charlie Glotzbach 33-34,
  Dave Marcis 35-48, Allison 49-81, Richard Petty 82, Allison 83-113, Dick Brooks 114,
  Bobby Isaac 115, Cale Yarborough 116-167, Petty 168-191, Isaac 192-193,
  Petty 194-199, Yarborough 200-201, Allison 202-285, Petty 286-289,
  Yarborough 290-291, Allison 292-304, Petty 305-318, Yarborough 319, Petty 320,
  Yarborough 321, Petty 322, Yarborough 323-355, Petty 356-492.
Cautions: 9 for 67 laps   Margin of Victory: 3-laps plus   Attendance: 38,000
*Relieved by Neil Castles

492 lap contest. Petty, leading by almost a lap, was dueling with third place Yarborough. Petty made a quick dive for pit road, but was nipped by Bobby Isaac. Petty's Plymouth wiggled into the path of Cale and the two cars tangled. "I guess I should have signaled or something," said Petty. "But I was in a hurry and didn't want to lose time in the pits. That's understandable, isn't it?"

Petty's car spun down pit road and stalled. However, he lost little time as another pit crew gave him a shove to his pit. Yarborough wasn't so fortunate. He lost two laps while the Wood Brothers pried torn metal from the car.

Allison won the pole with a record speed of 139.048 mph. He led five times for 162 laps. Two flat tires, ignition problems and a broken wheel knocked him out of contention. "I think I ran out of heart there toward the end," Allison sighed.

Dave Marcis finished sixth and emerged with a six point lead in the Grand National standings.

Richard Brickhouse, winner of the inaugural Talladega 500, qualified 10th in Tom Pistone's Ford. The Rocky Point, NC driver came down with the mumps two days before the race. Bunkie Blackburn was tabbed to replace Brickhouse, but he wrecked after 35 laps.

Petty's 102nd career win came at an average speed of 116.117 mph.

One member of the media asked Petty when he was going to retire from the sport. "I don't know," he replied. "I'll finish the rest of the year, then I'll think about next year."

Grand National Race No. 7
200 Laps at Savannah Speedway
Savannah, GA
"Savannah 200"
100 Miles on Half-mile Paved Track
March 15, 1970

Fin	St	No.	Driver	Team / Car	Laps	Money	Status
1	1	43	Richard Petty	Petty Ent '70 Plymouth	200	$1,000	Running
2	2	71	Bobby Isaac	K&K Insurance '69 Dodge	199	600	Running
3	3	48	James Hylton	Hylton Eng '69 Ford	196	400	Running
4	5	72	Benny Parsons	L G DeWitt '69 Ford	195	350	Running
5	6	30	Dave Marcis	Marcis '69 Dodge	195	325	Running
6	7	06	Neil Castles	Castles '69 Dodge	195	300	Running
7	8	64	Elmo Langley	Langley '69 Ford	193	275	Running
8	11	25	Jabe Thomas	Don Robertson '69 Plymouth	188	270	Running
9	9	34	Wendell Scott	Scott '69 Ford	187	265	Running
10	15	9	Roy Tyner	Tyner '70 Pontiac	186	260	Running
11	12	70	J D McDuffie	McDuffie '69 Buick	184	255	Running
12	14	24	Cecil Gordon	Gordon '68 Ford	180	250	Running
13	20	19	Henley Gray	Gray '69 Ford	176	245	Running
14	13	74	Bill Shirey	Shirey '69 Plymouth	171	240	Running
15	16	47	Bill Seifert	Seifert '69 Ford	91	235	Oil Leak
16	10	79	Frank Warren	Warren '69 Plymouth	73	230	Rear End
17	17	67	Dick May	Joyce Ronacher '69 Ford	66	225	Exhaust
18	18	26	Earl Brooks	Brooks '69 Ford	45	220	Oil Leak
19	4	22	Bobby Allison	Don Robertson '69 Plymouth	36	215	Brakes
20	19	12	Pete Hazelwood	'68 Chevrolet	8	210	Heating
21	21	04	Ken Meisenhelder	Meisenhelder '68 Chevrolet	1	205	Ignition

Time of Race: 1 hour, 21 minutes, 20 seconds
Average Speed: 82.418 mph
Pole Winner: Richard Petty - 85.874 mph
Lap Leaders: Richard Petty 1-125, Bobby Isaac 126-142, Petty 143-200.
Cautions: 1 for 4 laps   Margin of Victory: 1-lap plus   Attendance: 4,500

Race No. 7

Savannah 200 Falls
To Richard Petty

SAVANNAH, GA (Mar. 15) -- Richard Petty dominated the Savannah 200 at Savannah Speedway to gain his second win in a row.

Petty poked the nose of his Plymouth into the lead at the outset and led all but 17 laps. He wound up more than a lap in front of Bobby Isaac. James Hylton came in third with Benny Parsons fourth and Dave Marcis was fifth. Marcis' point lead was cut to just two points over Petty in the Grand National standings.

Petty led the first 125 laps when he made his only pit stop. Isaac led from lap 126-142, but Petty ran him down and was in the lead for the rest of the way.

"The car handled great and it feels good to win here again," said Petty, who most recently won on this half-mile paved oval in 1967.

Bobby Allison hitched a ride in a Don Robertson Plymouth and qualified fourth. The Hueytown, AL driver was out of the race after 36 laps with no brakes.

Only one caution flag for four laps broke the pace. Petty averaged 82.418 mph before 4,500 spectators.

Race No. 8

Allison Comes From Nowhere To Win Atlanta 500

HAMPTON, GA (Mar. 29) -- Bobby Allison came out of nowhere and nipped Cale Yarborough in a dramatic duel to win the Atlanta 500 at Atlanta International Raceway. It was the 17th career Grand National win for the Dodge Daytona driver, who was a full lap behind with 10 laps to go.

Roy Mayne #46 and Richard Petty through turn at Atlanta

Yarborough had taken the lead in the 244th lap and was pulling away from the field. Donnie Allison, running second, blew the engine in his Ford on lap 318 -- at the precise moment Cale had entered the pits for a splash-and-go.

The caution came out and Bobby Allison whipped his car into the lead lap.

Allison pitted under yellow and got two fresh tires under the direction of car owner and crew chief Mario Rossi. The green flag came back out on lap 323 and Allison darted to the inside of Yarborough and made the

Grand National Race No. 8
328 Laps at Atlanta Int'l Raceway
Hampton, GA
"Atlanta 500"
500 Miles on 1.522-mile Paved Track
March 29, 1970

Fin	St	No.	Driver	Team / Car	Laps	Money	Status
1	9	22	Bobby Allison	Mario Rossi '69 Dodge Day	328	$21,825	Running
2	1	21	Cale Yarborough	Wood Brothers '69 Mercury	328	11,375	Running
3	5	40	Pete Hamilton	Petty Ent '70 Plym SuperBird	326	6,550	Running
4	7	98	LeeRoy Yarbrough	Junior Johnson '69 Ford	325	4,300	Running
5	4	43	Richard Petty	Petty Ent '70 Plym SuperBird	321	3,375	Running
6	11	48	James Hylton	Hylton Eng '69 Ford	320	2,525	Running
7	8	27	Donnie Allison	Banjo Matthews'69 Ford	317	2,075	Engine
8	16	72	Benny Parsons	L G DeWitt '69 Ford	315	1,950	Running
9	18	07	Coo Coo Marlin	Cunningham-Kelley '69 Chev	308	1,725	Running
10	19	37	Dr Don Tarr	Tarr '69 Dodge Daytona	306	1,625	Running
11	14	64	Elmo Langley	Langley '69 Mercury	300	1,575	Running
12	21	39	Friday Hassler	James Hanley '69 Chevrolet	298	1,500	Running
13	15	79	Frank Warren	Warren '69 Plymouth	298	1,475	Running
14	22	18	Joe Frasson	Frasson '70 Dodge	295	1,400	Running
15	23	34	Wendell Scot	Scott '69 Ford	291	1,350	Running
16	30	76	Ben Arnold	Arnold '69 Ford	289	1,300	Running
17	24	45	Bill Seifert	Seifert '69 Ford	282	1,275	Running
18	26	62	Ron Keselowski	Kaye Eng '69 Dodge	281	1,250	Running
19	28	10	Bill Champion	Champion '69 Ford	273	1,225	Running
20	3	6	Buddy Baker	Cotton Owens '69 Dodge Day	263	1,250	Ignition
21	13	3	Jim Vandiver	Ray Fox '69 Dodge	261	1,205	Fuel pmp
22	34	47	Raymond Williams	Bill Seifert '68 Ford	256	1,165	Engine
23	38	8	Ed Negre	Negre '69 Ford	245	1,150	Running
24	27	86	John Sears	Dennis Gallion '69 Dodge	228	1,135	Oil pump
25	20	49	G C Spencer	Spencer '69 Plymouth	217	1,145	Engine
26	6	32	Dick Brooks	Brooks '70 Plym SuperBird	194	1,130	Engine
27	36	46	Roy Mayne	Tom Hunter '69 Chevrolet	179	1,090	Engine
28	10	71	Bobby Isaac	K&K Ins '69 Dodge Daytona	159	1,105	Engine
29	32	25	Jabe Thomas	Don Robertson '69 Plymouth	155	1,120	Engine
30	40	70	J D McDuffie	McDuffie '69 Buick	124	1,060	Engine
31	12	30	Dave Marcis	Marcis '69 Dodge Daytona	119	1,075	Crash
32	33	19	Henley Gray	Gray '69 Ford	114	1,040	Engine
33	31	68	Larry Baumel	Auto Lad '69 Ford	89	1,105	Clutch
34	37	65	Lennie Pond	Joe Phipps '69 Chevrolet	88	1,020	Gear shift
35	29	24	Cecil Gordon	Gordon '68 Ford	70	1,010	Clutch
36	35	54	Bill Dennis	Dennis '69 Chevrolet	40	1,025	Vibration
37	25	57	Johnny Halford	Ervin Pruitt '69 Dodge	33	1,000	Engine
38	2	99	Charlie Glotzbach	Nchls-G'smith '69 Dodge Day	29	1,100	Ignition
39	17	06	Neil Castles	Castles '69 Dodge Daytona	10	1,050	Ignition
40	39	08	E J Trivette	E C Reid '69 Chevrolet	2	1,000	Quit

Time of Race: 3 hours, 34 minutes, 38 seconds
Average Speed: 139.554 mph
Pole Winner: Cale Yarborough - 159.929 mph
Lap Leaders: Charlie Glotzbach 1-2, Buddy Baker 3-50, Richard Petty 51-55,
    James Hylton 56-61, Pete Hamilton 62-63, Baker 64-97, Donnie Allison 98-105,
    Petty 106-109, D.Allison 110-111, Cale Yarborough 112-147, D.Allison 148, Baker 149
    D.Allison 150-186, Yarborough 187-201, Baker 202-206, D.Allison 207-243,
    Yarborough 244-319, Bobby Allison 320, Yarborough 321-322, B.Allison 323-328.
Cautions:4 for 23 laps   Margin of Victory: 50 feet   Attendance: 22,000

pass.

Yarborough made a charge in the final laps, but wound up 50 feet short at the finish line.

Pete Hamilton came in third with LeeRoy Yarbrough fourth and Richard Petty fifth.

The outcome snapped a string of three consecutive Atlanta 500 victories by the Timmonsville, SC Mercury driver.

"That was really a big break," said Allison. "Cale pitted just as the yellow came out. That allowed me to make up the lap I was behind. I was scheduled for a regular stop four laps later."

Yarborough suffered his second straight superspeedway loss. "Leonard (Wood) made the decision not to put new rubber on the car. It's the breaks of the game. I couldn't catch him because he was stickin' better in the turns."

Dave Marcis, entering the race with the point lead, crashed hard on lap 119 after a tire let go. Petty took the point lead by 26 points over Allison.

Ignition problems continued to foil the Dodge teams. Neil Castles, Charlie Glotzbach and Buddy Baker were all kayoed by ignition failure.

Allison averaged a record 139.554 mph as a slim Easter Sunday crowd of 22,000 watched the race.

Race No. 9

Donnie Beats Bobby at Bristol; Jabe Behaves

BRISTOL, TN (Apr. 5) -- Donnie Allison took the lead on lap 457 and led the rest of the way to win the Southeastern 500 at Bristol International Speedway. It was the third career Grand National win for the 30 year-old Hueytown, AL Ford driver.

Bobby Allison finished three laps behind in second place. Cale Yarborough, who had passed Donnie on lap 323 and built up a big lead, saw his hopes dashed when the engine blew with 44 laps remaining. He still got paid for third place. James Hylton came in fourth and Dick Brooks wound up fifth.

Banjo Matthews and Donnie Allison won the Southeastern 500 at Bristol

Runner-up Bobby Allison rented a Plymouth owned by Don Robertson, whose regular driver is independent Jabe Thomas. Both were in Robertson Plymouths for the 500-lapper.

With Donnie leading in the final laps, Thomas wheeled his car down pit road and stopped next to Banjo Matthews, who owns Donnie's Ford. "How much will you pay me *not* to spin Donnie out," cracked Thomas. Matthews waved Thomas on. The next lap, Matthews held a pit board up that read: "50 cents".

Thomas came down pit road the next lap with his

hand out the window. Matthews gave Thomas two quarters, and he continued in the race, finishing 12th.

David Pearson won the pole in his first start since a kidney operation. The Spartanburg Ford driver led the first 39 laps, but fell out on lap 180 with a blown engine. Only 10 cars finished the race.

Richard Petty lost the point lead when he was pinched by Ed Negre and Yarborough in the 37th lap. Bobby Allison became the new point leader, holding an 18 point lead over Petty.

A standing room only crowd of 32,000 watched as Donnie won at an average speed of 87.543 mph.

Grand National Race No. 9
500 Laps at Bristol Int'l Speedway
Bristol, TN
"Southeastern 500"
266.5 Miles on .533-mile Paved Track
April 5, 1970

Fin	St	No.	Driver	Team / Car	Laps	Money	Status
1	2	27	Donnie Allison	Banjo Matthews '70 Ford	500	$6,670	Running
2	6	22	Bobby Allison	Don Robertson '69 Plymouth	497	3,820	Running
3	4	21	Cale Yarborough	Wood Brothers '70 Mercury	456	2,345	Engine
4	9	48	James Hylton	Hylton Eng '69 Ford	453	1,295	Running
5	7	32	Dick Brooks	Brooks '70 Plymouth	447	1,020	Oil pump
6	23	70	J D McDuffie	McDuffie '69 Buick	444	820	Running
7	27	19	Henley Gray	Gray '69 Ford	443	770	Running
8	24	24	Cecil Gordon	Gordon '68 Ford	440	670	Running
9	13	07	Coo Coo Marlin	Cunningham-Kelley '69 Chev	437	645	Running
10	26	04	Ken Meisenhelder	Meisenhelder '68 Chevrolet	411	595	Running
11	11	30	Dave Marcis	Marcis '69 Dodge	373	615	Running
12	19	25	Jabe Thomas	Don Robertson '69 Plymouth	344	545	Running
13	17	64	Elmo Langley	Langley '68 Ford	292	535	Crash
14	8	49	G C Spencer	Spencer '69 Plymouth	226	525	Engine
15	20	57	Johnny Halford	Ervin Pruitt '69 Dodge	217	515	Rear End
16	21	74	Bill Shirey	Shirey '69 Plymouth	207	505	Oil Leak
17	10	71	Bobby Isaac	K&K Insurance '69 Dodge	198	495	Engine
18	1	17	David Pearson	Holman-Moody '69 Ford	180	1,435	Engine
19	29	8	Ed Negre	Negre '69 Ford	105	475	Oil Leak
20	15	06	Neil Castles	Castles '69 Dodge	53	490	Engine
21	14	34	Wendell Scott	Scott '69 Ford	50	480	Engine
22	30	65	Joe Phipps	Phipps '69 Chevrolet	50	445	Flagged
23	22	68	Larry Baumel	Auto Lad '69 Ford	42	435	Quit
24	3	43	Richard Petty	Petty Ent '70 Plymouth	37	450	Crash
25	18	45	Bill Seifert	Seifert '69 Ford	34	415	Clutch
26	16	62	Ron Keselowski	Kaye Eng '69 Dodge	31	410	Engine
27	5	72	Benny Parsons	L G DeWitt '69 Ford	16	425	Crash
28	12	88	Bobby Watson	H B Ranier '70 Dodge	11	430	Oil Pump
29	28	9	Roy Tyner	Tyner '70 Pontiac	9	380	Oil Pump
30	25	79	Frank Warren	Warren '69 Plymouth	4	370	Engine

Time of Race: 3 hours, 2 minutes, 42 seconds
Average Speed: 87.543 mph
Pole Winner: David Pearson - 107.079 mph
Lap Leaders: David Pearson 1-39, James Hylton 40, Dick Brooks 41-76, Donnie Allison 77-173, Bobby Isaac 174, Cale Yarborough 175-184, D.Allison 185-197, Yarborough 198-207, D.Allison 208-322, Yarborough 323-456, D.Allison 457-500.
Cautions: 6 for 58 laps   Margin of Victory: 3-laps plus   Attendance: 32,000

Race No. 10
Fate Bakes Baker; Hamilton Annexes Alabama 500

TALLADEGA, AL (Apr. 12) -- Pete Hamilton took the lead as the heavy hand of fate swatted Buddy Baker

Grand National Race No. 10
188 Laps at Alabama Int'l Motor Speedway
Talladega, AL
"Alabama 500"
188 Laps on 2.66-mile Paved Track
April 12, 1970

Fin	St	No.	Driver	Team / Car	Laps	Money	Status
1	6	40	Pete Hamilton	Petty Ent '70 Plym SuperBird	188	$26,650	Running
2	1	71	Bobby Isaac	K&K Ins '69 Dodge Daytona	188	12,500	Running
3	2	17	David Pearson	Holman-Moody '69 Ford	187	8,675	Running
4	11	72	Benny Parsons	L G DeWitt '69 Ford	187	5,825	Running
5	21	21	Cale Yarborough	Wood Brothers '69 Mercury	183	4,425	Running
6	9	14	Freddy Fryar	Bill Ellis '70 Plym SuperBird	182	3,000	Running
7	8	43	Richard Petty	Petty Ent '70 Plym SuperBird	181	2,500	Running
8	22	48	James Hylton	Hylton Eng '69 Ford	180	2,300	Running
9	33	06	Neil Castles	Castles '69 Dodge Daytona	179	2,200	Running
10	38	07	Coo Coo Marlin	Cunningham-Kelley '69 Chev	177	2,000	Running
11	10	79	Frank Warren	Warren '69 Plymouth	176	1,885	Running
12	5	6	Buddy Baker	Cotton Owens '69 Dodge Day	175	1,860	Spin-fire
13	7	32	Dick Brooks	Brooks '70 Plym SuperBird	175	1,785	Running
14	36	39	Friday Hassler	James Hanley '69 Chevrolet	175	1,760	Running
15	16	25	Jabe Thomas	Don Robertson '69 Plymouth	174	1,710	Running
16	30	89	Butch Hirst	Morris Davis '69 Ford	169	1,685	Running
17	24	30	Dave Marcis	Marcis '69 Ford	168	1,685	Running
18	15	45	Bill Seifert	Seifert '69 Ford	167	1,635	Running
19	29	86	John Sears	Dennis Gallion '69 Dodge	167	1,610	Running
20	32	34	Wendell Scott	Scott '69 Ford	165	1,585	Running
21	18	24	Cecil Gordon	Gordon '68 Ford	164	1,560	Running
22	20	51	Dub Simpson	Bill Strong '69 Chevrolet	162	1,535	Running
23	35	76	Ben Arnold	Arnold '69 Ford	160	1,510	Running
24	39	7	Alton Jones	'68 Ford	155	1,485	Engine
25	26	62	Ron Keselowski	Kaye Eng '69 Dodge	153	1,460	Wtr pump
26	27	68	Larry Baumel	Auto Lad '69 Ford	150	1,435	Running
27	14	64	Elmo Langley	Langley '69 Ford	149	1,435	Engine
28	19	63	Jimmy Crawford	Crawford Ent '69 Chevrolet	143	1,385	Running
29	4	22	Bobby Allison	Mario Rossi '69 Dodge Day	126	1,410	Engine
30	25	10	Bill Champion	Champion '69 Ford	125	1,335	Oil Leak
31	3	99	Charlie Glotzbach	Nchls-G'smith '69 Dodge Day	117	1,385	Engine
32	17	47	Raymond Williams	Bill Seifert '68 Ford	107	1,285	Engine
33	23	31	Jim Vandiver	Vandiver Bros '69 Dodge Day	93	1,285	Heating
34	34	19	Henley Gray	Gray '69 Ford	78	1,285	Steering
35	40	96	E J Trivette	'68 Ford	73	1,210	Engine
36	37	84	Bobby Mausgrover	Bob Davis '69 Dodge	25	1,210	Engine
37	12	59	Richard Brickhouse	Tom Pistone '70 Ford	25	1,210	Engine
38	13	37	Dr Don Tarr	Tarr '69 Dodge Daytona	17	1,160	Engine
39	28	81	Dave Alonzo	'69 Dodge	10	1,110	Crash
40	31	74	Bill Shirey	Shirey '69 Plymouth	3	1,085	Engine

Time of Race: 3 hours, 16 minutes, 59 seconds
Average Speed: 152.321 mph
Pole Winner: Bobby Isaac - 199.658 mph
Lap Leaders: Buddy Baker 1, David Pearson 2, Baker 3, Bobby Isaac 4, Baker 5-13, Richard Brickhouse 14-15, Cale Yarborough 16-23, Baker 24-27, Charlie Glotzbach 28-29, Yarborough 30-33, Baker 34-36, Bobby Allison 37, Isaac 38, Baker 39, Isaac 40, Glotzbach 41-42, Baker 43-48, Allison 49-51, Baker 52-53, Pearson 54-59, Baker 60-73, Allison 74-76, Baker 77-78, Allison 79, Baker 80-81, Allison 82-84, Baker 85-86, Allison 87-115, Baker 116-139, Pete Hamilton 140, Baker 141-170, Hamilton 171-188.
Cautions: 6 for 42 laps   Margin of Victory: 44 seconds   Attendance: 36,000

out of contention and won the Alabama 500 at the Alabama International Motor Speedway.

Hamilton cruised the final 18 laps and finished 44 seconds in front of Bobby Isaac. David Pearson was third place with Benny Parsons fourth and Cale Yarborough fifth.

Hamilton didn't emerge from the pack until the final stages of the event. "You can't beat a Petty Plymouth or a Petty plan," said Hamilton. "Our plan was to sit back early in the race and get an idea what tire problems there might be. Once we found out tires weren't going to be a major problem, we upped our pace."

Pete Hamilton #40, Charlie Glotzbach #99, and Benny Parsons #72 at Talladega

Baker had held the upper hand most of the way, leading 14 times for 105 laps. Following a pit stop, he was running down leader Hamilton when a tire blew. Chunks of rubber slashed through the oil cooler. Oil splashed onto the hot exhaust pipes, setting Baker's car on fire.

Baker put his Dodge into a spin to blow out the flames. "It felt like it was going to take forever to stop," said Baker. "I could feel that heat and I wanted out of there."

Baker's fiery exit with 13 laps to go set the stage for Hamilton, who was a full lap ahead of pole winner Isaac.

Isaac made up the lap in the final few circuits when Hamilton eased up.

Fifth place Yarborough survived a scary incident midway through the race. A beer bottle was tossed out of the backstretch grandstands and hit the upper center

Bobby Allison leads Buddy Baker before half empty grandstands in Alabama 500

section of the front windshield. "If it would have hit another foot off center," said Cale, "it would have taken my head off. Something has got to be done about drunks in the grandstands."

Yarborough pitted and the Wood Brothers removed the broken glass. They sent Cale back onto the track while they located a replacement. Yarborough drove for

five laps without a windshield. "I had to cover my nose and mouth with one hand so I could breathe," said Cale.

The Alabama 500 was televised live in part by ABC-Sports. It was the first live network presentation since 1960, when CBS televised the Daytona pole position races.

Top contenders Charlie Glotzbach and Bobby Allison lost their chances due to blown engines. Missing from the field were two of Ford's top threats -- local star Donnie Allison and LeeRoy Yarbrough.

Hamilton averaged 152.321 mph before a slim turnout of 36,000.

Pete Hamilton in victory lane after winning the first Alabama 500

Race No. 11

Petty 'Bores' TV Audience In North Wilkesboro Romp

N.WILKESBORO, NC (Apr. 18) -- Richard Petty took the lead in the 52nd lap and sprinted to an easy victory in the Gwyn Staley Memorial at North Wilkesboro Speedway. The 400 lap event was run on Saturday afternoon to accommodate live television coverage on ABC Wide World of Sports.

Petty left little doubt once the TV cameras were plugged into New York. He led every lap that was shown on TV, and most of the time he was better than a lap up on the field. ABC executives were squirming in their seats by the lack of a good show.

"All the TV folks had to do was hold up a board down there and tell me how much they would pay for a show," said Richard. "I would have given them a show if the price had been right. But my understanding was that I would get paid more for winning the race than putting on a show."

Bobby Isaac led the first 51 laps from the pole, then

faded to a distant second. LeeRoy Yarbrough finished third, James Hylton was fourth and Dick Brooks fifth.

An interested observer in the pits was retired Fred Lorenzen, who spent most of the day in the Johnson pits. "I'm tired of doing nothing," said the former 'Golden Boy'. "If the right kind of deal came along, I'd like to race again."

Donnie Allison started second and was running fourth when his engine blew, sending him into a spin in the third turn.

Petty extended his lead in the Grand National point standings to 52 points over Isaac.

A crowd of 11,500 watched Petty take his 104th career win at an average speed of 94.246 mph.

Grand National Race No. 11
400 Laps at N.Wilkesboro Speedway
N.Wilkesboro, NC
"Gwyn Staley Memorial"
250 Miles on .625-mile Paved Track
April 18, 1970

Fin	St	No.	Driver	Team / Car	Laps	Money	Status
1	16	43	Richard Petty	Petty Ent '70 Plymouth	400	$6,025	Running
2	1	71	Bobby Isaac	K&K Insurance '69 Dodge	399	3,725	Running
3	3	98	LeeRoy Yarbrough	Junior Johnson '70 Ford	399	2,350	Running
4	4	48	James Hylton	Hylton Eng '69 Ford	396	1,500	Running
5	6	32	Dick Brooks	Brooks '69 Plymouth	394	1,250	Running
6	17	22	Bobby Allison	Don Robertson '69 Plymouth	388	1,025	Running
7	7	45	Bill Seifert	Seifert '69 Ford	379	975	Running
8	12	64	Elmo Langley	Langley '68 Ford	379	925	Running
9	9	24	Cecil Gordon	Gordon '68 Ford	377	930	Running
10	11	54	Bill Dennis	Dennis '69 Chevrolet	374	895	Running
11	19	37	Dr Don Tarr	Tarr '69 Dodge	374	910	Running
12	13	51	Dub Simpson	Bill Strong '69 Chevrolet	374	895	Running
13	22	79	Frank Warren	Warren '69 Plymouth	371	890	Running
14	21	10	Bill Champion	Champion '69 Ford	370	880	Running
15	20	39	Friday Hassler	James Hanley '69 Chevrolet	366	845	Running
16	28	47	Raymond Williams	Bill Seifert '68 Ford	362	835	Running
17	30	62	Ron Keselowski	Kaye Eng '69 Dodge	347	825	Running
18	24	4	Neil Castles	John Sears '69 Dodge	345	850	Running
19	14	19	Henley Gray	Gray '69 Ford	313	830	Quit
20	5	30	Dave Marcis	Marcis '69 Dodge	295	820	Engine
21	8	25	Jabe Thomas	Don Robertson '69 Plymouth	295	810	Axle
22	2	27	Donnie Allison	Banjo Matthews '69 Ford	236	825	Engine
23	27	04	Ken Meisenhelder	Meisenhelder '68 Chevrolet	235	765	Trans
24	15	34	Wendell Scott	Scott '69 Ford	234	755	Engine
25	25	57	Johnny Halford	Ervin Pruitt '69 Dodge	217	770	Clutch
26	29	8	Ed Negre	Negre '69 Dodge	95	740	Engine
27	23	5	Larry Manning	Buddy Arrington '69 Dodge	83	755	Ignition
28	18	72	Benny Parsons	L G DeWitt '69 Ford	48	745	Rear End
29	26	76	Ben Arnold	Arnold '69 Ford	36	710	Engine
30	10	49	G C Spencer	Spencer '69 Plymouth	32	725	Engine

Time of Race: 2 hours, 38 minutes, 41 seconds
Average Speed: 94.246 mph
Pole Winner: Bobby Isaac - 107.041 mph
Lap Leaders: Bobby Isaac 1-51, Richard Petty 52-400.
Cautions: 3 for 21 laps   Margin of Victory: 1 1/2 laps   Attendance: 11,500

Race No. 12

Independents Fade; Petty wins Columbia in Borrowed Car

COLUMBIA, SC (Apr. 30) -- Richard Petty, driving

a Plymouth owned by Don Robertson, overcame a series of bids by four little known independents and won the Columbia 200 at Columbia Speedway. It was the fourth win of the season for Petty, but the first of Robertson's career. Jabe Thomas is Robertson's regular driver.

Petty started seventh on the grid as independents stole the spotlight in qualifying. Rookie Larry Baumel of Sparta, WI put his Ford on the pole. Lining up next were Johnny Halford, Frank Warren and Cecil Gordon.

Halford, of Spartanburg, took the lead and held it the first three laps. Ron Keselowski of Troy, MI passed Halford on lap four and was leading when he spun and crashed in the 12th lap. Halford picked up the lead and held it until Warren passed him on lap 26. The Augusta, GA driver held his Plymouth in front until he made a scheduled pit stop.

He lost three laps in the pits while his crew worked on the brakes. Petty drove into the lead and was never headed.

Bobby Allison finished second. Bobby Isaac, Neil

Grand National Race No. 12
200 Laps at Columbia Speedway
Columbia, SC
"Columbia 200"
100 Miles on Half-mile Dirt Track
April 30, 1970

Fin	St	No.	Driver	Team / Car	Laps	Money	Status
1	7	43	Richard Petty	Petty Ent '70 Plymouth	200	$1,500	Running
2	5	22	Bobby Allison	Allison '69 Dodge	199	900	Running
3	9	71	Bobby Isaac	K&K Insurance '69 Dodge	197	500	Running
4	24	06	Neil Castles	Castles '69 Dodge	197	350	Running
5	11	48	James Hylton	Hylton Eng '69 Ford	195	325	Running
6	10	45	Bill Seifert	Seifert '69 Ford	194	300	Running
7	14	37	James Sears	Dr Don Tarr '69 Dodge	193	275	Running
8	22	70	J D McDuffie	McDuffie '69 Buick	192	270	Running
9	25	25	Joe Frasson	Frasson '69 Dodge	190	265	Running
10	13	25	Jabe Thomas	Don Robertson '69 Plymouth	187	260	Running
11	18	34	Wendell Scott	Scott '69 Ford	186	255	Running
12	19	47	Raymond Williams	Bill Seifert '68 Ford	183	250	Running
13	26	64	Elmo Langley	Langley '68 Ford	156	245	Rear End
14	3	79	Frank Warren	Warren '69 Plymouth	113	240	Brakes
15	2	57	Johnny Halford	Ervin Pruitt '69 Dodge	108	235	Heating
16	23	72	Benny Parsons	L G DeWitt '69 Ford	85	230	Rear End
17	16	30	Dave Marcis	Marcis '69 Dodge	54	225	Rear End
18	20	04	Ken Meisenhelder	Meisenhelder '68 Chevrolet	53	220	Rear End
19	17	74	Bill Shirey	Shirey '69 Plymouth	35	215	Quit
20	1	68	Larry Baumel	Auto Lad '69 Ford	30	210	Brakes
21	8	8	Ed Negre	Negre '69 Ford	30	205	Crash
22	21	67	Dick May	Joyce Ronacher '69 Ford	29	200	Crash
23	27	9	Roy Tyner	Tyner '69 Pontiac	29	200	Crash
24	12	4	John Sears	Sears '69 Dodge	25	200	Ignition
25	6	62	Ron Keselowski	Kaye Eng '69 Dodge	12	200	Crash
26	15	19	Henley Gray	Gray '69 Ford	8	200	Brakes
27	4	24	Cecil Gordon	Gordon '68 Ford	2	200	Trans

Time of Race: 1 hour, 35 minutes, 43 seconds
Average Speed: 62.685 mph
Pole Winner: Larry Baumel - 72.329 mph
Lap Leaders: Johnny Halford 1-3, Ron Keselowski 4-12, Halford 13-25,
  Frank Warren 26-96, Richard Petty 97-200.
Cautions: 6 for 30 laps   Margin of Victory: 1-lap plus   Attendance: 10,000.

Castles and James Hylton filled out the top five.

Warren got back on the track but was blackflagged when NAS-CAR officials noticed a glowing right rear hub on his car.

Baumel lost his brakes on lap 30, putting him out of the race. Halford retired with overheating problems on lap 108, ending his bid.

Petty averaged 62.685 mph before a crowd of 10,000.

Race No. 13

Petty Tears Down Darlington Walls; Pearson Wins

DARLINGTON, SC (May 9) -- David Pearson took the lead 33 laps from the finish and won the Rebel 400 at Darlington Raceway. Richard Petty survived a horrible tumble in the 176th lap -- just minutes after ABC-Sports picked up the live television coverage at 5:00 pm. Petty's Plymouth brushed the outside rail in the fourth turn, then socked the inside concrete wall with a head-on shot. The impact sent chunks of concrete in all directions, and Petty flipped four times. He was taken from the car unconscious and transported to Florence's McLeod Hospital. He was diagnosed as having a broken shoulder.

Pearson got the lead when Bobby Isaac slipped and hit the wall coming off turn two of lap 258. Isaac made a lengthy stay on pit road and returned to the fray running well off the pace. He wound up third behind runner-up Dick Brooks. Brooks, the 1969 Rookie of the Year, lost three laps early while his pit crew replaced a broken hub. He lost to Pearson by three laps. James Hylton came in fourth and Benny Parsons was fifth.

"I was laying back most of the way, watching my tires," said Pearson, who won for the 58th time in his career. "The hardest I ran all day was with Isaac, and that lasted only three or four laps."

Brooks enjoyed his best finish in Grand National racing. "My pit crew replaced the hub and I only lost three laps," said the Porterville, CA sophomore. "My crew chief Tim Ingram and the boys did a great job. If it hadn't been for that durned hub, it might be a different car going to victory circle."

Petty's exit was spectacular, but not the only wall-banger he experienced that week. After he had qualified eighth, Petty put his superspeedway SuperBird into the wall. The Petty Enterprises crew went back to Level Cross and brought back a short track Roadrunner. "I don't remember anything about the wreck," Petty said of his race day dive. "I missed the whole deal when I was knocked out."

Sequence photos of Richard Petty's spectacular crash at Darlington. Coming off the fourth turn the car clipped the outside wall and shot across the track, smashing head-on into the inside wall. The car then began a series of rolls. Top photo shows the beginning of the roll off the inside wall. In second photo, Richard's head can be seen partially out of the car. In center photo, Richards arm is outside the car. Photo four shows the car coming down hard on the left rear. Bottom photo shows car coming to rest upside down with Richard partially outside the car.

Grand National Race No.13
291 Laps at Darlington Raceway
Darlington, SC
"Rebel 400"
400 Miles on 1.366-mile Paved Track
May 9, 1970

Fin	St	No.	Driver	Team / Car	Laps	Money	Status
1	3	17	David Pearson	Holman-Moody '69 Ford	291	$15,650	Running
2	5	32	Dick Brooks	Brooks '70 Plym SuperBird	288	8,170	Running
3	9	71	Bobby Isaac	K&K Ins '69 Dodge Daytona	284	5,580	Running
4	13	48	James Hylton	Hylton Eng '69 Ford	282	3,350	Running
5	8	72	Benny Parsons	L G DeWitt '69 Ford	279	2,600	Running
6	17	5	Buddy Arrington	Arrington '69 Dodge	272	1,950	Running
7	26	37	Dr Don Tarr	Tarr '69 Dodge	270	1,675	Running
8	36	46	Roy Mayne	Tom Hunter '69 Chevrolet	267	1,500	Running
9	21	25	Jabe Thomas	Don Robertson '69 Plymouth	265	1,425	Running
10	34	54	Bill Dennis	Dennis '69 Chevrolet	261	1,350	Running
11	28	4	John Sears	Sears '69 Dodge	255	1,300	Running
12	23	19	Henley Gray	Gray '69 Ford	251	1,225	Running
13	7	27	Cale Yarborough	Banjo Matthews '69 Ford	250	1,200	Clutch
14	25	76	Ben Arnold	Arnold '69 Ford	242	1,225	Running
15	6	6	Buddy Baker	Cotton Owens '69 Dodge Day	234	1,150	Engine
16	29	34	Wendell Scott	Scott '69 Ford	233	1,100	Clutch
17	19	06	Neil Castles	Castles '69 Dodge	206	1,075	Clutch
18	12	43	Richard Petty	Petty Ent '70 Plymouth	176	1,050	Crash
19	4	40	Pete Hamilton	Petty Ent '70 Plym SuperBird	150	1,000	Engine
20	2	22	Bobby Allison	Mario Rossi '69 Dodge Day	146	1,050	Engine
21	18	39	Friday Hassler	James Hanley '69 Chevrolet	144	950	Oil Leak
22	1	99	Charlie Glotzbach	Nchls-G'smith '69 Dodge Day	137	1,050	Heating
23	20	10	Bill Champion	Champion '69 Ford	136	900	Engine
24	30	53	Paul Conners	'69 Dodge	134	890	Engine
25	16	49	G C Spencer	Spencer '69 Plymouth	116	875	Engine
26	10	98	LeeRoy Yarbrough	Junior Johnson '69 Ford	107	860	Crash
27	11	79	Frank Warren	Warren '69 Plymouth	96	850	Engine
28	35	84	Bobby Mausgrover	Bob Davis '69 Dodge	73	840	Engine
29	32	24	Cecil Gordon	Gordon '68 Ford	67	835	Engine
30	33	89	Butch Hirst	Morris Davis '69 Ford	55	830	Heating
31	27	64	Elmo Langley	Langley '69 Mercury	37	825	Clutch
32	14	30	Dave Marcis	Marcis '69 Dodge	34	870	Engine
33	22	23	Earl Brooks	Don Robertson '69 Plymouth	29	815	Vibration
34	31	68	Larry Baumel	Auto Lad '69 Ford	11	810	W'shield
35	15	31	Jim Vandiver	Vandiver Bros '69 Dodge Day	3	830	Engine
36	24	45	Bill Seifert	Seifert '69 Ford	3	800	Quit

Time of Race: 3 hours, 5 minutes, 7 seconds
Average Speed: 129.668 mph
Pole Winner: Charlie Glotzbach - 153.822 mph
Lap Leaders: Charlie Glotzbach 1-4, Bobby Allison 5-60, Pete Hamilton 61-62,
   Richard Petty 63-64, LeeRoy Yarbrough 65-66, B.Allison 67-81, David Pearson 82-109,
   Bobby Isaac 110, Petty 111, Hamilton 112, Pearson 113-131, B.Allison 132-145,
   Pearson 146-153, Isaac 154, Pearson 155, Isaac 156-180, Pearson 181-190,
   Isaac 191-237, Pearson 238-255, Isaac 256-258, Pearson 259-291.
Cautions: 4 for 37 laps   Margin of Victory: 3-laps plus   Attendance: 42,000

Petty scoffed off rumors of retirement. "I've always said that when I stop racing, it probably will be when I get hurt so badly I just can't race anymore. This wreck didn't hurt me that badly."

Petty would be confined to the sidelines for five races, doctors said. He still left Darlington with a nine point lead over Isaac in the standings.

Bobby Allison emerged as the driver to beat in the early going, but engine failure put his Dodge out after 146 laps. Cale Yarborough, filling in for Donnie Allison, lost the clutch in the final 40 laps.

Pearson averaged 129.668 before a crowd of 42,000.

Race No. 14

Isaac Takes Point Lead With Beltsville Victory

BELTSVILLE, MD (May 15) -- Bobby Isaac pushed his Dodge into the lead with 157 laps to go and won the Beltsville 300 before 5,800 spectators. The first win of the year for the 37 year-old Dodge driver vaulted him into the NASCAR point lead. Richard Petty, injured in a crash at Darlington six days earlier, was watching from the pits.

James Hylton won his third career pole and led the first 14 laps. He eventually finished second, one lap behind Isaac. Third place went to Bobby Allison. Neil Castles was fourth and Dave Marcis fifth.

Isaac started third on the grid, but had the lead by the 15th lap. He pulled away from the field before he made his first pit stop on lap 129. Allison, Hylton and Castles led for brief stints as pit stops continued to take place. Isaac picked up the lead on lap 144 and led the rest of the way.

Petty, attired in an all green outfit, greeted Isaac in victory lane.

Bill Seifert, independent out of Skyland, NC, qualified seventh. It was his best start since being injured in the Tab Prince crash at Daytona. Seifert went out on lap 82 with ignition failure.

Isaac averaged 76.370 mph for his 22nd career Grand National win.

Dick Brooks and Jabe Thomas ride through turn at Darlington. Brooks finished second in Rebel 400

Grand National Race No. 14
300 Laps at Beltsville Speedway
Beltsville, MD
"Beltsville 300"
150 Miles on Half-mile Paved Track
May 15, 1970

Fin	St	No.	Driver	Team / Car	Laps	Money	Status
1	3	71	Bobby Isaac	K&K Insurance '70 Dodge	300	$1,900	Running
2	1	48	James Hylton	Hylton Eng '69 Ford	299	1,300	Running
3	2	22	Bobby Allison	Allison '69 Dodge	298	900	Running
4	5	06	Neil Castles	Castles '69 Dodge	297	600	Running
5	4	30	Dave Marcis	Marcis '69 Dodge	294	475	Running
6	8	54	Bill Dennis	Dennis '69 Chevrolet	290	430	Running
7	9	64	Elmo Langley	Langley '68 Ford	289	400	Running
8	15	25	Jabe Thomas	Don Robertson '69 Plymouth	285	380	Running
9	14	34	Wendell Scott	Scott '69 Ford	284	360	Running
10	17	70	J D McDuffie	McDuffie '69 Buick	269	350	Running
11	20	65	Joe Phipps	Phipps '69 Chevrolet	267	340	Running
12	6	72	Benny Parsons	L G DeWitt '69 Ford	236	330	Rear End
13	19	19	Henley Gray	Gray '69 Ford	219	320	Running
14	13	10	Bill Champion	Champion '68 Ford	204	310	Steering
15	11	79	Frank Warren	Warren '69 Plymouth	197	300	Steering
16	18	04	Ken Meisenhelder	Meisenhelder '69 Chevrolet	130	290	Trans
17	10	24	Cecil Gordon	Gordon '68 Ford	125	285	Trans
18	26	77	John Kenney	Bob Freeman '68 Ford	113	280	Engine
19	25	97	Lee Gordon	Cecil Gordon '68 Ford	109	275	Ignition
20	7	45	Bill Seifert	Seifert '69 Ford	82	270	Ignition
21	22	82	John Jennings	'68 Ford	64	265	Rear End
22	12	4	John Sears	Sears '69 Dodge	45	260	Wtr Hose
23	21	67	Dick May	Joyce Ronacher '69 Ford	26	255	Quit
24	23	00	Harry Shipe	John Savoca '69 Ford	24	250	Trans
25	16	8	Ed Negre	Negre '69 Ford	12	200	Oil Leak
26	24	23	James Cox	Don Robertson '69 Plymouth	3	200	Quit

Time of Race: 1 hour, 17 minutes, 50 seconds
Average Speed: 76.370 mph
Pole Winner: James Hylton - 83.128 mph
Lap Leaders: James Hylton 1-14, Bobby Isaac 15-128, Bobby Allison 129-132,
   Hylton 133-137, Neil Castles 138-143, Isaac 144-300.
Cautions: 1 for 10 laps   Margin of Victory: 1-lap plus   Attendance: 5,800

Race No. 15

Isaac Outlasts Allison and Castles to Win Tidewater 300

HAMPTON, VA (May 18) -- Bobby Isaac took the lead from Neil Castles on lap 199 and sprinted to an easy win in the Tidewater 300 at Langley Field Speedway. It was the second win in a row for the Catawba, NC veteran.

Bobby Allison ran strong in the early going and finished second. Castles wound up third with James Hylton fourth and Benny Parsons fifth.

Dave Marcis qualified a strong second and challenged all the way until rear gearing failure put his Dodge behind the wall with 15 laps to go.

"I was watching Allison after all the pit stops," said Isaac. "When I saw he couldn't run as well as he had earlier, I took it easy. I didn't even know Castles was that close."

Castles, 36, of Charlotte, led from laps 174-198. He was foiled by a flat tire which forced an extra pit stop. "A fellow once told me you've got to do the best you can do, and that's all I did," said Castles. "But if that tire hadn't gone down, I'd have given Isaac one heck of a chase in the end."

Four drivers withdrew from the race as complaints over the pay-off structure rose again. James Cox quit after one lap and earned $200. Dr. Don Tarr drove 287 laps, finishing seventh. He won only $275.

Isaac averaged 73.245 mph on the .4-mile paved track.

Grand National Race No. 15
300 Laps at Langley Field Speedway
Hampton, VA
"Tidewater 300"
120 Miles on .4-mile Paved Track
May 18, 1970

Fin	St	No.	Driver	Team / Car	Laps	Money	Status
1	1	71	Bobby Isaac	K&K Insurance '70 Dodge	300	$1,700	Running
2	4	22	Bobby Allison	Allison '69 Dodge	298	1,035	Running
3	5	06	Neil Castles	Castles '69 Dodge	298	630	Running
4	3	48	James Hylton	Hylton Eng '69 Ford	296	440	Running
5	6	72	Benny Parsons	L G DeWitt '69 Ford	296	350	Running
6	7	25	Jabe Thomas	Don Robertson '69 Plymouth	287	325	Running
7	18	37	Dr Don Tarr	Tarr '69 Dodge	287	275	Running
8	10	64	Elmo Langley	Langley '68 Ford	286	295	Running
9	2	30	Dave Marcis	Marcis '69 Dodge	281	325	Rear End
10	15	34	Wendell Scott	Scott '69 Ford	280	260	Running
11	9	4	John Sears	Sears '69 Dodge	277	280	Running
12	20	77	John Kenney	Bob Freeman '68 Ford	255	250	Running
13	21	82	John Jennings	'68 Ford	245	245	Running
14	22	97	Lee Gordon	Cecil Gordon '68 Ford	235	240	Running
15	23	67	Dick May	Joyce Ronacher '69 Ford	219	235	Crash
16	16	70	J D McDuffie	McDuffie '69 Buick	186	230	Crash
17	12	79	Frank Warren	Warren '69 Plymouth	129	225	Carb
18	8	24	Cecil Gordon	Gordon '68 Ford	128	245	Rear End
19	11	8	Ed Negre	Negre '69 Ford	74	215	Engine
20	17	10	Bill Champion	Champion '68 Ford	58	210	Quit
21	14	19	Henley Gray	Gray '69 Ford	50	205	Quit
22	25	54	Bill Dennis	Dennis '69 Chevrolet	27	200	Oil Leak
23	13	45	Bill Seifert	Seifert '69 Ford	11	200	Wheel
24	24	04	Ken Meisenhelder	Meisenhelder '69 Chevrolet	2	200	Quit
25	19	23	James Cox	Don Robertson '69 Plymouth	1	200	Quit

Time of Race: 1 hour, 38 minutes, 18 seconds
Average Speed: 73.245 mph
Pole Winner: Bobby Isaac - 79.659 mph
Lap Leaders: Bobby Isaac 1-161, Bobby Allison 162-173, Neil Castles 174-198,
   Isaac 199-300.
Cautions: 2 for 11 laps   Margin of Victory: 2-laps plus   Attendance: 3,800

Race No. 16

Donnie, LeeRoy Team To Win World 600; Lorenzen Returns

CHARLOTTE, NC (May 24) -- LeeRoy Yarbrough, driving in relief of Donnie Allison, took the lead in the 363rd lap and hustled to victory in the World 600 at

Grand National Race No. 16
400 Laps at Charlotte Motor Speedway
Charlotte, NC
"World 600"
600 Miles on 1.5 mile Paved Track
May 24, 1970

Fin	St	No.	Driver	Team / Car	Laps	Money	Status
1	9	27	Donnie Allison*	Banjo Matthews '69 Ford	400	$39,750	Running
2	3	21	Cale Yarborough	Wood Brothers '69 Mercury	398	17,080	Running
3	14	72	Benny Parsons	L G DeWitt '69 Ford	396	11,445	Running
4	15	55	Tiny Lund**	John McConnell '69 Dodge Day	395	7,575	Running
5	13	48	James Hylton	Hylton Eng '69 Ford	395	6,200	Running
6	17	36	Bugs Stevens	Richard Brown '70 Plym S'Bird	392	4,400	Running
7	1	71	Bobby Isaac	K&K Ins '69 Dodge Daytona	390	6,250	Running
8	5	40	Pete Hamilton	Petty Ent '70 Plym SuperBird	388	3,550	Running
9	16	49	G C Spencer	Spencer '69 Plymouth	384	2,925	Running
10	18	31	Jim Vandiver	Vandiver Bros. '69 Dodge Day	374	2,400	Running
11	30	25	Jabe Thomas	Don Robertson '69 Plymouth	372	2,835	Running
12	23	18	Joe Frasson	Frasson '69 Dodge Daytona	366	2,200	Running
13	19	5	Buddy Arrington	Arrington '69 Dodge	365	2,150	Running
14	4	17	David Pearson	Holman-Moody '69 Ford	362	2,925	Clutch
15	27	10	Bill Champion	Champion '69 Ford	359	2,100	Running
16	26	06	Neil Castles	Castles '69 Dodge Daytona	354	2,075	Running
17	25	30	Dave Marcis	Marcis '69 Dodge Daytona	347	2,050	Engine
18	33	4	John Sears	Sears '69 Dodge	340	1,925	Running
19	36	19	Henley Gray	Gray '69 Ford	334	1,900	Running
20	11	43	Jim Paschal	Petty Ent '70 Plym SuperBird	325	1,800	Heating
21	39	70	J D McDuffie	McDuffie '69 Mercury	316	1,750	Battery
22	40	62	Ron Keselowski	Kaye Eng '69 Dodge	306	1,725	Crash
23	10	6	Buddy Baker	Cotton Owens '69 Dodge Day	297	1,750	Crash
24	6	28	Fred Lorenzen	R Howard '69 Dodge Daytona	252	1,825	Engine
25	7	99	Charlie Glotzbach	Nchls-G'smith '69 Dodge Day	252	1,775	Crash
26	20	90	Sonny Hutchins	Junie Donlavey '69 Ford	230	1,625	Crash
27	24	79	Frank Warren	Warren '69 Plymouth	190	2,600	Crash
28	29	45	Bill Seifert	Seifert '69 Ford	179	1,600	Clutch
29	8	98	LeeRoy Yarbrough	Junior Johnson '69 Mercury	177	1,650	Clutch
30	31	07	Coo Coo Marlin	Cunningham-Kelley '69 Chev	160	1,525	Engine
31	12	32	Dick Brooks	Brooks '70 Plym SuperBird	127	1,525	Crash
32	37	59	Richard Brickhouse	Tom Pistone '70 Ford	126	1,525	Crash
33	22	39	Friday Hassler	James Hanley '69 Chevrolet	103	1,450	Engine
34	32	16	Roy Mayne	Ken Spikes '70 Chevrolet	93	1,425	Trans
35	21	64	Elmo Langley	Langley '69 Mercury	92	1,400	Engine
36	28	76	Ben Arnold	Arnold '69 Ford	78	1,400	Engine
37	38	24	Cecil Gordon	Gordon '68 Ford	33	1,375	Engine
38	34	37	Dr Don Tarr	Tarr '69 Dodge	23	1,325	Brakes
39	2	22	Bobby Allison	Mario Rossi '69 Dodge Day	17	1,675	Engine
40	35	68	Larry Baumel	Auto Lad '69 Ford	6	1,275	Engine

Time of Race: 4 hours, 37 minutes, 36 seconds
Average Speed: 129.680 mph
Pole Winner: Bobby Isaac - 159.277 mph
Lap Leaders: Bobby Isaac 1-19, Charlie Glotzbach 20, James Hylton 21-23,
    Jim Vandiver 24-29, LeeRoy Yarbrough 30-79, Donnie Allison 80-81, Yarbrough 82-84,
    Hylton 85-90, D.Allison 91-99, Buddy Baker 100, Jim Paschal 101-111,
    David Pearson 112-116, Cale Yarborough 117, Pearson 118-119, D.Allison 120-147,
    Fred Lorenzen 148-172, Glotzbach 173-185, Lorenzen 186, Glotzbach 187-188,
    Lorenzen 189-193, Glotzbach 194-226, Lorenzen 227-238, Pearson 239-248,
    Lorenzen 249-252, D.Allison 253-300, Pearson 301, D.Allison 302-317,
    Pearson 318-362, D Allison 363-400.
Cautions: 10 for 66 laps   Margin of Victory: 2-laps plus   Attendance: 70,000
*Relieved by LeeRoy Yarbrough   **Relieved by Dick Brooks

David Pearson spins at Charlotte as Tiny Lund passes

laps in the pits just past the 100-lap mark, but made up five of them.

Third place went to Benny Parsons. Tiny Lund's Dodge, driven in relief by Dick Brooks, passed James Hylton in the final turn of the final lap to grab fourth place. Hylton got paid for fifth.

Pole sitter Bobby Isaac lost 11 laps on a pit stop to replace a distributor, but managed to finish seventh. Top Modified driver Bugs Stevens wound up sixth in his first Grand National start.

Fred Lorenzen drove a Dodge purchased by Charlotte promoter Richard Howard

Charlotte Motor Speedway as heat and fatigue took a heavy toll in NASCAR's longest race.

Yarbrough took over the driving chores when Allison pitted on lap 355. He was running in second place. Leader David Pearson came down pit road for his final routine stop on lap 363, but he was destined to stay there. The Holman-Moody team found parts of the clutch scattered on pit road.

Yarbrough coasted the rest of the way, finishing two laps ahead of Cale Yarborough. Cale had lost seven

Fred Lorenzen ended a three year, self-imposed exile. Driving a Richard Howard-owned, Mario Rossi prepared Dodge Daytona, Lorenzen started sixth and laid back in the early going. He forged to the front by lap 148 and was leading when his engine blew in the 252nd lap. "Everything was going so well," said a dejected Lorenzen. "I actually started thinking about winning. The worse part about it was that I took Charlie Glotzbach with me. That's one thing I didn't want to do -- cause someone else to be taken out."

Fred Lorenzen made his return to racing at Charlotte

Race No. 17

Bobby Isaac Master At Maryville

MARYVILLE, TN (May 28) -- Bobby Isaac of Catawba, NC led the entire distance and won the Maryville 200 at Smoky Mountain Raceway.

Isaac passed pole sitter Bobby Allison in the third turn of the first lap. The 37 year-old veteran kept Allison at bay for the first 50 laps. On lap 75, Allison blew a tire and lost three laps getting new rubber.

James Hylton drove his Ford to second place and Neil Castles was third. Dick Brooks came in fourth and Dave Marcis was fifth.

Allison was back in the running when his Dodge blew another tire, sending him into the guard rail. He was awarded 12th place in the field of 22.

Charlie Glotzbach was a surprise entrant. He hopped aboard Don Robertson's now famous 'rent-a-racer' Plymouth and chased Isaac, Marcis and Allison in the early going. Ignition failure on lap 128 put Glotzbach behind the wall.

As Lorenzen made his move to the front, the crowd of 70,000 rose to their feet and cheered.

Allison started ninth and was among the leaders the entire way. "The insulation in the floor board came apart and my feet were blistered from the heat. I was sure glad to see LeeRoy standing by to relieve me. Someday, I'll return the favor," he said.

Richard Brickhouse was shaken up when his Ford broke loose in turn two and was clobbered by Dick Brooks' Plymouth.

Jim Paschal subbed for Richard Petty in the Petty Enterprises Plymouth -- and he proved he wasn't rusty from a two year layoff. The 43 year-old High Point, NC driver led for 11 laps before overheating problems put him out after 325 laps.

Bobby Allison qualified second, but lost his chances when the engine let go on lap 17. The winged Dodge exploded in flames. Allison spun the car, putting out the fire -- but he hit the inside retaining wall.

Allison and Yarbrough averaged 129.680 mph in the $193,000 event.

Bugs Stevens finished 6th in the World 600 - his first Grand National start

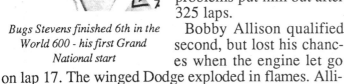

Grand National Race No. 17
200 Laps at Smoky Mountain Raceway
Maryville, TN
"Maryville 200"
104 Miles on .520-mile Paved Track
May 28, 1970

Fin	St	No.	Driver	Team / Car	Laps	Money	Status
1	2	71	Bobby Isaac	K&K Insurance '70 Dodge	200	$1,500	Running
2	6	48	James Hylton	Hylton Eng '69 Ford	199	900	Running
3	7	06	Neil Castles	Castles '69 Dodge	199	500	Running
4	4	32	Dick Brooks	Brooks '69 Plymouth	197	350	Running
5	3	30	Dave Marcis	Marcis '69 Dodge	195	325	Running
6	13	25	Jabe Thomas	Don Robertson '69 Plymouth	189	300	Running
7	12	4	John Sears	Sears '69 Dodge	189	275	Running
8	11	24	Cecil Gordon	Gordon '68 Ford	188	270	Running
9	10	34	Wendell Scott	Scott '69 Ford	187	265	Running
10	16	9	Henley Gray	Gray '69 Ford	178	260	Running
11	19	70	J D McDuffie	McDuffie '69 Buick	176	255	Running
12	1	22	Bobby Allison	Allison '69 Dodge	169	250	Crash
13	18	47	Raymond Williams	Bill Seifert '68 Ford	168	245	Running
14	5	23	Charlie Glotzbach	Don Robertson '69 Plymouth	128	240	Ignition
15	17	45	Bill Seifert	Seifert '69 Ford	118	235	Oil Press
16	8	39	Friday Hassler	James Hanley '69 Chevrolet	96	230	Engine
17	9	64	Elmo Langley	Langley '68 Ford	60	225	Engine
18	15	57	Johnny Halford	Ervin Pruitt '69 Dodge	53	220	Ignition
19	22	97	Lee Gordon	Cecil Gordon '68 Ford	34	215	Quit
20	20	12	Pete Hazelwood	'68 Chevrolet	20	210	Oil Leak
21	14	8	Ed Negre	Negre '69 Ford	12	205	Oil Leak
22	21	67	Dick May	Joyce Ronacher '69 Ford	10	200	Quit

Time of Race: 1 hour, 15 minutes, 35 seconds
Average Speed: 82.558 mph
Pole Winner: Bobby Allison - 92.094 mph
Lap Leaders: Bobby Isaac 1-200.
Cautions: 2 for 15 laps   Margin of Victory: 1-lap plus   Attendance: 7,300.

Isaac averaged 82.558 mph for his 24th career win. A crowd of 7,300 turned out. Just a few miles down the road, President Nixon was visiting the Billy Graham crusade in Knoxville.

Grand National Race No. 18
500 Laps at Martinsville Speedway
Martinsville, VA
"Virginia 500"
262.5 Miles on .525-mile Paved Track
May 31, 1970

Fin	St	No.	Driver	team / Car	Laps	Money	Status
1	2	71	Bobby Isaac	K&K Insurance '69 Dodge	377	$10,795	Running
2	3	22	Bobby Allison	Allison '69 Dodge	377	5,140	Running
3	4	21	Cale Yarborough	Wood Brothers '70 Mercury	376	3,100	Running
4	7	98	David Pearson	Junior Johnson '70 Ford	375	1,525	Running
5	9	32	Dick Brooks	Brooks '69 Plymouth	373	1,025	Running
6	18	49	G C Spencer	Spencer '69 Plymouth	370	1,000	Running
7	10	48	James Hylton	Hylton Eng '69 Ford	369	875	Running
8	19	25	Jabe Thomas	Don Robertson '69 Plymouth	365	825	Running
9	13	54	Bill Dennis	Dennis '69 Chevrolet	363	800	Running
10	17	24	Cecil Gordon	Gordon '68 Ford	359	775	Running
11	21	10	Bill Champion	Champion '68 Ford	358	790	Running
12	27	34	Wendell Scott	Scott '69 Ford	357	755	Running
13	23	4	John Sears	Sears '69 Dodge	356	745	Running
14	32	62	Ron Keselowski	Kaye Eng '69 Dodge	355	735	Running
15	35	47	Raymond Williams	Bill Seifert '68 Ford	352	725	Running
16	25	76	Ben Arnold	Arnold '69 Ford	337	715	Running
17	29	19	Henley Gray	Gray '69 Ford	333	705	Running
18	15	79	Frank Warren	Warren '69 Plymouth	329	695	Running
19	12	5	Buddy Arrington	Arrington '69 Dodge	273	685	H Gasket
20	26	46	Roy Mayne	Tom Hunter '69 Chevrolet	231	675	Running
21	33	70	J D McDuffie	McDuffie '69 Buick	141	665	Engine
22	11	06	Neil Castles	Castles '69 Dodge	132	655	Rear End
23	28	8	Ed Negre	Negre '69 Ford	116	645	Ignition
24	14	64	Elmo Langley	Langley '69 Ford	112	635	Oil Pan
25	36	23	James Cox	Don Robertson '69 Plymouth	110	625	Engine
26	1	27	LeeRoy Yarborough	Banjo Matthews '70 Ford	102	700	Clutch
27	37	77	John Kenney	Bob Freeman '68 Ford	99	605	Brakes
28	22	45	Bill Seifert	Seifert '69 Ford	74	595	Brakes
29	34	67	Dick May	Joyce Ronacher '69 Ford	73	685	Oil Leak
30	24	74	Bill Shirey	Shirey '69 Plymouth	61	575	Trans
31	31	04	Ken Meisenhelder	Meisenhelder '69 Chevrolet	51	570	Brakes
32	20	51	Dub Simpson	Bill Strong '69 Chevrolet	37	565	Ignition
33	5	30	Dave Marcis	Marcis '69 Dodge	37	560	Trans
34	39	92	Roy Tyner	Tyner '69 Pontiac	35	555	Engine
35	16	57	Johnny Halford	Ervin Pruitt '69 Dodge	30	550	Engine
36	6	39	Friday Hassler	James Hanley '69 Chevrolet	22	545	Engine
37	30	26	Earl Brooks	Brooks '69 Ford	19	535	Heating
38	8	72	Benny Parsons	L G DeWitt '69 Ford	19	535	Heating
39	38	33	Wayne Smith	Smith '69 Chevrolet	18	530	Brakes

Time of Race: 2 hours, 53 minutes, 20 seconds
Average Speed: 68.584 mph
Pole Winner: Donnie Allison - 82.609 mph (car driven by LeeRoy Yarbrough in race)
Fastest Qualifier: Richard Petty - 83.095 mph (car was withdrawn)
Lap Leaders: LeeRoy Yarbrough 19, Bobby Isaac 20-107, Yarbrough 108-158, Bobby Allison 159-242, Isaac 243-377.
Cautions: 7 for 46 laps   Margin of Victory: Under caution   Attendance: 17,000
* Race shortened to 377 laps due to rain

Race No. 18

Isaac Declared Winner in Rain-shortened Virginia 500

MARTINSVILLE, VA (May 31) -- Bobby Isaac dominated the proceedings and won the Virginia 500 at Martinsville Speedway. The scheduled 500-miler, twice postponed by rain, was hit a third time and red flagged after 377 laps.

Isaac, who has won four of his last five starts on the NASCAR Grand National trail, led for 223 laps and was almost a lap ahead of runner-up Bobby Allison. Third place went to Cale Yarborough, a lap back. David Pearson, driving the Junior Johnson Ford, was fourth. Fifth place went to Dick Brooks.

The lead changed hands only four times. LeeRoy Yarbrough, who shifted over to the Banjo Matthews Ford, led the first 19 laps. Isaac led for an 87 lap stretch before Yarborough took a brief lead. Allison was in front for 84 laps before Isaac went in front to stay on lap 243.

LeeRoy's Ford went behind the wall on lap 102 with clutch trouble.

Richard Petty had won the pole six weeks earlier. Donnie Allison had qualified second. Petty lost credit for winning the pole since his car was withdrawn. Allison got credit for winning the pole since the car he qualified competed in the race. Allison did not drive at Martinsville. He was practicing for his Indianapolis 500 debut.

Isaac averaged 68.584 mph and stretched his point lead to 31 points over James Hylton, who finished seventh.

Race No. 19

Scoring Flap Mars
Motor State 400

BROOKLYN, MI (June 7) -- An embarrassing scoring foul-up involving the first nine positions marred Cale Yarborough's sensational win in the Motor State

Charlie Glotzbach's Dodge Daytona goes up in flames at Michigan

Grand National Race No. 19
200 Laps at Michigan Int'l Speedway
Brooklyn, MI
"Motor State 400"
400 Miles on 2-mile Paved Track
June 7, 1970

Fin	St	No.	Driver	Team / Car	Laps	Money	Status
1	4	21	Cale Yarborough	Wood Brothers '69 Mercury	200	$14,675	Running
2	1	40	Pete Hamilton	Petty Ent '70 Plym SuperBird	200	7,120	Running
3	3	17	David Pearson	Holman-Moody '69 Ford	200	4,980	Running
4	8	98	LeeRoy Yarbrough	Junior Johnson '69 Ford	200	2,800	Running
5	6	71	Bobby Isaac	K&K Ins '69 Dodge Daytona	199	2,025	Running
6	16	31	Jim Vandiver	Vandiver Bros '69 Dodge Day	198	1,550	Running
7	5	6	Buddy Baker	Cotton Owens '69 Dodge Day	198	1,300	Running
8	12	48	James Hylton	Hylton Eng '69 Ford	196	1,200	Running
9	9	30	Dave Marcis	Marcis '69 Dodge Daytona	196	1,100	Running
10	11	72	Benny Parsons	L G DeWitt '69 Ford	193	1,000	Running
11	13	64	Elmo Langley	Langley '69 Mercury	189	975	Running
12	23	39	Friday Hassler	James Hanley '69 Chevrolet	188	950	Running
13	22	37	Dr Don Tarr	Tarr '69 Dodge	185	925	Running
14	21	25	Jabe Thomas	Don Robertson '69 Plymouth	185	900	Running
15	25	4	John Sears	Sears '69 Dodge	184	875	Running
16	27	45	Bill Seifert	Seifert '69 Ford	183	850	Running
17	7	22	Bobby Allison	Mario Rossi '69 Dodge Day	179	830	Running
18	28	57	Johnny Halford	Ervin Pruitt '69 Dodge	178	820	Running
19	39	47	Raymond Williams	Bill Seifert '68 Ford	176	805	Running
20	30	34	Wendell Scott	Scott '69 Ford	171	790	Running
21	26	54	Bill Dennis	Dennis '69 Chevrolet	165	775	Engine
22	18	18	Joe Frasson	Frasson '69 Dodge Daytona	156	785	Running
23	15	79	Frank Warren	Warren '69 Plymouth	151	745	Engine
24	10	99	Charlie Glotzbach	Nchls-G'smith '69 Dodge Day	149	730	Engine
25	20	76	Ben Arnold	Arnold '69 Ford	147	715	Engine
26	38	74	Bill Shirey	Shirey '69 Plymouth	146	700	Engine
27	14	05	Ron Grana	C J Grana '69 Ford	124	690	Engine
28	2	43	Richard Petty	Petty Ent '70 Plym SuperBird	109	755	Ignition
29	34	62	Ron Keselowski	Kaye Eng '69 Dodge	105	670	Engine
30	17	06	Neil Castles	Castles '69 Dodge Daytona	88	710	Engine
31	37	07	Coo Coo Marlin	Cunningham-Kelley '69 Chev	71	645	Engine
32	29	24	Cecil Gordon	Gordon '68 Ford	68	640	Heating
33	36	44	Harold Smith	Giachetti Bros '69 Chevrolet	30	635	Engine
34	33	19	Henley Gray	Gray '69 Ford	15	655	Heating
35	40	8	Ed Negre	Negre '69 Ford	9	625	Engine
36	24	03	Tommy Gale	Walt Valerio '69 Mercury	6	620	Engine
37	32	86	Dick Brooks	Dennis Gallion '69 Dodge	5	640	Quit
38	31	68	Larry Baumel	Auto Lad '69 Ford	5	660	Engine
39	35	5	Buddy Arrington	Arrington '69 Dodge	3	605	Engine
40	19	10	Bill Champion	Champion '69 Ford	1	600	Engine

Time of Race: 2 hours, 53 minutes, 2 seconds
Average Speed: 138.302 mph
Pole Winner: Pete Hamilton - 162.737 mph
Lap Leaders: Pete Hamilton 1, Bobby Isaac 2-13, Richard Petty 14-37, Hamilton 38-43,
Petty 44-81, Hamilton 82-83, LeeRoy Yarbrough 84-89, Petty 90-107, Hamilton 108-114,
Charlie Glotzbach 115-128, Hamilton 129-136, Cale Yarborough 137-186,
Hamilton 187, Yarbrough 188-196, Hamilton 197-198, Yarbrough 199-200.
Cautions: 3 for 28 laps   Margin of Victory: 0.3 seconds   Attendance: 47,600

Buddy Baker's
Dodge Daytona roars
through front stretch at Michigan

400 at Michigan International Speedway.

Yarborough, at one time two laps off the pace, burst back into contention and nipped Pete Hamilton by 0.3-seconds to gain his second win of the year. Hamilton was flagged in second place, but claimed he was at least one lap ahead of Cale. David Pearson got third place, LeeRoy Yarbrough fourth and Bobby Isaac fifth.

Dick Hutcherson, crew chief on Pearson's Ford, filed a protest with NASCAR with 56 miles remaining in the race. As the checkered flag fell, the top NAS-CAR executives Lin Kuchler and Joe Epton left aboard a jet and returned to Daytona.

Hutcherson was protesting the fact that Cale and Lee-Roy were being shown on the lead lap.

LeeRoy had fallen one lap behind, but mysteriously made up the lap during a caution flag. Occupants of pit road said he came into the pits and was flashed on by crew chief Herb Nab. Yarbrough outran the pace car to the first turn and made up a lap.

Yarbrough said he had an idea controversy would flare after the end of the race. "David had been pulling me all day long," he said. "Then I look up at the scoreboard and they have me leading the race. I had to laugh. I knew somebody sure had something fouled up."

Three days later NASCAR announced Cale's win had been upheld. Chief Scorer Epton said Yarborough made up one lap during the caution flag on lap 114, and made the other one up on lap 133 when Hamilton made four stops under yellow.

Richard Petty said Cale could not have possibly made up the second lap under the caution. "The cards say Cale had lapped Pete under caution without the pace car lapping Pete. That's impossible," said Petty.

Assistant Scorer Don Matlock presided over the stormy gathering at the track.

Officially, Cale took the lead in the 137th lap and was in the hunt the rest of the way. He and Hamilton traded the lead six times in the final 130 miles.

Charlie Glotzbach authored the most spectacular incident. The engine in Glotzbach's Dodge exploded on lap 149. The car caught fire as Glotzbach spun through the fourth turn. Afterwards, Glotzbach said, "If I hadn't been wearing this full face mask, things would have been a lot worse."

Petty made his first start since his May 9 injury at Darlington. Petty led three times for 80 laps and was holding down first place when ignition problems interrupted his bid for a comeback win.

Yarborough's 13th career win came at an average speed of 138.302 mph. A crowd of 47,600 was on hand in sunny weather.

Race No. 20

Petty Leaves No Doubt; Wins Falstaff 400 Easily

RIVERSIDE, CA (June 14) -- Richard Petty led all but four laps and breezed to an easy win in the Falstaff 400 at Riverside International Raceway. It was the fifth win of the year for the Randleman, NC Plymouth driver.

Petty led for 149 of the 153 laps on the 2.62-mile road course. A slim spectator turnout of 18,500 watched Petty finish a lap ahead of runner-up Bobby Allison. Allison started on the pole, but spun off the course in the opening lap. He righted his course and chased the rest of the 40 car field. He finally caught up and took the lead on lap 64.

Allison led four laps while Petty was in the pits. The Hueytown, AL Dodge driver was unable to match Petty in speed and settled for a distant second.

James Hylton finished in third place and pulled to within one point of standings leader Bobby Isaac, who departed on lap 119 and wound up 16th. John Soares, Jr. came in fourth and Dick Gulstrand was fifth.

Mel Larson of Phoenix made his return to Grand

Grand National Race No. 20
153 Laps at Riverside Int'l Raceway
Riverside, CA
"Falstaff 400"
400 Miles on 2.62-mile Paved Road Course
June 14, 1970

Fin	St	No.	Driver	Team / Car	Laps	Money	Status
1	2	43	Richard Petty	Petty Ent '70 Plym SuperBird	153	$18,840	Running
2	1	22	Bobby Allison	Mario Rossi '69 Dodge Day	152	9,365	Running
3	5	48	James Hylton	Hylton Eng '69 Ford	144	5,340	Running
4	25	08	John Soares, Jr.	John Soares '70 Plymouth	141	3,415	Running
5	11	44	Dick Gulstrand	James Good '68 Chevrolet	139	2,540	Running
6	4	7	Jack McCoy	Ernie Conn '69 Dodge Day	138	1,890	Running
7	27	06	Neil Castles	Castles '69 Dodge Daytona	138	1,315	Running
8	29	83	Joe Clark	'69 Chevrolet	136	1,215	Running
9	40	5	Mel Larson	Don Smith '69 Ford	133	1,115	Running
10	23	37	Dr Don Tarr	Tarr '69 Dodge	130	1,040	Running
11	17	25	Jabe Thomas	Don Robertson '69 Plymouth	129	990	Running
12	38	68	Don Simkins	'67 Olds	127	965	Running
13	15	8	Bob England	England '69 Chevrolet	123	940	Rear End
14	20	74	Bob Hale	'67 Pontiac	123	915	Running
15	12	00	Frank James	Jim Calder '69 Chevrolet	120	890	Running
16	3	71	Bobby Isaac	K&K Ins '69 Dodge Daytona	119	915	Rear End
17	10	64	Elmo Langley	Langley '69 Mercury	107	845	Engine
18	8	72	Benny Parsons	L G DeWitt '69 Ford	98	835	Trans
19	22	96	Ray Elder	Fred Elder '69 Dodge	97	1,270	Engine
20	36	33	Glen Francis	Bill Andersen '70 Chevrolet	95	805	Running
21	34	129	Jerry Griffin	'69 Ford	94	790	Running
22	14	0	Jerry Oliver	Cos Cancilla '70 Olds	92	775	Engine
23	39	78	Ed Howland	'69 Chevrolet	91	760	Crash
24	13	23	G T Tallas	Tallas '69 Ford	90	745	Engine
25	6	02	Dick Bown	Mike Ober '70 Plym SuperBird	81	730	Wheel
26	18	179	Randy Dodd	'69 Chevrolet	72	715	Engine
27	32	79	Frank Warren	Warren '69 Plymouth	70	705	Clutch
28	9	45	Scotty Cain	Bill Clinton '69 Ford	57	695	Engine
29	7	38	Jimmy Insolo	Marvin Rowley '68 Chevrolet	39	685	Wheel
30	21	86	Dick Brooks	Dennis Gallion '69 Dodge	29	750	Trans
31	31	24	Ray Johnstone	Johnstone '67 Chevrolet	26	660	Fan pulley
32	16	99	Pat Fay	Martin Fay '70 Ford	24	655	Engine
33	26	88	Don Noel	Noel-Lewin '67 Ford	20	650	Engine
34	24	30	Dave Marcis	Marcis '69 Dodge Daytona	16	645	Engine
35	28	34	Wendell Scott	Scott '69 Ford	15	640	Engine
36	19	07	Bill Scott	'67 Chevrolet	6	635	Engine
37	37	9	Bill Pratt	'67 Ford	5	630	Crash
38	30	32	Kevin Terris	Gary Sigman '70 Plymouth	4	625	Engine
39	35	61	Steve Froines	'69 Chevrolet	3	620	Engine
40	33	15	Paul Dorrity	Glen Dorrity '69 Chevrolet	0	615	Engine

Time of Race: 3 hours, 57 minutes, 51 seconds
Average Speed: 101.120 mph
Pole Winner: Bobby Allison - 111.621 mph
Lap Leaders: Richard Petty 1-63, Bobby Allison 64-67, Petty 68-153.
Cautions: 3 for 13 laps　　Margin of Victory: 1-lap plus　　Attendance: 18,500.

Richard Petty drove his winged SuperBird to victory in 400-miler at Riverside

National racing. It was his first start in 10 years. The former Convertible driver ran ninth in a Ford after starting in 40th spot.

Jack McCoy spins off course in Falstaff 400

Petty said his strategy was to get out front early and build up a big lead. "I wanted to get away from everybody else," he said, "so there would be no question who was leading. Last week, they didn't know who was leading at Michigan."

Petty added that he had only two drivers in the field to battle with. "The only guys I had to race were Allison and Isaac," said Petty. No factory backed Fords were entered.

Petty averaged 101.120 mph for his 106th career win. Despite missing five races in the 1970 season, Petty still ranked eighth in the point standings.

Race No. 21

Isaac All The Way in Hickory Hundred-miler

HICKORY, NC (June 20) -- Bobby Isaac started on the pole and never looked back as he won the Hickory 276 at Hickory Speedway by a wide margin.

Isaac's Dodge finished two laps ahead of runner-up Dick Brooks in the 100-miler on the .363-mile oval. Dave Marcis came in third, G.C. Spencer was fourth and Bill Seifert fifth.

Isaac increased his point lead from one to 13 points over James Hylton. Hylton's

Fin	St	No.	Driver	Team / Car	Laps	Money	Status
1	1	71	Bobby Isaac	K&K Insurance '69 Dodge	276	$2,200	Running
2	3	32	Dick Brooks	Brooks '69 Plymouth	274	1,500	Running
3	6	30	Dave Marcis	Marcis '69 Dodge	272	1,000	Running
4	11	49	G C Spencer	Spencer '69 Plymouth	269	700	Running
5	17	45	Bill Seifert	Seifert '69 Ford	268	600	Running
6	7	72	Benny Parsons	L G DeWitt '69 Ford	267	500	Running
7	18	64	Elmo Langley	Langley '68 Ford	267	400	Running
8	16	25	Jabe Thomas	Don Robertson '69 Plymouth	264	350	Running
9	21	10	Bill Champion	Champion '68 Ford	264	300	Running
10	14	34	Wendell Scott	Scott '69 Ford	261	280	Running
11	20	76	Ben Arnold	Arnold '68 Ford	259	275	Running
12	19	8	Ed Negre	Negre '69 Ford	252	270	Running
13	5	48	James Hylton	Hylton Eng '69 Ford	239	265	Throttle
14	12	74	Bill Shirey	Shirey '69 Plymouth	162	260	Engine
15	9	88	Bobby Allison	'69 Dodge	152	255	Oil Leak
16	22	79	Frank Warren	Warren '69 Plymouth	128	250	Clutch
17	4	27	Donnie Allison	Banjo Matthews '69 Ford	72	245	Crash
18	8	54	Bill Dennis	Dennis '69 Chevrolet	70	240	Crash
19	10	93	Morgan Shepherd	'69 Chevrolet	68	235	Rear End
20	13	26	Earl Brooks	Brooks '69 Ford	39	230	Ignition
21	2	06	Neil Castles	Castles '69 Dodge	33	225	Lug Bolt
22	15	24	Cecil Gordon	Gordon '68 Ford	32	220	Heating

Time of Race: 1 hour, 27 minutes, 11 seconds
Average Speed: 68.011 mph
Pole Winner: Bobby Isaac - 79.596 mph
Lap Leaders: Bobby Isaac 1-276.
Cautions: 2 for 14 laps   Margin of Victory: 2-laps plus   Attendance: 9,200

Ford fell victim to a broken throttle linkage and wound up 13th.

Donnie Allison and the factory backed Banjo Matthews Ford team were surprise entrants. They had passed up a number of superspeedway races earlier in the year, but were on hand for a 100-miler. Donnie crashed with rookie Bill Dennis in the 72nd lap, knocking both out of action.

Neil Castles, still looking for his first big league win, qualified second. The Charlotte Dodge driver was out after 33 laps with broken wheel studs.

Richard Petty was unable to compete in the race. His short

Bobby Isaac

track Roadrunner had been demolished at Darlington, and the Petty Enterprises team was behind schedule in getting it rebuilt.

Morgan Shepherd, local Hobby Stock driver, made his debut in the Grand Nationals. He qualified 10th and was running ninth when officials blackflagged him for smoking. He got credit for 19th in the field of 22.

Isaac averaged 68.011 mph before 9,200 spectators.

Race No. 22

Petty's Plymouth King at Kingsport

KINGSPORT, TN (June 26) -- Richard Petty drove his Plymouth into the lead in the 50th lap and led the rest of the way to win the Kingsport 100 at Kingsport Speedway.

Petty started on the pole and led the first 15 laps. Bobby Isaac made a move for the lead and paced the action for 34 laps. As he was heading the field on lap 49, Isaac blew a tire and hit the wall. Petty regained first place as Isaac limped to the pits.

James Hylton finished second and lopped six points off Isaac's point lead. Dave Marcis made a marvelous run into third place despite losing his brakes with 200 laps remaining. Fourth place went to Bobby Allison and Neil Castles was fifth. Isaac struggled to finish eighth.

Charlie Glotzbach was ticketed to drive the Don Robertson Plymouth in a rare short track appearance. Glotzbach started eighth and was running in the top five when a tire blew, sending him into the wall on lap 91.

Frank Warren and Elmo Langley crashed early, putting Warren out of action. Langley crashed later on lap 239.

Petty won the 100-miler at a 68.583 mph clip. A crowd of 6,200 was on hand.

Race No. 23

Isaac Wins 6th of Year on New Greenville Pavement

GREENVILLE, SC (June 27) -- Bobby Isaac won his third straight race at Greenville-Pickens Speedway in the Greenville 100. The triumph enabled Isaac to inch out to a 10 point lead over James Hylton in the

Grand National Race No. 22
297 Laps at Kingsport Speedway
Kingsport, TN
"Kingsport 100"
100 Miles on .337-mile Paved Track
June 26, 1970

Fin	St	No.	Driver	Team / Car	Laps	Money	Status
1	1	43	Richard Petty	Petty Ent '70 Plymouth	297	$1,500	Running
2	7	48	James Hylton	Hylton Eng '69 Ford	295	900	Running
3	5	30	Dave Marcis	Marcis '69 Dodge	293	500	Running
4	4	22	Bobby Allison	Allison '69 Dodge	292	350	Running
5	2	06	Neil Castles	Castles '69 Dodge	292	325	Running
6	13	34	Wendell Scott	Scott '69 Ford	283	300	Running
7	16	70	J D McDuffie	McDuffie '69 Buick	276	275	Running
8	3	71	Bobby Isaac	K&K Insurance '70 Dodge	271	270	Running
9	17	76	Ben Arnold	Arnold '68 Ford	260	265	Running
10	19	25	Jabe Thomas	Don Robertson '69 Plymouth	248	260	Running
11	11	64	Elmo Langley	Langley '68 Ford	229	255	Crash
12	9	24	Cecil Gordon	Gordon '68 Ford	217	250	Trans
13	6	72	Benny Parsons	L G DeWitt '69 Ford	195	245	Crash
14	12	10	Bill Champion	Champion '68 Ford	154	240	Brakes
15	8	2	Charlie Glotzbach	Don Robertson '69 Plymouth	91	235	Crash
16	20	79	Frank Warren	Warren '69 Plymouth	33	230	Crash
17	21	19	Lee Gordon	Henley Gray '68 Ford	26	25	Heating
18	22	57	Johnny Halford	Ervin Pruitt '69 Dodge	21	220	Rear End
19	10	26	Earl Brooks	Brooks '69 Ford	13	215	Quit
20	14	47	Raymond Williams	Bill Seifert '68 Ford	5	210	Quit
21	15	45	Bill Seifert	Seifert '69 Ford	5	205	Quit
22	18	74	Bill Shirey	Shirey '69 Plymouth	5	200	Heating

Time of Race: 1 hour, 46 minutes, 26 seconds
Average Speed: 68.583 mph
Pole Winner: Richard Petty - 75.056 mph
Lap Leaders: Richard Petty 1-15, Bobby Isaac 16-49, Petty 50-297.
Cautions: 2 for 14 laps   Margin of Victory: 2-laps plus   Attendance: 6,200

battle for the Grand National championship.

Isaac led all but 10 laps on the new half mile paved track. He beat runner-up Bobby Allison by a half lap. Dick Brooks came in third. Hylton was fourth as Benny Parsons took fifth spot.

Isaac led the first 123 laps, then made a scheduled pit stop. Richard Petty led for one lap and Allison for nine. Isaac got around his foes on lap 134 and led the rest of the way.

Petty was running second and closing on Isaac when a tire blew on his Plymouth, sending him into the wall. He was out of the race.

Isaac's 27th career victory came at an average speed of 75.345 mph.

Race No. 24

Pearson Blew; Donnie Flew in Firecracker 400

DAYTONA BEACH, FL (July 4) --Donnie Allison parlayed a wheezing engine and misfortune of his foes into a surprise victory in the Firecracker 400 at Daytona

Grand National Race No. 23
200 Laps at Greenville-Pickens Speedway
Greenville, SC
"Greenville 200"
100 Miles on Half-mile Paved Track
June 27, 1970

Fin	St	No.	Driver	Team / Car	Laps	Money	Status
1	1	71	Bobby Isaac	K&K Insurance '70 Dodge	200	$1,500	Running
2	3	22	Bobby Allison	Allison '69 Dodge	200	900	Running
3	4	32	Dick Brooks	Brooks '69 Plymouth	198	400	Running
4	8	48	James Hylton	Hylton Eng '69 Ford	197	350	Running
5	5	72	Benny Parsons	L G DeWitt '69 Ford	196	325	Running
6	17	64	Elmo Langley	Langley '68 Ford	191	300	Running
7	14	25	Jabe Thomas	Don Robertson '69 Plymouth	190	275	Running
8	19	10	Bill Champion	Champion '68 Ford	189	270	Running
9	10	8	Ed Negre	Negre '69 Ford	188	265	Running
10	25	04	Ken Meisenhelder	Meisenhelder '69 Chevrolet	185	260	Running
11	12	34	Wendell Scott	Scott '69 Ford	185	255	Running
12	24	70	J D McDuffie	McDuffie '69 Buick	184	250	Running
13	13	76	Ben Arnold	Arnold '68 Ford	183	245	Running
14	6	06	Neil Castles	Castles '69 Dodge	175	240	Rear End
15	18	45	Bill Seifert	Seifert '69 Ford	175	235	Running
16	28	97	Lee Gordon	Cecil Gordon '68 Ford	175	230	Running
17	7	57	Johnny Halford	Ervin Pruitt '69 Dodge	163	225	Oil Press
18	26	92	Roy Tyner	Tyner '70 Pontiac	162	220	Running
19	2	43	Richard Petty	Petty Ent '70 Plymouth	137	215	Crash
20	21	30	Dave Marcis	Marcis '69 Dodge	107	210	Running
21	22	47	Raymond Williams	Bill Seifert '69 Ford	63	205	Heating
22	11	79	Frank Warren	Warren '69 Plymouth	63	200	Rear End
23	23	19	Henley Gray	Gray '68 Ford	46	200	Heating
24	16	4	John Sears	L G DeWitt '68 Ford	40	200	Steering
25	9	26	Earl Brooks	Brooks '69 Ford	37	200	Brakes
26	15	24	Cecil Gordon	Gordon '68 Ford	34	200	Trans
27	29	12	Pete Hazelwood	'68 Ford	23	200	Oil Press
28	20	74	Bill Shirey	Shirey '69 Plymouth	10	200	Heating
29	27	82	John Jennings	'69 Ford	3	200	Heating

Time of Race: 1 hour, 33 minutes, 12 seconds
Average Speed: 75.345 mph
Pole Winner: Bobby Isaac - 82.327 mph
Lap Leaders: Bobby Isaac 1-123, Richard Petty 124, Bobby Allison 125-133,
Isaac 134-200.
Cautions: 2 for 10 Laps   Margin of Victory: Half-lap   Attendance: 7,000

Grand National Race No. 24
160 Laps at Daytona Int'l Speedway
Daytona Beach, FL
"Firecracker 400"
400 Miles on 2.5-mile Paved Track
July 4, 1970

Fin	St	No.	Driver	Team / Car	Laps	Money	Status
1	15	27	Donnie Allison	Banjo Matthews '69 Ford	160	$21,025	Running
2	8	6	Buddy Baker	Cotton Owens '69 Dodge Day	160	10,795	Running
3	9	22	Bobby Allison	Mario Rossi '69 Dodge Day	160	7,005	Running
4	6	99	Charlie Glotzbach	Nchls-G'smith '69 Dodge Day	159	3,825	Running
5	10	32	Dick Brooks	Brooks '70 Plym SuperBird	158	2,500	Running
6	21	36	Dr Don Tarr	Richard Brown '70 Plym S'Bird	157	2,050	Running
7	13	48	James Hylton	Hylton Eng '69 Ford	155	1,400	Running
8	5	17	David Pearson	Holman-Moody '69 Ford	154	1,700	Blew tire
9	2	71	Bobby Isaac	K&K Ins '69 Dodge Daytona	151	1,250	Running
10	23	06	Neil Castles	Castles '69 Dodge Daytona	148	1,075	Running
11	16	10	Bill Champion	Champion '69 Ford	147	1,040	Running
12	31	57	Johnny Halford	Ervin Pruitt '69 Dodge	146	990	Running
13	30	4	John Sears	Sears '69 Dodge	143	965	Running
14	18	5	Buddy Arrington	Arrington '69 Dodge	143	940	Running
15	25	76	Ben Arnold	Arnold '69 Ford	143	940	Running
16	27	70	J D McDuffie	McDuffie '69 Ford	142	890	Running
17	20	79	Frank Warren	Warren '69 Plymouth	141	865	Running
18	11	43	Richard Petty	Petty Ent '70 Plym S'Bird	139	965	Engine
19	33	24	Cecil Gordon	Gordon '68 Ford	135	820	Running
20	28	45	Bill Seifert*	Seifert '69 Ford	135	805	Running
21	26	68	Larry Baumel	Auto Lad '69 Ford	129	820	Running
22	14	30	Dave Marcis	Marcis '69 Dodge Daytona	122	810	Running
23	24	18	Joe Frasson	Frasson '69 Dodge Daytona	111	800	Oil Leak
24	36	16	Roy Mayne	Ken Spikes '70 Chevrolet	96	765	Oil Pump
25	3	98	LeeRoy Yarbrough	Junior Johnson '69 Mercury	90	830	Engine
26	39	34	Wendell Scott	Scott '69 Ford	88	745	Engine
27	38	89	Gary Depuis	Morris Davis '69 Ford	78	735	Crash
28	17	64	Elmo Langley	Langley '69 Mercury	59	725	Oil Leak
29	32	25	Jabe Thomas	Don Robertson '69 Plymouth	58	715	Oil Pan
30	4	40	Pete Hamilton	Petty Ent '70 Plym SuperBird	46	760	Ignition
31	7	72	Benny Parsons	L G DeWitt '69 Ford	43	700	Engine
32	12	28	Fred Lorenzen	Ray Fox '69 Dodge Daytona	30	765	Distrib
33	22	31	Jim Vandiver	O L Nixon '69 Dodge Daytona	27	735	Oil Line
34	19	07	Coo Coo Marlin	Cunningham-Kelley '69 Chev	25	680	Engine
35	1	21	Cale Yarborough	Wood Brothers '69 Mercury	23	875	Engine
36	29	39	Friday Hassler	James Hanley '69 Chevrolet	15	670	Steering
37	35	8	Ed Negre	Negre '69 Ford	6	665	Quit
38	34	84	Bobby Mausgrover	Bob Davis '69 Dodge	5	660	Engine
39	37	74	Bill Shirey	Shirey '69 Plymouth	0	655	Heating
40	40	19	Henley Gray	Gray '69 Ford	0	650	Quit

Time of Race: 2 hours, 27 minutes, 56 seconds
Average Speed: 162.235 mph
Pole Winner: Cale Yarborough - 191.640 mph
Lap Leaders: Pete Hamilton 1-2, Buddy Baker 3-9, Cale Yarborough 10-14,
Buddy Baker 15-18, Yarborough 19-22, Baker 23, Charlie Glotzbach 24-25,
Hamilton 26-33, LeeRoy Yarbrough 34-37, Benny Parsons 38, Yarbrough 39-45,
Baker 46-47, Glotzbach 48-52,
Yarbrough 53, David Pearson 54,
Yarbrough 55-56, Pearson 57-58,
Baker 59-64, Yarbrough 65-66,
Baker 67-72, Pearson 73,
Baker 74-86, Pearson 87,
Baker 88-94, Bobby Allison 95,
Baker 96, Pearson 97-102,
Baker 103-106, Bobby Isaac 107-110,
Baker 111-130, Pearson 131-153,
Donnie Allison 154-160.
Cautions: 3 for 17 laps
Margin of Victory: 15 seconds
Attendance: 55,700
*Relieved by Raymond Williams

International Speedway. It was the third win of the season for the Hueytown, AL Ford driver.

Allison started 15th after a poor week of practice and qualifying. After several engine related malfunctions,

Donnie Allison #27 leads brother Bobby in Firecracker 400

David Pearson limps off the banks at Daytona after blowing a tire late in the Firecracker 400

car owner Banjo Matthews borrowed an engine from Ford friend Junior Johnson.

Allison had worked his way up to second, but was 10 seconds behind leader David Pearson in the final laps. Then, with seven laps to go, the right front tire on Pearson's Ford literally exploded. The force of the blast ripped the right front quarter panel to pieces and damaged the suspension. "I've never seen a tire come apart like that," said Pearson, who was unable to get back in the race. "It's a good thing I was on the back-stretch and not in a corner when it came apart."

Allison scooted into the lead with seven laps left and outdistanced Buddy Baker's Dodge by 15 seconds. Bobby Allison finished third, Charlie Glotzbach was fourth and Dick Brooks fifth.

"David's bad luck was my good luck," said Allison. "I never could have caught him, and I was running as fast as I could. My car wasn't that fast. I could hardly keep sight of the leaders."

Baker was one of the contenders from start to finish, but he had problems with chunking tires near the end. "I felt I could outrun anyone on the track," said Baker. "But my right front tire started chunking. I still stood on it -- it was my only chance. Then the left front tire chunked. I had to settle for second place."

A number of competitors said the tire situation was dangerous. The recent Goodyear tire strike had affected the development and quality of the tires which were shipped to Daytona.

Pole winner Cale Yarborough blew an engine after 23 laps and parked his Mercury. Fred Lorenzen's Dodge was kayoed with distributor failure; LeeRoy Yarbrough took a trip to the showers after his engine blew; Pete Hamilton's Plymouth suffered ignition failure; and Richard Petty's engine blew late in the race.

Bobby Isaac's point lead was cut to four points. Isaac finished ninth and James Hylton was seventh.

Allison averaged 162.235 mph for his fifth career NASCAR Grand National victory.

Race No. 25

Bobby Pits, Petty Wins Malta; Hylton Leads Standings

MALTA, NY (July 7) -- Richard Petty took the lead five laps from the finish and won the Albany-Saratoga 250 at Albany-Saratoga Speedway. It was the seventh win of the season for the 33 year-old Plymouth driver.

Bobby Allison had picked up the lead in the 179th lap of the 250-lap contest on the .362-mile paved track. Allison appeared to have the muscle to hold off Petty, but he had to make a pit stop for fuel with five laps remaining.

Allison got back out of the pits a lap behind, but still held on to second place. Dave Marcis was third, Neil Castles was fourth and G.C. Spencer fifth.

James Hylton finished sixth and moved into the Grand National point lead. Bobby Isaac's Dodge ran into mechanical problems and finished 17th, 36 laps behind. The Catawba, NC driver had won the pole and led the first 47 laps, but he fell seven points behind Hylton in the battle for the national championship.

Petty averaged 68.589 mph. Isaac had won the pole with a speed of 73.213 mph, but official NASCAR

Grand National Race No. 25
250 Laps at Albany-Saratoga Speedway
Malta, NY
"Albany-Saratoga 250"
90.5 Miles on .362-mile Paved Track
July 7, 1970

Fin	St	No.	Driver	Team / Car	Laps	Money	Status
1	2	43	Richard Petty	Petty Ent '70 Plymouth	250	$1,500	Running
2	3	22	Bobby Allison	Allison '69 Dodge	249	900	Running
3	4	30	Dave Marcis	Marcis '69 Dodge	246	500	Running
4	10	06	Neil Castles	Castles '69 Dodge	243	350	Running
5	9	49	G C Spencer	Spencer '69 Plymouth	240	325	Running
6	5	48	James Hylton	Hylton Eng '69 Ford	238	300	Running
7	14	64	Elmo Langley	Langley '69 Mercury	235	275	Running
8	15	34	Wendell Scott	Scott '69 Ford	235	270	Running
9	20	18	Joe Frasson	Frasson '70 Plymouth	233	265	Running
10	17	45	Bill Seifert	Seifert '69 Ford	233	260	Running
11	23	78	Tom Usry	J D McDuffie '69 Buick	226	255	Running
12	16	8	Ed Negre	Negre '69 Ford	225	250	Running
13	22	24	Cecil Gordon	Gordon '68 Ford	225	245	Running
14	19	47	Raymond Williams	Bill Seifert '68 Ford	219	240	Running
15	25	77	John Kenney	Bob Freeman '69 Ford	217	235	Running
16	27	82	John Jennings	'69 Ford	216	230	Running
17	1	71	Bobby Isaac	K&K Insurance '69 Dodge	214	225	Running
18	21	0	Cliff Tyler	'69 Chevrolet	202	220	Flat Tire
19	12	79	Frank Warren	Warren '69 Plymouth	187	215	Rear End
20	24	67	Dick May	Joyce Ronacher '69 Ford	158	210	Running
21	13	4	John Sears	Sears '69 Dodge	155	205	Axle
22	26	04	Ken Meisenhelder	Meisenhelder '69 Ford	135	200	Flagged
23	6	70	J D McDuffie	McDuffie '69 Mercury	127	200	Ignition
24	8	25	Jabe Thomas	Don Robertson '69 Plymouth	127	200	Rear End
25	7	72	Benny Parsons	L G DeWitt '69 Ford	71	200	Trans
26	11	68	Larry Baumel	Auto Lad '69 Ford	32	200	Oil Leak
27	18	74	Bill Shirey	Shirey '69 Plymouth	2	200	Quit
28	28	23	James Cox	Don Robertson '69 Plymouth	2	200	Quit

Time of Race: 1 hour, 19 minutes, 10 seconds
Average Speed: 68.589 mph
Pole Winner: Bobby Isaac - 73.213 mph
Lap Leaders: Bobby Isaac 1-47, Richard Petty 48-178, Bobby Allison 179-245, Petty 246-250.
Cautions: 1 for 4 laps   Margin of Victory: 1-lap plus   Attendance: 9,500

Grand National Race No. 26
200 Laps at Thompson Speedway
Thompson, CT
"Thompson Speedway 200"
108.4 Miles on .542-mile Paved Track
July 9, 1970

Fin	St	No.	Driver	Team / Car	Laps	Money	Status
1	1	71	Bobby Isaac	K&K Insurance '69 Dodge	200	$2,500	Running
2	2	43	Richard Petty	Petty Ent '70 Plymouth	200	1,800	Running
3	5	72	Benny Parsons	L G DeWitt '69 Ford	198	1,100	Running
4	9	32	Richard Brooks	Brooks '69 Plymouth	198	900	Running
5	4	06	Neil Castles	Castles '69 Dodge	198	800	Running
6	10	30	Dave Marcis	Marcis '69 Dodge	197	700	Running
7	3	22	Bobby Allison	Allison '69 Dodge	196	650	Running
8	6	48	James Hylton	Hylton Eng '69 Ford	195	600	Running
9	14	25	Jabe Thomas	Don Robertson '69 Plymouth	189	550	Running
10	12	64	Elmo Langley	Langley '69 Mercury	188	500	Running
11	11	70	J D McDuffie	McDuffie '69 Mercury	187	475	Running
12	17	45	Bill Seifert	Seifert '69 Ford	183	450	Running
13	20	18	Joe Frasson	Frasson '70 Plymouth	183	425	Running
14	16	79	Frank Warren	Warren '69 Plymouth	183	400	Running
15	21	8	Ed Negre	Negre '69 Ford	182	390	Running
16	15	4	John Sears	Sears '69 Dodge	181	380	Running
17	13	24	Cecil Gordon	Gordon '68 Ford	176	370	Brakes
18	24	47	Raymond Williams	Bill Seifert '68 Ford	176	360	Running
19	29	04	Ken Meisenhelder	Meisenhelder '69 Chevrolet	172	350	Running
20	18	34	Wendell Scott	Scott '69 Ford	171	340	Running
21	7	49	G C Spencer	Spencer '69 Plymouth	156	330	Engine
22	19	10	Bill Champion	Champion '69 Ford	125	320	Steering
23	28	23	James Cox	Don Robertson '69 Plymouth	113	310	Heating
24	23	62	Ron Keselowski	Keselowski Auto '69 Dodge	101	300	Oil Leak
25	26	67	Dick May	Joyce Ronacher '69 Ford	57	250	Oil Leak
26	27	82	John Jennings	'69 Ford	54	250	Engine
27	25	77	John Kenney	Bob Freeman '68 Ford	37	250	Ignition
28	30	0	Cliff Tyler	'69 Chevrolet	21	250	Oil Leak
29	8	68	Larry Baumel	Auto Lad '69 Ford	10	250	Ignition
30	22	74	Bill Shirey	Shirey '69 Plymouth	5	250	Quit

Time of Race: 1 hour, 21 minutes,
Average Speed: 80.296 mph
Pole Winner: Bobby Isaac - 87.029 mph
Lap Leaders: Bobby Isaac 1-117, Richard Petty 118-128, Benny Parsons 129-135, Isaac 136-200.
Cautions: 1 for 7 laps   Margin of Victory: Attendance: 8,000

figures said he won the pole at 81.466 mph. Isaac toured the .362-mile track in 17.80 seconds in qualifying, which computes to 73.213 mph.

Race No. 26

Isaac Takes Thompson 200; Ties Hylton for Point Lead

THOMPSON, CT (July 9) -- Bobby Isaac took the lead from rookie Benny Parsons in the 136th lap and sped to victory in the Thompson Speedway 200 at Thompson Speedway. It was Isaac's seventh win of the year and it deadlocked him with James Hylton at the top of the Grand National point standings.

Richard Petty wound up second with Parsons third.

Dick Brooks came in fourth and Neil Castles fifth. Hylton managed to finish eighth.

Isaac won the pole for the 32nd time in his career and led the first 117 laps. Petty took the lead for 11 laps when Isaac went to the pits. Parsons led for seven laps as pit stop continued. Isaac resumed the lead once all the leaders had visited the pits.

The caution was out only once for seven laps, and Isaac averaged 80.296 mph.

Isaac, who found himself locked up in a ferocious title battle, aired complaints about the point structure. "I think the point system could use some revising," he said. "I don't like a system that rewards a 'stroker'. Our team is running hard, leading races and winning races. But if we have trouble or fall out of a race, all the points are lost. I don't think a person *not* running to win should be this close in the championship."

Race No. 27

Petty Overcomes Practice Crash to Win at Trenton

TRENTON, NJ (July 12) -- Richard Petty battled back from a practice crash and dominated the Schaefer 300 at Trenton Speedway. It was the eighth win of the year for Petty.

Petty took the lead for the final time in the 170th lap. He motored away from his rivals and finished 2.3-seconds in front of runner-up Bobby Allison. Charlie

Grand National Race No. 27
200 Laps at Trenton Speedway
Trenton, NJ
"Schaefer 300"
300 Miles on 1.5-mile Paved Track
July 12, 1970

Fin	St	No.	Driver	Team / Car	Laps	Money	Status
1	4	43	Richard Petty	Petty Ent '70 Plym SuperBird	200	$6,730	Running
2	2	22	Bobby Allison	Mario Rossi '69 Dodge Day	200	2,470	Running
3	3	99	Charlie Glotzbach	Nchls-G'smith '69 Dodge Day	200	1,720	Running
4	5	32	Dick Brooks	Brooks '70 Plymouth	198	1,320	Running
5	7	48	James Hylton	Hylton Eng '69 Ford	196	1,045	Running
6	12	30	Dave Marcis	Bobby Allison '69 Dodge	195	795	Running
7	6	72	Benny Parsons	L G DeWitt '69 Ford	194	760	Running
8	8	06	Neil Castles	Castles '69 Dodge	193	695	Running
9	11	49	G C Spencer	Spencer '69 Plymouth	189	645	Running
10	18	03	Tommy Gale	Walt Valerio '69 Mercury	184	620	Running
11	31	57	Johnny Halford	Ervin Pruitt '69 Dodge	180	570	Running
12	20	4	John Sears	Sears '69 Dodge	180	520	Running
13	23	64	Elmo Langley	Langley '69 Mercury	179	495	Running
14	24	18	Joe Frasson	Frasson '70 Plymouth	178	470	Running
15	17	79	Frank Warren	Warren '69 Plymouth	178	445	Running
16	16	47	Raymond Williams	Bill Seifert '68 Ford	176	420	Running
17	32	04	Ken Meisenhelder	Meisenhelder '69 Chevrolet	176	390	Running
18	36	37	Dr Don Tarr	Tarr '69 Dodge	175	380	Running
19	1	71	Bobby Isaac	K&K Ins '69 Dodge Daytona	170	500	Engine
20	33	65	Joe Phipps	Phipps '69 Chevrolet	169	370	Running
21	19	10	Bill Champion	Champion '69 Ford	166	365	Running
22	26	0	Cliff Tyler	'69 Chevrolet	153	360	Running
23	15	70	J D McDuffie	McDuffie '69 Mercury	153	355	Running
24	28	67	Dick May	Joyce Ronacher '69 Ford	100	350	No Tires
25	37	26	Wendell Scott	Earl Brooks '69 Ford	84	345	Wheel
26	22	2	Dr Ed Hessert	Don Robertson '69 Plymouth	60	240	Brakes
27	25	62	Ron Keselowski	Kaye Eng '69 Dodge	55	335	Oil Pan
28	14	45	Bill Seifert	Seifert '69 Ford	35	330	Brakes
29	29	82	John Jennings	'69 Ford	28	325	Engine
30	10	90	LeeRoy Yarbrough	Junie Donlavey '69 Ford	22	320	Engine
31	21	8	Ed Negre	Negre '69 Ford	18	315	Engine
32	27	25	Jabe Thomas	Don Robertson '69 Plymouth	15	315	Engine
33	9	68	Larry Baumel	Auto Lad '69 Ford	13	330	Engine
34	35	6	Buddy Baker	Cotton Owens '69 Dodge Day	10	315	Brakes
35	13	24	Cecil Gordon	Gordon '68 Ford	4	315	Engine
36	34	74	Bill Shirey	Shirey '69 Plymouth	3	315	Quit
37	30	77	John Kenney	Bob Freeman '68 Ford	1	315	Clutch

Time of Race: 2 hours, 29 minutes, 6 seconds
Average Speed: 120.724 mph
Pole Winner: Bobby Isaac - 131.749 mph
Lap Leaders: Bobby Isaac 1-4, Richard Petty 5-22, Charlie Glotzbach 23-24,
   Bobby Allison 25-57, Petty 58-77, Glotzbach 78-80, Dick Brooks 81-82,
   James Hylton 83, Petty 84-108, Glotzbach 109-125, Petty 126-165, Glotzbach 166-169,
   Petty 170-200.
Cautions: 3 for 13 laps   Margin of Victory: 2.3 seconds   Attendance: 21,000

Glotzbach, who led until Petty made his final move, wound up third. Dick Brooks came in fourth with James Hylton fifth.

Hylton's fifth place effort enabled him to take a 28 point lead over Bobby Isaac in the NASCAR point standings. Isaac started on the pole but lost an engine with 30 laps left.

Buddy Baker and Wendell Scott crashed in the tricky first turn during qualifying. Baker's Dodge Daytona was repaired by car owner Cotton Owens, but the Charlotte driver had to start near the rear of the 37 car field. Baker went only 10 laps before brake failure put him out.

Scott lost control of his Ford and plowed into the steel retaining barrier. His

Wendell Scott wiped out his Ford in a practice crash at Trenton

red Ford climbed on top of the rail before flipping back onto the racing surface. "That's the worst wreck I've ever been in," said the 48 year-old Danville, VA veteran. "My car is destroyed. It's my only ride. I don't know about my future plans."

Long time friend Earl Brooks invited Scott to drive his car in the race. Scott finished 25th in the race and was able to hold onto 12th place in the point standings.

Petty was in the lead on five occasions for a total of 134 laps. "After I wrecked the car (in practice), we picked up about a half second," he remarked. "The car ran a lot better after I ran into the wall."

Petty's 109th career win came at an average speed of 120.724 mph on the 1.5-mile kidney-shaped track. A crowd of 21,000 watched the 200 lap event.

Race No. 28

Allison-Marcis Tag Team Tops in Volunteer 500

BRISTOL, TN (July 19) -- Dave Marcis drove Bobby Allison's Dodge the final 130 laps and finished two laps ahead of the field in the wreck-marred Volunteer 500 at Bristol International Speedway.

The 500 lap event in Tennessee's "Thunder Valley" was a heat-searing contest. LeeRoy Yarbrough, who

Benny Parsons #72 and Dick Brooks #32 lead
eventual winner Bobby Allison at Bristol

the pace. G.C. Spencer was fourth and Richard Petty and Pete Hamilton formed the fifth place team.

"I saw what LeeRoy and Petty were doing (calling for relief)," said winner Allison. "I decided I was foolish to try it by myself. It was hot and I was getting tired. I saw Marcis in my pit and I couldn't think of anyone I'd rather have in my car."

Marcis enjoyed basking in the victory lane

Earl Brooks spins off track at Bristol after crash

had to call on relief from Donnie Allison, wound up in second place. Bobby Isaac finished third, nine laps off

Grand National Race   No. 28
500 Laps at Bristol Int'l Speedway
Bristol, TN
"Volunteer 500"
266.5 Miles on .533-mile Paved Track
July 19, 1970

Fin	St	No.	Driver	Team / Car	Laps	Money	Status
1	10	22	Bobby Allison*	Allison '69 Dodge	500	$4,850	Running
2	9	98	LeeRoy Yarbrough**	Junior Johnson '69 Ford	498	2,850	Running
3	3	71	Bobby Isaac	K&K Insurance '70 Dodge	491	2,075	Running
4	11	49	G C Spencer	Spencer '69 Plymouth	479	1,385	Running
5	6	43	Richard Petty***	Petty Ent '70 Plymouth	464	1,050	Engine
6	24	79	Frank Warren	Warren '69 Plymouth	454	850	Running
7	17	10	Bill Champion	Champion '68 Ford	449	825	Running
8	25	45	Elmo Langley	Langley '69 Ford	447	700	Running
9	19	70	J D McDuffie	McDuffie '69 Mercury	439	675	Running
10	23	24	Cecil Gordon	Gordon '68 Ford	429	625	Running
11	15	48	James Hylton	Hylton Eng '69 Ford	427	585	Running
12	30	19	Henley Gray	Gray '68 Ford	421	575	Running
13	12	39	Friday Hassler	James Hanley '69 Chevrolet	354	565	Engine
14	27	76	Ben Arnold	Arnold '68 Ford	319	595	Running
15	26	25	Jabe Thomas	Don Robertson '69 Plymouth	252	545	Rear End
16	22	4	John Sears	Sears '69 Dodge	235	535	Axle
17	1	21	Cale Yarborough	Wood Brothers '69 Mercury	221	1,125	Crash
18	28	34	Wendell Scott	Earl Brooks '69 Ford	149	515	Crash
19	5	72	Benny Parsons	L G DeWitt '69 Ford	136	530	Crash
20	20	26	Earl Brooks	Brooks '69 Ford	126	495	Engine
21	16	06	Neil Castles	Castles '69 Dodge	126	485	Crash
22	2	17	David Pearson	Holman-Moody '69 Ford	100	775	Crash
23	8	30	Dave Marcis	Marcis '69 Dodge	83	465	Engine
24	14	02	Dick Bown	Mike Ober '70 Plym SuperBird	75	480	Handling
25	4	27	Donnie Allison	Banjo Matthews '69 Ford	67	470	Engine
26	7	32	Dick Brooks	Brooks '69 Plymouth	51	440	Crash
27	13	28	Fred Lorenzen	Richard Howard '70 Dodge	48	470	Heating
28	29	33	Wayne Smith	Smith '69 Chevrolet	30	430	Heating
29	18	5	Buddy Arrington	Arrington '69 Dodge	5	430	Brakes
30	21	64	Bill Seifert	Elmo Langley '69 Ford	1	430	Engine

Time of Race: 3 hours, 8 minutes, 23 seconds
Average Speed: 84.880 mph
Pole Winner: Cale Yarborough - 107.375 mph
Lap Leaders: Cale Yarborough 1-81, Bobby Allison 82-91, Yarborough 92-103,
    B.Allison 104-125, Yarborough 126-139, B.Allison 140, Yarborough 141-163,
    B.Allison 164-208, Yarborough 209-221, B.Allison 222-500.
Cautions: 8 for 54 laps   Margin of Victory: 2-laps plus   Attendance: 22,500
*Relieved by Dave Marcis   **Relieved by Donnie Allison   ***Relieved by Pete Hamilton

Bobby Allison and Dave Marcis in Bristol's victory lane

celebration. "I was familiar with the car," said the 29 year-old Wausau, WI driver. "Bobby let me drive this car last week at Trenton. All I had to do here was keep it in front. Bobby put it in the lead."

Wrecks took out several contenders. Pole sitter Cale Yarborough had led 143 of the first 221 laps, but he blew a tire and crashed his Mercury while holding a big lead. Dick Brooks crashed on lap 51, knocking him out of the race. Wendell Scott, Benny Parsons and Neil Castles also wrecked.

David Pearson provided a scare when his Ford popped a tire and nailed the inside pit wall head-on. The impact was severe and there was little movement in the driver's compartment for a few minutes. "That was a hard lick," Pearson said afterwards. "I've always been told that if you hit something hard enough to knock your shoes off, you're dead. When I came to, I looked on the floorboard and saw my shoes laying there. I thought for sure I was dead."

Only 12 cars finished the event. A crowd of 22,500 watched Allison and Marcis average 84.880 mph.

Point leader James Hylton wound up 11th, 73 laps off the pace. His point lead was shaved to 12 points over Isaac.

Grand National Race No. 29
200 Laps at Smoky Mountain Raceway
Maryville, TN
"East Tennessee 200"
104 Miles on .520-mile Paved Track
July 24, 1970

Fin	St	No.	Driver	Team / Car	Laps	Money	Status
1	1	43	Richard Petty	Petty Ent '70 Plymouth	200	$1,500	Running
2	3	71	Bobby Isaac	K&K Insurance '69 Dodge	200	900	Running
3	10	32	Dick Brooks	Brooks '69 Plymouth	198	500	Running
4	6	48	James Hylton	Hylton Eng '69 Ford	196	350	Running
5	2	39	Friday Hassler	James Hanley '69 Chevrolet	196	325	Running
6	12	02	Dick Bown	Mike Ober '70 Plym SuperBird	190	300	Running
7	8	06	Neil Castles	Castles '69 Dodge	189	275	Running
8	26	25	Jabe Thomas	Don Robertson '69 Plymouth	186	270	Running
9	17	10	Bill Champion	Champion '68 Ford	185	265	Running
10	20	24	Cecil Gordon	Gordon '68 Ford	183	260	Running
11	23	4	John Sears	Sears '69 Dodge	183	255	Running
12	18	76	Ben Arnold	Arnold '68 Ford	182	250	Running
13	9	72	Benny Parsons	L G DeWitt '69 Ford	180	245	Wheel
14	27	45	Raymond Williams	Bill Seifert '69 Ford	180	240	Running
15	4	30	Dave Marcis	Marcis '69 Dodge	177	235	Oil Line
16	29	04	Ken Meisenhelder	Meisenhelder '69 Chevrolet	174	230	Running
17	5	22	Bobby Allison	Allison '69 Dodge	173	225	Running
18	21	79	Frank Warren	Warren '69 Plymouth	171	220	Fuel pump
19	30	97	Lee Gordon	Cecil Gordon '68 Ford	169	215	Running
20	16	64	Elmo Langley	Langley '69 Ford	107	210	Suspen
21	13	70	J D McDuffie	McDuffie '69 Mercury	80	205	Brakes
22	22	57	Johnny Halford	Ervin Pruitt '69 Dodge	66	200	Brakes
23	19	8	Ed Negre	Negre '69 Ford	55	200	Engine
24	7	49	G C Spencer	Spencer '69 Plymouth	51	200	Crash
25	24	34	Wendell Scott	Don Robertson '69 Plymouth	21	200	Oil Leak
26	14	26	Earl Brooks	Brooks '69 Ford	19	200	Oil Line
27	11	5	Buddy Arrington	Arrington '69 Dodge	15	200	Rear End
28	15	54	Bill Dennis	Dennis '69 Chevrolet	11	200	Wtr pump
29	28	60	Charlie Robertson	'69 Dodge	11	200	Trans
30	25	19	Henley Gray	Gray '69 Ford	7	200	Oil Leak

Time of Race: 1 hour, 13 minutes, 27 seconds
Average Speed: 84.956 mph
Pole Winner: Richard Petty - 91.264 mph
Lap Leaders: Richard Petty 1-127, Bobby Isaac 128-141, Dick Brooks 142-155, Petty 156-200.
Cautions: 2 for 7 laps   Margin of Victory: 1 car length   Attendance: 6,000

Race No. 29

Petty Edges Isaac By a Car Length at Maryville

MARYVILLE, TN (July 24) -- Richard Petty took the lead from Dick Brooks with 47 laps to go and held off Bobby Isaac to win the East Tennessee 200 at Smoky Mountain Raceway.

Petty, Isaac and Brooks were the three challengers in the 104-lap race on the .520-mile paved oval. Petty started on the pole and led the first 127 laps. Isaac led for 14 laps and Brooks was on top 14 laps before Petty got back in the lead for good.

Petty and Isaac battled bumper-to-bumper for the final 30 laps -- often running side-by-side. "That's as close as Isaac and myself have run this year," said Petty. "I got to racing Brooks and heated my tires up. That almost let Isaac slip by."

Brooks finished third and James Hylton was fourth. Hylton led the point chase by just 10 points over Isaac. Fifth place went to Friday Hassler.

Dave Marcis qualified fourth and ran behind Petty and Isaac in the early stages. A broken oil line put him out late in the race.

Hassler, of Chattanooga, TN, qualified second to Petty and made a strong run all evening. He was four laps off the pace in the end.

Petty averaged 84.956 mph before an audience of 6,000.

Race No. 30

Weary Isaac Takes Nashville; Blasts New Track

NASHVILLE, TN (July 25) -- Weary Bobby Isaac, driving on little sleep from a demanding schedule, stayed out of trouble and easily won the Nashville 420 at the new Fairgrounds Speedway.

Isaac, who admittedly drove a cautious pace, missed all the tire-related accidents and finished two laps ahead of runner-up Bobby Allison. Neil Castles came in third, Cecil Gordon was fourth and J.D. McDuffie fifth. Only nine cars in the starting field of 36 finished.

Blown tires triggered several crashes on the new .596-mile oval with imposing turns banked at 35 degrees. James Hylton lost the point lead when he crashed on lap 17. He fell 44 points behind Isaac in the

Grand National Race No. 30
420 Laps at Fairgrounds Speedway
Nashville, TN
"Nashville 420"
250 Miles on .596-mile Paved Track
July 25, 1970

Fin	St	No.	Driver	Team / Car	Laps	Money	Status
1	2	71	Bobby Isaac	K&K Insurance '69 Dodge	420	$3,310	Running
2	8	22	Bobby Allison	Allison '69 Dodge	418	1,910	Running
3	16	06	Neil Castles	Castles '69 Dodge	394	1,310	Running
4	15	24	Cecil Gordon	Gordon '68 Ford	391	1,010	Running
5	26	70	J D McDuffie	McDuffie '69 Mercury	385	910	Running
6	6	07	Coo Coo Marlin	Cunningham-Kelley '69 Chev	384	860	Running
7	10	76	Ben Arnold	Arnold '69 Ford	380	835	Running
8	23	25	Jabe Thomas	Don Robertson '69 Plymouth	365	810	Running
9	36	03	Eddie Yarboro	'69 Plymouth	338	800	Running
10	13	30	Dave Marcis	Marcis '69 Dodge	336	790	Crash
11	25	79	Frank Warren	Warren '69 Plymouth	318	780	Rear End
12	29	77	John Kenney	Bob Freeman '68 Ford	242	770	Crash
13	28	10	Bill Champion	Champion '69 Ford	221	760	Crash
14	7	39	Friday Hassler	James Hanley '69 Chevrolet	209	750	Ignition
15	34	74	Bill Shirey	Shirey '69 Plymouth	167	740	Quit
16	3	43	Richard Petty	Petty Ent '70 Plymouth	154	730	Crash
17	21	8	Ed Negre	Negre '69 Ford	151	720	Engine
18	19	67	Dick May	Joyce Ronacher '69 Ford	139	710	Crash
19	27	57	Johnny Halford	Ervin Pruitt '69 Dodge	111	700	Vibration
20	31	45	Raymond Williams	Bill Seifert '69 Ford	78	690	Engine
21	9	02	Dick Bown	Mike Ober '70 Plym SuperBird	63	680	Sway bar
22	12	72	Benny Parsons	L G DeWitt '69 Ford	59	670	Wheel
23	1	98	LeeRoy Yarbrough	Junior Johnson '70 Ford	45	660	Crash
24	30	19	Henley Gray	Gray '69 Ford	45	650	Quit
25	32	60	Charlie Roberts	'69 Dodge	39	640	Oil Leak
26	14	26	Earl Brooks	Brooks'69 Ford	35	635	Engine
27	24	4	John Sears	Sears '69 Dodge	34	625	Engine
28	5	48	James Hylton	Hylton Eng '69 Ford	17	615	Crash
29	17	34	Wendell Scott	Don Robertson '69 Plymouth	10	605	Oil Line
30	22	62	Ron Keselowski	Kaye Eng '69 Dodge	8	590	Engine
31	35	97	Lee Gordon	Cecil Gordon '68 Ford	7	570	Quit
32	11	5	Buddy Arrington	Arrington '69 Dodge	5	550	Rear End
33	18	54	Bill Dennis	Dennis '69 Chevrolet	5	530	Heating
34	33	64	Elmo Langley	Langley '69 Mercury	3	525	Engine
35	4	32	Dick Brooks	Brooks '70 Plymouth	1	520	Axle
36	20	49	G C Spencer	Spencer '69 Plymouth	1	515	Engine

Time of Race: 2 hours, 50 minutes 47 seconds
Average Speed: 87.943 mph
Pole Winner: LeeRoy Yarbrough - 114.115 mph
Lap Leaders: LeeRoy Yarbrough 1-16, Richard Petty 17-150,
    Friday Hassler 151-164, Bobby Isaac 165-167, Hassler 168-209,
    Isaac 210-420.
Cautions: 4 for 39 laps   Margin of Victory: 2-laps plus   Attendance: 17,000

Grand National point standings.

Isaac led the final 211 laps and won only $3,310 in the nationally televised event. "There was a tire problem because there wasn't enough time to make tests," said Isaac. "I just cooled it. Harry (Hyde, crew chief) and I decided to run cautiously when we heard about this track. The only time I ran hard was in qualifying."

LeeRoy Yarbrough started on the pole and led the first 16 laps. The race was only 45 laps off when Yarbrough blew a tire and slapped the wall.

Richard Petty led from lap 17-150, but crashed on lap 154 when a tire let go. Dave Marcis was running third when a blown tire sent his Dodge into the second turn wall. There were no serious injuries.

Hylton's mishap set off a verbal blast from the Inman, SC Ford driver. "This is the lousiest track in the country," Hylton steamed. "They topped Bristol with this one. The walls are too low, the track has gullies in it and the pit area is dangerous."

Chevrolet driver Friday Hassler forged to the front twice for 56 laps and was leading when ignition failure put him out of the race. Isaac took the lead at that point and was never headed.

ABC-Sports, which televised the event live, did so despite an injunction. ABC crewmen were warned not to broadcast the race by Chancellor Alfred Adams, who issued a temporary court order at the request of WMCM-TV in Nashville. The station contended it held rights for televising.

A spokesman for ABC said the network had not been notified of the injunction. "Besides," said the spokesman, "our contract is with NASCAR."

Race No. 31
Petty Marches Through Atlanta; Wins Dixie 500

HAMPTON, GA (Aug. 2) -- Richard Petty aired out his SuperBird and flew away from the field to win the Dixie 500 at Atlanta International Raceway. The Randleman, NC driver led all but 43 of the 328 laps and wound up a lap and 31 seconds in front of Cale Yarborough. LeeRoy Yarbrough, with relief assistance from Charlie Glotzbach, finished third. Buddy Baker came in fourth and Donnie Allison was fifth.

Dick Brooks spins into pit wall at Atlanta

*Dale Inman's quick service in pits helped Richard Petty
lap the field in Dixie 500*

James Hylton retook the point lead by finishing 10th.
Bobby Isaac went behind the wall after 83 laps and fell
31 laps behind. "I was just cruising, trying to finish,"
said Isaac. "If I had been going any slower, they would
have thought I was driving the pace car. We know
we're going to have to stroke it to have a chance to win
the championship. I hate to do that, but those are orders
from the top." Nord Krauskopf is President of K&K
Insurance Co., which owns and sponsors Isaac's
Dodges.

Fred Lorenzen won the pole in his winged Dodge,
but never led a lap. Lorenzen called for relief help from
Dave Marcis, but the engine let go 10 laps after Marcis
got in the car.

David Pearson led the first lap after starting fifth, but
was out of the race on lap 126. Pearson made a routine
pit stop. Crew chief Dick Hutcherson noticed fumes
were coming from the driver's compartment. "It was
terrible," said Hutcherson. "I looked at David and he
was glossy-eyed. I asked him 'Where are you David'?
He told me 'I'm somewhere in Atlanta. It's hot and the
fields are green'. I pulled him out and parked the car."

Dick Brooks was the only victim of a wreck. The 28
year-old Porterville, CA sophomore spun his Super-
Bird down pit road and backed into a concrete wall.

Petty averaged 142.712 mph before a crowd of
20,000.

The 500-miler was in danger of being canceled due to
Raceway financial problems. Atlanta International
Raceway, under Larry LoPatin's American Raceways,
Inc., had hit on hard times and there was not enough
money to post the $102,295 purse. Richard Howard,
General Manager of Charlotte Motor Speedway,
stepped in and posted the purse. The race went on as
scheduled.

Grand National Race No. 31
328 Laps at Atlanta Int'l Raceway
Hampton, GA
"Dixie 500"
500 Miles on 1.522-mile Paved Track
August 2, 1970

Fin	St	No.	Driver	Team / Car	Laps	Money	Status
1	6	43	Richard Petty	Petty Ent '70 Plym SuperBird	328	$19,600	Running
2	4	21	Cale Yarborough	Wood Brothers '69 Mercury	327	11,525	Running
3	7	98	LeeRoy Yarbrough*	Junior Johnson '69 Mercury	326	7,200	Running
4	2	6	Buddy Baker	Cotton Owens '69 Dodge Day	326	3,775	Running
5	11	27	Donnie Allison	Banjo Matthews '69 Ford	325	2,800	Running
6	10	40	Pete Hamilton	Petty Ent '70 Plym SuperBird	324	2,500	Running
7	29	22	Bobby Allison	Mario Rossi '69 Dodge Day	323	1,875	Running
8	12	72	Benny Parsons	L G DeWitt '69 Ford	323	1,850	Running
9	13	31	Jim Vandiver	O L Nixon '69 Dodge Daytona	316	1,800	Running
10	18	48	James Hylton	Hylton Eng '69 Ford	310	1,525	Running
11	26	39	Friday Hassler	James Hanley '69 Chevrolet	307	1,475	Running
12	34	4	John Sears	Sears '69 Dodge	304	1,400	Running
13	17	64	Elmo Langley	Langley '69 Mercury	303	1,375	Running
14	27	46	Roy Mayne	Tom Hunter '69 Chevrolet	300	1,325	Running
15	32	07	Coo Coo Marlin	Cunningham-Kelley '69 Chev	300	1,255	Running
16	21	76	Ben Arnold	Arnold '69 Ford	299	1,225	Running
17	37	57	Johnny Halford	Ervin Pruitt '69 Dodge	297	1,150	Running
18	28	5	Buddy Arrington	Arrington '69 Dodge	295	1,125	Running
19	31	02	Dick Bown	Mike Ober '70 Plym SuperBird	292	1,060	Running
20	39	45	Bill Seifert	Seifert '69 Ford	292	1,000	Running
21	15	06	Neil Castles	Castles '69 Dodge Daytona	287	1,000	Running
22	1	28	Fred Lorenzen**	Ray Fox '69 Dodge Daytona	284	1,550	Engine
23	22	8	Ed Negre	Negre '69 Ford	279	950	Running
24	40	25	Jabe Thomas	Don Robertson '69 Plymouth	278	900	Running
25	24	68	Larry Baumel	Auto Lad '69 Ford	244	915	Engine
26	9	32	Dick Brooks	Brooks '70 Plym SuperBird	219	930	Crash
27	23	49	G C Spencer	Spencer '69 Plymouth	196	895	Engine
28	19	34	Joe Frasson	Frasson '69 Dodge Daytona	183	880	Engine
29	14	30	Dave Marcis	Marcis '69 Dodge Daytona	165	875	Ignition
30	20	79	Frank Warren	Warren '69 Plymouth	164	865	Gr Seal
31	36	34	Wendell Scott	Don Robertson '69 Plymouth	136	830	Engine
32	5	17	David Pearson	Holman-Moody '69 Ford	126	1,370	Engine
33	8	99	Charlie Glotzbach	Nchls-G'smith '69 Dodge Day	108	860	Engine
34	35	54	Bill Dennis	Dennis '69 Chevrolet	93	800	Engine
35	3	71	Bobby Isaac	K&K Ins '69 Dodge Daytona	83	840	Engine
36	38	26	Earl Brooks	Brooks '69 Ford	77	780	Engine
37	25	24	Cecil Gordon	Gordon '68 Ford	69	795	Frame
38	30	10	Bill Champion	Champion '69 Ford	53	770	Suspen
39	33	16	J D McDuffie	Ken Spikes '70 Chevrolet	30	755	Vibration
40	16	36	Bugs Stevens	Richard Brown '70 Plym S'Bird	24	775	Engine

Time of Race: 3 hours, 29 minutes, 53 seconds
Average Speed: 142.712 mph
Pole Winner: Fred Lorenzen - 157.625 mph
Lap Leaders: David Pearson 1, Buddy Baker 2-16, LeeRoy Yarbrough 17,
    Richard Petty 18-56, Yarbrough 57-60, Petty 61-116, Yarbrough 117-123,
    Petty 124-175, Yarbrough 176-180, Petty 181-328.
Cautions: 1 for 10 laps   Margin of Victory: 1 lap and 31 seconds   Attendance: 20,000
*Relieved by Charlie Glotzbach   **Relieved by Dave Marcis

Race No. 32

Isaac Outduels Petty to Win On Columbia Dirt

COLUMBIA, SC (Aug. 6) -- Bobby Isaac drove his
Dodge around a spinning Richard Petty in the 96th lap
and went on to win the Sandlapper 200 at Columbia

Speedway. It was the ninth win of the year for the shaggy-haired veteran.

Petty finished 6.0-seconds behind Isaac's fleet Dodge. Bobby Allison came in third, John Sears was fourth and Neil Castles fifth. It was a 1-2-3-4-5 sweep for Chrysler products.

Petty won the pole and led the first 95 laps. Rookie Ron Keselowski qualified second and ran with the leaders until he wrecked on lap 72. Petty looped his car while leading in turn one and Isaac grabbed the lead for keeps.

"We changed all four tires on the yellow flag and I wasn't worried about running hard," said Isaac. "The way the tires have been this year, we figured we'd change 'em all."

Frank Warren started third on the grid, but lost control of his Plymouth on lap 21 and hit the guard rails. Dave Marcis, and Benny Parsons also crashed on the half-mile dirt track.

Isaac averaged 67.101 mph for his 30th career Grand National win.

Grand National Race No. 32
200 Laps at Columbia Speedway
Columbia, SC
"Sandlapper 200"
100 Miles on Half-mile Dirt Track
August 6, 1970

Fin	St	No.	Driver	Team / Car	Laps	Money	Status
1	7	71	Bobby Isaac	K&K Insurance '70 Dodge	200	$1,500	Running
2	1	43	Richard Petty	Petty Ent '70 Plymouth	200	900	Running
3	11	22	Bobby Allison	Allison '69 Dodge	199	500	Running
4	8	4	John Sears	Sears '69 Dodge	197	350	Running
5	4	06	Neil Castles	Castles '69 Dodge	196	325	Running
6	9	64	Elmo Langley	Langley '69 Ford	193	300	Running
7	10	25	Jabe Thomas	Don Robertson '69 Plymouth	191	275	Running
8	20	26	Earl Brooks	Brooks '69 Ford	190	270	Running
9	6	48	James Hylton	Hylton Eng '70 Ford	188	265	Running
10	13	82	Roy Tyner	'68 Ford	188	260	Running
11	25	04	Ken Meisenhelder	Meisenhelder '69 Chevrolet	172	255	Running
12	21	34	Wendell Scott	Don Robertson '69 Plymouth	168	250	Flat tire
13	23	74	Bill Shirey	Shirey '69 Plymouth	92	245	Engine
14	2	62	Ron Keselowski	Kaye Eng '69 Dodge	72	240	Crash
15	18	51	Dave Marcis	Bill Strong '69 Chevrolet	70	235	Crash
16	12	72	Benny Parsons	L G DeWitt '69 Ford	68	230	Crash
17	17	32	Dick Brooks	Brooks '70 Plymouth	50	225	Brakes
18	14	8	Ed Negre	Negre '69 Ford	37	220	Trans
19	15	45	Bill Seifert	Seifert '69 Ford	30	215	Vibration
20	22	67	Dick May	Joyce Ronacher '69 Ford	24	210	Heating
21	3	79	Frank Warren	Warren '69 Plymouth	21	205	Crash
22	16	87	Leroy Carrigg	'68 Ford	19	200	Crash
23	24	70	J D McDuffie	McDuffie '69 Buick	16	200	Engine
24	19	24	Cecil Gordon	Gordon '69 Ford	4	200	Quit
25	5	10	Bill Champion	Champion '69 Ford	1	200	Quit

Time of Race: 1 hour, 29 minutes, 25 seconds
Average Speed: 67.101 mph
Pole Winner: Richard Petty - 72.695 mph
Lap Leaders: Richard Petty 1-95, Bobby Isaac 96-200.
Cautions: 3 for 22 laps   Margin of Victory: 6 seconds   Attendance: 6,800

Grand National Race No. 33
300 Laps at Int'l Raceway Park
Ona, WV
"West Virginia 300"
131.1 Miles on .437-mile Paved Track
August 11, 1970

Fin	St	No.	Driver	Team / Car	Laps	Money	Status
1	3	43	Richard Petty	Petty Ent '70 Plymouth	300	$1,700	Running
2	7	48	James Hylton	Hylton Eng '70 Ford	292	1,100	Running
3	5	06	Neil Castles	Castles '69 Dodge	290	600	Running
4	6	4	John Sears	Sears '69 Dodge	290	480	Running
5	15	97	Dave Marcis	Cecil Gordon '68 Ford	283	425	Running
6	14	24	Cecil Gordon	Gordon '68 Ford	282	400	Running
7	11	64	Elmo Langley	Langley '69 Ford	282	350	Running
8	20	62	Ron Keselowski	Kaye Eng '69 Dodge	276	340	Running
9	25	33	Pop McGinnis	'69 Mercury	274	330	Running
10	2	71	Bobby Isaac	K&K Insurance '70 Dodge	267	320	Rear End
11	1	22	Bobby Allison	Allison '69 Dodge	263	310	Running
12	18	8	Ed Negre	Negre '69 Ford	259	300	Running
13	12	25	Jabe Thomas	Don Robertson '69 Plymouth	234	290	Rear End
14	17	79	Frank Warren	Warren '69 Plymouth	142	280	Radiator
15	10	34	Wendell Scott	Don Robertson '69 Plymouth	50	270	Oil Leak
16	13	45	Bill Seifert	Seifert '69 Ford	42	260	Trans
17	9	26	Earl Brooks	Brooks '69 Ford	41	250	Quit
18	16	19	Henley Gray	Gray '69 Ford	33	240	Exhaust
19	23	68	Larry Baumel	Auto Lad '69 Ford	21	235	Quit
20	22	87	Leroy Carrigg	'69 Ford	9	230	Quit
21	4	86	Buddy Baker	Neil Castles '69 Dodge Daytona	7	225	Brakes
22	21	54	Bill Dennis	Dennis '69 Chevrolet	7	220	Fan Belt
23	8	72	Benny Parsons	L G DeWitt '69 Ford	4	215	Quit
24	24	04	Ken Meisenhelder	Meisenhelder '69 Chevrolet	4	210	Quit
25	26	82	Bobby Boyles	'68 Ford	3	200	Flagged
26	19	47	Raymond Williams	Bill Seifert '70 Ford	3	200	Quit

Time of Race: 1 hour, 40 minutes, 30 seconds
Average Speed: 78.358 mph
Pole Winner: Bobby Allison - 83.970 mph
Lap Leaders: Bobby Allison 1-26, Bobby Isaac 27-40, Richard Petty 41-45, Isaac 46-65, Petty 66-300.
Cautions: 1 for 2 laps   Margin of Victory: 8-laps plus   Attendance: 8,600

Race No. 33

Isaac, Allison Falter; Petty Wins West Virginia 300

ONA, WV (Aug. 11) -- Richard Petty took the lead in the 66th lap and sprinted to a big win in the West Virginia 300 at International Raceway Park. It was the 11th win of the year for NASCAR's all-time race winner.

Petty was locked in a dog-fight with Bobby Isaac and Bobby Allison for the first half of the race. Both of Petty's rivals fell victim to mechanical problems. Isaac departed on lap 267 with rear gearing failure; and Allison spent about 40 laps in the pits having a universal joint repaired. Isaac got credit for 10th in the final rundown. Allison was 11th.

James Hylton finished second to Petty and upped his

point lead to 31 over Isaac. Neil Castles was third, John Sears fourth and Dave Marcis fifth.

Buddy Baker qualified a Neil Castles Dodge Daytona

Buddy Baker drove Neil Castles' Dodge Daytona at Ona, WV

fourth, but left early with brake failure.

One caution for two laps plus a red flag for a power blackout interrupted the 131.1-mile event. As the leaders were completing their 45th lap, all the lights went out. "I was going into the first turn and suddenly the track went dark," said Petty. "I tried to keep from running over anyone. I scraped another car, but whose I don't know."

Pop McGinnis of Huntington, WV -- a regular on the Grand National circuit in 1953 -- came out of retirement and finished ninth in a Mercury.

Petty's eight lap victory over Hylton was achieved at a speed of 78.358 mph. A crowd of 8,600 was on hand.

Race No. 34

Glotzbach Makes Up Deficit; Wins Yankee 400

BROOKLYN, MI (Aug. 16) -- Charlie Glotzbach of Georgetown, IN overcame a 7-second deficit, ran down Cale Yarborough and won the Yankee 400 at Michigan International Speedway. It was the second win of the season for the 32 year-old Dodge Daytona driver.

Glotzbach drove his Nichels-Goldsmith Dodge

Grand National Race No. 34
197 Laps at Michigan Int'l Speedway
Brooklyn, MI
"Yankee 400"
400 Miles on 2.04-mile Paved Track
August 16, 1970

Fin	St	No.	Driver	Team / Car	Laps	Money	Status
1	1	99	Charlie Glotzbach	Nchls-G'smith '69 Dodge Day	197	$14,275	Running
2	6	22	Bobby Allison	Mario Rossi '69 Dodge Day	197	6,845	Running
3	9	32	Dick Brooks	Brooks '70 Plym SuperBird	196	4,430	Running
4	2	71	Bobby Isaac	K&K Ins '69 Dodge Daytona	196	2,800	Running
5	12	40	Pete Hamilton	Petty Ent '70 Plym SuperBird	196	1,975	Running
6	7	6	Buddy Baker	Cotton Owens '69 Dodge Day	195	1,475	Running
7	4	98	LeeRoy Yarbrough	Junior Johnson '69 Mercury	196	1,350	Running
8	14	72	Benny Parsons	L G DeWitt '69 Ford	192	1,200	Running
9	13	48	James Hylton	Hylton Eng '69 Ford	190	1,100	Running
10	5	21	Cale Yarborough	Wood Brothers '69 Mercury	188	1,050	Engine
11	17	18	Joe Frasson	Frasson ' 69 Dodge Daytona	187	975	Running
12	23	06	Neil Castles	Castles '69 Dodge Daytona	183	950	Running
13	15	64	Elmo Langley	Langley '69 Mercury	183	925	Running
14	3	43	Richard Petty	Petty Ent '70 Plym SuperBird	183	975	Running
15	27	47	Raymond Williams	Bill Seifert '70 Ford	183	875	Running
16	25	45	Bill Seifert	Seifert '69 Ford	182	850	Running
17	31	07	Coo Marlin	Cunningham-Kelley '69 Chev	182	880	Running
18	26	25	Jabe Thomas	Don Robertson '69 Plymouth	180	820	Running
19	21	79	Frank Warren	Warren '69 Plymouth	179	805	Running
20	36	54	Bill Dennis	Dennis '69 Chevrolet	177	790	Running
21	30	01	Bob Senneker	Tire City '69 Mercury	175	775	Running
22	33	34	Wendell Scott	Don Robertson '69 Plymouth	170	785	Running
23	19	8	Ed Negre	Negre '69 Ford	140	745	Running
24	28	4	John Sears	Sears '69 Dodge	136	730	Ignition
25	29	26	Earl Brooks	Brooks '69 Ford	131	715	Oil pump
26	16	10	Bill Champion	Champion '69 Ford	123	700	Oil Leak
27	34	74	Bill Shirey	Shirey '69 Plymouth	104	690	Oil Leak
28	8	27	Donnie Allison	Banjo Matthews '69 Ford	101	680	Engine
29	22	68	Larry Baumel	Auto Lad '69 Ford	74	670	Heating
30	18	76	Ben Arnold	Arnold '69 Ford	27	660	Exhaust
31	39	86	Roy Tyner	Neil Castles '69 Dodge	26	645	Battery
32	20	5	Buddy Arrington	Arrington '69 Dodge	22	640	Alternator
33	40	44	Harold Fagan	Giachetti Brothers '69 Chev	16	635	Trans
34	24	39	Friday Hassler	James Hanley '69 Chevrolet	13	630	Engine
35	35	19	Henley Gray	Gray '69 Ford	11	625	Engine
36	38	87	Leroy Carrigg	'69 Ford	11	620	Fuel pump
37	11	17	David Pearson	Holman-Moody '69 Ford	5	1,015	Ignition
38	32	62	Ron Keselowski	Kaye Eng'69 Dodge	5	635	Rear End
39	10	30	Dave Marcis	Marcis '69 Dodge Daytona	3	605	Engine
40	37	24	Cecil Gordon	Gordon '68 Ford	0	600	Engine

Time of Race: 2 hours, 48 minutes, 32 seconds
Average Speed: 147.571 mph
Pole Winner: Charlie Glotzbach - 157.363 mph
Lap Leaders: Charlie Glotzbach 1-7, Richard Petty 8, Glotzbach 9-19,
    Cale Yarborough 20-26, Glotzbach 27-37, Yarborough 38-41, Bobby Isaac 42,
    LeeRoy Yarbrough 43-44, Donnie Allison 45-47, Glotzbach 48-78, Yarborough 79-86,
    Bobby Allison 87-92, Glotzbach 93-119, B.Allison 120-139, Yarborough 140-142,
    Glotzbach 143-162, Benny Parsons 163-184, Yarborough 185-188, Glotzbach 189-197.
Cautions: 1 for 9 laps   Margin of Victory: Under Caution   Attendance: 34,500

around Yarborough's Mercury with nine laps left in the 197-lap event. Yarborough's lead was sliced to a single car length when the engine let go in the Wood Brothers Mercury. Glotzbach followed the pace car home as the winner as the event ended under caution.

"I would have rather won it under green," said Glotzbach. "But it all pays the same. I was running faster than Cale was most of the day. I think I could have caught him if he hadn't blown."

Glotzbach led seven times for 116 laps. Bobby Allison was flagged in second place and Dick Brooks was

Buddy Baker #6 and Dick Brooks race in Yankee 400.
Brooks finished 3rd; Baker 6th

third. Bobby Isaac came in fourth and Pete Hamilton finished fifth. Point leader James Hylton came in ninth and escaped with a 16 point lead in the NASCAR standings.

Allison had made a pit stop to get four new tires on his Dodge. He was ready for a restart, which never came. It took safety workers nine laps to clean up the oil from Yarborough's blown engine. "I felt like I would have won the race," said Allison. "They sure took their time getting the job done. We passed four laps and the clean-up crew was just standing around."

NASCAR's Lin Kuchler explained the long clean-up period. "We thought we could get it cleaned up and let them go," he said. "But they found engine parts in the high speed groove. We let them finish under yellow rather than endangering the drivers."

Glotzbach averaged 147.571 mph before a crowd of 34,500.

Race No. 35

Pete and Plymouth Perfect at Talladega

TALLADEGA, AL (Aug. 23) -- Pete Hamilton led 153 of the 188-lap Talladega 500 and gained his third win of the season at Alabama International Motor Speedway. The 28 year-old Plymouth driver averaged 158.517 mph -- the fastest 500-mile stock car race ever run.

Hamilton outran Bobby Isaac in the last 38 laps

Grand National Race No. 35
188 Laps at Alabama Int'l Motor Speedway
Talladega, AL
"Talladega 500"
500 Miles on 2.66-mile Paved Track
August 23, 1970

Fin	St	No.	Driver	Team / Car	Laps	Money	Status
1	4	40	Pete Hamilton	Petty Ent '70 Plym SuperBird	188	$23,165	Running
2	1	71	Bobby Isaac	K&K Ins '69 Dodge Daytona	188	11,490	Running
3	3	99	Charlie Glotzbach	Nchls-G'smith '69 Dodge Day	187	7,380	Running
4	2	17	David Pearson	Holman-Moody '69 Ford	184	5,540	Running
5	7	6	Buddy Baker	Cotton Owens '69 Dodge Day	184	3,915	Running
6	9	21	Cale Yarborough	Wood Brothers '69 Mercury	183	3,015	Running
7	5	43	Richard Petty	Petty Ent '70 Plym SuperBird	183	2,540	Running
8	11	77	Ramo Stott	Stott '70 Plym SuperBird	182	2,015	Running
9	13	31	Jim Vandiver	O L Nixon '69 Dodge Daytona	180	1,915	Running
10	10	48	James Hylton	Hylton Eng '69 Ford	179	1,865	Running
11	12	18	Joe Frasson	Frasson '69 Dodge Daytona	178	1,815	Running
12	25	64	Elmo Langley	Langley '69 Mercury	177	1,765	Running
13	6	22	Bobby Allison	Mario Rossi '69 Dodge Day	175	1,715	Running
14	39	07	Coo Coo Marlin	Cunningham-Kelley '69 Chev	173	1,665	Running
15	18	39	Friday Hassler	James Hanley '69 Chevrolet	172	1,575	Running
16	41	25	Jabe Thomas	Don Robertson '69 Plymouth	172	1,670	Running
17	33	10	Bill Champion	Champion '69 Ford	171	1,515	Running
18	28	4	John Sears	Sears '69 Dodge	170	1,465	Running
19	32	76	Ben Arnold	Arnold '69 Ford	168	1,415	Running
20	17	57	Johnny Halford	Ervin Pruitt '69 Dodge	167	1,315	Running
21	19	24	Cecil Gordon	Gordon '69 Ford	166	1,290	Running
22	44	34	Wendell Scott	Don Robertson '69 Plymouth	165	1,290	Running
23	42	44	Harold Fagan	Giachetti Brothers '69 Chev	163	1,290	Running
24	15	79	Frank Warren	Warren '69 Plymouth	159	1,215	Ignition
25	34	19	Henley Gray	Gray '69 Ford	159	1,190	Running
26	36	26	Earl Brooks	Brooks '69 Ford	158	1,165	Running
27	50	97	Bill Dennis	Cecil Gordon '68 Ford	158	1,140	Running
28	37	65	Joe Phipps	Phipps '69 Chevrolet	157	1,115	Running
29	16	68	Larry Baumel	Auto Lad '69 Ford	154	1,090	Running
30	38	87	Leroy Carrigg	'68 Ford	152	1,065	Running
31	30	62	Ron Keselowski	Kaye Eng '69 Dodge	151	1,040	Running
32	21	30	Dave Marcis	Marcis '69 Dodge Daytona	148	1,115	Ignition
33	46	7	Ken Meisenhelder	Meisenhelder '69 Chevrolet	148	990	Running
34	48	46	Roy Mayne	Tom Hunter '69 Chevrolet	146	965	Engine
35	24	72	Benny Parsons	L G DeWitt '69 Ford	130	965	Engine
36	31	47	Raymond Williams	Bill Seifert '69 Ford	128	915	Crash
37	49	16	Ken Spikes	Spikes '70 Chevrolet	116	890	Running
38	47	33	Wayne Smith	Smith '69 Chevrolet	102	865	Heating
39	23	55	Tiny Lund	John McConnell '69 Dodge Day	101	865	Heating
40	8	32	Dick Brooks	Brooks '70 Plym SuperBird	94	815	Engine
41	29	70	J D McDuffie	McDuffie '69 Mercury	73	750	Oil Leak
42	14	5	Buddy Arrington	Arrington '69 Dodge	64	700	Ignition
43	20	60	Charlie Roberts	'69 Dodge	45	630	Engine
44	45	74	Bill Shirey	Shirey '69 Plymouth	34	610	Oil Leak
45	26	8	Ed Negre	Negre '69 Ford	29	590	Engine
46	27	37	Dr Don Tarr	Tarr '69 Dodge	25	565	Engine
47	40	45	Bill Seifert	Seifert '69 Ford	13	550	Steering
48	43	59	Richard Brickhouse	Tom Pistone '70 Ford	11	565	Engine
49	22	28	Fred Lorenzen	Ray Fox '69 Dodge Daytona	9	580	Engine
50	35	06	Neil Castles	Castles '69 Dodge Daytona	5	515	Suspen

Time of Race: 3 hours, 9 minutes, 17 seconds
Average Speed: 158.517 mph
Pole Winner: Bobby Isaac - 186.834 mph
Lap Leaders: Charlie Glotzbach 1, Buddy Baker 2, Bobby Isaac 3-5, Baker 6, Isaac 7-9, Cale Yarborough 10, Glotzbach 11, James Hylton 12, Dr Don Tarr 13-17, Baker 18-19, Pete Hamilton 20-27, Glotzbach 28, Tiny Lund 29-32, Yarborough 33, Hamilton 34-35, Glotzbach 36-38, Hamilton 39-64, Bobby Allison 65, Hamilton 66-147, Isaac 148-151, Hamilton 152, Isaac 153-154, Hamilton 155-188.
Cautions: 4 for 30 laps   Margin of Victory: 10 seconds   Attendance: 38,000

following the fourth and final caution period. "Some of the guys could run as fast as I could with fresh rubber," said Hamilton. "But their tires wore down a little and I could run the turns deeper. I knew I had them

Pete Hamilton - won another 500-miler at Talladega

Race No. 36

Petty Waxes Winston-Salem Field for 12th of Year

WINSTON-SALEM, NC (Aug. 28) -- Richard Petty swept past Bobby Isaac in the 64th lap and had little trouble disposing the field in the Myers Brothers Memorial at Bowman Gray Stadium.

Petty won the pole but followed Isaac for the first 63 laps. The brakes on Isaac's Dodge locked up and he grazed the wall. Petty took the opening into first place and led the rest of the way.

Petty beat Bobby Allison by a half lap to win the $1,000 top prize. Isaac faded to third, James Hylton was fourth and Benny Parsons fifth.

"My brakes locked up," explained Isaac, "That's how they got past. After that, the brakes would give me trouble every two or three laps. I couldn't run. I had to take what I could get."

Isaac gained a single point over Hylton to raise his point lead to nine.

Petty's 113th Grand National triumph came at 51.527 mph. A crowd of 8,500 watched the caution free event.

covered."

Isaac finished second, 10-seconds behind. The Catawba, NC speedster was back on top of the tight point race by eight markers over James Hylton, who finished 10th. Charlie Glotzbach came in third place with David Pearson fourth and Buddy Baker fifth.

"Pete hooked up in a draft with Glotzbach and I couldn't keep up," said Isaac. "Pete was awfully fast today."

Although more tire problems were forecast, most of the top contenders experienced good tire wear. "I think we all owe thanks to Goodyear for the tire they came up with," said Isaac. "We thought there would be more problems than there were."

Baker and Cale Yarborough, who finished sixth, encountered some degree of tire troubles. "I had a right rear chunking and I couldn't run strong at the end," said Baker. "We can't seem to go a whole race trouble-free."

Glen Wood said, "We can't keep tires on our car when we tried to run with Hamilton. He ran the tires right off our car."

Isaac won his third straight Talladega pole at a speed of 186.834 mph. Speeds were down due to a NASCAR imposed carburetor restrictor plate on superspeedways.

A disappointing crowd of 38,000 turned out in warm, muggy weather.

Grand National Race No. 36
250 Laps at Bowman Gray Stadium
Winston-Salem, NC
"Myers Brothers Memorial"
62.5 Miles on Quarter-mile Paved Track
August 28, 1970

Fin	St	No.	Driver	Team / Car	Laps	Money	Status
1	1	43	Richard Petty	Petty Ent '70 Plymouth	250	$1,000	Running
2	3	22	Bobby Allison	Allison '69 Dodge	250	600	Running
3	2	71	Bobby Isaac	K&K Insurance '70 Dodge	247	400	Running
4	4	48	James Hylton	Hylton Eng '69 Ford	246	350	Running
5	12	72	Benny Parsons	L G DeWitt '69 Ford	243	325	Running
6	5	06	Neil Castles	Castles '69 Dodge	243	300	Running
7	6	70	J D McDuffie	McDuffie '69 Mercury	238	275	Running
8	14	64	Elmo Langley	Langley '68 Ford	238	270	Running
9	11	54	Bill Dennis	Dennis '69 Chevrolet	234	265	Running
10	21	25	Jabe Thomas	Don Robertson '69 Plymouth	230	260	Running
11	13	34	Wendell Scott	Don Robertson '69 Plymouth	228	255	Running
12	20	04	Ken Meisenhelder	Meisenhelder '69 Chevrolet	227	250	Running
13	9	74	Bill Shirey	Shirey '69 Plymouth	224	245	Running
14	17	97	Dave Marcis	Cecil Gordon '68 Ford	137	240	Running
15	22	19	Henley Gray	Gray '69 Ford	120	235	Quit
16	16	10	Bill Champion	Champion '68 Ford	117	230	Quit
17	19	4	John Sears	Sears '69 Dodge	61	225	Quit
18	8	24	Cecil Gordon	Gordon '68 Ford	46	220	Axle
19	15	45	Bill Seifert	Seifert '69 Ford	40	215	Trans
20	18	79	Frank Warren	Warren '69 Plymouth	21	210	Trans
21	7	8	Ed Negre	Negre '69 Ford	10	205	Heating
22	10	26	Earl Brooks	Brooks '69 Ford	3	200	Clutch

Time of Race: 1 hour, 12 minutes, 13 seconds
Average Speed: 51.527 mph
Pole Winner: Richard Petty - 54.553 mph
Lap Leaders: Bobby Isaac 1-63, Richard Petty 64-250.
Cautions: None   Margin of Victory: Half-lap   Attendance: 8,500

Race No. 37

Petty Hurries to Halifax County 100 Victory

S.BOSTON, VA (Aug. 29) -- Richard Petty passed Benny Parsons in the 103rd lap and sped to victory in the Halifax County 100 at South Boston Speedway. It was the 13th win of the year for the 6'2", 195-pound veteran.

Bobby Isaac qualified second, but started 24th. Crew chief Harry Hyde opted to change to a softer tire compound as the cars were lining up. Once the change took place, Isaac had to start at the back.

Isaac overtook all of his rivals except Petty. He finished 13.0-seconds behind the winner. Bobby Allison came across the line in third place and Benny Parsons was fourth. James Hylton took fifth place.

Earl Brooks started fourth in his Ford and ran a surprisingly strong race. He was running in the top 10 when his engine blew on lap 87.

Petty led all but 10 of the 281 laps on the .357-mile paved oval. He averaged 73.060 mph before a crowd of 5,800.

Grand National Race No. 37
281 Laps at South Boston Speedway
South Boston, VA
"Halifax County 100"
100 Miles on .357-mile Paved Track
August 29, 1970

Fin	St	No.	Driver	Team / Car	Laps	Money	Status
1	1	43	Richard Petty	Petty Ent '70 Plymouth	281	1,500	Running
2	24	71	Bobby Isaac	K&K Insurance '70 Dodge	281	900	Running
3	3	22	Bobby Allison	Allison '69 Dodge	280	500	Running
4	2	72	Benny Parsons	L G DeWitt '69 Ford	279	350	Running
5	7	48	James Hylton	Hylton Eng '70 Ford	277	325	Running
6	5	06	Neil Castles	Castles '69 Dodge	276	300	Running
7	8	70	J D McDuffie	McDuffie '69 Mercury	273	275	Running
8	16	64	Elmo Langley	Langley '68 Ford	272	270	Running
9	19	25	Jabe Thomas	Don Robertson '69 Plymouth	272	265	Running
10	10	4	John Sears	Sears '69 Dodge	272	260	Running
11	11	24	Cecil Gordon	Gordon '68 Ford	267	255	Running
12	18	68	Larry Baumel	Auto Lad '69 Ford	260	250	Running
13	6	74	Bill Shirey	Shirey '69 Plymouth	258	245	Running
14	17	79	Frank Warren	Warren '69 Plymouth	178	240	Suspen
15	9	10	Bill Champion	Champion '69 Ford	161	235	Trans
16	15	8	Ed Negre	Negre '69 Ford	150	230	Oil Pan
17	14	34	Wendell Scott	Don Robertson '69 Plymouth	125	225	Oil Leak
18	13	45	Bill Seifert	Seifert '69 Ford	97	220	Clutch
19	4	26	Earl Brooks	Brooks '69 Ford	87	215	Engine
20	21	19	Henley Gray	Gray '69 Ford	80	210	Oil Pan
21	20	04	Ken Meisenhelder	Meisenhelder '69 Chevrolet	54	205	Quit
22	12	54	Bill Dennis	Dennis '69 Chevrolet	24	200	Heating
23	22	77	John Kenney	Bob Freeman '68 Ford	19	200	Quit
24	23	33	Dave Marcis	Wayne Smith '69 Chevrolet	3	200	Quit

Time of Race: 1 hour, 22 minutes, 23 seconds
Average Speed: 73.060 mph
Pole Winner: Richard Petty - 81.187 mph
Lap Leaders: Richard Petty 1-92, Benny Parsons 93-102, Petty 103-281.
Cautions: 1 for 10 laps   Margin of Victory: 13 seconds   Attendance: 5,800.

Race No. 38

Following Family Footsteps, Baker Wins Southern 500

DARLINGTON, SC (Sept. 7) -- Buddy Baker, hulking 29 year-old Dodge driver, led the final 65 laps and won the storied Southern 500 at Darlington Raceway. Baker's third career win came in the nation's oldest superspeedway stock car race, an event his dad Buck won three times.

Buddy Baker won Southern 500

Bobby Isaac finished second, a lap down. He decided to forego a caution flag pit stop with 17 laps to go but lost a lap when he had to pit for gas 10 laps later.

Third place went to Pete Hamilton. David Pearson took fourth and Richard Petty fifth.

Isaac increased his point lead to 27 over James Hylton, who finished seventh.

Baker started second and was always in the lead pack. He survived a near spin-out with nine laps to go, but gathered his car up and went on to win. "I've been dreaming of winning this race since I was nine years old," said Baker.

Car owner Cotton Owens, who was inducted into the Hall of Fame two nights earlier, said it was his biggest win as a team owner. "We needed a win," he said. "It's been almost two years since I won a race. It's just great to have this weekend topped off like this."

Cale Yarborough posed as a late race threat, but he got tangled up in traffic and spun into the inside guard rail. The crash occurred with just 36 laps remaining. Donnie Allison crashed his Ford a few laps later.

Dr. Don Tarr, practicing physician from Miami, wrecked his Dodge on lap 11. He suffered a broken finger in the mishap.

Fred Lorenzen was assigned to drive Junior Johnson's Ford. The Elmhurst, IL driver started ninth, but

Charlie Glotzbach #99 and Bobby Isaac battle in Southern 500

failed to lead a lap. He crashed into the first turn wall on lap 209 and retired for the day.

Baker averaged 128.817 mph before 69,500 spectators.

Race No. 39

Isaac Prevails in Heated Hickory Chase

HICKORY, NC (Sept. 11) -- Bobby Isaac overtook Richard Petty in the 250th lap and won the Buddy Shuman Memorial at Hickory Speedway. It was the 10th win of the year for the 38 year-old Dodge pilot.

Isaac led most of the way, but had to deal with Petty's speedy Plymouth in the final laps. Isaac led Petty across the finish line by eight car lengths in the 276-lap chase on the .363-mile oval. Bobby Allison took third place with Dick Brooks fourth and James Hylton fifth.

Petty led the first five laps, but Isaac raced ahead for a 225 lap stretch. Petty made a late charge, passing Isaac on lap 231. Isaac dogged Petty's heels until he made the decisive pass with 27 laps to go.

Only one caution flag interrupted the race. Bobby and Donnie Allison snagged bumpers. Donnie spun off the backstretch. Both continued with Donnie finishing sixth.

A crowd of 6,000 watched Isaac win at an average speed of 73.365 mph.

Grand National Race No. 38
367 Laps at Darlington Raceway
Darlington, SC
"Southern 500"
500 Miles on 1.366-mile Paved Track
September 7, 1970

Fin	St	No.	Driver	Team / Car	Laps	Money	Status
1	2	6	Buddy Baker	Cotton Owens '69 Dodge Day	367	$27,450	Running
2	5	71	Bobby Isaac	K&K Ins '69 Dodge Daytona	366	11,825	Running
3	6	40	Pete Hamilton	Petty Ent '70 Plym SuperBird	364	7,000	Running
4	1	17	David Pearson	Holman-Moody '69 Ford	363	6,175	Running
5	10	43	Richard Petty	Petty Ent '70 Plym SuperBird	362	3,100	Running
6	4	99	Charlie Glotzbach	Nchls-G'smith '69 Dodge Day	360	2,150	Running
7	14	48	James Hylton	Hylton Eng '69 Ford	356	2,500	Running
8	13	32	Dick Brooks*	Brooks '70 Plym SuperBird	354	2,025	Running
9	11	49	G C Spencer	Spencer '69 Plymouth	350	1,750	Running
10	3	22	Bobby Allison	Mario Rossi '69 Dodge Day	348	1,700	Running
11	8	27	Donnie Allison	Banjo Matthews '69 Ford	346	4,100	Crash
12	18	39	Friday Hassler	James Hanley '69 Chevrolet	341	1,550	Running
13	17	61	Hoss Ellington	Ellington '69 Ford	339	1,525	Running
14	12	5	Buddy Arrington	Arrington '69 Dodge	338	1,500	Running
15	19	18	Joe Frasson	Frasson '69 Dodge Daytona	337	1,475	Running
16	33	4	John Sears	Sears '69 Dodge	336	1,445	Running
17	37	34	Wendell Scott	Don Robertson '69 Plymouth	336	1,420	Running
18	36	46	Roy Mayne	Tom Hunter '69 Chevrolet	336	1,395	Running
19	24	10	Bill Champion	Champion '69 Ford	332	1,370	Lug Bolts
20	7	21	Cale Yarborough	Wood Brothers '69 Mercury	331	1,720	Crash
21	21	64	Elmo Langley	Langley '69 Mercury	322	1,320	Running
22	38	24	Cecil Gordon	Gordon '68 Ford	318	1,295	Running
23	34	57	Johnny Halford	Ervin Pruitt '69 Dodge	313	1,270	Running
24	27	76	Ben Arnold	Arnold '69 Ford	311	1,245	Running
25	32	79	Frank Warren	Warren '69 Plymouth	310	1,220	Lug Bolts
26	30	70	J D McDuffie	McDuffie '69 Mercury	301	1,195	Ignition
27	39	19	Henley Gray	Gray '69 Ford	300	1,170	Lug Bolts
28	20	06	Neil Castles	Castles '69 Dodge Daytona	274	1,145	Engine
29	29	62	Dave Marcis**	Kaye Eng '69 Dodge	255	1,145	Wheel
30	28	68	Larry Baumel	Auto Lad '69 Ford	242	1,145	Engine
31	23	25	Jabe Thomas	Don Robertson '69 Plymouth	235	1,070	Engine
32	35	33	Wayne Smith	Smith '69 Chevrolet	212	1,045	Engine
33	9	98	Fred Lorenzen	Junior Johnson '69 Ford	209	1,020	Crash
34	31	38	H B Bailey	Bailey '69 Pontiac	180	995	Rear End
35	26	45	Bill Seifert	Seifert '69 Ford	154	970	Steering
36	22	8	Ed Negre	Negre '69 Ford	150	945	Engine
37	40	26	Earl Brooks	Brooks '69 Ford	47	920	Ignition
38	25	36	Bugs Stevens	Richard Brown '70 Plym S'Bird	42	970	Engine
39	15	72	Benny Parsons	L G DeWitt '69 Ford	39	895	Crash
40	16	37	Dr Don Tarr	Tarr '69 Dodge	11	845	Crash

Time of Race: 3 hours, 55 minutes, 3 seconds
Average Speed: 128.817 mph
Pole Winner: David Pearson - 150.555 mph
Lap Leaders: David Pearson 1-14, Bobby Isaac 15-34, Charlie Glotzbach 35,
 Donnie Allison 36-50, Cale Yarborough 51-57, Isaac 58-84, D.Allison 85-86,
 Pearson 87, James Hylton 88-89, Dick Brooks 90-97, D.Allison 98-208, Baker 209,
 D.Allison 210-232, Baker 233, Yarborough 234-247, Baker 248, Yarborough 249-250,
 Baker 251-270, Isaac 271-302, Baker 303-367.
Cautions: 9 for 50 laps   Margin of Victory: 1 Lap and four car lengths   Attendance: 69,500

Race No. 40

Petty Routs Field at Richmond for No. 115

RICHMOND, VA (Sept. 13) -- Richard Petty stormed past Donnie Allison in the 17th lap and easily pulled away from the field to win an uncontested Capital City 500 at Richmond Fairgrounds Raceway. The

Grand National Race No. 39
276 Laps at Hickory Speedway
Hickory, NC
"Buddy Shuman Memorial"
100 Miles on .363-mile Paved Track
September 11, 1970

Fin	St	No.	Driver	Team / Car	Laps	Money	Status
1	1	71	Bobby Isaac	K&K Insurance '70 Dodge	276	$2,200	Running
2	2	43	Richard Petty	Petty Ent '70 Plymouth	276	1,500	Running
3	3	22	Bobby Allison	Allison '69 Dodge	276	1,000	Running
4	7	32	Dick Brooks	Brooks '69 Plymouth	273	700	Running
5	6	48	James Hylton	Hylton Eng '69 Ford	273	600	Running
6	4	27	Donnie Allison	Banjo Matthews '70 Ford	272	500	Running
7	8	49	G C Spencer	Spencer '69 Plymouth	272	400	Running
8	13	06	Neil Castles	Castles '69 Dodge	271	350	Running
9	10	4	John Sears	Sears '69 Dodge	268	300	Running
10	18	64	Elmo Langley	Langley '68 Ford	267	280	Running
11	14	70	J D McDuffie	McDuffie '69 Mercury	267	275	Running
12	17	10	Bill Champion	Champion '68 Ford	267	270	Running
13	12	26	Dave Marcis	Earl Brooks '69 Ford	240	265	Rear End
14	15	93	Morgan Shepherd	'69 Chevrolet	173	260	Rear End
15	5	72	Benny Parsons	L G DeWitt '69 Ford	164	255	Engine
16	9	25	Jabe Thomas	Don Robertson '69 Plymouth	131	250	Axle
17	16	74	Bill Shirey	Shirey '69 Plymouth	93	245	Clutch
18	21	45	Bill Seifert	Seifert '69 Ford	78	240	Ignition
19	11	34	Wendell Scott	Scott '69 Ford	46	235	Steering
20	19	79	Frank Warren	Warren '69 Plymouth	36	230	Vibration
21	22	57	Johnny Halford	Ervin Pruitt '69 Dodge	29	225	Rear End
22	20	24	Henley Gray	Cecil Gordon '68 Ford	24	220	Brakes

Time of Race: 1 hour, 21 minutes, 47 seconds
Average Speed: 73.365 mph
Pole Winner: Bobby Isaac - 78.411 mph
Lap Leaders: Richard Petty 1-5, Bobby Isaac 6-230, Petty 231-239, Isaac 240-276
Cautions: 1 for 5 laps   Margin of Victory: 8 car lengths   Attendance: 6,000

Grand National Race No. 40
500 Laps at Richmond Fairgrounds Raceway
Richmond, VA
"Capital City 500"
271 Miles on .542-mile Paved Track
September 13, 1970

Fin	St	No.	Driver	Team / Car	Laps	Money	Status
1	1	43	Richard Petty	Petty Ent '70 Plymouth	500	$4,675	Running
2	7	22	Bobby Allison	Allison '69 Dodge	498	2,550	Running
3	3	27	Donnie Allison	Banjo Matthews '70 Ford	497	1,800	Running
4	4	71	Bobby Isaac*	K&K Insurance '69 Dodge	496	1,175	Running
5	9	90	Sonny Hutchins	Junie Donlavey '69 Ford	492	950	Running
6	6	72	Benny Parsons	L G DeWitt '69 Ford	492	675	Running
7	8	49	G C Spencer	Spencer '69 Plymouth	491	625	Running
8	5	48	James Hylton	Hylton Eng '69 Ford	489	600	Running
9	2	32	Dick Brooks	Brooks '70 Plymouth	481	655	Running
10	13	25	Jabe Thomas	Don Robertson '69 Plymouth	481	570	Running
11	19	45	Bill Seifert	Seifert '69 Ford	476	560	Running
12	14	64	Elmo Langley	Langley '69 Ford	476	550	Running
13	20	24	Cecil Gordon	Gordon '68 Ford	471	540	Running
14	24	76	Ben Arnold	Arnold '69 Ford	470	505	Running
15	17	70	J D McDuffie	McDuffie '69 Mercury	468	520	Running
16	21	34	Wendell Scott	Don Robertson '69 Plymouth	467	485	Running
17	23	92	Roy Tyner	Tyner '69 Ford	462	475	Running
18	25	19	Henley Gray	Gray '69 Ford	451	465	Running
19	27	57	Johnny Halford	Ervin Pruitt '69 Dodge	396	455	Engine
20	15	26	Dave Marcis	Earl Brooks '69 Ford	394	470	Heating
21	29	04	Ken Meisenhelder	Meisenhelder '69 Chevrolet	376	435	Engine
22	18	79	Frank Warren	Warren '69 Plymouth	359	450	Engine
23	12	06	Neil Castles	Castles '69 Dodge	340	440	Rear End
24	30	10	Bill Champion	Champion '69 Ford	154	405	Mtr mount
25	11	4	John Sears	Sears '69 Dodge	148	420	Axle
26	22	5	Buddy Arrington	Arrington '69 Dodge	138	390	Rear End
27	10	54	Bill Dennis	Dennis '69 Chevrolet	41	405	Engine
28	16	8	Ed Negre	Negre '69 Ford	21	395	Engine
29	26	87	Leroy Carrigg	'68 Ford	4	360	Clutch
30	28	74	Bill Shirey	Shirey '69 Plymouth	0	350	Quit

Time of Race: 3 hours, 19 minutes, 34 seconds
Average Speed: 81.476 mph
Pole Winner: Richard Petty - 87.014 mph
Lap Leaders: Richard Petty 1-4, Donnie Allison 5-16, Petty 17-500.
Cautions: 2 for 9 laps   Margin of Victory: 2-laps plus   Attendance: 11,000
*Relieved by Dave Marcis

two lap victory was Petty's 14th of the season.

Bobby Allison came in second place with Donnie Allison third. Fourth place went to Bobby Isaac with relief help from Dave Marcis. Sonny Hutchins finished fifth.

Petty started on the pole and led 488 of the 500 laps on the .542-mile oval. "The car worked perfectly today," said Petty. "The deal was that if I stayed out of trouble, I'd win."

Point contender James Hylton finished eighth and fell 39 points behind Isaac.

The 271-miler was an uneventful contest with only two cautions breaking the action. Petty averaged 81.476 mph before a crowd of 11,000.

Race No. 41

Petty Leads Chrysler Sweep In Mason-Dixon 500

DOVER, DE (Sept. 20) -- Richard Petty broke out of a tight battle and easily won the Mason-Dixon 300 at Dover Downs International Speedway. It was the fifth win in the last 11 Grand National races for the lanky Petty.

Richard Petty won Mason-Dixon 300 at Dover

Bobby Allison finished second, 27-seconds behind the winged Petty Plymouth. Charlie Glotzbach took third place, David Pearson was fourth and Benny Parsons fifth.

Petty took the lead for the final time on lap 269 of the 300 lapper. "I ran with the crowd in the beginning to see what my tires would do," said Petty, who sprinted away from the pack in the final laps. "After my first pit stop, we weren't having any tire problems so I could run flat out the rest of the way."

Third fastest qualifier Buddy Baker wrecked his Dodge in the last 20 laps.

Point leader Bobby Isaac finished sixth, picking up two points on James Hylton, who followed in seventh. Isaac's point lead stood at 41 with seven races left on the 1970 slate.

Glotzbach came from the rear of the field to finish third. He had missed qualifying due to a blown engine. "We lost a lap and couldn't seem to make it up," said Glotzbach. "We could run with Petty, but couldn't pass

him."

Petty averaged 112.103 mph before a track record 20,000 spectators.

Race No. 42

Final Dirt Track Grand National to Richard Petty

RALEIGH, NC (Sept. 30) -- Richard Petty took the lead in the 89th lap and led the rest of the way to win the Home State 200 at State Fairgrounds Speedway. The 100-miler would turn out to be the final Grand National race staged on a dirt track.

Petty was driving a Plymouth owned by Don Robertson -- the second time Petty has driven a Robertson Plymouth to victory lane. Neil Castles finished second, two laps behind. Bobby Isaac, running a conservative race, came in third. James Hylton captured fourth place

---

Grand National Race No. 41
300 Laps at Dover Downs Int'l
Speedway
Dover, DE
"Mason-Dixon 300"
300 Miles on 1-mile Paved Track
September 20, 1970

Fin	St	No.	Driver	Team / Car	Laps	Money	Status
1	2	43	Richard Petty	Petty Ent '70 Plym SuperBird	300	$6,195	Running
2	4	22	Bobby Allison	Mario Rossi '69 Dodge Day	300	3,095	Running
3	36	99	Charlie Glotzbach	Nchls-G'smith '69 Dodge Day	299	2,170	Running
4	5	17	David Pearson	Holman-Moody '70 Ford	296	1,885	Running
5	6	72	Benny Parsons	L G DeWitt '69 Ford	296	1,280	Running
6	1	71	Bobby Isaac	K&K Ins '69 Dodge Daytona	291	1,170	Running
7	25	48	James Hylton	Hylton Eng '69 Ford	289	920	Running
8	14	10	Bill Champion	Champion '69 Ford	285	920	Running
9	29	68	Larry Baumel	Auto Lad '69 Ford	285	880	Running
10	11	24	Cecil Gordon	Gordon '68 Ford	281	830	Running
11	3	6	Buddy Baker	Cotton Owens '69 Dodge Day	280	845	Crash
12	32	54	Bill Dennis	Dennis '69 Chevrolet	278	710	Running
13	12	79	Frank Warren	Warren '69 Plymouth	277	675	Running
14	13	4	John Sears	Sears '69 Dodge	275	645	Running
15	19	06	Neil Castles	Castles '69 Dodge	272	610	Running
16	16	74	Bill Shirey	Shirey '69 Plymouth	268	600	Running
17	31	58	Buck Baker	'69 Chevrolet	267	610	Running
18	27	65	Joe Phipps	Phipps '69 Chevrolet	266	580	Running
19	8	64	Elmo Langley	Langley '69 Mercury	262	620	Engine
20	21	26	Earl Brooks	Brooks '69 Ford	253	560	Ignition
21	18	76	Ben Arnold	Arnold '69 Ford	252	550	Running
22	20	87	Leroy Carrigg	'69 Ford	245	540	Running
23	7	30	Dave Marcis	Marcis '69 Dodge Daytona	203	585	Suspen
24	17	18	Joe Frasson	Frasson '70 Plymouth	199	510	Oil Leak
25	23	70	J D McDuffie	McDuffie '69 Mercury	116	505	Engine
26	15	19	Henley Gray	Gray '69 Ford	95	525	Radiator
27	30	03	Tommy Gale	Walt Valerio '69 Mercury	88	520	Engine
28	10	8	Ed Negre	Negre '69 Ford	82	530	Heating
29	34	0	Cliff Tyler	'69 Chevrolet	79	485	Crash
30	24	45	Bill Seifert	Seifert '69 Ford	74	480	Crash
31	33	92	Roy Tyner	Tyner '69 Ford	42	470	Engine
32	28	67	Dick May	Joyce Ronacher '69 Ford	17	465	Oil Leak
33	22	84	Raymond Williams	Bob Davis '69 Ford	14	460	Vibration
34	26	77	John Kenney	Bob Freeman '68 Ford	6	455	Trans
35	9	25	Jabe Thomas	Don Robertson '69 Plymouth	2	495	Engine
36	35	34	Wendell Scott	Scott '69 Ford	1	445	Engine

Time of Race: 2 hours, 40 minutes, 34 seconds
Average Speed: 112.103 mph
Pole Winner: Bobby Isaac - 129.538 mph
Lap Leaders: Buddy Baker 1-81, Charlie Glotzbach 82-93, Richard Petty 94-171,
   Baker 172, Glotzbach 173, Baker 174, Glotzbach 175-183, Petty 184-259,
   Glotzbach 260-268, Petty 269-300.
Cautions: 4 for 27 laps   Attendance: 20,000

Grand National Race No. 42
200 Laps at State Fairgrounds
Speedway
Raleigh, NC
"Home State 200"
100 Miles on Half-mile Dirt Track
September 30, 1970

Fin	St	No.	Driver	Team / Car	Laps	Money	Status
1	6	43	Richard Petty	Don Robertson '69 Plymouth	200	$1,000	Running
2	5	06	Neil Castles	Castles '69 Dodge	198	600	Running
3	3	71	Bobby Isaac	K&K Insurance '69 Dodge	195	400	Running
4	8	48	James Hylton	Hylton '70 Ford	193	350	Running
5	11	97	Cecil Gordon	Gordon '68 Ford	186	325	Running
6	7	22	Bobby Allison	Allison '70 Dodge	183	300	Running
7	9	26	Dave Marcis	Earl Brooks '69 Ford	182	275	Running
8	18	76	Ben Arnold	Arnold '68 Ford	179	270	Running
9	15	88	Bill Hollar	'69 Ford	179	265	Running
10	22	25	Jabe Thomas	Don Robertson '69 Plymouth	173	260	Running
11	19	74	Bill Shirey	Shirey '69 Plymouth	166	255	Running
12	20	77	John Kenney	Bob Freeman '68 Ford	164	250	Running
13	21	45	Bill Seifert	Seifert '69 Ford	97	245	Steering
14	2	72	Benny Parsons	L G DeWitt '69 Ford	96	240	Engine
15	17	24	Henley Gray	Gray '69 Ford	96	235	Heating
16	10	8	Ed Negre	Negre '69 Ford	94	230	Heating
17	14	10	Bill Champion	Champion '69 Ford	87	225	Engine
18	4	64	Elmo Langley	Langley '69 Ford	86	220	Heating
19	12	70	J D McDuffie	McDuffie '69 Buick	77	215	D Shaft
20	13	34	Wendell Scott	Scott '69 Ford	68	210	Trans
21	16	79	Frank Warren	Warren '69 Plymouth	61	205	Ignition
22	23	87	Leroy Carrigg	'68 Ford	29	200	Wtr Hose
23	1	4	John Sears	Sears '69 Dodge	16	200	Engine

Time of Race: 1 hour, 27 minutes, 45 seconds
Average Speed: 68.376 mph
Pole Winner: John Sears - 71.380 mph
Lap Leaders: John Sears 1-10, Benny Parsons 11-88, Richard Petty 89-200.
Cautions: 1 for 4 laps   Margin of Victory: 2-laps plus   Attendance: 6,000

with Cecil Gordon fifth.

John Sears won his second career pole position and led the first 10 laps. Benny Parsons passed Sears and led for 78 laps before Petty moved in front for good.

Sears fell out with a broken exhaust pipe, leaving him last in the 23 car field. Parsons went 96 laps before the engine blew in his Ford.

Petty averaged 68.376 mph before a crowd of 6,000.

"The dirt tracks are rapidly becoming a thing of the past," said Petty. "I hope a few dirt tracks are kept on the schedule. This is where our brand of racing started."

Race No. 43

Isaac Gambles, Wins Wilkes 400; Turner Dies in Air Crash

N.WILKESBORO, NC (Oct. 4) -- Bobby Isaac gambled on a late pit stop and nipped Richard Petty in the final laps to win the Wilkes 400 at North Wilkesboro Speedway. It was the 11th win of the season for the current Grand National point leader.

Isaac and Petty waged a tight battle that kept the crowd of 8,800 on its feet much of the time. Isaac lost a lap while pitting under the yellow flag with less than 100 laps to go. "The jack sunk in the pavement and we lost a lap," Isaac said later.

Once the green flag came out, Isaac passed Petty to unlap himself. When Bub Strickler spun with 25 laps to go, Isaac retreated to the pits to get new tires.

Crew chief Harry Hyde elected to put soft tires all

Bobby Isaac

the way around on Isaac's Dodge. Petty stayed on the track and did not pit.

Isaac scooted around Petty with 12 laps to go and won by six car lengths. Donnie Allison came in third,

Grand National Race No. 43
400 Laps at N.Wilkesboro Speedway
N.Wilkesboro, NC
"Wilkes 400"
250 Miles on .625-mile Paved Track
October 4, 1970

Fin	St	No.	Driver	Team / Car	Laps	Money	Status
1	1	71	Bobby Isaac	K&K Insurance '70 Dodge	400	$5,825	Running
2	3	43	Richard Petty	Petty Ent '70 Plymouth	400	2,850	Running
3	2	98	Donnie Allison	Junior Johnson '70 Ford	399	1,975	Running
4	4	22	Bobby Allison	Mario Rossi '70 Dodge	395	1,250	Running
5	8	48	James Hylton	Hylton Eng '70 Ford	393	900	Running
6	11	72	Benny Parsons	L G DeWitt '69 Ford	393	650	Running
7	9	06	Neil Castles	Castles '69 Dodge	392	700	Running
8	10	20	Clyde Lynn	Lynn '70 Ford	386	625	Running
9	5	39	Friday Hassler	James Hanley '69 Chevrolet	385	580	Running
10	12	25	Jabe Thomas	Don Robertson '69 Plymouth	383	570	Running
11	7	64	Elmo Langley	Langley '69 Ford	383	560	Running
12	14	79	Frank Warren	Warren '69 Plymouth	382	550	Running
13	20	26	Dave Marcis	Earl Brooks '69 Ford	379	540	Running
14	17	24	Cecil Gordon	Gordon '68 Ford	376	530	Running
15	26	34	Wendell Scott	Scott '69 Ford	366	520	Running
16	30	88	Bill Hollar	'69 Ford	358	485	Running
17	27	87	Leroy Carrigg	'68 Ford	352	500	Running
18	22	54	Bill Dennis	Dennis '69 Chevrolet	346	490	Engine
19	28	58	Bub Strickler	'70 Chevrolet	316	455	Engine
20	24	45	Bill Seifert	Seifert '69 Ford	273	470	Ignition
21	18	70	J D McDuffie	McDuffie '69 Mercury	235	460	Axle
22	13	8	Ed Negre	Negre '69 Ford	223	450	Alternator
23	25	46	Roy Mayne	Tom Hunter '69 Chevrolet	212	440	Suspen
24	16	4	John Sears	Sears '69 Dodge	202	430	Steering
25	23	10	Bill Champion	Champion 68 Ford	186	420	D Shaft
26	6	32	Dick Brooks	Brooks '69 Plymouth	176	415	Engine
27	19	57	Johnny Halford	Ervin Pruitt '69 Dodge	113	405	Engine
28	21	5	Buddy Arrington	Arrington '69 Dodge	95	395	Engine
29	29	33	Wayne Smith	Smith '69 Chevrolet	92	360	Steering
30	15	49	G C Spencer	Spencer '69 Plymouth	63	375	Crash

Time of Race: 2 hours, 46 minutes, 20 seconds
Average Speed: 90.162 mph
Pole Winner: Bobby Isaac - 105.406 mph
Lap Leaders: Bobby Isaac 1-4, Donnie Allison 5-9, Isaac 10-131, Richard Petty 132-178, Isaac 179-180, Petty 181-190, Isaac 191-227, Petty 228-350, Isaac 351, Petty 352, Isaac 353, Petty 354-388, Isaac 389-400.
Cautions: 4 for 32 laps   Margin of Victory: 6 car lengths   Attendance: 8,800

Bobby Allison was fourth and James Hylton fifth.

"We didn't have any idea if the softer compound would work or not," said Isaac. "But it was our only chance to beat Petty. He's a good man to race against. He doesn't hog the track or try to wreck you. He's a clean driver."

Isaac stretched his lead to 50 points over Hylton in the Grand National standings.

Donnie Allison was driving Junior Johnson's Ford. LeeRoy Yarbrough, Johnson's regular driver, was negotiating for a full time Indy Car ride with car owner Jack Brabham.

Isaac's 32nd career victory came at an average speed of 90.162 mph.

Curtis Turner

The legendary Curtis Turner was killed when his Aero Commander 500 crashed near DuBois, PA while flying home to Roanoke, VA. Turner and companion Clarence King, a golf pro, were found dead in the wreckage.

Race No. 44

Crashes Clear Way; LeeRoy Wins National 500

CHARLOTTE, NC (Oct. 11) -- Wrecks took out a number of contenders in the National 500, opening the door for LeeRoy Yarbrough to capture his first victory of the 1970 Grand National season.

Yarbrough took the lead 12 laps from the finish and was in front when the 500-miler at Charlotte Motor Speedway ended under the caution flag. Bobby Allison came in second with Fred Lorenzen third. Benny Parsons came in fourth and fifth place went to Bobby Isaac.

Isaac had made a tremendous comeback -- coming from two laps behind to take the lead with 14 laps remaining. However, just as Isaac raced past Yarbrough, the engine erupted in his Dodge. "This is a hard loss to take," said Isaac. "For awhile, everything had been working great. The caution flag fell right and I got back into the lead lap. I think I would have won the race."

Yarbrough, the sensation of 1969, rolled his Junior

Grand National Race No. 44
334 Laps at Charlotte Motor Speedway
Charlotte, NC
"National 500"
500 Miles on 1.5-mile Paved Track
October 11, 1970

Fin	St	No.	Driver	Team / Car	Laps	Money	Status
1	5	98	LeeRoy Yarbrough	Junior Johnson '69 Mercury	334	$23,700	Running
2	10	22	Bobby Allison	Mario Rossi '69 Dodge Day	334	10,950	Running
3	3	4	Fred Lorenzen	Ray Fox '69 Dodge Daytona	333	6,400	Running
4	15	72	Benny Parsons	L G DeWitt '69 Ford	329	3,955	Running
5	9	71	Bobby Isaac	K&K Ins '69 Dodge Daytona	323	3,330	Engine
6	18	64	Elmo Langley	Langley '69 Mercury	321	2,265	Running
7	19	10	Bill Champion	Champion '69 Ford	320	2,065	Running
8	20	5	Buddy Arrington	Arrington '69 Dodge	319	1,965	Running
9	36	46	Roy Mayne	Tom Hunter '69 Chevrolet	317	1,955	Running
10	22	39	Friday Hassler	James Hanley '69 Chevrolet	315	1,765	Engine
11	26	49	G C Spencer	Spencer '69 Plymouth	313	1,730	Running
12	31	25	Jabe Thomas	Don Robertson '69 Plymouth	310	1,655	Running
13	34	47	Bill Seifert	Seifert '70 Ford	307	1,605	Running
14	23	90	Bill Dennis	Junie Donlavey '69 Mercury	304	1,590	Running
15	39	70	J D McDuffie	McDuffie '69 Mercury	302	1,565	Running
16	38	68	Larry Baumel	Auto Lad '69 Ford	300	1,775	Running
17	30	24	Cecil Gordon*	Gordon '68 Ford	300	1,760	Running
18	13	27	Donnie Allison	Banjo Matthews '69 Ford	296	1,796	Engine
19	17	18	Joe Frasson	Frasson '69 Dodge Daytona	295	1,705	Running
20	28	8	Henley Gray**	Ed Negre '69 Ford	294	1,654	Running
21	40	4	John Sears	Sears '69 Dodge	291	1,591	Running
22	21	76	Ben Arnold	Arnold '69 Ford	258	1,568	Fuel pump
23	2	43	Richard Petty	Petty Ent '70 Plym SuperBird	239	2,039	Crash
24	6	40	Pete Hamilton	Petty Ent '70 Plym SuperBird	226	2,001	Crash
25	25	36	Butch Hirst	R Brown '70 Plym SuperBird	224	1,499	Suspen
26	3	6	Buddy Baker	Cotton Owens '69 Dodge Day	163	1,738	Crash
27	32	06	Neil Castles	Castles '69 Dodge Daytona	163	1,338	Crash
28	24	79	Frank Warren	Warren '69 Plymouth	158	1,318	Engine
29	16	48	James Hylton	Hylton Eng '69 Ford	125	1,260	Crash
30	11	32	Dick Brooks	Brooks '70 Plym SuperBird	122	1,247	Engine
31	27	37	Dr Don Tarr	Tarr '69 Dodge	122	1,212	Crash
32	33	42	Marty Robbins***	Robbins '69 Dodge Daytona	105	1,160	Engine
33	14	31	Jim Vandiver	O L Nixon '69 Dodge Daytona	105	1,185	Crash
34	29	07	Coo Coo Marlin	Cunningham-Kelley '69 Chev	94	1,109	W bear
35	37	57	Johnny Halford	Ervin Pruitt '69 Dodge	84	1,114	Engine
36	12	30	Dave Marcis	Marcis '69 Dodge Daytona	54	1,034	Engine
37	1	99	Charlie Glotzbach	Nchls-G'smith '69 Dodge Day	44	1,449	Crash
38	35	61	Hoss Ellington	Ellington '69 Ford	33	938	Steering
39	7	17	David Pearson	Holman-Moody '69 Ford	13	1,418	Crash
40	8	21	Cale Yarborough	Wood Brothers '69 Mercury	10	890	Crash

Time of Race: 4 hours, 3 minutes, 28 seconds
Average Speed: 123.246 mph
Pole Winner: Charlie Glotzbach - 157.273 mph
Lap Leaders: Charlie Glotzbach 1-2, Buddy Baker 3-20, Richard Petty 21-60, LeeRoy Yarbrough 61-66, Fred Lorenzen 67-69, Petty 70-73, Pete Hamilton 74-81, Baker 82, Petty 83-89, Bobby Allison 90-97, Yarbrough 98-107, B.Allison 108-109, Hamilton 110-120, Petty 121-133, Baker 134, Hamilton 135-174, Yarbrough 175, Hamilton 176, B.Allison 177, Hamilton 178-226, Yarbrough 227-309, B.Allison 310-320, Bobby Isaac 321-322, Yarbrough 323-334.
Cautions: 8 for 63 laps
Margin of Victory: Under Caution
Attendance: 50,000
*Relieved by Henley Gray
**Relieved by Ed Negre
***Relieved by Dave Marcis

David Pearson heads for the wall after hooking fenders with Cale Yarborough #21 at Charlotte.
Pete Hamilton ducks to safety

Johnson Mercury home first to end a 12 month dry spell. "This is the first race this year that something small didn't bother us," said the 32 year-old Yarbrough. "No little wire broke, no tire troubles, nothing trivial. This is the way things went last year. It feels damn good to have them going that way again."

Ford contenders David Pearson and Cale Yarborough were taken out in a ninth lap crash. Pole sitter Charlie Glotzbach wrecked on lap 44; and team-mates Richard Petty and Pete Hamilton crashed within a 13 lap span. Buddy Baker, Neil Castles, Dr. Don Tarr, James Hylton and Jim Vandiver also wrecked.

Hylton, Tarr and Vandiver became entangled in a spectacular pile-up off the second turn on lap 126. Tarr's Dodge slapped the guard rail and bounced in front of Hylton's Ford. Vandiver hit both cars on the backstretch. "This takes me out of the point race," said Hylton. "My car is a total wipe-out."

Isaac came away with an 85 point lead over Bobby Allison as Hylton faded to third, 122 points behind Isaac.

Yarbrough averaged 123.246 mph before a crowd of 50,000. It was Yarbrough's 14th career Grand National win.

Race No. 45

Petty Masters Martinsville; Independents Stage Park-out

MARTINSVILLE, VA (Oct. 18) -- Richard Petty led all but 20 laps and won the Old Dominion 500 at Martinsville Speedway; an event marred by a wholesale independent driver park-out.

Petty took the lead in the 18th lap and was in front for all but three of the remaining laps. He beat runner-up Bobby Allison by a full lap en route to the $8,775 first prize. Cale Yarborough came in third, Bobby Isaac was fourth and Donnie Allison fifth.

A dozen independent racers parked their cars in protest of the prize distribution. The difference between 30th and 10th was only $350.

The real fly in the ointment was qualifying bonus awards posted by Clay Earles, Speedway President. After being advised by sanctioning NASCAR to refrain from paying any appearance money to top teams, Earles tossed in an extra $10,000 to the top qualifiers. Most of the money was gobbled up by the factory teams.

"We were threatened with this, but I had a talk with

them at the driver's meeting," said Earles. "I asked them not to do this -- that it would hurt them more than me. But they went ahead anyway.

"And you know," Earles continued, "I think it made a better race. With all those strokers off the track, there was better racing. What I would like to do here is to have just the top 10 Grand National drivers -- nobody else -- in a race. This thing today has got me thinking more about it."

Only 10 cars finished the race.

Dick Brooks was irate when he was eliminated in a 61st lap crash. "I made a clean pass on LeeRoy (Yarbrough)," said Brooks. "But he cut me off -- on the straightaway. I think it is unfortunate when someone has to resort to things like that."

A crowd of 22,000 watched Petty take his 118th career at a speed of 72.235 mph.

Grand National Race No. 45
500 Laps at Martinsville Speedway
Martinsville, VA
"Old Dominion 500"
262.5 Miles on .525-mile Paved Track
October 18, 1970

Fin	St	No.	Driver	Team / Car	Laps	Money	Status
1	4	43	Richard Petty	Petty Ent '70 Plymouth	500	$8,775	Running
2	1	22	Bobby Allison	Mario Rossi '69 Dodge	499	6,175	Running
3	3	21	Cale Yarborough	Wood Brothers '70 Mercury	498	4,100	Running
4	2	71	Bobby Isaac	K&K Insurance '70 Dodge	498	3,525	Running
5	6	27	Donnie Allison	Banjo Matthews '69 Ford	497	2,125	Running
6	11	17	David Pearson	Holman-Moody '70 Ford	496	1,275	Running
7	7	98	LeeRoy Yarbrough	Junior Johnson '70 Ford	490	1,875	Running
8	14	48	James Hylton	Hylton Eng '69 Ford	487	925	Running
9	10	72	Benny Parsons	L G DeWitt '69 Ford	485	1,400	Running
10	17	70	J D McDuffie	McDuffie '69 Mercury	467	875	Running
11	30	18	Joe Frasson	Frasson '70 Dodge	445	850	Rear End
12	13	5	Buddy Arrington	Arrington '69 Dodge	396	825	Engine
13	27	54	Bill Dennis	Dennis '69 Chevrolet	297	800	Engine
14	22	10	Bill Champion	Champion '68 Ford	76	775	Steering
15	19	26	Earl Brooks	Brooks '69 Ford	74	750	Engine
16	9	32	Dick Brooks	Brooks '69 Plymouth	60	1,425	Crash
17	28	46	Roy Mayne	Tom Hunter '69 Chevrolet	38	700	Quit
18	23	76	Ben Arnold	Arnold '69 Ford	33	675	Quit
19	25	25	Jabe Thomas*	Don Robertson '69 Plymouth	22	650	Quit
20	8	39	Friday Hassler	James Hanley '69 Chevrolet	20	1,425	Heating
21	20	45	Bill Seifert	Seifert '69 Ford	16	615	Quit
22	21	8	Ed Negre	Negre '69 Ford	11	605	Quit
23	29	79	Frank Warren	Warren '69 Plymouth	9	595	Heating
24	26	57	Johnny Halford	Ervin Pruitt '69 Dodge	5	585	Quit
25	5	30	Dave Marcis	Marcis '69 Dodge Daytona	5	1,775	Quit
26	18	24	Cecil Gordon	Gordon '68 Ford	5	565	Quit
27	15	49	James Cox	Don Robertson '69 Plymouth	4	555	Quit
28	16	4	John Sears	Sears '69 Dodge	3	545	Quit
29	24	64	Elmo Langley	Langley '68 Ford	2	535	Quit
30	12	06	Neil Castles	Castles '69 Dodge	2	525	Quit

Time of Race: 3 hours, 38 minutes, 16 seconds
Average Speed: 72.235 mph
Pole Winner: Bobby Allison - 82.167 mph
Lap Leaders: Bobby Allison 1-17, Richard Petty 18-62, Bobby Isaac 63, Petty 64-212, Donnie Allison 213-214, Petty 215-500.
Cautions: 5 for 32 laps   Margin of Victory: 1-lap plus   Attendance: 22,000
*Relieved by Wendell Scott

Race No. 46

Petty Pulls Away for 18th Win of Year

MACON, GA (Nov. 8) -- Richard Petty passed Bobby Isaac in the 445th lap and pulled away for an easy win in the Georgia 500 at Middle Georgia Raceway. It was the 18th win of the season for the Randleman, NC Plymouth pilot.

Isaac finished second, 14-seconds behind. Dick Brooks came in third, Bobby Allison was fourth and John Sears fifth.

Isaac and Brooks dueled Petty most of the way. Brooks, a sophomore out of Porterville, CA, led on

three occasions for 130 laps. He fell two laps off the pace due to long pit stops.

Petty led the first 36 laps and was running with the leaders when he made a green flag pit stop for tires. He lost one lap in the process and got trapped a full lap behind when Wendell Scott blew his engine on lap 265. Ironically, it was another spin by Scott on lap 402 -- while driving in relief of Jabe Thomas -- that got Petty back on the lead lap.

Petty and Isaac swapped the lead three times in the final 80 laps. Petty averaged 83.284 mph before a disappointing crowd of 6,500.

Race No. 47

Yarborough Makes American 500 Last Fling; Isaac Champ

ROCKINGHAM, NC (Nov.15) -- Cale Yarborough held off David Pearson in a stretch duel and won the American 500 at North Carolina Motor Speedway. It was the 14th career win for the muscular Timmonsville, SC Mercury driver, who hinted that he may switch to USAC Indy Cars in 1971.

"I'll be driving a race car of some kind next year," said Yarborough. "I don't know if it will be in NASCAR or USAC. Gene White has already offered me his Indy Car ride next year. If I'm in another part of the country next year, I wish to thank the Southern fans for their support during my career."

Pearson chased Yarborough for the final 43 laps. He finished 4.0-seconds behind Yarborough. Bobby Allison came in third, Donnie Allison was fourth and Buddy Baker fifth.

Bobby Isaac started fifth and cruised to a seventh place finish, 11 laps behind. "I wasn't worried about how many laps I was behind," said the new NASCAR champion. "I just wanted to run fast enough to stay behind the factory cars and in front of the independents. I wanted to make sure we finished and

Richard Petty spins to the apron at Rockingham

wrapped this championship up. I hate to stroke, but it's been worth it."

Pole sitter Charlie Glotzbach led the first 81 laps and

Grand National Race No. 46
500 Laps at Middle Georgia Raceway
Macon, GA
"Georgia 500"
274 Miles on .548-mile Paved Track
November 8, 1970

Fin	St	No.	Driver	Team / Car	Laps	Money	Status
1	1	43	Richard Petty	Petty Ent '70 Plymouth	500	$3,275	Running
2	5	71	Bobby Isaac	K&K Insurance '70 Dodge	500	1,800	Running
3	4	32	Dick Brooks	Brooks '69 Plymouth	498	1,150	Running
4	2	22	Bobby Allison	Allison '69 Dodge	497	925	Running
5	7	4	John Sears	Sears '69 Dodge	487	700	Running
6	8	48	James Hylton	Hylton Eng '70 Ford	485	650	Running
7	3	72	Benny Parsons	L G DeWitt '69 Ford	485	675	Running
8	9	64	Elmo Langley	Langley '69 Ford	483	600	Running
9	11	25	Jabe Thomas*	Don Robertson '69 Plymouth	482	580	Running
10	16	24	Cecil Gordon	Gordon '68 Ford	475	570	Running
11	6	06	Neil Castles	Castles '69 Dodge	475	560	Running
12	21	76	Ben Arnold	Arnold '69 Ford	473	525	Running
13	13	10	Bill Champion	Champion '69 Ford	461	540	Running
14	27	16	Jimmy Watson	Ken Spikes '70 Chevrolet	451	505	Running
15	29	39	Friday Hassler	James Hanley '69 Chevrolet	449	495	Running
16	24	19	Henley Gray	Gray '69 Ford	448	485	Running
17	28	74	Bill Shirey	Shirey '69 Plymouth	423	475	Running
18	23	77	Roy Mayne	Bob Freeman '69 Ford	405	465	Engine
19	25	58	Jim Vandiver	'70 Chevrolet	285	455	Rear End
20	19	93	Morgan Shepherd	'69 Chevrolet	281	470	Radiator
21	22	34	Wendell Scott	Scott '69 Ford	265	435	Engine
22	14	8	Joe Frasson	Ed Negre '69 Ford	223	450	Oil Leak
23	30	87	Leroy Carrigg	'68 Ford	181	415	Engine
24	10	26	Dave Marcis	Earl Brooks '69 Ford	131	430	Engine
25	17	54	Bill Dennis	Dennis '69 Chevrolet	105	420	Ignition
26	26	89	Rod Eulenfeld	Morris Davis '69 Ford	80	390	Fire
27	12	79	Frank Warren	Warren '69 Plymouth	78	405	Suspen
28	20	02	E J Trivette	Crawford Ent '69 Chevrolet	68	395	Rear End
29	15	67	Dick May	Joyce Ronacher '69 Ford	54	385	Suspen
30	18	68	Larry Baumel	Auto Lad '69 Ford	4	375	Engine

Time of Race: 3 hours, 17 minutes, 33 seconds
Average Speed: 83.284 mph
Pole Winner: Richard Petty - 94.064 mph
Lap Leaders: Richard Petty 1-36, Dick Brooks 37-84, Petty 85, Brooks 86-138,
     Bobby Isaac 139-140, Brooks 141-172, Bobby Allison 173-200, Isaac 201-403,
     Petty 404-410, Isaac 411-412, Petty 413-425, Isaac 426-444, Petty 445-500.
Cautions: 5 for 35 laps   Margin of Victory: 14 seconds   Attendance: 6,500
*Relieved by Wendell Scott

was in contention when the engine blew in his Dodge on lap 324. Pete Hamilton, who had side-stepped a call from the Army, drove in his last race for Petty Enterprises. The Dedham, MA driver crashed late in the race.

Just a few days later, he received word from Chrysler that Buddy Baker was taking his place on the Petty team. "We wanted to keep Hamilton," said Petty. "But Chrysler called the shots."

Bobby Allison's neatly outfitted pit crew goes to work in American 500

Buddy Young of Fairfax, VA, who was seriously injured in a January crash at Riverside, got back into the saddle at Rockingham. He drove a back-up L.G. De-Witt Ford and finished 10th -- with the number 13 on the doors. "It sure was good to get the feel of driving again," said Young. "I hope I can line something up next year. I'm ready to race."

Although Young had hoped to get back into racing full time, he would never again compete in a NASCAR Grand National event.

Yarborough drove his Wood Brothers Mercury into victory lane after averaging 117.811 mph. Only 20,000 fans showed up. The race had been postponed twice by rain.

Race No. 48

Allison Noses Out Parsons To Win '70 Finale at Hampton

HAMPTON, VA (Nov. 22) -- Bobby Allison passed Benny Parsons in the 202nd lap and led the rest of the way to win the Tidewater 300 at Langley Field

---

Grand National Race No. 47
492 Laps at North Carolina Motor Speedway
Rockingham, NC
"American 500"
500 Miles on 1.017-mile Paved Track
November 15, 1970

Fin	St	No.	Driver	Team / Car	Laps	Money	Status
1	2	21	Cale Yarborough	Wood Brothers '69 Mercury	492	$20,445	Running
2	6	17	David Pearson	Holman-Moody '69 Ford	492	11,170	Running
3	3	22	Bobby Allison	Mario Rossi '69 Dodge Day	489	6,195	Running
4	16	27	Donnie Allison	Banjo Matthews '69 Ford	486	3,045	Running
5	9	6	Buddy Baker	Cotton Owens '69 Dodge Day	485	2,190	Running
6	7	43	Richard Petty	Petty Ent '70 Plym SuperBird	481	1,920	Running
7	5	71	Bobby Isaac	K&K Ins '69 Dodge Daytona	478	2,020	Running
8	22	48	James Hylton	Hylton Eng '70 Ford	469	1,245	Running
9	21	39	Friday Hassler	James Hanley '69 Chevrolet	464	1,145	Running
10	14	13	Buddy Young	L G DeWitt '69 Ford	464	1,170	Running
11	20	18	Joe Frasson	Frasson '69 Dodge Daytona	458	1,270	Running
12	30	06	Neil Castles	Castles '69 Dodge Daytona	457	1,045	Running
13	28	64	Elmo Langley	Langley '69 Mercury	455	1,020	Running
14	34	25	Jabe Thomas	Don Robertson '69 Plymouth	450	995	Running
15	10	40	Pete Hamilton	Petty Ent '70 Plym SuperBird	449	1,145	Crash
16	17	31	Jim Vandiver	O L Nixon '69 Dodge Daytona	448	1,045	Running
17	32	76	Ben Arnold	Arnold '69 Ford	436	895	Running
18	38	70	J D McDuffie	McDuffie '69 Mercury	435	895	Running
19	24	45	Raymond Williams	Bill Seifert '69 Ford	428	870	Running
20	39	34	Wendell Scott	Scott '69 Ford	427	845	Engine
21	31	24	Cecil Gordon	Gordon '68 Ford	420	795	Running
22	29	57	Johnny Halford	Ervin Pruitt '69 Dodge	420	795	Running
23	19	36	Roy Mayne*	R Brown '70 Plym SuperBird	420	795	Running
24	33	68	Larry Baumel	Auto Lad '69 Ford	402	745	Running
25	18	10	Bill Champion	Champion '69 Ford	395	795	Fan pulley
26	40	79	Frank Warren	Warren '69 Plymouth	384	695	Running
27	27	61	Hoss Ellington	Ellington '69 Ford	356	670	Rear End
28	37	19	Henley Gray	Gray '69 Ford	347	645	Running
29	11	98	LeeRoy Yarbrough	Junior Johnson '69 Mercury	343	695	Engine
30	26	4	John Sears	Sears '69 Dodge	336	595	Ignition
31	1	99	Charlie Glotzbach	Nchls-G'smith '69 Dodge Day	324	2,160	Engine
32	8	30	Dave Marcis	Marcis '69 Dodge Daytona	273	955	Crash
33	12	72	Benny Parsons	L G DeWitt '69 Ford	119	695	Rear End
34	23	47	Bill Seifert	Seifert '70 Ford	117	545	D Shaft
35	13	55	Tiny Lund	J McConnell '69 Dodge Day	87	565	Engine
36	36	74	Bill Shirey	Shirey '69 Plymouth	81	585	Engine
37	15	90	Bill Dennis	Junie Donlavey '69 Mercury	53	630	Trans
38	35	92	Roy Tyner	Tyner '69 Ford	52	550	Clutch
39	4	32	Dick Brooks	Brooks '70 Plym SuperBird	43	1,320	Engine
40	25	5	Buddy Arrington	Arrington '69 Dodge	10	540	Rear End

Time of Race: 4 hours, 14 minutes, 24 seconds
Average Speed: 117.811 mph
Pole Winner: Charlie Glotzbach - 136.498 mph
Lap Leaders: Charlie Glotzbach 1-81, Cale Yarborough 82-85, David Pearson 86-188, Yarborough 189-190, Pearson 191-255, LeeRoy Yarborough 256, Richard Petty 257-280, Yarborough 281-282, Yarbrough 283, Yarborough 284-325, Pearson 326-329, Yarborough 330-441, Pearson 442-449, Yarborough 450-492.
Cautions: 7 for 46 laps   Margin of Victory: 4 seconds   Attendance: 20,000
*Relieved by Butch Hirst

Speedway. It was the third win of the season for the 32 year-old Dodge driver.

Parsons, who won the pole for the first time in his career, finished 100 yards behind Allison. Pete Hamilton, driving the Dick Brooks Plymouth, was third. John Sears came in fourth and James Hylton fifth.

Bobby Isaac, newly crowned Grand National champion, qualified second, but went out of the race on lap 106 with rear end problems.

Allison wound up 51 points behind Isaac in the final

point tally. Curiously, he missed one race -- the Richmond 500 on March 1. "I didn't have a short track car at the time," said Allison. "If I'd have been able to make that race, maybe things would have turned out differently."

In retrospect, had Allison been able to finish 25th at Richmond, he would have won the title.

Bill Dennis of Glen Allen, VA qualified a strong third in Junie Donlavey's Mercury. Dennis went 28 laps before the engine blew. He did, however, win the 1970 Grand National Rookie of the Year award in a close voting over Joe Frasson and Jim Vandiver.

Parsons led the first 34 laps before Allison made his move. Parsons worked his way back up to the front for 12 more laps, but was unable to handle Allison in the final battle. "I just couldn't quite keep up with Bobby," said Parsons. "Nevertheless, this is a good way to end the year."

Allison averaged 69.584 mph before a slim audience of 3,200.

Grand National Race No. 48
300 Laps at Langley Field Speedway
Hampton, VA
"Tidewater 300"
118.5 Miles on .395-mile Paved Track
November 22, 1970

Fin	St	No.	Driver	Team / Car	Laps	Money	Status
1	4	22	Bobby Allison	Allison '70 Dodge	300	$1,635	Running
2	1	72	Benny Parsons	L G DeWitt '69 Ford	300	1,100	Running
3	17	32	Pete Hamilton	Dick Brooks '69 Plymouth	299	600	Running
4	7	4	John Sears	Sears '69 Dodge	298	425	Running
5	5	48	James Hylton	Hylton Eng '70 Ford	297	355	Running
6	6	06	Neil Castles	Castles '69 Dodge	295	325	Running
7	11	64	Elmo Langley	Langley '69 Mercury	293	275	Running
8	8	70	J D McDuffie	McDuffie '69 Mercury	293	295	Running
9	14	79	Frank Warren	Warren '69 Plymouth	290	265	Running
10	10	25	Jabe Thomas	Don Robertson '69 Plymouth	290	285	Running
11	9	39	Friday Hassler	James Hanley '69 Chevrolet	289	280	Running
12	15	10	Bill Champion	Champion '69 Ford	287	250	Running
13	20	8	Joe Frasson	Ed Negre '69 Ford	285	245	Running
14	25	97	Jim Vandiver	Cecil Gordon '68 Ford	281	240	Running
15	26	19	Henley Gray	Gray '69 Ford	273	235	Running
16	19	74	Bill Shirey	Shirey '69 Plymouth	273	230	Running
17	29	78	Rodney Bruce	J D McDuffie '69 Buick	261	225	Running
18	27	88	Bill Hollar	'69 Ford	255	220	Running
19	22	34	Wendell Scott	Scott '69 Ford	237	215	Running
20	16	26	Dave Marcis	Earl Brooks '69 Ford	205	210	Running
21	24	65	Joe Phipps	Phipps '69 Chevrolet	196	205	Trans
22	30	02	Jimmy Crawford	Crawford Ent '69 Plymouth	108	200	Ignition
23	2	71	Bobby Isaac	K&K Insurance '69 Dodge	106	260	Rear End
24	13	24	Cecil Gordon	Gordon '68 Ford	87	200	Rear End
25	12	54	Ben Arnold	Bill Dennis '69 Chevrolet	66	200	Engine
26	23	92	Roy Tyner	Tyner '69 Ford	51	200	Handling
27	3	90	Bill Dennis	Junie Donlavey '69 Mercury	28	240	Engine
28	18	68	Larry Baumel	Auto Lad '69 Ford	17	200	Trans
29	21	37	Dr Don Tarr	Tarr '69 Dodge	4	200	Engine
30	28	67	Dick May	Joyce Ronacher '69 Ford	2	200	Engine

Time of Race: 1 hour, 40 minutes, 45 seconds
Average Speed: 69.584 mph
Pole Winner: Benny Parsons - 78.239 mph
Lap Leaders: Benny Parsons 1-34, Bobby Allison 35-189, Parsons 190-201,
    Bobby Allison 202-300.
Cautions: 2 for 10 laps   Margin of Victory: 100 Yards   Attendance: 3,200

1970 NASCAR Season
Final Point Standings - Grand National Division

Rank	Driver	Points	Starts	Wins	Top 5	Top 10	Winnings
1	Bobby Isaac	3,911	47	11	32	38	$199,600
2	Bobby Allison	3,860	46	3	30	35	149,745
3	James Hylton	3,788	47	1	22	39	78,201
4	Richard Petty	3,447	40	18	27	31	151,124
5	Neil Castles	3,158	47	0	12	24	49,746
6	Elmo Langley	3,154	47	0	1	19	45,193
7	Jabe Thomas	3,120	46	0	0	23	42,958
8	Benny Parsons	2,993	45	0	12	23	59,402
9	Dave Marcis	2,820	47	0	7	15	41,111
10	Frank Warren	2,697	46	0	0	2	35,161
11	Cecil Gordon	2,514	44	0	2	11	32,713
12	John Sears	2,465	40	0	4	7	32,675
13	Dick Brooks	2,460	34	0	15	18	53,754
14	Wendell Scott	2,425	41	0	0	9	28,518
15	Bill Champion	2,350	38	0	0	6	30,943
16	J.D. McDuffie	2,079	36	0	1	10	24,905
17	Ben Arnold	1,997	29	0	0	3	25,805
18	Bill Seifert	1,962	39	0	1	4	25,647
19	Henley Gray	1,871	34	0	0	2	23,130
20	Friday Hassler	1,831	26	0	1	6	27,535
21	Pete Hamilton	1,819	16	3	10	12	131,406
22	Joe Frasson	1,723	22	0	0	2	20,172
23	David Pearson	1,716	19	1	9	11	87,118
24	Buddy Baker	1,555	18	1	6	8	63,510
25	Bill Dennis	1,432	25	0	0	5	15,630
26	Ed Negre	1,413	31	0	0	1	14,580
27	G.C. Spencer	1,410	20	0	3	9	17,915
28	Charlie Glotzbach	1,358	19	3	7	8	50,649
29	Roy Mayne	1,333	16	0	0	3	16,910
30	Bill Shirey	1,244	29	0	0	1	12,215
31	Raymond Williams	1,204	22	0	0	0	12,535
32	Larry Baumel	1,138	23	0	0	1	16,645
33	Buddy Arrington	1,087	19	0	0	2	16,845
34	Cale Yarborough	1,016	19	3	11	13	115,875
35	Dr. Don Tarr	995	17	0	0	5	16,592
36	Johnny Halford	975	25	0	0	0	15,645
37	Earl Brooks	884	21	0	0	1	10,340
38	Coo Coo Marlin	876	13	0	0	4	14,799
39	Ron Keselowski	855	17	0	0	1	11,985
40	Donnie Allison	841	19	3	10	12	96,081
41	Ken Meisenhelder	812	19	0	0	2	7,020
42	Roy Tyner	631	14	0	0	3	5,565
43	LeeRoy Yarbrough	625	19	1	7	11	61,930
44	Dick May	551	15	0	0	0	4,510
45	Jim Vandiver	519	14	0	0	5	16,080
46	John Kenney	457	11	0	0	0	4,115
47	Dub Simpson	367	6	0	0	1	4,510
48	Leroy Carrigg	355	9	0	0	0	4,130
49	Joe Phipps	325	7	0	0	0	4,090
50	Wayne Smith	300	8	0	0	0	4,505

The 1971 Season

A Pivotal Year; NASCAR Loses Factories and Drivers, Gains Winston

Volume three of a four volume series . . Big Bucks and Boycotts   1965 - 1971

1971

Chrysler Corp. had unexpectedly announced their factory backed efforts in 1971 would be severely reduced. Bobby Isaac and Bobby Allison had finished first and second in the 1970 Grand National point standings, and both lost their factory sponsorship for 1971.

Chrysler's Gayle Porter said, "We had to cut back. There was no alternative."

Chrysler cut back from six teams to two for the 1971 NASCAR season -- and both teams would operate out of the Petty Enterprises complex. Richard Petty and Buddy Baker would be the drivers.

On November 19, 1970, Ford Motor Co. dropped a bombshell. Matthew McLaughlin, Ford Sales Vice-President, announced that his company was getting out of stock car racing -- entirely. "We believe our racing activities have served their purpose, and we propose now to concentrate our promotional efforts on direct merchandising and sale of our products through franchized dealers. Accordingly, effective immediately we are withdrawing from all forms of motorsports competition."

Two Ford factory teams, under the direction of Jacques Passino, were engaged in a shake down session at Riverside as McLaughlin made his announcement. They were forced to pack up their equipment and come home -- immediately.

Passino, 50, who had been among the leaders of Ford's racing efforts, was shocked by the sudden pull out. Rather than being reassigned by Ford, he quit. "Although Ford has severed its ties with racing," said Passino, "I still feel the race track, which has proven to be the real test track for automobile production, will be the same -- even more so in the future.

A year ago, auto racing drew 53 million spectators and millions more saw it on television. I feel auto racing is on the way to being the number one sport in the United States and I wanted to be a part of the future. I have considered the other areas offered to me at Ford in manufacturing and merchandising, but I wanted to devote my energies to performance. Effectively immediately, I hereby resign from Ford Motor Co."

Jacques Passino -- When Ford withdrew its factory support, he quit the company

Passino had been part of Ford's racing effort since the summer of 1962 when openly, they said they would support stock car racing. "I was told to pack my bags, move down South and not to come home until Ford was a winner," reflected Passino. "I thought I may never get to see my wife again. Fortunately we did win and I was able to come home."

On the heels of Ford's retreat, Cale Yarborough announced he was jumping to the USAC Indy Car circuit. "I have been offered one of Gene White's Indy Cars," said Cale. "It seems like the best route to go. The Ford withdrawal had a lot to do with my decision."

Ford car owners Junior Johnson and Banjo Matthews were concerned about their future. "I can't race without a sponsor," said Johnson. "I've sold one car, in the process of selling another and hope to sell the third car. After that, I'm out of racing."

"I still have three cars," said Matthews. "But I can't race without some backing. If someone isn't footing the bills, the car owner is wasting his time and he's not going to make any money."

The Wood Brothers and Holman-Moody, Ford's other factory backed teams in 1970, said they would run if they could locate sponsors or where track promoters were willing to give them a sizeable appearance fee.

* * *

Two weeks after Ford pulled up stakes, NASCAR and R.J. Reynolds Tobacco Co. formed what would turn out to be the most fruitful and important relationship in the history of stock car racing. Beginning in 1971, the Winston brand of cigarettes would sponsor a 500-mile race at Talladega -- and a special point fund worth $100,000.

R.A. Rechholtz, Vice President of Marketing for R.J. Reynolds, said his company decided to sponsor the Winston 500 at Alabama International Motor Speedway "because it is the fastest race track in the world and destined , we feel, to be the number one motorsports facility of the future; which is appropriate for Winston, being the number one cigarette brand in the United States.

"We are very excited about starting our association with NASCAR," Rechholtz added. "We intend to work closely with them in making 1971 the best year ever for the sport of stock car racing."

The Winston Cup point money would be channeled to the Grand National drivers at three intervals during the 1971 season. A $25,000 pay-off going to the top 10 drivers in the Winston Cup point standings would be distributed following the World 600 on May 30. The second leg, worth an additional $25,000, would be given out after the Labor Day Southern 500. The big chunk of point money -- $50,000, would be paid to the top 20 drivers after the conclusion of the season.

"The $100,000 posted by Reynolds for the Winston Cup will assure the Grand National division of one of the largest point funds in automobile racing history," said NASCAR President Bill France. "It will be the largest point fund in NASCAR's 23 year history. Our agreement with Winston calls for having advertising and promotional support on a nation-wide scale."

Curiously, only the events of 250 miles or more would comprise the *"Winston Cup Series"* , although the three payments would be determined by points from all races, including the 100-milers on the short tracks.

One of the first steps by R.J. Reynolds was to place a large number of ads in daily newspapers in areas where the Winston Cup Grand National drivers were scheduled to race. The ads would promote the event -- along with the Winston product. Billboards also went up along interstates and major highways. "No doubt about it," said Richmond Fairgrounds Raceway promoter Paul Sawyer, "all of this has helped us attract a large crowd for our (Richmond 500) race."

R.M. Odear, Winston Product Manager, said the newspaper advertisements and billboards would only be directed to the events on the Winston Cup Series. Any race shorter than 250 miles was not included in the promotions. "Everything we do to promote the Winston Cup also promotes all Grand National races," said Odear. "We intend on making our presence felt this season and let everyone in racing know we're in it in a big way."

Winston's plunge into stock car racing was one of the few high water marks in an otherwise troubled year.

* * *

The carburetor plates introduced by NASCAR in August of 1970 were spawning epic controversy. The heavy hitting Ford 'Boss' 429 engines and the Chrysler 426 hemi power plants, were severely restricted under the 1971 rules. The big engines, specifically designed for racing, could compete with a 1 1/4-inch carburetor opening. In an effort to equalize competition and make racing more affordable to the independents, of which there were many, NASCAR allowed the 427 c.i. Ford wedge engine to utilize a 1 1/2-inch opening. The Chrysler wedge engine could operate with an opening of 1 5/8 inches. The larger the holes in the carburetor, the more horsepower that could be attained.

By early spring, the Wood Brothers and Holman-Moody made the switch from the heavily restricted 429 to the conventional 427 wedge. Most of the independents, who had used the bigger engine in 1970, couldn't afford the costly conversion to the 427. "It's hurting all of us independents," said privateer Jabe Thomas. "That plate has made finishers out of a lot of those hot dogs. Buddy Baker used to always blow up. Now he's finishing, and knocking us poor boys down another notch. And none of us can afford to switch over to wedge engines."

Through the first half of the year, no Chrysler car had opted to use the old wedge engine, even though it was allowed the largest opening of all the engines.

As the season progressed, the Chrysler teams were complaining the loudest -- claiming their choked down hemis couldn't keep up with the "new" 427 c.i. Fords. "We're being played with," said Richard Petty. "When the Fords want to go, they drive off from us."

In the Yankee 400 at Michigan International Speedway, Bobby Allison, who left his self-owned Dodge to join Holman-Moody in May, and Petty's factory backed Plymouth were locked in a tight battle. As the pair whipped off the fourth turn for the final time, Petty backed off and gave the win to Allison. "I know when I'm being played with," said Petty. "I just decided to stay out of the pictures at the finish. I didn't have a chance."

During the course of the season, many former top car owners had thrown in the towel. Mario Rossi, L.G. DeWitt, Junior Johnson and Banjo Matthews had pulled off the circuit. Defending champion Bobby Isaac had been taken off the tour by his car owner Nord Krauskopf, who parked the champion's cars in protest of the carburetor plate rules.

Petty objected to the concept of having three different size plates. "When you have two or three different size plates," said Petty, "it's easy to wonder if someone else doesn't have the right size plate. When you beat a guy at one track, then he turns around and blows your doors off a few days later, it's easy to suspect he's got a different size plate."

Petty was in favor of a uniform size carburetor plate for all competitors. "Everyone's got four tires, a 22 gallon gas tank and one four-barrel carburetor -- all the same. So everyone should have the same size plate," said Petty.

Adding fuel to the fire was the fact that David Pearson had won a 125-mile qualifying race at Daytona using a 'cheater' plate. NASCAR allowed him to keep the victory. They said they were unable to determine if the plate had been used in the race.

Bobby Allison, who had hopped aboard the Holman-Moody Mercury when Pearson quit in May, immediately went on a tear. He won the World 600 at Charlotte, the Mason-Dixon 500 at Dover, both 400-milers at Michigan and the Talladega 500 -- all within three months. "If Richard Petty wins a race by 10 laps," said Allison, "everybody says it is because of superior driving. If I win by a half car length, they say I'm cheating."

The whole carburetor plate situation had gotten out of hand. So much that NAS-CAR's Vice President Lin Kuchler had to make an official statement, clairifying the rules. "The carburetor rule does not specify brand names of cars," said Kuchler. "It goes by types of engines. The controversy has erupted because of the misunderstanding that one brand is handicapped by the rule more than another brand."

The car owners could use any type of engine they wanted, Kuchler added.

"The rule was written not to handicap any one manufacturer," said Kuchler, "but to improve competition by making it possible for the less expensive wedge-type engines to compete with the 429 Ford 'Boss' and the 426 Chrysler hemi. We feel the rule has accomplished our goal

NASCAR's Executive Vice-President, Lin Kuchler

because our races have been the closest in history with more drivers leading and more lead changes than any time I can remember. We also have more different brands competing than we have had in recent years. That is what the spectators want."

Bill France had a short statement of his own. "The restrictor plates have made for better racing at lesser costs for most drivers. The wedge engines cost half what the hemis do. Therefore, we see no need for a change at this time."

By the July 4 Firecracker 400, four of the leading Chrysler teams had made the time-consuming change over the wedge engine, which had the largest size plate allowed under NASCAR rules. Bobby Isaac was brought back into racing by Krauskopf, who reluctantly gave in to the wishes of crew chief Harry Hyde. Hyde had wanted to go to Daytona to do some "experimenting" with the wedge.

The teams owned by Petty Enterprises (two cars), K&K Insurance and Cotton Owens brought wedge engines to Daytona. Their drivers, Isaac, Petty, Buddy Baker and Pete Hamilton promptly finished 1-2-3-4.

Now, this brought outcries from the Ford people. Glen Wood pulled his Mercury off the tour following the Dixie 500 at Atlanta.

In the August 1 event at Atlanta, Bobby Allison and Richard Petty had embarrassed the entire field. The two rivals put on a dazzling show - nine laps ahead of everybody else. Petty edged Allison at the wire. Third place finisher Benny Parsons was nine laps behind. The Wood Brothers Mercury, with Donnie Allison aboard, was 11 laps back.

Shortly after the Atlanta contest, NASCAR changed the carburetor rules. The controversial carburetor plate would be replaced by limiting carburetor base openings.

The new regulation served the same purpose -- reducing speeds -- and NASCAR was hopeful it would eliminate the dissent that has prevailed since the introduction of the restrictor plate.

"I think the restrictor plate was one of the greatest things NASCAR has ever done," stressed France. "And if the new carburetor base opening formula doesn't work out satisfactorily, here comes the restrictor plate back again."

The new regulations, which went into effect on September 15, called for a "sleeve" in each of the four discharge holes, thus limiting the amount of air and gas to pass into the carburetor.

There were four different size base openings outlined in the new specifications.

The results were basically the same. Bobby Allison and Richard Petty continued to do most of the winning.

Junior Johnson sold his Ford equipment and built a Chevrolet

And, when a Chrysler product won, the Ford people grumbled. When a Ford product won, the Chrysler people complained.

It was the same thing which had been going on all year long.

*   *   *

Trying to muscle up toward the leading Fords and Chryslers was a little white Chevrolet built by Junior Johnson. Johnson had liquidated all of his Ford equipment and was virtually out of racing.

Richard Howard, General Manager of Charlotte Motor Speedway, was concerned about the prospects of a poor spectator turnout for the May 30th World 600. Several of the leading independents had quit when they ran out of good equipment. Those remaining were racing with tired machinery. Except for the three or four teams that had the means to get new parts, everyone was lagging behind.

Howard had an idea. What if a competitive Chevrolet came back on the scene? It would fill a void that had existed since 1963.

At Daytona in February, Junior Johnson was seen huddled with some General Motors representatives. There was speculation that Johnson would begin a gradual shift over to General Motors once he got rid of his Ford equipment.

The white Chevy #3 that Charlie Glotzbach drove in 1971

In March, Howard said publicly that he wanted a potential winning Chevrolet in his World 600 field -- and he would like Junior Johnson to build and *drive* it.

"Junior would bring several thousand spectators if he drives," said Howard. "And even as a builder of a Chevy, he'd be valuable to our promotion."

Johnson decided against driving, but he worked out an arrangement with Howard to build a Chevrolet. On April 8, Howard said, "I have made a deal with Junior to build the Chevy. And it could be the most competitive Chevy to race since General Motors quit backing stock car racing. I wish Junior would drive it, but if he won't, we'll have a good man behind the wheel".

Charlie Glotzbach was selected to drive the Howard-Johnson Chevrolet. "I like Charlie," said Johnson. "He'll make a car go. When he goes out of a race, you know it went out wide open."

In shake down runs a week before the World 600, Glotzbach was turning in some very impressive speeds on the 1.5-mile Charlotte Motor Speedway. It appeared that Howard had a competitive Chevy.

Glotzbach went out and won the pole for the World 600 with a speed of 157.788 mph.

Richard Howard brought Chevrolet back to NASCAR racing

And presto, 78,000 spectators showed up on race day.

Glotzbach didn't disappoint them. He led the 600 on four occasions for 87 laps. While running second on lap 234, Glotzbach plowed into the front stretch wall after he swerved to keep from hitting Speedy Thompson in the rear. Glotzbach said Thompson had pulled out in front of him.

Within moments, Richard Howard made an appearance in the press box. Track publicist Bob Latford introduced him, "And now, we'll have a word from the car owner."

Howard took the microphone and told the members of the media, "I just want to let everybody know that we're real happy with the way the car ran today. And we're going to build another one for the National 500 in October."

True to his word, Howard put up the money for Johnson to rebuild the car before the return trip to Charlotte. Johnson did so, and took the car wherever promoters were willing to pay for it. The new team was able to make 13 races during the last half of the 1971 season.

Glotzbach drove in the Firecracker 400, but went out with a blown engine. The third start for the car produced a popular victory. Glotzbach and relief driver Friday Hassler teamed up to win the Volunteer 500 at Bristol.

The car was always fast -- never qualifying below fourth position. When it finished, it was among the leaders. Glotzbach and Johnson finished six of the 13 races, and each time they made the distance, they finished in the top five.

* * *

Toward the end of the year, NASCAR made a major procedural rule change. Effective August 6, 1971, the smaller Grand American automobiles -- Mustangs, Camaros and AMC Javelins -- would be allowed to compete in all Winston Cup Grand National events on the short tracks.

"The Grand Americans have not joined the Grand Nationals," said Kuchler. "We feel it will benefit the sport and the fans to see the smaller cars run against the Grand Nationals on short tracks."

Actually, NASCAR made the change to provide a schedule for the failing Grand American tour formerly called the Grand Touring Circuit. The compact car series had floundered and was virtually out of business half way through the season. The "mixed" races would also spice up competition for the Grand Nationals on the short tracks.

The Winston Cup Grand National regulars weren't too pleased with the latest ruling. "If the small cars win," said Petty, "it will damage the prestige of the Grand Nationals."

In the Myers Brothers Memorial event at Winston-Salem, NC -- the first meeting of the two divisions, the Grand Americans ran circles around the bigger Grand Nationals. Bobby Allison won in a Mustang, followed by Petty's Plymouth. The next five spots were taken by Grand Americans. "I figured something like this would happen," said Petty. "They'll probably win all these races".

One independent driver, who requested anonymity, said, "The Grand Americans spoil the image of the Grand Nationals. They race for a hobby; we race for a living."

In the next meeting, Petty beat Allison's Mustang at Ona, WV to even the score. After the second race, Allison elected not to drive the Mustang anymore. "I didn't get credit for a Grand National win," said Allison. "In fact, nobody got credit for a win. You look in the Grand National record and nobody won the Myers Brothers Memorial."

What Allison said was true. NASCAR gave Allison credit for a Grand American win. There was no Winston Cup Grand National race winner for that particular event.

Nor was there an official winner in the Motor Trend

Richard Petty won the first 'Winston Cup' in 1971.
Miss Winston, Marilyn Chilton, is shown with the 3-time champion

500 at Riverside staged back in January. Ray Elder, who was competing for Winston West points in that event, got credit for a Winston West victory when he won on the 2.62-mile road course in 1971 (and again in June of 1972). According to the Official NASCAR Record Book from 1972-1975, Ray Elder had zero Winston Cup victories. However, that was to be adjusted in 1976 -- and sanctioning NASCAR properly gave him credit for the two races he won.

They never did that with Bobby Allison's victory at Winston-Salem in a Mustang, which occurred under the same circumstances in the same year. Tiny Lund, who won two late 1971 events in a Camaro, never was acknowledged by sanctioning NASCAR for his fourth and fifth career Winston Cup triumphs.

There were six "mixed" races run in late 1971. The Winston Cup Grand National cars won three, and the Grand Americans won three. Under the NASCAR rules, eight events were to be opened to the compact cars. But Martinsville promoter Clay Earles and Richmond owner Paul Sawyer refused to allow the Grand Americans to enter their races.

"I'm not going to allow the Grand Americans to put me out of business," huffed Earles. "I have nothing against the Grand American boys, but I think they

Richard Petty won 21 races in 1971 and became NASCAR champion for the third time

should run as a separate division and not intermingle with the bigger Grand National cars.

"I'm doing this for the good of Martinsville Speedway," Earles continued. "As manager of the track, it is my duty to manage it to the best of my ability. We've scheduled a Grand National race and that's what we'll run".

Bobby Isaac won the Old Dominion 500 in a Dodge.

At North Wilkesboro, the Grand Americans were permitted to enter. But a number of Winston Cup car owners didn't like it. "If these little cars hold together," said Ralph Moody, "there might be three or four of them several laps ahead of the field."

Junior Johnson agreed. "They use less tires and less gasoline," said Johnson. "They also have a better power-to-weight ratio. How much could you ask for?" queried Johnson.

Tiny Lund won the Wilkes 400 in a Camaro.

Richard Petty enjoyed a banner year in 1971, winning 21 races in 46 starts. Including the point money and the Winston Cup bonus, his winnings came to a record $351,071. He became the first man to top the $300,000 plateau in winnings.

The 1971 season was also the last year that the Winston Cup Grand National schedule consisted of 48-50 events. Winston only recognized the 'major' events as part of the Winston Cup Series in 1971. By 1972, all of the others had been removed from the tour.

Race No. 1

Elder Surprise Winner in Motor Trend 500

RIVERSIDE, CA (Jan. 10) -- Part-time racer and full-time farmer Ray Elder authored a major surprise by wheeling his family owned Dodge to victory in the Motor Trend 500 at Riverside International Raceway. It was the first big win for the 28 year-old Caruthers, CA

Ray Elder

driver.

Elder drove past Bobby Allison with 12 laps remaining and pulled away to a 10.5-second triumph. Benny Parsons was two laps behind the leaders in third place. Bobby Isaac, with relief help from David Pearson, was fourth. Fifth place went to James Hylton.

"I can't believe this," said a jubilant Elder from victory lane. "Only thing is I owe most of this money to the bank."

The 191 lap event on the 2.62-mile road course was the first NASCAR race run under the new Winston Cup Grand National banner. The premier stock car racing series received support from R.J. Reynolds Tobacco Co. for the 1971 season.

Richard Petty, driving a Plymouth, started on the pole and led the first three laps. Petty lost the lead to Allison and Pearson, then led for a 59 lap stretch after retaking the lead. Engine failure put him out on lap 107.

Pearson had the fastest time trial, but had to start back in 16th place. By the fifth lap, the three-time champ had moved into the lead. Pearson was taken out on lap 25 when the engine in his Holman-Moody Ford blew. "I was long gone until the engine blew," said Pearson.

Elder, driving the only car among the leaders shod with Firestone tires, led for a total of 61 laps. He had started third on the grid.

A relatively small crowd of 23,000 watched Elder win at an average speed of 100.783 mph.

Winston Cup GN Race No. 1
191 Laps at Riverside Int'l Raceway
Riverside, CA
"Motor Trend 500"
500 Miles on 2.62-mile Paved Road Course
January 10, 1971

Fin	St	No.	Driver	Team / Car	Laps	Money	Status
1	3	96	Ray Elder	Fred Elder '70 Dodge	191	$18,715	Running
2	2	12	Bobby Allison	Allison '70 Dodge	191	9,215	Running
3	7	72	Benny Parsons	L G DeWitt '69 Ford	189	6,390	Running
4	4	71	Bobby Isaac*	K&K Insurance '71 Dodge	189	4,540	Running
5	5	48	James Hylton	Hylton Eng '70 Ford	185	2,915	Running
6	9	39	Friday Hassler	Hassler '69 Chevrolet	184	2,040	Running
7	10	32	Kevin Terris	Dean Barnicle '70 Plymouth	184	1,785	Running
8	22	26	Carl Joiner	Dean Thorne '69 Chevrolet	169	1,615	Running
9	17	19	Henley Gray	Gray '69 Ford	169	1,640	Running
10	13	24	Cecil Gordon	Gordon '69 Ford	167	1,415	Running
11	29	23	G T Tallas	Tallas '69 Ford	157	1,315	Engine
12	8	04	Hershel McGriff	Beryl Jackson '70 Plymouth	156	1,290	Ignition
13	40	18	Bob England	England '70 Chevrolet	155	1,240	Engine
14	27	4	Dick Kranzler	Kranzler '70 Chevrolet	143	1,215	Running
15	34	70	J D McDuffie	McDuffie '69 Mercury	140	1,190	Engine
16	6	02	Dick Bown	Mike Ober '70 Plymouth	133	1,215	Steering
17	19	64	Elmo Langley	Langley '69 Mercury	130	1,190	Engine
18	31	7	Jack McCoy	Ernie Conn '70 Dodge	126	1,235	Engine
19	26	82	Ron Gautsche	Gautsche '69 Ford	118	1,125	Lug Bolt
20	1	43	Richard Petty	Petty Ent '70 Plymouth	107	1,515	Engine
21	15	08	John Soares, Jr.	Soares '70 Plymouth	101	1,105	Engine
22	30	00	Frank James	Jim Calder '69 Chevrolet	97	1,095	Trans
23	33	5	Ron Grable	'70 Ford	77	1,160	Engine
24	14	44	Dick Gulstrand	James Good '68 Chevrolet	76	1,075	A Frame
25	11	38	Jimmy Insolo	Marvin Rowley 69 Chevrolet	75	1,065	Engine
26	12	10	Bill Champion	Champion '69 Ford	58	1,055	Trans
27	24	95	Robert Kauf	Paul Stockwell '69 Chevrolet	56	1,045	Trans
28	25	15	Paul Dorrity	Glen Dorrity '71 Chevrolet	50	1,035	Engine
29	23	6	Jerry Oliver	Cos Cancilla '70 Olds	47	1,025	Engine
30	37	79	Frank Warren	Warren '69 Plymouth	40	1,015	Trans
31	38	107	Mike Kittlekow	'69 Chevrolet	38	1,015	Clutch
32	32	77	Ron Johnstone	Johnstone '69 Plymouth	36	1,095	Crash
33	18	88	Don Noel	Noel - Lewin '70 Ford	27	1,090	Engine
34	39	33	Glenn Francis	Bill Andersen '70 Chev	27	1,015	Engine
35	16	17	David Pearson	Holman-Moody '70 Ford	25	1,165	Engine
36	20	83	Joe Clark	'69 Chevrolet	21	1,065	Trans
37	35	148	Herry Schilling	Thomas Hynes '69 Dodge	18	1,065	Engine
38	36	177	Roy Collins	'69 Dodge	7	1,040	Engine
39	28	07	Ivan Baldwin	Baldwin '69 Chevrolet	2	1,015	Engine
40	21	99	Pat Fay	'71 Ford	1	1,015	Engine

Time of Race: 4 hours, 57 minutes, 55 seconds
Average Speed: 100.783 mph
Pole Winner: Richard Petty - 107.084 mph
Fastest Qualifier: David Pearson - 109.015 mph
Lap Leaders: Richard Petty 1-3, Bobby Allison 4, David Pearson 5-24, Petty 25-83,
    Ray Elder 84-106, Allison 107-119, Elder 120-135, Allison 136-149, Elder 150-165,
    Allison 166-179, Elder 180-191.
Cautions: 1 for 9 laps   Margin of Victory: 10.5 seconds   Attendance: 23,000
*Relieved by David Pearson

Race No. 2

Foyt Slows, Hamilton Wins Daytona 125 By Inches

DAYTONA BEACH, FL (Feb. 11) -- A cautious A.J. Foyt cracked the throttle in the final lap and Pete Hamilton sneaked past to win the first 125-mile race at Daytona International Speedway. It was the first start for the new Hamilton-Cotton Owens team.

Foyt had taken the lead from Fred Lorenzen in the 43rd lap and led Hamilton by four car lengths entering the final lap. Sophomore driver Ron Keselowski flipped his Dodge in the last lap -- just ahead of the leaders. Foyt lifted, allowing Hamilton to make up the gap and produce a race-winning pass.

Hamilton got to the finish line first by about three feet. "If his (Keselowski) car came back onto the banking," Foyt explained, "I wanted to be able to go either underneath him or around him. If I hadn't lifted, I would have been committed to going around the top of him."

Keselowski's car stayed on the apron, and he climbed out unhurt.

Richard Petty finished third, LeeRoy Yarbrough was fourth and Lorenzen fifth.

Cotton Owens and Pete Hamilton won Daytona 125, their first joint effort

Internationally acclaimed Pedro Rodriguez was assigned to drive a Bill Ellis Chevrolet. The Mexican star, who first competed in NASCAR in 1959, went only 16 laps before his engine blew.

Cale Yarborough, who left NASCAR to join USAC, drove a Ray Fox Plymouth in a one shot deal. He finished seventh.

The caution free event was run at an average speed of 175.029 mph. A crowd of 20,000 dotted the grandstands.

Race No. 3

Pearson Wins Second 125 In Hepped Up (?) Mercury

DAYTONA BEACH, FL (Feb. 11) -- David Pearson whisked around Buddy Baker with six laps left and scored a two car length win in the second 125-mile qualifier at Daytona International Speedway. It was the 59th career win for the 36 year-old veteran.

Baker finished a close second and Dick Brooks was third. Brooks was driving a winged Dodge equipped with a small 305 c.i. engine under the new NASCAR rules. Bill Dennis came in fourth and Benny Parsons

was fifth.

Pearson started fourth and grabbed the lead in the opening lap. The wily 'Silver Fox' backed off and was content to run behind the Baker-Bobby Isaac battle. In the closing laps, Pearson came out of the pack and marched confidently toward the checkered flag.

Two days later, the Holman-Moody team was quietly fined $500 for having an illegal carburetor restrictor plate. NASCAR was unable to determine if the illegal gadget was used in the 125-miler.

Pearson's team was fined an additional $200 for another infraction earlier in the week.

Isaac started on the pole and led on six occasions before blowing a left front tire with four laps remaining. His green flag pit stop dropped him to 11th in the final rundown.

NASCAR regular Charlie Glotzbach was slated to drive a Nichels-Goldsmith Pontiac, but refused to accept the ride. "Two days before I came to Daytona, (Ray) Nichels tells me they are going to give the Ply-

Winston Cup GN Race No. 2
50 Laps at Daytona Int'l Speedway
Daytona Beach, FL
125 Miles on 2.5-mile Paved Track
February 11, 1971

Fin	St	No.	Driver	Team / Car	Laps	Money	Status
1	2	6	Pete Hamilton	Cotton Owens '71 Plym	50	$1,300	Running
2	1	21	A J Foyt	Wood Brothers '69 Mercury	50	800	Running
3	3	43	Richard Petty	Petty Ent '71 Plymouth	50	550	Running
4	5	98	LeeRoy Yarbrough	Junior Johnson '69 Mercury	50	500	Running
5	4	99	Fred Lorenzen	Nichels-Goldsmith '71 Plym	50	450	Running
6	6	27	Donnie Allison	Banjo Matthews 69 Mercury	50	400	Running
7	16	3	Cale Yarborough	Ray Fox '71 Plymouth	49	345	Running
8	10	48	James Hylton	Hylton Eng '69 Ford	48	335	Running
9	7	2	Dave Marcis	Marcis '69 Dodge	48	325	Running
10	17	24	Cecil Gordon	Gordon '69 Mercury	47	310	Running
11	22	4	John Sears	Sears '69 Dodge	47	300	Running
12	20	55	Tiny Lund	John McConnell '69 Dodge	47	290	Running
13	12	18	Joe Frasson	Frasson '70 Dodge	47	280	Running
14	13	10	Bill Champion	Champion '69 Ford	47	270	Running
15	21	68	Larry Baumel	Auto Lad '69 Ford	47	260	Running
16	23	95	Leonard Blanchard	Blanchard '71 Ford	46	255	Running
17	19	39	Friday Hassler	Hassler '69 Chevrolet	46	245	Running
18	11	40	Marv Acton	Dick Brooks '70 Plymouth	46	235	Running
19	9	79	Frank Warren	Warren '69 Plymouth	46	225	Running
20	14	59	Vic Elford	Tom Pistone '71 Ford	46	220	Running
21	24	63	Charlie Roberts	Roberts '69 Dodge	46	215	Running
22	18	88	Ron Keselowski	Roger Lubinski '70 Dodge	45	210	Crash
23	27	23	Fritz Schultz	Don Robertson '70 Plymouth	45	205	Running
24	30	58	Robert Brown	Allan Brown '71 Chevrolet	44	200	Running
25	26	26	Earl Brooks	Brooks '69 Ford	42	---	Running
26	33	67	Dick May	Joyce Ronacher '69 Ford	41	---	Running
27	15	74	Bill Shirey	Shirey '69 Plymouth	41	---	Running
28	25	84	Bobby Mausgrover	Bob Davis '69 Dodge	39	---	Running
29	29	78	Dick Poling	Frank Warren '69 Dodge	21	---	Clutch
30	32	14	Pedro Rodriguez	Bill Ellis '71 Chevrolet	16	---	Engine
31	8	45	Bill Seifert	Seifert '70 Ford	7	---	Engine
32	28	87	Butch Hirst	Universal Air Lift '69 Olds	2	---	D Shaft
33	31	80	Joe Hines	Hines '69 Chevrolet	1	---	Engine

Time of Race: 42 minutes, 51 seconds
Average Speed: 175.029 mph
Pole Winner: A J Foyt 182.744 mph
Lap Leaders: A J Foyt 1-23, Pete Hamilton 24-26, Foyt 27, Hamilton 28-29, Foyt 30-31, Richard Petty 32-36, Donnie Allison 37, Fred Lorenzen 38-42, Foyt 43-49, Hamilton 50.
Cautions: None   Margin of Victory: 3 feet   Attendance: 20,000

mouth they had built for me to Fred Lorenzen," said Glotzbach. "The Pontiac won't run. I want nothing else out of a race but to win. I can not feel competitive in a car that is 12 1/2 mph off the pace. I quit."

Lorenzen, who finished fifth, got the STP sponsorship and took his deal to Nichels, who promptly saddled him in his primary Plymouth.

Winston Cup GN Race No. 3
50 Laps at Daytona Int'l Speedway
Daytona Beach, FL
125 Miles on 2.5-mile Paved Track
February 11, 1971

Fin	St	No.	Driver	Team / Car	Laps	Money	Status
1	4	17	David Pearson	Holman-Moody '69 Mercury	50	$1,200	Running
2	2	11	Buddy Baker	Petty Ent '71 Dodge	50	800	Running
3	5	22	Dick Brooks	Mario Rossi '69 Dodge Daytona	50	550	Running
4	16	90	Bill Dennis	Junie Donlavey '69 Mercury	50	500	Running
5	9	72	Benny Parsons	L G DeWitt '69 Ford	50	450	Running
6	21	7	Ramo Stott	Stott '71 Plymouth	50	400	Running
7	15	64	Elmo Langley	Langley '69 Mercury	49	345	Running
8	11	60	Maynard Troyer	Nagle Racers '69 Ford	49	335	Running
9	13	03	Tommy Gale	Larry Jackson '69 Mercury	49	325	Running
10	12	44	Red Farmer	Giachetti Bros '71 Ford	49	310	Running
11	1	71	Bobby Isaac	K&K Insurance '71 Dodge	49	500	Running
12	7	20	Jim Hurtubise	Jimmy McCain '70 Ford	49	290	Running
13	22	07	Coo Coo Marlin	Cunningham-Kelley '69 Chev	48	280	Running
14	10	76	Ben Arnold	Arnold '69 Ford	48	270	Running
15	23	06	Neil Castles	Castles '70 Dodge	48	260	Running
16	14	16	Dub Simpson	Ken Spikes '71 Chevrolet	48	255	Running
17	6	31	Jim Vandiver	O L Nixon '69 Dodge	48	245	Running
18	24	46	Roy Mayne	Tom Hunter '69 Chevrolet	47	235	Running
19	20	19	Henley Gray	Gray '69 Ford	47	225	Running
20	19	34	Wendell Scott	Scott '69 Ford	47	220	Running
21	27	56	E J Trivette	Gary Baird '71 Chevrolet	46	215	Running
22	17	04	Freddy Fryar	Bob Davis '69 Dodge	46	210	Running
23	28	30	Walter Ballard	Vic Ballard '71 Ford	46	205	Running
24	3	12	Bobby Allison	Allison '70 Dodge	46	200	Running
25	18	02	Jimmy Crawford	Crawford Ent '69 Plymouth	43	---	Running
26	31	8	Ed Negre	Negre '69 Dodge	43	---	Running
27	29	88	Bill Hollar	Earl Brooks '69 Ford	42	---	Running
28	8	25	Jabe Thomas	Don Robertson '70 Plymouth	27	---	Vibration
29	25	38	Blackie Wangerin	Wangerin '69 Ford	16	---	Engine
30	26	70	J D McDuffie	McDuffie '69 Mercury	7	---	Radiator
31	30	41	Ken Meisenhelder	Meisenhelder '69 Chevrolet	1	---	Flagged

Time of Race: 44 minutes, 27 seconds
Average Speed: 168.728 mph
Pole Winner: Bobby Isaac - 180.050 mph
Lap Leaders: David Pearson 1-3, Buddy Baker 4-5, Bobby Isaac 6, Baker 7, Isaac 8, Baker 9-10, Isaac 11, Baker 12-14, Isaac 15-17, Baker 18-19, Isaac 20, Baker 21, Isaac 22-24, Baker 25-26, Dick Brooks 27, Pearson 28-30, Baker 31-39, Pearson 40-43, Baker 44, Pearson 45-50.
Cautions: 1 for 3 laps   Margin of Victory: 2 car lengths   Attendance: 20,000

Race No. 4

Foyt Runs Out of Gas; Petty Gets 3rd Daytona 500 Win

DAYTONA BEACH, FL (Feb. 14) -- Richard Petty held off running-mate Buddy Baker in the final laps and won the Daytona 500 at Daytona International Speedway. The $45,450 triumph was the 120th of Pet-

Winston Cup GN Race No. 4
200 Laps at Daytona Int'l Speedway
Daytona Beach, FL
"Daytona 500"
500 Miles on 2.5-mile Paved Track
February 14, 1971

Fin	St	No.	Driver	Team / Car	Laps	Money	Status
1	5	43	Richard Petty	Petty Ent '71 Plymouth	200	$45,450	Running
2	6	11	Buddy Baker	Petty Ent '71 Dodge	200	16,100	Running
3	1	21	A J Foyt	Wood Brothers '69 Mercury	200	14,500	Running
4	4	17	David Pearson	Holman-Moody '69 Mercury	199	4,225	Running
5	9	99	Fred Lorenzen	Nichels-Goldsmith '71 Plym	199	3,825	Running
6	32	31	Jim Vandiver	O L Nixon '69 Dodge	198	3,475	Running
7	8	22	Dick Brooks	Mario Rossi '69 Dodge Daytona	198	3,125	Running
8	24	20	Jim Hurtubise	Jimmy McClain '70 Ford	197	2,800	Running
9	15	48	James Hylton	Hylton Eng '69 Ford	197	2,600	Running
10	2	71	Bobby Isaac	K&K Insurance '71 Dodge	197	3,950	Running
11	14	7	Ramo Stott	Stott '71 Plymouth	195	2,350	Running
12	25	18	Joe Frasson	Frasson '70 Dodge	194	2,200	Running
13	36	25	Pedro Rodriguez*	Don Robertson '70 Plymouth	194	1,975	Running
14	16	64	Elmo Langley	Langley '69 Mercury	193	1,850	Running
15	34	04	Freddy Fryar	Bob Davis '69 Dodge	192	1,800	Running
16	27	10	Bill Champion	Champion '69 Ford	191	1,700	Running
17	19	24	Cecil Gordon	Gordon '69 Mercury	187	1,750	Running
18	31	12	Bobby Allison	Allison '70 Dodge	187	1,600	Running
19	38	40	Marv Acton	Dick Brooks '70 Plymouth	186	1,550	Running
20	26	07	Coo Coo Marlin	Cunningham-Kelley '69 Chev	184	1,500	Running
21	20	03	Tomy Gale	Larry Jackson '69 Mercury	183	1,475	Running
22	29	68	Larry Baumel	Auto Lad '69 Ford	179	1,525	Running
23	28	76	Ben Arnold	Arnold '69 Ford	179	1,425	Running
24	37	79	Frank Warren	Warren '69 Plymouth	178	1,400	Running
25	17	2	Dave Marcis	Marcis '69 Dodge	173	1,375	Engine
26	11	27	Donnie Allison	Banjo Matthews '69 Mercury	170	1,350	Crash
27	10	90	Bill Dennis	Junie Donlavey '69 Mercury	162	1,525	Clutch
28	3	6	Pete Hamilton	Cotton Owens '71 Plymouth	157	2,050	Engine
29	21	4	John Sears	Sears '69 Dodge	126	1,275	Engine
30	35	45	Bill Seifert	Seifert '70 Ford	111	1,250	Steering
31	40	19	Henley Gray	Gray '69 Ford	93	1,225	Steering
32	22	44	Red Farmer	Giachetti Bros '71 Ford	91	1,200	Engine
33	13	3	Cale Yarborough	Ray Fox '71 Plymouth	61	1,375	Engine
34	7	98	LeeRoy Yarbrough	Junior Johnson '69 Mercury	45	1,150	Oil Line
35	12	72	Benny Parsons	L G DeWitt '69 Ford	39	1,125	Ignition
36	33	39	Friday Hassler	Hassler '69 Chevrolet	38	1,200	Engine
37	30	06	Neil Castles	Castles '69 Dodge	24	1,075	Ignition
38	18	60	Maynard Troyer	Nagle Racers '69 Ford	9	1,050	Crash
39	23	55	Tiny Lund	John McConnell '69 Dodge	7	1,025	Ignition
40	39	88	Ron Keselowski	Roger Lubinski '70 Dodge	1	1,000	Quit

Time of Race: 3 hours, 27 minutes, 40 seconds
Average Speed: 144.462 mph
Pole Winner: A J Foyt - 182.744 mph
Lap Leaders: A J Foyt 1-3, David Pearson 4, Foyt 5-6, Buddy Baker 7-8, Bobby Isaac 9-11, LeeRoy Yarbrough 12-15, James Hylton 16-19, Baker 20, Pete Hamilton 21, Pearson 22, Hamilton 23, Baker 24, Pearson 25, Isaac 26, Baker 27, Isaac 28-34, Baker 35, Isaac 36-56, Hamilton 57-58, Richard Petty 59, Dick Brooks 60-61, Petty 62-63, Brooks 64, Petty 65-68, Bobby Allison 69-73, Hamilton 74, Pearson 75, Isaac 76-80, Foyt 81-91, Donnie Allison 92-93, Pearson 94-95, Brooks 96, Hamilton 97 Brooks 98, Foyt 99-102, Petty 103-108, B.Allison 109, Petty 110-122, B.Allison 123, Foyt 124-129, Petty 130-151, Foyt 152-161, D.Allison 162-165, Baker 166, D.Allison 167-170, Baker 171-173, Petty 174-175, Baker 176-181, Petty 182-200.
Cautions: 7 for 44 laps   Margin of Victory: 10 seconds   Attendance: 80,000
*Jabe Thomas drove one pace lap. Rodriguez drove entire race. Thomas got credit for points.

ty's career.

Baker, driving the Petty Enterprises Dodge, finished second, 10-seconds behind. A.J. Foyt, who had the Wood Brothers Mercury under him, fell to third place after running out of gas with 39 laps to go. David Pearson came in fourth and Fred Lorenzen was fifth.

Foyt had led on six occasions for 36 laps when his car sputtered on the backstretch -- out of gas. By the

Fred Lorenzen had a new STP Plymouth at Daytona

foot-stomping crowd of 80,000. When Petty took the lead for the final time on lap 182, both of the factory backed drivers received a message from their pit crews. Both signs said 'yes'. "The deal was if we had to run together," explained Petty, "I would run just fast enough to see who could lead. It was 'yes' for him (Baker) to stay behind and 'yes' for me to stay in front."

When the final caution came out for Pete Hamilton's blown engine, Donnie Allison scrambled his way to the front. But on the final lap of yellow, Allison's

time the tough Texan made it back around to the pits, he was a lap behind. The caution came out three laps later, keeping A.J. a lap behind the leaders.

In the final 20 laps, Foyt unlapped himself, but couldn't make up the 2.5-mile deficit. Glen and Leonard Wood did not rule out sabotage. They said a fuel line had been twisted and tampered with, thus prevent-

Mercury darted into the wall. "The brakes locked up," said Donnie.

Dick Brooks and crew chief Mario Rossi entered the only winged Dodge, free of engine restrictions but limit-

Dick Brooks drove a Dodge Daytona powered by a 305 c.i engine

ed to 305 cubic inches. The Porterville, CA driver led

Richard Petty gets quick pit service in Daytona 500

ing the full load of fuel to be consumed.

Petty was proud that his cars finished 1-2. "There's no way to be more pleased," he said. "This is probably three times better than the other two. We've put a helluva lot of work into it, so we deserved to win."

Petty and Baker were left to battle it out before the

LeeRoy Yarbrough makes pit stop

for five laps, but the rear end scooted out from under him two laps short of the half-way point. Brooks gathered the car up, but was popped by Hamilton. Brooks spun and lost two laps in the mishap.

Rookie Maynard Troyer survived a nasty spill on lap nine. Troyer's Ford blew an engine and spun off the second turn. When the car hit the apron, it began a series of turnovers. Troyer flipped 16 times and was taken to Halifax Hospital where his condition was listed "serious".

Cale Yarborough went out early with engine problems in his Ray Fox Plymouth. "This was my 13th Daytona 500, and I started 13th," said Cale. "I knew this wasn't going to be my day."

Petty averaged 144.462 mph.

Race No. 5

A.J. Wins Ontario 500 -- NASCAR's 1,000th Race

ONTARIO, CA (Feb. 28) -- A.J. Foyt drove his Mercury into the lead 14 laps from the finish and outran Buddy Baker to win the Miller High Life 500 at the new Ontario Motor Speedway. The richest event ever in NASCAR ($207,675) was also the 1,000th Winston Cup Grand National race run, a newsy footnote that was overlooked by everyone including the sanctioning body.

Baker finished 8.5-seconds behind in his Petty Dodge. Richard Petty crossed the finish line third. His engine blew as he drove under the checkered flag. Bobby Isaac was foiled by three green flag pit stops and wound up fourth. Fifth place went to Dick Brooks.

Although the grandstands were only about 60% full, Speedway management said 78,810 spectators had gone through the turnstiles.

Foyt, Petty and Baker were poised for a last lap shoot-out. However, Petty overshot his pit on the final stop, which removed him from the hunt. Baker nearly spun out in the first turn late in the going, which let Foyt slip away.

"This is one of the best races I've ever driven," boasted A.J. "They said this speedway wasn't built for stock car racing. But let me tell you, it's a wild race track for any type of machinery."

Fred Lorenzen's Plymouth gave Foyt fits in the middle stages of the event. The Elmhurst, IL veteran, still looking for his first win since ending a self-imposed 3-year retirement in May of 1970, led seven times for 42 laps. He was leading in the 142nd lap when the engine blew in flame, catching the entire car on fire. Lorenzen dived into the pit wall to put out the flames.

Winston Cup GN Race No. 5
200 Laps at Ontario Motor Speedway
Ontario, CA
"Miller High Life 500"
500 Miles on 2.5-mile Paved Track
February 28, 1971

Fin	St	No.	Driver	Team / Car	Laps	Money	Status
1	1	21	A J Foyt	Wood Brothers '69 Mercury	200	$51,850	Running
2	6	11	Buddy Baker	Petty Ent '71 Dodge	200	15,325	Running
3	3	43	Richard Petty	Petty Ent '71 Plymouth	200	12,825	Running
4	2	71	Bobby Isaac	K&K Insurance '71 Dodge	199	9,325	Running
5	21	22	Dick Brooks	Mario Rossi '70 Dodge	198	5,025	Running
6	22	98	LeeRoy Yarbrough	Junior Johnson '69 Mercury	197	4,100	Running
7	7	96	Ray Elder	Fred Elder '70 Dodge	196	3,650	Running
8	10	55	Tiny Lund	John McConnell '69 Dodge	194	2,680	Running
9	8	72	Benny Parsons	L G DeWitt '69 Mercury	194	2,625	Running
10	12	48	James Hylton	Hylton Eng '69 Mercury	194	2,250	Running
11	14	64	Elmo Langley	Langley '69 Mercury	191	2,175	Running
12	46	40	Marv Acton	Dick Brooks '70 Plymouth	190	2,100	Running
13	23	7	Jack McCoy	Ernie Conn '71 Dodge	190	2,085	Running
14	18	45	Bill Seifert	Seifert '69 Ford	187	2,000	Running
15	28	28	Carl Joiner	Dean Thorne '69 Chevrolet	185	1,950	Running
16	9	39	Friday Hassler	Hassler '69 Chevrolet	185	1,975	Running
17	34	38	Jimmy Insolo	'69 Chevrolet	183	1,875	Running
18	19	25	Jabe Thomas	Don Robertson '70 Plymouth	179	1,875	Running
19	16	24	Cecil Gordon	Gordon '69 Ford	179	1,850	Running
20	44	75	Bobby Wawak	Wawak '69 Dodge	179	1,800	Running
21	38	0	Frank James	Jim Calder '69 Chevrolet	177	1,775	Running
22	50	5	Ron Hornaday	'70 Ford	177	1,750	Running
23	30	26	Earl Brooks	Brooks '69 Ford	176	1,750	Running
24	49	44	Dick Gulstrand	'69 Chevrolet	175	1,700	Running
25	14	14	Harry Schilling	'69 Dodge	173	1,675	Running
26	40	87	Ivan Baldwin	'69 Chevrolet	172	1,650	Running
27	15	2	Dick Bown	Mike Ober '70 Plymouth	169	1,650	Engine
28	13	41	Hershel McGriff	Robert Koehler '70 Plymouth	163	1,775	Engine
29	34	19	Henley Gray	Gray '69 Ford	151	1,575	Engine
30	5	99	Fred Lorenzen	Nichels-Goldsmith '71 Plym	142	8,050	Engine
31	4	6	Pete Hamilton	Cotton Owens '71 Plymouth	117	1,800	Engine
32	47	90	Pay Fay	'71 Ford	111	1,500	Flagged
33	20	77	Ray Johnstone	'69 Plymouth	96	1,500	Ignition
34	36	83	Marty Kinerk	'69 Chevrolet	91	1,450	Heating
35	42	70	J D McDuffie	McDuffie '69 Mercury	91	1,475	Engine
36	25	76	Jim McElreath	'70 Dodge	88	1,440	Rear End
37	48	27	John Steele	'69 Ford	79	1,375	Engine
38	26	8	John Soares, Jr.	Soares '70 Plymouth	78	1,385	Engine
39	41	12	Bobby Allison	Allison '70 Dodge	76	1,400	Ignition
40	27	46	Red Farmer	'69 Ford	73	1,325	Clutch
41	51	81	Bob England	England '70 Chevrolet	63	1,275	Rear End
42	32	32	Kevin Terris	Dean Barnicle '70 Plymouth	41	1,260	Engine
43	31	63	Bill Champion	'69 Dodge	41	1,250	Engine
44	24	88	Don Noel	'70 Ford	38	1,250	Engine
45	37	23	G T Tallas	Tallas '69 Ford	32	1,175	Heating
46	35	9	Bill Osborne	'71 Ford	24	1,150	Engine
47	11	20	Pedro Rodriguez	Jimmy McCain '70 Ford	18	1,175	Elect
48	29	4	Dick Kranzler	Kranzler '70 Chevrolet	13	1,125	Heating
49	39	82	Ron Gautsche	Gautsche '69 Ford	10	1,075	Engine
50	17	79	Frank Warren	Warren '69 Dodge	4	1,075	Engine
51	43	17	Dean Dalton	Dalton '69 Ford	2	1,050	Flagged

Time of Race: 3 hours, 43 minutes, 36 seconds
Average Speed: 134.168 mph
Pole Winner: A J Foyt - 151.711 mph
Lap Leaders: Richard Petty 1, A J Foyt 2-7, Bobby Isaac 8-17, Tiny Lund 18-21, Buddy Baker 22, Fred Lorenzen 23-24, Foyt 25-29, Lorenzen 30-43, Foyt 44-68, Hershel McGriff 69, Baker 70, Foyt 71-73, Isaac 74-80, Lorenzen 81-93, Foyt 94-98, Lorenzen 99, Foyt 100, Lorenzen 101, Foyt 102, Lorenzen 103-110, Foyt 111-139, Lorenzen 140-142, Petty 143-144, Baker 145, Foyt 146-174, Petty 175-184, Baker 185-186, Foyt 187-200.
Cautions: 5 for 21 laps   Margin of Victory: 8.5 seconds   Attendance: 78,810

"It was getting hot in there," he said. "All I could do to stop it was take it to the wall."

Fifty-one cars started the race and 27 finished. The field was started three-abreast -- the first time NAS-

Fred Lorenzen ran strong at Ontario until the engine in his Plymouth blew

CAR has used that starting alignment since the 1960 Southern 500 at Darlington.

Foyt pocketed $51,850 for his 134.168 mph victory.

David Pearson and the Holman-Moody team did not enter. Crew chief Ralph Moody said a West coast trip was too costly and his team had not been able to get a car properly prepared for the new track.

Race No. 6

Penalized Petty Romps in Controversial Richmond 500

RICHMOND, VA (Mar. 7) -- Richard Petty started at the rear of the field, cut through the traffic swiftly and won the controversial Richmond 500 going away. It was the second win of the year for Petty, whose team is the only one with admitted factory help.

Bobby Isaac finished second, two laps down at the .542-mile Richmond Fairgrounds Raceway. Benny Parsons was third, Bobby Allison fourth and pole sitter Dave Marcis fifth.

Petty's decisive triumph created an uproar along pit road. Originally, Petty's Plymouth had not earned a starting berth in the 25 car field. NASCAR officials discovered a number of areas where work on the car was needed to pass inspection. The engine was set back several inches, the wheelbase had been altered and the fuel tank was too low. The Fords of James Hylton and Benny Parsons had similar infractions. Allison's Dodge did not arrive in time and missed qualifications.

Promoters Paul Sawyer and Ken Campbell were faced with the probability that four top drivers would not be in the field. The 25 car grid had been formed without Petty, Parsons, Hylton and Allison.

After a closed door deliberation with the promoters,

Winston Cup GN Race No. 6
500 Laps at Richmond Fairgrounds Raceway
Richmond, VA
"Richmond 500"
271 Miles on .542-mile Paved Track
March 7, 1971

Fin	St	No.	Driver	Team / Car	Laps	Money	Status
1	30	43	Richard Petty	Petty Ent '70 Plymouth	500	$4,425	Running
2	3	71	Bobby Isaac	K&K Insurance '70 Dodge	498	2,850	Running
3	28	72	Benny Parsons	L G DeWitt '69 Ford	492	1,525	Running
4	29	12	Bobby Allison	Allison '69 Dodge	491	1,125	Running
5	1	2	Dave Marcis	Marcis '69 Dodge	490	1,075	Running
6	9	64	Elmo Langley	Langley '69 Mercury	480	625	Running
7	11	06	Neil Castles	Castles '69 Dodge	479	575	Running
8	4	10	Bill Champion	Champion '69 Ford	472	600	Running
9	14	24	Cecil Gordon	Gordon '69 Ford	466	535	Running
10	27	48	James Hylton	Hylton Eng '70 Ford	463	525	Running
11	8	20	Clyde Lynn	Lynn '69 Ford	461	515	Running
12	5	25	Jabe Thomas	Don Robertson '69 Plymouth	460	530	Running
13	33	50	Al Grinnan	'69 Chevrolet	459	495	Running
14	6	4	John Sears	Sears '69 Dodge	454	485	Running
15	24	56	E J Trivette	Gary Baird '71 Chevrolet	445	475	Running
16	21	74	Bill Shirey	Shirey '69 Plymouth	443	450	Running
17	25	13	Eddie Yarboro	Yarboro '69 Dodge	430	445	Running
18	15	26	Earl Brooks	Brooks '69 Ford	396	440	Crash
19	16	19	Henley Gray	Gray '69 Ford	371	435	Throttle
20	19	70	J D McDuffie	McDuffie '69 Buick	210	425	Engine
21	13	8	Ed Negre	Negre '69 Ford	174	395	Ignition
22	12	51	Dub Simpson	Bill Strong '69 Chevrolet	158	385	Rear End
23	7	34	Wendell Scott	Scott '69 Ford	133	375	Rear End
24	18	28	Bill Hollar	Earl Brooks '69 Ford	52	365	Engine
25	26	67	Dick May	Ron Ronacher '69 Ford	47	355	Oil Leak
26	17	65	Joe Phipps	Phipps '69 Chevrolet	44	355	Ignition
27	2	90	Bill Dennis	Junie Donlavey '69 Mercury	35	455	Rear End
28	20	79	Frank Warren	Warren '69 Plymouth	35	355	Trans
29	10	88	Ron Keselowski	Roger Lubinski '69 Dodge	5	355	Engine
30	22	30	Walter Ballard	Vic Ballard '71 Plymouth	2	355	Crash

Time of Race: 3 hours, 23 minutes, 20 seconds
Average Speed: 79.836 mph
Pole Winner: Dave Marcis - 87.178 mph
Lap Leaders: Dave Marcis 1-8, Bobby Isaac 9-76, Bobby Allison 77-112, Isaac 113-134, Petty 135-215, Isaac 216-233, Petty 234-500.
Cautions: 3 for 18 laps   Margin of Victory: 2-laps plus   Attendance: 14,500

NASCAR officials announced the starting field would be stretched to 30 cars. The automobiles nabbed at the inspection station could start in the rear if they were corrected by mechanics.

Petty told NASCAR Chief Inspector Bill Gazaway that his car could not be rendered 'legal' to compete in the Richmond 500. "This car was legal last year," claimed Petty. "There was no engine placement rule last year. So I didn't change it and got caught. I admit that."

NASCAR adjusted the rules again and allowed Petty to start last in the 30 car field. Gazaway ordered that the Petty car must start with a smaller carburetor restrictor plate. Isaac's Dodge was found to have its fuel tank an inch and a half too low; and it was placed with the same restrictor plate penalty. So was Bobby Allison's Dodge.

NASCAR's ruling produced an uproar from Harry Hyde, crew chief on Isaac's car. "I would not expect a police officer to write the same ticket for a car with a faulty windshield wiper as he would some drunk who runs a stop sign and kills someone," steamed Hyde. "If I was in the same position as Petty, they would have sent me home."

Petty scrambled through the field and was fifth by the 30th lap. He grabbed the lead for the first time on lap 135 and led all but 18 laps from there on out.

After the race, Nord Krauskopf, owner of Isaac's fleet of Dodges, threatened to quit the NASCAR circuit. "I don't want to do anything bad for racing," said Krauskopf, "but it's become an intolerable situation. I've advised promoters Ned Jarrett (Hickory) and Larry Carrier (Bristol) by wire that our entries for their events have been withdrawn."

Isaac came away from Richmond with an eight point lead in the Winston Cup point standings.

Race No. 7

Petty Snakes Through Wreck; Wins Carolina 500

ROCKINGHAM, NC (Mar. 14) -- Richard Petty zigzagged through a late race wreck and won the Carolina 500 at North Carolina Motor Speedway. It was Petty's 12th career superspeedway win, tying him with Fred Lorenzen for second place on the all-time list. The late Fireball Roberts still leads with 13 big track wins.

The crash was triggered by Bobby Wawak's blowing a tire on the backstretch. Fred Lorenzen, Wendell Scott, LeeRoy Yarbrough, Elmo Langley and Ben

Richard Petty won the Carolina 500 at Rockingham

Winston Cup GN Race No. 7
492 Laps at North Carolina Motor Speedway
Rockingham, NC
"Carolina 500"
500 Miles on 1.017-mile Paved Track
March 14, 1971

Fin	St	No.	Driver	Team / Car	Laps	Money	Status
1	2	43	Richard Petty	Petty Ent '71 Plymouth	492	$17,315	Running
2	3	71	Bobby Isaac	K&K Insurance '71 Dodge	492	11,240	Running
3	10	11	Buddy Baker	Petty Ent '71 Dodge	492	5,065	Running
4	1	99	Fred Lorenzen	Nichels-Goldsmith '71 Plym	488	3,815	Crash
5	13	22	Dick Brooks	Mario Rossi '69 Dodge	488	1,875	Running
6	16	98	LeeRoy Yarbrough	Junior Johnson '69 Mercury	486	1,565	Crash
7	27	18	Joe Frasson	Frasson '69 Dodge	474	1,340	Running
8	8	55	Tiny Lund	John McConnell '69 Dodge	471	1,415	Running
9	11	64	Elmo Langley	Langley '69 Mercury	470	1,215	Crash
10	14	90	Bill Dennis	Junie Donlavey '69 Mercury	462	1,165	Running
11	18	76	Ben Arnold	Arnold '69 Ford	455	1,090	Running
12	22	25	Jabe Thomas	Don Robertson '69 Plymouth	454	1,040	Running
13	12	24	Cecil Gordon	Gordon '69 Mercury	446	1,090	Running
14	31	88	J D McDuffie	Roger Lubinski '69 Dodge	441	1,015	Running
15	35	34	Wendell Scott	Scott '69 Ford	439	965	Crash
16	25	8	Ed Negre	Negre '69 Ford	438	940	Running
17	28	79	Frank Warren	Warren '69 Plymouth	437	915	Running
18	15	48	James Hylton	Hylton Eng '70 Mercury	436	965	Suspen
19	40	75	Bobby Wawak	Wawak '69 Dodge	436	865	Crash
20	29	68	Larry Baumel	Auto Lad '69 Ford	413	840	Running
21	32	45	Bill Seifert	Seifert '70 Ford	384	815	Heating
22	34	56	E J Trivette	Gary Baird '71 Chevrolet	368	790	Running
23	18	10	Bill Champion	Champion 69 Ford	366	840	Running
24	6	6	Pete Hamilton	Cotton Owens '71 Plymouth	339	1,115	Radiator
25	9	72	Benny Parsons	L G DeWitt '69 Mercury	304	790	Crash
26	17	49	G C Spencer	Spencer '69 Plymouth	301	790	Engine
27	21	42	Ray Hendrick	L G DeWitt '70 Ford	295	665	Crash
28	30	46	Roy Mayne	Tom Hunter '69 Chevrolet	282	640	Engine
29	37	63	Charlie Roberts	Roberts '69 Dodge	265	615	Engine
30	5	12	Bobby Allison	Allison '69 Dodge	231	1,065	Engine
31	7	39	Friday Hassler	Hassler '69 Chevrolet	186	860	Radiator
32	24	40	Marv Acton	Dick Brooks '69 Plymouth	162	580	Crash
33	23	4	John Sears	Sears '69 Dodge	148	575	Lug Bolts
34	4	2	Dave Marcis	Marcis '69 Dodge	132	1,145	Engine
35	39	67	Dick May	Ron Ronacher '69 Ford	98	565	Suspen
36	20	06	Neil Castles	Castles '69 Dodge	95	560	Heating
37	33	19	Henley Gray	Gray '69 Ford	72	555	Heating
38	38	51	Dub Simpson	Bill Strong '69 Chevrolet	28	550	Trans
39	36	44	James Sears	Giachetti Bros '71 Ford	9	545	Brakes
40	26	47	Raymond Williams	Bill Seifert '70 Ford	5	540	Crash

Time of Race: 4 hours, 12 minutes, 55 seconds
Average Speed: 118.696 mph
Pole Winner: Fred Lorenzen - 133.892 mph
Lap Leaders: Fred Lorenzen 1-15, Bobby Isaac 16-28, Lorenzen 29, G C Spencer 30-41, Richard Petty 42-98, Isaac 99-128, LeeRoy Yarbrough 129-130, Buddy Baker 131-215, Yarbrough 216-233, Baker 234-306, Pete Hamilton 307-313, Petty 314, Baker 315-332, Yarbrough 333-334, Petty 335-422, Baker 423-425, Isaac 426-437, Petty 438-468, Baker 469-471, Petty 472-492.
Cautions: 7 for 36 laps   Margin of Victory: Under caution   Attendance: 33,000

Arnold were all involved in the melee. Petty gunned his car through an opening, followed closely by Isaac. As Lorenzen tried to follow, the hole closed. The entire right side of Lorenzen's Nichels-Goldsmith mount was sheared off, with pieces of the car and roll cage scattered over the backstretch. Lorenzen was badly shaken after the incident. No other injuries were reported. NASCAR officials said they were "concerned" because the roll bars had apparently been constructed with light weight materials.

NASCAR steward Bill Blackwell ran onto the track

to wave a yellow flag. Instantly, Arnold's Ford went into a slide, nearly hitting Blackwell. Blackwell dove out of the way and was treated at the speedway hospital for arm lacerations.

Benny Parsons and Modified star Ray Hendrick were eliminated in earlier crashes. Both drivers were behind the wheel of cars owned by Speedway President L.G. DeWitt.

Petty led on five occasions for 198 laps. Pole sitter Lorenzen led the first 15 laps, then fell off the pace due to a cut tire. Isaac wound up second to Petty as the race ended under the caution flag. Buddy Baker finished third with Lorenzen fourth. Dick Brooks was fifth.

Petty cut Isaac's point lead to five after the first seven races. However, Isaac's car had been pulled from the entry list at Hickory and Bristol.

A crowd of 33,000 watched Petty win his 122nd race at an average speed of 118.696 mph.

Race No. 8

Petty Takes Standings Lead With Victory at Hickory

HICKORY, NC (Mar. 21) -- Richard Petty passed Neil Castles in the 116th lap and drove to victory in the Hickory 276 at Hickory Speedway. It was the third win in a row for the factory backed Plymouth driver and it moved him into the Winston Cup point lead.

Surprise entry David Pearson finished second in a Ford owned by the Giachetti Brothers. Benny Parsons came in third, James Hylton was fourth and Elmo Langley fifth. Castles wound up sixth.

Bobby Allison led the first 47 laps from the pole. Bill Champion blew an engine in his Ford and Allison ran over the debris. Allison's Dodge darted into the guard rail, putting him out of the race.

Independent Dave Marcis put his Dodge into the lead for 106 laps before pitting. After everyone had made their appearance on pit road, Petty led Marcis by a car length.

Marcis gave Petty a run for the money, but the Wisconsin driver lost 15 laps in the pits when his engine overheated. Marcis eventually finished 10th, 17 laps off the pace.

Petty pushed his way to a 45 point lead over the idle Bobby Isaac with his 67.700 mph win.

Winston Cup GN Race No. 8
276 Laps at Hickory Speedway
Hickory, NC
"Hickory 276"
100 Miles on .363-mile Paved Track
March 21, 1971

Fin	St	No.	Driver	Team / Car	Laps	Money	Status
1	4	43	Richard Petty	Petty Ent '71 Plymouth	276	$2,200	Running
2	3	44	David Pearson	Giachetti Bros '71 Ford	275	1,500	Running
3	9	72	Benny Parsons	L G DeWitt '70 Ford	273	1,000	Running
4	12	48	James Hylton	Hylton Eng '70 Ford	273	700	Running
5	5	64	Elmo Langley	Langley '69 Mercury	273	600	Running
6	7	06	Neil Castles	Castles '70 Dodge	270	500	Running
7	8	49	G C Spencer	Spencer '69 Plymouth	266	400	Running
8	13	25	Jabe Thomas	Don Robertson '70 Plymouth	265	350	Running
9	15	4	John Sears	Sears '69 Dodge	261	310	Running
10	2	2	Dave Marcis	Marcis '69 Dodge	259	290	Running
11	14	24	Cecil Gordon	Gordon '69 Mercury	257	280	Running
12	19	74	Bill Shirey	Shirey '69 Plymouth	255	275	Running
13	17	79	Frank Warren	Warren '69 Dodge	236	270	Rear End
14	6	22	Dick Brooks	Mario Rossi '70 Dodge	211	265	Rear End
15	21	34	Wendell Scott	Scott '69 Ford	151	260	Trans
16	22	26	Earl Brooks	Brooks '69 Ford	112	255	Trans
17	18	19	Henley Gray	Gray '69 Ford	100	250	Lug Bolts
18	10	93	Richard Brown	Harold Furr '69 Chevrolet	99	245	Rear End
19	16	8	Ed Negre	Negre '69 Ford	73	240	Clutch
20	1	12	Bobby Allison	Allison '71 Dodge	49	235	Crash
21	11	10	Bill Champion	Champion '69 Ford	47	230	Engine
22	20	41	Ken Meisenhelder	Meisenhelder '69 Chevrolet	17	225	Heating

Time of Race: 1 hour, 28 minutes, 32 seconds
Average Speed: 67.700 mph
Pole Winner: Bobby Allison - 79.001 mph
Lap Leaders: Bobby Allison 1-47, Dave Marcis 48-104, David Pearson 105,
    Neil Castles 106-115, Richard Petty 116-276.
Cautions: 3 for 22 laps   Margin of Victory: 1-lap plus   Attendance: 7,200

Race No. 9

Pearson Holds Off Furious Petty Rally to Win at Bristol

BRISTOL, TN (Mar. 28) -- David Pearson overcame an early mental lapse and near disaster to win the

David Pearson takes checkered flag at Bristol

Winston Cup GN Race No. 9
500 Laps at Bristol Int'l Speedway
Bristol, TN
"Southeastern 500"
276 Miles on .533-mile Paved Track
March 28, 1971

Fin	St	No.	Driver	Team / Car	Laps	Money	Status
1	1	17	David Pearson	Holman-Moody '71 Ford	500	$6,120	Running
2	2	43	Richard Petty	Petty Ent '71 Plymouth	500	3,570	Running
3	7	22	Dick Brooks	Mario Rossi '70 Dodge	489	2,245	Running
4	3	12	Bobby Allison	Allison '71 Dodge	487	1,320	Running
5	4	72	Benny Parsons*	L G DeWitt '70 Ford	485	1,045	Running
6	8	39	Friday Hassler	Hassler '69 Chevrolet	483	845	Running
7	5	64	Elmo Langley	Langley '69 Mercury	469	795	Running
8	18	25	Jabe Thomas	Don Robertson '70 Plymouth	448	670	Running
9	16	19	Henley Gray	Gray '69 Ford	443	620	Running
10	30	06	Neil Castles	Castles '70 Dodge	439	595	Running
11	10	2	Dave Marcis	Marcis '69 Dodge	413	580	Heating
12	25	79	Frank Warren	Warren '69 Plymouth	398	545	Running
13	17	4	John Sears	Sears '69 Dodge	367	535	Trans
14	11	24	Cecil Gordon	Gordon '69 Mercury	366	525	Engine
15	24	34	Wendell Scott	Scott '69 Ford	340	515	Engine
16	28	26	Earl Brooks	Brooks '69 Ford	267	505	Trans
17	19	95	Paul Tyler	Tyler '69 Ford	248	495	Rear End
18	26	58	Robert Brown	Allan Brown '71 Chevrolet	228	485	Oil Leak
19	9	48	James Hylton	Hylton Eng '70 Ford	180	500	Crash
20	21	45	Bill Seifert	Seifert '70 Ford	152	465	Ignition
21	29	67	Dick May	Ron Ronacher '69 Ford	130	455	Oil Leak
22	15	10	Bill Champion	Champion '69 Ford	111	445	Crash
23	14	7	Ed Negre	Dean Dalton '69 Ford	106	435	Crash
24	20	68	Larry Baumel	Auto Lad '69 Ford	92	425	Engine
25	22	30	Walter Ballard	Vic Ballard '71 Ford	60	415	Heating
26	13	74	Bill Shirey	Shirey '69 Plymouth	58	410	Engine
27	6	49	G C Spencer	Spencer '69 Plymouth	47	425	Crash
28	12	88	Ron Keselowski	Roger Lubinski '70 Dodge	32	390	Ignition
29	23	41	Ken Meisenhelder	Meisenhelder '69 Chevrolet	32	380	Heating
30	27	70	J D McDuffie	McDuffie '71 Chevrolet	18	370	Oil Line

Time of Race: 2 hours, 52 minutes, 23 seconds
Average Speed: 91.704 mph
Pole Winner: David Pearson - 105.525 mph
Lap Leaders: David Pearson 1-48, Bobby Allison 49-69, James Hylton 70, Allison 71-127, Hylton 128-180, Dick Brooks 181-182, Richard Petty 183-331, Pearson 332-336, Petty 337-420, Pearson 421-500..
Cautions: 5 for 45 laps　　Margin of Victory: 4 seconds　　Attendance: 25,000
*Relieved by G C Spencer

David Pearson won Southeastern 500, but quit the Holman-Moody Ford team 5 weeks later

passed Allison on lap 128 and was holding down first place when he tangled with Pearson on lap 180. Pearson was attempting to make a pass for the lead and hooked Hylton's Ford. Both spun down the front stretch. Hylton piled head-on into the pit wall. Pearson spun and recovered.

"He ran me over," hollered Hylton. "There's no excuse for it."

"I hated to run into Hylton," Pearson said later. "His car was running the best it has in a long time. He was running strong, but suddenly he backed off and I was on him."

Southeastern 500 at Bristol International Speedway. It was the 60th career win for Pearson, who ranks second to Richard Petty in the all-time Winston Cup Grand National victory column.

Petty was 4.0-seconds behind when the checkered flag fell. Dick Brooks came in third, Bobby Allison was fourth and Benny Parsons fifth.

Pearson started on the pole and led the first 48 laps. When a car spun in the first turn, Pearson quickly ducked on pit road -- thinking the caution flag would come out. The Holman-Moody crew waved Pearson on and he returned to the track running sixth, one lap down.

Allison and James Hylton each enjoyed fine drives. Allison led twice for 78 laps, but faded due to mechanical problems. Hylton

G.C. Spencer bounces off guard rail at Bristol

Crew chief and part owner Ralph Moody said, "I'll see to it that Hylton's car get fixed real cheap."

Petty was leading by a lap and a half when a wheel came off his Plymouth on lap 420. He coasted all the way around the track and pitted for a replacement. When he got back on the track, he was over a lap behind.

Petty gobbled up lost time and dramatically closed on Pearson in the final duel.

Petty extended his point lead to 106 points over Elmo Langley. Langley finished seventh.

Pearson averaged 91.704 mph before a standing room only crowd of 25,000.

A.J. Foyt passes Richard Petty late in Atlanta 500

Race No. 10

Foyt Flings Past Petty; Wins Atlanta 500

Coo Coo Marlin leads pack off 4th turn at Atlanta

HAMPTON, GA (Apr. 4) -- A.J. Foyt sped past Richard Petty with 13 laps remaining and won the Atlanta 500 before a sun-splashed crowd of 52,000 and a network

Winston Cup GN Race No. 10
328 Laps at Atlanta Int'l Raceway
Hampton, GA
"Atlanta 500"
500 Miles on 1.522-mile Paved Track
April 4, 1971

Fin	St	No.	Driver	Team / Car	Laps	Money	Status
1	1	21	A J Foyt	Wood Brothers '69 Mercury	328	$19,200	Running
2	3	43	Richard Petty	Petty Ent '71 Plymouth	328	10,700	Running
3	16	6	Pete Hamilton	Cotton Owens '71 Plymouth	327	6,975	Running
4	6	17	David Pearson	Holman-Moody '70 Ford	327	4,490	Running
5	2	71	Bobby Isaac	K&K Insurance '71 Dodge	327	3,500	Running
6	4	11	Buddy Baker	Petty Ent '71 Dodge	325	3,000	Running
7	12	38	Charlie Glotzbach	John McCarthy '70 Dodge	319	2,500	Running
8	11	31	Jim Vandiver	O L Nixon '70 Dodge	319	2,000	Running
9	22	48	James Hylton	Hylton Eng '69 Ford	315	1,750	Running
10	15	12	Bobby Allison	Allison '71 Dodge	315	1,600	Running
11	9	2	Dave Marcis	Marcis '69 Dodge	315	1,550	Running
12	20	39	Friday Hassler	Hassler '69 Chevrolet	313	1,500	Running
13	14	18	Joe Frasson	Frasson '70 Dodge	313	1,450	Running
14	31	22	Dick Brooks	Mario Rossi '70 Dodge	310	1,400	Running
15	26	07	Coo Coo Marlin	Cunningham-Kelley '69 Chev	310	1,350	Running
16	25	46	Roy Mayne	Tom Hunter '69 Chevrolet	310	1,300	Running
17	10	24	Cecil Gordon	Gordon '69 Mercury	307	1,275	Running
18	13	64	Elmo Langley	Langley '69 Mercury	307	1,250	Running
19	28	88	Ron Keselowski	Roger Lubinski '70 Dodge	306	1,225	Running
20	35	60	Maynard Troyer	Nagle Racers '69 Ford	306	1,200	Fuel Pmp
21	21	79	Frank Warren	Warren '69 Dodge	306	1,180	Running
22	32	03	Tommy Gale	Larry Jackson '69 Mercury	303	1,165	Running
23	36	7	Dean Dalton	Dalton '69 Ford	294	1,150	Running
24	37	53	Rod Eulenfeld	Hopper-Crews '69 Ford	293	1,135	Running
25	39	70	J D McDuffie	McDuffie '71 Chevrolet	288	1,120	Running
26	29	76	Ben Arnold	Arnold '69 Ford	288	1,105	Running
27	24	10	Bill Champion	Champion '69 Ford	251	1,090	Clutch
28	8	45	LeeRoy Yarbrough	Bill Seifert '70 Ford	246	1,080	Heating
29	7	3	Cale Yarborough	Ray Fox '71 Plymouth	245	1,070	Crash
30	34	19	Henley Gray	Gray '69 Ford	194	1,060	Heating
31	18	90	Bill Dennis	Junie Donlavey '69 Mercury	185	1,050	Heating
32	40	4	John Sears	Sears '69 Dodge	139	1,040	Trans
33	30	25	Jabe Thomas	Don Robertson '70 Plymouth	111	1,035	Engine
34	27	06	Neil Castles	Castles '70 Dodge	97	1,030	Engine
35	5	99	Fred Lorenzen	Nichels-Goldsmith '71 Plym	85	1,025	Ignition
36	19	72	Benny Parsons	L G DeWitt '69 Ford	80	1,020	Engine
37	23	49	Earl Brooks*	G C Spencer '69 Plymouth	67	1,015	Engine
38	17	20	Jim Hurtubise	Jimmy McCain '70 Ford	44	1,010	Fuel pmp
39	33	30	Walter Ballard	Vic Ballard '71 Ford	44	1,005	Trans
40	38	16	Dub Simpson	Bill Strong '69 Chevrolet	7	1,000	Quit

Time of Race: 3 hours, 42 minutes, 16 seconds
Average Speed: 131.375 mph
Pole Winner: A J Foyt - 155.152 mph
Lap Leaders: A J Foyt 1-36, Richard Petty 37-51, Pete Hamilton 52, Petty 53, David Pearson 54-60, Cale Yarborough 61-64, Pearson 65-71, Yarborough 72, Hamilton 73-85, Richard Petty 86-105, Bobby Isaac 106, Yarborough 107, Pearson 108-120, Foyt 121-165, Petty 166-168, Yarborough 169-175, Foyt 176-222, Petty 223-230, Pearson 231-239, Foyt 240-248, Petty 249, Foyt 250-304, Petty 305-315, Foyt 316-328.
Cautions: 4 for 31 laps   Margin of Victory: 1.8 seconds   Attendance: 52,000
*Relieved by G C Spencer

television audience. It was the second win of the year for the 36 year-old Mercury driver.

Essentially, the 500 miler at Atlanta International Raceway was a private battle between Foyt and Petty. Foyt led for a total of 205 of the 328 laps on the 1.522-mile oval. He shook the pesky Petty in the final 10 laps

Georgia Governor Jimmy Carter invited the NASCAR drivers to dinner before the Atlanta 500

and won by 1.8 seconds. Pete Hamilton came in third, David Pearson was fourth and Bobby Isaac fifth.

Foyt won the pole at 155.152 mph using an old 427 c.i. Wedge engine. "The restrictor plates choked the 429 off too much," said A.J. "The Wood boys felt this was the way to go. It turns out they were right."

Foyt and Petty shook loose from the rest of the pack and engaged in a crowd pleasing duel. "One thing about Petty," said Foyt. "He'll run you wheel to wheel, and when you've beaten him and the other NASCAR drivers,

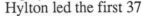

A.J. Foyt #21 leads Charlie Glotzbach and LeeRoy Yarbrough in Atlanta 500

you've beaten the best."

LeeRoy Yarbrough, who accepted an offer to drive an independent Ford owned by Bill Seifert, qualified eighth. He went out with overheating problems after 246 laps.

Cale Yarborough put his Ray Fox Plymouth into the wall on lap 245 and Fred Lorenzen went out early with ignition failure.

Foyt's fifth career Grand National win came at an average speed of 131.375 mph.

Race No. 11

Petty Nips Upstart Parsons On New Columbia Pavement

COLUMBIA, SC (Apr. 8) -- Richard Petty nosed past Benny Parsons with two laps to go and inched across the finish line first to win the Sandlapper 200 at the newly paved Columbia Speedway.

Parsons led the parade for the inspired independents. Parsons finished only three car length behind to register his second career runner-up finish. Dick Brooks came in third, pole sitter James Hylton was fourth and Elmo Langley fifth.

Hylton led the first 37

Neil Castles drove the "Free Lt. Calley Special" at Columbia

Winston Cup GN Race No. 11
200 Laps at Columbia Speedway
Columbia, SC
"Sandlapper 200"
100 Miles on Half-mile Paved Track
April 8, 1971

Fin	St	No.	Driver	Team / Car	Laps	Money	Status
1	4	43	Richard Petty	Petty Ent '71 Plymouth	200	$1,700	Running
2	3	72	Benny Parsons	L G DeWitt '69 Ford	200	1,200	Running
3	2	22	Dick Brooks	Mario Rossi '70 Dodge	200	800	Running
4	1	48	James Hylton	Hylton Eng '60 Ford	198	550	Running
5	6	20	Elmo Langley	Clyde Lynn '70 Ford	198	425	Running
6	9	38	Charlie Glotzbach	John McCarthy '70 Dodge	198	360	Running
7	5	12	Bobby Allison	Allison '71 Dodge	197	325	Running
8	13	10	Bill Champion	Champion '69 Ford	193	300	Running
9	7	06	Neil Castles	Castles '70 Dodge	192	285	Running
10	12	79	Frank Warren	Warren '69 Dodge	191	280	Running
11	14	24	Cecil Gordon	Gordon '69 Mercury	188	275	Running
12	26	28	Earl Brooks	Brooks '69 Ford	182	270	Running
13	10	30	Walter Ballard	Vic Ballard '71 Ford	174	265	Running
14	18	34	Wendell Scott	Scott '69 Ford	172	260	Running
15	25	70	J D McDuffie	McDuffie '71 Chevrolet	135	255	Engine
16	8	32	Marv Acton	Dick Brooks '70 Plymouth	115	250	Crash
17	17	25	Jabe Thomas	Don Robertson '69 Plymouth	68	245	Oil Leak
18	23	67	Dick May	Ron Ronacher '69 Ford	63	240	Trans
19	24	81	Ken Meisenhelder	'69 Ford	44	235	Oil Leak
20	16	19	Henley Gray	Gray '69 Ford	42	230	Engine
21	15	4	John Sears	Sears '69 Dodge	39	225	Rear End
22	19	7	Dean Dalton	Dalton '69 Ford	10	220	Trans
23	21	56	E J Trivette	Gary Baird '71 Chevrolet	10	215	Brakes
24	11	8	Ed Negre	Negre '69 Ford	8	210	Oil Leak
25	20	74	Bill Shirey	Shirey '69 Plymouth	8	205	Clutch
26	22	88	Ron Keselowski	Roger Lubinski '70 Dodge	7	200	Quit

Time of Race: 1 hour, 18 minutes, 25 seconds
Average Speed: 76.514 mph
Pole Winner: James Hylton - 84.229 mph
Lap Leaders: James Hylton 1-37, Benny Parsons 38-118, Richard Petty 119-121,
 Dick Brooks 122-123, Petty 124-197, Parsons 198, Petty 199-200.
Cautions: 2 for 10 laps   Margin of Victory: 3 car lengths   Attendance: 4,500.

laps before Parsons set sail. Parsons pitted his Ford on lap 119, giving the lead to Petty. Petty pitted a lap later and the Level Cross unit put King Richard back on the track first.

Parsons chased Petty the rest of the way. He briefly snatched the lead with two laps to go, but Petty got back around a lap later. The crowd of 4,500 cheered the finish.

Neil Castles finished ninth in his Dodge. Inscribed on the quarter panels of his car was *"The Free Lt. Calley Special"*, airing an opinion about the arraignment of Lt. William Calley, who was convicted for his part in the Meylai Massacre in Viet Nam.

Race No. 12

Isaac Wins Greenville; Live Flag-to-Flag TV Coverage

GREENVILLE, SC (Apr. 10) -- Bobby Isaac took the lead from David Pearson in the 20th lap and sped to victory in the Greenville 200 at Greenville-Pickens Speedway. The 100-mile event was televised live from start-to-finish by ABC-Sports.

Pearson finished two laps behind in second place and Dick Brooks was third. Dave Marcis finished fourth with Benny Parsons fifth.

The starting time was pushed up to 5:00 pm to accommodate the live TV coverage. A record 62 entries, 47 of which attempted qualifications, tried to get in the 26 car field. Most notable non-qualifier was LeeRoy Yarbrough.

Isaac earned $1,430 from a record $20,000 purse -- the richest 100-miler in NASCAR history. "I didn't even know I was going to race here until this morning," said Isaac. "Mr. Krauskopf called this morning and told us to run. The television coverage had a lot to do with that."

A record trackside gallery of 15,000 jammed the grandstands and infield to watch the race.

Richard Petty struggled to finish seventh, four laps behind. It was the worst effort of the year for the current Winston Cup point leaders.

Isaac averaged 78.159 mph.

Winston Cup GN Race No. 12
200 Laps at Greenville-Pickens
Speedway
Greenville, SC
"Greenville 200"
100 Miles on Half-mile Paved Track
April 10, 1971

Fin	St	No.	Driver	Team / Car	Laps	Money	Status
1	2	71	Bobby Isaac	K&K Insurance '71 Dodge	200	$1,430	Running
2	1	17	David Pearson	Holman-Moody '70 Ford	198	1,030	Running
3	9	22	Dick Brooks	Mario Rossi '70 Dodge	198	830	Running
4	12	2	Dave Marcis	Marcis '69 Dodge	198	780	Running
5	3	72	Benny Parsons	L G DeWitt '70 Ford	198	755	Running
6	14	48	James Hylton	Hylton Eng '71 Ford	196	730	Running
7	4	43	Richard Petty	Petty Ent '71 Plymouth	196	705	Running
8	21	39	Friday Hassler	Hassler '69 Chevrolet	195	700	Running
9	8	06	Neil Castles	Castles '70 Dodge	195	695	Running
10	24	20	Elmo Langley	Clyde Lynn '70 Mercury	193	690	Running
11	13	30	Walter Ballard	Vic Ballard '71 Ford	191	685	Running
12	7	24	Cecil Gordon	Gordon '69 Mercury	190	680	Running
13	22	10	Bill Champion	Champion '69 Ford	184	675	Running
14	19	25	Jabe Thomas	Don Robertson '69 Plymouth	182	670	Running
15	25	76	Ben Arnold	Arnold '69 Ford	178	665	Running
16	26	68	Larry Baumel	Auto Lad '69 Ford	177	655	Running
17	23	49	Ed Negre*	G C Spencer '69 Plymouth	103	650	Vibration
18	15	38	Charlie Glotzbach	John McCarthy '69 Dodge	85	645	Heating
19	18	45	Bill Seifert	Seifert '70 Ford	60	640	Engine
20	5	12	Bobby Allison	Allison '69 Dodge	56	635	Oil Leak
21	20	34	Wendell Scott	Scott '69 Ford	56	620	Oil Leak
22	16	46	Roy Mayne	Tom Hunter '69 Chevrolet	26	625	Engine
23	17	88	Frank Warren	Roger Lubinski '70 Dodge	25	625	Heating
24	6	90	Bill Dennis	Junie Donlavey '69 Mercury	11	625	Heating
25	10	32	Marv Acton	Dick Brooks '70 Plymouth	7	625	Oil Leak
26	11	47	Raymond Williams	Bill Seifert '70 Ford	4	625	Fender

Time of Race: 1 hour, 16 minutes, 46 seconds
Average Speed: 78.159 mph
Pole Winner: David Pearson - 82.557 mph
Lap Leaders: David Pearson 1-19, Bobby Isaac 20-200.
Cautions: 1 for 5 laps   Margin of Victory: 2-laps plus   Attendance: 15,000
*Relieved by G C Spencer

Race No. 13

Petty Edges Parsons and Hassler for Win at Maryville

MARYVILLE, TN (Apr. 15) -- Richard Petty passed Benny Parsons in the 154th lap and gained a narrow decision in the Maryville 200 at Smoky Mountain Raceway. It was the sixth win of the season for the red hot Plymouth driver.

Parsons finished 8.0-seconds behind. Friday Hassler, who won his first career pole in a Chevrolet, wound up third. Elmo Langley came in fourth and Dick Brooks was fifth.

Hassler, 35 year-old veteran out of Chattanooga, TN, led the first 52 laps with Petty in hot pursuit. Petty got around Hassler on lap 53 and led until Parsons passed him on lap 140. Parsons set the pace for 14 laps until Petty grabbed the lead for good.

A crowd of 4,200 watched Petty set a race record of 88.697 mph.

Petty increased his point lead to 139 over James Hylton.

Winston Cup GN Race No. 13
200 Laps at Smoky Mountain Raceway
Maryville, TN
"Maryville 200"
104 Miles on .520-mile Paved Track
April 15, 1971

Fin	St	No.	Driver	Team / Car	Laps	Money	Status
1	2	43	Richard Petty	Petty Ent '71 Plymouth	200	$1,000	Running
2	5	72	Benny Parsons	L G DeWitt '70 Ford	200	600	Running
3	1	39	Friday Hassler	Hassler '69 Chevrolet	199	400	Running
4	7	64	Elmo Langley	Langley '70 Ford	196	350	Running
5	4	22	Dick Brooks	Mario Rossi '70 Dodge	196	325	Running
6	6	48	James Hylton	Hylton Eng '70 Ford	196	300	Running
7	10	38	Charlie Glotzbach	John McCarthy '70 Dodge	194	275	Running
8	8	49	G C Spencer	Spencer '69 Plymouth	191	270	Running
9	12	24	Cecil Gordon	Gordon '69 Mercury	186	265	Running
10	11	10	Bill Champion	Champion '69 Ford	186	260	Running
11	13	19	Henley Gray	Gray '69 Ford	180	255	Running
12	14	30	Walter Ballard	Vic Ballard '71 Ford	179	250	Running
13	26	25	Jabe Thomas	Don Robertson '70 Plymouth	176	245	Running
14	20	79	Frank Warren	Warren '69 Dodge	174	240	Running
15	17	7	Dean Dalton	Dalton '69 Ford	168	235	Running
16	27	28	Bill Hollar	Earl Brooks '69 Ford	154	230	Fuel pump
17	18	45	Bill Seifert	Seifert '69 Ford	143	225	Crash
18	21	70	J D McDuffie	McDuffie '71 Chevrolet	136	220	Crash
19	22	26	Earl Brooks	Brooks '69 Ford	124	215	Rear End
20	25	67	Dick May	Ron Ronacher '69 Ford	124	210	No Gas
21	9	2	Dave Marcis	Marcis '69 Dodge	99	205	Steering
22	23	58	Bob Brown	Allan Brown '71 Chevrolet	86	200	Engine
23	16	4	John Sears	Sears '69 Dodge	78	200	Quit
24	24	34	Wendell Scott	Scott '69 Ford	55	200	Heating
25	19	56	E J Trivette	Gary Baird '71 Chevrolet	45	200	Rock Arm
26	3	06	Neil Castles	Castles '70 Dodge	33	200	Heating
27	15	8	Ed Negre	Negre '69 Ford	32	200	Oil Leak
28	28	74	Bill Shirey	Shirey '69 Plymouth	16	200	Ignition
29	29	41	D K Ulrich	Ulrich '70 Ford	3	200	Heating
30	30	02	Jimmy Crawford	Crawford Ent '69 Plymouth	1	200	Ignition

Time of Race: 1 hour, 10 minutes, 21 seconds
Average Speed: 88.697 mph
Pole Winner: Friday Hassler - 91.464 mph
Lap Leaders: Friday Hassler 1-52, Richard Petty 53-139, Benny Parsons 140-153, Petty 154-200.
Cautions: 1 for 3 laps   Margin of Victory: 8 seconds   Attendance: 4,200

Race No. 14
Petty Sails On; Wins Non-Stop Gwyn Staley Memorial

N.WILKESBORO, NC (Apr. 18) -- Richard Petty continued his winning ways by coming on strong in the end to win the Gwyn Staley Memorial at North Wilkesboro Speedway. It was the seventh win of the season for the Randleman, NC star.

Petty took a back seat during the first half of the 250-miler. Pole sitter Bobby Isaac led 204 of the first 205 laps, but a metal object from the track busted his windshield. Isaac fell two laps off the pace, but made up half the deficit when his engine blew.

Petty took the lead for the final time when he got around Dick Brooks with 126 laps to go. Brooks eventually fell four laps off the pace. He finished third behind David Pearson. Fourth place went to Benny Parsons with Bobby Allison fifth.

Charlie Glotzbach qualified ninth in a Chevrolet owned by Junior Fields. The car was turned over to the Junior Johnson-Herb Nab crew for preparation. Glotzbach roared through the field and was running fourth when the transmission broke.

The 400 lapper on the .625-mile oval was run without a caution flag. Petty averaged a record 98.479 mph before a crowd of 10,000.

Winston Cup GN Race No. 14
400 Laps at N.Wilkesboro Speedway
N.Wilkesboro, NC
"Gwyn Staley Memorial"
250 Miles on .625-mile Paved Track
April 18, 1971

Fin	St	No.	Driver	Team / Car	Laps	Money	Status
1	3	43	Richard Petty	Petty Ent '71 Plymouth	400	$4,545	Running
2	2	17	David Pearson	Holman-Moody '70 Ford	399	2,570	Running
3	5	22	Dick Brooks	Mario Rossi '70 Dodge	396	1,745	Running
4	4	72	Benny Parsons	L G DeWitt '70 Ford	394	1,145	Running
5	5	12	Bobby Allison	Allison '71 Dodge	394	895	Running
6	13	48	James Hylton	Hylton Eng '70 Mercury	386	645	Running
7	10	90	Bill Dennis	Junie Donlavey '69 Mercury	379	645	Running
8	11	10	Bill Champion	Champion '69 Ford	379	595	Running
9	19	49	G C Spencer	Spencer '69 Plymouth	379	550	Running
10	17	24	Cecil Gordon	Gordon '69 Mercury	374	565	Running
11	12	25	Jabe Thomas	Don Robertson '70 Plymouth	364	555	Running
12	25	79	Frank Warren	Warren '69 Plymouth	358	520	Running
13	1	71	Bobby Isaac	K&K Insurance '71 Dodge	355	1,260	Engine
14	27	74	Bill Shirey	Shirey '69 Plymouth	348	500	Running
15	8	64	Elmo Langley	Langley '70 Ford	306	515	Oil Line
16	7	93	Richard Brown	Harold Furr '69 Chevrolet	281	505	Clutch
17	15	30	Walter Ballard	Vic Ballard '71 Ford	249	495	Heating
18	30	28	Ed Negre	Earl Brooks '69 Ford	243	460	Suspen
19	24	63	Charlie Roberts	Roberts '69 Dodge	241	450	Engine
20	27	70	J D McDuffie	McDuffie '69 Mercury	191	440	Rear End
21	16	34	Wendell Scott	Scott '69 Ford	96	455	Axle
22	23	51	Dub Simpson	Bill Strong '69 Chevrolet	96	420	Battery
23	20	88	Ron Keselowski	Roger Lubinski '70 Dodge	94	410	Engine
24	29	47	Raymond Williams	Bill Seifert '70 Ford	92	400	Heating
25	18	46	Roy Mayne	Tom Hunter '69 Chevrolet	54	390	Engine
26	9	91	Charlie Glotzbach	Junior Fields '71 Chevrolet	29	485	Trans
27	28	26	Earl Brooks	Brooks '69 Ford	28	375	Engine
28	24	84	Clyde Lynn	Elmo Langley '69 Mercury	15	365	Vibration
29	14	45	Bill Seifert	Seifert '70 Ford	14	380	Heating
30	26	62	Dick Poling	Kaye Eng '70 Dodge	2	345	Oil Leak

Time of Race: 2 hours, 32 minutes, 19 seconds
Average Speed: 98.479 mph
Pole Winner: Bobby Isaac - 106.217 mph
Lap Leaders: Bobby Isaac 1-133, David Pearson 134, Isaac 135-205,
    Richard Petty 206-265, Pearson 266-268, Dick Brooks 269-274, Petty 275-400.
Cautions: None   Margin of Victory: 1-lap plus   Attendance: 10,000

Race No. 15
Another Uproar -- Petty Wins Martinsville Without Gas Cap

MARTINSVILLE, VA (Apr. 25) -- Richard Petty, his fuel cap dangling at the end of its chain, crossed the finish line 1.6 seconds ahead of David Pearson to win the protested Virginia 500 at Martinsville Speedway. It took five days for sanctioning NASCAR to announce that Petty had been officially declared the winner.

Pearson and car owner Ralph Moody protested Petty's triumph. The protest revolved around an unannounced change in the rules. Rule 22, Section 9 of the 1971 NASCAR rule book states "No car will be permitted on the race track at any time unless the gas tank cap remains in the closed position on the filler spout. Any car observed without gas cap in closed position *may* be flagged to the pits and kept in the pits until the gas cap is in its proper position."

In 1970 the rule book said that any car in violation of the rule *will* be flagged to the pits.

Petty was holding a 13 second lead over Pearson with 18 laps to go. Petty hustled down pit road to take on enough gas to finish the race. In haste he pulled out of the pits before his crew could put the cap securely in place.

Petty returned to the track just ahead of Pearson. Starter Johnny Bruner, Jr. noticed Petty's gas cap swinging on the chain and he reached for the black flag. NASCAR Competition Director Lin Kuchler, the senior official present, advised Bruner that Petty was not to be black-flagged. "The fans come to see a race decided on the track, not on a technicality," said Kuchler.

Bobby Isaac finished in third place with Dave Marcis and James Hylton filling out the top five.

Donnie Allison, taking his first ride in the Wood Brothers Mercury, led five times for 367 laps. He engaged in a crowd-pleasing 13 lap side-by-side duel with Petty before he gained the upper hand. Allison was leading when his engine expired on lap 412.

A crowd of 20,000 watched Petty notch his eighth win of the year at an average speed of 77.707 mph.

Race No. 16

Donnie Blows; Baker Wins Rebel 400 by 7 laps

DARLINGTON, SC (May 2) -- Buddy Baker drove his Petty Enterprises Dodge around Donnie Allison's ailing Mercury eleven laps from the finish and won the Rebel 400 at Darlington Raceway. It was the first win of the season for the 30 year-old Charlotte driver.

Dick Brooks finished second, seven laps behind. Dave Marcis was third, Allison fourth and Jim Vandiver fifth.

Allison, of Hueytown, AL, held command for most of the way. He was in front six times for 250 of the 293 laps. He had worked his way into a healthy lead

Donnie Allison leads Bobby Isaac in Martinsville's Virginia 500

Winston Cup GN Race No. 15
500 Laps at Martinsville Speedway
Martinsville, VA
"Virginia 500"
262.5 Miles on .525-mile Paved Track
April 25, 1971

Fin	St	No.	Driver	Team / Car	Laps	Money	Status
1	3	43	Richard Petty	Petty Ent '71 Plymouth	500	$5,075	Running
2	5	17	David Pearson	Holman-Moody '71 Ford	500	2,550	Running
3	2	71	Bobby Isaac	K&K Insurance '71 Dodge	492	2,350	Out of gas
4	8	2	Dave Marcis	Marcis '69 Dodge	486	1,525	Running
5	15	48	James Hylton	Hylton Eng '70 Ford	483	1,225	Running
6	4	12	Bobby Allison	Allison '71 Dodge	482	1,050	Running
7	16	24	Cecil Gordon	Gordon '69 Mercury	471	925	Running
8	27	88	Ron Keselowski	Roger Lubinski '70 Dodge	470	850	Running
9	20	06	Neil Castles	Castles '70 Dodge	466	825	Running
10	28	45	Bill Seifert	Seifert '71 Ford	465	750	Running
11	26	46	Roy Mayne	Tom Hunter '69 Chevrolet	460	725	Running
12	18	20	Elmo Langley	Clyde Lynn '70 Ford	449	725	Running
13	21	19	Henley Gray	Gray '69 Ford	444	675	Running
14	19	7	Bill Dennis	Dean Dalton '69 Ford	434	675	Running
15	1	21	Donnie Allison	Wood Brothers '71 Mercury	413	775	Engine
16	7	72	Benny Parsons	L G DeWitt '70 Ford	367	625	Engine
17	25	34	Wendell Scott	Scott '69 Ford	362	575	Engine
18	17	25	Jabe Thomas	Don Robertson '70 Plymouth	337	575	Engine
19	23	70	J D McDuffie	McDuffie '69 Mercury	330	525	Clutch
20	6	99	Fred Lorenzen	Nichels-Goldsmith '71 Plym	329	525	Heating
21	24	4	John Sears	Sears '69 Dodge	164	475	Ignition
22	30	68	Larry Baumel	Auto Lad '69 Ford	146	450	Trans
23	11	22	Dick Brooks	Mario Rossi '70 Dodge	133	450	Engine
24	12	10	Bill Champion	Champion '71 Ford	111	425	Engine
25	22	30	Walter Ballard	Vic Ballard '71 Ford	99	375	Clutch
26	14	51	Dub Simpson	Bill Strong '69 Chevrolet	92	375	Rear End
27	9	64	Earl Brooks	Brooks '69 Ford	67	350	Rear End
28	29	74	Bill Shirey	Shirey '69 Plymouth	37	300	Engine
29	10	79	Frank Warren	Warren '69 Plymouth	18	300	Engine
30	13	49	Ed Negre	G C Spencer '69 Plymouth	0	275	Trans

Time of Race: 3 hours, 22 minutes, 41 seconds
Average Speed: 77.707 mph
Pole Winner: Donnie Allison - 82.529 mph
Lap Leaders: Donnie Allison 1-132, Richard Petty 133-147, D.Allison 148-186,
　　Fred Lorenzen 187, D.Allison 188-328, Petty 329-335, David Pearson 336-349,
　　D.Allison 350-371, Petty 372-379, D.Allison 380-412, Petty 413-500.
Cautions: 1 for 3 laps　　Margin of Victory: 1.6 seconds　　Attendance: 20,000

Winston Cup GN Race No. 16
293 Laps at Darlington Raceway
Darlington, SC
"Rebel 400"
400 Miles on 1.366-mile Paved Track
May 2, 1971

Fin	St	No.	Driver	Team / Car	Laps	Money	Status
1	5	11	Buddy Baker	Petty Ent '71 Dodge	293	$16,065	Running
2	11	22	Dick Brooks	Mario Rossi '70 Dodge	286	8,165	Running
3	14	2	Dave Marcis	Marcis '69 Dodge	286	5,540	Running
4	1	21	Donnie Allison	Wood Brothers '71 Mercury	283	4,090	Engine
5	15	31	Jim Vandiver	O L Nixon '70 Dodge	276	2,215	Running
6	16	49	G C Spencer	Spencer '69 Plymouth	268	1,725	Running
7	34	70	J D McDuffie	McDuffie '69 Mercury	265	1,400	Running
8	13	39	Friday Hassler	Hassler '69 Chevrolet	264	1,350	Running
9	27	76	Ben Arnold	Arnold '69 Ford	261	1,175	Running
10	10	64	Elmo Langley	Langley '69 Mercury	258	1,100	Running
11	31	19	Henley Gray	Gray '69 Ford	256	1,225	Running
12	17	10	Bill Champion	Champion '70 Ford	255	975	Running
13	23	34	Wendell Scott	Scott '69 Ford	252	950	Running
14	32	49	Ed Negre	Negre '69 Ford	247	925	Running
15	18	24	Cecil Gordon	Gordon '69 Mercury	245	900	Engine
16	21	30	Walter Ballard	Vic Ballard '71 Ford	219	850	Rear End
17	19	95	Paul Tyler	Tyler '69 Mercury	215	825	Suspen
18	3	99	Fred Lorenzen	Nichels-Goldsmith '71 Plym	205	1,000	Engine
19	22	7	Dean Dalton	Dalton '69 Ford	201	750	Engine
20	4	43	Richard Petty	Petty Ent '71 Plymouth	185	925	Engine
21	7	12	Bobby Allison	Allison '71 Dodge	177	700	Engine
22	29	18	Joe Frasson	Frasson '70 Dodge	159	675	Lug Bolts
23	8	72	Benny Parsons	L G DeWitt '70 Mercury	132	650	Engine
24	26	48	James Hylton	Hylton Eng '69 Ford	122	640	Engine
25	6	71	Bobby Isaac	K&K Insurance '71 Dodge	119	625	Suspen
26	36	5	Earl Brooks	Doc Faustina '70 Plymouth	97	610	Fire
27	28	25	Jabe Thomas	Don Robertson '69 Plymouth	69	650	Ignition
28	30	47	Raymond Williams	Bill Seifert '70 Ford	60	615	Brakes
29	25	93	Richard Brown	Harold Furr '70 Chevrolet	52	660	Crash
30	20	45	Bill Seifert	Seifert '69 Ford	48	580	Ignition
31	2	17	David Pearson	Holman-Moody '71 Mercury	30	1,075	Steering
32	35	63	Frank Warren*	Charlie Roberts '69 Dodge	26	570	Oil Leak
33	24	46	Roy Mayne	Tom Hunter '69 Chevrolet	23	565	Engine
34	12	91	Charlie Glotzbach	Junior Fields '71 Chevrolet	13	560	Mtr Mount
35	9	6	Pete Hamilton	Cotton Owens '71 Plymouth	3	555	Engine
36	33	06	Neil Castles	Castles '70 Dodge	2	550	Engine

Time of Race: 3 hours, 3 minutes, 46 seconds
Average Speed: 130.678 mph
Pole Winner: Donnie Allison - 149.826 mph
Lap Leaders: David Pearson 1-3, Donnie Allison 4-15, Dave Marcis 16-23, D.Allison 24-66,
　　Bobby Allison 67, D.Allison 68-109, Richard Petty 110, D.Allison 111-153,
　　Petty 154-162, D.Allison 163-251, Buddy Baker 252-267, D.Allison 268-282,
　　Baker 283-293.
Cautions: 5 for 30 laps　　Margin of Victory: 7-laps plus　　Attendance: 25,000
*Relieved by Charlie Roberts

when smoke poured from the headers. "The engine just stopped," said Donnie. "We had a fine race. He (Baker) is to be congratulated."

Baker, who won for only the fourth time in a career spanning 13 seasons, said, "I know how he feels. It's happened to me many times. It would have been a three

Donnie Alliston leads David Pearson, Richard Petty and Fred Lorenzen at Darlington.
Donnie led most of the way but blew his engine late in the Rebel 400

car race if Donnie and Richard (Petty) could have stayed in."

Petty started fourth and led nine laps before he went to the sidelines with a blown engine.

Fred Lorenzen started third and went 205 laps before the engine in his Plymouth blew.

After the race, David Pearson and the famed Holman-Moody team split. "Pearson told us he would not drive at Talladega unless he gets $1,500 appearance money," said John Holman. "We cannot justify this. Ralph is talking with three other drivers about driving our car."

The three-time Grand National champion said he knew Holman-Moody was getting $3,000 in appearance money at Talladega. "I just wanted my customary half," said Pearson. "We've always split everything 50/50. Now they want to keep it all."

Pearson was expected to shift over to a new Pontiac prepared by Ray Nichels and funded by the mysterious Chris Vallo. Vallo said he gave Nichels a $1 million check to start the Pontiac project.

Race No. 17

Parsons Finds Golden Nugget In South Boston 100

S. BOSTON, VA (May 9) -- After nearly eight years of panning, Benny Parsons sifted a nugget of victory from NASCAR Winston Cup Grand National racing's stream. The 29 year-old Ellerbe, NC Ford driver, who tried unsuccessfully to hop aboard the major leagues of stock car racing in 1964, finally made that elusive first trip to victory lane in the Halifax 100 at South Boston Speedway.

Parsons took the lead in the 248th lap when engine

Winston Cup GN Race No. 17
281 Laps at South Boston Speedway
South Boston, VA
"Halifax County 100"
100 Miles on .357-mile Paved Track
May 9, 1971

Fin	St	No.	Driver	Team / Car	Laps	Money	Status
1	2	72	Benny Parsons	L G DeWitt '70 Ford	281	$1,500	Running
2	3	43	Richard Petty	Petty Ent '71 Plymouth	280	900	Running
3	9	48	James Hylton	Hylton Eng '71 Ford	277	500	Running
4	10	30	Walter Ballard	Vic Ballard '71 Ford	273	350	Running
5	17	24	Cecil Gordon	Gordon '69 Mercury	273	325	Running
6	8	10	Bill Champion	Champion '71 Ford	270	300	Running
7	13	70	J D McDuffie	McDuffie '71 Chevrolet	270	275	Running
8	26	79	Frank Warren	Warren '69 Dodge	269	270	Running
9	12	25	Jabe Thomas	Don Robertson '70 Plymouth	267	265	Running
10	11	34	Wendell Scott	Scott '69 Ford	263	260	Running
11	23	19	Henley Gray	Gray '69 Ford	257	255	Running
12	28	8	Ed Negre	Negre '69 Ford	255	250	Running
13	1	71	Bobby Isaac	K&K Insurance '71 Dodge	247	245	Engine
14	24	67	Dick May	Ron Ronacher '69 Ford	185	240	Quit
15	15	74	Bill Shirey	Shirey '69 Plymouth	134	235	Quit
16	19	7	Dean Dalton	Dalton '69 Ford	109	230	Engine
17	16	4	John Sears	Sears '69 Dodge	103	225	Ignition
18	21	41	D K Ulrich	Ulrich '70 Ford	77	220	Quit
19	7	06	Neil Castles	Castles '70 Dodge	60	215	Rear End
20	18	68	Larry Baumel	Auto Lad '69 Ford	56	210	Heating
21	20	96	Richard Childress	Tom Garn '71 Chevrolet	37	205	Engine
22	14	20	Clyde Lynn	Lynn '70 Ford	32	200	Engine
23	27	63	Charlie Roberts	Roberts '69 Dodge	25	200	Quit
24	5	64	Elmo Langley	Langley '71 Ford	24	200	Engine
25	22	26	Earl Brooks	Brooks '69 Ford	20	200	Heating
26	25	85	Ronnie Daniels	Daniels '70 Chevrolet	16	200	Heating
27	6	2	Dave Marcis	Marcis '69 Dodge	9	200	Rear End
28	4	90	Bill Dennis	Junie Donlavey '69 Mercury	6	200	D Shaft

Time of Race: 1 hour, 23 minutes, 17 seconds
Average Speed: 72.271 mph
Pole Winner: Bobby Isaac - 81.548 mph
Lap Leaders: Bobby Isaac 1-181, Benny Parsons 182-189, Richard Petty 190-212, Isaac 213-247, Parsons 248-281.
Cautions: 2 for 14 laps   Margin of Victory: 1-lap plus   Attendance: 1,400

Benny Parsons (r) chats with Henley Gray. Parsons won his first Winston Cup Grand National race at South Boston, VA

failure put leader Bobby Isaac out of the race. Parsons held Richard Petty in check the rest of the way.

Petty finished a lap behind in second place. James Hylton was third, rookie Walter Ballard came in fourth and Cecil Gordon was fifth.

"We got a little luck today," said Parsons. "But I figure we had it coming. We had been close before. This sure feels good."

A slim Mother's Day turnout of 1,400 watched Parsons win at an average speed of 72.271 mph. Only 12 cars finished in the starting field of 28. Four drivers withdrew. Bill Dennis left after six laps with a broken drive shaft and earned $200. Dick May drove 185 laps before he parked his Ford, winning $240.

Race No. 18

Donnie Beats Bobby at Talladega; Marcis Shines

TALLADEGA, AL (May 16) -- Donnie Allison sped across the finish line six car lengths ahead of his brother Bobby to win the Winston 500 at Alabama International Motor Speedway. It was the fourth time the Hueytown, AL brothers have finished 1-2 in a Winston Cup Grand National race -- and each time Donnie has come out on top.

Donnie prevailed in a one lap shoot-out for the $31,140 top prize. The seventh and final caution period had ended just as the white flag was waved. Donnie gunned his Wood Brothers Mercury ahead by several car lengths. Buddy Baker, running second, did not attempt to make a pass for the lead -- and Bobby sneaked past to gain runner-up honors.

Pete Hamilton was fourth, a lap behind. Fred Lorenzen was fifth.

The 188-lap contest was strictly a four car duel. Dave Marcis, a last minute substitute for Bobby Isaac, who reportedly fell ill with a kidney stone two days before the race, responded brilliantly in the potent K&K Insurance Dodge. Marcis led for 38 laps and was holding down first place with nine laps to go.

As the four leaders stormed around the front chute, Marcis' Dodge fluttered. After dropping from first to fourth, the engine blew in flame, sending the car out of control. Marcis grazed the turn two wall before coming to a halt in the infield. "I just hope I get another chance to run up front," said the 30 year-old Wausau, WI driver. "It was really fun. I wish that engine had lasted eight more laps."

For winner Donnie Allison, it was his first win since replacing A.J. Foyt in the Wood Brothers car. "I had the other two races won (at Martinsville and Darlington), but we didn't finish," he said. "I was determined not to let this one slip away. I wanted to lead that last

Dave Marcis drove the K&K Insurance Dodge at Talladega

Winston Cup GN Race No. 18
188 Laps at Alabama Int'l Motor Speedway
Talladega, AL
"Winston 500"
500 Miles on 2.66-mile Paved Track
May 16, 1971

Fin	St	No.	Driver	Team / Car	Laps	Money	Status
1	1	21	Donnie Allison	Wood Brothers '69 Mercury	188	$31,140	Running
2	3	12	Bobby Allison	Holman-Moody '69 Mercury	188	19,225	Running
3	7	11	Buddy Baker	Petty Ent '71 Dodge	188	9,825	Running
4	6	6	Pete Hamilton	Cotton Owens '71 Plymouth	187	5,825	Running
5	4	99	Fred Lorenzen	Nichels-Goldsmith '71 Plym	187	3,950	Running
6	27	31	Jim Vandiver	O L Nixon '69 Dodge	186	2,800	Running
7	10	48	James Hylton	Hylton Eng '70 Ford	185	2,500	Running
8	9	90	Bill Dennis	Junie Donlavey '69 Mercury	183	2,250	Running
9	2	71	Dave Marcis	K&K Insurance '71 Dodge	181	6,025	Engine
10	32	68	Larry Baumel	Auto Lad '69 Ford	178	2,000	Running
11	36	25	Jabe Thomas	Don Robertson '70 Plymouth	178	1,975	Running
12	22	2	Bill Seifert	Dave Marcis '69 Dodge	177	1,950	Running
13	13	24	Cecil Gordon	Gordon '69 Mercury	176	1,925	Running
14	20	76	Ben Arnold	Arnold '69 Ford	175	1,900	Running
15	38	4	John Sears	Sears '69 Dodge	174	1,875	Running
16	17	39	Friday Hassler	Hassler '69 Chevrolet	174	1,850	Running
17	15	88	Ron Keselowski	Roger Lubinski '70 Dodge	173	1,825	Running
18	44	5	Doc Faustina	Faustina '70 Plymouth	170	1,800	Running
19	47	34	Wendell Scott	Scott '69 Ford	170	1,775	Running
20	39	7	Dean Dalton	Dalton '69 Ford	169	1,750	Running
21	16	60	Maynard Troyer	Nagle Racers '69 Mercury	167	1,725	Running
22	24	30	Walter Ballard	Vic Ballard '71 Ford	167	1,700	Running
23	31	18	Joe Frasson	Frasson '70 Dodge	166	1,675	Running
24	42	8	Ed Negre	Negre '69 Ford	165	1,650	Running
25	46	77	Charlie Roberts	Bob Freeman '70 Ford	160	1,625	Running
26	46	32	Kevin Terris	Dean Barnicle '70 Plymouth	150	1,600	Heating
27	43	0	George Altheide	'70 Dodge	135	1,575	Engine
28	26	64	Elmo Langley	Langley '69 Mercury	133	1,550	Spindle
29	29	20	Bill Ward	Jimmy McCain '71 Ford	108	1,525	Engine
30	11	79	Frank Warren	Warren '69 Dodge	97	1,500	Engine
31	37	05	David Sisco	Charlie McGee '70 Chevrolet	85	1,475	Fan pulle
32	48	63	Ray Mulligan	Charlie Roberts '69 Dodge	83	1,450	Engine
33	18	70	J D McDuffie	McDuffie '69 Mercury	81	1,425	Fuel Line
34	33	46	Roy Mayne	Tom Hunter '69 Chevrolet	68	1,400	Engine
35	34	36	Jimmy Crawford	Crawford Ent '70 Dodge	66	1,375	Eng/crash
36	50	26	Earl Brooks	Brooks '69 Ford	58	1,350	Engine
37	14	03	Tommy Gale	Larry Jackson '69 Mercury	53	1,325	Engine
38	5	43	Richard Petty	Petty Ent '71 Plym	42	1,300	Crash
39	35	07	Coo Coo Marlin	Cunningham-Kelley '69 Chev	39	1,275	Engine
40	45	19	Henley Gray	Gray '69 Ford	35	1,250	Engine
41	19	47	Raymond Williams	Bill Seifert '71 Ford	31	1,225	Heating
42	12	10	Bill Champion	Champion '70 Ford	25	1,200	Engine
43	8	33	David Pearson	C V Enterprises '71 Pontiac	19	1,175	Engine
44	21	93	Richard Brown	Harold Furr '69 Chevrolet	17	1,150	Engine
45	28	95	Paul Tyler	Tyler '69 Mercury	15	1,125	Heating
46	41	45	Dub Simpson	Bill Seifert '69 Mercury	11	1,100	Engine
47	23	86	Bobby Mausgrover	Neil Castles '69 Dodge	9	1,075	Trans
48	30	72	Benny Parsons	L G DeWitt '69 Mercury	6	1,050	Engine
49	40	06	Neil Castles	Castles '70 Dodge	4	1,025	Ignition
50	25	35	Bub Strickler	'69 Ford	1	1,000	Engine

Time of Race: 3 hours, 23 minutes, 32 seconds
Average Speed: 147.419 mph
Pole Winner: Donnie Allison - 185.869 mph
Lap Leaders: Donnie Allison 1-2, Buddy Baker 3, D.Allison 4-5, Bobby Allison 6-15,
    D.Allison 16-21, B.Allison 22-26, D.Allison 27-30, Baker 31-34, Dave Marcis 35-37,
    B.Allison 38-44, Marcis 45-46, B.Allison 47-49, D.Allison 50-53, Baker 54-55,
    B.Allison 56-72, D.Allison 73, Marcis 74, D.Allison 75-86, B.Allison 87, Baker 88,
    D.Allison 89-92, Baker 93, B.Allison 94-96, Marcis 97-102, B.Allison 103,
    D.Allison 104-110, B.Allison 111-113, D.Allison 114-116, B.Allison 117-123,
    D.Allison 124-125, Marcis 126-128, D.Allison 129-130, Marcis 131-138,
    B.Allison 139-142, Baker 143-144, B.Allison 145-150, D.Allison 151-156,
    Marcis 157-158, B.Allison 159-161, D.Allison 162, Marcis 163-166,
    D.Allison 167, Marcis 168-174, Baker 175-178, Marcis 179-180,
    D.Allison 181-188.
Cautions: 7 for 45 laps
Margin of Victory: 6 car lengths
Attendance: 29,000

lap from start to finish and not worry about having to draft anybody."

Ironically, it was Donnie's first start at the world's fastest speedway. He was part of the PDA walkout in 1969, and did not compete in either 1970 race.

Richard Petty picked up the Pepsi Cola sponsorship. He backed his Plymouth into the wall on lap 42. "A tire went down," he said. "I had no control over it."

David Pearson made his debut in the C V Enterprises Pontiac. He started eighth but left after 19 laps with a blown engine.

The second half of the event was televised live by ABC-Sports. The national telecast contributed to a slim trackside audience of 29,000.

Race No. 19

Independents Boycott Asheville 300; Petty Wins

ASHEVILLE, NC (May 21) -- Richard Petty passed Elmo Langley in the 206th lap and went on to win the Asheville 300 at the New Asheville Speedway. By the time the checkered flag fell, there were only five cars on the track. Most of the independents staged a post green flag boycott.

Petty, the only factory backed driver in the field, had received $2,000 in appearance money from promoter George Ledford. A number of independents requested a smaller 'deal', but Ledford refused to pay anyone other than Petty. "We've got who we need," Ledford was reported to have said.

Of the 12 cars that failed to finish, seven of them quit. Led by James Hylton, who ranks second to Petty in the Winston Cup point standings, the independents voiced their opinion in the form of a walk-out. Hylton and Neil Castles pulled out after one lap. They were followed a short time later by John Sears, Bill Shirey, Frank Warren, Earl Brooks and Dick May.

Langley finished the race four laps behind Petty. Cecil Gordon came in third with Jabe Thomas fourth and Bill Champion fifth.

Petty, who won for the 128th time in his career, offered his opinion on the future of short distance, short track races. "I think Grand National racing will work itself out of short track racing into nothing but a large track circuit," he said. "I think for it to be what it started out to be -- the very best in racing -- then NASCAR is going to have to work up a circuit with 25 races or something like that."

A crowd of 4,500 jeered the finish as only Petty and four other straggling cars were on the track -- running some 41 laps apart.

A week later, promoter Ledford resigned from his position at the track.

Winston Cup GN Race No. 19
300 Laps at New Asheville Speedway
Asheville, NC
"Asheville 300"
100 Miles on .333-mile Paved Track
May 21, 1971

Fin	St	No.	Driver	Team / Car	Laps	Money	status
1	1	43	Richard Petty	Petty Ent '71 Plymouth	300	$1,500	Running
2	2	64	Elmo LAngley	Langley '69 Mercury	296	900	Running
3	3	24	Cecil Gordon	Gordon '69 Mercury	284	500	Running
4	10	25	Jabe Thomas	Don Robertson '69 Plymouth	281	350	Running
5	7	10	Bill Champion	Champion '69 Ford	259	325	Running
6	15	67	Dick May	Ron Ronacher '69 Ford	155	300	Quit
7	17	70	J D McDuffie	McDuffie '69 Mercury	130	275	Engine
8	14	26	Earl Brooks	Brooks '69 Ford	124	270	Quit
9	12	79	Frank Warren	Warren '69 Plymouth	110	265	Quit
10	9	74	Bill Shirey	Shirey '69 Plymouth	79	260	Quit
11	13	4	John Sears	Sears '69 Dodge	74	255	Quit
12	8	72	Benny Parsons	L G DeWitt '70 Ford	33	250	Engine
13	11	30	Walter Ballard	Vic Ballard '71 Ford	32	245	Engine
14	6	34	Wendell Scott	Scott '69 Ford	15	240	Ignition
15	16	8	Ed Negre	Negre '69 Ford	9	235	Brakes
16	5	06	Neil Castles	Castles '70 Dodge	1	230	Quit
17	4	48	James Hylton	Hylton Eng '71 Ford	1	225	Quit

Time of Race: 1 hour, 24 minutes, 14 seconds
Average Speed: 71.231 mph
Pole Winner: Richard Petty - 79.598 mph
Lap Leaders: Richard Petty 1-13, Elmo Langley 14-56, Petty 57-200, Langley 201-205, Petty 206-300.
Cautions: None   Margin of Victory: 4-laps plus   Attendance: 4,500

Race No. 20

Isaac Cruises to Kingsport 300 Victory

KINGSPORT, TN (May 23) -- Bobby Isaac outran and outlasted Richard Petty to win the Kingsport 300 at Kingsport Speedway. It was the 34th career Grand National win for Isaac, moving him out of a tie with Fireball Roberts, who won 33 times.

Isaac and Petty battled for the lead -- far ahead of the trailing independents. Isaac led for 294 of the 300 laps on the .337-mile oval. Petty departed on lap 163 with rear end failure, which let Isaac scoot home free.

Isaac's K&K Insurance Dodge beat runner-up Elmo Langley by five laps. James Hylton was third, two more laps back. Cecil Gordon was fourth, 17 laps behind and fifth place Bill Champion was 18 laps back.

"There wasn't much going on after Petty fell out," said Isaac. "I wasn't even running hard at the end of the race."

Isaac covered the 101 miles at a 63.242 mph clip.

Winston Cup GN Race No. 20
300 Laps at Kingsport Speedway
Kingsport, TN
"Kingsport 300"
101 Miles on .337-mile Paved Track
May 23, 1971

Fin	St	No.	Driver	Team / Car	Laps	Money	Status
1	1	71	Bobby Isaac	K&K Insurance '71 Dodge	300	$1,800	Running
2	6	64	Elmo Langley	Langley '71 Ford	295	1,100	Running
3	3	48	James Hylton	Hylton Eng '71 Ford	293	800	Running
4	9	24	Cecil Gordon	Gordon '69 Mercury	283	600	Running
5	4	10	Bill Champion	Champion '69 Ford	282	500	Running
6	7	34	Wendell Scott	Scott '69 Ford	281	400	Running
7	12	30	Walter Ballard	Vic Ballard '71 Ford	280	390	Running
8	11	25	Jabe Thomas	Don Robertson '70 Plymouth	277	380	Running
9	17	74	Bill Shirey	Shirey '69 Plymouth	274	370	Running
10	16	45	Bill Seifert	Seifert '70 Ford	260	360	Running
11	25	79	Frank Warren	Warren '69 Dodge	259	350	Running
12	10	4	John Sears	Sears '69 Dodge	238	340	Ignition
13	13	8	Ed Negre	Negre '69 Ford	211	330	Running
14	18	67	Dick May	Ron Ronacher '69 Ford	200	320	Trans
15	21	41	Ken Meisenhelder	Meisenhelder '69 Chevrolet	194	310	Rear End
16	14	40	D K Ulrich	Ulrich '70 Ford	186	300	Crash
17	2	43	Richard Petty	Petty Ent '71 Plymouth	166	290	Rear End
18	8	06	Neil Castles	Castles '70 Dodge	138	280	Brakes
19	22	77	Charlie Roberts	Roberts '70 Ford	138	270	Quit
20	23	19	Henley Gray	Gray '69 Ford	87	260	Battery
21	15	26	Earl Brooks	Brooks '69 Ford	85	250	Wiring
22	20	96	Richard Childress	Tom Garn '71 Chevrolet	72	240	Fire
23	5	72	Benny Parsons	L G DeWitt '70 Ford	46	230	Heating
24	19	70	J D McDuffie	McDuffie '69 Chevrolet	26	220	Oil Leak
25	24	28	Bill Hollar	Earl Brooks '69 Ford	1	200	Clutch

Time of Race: 1 hour, 32 minutes, 35 seconds
Average Speed: 63.242 mph
Pole Winner: Bobby Isaac - 75.167 mph
Lap Leaders: Bobby Isaac 1-82, Richard Petty 83-88, Isaac 89-300.
Cautions: 6 for 35 laps   Margin of Victory: 5-laps plus   Attendance: 3,800

Winston Cup GN Race No. 21
400 Laps at Charlotte Motor Speedway
Charlotte, NC
"World 600"
600 Miles on 1.5-mile Paved Track
May 30, 1971

Fin	St	No.	Driver	Team / Car	Laps	Money	Status
1	2	12	Bobby Allison	Holman-Moody '69 Mercury	400	$28,400	Running
2	13	21	Donnie Allison	Wood Brothers '69 Mercury	400	14,900	Running
3	6	6	Pete Hamilton	Cotton Owens '71 Plymouth	399	10,425	Running
4	5	43	Richard Petty	Petty Ent '71 Plymouth	398	7,175	Running
5	4	99	Fred Lorenzen	Nichels-Goldsmith '71 Plym	395	5,600	Running
6	8	11	Buddy Baker	Petty Ent '71 Dodge	394	4,125	Running
7	15	72	Benny Parsons	L G DeWitt '69 Mercury	392	3,600	Running
8	25	39	Friday Hassler	Hassler '70 Chevrolet	391	3,125	Running
9	12	2	Dave Marcis	Marcis '69 Dodge	390	2,550	Running
10	7	22	Dick Brooks	Mario Rossi '70 Dodge	390	2,400	Running
11	10	31	Jim Vandiver	O L Nixon '70 Dodge	386	2,175	Running
12	11	14	Jim Paschal	Bill Ellis '71 Chevrolet	386	2,050	Running
13	17	48	James Hylton	Hylton Eng '71 Ford	385	1,975	Running
14	16	90	Bill Dennis	Junie Donlavey '69 Mercury	382	1,925	Running
15	19	42	Marty Robbins	Robbins '69 Dodge	376	1,800	Running
16	9	91	Speedy Thompson	Junior Fields '71 Chevrolet	376	1,800	Running
17	18	24	Cecil Gordon	Gordon '69 Mercury	374	1,700	Running
18	37	06	Neil Castles	Castles '70 Dodge	370	1,675	Running
19	27	10	Bill Champion	Champion '71 Ford	363	1,625	Running
20	39	04	Ed Negre	Bob Davis '70 Plymouth	354	1,525	Running
21	30	5	Earl Brooks	Doc Faustina '70 Plymouth	353	1,485	Running
22	24	92	Larry Smith	Harley Smith '69 Ford	352	1,425	Running
23	35	79	Frank Warren	Warren '69 Dodge	349	1,375	Running
24	32	70	J D McDuffie	McDuffie '69 Mercury	333	1,325	Running
25	26	93	Richard Brown	Harold Furr '71 Chevrolet	330	1,350	Crash
26	34	07	Jabe Thomas	Cunningham-Kelley '69 Chev	292	1,230	W Bearing
27	21	64	Elmo Langley	Langley '69 Mercury	282	1,195	Clutch
28	1	3	Charlie Glotzbach	Richard Howard '71 Chevrolet	234	1,735	Crash
29	31	45	Bill Seifert	Seifert '69 Ford	232	1,125	Vibration
30	28	88	Ron Keselowski	Roger Lubinski '70 Dodge	213	1,115	Suspen
31	33	47	Raymond Williams	Bill Seifert '71 Ford	211	1,055	Engine
32	3	71	Bobby Isaac	K&K Insurance '71 Dodge	160	1,905	Radiator
33	36	02	Dick Bown	Mike Ober '70 Plymouth	110	1,015	Suspen
34	14	33	David Pearson	C V Enterprises '71 Pontiac	94	1,055	Oil Leak
35	23	18	Joe Frasson	Frasson '70 Dodge	79	920	Oil Pan
36	20	49	G C Spencer	Spencer '69 Plymouth	60	860	Engine
37	22	60	Maynard Troyer	Nagle Racers '69 Mercury	39	850	Steering
38	40	55	Ben Arnold	'69 Mercury	33	790	Oil Line
39	38	77	Charlie Roberts	Bob Freeman '70 Ford	17	795	Engine
40	29	30	Walter Ballard	Vic Ballard '71 Ford	11	800	Crash

Time of Race: 4 hours, 16 minutes, 20 seconds
Average Speed: 140.422 mph
Pole Winner: Charlie Glotzbach - 157.788 mph
Lap Leaders: Bobby Allison 1-5, Charlie Glotzbach 6-16, Dave Marcis 17-23,
   James Hylton 24, B.Allison 25-76, Buddy Baker 77-78, B.Allison 79-91, Glotzbach 92-97,
   B.Allison 98-136, Glotzbach 137-174, B.Allison 175-194, Glotzbach 195-226,
   B.Allison 227-400.
Cautions: 3 for 24 laps   Margin of Victory: 33.9 seconds   Attendance: 78,000
Relief Drivers: Ben Arnold relieved Marty Robbins; Hershel McGriff relieved Ed Negre;
   Billy Scott relieved Earl Brooks; Coo Coo Marlin relieved Jabe Thomas;
   Tiny Lund relieved Ben Arnold. Jim Paschal and
   Speedy Thompson also had relief drivers.

Race No. 21

Glotzbach's Chevy Crashes; Bobby Allison Wins 600

CHARLOTTE, NC (May 30) -- Bobby Allison took the lead just after the half way point and drove his Holman-Moody Mercury to a convincing victory in the World 600 at Charlotte Motor Speedway. It was the second start and first win for Allison since he joined Holman-Moody two weeks earlier.

Donnie Allison finished second, 33.9-seconds behind his brother. The younger Allison had just returned from Indianapolis where he finished sixth in the Indy 500. Third place went to Pete Hamilton, Richard Petty was fourth and Fred Lorenzen fifth.

Charlie Glotzbach was seated in the Richard Howard-owned, Junior Johnson prepared Chevrolet and won the pole at 157.788 mph. The throttle-stomping

Georgetown, IN veteran led four times for 87 laps, bringing cheers from the record crowd of 78,000.

Glotzbach was running in second place when he crashed heavily on the front chute on lap 234. "I came flying down toward the start-finish line and came up on Speedy Thompson," explained Glotzbach. "He was behind another car, but he whipped out in front of me. I got in the loose stuff and I lost it."

Thompson was ending a nine year retirement from

Winston Cup Grand National racing. Ironically, it was Glotzbach who lined Thompson up with car owner Junior Fields to drive his car in the 600. Thompson, who said, "I never saw Charlie; I didn't know I got in the way", continued and wound up 16th.

Charlie Glotzbach put the Junior Johnson Chevrolet on the pole for the World 600

The two Mercurys which dominated the race, were powered by 427 c.i. Ford Tunnelport engine; an outdated power plant but one that is allowed to have a larger carburetor plate opening. The difference in the plate openings brought a sharp response from Richard Petty, who said the rule rendered his Plymouth "uncompetitive. It was never more obvious that they had the advantage," said Petty. "When the green flag dropped, they drove off."

Allison started second and led for a total of 263 laps. "Getting this ride with Holman-Moody has to be the best thing that has ever happened to me," said the delighted winner. "The pit work today was just excellent. I look for some good things to happen the rest of the year."

Allison averaged a record 140.422 mph. He moved up to sixth place in the point standings. Petty held a firm grip of 106 points in the Winston Cup point standings.

Race No. 22

Allison Shuns Relief; Takes Torrid Mason-Dixon 500

DOVER, DE (June 6) -- Bobby Allison repelled a late challenge from Fred Lorenzen and won the blazing hot Mason-Dixon 500 at Dover Downs International Speedway. It was the second straight superspeedway triumph for the 33 year-old Hueytown, AL speedster.

Air temperatures reached 93 degrees and Allison was the only one of the first four finishers not to call on relief. "It's the toughest race I can remember running," said Allison. "I guess I come from further South than most of the drivers. I guess I can stand the heat more than some of them."

Lorenzen, who was later relieved by Bobby Isaac,

Winston Cup GN Race No. 22
500 Laps at Dover Downs Int'l Speedway
Dover, DE
"Mason-Dixon 500"
500 Miles on 1-mile Paved Track
June 6, 1971

Fin	St	No.	Driver	Team / Car	Laps	Money	Status
1	2	12	Bobby Allison	Holman-Moody '69 Mercury	500	$15,720	Running
2	21	99	Fred Lorenzen	Nichels-Goldsmith '71 Plym	499	9,045	Running
3	1	43	Richard Petty	Petty Ent '71 Plymouth	498	5,020	Running
4	3	71	Bobby Isaac	K&K Insurance '71 Dodge	496	3,495	Running
5	23	49	G C Spencer	Spencer '69 Plymouth	486	2,020	Running
6	16	48	James Hylton	Hylton Eng '71 Ford	477	1,645	Running
7	11	64	Elmo Langley	Langley '71 Ford	475	1,495	Running
8	9	10	Bill Champion	Champion '71 Ford	475	1,395	Running
9	27	77	Charlie Roberts	Bob Freeman '70 Ford	474	1,295	Running
10	28	30	Walter Ballard	Vic Ballard '71 Ford	469	1,245	Running
11	26	45	Bill Seifert	Seifert '69 Ford	460	1,195	Running
12	29	70	J D McDuffie	McDuffie '69 Mercury	456	1,145	Running
13	32	7	Dean Dalton	Dalton '69 Ford	451	1,095	Running
14	30	86	Bobby Mausgrover	Neil Castles '69 Dodge	450	1,070	Running
15	10	25	Jabe Thomas	Don Robertson '70 Plymouth	448	1,045	Running
16	13	8	Ed Negre	Negre '69 Ford	427	1,020	Running
17	18	28	Bill Hollar	Earl Brooks '69 Ford	395	995	Running
18	37	96	Richard Childress	Tom Garn '71 Chevrolet	394	970	Running
19	38	40	D K Ulrich	Ulrich '70 Ford	357	945	Engine
20	14	79	Frank Warren	Warren '69 Dodge	349	920	Running
21	35	41	Ken Meisenhelder	Meisenhelder '69 Chevrolet	312	895	Oil Leak
22	4	11	Buddy Baker	Petty Ent '71 Dodge	253	920	Engine
23	22	72	Benny Parsons	L G DeWitt '60 Mercury	225	895	Engine
24	36	26	Earl Brooks	Brooks '69 Ford	196	820	Clutch
25	17	4	John Sears	Sears '69 Dodge	141	795	Lug Bolts
26	7	6	Pete Hamilton	Cotton Owens '71 Plymouth	138	770	Engine
27	34	34	Wendell Scott	Scott '69 Ford	137	745	Engine
28	6	24	Cecil Gordon	Gordon '69 Mercury	135	720	Engine
29	20	74	Bill Shirey	Shirey '69 Plymouth	121	695	Quit
30	31	67	Dick May	Ron Ronacher '69 Ford	98	670	Throttle
31	19	19	Henley Gray	Gray '69 Ford	88	640	Ignition
32	39	81	A J Cox	Cox '69 Plymouth	82	615	Engine
33	25	95	Paul Tyler	Tyler '69 Mercury	58	590	Engine
34	8	88	Ron Keselowski	Roger Lubinski '70 Dodge	57	580	Engine
35	33	47	Raymond Williams	Bill Seifert '71 Ford	55	575	Engine
36	15	91	L D Fields	Junior Fields '71 Chevrolet	31	570	Engine
37	40	65	Joe Phipps	Phipps '69 Chevrolet	29	565	Oil Leak
38	24	06	Neil Castles	Castles '70 Dodge	22	560	Fuel pump
39	5	39	Friday Hassler	Hassler '70 Chevrolet	18	580	Engine
40	12	68	Larry Baumel	Auto Lad '69 Ford	9	550	Suspen

Time of Race: 4 hours, 3 minutes, 40 seconds
Average Speed: 123.119 mph
Pole Winner: Richard Petty - 129.486 mph
Lap Leaders: Richard Petty 1, Bobby Isaac 2-54, Pete Hamilton 55-82, Bobby Allison 83-85, Buddy Baker 86-88, Hamilton 89-90, Allison 91-102, Hamilton 103-137, Petty 138-164, Baker 165-183, Petty 184-185, Allison 186-226, Fred Lorenzen 227-272, Allison 273-276, Lorenzen 277-281, Allison 282-290, Lorenzen 291-313, Allison 314-372, Lorenzen 373-380, Allison 381-457, Lorenzen 458-460, Allison 461-500.
Cautions: None
Margin of Victory: 1-lap plus
Attendance: 25,000
Relief Drivers: Bobby Isaac relieved Fred Lorenzen; Buddy Baker relieved Richard Petty; Pete Hamilton relieved Bobby Isaac; Dick May relieved Bobby Mausgrover; Henley Gray relieved Jabe Thomas.

put on a charge from 21st starting position. Isaac punched the car into the lead in the late stages, but Allison roared home a lap and a half in front. Lorenzen got credit for finishing second. Richard Petty's Plymouth, with Buddy Baker at the helm, took third. Isaac's Dodge, which was driven in the second half of the race by Pete Hamilton, came in fourth. G.C. Spencer was

Bobby Allison flashes under the checkered flag at Dover

fifth.

The 500-miler was run without a caution flag -- the first time since the 1963 Southern 500 at Darlington that a 500-miler had been uninterrupted by the yellow flag.

Allison kept his red and gold Mercury on top for 245 laps. Petty had won the pole for the 97th time in his career.

A crowd of 25,000 watched Allison average 123.119 mph.

Race No. 23

Allison Mans Mercury To Michigan 400 Victory

BROOKLYN, MI (June 13) -- Bobby Allison toyed with Bobby Isaac until the final two laps, then pulled away for his third straight superspeedway win at Michigan International Speedway. Allison's victory in the Motor State 400 moved the Hueytown, AL driver into fifth place in the point standings.

Isaac led briefly near the end of the 197-lap event on the 2.04-mile oval. But he was no match for Allison in the last two laps. He finished two car lengths behind. Pete Hamilton came in third, Donnie Allison was fourth and Buddy Baker fifth.

Winston Cup GN Race No.23
197 Laps at Michigan Int'l Speedway
Brooklyn, MI
"Motor State 400"
400 Miles on 2.04-mile Paved Track
June 13, 1971

Fin	St	No.	Driver	Team / Car	Laps	Money	Status
1	1	12	Bobby Allison	Holman-Moody '69 Mercury	197	$14,945	Running
2	4	71	Bobby Isaac	K&K Insurance '71 Dodge	197	7,620	Running
3	3	6	Pete Hamilton	Cotton Owens '71 Plymouth	197	4,920	Running
4	2	21	Donnie Allison	Wood Brothers '69 Mercury	197	2,945	Running
5	5	11	Buddy Baker	Petty Ent '71 Dodge	195	1,945	Running
6	7	43	Richard Petty	Petty Ent '71 Plymouth	194	1,495	Running
7	6	99	Fred Lorenzen	Nichels-Goldsmith '71 Plym	193	1,320	Running
8	10	22	Dick Brooks	Mario Rossi '70 Dodge	193	1,220	Running
9	9	2	Dave Marcis	Marcis '69 Dodge	191	1,120	Running
10	14	88	Ron Keselowski	Roger Lubinski '70 Dodge	189	1,020	Running
11	18	76	Ben Arnold	Arnold '69 Ford	188	1,020	Running
12	22	48	James Hylton	Hylton Eng '69 Mercury	188	970	Running
13	13	06	Neil Castles	Castles '70 Dodge	188	945	Running
14	28	5	Ron Grana	C J Grana '70 Chevrolet	187	920	Running
15	25	18	Joe Frasson	Frasson '70 Dodge	185	895	Running
16	21	25	Jabe Thomas	Don Robertson '70 Plymouth	185	870	Running
17	24	30	Walter Ballard	Vic Ballard '71 Ford	185	850	Running
18	39	03	Tommy Gale	Larry Jackson '69 Mercury	185	840	Running
19	12	24	Cecil Gordon	Gordon '69 Mercury	184	825	Running
20	36	7	Dean Dalton	Dalton '69 Ford	183	810	Running
21	26	19	Henley Gray	Gray '69 Ford	180	795	Running
22	35	64	Elmo Langley	Langley '69 Mercury	179	780	Running
23	40	8	Ed Negre	Negre '69 Ford	174	765	Running
24	20	0	George Altheide	'70 Plymouth	164	750	Running
25	38	70	J D McDuffie	McDuffie '69 Mercury	156	735	Running
26	30	95	Paul Tyler	Tyler '69 Mercury	128	720	Engine
27	32	07	Coo Coo Marlin	Cunningham-Kelley '69 Chev	122	760	Engine
28	11	72	Benny Parsons	L G DeWitt '70 Mercury	121	700	Engine
29	31	79	Frank Warren	Warren '69 Dodge	118	690	Engine
30	15	60	Maynard Troyer	Nagle Racers '69 Mercury	85	680	Valve
31	33	10	Bill Champion	Champion '71 Ford	79	685	Valve
32	8	39	Friday Hassler	Hassler '70 Chevrolet	76	655	Rock Arm
33	19	33	David Pearson	C V Enterprises '71 Pontiac	68	650	Ignition
34	17	90	Bill Dennis	Junie Donlavey '69 Mercury	65	695	Engine
35	23	47	Raymond Williams	Williams '71 Ford	42	640	Oil Leak
36	34	4	John Sears	Sears '69 Dodge	28	660	H Gasket
37	29	86	Bobby Mausgrover	Neil Castles '69 Dodge	17	630	Piston
38	37	45	Bill Seifert	Seifert '70 Ford	16	625	Oil Press
39	16	77	Charlie Roberts	Roberts '70 Ford	1	620	D Shaft
40	27	67	Dick May	Ron Ronacher '69 Ford	0	615	Clutch

Time of Race: 2 hours, 41 minutes, 13 seconds
Average Speed: 149.567 mph
Pole Winner: Bobby Allison - 161.190 mph
Lap Leaders: Bobby Allison 1-7, Donnie Allison 8, B.Allison 9, D.Allison 10-13,
    Bobby Isaac 14-18, D.Allison 19-22, Isaac 23-26, D.Allison 27-45, Pete Hamilton 46-47
    Fred Lorenzen 48-50, D.Allison 51-94, Isaac 95-97, D.Allison 98-99, Hamilton 100-105,
    D.Allison 106-114, B.Allison 115-121, D.Allison 122-123, B.Allison 124,
    D.Allison 125-127, Isaac 128, B.Allison 129-133, D.Allison 134-135, B.Allison 136-146,
    D.Allison 147-149, Isaac 150, Hamilton 151-156, B.Allison 157-173, Isaac 174-179,
    B.Allison 180-188, Isaac 189-192, B.Allison 193-194, Isaac 195, B.Allison 196-197.
Cautions: 2 for 13 laps   Margin of Victory: 2 car lengths   Attendance: 37,583

After the race, Nord Krauskopf, Isaac's car owner, said he was pulling the defending Grand National champion off the tour. "We have had it with the carburetor plate," said the insurance tycoon. "We will not run again until August 1. At that time we will make an assessment of the program and make a final decision later. There comes a time when you can no longer let people take advantage of you."

Krauskopf's complaint centered around the NASCAR rules, which permit different size carburetor openings for different engines. "The 426 c.i. Hemi engine we use is restricted to 1 1/4 inch opening," said Krauskopf, "whereas the Fords are allowed to have a 1 1/2 inch plate. It's not fair."

Isaac and rival Richard Petty agreed. "When it came time for them (Mercurys) to run," said Isaac, "they took off. I was just being played with."

Petty chided, "The Ford engine gets 44% more air than our 426. There's no way we can run with them."

Allison said the opposition was just letting off steam. "Some people just go crying around when they're not in front," he said. "I've lost a lot of races and been beaten badly, but I didn't need any excuses."

Neil Castles said he was going to shift over to the USAC stock car tour. He entered a Dodge Daytona in the USAC event at Milwaukee a few days after the Michigan race.

Allison averaged 149.567 mph before a crowd of 37,583.

Race No. 24

Allison's Dodge Dominant At Riverside

RIVERSIDE, CA (June 20) --Bobby Allison pushed his Dodge around Ray Elder with 34 laps remaining and drove to a big victory in the Winston Golden State 400 at Riverside International Raceway. It was the fourth win in a row for Allison.

Elder finished second, 59.3 seconds behind the winner. Cecil Gordon came in third, James Hylton was fourth and Jerry Oliver fifth.

Allison used the latest in technology in his independently owned Dodge. "I was wired for sound," said Allison. "I had a radio hook-up with my brother Eddie in the pits and it helped a lot. There was one wreck which had the track almost blocked. The caution never came out. My crew hollered at me about the wreck, so I was on my toes. I got by without any trouble. If I hadn't known about it, I might have plowed right into it."

Allison led for 136 of the 153 laps. Hershel McGriff, Richard Petty and Elder led briefly, but could not match Allison's speed.

Kevin Terris finished seventh in a Plymouth. Terris, the Winston West Rookie of the Year in 1970, got out of the car after 90 miles. He turned the wheel over to Dick Bown, who later called on relief from Cliff Garner. Garner pitted on lap 113 and turned the wheel over to McGriff. NASCAR officials stepped in and disallowed the fourth driver. Garner, weary from the 101 degree heat, finished the race, eight laps behind.

A slim crowd of 18,700 watched Allison win his 23rd career race at an average speed of 93.427 mph.

Winston Cup GN Race No. 24
153 Laps at Riverside Int'l Raceway
Riverside, CA
"Winston Golden State 400"
400 Miles on 2.62-mile Paved Road Course
June 20, 1971

Fin	St	No.	Driver	Team / Car	Laps	Money	Status
1	1	12	Bobby Allison	Allison '70 Dodge	153	$14,395	Running
2	3	96	Ray Elder	Fred Elder '71 Dodge	153	7,695	Running
3	11	24	Cecil Gordon	Gordon '69 Mercury	147	4,595	Running
4	8	48	James Hylton	Hylton Eng '70 Ford	146	2,870	Running
5	31	6	Jerry Oliver	Cos Cancilla '70 Dodge	145	1,945	Running
6	25	08	John Soares, Jr	Soares '71 Plymouth	145	1,495	Running
7	7	32	Kevin Terris	Dean Barnicle '70 Plymouth	144	1,320	Running
8	22	1	Scotty Cain	'69 Ford	143	1,270	Running
9	14	99	Pay Fay	'71 Ford	136	1,120	Running
10	19	00	Frank James	Jim Calder '69 Chevrolet	135	1,020	Running
11	9	7	Jack McCoy	Ernie Conn '71 Dodge	127	995	Engine
12	37	18	Bob England	England '70 Chevrolet	126	970	Suspen
13	2	43	Richard Petty	Petty Ent '71 Plymouth	110	1,020	Engine
14	21	70	J D McDuffie	McDuffie '69 Mercury	107	995	Running
15	29	88	Don Noel	'71 Ford	99	895	Flagged
16	39	07	Ivan Baldwin	'71 Chevrolet	98	870	Flagged
17	12	38	Jimmy Insolo	Marvin Rowley '69 Chevrolet	91	850	Engine
18	15	19	Henley Gray	Gray '69 Ford	90	840	Axle
19	24	77	Charlie Roberts	Roberts '70 Ford	89	825	Crash
20	20	74	Ray Johnstone	'69 Plymouth	79	810	Rear End
21	6	04	Hershel McGriff	Beryl Jackson '70 Plymouth	78	795	Engine
22	4	72	Benny Parsons	L G DeWitt '70 Mercury	76	780	Crash
23	30	4	Dick Kranzler	Kranzler '71 Chevrolet	59	765	Radiator
24	32	62	Tru Cheek	'69 Chevrolet	57	750	Suspen
25	26	82	Ron Gautsche	Gautsche '69 Ford	48	735	Heating
26	35	9	Bill Osborne	'71 Ford	37	720	Engine
27	10	64	Elmo Langley	Langley '69 Mercury	35	710	Engine
28	28	83	John Lyons	'69 Chevrolet	35	700	Crash
29	17	91	John Anderson	'69 Chevrolet	34	690	Engine
30	33	55	Jerry Barnett	'70 Chevrolet	32	680	Engine
31	23	26	Carl Joiner	Dean Thorne '69 Chevrolet	31	685	Wtr pump
32	27	34	Harry Schilling	'69 Dodge	31	655	Oil Leak
33	38	15	Paul Dorrity	'71 Chevrolet	24	650	Engine
34	18	01	Pete Torres	'69 Ford	19	645	Engine
35	34	47	J R Skinner	'71 Ford	17	640	Engine
36	13	79	Frank Warren	Warren '69 Dodge	10	635	Engine
37	36	95	Bob Kauf	Paul Stockwell '70 Chevrolet	8	630	Engine
38	40	8	Ed Negre	Negre '69 Ford	6	625	Steering
39	5	02	Dick Bown	Mike Ober '71 Plymouth	2	620	Engine
40	16	10	Mike James	Jim Calder '69 Chevrolet	1	615	Engine

Time of Race: 4 hours, 17 minutes, 5 seconds
Average Speed: 93.427 mph
Pole Winner: Bobby Allison - 107.315 mph
Lap Leaders: Bobby Allison 1-15, Hershel McGriff 16, Allison 17-33, Richard Petty 34-35, McGriff 36, Ray Elder 37-38, Petty 39-40, Allison 41-44, McGriff 45, Benny Parsons 46-51, Allison 52-116, Elder 117, Allison 118-153.
Cautions: 6 for 32 laps   Margin of Victory: 59.3 seconds   Attendance: 18,700
Relief Drivers: Dick Bown and Cliff Garner relieved Kevin Terris; Dick Gulstrand relieved Jimmy Insolo; Sam Beler relieved John Lyons, Bill Butts relieved Jerry Barnett.

Race No. 25

Allison Grabs 5th Straight In Space City 300

HOUSTON, TX (June 23) -- Bobby Allison nudged past James Hylton in the 157th lap and sped to victory

Winston Cup GN Race No. 25
300 Laps at Meyer Speedway
Houston, TX
"Space City 300"
150 Miles on Half-mile Paved Track
June 23, 1971

Fin	St	No.	Driver	Team / Car	Laps	Money	Status
1	1	12	Bobby Allison	Allison '70 Dodge	300	$2,200	Running
2	14	48	James Hylton	Hylton Eng '70 Ford	298	1,500	Running
3	11	30	Walter Ballard	Vic Ballard '71 Ford	292	1,000	Running
4	3	64	Elmo Langley	Langley '69 Mercury	290	700	Running
5	36	36	Frank Warren	H B Bailey '70 Pontiac	289	650	Running
6	7	24	Cecil Gordon	Gordon '69 Mercury	286	550	Running
7	2	43	Richard Petty	Petty Ent '71 Plymouth	279	475	Running
8	10	19	Henley Gray	Gray '69 Ford	270	450	Running
9	8	77	Charlie Roberts	Roberts '70 Ford	254	425	Running
10	6	70	J D McDuffie	McDuffie '69 Mercury	249	400	Running
11	4	8	Ed Negre	Negre '69 Ford	239	370	Running
12	12	00	Ronnie Chumley	'69 Ford	136	360	Trans
13	9	14	Fred Hill	'69 Ford	116	350	Rear End
14	13	3	Pete Arnold	'70 Ford	58	340	Steering

Time of Race: 2 hours, 2 minutes, 28 seconds
Average Speed: 73.489 mph
Pole Winner: Bobby Allison 78.226 mph
Lap Leaders: Richard Petty 1-4, Bobby Allison 5-8, Petty 9-42, Allison 43-147,
    James Hylton 148-156, Allison 157-300.
Cautions: None   Margin of Victory: 2-laps plus   Attendance: 9,000

Race No. 26

Allison Crashes New Ford; Petty Wins Pickens 200

GREENVILLE, SC (June 26) -- Bobby Allison's bid for his sixth win of the season was foiled by a blown engine, and Richard Petty snared his 10th win of the year in the Pickens 200.

Allison was unveiling a new 1971 Holman-Moody Ford at Greenville-Pickens Speedway. He led all but one of the first 107 laps when his engine blew, sending him into the guard rail. He had to settle for 20th place in the final order.

Petty took over and held off Tiny Lund's surprising effort to win the 200 lapper. Lund finished second, Bill

in the Space City 300 at Meyer Speedway in Houston. It was the fifth straight win for Allison, and his second in his own Dodge.

"Holman-Moody didn't enter their car on this Westward trip," said Allison. "I went back to my Dodge. It's funny, earlier in the year, my Dodge wouldn't finish a race. It kept breaking down. I'm not doing anything different now. Sometimes it's strange how your luck turns around."

Hylton finished in second place and trimmed Richard Petty's point lead to 101 points. Leading rookie driver Walter Ballard came in third with Elmo Langley fourth and Frank Warren fifth.

Petty struggled to finish seventh, 21 laps behind.

Only 14 cars entered the race and 11 were running at the finish.

In other news, L.G. DeWitt, car owner for Benny Parsons, announced he was pulling his cars off the Winston Cup tour. "We've had a lot of problems and it looks like we can't get things to go right for us," said DeWitt. "I just decided to quit."

Mario Rossi, owner of the Dodge Dick Brooks had driven in 1971, also tossed in the towel. "I find it financially unfeasible to independently support a car on the Grand National circuit," said Rossi. "I'm in the process of selling my race car and all related parts."

Winston Cup GN Race No. 26
200 Laps at Greenville-Pickens Speedway
Greenville, SC
"Pickens 200"
100 Miles on Half-mile Paved Track
June 26, 1971

Fin	St	No.	Driver	Team / Car	Lap	Money	Status
1	2	43	Richard Petty	Petty Ent' 71 Plymouth	200	$1,500	Running
2	4	55	Tiny Lund	John McConnell '70 Dodge	199	900	Running
3	3	90	Bill Dennis	Junie Donlavey '69 Mercury	199	500	Running
4	8	64	Elmo Langley	Langley '71 Ford	197	350	Running
5	16	30	Walter Ballard	Vic Ballard '71 Ford	197	325	Running
6	12	45	Bill Seifert	Seifert '69 Ford	194	300	Running
7	18	79	Frank Warren	Warren '69 Dodge	189	275	Running
8	21	34	Wendell Scott	Scott '69 Ford	189	270	Running
9	13	24	Cecil Gordon	Gordon '69 Mercury	189	265	Running
10	27	7	Dean Dalton	Dalton '69 Ford	188	260	Running
11	7	32	Marv Acton	Dick Brooks '69 Plym	187	255	Running
12	15	48	James Hylton	Hylton Eng '70 Ford	187	250	Running
13	26	25	Jabe Thomas	Don Robertson '70 Plymouth	183	245	Running
14	6	10	Bill Champion	Champion '71 Ford	180	240	Fuel pmp
15	25	13	Eddie Yarboro	Yarboro '69 Plymouth	179	235	Running
16	10	8	Ed Negre	Negre '69 Ford	169	230	Running
17	24	41	Ken Meisenhelder	Meisenhelder '69 Chevrolet	160	225	Running
18	19	26	Earl Brooks	Brooks '69 Ford	123	220	Trans
19	14	06	Neil Castles	Castles '70 Dodge	108	215	Crash
20	1	12	Bobby Allison	Holman-Moody '71 Ford	108	210	Engine
21	23	19	Henley Gray	Gray '69 Ford	100	205	Ignition
22	17	74	Bill Shirey	Shirey '69 Plymouth	92	200	Engine
23	11	96	Richard Childress	Tom Garn '71 Chevrolet	77	200	Alternator
24	9	70	J D McDuffie	McDuffie '69 Mercury	60	200	Rear End
25	22	67	Dick May	Ron Ronacher '69 Ford	60	200	Heating
26	20	40	D K Ulrich	Ulrich '70 Ford	32	200	Oil Leak
27	5	4	John Sears	Sears '69 Ford	31	200	Heating
28	28	58	Bob Brown	Allan Brown '71 Chevrolet	31	200	Fuel pmp
29	29	05	Ernest Eury	'69 Chevrolet	1	200	Flagged

Time of Race: 1 hour, 23 minutes,
Average Speed: 74.297 mph
Pole Winner: Bobby Allison - 81.555 mph
Lap Leaders: Bobby Allison 1-47, Bill Dennis 48, Allison 49-107, Richard Petty 108-109,
    Tiny Lund 110, Petty 111, Lund 112-114, Petty 115-200.
Cautions: 3 for 15 laps   Margin of victory: 1lap plus Under Caution   Attendance: 4,000

Dennis was third and Elmo Langley fourth. Fifth place went to Walter Ballard.

"The only thing that bothered me was when Bobby's engine blew," said Petty. "I was lucky to miss him. I was just a matter of inches behind him. I still don't know how I got by."

Neil Castles decided against moving over to the USAC stock car tour, as he had announced the preceding week. Sour luck continued for the Charlotte Dodge driver when he wrecked on lap 108.

Petty averaged 74.297 mph for his 129th career win.

Race No. 27

Bobby Isaac Enters Late; Wins Firecracker 400 With New Wedge Engine

DAYTONA BEACH, FL (July 4) -- Bobby Isaac, an 11th hour entrant, started deep in the field and came on strong to win the Firecracker 400 at Daytona International Speedway. It was only the second career superspeedway triumph for the 38 year-old Dodge driver.

Bobby Isaac and K&K Insurance crew celebrate Firecracker 400 victory

Isaac beat runner-up Richard Petty by four seconds to gain his third win of the season. He ran the final five laps with two of the three hood pins broken. The right side of the hood was flapping in the breeze as Isaac crossed under the checkered flag.

Isaac and crew chief Harry Hyde did not show up at the track until 48 hours before the start of the race. Isaac had been pulled off the NASCAR tour when car owner Nord Krauskopf engaged in a cold war with the

Winston Cup GN Race No. 27
160 Laps at Daytona Int'l Speedway
Daytona Beach, FL
"Firecracker 400"
400 Miles on 2.5-mile Paved Track
July 4, 1971

Fin	St	No.	Driver	Team / Car	Laps	Money	Status
1	21	71	Bobby Isaac	K&K Insurance '71 Dodge	160	$16,450	Running
2	4	43	Richard Petty	Petty Ent '71 Plymouth	160	8,825	Running
3	2	11	Buddy Baker	Petty Ent '71 Dodge	160	6,325	Running
4	8	6	Pete Hamilton	Cotton Owens '71 Plymouth	160	3,275	Running
5	1	21	Donnie Allison	Wood Brothers '69 Mercury	160	2,200	Running
6	5	12	Bobby Allison	Holman-Moody '69 Mercury	159	1,600	Running
7	6	99	Fred Lorenzen	Nichels-Goldsmith '71 Plym	158	1,375	Running
8	7	17	David Pearson	C V Enterprises '71 Plymouth	157	1,250	Running
9	20	48	James Hylton	Hylton Eng '71 Ford	155	1,150	Running
10	11	39	Friday Hassler	Hassler '70 Chevrolet	154	1,175	Running
11	9	90	Bill Dennis	Junie Donlavey '69 Mercury	152	1,015	Running
12	32	53	Bobby Brack	Hopper-Crews '69 Ford	151	990	Running
13	13	88	Ron Keselowski	Roger Lubinski '70 Dodge	151	1,015	Running
14	15	60	Maynard Troyer	Nagle Racers '69 Mercury	151	965	Running
15	12	18	Joe Frasson	Frasson '70 Dodge	151	990	Running
16	39	46	Roy Mayne	Tom Hunter '69 Chevrolet	150	885	Running
17	18	24	Cecil Gordon	Gordon '69 Mercury	149	860	Running
18	26	25	Jabe Thomas	Don Robertson '70 Plymouth	149	860	Running
19	22	79	Frank Warren	Warren '69 Dodge	148	865	Running
20	16	0	George Altheide	'70 Dodge	148	825	Running
21	34	92	Larry Smith	Harley Smith '69 Ford	147	790	Running
22	35	7	Dean Dalton	Dalton '69 Ford	147	780	Running
23	29	76	Ben Arnold	Arnold '69 Ford	147	770	Running
24	23	45	Bill Seifert	Seifert '71 Ford	145	785	Running
25	30	47	Raymond Williams	Williams '71 Ford	145	750	Running
26	38	86	Bill Champion*	Neil Castles '69 Dodge	141	740	Running
27	14	64	Elmo Langley**	Langley '69 Mercury	120	755	Heating
28	40	68	Larry Baumel	Auto Lad '69 Ford	116	720	Running
29	37	77	Charlie Roberts	Roberts '70 Ford	103	710	D Shaft
30	28	4	John Sears	Sears '69 Dodge	94	705	Engine
31	36	07	Coo Coo Marlin	Cunningham-Kelley '69 Chev	93	695	Engine
32	19	30	Walter Ballard	Vic Ballard '71 Ford	85	685	Engine
33	24	55	Tiny Lund	'69 Mercury	80	705	Crash
34	31	2	Dave Marcis	Marcis '69 Dodge	70	675	Ignition
35	33	70	J D McDuffie	McDuffie '69 Mercury	49	670	Trans
36	17	91	Ed Negre	Junior Fields '71 Chevrolet	44	665	Battery
37	3	3	Charlie Glotzbach	Richard Howard '71 Chevrolet	43	735	Engine
38	10	52	A J Foyt	Holman-Moody '69 Mercury	33	655	Quit
39	27	06	Neil Castles	Castles '70 Dodge	19	650	Sway Bar
40	25	15	Dr Don Tarr	'70 Ford	18	670	Engine

Time of Race: 2 hours, 28 minutes, 12 seconds
Average Speed: 161.947 mph
Pole Winner: Donnie Allison - 183.228 mph
Lap Leaders: Charlie Glotzbach 1, Buddy Baker 2, Donnie Allison 3-4, Baker 5, D.Allison 6, Bobby Allison 7, Baker 8, B.Allison 9-10, Baker 11-12, B.Allison 13, Baker 14-20, D.Allison 21, Baker 22-29, B.Allison 30-31, Baker 32-38, Friday Hassler 39-42, Richard Petty 43-61, Bobby Isaac 62-71, Petty 72, Baker 73-74, Petty 75-86, Baker 87-88, Pete Hamilton 89-91, Petty 92-95, Isaac 96, Petty 97-98, Isaac 99-102, Petty 103, Baker 104-106, Isaac 107-125, Petty 126-132, Baker 133, Hamilton 134-135, Isaac 136-160.
Cautions: 2 for 11 laps   Margin of Victory: 4 seconds   Attendance: 63,000
*Relieved by Bobby Mausgrover   **Relieved by Bill Champion

sanctioning body over carburetor plate sizes.

Hyde built a Chrysler Wedge engine for the Firecracker. "I had begged Nord earlier to let me come down here and experiment with the wedge engine," said Hyde. "But there were a lot of people reluctant to try it. I didn't get word that we were racing until Friday at 2:00 am."

Isaac overcame a 30 second pit stop to take the lead on lap 136 of the 160 lap contest. He built up a lead of

10 seconds with five laps to go. Then a hood pin broke.

NASCAR officials reached for the black flag, but didn't wave it at Isaac. "I wasn't worried about the black flag," said Isaac. "I knew if I made a pit stop, I'd lose. So I gave it our best shot. That was to stay out there on the track and hope the hood didn't fly off."

Buddy Baker finished in third place with Pete Hamilton fourth. Fifth place went to pole sitter Donnie Allison. The cars of Petty, Baker and Hamilton were also equipped with a Chrysler wedge engine.

Allison's car owner Glen Wood, levied a blast at the latest rules. "The Chrysler Wedge is allowed to have a 1 5/8 inch opening," cried Wood. "But we are only allowed to have 1 1/2 inches. We're getting a raw deal,"

Junior Johnson, manager of Richard Howard's Chevrolet team, said his engine should have the largest opening. "We've got the most stock engine out there," said Johnson. "But they have a bigger plate."

NASCAR President Bill France rifled a shot of his own at the complaint-plagued 1971 season. "When everybody's complaining," said Big Bill, "the rules must be all right."

Isaac won the 400-miler at an average speed of 161.947 mph.

David Pearson drove a C V Enterprises Plymouth and finished eighth. He was under strict orders from Chris Vallo not to win the race in a Plymouth. "Our Pontiac is not ready," said Vallo. "So we had to run a Plymouth. I told David if he was leading the race, I'd pull his pit crew out. He couldn't have won the race if he didn't have anyone in the pits."

Race No. 28

Glotzbach and Hassler Win at Bristol in Howard Chevrolet

BRISTOL, TN (July 11) -- Charlie Glotzbach and relief driver Friday Hassler shared the glory as Chevrolet returned to the winner's circle for the first time in three years.

The Chevrolet, owned by Charlotte Motor Speedway General Manager Richard Howard and prepared by Junior Johnson, led for 411 of the 500 laps in the Volunteer 500 at Bristol International Speedway.

Glotzbach took the lead from Richard Petty in the 44th lap and led through lap 255. When Glotzbach wheeled the white Chevy down pit road, Friday Hassler was standing by. Hassler drove the car the rest of the distance.

Hassler lost the lead to Bobby Allison on three occa-

Winston Cup GN Race No. 28
500 Laps at Bristol Int'l Speedway
Bristol, TN
"Volunteer 500"
266.5 Miles on .533-mile Paved Track
July 11, 1971

Fin	St	No.	Driver	Team / Car	Laps	Money	Status
1	2	3	Charlie Glotzbach	Richard Howard '71 Chevrolet	500	$5,675	Running
2	3	12	Bobby Allison	Holman-Moody '70 Ford	497	3,450	Running
3	1	43	Richard Petty	Petty Ent '71 Plymouth	494	2,575	Running
4	10	24	Cecil Gordon	Gordon '69 Mercury	477	1,200	Running
5	8	48	James Hylton	Hylton Eng '70 Ford	473	1,025	Running
6	12	67	Elmo Langley	Ron Ronacher '69 Ford	465	865	Running
7	15	77	Frank Warren	Charlie Roberts '71 Ford	464	800	Running
8	9	10	Bill Champion	Champion '71 Ford	454	675	Running
9	18	70	J D McDuffie	McDuffie '69 Mercury	450	625	Running
10	30	25	Jabe Thomas	Don Robertson '70 Plymouth	445	600	Running
11	15	30	Walter Ballard	Vic Ballard '71 Ford	445	580	Running
12	24	19	Henley Gray	Gray '69 Ford	432	550	Running
13	29	4	John Sears	Sears '69 Dodge	420	540	Running
14	7	07	Coo Coo Marlin	Cunningham-Kelley '69 Chev	369	530	Heating
15	13	32	Bill Dennis	Dick Brooks '69 Plymouth	328	545	Lug Boit
16	18	37	Dr Don Tarr	Tarr '71 Dodge	238	510	Alternator
17	5	88	Ron Keselowski	Roger Lubinski '70 Dodge	262	525	Spindle
18	26	26	Earl Brooks	Brooks '69 Ford	168	490	Rear End
19	23	7	Dean Dalton	Dalton '69 Ford	167	480	Lug Bolt
20	16	41	Ken Meisenhelder	Meisenhelder '69 Chevrolet	131	470	Vibration
21	11	39	Friday Hassler	Hassler '70 Chevrolet	104	520	W Bearing
22	25	95	Paul Tyler	Tyler '69 Mercury	70	450	Rear End
23	17	45	Bill Seifert	Seifert '71 Ford	63	440	Heating
24	6	49	G C Spencer	Spencer '69 Plymouth	59	430	Engine
25	27	8	Ed Negre	Negre '69 Ford	40	420	Engine
26	28	38	Wayne Smith	Smith '69 Chevrolet	18	415	Crash
27	22	47	Raymond Williams	Williams '71 Ford	18	405	Quit
28	4	91	Richard Brown	Junior Fields '71 Ford	12	420	Trans
29	20	64	Dick May	Elmo Langley '71 Ford	6	385	Quit
30	21	74	Bill Shirey	Shirey '69 Plymouth	5	375	Ignition

Time of Race: 2 hours, 38 minutes, 12 seconds
Average Speed: 101.074 mph
Pole Winner: Richard Petty - 104.589 mph
Lap Leaders: Richard Petty 1-43, Charlie Glotzbach 44-255, Bobby Allison 256-280, Glotzbach 281-282, Allison 283-297, Glotzbach 298-350, Allison 351-356, Glotzbach 357-500.
Cautions: None   Margin of Victory: 3-laps plus   Attendance: 20,500
Relief Drivers: Friday Hassler relieved Charlie Glotzbach; James Hylton relieved by Bobby Allison; Buddy Baker relieved Richard Petty; G C Spencer relieved James Hylton; Charlie Roberts relieved Frank Warren; Marv Acton relieved Bill Dennis.

sions, but fought back and won by three laps. Allison's Ford, with James Hylton at the wheel, came in second. Petty and Buddy Baker teamed to take third place honors. Cecil Gordon was fourth and Hylton's car, with G.C. Spencer manning the controls, came in fifth.

Victory for the Johnson-tuned car came in its third start. "I thought we'd win all the races," said Johnson. "We take the car where the promoter is willing to pay for it. But if we get to winning most of the races, that

Friday Hassler provided a crucial assist and earned a trip to victory lane

Charlie Glotzbach and chassis man Herb Nab. The Chevrolet team got its first win at Bristol

Hassler averaged 101.074 mph in the caution-free event. A crowd of 20,500 was on hand.

Race No. 29

Petty Overcomes Deficit; Beats Marcis at Malta

MALTA, NY (July 14) -- Richard Petty battled back from a lap behind, passed Dave Marcis and won the Albany-Saratoga 250 at Albany-Saratoga Speedway.

Petty fell a lap off the pace when he made a green flag pit stop and got caught by the caution light. The Randleman, NC Plymouth driver fought back, passed Marcis on lap 156 and led the rest of the way. J.D. McDuffie enjoyed his best Winston Cup Grand National finish by taking third place. James Hylton was fourth and Elmo Langley fifth.

"You never give up," said Petty, who won for the 11th time in 1971. "You may give out, but never give up. We had a good car and I knew I could make it up."

A big field of 34 cars started the 250 lapper on the .362-mile paved oval. Petty led the first 58 laps before McDuffie drove into first place. McDuffie held the lead for five laps before Pete Hamilton assumed command. Marcis gained the upper hand on lap 68 and led most of the way while Petty was making his catch-up run.

Hamilton qualified second in a lightly regarded Chevrolet and led twice for five laps. The Dedham, MA

driver went out on lap 82 with transmission failure.

Petty averaged 66.748 mph. A crowd of 7,000 watched from the bleachers.

Race No. 30

Scoring Error Shaves Islip 250; Petty Still Wins

ISLIP, NY (July 15) -- An embarrassing scoring mistake shaved 20 laps off the scheduled Islip 250, but it didn't matter to Richard Petty. Petty led all the way and was in front when the checkered flag was mistakenly dropped at 230 laps.

"Don't tell nobody about them 20 laps they forgot to

Winston Cup GN Race No. 29
250 Laps at Albany-Saratoga Speedway
Malta, NY
"Albany-Saratoga 250"
90.5 Miles on .362-mile Paved Track
July 14, 1971

Fin	St	No.	Driver	Team / Car	Laps	Money	Status
1	1	43	Richard Petty	Petty Ent '71 Plymouth	250	$1,500	Running
2	4	2	Dave Marcis	Marcis '69 Dodge	248	900	Running
3	6	70	J D McDuffie	McDuffie '69 Mercury	244	500	Running
4	9	48	James Hylton	Hylton Eng '71 Ford	243	350	Running
5	18	67	Elmo Langley	Ron Ronacher '69 Ford	242	325	Running
6	8	10	Bill Champion	Champion '71 Ford	240	300	Running
7	10	34	Wendell Scott	Scott '69 Ford	240	275	Running
8	19	24	Cecil Gordon	Gordon '69 Mercury	240	270	Running
9	26	88	Ron Keselowski	Roger Lubinski '70 Dodge	239	265	Running
10	25	8	Ed Negre	Negre '69 Ford	239	260	Running
11	23	77	Charlie Roberts	Roberts '70 Ford	236	255	Running
12	22	19	Henley Gray	Gray '69 Ford	235	250	Running
13	11	30	Walter Ballard	Vic Ballard '71 Ford	233	245	Running
14	13	74	Bill Shirey	Shirey '69 Plymouth	221	240	Running
15	33		Jerry Churchill	'69 Ford	216	235	Running
16	29	45	Bill Seifert	Seifert '70 Ford	207	230	Rear End
17	28	41	Ken Meisenhelder	Meisenhelder '69 Chevrolet	191	225	Ignition
18	15	23	Jabe Thomas	Don Robertson '69 Plymouth	189	220	Vibration
19	31	28	Bill Hollar	Earl Brooks '69 Ford	165	215	Brakes
20	3	12	Bobby Allison	Holman-Moody '69 Mercury	144	210	Engine
21	7	39	Friday Hassler	Hassler '70 Chevrolet	130	205	Vibration
22	14	68	Larry Baumel	Auto Lad '69 Ford	130	200	Engine
23	27	64	Dick May	Elmo Langley '69 Mercury	123	100	Brakes
24	5	49	G C Spencer	Spencer '69 Plymouth	105	100	Rear End
25	20	79	Frank Warren	Warren '69 Dodge	97	100	Axle
26	30	6	Dr Ed Hessert	Neil Castles '69 Dodge	94	100	Suspen
27	2	91	Pete Hamilton	Junior Fields '71 Plymouth	82	100	Trans
28	17	96	Richard Childress	Tom Garn '70 Chevrolet	75	100	Trans
29	21	86	Bobby Mausgrover	Neil Castles '69 Dodge	53	100	Brakes
30	16	4	John Sears	Sears '69 Dodge	36	100	Engine
31	12	62	Rene Charland	Kaye Eng '69 Dodge	33	100	Brakes
32	32	40	D K Ulrich	Ulrich '70 Ford	27	100	Flat tire
33	24	06	Neil Castles	Castles '70 Dodge	13	100	Trans
34	34	25	James Cox	Don Robertson '69 Plymouth	1	100	Quit

Time of Race: 1 hour, 21 minutes, 21 seconds
Average Speed: 66.748 mph
Pole Winner: Richard Petty - 74.896 mph
Lap Leaders: Richard Petty 1-58, J D McDuffie 59-63, Pete Hamilton 64-67,
    Dave Marcis 68-69, Hamilton 70, Petty 71-98, Marcis 99-155, Petty 156-250.
Cautions: 2 for 10 laps   Margin of Victory: 2-laps plus   Attendance: 7,000

Winston Cup GN Race No. 30
250 Laps at Islip Speedway
Islip, NY
"Islip 250"
50 Miles on .2-mile Paved Track
July 15, 1971

Fin	St	No.	Driver	Team / Car	Laps	Money	Status
1	1	43	Richard Petty	Petty Ent '71 Plymouth	230	$1,500	Running
2	4	39	Friday Hassler	Hassler '70 Chevrolet	228	900	Running
3	9	67	Elmo Langley	Langley '69 Mercury	224	500	Running
4	2	12	Bobby Allison	Holman-Moody '69 Mercury	223	350	Running
5	14	49	G C Spencer	Spencer '69 Plymouth	222	325	Running
6	7	48	James Hylton	Hylton Eng '71 Ford	222	300	Running
7	6	6	Neil Castles	Castles '69 Dodge	221	275	Running
8	12	24	Cecil Gordon	Gordon '69 Mercury	220	270	Running
9	8	23	Jabe Thomas	Don Robertson '69 Plymouth	217	265	Running
10	21	30	Walter Ballard	Ballard '71 Ford	215	260	Running
11	17	34	Wendell Scott	Scott '69 Ford	211	255	Running
12	25	40	D K Ulrich	Ulrich '70 Ford	205	250	Running
13	15	19	Henley Gray	Gray '69 Ford	200	245	Brakes
14	18	28	Bill Hollar	Earl Brooks '69 Ford	200	240	Running
15	22	68	Larry Baumel	Auto Lad '69 Ford	142	235	Trans
16	16	70	J D McDuffie	McDuffie '69 Mercury	132	230	Rear End
17	27	73	Jerry Churchill	'69 Ford	119	225	Engine
18	23	45	Bill Seifert	Seifert '70 Ford	113	220	Trans
19	11	8	Ed Negre	Negre '69 Ford	106	215	Battery
20	26	86	Bobby Mausgrover	Neil Castles '69 Dodge	102	210	Brakes
21	5	10	Champion	Champion 71 Ford	71	205	Ignition
22	10	4	John Sears	Sears '69 Dodge	48	200	Axle
23	3	91	Pete Hamilton	Junior Fields '71 Chevrolet	36	100	Heating
24	19	41	Ken Meisenhelder	Meisenhelder '69 Chevrolet	27	100	Heating
25	13	74	Bill Shirey	Shirey '69 Plymouth	13	100	Quit
26	28	62	Bennis Listman	Kaye Eng '69 Dodge	6	100	Quit
27	24	64	Dick May	Elmo Langley '69 Mercury	3	100	Quit
28	29	89	George Wiltshire	'70 Plymouth	2	100	Quit
29	20	77	Charlie Roberts	Roberts '70 Ford	2	100	Quit
30	30	25	James Cox	Don Robertson '69 Plymouth	1	100	Quit
31	31	96	Richard Childress	Tom Garn '70 Chevrolet	1	100	Oil Leak
32	32	06	Harold Fagan	Neil Castles '70 Dodge	1	100	Quit
33	33	79	Frank Warren	Warren '69 Dodge	0	10	Engine

Time of Race: 55 minutes, 17 seconds
Average Speed: 49.925 mph
Pole Winner: Richard Petty - 46.133 mph
Lap Leaders: Richard Petty 1-230.
Cautions: None
Margin of Victory: 2-laps plus
Attendance: 6,200
*Race was shortned to 230 laps due to scoring error.

run," cracked a weary Petty. "It seemed like we ran 500 laps out there. This has to be the smallest track in the country. You relax one moment and you've run over three cars."

Petty beat runner-up Friday Hassler by two laps at the .2-mile Islip Speedway. Elmo Langley came in third with Bobby Allison fourth and G.C. Spencer fifth.

Black driver George Wiltshire drove two laps then parked his Plymouth. The native New Yorker became the fourth black driver in the history of NASCAR Winston Cup Grand National racing.

Seven drivers withdrew from the race -- each earning $100.

Petty won the pole at 46.133 mph. He averaged 49.925 mph for the caution-free race -- almost four mph faster than his qualifying time.

A crowd of 6,200 watched Petty win the second leg of the annual Northern tour.

Race No. 31

Petty Holds off Baker to Win Northern 300 at Trenton

TRENTON, NJ (July 18) -- Richard Petty outran a determined Buddy Baker to win the Northern 300 at Trenton Speedway. It was the third straight win for the 34 year-old Plymouth jockey.

Baker, driving a Dodge owned by Neil Castles, was

Winston Cup GN Race No. 31
200 Laps at Trenton Speedway
Trenton, NJ
"Northern 300"
300 Miles on 1.5-mile Paved Track
July 18, 1971

Fin	St	No.	Driver	Team / Car	Laps	Money	Status
1	2	43	Richard Petty	Petty Ent '71 Plymouth	200	$6,760	Running
2	6	06	Buddy Baker	Castles '70 Dodge	200	2,980	Running
3	4	12	Bobby Allison	Holman-Moody '71 Ford	199	2,055	Running
4	5	2	Dave Marcis	Marcis '69 Dodge	198	1,370	Running
5	3	6	Pete Hamilton	Cotton Owens '71 Plymouth	198	1,075	Running
6	1	39	Friday Hassler	Hassler '70 Chevrolet	193	920	Running
7	9	90	Bill Dennis	Junie Donlavey '69 Mercury	193	735	Running
8	8	60	Maynard Troyer	Nagle Racers '69 Mercury	191	695	Running
9	10	48	James Hylton	Hylton Eng '71 Ford	190	645	Running
10	36	91	Bill Chevalier	Junior Fields '71 Chevrolet	188	620	Running
11	12	24	Cecil Gordon	Gordon '69 Mercury	187	570	Running
12	21	30	Walter Ballard	Vic Ballard '71 Ford	185	520	Running
13	7	10	Bill Champion	Champion '71 Ford	184	520	Running
14	32	41	Ken Meisenhelder	Meisenhelder '69 Chevrolet	183	470	Running
15	23	67	Elmo Langley	Ron Ronacher '69 Ford	183	445	Running
16	31	47	Raymond Williams	Williams '71 Ford	183	420	Running
17	30	70	J D McDuffie	McDuffie '69 Mercury	181	390	Running
18	19	8	Ed Negre	Negre '69 Ford	181	380	Running
19	25	34	Wendell Scott	Scott '69 Ford	178	375	Running
20	34	86	Bobby Mausgrover	Neil Castles '69 Dodge	177	370	Running
21	38	13	Eddie Yarboro	Yarboro '69 Plymouth	173	365	Running
22	37	40	D K Ulrich	Ulrich '70 Ford	171	360	Trans
23	35	74	Bill Shirey	Shirey '69 Plymouth	167	355	Running
24	26	03	Tommy Gale	Larry Jackson '69 Mercury	163	350	Engine
25	24	45	Bill Seifert	Seifert '71 Ford	148	345	Suspen
26	28	26	Earl Brooks	Brooks '69 Ford	144	340	Lug Bolt
27	13	88	Ron Keselowski	Roger Lubinski '70 Dodge	121	335	Steering
28	22	5	Doc Faustina	Faustina '70 Plymouth	104	330	Vibration
29	15	25	Jabe Thomas	Don Robertson '70 Plymouth	98	325	Battery
30	29	4	John Sears	Sears '69 Dodge	97	320	Ignition
31	14	49	G C Spencer	Spencer '69 Plymouth	72	315	Engine
32	20	68	Larry Baumel	Auto Lad '69 Ford	54	315	Brakes
33	17	19	Henley Gray	Gray '69 Ford	47	315	Carb
34	16	64	Dick May	Elmo Langley '69 Mercury	44	315	Engine
35	11	77	Charlie Roberts	Roberts '70 Ford	43	315	Fly wheel
36	40	96	Richard Childress	Tom Garn '70 Chevrolet	34	315	Engine
37	27	79	Frank Warren	Warren '69 Dodge	29	315	Engine
38	18	15	Dr Ed Hessert	Hessert '70 Plymouth	14	315	Crash
39	33	23	Neil Castles	Don Robertson '69 Plymouth	2	315	Brakes
40	39	73	Jerry Churchill	'69 Ford	2	315	Quit

Time of Race: 2 hours, 29 minutes, 34 seconds
Average Speed: 120.347 mph
Pole Winner: Friday Hassler - 129.134 mph
Lap Leaders: Richard Petty 1, Bobby Allison 2-18, Buddy Baker 19-47, Allison 48-55,
   Baker 56,56, Petty 57-63, Marcis 64-65, Pete Hamilton 66-73, Petty 74-105,
   Baker 106-109, Petty 110-119, Hamilton 120-122, Petty 123-200.
Cautions: 3 for 12 laps   Margin of Victory: 23 seconds   Attendance: 15,000

23 seconds behind Petty at the stripe. Bobby Allison came in third, Dave Marcis was fourth and Pete Hamilton fifth.

Hamilton had third place locked up, but had to pit when Baker knocked Hamilton on pit road. "I didn't mean to do it," said Baker. "I had lost all my brakes."

Hamilton's brief excursion on pit road dropped him two positions. Pole sitter Friday Hassler finished sixth.

Petty led for 128 of the 200 laps on the 1.5-mile course. "I expected to get a lot of tough competition from Allison, Hamilton and Hassler," said Petty. "But I'll have to admit it really surprised me to see Buddy run that strong. He was really going out there."

A crowd of 15,000 watched Petty take his 132nd career win at an average speed of 120.347 mph.

Winston Cup GN Race No. 32
420 Laps at Fairgrounds Speedway
Nashville, TN
"Nashville 420"
250 Miles on .596-mile Paved Track
July 24, 1971

Fin	St	No.	Driver	Team / Car	Laps	Money	Status
1	1	43	Richard Petty	Petty Ent '71 Plymouth	420	$4,325	Running
2	10	48	James Hylton	Hylton Eng '70 Ford	416	2,415	Running
3	9	72	Benny Parsons	L G DeWitt '70 Mercury	416	1,600	Running
4	11	26	Earl Brooks	Brooks '69 Ford	411	1,160	Running
5	7	70	J D McDuffie	McDuffie '69 Mercury	403	1,025	Running
6	25	30	Walter Ballard	Vic Ballard '71 Ford	398	815	Running
7	19	23	Jabe Thomas	Don Robertson '69 Plymouth	385	765	Running
8	29	19	Henley Gray	Gray '69 Ford	379	740	Running
9	8	76	Ben Arnold	Arnold '69 Ford	375	715	Running
10	27	28	Bill Hollar	Earl Brooks '69 Ford	375	690	Running
11	6	8	Ed Negre	Negre '69 Ford	374	665	Throttle
12	20	41	Ken Meisenhelder	Meisenhelder '69 Chevrolet	359	640	Running
13	5	7	Dean Dalton	Dalton '69 Ford	329	590	Engine
14	21	73	Jerry Churchill	'69 Ford	323	540	Running
15	24	79	Frank Warren	Warren '69 Dodge	249	490	Running
16	3	24	Cecil Gordon	Gordon '69 Mercury	236	415	Running
17	4	64	Elmo Langley	Langley '71 Ford	167	340	Wtr pump
18	13	10	Bill Champion	Champion '70 Ford	154	290	Rear End
19	12	05	David Sisco	Charlie McGee '70 Chevrolet	141	265	Crash
20	26	34	Wendell Scott	Scott '69 Ford	121	250	Engine
21	18	96	Richard Childress	Tom Garn '70 Chevrolet	108	250	Engine
22	16	74	Bill Shirey	Shirey '69 Plymouth	102	250	Throttle
23	15	58	Bob Brown	Allan Brown '70 Chevrolet	73	250	Suspen
24	17	40	D K Ulrich	Ulrich '70 Ford	60	250	Flat tire
25	22	07	Coo Coo Marlin	Cunningham-Kelley '69 Chev	51	250	Crash
26	14	38	Wayne Smith	Smith '69 Chevrolet	49	245	Engine
27	2	12	Bobby Allison	Allison '70 Dodge	22	295	Suspen
28	28	25	Bill Seifert	Don Robertson '70 Plymouth	9	240	Quit
29	23	67	Dick May	Ron Ronacher '69 Ford	5	215	Suspen

Time of Race: 2 hours, 47 minutes, 30 seconds
Average Speed: 89.667 mph
Pole Winner: Richard Petty - 114.628 mph
Lap Leaders: Richard Petty 1, Bobby Allison 2-21, Petty 22-420.
Cautions: 4 for 46 laps   Margin of Victory: 4-laps plus   Attendance: 10,000

Race No. 32

Petty on Tear; Racks Up 4th in Row at Nashville

NASHVILLE, TN (July 24) -- Richard Petty continued his hot streak by racking up his fourth win in a row at Fairgrounds Speedway.

Petty started on the pole and led for 400 of the 420 laps in the Nashville 420. Finishing four laps behind in second was James Hylton. Benny Parsons came in third as car owner L.G. DeWitt ended a six week retirement. Earl Brooks finished fourth and J.D. McDuffie was fifth.

There was little suspense for the crowd of 10,000 after the first 100 laps. Petty had lapped the entire field by then.

"I'm tired," said Petty after climbing out of his Plymouth. "This track beats you to death. I didn't have any particular trouble, but it seems there were a lot of spinning race cars out there. I was lucky to get past them all."

Bobby Allison passed Petty -- the only driver to do so -- on lap two. Allison kept his Dodge in front until the 21st lap when he went out with a suspension problems.

Third fastest qualifier Cecil Gordon made several unscheduled pit stops and finished 16th, 184 laps behind Petty.

Petty averaged 89.667 mph in winning his 133rd Winston Cup Grand National race.

Race No. 33

Petty Nips Allison at Atlanta; Wood Brothers Quit Tour

HAMPTON, GA (Aug. 1) -- Richard Petty squeezed out a narrow victory over Bobby Allison in the Dixie 500 at Atlanta International Raceway. It was Petty's fifth win in a row and it moved him 187 points ahead of James Hylton in the Winston Cup point standings.

After the event, which Petty and Allison were nine laps up on the field, Glen Wood said he was pulling his cars off the Winston Cup Grand National tour in a dispute over the carburetor plate rules.

Petty and Allison engaged in a heated battle for first place for the entire 500 miles -- and the two cars swapped paint on several occasions. "It was nothing intentional," said Petty. "Once he slipped when he was trying to get inside me. That little fender banging was

Dick Poling #62, Pete Hamilton #6, Marty Robbins #42 and Benny Parsons at Atlanta

accidental."

Allison gave chase to Petty in the final 31 laps, but fell two car lengths short at the finish line. "There at the

Dave Marcis' Dodge speeds down the front chute in Dixie 500

last I couldn't get the breaks I was looking for in traffic. But then you make your own breaks in this game. I'm not making excuses. He won the race."

Benny Parsons finished third, nine laps behind. Charlie Glotzbach was fourth and Friday Hassler fifth. Donnie Allison, with relief help from Dave Marcis,

Buddy Baker #11 moves over for thrilling Petty-Allison shootout in Atlanta

Winston Cup GN Race No. 33
328 Laps at Atlanta Int'l Raceway
Hampton, GA
"Dixie 500"
500 Miles on 1.5-mile Paved Track
August 1, 1971

Fin	St	No.	Driver	Team / Car	Laps	Money	Status
1	3	43	Richard Petty	Petty Ent '71 Plymouth	328	$20,220	Running
2	5	12	Bobby Allison	Holman-Moody '69 Mercury	328	9,530	Running
3	18	72	Benny Parsons	L G DeWitt '69 Mercury	319	6,225	Running
4	2	3	Charlie Glotzbach	Richard Howard '71 Chevrolet	318	4,525	Running
5	20	39	Friday Hassler	Hassler '70 Chevrolet	317	3,375	Running
6	6	21	Donnie Allison*	Wood Brothers '69 Mercury	316	3,025	Running
7	26	88	Ron Keselowski	Roger Lubinski '70 Dodge	313	2,800	Running
8	12	79	Frank Warren	Warren '69 Dodge	312	2,525	Running
9	15	48	James Hylton	Hylton Eng '70 Ford	312	2,275	Running
10	24	10	Bill Champion	Champion '70 Ford	312	2,000	Running
11	23	91	Richard Brown	Junior Fields '71 Chevrolet	309	1,750	Running
12	19	24	Cecil Gordon	Gordon '69 Mercury	309	1,525	Running
13	17	42	Marty Robbins	Robbins '69 Dodge	309	1,350	Running
14	27	25	Jabe Thomas	Don Robertson '70 Plymouth	306	1,200	Running
15	10	45	Bill Seifert	Seifert '71 Ford	304	1,125	Running
16	32	53	Bobby Brack	Hopper-Crews '69 Ford	302	1,000	Engine
17	38	70	J D McDuffie	McDuffie '69 Mercury	299	900	Running
18	21	30	Walter Ballard	Vic Ballard '71 Ford	295	800	Running
19	13	76	Ben Arnold	Arnold '69 Ford	294	725	Running
20	39	19	Henley Gray	Gray '69 Ford	293	650	Running
21	40	34	Wendell Scott	Scott '69 Ford	290	600	Running
22	35	5	Dick May	Doc Faustina '70 Plymouth	268	590	Running
23	37	46	Earl Brooks	Tom Hunter '69 Chevrolet	264	585	Engine
24	4	6	Pete Hamilton	Cotton Owens '71 Plymouth	249	745	Engine
25	1	11	Buddy Baker	Petty Ent '71 Dodge	231	1,960	Engine
26	33	62	Dick Poling	Kaye Eng '69 Dodge	226	570	Running
27	16	49	G C Spencer	Spencer '69 Plymouth	164	665	Wheel
28	28	95	Paul Tyler	Tyler '69 Mercury	149	560	Engine
29	29	4	John Sears	Sears '69 Dodge	136	555	Lug Bolt
30	25	90	Bill Dennis	Junie Donlavey '69 Mercury	131	550	Vibration
31	14	06	Neil Castles	Castles '70 Dodge	92	570	Suspen
32	30	77	Charlie Roberts	Roberts '70 Ford	90	540	Engine
33	7	71	Bobby Isaac	K&K Insurance '71 Dodge	86	560	Oil Cooler
34	22	07	Coo Coo Marlin	Cunningham-Kelley '69 Chev	82	530	Engine
35	11	18	Joe Frasson	Frasson '70 Dodge	66	550	Wheel
36	36	8	Ed Negre	Negre '69 Ford	62	520	Trans
37	31	93	Dub Simpson	Harold Furr '71 Chevrolet	60	515	Engine
38	34	47	Raymond Williams	Williams '71 Ford	40	510	Trans
39	8	2	Dave Marcis	Marcis '69 Dodge	38	530	Suspen
40	9	64	Elmo Langley	Langley '69 Mercury	36	525	Engine

Time of Race: 3 hours, 52 minutes, 5 seconds
Average Speed: 129.061 mph
Pole Winner: Buddy Baker - 155.796 mph
Lap Leaders:Buddy Baker 1-25, Richard Petty 26-39, Baker 40, Pete Hamilton 41, Baker 42, Bobby Allison 43-58, Baker 59-69, Petty 70, Baker 71-75, B.Allison 76-77, Baker 78-79, Petty 80-84, Hamilton 85-92, Petty 93-139, B.Allison 140-149, Petty 150-169, Baker 170, Petty 171, B.Allison 172-176, Petty 177-189, Baker 190-218, Petty 219-226, Baker 227-228, Hamilton 229-235, B.Allison 236-247, Petty 248-288, B.Allison 289-297, Petty 298-328.
Cautions: 5 for 48 laps　　Margin of Victory: 2 car lengths　　Attendance: 22,500
*Relieved by Dave Marcis

finished a disappointing sixth, 12 laps off the pace.

Wood, owner of the Mercury Donnie Allison was driving, said he was pulling out of NASCAR racing. "This will be the last race for my car," said Wood. "I have made up my mind that I'm not going to fight unfair rules any longer. The Chrysler Wedge has won the last five or six races and it's because they get a larger opening on their carburetor plate. Unless NASCAR changes the rules, we will not race again."

NASCAR Vice-President Lin Kuchler said that

Wood's complaint would be studied. "I don't think any sanctioning body should change the rules just because one person doesn't like them," he responded. "I have much respect for Glen Wood, but whatever he does, he does of his own choice."

A poor spectator turnout of 22,500 watched Petty win at an average speed of 129.061 mph.

Race No. 34
Bobby Allison Wins Myers Brothers Memorial in Mustang

WINSTON-SALEM, NC (Aug. 6) -- Bobby Allison wheeled his Mustang around Richard Petty in the 113th lap and led the rest of the way to win the Myers Brothers Memorial event at Bowman Gray Stadium. It was the first meeting of Grand National and Grand American cars, a new NASCAR ruling designed to perk up interest in both divisions.

"We feel it will benefit the sport and the fans to see the smaller cars run against the Grand Nationals on the shorter tracks," said NASCAR Vice President and Competition Director Lin Kuchler. "The record book shows the Grand American qualifying and race speeds are comparable to the Grand National speeds."

Bobby Allison won at Winston-Salem in a Mustang

The first confrontation of the big Winston Cup Grand Nationals and the smaller sedans was a box office bonanza, but a major headache for the GN cars and drivers.

Allison led the charge that saw the Grand American cars sweep six of the first seven spots. "On a track like this, we had the decided advantage," said winner Allison. "We could get in and out of the corners quicker."

Petty finished second and denounced the idea of mixing the two divisions. "I figured something like this would happen," said Petty. "They'll probably win all these races. They ought to keep the two divisions separate. Grand National racing isn't supposed to be filled with Mustangs and Camaros."

Jim Paschal finished third, Buck Baker fourth, Dave Marcis fifth, Tiny Lund sixth and Wayne Andrews seventh -- all in Grand American cars.

Hometown ace Max Berrier was slated to drive a Toy Bolton Camaro, but the car didn't show up. Bolton told promoter Joe Hawkins that a number of Grand National drivers had telephoned him with the message that his car "might be wrecked if I brought it to the track."

Allison averaged 44.792 mph for his 25th career victory.

Winston Cup GN Race No. 34
250 Laps at Bowman Gray Stadium
Winston-Salem, NC
"Myers Brothers Memorial"
62.5 Miles on Quarter-mile Paved Track
August 6, 1971

Fin	St	No.	Driver	Team / Car	Laps	Money	Status
1	2	49	Bobby Allison	Rollins Leasing '70 Mustang	250	$1,000	Running
2	1	43	Richard Petty	Petty Ent '70 Plymouth	250	600	Running
3	3	14	Jim Paschal	Cliff Stewart '70 AMC Javelin	249	400	Running
4	9	87	Buck Baker	Baker '71 Firebird	247	350	Running
5	15	11	Dave Marcis	James Rupe '69 Camaro	244	325	Running
6	19	55	Tiny Lund	Ronnie Hopkins '69 Camaro	243	500	Running
7	4	15	Wayne Andrews	Reid Shaw '71 Mustang	242	275	Running
8	21	25	Jabe Thomas	Don Robertson '70 Plymouth	240	270	Running
9	17	86	David Ray Boggs	Boggs '71 Firebird	238	265	Running
10	18	30	Walter Ballard	Vic Ballard '71 Ford	238	260	Running
11	16	10	Bill Champion	Champion '70 Ford	234	255	Running
12	22	2	Randy Hutchison	Warren Prout '69 Camaro	230	250	Running
13	14	70	J D McDuffie	McDuffie '69 Mercury	225	245	Running
14	5	44	Ken Rush	'69 Camaro	117	240	Crash
15	12	64	Elmo Langley	Langley '69 Mercury	109	235	Ignition
16	7	21	Tommy Andrews	Andrews '69 Mustang	103	230	Engine
17	26	8	Ed Negre	Negre '69 Ford	97	225	Carb
18	25	06	Neil Castles	Castles '70 Dodge	94	220	Battery
19	28	28	Bill Hollar	Earl Brooks '69 Ford	83	215	Brakes
20	20	41	Ken Meisenhelder	Meisenhelder '69 Chevrolet	56	210	Heating
21	29	96	Richard Childress	Tom Garn '70 Chevrolet	40	205	Engine
22	8	48	James Hylton	Hylton Eng '70 Ford	38	200	Steering
23	10	79	Frank Warren	Warren '69 Dodge	18	200	Trans
24	11	24	Cecil Gordon	Gordon '69 Mercury	13	200	Quit
25	24	34	Wendell Scott	Scott '69 Ford	9	200	Clutch
26	6	26	Earl Brooks	Brooks '69 Ford	8	200	Trans
27	27	73	Jerry Churchill	'69 Ford	3	200	Heating
28	13	45	Bill Seifert	Seifert '69 Ford	1	200	Quit
29	23	74	Bill Shirey	Shirey '69 Plymouth	1	200	Quit

Time of Race: 1 hour, 23 minutes, 47 seconds
Average Speed: 44.792 mph
Pole Winner: Richard Petty - 55.283 mph
Lap Leaders: Richard Petty 1-112, Bobby Allison 113-250.
Cautions: 6 for 36 laps   Margin of Victory: 3 seconds   Attendance: 14,000

Race No. 35
Petty, Allison Feud; Petty Wins West Virginia 500

ONA, WV (Aug. 8) -- Richard Petty booted Bobby Allison out of the lead on lap 424 and drove his Plymouth to victory in the West Virginia 500 at International Speedway Park. It was the second meeting of Grand National and Grand American cars on a short track.

Petty and Allison both employed rough tactics on the .455-mile paved oval. Both cars had collected the scars of close battle when the 500 lapper ended.

"It got kinda hot out there," said Petty. "Allison really put the pressure on. That's racing. I drove to win and he was driving to win."

Allison figured he would have notched his second straight win until he was pinched into the lapped Ford of Wendell Scott. "After that, I just drove as hard as I could," said Allison. "But the car was bent out of shape pretty bad and I had to take second place."

James Hylton came in third, Tiny Lund was fourth and Cecil Gordon fifth.

Elmo Langley qualified a strong third, but ignition failure knocked his Ford out after 141 laps.

A crowd of 10,000 watched Petty win his 16th race of the year at an average speed of 83.805 mph.

Winston Cup GN Race No. 35
500 Laps at Int'l Raceway Park
Ona, WV
"West Virginia 500"
219 Miles on .455-mile Paved Track
August 8, 1971

Fin	St	No.	Driver	Team / Car	Laps	Money	Status
1	2	43	Richard Petty	Petty Ent '71 Plymouth	500	$2,300	Running
2	1	49	Bobby Allison	Rolins Leasing '70 Mustang	498	1,500	Running
3	5	48	James Hylton	Hylton Eng '71 Ford	495	950	Running
4	6	55	Tiny Lund	Ronnie Hopkins '70 Camaro	493	750	Running
5	14	24	Cecil Gordon	Gordon '69 Mercury	482	650	Running
6	4	14	Jim Paschal	Cliff Stewart '70 AMC Javelin	477	550	Engine
7	17	41	Gary Myers	Norris Reed '70 Mustang	474	500	Running
8	25	30	Walter Ballard	Vic Ballard '71 Ford	468	490	Running
9	11	10	Bill Champion	Champion '70 Ford	468	480	Running
10	26	25	Jabe Thomas	Don Robertson '70 Plymouth	467	470	Running
11	16	26	Earl Brooks	Brooks '69 Ford	459	460	Running
12	28	70	J D McDuffie	McDuffie '69 Mercury	452	450	Running
13	27	34	Wendell Scott	Scott '69 Ford	432	440	Running
14	12	86	David Ray Boggs	Boggs '71 Firebird	422	430	Running
15	7	33	Joe Dean Huss	Jack Balmer '69 Camaro	417	420	Running
16	9	87	Buck Baker	Baker '71 Firebird	413	410	Engine
17	30	2	Randy Hutchison	Warren Prout '71 Camaro	364	400	Crash
18	10	06	Neil Castles	Castles '70 Dodge	312	390	Engine
19	22	7	Jimmy Vaughn	Vaughn '69 Camaro	266	380	Oil Leak
20	31	4	John Sears	Sears '69 Dodge	224	370	Ignition
21	34	50	Gordon Burkett	'69 Chevrolet	220	360	Crash
22	32	8	Ed Negre	Negre '69 Ford	214	350	Carb
23	15	15	Wayne Andrews	Reid Shaw '71 Mustang	206	340	Heating
24	13	45	Bill Seifert	Seifert '69 Ford	187	330	Driver ill
25	3	64	Elmo Langley	Langley '71 Ford	141	320	Ignition
26	8	11	Junior Spencer	James Rupe '69 Camaro	112	310	Ignition
27	23	3	Charlie Glotzbach	Richard Howard '71 Chevrolet	100	300	Heating
28	20	5	Pee Wee Wentz	Jerry Wentz '69 Camaro	100	300	Engine
29	29	47	Raymond Williams	Williams '71 Ford	48	300	Heating
30	19	94	Al Straub	Straub '71 Mustang	48	300	Heating
31	33	79	Frank Warren	Warren '69 Dodge	47	300	Heating
32	24	74	Bill Shirey	Shirey '69 Plymouth	31	300	Quit
33	18	19	Henley Gray	Gray '69 Ford	25	300	Suspen
34	21	78	Paul Tyler	Keith Christensen '69 Camaro	11	300	Engine
35	35	73	Jerry Churchill	'69 Ford	1	300	Quit

Time of Race: 2 hours, 57 minutes, 50 seconds
Average Speed: 83.805 mph
Pole Winner: Bobby Allison - 84.053 mph
Lap Leaders: Bobby Allison 1-29, Richard Petty 30-52, Allison 53-54, Tiny Lund 55-74, Allison 75-147, Petty 148-233, Allison 234-297, Petty 298-299, Allison 300-315, Petty 316-348, Allison 349-361, Petty 362-419, Allison 420-423, Petty 424-500.
Cautions: 5 for 38 laps   Margin of Victory: 2-laps plus   Attendance: 10,000

Race No. 36

Allison Wins Yankee 400; Petty Backs Out of Photo Finish

BROOKLYN, MI (Aug. 15) -- Bobby Allison passed Richard Petty with three laps to go and breezed uncontested to the finish line to win the Yankee 400. It was the seventh win of the season for the Hueytown, AL Mercury driver.

Petty was nipping at the heels in the final lap of the 400-miler at Michigan International Speedway. But he backed out of the throttle as he came off the fourth turn. "He was a half-second to three-quarters of a second faster than I was," said Pet-

Bobby Allison won the Yankee 400 in Holman-Moody Mercury

ty. "It wouldn't have made any difference. I know when I'm being played with. I just wanted to stay out of the pictures at the finish line."

Allison said he was surprised when he looked in the mirror and saw Petty fading fast. "I figured he would try to come around me off number four, but he disappeared," said Allison.

Buddy Baker finished third, a lap behind. He was upset with crew chief Maurice Petty for telling him to keep away from the Allison-Petty shoot-out. Baker was dicing it out with the two leaders, trying to get his lap back. Richard motioned for Baker to back off and let him battle freely with Allison. At first Baker refused to let off the throttle.

Three laps later, Maurice held up a pit board that said *"BACK OFF!"* Baker made a hand gesture to Maurice and followed instructions.

Maynard Troyer's surprising run netted him fourth place. Joe Frasson came in fifth.

The Wood Brothers did not enter the 400-miler, but they said they would return at Talladega. NASCAR announced new carburetor rules after Wood complained about the situation at Atlanta.

Allison's Holman-Moody Mercury was out front for 154 of the 197 laps on the 2.04-mile oval. He averaged 149.862 mph before one of the smallest crowd in the history of Michigan International Speedway -- 26,000.

Winston Cup GN Race No. 36
197 Laps at Michigan Int'l Speedway
Brooklyn, MI
"Yankee 400"
400 Miles on 2.04-mile Paved Track
August 15, 1971

Fin	St	No.	Driver	Team / Car	Laps	Money	Status
1	2	12	Bobby Allison	Holman-Moody '69 Mercury	197	$15,395	Running
2	6	43	Richard Petty	Petty Ent '71 Plymouth	197	7,870	Running
3	5	11	Buddy Baker	Petty Ent '71 Dodge	196	4,700	Running
4	10	60	Maynard Troyer	Nagle Racers '69 Mercury	193	2,870	Running
5	16	18	Joe Frasson	Frasson '70 Dodge	192	2,020	Running
6	7	24	Cecil Gordon	Gordon '69 Mercury	190	1,495	Running
7	14	88	Ron Keselowski	Roger Lubinski '70 Dodge	189	1,320	Running
8	26	48	James Hylton	Hylton Eng '69 Ford	188	1,220	Running
9	9	25	Jabe Thomas	Don Robertson '70 Plymouth	187	1,120	Running
10	21	06	Neil Castles	Castles '70 Dodge	186	1,020	Running
11	39	44	Tommy Gale	Giachetti Bros '70 Ford	185	1,045	Running
12	31	32	Marv Acton	Dick Brooks '70 Plymouth	184	1,020	Running
13	35	76	Ben Arnold	Arnold '69 Ford	184	945	Running
14	11	79	Frank Warren	Warren '69 Dodge	184	920	Running
15	17	90	Bill Dennis	Junie Donlavey '69 Mercury	184	995	Running
16	18	18	Richard Brown	Junior Fields '71 Chevrolet	183	895	Running
17	37	47	Raymond Williams	Williams '71 Ford	183	850	Running
18	29	70	J D McDuffie	McDuffie '69 Mercury	183	840	Running
19	28	77	Charlie Roberts	Roberts '70 Ford	181	825	Running
20	33	30	Walter Ballard	Vic Ballard '71 Ford	181	810	Running
21	12	64	Elmo Langley	Langley '69 Mercury	180	795	Running
22	22	0	George Altheide	'70 Dodge	177	780	Running
23	40	34	Wendell Scott	Scott '69 Ford	174	765	Running
24	26	26	Earl Brooks	Brooks '69 Ford	174	750	Running
25	34	86	Bobby Mausgrover	Neil Castles '69 Dodge	167	760	Running
26	20	10	Bill Champion	Champion '70 Ford	166	720	Running
27	4	3	Charlie Glotzbach	Richard Howard '71 Chevrolet	129	710	Engine
28	27	7	Dean Dalton	Dalton '69 Ford	125	700	Engine
29	38	45	Bill Seifert	Seifert '69 Ford	110	690	Fuel pump
30	25	83	Johnny Halford	'69 Plymouth	94	680	Ignition
31	1	6	Pete Hamilton	Cotton Owens '71 Plymouth	87	785	Engine
32	36	84	Dick May	Ralph Davis '69 Dodge	84	655	Heating
33	32	07	Coo Coo Marlin	Cunningham-Kelley '69 Chev	76	675	Engine
34	15	4	John Sears	Sears '69 Dodge	49	645	Clutch
35	19	5	Dave Marcis	Doc Faustina '70 Plymouth	45	640	Heating
36	24	8	Ed Negre	Negre '69 Ford	40	635	Fuel pump
37	23	19	Henley Gray	Gray '69 Ford	38	630	Suspen
38	8	72	Benny Parsons	L G DeWitt '69 Mercury	29	625	Engine
39	3	71	Bobby Isaac	K&K Insurance '71 Dodge	11	1,070	Wtr pump
40	13	39	Friday Hassler	Hassler '70 Chevrolet	7	615	Engine

Time of Race: 2 hours, 40 minutes, 54 seconds
Average Speed: 149.862 mph
Pole Winner: Pete Hamilton - 161.901 mph
Lap Leaders: Pete Hamilton 1, Bobby Isaac 2, Bobby Allison 3-30, Hamilton 31-32,
    Allison 33-39, Hamilton 40, Charlie Glotzbach 41-42, Richard Petty 43,
    Glotzbach 44, Allison 45, Hamilton 46, Allison 47-48, Hamilton 49, Allison 50-83,
    Glotzbach 84-85, Petty 86-88, Allison 89-127, Petty 128-134, Allison 135-145,
    Petty 146, Allison 147-149, Petty 150-157, Allison 158-167, Petty 168, Allison 169-170,
    Petty 171, Allison 172-183, Petty 184, Allison 185-187, Petty 188-194, Allison 195-197.
Cautions: 2 for 12 laps   Margin of Victory: 3 seconds   Attendance: 26,000

Race No. 37

Petty-Allison at War; Bobby Wins Wild Talladega 500

TALLADEGA, AL (Aug. 22) -- Bobby Allison survived a last lap scramble and rode home first in the spine-tingling finish to the Talladega 500 at Alabama

Winston Cup GN Race No. 37
188 Laps at Alabama Int'l Motor Speedway
Talladega, AL
"Talladega 500"
500 Miles on 2.66-mile Paved Track
August 22, 1971

Fin	St	No.	Driver	Team / Car	Laps	Money	Status
1	2	12	Bobby Allison	Holman-Moody '69 Mercury	188	$19,565	Running
2	5	43	Richard Petty	Petty Ent '71 Plymouth	188	10,040	Running
3	4	6	Pete Hamilton	Cotton Owens '71 Plymouth	187	6,265	Crash
4	8	99	Fred Lorenzen	Nichels-Goldsmith '71 Plym	184	4,290	Running
5	14	48	James Hylton	Hylton Eng '69 Mercury	183	4,340	Running
6	11	45	Bill Seifert	Seifert '69 Ford	181	2,515	Running
7	20	15	Dr Don Tarr	'70 Ford	181	2,265	Running
8	39	88	Ron Keselowski	Roger Lubinski '70 Dodge	179	2,015	Running
9	31	25	Jabe Thomas	Don Robertson '70 Plymouth	179	1,865	Running
10	19	92	Larry Smith	Harley Smith '69 Ford	179	1,775	Running
11	13	64	Elmo Langley	Langley '69 Mercury	179	1,490	Running
12	25	10	Bill Champion	Champion '70 Ford	178	1,465	Running
13	38	46	Roy Mayne	Tom Hunter '69 Chevrolet	178	1,440	Running
14	32	03	Tommy Gale	Larry Jackson '69 Mercury	176	1,415	Running
15	14	79	Frank Warren	Warren '69 Dodge	175	1,390	Running
16	46	05	David Sisco	Charlie McGee '69 Chevrolet	173	1,365	Running
17	30	20	Bill Ward	Jimmy McCain '70 Ford	173	1,340	Running
18	33	47	Raymond Williams	Williams '70 Ford	169	1,315	Running
19	36	4	John Sears	Sears '69 Dodge	163	1,290	Running
20	50	26	Earl Brooks	Brooks '69 Ford	162	1,265	Running
21	27	70	J D McDuffie	McDuffie '69 Mercury	161	1,240	Running
22	23	30	Walter Ballard	Vic Ballard '71 Ford	156	1,240	Running
23	3	3	Charlie Glotzbach	Richard Howard '71 Chevrolet	155	1,265	Engine
24	26	77	Charlie Roberts	Roberts '70 Ford	155	1,165	Engine
25	48	7	Dean Dalton	Dalton '69 Ford	155	1,140	Running
26	49	96	Wendell Scott*	Tom Garn '70 Chevrolet	153	1,115	Running
27	43	84	Dick May	Ralph Davis '69 Ford	153	1,115	Running
28	40	8	Ed Negre	Negre '69 Ford	151	1,065	Running
29	37	68	Larry Baumel	Auto Lad '69 Ford	148	1,040	Axle
30	28	32	Marv Acton	Dick Brooks '70 Plymouth	146	1,015	Engine
31	45	94	Harry Gailey	'69 Ford	141	990	Running
32	15	18	Joe Frasson	Frasson '70 Dodge	105	965	Crash
33	44	53	Bobby Brack	Hopper-Crews '69 Ford	105	965	Crash
34	29	5	Dave Marcis	Doc Faustina '70 Plymouth	101	915	Crash
35	17	76	Ben Arnold	Arnold '69 Ford	97	890	Engine
36	7	11	Buddy Baker	Petty Ent '71 Dodge	95	865	Engine
37	9	39	Friday Hassler	Hassler '70 Chevrolet	86	840	W'shield
38	12	24	Cecil Gordon	Gordon '69 Mercury	63	815	Crash
39	6	52	Rolf Stommelen	Holman-Moody '69 Mercury	53	790	Frame
40	24	93	Dub Simpson	Harold Furr '71 Chevrolet	49	790	Fuel line
41	1	21	Donnie Allison	Wood Brothers '69 Mercury	44	790	Engine
42	34	07	Coo Coo Marlin	Cunningham-Kelley '69 Chev	42	715	Axle
43	42	19	Henley Gray	Gray '69 Ford	39	740	Engine
44	10	60	Maynard Troyer	Nagle Racers '69 Mercury	33	665	Oil Leak
45	35	86	Bobby Mausgrover	Neil Castles '69 Dodge	27	640	Engine
46	47	63	Johnny Barnes	'69 Dodge	23	615	Oil Pan
47	21	72	Benny Parsons	L G DeWitt '69 Mercury	10	690	Engine
48	22	90	Bill Dennis	Junie Donlavey '69 Mercury	10	615	Engine
49	16	91	Richard Brown	Junior Fields '71 Chevrolet	5	540	Engine
50	18	06	Neil Castles	Castles '70 Dodge	1	515	Ignition

Time of Race: 3 hours, 25 minutes, 38 seconds
Average Speed: 145.945 mph
Pole Winner: Donnie Allison - 187.323 mph
Lap Leaders: Donnie Allison 1-4, Pete Hamilton 5-7, D.Allison 8, Buddy Baker 9,
    Bobby Allison 10-11, Baker 12-13, D.Allison 14, Baker 15, D.Allison 16, B.Allison 17-19,
    D.Allison 20-21, Baker 22, D.Allison 23-25, Baker 26-30, D.Allison 31-33,
    Charlie Glotzbach 34, D.Allison 35-38, Hamilton 39, Richard Petty 40, D.Allison 41-44,
    Hamilton 45-48, Petty 49-51, Hamilton 52-55, Glotzbach 56-57, Hamilton 58-70,
    Glotzbach 71, B.Allison 72-86, Hamilton 87, Petty 88, Hamilton 89, B.Allison 90-97,
    Petty 98, B.Allison 99-104, Petty 105-106, Hamilton 107-108, B.Allison 109-116,
    Hamilton 117-118, Petty 119-120, B.Allison 121-125, Petty 126-127, B.Allison 128-129,
    Hamilton 130, B.Allison 131-133, Hamilton 134, B.Allison 135-152, Glotzbach 153,
    Hamilton 154, B.Allison 155-157, Petty 158, B.Allison 159-175, Petty 176-177,
    Hamilton 178, B.Allison 179, Hamilton 180, B.Allison 181-188.
Cautions: 5 for 43 laps   Margin of Victory: 2.1 seconds   Attendance: 46,700
*Relieved by Richard Childress

International Motor Speedway. Following the frantic action on the track, Allison and rival Richard Petty exchanged verbal barbs in the press box.

Allison, Petty and Pete Hamilton battled virtually from start to finish in the 500 miler at the world's fastest speedway. Allison ducked the nose of his Mercury under Hamilton with eight laps to go and kept a one car length cushion entering the final lap.

Allison rode under the white flag with Petty and Hamilton tucked in his draft. On the backstretch, Allison darted to the inside in an effort to break the draft. Petty made a stab at the lead as the trio hit the third turn. The Plymouths of Petty and Hamilton came together.

Hamilton spun off the track and became disabled in the fourth turn. Petty's car wobbled before he got it under control. Allison raced on and got to the finish line 2.1-seconds ahead of Petty. Hamilton got credit for taking third place. Fred Lorenzen was fourth, four laps down. James

Petty #43, Hamilton #6 and Allison in Talladega showdown

Hylton finished fifth.

Petty blamed Allison for the last lap skirmish. "Everybody wants to win," he said, "but different folks go about it in different ways. I've been racing 13 years and the only cat I've ever had any trouble with is Bobby Allison. He came along and won some races a couple of years ago. He's been charged up ever since. There's an awful lot of red paint on the side of my car."

Allison admitted that he and Petty "came together several times during the last 10 laps, but there was nothing intentional on my part or his. Our cars were about equal in speed and we both had a desire to win."

Rolf Stommelen, noted road racer from Germany, got only four laps of practice before he went out and registered the sixth fastest qualification. "I've never seen any of them foreign road racers come over here and get the knack of stock cars that quickly," said an admiring Petty. Stommelen departed on lap 53 with suspension damage.

A crowd of 46,700 watched Allison average 145.945 mph. The event was interrupted for an hour and a half due to rain. During the break, Lorenzen announced he was quitting the Nichels-Goldsmith Plymouth. "The car won't run because there is a lack of communication between myself and the crew," said the 'Golden Boy'. "No more Chrysler products."

Race No. 38

Petty Passes Lund For Sandlapper 200 Victory

COLUMBIA, SC (Aug. 27) -- Richard Petty passed Tiny Lund with 13 laps to go and scored a close victory in Columbia Speedway's Sandlapper 200. It was the third meeting of Grand National and Grand American cars in so-called 'mixed' races.

Lund drove his Camaro into second place, 10 car lengths behind Petty's Plymouth. Jim Paschal finished third, James Hylton was fourth and Jabe Thomas fifth.

Bobby Allison, who won the first mixed race in a Mustang, did not enter. "The race procedure has been inconsistent," said Allison. "I found out that I didn't get credit for a Grand National victory at Winston-

Winston Cup GN Race No. 38
200 Laps at Columbia Speedway
Columbia, SC
"Sandlapper 200"
100 Miles on Half-mile Paved Track
August 27, 1971

Fin	St	No.	Driver	Team / Car	Laps	Money	Status
1	1	43	Richard Petty	Petty Ent '70 Plymouth	200	$1,500	Running
2	3	55	Tiny Lund	Ronnie Hopkins '69 Camaro	200	900	Running
3	4	14	Jim Paschal	Cliff Stewart '70 AMC Javelin	200	500	Running
4	6	48	James Hylton	Hylton Eng '70 Ford	197	350	Running
5	21	25	Jabe Thomas	Don Robertson '70 Plymouth	196	325	Running
6	5	15	Wayne Andrews	Reid Shaw '71 Mustang	196	300	Running
7	10	64	Elmo Langley	Langley '71 Ford	194	275	Running
8	14	30	Walter Ballard	Vic Ballard '71 Ford	193	270	Running
9	11	2	Randy Hutchison	Warren Prout '69 Camaro	193	265	Running
10	23	41	Ken Meisenhelder	Meisenhelder '69 Chevrolet	190	260	Running
11	18	10	Bill Champion	Champion '70 Ford	189	255	Running
12	34	34	Wendell Scott	Scott '69 Ford	186	250	Running
13	9	24	Cecil Gordon	Gordon '69 Mercury	182	245	Running
14	13	4	John Sears	Sears '69 Dodge	179	240	Running
15	30	73	Bill Seifert	Seifert '69 Ford	179	235	Running
16	7	74	Bill Shirey	Shirey '69 Plymouth	178	230	Running
17	8	87	Buck Baker	Baker '71 Firebird	165	225	Running
18	15	7	Jimmy Vaughn	Vaughn '69 Camaro	162	220	Crash
19	24	70	J D McDuffie	McDuffie '69 Mercury	159	215	Crash
20	20	79	Frank Warren	Warren '69 Plymouth	152	210	Steering
21	25	8	Ed Negre	Negre '69 Ford	143	205	Ignition
22	19	17	Ernie Shaw	Shaw '68 Mustang	109	200	Clutch
23	26	40	D K Ulrich	Ulrich '70 Ford	68	200	Brakes
24	2	36	H B Bailey	Bailey '71 Firebird	55	200	Crash
25	29	86	Bobby Mausgrover	Neil Castles '69 Dodge	51	200	Hub
26	17	26	Earl Brooks	Brooks '69 Ford	21	200	Heating
27	28	96	Richard Childress	Tom Garn '70 Chevrolet	17	200	Heating
28	16	19	Henley Gray	Gray '69 Ford	12	200	Engine
29	27	32	Marv Acton	Dick Brooks '70 Plymouth	11	200	Ignition
30	22	62	Ron Keselowski	Kaye Eng '71 Dodge	0	200	Crash

Time of Race: 1 hour, 34 minutes, 24 seconds
Average Speed: 64.831 mph
Pole Winner: Richard Petty - 85.137 mph
Lap Leaders: Richard Petty 1, H B Bailey 2-12, Petty 13-51, Jim Paschal 52-66, Petty 67-123, Tiny Lund 124-187, Petty 188-200.
Cautions: 6 for 41 laps   Margin of Victory: 10 car lengths   Attendance: 8,000

Salem. In fact, nobody got credit for winning. I don't understand NASCAR sanctioning a race and not having a winner. Plus, there have been some ill feelings on the part of Grand National drivers toward the drivers who switched to Grand American cars."

Petty started on the pole and led for a single lap before H.B. Bailey took command. Bailey, a part timer from Houston, led for 11 laps but later crashed on lap 55. Petty, Paschal and Lund swapped the lead five times before Petty eventually gained the upper hand.

Petty averaged 64.831 mph before 8,000 spectators.

Race No. 39

Dave Marcis Foiled Again; Tiny Lund Wins at Hickory

HICKORY, NC (Aug. 28) -- Tiny Lund passed a faltering Dave Marcis in the 153rd lap and sped to victory in the Buddy Shuman Memorial at Hickory Speedway. It was Lund's first big league win since 1966 when he won at Beltsville, MD.

Marcis started on the pole for the second time in 1971 and took off like a shot. The Wausau, WI driver had lapped everyone on the track except Lund, Elmo Langley and Richard Petty by the 95th lap.

Despite making a pit stop, Marcis continued to hold his lead. Lund began closing in just past the half way point and made the pass on lap 153. Marcis fell off the pace 20 laps later and was behind the wall with rear gearing failure.

Langley, driving one of the best races of his career, chased Lund the rest of the way but had to settle for

Buck Baker pits his Firebird at Hickory

Winston Cup GN Race No. 39
276 Laps at Hickory Speedway
Hickory, NC
"Buddy Shuman Memorial"
100 Miles on .363-mile Paved Track
August 28, 1971

Fin	St	No.	Driver	Team / Car	Laps	Money	Status
1	3	55	Tiny Lund	Ronnie Hopkins '69 Camaro	276	$1,500	Running
2	2	64	Elmo Langley	Langley '71 Ford	276	900	Running
3	4	43	Richard Petty	Petty Ent '71 Plymouth	276	500	Running
4	6	12	Bobby Allison	Allison '70 Dodge	276	350	Running
5	7	15	Wayne Andrews	Reid Shaw '71 Mustang	274	325	Running
6	18	48	James Hylton	Hylton Eng '70 Ford	274	300	Running
7	10	06	Frank Warren	Warren '69 Dodge	273	275	Running
8	11	91	Ed Negre	Junior Fields '71 Chevrolet	269	270	Running
9	8	10	Bill Champion	Champion '70 Ford	268	265	Running
10	13	25	Jabe Thomas	Don Robertson '70 Plymouth	264	260	Running
11	14	4	John Sears	Sears '69 Dodge	261	255	Running
12	9	24	Cecil Gordon	Gordon '69 Mercury	260	250	Running
13	20	87	Buck Baker	Baker '71 Firebird	258	245	Running
14	13	36	H B Bailey	Bailey '71 Firebird	254	240	Running
15	5	14	Jim Paschal	Cliff Stewart '70 AMC Javelin	233	235	Engine
16	1	2	Dave Marcis	Marcis '69 Dodge	173	230	Rear End
17	22	34	Wendell Scott	Scott '69 Ford	151	225	Oil Pan
18	19	21	Tommy Andrews	Andrews '69 Mustang	148	220	Heating
19	17	74	Bill Shirey	Shirey '69 Plymouth	80	215	Rear End
20	16	02	Randy Hutchison	Warren Prout '69 Camaro	75	210	Oil Leak
21	21	30	Walter Ballard	Vic Ballard '71 Ford	74	205	Clutch
22	15	95	Dick Brooks	'69 Camaro	30	200	Heating

Time of Race: 1 hour, 22 minutes, 25 seconds
Average Speed: 72.937 mph
Pole Winner: Dave Marcis - 80.147 mph
Lap Leaders: Dave Marcis 1-152, Tiny Lund 153-276.
Cautions: 2 for 7 laps   Margin of Victory: 3/4 lap   Attendance: 11,662

second place. Petty came in third. Bobby Allison was fourth in his Dodge and Wayne Andrews finished fifth.

Lund, driving a Camaro owned by Ronnie Hopkins, gave credit to his pit crew. "They did a real good job preparing the car," said the 41 year-old Harlan, IA native. "All I had to do was drive it."

Lund's fourth career win came at an average speed of 72.937 mph. A capacity crowd of 11,662 watched the race under the lights.

Race No. 40

Allison Virtually All the Way In Southern 500 Cakewalk

DARLINGTON, SC (Sept. 6) -- Bobby Allison's red and gold Mercury was the class of the field as he stormed to a one lap victory in the Southern 500 at Darlington Raceway. The Hueytown, AL veteran led for 329 of the 367 laps.

Richard Petty lost all hopes of catching the fleet Allison when he ducked onto pit road under caution to get a drink of water. His pit crew thought he was going to top off the tank, so they unfastened the gas cap. Petty roared back onto the track and was blackflagged.

Despite the late race incident, Petty finished second. Buddy Baker was third and Bobby Isaac fourth with relief help from Pete Hamilton. Fifth place went to Dave Marcis, who took over the Nichels-Goldsmith Plymouth vacated by Fred Lorenzen.

Lorenzen was saddled in the Wood Brothers Mercury since regular driver Donnie Allison was competing in a USAC Indy Car race at Ontario, CA. On Thursday, Lorenzen was seriously injured when he lost control of

the car exiting turn four. The maroon and white Mercury climbed the outside retaining wall, then spun and clobbered the concrete pit wall. He suffered a compound dislocation of the left ankle and a broken bone in his left foot, a mild concussion, facial lacerations and a gashed throat. He underwent surgery the following day.

Allison, Petty and Isaac were the only leaders in the race. "I would say this has been the best day I've ever had," said the winner. "Winning this race has to rank as one of my greatest thrills."

Petty said his pit road miscue didn't change the outcome. "It wouldn't have made any difference. He was so much faster -- he was just laughing at us."

David Pearson's woes continued with his highly publicized C V Enterprises Pontiac. Pearson started 13th, but pulled out of the race with engine failure on lap 50. "It was the head gasket," said the three-time Grand National champion. "It's the same problem we've had all year long."

Allison's 28th career Grand National triumph came at a record speed of 131.398 mph.

Winston Cup GN Race No. 40
367 Laps at Darlington Raceway
Darlington, SC
"Southern 500"
500 Miles on 1.366-mile Paved Track
September 6, 1971

Fin	St	No.	Driver	Team / Car	Laps	Money	Status
1	1	12	Bobby Allison	Holman-Moody '69 Mercury	367	$22,450	Running
2	6	43	Richard Petty	Petty Ent '71 Plymouth	366	10,050	Running
3	4	11	Buddy Baker	Petty Ent '71 Dodge	363	6,575	Running
4	7	71	Bobby Isaac*	K&K Insurance '71 Dodge	361	4,625	Running
5	5	99	Dave Marcis	Nichels-Goldsmith '71 Plym	355	3,600	Running
6	9	48	James Hylton	Hylton Eng '69 Mercury	343	3,050	Running
7	18	42	Marty Robbins**	Robbins '69 Dodge	339	2,550	Running
8	22	4	John Sears	Sears '69 Dodge	338	2,350	Running
9	11	24	Cecil Gordon	Gordon '69 Mercury	337	2,150	Running
10	37	40	Roy Mayne	D K Ulrich '71 Ford	320	2,050	Running
11	25	76	Ben Arnold	Arnold '69 Ford	316	1,850	Running
12	30	19	Henley Gray	Gray '69 Ford	315	1,575	Running
13	32	26	Earl Brooks	Brooks '69 Ford	313	1,430	Running
14	34	47	Raymond Williams	Williams '71 Ford	313	1,350	Running
15	36	13	Eddie Yarboro	Yarboro '69 Plymouth	303	1,200	Running
16	8	72	Benny Parsons	L G DeWitt '69 Mercury	276	1,545	Engine
17	20	8	Ed Negre	Negre '69 Ford	274	945	Running
18	35	68	Larry Baumel	Auto Lad '69 Ford	267	895	Running
19	10	90	Bill Dennis***	Junie Donlavey '69 Mercury	264	845	Battery
20	40	34	Wendell Scott	Scott '69 Ford	242	820	Running
21	15	49	G C Spencer	Spencer '69 Plymouth	223	820	Crash
22	21	7	Dean Dalton	Dalton '69 Ford	217	770	Engine
23	12	18	Joe Frasson	Frasson '70 Dodge	216	745	Battery
24	3	3	Charlie Glotzbach	Richard Howard '71 Chevrolet	214	785	Crash
25	23	84	Dick May	Ralph Davis '69 Dodge	204	725	Engine
26	19	10	Bill Champion	Champion '70 Ford	194	720	Rear End
27	27	32	Marv Acton	Dick Brooks '70 Plymouth	187	790	Hood Pin
28	33	74	Bill Shirey	Shirey '69 Plymouth	170	710	Engine
29	14	30	Walter Ballard	Vic Ballard '71 Ford	167	755	Engine
30	2	6	Pete Hamilton	Cotton Owens '71 Plymouth	156	800	Heating
31	28	79	Frank Warren	Warren '69 Dodge	149	695	Engine
32	17	45	Bill Seifert	Seifert '69 Ford	111	685	Engine
33	16	39	Friday Hassler	Hassler '70 Chevrolet	96	680	Engine
34	24	64	Elmo Langley	Langley '69 Mercury	81	675	Engine
35	13	17	David Pearson	C V Enterprises '71 Pontiac	50	795	Engine
36	29	86	Bobby Mausgrover	Neil Castles '69 Dodge	44	715	Suspen
37	38	06	Neil Castles	Castles '70 Dodge	41	660	Suspen
38	26	25	Jabe Thomas	Don Robertson '70 Plymouth	13	655	Engine
39	39	66	Dick Brooks	Ferguson-Stephens '71 Pont	8	650	Heating
40	31	91	J D McDuffie	Junior Fields '71 Chevrolet	2	645	Steering

Time of Race: 3 hours, 48 minutes, 55 seconds
Average Speed: 131.398 mph
Pole Winner: Bobby Allison - 147.915 mph
Lap Leaders: Bobby Allison 1-16, Bobby Isaac 17-40, Allison 41-89, Richard Petty 90-91, Allison 92-121, Isaac 122, Allison 123-155, Petty 156-157, Allison 158-239, Petty 240, Allison 241-293, Petty 294, Allison 295-301, Petty 302-308, Allison 309-367.
Cautions: 5 for 32 laps   Margin of Victory: 1 lap and 3 seconds   Attendance: 70,000
*Relieved by Pete Hamilton   **Relieved by Dick Brooks   ***Relieved by Dick Brooks

---

Race No. 41
Martinsville Money to Isaac's Dodge

MARTINSVILLE, VA (Sept. 26) -- Bobby Isaac led all but 55 laps en route to a wide victory in the Old Dominion 500 at Martinsville Speedway. It was the fourth win of the season for the 39 year-old Dodge driver.

Isaac took the lead for the final time in the 337th lap. Bobby Allison's Ford wound up a lap behind in second. Richard Petty was third, Charlie Glotzbach fourth and Donnie Allison fifth.

The 262.5-mile contest was the first under new NASCAR rules, which utilized carburetor restrictor sleeves rather than the controversial plate.

Some of the Ford teams were grumbling, but Isaac put things into a different perspective. "You can't use Martinsville as a true indicator," he said. "This is strictly a handling track, not a horsepower track. If you handle well here, you run well."

Ralph Moody, crew chief on Allison's Ford, hinted at withdrawal from the Winston Cup Series. "We knew what would happen and we tried to tell NASCAR that," said Moody. "We are not going to be competitive. There's no way we can go spend money just to run 10th."

Glen Wood, who earlier said he was quitting NASCAR due to unfair carburetor plate rules, was still irritated. "I still don't think the rules are fair," complained Wood.

Winston Cup GN Race No. 41
500 Laps at Martinsville Speedway
Martinsville, VA
"Old Dominion 500"
262.5 Miles on .525-mile Paved Track
September 26, 1971

Fin	St	No.	Driver	Team / Car	Laps	Money	Status
1	1	71	Bobby Isaac	K&K Insurance '71 Dodge	500	$6,250	Running
2	3	12	Bobby Allison	Holman-Moody '71 Ford	499	2,600	Running
3	2	43	Richard Petty	Petty Ent '71 Plymouth	499	2,200	Running
4	4	3	Charlie Glotzbach	Richard Howard '71 Chevrolet	496	1,575	Running
5	5	21	Donnie Allison	Wood Brothers '71 Mercury	495	1,250	Running
6	8	72	Benny Parsons	L G DeWitt '69 Mercury	488	1,025	Running
7	12	64	Elmo Langley	Langley '71 Ford	486	925	Running
8	15	90	Bill Dennis	Junie Donlavey '69 Mercury	483	875	Running
9	17	48	James Hylton	Hylton Eng '70 Ford	483	825	Running
10	16	55	Earl Brooks	'70 Dodge	481	775	Running
11	10	10	Bill Champion	Champion '71 Ford	476	750	Running
12	13	24	Cecil Gordon	Gordon '69 Mercury	475	725	Running
13	30	25	Jabe Thomas	Don Robertson '70 Plymouth	473	675	Running
14	21	5	Buddy Arrington	Arrington '70 Dodge	472	650	Running
15	20	4	Joe Frasson	Frasson '70 Dodge	471	650	Running
16	14	30	Walter Ballard	Vic Ballard '71 Ford	470	625	Running
17	6	91	Ed Negre	Junior Fields '71 Chevrolet	468	600	Running
18	9	2	Dave Marcis	Marcis '69 Dodge	468	575	Running
19	19	45	Bill Seifert	Seifert '69 Ford	460	550	Running
20	27	4	John Sears	Sears '69 Dodge	458	500	Running
21	23	7	Dean Dalton	Dalton '69 Ford	451	475	Running
22	28	06	Neil Castles	Castles '70 Dodge	445	450	Running
23	25	13	Wendell Scott	Eddie Yarboro '69 Plymouth	251	425	Engine
24	29	74	Bill Shirey	Shirey '69 Plymouth	251	400	Engine
25	18	79	Frank Warren	Warren '69 Dodge	185	400	D Shaft
26	11	66	Dick Brooks	Ferguson-Stephens '71 Pont	166	375	Running
27	24	78	Henley Gray	'71 Chevrolet	119	325	Brakes
28	7	39	Friday Hassler	Hassler '70 Chevrolet	114	325	Rear End
29	22	01	Earle Canavan	Canavan '71 Plymouth	94	275	Oil Leak
30	26	70	J D McDuffie	McDuffie '69 Mercury	58	250	Rear End

Time of Race: 3 hours, 33 minutes, 59 seconds
Average Speed: 73.681 mph
Pole Winner: Bobby Isaac - 83.635 mph
Lap Leaders: Bobby Isaac 1-132, Bobby Allison 133-149, Isaac 150-175, B.Allison 176,
Richard Petty 177, B.Allison 178-206, Isaac 207, B.Allison 208, Isaac 209-330,
B.Allison 331-336, Isaac 337-500.
Cautions: 3 for 33 laps   Margin of Victory: 1-lap plus   Attendance: 20,500

Winston Cup GN Race No. 42
334 Laps at Charlotte Motor Speedway
Charlotte, NC
"National 500"
500 Miles on 1.5-mile Paved Track
October 10, 1971

Fin	St	No.	Driver	Team / Car	Laps	Money	Status
1	3	12	Bobby Allison	Holman-Moody '69 Mercury	238	$18,450	Running
2	8	71	Bobby Isaac	K&K Insurance '71 Dodge	238	10,525	Running
3	4	21	Donnie Allison	Wood Brothers '69 Mercury	238	6,050	Running
4	5	43	Richard Petty	Petty Ent '71 Plymouth	238	4,025	Running
5	1	3	Charlie Glotzbach	Richard Howard '71 Chevrolet	238	2,975	Running
6	2	11	Buddy Baker	Petty Ent '71 Dodge	237	2,000	Running
7	6	6	Pete Hamilton	Cotton Owens '71 Plymouth	234	1,650	Running
8	14	39	Friday Hassler	Hassler '70 Chevrolet	233	1,575	Running
9	9	48	James Hylton	Hylton Eng '69 Mercury	231	1,500	Running
10	11	72	Benny Parsons	L G DeWitt '69 Mercury	226	1,500	Running
11	21	18	Joe Frasson	Frasson '70 Dodge	225	1,385	Running
12	28	25	Jabe Thomas	Don Robertson '70 Plymouth	225	1,360	Running
13	24	79	Frank Warren	Warren '69 Dodge	225	1,335	Running
14	31	64	Elmo Langley*	Langley '69 Mercury	225	1,300	Running
15	12	24	Cecil Gordon	Gordon '69 Mercury	225	1,300	Running
16	42	10	Bill Champion**	Champion '70 Mercury	224	1,324	Running
17	20	45	Bill Seifert	Seifert '71 Mercury	224	1,219	Running
18	36	57	David Ray Boggs	Boggs '69 Dodge	224	1,184	Running
19	16	91	Ed Negre	Junior Fields '71 Chevrolet	223	1,173	Running
20	30	30	Walter Ballard	Vic Ballard '71 Ford	223	1,148	Running
21	39	26	Earl Brooks	Brooks '69 Ford	222	1,097	Running
22	27	47	J D McDuffie	Raymond Williams '71 Ford	222	1,117	Running
23	29	76	Ben Arnold	Arnold '69 Ford	221	1,091	Running
24	32	53	Bobby Brack	Hopper-Crews '69 Ford	218	1,073	Running
25	19	92	Larry Smith	Harley Smith '69 Ford	218	1,068	Running
26	40	83	Johnny Halford	'69 Plymouth	214	1,039	Running
27	22	19	Henley Gray	Gray '70 Ford	213	1,033	Running
28	35	87	Cale Yarborough	'69 Mercury	209	1,054	Heating
29	37	4	John Sears	Sears '69 Dodge	206	981	Running
30	23	27	A J Foyt	Banjo Matthews '71 Chevrolet	184	974	Steering
31	26	31	Stick Elliott	O L Nixon '69 Dodge	163	923	D Shaft
32	10	99	Dave Marcis	Nichels-Goldsmith '71 Plym	152	907	Steering
33	33	01	Earle Canavan	Canavan '71 Plymouth	120	865	Crash
34	7	98	LeeRoy Yarbrough	Richard Howard '71 Chevrolet	120	865	Crash
35	18	60	Maynard Troyer	Nagle Racers '69 Mercury	115	840	Engine
36	17	49	Neil Castles	G C Spencer '69 Plymouth	114	834	Lug Bolt
37	15	42	Marty Robbins	Robbins '69 Dodge	97	812	Steering
38	41	55	Tiny Lund	'69 Mercury	95	770	Alternator
39	38	66	Dick Brooks	Ferguson-Stephens '71 Pont	76	796	Running
40	13	90	Bill Dennis	Junie Donlavey '69 Mercury	73	788	D Shaft
41	25	07	Wendell Scott***	Cunningham-Kelley '69 Chev	64	714	W Bearing
42	34	5	Jim Vandiver	Doc Faustina '70 Plymouth	10	640	Crash

Time of Race: 2 hours, 49 minutes, 38 seconds
Average Speed: 126.140 mph
Pole Winner: Charlie Glotzbach - 157.085 mph
Fastest Qualifier: A J Foyt - 158.492 mph
Lap Leaders: Charlie Glotzbach 1-11, Buddy Baker 12-23, Glotzbach 24-63, Baker 64-69,
Glotzbach 70-125, Richard Petty 126-134, Glotzbach 135, Bobby Isaac 136-157,
Bobby Allison 158-165, Glotzbach 166-176, B.Allison 177-238.
Cautions: 6 for 37 laps   Margin of Victory: 5 seconds   Attendance: 52,000
Race was shortened to 238 laps due to rain and darkness
*Relieved by Dick May   **Relieved by Henley Gray   ***Relieved by Coo Coo Marlin

Although NASCAR had said that Grand American cars were eligible to enter the race, track promoter Clay Earles would not accept the entry forms from any Grand American regular. "We've scheduled a Grand National race," said Earles, "and that's what we'll run. I don't think the Grand Americans should intermingle with the larger Grand Nationals. I'm not going to let the Grand Americans put me out of business."

Isaac's 36th career win came at an average speed of 73.681 mph.

Race No. 42

Allison Gets 4th Straight Superspeedway Win in Charlotte's National 500

CHARLOTTE, NC (Oct. 10) -- Bobby Allison had his Mercury out front when a surprise checkered flag ended the National 500 at Charlotte Motor Speedway after 347 miles. It was the fourth straight superspeedway win for Allison and his seventh of the year.

Flagman Roby Combs flashed the white flag as Allison motored around on his 237th lap. He drove the final lap and finished 5.0-seconds ahead of runner-up Bobby Isaac. Donnie Allison was third, Richard Petty fourth and Charlie Glotzbach fifth.

"The white flag surprised me," said Allison. "But it had begun to rain again -- and it was getting dark. I

Charlie Glotzbach won the pole and finished 5th in National 500

suppose it was the best thing to do. I had a pretty good lead and I was pulling away. I don't think it hurt anyone."

NASCAR Vice President Lin Kuchler explained the quick ending. "We felt that if a downpour came, we might endanger the drivers if we gave them a five lap notice. He had a big lead, so we decided to give the white and then the checkered."

Allison took the lead from Glotzbach with what amounted to 62 laps left. The lead changed hands only 10 times among five drivers.

Runner-up Isaac was not upset with the outcome. "I can't grumble. There's no use racing on the wet track until somebody got hurt. I like to race as well as anybody, but not when the track is as slick as this one was getting."

LeeRoy Yarbrough, on the comeback trail after being injured at Indianapolis, drove a Richard Howard Chevrolet. He started a respectable seventh, but crashed at the end of the backstretch on lap 120.

Allison averaged 126.140 mph before an audience of 52,000.

Race No. 43
Four Minute Pit Stop Ruins Allison; Petty Tops at Dover

DOVER, DE (Oct. 17) -- A four minute pit stop knocked Bobby Allison from the lead and Richard Petty seized the opportunity to win the Delaware 500 at Dover Downs International Speedway. It was the 18th victory of the season for Petty.

Charlie Glotzbach's Chevrolet crossed the finish line in second place, a lap behind. Bobby Isaac was third, Allison managed to finish fourth and Bill Dennis was fifth.

Allison started on the pole and was virtually untouchable. He led the first 142 laps and lost the lead briefly when he made a pit stop. Allison was back on top and had stretched his advantage to better than two laps when misfortune struck on lap 399.

As the Holman-Moody crew were changing the right front tire, they snapped off a log bolt. Before the frantic crew could replace it, he was almost four laps be-

Winston Cup GN Race No. 43
500 Laps at Dover Downs Int'l Speedway
Dover, DE
"Delaware 500"
500 Miles on 1-mile Paved Track
October 17, 1971

Fin	St	No.	Driver	Team / Car	Laps	Money	Status
1	4	43	Richard Petty	Petty Ent '71 Plymouth	500	$14,570	Running
2	3	98	Charlie Glotzbach	Richard Howard '71 Chevrolet	499	7,945	Running
3	2	71	Bobby Isaac	K&K Insurance '71 Dodge	499	4,970	Running
4	1	12	Bobby Allison	Holman-Moody '69 Mercury	498	2,695	Running
5	12	90	Bill Dennis	Junie Donlavey '69 Mercury	483	1,595	Running
6	10	57	David Ray Boggs	Boggs '69 Dodge	480	1,295	Running
7	6	91	Richard Brown	Junior Fields '71 Chevrolet	477	1,195	Running
8	17	64	Elmo Langley	Langley '69 Mercury	476	1,095	Running
9	18	30	Walter Ballard	Vic Ballard '71 Ford	473	1,070	Running
10	7	48	James Hylton	Hylton Eng '69 Mercury	466	1,045	Running
11	9	24	Cecil Gordon	Gordon '69 Mercury	465	1,020	Running
12	11	95	Paul Tyler	Tyler '69 Ford	464	995	Running
13	14	79	Frank Warren	Warren '69 Dodge	460	970	Running
14	26	47	Raymond Williams	Williams '71 Ford	459	945	Running
15	19	8	Ed Negre	Negre '69 Ford	458	920	Running
16	29	19	Henley Gray	Gray '69 Ford	442	895	Running
17	39	08	John Soares, Jr.	Soares '69 Dodge	440	870	Running
18	16	25	Jabe Thomas	Don Robertson '70 Plymouth	436	860	Fuel pump
19	35	40	Dick May	D K Ulrich '71 Ford	436	855	Running
20	28	34	Wendell Scott	Scott '69 Ford	392	845	Clutch
21	38	4	John Sears	Sears '69 Dodge	374	835	Engine
22	22	06	Neil Castles	Castles '69 Dodge	369	810	Alternator
23	36	03	Tommy Gale	Larry Jackson '69 Mercury	319	785	Engine
24	37	41	Ken Meisenhelder	Meisenhelder '69 Chevrolet	297	760	Rear End
25	33	74	Bill Shirey	Shirey '69 Plymouth	280	735	Engine
26	31	70	J D McDuffie	McDuffie '69 Mercury	266	710	Heating
27	15	10	Bill Champion	Champion '69 Ford	266	685	Steering
28	5	60	Maynard Troyer	Nagle Racers '69 Mercury	266	695	W Bearing
29	22	72	Benny Parsons	L G DeWitt '69 Mercury	229	705	Engine
30	25	5	Richard Childress	Doc Faustina '70 Plymouth	180	645	Steering
31	21	99	Fred Lorenzen	Nichels-Goldsmith '71 Plym	115	705	Engine
32	27	26	Earl Brooks	Brooks '69 Ford	15	620	Oil Pan
33	8	39	Friday Hassler	Hassler '70 Chevrolet	114	610	Engine
34	23	49	G C Spencer	Spencer '69 Plymouth	102	625	Axle
35	30	68	Larry Baumel	Auto Lad '69 Ford	91	590	Heating
36	40	23	James Cox	Don Robertson '69 Plymouth	87	580	Engine
37	13	1	Charlie Roberts	Roberts '69 Ford	68	570	Crash
38	34	45	Bill Seifert	Seifert '69 Ford	62	560	Frame
39	24	51	Dub Simpson	Bill Strong '69 Chevrolet	26	550	Oil Pan
40	32	7	Dean Dalton	Dalton '69 Ford	10	540	Oil Leak

Time of Race: 4 hours, 3 minutes, 25 seconds
Average Speed: 123.254 mph
Pole Winner: Bobby Allison - 132.811 mph
Lap Leaders: Bobby Allison 1-142, Charlie Glotzbach 143-147, Allison 148-399, Richard Petty 400-500.
Cautions: 2 for 9 laps   Margin of Victory: 1-lap plus   Attendance: 18,000
Relief Drivers: David Pearson relieved Bobby Isaac; Maynard Troyer relieved Bill Dennis; Bill Seifert relieved Elmo Langley; Dean Dalton relieved Henley Gray; Doc Faustina relieved Richard Childress.

hind. He made up two of those laps en route to fourth place.

"I couldn't have caught Allison," said an exhausted Petty. "Nobody could. I was about equal with Glotzbach and Isaac, and the breaks fell in place for me. That's what it takes to win sometimes."

There were only three lead changed in the 500-miler. A crowd of 18,000 was on hand.

Fred Lorenzen made his first start since being seriously injured at Darlington six weeks earlier. He was back behind the wheel of the Nichels-Goldsmith

Winston Cup GN Race No. 44
492 Laps at North Carolina Motor Speedway
Rockingham, NC
"American 500"
500 Miles on 1.017-mile Paved Track
October 24, 1971

Fin	St	No.	Driver	Team / Car	Laps	Money	Status
1	5	43	Richard Petty	Petty Ent '71 Plymouth	492	$17,120	Running
2	2	11	Buddy Baker	Petty Ent '71 Dodge	492	9,745	Running
3	4	12	Bobby Allison*	Holman-Moody '71 Mercury	488	6,320	Running
4	7	6	Pete Hamilton	Cotton Owens '71 Plymouth	487	4,195	Running
5	6	71	Bobby Isaac	K&K Insurance '71 Dodge	483	3,920	Running
6	11	72	Benny Parsons	L G DeWitt '69 Mercury	482	2,570	Running
7	27	48	James Hylton	Hylton Eng '69 Mercury	476	1,045	Running
8	15	18	Joe Frasson	Frasson '70 Dodge	471	1,670	Running
9	23	90	Bill Dennis	Junie Donlavey '69 Mercury	471	1,445	Running
10	13	39	Friday Hassler	Hassler '70 Chevrolet	468	1,270	Running
11	19	24	Cecil Gordon	Gordon '69 Mercury	464	1,070	Running
12	26	55	Tiny Lund	'69 Mercury	461	1,045	Running
13	21	76	Ben Arnold	Arnold '69 Ford	459	1,020	Running
14	25	47	Raymond Williams	Williams '71 Ford	457	995	Running
15	40	45	Bill Seifert	Seifert '69 Ford	453	970	Running
16	28	8	Ed Negre	Negre '69 Ford	446	945	Running
17	31	91	Richard Brown	Junior Fields '71 Chevrolet	445	1,020	Running
18	37	19	Henley Gray	Gray '69 Ford	440	895	Running
19	34	57	David Ray Boggs	Boggs '69 Dodge	439	870	Running
20	17	31	Stick Elliott	O L Nixon '69 Dodge	435	895	Running
21	36	34	Wendell Scott	Scott '69 Ford	421	820	Running
22	38	30	Walter Ballard	Vic Ballard '71 Ford	397	795	Engine
23	22	4	John Sears	Sears '69 Dodge	389	770	Running
24	35	70	J D McDuffie	McDuffie '69 Mercury	342	745	Suspen
25	30	10	Bill Champion	Champion '69 Ford	333	720	Oil Leak
26	41	26	Earl Brooks	Brooks '69 Ford	297	670	Suspen
27	39	06	Neil Castles	Castles '69 Dodge	254	670	Engine
28	9	2	Dave Marcis	Marcis '69 Dodge	227	670	Engine
29	32	64	Elmo Langley	Langley '69 Mercury	216	670	Engine
30	24	25	Jabe Thomas	Don Robertson '70 Plymouth	174	595	Crash
31	16	49	G C Spencer	Spencer '69 Plymouth	171	710	Crash
32	20	53	Bobby Brack	Hopper-Crews '69 Ford	170	580	Crash
33	29	95	Paul Tyler	Tyler '69 Ford	163	575	Crash
34	10	27	A J Foyt	Banjo Matthews '71 Chevrolet	139	595	Crash
35	18	79	Frank Warren	Warren '69 Plymouth	112	590	Engine
36	8	99	David Pearson	Nichels-Goldsmith '71 Plym	92	585	Crash
37	1	3	Charlie Glotzbach	Richard Howard '71 Chevrolet	84	1,130	Crash
38	12	07	Coo Coo Marlin	Cunningham-Kelley '69 Chev	79	575	Engine
39	3	21	Donnie Allison	Wood Brothers '69 Mercury	63	820	Heating
40	33	13	Eddie Yarboro	Yarboro '69 Plymouth	36	565	Engine
41	14	60	Maynard Troyer	Nagle Racers '69 Mercury	13	545	Engine

Time of Race: 4 hours, 24 minutes, 43 seconds
Average Speed: 113.405 mph
Pole Winner: Charlie Glotzbach - 135.167 mph
Lap Leaders: Charlie Glotzbach 1, Buddy Baker 2-6, Glotzbach 7-82, Baker 83,
    Bobby Allison 84, Baker 85-86, Pete Hamilton 87-100, Baker 101-146,
    Hamilton 147-148, Baker 149-233, Richard Petty 234-235, Baker 236-293,
    Petty 294-337, Baker 338-349, Petty 350-492.
Cautions: 9 for 58 laps   Margin of Victory: Attendance: 25,000
*Relieved by Donnie Allison

Plymouth, which had been vacated by Dave Marcis. Marcis drove the car twice, then went back to his independent Dodge. Lorenzen qualified 21st and left the race after 115 laps with a blown engine.

Rookie Maynard Troyer qualified a strong fifth, but departed on lap 266 with a burned wheel bearing.

Petty's 137th career win came at an average speed of 123.254 mph.

Race No. 44

Petty Wins American 500; Baker Hopping Mad

ROCKINGHAM, NC (Oct. 24) -- The 1971 Winston Cup Grand National season was once again hit by a controversial turn of events. Richard Petty won the American 500 at North Carolina Motor Speedway, but his team mate Buddy Baker yelled foul.

Baker was holding down a lap lead on Petty when

Buddy Baker thought his Dodge finished first at Rockingham

Dave Marcis' engine blew in the 232nd lap. Baker rode under the yellow flag, then moments later Petty passed him to get back in the lead lap. NASCAR officials didn't notice the illegal pass. Petty won the late race shoot-out to register his 19th win of the year.

"I didn't think nothin' about it," Petty said afterwards. "Undoubtedly, NASCAR didn't think much about it either or they would have blackflagged me."

"When they gave the white flag to Richard," said Baker, "I nearly jumped out of my car. I know I won the race. He passed me under caution."

Bobby Allison finished in third place, Pete Hamilton was fourth and Bobby Isaac fifth.

In the driver's lounge after the race, Allison spoke to Baker, "I feel sorry for you," he said. "I asked (Johnny) Bruner (NASCAR Field Manager) how they keep coming up with new rules to give him (Petty) races."

Baker listened for a moment then vented his frustrations on a dressing room door. He put his fist through it.

Charlie Glotzbach won the pole for the third time this year and led twice for 77 laps. He had just been passed by Baker when a tire blew, sending his Chevrolet into the wall.

USAC driver A.J. Foyt started 10th, but wrecked his Chevrolet on lap 139. David Pearson, latest driver in the Nichels-Goldsmith Plymouth, crashed on lap 92.

A crowd of 25,000 watched Petty take his 15th superspeedway victory at an average speed of 113.405 mph.

Race No. 45

Allison Beats Weak Field In Georgia 500

MACON, GA (Nov. 7) -- Bobby Allison drove his Holman-Moody Ford past Tiny Lund in the 195th lap

Winston Cup GN Race No. 45
500 Laps at Middle Georgia Raceway
Macon, GA
"Georgia 500"
274 Miles on .548-mile Paved Track
November 7, 1971

Fin	St	No.	Driver	Team / Car	Laps	Money	Status
1	1	12	Bobby Allison	Holman-Moody '71 Ford	500	$3,275	Running
2	4	55	Tiny Lund	Ronnie Hopkins '70 Camaro	499	2,000	Running
3	2	39	Friday Hassler	Hassler '70 Chevrolet	490	1,200	Running
4	12	06	Neil Castles	Castles '70 Dodge	486	800	Running
5	11	10	Bill Champion	Champion '71 Ford	483	700	Running
6	28	26	Earl Brooks	Brooks '69 Ford	476	625	Running
7	21	70	J D McDuffie	McDuffie '71 Chevrolet	474	600	Running
8	31	43	Ernie Shaw	'68 Mustang	469	575	Running
9	14	21	Frank Sessoms	Sessoms '68 Camaro	468	580	Running
10	15	79	Frank Warren	Warren '69 Plymouth	468	570	Running
11	6	25	Jabe Thomas	Don Robertson '70 Plymouth	463	560	Running
12	13	30	Walter Ballard	Vic Ballard '71 Ford	455	550	Crash
13	9	15	Wayne Andrews	Reid Shaw '71 Mustang	454	540	Ignition
14	27	34	Wendell Scott	Scott '69 Ford	454	505	Running
15	16	05	David Sisco	Charlie McGee '71 Chevrolet	454	520	Running
16	18	33	Joe Dean Huss	Jack Balmer '69 Camaro	451	510	Engine
17	8	4	John Sears	Sears '69 Dodge	419	500	Engine
18	24	87	Buck Baker	Baker '71 Firebird	305	465	Heating
19	20	22	Randy Hutchison	Warren Prout '69 Camaro	301	480	Alternator
20	5	32	Dick Brooks	Brooks '70 Plymouth	279	495	Trans
21	17	8	Ed Negre	Negre '69 Ford	243	460	Oil Leak
22	7	36	H B Bailey	Bailey '71 Firebird	231	450	Engine
23	26	37	G C Spencer	Dr Don Tarr '70 Dodge	209	415	Suspen
24	3	14	Jim Paschal	Cliff Stewart '70 AMC Javelin	201	480	Trans
25	23	45	Bill Seifert	Seifert '69 Ford	198	395	Clutch
26	32	88	Bob Williams	T C Hunt '68 Camaro	178	390	Engine
27	25	19	Henley Gray	Gray '69 Ford	155	380	Heating
28	29	86	David Ray Boggs	Boggs '71 Firebird	115	370	Engine
29	22	51	Dub Simpson	Bill Strong '69 Chevrolet	46	360	Clutch
30	19	01	Earle Canavan	Canavan '71 Plymouth	31	375	Oil Leak
31	30	16	Jimmy Watson	Ken Spikes '71 Chevrolet	29	350	Oil Leak
32	10	90	Bill Dennis	Junie Donlavey '69 Mercury	1	375	D Shaft

Time of Race: 3 hours, 23 minutes, 19 seconds
Average Speed: 80.859 mph
Pole Winner: Bobby Allison - 95.334 mph
Lap Leaders: Friday Hassler 1-6, Bobby Allison 7-53, Hassler 54-59, Jim Paschal 60-75, Allison 76-140, Paschal 141-159, Tiny Lund 160-194, Allison 195-500.
Cautions: 7 for 44 laps   Margin of Victory: 1-lap plus   Attendance: 7,300

and led the rest of the way to win the Georgia 500 at Middle Georgia Raceway. It was the 11th win of the season for Allison.

Richard Petty and four of the five leading contenders in the point standings, did not show up. Promoter Ralph Brawner said he was not going to issue appearance money to any driver, so the leading drivers got together and staged a mini-boycott.

Brawner was excited that a crowd of 7,300 showed up for the 274-miler on the .548-mile track. Dick Brooks perhaps summed it up best, "Financially it was a success, but artistically it stunk," he said.

Lund finished second, a lap behind. Friday Hassler, who once again turned in a fine driving effort, came in third. Neil Castles came in fourth and Bill Champion was fifth.

Some of the boycotting drivers were present without their cars. There was some speculation that they had planned to interrupt the proceedings.

Jim Paschal, driving Cliff Stewart's Javelin, led for 16 laps. The High Point, NC veteran went out on lap 201 with transmission failure.

Allison, who said the Holman-Moody team entered the '71 Ford to do some experimental testing, averaged 80.859 mph.

Race No. 46

Petty Wraps Up Championship With Richmond Win

RICHMOND, VA (Nov. 14) -- Richard Petty led the final 299 laps and won the Capital City 500 at Richmond Fairgrounds Raceway with ease. Petty also wrapped up the 1971 Winston Cup Grand National driving title.

All Petty needed to do was start the race to clinch the championship. "I've never entered a race in my life that I didn't try to win," he reasoned. "I want to have pleasant memories in a few years when I think back to this day. So winning the race is more important that winning the title."

Bobby Allison finished a lap behind in second place. Pete Hamilton was third, Charlie Glotzbach fourth and Elmo Langley fifth.

Petty started 11th on the grid and worked his way into contention early. He took the lead for the first time on lap 138, but was seldom pushed after that.

Home statesman Bill Dennis won the pole and led most of the early stages. Driving the Junie Donlavey Mercury, Dennis passed Glotzbach in the sixth lap and led through lap 51. A long pit stop removed him from the hunt. Dennis wound up 14th, 60 laps behind Petty.

A crowd of 13,000 watched the 271-miler. Petty's 20th win of the year came at a 80.025 mph clip.

Winston Cup GN Race No. 46
500 Laps at Richmond Fairgrounds Raceway
Richmond, VA
"Capital City 500"
271 Miles on .542-mile Paved Track
November 14, 1971

Fin	St	No.	Driver	Team / Car	Laps	Money	Status
1	11	43	Richard Petty	Petty Ent '71 Plymouth	500	$4,450	Running
2	10	12	Bobby Allison	Holman-Moody '71 Ford	499	2,585	Running
3	3	6	Pete Hamilton	Cotton Owens '71 Plymouth	490	1,750	Running
4	2	98	Charlie Glotzbach	Richard Howard '71 Chevrolet	487	1,175	Running
5	12	64	Elmo Langley	Langley '71 Ford	480	965	Running
6	5	06	Neil Castles	Castles '70 Dodge	480	650	Running
7	19	48	James Hylton	Hylton Eng '69 Ford	476	575	Running
8	16	4	John Sears	Sears '69 Dodge	472	550	Running
9	14	24	Cecil Gordon	Gordon '69 Mercury	471	560	Running
10	4	79	Frank Warren	Warren '69 Dodge	457	550	Running
11	8	30	Walter Ballard	Vic Ballard '71 Ford	445	515	Running
12	29	13	Eddie Yarboro	Yarboro '69 Plymouth	442	505	Running
13	25	23	James Cox	Don Robertson '69 Plymouth	442	495	Running
14	1	90	Bill Dennis	Junie Donlavey '69 Mercury	440	985	Running
15	21	19	Henley Gray	Gray '69 Ford	435	475	Running
16	15	25	Jabe Thomas	Don Robertson '70 Plymouth	433	450	Running
17	17	28	Bill Hollar	Earl Brooks '69 Ford	416	445	Running
18	20	8	Ed Negre	Negre '69 Ford	415	440	Running
19	9	70	J D McDuffie	McDuffie '71 Chevrolet	384	435	Running
20	26	96	Richard Childress	Tom Garn '70 Chevrolet	359	425	Running
21	28	80	Phil Finney	Finney '69 Chevrolet	357	400	Running
22	27	40	D K Ulrich	Ulrich '71 Ford	314	390	Rear End
23	18	26	Earl Brooks	Brooks '69 Ford	309	380	Running
24	22	86	Bobby Mausgrover	Neil Castles '69 Dodge	282	370	Suspen
25	13	72	Benny Parsons	L G DeWitt '71 Ford	253	385	Engine
26	7	45	Bill Seifert	Seifert '69 Ford	188	350	Rear End
27	23	62	Bill Shirey	Kaye Eng '69 Dodge	118	325	Oil Leak
28	24	34	Wendell Scott	Scott '69 Ford	103	300	Engine
29	6	10	Bill Champion	Champion '71 Ford	59	285	Engine
30	30	50	Gordon Burkett	'69 Chevrolet	43	275	Engine

Time of Race: 3 hours, 23 minutes, 11 seconds
Average Speed: 80.025 mph
Pole Winner: Bill Dennis -
Fastest Qualifier: Bobby Allison - 87.584 mph
Lap Leaders: Charlie Glotzbach 1-5, Dennis 6-51, Glotzbach 52-65, Allison 66-137, Richard Petty 138-167, Allison 168-190, Petty 191, Allison 192-201, Petty 202-500.
Cautions: 4 for 24 laps   Margin of Victory: 1-lap plus   Attendance: 13,000

Winston Cup GN Race No. 47
400 Laps at N.Wilkesboro Speedway
N.Wilkesboro, NC
"Wilkes 400"
250 Miles on .625-mile Paved Track
November 21, 1971

Fin	St	No.	Driver	Team / Car	Laps	Money	Status
1	6	55	Tiny Lund	Ronnie Hopkins '70 Camaro	400	$3,875	Running
2	1	3	Charlie Glotzbach	Richard Howard '71 Chevrolet	400	3,525	Running
3	2	43	Richard Petty	Petty Ent '70 Plymouth	400	1,650	Running
4	5	2	Dave Marcis	Marcis '69 Dodge	398	1,175	Running
5	11	72	Benny Parsons	L G DeWitt '71 Ford	394	1,000	Running
6	14	87	Buck Baker	Baker '71 Firebird	387	650	Running
7	22	48	James Hylton	Hylton Eng '71 Ford	385	600	Running
8	15	21	Frank Sessoms	Sessoms '68 Camaro	384	600	Running
9	10	24	Cecil Gordon	Gordon '69 Mercury	382	655	Running
10	9	64	Elmo Langley	Langley '71 Ford	382	695	Running
11	13	10	Bill Champion	Champion '71 Ford	380	585	Running
12	18	06	Neil Castles	Castles '70 Dodge	377	550	Running
13	31	30	Walter Ballard	Vic Ballard '71 Ford	375	515	Running
14	25	33	Joe Dean Huss	Jack Balmer '69 Camaro	374	505	Running
15	30	70	J D McDuffie	McDuffie '71 Chevrolet	372	520	Running
16	29	8	Ed Negre	Negre '69 Ford	362	485	Running
17	28	26	Wendell Scott	Scott '69 Ford	352	475	Running
18	16	4	John Sears	Sears '69 Dodge	343	490	Running
19	26	74	Jabe Thomas	Bill Shirey '69 Plymouth	339	455	Running
20	20	11	Bob Williams	James Rupe '69 Camaro	297	445	Engine
21	3	12	Bobby Allison	Holman-Moody '71 Ford	173	510	Engine
22	23	79	Frank Warren	Warren '69 Dodge	171	450	Rear End
23	27	59	Jimmy Vaughn	Vaughn '70 Mustang	147	415	Engine
24	8	90	Bill Dennis	Junie Donlavey '69 Mercury	106	430	Oil Leak
25	24	47	Raymond Williams	Williams '71 Ford	96	395	Vibration
26	17	45	Bill Seifert	Seifert '69 Ford	87	415	Electrical
27	12	22	Randy Hutchison	Warren Prout '69 Camaro	70	405	Engine
28	21	13	Eddie Yarboro	Yarboro '69 Plymouth	61	370	Clutch
29	19	01	Earle Canavan	Canavan '71 Plymouth	17	385	Engine
30	4	91	Richard Brown	Junior Fields '71 Chevrolet	12	475	Oil Leak
31	7	25	James Cox	Don Robertson '70 Plymouth	0	375	Engine

Time of Race: 2 hours, 35 minutes, 58 seconds
Average Speed: 96.174 mph
Pole Winner: Charlie Glotzbach - 107.558 mph
Lap Leaders: Charlie Glotzbach 1-41, Bobby Allison 42-48, Richard Petty 49-74, Allison 75, Tiny Lund 76, Allison 77-79, Richard Petty 80-359, Glotzbach 360-394, Lund 395-400.
Cautions: 3 for 19 laps   Margin of Victory: 6 seconds   Attendance: 9,500

Race No. 47

Petty, Glotzbach Falter; Lund Wins Wilkesboro in Camaro

N.WILKESBORO, NC (Nov. 21) -- Tiny Lund roared from a four lap deficit, took the lead with six laps remaining and won the twice postponed Wilkes 400 at North Wilkesboro Speedway. It was the second win of the year for Lund and the Ronnie Hopklins team in 'mixed' races.

Richard Petty was well on his way to his 21st win of the season, holding a two lap lead with 70 laps to go. Lund was third, four laps back.

A broken valve spring crippled Petty's Plymouth and Glotzbach ran him down within 10 laps. Glotzbach led

Tiny Lund

through the 394th lap when Lund made the winning pass.

Team manager Junior Johnson inspected his Chevrolet and determined that a piece in the rear suspension had broken off, causing the right rear wheel to wobble. "It would have probably fallen off in a few more laps," he said.

Lund scoffed at some opinions that the Grand American cars have an advantage on the short tracks. "That's the only talk I've heard lately," said Lund. "There are some advantages, yes, but some disadvantages too. We have to use a narrower tire, and we had to use a three man pit crew. The Grand Nationals are allowed five men over the wall on pit stops."

Glotzbach finished second, 6.0-seconds behind Lund's Camaro. Petty managed to go the full 400 laps on a sour engine to salvage third. Dave Marcis came in fourth and Benny Parsons was fifth.

Richard Brown of Claremont, NC qualified the Junior Fields Chevrolet fourth fastest. It was the major surprise in time trials. Brown went only 12 laps before an oil leak sidelined him.

Bobby Allison left the race after 173 laps with a blown engine.

Lund averaged 96.174 before a crowd of 9,500.

Race No. 48

King Richard Tops Off '71 Season with Texas 500 Win

COLLEGE STATION, TX (Dec. 12) -- Richard Petty tied down his 21st win of the year by taking first place in the Texas 500 at Texas World Speedway. The Randleman, NC Plymouth ace wound up winning his third Winston Cup Grand National championship by 364 points over James Hylton.

Petty took the lead with 20 laps to go and outdistanced Buddy Baker by 18 seconds. Bobby Allison

Richard Petty topped off fantastic 1971 season with Texas 500 victory

Winston Cup GN Race No. 48
250 Laps at Texas World Speedway
College Station, TX
"Texas 500"
500 Miles on 2-mile Paved Track
December 12, 1971

Fin	St	No.	Driver	Team / Car	Laps	Money	Status
1	3	43	Richard Petty	Petty Eng '71 Plymouth	250	$13,395	Running
2	4	11	Buddy Baker	Petty Ent '71 Dodge	250	6,805	Running
3	5	12	Bobby Allison	Holman-Moody '71 Mercury	248	5,125	Running
4	1	6	Pete Hamilton	Cotton Owens '71 Plymouth	245	3,865	Running
5	8	90	Bill Dennis	Junie Donlavey '69 Mercury	239	3,100	Running
6	10	18	Joe Frasson	Frasson '70 Dodge	238	2,540	Running
7	15	24	Cecil Gordon	Gordon '69 Mercury	234	2,035	Running
8	14	91	Richard Brown	Junior Fields '71 Chevrolet	232	1,535	Running
9	30	76	Ben Arnold	Arnold '69 Ford	232	1,045	Running
10	22	25	Jabe Thomas	Don Robertson '70 Plymouth	231	965	Running
11	21	9	Ramo Stott	Stott '70 Dodge	231	965	Running
12	12	48	James Hylton	Hylton Eng '71 Ford	230	835	Running
13	35	10	Bill Champion	Champion '71 Ford	219	765	Running
14	32	26	Earl Brooks	Brooks '69 Ford	216	745	Running
15	37	0	George Altheide	'70 Dodge	216	690	Running
16	25	45	Bill Seifert	Seifert '69 Ford	212	685	Running
17	43	28	Bill Hollar	Earl Brooks '69 Ford	212	680	Running
18	33	47	Raymond Williams	Williams '71 Ford	211	675	Running
19	44	70	J D McDuffie	McDuffie '69 Mercury	211	720	Running
20	16	06	Neil Castles	Castles '70 Dodge	209	665	Running
21	49	34	Wendell Scott	Scott '69 Ford	209	660	Running
22	39	63	Charlie Roberts	Roberts '69 Dodge	208	655	Running
23	40	19	Henley Gray	Gray '69 Ford	196	650	Running
24	24	4	John Sears	Sears '69 Dodge	194	685	Fuel pmp
25	20	42	Marty Robbins	Robbins '71 Dodge	174	640	Engine
26	9	39	Friday Hassler	Hassler '70 Chevrolet	164	665	Valve
27	29	00	Ronnie Chumley	'69 Mercury	155	630	Engine
28	46	74	Bill Shirey	Shirey '69 Plymouth	144	625	Out of gas
29	47	81	Bob England	England '70 Chevrolet	133	620	Vibration
30	31	5	Doc Faustina	Faustina '70 Plymouth	128	615	Oil Leak
31	38	55	Tiny Lund	'69 Mercury	118	610	Engine
32	19	87	Jackie Oliver	'69 Mercury	117	605	Engine
33	18	53	H B Bailey	Hopper-Crews '69 Ford	117	600	Engine
34	28	01	Earle Canavan	Canavan '71 Plymouth	113	630	Engine
35	41	7	Dean Dalton	Dalton '69 Ford	111	665	Lug Bolt
36	13	79	Frank Warren	Warren '69 Dodge	98	605	Valve
37	34	27	Jerry Barnette	'71 Dodge	86	580	Crash
38	2	72	Benny Parsons	L G DeWitt '71 Chevrolet	82	675	Engine
39	23	30	Walter Ballard	Vic Ballard '71 Ford	79	615	Engine
40	11	2	Dave Marcis	Marcis '69 Dodge	73	585	Engine
41	27	64	Elmo Langley	Langley '71 Ford	69	560	Oil Press
42	26	57	David Ray Boggs	Boggs '69 Dodge	67	555	Engine
43	36	37	Dr Don Tarr	Tarr '70 Dodge	59	550	Lug Bolt
44	42	8	Ed Negre	Negre '69 Ford	34	545	Engine
45	45	40	D K Ulrich	Ulrich '71 Ford	26	540	Clutch
46	17	96	Ray Elder	Fred Elder '71 Dodge	24	535	Engine
47	48	61	Jimmy Finger	Bierschwale-Burke '69 Ford	18	530	Engine
48	6	17	David Pearson	C V Enterprises '71 Pontiac	15	575	Heating
49	7	71	Bobby Isaac	K&K Insurance '71 Dodge	1	1,020	Engine

Time of Race: 3 hours, 28 minutes, 20 seconds
Average Speed: 144.000 mph
Pole Winner: Pete Hamilton - 170.830 mph
Lap Leaders: Richard Petty 1-16, Buddy Baker 17-47, Pete Hamilton 48-51,
   Bobby Allison 52, Petty 53-77, Allison 78-88, Petty 89-95, Baker 96-99, Baker 100,
   Petty 101-113, Baker 114-133, Allison 134, Petty 135, Allison 136-139, Petty 140-164,
   Allison 165-172, Hamilton 173-180, Petty 181, Allison 182-222, Petty 223-225,
   Allison 226-230, Petty 231-250.
Cautions: 3 for 28 laps   Margin of Victory: 18 seconds   Attendance: 18,600

tried to get the lead back with 11 laps remaining, but smoke poured from under the car. He limped the rest of the way and finished third, two laps off the pace.

Pole sitter Pete Hamilton came in fourth and Bill Dennis was fifth.

Benny Parsons qualified a strong second, but went

out on lap 82 with a blown engine.

A number of USAC drivers had lined up rides, including A.J. Foyt, Lloyd Ruby, Jim McElreath and Roger McCluskey. However, USAC Executive Director William J. Smythe warned all USACers that if they competed in the Texas 500, they would "face severe penalties".

Texan Johnny Rutherford had been asked to drive the pace car, but he had to back out in fear of a severe USAC reprimand.

Bobby Isaac, winner of the only other NASCAR race at the two-mile oval in 1969, was the first driver out of the race. The engine blew in Isaac's Dodge after one lap. Oil splashed onto the headers, catching the car on fire. Isaac scrambled out unhurt.

David Pearson lasted only 15 laps in the C V Enterprises Pontiac. Shortly before the Texas event, car builder Ray Nichels filed an $8 million suit against money man Chris Vallo for fraud and misrepresentation.

Petty's 140th career victory came at an average speed of 144.000. A small crowd of 18,600 showed up at the financially plagued facility.

1971 NASCAR Season
Final Point Standings - Winston Cup Grand National Division

Rank	Driver	Points	Starts	Wins	Top 5	Top 10	Winnings
1	Richard Petty	4,435	46	21	38	41	$351,071
2	James Hylton	4,071	46	0	14	37	90,282
3	Cecil Gordon	3,677	46	0	6	21	69,080
4	Bobby Allison	3,636	42	11	27	31	254,316
5	Elmo Langley	3,356	46	0	11	23	57,037
6	Jabe Thomas	3,200	44	0	2	15	48,241
7	Bill Champion	3,058	45	0	3	14	43,769
8	Frank Warren	2,886	47	0	1	10	40,072
9	J.D. McDuffie	2,862	43	0	2	8	35,578
10	Walter Ballard	2,633	41	0	3	11	30,974
11	Benny Parsons	2,611	35	1	13	18	55,896
12	Ed Negre	2,528	43	0	0	2	29,738
13	Bill Seifert	2,403	37	0	0	4	33,220
14	Henley Gray	2,392	39	0	0	4	31,789
15	Buddy Baker	2,358	19	1	13	16	115,150
16	Friday Hassler	2,277	29	0	4	13	37,305
17	Earl Brooks	2,205	35	0	1	3	25,360
18	Bill Dennis	2,181	28	0	4	10	29,420
19	Wendell Scott	2,180	37	0	0	4	21,701
20	John Sears	2,167	37	0	0	3	26,735
21	Dave Marcis	2,049	28	0	8	13	37,582
22	Neil Castles	2,036	38	0	1	10	22,939
23	Bobby Isaac	1,819	25	4	16	17	106,526
24	Pete Hamilton	1,739	22	1	11	12	60,440
25	Joe Frasson	1,619	17	0	1	4	20,975
26	Ben Arnold	1,618	18	0	0	3	18,491
27	Ron Keselowski	1,446	20	0	0	6	17,680
28	Bill Shirey	1,303	27	0	0	2	9,160
29	Donnie Allison	1,280	13	1	7	9	69,995
30	Dean Dalton	1,276	20	0	0	1	13,910
31	Raymond Williams	1,270	20	0	0	0	14,585
32	Dick May	1,090	22	0	0	1	9,225
33	Charlie Roberts	1,053	20	0	0	2	12,470
34	G.C. Spencer	1,008	18	0	2	6	11,470
35	Richard Brown	967	13	0	0	2	11,940
36	Dick Brooks	939	20	0	9	12	32,921
37	Larry Baumel	904	16	0	0	1	10,910
38	Maynard Troyer	879	13	0	1	3	13,115
39	Roy Mayne	852	11	0	0	1	10,330
40	Ken Meisenhelder	797	15	0	0	1	5,405
41	Tommy Gale	729	9	0	0	1	8,800
42	Charlie Glotzbach	699	19	1	7	10	38,605
43	Bill Hollar	644	11	0	0	1	4,275
44	Marv Acton	627	11	0	0	0	8,620
45	Fred Lorenzen	611	15	0	7	9	45,100
46	Richard Childress	601	12	0	0	0	3,855
47	Paul Tyler	561	9	0	0	0	6,360
48	Jim Vandiver	553	7	0	0	3	13,575
49	Coo Coo Marlin	527	12	0	0	0	9,085
50	Eddie Yarboro	497	7	0	0	0	3,685